THE
OLD TESTAMENT

THE
JOSEPH SMITH NEW TRANSLATION
OF THE HOLY BIBLE

RESTORATION EDITION

[PREVIEW TWO]

Restoration Scriptures Preview by Chris Hamill is licensed under a Creative Commons Attribution-Non Commercial-ShareAlike 4.0 International License. Permissions beyond the scope of this license may be available at scriptures.info.

FOREWORD

This volume is one of three, which together constitute a unified effort by two independent bodies of volunteers, separately driven to approach the scriptures anew.

Initially the members of these two groups felt individually inspired to revisit the scriptures in an effort to prune away some of the uninspired alterations of man, that they might have a more correct version of scripture to aid their study. These individuals were led to one another and agreed to combine and harmonize their efforts. What began as two wholly separate groups, each forming at the same time, both unknown to one another, resulted in two separate projects that completed at the same time, and what was learned from their independent efforts identified issues that needed to be addressed.

On the last day of 2016, less than two weeks after discovering each other, these two groups held a meeting, facilitated by Denver Snuffer, and determined to unify their efforts, each bringing to the table differing components for a greater outcome than either project possessed alone. On the first day of the new year, the two became one as work began, preparing what would become this edition of the scriptures. Moving forward, the united team has worked closely with each other, with the Lord, and with his servant to produce a more accurate record that is true to the Lord's intent and to the Restoration.

In September 1832, the saints were condemned by the Lord and commanded to *"repent and remember the new covenant, even the Book of Mormon and the former commandments which I have given them, not only to say, but to do according to that which I have written."*

We often see this as the Lord rebuking the saints for failing to *do* according to that which He has written, yet assume that the saints have been correctly *saying* what He has written. But the saints did not say, and have failed to accurately preserve, what the revelations God provided to them said, because even their texts were corrupted. This means that the first step towards emerging from condemnation is to try and do exactly what is being accomplished through this scriptural work now underway. While the full purpose was initially unknown, this project has begun a best effort to repent and remember the new covenant. If done right, we will at least accomplish the first step: Recovering what the Lord provided so we can "say" what He revealed. Then the challenges increase as we are called upon "to do according to that" which God has revealed.

Great effort has been put into honoring the work of Joseph Smith in this collection. This includes the use of his New Translation as the text for the Bible, and stripping away most alterations to his revelations which were made by others. We believe his work is to be honored above any who would claim to be his successors.

Punctuation has been heavily reduced, as its presence can directly influence the interpretation of scriptural statements. The removal of such punctuation allows for a freer text with greater possibilities for interpretation and understanding, as guided by the Lord.

Traditional versing has been entirely removed from this collection, and chaptering and paragraphing has been reduced and revised. The purpose of this is to offset the divorcing of statements from their greater context, which often occurs when a scriptural text is poorly divided into smaller chapters and verses.

Additional, work-specific changes, if any, can be found in the introductions to each work.

The hand of the Lord has been present in the process of preparing these scriptures. May His Spirit guide you and testify to you as you receive them.

INTRODUCTION

This edition of The Old Testament is drawn from Joseph Smith's New Translation of the Holy Bible. In addition to the written edits made by Joseph, we have included a number of other textual adjustments that Joseph stated should be made, from public discourses which never became part of his written New Translation.

In line with what Joseph did with his New Translation, the Song of Solomon has been removed, as Joseph declared that it was not an inspired writing.

The Book of Proverbs is a collection of wisdom writings that was compiled over time. In accordance with that pattern, additional wisdom writings have been included at the end of that book, comprised of the Proverbs of Joseph Smith, Jr. and the Proverbs of Denver Snuffer, Jr.

CONTENTS

GENESIS	1
EXODUS	64
LEVITICUS	106
NUMBERS	137
DEUTERONOMY	181
JOSHUA	216
JUDGES	241
RUTH	265
1 SAMUEL	269
2 SAMUEL	301
1 KINGS	328
2 KINGS	360
1 CHRONICLES	390
2 CHRONICLES	417
EZRA	452
NEHEMIAH	462
ESTHER	476
JOB	483
PSALMS	506
PROVERBS	570
ECCLESIASTES	598
ISAIAH	605
JEREMIAH	654
LAMENTATIONS	708
EZEKIEL	712
DANIEL	762
HOSEA	777
JOEL	784
AMOS	787
OBADIAH	792
JONAH	793
MICAH	795
NAHUM	799
HABAKKUK	800
ZEPHANIAH	802
HAGGAI	805
ZECHARIAH	806
MALACHI	814

GENESIS

THE words of God which he spake unto Moses, at a time when Moses was caught up into an exceeding high mountain, and he saw God face to face, and he talked with him, and the glory of God was upon Moses, therefore Moses could endure his presence. And God spake unto Moses, saying, Behold, I am the Lord God Almighty, and endless is my name, for I am without beginning of days or end of years, and is not this endless? And behold, thou art my son, wherefore look, and I will show thee the workmanship of mine hands, but not all, for my works are without end, and also my words, for they never cease, wherefore, no man can behold all my works except he behold all my glory, and no man can behold all my glory, and afterwards remain in the flesh, on the Earth. And I have a work for thee, Moses, my son, and thou art in the similitude of mine Only Begotten, and my Only Begotten is and shall be the Savior, for he is full of grace and truth, but there is no God beside me, and all things are present with me, for I know them all. And now, behold, this one thing I show unto thee, Moses, my son, for thou art in the world, and now I show it unto thee.

And it came to pass, that Moses looked and beheld the world upon which he was created. And as Moses beheld the world, and the ends thereof, and all the children of men, which are and which were created, of the same he greatly marvelled, and wondered. And the presence of God withdrew from Moses, that his glory was not upon Moses, and Moses was left unto himself, and as he was left unto himself, he fell unto the earth. And it came to pass, that it was for the space of many hours before Moses did again receive his natural strength like unto man, and he said unto himself, Now, for this cause, I know that man is nothing, which thing I never had supposed, but now mine eyes have beheld God, but not mine natural but my spiritual eyes, for mine natural eyes could not have beheld, for I should have withered and died in his presence, but his glory was upon me, and I beheld his face, for I was transfigured before him.

And now it came to pass, that when Moses had said these words, behold, Satan came tempting him, saying, Moses, son of man, worship me. And it came to pass that Moses looked upon Satan, and said, Who art thou, for behold I am a son of God, in the similitude of his Only Begotten, and where is thy glory, that I should worship thee? For, behold, I could not look upon God except his glory should come upon me, and I were transfigured before him. But I can look upon thee in the natural man. Is it not so surely? Blessed be the name of my God, for his Spirit hath not altogether withdrawn from me, or else where is thy glory, for it is darkness unto me, and I can judge between thee and God, for God said unto me, Worship God, for him only shalt thou serve. Get thee hence, Satan, deceive me not, for God said unto me, Thou art after the similitude of mine Only Begotten. And he also gave unto me commandment, when he called unto me out of the burning bush, saying, Call upon God in the name of mine Only Begotten, and worship me. And again, Moses said, I will not cease to call upon God. I have other things to inquire of him, for his glory has been upon me, and it is glory unto me, wherefore, I can judge between him and thee. Depart hence, Satan.

And now, when Moses had said these words, Satan cried with a loud voice, and went upon the Earth, and commanded, saying, I am the Only Begotten, worship me. And it came to pass, that Moses began to fear exceedingly, and as he began to fear, he saw the bitterness of hell, nevertheless, calling upon God he received strength, and he commanded, saying, Depart hence, Satan, for this one God only will I worship, which is the God of glory. And now, Satan began to tremble, and the Earth shook, and Moses received strength and called upon

God in the name of his Son, saying to Satan, Depart hence. And it came to pass, that Satan cried with a loud voice, with weeping, and wailing, and gnashing of teeth, and departed hence, yea, from the presence of Moses, that he beheld him not. And now, of this thing Moses bore record, but because of wickedness, it is not had among the children of men.

And it came to pass, that when Satan had departed from the presence of Moses, that Moses lifted up his eyes unto Heaven, being filled with the Holy Ghost, which beareth record of the Father and the Son, and calling upon the name of God, he beheld again his glory, for it rested upon him, and he heard a voice, saying, Blessed art thou, Moses, for I, the Almighty, have chosen thee, and thou shalt be made stronger than many waters, for they shall obey thy command even as if thou wert God. And lo, I am with thee, even unto the end of thy days, for thou shalt deliver my people from bondage, even Israel my chosen.

And it came to pass, as the voice was still speaking, he cast his eyes and beheld the Earth, yea, even all the face of it, and there was not a particle of it which he did not behold, discerning it by the Spirit of God. And he beheld also the inhabitants thereof, and there was not a soul which he beheld not, and he discerned them by the Spirit of God, and their numbers were great, even as numberless as the sand upon the seashore. And he beheld many lands, and each land was called Earth, and there were inhabitants on the face thereof. And it came to pass, that Moses called upon God, saying, Tell me, I pray thee, why these things are so, and by what thou madest them? And behold the glory of God was upon Moses, so that Moses stood in the presence of God, and he talked with him face to face. And the Lord God said unto Moses, For mine own purpose have I made these things. Here is wisdom, and it remaineth in me. And by the word of my power have I created them, which is mine Only Begotten Son, who is full of grace and truth. And worlds without number have I created, and I also created them for mine own purpose, and by the Son I created them, which is mine Only Begotten. And the first man of all men have I called Adam, which is many. But only an account of this Earth, and the inhabitants thereof, give I unto you, for behold there are many worlds which have passed away by the word of my power, and there are many also which now stand, and numberless are they unto man, but all things are numbered unto me, for they are mine, and I know them. And it came to pass, that Moses spake unto the Lord, saying, Be merciful unto thy servant, O God, and tell me concerning this Earth, and the inhabitants thereof, and also the heavens, and then thy servant will be content. And the Lord God spake unto Moses, saying, The heavens, they are many and they can not be numbered unto man, but they are numbered unto me, for they are mine, and as one Earth shall pass away, and the heavens thereof, even so shall another come, and there is no end to my works, neither to my words, for this is my work and my glory, to bring to pass the immortality, and Eternal life of man. And now, Moses, my son, I will speak unto you concerning this Earth upon which thou standest, and thou shalt write the things which I shall speak. And in a day when the children of men shall esteem my words as naught, and take many of them from the book which thou shalt write, behold I will raise up another like unto thee, and they shall be had again among the children of men, among even as many as shall believe. These words were spoken unto Moses in the mount, the name of which shall not be known among the children of men. And now they are spoken unto you. Amen.

2 AND it came to pass, that the Lord spake unto Moses, saying, Behold, I reveal unto you concerning this Heaven and this Earth, write the words which I speak.

I am the Beginning and the End, the Almighty God. By mine Only Begotten I created these things. Yea, in the beginning I organized the Heaven, and the Earth upon which thou standest. And the Earth was empty, and desolate, and I caused darkness to come up upon the face of the deep. And my Spirit moved upon the face of the waters, for I am God. And I, God, said, Let there be light, and there was light. And I, God, saw the light, and that light was good. And I, God, divided the light from the darkness. And I, God, called the light day, and the darkness I called night. And this I did by the word of my power, and it was done as I spake. And the evening and the morning were the first day.

And again, I, God, said, Let there be a firmament in the midst of the waters, and it was so, even as I spake. And I said, Let it divide the waters from the waters, and it was done. And I, God, made the firmament, and divided the waters, yea, the great waters under the firmament, from the waters which were above the firmament, and it was so, even as I spake. And I, God, called the firmament Heaven. And the evening and the morning were the second day.

And I, God, said, Let the waters under the Heaven be gathered together unto one place, and it was so. And I, God, said, Let there be dry land, and it was so. And I, God, called the dry land Earth, and the gathering together of the waters called I the sea. And I, God, saw that all things which I had made were good. And I, God, said, Let the Earth bring forth grass, the herb yielding seed, the fruit tree yielding fruit after his kind, and the tree yielding fruit, whose seed should be in itself, upon the Earth, and it was so, even as I spake. And the Earth brought forth grass, every herb yielding seed after his kind, and the tree yielding fruit, whose seed should be in itself, after his kind. And I, God, saw that all things which I had made were good. And the evening and the morning were the third day.

And I, God, said, Let there be lights in the firmament of the Heaven, to divide the day from the night, and let them be for signs and for seasons, and for days and for years, and let them be for lights in the firmament of the Heaven, to give light upon the Earth, and it was so. And I, God, made two great lights, the greater light to rule the day, and the lesser light to rule the night, and the greater light was the sun, and the lesser light was the moon. And the stars also were made, even according to my word, and I, God, set them in the firmament of the Heaven, to give light upon the Earth, and the sun to rule over the day, and the moon to rule over the night, and to divide the light from the darkness. And I, God, saw that all things which I had made were good. And the evening and the morning were the fourth day.

And I, God, said, Let the waters bring forth abundantly, the moving creature that hath life, and fowl which may fly above the Earth, in the open firmament of Heaven. And I, God, created great whales, and every living creature that moveth, which the waters brought forth abundantly, after their kind, and every winged fowl, after his kind. And I, God, saw that all things which I had created were good, and I, God, blessed them, saying, Be fruitful, and multiply, and fill the waters in the sea, and let fowl multiply in the Earth. And the evening and the morning were the fifth day.

And I, God, said, Let the Earth bring forth the living creature, after his kind, cattle and creeping things, and beasts of the Earth, after their kind, and it was so. And I, God, made the beasts of the Earth, after their kind, and cattle after their kind, and everything which creepeth upon the Earth, after his kind. And I, God, saw that all these things were good. And I, God, said unto mine Only Begotten, which was with me from the beginning, Let us make man in our image, after our likeness, and it was so. And I, God, said, Let them have dominion over the fishes of the sea, and over the fowl of the air, and over the cattle, and over all the Earth, and over every creeping thing that creepeth upon the Earth. And I, God, created man in mine own image, in the image of mine Only Begotten created I him, male and female created I them. And I, God, blessed them and said unto them, Be fruitful, and multiply, and replenish the Earth, and subdue it, and have dominion over the fish of the sea, and over the fowl of the air, and over every living thing that moveth upon the Earth. And I, God, said unto man, Behold, I have given you every herb, bearing seed, which is upon the face of all the Earth, and every tree in the which shall be the fruit of a tree, yielding seed, to you it shall be for meat. And to every beast of the Earth, and to every fowl of the air, and to everything that creepeth upon the Earth, wherein I grant life, there shall be given every clean herb for meat, and it was so, even as I spake. And I, God, saw everything that I had made, and behold, all things which I had made were very good. And the evening and the morning were the sixth day.

Thus the Heaven and the Earth were finished, and all the host of them. And on the seventh day, I, God, ended my work, and all things which I had made, and I rested on the seventh day from all my work, and all things which I had made were finished. And I, God, saw that they were good. And I, God, blessed the seventh day, and sanctified it, because that in it I had rested from all my work, which I, God, had created and made.

And now, behold, I say unto you, that these are the generations of the Heaven, and of the Earth, when they were created in the day that I the Lord God made the Heaven and the Earth, and every plant of the field before it was in the Earth, and every herb of the field before it grew, For I, the Lord God, created all things of which I have spoken spiritually, before they were naturally upon the face of the Earth, for I, the Lord God, had not caused it to rain upon the face of the Earth. And I, the Lord God, had created all the children of men, and not yet a man to till the ground, for in Heaven created I them, and there was not yet flesh upon the Earth, neither in the water, neither in the air, But I, the Lord God, spake, and there went up a mist from the Earth, and watered the whole face of the ground. And I, the Lord God, formed man from the dust of the ground, and breathed into Adam his spirit or the breath of life, and man became a living soul, the first flesh upon the Earth, the first man also, Nevertheless, all things were before created, but spiritually were they created and made, according to my word.

And I, the Lord God, planted a garden eastward in Eden, and there I put the man whom I had formed. And out of the ground, made I, the Lord God, to grow every tree naturally, that is pleasant to the sight of man, and man could behold it, and it became also a living soul, for it was spiritual in the day that I created it, for it remaineth in the sphere in which I, God, created it, yea, even all things which I prepared for the use of man, and man saw that it was good for food. And I, the Lord God, planted the tree of life also, in the midst of the garden, and also the tree of knowledge of good and evil. And I, the Lord God, caused a river to go out of Eden, to water the garden, and from thence it was parted, and became into four heads. And I, the Lord God, called the name of the first Pison, and it compasseth the whole land of Havilah, where I, the Lord, created much gold, and the gold of that land was good, and there was bdellium, and the onyx stone. And the name of the second river was called Gihon, the same that compasseth the whole land of Ethiopia. And the name of the third river was Hiddekel, that which goeth toward the east of Assyria. And the fourth river was Euphrates.

And I, the Lord God, took the man, and put him into the garden of Eden, to dress it, and to keep it. And I, the Lord God, commanded the man, saying, Of every tree of the garden thou mayest freely eat, but of the tree of the knowledge of good and evil, thou shalt not eat of it. Nevertheless, thou mayest choose for thyself, for it is given unto thee, but remember that I forbid it, for in the day thou eatest thereof thou shalt surely die. And I, the Lord God, said unto mine Only Begotten, that it was not good that the man should be alone, Wherefore, I will make an help meet for him. And out of the ground, I the Lord God, formed every beast of the field, and every fowl of the air, and commanded that they should come unto Adam, to see what he would call them. And they were also living souls, for

I, God, breathed into them the breath of life, and commanded that whatsoever Adam called every living creature, that should be the name thereof. And Adam gave names to all cattle, and to the fowl of the air, and to every beast of the field, but as for Adam, there was not found an help meet for him.

And I, the Lord God, caused a deep sleep to fall upon Adam, and he slept, and I took one of his ribs, and closed up the flesh in the stead thereof, and the rib, which I, the Lord God had taken from man, made I a woman, and brought her unto the man. And Adam said, This I know now is bone of my bones, and flesh of my flesh. She shall be called woman, because she was taken out of man. Therefore shall a man leave his father and his mother, and shall cleave unto his wife, and they shall be one flesh. And they were both naked, the man and his wife, and were not ashamed.

And I, the Lord God, spake unto Moses, saying, That Satan whom thou hast commanded in the name of mine Only Begotten, is the same which was from the beginning, And he came before me, saying, Behold I, send me, I will be thy Son, and I will redeem all mankind, that one soul shall not be lost, and surely I will do it, wherefore, give me thine honor. But behold, my beloved Son, which was my beloved and chosen from the beginning, said unto me: Father, thy will be done, and the glory be thine forever. Wherefore, because that Satan rebelled against me, and sought to destroy the agency of man, which I, the Lord God, had given him, and also that I should give unto him mine own power, by the power of mine Only Begotten I caused that he should be cast down, and he became Satan. Yea, even the devil, the father of all lies, to deceive, and to blind men, and to lead them captive at his will, even as many as would not hearken unto my voice.

And now, the serpent was more subtle than any beast of the field, which I, the Lord God, had made. And Satan put it into the heart of the serpent, for he had drawn away many after him, and he sought also to beguile Eve, for he knew not the mind of God, wherefore, he sought to destroy the world. And he said unto the woman, Yea, hath God said, Ye shall not eat of every tree of the garden. And he spake by the mouth of the serpent. And the woman said unto the serpent, We may eat of the fruit of the trees of the garden, but of the fruit of the tree which thou beholdest in the midst of the garden, God hath said, Ye shall not eat of it, neither shall ye touch it, lest ye die. And the serpent said unto the woman, Ye shall not surely die, for God doth know, that in the day ye eat thereof, then your eyes shall be opened, and ye shall be as gods, knowing good and evil. And when the woman saw that the tree was good for food, and that it became pleasant to the eyes, and a tree to be desired to make her wise, she took of the fruit thereof, and did eat, and gave also unto her husband with her, and he did eat. And the eyes of them both were opened, and they knew that they had been naked, and they sewed fig leaves together, and made themselves aprons. And they heard the voice of the Lord God, as they were walking in the garden, in the cool of the day. And Adam and his wife went to hide themselves from the presence of the Lord God, amongst the trees of the garden. And I, the Lord God, called unto Adam, and said unto him, Where goest thou? And he said, I heard thy voice, in the garden, and I was afraid, because I beheld that I was naked, and I hid myself. And I, the Lord God, said unto Adam, Who told thee that thou wast naked? Hast thou eaten of the tree whereof I commanded thee that thou shouldst not eat, if so thou shouldst surely die? And the man said, The woman whom thou gavest me, and commanded that she should remain with me, she gave me of the fruit of the tree, and I did eat. And I, the Lord God, said unto the woman, What is this thing which thou hast done? And the woman said, The serpent beguiled me, and I did eat.

And I, the Lord God, said unto the serpent, Because thou hast done this, thou shalt be cursed above all cattle, and above every beast of the field, upon thy belly shalt thou go, and dust shalt thou eat all the days of thy life, And I will put enmity between thee and the woman, between thy seed and her seed, and he shall bruise thy head, and thou shalt bruise his heel. Unto the woman, I, the Lord God, said, I will greatly multiply thy sorrow, and thy conception, in sorrow thou shalt bring forth children, and thy desire shall be to thy husband, and he shall rule over thee. And unto Adam, I, the Lord God, said, Because thou hast hearkened unto the voice of thy wife, and hast eaten of the fruit of the tree, of which I commanded thee, saying, Thou shalt not eat of it, cursed shall be the ground for thy sake, in sorrow shalt thou eat of it all the days of thy life, Thorns also and thistles shall it bring forth to thee, and thou shalt eat the herb of the field, By the sweat of thy face shalt thou eat bread, until thou shalt return unto the ground, for thou shalt surely die, for out of it wast thou taken, for dust thou wast, and unto dust shalt thou return. And Adam called his wife's name Eve, because she was the mother of all living, for thus have I, the Lord God, called the first of all women, which are many. Unto Adam, and also unto his wife, did I, the Lord God, make coats of skins, and clothed them.

And I, the Lord God, said unto mine Only Begotten, Behold, the man is become as one of us, to know good and evil, and now, lest he put forth his hand, and partake also of the tree of life, and eat, and live forever, Therefore, I, the Lord God, will send him forth from the garden of Eden, to till the ground from whence he was taken, For, as I, the Lord God, liveth, even so my words cannot return void, for, as they go forth out of my mouth, they must be fulfilled. So I drove out the man, and I placed at the east of the garden of Eden, cherubim, and a flaming sword, which turned every way, to keep the way of the tree of life. (And these are the words which I spake unto my servant Moses. And they are true, even as I will. And I have spoken them unto you. See thou show them unto no man, until I command you, except they that believe.) Amen.

3 AND it came to pass, that after I, the Lord God, had driven them out, that Adam began to till the Earth, and to have dominion over all the beasts of the field, and to eat his bread by the sweat of his brow, as I, the Lord had commanded him, and Eve also, his wife, did labor with him. And Adam knew his wife, and she bare unto him sons and daughters, and they began to multiply, and to replenish the Earth. And from that time forth, the sons and daughters of Adam began to divide, two and two, in the land, and to till the land, and to tend flocks, and they also begat sons and daughters.

And Adam called upon the name of the Lord, and Eve also, his wife, and they heard the voice of the Lord, from the way towards the garden of Eden, speaking unto them, and they saw him not, for they were shut out from his presence. And he gave unto them commandments, that they should worship the Lord their God, and should offer the firstlings of their flocks for an offering unto the Lord. And Adam was obedient unto the commandments of the Lord.

And after many days, an Angel of the Lord appeared unto Adam, saying, Why dost thou offer sacrifices unto the Lord? And Adam said unto him, I know not, save the Lord commanded me. And then the angel spake, saying, This thing is a similitude of the sacrifice of the Only Begotten of the Father, which is full of grace and truth, Wherefore, thou shalt do all that thou doest, in the name of the Son. And thou shalt repent, and call upon God, in the name of the Son for evermore.

And in that day, the Holy Ghost fell upon Adam, which beareth record of the Father and the Son, saying, I am the Only Begotten of the Father from the beginning, henceforth and forever, that, as thou hast fallen, thou mayest be redeemed, and all mankind, even as many as will. And in that day Adam blessed

God, and was filled, and began to prophesy concerning all the families of the Earth, saying, Blessed be the name of God, for, because of my transgression my eyes are opened, and in this life I shall have joy, and again, in the flesh I shall see God. And Eve, his wife, heard all these things and was glad, saying, Were it not for our transgression, we should never had seed, and should never had known good and evil, and the joy of our redemption, and the Eternal life which God giveth unto all the obedient. And Adam and Eve blessed the name of God, and they made all things known unto their sons and their daughters.

And Satan came among them, saying, I am also a son of God, and he commanded them, saying, Believe it not. And they believed it not, and they loved Satan more than God. And men began from that time forth to be carnal, sensual and devilish. And the Lord God called upon men, by the Holy Ghost, everywhere, and commanded them that they should repent, And as many as believed in the Son, and repented of their sins, should be saved. And as many as believed not, and repented not, should be damned. And the words went forth out of the mouth of God, in a firm decree, wherefore they must be fulfilled. And Adam ceased not to call upon God, and Eve also his wife.

And Adam knew Eve his wife, and she conceived and bare Cain, and said, I have gotten a man from the Lord, wherefore he may not reject his words. But, behold, also Cain hearkened not saying, Who is the Lord, that I should know him? And she again conceived, and bare his brother Abel. And Abel hearkened unto the voice of the Lord. And Abel was a keeper of sheep, but Cain was a tiller of the ground. And Cain loved Satan more than God. And Satan commanded him, saying, Make an offering unto the Lord. And in process of time it came to pass, that Cain brought of the fruit of the ground an offering unto the Lord. And Abel, he also brought, of the firstlings of his flock, and of the fat thereof, and the Lord had respect unto Abel, and to his offering, but unto Cain, and to his offering, he had not respect. Now Satan knew this, and it pleased him. And Cain was very wroth, and his countenance fell. And the Lord said unto Cain, Why art thou wroth? Why is thy countenance fallen? If thou doest well thou shalt be accepted, and if thou doest not well, sin lieth at the door, and Satan desireth to have thee, and except thou shalt hearken unto my commandments, I will deliver thee up, and it shall be unto thee according to his desire, and thou shalt rule over him, for from this time forth thou shalt be the father of his lies. Thou shalt be called Perdition, for thou wast also before the world, and it shall be said in time to come, that these abominations were had from Cain, for he rejected the greater counsel, which was had from God, and this is a cursing which I will put upon thee, except thou repent. And Cain was wroth, and listened not any more to the voice of the Lord, neither to Abel his brother, who walked in holiness before the Lord. And Adam also, and his wife, mourned before the Lord, because of Cain and his brethren. And it came to pass, that Cain took one of his brother's daughters to wife, and they loved Satan more than God. And Satan said unto Cain, Swear unto me by thy throat, and if thou tell it thou shalt die, and swear thy brethren by their heads, and by the living God, that they tell it not, for if they tell it they shall surely die, and this that thy father may not know it, and this day I will deliver thy brother Abel into thine hands. And Satan swear unto Cain, that he would do according to his commands. And all these things were done in secret. And Cain said, Truly I am Mahan, the master of this great secret, that I may murder and get gain. Wherefore Cain was called Master Mahan, and he gloried in his wickedness. And Cain went into the field, and Cain talked with Abel his brother, and it came to pass, that while they were in the field, Cain rose up against Abel his brother, and slew him. And Cain gloried in that which he had done, saying, I am free, surely the flocks of my brother falleth into my hands. And the Lord said unto Cain,

Where is Abel, thy brother? And he said, I know not, am I my brother's keeper? And the Lord said, What hast thou done? The voice of thy brother's blood cries unto me from the ground. And now, thou shalt be cursed from the Earth, which hath opened her mouth to receive thy brother's blood from thy hand. When thou tillest the ground, it shall not henceforth yield unto thee her strength, a fugitive and a vagabond shalt thou be in the Earth. And Cain said unto the Lord, Satan tempted me, because of my brother's flock, and I was wroth also, for his offering thou didst accept, and not mine. My punishment is greater than I can bear. Behold, thou hast driven me out this day from the face of the Lord, and from thy face shall I be hid, and I shall be a fugitive and a vagabond in the Earth, and it shall come to pass, that he that findeth me shall slay me, because of mine iniquities, for these things are not hid from the Lord. And I, the Lord, said unto him, Whosoever slayeth thee, vengeance shall be taken on him sevenfold, and I, the Lord, set a mark upon Cain, lest any finding him should kill him.

And Cain was shut out from the presence of the Lord, and with his wife and many of his brethren, dwelt in the land of Nod, on the east of Eden. And Cain knew his wife, and she conceived and bare Enoch, and he also begat many sons and daughters. And he builded a city, and he called the name of the city after the name of his son Enoch. And unto Enoch was born Irad, and other sons and daughters, and Irad begat Mehujael, and other sons and daughters. And Mehujael begat Methusael, and other sons and daughters. And Methusael begat Lamech. And Lamech took unto himself two wives, the name of one being Adah, and the name of the other, Zillah. And Adah bare Jabal, he was the father of such as dwell in tents, and they were keepers of cattle, and his brother's name was Jubal, who was the father of all such as handle the harp and organ. And Zillah, she also bare Tubal Cain, an instructor of every artificer in brass and iron, and the sister of Tubal Cain was called Naamah. And Lamech said unto his wives, Adah and Zillah, Hear my voice, ye wives of Lamech, hearken unto my speech, for I have slain a man to my wounding, and a young man to my hurt. If Cain shall be avenged sevenfold, truly Lamech shall be seventy and sevenfold. For, Lamech having entered into a covenant with Satan, after the manner of Cain, wherein he became Master Mahan, master of that great secret which was administered unto Cain by Satan. And Irad, the son of Enoch, having known their secret, began to reveal it unto the sons of Adam, wherefore, Lamech, being angry, slew him, not like unto Cain his brother Abel for the sake of getting gain, but he slew him for the oath's sake, For, from the days of Cain, there was a secret combination, and their works were in the dark, and they knew every man his brother. Wherefore the Lord cursed Lamech and his house, and all they that had covenanted with Satan, for they kept not the commandments of God. And it displeased God, and he ministered not unto them. And their works were abominations, and began to spread among all the sons of men. And it was among the sons of men. And among the daughters of men, these things were not spoken, because that Lamech had spoken the secret unto his wives, and they rebelled against him, and declared these things abroad, and had not compassion. Wherefore Lamech was despised, and cast out, and came not among the sons of men, lest he should die. And thus the works of darkness began to prevail among all the sons of men.

And God cursed the Earth with a sore curse, and was angry with the wicked, with all the sons of men whom he had made, for they would not hearken unto his voice, nor believe on his Only Begotten Son, even him whom he declared should come in the meridian of time, who was prepared from before the foundation of the world. And thus the gospel began to be preached from the beginning, being declared by holy angels, sent forth from the presence of God, and by his own voice, and by the gift of the Holy Ghost. And thus all things were confirmed unto

Adam by an holy ordinance, and the gospel preached, and a decree sent forth that it should be in the world until the end thereof, and thus it was. Amen.

And Adam hearkened unto the voice of God, and called upon his sons to repent. And Adam knew his wife again, and she bare a son, and he called his name Seth. And Adam glorified the name of God, for he said, God hath appointed me another seed instead of Abel whom Cain slew. And God revealed himself unto Seth, and he rebelled not, but offered an acceptable sacrifice like unto his brother Abel. And to him also was born a son, and he called his name Enos. And then began these men to call upon the name of the Lord, and the Lord blessed them, and a book of remembrance was kept in the which was recorded in the language of Adam, for it was given unto as many as called upon God, to write by the Spirit of inspiration, And by them their children were taught to read and write, having a language which was pure and undefiled. Now this same priesthood which was in the beginning, shall be in the end of the world also. Now this prophecy Adam spake, as he was moved upon by the Holy Ghost. And a genealogy was kept of the children of God. And this was the book of the generations of Adam, saying, In the day that God created man, (in the likeness of God made he him,) in the image of his own body, male and female created he them, and blessed them, and called their name Adam, in the day when they were created, and became living souls, in the land, upon the footstool of God.

And Adam lived one hundred and thirty years, and begat a son in his own likeness, after his own image, and called his name Seth. And the days of Adam, after he had begotten Seth, were eight hundred and seventy years. And he begat many sons and daughters. And all the days that Adam lived were one thousand years, and he died.

Seth lived one hundred and five years, and begat Enos, and prophesied in all his days, and taught his son Enos in the ways of God. Wherefore Enos prophesied also. And Seth lived after he begat Enos, eight hundred and seven years, and begat many sons and daughters.

And the children of men were numerous upon all the face of the land. And in those days, Satan had great dominion among men, and raged in their hearts, and from thenceforth came wars and bloodshed. And a man's hand was against his own brother in administering death, because of secret works, seeking for power. And all the days of Seth were nine hundred and twelve years, and he died.

And Enos lived ninety years, and begat Cainan. And Enos, and the residue of the people of God, came out from the land which was called Shulon, and dwelt in a land of promise, which he called after his own son, whom he had named Cainan. And Enos lived, after he begat Cainan, eight hundred and fifteen years, and begat many sons and daughters. And all the days of Enos were nine hundred and five years, and he died.

And Cainan lived seventy years, and begat Mahalaleel. And Cainan lived after he begat Mahalaleel, eight hundred and forty years, and begat sons and daughters. And all the days of Cainan were nine hundred and ten years, and he died.

And Mahalaleel lived sixty-five years, and begat Jared. And Mahalaleel lived after he begat Jared, eight hundred and thirty years, and begat sons and daughters. And all the days of Mahalaleel were eight hundred and ninety-five years, and he died.

And Jared lived one hundred and sixty-two years, and begat Enoch. And Jared lived, after he begat Enoch, eight hundred years, and begat sons and daughters. And Jared taught Enoch in all the ways of God.

And this is the genealogy of the sons of Adam, who was the son of God, with whom God himself conversed. And they were preachers of righteousness, and spake and prophesied, and called upon all men everywhere to repent. And faith was taught unto the children of men.

And it came to pass, that all the days of Jared were nine hundred and sixty-two years, and he died.

And Enoch lived sixty-five years, and begat Methuselah.

4 AND it came to pass that Enoch journeyed in the land, among the people, and as he journeyed the Spirit of God descended out of Heaven, and abode upon him, And he heard a voice from Heaven, saying, Enoch, my son, prophesy unto this people, and say unto them, Repent, for thus saith the Lord, I am angry with this people, and my fierce anger is kindled against them, for their hearts have waxed hard, and their ears are dull of hearing, and their eyes cannot see afar off. And for these many generations, even since the day that I created them, have they gone astray, and have denied me, and have sought their own counsels in the dark, and in their own abominations have they devised murder, and have not kept the commandments which I gave unto their father Adam. Wherefore, they have forsworn themselves, and by their oaths they have brought upon themselves death. And an hell I have prepared for them, if they repent not, And this is a decree which I have sent forth in the beginning of the world, from mine own mouth, from the foundation thereof, and by the mouths of my servants, thy fathers, have I decreed it, even as it shall be sent forth in the world, unto the end thereof.

And when Enoch had heard these words, he bowed himself to the earth, before the Lord, and spake before the Lord, saying, Why is it that I have found favor in thy sight, and am but a lad, and all the people hate me, for I am slow of speech, wherefore am I thy servant? And the Lord said unto Enoch, Go forth, and do as I have commanded thee, and no man shall pierce thee. Open thy mouth, and it shall be filled, and I will give thee utterance, for all flesh is in my hands, and I will do as seemeth me good. Say unto this people, choose ye this day to serve the Lord God who made you. Behold, my Spirit is upon you, wherefore all thy words will I justify, and the mountains shall flee before you, and the rivers shall turn from their course, and thou shalt abide in me, and I in you, therefore walk with me.

And the Lord spake unto Enoch, and said unto him, Anoint thine eyes with clay, and wash them, and thou shalt see, and he did so. And he beheld the spirits that God had created, and he beheld also things which were not visible to the natural eye, and from thenceforth came the saying abroad in the land, A seer hath the Lord raised up unto his people.

And it came to pass, that Enoch went forth in the land, among the people, standing upon the hills, and the high places, and cried with a loud voice, testifying against their works. And all men were offended because of him, and they came forth to hear him upon the high places, saying unto the tent-keepers, Tarry ye here and keep the tents while we go yonder to behold the seer, for he prophesieth, and there is a strange thing in the land, a wild man hath come among us. And it came to pass when they heard him, no man laid hands on him, for fear came on them all that heard him, for he walked with God.

And there came a man unto him, whose name was Mahijah, and said unto him, Tell us plainly who thou art, and from whence thou comest. And he said unto them, I came out from the land of Cainan, the land of my fathers, a land of righteousness unto this day, and my father taught me in all the ways of God. And it came to pass, as I journeyed from the land of Cainan by the sea east, I beheld a vision, and lo, the heavens I saw, and the Lord spake with me, and gave me commandment, wherefore for this cause, to keep the commandment, I speak forth these words. And Enoch continued his speech, saying, The Lord which spake with me, the same is the God of Heaven, and he is my God and your God, and ye are my brethren, and why counsel ye yourselves, and deny the God of Heaven? The heavens he made, the Earth is his footstool, and the foundation thereof is his, behold, he laid it, and hosts of men hath he brought in upon the face thereof. And death hath come upon our fathers, nevertheless, we know them, and cannot deny, and even the first of all we know, even Adam, for a book of remembrance we have written among us, according to the pattern given by the finger of God, and it is given in our own language.

And as Enoch spake forth the words of God, the people trembled and could not stand in his presence.

And he said unto them, Because that Adam fell, we are, and by his fall came death, and we are made partakers of misery and woe. Behold, Satan hath come among the children of men, and tempteth them to worship him, and men have become carnal, sensual, and devilish, and are shut out from the presence of God. But God hath made known unto our fathers, that all men must repent. And he called upon our father Adam, by his own voice, saying, I am God, I made the world, and men before they were in the flesh. And he also said unto him, If thou wilt, turn unto me and hearken unto my voice, and believe, and repent of all thy transgressions, and be baptized, even in water, in the name of mine Only Begotten Son, who is full of grace and truth, which is Jesus Christ, the only name which shall be given under Heaven, whereby salvation shall come unto the children of men, and ye shall receive the gift of the Holy Ghost, asking all things in his name, and whatsoever ye shall ask it shall be given you. And our father Adam spake unto the Lord, and said, Why is it that men must repent, and be baptized in water? And the Lord said unto Adam, Behold, I have forgiven thee thy transgression in the garden of Eden. Hence came the saying abroad among the people, that the Son of God hath atoned for original guilt, wherein the sins of the parents cannot be answered upon the heads of the children, for they are whole from the foundation of the world. And the Lord spake unto Adam, saying, Inasmuch as thy children are conceived in sin, even so, when they begin to grow up sin conceiveth in their hearts, and they taste the bitter, that they may know to prize the good. And it is given unto them to know good from evil, wherefore, they are agents unto themselves. And I have given unto you another law and commandment, wherefore teach it unto your children, that all men, everywhere, must repent, or they can in no wise inherit the kingdom of God. For no unclean thing can dwell there, or dwell in his presence, for, in the language of Adam, Man of Holiness is his name, and the name of his Only Begotten is the son of Man, even Jesus Christ, a righteous judge, who shall come in the meridian of time. Therefore I give unto you a commandment, to teach these things freely unto your children, saying, that by reason of transgression cometh the fall, which fall bringeth death, and inasmuch as ye were born into the world by water and blood, and the spirit, which I have made, and so become of dust a living soul, Even so ye must be born again, into the kingdom of Heaven, of water, and of the Spirit, and be cleansed by blood, even the blood of mine Only Begotten, that ye may be sanctified from all sin, and enjoy the words of Eternal life in this world, and Eternal life in the world to come, even immortal glory. For, by the water ye keep the commandment, by the Spirit ye are justified, and by the blood ye are sanctified. Therefore it is given to abide in you, the record of Heaven, the Comforter, the peaceable things of immortal glory, the truth of all things, that which quickeneth all things which maketh alive all things, that which knoweth all things, and hath all power according to wisdom, mercy, truth, justice and judgment. And now, behold, I say unto you, This is the plan of salvation unto all men, through the blood of mine Only Begotten, who shall come in the meridian of time. And, behold, all things have their likeness, and all things are created and made to bear record of me, both things which are temporal, and things which are spiritual, things which are in the heavens above, and things which are on the Earth, and things which are in the Earth, and things which are under the Earth, both above and beneath, all things bear record of me. And it came to pass, when the Lord had spoken with Adam our father, that Adam cried unto the Lord, and he was caught away by the Spirit of the Lord, and was carried down into the water, and was laid under the water, and was brought forth out of the water, and thus he was baptized. And the Spirit of God descended upon him, and thus he was born of the Spirit, and became quickened in the inner man. And he heard a voice out of Heaven, saying, Thou art baptized with fire and with the Holy Ghost, this is the record of the Father and the Son, from henceforth and forever, And thou art after the order of him who was without beginning of days or end of years, from all eternity to all eternity. Behold, thou art one in me, a son of God, and thus may all become my sons. Amen.

And it came to pass, that Enoch continued his speech, saying, Behold, our father Adam taught these things, and many have believed, and become the sons of God, and many have believed not, and have perished in their sins, and are looking forth with fear, in torment, for the fiery indignation of the wrath of God to be poured out upon them.

And from that time forth, Enoch began to prophesy, saying unto the people, that, as I was journeying, and stood in the place Mahujah, and cried unto the Lord, there came a voice out of Heaven, saying, Turn ye and get ye upon the mount Simeon. And it came to pass, that I turned and went up on the mount, and as I stood upon the mount, I beheld the heavens open, and I was clothed upon with glory. And I saw the Lord, and he stood before my face, and he talked with me, even as a man talketh one with another, face to face, and he said unto me, Look, and I will show unto thee the world for the space of many generations. And it came to pass, that I beheld in the valley of Shum, and, lo! a great people which dwelt in tents, which were the people of Shum. And again the Lord said unto me, Look, and I looked towards the north, and I beheld the people of Canaan, which dwelt in tents. And the Lord said unto me, Prophesy, and I prophesied saying, Behold, the people of Cainan which are numerous, shall go forth in battle array against the people of Shum, and shall slay them, that they shall be utterly destroyed. And the people of Canaan shall divide themselves in the land, and the land shall be barren and unfruitful, and none other people shall dwell there, but the people of Canaan, for, behold, the Lord shall curse the land with much heat, and the barrenness thereof shall go forth forever. And there was a blackness came upon all the children of Canaan, that they were despised among all people. And it came to pass, that the Lord said unto me, Look, and I looked, and I beheld the land of Sharon, and the land of Enoch, and the land of Omner, and the land of Heni, and the land of Shem, and the land of Haner, and the land of Hanannihah, and all the inhabitants thereof. And the Lord said unto me, Go forth to this people, and say unto them, Repent, lest I come out and smite them with a curse, and they die. And he gave unto me a commandment, that I should baptize in the name of the Father, and of the Son, who is full of grace and truth, and the Holy Ghost which beareth record of the Father and the Son.

And it came to pass, that Enoch continued to call upon all the people, save it were the people of Canaan, to repent. And so great was the faith of Enoch, that he led the people of God, and their enemies came to battle against them, and he spake the word of the Lord, and the Earth trembled, and the mountains fled, even according to his command. And the rivers of water were turned out of their course, and the roar of the lions was heard out of the wilderness. And all nations feared greatly, so powerful was the word of Enoch, and so great was the power of the language which God had given him. There also came up a land out of the depths of the sea, and so great was the fear of the enemies of the people of God, that they fled and stood afar off, and went upon the land which came up out of the depths of the sea. And the giants of the land also stood afar off, and there went forth a curse upon all the people which fought against God.

And from that time forth, there were wars, and bloodshed among them, but the Lord came and dwelt with his people, and they dwelt in righteousness. And the fear of the Lord was upon all nations, so great was the glory of the Lord which was upon his people. And the Lord blessed the land, and they were blessed upon the mountains, and upon the high places, and did flourish. And the Lord called his people, Zion, because they were of one heart and of one mind, and dwelt in righteousness, and there were no poor among them. And Enoch continued his preaching in righteousness unto the people of God. And it came to pass in his days, that he built a city that was called the city of Holiness, even Zion.

And it came to pass, that Enoch talked with the Lord, and he said unto the Lord, Surely, Zion shall dwell in safety forever. But the Lord said unto Enoch, Zion have I blessed, but the residue of the people have I cursed. And it came to pass, that the Lord showed unto Enoch all the inhabitants of the Earth, and he beheld, and lo! Zion in process of time was taken up into Heaven. And the Lord said unto Enoch, Behold mine abode forever. And Enoch also beheld the residue of the people which were the sons of Adam, and they were a mixture of all the seed of Adam, save it were the seed of Cain, for the seed of Cain were black, and had not place among them. And after that Zion was taken up into Heaven, Enoch beheld, and lo, all the nations of the Earth were before him, and there came generation upon generation. And Enoch was high and lifted up, even in the bosom of the Father and the Son of Man, and, behold, the powers of Satan were upon all the face of the Earth, and he saw angels descending out of Heaven, and he heard a loud voice, saying, Woe! woe! be unto the inhabitants of the Earth! And he beheld Satan, and he had a great chain in his hand, and it veiled the whole face of the Earth with darkness, and he looked up and laughed, and his angels rejoiced. And Enoch beheld angels descending out of Heaven, bearing testimony of the Father, and of the Son. And the Holy Ghost fell on many, and they were caught up by the powers of Heaven into Zion.

And it came to pass, Enoch looked upon the residue of the people, and wept, and he beheld and lo, the heavens wept also, and shed forth their tears as the rain upon the mountains? And Enoch said unto the Lord, How is it that thou canst weep, seeing thou art holy, and from all eternity to all eternity? And were it possible that man could number the particles of the Earth, yea, and millions of Earths like this, it would not be a beginning to the number of thy creations, And thy curtains are stretched out still, and thou art there, and thy presence is there, and also, thou art just, thou art merciful and kind forever, Thou hast taken Zion to thine own bosom, from all thy creations, from all eternity to all eternity, and naught but peace, justice, and truth is the habitation of thy throne, and mercy shall go before thy face and have no end. How is it that thou canst weep?

The Lord said unto Enoch, Behold, these thy brethren, they are the workmanship of mine own hands, and I gave unto them their intelligence. And in the garden of Eden man had agency, and unto thy brethren have I said, and also gave commandment, that they should love one another, and that they should serve me, their God. But, behold, they are without affection, and they hate their own blood, and the fire of mine indignation is kindled against them, and in my hot displeasure will I send in the floods upon them, for my fierce anger is kindled against them. Behold, I am God, Man of Holiness is my name, Man of Counsel is my name, and Endless and Eternal is my name also. Wherefore I can stretch forth my hands and hold all the creations which I have made, and mine eye can pierce them also. And among all the workmanship of my hands there has not been so great wickedness as among thy brethren, but, behold, their sins shall be upon the heads of their fathers, Satan shall be their father, and misery shall be their doom, and the whole heavens shall weep over them, even all the workmanship of my hands. Wherefore should not the heavens weep, seeing these shall suffer? But, behold, these which thine eyes are upon shall perish in the floods, and, behold, I will shut them up, a prison have I prepared for them, and he whom I have chosen hath pleaded before my face, Wherefore he suffereth for their sins, inasmuch as they will repent, in the day that my chosen shall return unto me, and until that day they shall be in torment. Wherefore for this shall the heavens weep, yea, and all the workmanship of my hands. And it came to pass, that the Lord spake unto Enoch, and told Enoch all the doings of the children of men. Wherefore Enoch knew and looked upon their wickedness, and their misery, and wept, and stretched forth his arms, and he beheld eternity, and his bowels yearned, and all eternity shook. And Enoch saw Noah also, and his family, that the posterity of all the sons of Noah should be saved with a temporal salvation. Wherefore Enoch saw that Noah built an ark, and the Lord smiled upon it, and held it in his own hand, but upon the residue of the wicked came the floods and swallowed them up.

And as Enoch saw thus, he had bitterness of soul, and wept over his brethren, and said unto the heavens, I will refuse to be comforted. But the Lord said unto Enoch, Lift up your heart and be glad, and look. And it came to pass, that Enoch looked, and from Noah he beheld all the families of the Earth, and he cried unto the Lord, saying, When shall the day of the Lord come? When shall the blood of the righteous be shed, that all they that mourn may be sanctified, and have Eternal life? And the Lord said, It shall be in the meridian of time, in the days of wickedness and vengeance. And, behold, Enoch saw the day of the coming of the Son of Man, even in the flesh, and his soul rejoiced, saying, The righteous is lifted up, and the Lamb is slain from the foundation of the world, and through faith I am in the bosom of the Father, and behold, Zion is with me!

And it came to pass, that Enoch looked upon the Earth, and he heard a voice from the bowels thereof, saying, Woe! woe! is me, the mother of men! I am pained, I am weary, because of the wickedness of my children! When shall I rest, and be cleansed from the filthiness which has gone forth out of me? When will my Creator sanctify me, that I may rest, and righteousness for a season abide upon my face? And when Enoch heard the Earth mourn, he wept, and cried unto the Lord, saying, O Lord, wilt thou not have compassion upon the Earth? wilt thou not bless the children of Noah? And it came to pass, that Enoch continued his cry unto the Lord, saying, I ask thee, O Lord, in the name of thine Only Begotten, even Jesus Christ, that thou wilt have mercy upon Noah, and his seed, that the Earth might never more be covered by the floods. And the Lord could not withhold, and he covenanted with Enoch, and sware unto him with an oath, that he would stay the floods, that he would call upon the children of Noah, and he sent forth an unalterable decree, that a remnant of his seed should always be found among all nations, while the Earth should stand. And the Lord said, Blessed is he through whose seed Messiah shall come, for he saith, I am Messiah, the King of Zion, the Rock of Heaven, which is broad as eternity, and whoso cometh in at the gate, and climbeth up by me shall never fall. Wherefore blessed are they of whom I have spoken, for they shall come forth with songs of everlasting joy.

And it came to pass, that Enoch cried unto the Lord, saying, When the Son of Man cometh in the flesh shall the Earth rest? I pray thee show me these things. And the Lord said unto Enoch, Look, and he looked, and beheld the Son of Man lifted up on the cross, after the manner of men. And he heard a loud voice, and the heavens were veiled, and all the creations of God mourned, and the Earth groaned, and the rocks were rent, and the saints arose, and were crowned at the right hand of the Son of Man, with crowns of glory. And as many of the spirits as were in prison came forth and stood on the right hand of God. And the remainder were reserved in chains of darkness until the judgment of the great day.

And again Enoch wept, and cried unto the Lord, saying, When shall the Earth rest? And Enoch beheld the Son of Man ascend up unto the Father, and he called unto the Lord, saying, Wilt thou not come again upon the Earth? for inasmuch as thou art God, and I know thee, and thou hast sworn unto me, and commanded me that I should ask in the name of thine Only Begotten, thou hast made me, and given unto me a right to thy throne, and not of myself, but through thine own grace, and wherefore I ask thee if thou wilt not come again on the Earth? And the Lord said unto Enoch, As I live, even so will I come in the last days, in the days of wickedness and vengeance, to fulfill the oath which I made unto you concerning the children of Noah. And the day shall come that the Earth shall rest. But before that day the heavens shall be darkened, and a veil of darkness shall cover the Earth, and the heavens shall shake, and also the Earth. And great tribulations shall be among the children of men, but my people will I preserve, and righteousness will I send down out of Heaven, and truth will I send forth out of the Earth, to bear testimony of mine Only Begotten, his resurrection from the dead, yea, and also the resurrection of all men. And righteousness and truth will I cause to sweep the Earth as with a flood, to gather out mine own elect from the four quarters of the Earth, unto a place which I shall prepare, an holy city, that my people may gird up their loins, and be looking forth for the time of my coming, for there shall be my tabernacle, and it shall be called Zion, a New Jerusalem. And the Lord said unto Enoch, Then shalt thou and all thy city meet them there, and we will receive them into our bosom, and they shall see us, and we will fall upon their necks, and they shall fall upon our necks, and we will kiss each other, And there shall be mine abode, and it shall be Zion, which shall come forth out of all the creations which I have made, and for the space of a thousand years shall the Earth rest.

And it came to pass, that Enoch saw the day of the coming of the Son of Man, in the last days, to dwell on the Earth, in righteousness, for the space of a thousand years. But before that day, he saw great tribulation among the wicked, and he also saw the sea, that it was troubled, and men's hearts failing them, looking forth with fear for the judgment of the Almighty God, which should come upon the wicked. And the Lord showed Enoch all things, even unto the end of the world. And he saw the day of the righteous, the hour of their redemption, and received a fullness of joy. And all the days of Zion, in the days of Enoch, were three hundred and sixty-five years. And Enoch and all his people walked with God, and he dwelt in the midst of Zion. And it came to pass, that Zion was not, for God received it up into his own bosom, and from thence went forth the saying, Zion is fled. And all the days of Enoch were four hundred and thirty years.

5 AND it came to pass, that Methuselah, the son of Enoch, was not taken, that the covenants of the Lord might be fulfilled which he made to Enoch, for he truly covenanted with Enoch, that Noah should be of the fruit of his loins. And it came to pass, that Methuselah prophesied that from his loins should spring all the kingdoms of the Earth, (through Noah,) and he took glory unto himself.

And there came forth a great famine into the land, and the Lord cursed the Earth with a sore curse, and many of the inhabitants thereof died.

And it came to pass, that Methuselah lived one hundred and eighty-seven years, and begat Lamech, and Methuselah lived after he begat Lamech, seven hundred and eighty-two years, and begat sons and daughters. And all the days of Methuselah were nine hundred and sixty-nine years, and he died.

And Lamech lived one hundred and eighty-two years, and begat a son, and he called his name Noah, saying, This son shall comfort us concerning our work, and toil of our hands, because of the ground which the Lord hath cursed. And Lamech lived after he begat Noah, five hundred and ninety-five years, and begat sons and daughters. And all the days of Lamech were seven hundred and seventy-seven years, and he died.

And Noah was four hundred and fifty years old, and begat Japheth, and forty-two years afterwards, he begat Shem, of her who was the mother of Japheth, and when he was five hundred years old, he begat Ham. And Noah and his sons hearkened unto the Lord, and gave heed, and they were called the sons of God.

And when these men began to multiply on the face of the Earth, and daughters were born unto them, the sons of men saw that their daughters were fair, and they took them wives even as they chose. And the Lord said unto Noah, The daughters of thy sons have sold themselves, for behold, mine anger is kindled against the sons of men, for they will not hearken to my voice. And it came to pass, that Noah prophesied, and taught the things of God, even as it was in the beginning.

And the Lord said unto Noah, My Spirit shall not always strive with man, for he shall know that all flesh shall die, yet his days shall be an hundred and twenty years, and if men do not repent, I will send in the floods upon them.

And in those days there were giants on the Earth, and they sought Noah to take away his life, But the Lord was with Noah, and the power of the Lord was upon him, and the Lord ordained Noah after his own order, and commanded him that he should go forth and declare his gospel unto the children of men, even as it was given unto Enoch.

And it came to pass that Noah called upon the children of men, that they should repent, but they hearkened not unto his words. And also, after that they had heard him, they came up before him, saying, Behold, we are the sons of God, have we not taken unto ourselves the daughters of men? And are we not eating and drinking, and marrying and given in marriage? And our wives bear unto us children, and the same are mighty men, which are like unto them of old, men of great renown. And they hearkened not unto the words of Noah. And God saw that the wickedness of man had become great in the Earth, and every man was lifted up in the imagination of the thoughts of his heart, being only evil continually.

And it came to pass, that Noah continued his preaching unto the people, saying, Hearken and give heed unto my words, believe and repent of your sins and be baptized in the name of Jesus Christ, the Son of God, even as our fathers did, and ye shall receive the Holy Ghost, that ye may have all things made manifest, And if you do not this, the floods will come in upon you, nevertheless, they hearkened not.

And it repented Noah, and his heart was pained, that the Lord had made man on the Earth, and it grieved him at his heart. And the Lord said, I will destroy man whom I have created, from the face of the Earth, both man and beast, and the creeping things, and the fowls of the air. For it repenteth Noah that I have created them, and that I have made them, and he hath called upon me, for they have sought his life. And thus Noah found grace in the eyes of the Lord, for Noah was a just man, and perfect in his generation, and he walked with God, and also his three sons, Shem, Ham, and Japheth.

The Earth was corrupt before God, and it was filled with violence. And God looked upon the Earth, and behold, it was corrupt, for all flesh had corrupted its way upon the Earth. And God said unto Noah, The end of all flesh is come before me, for the Earth is filled with violence, and behold, I will destroy all flesh from off the Earth. Make thee therefore, an ark of gopher wood, rooms shalt thou make in the ark, and thou shalt pitch it within and without with pitch, And the length of the ark thou shalt make three hundred cubits, the breadth of it fifty cubits, and the height of it thirty cubits. And windows shalt thou make to the ark, and in a cubit shalt thou finish it above, and the door of the ark shalt thou set in the side thereof, lower, second, and third chambers shalt thou make in it. And behold, I, even I will bring in a flood of water upon the Earth, to destroy all flesh, wherein is the breath of life, from under Heaven, every thing that liveth on the Earth shall die. But with thee will I establish my covenant, even as I have sworn unto thy father, Enoch, that of thy posterity shall come all nations. And thou shalt come into the ark, thou and thy sons, and thy wife, and thy sons' wives with them. And of every living thing of all flesh, two of every kind shalt thou bring into the ark, to keep alive with thee, they shall be male and female. Of fowls after their kind, and of cattle after their kind, of every creeping thing of the Earth after his kind, two of every kind shalt thou take into the ark, to keep alive. And take thou unto thee of all food that is eaten, and thou shalt gather fruit of every kind unto thee in the ark, and it shall be for food for thee, and for them. Thus did Noah, according to all that God commanded him.

And the Lord said unto Noah, Come thou and all thy house, into the ark, for thee only have I seen righteous before me, in this generation. Of every clean beast thou shalt take to thee by sevens, the male and his female, and of beasts that are not clean by two, the male and his female, Of fowls also of the air, by sevens, the male and his female, to keep seed alive upon the face of the Earth. For yet seven days, and I will cause it to rain upon the Earth forty days, and forty nights, and every living substance that I have made will I destroy from off the face of the Earth. And Noah did according to all that the Lord commanded him. And Noah was six hundred years old when the flood of waters was upon the Earth.

And Noah went in, and his sons, and his wife, and his sons' wives with him, into the ark, because of the waters of the flood. Of clean beasts, and of beasts that were not clean, and of fowls, and of every thing that creepeth upon the Earth, there went in two and two, unto Noah into the ark, the male and the female, as God had commanded Noah.

And it came to pass, after seven days, that the waters of the flood were upon the Earth. In the six hundredth year of Noah's life, in the second month, and the seventeenth day of the month, the same day were all the fountains of the great deep broken up, and the windows of Heaven were opened, and the rain was upon the Earth forty days and forty nights. In the selfsame day entered Noah, and Shem, and Ham, and Japheth, the sons of Noah, and Noah's wife, and the three wives of his sons with them into the ark, they, and every beast after his kind, and all the cattle after their kind, and every creeping thing that creepeth on the Earth, after his kind, and every fowl after his kind, and every bird of every sort, And they went unto Noah, into the ark, two and two of all flesh, wherein is the breath of life, and they that went in, went in male and female of all flesh, as God had commanded him, and the Lord shut him in. And the flood was forty days upon the Earth, and the waters increased, and bare up the ark, and it was lifted up above the Earth. And the waters prevailed and increased greatly upon the Earth, and the ark went upon the face of the waters. And the waters prevailed exceedingly upon the face of the Earth, and all the high hills, under the whole heavens were covered. Fifteen cubits and upward did the waters prevail, and the mountains were covered. And all flesh died that moved upon the face of the Earth, both of fowl, and of cattle, and of beasts, and of every creeping thing that creepeth upon the Earth, and every man. All in whose nostrils the Lord had breathed the breath of life, of all that were on the dry land, died.

And every living substance was destroyed, which was upon the face of the ground, both man, and cattle, and the creeping things, and the fowls of the air, and they were destroyed from the Earth, And Noah only remained, and they that were with him in the ark. And the waters prevailed on the Earth one hundred and fifty days. And God remembered Noah, and all that were with him in the ark. And God made a wind to pass over the Earth, and the waters assuaged. The fountains also of the deep, and the windows of Heaven were stopped, and the rain from Heaven was restrained, and the waters returned from off the Earth. And after the end of the hundred and fifty days, the waters were abated. And the ark rested in the seventh month, on the seventeenth day of the month, upon the mountain of Ararat. And the waters decreased until the tenth month, and in the tenth month, on the first day of the month, were the tops of the mountains seen.

And it came to pass, at the end of forty days, that Noah opened the window of the ark which he had made, and he sent forth a raven, which went forth to and fro, until the waters were dried up from off the Earth. He also sent forth a dove from him, to see if the waters were abated from off the face of the ground, but the dove found no rest for the sole of her foot, and she returned unto him into the ark, for the waters had not receded from off the face of the whole Earth, then he put forth his hand and took her, and pulled her in unto him into the ark. And he stayed yet other seven days, and again he sent forth the dove out of the ark, and the dove came in to him in the evening, and lo, in her mouth an olive leaf plucked off, so Noah knew that the waters were abated from off the Earth. And he stayed yet other seven days, and sent forth a dove, which returned not again unto him any more.

And it came to pass, in the six hundred and first year, in the first month, the first day of the month, the waters were dried up from off the Earth. And Noah removed the covering of the ark, and looked, and behold, the face of the ground was dry. And in the second month, on the seven and twentieth day of the month, was the Earth dried.

And God spake unto Noah, saying, Go forth out of the ark, thou and thy wife, and thy sons, and thy sons' wives with thee. Bring forth with thee every living thing that is with thee, of all flesh, both of fowl, and of cattle, and of every creeping thing that creepeth upon the Earth, that they may breed abundantly in the Earth, and be fruitful and multiply upon the Earth. And Noah went forth, and his sons, and his wife, and his sons' wives with him. And every beast, every creeping thing, and every fowl upon the Earth, after their kinds, went forth out of the ark. And Noah builded an altar unto the Lord, and took of every clean beast, and of every clean fowl, and offered burnt offerings on the altar, and gave thanks unto the Lord, and rejoiced in his heart.

And the Lord spake unto Noah, and he blessed him. And Noah smelled a sweet savor, and he said in his heart, I will call on the name of the Lord, that he will not again curse the ground any more for man's sake, for the imagination of man's heart is evil from his youth, and that he will not again smite any more every thing living, as he hath done, while the Earth remaineth, And, that seedtime and harvest, and cold and heat, and summer and winter, and day and night, may not cease with man.

And God blessed Noah and his sons, and said unto them, Be fruitful and multiply, and replenish the Earth. And the fear of you, and the dread of you shall be upon every beast of the Earth, and upon every fowl of the air, upon all that moveth upon the Earth, and upon all the fishes of the sea, into your hand are they delivered. Every moving thing that liveth shall be meat for you, even as the green herb have I given you all things. But, the blood of all flesh which I have given you for meat, shall be shed upon the ground, which taketh life thereof, and the blood ye shall not eat. And surely, blood shall not be shed, only for meat, to save your lives, and the blood of every beast will I require at your hands. And whoso sheddeth man's blood, by man shall his blood be shed, for man shall not shed the blood of man. For a commandment I give, that every man's brother shall preserve the life of man, for in mine own image have I made man. And a commandment I give unto you, Be ye fruitful and multiply, bring forth abundantly on the Earth, and multiply therein.

And God spake unto Noah, and to his sons with him, saying, And I, behold, I will establish my covenant with you, which I made unto your father Enoch, concerning your seed after you. And it shall come to pass, that every living creature that is with you, of the fowl, and of the cattle, and of the beast of the Earth that is with you, which shall go out of the ark, shall not altogether perish, neither shall all flesh be cut off any more by the waters of a flood, neither shall there any more be a flood to destroy the Earth. And I will establish my covenant with you, which I made unto Enoch, concerning the remnants of your posterity. And God made a covenant with Noah, and said, This shall be the token of the covenant I make between me and you, and for every living creature with you, for perpetual generations, I will set my bow in the cloud, and it shall be for a token of a covenant between me and the Earth. And it shall come to pass, when I bring a cloud over the Earth, that the bow shall be seen in the cloud, and I will remember my covenant, which I have made between me and you, for every living creature of all flesh. And the waters shall no more become a flood to destroy all flesh. And the bow shall be in the cloud, and I will look upon it, that I may remember the everlasting covenant, which I made unto thy father Enoch, that, when men should keep all my commandments, Zion should again come on the Earth, the city of Enoch which I have caught up unto myself. And this is mine everlasting covenant, that when thy posterity shall embrace the truth, and look upward, then shall Zion look downward, and all the heavens shall shake with gladness, and the Earth shall tremble with joy, And the general assembly of the church of the firstborn shall come down out of Heaven, and possess the Earth, and shall have place until the end come. And this is mine everlasting covenant, which I made with thy father Enoch. And the bow shall be in the cloud, and I will establish my covenant unto thee, which I have made between me and thee, for every living creature of all flesh that shall be upon the Earth. And God said unto Noah, This is the token of the covenant which I have established between me and thee, for all flesh that shall be upon the Earth.

And the sons of Noah that went forth of the ark, were Shem, and Ham, and Japheth, and Ham was the father of Canaan. These were the three sons of Noah, and of them was the whole Earth overspread.

And Noah began to till the earth, and he was an husbandman, and he planted a vineyard, and he drank of the wine, and was drunken, and he was uncovered within his tent, And Ham, the father of Canaan, saw the nakedness of his father, and told his brethren without, and Shem and Japheth took a garment and laid upon both their shoulders, and went backward and covered the nakedness of their father, and they saw not their father's nakedness. And Noah awoke from his wine, and knew what his youngest son had done unto him, and he said, Cursed be Canaan, a servant of servants shall he be unto his brethren. And he said, Blessed be the Lord God of Shem, and Canaan shall be his servant, and a veil of darkness shall cover him, that he shall be known among all men. God shall enlarge Japheth, and he shall dwell in the tents of Shem, and Canaan shall be his servant. And Noah lived after the flood, three hundred and fifty years. And all the days of Noah were nine hundred and fifty years, and he died.

6 NOW these were the generations of the sons of Noah, Shem, Ham, and Japheth, and unto them were sons born after the flood.

The sons of Japheth, Gomer, and Magog, Madai, and Javan, and Tubal, and Meschech, and Tiras. And these are the sons of Gomer, Ashkenaz and

Riphath, and Togarmah. And the sons of Javan, Elishah, and Tarshish, Kittim, and Dodanim. By these were the isles of the Gentiles divided in their lands, every one after the same tongue, after their families, in their nations.

And the sons of Ham, Cush, and Mizraim, and Phut, and Canaan. And the sons of Cush, Seba, and Havilah, and Sabtah, and Raamah, and Sabtecha. And the sons of Raamah, Sheba, and Dedan. And Cush begat Nimrod, he began to be a mighty one in the Earth. He was a mighty hunter in the land. Wherefore, it is said, Even as Nimrod, the mighty hunter in the land. And he began a kingdom, and the beginning of his kingdom was Babel, and Erech, and Accad, and Calneh, in the land of Shinar. Out of that land went forth Asshur, and builded Nineveh, and the city Rehoboth, and Calah, and Resen between Nineveh and Calah, the same was a great city. And Mizraim begat Ludim, and Anamim, and Lehabim, and Naphtuhim, and Pathrusim, and Casluhim, out of whom came Philistim and Caphtorim. And Canaan begat Sidon, his firstborn, and Heth, and the Jebusite, and the Amorite, and Girgashite, and the Hivite, and the Arkite, and the Sinite, and the Arvadite, and Zemarite, and the Hamathite, and afterward were the families of the Canaanites spread abroad. And the borders of the Canaanites were from Sidon, as thou comest to Gerar unto Gaza, as thou goest unto Sodom and Gomorrah, and Admah, and Zeboiim even unto Lasha. These were the sons of Ham, after their families, after the same tongue, in their countries, and in their nations.

Unto Shem also, which was the elder, children were born, and he was the father of Eber, and even to him were children born. And these are the children of Shem, Eber, and Elam, and Asshur, and Arphaxad, and Lud, and Aram. And these were the children of Aram, Us, and Hul, and Gether, and Mash. And Arphaxad begat Salah, and Salah begat Eber. And unto Eber were born two sons, the name of one, Peleg, the other Joktan. And Peleg was a mighty man, for in his days was the Earth divided. And Joktan begat Almodad, and Sheleph, and Hazarmaveth, and Jerah, and Hadoram, and Uzal, and Diklah, and Obal, and Abimael, and Sheba, and Ophar, and Havilah, and Jobab, and these were the sons of Joktan. And their dwelling was from Mesha, as thou goest unto Sephar, a mount of the east. These were the sons of Shem, after their families, after their tongues, in their lands, after their nations.

These were the families of the sons of Noah, after their generations, in their nations, and by these were the nations divided on the Earth, after the flood.

And the whole Earth was of the same language, and of the same speech. And it came to pass, that many journeyed from the east, and as they journeyed from the east, they found a plain in the land of Shinar, and dwelt there in the plain of Shinar. And they said one to another, Come, go to, let us make brick, and burn them thoroughly. And they had brick for stone, and they had slime for mortar. And they said, Come, go to, let us build us a city, and a tower whose top will be high, nigh unto Heaven, and let us make us a name, lest we be scattered abroad upon the face of the whole Earth. And the Lord came down, beholding the city and the tower which the children of men were building, And the Lord said, Behold, the people are the same, and they all have the same language, and this tower they begin to build, and now, nothing will be restrained from them, which they have imagined, except I, the Lord, confound their language, that they may not understand one another's speech. So I, the Lord, will scatter them abroad from thence, upon all the face of the land, and unto every quarter of the Earth. And they were confounded, and left off to build the city, and they hearkened not unto the Lord, therefore, is the name of it called Babel, because the Lord was displeased with their works, and did there confound the language of all the Earth, and from thence did the Lord scatter them abroad upon the face thereof.

And these were the generations of Shem. And Shem being an hundred years old, begat Arphaxad two years after the flood, and Shem lived after he begat Arphaxad five hundred years, and begat sons and daughters. And Arphaxad lived five and thirty years, and begat Salah, and Arphaxad lived after he begat Salah, four hundred and three years, and begat sons and daughters. And Salah lived thirty years, and begat Eber, and Salah lived after he begat Eber four hundred and three years, and begat sons and daughters. And Eber lived four and thirty years, and begat Peleg, and Eber lived after he begat Peleg four hundred and thirty years, and begat sons and daughters. And Peleg lived thirty years, and begat Reu, and Peleg lived after he begat Reu, two hundred and nine years, and begat sons and daughters. And Reu lived two and thirty years, and begat Serug, and Reu lived after he begat Serug two hundred and seven years, and begat sons and daughters. And Serug lived thirty years, and begat Nahor, and Serug lived after he begat Nahor two hundred years, and begat sons and daughters. And Nahor lived nine and twenty years, and begat Terah, and Nahor lived after he begat Terah and hundred and nineteen years, and begat sons and daughters. And Terah lived seventy years, and begat Abram, Nahor and Haran. Now these were the generations of Terah, Terah begat Abram, Nahor and Haran, and Haran begat Lot. And Haran died before his father Terah, in the land of his nativity, in Ur of the Chaldees. And Abram and Nahor took them wives, and the name of Abram's wife was Sarai, and the name of Nahor's wife, Milcah, the daughter of Haran, the father of Milcah and the father of Iscah, but Sarai was barren, and she bear no child. And Terah took Abram his son, and Lot the son of Haran, his son's son, and Sarai his daughter-in-law, his son Abram's wife, and went forth with them from Ur of the Chaldees, to go into the land of Canaan, and they came unto Haran, and dwelt there. And the days of Terah were two hundred and five years, and Terah died in Haran.

7 NOW, the Lord had said unto Abram, Get thee out of thy country, and from thy kindred, and from thy father's house, unto a land that I will show thee, And I will make of thee a great nation, and I will bless thee, and make thy name great, and thou shalt be a blessing, and I will bless them that bless thee, and curse them that curse thee, and in thee shall the families of the Earth be blessed.

So Abram departed, as the Lord had spoken unto him, and Lot went with him. And Abram was seventy and five years old when he departed out of Haran. And Abram took Sarai, his wife, and Lot, his brother's son, and all their substance that they had gathered, and the souls that they had gotten in Haran, and they went forth to go into the land of Canaan, and into the land of Canaan they came. And Abram passed through the land unto the place of Sichem, and the plain of Moreh. And the Canaanites were then in the land.

And the Lord appeared unto Abram, and said, Unto thy seed will I give this land. And there builded he an altar unto the Lord, who appeared unto him. And he removed from thence unto a mountain on the east of Beth-el, and pitched his tent, leaving Beth-el on the west, and Hai was on the east. And there he builded an altar unto the Lord, and called upon the name of the Lord. And Abram journeyed, going on still toward the south. And there was a famine in the land, and Abram went down into Egypt to sojourn there, for the famine became grievous in the land.

And it came to pass, when he was come near to enter into Egypt, that he said unto Sarai his wife, Behold, now I know thee to be a fair woman to look upon, therefore it shall come to pass, when the Egyptians shall see thee, that they shall say, This is his wife, and they will kill me, but they will save thee alive, say I pray thee unto them, I am his sister, that it may be well with me for thy sake, and my soul shall live because of thee. And it came to pass, that when Abram was come into Egypt, the Egyptians beheld the woman, that she was very fair. The princes also of Pharaoh saw her, and commanded her to be brought before Pharaoh, and the woman was taken into Pharaoh's house. And he entreated Abram well for her sake, and he had sheep, and oxen, and he asses, and menservants, and maidservants, and she asses, and camels.

And the Lord plagued Pharaoh and his house with great plagues, because of Sarai, Abram's wife. And Pharaoh called Abram, and said, What hast thou done unto me in this thing? Why didst thou not tell me that she was thy wife? Why saidst thou, She is my sister? so I might have taken her unto me to wife, now therefore, behold I say unto thee, Take thy wife and go thy way. And Pharaoh commanded men concerning him, and they sent him away, and his wife, and all that he had. And Abram went up out of Egypt, he, and his wife, and all that he had, and Lot with him, unto the south. And Abram was very rich in cattle, in silver, and in gold.

And he went on his journey from the south, even to Bethel, unto the place where his tent had been at the beginning, between Bethel and Hai, unto the place of the altar, which he had made there at the first, and there Abram called on the name of the Lord. And Lot also, which went with Abram, had flocks, and herds, and tents.

And the land was not able to bear them, that they might dwell together, for their substance was great, so that they could not dwell together. And there was a strife between the herdmen of Abram's cattle, and the herdmen of Lot's cattle, that they could not dwell together. And the Canaanite, and the Perizzite dwelled then in the land.

And Abram said unto Lot, Let there be no strife, I pray thee, between me and thee, and between my herdmen and thy herdmen, for we are brethren. Is not the whole land before thee? Separate thyself, I pray thee, from me, if thou go to the left hand, then I will go to the right, if thou go to the right hand, then I will go to the left.

And Lot lifted up his eyes, and beheld all the plain of Jordan, that it was well watered everywhere, before the Lord destroyed Sodom and Gomorrah, like as the garden of the Lord, like the land of Egypt. Then Lot chose him all the plain of Jordan, and Lot journeyed east, and they separated themselves the one from the other. Abram dwelled in the land of Canaan, and Lot dwelled in the cities of the plain, and pitched his tent toward Sodom. But the men of Sodom becoming sinners, and exceedingly wicked before the Lord, the Lord was angry with them.

And the Lord said unto Abram, after that Lot was separated from him, Lift up now thine eyes, and look from the place where thou art, northward, and southward, and eastward, and westward, And remember the covenant which I make with thee, for it shall be an everlasting covenant, and thou shalt remember the days of Enoch thy father, For all the land which thou seest, will I give thee, and to thy seed for ever, and I will make thy seed as the dust of the Earth, so that if a man can number the dust of the Earth, thy seed shall also be numbered. Arise, walk through the land in the length of it, and in the breadth of it, for I will give it unto thee. Then Abram removed his tent, and came and dwelt in the plain of Mamre, which was in Hebron, and built there an altar unto the Lord.

And it came to pass, in the days of Amraphel king of Shinar, and Arioch king of Ellasar, and Chedorlaomer king of Elam, and Tidal king of nations, That these kings made war with Bera king of Sodom, and with Birsha king of Gomorrah, Shinab king of Admah, and Shemeber king of Zeboiim, and the king of Bela, which is Zoar. All these were joined together in the vale of Siddim, which is the salt sea, Twelve years they served Chedorlaomer, and in the thirteenth year they rebelled. And in the fourteenth year came Chedorlaomer, and the kings that were with him, and smote the Rephaims in Ashteroth Karnaim, and the Zuzims in

Ham, and the Emims in Shaveh Kiriathaim, and the Horites in their mount Seir, unto Elparan, which was by the wilderness. And they returned and came to Enmishpat, which is Kadesh, and smote all the country of the Amalekites, and also the Amorites, in Hazezontamar. And there went out the king of Sodom, and the king of Gomorrah, and the king of Admah, and the king of Zeboiim, and the king of Bela, which is Zoar, And they joined battle with them in the vale of Siddim, with Chedorlaomer king of Elam, and with Tidal king of nations, and Amraphel king of Shinar, and Arioch king of Ellasar, four kings with five. And the vale of Siddim was filled with slime pits, and the kings of Sodom and Gomorrah fled and fell there, and they that remained fled to the mountain which was called Hanabal. And they took all the goods of Sodom and Gomorrah, and all their victuals, and went their way. And they took Lot, Abram's brother's son, who dwelt in Sodom, and his goods and departed. And there came one that had escaped, and told Abram the Hebrew, the man of God, for he dwelt in the plain of Mamre the Amorite, brother of Eschol, and brother of Aner, and these were confederate with Abram.

And when Abram heard that Lot, his brother's son, was taken captive, he armed his trained men, and they which were born in his own house, three hundred and eighteen, and pursued unto Dan. And he divided himself against them, he and his men, by night, and smote them, and pursued them unto Hobah, which was on the left hand of Damascus. And he brought back Lot, his brother's son, and all his goods, and the women also, and the people. And the king of Sodom also went out to meet him after his return from the slaughter of Chedorlaomer, and of the kings that were with him, at the valley of Shaveh, which was the king's dale.

And Melchizedek, king of Shalom, brought forth bread and wine, and he break bread and blest it, and he blest the wine, he being the priest of the Most High God, and he gave to Abram, and he blessed him, and said, Blessed Abram, thou art a man of the Most High God, possessor of Heaven and of Earth, and blessed is the name of the Most High God, which hath delivered thine enemies into thine hand.

And Abram gave him tithes of all he had taken.

And the king of Sodom said to Abram, Give me the persons, and take the goods to thyself.

And Abram said to the king of Sodom, I have lifted up my hand unto the Lord, the Most High God, the possessor of Heaven and Earth. And have sworn that I will not take of thee from a thread even to a shoe-latchet, and that I will not take anything that is thine, (lest thou shouldst say, I have made Abram rich,) Save only that which the young men have eaten, and the portion of the men which went with me, Ener, Eschol, and Mamre, let them take their portion.

And Melchizedek lifted up his voice and blessed Abram.

Now Melchizedek was a man of faith, who wrought righteousness, and when a child he feared God, and stopped the mouths of lions, and quenched the violence of fire. And thus, having been approved of God, he was ordained an high priest after the order of the covenant which God made with Enoch, It being after the order of the Son of God, which order came, not by man, nor the will of man, neither by father nor mother, neither by beginning of days nor end of years, but of God, And it was delivered unto men by the calling of his own voice, according to his own will, unto as many as believed on his name.

For God having sworn unto Enoch and unto his seed with an oath by himself, that every one being ordained after this order and calling should have power, by faith, to break mountains, to divide the seas, to dry up waters, to turn them out of their course, To put at defiance the armies of nations, to divide the Earth, to break every band, to stand in the presence of God, to do all things according to his will, according to his command, subdue principalities and powers, and this by the will of the Son of God which was from before the foundation of the world. And men having this faith, coming up unto this order of God, were translated and taken up into Heaven.

And now, Melchizedek was a priest of this order, therefore he obtained peace in Salem, and was called the Prince of peace. And his people wrought righteousness, and obtained Heaven, and sought for the city of Enoch which God had before taken, separating it from the Earth, having reserved it unto the latter days, or the end of the world, And hath said, and sworn with an oath, that the heavens and the Earth should come together, and the sons of God should be tried so as by fire. And this Melchizedek, having thus established righteousness, was called the king of Heaven by his people, or, in other words, the King of peace.

And he lifted up his voice, and he blessed Abram, being the high priest, and the keeper of the storehouse of God, Him whom God had appointed to receive tithes for the poor. Wherefore, Abram paid unto him tithes of all that he had, of all the riches which he possessed, which God had given him more than that which he had need.

And it came to pass, that God blessed Abram, and gave unto him riches, and honor, and lands for an everlasting possession, according to the covenant which he had made, and according to the blessing wherewith Melchizedek had blessed him.

And it came to pass, that after these things, the word of the Lord came unto Abram in a vision, saying, Fear not, Abram, I will be thy shield, I will be thy exceeding great reward. And according to the blessings of my servant, I will give unto thee. And Abram said, Lord God, what wilt thou give me, seeing I go childless, and Eliezer of Damascus was made the steward of my house? And Abram said, Behold, to me thou hast given no seed, and lo, one born in my house is mine heir. And behold, the word of the Lord came unto him again, saying, This shalt not be thine heir, but he that shall come forth out of thine own bowels shall be thine heir. And he brought him forth abroad, and he said, Look now toward Heaven, and tell the stars, if thou be able to number them. And he said unto him, so shall thy seed be. And Abram said, Lord God, how wilt thou give me this land for an everlasting inheritance? And the Lord said, Though thou wast dead, yet am I not able to give it thee? And if thou shalt die, yet thou shalt possess it, for the day cometh, that the Son of Man shall live, but how can he live if he be not dead? he must first be quickened.

And it came to pass that Abram looked forth and saw the days of the Son of Man, and was glad, and his soul found rest, and he believed in the Lord, and the Lord counted it unto him for righteousness. And the Lord said unto him, I, the Lord, brought thee out of Ur, of the Chaldees, to give thee this land to inherit it. And Abram said, Lord, whereby shall I know that I shall inherit it? yet he believed God. And the Lord said unto him, Take me a heifer of three years old, and a she goat of three years old, and a ram of three years old, and a turtle-dove, and a young pigeon. And he took unto him all these, and he divided them in the midst, and he laid each piece one against the other, but the birds divided he not. And when the fowls came down upon the carcasses, Abram drove them away. And when the sun was going down, a deep sleep fell upon Abram, and, lo, a great horror of darkness fell upon him. And the Lord spake, and he said unto Abram, Know of a surety that thy seed shall be a stranger in a land which shall not be theirs, and shall serve strangers, and they shall be afflicted, and serve them four hundred years, and also that nation whom they shall serve will I judge, and afterwards shall they come out with great substance. And thou shalt die, and go to thy fathers in peace, thou shalt be buried in a good old age. But in the fourth generation they shall come hither again, for the iniquity of the Amorites is not yet full.

And it came to pass, that when the sun went down, and it was dark, behold, a smoking furnace, and a burning lamp which passed between those pieces which Abram had divided. And in that same day the Lord made a covenant with Abram, saying, Unto thy seed have I given this land, from the river of Egypt unto the great river Euphrates, The Kenites, and the Kenazites, and the Kadmonites, and Hittites, and the Perizzites, and the Rephaims, and the Amorites, and the Canaanites, and the Girgashites, and the Jebusites.

Now Sarai, Abram's wife, bare him no children. And she had a handmaid, an Egyptian, whose name was Hagar. And Sarai said unto Abram, Behold, now, the Lord hath restrained me from bearing, I pray thee go in unto my maid, it may be that I may obtain children by her. And Abram hearkened unto the voice of Sarai. And Sarai, Abram's wife, took Hagar her maid, the Egyptian, after Abram had dwelt ten years in the land of Canaan, and gave her to her husband, Abram, to be his wife. And he went in unto Hagar, and she conceived, and when she saw that she had conceived, her mistress was despised in her eyes. And Sarai said unto Abram, My wrong is upon thee, I have given my maid into thy bosom, and when she saw that she had conceived, I was despised in her eyes, the Lord judge between me and thee. But Abram said unto Sarai, Behold, thy maid is in thy hands, do to her as it pleaseth thee. And when Sarai dealt hardly with her, she fled from her face. And an Angel of the Lord found her by a fountain of water in the wilderness, by the fountain in the way to Shur. And he said, Hagar, Sarai's maid, whence comest thou, and whither wilt thou go? and she said, I flee from the face of my mistress Sarai. And the Angel of the Lord said unto her, Return to thy mistress, and submit thyself unto her hands. And the Angel of the Lord said unto her, The Lord will multiply thy seed exceedingly, so that it shall not be numbered for multitude. And the Angel of the Lord said unto her, Behold, thou art with child, and shalt bear a son, and shall call his name Ishmael: because the Lord hath heard thy afflictions. And he will be a wild man, and his hand will be against every man, and every man's hand against him, and he shall dwell in the presence of all his brethren. And she called the name of the Angel of the Lord. And he spake unto her, saying, Knowest thou that God seest thee? And she said, I know that God seest me, for I have also here looked after him.

And there was a well between Kadesh and Bered, near where Hagar saw the angel. And the name of the angel was Beer-la-hai-roi, wherefore the well was called Beer-la-hai-roi for a memorial. And Hagar bear Abram a son, and Abram called his son's name, which Hagar bear, Ishmael. And Abram was four-score and six years old, when Hagar bare Ishmael to Abram. And when Abram was ninety and nine years old, the Lord appeared to Abram, and said unto him, I, the Almighty God, give unto thee a commandment, that thou shalt walk uprightly before me, and be perfect. And I will make my covenant between me and thee, and I will multiply thee exceedingly.

And it came to pass, that Abram fell on his face, and called upon the name of the Lord. And God talked with him, saying, My people have gone astray from my precepts, and have not kept mine ordinances, which I gave unto their fathers, And they have not observed mine anointing, and the burial, or baptism wherewith I commanded them, But have turned from the commandment, and taken unto themselves the washing of children, and the blood of sprinkling, And have said that the blood of the righteous Abel was shed for sins, and have not known wherein they are accountable before me. But as for thee, behold, I will make my covenant with thee, and thou shalt be a father of many nations. And this covenant I make, that thy children may be known among all nations. Neither shall thy name any more be called Abram, but thy name shall be called Abraham, for, a father of many nations have I made thee. And I will make thee exceedingly fruitful, and I will make nations of thee, and kings shall come of thee, and of thy seed. And I will establish a covenant of circumcision with thee, and it shall be my covenant between me and thee, and thy seed after thee, in their generations, that thou mayest know for ever that children are not accountable before me until they are eight years old. And thou shalt observe to keep all my covenants wherein I covenanted with thy fathers, and thou shalt keep the commandments which I have given thee with mine own mouth, and I will be a God unto thee and thy seed after thee. And I will give unto thee and thy seed after thee, a land wherein thou art a stranger, all the land of Canaan, for an everlasting possession, and I will be their God. And God said unto Abraham, Therefore thou shalt keep my covenant, thou and thy seed after thee, in their generations. And this shall be my covenant which ye shall keep between me and thee and thy seed after thee, every man-child among you shall be circumcised. And ye shall circumcise the flesh of your foreskin, and it shall be a token of the covenant betwixt me and you. And he that is eight days old shall be circumcised among you, every man-child in your generations, He that is born in the house, or bought with money of any stranger, which is not of thy seed. He that is born in thy house, and he that is bought with thy money, must needs be circumcised, and my covenant shall be in your flesh for an everlasting covenant. And the uncircumcised man-child, whose flesh of his foreskin is not circumcised, that soul shall be cut off from his people, he hath broken my covenant.

And God said unto Abraham, as for Sarai thy wife, thou shalt not call her name Sarai, but Sarah thou shalt call her name. And I will bless her, and I will give thee a son of her, yea, I will bless her, and she shall be blessed, The mother of nations, kings and people shall be of her.

Then Abraham fell on his face and rejoiced, and said in his heart, There shall a child be born unto him that is an hundred years old, and Sarah that is ninety years old shall bear.

And Abraham said unto God, O that Ishmael might live uprightly before thee! And God said, Sarah thy wife shall bare thee a son, and thou shalt call his name Isaac, and I will establish my covenant with him also, for an everlasting covenant with his seed after him. And as for Ishmael, I have heard thee, Behold, I have blessed him, and will make him fruitful, and will multiply him exceedingly, Twelve princes shall he beget, and I will make him a great nation. But my covenant will I establish with Isaac, whom Sarah shall bear unto thee at this set time in the next year.

And he left off talking with him, and God went up from Abraham. And Abraham took Ishmael his son, and all that were born in his house, and all that were bought with his money, every male among the men of Abraham's house, and circumcised the flesh of their foreskin in the selfsame day, as God had said unto him. And Abraham was ninety and nine years old when he was circumcised in the flesh of his foreskin. And Ishmael was thirteen years old when he was circumcised in the flesh of his foreskin. In the selfsame day Abraham was circumcised, and Ishmael his son, and all the men of his house, which were born in his house, and bought with money of strangers, were also circumcised with him.

And the Lord appeared unto Abraham in the plains of Mamre. And he sat in his tent door in the heat of the day, And he lifted up his eyes and looked, and lo, three men stood by him, and when he saw, he ran to meet them from his tent door, and bowed himself toward the ground, and said, My brethren, if now I have found favor in your sight, pass not away I pray you from thy servant. Let a little water I pray you be fetched, and wash your feet, and rest yourselves under the tree, and I will fetch a morsel of bread, and comfort ye your hearts, after that you shall pass on, for therefore are ye come to your servant. And they said, So do, as thou hast said. And Abraham hastened into the tent unto Sarah, and said, Make ready quickly three measures of fine meal, knead, and make cakes upon the hearth. And Abraham ran unto the herd, and fetched a calf, tender and good, and gave it unto a young man, and he hasted to dress it. And he took butter and milk, and the calf which he had dressed, and set them before them, and he stood by them under the tree, and they did eat. And they said unto him, Where is Sarah thy wife? And he said, Behold, in the tent. And one of them blessed Abraham, and he said, I will certainly return unto thee from my journey, and lo, according to the time of life, Sarah thy wife shall have a son. And Sarah heard him, in the tent door.

And now Abraham and Sarah being old, and stricken in age, therefore it had ceased to be with Sarah after the manner of women, Therefore Sarah laughed within herself, saying, After I have waxed old shall I have pleasure, my lord being old also? And the Angel of the Lord said unto Abraham, Wherefore did Sarah laugh, saying, Shall I of a surety bear a child, which am old? Is anything too hard for the Lord? At the time appointed, behold, I will return unto thee from my journey, which the Lord hath sent me, and according to the time of life thou mayest know that Sarah shall have a son. Then Sarah denied, saying, I laughed not, for she was afraid. And he said, Nay, but thou didst laugh.

And the angels rose up from thence, and looked toward Sodom, and Abraham went with them to bring them on the way. And the Angel of the Lord, said, Shall I hide from Abraham that thing which the Lord will do for him, seeing that Abraham shall surely become a great and mighty nation, and all the nations of the Earth shall be blessed in him? For I know him, that he will command his children, and his household after him, and they shall keep the way of the Lord, to do justice and judgment, that the Lord may bring upon Abraham that which he has spoken of him. And the Angel of the Lord said unto Abraham, The Lord said unto us, Because the cry of Sodom and Gomorrah is great, and because their sin is very grievous, I will destroy them. And I will send you, and ye shall go down now, and see that their iniquities are rewarded unto them. And ye shall have all things done altogether according to the cry of it, which is come unto me. And if ye do it not, it shall be upon your heads, for I will destroy them, and you shall know that I will do it, for it shall be before your eyes.

And the angels which were holy men, and were sent forth after the order of God, turned their faces from thence and went toward Sodom. But Abraham stood yet before the Lord, remembering the things which had been told him.

And Abraham drew near to Sodom, and said unto the Lord, calling upon his name, saying, Wilt thou destroy the righteous with the wicked? Wilt thou not spare them? Peradventure there may be fifty righteous within the city, wilt thou also destroy and not spare the place for the fifty righteous that may be therein? O may that be far from thee to do after this manner, to slay the righteous with the wicked, and that the righteous should be as the wicked. O God, may that be far from thee, for shall not the Judge of all the Earth do right? And the Lord said unto Abraham, If thou findest in Sodom, fifty righteous within the city, then I will spare all the place for their sakes. And Abraham answered and said, Behold, now, I have taken upon me to speak unto the Lord, which is able to destroy the city, and lay all the people in dust and ashes, Will the Lord spare them peradventure there lack five of the fifty righteous, wilt thou destroy all the city for their wickedness, if I find there forty and five righteous? And he said, I will not destroy, but spare them. And he spake unto him again, and said, Peradventure there should be forty found there? And he said, I will not destroy it for forty's sake. And he said again unto the Lord, O, let not the Lord be angry, and I will speak: Peradventure there shall thirty be found there? And he said, I will not destroy them if thou shalt find thirty there. And he said, Behold now, I have taken upon me to speak unto the Lord, wilt thou destroy them if peradventure there shall twenty be found there? And he said, I will not destroy them for twenty's sake. And Abraham said unto the Lord, O, let not the Lord be angry, and I will speak yet but this once, peradventure ten shall be found there? And the Lord said, I will not destroy them for ten's sake. And the Lord ceased speaking with Abraham. And as soon as he had left communing with the Lord, Abraham went his way. And it came to pass that Abraham returned unto his tent.

And it came to pass, that there came three angels to Sodom in the evening, and Lot sat in the door of his house, in the city of Sodom. And Lot, seeing the angels, rose up to meet them, and he bowed himself with his face toward the ground, And he said, Behold now, my lords, turn in, I pray you, into your servant's house, and tarry all night, and wash your feet, and ye shall rise up early, and go on your ways. And they said, Nay, but we will abide in the street all night. And he pressed upon them greatly, and they turned in unto him, and entered into his house, and he made them a feast, and did bake unleavened bread, and they did eat. But before they lay down to rest, the men of the city of Sodom compassed the house round, even men which were both old and young, even the people from every quarter, And they called unto Lot, and said unto him, Where are the men which came in unto thee this night? bring them out unto us, that we may know them. And Lot went out of the door, unto them, and shut the door after him, and said, I pray you, brethren, do not so wickedly. And they said unto him, Stand back. And they were angry with him. And they said among themselves, This one man came in to sojourn among us, and he will needs now make himself to be a judge, now we will deal worse with him than with them. Wherefore they said unto the man, We will have the men, and thy daughters also, and we will do with them as seemeth us good. Now this was after the wickedness of Sodom.

And Lot said, Behold now, I have two daughters which have not known man, let me, I pray you, plead with my brethren that I may not bring them out unto you, and ye shall not do unto them as seemeth good in your eyes, For God will not justify his servant in this thing, wherefore, let me plead with my brethren, this once only, that unto these men ye do nothing, that they may have peace in my house, for therefore came they under the shadow of my roof. And they were angry with Lot and came near to break the door, but the angels of God, which were holy men, put forth their hand and pulled Lot into the house unto them, and shut the door. And they smote the men with blindness, both small and great, that they could not come at the door. And they were angry, so that they wearied themselves to find the door, and could not find it.

And these holy men said unto Lot, Hast thou any here besides thy sons-in-law, and thy son's sons and thy daughters? And they commanded Lot, saying, Whatsoever thou hast in the city, thou shalt bring out of this place, for we will destroy this place, Because the cry of them is waxen great, and their abominations have come up before the face of the Lord, and the Lord hath sent us to destroy it. And Lot went out and spake unto his sons-in-law, which married his daughters, and said, Up, get ye out of this place, for the Lord will destroy this city. But he seemed as one that mocked, unto his sons-in-law. And when the morning came, the angels hastened Lot, saying, Arise, take thy wife, and thy two daughters which are here, lest thou be consumed in the iniquity of the city. And while he lingered the angels laid hold upon his hand, and upon the hand of his wife, and upon the hand of his two daughters, the Lord being merciful unto them, and they brought them forth, and set them down without the city.

And it came to pass, when they had brought them forth abroad that they said unto them, Escape for your lives, look not behind you, neither stay you in all the plain, escape to the mountain lest you be consumed. And Lot said unto one of them, Oh, not so my Lord! behold now, thy servant has found grace in thy sight, and thou hast magnified thy mercy which thou hast showed unto me in saving my life, and I cannot escape to the mountain, lest some evil overtake me, and I die. Behold now, here is another city, and this is near to flee unto and it is a little one, oh, let me escape thither, and may the Lord not destroy it, and my soul shall live. And the angel said unto him, See, I have accepted thee concerning this thing also, that I will not overthrow this city, for the which thou hast spoken, haste thee, escape thither, for I cannot do anything until thou be come thither. And the name of the city was called Zoar. Therefore the sun was risen upon the Earth when Lot entered into Zoar. And the Lord did not destroy Sodom until Lot had entered into Zoar. And then, when Lot had entered into Zoar, the Lord rained upon Sodom, and upon Gomorrah, for the angels called upon the name of the Lord for brimstone and fire from the Lord out of Heaven. And thus they overthrew those cities and all the plain, and all the inhabitants of the cities, and that which grew upon the ground. But it came to pass, when Lot fled, his wife looked back from behind him, and became a pillar of salt.

And Abraham got up early in the morning to the place where he stood before the Lord, and he looked toward Sodom and Gomorrah, and toward all the land of the plain, and behold, lo, the smoke of the country went up as the smoke of a furnace. And it came to pass, when God had destroyed the cities of the plain, that God spake unto Abraham, saying, I have remembered Lot, and sent him out of the midst of the overthrow, that thy brother might not be destroyed, when I overthrew the city in the which thy brother Lot dwelt. And Abraham was comforted.

And Lot went up out of Zoar, and dwelt in the mountain, and his two daughters with him, for he feared to dwell in Zoar. And he dwelt in a cave, he and his two daughters. And the firstborn dealt wickedly, and said unto the younger, Our father has become old, and we have not a man on the Earth to come in unto us, to live with us after the manner of all that live on the Earth, Therefore come, let us make our father drink wine, and we will lie with him, that we may preserve seed of our father. And they did wickedly, and made their father drink wine that night, and the firstborn went in and lay with her father, and he perceived not when she lay down, nor when she arose. And it came to pass on the morrow, that the firstborn said unto the younger, Behold, I lay yesternight with my father, let us make him drink wine this night also, and go thou in and lie with him, that we may preserve seed of our father. And they made their father drink wine that night also, and the younger arose, and lay with him, and he perceived not when she lay down, nor when she arose. Thus were both the daughters of Lot with child by their father. And the firstborn bare a son, and called his name Moab, the father of the Moabites, the same which are unto this day. And the younger, she also bare a son, and called his name Ben-ammi, the father of the children which are Ammonites, the same which are unto this day.

And Abraham journeyed from thence toward the south country, and dwelt between Kadesh and Shur, and sojourned in Gerar. And Abraham said again of Sarah his wife, She is my sister. And Abimelech, king of Gerar, sent and took Sarah. But God came to Abimelech in a dream by night, and said unto him, Behold, thou hast taken a woman which is not thine own, for she is Abraham's wife. And the Lord said unto him, Thou shalt return her unto Abraham, for if thou do it not thou shalt die. And Abimelech had not come near her, for the Lord had not suffered him. And he said, Lord, wilt thou slay me, and also a righteous nation? Behold, said he not unto me, She is my sister? And she, even she herself said, He is my brother, and in the integrity of my heart and innocency of my hands have I done this. And God said unto him in a dream, Yea, I know that thou didst do this in the integrity of thy heart, for I also withheld thee from sinning against me, therefore suffered I not thee to touch her. Now, therefore, restore the man's wife to him, for he is a prophet, and he shall pray for thee, and thou shalt live, and if thou restore her not to him, know thou that thou shalt surely die, thou and all that are thine. Therefore, Abimelech arose early in the morning, and called his servants, and told all these things in their ears, and the men were sore afraid. Then Abimelech called Abraham, and said unto him, What hast thou done unto us? and in what have I offended thee that thou hast brought on me and on my kingdom a great sin? Thou hast done things unto me that ought not to be done. And Abimelech said unto Abraham, What sawest thou, that thou hast done this thing? And Abraham said, Because I thought assuredly the fear of God was not in this place, and they would slay me for my wife's sake, And yet indeed she was my sister, she was the daughter of my father, but not the daughter of my mother, and she became my wife. And it came to pass, when God caused me to wander from my father's house, that I said unto her, This shall be thy kindness which thou shalt show unto me, at every place whither we shall come, say of me, He is my brother. And Abimelech took sheep and oxen, and menservants, and womenservants, and gave unto Abraham, and restored unto him Sarah his wife. And Abimelech said, Behold, my land lieth before thee, dwell where it pleaseth thee. And unto Sarah he said, Behold, I have given thy brother a thousand pieces of silver, behold, he shall give unto thee a covering of the eyes, and it shall be a token unto all that thou mayest not be taken again from Abraham thy husband. And thus she was reproved. So Abraham prayed unto God, and God healed Abimelech, and his wife, and his maidservants, and they bare unto him children. For because of Sarah, Abraham's wife, the Lord had fast closed up all the wombs of the house of Abimelech.

And the Lord visited Sarah as he had said, and the Lord did unto Sarah as he had spoken by the mouth of his angels, for Sarah conceived and bear Abraham a son in his old age, at the set time of which the angels of God had spoken to him. And Abraham called the name of his son that was born unto him, whom Sarah bear unto him, Isaac. And Abraham circumcised his son Isaac, he being eight days old, as God had commanded him. And Abraham was an hundred years old, when his son Isaac was born unto him. And Sarah said, God has made me to rejoice, and also all that know me will rejoice with me. And she said unto Abraham, Who would have said that Sarah should have given children suck? For I was barren, but the Lord promised, and I have borne unto Abraham a son in his old age.

And the child grew, and was weaned. And the day that Isaac was weaned, Abraham made a great feast, and Sarah saw the son of Hagar the Egyptian, which Hagar had borne unto Abraham, mocking, and she was troubled. Wherefore she said unto Abraham, Cast out this bondwoman and her son, for the son of this bondwoman shall not be heir with my son, Isaac. And this thing was very grievous unto Abraham because of his son. And God said unto Abraham, Let it not be grievous in thy sight, because of the lad, and because of thy bondwoman, in all that Sarah has said unto thee, hearken unto her voice, for in Isaac shall thy seed be called. And also of the son of the bondwoman will I make a nation, because he is thy seed.

And Abraham rose up early in the morning, and took bread, and a bottle of water, and gave unto Hagar, and she took the child, and he sent her away, and she departed, and wandered in the wilderness of Beersheba. And it came to pass that the water was spent in the bottle, and she cast the child under one of the shrubs, and she went and sat her down over against the child, a good way off, as it were a bowshot, for she said, Let me not see the death of the child. And she sat over against the child, and lifted up her voice and wept. And God heard the voice of the lad, and the Angel of the Lord called to Hagar out of Heaven, and said unto her, What aileth thee, Hagar? fear not, for God hath heard the voice of the lad where he lieth, arise, lift up the lad, and hold him in thine hand, for I will make of him a great nation. And God opened her eyes, and she saw a well of water, and she went and filled the bottle with water and gave the lad drink. And God was with the lad, and he grew, and dwelt in the wilderness, and became an archer, and he dwelt in the wilderness of Paran, he and his mother. And he took him a wife out of the land of Egypt.

And it came to pass at the time, that Abimelech and Phicol the chief captain of his host spake unto Abraham, saying, God is with thee in all that thou doest. Now therefore, sware unto me here, that, by the help of God thou wilt not deal falsely with me, nor with my son, nor with my son's son, but, that according to the kindness that I have shown unto thee, thou shalt do unto me, and to the land wherein thou hast sojourned. And Abraham said, I will swear. And Abraham reproved Abimelech, because of a well of water which Abimelech's servants had violently taken away. And Abimelech said, Thou didst not tell me, and I know not who hath done this thing, neither yet have I heard that it was done until this day. And Abraham took sheep and oxen, and gave them unto Abimelech, and both of them made a covenant. And Abraham set seven ewe lambs of the flock by themselves. And Abimelech said unto Abraham, What wilt thou do with these seven ewe lambs which thou hast set by themselves? And he said, Seven ewe lambs shalt thou take at my hand, that they may be a witness unto me that I have digged this well. And because they sware, both of them, wherefore he called that place Beer-sheba, And thus they made a covenant at Beer-sheba, Then Abimelech, and Phicol, the chief captain of his hosts, rose up, and they planted a grove in Beer-sheba, and called there on the name of the Lord, and they returned unto the land of the Philistines.

And Abraham worshiped the everlasting God, and sojourned in the land of the Philistines many days.

And it came to pass after these things, that God did try Abraham and said unto him, Abraham, and Abraham said, Behold, here am I. And the Lord said, Take now thy son, thine only Isaac, whom thou lovest, and get thee into the land of Moriah, and offer him there for a burnt offering, upon one of the mountains of which I will tell thee. And Abraham rose up early in the morning and saddled his ass, and took two of his young men with him, and Isaac his son, And clave the wood for the burnt offering, and rose up, and went unto the place of which God had told him. Then on the third day, Abraham lifted up his eyes and saw the place afar off. And Abraham said unto his young men, Abide you here with the ass, and I and the lad will go yonder and worship, and come to you again. And Abraham took the wood of the burnt offering, and laid it upon his back, and he took the fire in his hand, and a knife, and Isaac his son, and they went both of them together. And Isaac spake unto Abraham his father, and said, My father! And he said, Here am I, my son. And he said, Behold the fire and the wood, but where is the lamb for a burnt offering? And Abraham said, My son, God will provide himself a lamb for a burnt offering. So they went both of them together, and they came to the place of which God had told him. And Abraham built an altar there, and laid the wood in order, and bound Isaac his son, and laid him on the altar, upon the wood. And Abraham stretched forth his hand and took the knife to slay his son. And the Angel of the Lord called unto him out of Heaven, and said, Abraham! Abraham! And Abraham said, Here am I. And the angel said, Lay not thine hand upon the lad, neither do thou anything unto him, For now I know that thou fearest God, seeing thou hast not withheld thy son, thine only Isaac from me. And Abraham lifted up his eyes and looked, and behold, behind a thicket, there was a ram caught in it by his horns. And Abraham went and took the ram, and offered him up for a burnt offering, in the stead of his son. And Abraham called the name of that place Jehovah-jireh, as it is said unto this day, In the mount of the Lord it shall be seen.

And the Angel of the Lord called unto Abraham out of Heaven the second time, and said, Thus saith the Lord, I have sworn by myself, that because thou hast done this thing, and hast not withheld thy son, thine only Isaac from me, That in blessing I will bless thee, and in multiplying I will multiply thy seed as the stars of Heaven, and as the sand which is upon the seashore. And thy seed shall possess the gate of his enemies, and in thy seed shall all the nations of the Earth be blessed, because thou hast obeyed my voice.

So Abraham returned unto his young men, and they rose up and went to Beer-sheba, and Abraham dwelt at Beer-sheba.

And it came to pass after these things, that it was told Abraham, saying, Behold, Milcah, she hath also borne children unto thy brother Nahor, Huz is his firstborn, and Buz is his brother. And Kemuel is the father of Aram, and Chesed, and Haza, and Bildash, and Jidlaph, and Bethuel, And Bethuel begat Rebekah. These eight Milcah did bear to Nahor, Abraham's brother, and his concubine, whose name was Reumah, she bare also Tebah, and Gaham, Thahash, and Maachah.

And Sarah was an hundred and twenty-seven years old, and she died, and thus ended the years of the life of Sarah. And Sarah died in Kirjatharba, the same is now called Hebron, in the land of Canaan. And Abraham came to mourn for Sarah, and to weep for her, his wife which was dead. And Abraham stood up from before his dead, and spake unto the sons of Heth, saying, I am a stranger and a sojourner with you, give me a possession of a burying-place with you, that I may bury my dead out of my sight. And the children of Heth answered Abraham, saying unto him, Hear us, my lord, thou art a mighty prince among us, in the choicest of our sepulchers bury thou thy dead, none of us shall withhold from thee his sepulcher, but that thou mayest bury thy dead. And Abraham stood up, and bowed himself to the people of the land, and to the children of Heth, and he communed with them, saying, If it be your mind that I should bury my dead out of my sight, hear me, and entreat Ephron the son of Zohar for me, that he may give me the cave of Machpelah, which he hath in the end of his field, For, as much money as it is worth he shall have, if he will give it me for a possession of a burying-place among you.

And Ephron dwelt among the children of Heth. And Ephron, the Hittite, answered Abraham in the audience of the children of Heth, among all of them that went in at the gates of the city, saying, Hearken, my lord, and hear me, the field I give thee, and the cave that is therein, I give it thee in the presence of the sons of my people, and I give it thee, therefore, bury thy dead. And Abraham bowed himself down before the people of the land, and he spake unto Ephron in the audience of the people of the land, saying, I pray thee, hear me, If thou wilt take it of me, I will give thee money for the field, and I will bury my dead there, but I will give thee money for it. And Ephron answered Abraham, saying unto him, My lord, hearken unto me, the land thou shalt have for four hundred shekels of silver, what shall that be betwixt me and thee? Bury therefore thy dead. And Abraham hearkened unto Ephron, and Abraham weighed unto Ephron the silver which he had named in the audience of the sons of Heth, four hundred shekels of silver, which was current with the merchant. And the field of Ephron, which was in Machpelah, which was before Mamre, the field, and the cave which was therein, and all the trees that were in the field, and that were in all the borders round about, were made sure unto Abraham for a possession, in the presence of the children of Heth, before all that went in at the gate of the city. And after this, Abraham buried Sarah his wife in the cave of the field of Machpelah, which is before Mamre, the same is called Hebron, in the land of Canaan. And the field and the cave that was therein, were made sure unto Abraham for a possession of a burying-place by the sons of Heth.

And now Abraham was old, being well stricken in age, and the Lord had blessed Abraham in all things. And Abraham said unto his eldest servant of his house, that ruled over all that he had, Put forth I pray thee thy hand under my hand, and I will make thee swear before the Lord, the God of Heaven, and the God of the Earth, that thou shalt not take a wife unto my son, of the daughters of the Canaanites among whom I dwell, but thou shalt go unto my country, and to my kindred and take a wife unto my son Isaac. And the servant said unto him, Perhaps the woman will not be willing to follow me unto this land, then I must needs bring thy son again unto the land from whence thou camest. And Abraham said unto him, Beware thou that thou bring not my son thither again. The Lord God of Heaven which took me from my father's house, and from the land of my kindred, and which spake unto me, and that swear unto me, saying, Unto thee will I give this land, He shall send his angel before thee, and thou shalt take a wife unto my son from thence. And if the woman will not be willing to follow thee, then thou shalt be clear from this thine oath, only bring not my son thither again. And the servant put his hand under the hand of Abraham his master, and sware to him concerning that matter.

And the servant took ten camels of his master, and departed, for all the goods of his master were in his hand. And he arose and went to Mesopotamia, unto the city of Nahor. And he made his camels to kneel down without the city, by a well of water, at evening, the time that women go out to draw water. And he said, O Lord God of my master Abraham, I pray thee this day, that thou wouldst show kindness unto my master Abraham, and send me good speed. Behold, I stand by the well of water, and the daughters of the men of the city come out to draw water, And let it come to pass, that the damsel to whom I shall say, Let down thy pitcher I pray thee, that I may drink, and she shall say, Drink, and I will give thy camels drink also, let her be the one whom thou hast appointed for thy servant Isaac, and thereby shall I know that thou hast showed kindness unto my master.

And it came to pass, before he had done speaking, that behold, Rebekah came out, who was born to Bethuel, son of Milcah, the wife of Nahor, Abraham's brother, with her pitcher upon her shoulder. And the damsel being a virgin, very fair to look upon, such as the servant of Abraham had not seen, neither had any man known the like unto her, and she went down to the well, and filled her pitcher, and came up.

And the servant ran to meet her, and said, Let me, I pray thee, drink a little water of thy pitcher. And she said, Drink, my lord, and she hasted and let down her pitcher upon her hand, and gave him drink. And when she had done giving him drink, she said, I will draw for thy camels also, until they have done drinking. And she hasted, and emptied her pitcher into the trough, and ran again unto the well to draw, and drew for all his camels. And the man, wondering at her, held his peace, pondering in his heart whether the Lord had made his journey prosperous or not.

And it came to pass, as the camels had done drinking, that the man took a gold earring of half a shekel weight, and two bracelets for her hands of ten shekels weight of gold, and said, Whose daughter art thou? tell me, I pray thee, and is there room in thy father's house for us to lodge in? And she said unto him, I am the daughter of Bethuel, the son of Milcah, which she bare unto Nahor. She said moreover, unto him, We have both straw and provender enough, and room to lodge in. And the man bowed down his head and worshiped the Lord. And he said, Blessed is the Lord God of my master Abraham, who hath not left my master destitute of his mercy and his truth, and when I was in the way, the Lord led me to the house of my master's brethren.

And the damsel ran to the house, and told her mother these things. And Rebekah had a brother, whose name was Laban, and Laban ran out to the man, unto the well. And it came to pass when he saw the earrings, and bracelets upon his sister's hands, and when he heard the word of Rebekah his sister, saying, Thus spake the man unto me, and I came unto the man, and behold, he stood by the camels at the well. And he said, Come in, thou blessed of the Lord, wherefore standest thou without? for I have prepared the house, and room for the camels. And the man came into the house. And he unburdened his camels, and gave straw and provender for the camels, and water to wash his feet, and the men's feet that came with him. And there was set before him food to eat, but he said, I will not eat until I have told mine errand. And Laban said, Speak on. And he said, I am Abraham's servant, And the Lord hath blessed my master greatly, and he is become great, and he hath given him flocks, and herds, and silver, and gold, and menservants, and maidservants, and camels, and asses. And Sarah, my master's wife, bare a son to my master when she was old, and unto him hath he given all that he hath. And my master made me swear, saying, Thou shalt not take a wife to my son of the daughters of the Canaanites, in whose land I dwell, But thou shalt go unto my father's house, and to my kindred, and take a wife unto my son. And I said unto my master, Perhaps the woman will not follow me. And he said unto me, The Lord, before whom I walk, will send his angel with thee, and he will prosper thy way, And thou shalt take a wife for my son, of my kindred, and of my father's house, then shalt thou be clear of my oath. When thou comest to my kindred, and if they give thee not a wife for my son, thou shalt be clear from my oath. And I came this day unto the well, and said, O Lord God of my master Abraham, if now thou wilt prosper my way which I go, Behold, I stand by the well of water, and it shall come to pass, that when the virgin cometh forth to draw water, and I say to her, Give me I pray thee a little water of thy pitcher to drink, And if she say to me, Both drink thou, and I will also draw for thy camels, the same is the woman whom the Lord hath appointed out for my master's son. And before I had done speaking in my heart, behold, Rebekah came forth with her pitcher on her shoulder, and she went down unto the well and drew water. And I said unto her, Let me drink I pray thee, And she made haste, and let down her pitcher from her shoulder, and said, Drink, and I will give thy camels drink also, so I drank, and she made the camels drink also. And I asked her and said, Whose daughter art thou? And she said, The daughter of Bethuel, Nahor's son, whom Milcah bare unto him. And I gave the earrings unto her, to put into her ears, and the bracelets upon her hands. And I bowed down my head, and worshiped the Lord, and blessed the Lord God of my master Abraham, who had led me in the right way to take my master's brother's daughter unto his son. And now, if thou wilt deal kindly and truly with my master, tell me, and if not, tell me, that I may turn to the right hand or to the left. Then Laban and Bethuel answered, and said, The thing proceedeth from the Lord, we cannot speak unto thee bad or good. Behold, Rebekah is before thee, take her and go, and let her be thy master's son's wife, as the Lord hath spoken.

And it came to pass that when Abraham's servant heard these words, he worshiped the Lord, bowing himself to the earth. And the servant brought forth jewels of silver, and jewels of gold, and raiment, and gave to Rebekah. He gave also to her brother, and to her mother, precious things. And they did eat and drink, he and the men that were with him, and tarried all night. And they arose up in the morning, and he said, Send me away unto my master. And her brother, and her mother, said, Let the damsel abide with us at the least ten days, after that she shall go. And he said unto them, Hinder me not, seeing the Lord hath prospered my way, send me away, that I may go unto my master. And they said, We will call the damsel and inquire at her mouth. And they called Rebekah, and said unto her, Wilt thou go with this man? And she said, I will go. And they sent away Rebekah their sister, and her nurse, and Abraham's servant, and his men. And they blessed Rebekah, and said unto her, O thou, our sister, be thou blessed of thousands -- of millions, and let thy seed possess the gate of those who hate them.

And Rebekah arose, and her damsels, and they rode upon the camels, and followed the man, and the servant took Rebekah and went his way.

And Isaac came from the way of the well La-hai-roi, for he dwelt in the south country. And Isaac went out to meditate in the field at eventide, and he lifted up his eyes and saw and beheld the camels coming. And Rebekah lifted up her eyes, and when she saw Isaac, she lighted off the camel, for she said unto the servant, What man is this that walketh in the field to meet us? And the servant said, It is my master, therefore she took a veil and covered herself. And the servant told Isaac all things that he had done. And Isaac brought her into his mother Sarah's tent, and took Rebekah, and she became his wife, and he loved her. And Isaac was comforted after his mother's death.

Then again Abraham took a wife, and her name was Keturah. And she bare him Zimran, and Jokshan, and Medan, and Midian, and Ishbak, and Shuah. And Jokshan begat Sheba, and Dedan. And the sons of Dedan were Asshurim, and Letushim, and Leummim. And the sons of Midian, Ephah, and Epher, and Hanoch, and Abidah, and Eldaah. All these were the children of Keturah. And Abraham gave all that he had unto Isaac. But unto the sons of the concubines, which Abraham had, Abraham gave gifts, and sent them away from Isaac his son, while he yet lived, eastward, unto the east country.

And these are the number of the years of Abraham's life, which he lived, a hundred threescore and fifteen years. Then Abraham gave up the ghost, and died in a good old age, an old man, and full of years, and was gathered to his people. And his sons Isaac and Ishmael buried him in the cave of Machpelah, in the field of Ephron the son of Zohar the Hittite, which is before Mamre, The field which Abraham purchased of the sons of Heth, there was Abraham buried, and Sarah his wife.

And it came to pass after the death of Abraham, that God blessed his son Isaac, and Isaac dwelt by the well La-hai-roi.

Now these are the generations of Ishmael, Abraham's son, whom Hagar the Egyptian, Sarah's handmaid, bare unto Abraham, And these are the names of the sons of Ishmael, by their names, according to their generations, the firstborn of Ishmael, Nebajoth, and Kedar, and Adbeel, and Mibsam. And Mishma, and Dumah, and Massa. Hadar, and Tema, Jetur, Naphish, and Kedemah, These are the sons of Ishmael, and these are their names, by their towns, and by their castles, twelve princes according to their nations. And these are the number of the years of the life of Ishmael, a hundred and thirty and seven years, and he gave up the ghost and died, and was gathered unto his people. And they dwelt from Havilah unto Shur, that is before Egypt, as thou goest toward Assyria, and he died in the presence of all his brethren.

And these are the generations of Isaac, Abraham's son, Abraham begat Isaac, And Isaac was forty years old when he took Rebekah to wife, the daughter of Bethuel the Syrian of Padan-aram, the sister to Laban the Syrian.

And Isaac entreated the Lord for his wife, that she might bare children, because she was barren. And the Lord was entreated of him, and Rebekah his wife conceived. And the children struggled together within her womb, and she said, If I am with child, why is it thus with me? And she went to inquire of the Lord. And the Lord said unto her, Two nations are in thy womb, and two manner of people shall be separated from thy bowels, and the one people shall be stronger than the other people, and the elder shall serve the younger.

And when her days to be delivered were fulfilled, behold, there were twins in her womb. And the first came out red, all over like a hairy garment, and they called his name Esau. And after that came his brother out, and his hand took hold on Esau's heel, and his name was called Jacob, and Isaac was threescore years old when she bare them.

And the boys grew, and Esau was a cunning hunter, a man of the field, and Jacob was a plain man, dwelling in tents. And Isaac loved Esau, because he did eat of his venison, but Rebekah loved Jacob. And Jacob sod pottage, and Esau came from the field, and he was faint, And Esau said to Jacob, Feed me, I pray thee, with that same red pottage, for I am faint, therefore was his name called Edom. And Jacob said, Sell me this day thy birthright. And Esau said, Behold, I am at the point of dying, and what shall this birthright profit me? And Jacob said, Swear to me this day, and he swore unto him, and he sold his birthright unto Jacob. Then Jacob gave Esau bread and pottage of lentiles, and he did eat and drink, and rose up, and went his way. Thus Esau despised his birthright.

And there was a famine in the land, besides the first famine that was in the days of Abraham. And Isaac went unto Abimelech king of the Philistines unto Gerar. And the Lord appeared unto him, and said, Go not down into Egypt, dwell in the land which I shall tell thee of. Sojourn in this land, and I will be with thee, and will bless thee, for unto thee, and unto thy seed, I will give all these countries, and I will perform the oath which I sware unto Abraham thy father, And I will make thy seed to multiply as the stars of Heaven, and will give unto thy seed all these countries, and in thy seed shall all the nations of the Earth be blessed, Because that Abraham obeyed my voice, and kept my charge, my commandments, my statutes, and my laws.

And Isaac dwelt in Gerar. And the men of the place asked him concerning his wife, and he said, She is my sister, for he feared to say, She in my wife, lest, the men of the place should kill him for to get Rebekah, because she was fair to look upon.

And it came to pass, when he had been there a long time, that Abimelech king of the Philistines looked out at a window, and saw, and, behold, Isaac was sporting with Rebekah his wife. And Abimelech called Isaac, and said, Behold, of a surety Rebekah is thy wife, and how saidst thou she is thy sister? And Isaac said unto him, I said it because I feared lest I die for her. And Abimelech said, What is this thou hast done unto us? one of the people might lightly have lain with thy wife, and thou shouldest have brought guiltiness upon us. And Abimelech charged all his people, saying, He that thoucheth this man or his wife shall surely be put to death.

Then Isaac sowed in that land, and received in the same year a hundredfold, and the Lord blessed him. And the man waxed great, and went forward, and grew until he became very great, For he had possession of flocks, and possession of herds, and great store of servants, and the Philistines envied him. For all the wells which his father's servants had digged in the days of Abraham his father, the Philistines had stopped them, and filled them with earth.

And Abimelech said unto Isaac, Go from us, for thou art much mightier than we. And Isaac departed thence, and pitched his tent in the valley of Gerar, and dwelt there.

And Isaac digged again the wells of water, which they had digged in the days of Abraham his father, for the Philistines had stopped them after the death of Abraham, and he called their names after the names by which his father had called them. And Isaac's servants digged in the valley, and found there a well of springing water.

And the herdman of Gerar did strive with Isaac's herdmen, saying, The water is ours, and he called the name of the well Esek, because they strove with him. And they digged another well, and strove for that also, and he called the name of it Sitnah. And he removed from thence, and digged another well, and for that they strove not, and he called the name of it Rehoboth, and he said, For now the Lord hath made room for us, and we shall be fruitful in the land. And he went up from thence to Beer-sheba. And the Lord appeared unto him the same night, and said, I am the God of Abraham thy father, fear not, for I am with thee, and will bless thee, and multiply thy seed for my servant Abraham's sake. And he builded an altar there, and called upon the name of the Lord, and pitched his tent there, and there Isaac's servants digged a well.

Then Abimelech went to him from Gerar, and Ahuzzath one of his friends, and Phichol the chief captain of his army. And Isaac said unto them, Wherefore come ye to me, seeing ye hate me, and have sent me away from you? And they said, We saw certainly that the Lord was with thee, and we said, Let there be now an oath betwixt us, even betwixt us and thee, and let us make a covenant with thee, That thou wilt do us no hurt, as we have not touched thee, and as we have done unto thee nothing but good, and have sent thee away in peace, thou art now the blessed of the Lord. And he made them a feast, and they did eat and drink. And they rose up betimes in the morning, and sware one to another, and Isaac sent them away, and they departed from him in peace. And it came to pass the same day, That Isaac's servants came, and told him concerning the well which they had digged, and said unto him, We have found water. And he called it Sheba, therefore the name of the city is Beer-sheba unto this day.

And Esau was forty years old when he took to wife Judith the daughter of Beeri the Hittite, and Bashemath the daughter of Elon the Hittite, Which was a grief of mind unto Isaac and to Rebekah.

And it came to pass, that when Isaac was old, and his eyes were dim, so that he could not see, he called Esau his eldest son, and said unto him, My son, and he said unto him, Behold, here am I. And he said, Behold, now, I am old, I know not the day of my death, Now therefore take, I pray thee, thy weapons, thy quiver and thy bow, and go out to the field, and take me some venison, And make me savory meat, such as I love, and bring it to me, that I may eat, that my soul may bless thee before I die.

And Rebekah heard when Isaac spake to Esau his son. And Esau went to the field to hunt for venison, and to bring it. And Rebekah spake unto Jacob her son, saying, Behold, I heard thy father speak unto Esau thy brother, saying, Bring me venison, and make me savory meat, that I may eat, and bless thee before the Lord before my death. Now therefore, my son, obey my voice according to that which I command thee. Go now to the flock, and fetch me from thence two good kids of the goats, and I will make them savory meat for thy father, such as he loveth, And thou shalt bring it to thy father, that he may eat, and that he may bless thee before his death. And Jacob said to Rebekah his mother, Behold, Esau my brother is a hairy man, and I am a smooth man, My father peradventure will feel me, and I shall seem to him as a deceiver, and I shall bring a curse upon me, and not a blessing. And his mother said unto him, Upon me be thy curse, my son, only obey my voice, and go fetch me them.

And he went, and fetched, and brought them to his mother, and his mother made savory meat, such as his father loved. And Rebekah took goodly raiment of her eldest son Esau, which were with her in the house, and put them upon Jacob her younger son, And she put the skins of the kids of the goats upon his hands, and upon the smooth of his neck, And she gave the savory meat and the bread, which she had prepared, into the hand of her son Jacob.

And he came unto his father, and said, My father, and he said, Here am I, who art thou, my son? And Jacob said unto his father, I am Esau thy firstborn, I have done according as thou badest me, arise, I pray thee, sit and eat of my venison, that thy soul may bless me. And Isaac said unto his son, How is it that thou hast found it so quickly, my son? And he said, Because the Lord thy God brought it to me. And Isaac said unto Jacob, Come near, I pray thee, that I may feel thee, my son, whether thou be my very son Esau or not. And Jacob went near unto Isaac his father, and he felt him and said, The voice is Jacob's voice, but the hands are the hands of Esau. And he discerned him not, because his hands were hairy, as his brother Esau's hands, so he blessed him. And he said, Art thou my very son Esau? And he said, I am. And he said, Bring it near to me, and I will eat of my son's venison, that my soul may bless thee. And he brought it near to him, and he did eat, and he brought him wine, and he drank. And his father Isaac said unto him, Come near now, and kiss me, my son. And he came near, and kissed him, and he smelled the smell of his raiment, and blessed him, and said, See, the smell of my son is as the smell of a field which the Lord hath blessed, Therefore God give thee of the dew of Heaven, and the fatness of the Earth, and plenty of corn and wine, Let people serve thee, and nations bow down to thee, be lord over thy brethren, and let thy mother's sons bow down to thee, cursed be every one that curseth thee, and blessed be he that blesseth thee. And it came to pass, as soon as Isaac had made an end of blessing Jacob, and Jacob was yet scarce gone out from the presence of Isaac his father, that Esau his brother came in from his hunting.

And he also had made savory meat, and brought it unto his father, and said unto his father, Let my father arise, and eat of his son's venison, that thy soul may bless me. And Isaac his father said unto him, Who art thou? And he said, I am thy son, thy firstborn, Esau. And Isaac trembled very exceedingly, and said, Who? where is he that hath taken venison, and brought it me, and I have eaten of all before thou camest, and have blessed him? Yea, and he shall be blessed. And when Esau heard the words of his father, he cried with a great and exceeding bitter cry, and said unto his father, Bless me, even me also, O my father. And he said, Thy brother came with subtilty, and hath taken away thy blessing. And he said, Is not he rightly named Jacob? for he hath supplanted me these two times, he took away my birthright, and, behold, now he hath taken away my blessing. And he said, Hast thou not reserved a blessing for me? And Isaac answered and said unto Esau, Behold, I have made him thy lord, and all his brethren have I given to him for servants, and with corn and wine have I sustained him, and what shall I do now unto thee, my son? And Esau said unto his father, Hast thou but one blessing, my father? bless me, even me also, O my father. And Esau lifted up his voice, and wept. And Isaac his father answered and said unto him, Behold, thy dwelling shall be the fatness of the Earth, and of the dew of Heaven from above, And by thy sword shalt thou live, and shalt serve thy brother, and it shall come to pass when thou shalt have the dominion, that thou shalt break his yoke from off thy neck.

And Esau hated Jacob because of the blessing wherewith his father blessed him, and Esau said in his heart, The days of mourning for my father are at hand, then will I slay my brother Jacob. And these words of Esau her elder son were told to Rebekah, and she sent and called Jacob her younger son, and said unto him, Behold, thy brother Esau, as touching thee, doth comfort himself, purposing to kill thee. Now therefore, my son, obey my voice, and arise, flee thou to Laban my brother, to Haran, And tarry with him a few days, until thy brother's fury turn away, Until thy brother's anger turn away from thee, and he forget that which thou hast done to him, then I will send, and fetch thee from thence, why should I be deprived also of you both in one day? And Rebekah said to Isaac, I am weary of my life because of the daughters of Heth, if Jacob take a wife of the daughters of Heth, such as these which are of the daughters of the land, what good shall my life do me?

And Isaac called Jacob, and blessed him, and charged him, and said unto him, Thou shalt not take a wife of the daughters of Canaan. Arise, go to Padan-aram, to the house of Bethuel thy mother's father, and take thee a wife from thence of the daughters of Laban thy mother's brother. And God Almighty bless thee, and make thee fruitful, and multiply thee, that thou mayest be a multitude of people, And give thee the blessing of Abraham, to thee, and to thy seed with thee, that thou mayest inherit the land wherein thou art a stranger, which God gave unto Abraham. And Isaac sent away Jacob, and he went to Padan-aram unto Laban, son of Bethuel the Syrian, the brother of Rebekah, Jacob's and Esau's mother.

When Esau saw that Isaac had blessed Jacob, and sent him away to Padan-aram, to take him a wife from thence, and that as he blessed him he gave him a charge, saying, Thou shalt not take a wife of the daughters of Canaan, And that Jacob obeyed his father and his mother, and was gone to Padan-aram, And Esau seeing that the daughters of Canaan pleased not Isaac his father, Then went Esau unto Ishmael, and took unto the wives which he had Mahalath the daughter of Ishmael Abraham's son, the sister of Nebajoth, to be his wife.

And Jacob went out from Beer-sheba, and went toward Haran. And he lighted upon a certain place, and tarried there all night, because the sun was set, and he took of the stones of that place, and put them for his pillows, and lay down in that place to sleep. And he dreamed, and behold a ladder set up on the Earth, and the top of it reached to Heaven, and behold the angels of God ascending and descending upon it. And, behold, the Lord stood above it, and said, I am the Lord God of Abraham thy father, and the God of Isaac, the land whereon thou liest, to thee will I give it, and to thy seed, And thy seed shall be as the dust of the Earth, and thou shalt spread abroad to the west, and to the east, and to the north, and to the south, and in thee and in thy seed shall all the families of the Earth be blessed. And, behold, I am with thee, and will keep thee in all places whither thou goest, and will bring thee again into this land, for I will not leave thee, until I have done that which I have spoken to thee of.

And Jacob awaked out of his sleep, and he said, Surely the Lord is in this place, and I knew it not. And he was afraid, and said, How dreadful is this place! This is none other but the house of God and this is the gate of Heaven. And Jacob rose up early in the morning, and took the stone that he had put for his pillows, and set it up for a pillar, and poured oil upon the top of it. And he called the name of that place Beth-el, but the name of that city was called Luz at the first. And Jacob vowed a vow, saying, If God will be with me, and will keep me in this way that I go, and will give me bread to eat, and raiment to put on, So that I come again to my father's house in peace, then shall the Lord be my God, And the place of this stone which I have set for a pillar, shall be the place of God's house, and of all that thou shalt give me I will surely give the tenth unto thee.

Then Jacob went on his journey, and came into the land of the people of the east. And he looked, and behold a well in the field, and, lo, there were three flocks of sheep lying by it, for out of that well they watered the flocks, and a great stone was upon the well's mouth. And thither were all the flocks gathered, and they rolled the stone from the well's mouth, and watered the sheep, and put the stone again upon the well's mouth in his place. And Jacob said unto them, My brethren, from whence are ye? And they said, From Haran. And he said unto them, Know ye Laban the son of Nahor? And they said, We know him. And he said unto them, Is he well? And they said, He is well, and, behold, Rachel, his daughter cometh with the sheep. And he said, Lo, it is yet high day, neither is it time that the cattle should be gathered together, water ye the sheep, and go and feed them. And they said, We cannot, until all the flocks be gathered together, and till they roll the stone from the well's mouth, then we water the sheep. And while he yet spake with them, Rachel came with her father's sheep, for she kept them. And it came to pass, when Jacob saw Rachel the daughter of Laban his mother's brother, and the sheep of Laban his mother's brother, that Jacob went near, and rolled the stone from the well's mouth, and watered the flock of Laban his mother's brother. And Jacob kissed Rachel, and lifted up his voice, and wept. And Jacob told Rachel that he was her father's brother, and that he was Rebekah's son, and she ran and told her father.

And it came to pass, when Laban heard the tidings of Jacob his sister's son, that he ran to meet him, and embraced him, and kissed him, and brought him to his house. And he told Laban all these things. And Laban said to him, Surely thou art my bone and my flesh. And he abode with him the space of a month. And Laban said unto Jacob, Because thou art my brother, shouldest thou therefore serve me for naught? Tell me, what shall thy wages be? And Laban had two daughters, the name of the elder was Leah, and the name of the younger was Rachel. Leah was tender-eyed, but Rachel was beautiful and well-favored. And Jacob loved Rachel, and said, I will serve thee seven years for Rachel thy younger daughter. And Laban said, It is better that I give her to thee, than that I should give her to another man, abide with me.

And Jacob served seven years for Rachel, and they seemed unto him but a few days, for the love he had to her. And Jacob said unto Laban, Give unto me my wife, that I may go and take her, for my days of serving thee are fulfilled. And Laban gave her to Jacob, and gathered together all the men of the place, and made a feast. And it came to pass in the evening, that he took Leah his daughter, and brought her to Jacob, and she went in and slept with him. And Laban gave unto his daughter Leah, Zilpah, his handmaid, to be a handmaid for her. And it came to pass, that in the morning, behold, it was Leah, and he said to Laban, What is this thou hast done unto me? Did not I serve with thee for Rachel? Wherefore then hast thou beguiled me? And Laban said, It must not be so done in our country, to give the younger before the firstborn. Fulfill her week, and we will give thee this also for the service which thou shalt serve with me yet seven other years. And Jacob did so, and fulfilled her week, and he gave him Rachel his daughter to wife also. And Laban gave to Rachel his daughter, Bilhah, his handmaid, to be her maid. And he went in also and slept with Rachel, and he loved Rachel also, more than Leah, and served with Laban yet seven other years.

And when the Lord saw that Leah was hated, he opened her womb, but Rachel was barren. And Leah conceived, and bare a son, and she called his name Reuben, for she said, Surely the Lord hath looked upon my affliction, now therefore my husband will love me. And she conceived again, and bare a son, and said, Because the Lord hath heard that I was hated, he hath therefore given me this son also, and she called his name Simeon. And she conceived again, and bare a son, and said, Now this time will my husband be joined unto me, because I have borne him three sons, therefore was his name called Levi. And she conceived again, and bare a son, and she said, Now will I praise the Lord, therefore she called his name Judah, and left bearing.

And when Rachel saw that she bare Jacob no children, Rachel envied her sister, and said unto Jacob, Give me children, or else I die. And Jacob's anger was kindled against Rachel, and he said, Am I in God's stead, who hath withheld from thee the fruit of the womb? And she said, Behold my maid Bilhah, go in and lie with her, and she shall bear upon my knees, that I may also have children by her. And she gave him Bilhah her handmaid to wife, and Jacob went and lay with her. And Bilhah conceived, and bare Jacob a son. And Rachel said, God hath judged me, and hath also heard my voice, and hath given me a son, therefore called she his name Dan. And Bilhah, Rachel's maid conceived again and bare Jacob a second son. And Rachel said, With great wrestlings have I wrestled with my sister, and I have prevailed, and she called his name Naphtali. When Leah saw that she had left bearing, she took Zilpah her maid, and gave her unto Jacob to wife. And Zilpah Leah's maid bare Jacob a son. And Leah said, A troop cometh, and she called his name Gad. And Zilpah Leah's maid bare Jacob a second son. And Leah said, Happy am I, for the daughters will call me blessed, and she called his name Asher. And Reuben went in the days of wheat harvest, and found mandrakes in the field, and brought them unto his mother Leah. Then Rachel said to Leah, Give me, I pray thee, of thy son's mandrakes. And she said unto her, Is it a small matter that thou hast taken my husband? And wouldest thou take away my son's mandrakes also? And Rachel said, Therefore he shall lie with thee tonight for thy son's mandrakes. And Jacob came out of the field in the evening, and Leah went out to meet him, and said, Thou must come in and lie with me, for surely I have hired thee with my son's mandrakes. And he lay with her that night. And God hearkened unto Leah, and she conceived, and bare Jacob the fifth son. And Leah said, God hath given me my hire, because I have given my maiden to my husband, and she called his name Issachar. And Leah conceived again, and bare Jacob the sixth son. And Leah said, God hath endued me with a good dowry, now will my husband dwell with me, because I have borne him six sons, and she called his name Zebulun. And afterwards she bare a daughter, and called her name Dinah. And God remembered Rachel, and God hearkened to her, and opened her womb. And she conceived, and bare a son, and said, God hath taken away my reproach, And she called his name Joseph, and said, The Lord shall add to me another son.

And it came to pass, when Rachel had borne Joseph, that Jacob said unto Laban, Send me away, that I may go unto mine own place, and to my country. Give me my wives and my children, for whom I have served thee, and let me go, for thou knowest my service which I have done thee. And Laban said unto him, I pray thee, if I have found favor in thine eyes, tarry, for I have learned by experience that the Lord hath blessed me for thy sake. And he said, Appoint me thy wages, and I will give it. And he said unto him, Thou knowest how I have served thee and how thy cattle was with me. For it was little which thou hadst before I came, and it is now increased unto a multitude, and the Lord hath blessed thee since my coming, and now, when shall I provide for mine own house also? And he said, What shall I give thee? And Jacob said, Thou shalt not give me anything, if thou wilt do this thing for me, I will again feed and keep thy flock. I will pass through all thy flock today, removing from thence all the speckled and spotted cattle, and all the brown cattle among the sheep, and the spotted and speckled among the goats, and of such shall be my hire. So shall my righteousness answer for me in time to come, when it shall come for my hire before thy face, every one that is not speckled and spotted among the goats, and brown among the sheep, that shall be counted stolen with me. And Laban said, Behold, I would it might be according to thy word.

And he removed that day the he goats that were ringstreaked and spotted, and all the she goats that were speckled and spotted, and every one that had some white in it, and all the brown among the sheep, and gave them into the hand of his sons. And he set three days' journey betwixt himself and Jacob, and Jacob fed the rest of Laban's flocks. And Jacob took him rods of green poplar, and of the hazel and chestnut tree, and pilled white streaks in them, and made the white appear which was in the rods. And he set the rods which he had pilled before the flocks in the gutters in the watering troughs when the flocks came to drink, that they should conceive when they came to drink. And the flocks conceived before the rods, and brought forth cattle ringstreaked, speckled, and spotted. And Jacob did separate the lambs, and set the faces of the flocks toward the ringstreaked, and all the brown in the flock of Laban, and he put his own flocks by themselves, and put them not unto Laban's cattle.

And it came to pass, whensoever the stronger cattle did conceive, that Jacob laid the rods before the eyes of the cattle in the gutters, that they might conceive among the rods. But when the cattle were feeble, he put them not in, so the feebler were Laban's, and the stronger Jacob's. And the man increased exceedingly, and had much cattle, and maidservants, and menservants, and camels, and asses.

And he heard the words of Laban's sons, saying, Jacob hath taken away all that was our father's, and of that which was our father's hath he gotten all this glory. And Jacob beheld the countenance of Laban, and, behold, it was not toward him as before.

And the Lord said unto Jacob, Return unto the land of thy fathers, and to thy kindred, and I will be with thee.

And Jacob sent and called Rachel and Leah to the field unto his flock, And said unto them, I see your father's countenance, that it is not toward me as before, but the God of my father hath been with me. And ye know that with all my power I have served your father. And your father hath deceived me, and changed my wages ten times, but God suffered him not to hurt me. If he said thus, The speckled shall be thy wages, then all the cattle bare speckled, and it he said thus, The ringstreaked shall be thy hire, then bare all the cattle ringstreaked. Thus God hath taken away the cattle of your father, and given them to me. And it came to pass at the time that the cattle conceived, that I lifted up mine eyes, and saw in a dream, and, behold, the rams which leaped upon the cattle were ringstreaked, speckled, and grizzled. And the angel of God spake unto me in a dream, saying, Jacob, and I said, Here am I. And he said, Lift up now thine eyes, and see, all the rams which leap upon the cattle are ringstreaked, speckled, and grizzled, for I have seen all that Laban doeth unto thee. I am the God of Beth-el, where thou anointedst the pillar, and where thou vowedst a vow unto me, now arise, get thee out from this land, and return unto the land of thy kindred.

And Rachel and Leah answered and said unto him, Is there yet any portion or inheritance for us in our father's house? Are we not counted of him strangers? For he hath sold us, and hath quite devoured also our money. For all the riches which God hath taken from our father, that is ours, and our children's, now then whatsoever God hath said unto thee, do. Then Jacob rose up and set his sons and his wives upon camels, And he carried away all his cattle, and all his goods which he had gotten, the cattle of his getting, which he had gotten in Padan- aram, for to go to Isaac his father in the land of Canaan. And Laban went to shear his sheep, and Rachel had stolen the images that were her father's. And Jacob stole away unawares to Laban the Syrian, in that he told him not that he fled.

So he fled with all that he had, and he rose up, and passed over the river, and set his face toward the mount Gilead.

And it was told Laban on the third day, that Jacob had fled. And he took his brethren with him, and pursued after him seven days' journey, and they overtook him in the mount Gilead. And God came to Laban the Syrian in a dream by night, and said unto him, Take heed that thou speak not to Jacob either good or bad. Then Laban overtook Jacob.

Now Jacob had pitched his tent in the mount, and Laban with his brethren pitched in the mount of Gilead. And Laban said to Jacob, What hast thou done, that thou hast stolen away unawares to me, and carried away my daughters, as captives taken with the sword? Wherefore didst thou flee away secretly, and steal away from me, and didst not tell me, that I might have sent thee away with mirth, and with songs, with tabret, and with harp? And hast not suffered me to kiss my sons and my daughters? thou hast now done foolishly in so doing. It is in the power of my hand to do you hurt, but the God of your father spake unto me yesternight, saying, Take thou heed that thou speak not to Jacob either good or bad. And now, though thou wouldest needs be gone, because thou sore longedst after thy father's house, yet wherefore hast thou stolen my gods? And Jacob answered and said to Laban, Because I was afraid, for I said, Peradventure thou wouldest take by force thy daughters from me. With whomsoever thou findest thy gods, let him not live, before our brethren discern thou what is thine with me, and take it to thee. For Jacob knew not that Rachel had stolen them. And Laban went into Jacob's tent, and into Leah's tent, and into the two maidservants' tents, but he found them not. Then went he out of Leah's tent, and entered into Rachel's tent.

Now Rachel had taken the images, and put them in the camel's furniture, and sat upon them. And Laban searched all the tent, but found them not. And she said to her father, Let it not displease my lord that I cannot rise up before thee, for the custom of women is upon me. And he searched, but found not the images. And Jacob was wroth, and chode with Laban, and Jacob answered and said to Laban, What is my trespass? What is my sin, that thou hast so hotly pursued after me? Whereas thou hast searched all my stuff, what hast thou found of all thy household stuff? Set it here before my brethren and thy brethren that they may judge betwixt us both. This twenty years have I been with thee, thy ewes and thy she goats have not cast their young, and the rams of thy flock have I not eaten. That which was torn of beasts I brought not unto thee, I bare the loss of it, of my hand didst thou require it, whether stolen by day, or stolen by night. Thus I was, in the day the drought consumed me, and the frost by night, and my sleep departed from mine eyes. Thus have I been twenty years in thy house, I served thee fourteen years for thy two daughters, and six years for thy cattle, and thou hast changed my wages ten times. Except the God of my father, the God of Abraham, and the fear of Isaac, had been with me, surely thou hadst sent me away now empty. God hath seen my affliction and the labor of my hands, and rebuked thee yesternight.

And Laban answered and said unto Jacob, These daughters are my daughters, and these children are my children, and these cattle are my cattle, and all that thou seest is mine, and what can I do this day unto these my daughters, or unto their children which they have borne? Now therefore come thou, let us make a covenant, I and thou, and let it be for a witness between me and thee. And Jacob took a stone, and set it up for a pillar. And Jacob said unto his brethren, Gather stones, and they took stones, and made a heap, and they did eat there upon the heap. And Laban called it Jegarsahadutha, but Jacob called it Galeed. And Laban said, This heap is a witness between me and thee this day. Therefore was the name of it called Galeed, And Mizpah, for he said, The Lord watch between me and thee, when we are absent one from another. If thou shalt afflict my daughters, or if thou shalt take other wives beside my daughters, no man is with us, see, God is witness betwixt me and thee. And Laban said to Jacob, Behold this heap, and behold this pillar, which I have cast betwixt me and thee, This heap be witness, and this pillar be witness, that I will not pass over this heap to thee, and that thou shalt not pass over this heap and this pillar unto me, for harm. The God of Abraham, and the God of Nahor, the God of their father, judge betwixt us. And Jacob sware by the fear of his father Isaac. Then Jacob offered sacrifice upon the mount, and called his brethren to eat bread, and they did eat bread, and tarried all night in the mount. And early in the morning Laban rose up, and kissed his sons and his daughters, and blessed them, and Laban departed, and returned unto his place.

And Jacob went on his way, and the angels of God met him. And when Jacob saw them, he said, This is God's host, and he called the name of that place Mahanaim. And Jacob sent messengers before him to Esau his brother unto the land of Seir, the country of Edom. And he commanded them, saying, Thus shall ye speak unto my lord Esau, Thy servant Jacob saith thus, I have sojourned with Laban and stayed there until now, and I have oxen, and asses, flocks, and menservants, and womenservants, and I have sent to tell my lord, that I may find grace in thy sight.

And the messengers returned to Jacob, saying, We came to thy brother Esau, and also he cometh to meet thee, and four hundred men with him. Then Jacob was greatly afraid and distressed, and he divided the people that was with him, and the flocks, and herds, and the camels, into two bands, And said, If Esau come to the one company, and smite it, then the other company which is left shall escape. And Jacob said, O God of my father Abraham, and God of my father Isaac, the Lord which saidst unto me, Return unto thy country and to thy kindred and I will deal well with thee. I am not worthy of the least of all the mercies and of all the truth which thou hast showed unto thy servant, for with my staff I passed over this Jordan and now I am become two bands. Deliver me, I pray thee, from the hand of my brother, from the hand of Esau, for I fear him, lest he will come and smite me and the mothers with the children. And thou saidst, I will surely do thee good and make thy seed as the sand of the sea which cannot be numbered for multitude.

And he lodged there that same night and took of that which came to his hand a present for Esau his brother, two hundred she goats and twenty he goats, two hundred ewes and twenty rams, thirty milch camels with their colts, forty kine and ten bulls, twenty she asses and ten foals. And he delivered them into the hand of his servants, every drove by themselves, and said unto his servants, Pass over before me and put a space betwixt drove and drove. And he commanded the foremost, saying, When Esau my brother meeteth thee, and asketh thee, saying, Whose art thou? And whither goest thou? And whose are these before thee? And thou shalt say, They be thy servant Jacob's, it is a present sent unto my lord Esau, and behold, also he is behind us.

And so commanded he the second and the third, and all that followed the droves, saying, On this manner shall ye speak unto Esau, when ye find him. And say ye moreover, Behold, thy servant Jacob is behind us. For he said I will appease him with the present that goeth before me, and afterward I will see his face, peradventure he will accept of me. So went the present over before him, and himself lodged that night in the company.

And he rose up that night, and took his two wives, and his two womenservants, and his eleven sons, and passed over the ford Jabbok. And he took them, and sent them over the brook, and sent over that he had.

And Jacob was left alone and there wrestled a man with him until the breaking of the day. And when he saw that he prevailed not against him, he touched the hollow of his thigh, and the hollow of Jacob's thigh was out of joint, as he wrestled with him. And he said, Let me go, for the day breaketh. And he said, I will not let thee go, except thou bless me. And he said unto him, What is thy name? And he said, Jacob. And he said, Thy name shall be called no more Jacob, but Israel, for as a prince hast thou power with God and with men and hast prevailed. And Jacob asked him and said, Tell me, I pray thee, thy name. And he said, Wherefore is it that thou dost ask after my name? And he blessed him there. And Jacob called the name of the place Peniel, for I have seen God face to face and my life is preserved. And as he passed over Penuel the sun rose upon him and he halted upon his thigh. Therefore the children of Israel eat not of the sinew which shrank, which is upon the hollow of the thigh, unto this day, because he touched the hollow of Jacob's thigh in the sinew that shrank.

And Jacob lifted up his eyes, and looked, and, behold, Esau came, and with him four hundred men. And he divided the children unto Leah, and unto Rachel, and unto the two handmaids. And he put the handmaids and their children foremost, and Leah and her children after, and Rachel and Joseph hindermost.

And he passed over before them and bowed himself to the ground seven times until he came near to his brother.

And Esau ran to meet him and embraced him and fell on his neck and kissed him, and they wept. And he lifted up his eyes and saw the women and the children, and said, Who are those with thee? And he said, The children which God hath graciously given thy servant. Then the handmaidens came near, they and their children, and they bowed themselves. And Leah also with her children came near and bowed themselves, and after came Joseph near and Rachel, and they bowed themselves. And he said, What meanest thou by all this drove which I met? And he said, These are to find grace in the sight of my lord. And Esau said, I have enough, my brother, keep that thou hast unto thyself. And Jacob said, Nay, I pray thee, if now I have found grace in thy sight, then receive my present at my hand, for therefore I have seen thy face, as though I had seen the face of God, and thou wast pleased with me. Take, I pray thee, my blessing that is brought to thee, because God hath dealt graciously with me and because I have enough. And he urged him, and he took it.

And he said, Let us take our journey, and let us go, and I will go before thee. And he said unto him, My lord knoweth that the children are tender, and the flocks and herds with young are with me, and if men should overdrive them one day, all the flock will die. Let my lord, I pray thee, pass over before his servant, and I will lead on softly, according as the cattle that goeth before me and the children be able to endure, until I come unto my lord unto Seir. And Esau said, Let me now leave with thee some of the folk that are with me. And he said, What needeth it? Let me find grace in the sight of my lord. So Esau returned that day on his way unto Seir. And Jacob journeyed to Succoth and built him a house and made booths for his cattle, therefore the name of the place is called Succoth.

And Jacob came to Shalem, a city of Shechem, which is in the land of Canaan, when he came from Padan-aram, and pitched his tent before the city. And he bought a parcel of a field, where he had spread his tent, at the hand of the children of Hamor, Shechem's father, for a hundred pieces of money.

And he erected there an altar, and called it El-Elohe-Israel.

And Dinah the daughter of Leah, which she bare unto Jacob, went out to see the daughters of the land. And when Shechem the son of Hamor the Hivite, prince of the country, saw her, he took her, and lay with her, and defiled her. And his soul clave unto Dinah the daughter of Jacob, and he loved the damsel, and spake kindly unto the damsel. And Shechem spake unto his father Hamor, saying, Get me this damsel to wife. And Jacob heard that he had defiled Dinah his daughter, now his sons were with his cattle in the field, and Jacob held his peace until they were come. And Hamor the father of Shechem went out unto Jacob to commune with him. And the sons of Jacob came out of the field when they heard it, and the men were grieved, and they were very wroth, because he had wrought folly in Israel in lying with Jacob's daughter, which thing ought not to be done. And Hamor communed with them, saying, The soul of my son Shechem longeth for your daughter, I pray you give her him to wife. And make ye marriages with us, and give your daughters unto us, and take our daughters unto you. And ye shall dwell with us, and the land shall be before you, dwell and trade ye therein, and get you possessions therein. And Shechem said unto her father and unto her brethren, Let me find grace in your eyes, and what ye shall say unto me I will give. Ask me never so much dowry and gift, and I will give according as ye shall say unto me, but give me the damsel to wife. And the sons of Jacob answered Shechem and Hamor his father deceitfully, and said, because he had defiled Dinah their sister, and they said unto them, We cannot do this thing, t*o give our sister to one that is uncircumcised, for that were a reproach unto us, But in this will we consent unto you, If ye will be as we be, that every male of you be circumcised, Then will we give our daughters unto you, and we will take your daughters to us, and we will dwell with you, and we will become one people. But if ye will not hearken unto us, to be circumcised, then will we take our daughter, and we will be gone. And their words pleased Hamor and Shechem Hamor's son. And the young man deferred not to do the thing, because he had delight in Jacob's daughter, and he was more honorable than all the house of his father. And Hamor and Shechem his son came unto the gate of their city, and communed with the men of their city, saying, These men are peaceable with us, therefore let them dwell in the land, and trade therein, for the land, behold, it is large enough for them, let us take their daughters to us for wives, and let us give them our daughters. Only herein will the men consent unto us for to dwell with us, to be one people, if every male among us be circumcised, as they are circumcised. Shall not their cattle and their substance and every beast of theirs be ours? Only let us consent unto them and they will dwell with us. And unto Hamor and unto Shechem his son hearkened all that went out of the gate of his city, and every male was circumcised, all that went out of the gate of his city. And it came to pass on the third day, when they were sore, that two of the sons of Jacob, Simeon and Levi, Dinah's brethren, took each man his sword, and came upon the city boldly, and slew all the males. And they slew Hamor and Shechem his son with the edge of the sword, and took Dinah out of Shechem's house, and went out. The sons of Jacob came upon the slain, and spoiled the city, because they had defiled their sister. They took their sheep, and their oxen, and their asses, and that which was in the city, and that which was in the field, And all their wealth, and all their little ones, and their wives took they captive, and spoiled even all that was in the house. And Jacob said to Simeon and Levi, Ye have troubled me to make me to stink among the inhabitants of the land, among the Canaanites and the Perizzites, and I being few in number, they shall gather themselves together against me, and slay me, and I shall be destroyed, I and my house. And they said, Should he deal with our sister as with a harlot?

And God said unto Jacob, Arise, go up to Beth-el, and dwell there, and make there an altar unto God, that appeared unto thee when thou fleddest from the face of Esau thy brother.

Then Jacob said unto his household, and to all that were with him, Put away the strange gods that are among you and be clean and change your garments, and let us arise and go up to Beth-el, and I will make there an altar unto God who answered me in the day of my distress and was with me in the way which I went. And they gave unto Jacob all the strange gods which were in their hand and all their earrings which were in their ears and Jacob hid them under the oak which was by Shechem.

And they journeyed, and the terror of God was upon the cities that were round about them, and they did not pursue after the sons of Jacob.

So Jacob came to Luz which is in the land of Canaan, that is, Beth-el, he and all the people that were with him. And he built there an altar, and called the place El-beth-el, because there God appeared unto him when he fled from the face of his brother. But Deborah Rebekah's nurse died, and she was buried beneath Beth-el under an oak, and the name of it was called Allonbachuth. And God appeared unto Jacob again, when he came out of Padanaram, and blessed him. And God said unto him, Thy name is Jacob, thy name shall not be called any more Jacob, but Israel shall be thy name, and he called his name Israel. And God said unto him, I am God Almighty, be fruitful and multiply, a nation and a company of nations shall be of thee, and kings shall come out of thy loins, And the land which I gave Abraham and Isaac, to thee I will give it, and to thy seed after thee will I give the land. And God went up from him in the place where he talked with him.

And Jacob set up a pillar in the place where he talked with him, even a pillar of stone, and he poured a drink offering thereon, and he poured oil thereon. And Jacob called the name of the place where God spake with him, Beth-el.

And they journeyed from Beth-el, and there was but a little way to come to Ephrath, and Rachel travailed, and she had hard labor. And it came to pass, when she was in hard labor, that the midwife said unto her, Fear not, thou shalt have this son also. And it came to pass, as her soul was in departing, (for she died,) that she called his name Ben-oni, but his father called him Benjamin. And Rachel died, and was buried in the way to Ephrath, which is Bethlehem. And Jacob set a pillar upon her grave, that is the pillar of Rachel's grave unto this day.

And Israel journeyed, and spread his tent beyond the tower of Edar. And it came to pass, when Israel dwelt in that land, that Reuben went and lay with Bilhah his father's concubine, and Israel heard it. Now the sons of Jacob were twelve. The sons of Leah, Reuben, Jacob's firstborn, and Simeon, and Levi, and Judah, and Issachar, and Zebulun, The sons of Rachel, Joseph, and Benjamin, And the sons of Bilhah, Rachel's handmaid, Dan, and Naphtali, And the sons of Zilpah, Leah's handmaid, Gad, and Asher. These are the sons of Jacob, which were born to him in Padan-aram.

And Jacob came unto Isaac his father unto Mamre, unto the city of Arba, which is Hebron, where Abraham and Isaac sojourned.

And the days of Isaac were a hundred and fourscore years. And Isaac gave up the ghost, and died, and was gathered unto his people, being old and full of days, and his sons Esau and Jacob buried him.

8 NOW these are the generations of Esau, who is Edom. Esau took his wives of the daughters of Canaan, Adah the daughter of Elon the Hittite, and Aholibamah the daughter of Anah the daughter of Zibeon the Hivite, And Bashemath Ishmael's daughter, sister of Nebajoth. And Adah bare to Esau Eliphaz, and Bashemath bare Reuel, And Aholibamah bare Jeush, and Jaalam, and Korah, these are the sons of Esau, which were born unto him in the land of Canaan.

And Esau took his wives, and his sons, and his daughters, and all the persons of his house, and his cattle, and all his beasts, and all his substance, which he had got in the land of Canaan, and went into the country from the face of his brother Jacob. For their riches were more than that they might dwell together, and the land wherin they were strangers could not bear them because of their cattle. Thus dwelt Esau in mount Seir, Esau is Edom.

And these are the generations of Esau the father of the Edomites in mount Seir, These are the names of Esau's sons, Eliphaz the son of Adah the wife of Esau, Reuel the son of Bashemath the wife of Esau. And the sons of Eliphaz were Teman, Omar, Zepho, and Gatam, and Kenaz. And Timna was concubine to Eliphaz Esau's son, and she bare to Eliphaz Amalek, these were the sons of Adah Esau's wife. And these are the sons of Reuel, Nahath, and Zerah, Shammah, and Mizzah, these were the sons of Bashemath Esau's wife. And these were the sons of Aholibamah, the daughter of Anah the daughter of Zibeon, Esau's wife, and she bare to Esau Jeush, and Jaalam, and Korah. These were dukes of the sons of Esau, the sons of Eliphaz the firstborn son of Esau, duke Teman, duke Omar, duke Zepho, duke Kenaz, Duke Korah, duke Gatam, and duke Amalek, these are the dukes that came of Eliphaz in the land of Edom, these were the sons of Adah. And these are the sons of Reuel Esau's son, duke Nahath, duke Zerah, duke Shammah, duke Mizzah, these are the dukes that came of Reuel in the land of Edom, these are the sons of Bashemath Esau's wife. And these are the sons of Aholibamah Esau's wife, duke Jeush, duke Jaalam, duke Korah, these were the dukes that came of Aholibamah the daughter of Anah, Esau's wife. These are the sons of Esau, who is Edom, and these are their dukes. These are the sons of Seir the Horite, who inhabited the land, Lotan, and Shobal, and Zibeon, and Anah, And Dishon, and Ezer, and Dishan, these are the dukes of the Horites, the children of Seir in the land of Edom. And the children of Lotan were Hori and Hemam, and Lotan's sister was Timna. And the children of Shobal were these, Alvan, and Manahath, and Ebal, Shepho, and Onam. And these are the children of Zibeon, both Ajah, and Anah, this was that Anah that found the mules in the wilderness, as he fed the asses of Zibeon his father. And the children of Anah were these, Dishon, and Abholibamah the daughter of Anah. And these are the children of Dishon, Hemdan, and Eshban, and Ithran, and Cheran. The children of Ezer are these, Bilhan, and Zaavan, and Akan. The children of Dishan are these, Uz, and Aran. These are the dukes that came of the Horites, duke Lotan, duke Shobal, duke Zibeon, duke Anah, Duke Dishon, duke Ezer, duke Dishan, these are the dukes that came of Hori, among their dukes in the land of Seir. And these are the kings that reigned in the land of Edom, before there reigned any king over the children of Israel. And Bela the son of Beor reigned in Edom, and the name of his city was Dinhabah.

And Bela died, and Jobab the son of Zerah of Bozrah reigned in his stead. And Jobab died, and Husham of the land of Temani reigned in his stead. And Husham died, and Hadad the son of Bedad, who smote Midian in the field of Moab, reigned in his stead, and the name of his city was Avith. And Hadad died, and Samlah of Masrekah reigned in his stead. And Samlah died, and Saul of Rehoboth by the river reigned in his stead. And Saul died, and Baal-hanan the son of Achbor reigned in his stead. And Baal-hanan the son of Achbor died, and Hadar reigned in his stead, and the name of his city was Pau, and his wife's name was Mehetabel, the daughter of Matred, the daughter of Mezahab.

And these are the names of the dukes that came of Esau, according to their families, after their places, by their names, duke Timnah, duke Alvah, duke Jetheth, Duke Aholibamah, duke Elah, duke Pinon, Duke Kenaz, duke Teman, duke Mibzar, Duke Magdiel, duke Iram, these be the dukes of Edom, according to their habitations in the land of their possession, he is Esau the father of the Edomites.

9 AND Jacob dwelt in the land wherein his father was a stranger, in the land of Canaan. And this is the history of the generations of Jacob. Joseph, being seventeen years old, was feeding the flock with his brethren, and the lad was with the sons of Bilhah, and with the sons of Zilpah, his father's wives, and Joseph brought unto his father their evil report. Now Israel loved Joseph more than all his children, because he was the son of his old age, and he made him a coat of many colors. And when his brethren saw that their father loved him more than all his brethren, they hated him, and could not speak peaceably unto him.

And Joseph dreamed a dream, and he told it his brethren, and they hated him yet the more. And he said unto them, Hear, I pray you, this dream which I have dreamed, For, behold, we were binding sheaves in the field, and, lo, my sheaf arose, and also stood upright, and, behold, your sheaves stood round about, and made obeisance to my sheaf. And his brethren said to him, Shalt thou indeed reign over us? or shalt thou indeed have dominion over us? And they hated him yet the more for his dreams, and for his words. And he dreamed yet another dream, and told it his brethren, and said, Behold, I have dreamed a dream more, and behold, the sun and the moon and the eleven stars made obeisance to me. And he told it to his father, and to his brethren, and his father rebuked him, and said unto him, What is this dream that thou hast dreamed? Shall I and thy mother and thy brethren indeed come to bow down ourselves to thee to the earth? And his brethren envied him, but his father observed the saying. And his brethren went to feed their father's flock in Shechem.

And Israel said unto Joseph, Do not thy brethren feed the flock in Shechem? come, and I will send thee unto them. And he said to him, Here am I. And he said to him, Go, I pray thee, see whether it be well with thy brethren, and well with the flocks, and bring me word again. So he sent him out of the vale of Hebron, and he came to Shechem.

And a certain man found him, and, behold, he was wandering in the field, and the man asked him, saying, What seekest thou? And he said, I seek my brethren, tell me, I pray thee, where they feed their flocks. And the man said, They are departed hence, for I heard them say, Let us go to Dothan. And Joseph went after his brethren and found them in Dothan.

And when they saw him afar off, even before he came near unto them, they conspired against him to slay him. And they said one to another, Behold, this dreamer cometh. Come now therefore, and let us slay him, and cast him into some pit, and we will say, Some evil beast hath devoured him, and we shall see what will become of his dreams. And Reuben heard it, and he delivered him out of their hands, and said, Let us not kill him. And Reuben said unto them, Shed no blood, but cast him into this pit that is in the wilderness, and lay no hand upon him, that he might rid him out of their hands, to deliver him to his father again.

And it came to pass, when Joseph was come unto his brethren, that they stripped Joseph out of his coat, his coat of many colors that was on him, And they took him, and cast him into a pit, and the pit was empty, there was no water in it.

And they sat down to eat bread, and they lifted up their eyes and looked, and, behold, a company of Ishmaelites came from Gilead, with their camels bearing spicery and balm and myrrh, going to carry it down to Egypt. And Judah said unto his brethren, What profit is it if we slay our brother, and conceal his blood? Come, and let us sell him to the Ishmaelites, and let not our hand be upon him, for he is our brother and our flesh, and his brethren were content.

Then there passed by Midianites merchantmen, and they drew and lifted up Joseph out of the pit, and sold Joseph to the Ishmaelites for twenty pieces of silver, and they brought Joseph into Egypt. And Reuben returned unto the pit, and, behold, Joseph was not in the pit, and he rent his clothes. And he returned unto his brethren, and said, The child is not, and I, whither shall I go? And they took Joseph's coat, and killed a kid of the goats, and dipped the coat in the blood, And they sent the coat of many colors, and they brought it to their father, and said, This have we found, know now whether it be thy son's coat or no. And he knew it, and said, It is my son's coat, an evil beast hath devoured him, Joseph is without doubt rent in pieces. And Jacob rent his clothes, and put sackcloth upon his loins, and mourned for his son many days. And all his sons and all his daughters rose up to comfort him, but he refused to be comforted, and he said, For I will go down into the grave unto my son mourning. Thus his father wept for him.

And the Midianites sold him into Egypt unto Potiphar, an officer of Pharaoh's, and captain of the guard.

And it came to pass at that time, that Judah went down from his brethren, and turned into a certain Adullamite, whose name was Hirah. And Judah saw there a daughter of a certain Canaanite, whose name was Shuah, and he took her, and went in and lay with her. And she conceived, and bare a son, and he called his name Er. And she conceived again, and bare a son, and she called his name Onan. And she yet again conceived, and bare a son, and called his name Shelah, and he was at Chezib, when she bare him. And Judah took a wife for

Er his firstborn, whose name was Tamar. And Er, Judah's firstborn, was wicked in the sight of the Lord, and the Lord slew him. And Judah said unto Onan, Go and marry thy brother's wife, and raise up seed unto thy brother. And Onan knew that the seed should not be his, and it came to pass, when he married his brother's wife, that he would not lie with her, lest he should raise up seed unto his brother. And the thing which he did displeased the Lord, wherefore he slew him also. Then said Judah to Tamar his daughter-in-law, Remain a widow at thy father's house, till Shelah my son be grown, for he said, Lest peradventure he die also, as his brethren did. And Tamar went and dwelt in her father's house. And in process of time the daughter of Shuah Judah's wife died, and Judah was comforted, and went up unto his sheepshearers to Timnath, he and his friend Hirah the Adullamite. And it was told Tamar, saying, Behold, thy father-in-law goeth up to Timnath to shear his sheep. And she put her widow's garments off from her, and covered her with a veil, and wrapped herself, and sat in an open place, which is by the way to Timnath, for she saw that Shelah was grown, and she was not given unto him to wife. When Judah saw her, he thought her to be a harlot, because she had covered her face. And he turned unto her by the way, and said, Go to, I pray thee, let me come in and lie with thee, (for he knew not that she was his daughter-in-law,) and she said, What wilt thou give me, that thou mayest come in and lie with me? And he said, I will send thee a kid from the flock. And she said, Wilt thou give me a pledge, till thou send it? And he said, What pledge shall I give thee? And she said, Thy signet, and thy bracelets, and thy staff that is in thine hand. And he gave it her, and came in and slept with her, and she conceived by him. And she arose, and went away, and laid by her veil from her, and put on the garments of her widowhood. And Judah sent the kid by the hand of his friend the Adullamite, to receive his pledge from the woman's hand, but he found her not. Then he asked the men of that place, saying, Where is the harlot, that was openly by the wayside? And they said, There was no harlot in this place. And he returned to Judah, and said, I cannot find her, and also the men of the place said, that there was no harlot in this place. And Judah said, Let her take it to her, lest we be shamed, behold, I sent this kid, and thou hast not found her. And it came to pass about three months after, that it was told Judah, saying, Tamar thy daughter-in-law hath played the harlot, and also, behold, she is with child by whoredom. And Judah said, Bring her forth, and let her be burnt. When she was brought forth, she sent to her father-in-law, saying, Buy the man, whose these are, am I with child, and she said, Discern, I pray thee, whose are these, the signet, and bracelets, and staff. And Judah acknowledged them, and said, She hath been more righteous than I, because that I gave her not to Shelah my son. And he knew her again no more. And it came to pass in the time of her travail, that, behold, twins were in her womb. And it came to pass, when she travailed, that the one put out his hand, and the midwife took and bound upon his hand a scarlet thread saying, This came out first. And it came to pass, as he drew back his hand, that, behold, his brother came out, and she said, How hast thou broken forth? this breach be upon thee, therefore his name was called Pharez. And afterward came out his brother, that had the scarlet thread upon his hand, and his name was called Zarah.

And Joseph was brought down to Egypt, and Potiphar, an officer of Pharaoh, captain of the guard, an Egyptian, bought him of the hands of the Ishmaelites, which had brought him down thither. And the Lord was with Joseph, and he was a prosperous man, and he was in the house of his master the Egyptian. And his master saw that the Lord was with him, and that the Lord made all that he did to prosper in his hand. And Joseph found grace in his sight, and he served him, and he made him overseer over his house, and all that he had he put into his hand.

And it came to pass from the time that he had made him overseer in his house, and over all that he had, that the Lord blessed the Egyptian's house for Joseph's sake, and the blessing of the Lord was upon all that he had in the house, and in the field. And he left all that he had in Joseph's hand, and he knew not aught he had, save the bread which he did eat. And Joseph was a goodly person, and well favored.

And it came to pass after these things, that his master's wife cast her eyes upon Joseph, and she said, Lie with me. But he refused, and said unto his master's wife, Behold, my master knoweth not what is with me in the house, and he hath committed all that he hath to my hand, There is none greater in this house than I, neither hath he kept back anything from me but thee, because thou art his wife, how then can I do this great wickedness, and sin against God? And it came to pass, as she spake to Joseph day by day, that he hearkened not unto her, to lie by her, or to be with her. And it came to pass about this time, that Joseph went into the house to do his business, and there was none of the men of the house there within. And she caught him by his garment, saying, Lie with me, and he left his garment in her hand, and fled, and got him out. And it came to pass, when she saw that he had left his garment in her hand, and was fled forth, that she called unto the men of her house, and spake unto them, saying, See, he hath brought in a Hebrew unto us to mock us, he came in unto me to lie with me, and I cried with a loud voice, And it came to pass, when he heard that I lifted up my voice and cried, that he left his garment with me, and fled, and got him out. And she laid up his garment by her, until his lord came home. And she spake unto him according to these words, saying, The Hebrew servant, which thou hast brought unto us, came in unto me to mock me, And it came to pass, as I lifted up my voice and cried, that he left his garment with me, and fled out. And it came to pass, when his master heard the words of his wife, which she spake unto him, saying, After this manner did thy servant to me, that his wrath was kindled. And Joseph's master took him, and put him into the prison, a place where the king's prisoners were bound, and he was there in the prison. But the Lord was with Joseph, and showed him mercy, and gave him favor in the sight of the keeper of the prison. And the keeper of the prison committed to Joseph's hand all the prisoners that were in the prison, and whatsoever they did there, he was the overseer of it. The keeper of the prison looked not to anything that was under his hand, because the Lord was with him, and that which he did, the Lord made it to prosper.

And it came to pass after these things, that the butler of the king of Egypt and his baker had offended their lord the king of Egypt. And Pharaoh was wroth against two of his officers, against the chief of the butlers, and against the chief of the bakers. And he put them in ward in the house of the captain of the guard, into the prison, the place where Joseph was bound. And the captain of the guard charged Joseph with them, and he served them, and they continued a season in ward.

And they dreamed a dream both of them, each man his dream in one night, each man according to the interpretation of his dream, the butler and the baker of the king of Egypt, which were bound in the prison. And Joseph came in unto them in the morning, and looked upon them, and, behold, they were sad. And he asked Pharaoh's officers that were with him in the ward of his lord's house, saying, Wherefore look ye so sadly today? And they said unto him, We have dreamed a dream, and there is no interpreter of it. And Joseph said unto them, Do not interpretations belong to God? Tell me them, I pray you. And the chief butler told his dream to Joseph, and said to him, In my dream, behold, a vine was before me, And in the vine were three branches, and it was as though it budded, and her blossoms shot forth, and the clusters thereof brought forth ripe grapes, And Pharaoh's cup was in my hand, and I took the grapes, and pressed them into Pharaoh's cup, and I gave the cup into Pharaoh's hand. And Joseph said unto him, This is the interpretation of it, The three branches are three days, Yet within three days shall Pharaoh lift up thine head, and restore thee unto thy place, and thou shalt deliver Pharaoh's cup into his hand, after the former manner when thou wast his butler. But think on me when it shall be well with thee, and show kindness, I pray thee, unto me, and make mention of me unto Pharaoh, and bring me out of this house, For indeed I was stolen away out of the land of the Hebrews, and here also have I done nothing that they should put me into the dungeon. When the chief baker saw that the interpretation was good, he said unto Joseph, I also was in my dream, and, behold, I had three white baskets on my head, And in the uppermost basket there was of all manner of bakemeats for Pharaoh, and the birds did eat them out of the basket upon my head. And Joseph answered and said, This is the interpretation thereof, The three baskets are three days, Yet within three days shall Pharaoh lift up thy head from off thee, and shall hang thee on a tree, and the birds shall eat thy flesh from off thee.

And it came to pass the third day, which was Pharaoh's birthday, that he made a feast unto all his servants, and he lifted up the head of the chief butler and of the chief baker among his servants. And he restored the chief butler unto his butlership again, and he gave the cup into Pharaoh's hand, But he hanged the chief baker, as Joseph had interpreted to them. Yet did not the chief butler remember Joseph, but forgat him.

And it came to pass at the end of two full years, that Pharaoh dreamed, and, behold, he stood by the river. And, behold, there came up out of the river seven well-favored kine and fat-fleshed, and they fed in a meadow. And, behold, seven other kine came up after them out of the river, ill-favored and lean-fleshed, and stood by the other kine upon the brink of the river. And the ill-favored and lean-fleshed kine did eat up the seven well-favored and fat kine. So Pharaoh awoke. And he slept and dreamed the second time, and, behold, seven ears of corn came up upon one stalk, rank and good. And, behold, seven thin ears and blasted with the east wind sprung up after them. And the seven thin ears devoured the seven rank and full ears. And Pharaoh awoke, and, behold, it was a dream.

And it came to pass in the morning that his spirit was troubled, and he sent and called for all the magicians of Egypt, and all the wise men thereof, and Pharaoh told them his dream, but there was none that could interpret them unto Pharaoh. Then spake the chief butler unto Pharaoh, saying, I do remember my faults this day, Pharaoh was wroth with his servants, and put me in ward in the captain of the guard's house, both me and the chief baker, And we dreamed a dream in one night, I and he, we dreamed each man according to the interpretation of his dream. And there was there with us a young man, a Hebrew, servant to the captain of the guard, and we told him, and he interpreted to us our dreams, to each man according to his dream he did interpret. And it came to pass, as he interpreted to us, so it was, me he restored unto mine office, and him he hanged.

Then Pharaoh sent and called Joseph, and they brought him hastily out of the dungeon, and he shaved himself, and changed his raiment, and came in unto Pharaoh. And Pharaoh said unto Joseph, I have dreamed a dream, and there is none that can interpret it, and I have heard say of thee that thou canst understand a dream to interpret it. And Joseph answered Pharaoh, saying, It is not in me, God shall give Pharaoh an answer of peace. And Pharaoh said unto Joseph, In my dream, behold, I stood upon the bank of the river, And, behold, there came up out of the river seven kine, fat- fleshed and well-favored, and they fed in a meadow, And, behold, seven other kine came up after them, poor and very ill-favored and lean-fleshed, such as I never saw in all the land of Egypt for badness, And the lean in the ill-favored kine did eat up the first seven fat kine,

And when they had eaten them up, it could not be known that they had eaten them, but they were still ill-favored, as at the beginning. So I awoke. And I saw in my dream, and, behold, seven ears came up in one stalk, full and good, And, behold, seven ears, withered, thin, and blasted with the east wind, sprung up after them, And the thin ears devoured the seven good ears, and I told this unto the magicians, but there was none that could declare it to me. And Joseph said unto Pharaoh, The dream of Pharaoh is one, God hath showed Pharaoh what he is about to do. The seven good kine are seven years, and the seven good ears are seven years, the dream is one. And the seven thin and ill-favored kine that came up after them are seven years, and the seven empty ears blasted with the east wind shall be seven years of famine. This is the thing which I have spoken unto Pharaoh, What God is about to do he showeth unto Pharaoh. Behold, there come seven years of great plenty throughout all the land of Egypt, And there shall arise after them seven years of famine, and all the plenty shall be forgotten in the land of Egypt, and the famine shall consume the land, And the plenty shall not be known in the land by reason of that famine following, for it shall be very grievous. And for that the dream was doubled unto Pharaoh twice, it is because the thing is established by God, and God will shortly bring it to pass. Now therefore let Pharaoh look out a man discreet and wise, and set him over the land of Egypt. Let Pharaoh do this, and let him appoint officers over the land, and take up the fifth part of the land of Egypt in the seven plenteous years. And let them gather all the food of those good years that come, and lay up corn under the hand of Pharaoh, and let them keep food in the cities. And that food shall be for store to the land against the seven years of famine, which shall be in the land of Egypt, that the land perish not through the famine.

And the thing was good in the eyes of Pharaoh and in the eyes of all his servants. And Pharaoh said unto his servants, Can we find such a one as this is, a man in whom the Spirit of God is? And Pharaoh said unto Joseph, Forasmuch as God hath showed thee all this, there is none so discreet and wise as thou art. Thou shalt be over my house and according unto thy word shall all my people be ruled, only in the throne will I be greater than thou. And Pharaoh said unto Joseph, See, I have set thee over all the land of Egypt. And Pharaoh took off his ring from his hand and put it upon Joseph's hand and arrayed him in vestures of fine linen and put a gold chain about his neck. And he made him to ride in the second chariot which he had and they cried before him, Bow the knee, and he made him ruler over all the land of Egypt. And Pharaoh said unto Joseph, I am Pharaoh, and without thee shall no man lift up his hand or foot in all the land of Egypt. And Pharaoh called Joseph's name Zaphnath-paaneah and he gave him to wife Asenath the daughter of Poti-pherah priest of On.

And Joseph went out over all the land of Egypt. And Joseph was thirty years old when he stood before Pharaoh king of Egypt. And Joseph went out from the presence of Pharaoh and went throughout all the land of Egypt. And in the seven plenteous years the earth brought forth by handfuls. And he gathered up all the food of the seven years which were in the land of Egypt and laid up the food in the cities, the food of the field, which was round about every city, laid he up in the same. And Joseph gathered corn as the sand of the sea, very much, until he left numbering, for it was without number. And unto Joseph were born two sons before the years of famine came, which Asenath the daughter of Poti-pherah priest of On bare unto him. And Joseph called the name of the firstborn Manasseh, For God, said he, hath made me forget all my toil and all my father's house. And the name of the second called he Ephraim, For God hath caused me to be fruitful in the land of my affliction. And the seven years of plenteousness that was in the land of Egypt were ended.

And the seven years of dearth began to come, according as Joseph had said, and the dearth was in all lands, but in all the land of Egypt there was bread. And when all the land of Egypt was famished, the people cried to Pharaoh for bread, and Pharaoh said unto all the Egyptians, Go unto Joseph, what he saith to you, do.

And the famine was over all the face of the Earth, and Joseph opened all the storehouses, and sold unto the Egyptians, and the famine waxed sore in the land of Egypt. And all the countries came into Egypt to Joseph for to buy corn, because that the famine was so sore in all lands.

Now when Jacob saw that there was corn in Egypt, Jacob said unto his sons, Why do ye look one upon another? And he said, Behold, I have heard that there is corn in Egypt, get you down thither and buy for us from thence that we may live and not die. And Joseph's ten brethren went down to buy corn in Egypt. But Benjamin, Joseph's brother, Jacob sent not with his brethren, for he said, Lest peradventure mischief befall him.

And the sons of Israel came to buy corn among those that came, for the famine was in the land of Canaan. And Joseph was the governor over the land, and he it was that sold to all the people of the land, and Joseph's brethren came and bowed down themselves before him with their faces to the earth. And Joseph saw his brethren and he knew them, but made himself strange unto them and spake roughly unto them, and he said unto them, Whence come ye? And they said, From the land of Canaan to buy food. And Joseph knew his brethren, but they knew not him. And Joseph remembered the dreams which he dreamed of them, and said unto them, Ye are spies, to see the nakedness of the land ye are come. And they said unto him, Nay my lord, but to buy food are thy servants come. We are all one man's sons, we are true men, thy servants are no spies. And he said unto them, Nay, but to see the nakedness of the land ye are come. And they said, Thy servants are twelve brethren, the sons of one man in the land of Canaan, and, behold, the youngest is this day with our father, and one is not. And Joseph said unto them, That is it that I spake unto you, saying, Ye are spies, Hereby ye shall be proved, By the life of Pharaoh ye shall not go forth hence, except your youngest brother come hither. Send one of you and let him fetch your brother and ye shall be kept in prison that your words may be proved, whether there be any truth in you, or else by the life of Pharaoh surely ye are spies. And he put them all together into ward three days.

And Joseph said unto them the third day, This do and live, for I fear God. If ye be true men, let one of your brethren be bound in the house of your prison, go ye, carry corn for the famine of your houses, But bring your youngest brother unto me so shall your words be verified and ye shall not die. And they did so. And they said, one to another, We are verily guilty concerning our brother in that we saw the anguish of his soul when he besought us, and we would not hear, therefore is this distress come upon us. And Reuben answered them saying, Spake I not unto you saying, Do not sin against the child and ye would not hear? Therefore behold, also his blood is required. And they knew not that Joseph understood them, for he spake unto them by an interpreter. And he turned himself about from them and wept, and returned to them again and communed with them, and took from them Simeon and bound him before their eyes.

Then Joseph commanded to fill their sacks with corn and to restore every man's money into his sack, and to give them provision for the way, and thus did he unto them. And they laded their asses with the corn and departed thence.

And as one of them opened his sack to give his ass provender in the inn, he espied his money, for behold, it was in his sack's mouth. And he said unto his brethren, My money is restored and lo, it is even in my sack. And their heart failed them and they were afraid saying one to another, What is this that God hath done unto us? And they came unto Jacob their father unto the land of Canaan and told him all that befell unto them, saying, The man who is the lord of the land spake roughly to us and took us for spies of the country. And we said unto him, We are true men, we are no spies, We be twelve brethren, sons of our father, one is not, and the youngest is this day with our father in the land of Canaan. And the man, the lord of the country, said unto us, Hereby shall I know that ye are true men, leave one of your brethren here with me and take food for the famine of your households and be gone and bring your youngest brother unto me. Then shall I know that ye are no spies, but that ye are true men, so will I deliver you your brother and ye shall traffic in the land. And it came to pass as they emptied their sacks, that behold, every man's bundle of money was in his sack, and when both they and their father saw the bundles of money they were afraid. And Jacob their father said unto them, Me have ye bereaved of my children, Joseph is not, and Simeon is not, and ye will take Benjamin away, all these things are against me. And Reuben spake unto his father saying, Slay my two sons if I bring him not to thee, deliver him into my hand and I will bring him to thee again. And he said, My son shall not go down with you, for his brother is dead and he is left alone. If mischief befall him by the way in the which ye go, then shall ye bring down my gray hairs with sorrow to the grave.

And the famine was sore in the land. And it came to pass, when they had eaten up the corn which they had brought out of Egypt, their father said unto them, Go again, buy us a little food. And Judah spake unto him, saying, The man did solemnly protest unto us, saying, Ye shall not see my face except your brother be with you. If thou wilt send our brother with us, we will go down and buy thee food. But if thou wilt not send him, we will not go down, for the man said unto us, Ye shall not see my face except your brother be with you. And Israel said, Wherefore dealt ye so ill with me, as to tell the man whether ye had yet a brother? And they said, The man asked us straitly of our state, and of our kindred, saying, Is your father yet alive? Have ye another brother? And we told him according to the tenor of these words. Could we certainly know that he would say, Bring your brother down? And Judah said unto Israel his father, Send the lad with me and we will arise and go that we may live and not die, both we, and thou, and also our little ones. I will be surety for him, of my hand shalt thou require him, if I bring him not unto thee, and set him before thee, then let me bear the blame forever. For except we have lingered, surely now we had returned this second time. And their father Israel said unto them, If it must be so now, do this, take of the best fruits in the land in your vessels, and carry down the man a present, a little balm, and a little honey, spices and myrrh, nuts and almonds. And take double money in your hand, and the money that was brought again in the mouth of your sacks, carry it again in your hand, peradventure it was an oversight. Take also your brother, and arise, go again unto the man, And God Almighty give you mercy before the man, that he may send away your other brother, and Benjamin. If I be bereaved of my children, I am bereaved.

And the men took that present, and they took double money in their hand, and Benjamin, and rose up, and went down to Egypt, and stood before Joseph. And when Joseph saw Benjamin with them, he said to the ruler of his house, Bring these men home, and slay, and make ready, for these men shall dine with me at noon. And the man did as Joseph bade, and the man brought the men into Joseph's house. And the men were afraid because they were brought into Joseph's house, and they said, Because of the money that was returned in our sacks at the first time are we brought in, that he may seek occasion against us, and fall upon us, and take us for bondmen, and our asses. And they came near to the steward of Joseph's house, and they communed with him, at the door of the house, And said, O sir, we came indeed down at the first time to buy food, And it came to pass, when we came to the inn, that we opened our sacks, and, behold, every man's money was in the mouth of his sack, our money in full weight, and we have brought it again in our hand. And other money have we brought down in our hands to buy food, we cannot tell who put our money in our sacks. And he said, Peace be to you, fear not, your God, and the God of your father, hath given you treasure in your sacks, I had your money. And he brought Simeon out unto them. And the man brought the men into Joseph's house, and gave them water, and they washed their feet, and he gave their asses provender. And they made ready the present against Joseph came at noon, for they heard that they should eat bread there. And when Joseph came home, they brought him the present which was in their hand into the house and bowed themselves to him to the earth. And he asked them of their welfare and said, Is your father well, the old man of whom ye spake? Is he yet alive? And they answered, Thy servant our father is in good health, he is yet alive. And they bowed down their heads and made obeisance. And he lifted up his eyes, and saw his brother Benjamin, his mother's son, and said, Is this your younger brother of whom ye spake unto me? And he said, God be gracious unto thee my son. And Joseph made haste, for his bowels did yearn upon his brother, and he sought where to weep, and he entered into his chamber and wept there. And he washed his face and went out and refrained himself, and said, Set on bread. And they set on for him by himself, and for them by themselves, and for the Egyptians, which did eat with him, by themselves, because the Egyptians might not eat bread with the Hebrews, for that is an abomination unto the Egyptians. And they sat before him, the firstborn according to his birthright, and the youngest according to his youth, and the men marveled one at another. And he took and sent messes unto them from before him, but Benjamin's mess was five times so much as any of theirs. And they drank, and were merry with him.

And he commanded the steward of his house, saying, Fill the men's sacks with food, as much as they can carry, and put every man's money in his sack's mouth, And put my cup, the silver cup, in the sack's mouth of the youngest, and his corn money. And he did according to the word that Joseph had spoken. As soon as the morning was light the men were sent away, they and their asses.

And when they were gone out of the city, and not yet far off Joseph said unto his steward, Up, follow after the men and when thou dost overtake them, say unto them, Wherefore have ye rewarded evil for good? Is not this it in which my lord drinketh, and whereby indeed he divineth? Ye have done evil in so doing. And he overtook them, and he spake unto them these same words. And they said unto him, Wherefore saith my lord these words? God forbid that thy servants should do according to this thing. Behold, the money, which we found in our sacks' mouths we brought again unto thee of the land of Canaan, how then should we steal out of thy lord's house silver or gold? With whomsoever of thy servants it be found, both let him die, and we also will be my lord's bondmen. And he said, Now also let it be according unto your words, he with whom it is found shall be my servant, and ye shall be blameless. Then they speedily took down every man his sack to the ground, and opened every man his sack. And he searched, and began at the eldest, and left at the youngest, and the cup was found in Benjamin's sack. Then they rent their clothes and laded every man his ass and returned to the city.

And Judah and his brethren came to Joseph's house, for he was yet there, and they fell before him on the ground. And Joseph said unto them, What deed is this that ye have done? Knew ye not that such a man as I can certainly divine? And Judah said, What shall we say unto my lord? What shall we speak? Or how shall we clear ourselves? God hath found out the iniquity of thy servants, behold, we are my lord's servants, both we, and he also with whom the cup is found. And he said, God forbid that I should do so, but the man in whose hand the cup is found, he shall be my servant, and as for you, get you up in peace unto your father. Then Judah came near unto him, and said, O my lord, let thy servant, I pray thee, speak a word in my lord's ears, and let not thine anger burn against thy servant, for thou art even as Pharaoh. My lord asked his servants, saying, Have ye a father, or a brother? And we said unto my lord, We have a father, an old man, and a child of his old age, a little one, and his brother is dead, and he alone is left of his mother, and his father loveth him. And thou saidst unto thy servants, Bring him down unto me, that I may set mine eyes upon him. And we said unto my lord, The lad cannot leave his father, for if he should leave his father, his father would die. And thou saidst unto thy servants, Except your youngest brother come down with you, ye shall see my face no more. And it came to pass when we came up unto thy servant my father, we told him the words of my lord. And our father said, Go again, and buy us a little food. And we said, We cannot go down, if our youngest brother be with us, then will we go down, for we may not see the man's face, except our youngest brother be with us. And thy servant my father said unto us, Ye know that my wife bare me two sons, And the one went out from me, and I said, Surely he is torn in pieces, and I saw him not since. And if ye take this also from me, and mischief befall him, ye shall bring down my gray hairs with sorrow to the grave. Now therefore when I come to thy servant my father, and the lad be not with us, seeing that his life is bound up in the lad's life, It shall come to pass, when he seeth that the lad is not with us, that he will die, and thy servants shall bring down the gray hairs of thy servant our father with sorrow to the grave. For thy servant became surety for the lad unto my father, saying, If I bring him not unto thee, then I shall bear the blame to my father forever. Now therefore, I pray thee, let thy servant abide instead of the lad a bondman to my lord, and let the lad go up with his brethren. For how shall I go up to my father, and the lad be not with me? Lest peradventure I see the evil that shall come on my father. Then Joseph could not refrain himself before them all that stood by him, and he cried, Cause every man to go out from me. And there stood no man with him, while Joseph made himself known unto his brethren. And he wept aloud, and the Egyptians and the house of Pharaoh heard. And Joseph said unto his brethren, I am Joseph, doth my father yet live? And his brethren could not answer him for they were troubled at his presence. And Joseph said unto his brethren, Come near to me, I pray you. And they came near. And he said, I am Joseph your brother, whom ye sold into Egypt. Now therefore be not grieved, nor angry with yourselves that ye sold me hither, for God did send me before you to preserve life. For these two years hath the famine been in the land and yet there are five years in the which there shall neither be earing nor harvest. And God sent me before you to preserve you a posterity in the Earth and to save your lives by a great deliverance. So now it was not you that sent me hither, but God, and he hath made me a father to Pharaoh, and lord of all his house, and a ruler throughout all the land of Egypt. Haste ye, and go up to my father, and say unto him, Thus saith thy son Joseph, God hath made me lord of all Egypt, come down unto me, tarry not, and thou shalt dwell in the land of Goshen, and thou shalt be near unto me, thou, and thy children, and thy children's children, and thy flocks, and thy herds, and all that thou hast, and there will I nourish thee, for yet there are five years of famine, lest thou, and thy household, and all that thou hast, come to poverty. And, behold, your eyes see, and the eyes of my brother Benjamin, that it is my mouth that speaketh unto you. And ye shall tell my father of all my glory in Egypt, and of all that ye have seen, and ye shall haste and bring down my father hither.

And he fell upon his brother Benjamin's neck, and wept, and Benjamin wept upon his neck. Moreover he kissed all his brethren, and wept upon them, and after that his brethren talked with him.

And the fame thereof was heard in Pharaoh's house, saying, Joseph's brethren are come, and it pleased Pharaoh well, and his servants. And Pharaoh said unto Joseph, Say unto thy brethren, This do ye, lade your beasts, and go, get you unto the land of Canaan, And take your father and your households and come unto me, and I will give you the good of the land of Egypt, and ye shall eat the fat of the land. Now thou art commanded, this do ye, take you wagons out of the land of Egypt for your little ones, and for your wives, and bring your father, and come. Also regard not your stuff, for the good of all the land of Egypt is yours. And the children of Israel did so, and Joseph gave them wagons, according to the commandment of Pharaoh, and gave them provision for the way. To all of them he gave each man changes of raiment, but to Benjamin he gave three hundred pieces of silver and five changes of raiment. And to his father he sent after this manner, ten asses laden with the good things of Egypt, and ten she asses laden with corn, and bread and meat for his father by the way. So he sent his brethren away, and they departed, and he said unto them, See that ye fall not out by the way.

And they went up out of Egypt, and came into the land of Canaan unto Jacob their father, And told him saying, Joseph is yet alive, and he is governor over all the land of Egypt. And Jacob's heart fainted, for he believed them not. And they told him all the words of Joseph, which he had said unto them, and when he saw the wagons which Joseph had sent to carry him, the spirit of Jacob their father revived. And Israel said, It is enough, Joseph my son is yet alive, I will go and see him before I die.

And Israel took his journey with all that he had and came to Beer-sheba and offered sacrifices unto the God of his father Isaac. And God spake unto Israel in the visions of the night, and said, Jacob, Jacob. And he said, Here am I. And he said, I am God, the God of thy father, fear not to go down into Egypt, for I will there make of thee a great nation. I will go down with thee into Egypt and I will also surely bring thee up again and Joseph shall put his hand upon thine eyes.

And Jacob rose up from Beer-sheba, and the sons of Israel carried Jacob their father, and their little ones, and their wives, in the wagons which Pharaoh had sent to carry him. And they took their cattle, and their goods, which they had gotten in the land of Canaan, and came into Egypt, Jacob, and all his seed with him, His sons, and his sons' sons with him, his daughters, and his sons' daughters, and all his seed brought he with him into Egypt.

10 AND these are the names of the children of Israel, which came into Egypt, Jacob and his sons, Reuben, Jacob's firstborn. And the sons of Reuben, Hanoch, and Phallu, and Hezron, and Carmi. And the sons of Simeon, Jemuel, and Jamin, and Ohad, and Jachin, and Zohar, and Shaul the son of a Canaanitish woman. And the sons of Levi, Gershon, Kohath, and Merari. And the sons of Judah, Er, and Onan, and Shelah, and Pharez, and Zarah, but Er and Onan died in the land of Canaan. And the son of Pharez were Hezron and Hamul. And the sons of Issachar, Tola, and Phuvah, and Job, and Shimron. And the sons of Zebulun, Sered, and Elon, and Jahleel. These be the sons of Leah, which she bare unto Jacob in Padanaram, with his daughter Dinah, all the souls of his sons and his daughters were thirty and three. And the sons of Gad, Ziphion, and Haggi, Shuni, and Ezbon, Eri, and Arodi, and Areli. And the sons of Asher, Jimnah, and Ishuah, and Isui, and Beriah, and Serah their sister, and the sons of Beriah, Heber, and Malchiel. These are the sons of Zilpah, whom Laban gave to Leah his daughter, and these she bare unto Jacob, even sixteen souls. The sons of Rachel Jacob's wife, Joseph and Benjamin. And unto Joseph in the land of Egypt were born Manasseh and Ephraim, which

Asenath the daughter of Poti-pherah priest of On bare unto him. And the sons of Benjamin were Belah, and Becher, and Ashbel, Gera, and Naaman, Ehi, and Rosh, Muppim, and Huppim, and Ard. These are the sons of Rachel, which were born to Jacob, all the souls were fourteen. And the sons of Dan, Hushim. And the sons of Naphtali, Jahzeel, and Guni, and Jezer, and Shillem. These are the sons of Bilhah, which Laban gave unto Rachel his daughter, and she bare these unto Jacob, all the souls were seven. All the souls that came with Jacob into Egypt, which came out of his loins, besides Jacob's sons' wives, all the souls were threescore and six, And the sons of Joseph, which were borne him in Egypt, were two souls, all the souls of the house of Jacob, which came into Egypt, were threescore and ten.

And he sent Judah before him unto Joseph, to direct his face unto Goshen, and they came into the land of Goshen. And Joseph made ready his chariot, and went up to meet Israel his father, to Goshen, and presented himself unto him, and he fell on his neck, and wept on his neck a good while. And Israel said unto Joseph, Now let me die, since I have seen thy face, because thou art yet alive. And Joseph said unto his brethren and unto his father's house, I will go up, and show Pharaoh, and say unto him, My brethren and my father's house, which were in the land of Canaan, are come unto me. And the men are shepherds, for their trade hath been to feed cattle, and they have brought their flocks, and their herds, and all that they have. And it shall come to pass, when Pharaoh shall call you, and shall say, What is your occupation? That ye shall say, Thy servants' trade hath been about cattle from our youth even until now, both we, and also our fathers, that ye may dwell in the land of Goshen, for every shepherd is an abomination unto the Egyptians.

Then Joseph came and told Pharaoh, and said, My father and my brethren, and their flocks, and their herds, and all that they have, are come out of the land of Canaan, and, behold, they are in the land of Goshen. And he took some of his brethren, even five men, and presented them unto Pharaoh. And Pharaoh said unto his brethren, What is your occupation? And they said unto Pharaoh, Thy servants are shepherds, both we, and also our fathers. They said moreover unto Pharaoh, For to sojourn in the land are we come, for thy servants have no pasture for their flocks, for the famine is sore in the land of Canaan, now therefore, we pray thee, let thy servants dwell in the land of Goshen. And Pharaoh spake unto Joseph, saying, Thy father and thy brethren are come unto thee, The land of Egypt is before thee, in the best of the land make thy father and brethren to dwell, in the land of Goshen let them dwell, and if thou knowest any men of activity among them, then make them rulers over my cattle.

And Joseph brought in Jacob his father, and set him before Pharaoh, and Jacob blessed Pharaoh. And Pharaoh said unto Jacob, How old art thou? And Jacob said unto Pharaoh, The days of the years of my pilgrimage are a hundred and thirty years, few and evil have the days of the years of my life been and have not attained unto the days of the years of the life of my fathers in the days of their pilgrimage. And Jacob blessed Pharaoh, and went out from before Pharaoh.

And Joseph placed his father and his brethren, and gave them a possession in the land of Egypt, in the best of the land, in the land of Rameses, as Pharaoh had commanded. And Joseph nourished his father, and his brethren, and all his father's household, with bread, according to their families.

And there was no bread in all the land, for the famine was very sore, so that the land of Egypt and all the land of Canaan fainted by reason of the famine. And Joseph gathered up all the money that was found in the land of Egypt, and in the land of Canaan, for the corn which they bought, and Joseph brought the money into Pharaoh's house.

And when money failed in the land of Egypt, and in the land of Canaan, all the Egyptians came unto Joseph, and said, Give us bread, for why should we die in thy presence? for the money faileth. And Joseph said, Give your cattle, and I will give you for your cattle, if money fail. And they brought their cattle unto Joseph, and Joseph gave them bread in exchange for horses, and for the flocks, and for the cattle of the herds, and for the asses, and he fed them with bread for all their cattle for that year.

When that year was ended, they came unto him the second year, and said unto him, We will not hide it from my lord, how that our money is spent, my lord also hath our herds of cattle, there is not aught left in the sight of my lord, but our bodies and our lands, Wherefore shall we die before thine eyes, both we and our land? buy us and our land for bread, and we and our land will be servants unto Pharaoh, and give us seed, that we may live, and not die, that the land be not desolate.

And Joseph bought all the land of Egypt for Pharaoh, for the Egyptians sold every man his field, because the famine prevailed over them, so the land became Pharaoh's. And as for the people, he removed them to cities from one end of the borders of Egypt even to the other end thereof. Only the land of the priests bought he not, for the priests had a portion assigned them of Pharaoh, and did eat their portion which Pharaoh gave them, wherefore they sold not their lands.

Then Joseph said unto the people, Behold, I have bought you this day and your land for Pharaoh, lo, here is seed for you, and ye shall sow the land. And it shall come to pass in the increase, that ye shall give the fifth part unto Pharaoh, and four parts shall be your own, for seed of the field, and for your food, and for them of your households, and for food for your little ones. And they said, Thou hast saved our lives, let us find grace in the sight of my lord, and we will be Pharaoh's servants. And Joseph made it a law over the land of Egypt unto this day, that Pharaoh should have the fifth part, except the land of the priests only, which became not Pharaoh's.

And Israel dwelt in the land of Egypt, in the country of Goshen, and they had possessions therein, and grew, and multiplied exceedingly. And Jacob lived in the land of Egypt seventeen years, so the whole age of Jacob was a hundred forty and seven years. And the time drew nigh that Israel must die, and he called his son Joseph, and said unto him, If now I have found grace in thy sight, put, I pray thee, thy hand under my thigh, and deal kindly and truly with me, bury me not, I pray thee, in Egypt, But I will lie with my fathers, and thou shalt carry me out of Egypt and bury me in their burying-place. And he said, I will do as thou hast said. And he said, Swear unto me. And he sware unto him. And Israel bowed himself upon the bed's head.

And it came to pass after these things, that it was told Joseph, saying, Behold, thy father is sick, and he took with him his two sons, Manasseh and Ephraim. And it was told Jacob, saying, Look, and behold, thy son Joseph cometh unto thee, and Israel strengthened himself and sat upon the bed. And Jacob said unto Joseph, God Almighty appeared unto me at Luz in the land of Canaan and blessed me and said unto me, Behold, I will make thee fruitful and multiply thee, saith the Lord, and I will make of thee a multitude of people and will give this land to thy seed after thee for an everlasting possession. And now of thy two sons, Ephraim and Manasseh, which were born unto thee in the land of Egypt before I came unto thee into Egypt, behold, they are mine, and the God of my fathers shall bless them, even as Reuben and Simeon they shall be blessed, for they are mine, wherefore they shall be called after my name. (Therefore they were called Israel.) And thy issue which thou begettest after them shall be thine and shall be called after the name of their brethren in their inheritance in the tribes, therefore they were called the tribes of Manasseh and of Ephraim. And Jacob said unto Joseph,

When the God of my fathers appeared unto me in Luz in the land of Canaan, he sware unto me that he would give unto me and unto my seed the land for an everlasting possession. Therefore, O my son, he hath blessed me in raising thee up to be a servant unto me, in saving my house from death, in delivering my people, thy brethren, from famine which was sore in the land. Wherefore, the God of thy fathers shall bless thee and the fruit of thy loins that they shall be blessed above thy brethren and above thy father's house. For thou hast prevailed and thy father's house hath bowed down unto thee, even as it was shown unto thee before thou wast sold into Egypt by the hands of thy brethren. Wherefore, thy brethren shall bow down unto thee, from generation to generation, unto the fruit of thy loins forever. For thou shalt be a light unto my people to deliver them in the days of their captivity from bondage and to bring salvation unto them when they are altogether bowed down under sin. And therefore, as for me when I came from Padan, Rachel died by me in the land of Canaan, in the way when we were yet but a little way to come unto Ephrath, and I buried her there in the way of Ephrath, the same is called Bethlehem.

And Israel beheld Joseph's sons, and said, Who are these? And Joseph said unto his father, They are my sons, whom God hath given me in this land. And he said, Bring them, I pray thee, unto me, and I will bless them. Now the eyes of Israel were dim for age, so that he could not see well. And he brought them near unto him and he kissed them and embraced them. And Israel said unto Joseph, I had not thought to see thy face, and lo, God hath showed me also thy seed. And Joseph brought them out from between his knees, and he bowed himself with his face to the earth. And Joseph took them both, Ephraim in his right hand toward Israel's left hand, and Manasseh in his left hand toward Israel's right hand, and brought them near unto him. And Israel stretched out his right hand and laid it upon Ephraim's head, who was the younger, and his left hand upon Manasseh's head guiding his hands wittingly, for Manasseh was the firstborn. And he blessed Joseph, and said, God, before whom my fathers Abraham and Isaac did walk, the God which fed me all my life long unto this day, The Angel which redeemed me from all evil, bless the lads, and let my name be named on them and the name of my fathers Abraham and Isaac, and let them grow into a multitude in the midst of the Earth. And when Joseph saw that his father laid his right hand upon the head of Ephraim, it displeased him, and he held up his father's hand, to remove it from Ephraim's head unto Manasseh's head. And Joseph said unto his father, Not so, my father, for this is the firstborn, put thy right hand upon his head. And his father refused and said, I know it, my son, I know it, he also shall become a people and he also shall be great, but truly his younger brother shall be greater than he, and his seed shall become a multitude of nations. And he blessed them that day saying, In thee shall Israel bless, saying, God make thee as Ephraim and as Manasseh and he set Ephraim before Manasseh. And Israel said unto Joseph, Behold, I die, but God shall be with you and bring you again unto the land of your fathers. Moreover I have given to thee one portion above thy brethren, which I took out of the hand of the Amorite with my sword and with my bow. And Jacob called unto his sons and said, Gather yourselves together that I may tell you what shall befall you in the last days. Gather yourselves together, and hear, ye sons of Jacob and hearken unto Israel your father. Reuben, thou art my firstborn, my might, and the beginning of my strength, the excellency of dignity, and the excellency of power, Unstable as water, thou shalt not excel, because thou wentest up to thy father's bed, then defiledst thou it, he went up to my couch. Simeon and Levi are brethren, instruments of cruelty are in their habitations. O my soul, come not thou into their secret, unto their assembly, mine honor, be not thou united, for in their anger they slew a man, and in their self-will they digged down a wall. Cursed be their anger, for it was fierce, and their wrath, for it was cruel, I will divide them in Jacob and scatter them in Israel. Judah, thou art he whom thy brethren shall praise, thy hand shall be in the neck of thine enemies, thy father's children shall bow down before thee. Judah is a lion's whelp, from the prey, my son, thou art gone up, he stooped down, he couched as a lion, and as an old lion, who shall rouse him up? The sceptre shall not depart from Judah, nor a lawgiver from between his feet, until Shiloh come, and unto him shall the gathering of the people be. Binding his foal unto the vine, and has ass's colt unto the choice vine, he washed his garments in wine, and his clothes in the blood of grapes, His eyes shall be red with wine, and his teeth white with milk. Zebulun shall dwell at the haven of the sea, and shall be for a haven of ships, and his border shall be unto Zidon. Issachar is a strong ass couching down between two burdens, And he saw that rest was good, and the land that it was pleasant, and bowed his shoulder to bear, and became a servant unto tribute. Dan shall judge his people, as one of the tribes of Israel. Dan shall be a serpent by the way, an adder in the path that biteth the horse heels, so that his rider shall fall backward. I have waited for thy salvation, O Lord. Gad, a troop shall overcome him, but he shall overcome at the last. Out of Asher his bread shall be fat, and he shall yield royal dainties. Naphtali is a hind let loose, he giveth goodly words. Joseph is a fruitful bough, even a fruitful bough by a well, whose branches run over the wall. The archers have sorely grieved him and shot at him and hated him, but his bow abode in strength and the arms of his hands were made strong by the hands of the mighty God of Jacob, (from thence is the shepherd, the stone of Israel,) Even by the God of thy father who shall help thee, and by the Almighty who shall bless thee with blessings of Heaven above, blessings of the deep that lieth under, blessings of the breasts, and of the womb. The blessings of thy father have prevailed above the blessings of my progenitors unto the utmost bound of the everlasting hills, they shall be on the head of Joseph, and on the crown of the head of him that was separate from his brethren. Benjamin shall raven as a wolf, in the morning he shall devour the prey, and at night he shall divide the spoil. All these are the twelve tribes of Israel, and this is it that their father spake unto them, and blessed them, every one according to his blessing he blessed them. And he charged them, and said unto them, I am to be gathered unto my people, bury me with my fathers in the cave that is in the field of Ephron the Hittite, In the cave that is in the field of Machpelah, which is before Mamre, in the land of Canaan, which Abraham bought with the field of Ephron the Hittite for a possession of a burying-place. There they buried Abraham and Sarah his wife, there they buried Isaac and Rebekah his wife, and there I buried Leah. The purchase of the field and of the cave that is therein was from the children of Heth. And when Jacob had made an end of commanding his sons, he gathered up his feet into the bed, and yielded up the ghost, and was gathered unto his people.

    And Joseph fell upon his father's face, and wept upon him, and kissed him. And Joseph commanded his servants the physicians to embalm his father, and the physicians embalmed Israel. And forty days were fulfilled for him, for so are fulfilled the days of those which are embalmed, and the Egyptians mourned for him threescore and ten days. And when the days of his mourning were past, Joseph spake unto the house of Pharaoh, saying, If now I have found grace in your eyes, speak, I pray you, in the ears of Pharaoh, saying, My father made me swear, saying, Lo, I die, in my grave which I have digged for me in the land of Canaan, there shalt thou bury me. Now therefore let me go up, I pray thee, and bury my father, and I will come again. And Pharaoh said, Go up, and bury thy father, according as he made thee swear. And Joseph went up to bury his father, and with him went up all the servants of Pharaoh, the elders of his house, and all the elders of the land of Egypt, And all the house of Joseph, and his brethren, and his father's house, only their little ones, and their flocks, and their herds, they left in the land of Goshen. And there went up with him both chariots and horsemen, and it was a very great company. And they came to the threshing floor of Atad, which is beyond Jordan, and there they mourned with a great and very sore lamentation, and he made a mourning for his father seven days. And when the inhabitants of the land, the Canaanites, saw the mourning in the floor of Atad, they said, This is a grievous mourning to the Egyptians, wherefore the name of it was called Abel-mizraim, which is beyond Jordan. And his sons did unto him according as he commanded them, For his sons carried him into the land of Canaan, and buried him in the cave of the field of Machpelah, which Abraham bought with the field for a possession of a burying-place of Ephron the Hittite, before Mamre. And Joseph returned into Egypt, he, and his brethren, and all that went up with him to bury his father, after he had buried his father.

And when Joseph's brethren saw that their father was dead, they said, Joseph will peradventure hate us, and will certainly requite us all the evil which we did unto him. And they sent a messenger unto Joseph, saying, Thy father did command before he died, saying, So shall ye say unto Joseph, Forgive, I pray thee now, the trespass of thy brethren and their sin, for they did unto thee evil, and now we pray thee, forgive the trespass of the servants of the God of thy father. And Joseph wept when they spake unto him. And his brethren also went and fell down before his face, and they said, Behold, we be thy servants. And Joseph said unto them, Fear not, for am I in the place of God? But as for you, ye thought evil against me, but God meant it unto good, to bring to pass, as it is this day, to save much people alive. Now therefore fear ye not, I will nourish you, and your little ones. And he comforted them, and spake kindly unto them.

And Joseph dwelt in Egypt, he, and his father's house, and Joseph lived a hundred and ten years. And Joseph saw Ephraim's children of the third generation, the children also of Machir the son of Manasseh were brought up upon Joseph's knees.

And Joseph said unto his brethren, I die, and go unto my fathers, and I go down to my grave with joy. The God of my father Jacob be with you, to deliver you out of affliction in the days of your bondage, for the Lord hath visited me, and I have obtained a promise of the Lord, that out of the fruit of my loins, the Lord God will raise up a righteous branch out of my loins, and unto thee, whom my father Jacob hath named Israel, a prophet, (not the Messiah who is called Shilo,) and this prophet shall deliver my people out of Egypt in the days of thy bondage.

And it shall come to pass that they shall be scattered again and a branch shall be broken off and shall be carried into a far country, nevertheless they shall be remembered in the covenants of the Lord when the Messiah cometh, for he shall be made manifest unto them in the latter days, in the Spirit of power, and shall bring them out of darkness into light, out of hidden darkness and out of captivity unto freedom.

A seer shall the Lord my God raise up, who shall be a choice seer unto the fruit of my loins. Thus saith the Lord God of my fathers unto me, A choice seer will I raise up out of the fruit of thy loins, and he shall be esteemed highly among the fruit of thy loins, and unto him will I give commandment that he shall do a work for the fruit of thy loins, his brethren. And he shall bring them to the knowledge of the covenants which I have made with thy fathers, and he shall do whatsoever work I shall command him. And I will make him great in mine eyes, for he shall do my work, and he shall be great like unto him whom I have said I would raise up unto you to deliver my people, O house of Israel, out of the land of Egypt, for a seer will I raise up to deliver my people out of the land of Egypt, and he shall be called Moses. And by this name he shall know that he is of thy house, for he shall be nursed by the king's daughter and shall be called her son.

And again, a seer will I raise up out of the fruit of thy loins, and unto him will I give power to bring forth my word unto the seed of thy loins, and not to the bringing forth of my word only, saith the Lord, but to the convincing them of my word, which shall have already gone forth among them in the last days, Wherefore the fruit of thy loins shall write, and the fruit of the loins of Judah shall write, and that which shall be written by the fruit of thy loins, and also that which shall be written by the fruit of the loins of Judah, shall grow together unto the confounding of false doctrines, and laying down of contentions, and establishing peace among the fruit of thy loins, and bringing them to a knowledge of their fathers in the latter days, and also to the knowledge of my covenants, saith the Lord. And out of weakness shall he be made strong in that day when my work shall go forth among all my people, which shall restore them, who are of the house of Israel, in the last days.

And that seer will I bless, and they that seek to destroy him shall be confounded, for this promise I give unto you, for I will remember you from generation to generation, and his name shall be called Joseph, and it shall be after the name of his father, and he shall be like unto you, for the thing which the Lord shall bring forth by his hand shall bring my people unto salvation.

And the Lord sware unto Joseph that he would preserve his seed forever, saying, I will raise up Moses, and a rod shall be in his hand, and he shall gather together my people, and he shall lead them as a flock, and he shall smite the waters of the Red Sea with his rod. And he shall have judgment, and shall write the word of the Lord. And he shall not speak many words, for I will write unto him my law by the finger of mine own hand. And I will make a spokesman for him, and his name shall be called Aaron. And it shall be done unto thee in the last days also, even as I have sworn.

Therefore, Joseph said unto his brethren, God will surely visit you, and bring you out of this land, unto the land which he sware unto Abraham, and unto Isaac, and to Jacob. And Joseph confirmed many other things unto his brethren, and took an oath of the children of Israel, saying unto them, God will surely visit you, and ye shall carry up my bones from hence.

So Joseph died when he was an hundred and ten years old, and they embalmed him, and they put him in a coffin in Egypt, and he was kept from burial by the children of Israel, that he might be carried up and laid in the sepulcher with his father. And thus they remembered the oath which they sware unto him.

EXODUS

NOW these are the names of the children of Israel, which came into Egypt, every man according to his household who came with Jacob: Reuben, Simeon, Levi and Judah, Issachar, Zebulun and Benjamin, Dan and Naphtali, Gad and Asher. And all the souls that came out of the loins of Jacob were seventy souls, for Joseph was in Egypt already. And Joseph died, and all his brethren, and all that generation.

And the children of Israel were fruitful, and increased abundantly, and multiplied, and waxed exceeding mighty, and the land was filled with them. Now there arose up a new king over Egypt which knew not Joseph. And he said unto his people, Behold, the people of the children of Israel are more and mightier than we. Come on, let us deal wisely with them, lest they multiply, and it come to pass that, when there falleth out any war, they join also unto our enemies and fight against us and so get them up out of the land. Therefore they did set over them taskmasters to afflict them with their burdens. And they built for Pharaoh treasure cities: Pithom and Raamses. But the more they afflicted them, the more they multiplied and grew. And they were grieved because of the children of Israel. And the Egyptians made the children of Israel to serve with rigor and they made their lives bitter with hard bondage, in mortar, and in brick, and in all manner of service in the field, all their service wherein they made them serve was with rigor.

And the king of Egypt spake to the Hebrew midwives, of which the name of the one was Shiphrah and the name of the other Puah, and he said, When ye do the office of a midwife to the Hebrew women and see them upon the stools, if it be a son, then ye shall kill him, but if it be a daughter, then she shall live. But the midwives feared God and did not as the king of Egypt commanded them, but saved the men children alive. And the king of Egypt called for the midwives and said unto them, Why have ye done this thing and have saved the men children alive? And the midwives said unto Pharaoh, Because the Hebrew women are not as the Egyptian women, for they are lively and are delivered ere the midwives come in unto them. Therefore God dealt well with the midwives, and the people multiplied, and waxed very mighty. And it came to pass because the midwives feared God that he made them houses. And Pharaoh charged all his people saying, Every son that is born ye shall cast into the river and every daughter ye shall save alive.

And there went a man of the house of Levi and took to wife a daughter of Levi, and the woman conceived and bare a son. And when she saw him that he was a goodly child, she hid him three months. And when she could not longer hide him she took for him an ark of bulrushes, and daubed it with slime and with pitch, and put the child therein, and she laid it in the flags by the river's brink. And his sister stood afar off to wit what would be done to him.

And the daughter of Pharaoh came down to wash herself at the river and her maidens walked along by the river's side, and when she saw the ark among the flags she sent her maid to fetch it. And when she had opened it she saw the child and behold, the babe wept. And she had compassion on him and said, This is one of the Hebrews' children. Then said his sister to Pharaoh's daughter, Shall I go and call to thee a nurse of the Hebrew women, that she may nurse the child for thee? And Pharaoh's daughter said to her, Go. And the maid went and called the child's mother. And Pharaoh's daughter said unto her, Take this child away and nurse it for me and I will give thee thy wages. And the woman took the child and nursed it. And the child grew and she brought him unto Pharaoh's daughter and he became her son. And she called his name Moses and she said, Because I drew him out of the water.

And it came to pass in those days, when Moses was grown, that he went out unto his brethren and looked on their burdens, and he spied an Egyptian smiting a Hebrew, one of his brethren. And he looked this way and that way and when he saw that there was no man, he slew the Egyptian and hid him in the sand. And when he went out the second day behold, two men of the Hebrews strove together, and he said to him that did the wrong, Wherefore smitest thou thy fellow? And he said, Who made thee a prince and a judge over us? Intendest thou to kill me as thou killedst the Egyptian? And Moses feared and said, Surely this thing is known.

Now when Pharaoh heard this thing he sought to slay Moses. But Moses fled from the face of Pharaoh and dwelt in the land of Midian, and he sat down by a well. Now the priest of Midian had seven daughters, and they came and drew water and filled the troughs to water their father's flock. And the shepherds came and drove them away, but Moses stood up and helped them and watered their flock. And when they came to Reuel their father, he said, How is it that ye are come so soon today? And they said, An Egyptian delivered us out of the hand of the shepherds, and also drew water enough for us, and watered the flock. And he said unto his daughters, And where is he? Why is it that ye have left the man? Call him that he may eat bread. And Moses was content to dwell with the man, and he gave Moses Zipporah his daughter. And she bare him a son and he called his name Gershom, for he said, I have been a stranger in a strange land.

2 AND it came to pass in process of time that the king of Egypt died and the children of Israel sighed by reason of the bondage, and they cried and their cry came up unto God by reason of the bondage. And God heard their groaning and God remembered his covenant with Abraham, with Isaac, and with Jacob. And God looked upon the children of Israel and God had respect unto them.

Now Moses kept the flock of Jethro his father-in-law, the priest of Midian, and he led the flock to the back side of the desert and came to the mountain of God even to Horeb. And again the presence of the Lord appeared unto him in a flame of fire in the midst of a bush, and he looked and behold, the bush burned with fire and the bush was not consumed. And Moses said, I will now turn aside and see this great sight, why the bush is not consumed.

And when the Lord saw that he turned aside to see, God called unto him out of the midst of the bush and said, Moses, Moses. And he said, Here am I. And he said, Draw not nigh hither. Put off thy shoes from off thy feet, for the place whereon thou standest is holy ground. Moreover he said, I am the God of thy father, the God of Abraham, the God of Isaac, and the God of Jacob. And Moses hid his face, for he was afraid to look upon God. And the Lord said, I have surely seen the affliction of my people which are in Egypt and have heard their cry by reason of their taskmasters, for I know their sorrows, and I am come down to deliver them out of the hand of the Egyptians, and to bring them up out of that land unto a good land and a large, unto a land flowing with milk and honey, unto the place of the Canaanites, and the Hittites, and the Amorites, and the Perizzites, and the Hivites, and the Jebusites. Now therefore behold, the cry of the children of Israel is come unto me and I have also seen the oppression wherewith the Egyptians oppress them. Come now therefore, and I will send thee unto Pharaoh that thou mayest bring forth my people the children of Israel out of Egypt.

And Moses said unto God, Who am I that I should go unto Pharaoh and that I should bring forth the children of Israel out of Egypt? And he said, Certainly I will be with thee, and this shall be a token unto thee that I have sent thee, when thou hast brought forth the people out of Egypt ye shall serve God upon this mountain.

And Moses said unto God, Behold, when I come unto the children of Israel and shall say unto them, The God of your fathers hath sent me unto you, and they shall say to me, What is his name? What shall I say unto them? And God said unto Moses, I AM THAT I AM, and he said, Thus shalt thou say unto the children of Israel, I AM hath sent me unto you. And God said moreover unto Moses, Thus shalt thou say unto the children of Israel, The Lord God of your fathers, the God of Abraham, the God of Isaac, and the God of Jacob, hath sent me unto you. This is my name for ever and this is my memorial unto all generations. Go, and gather the elders of Israel together and say unto them, The Lord God of your fathers, the God of Abraham, of Isaac, and of Jacob, appeared unto me saying, I have surely visited you, and seen that which is done to you in Egypt, and I have said, I will bring you up out of the affliction of Egypt unto the land of the Canaanites, and the Hittites, and the Amorites, and the Perizzites, and the Hivites, and the Jebusites, unto a land flowing with milk and honey. And they shall hearken to thy voice and thou shalt come, thou and the elders of Israel, unto the king of Egypt, and ye shall say unto him, The Lord God of the Hebrews hath met with us, and now let us go, we beseech thee, three days' journey into the wilderness that we may sacrifice to the Lord our God. And I am sure that the king of Egypt will not let you go, no, not by a mighty hand. And I will stretch out my hand and smite Egypt with all my wonders which I will do in the midst thereof, and after that he will let you go. And I will give this people favor in the sight of the Egyptians, and it shall come to pass that, when ye go, ye shall not go empty, but every woman shall borrow of her neighbor and of her that sojourneth in her house, jewels of silver, and jewels of gold, and raiment, and ye shall put them upon your sons, and upon your daughters, and ye shall spoil the Egyptians.

And Moses answered and said, But behold, they will not believe me nor hearken unto my voice, for they will say, The Lord hath not appeared unto thee. And the Lord said unto him, What is that in thine hand? And he said, A rod. And he said, Cast it on the ground. And he cast it on the ground, and it became a serpent, and Moses fled from before it. And the Lord said unto Moses, Put forth thine hand and take it by the tail. And he put forth his hand and caught it, and it became a rod in his hand that they may believe that the Lord God of their fathers, the God of Abraham, the God of Isaac, and the God of Jacob, hath appeared unto thee. And the Lord said furthermore unto him, Put now thine hand into thy bosom. And he put his hand into his bosom and when he took it out, behold, his hand was leprous as snow. And he said, Put thy hand into thy bosom again. And he put his hand into his bosom again, and plucked it out of his bosom and behold, it was turned again as his other flesh. And it shall come to pass, if they will not believe thee, neither hearken to the voice of the first sign, that they will believe the voice of the latter sign. And it shall come to pass if they will not believe also these two signs, neither hearken unto thy voice, that thou shalt take of the water of the river and pour it upon the dry land, and the water which thou takest out of the river shall become blood upon the dry land.

And Moses said unto the Lord, O my Lord, I am not eloquent, neither heretofore nor since thou hast spoken unto thy servant, but I am slow of speech, and of a slow tongue. And the Lord said unto him, Who hath made man's mouth? Or who maketh the dumb, or deaf, or the seeing, or the blind? Have not I the Lord? Now therefore go, and I will be with thy mouth and teach thee what thou shalt say. And he said, O my Lord, send, I pray thee, by the hand of him whom thou wilt send. And the anger of the Lord was kindled against Moses and he said, Is not Aaron the Levite thy brother? I know that he can speak well. And also behold, he cometh forth to meet thee, and when he seeth thee he will be glad in his heart. And thou shalt speak unto him and put words in his mouth, and I will be with thy mouth and with his mouth, and will teach you what ye shall do. And he shall be thy spokesman unto the people, and he shall be, even he shall be to thee instead of a mouth and thou shalt be to him instead of God. And thou shalt take this rod in thine hand wherewith thou shalt do signs.

And Moses went and returned to Jethro his father-in-law, and said unto him, Let me go, I pray thee, and return unto my brethren which are in Egypt and see whether they be yet alive. And Jethro said to Moses, Go in peace. And the Lord said unto Moses in Midian, Go, return into Egypt, for all the men are dead which sought thy life. And Moses took his wife and his sons and set them upon an ass, and he returned to the land of Egypt, and Moses took the rod of God in his hand.

And the Lord said unto Moses, When thou goest to return into Egypt see that thou do all those wonders before Pharaoh which I have put in thine hand and I will prosper thee, but Pharaoh will harden his heart and he will not let the people go. And thou shalt say unto Pharaoh, Thus saith the Lord, Israel is my son, even my firstborn. And I say unto thee, Let my son go that he may serve me and if thou refuse to let him go behold, I will slay thy son, even thy firstborn.

And it came to pass that the Lord appeared unto him as he was in the way by the inn. The Lord was angry with Moses and his hand was about to fall upon him to kill him, for he had not circumcised his son. Then Zipporah took a sharp stone and circumcised her son, and cast the stone at his feet, and said, Surely thou art a bloody husband unto me. And the Lord spared Moses and let him go because Zipporah his wife circumcised the child. And she said, Thou art a bloody husband. And Moses was ashamed, and hid his face from the Lord, and said, I have sinned before the Lord.

And the Lord said unto Aaron, Go into the wilderness to meet Moses, and he went and met him in the mount of God, in the mount where God appeared unto him, and Aaron kissed him. And Moses told Aaron all the words of the Lord who had sent him and all the signs which he had commanded him. And Moses and Aaron went and gathered together all the elders of the children of Israel, and Aaron spake all the words which the Lord had spoken unto Moses, and did the signs in the sight of the people. And the people believed. And when they heard that the Lord had visited the children of Israel and that he had looked upon their affliction, then they bowed their heads and worshiped.

And afterward Moses and Aaron went in and told Pharaoh, Thus saith the Lord God of Israel, Let my people go, that they may hold a feast unto me in the wilderness. And Pharaoh said, Who is the Lord that I should obey his voice to let Israel go? I know not the Lord, neither will I let Israel go. And they said, The God of the Hebrews hath met with us. Let us go, we pray thee, three days' journey into the desert and sacrifice unto the Lord our God, lest he fall upon us with pestilence or with the sword. And the king of Egypt said unto them, Wherefore do ye, Moses and Aaron, lead the people from their works? Get you unto your burdens. And Pharaoh said, Behold, the people of the land now are many and ye make them rest from their burdens.

And Pharaoh commanded the same day the taskmasters of the people and their officers saying, Ye shall no more give the people straw to make brick as heretofore; let them go and gather straw for themselves. And the tale of the bricks, which they did make heretofore, ye shall lay upon them; ye shall not diminish aught thereof, for they be idle, therefore they cry saying, Let us go and sacrifice to our God. Let there more work be laid upon the men that they may labor therein and let them not regard vain words. And the taskmasters of the people went out, and their officers, and they spake to the people saying, Thus saith Pharaoh, I will not give you straw. Go ye, get your straw where ye can find it, yet not aught of your work shall be diminished. So the people were scattered abroad throughout all the land of Egypt to gather stubble instead of straw. And the taskmasters hasted them saying, Fulfill your works, your daily tasks, as when there was straw. And the officers of the children of Israel, which Pharaoh's taskmasters had set over them, were beaten and demanded, Wherefore have ye not fulfilled your task in making brick, both yesterday and today, as heretofore?

Then the officers of the children of Israel came and cried unto Pharaoh saying, Wherefore dealest thou thus with thy servants? There is no straw given unto thy servants, and they say to us, Make brick and behold, thy servants are beaten, but the fault is in thine own people. But he said, Ye are idle, ye are idle, therefore ye say, Let us go and do sacrifice to the Lord. Go therefore now and work, for there shall no straw be given you, yet shall ye deliver the tale of bricks. And the officers of the children of Israel did see that they were in evil case after it was said, Ye shall not diminish aught from your bricks of your daily task. And they met Moses and Aaron who stood in the way as they came forth from Pharaoh, and they said unto them, The Lord look upon you and judge because ye have made our savor to be abhorred in the eyes of Pharaoh, and in the eyes of his servants, to put a sword in their hand to slay us.

And Moses returned unto the Lord and said, Lord, wherefore hast thou so evil entreated this people? Why is it that thou hast sent me? For since I came to Pharaoh to speak in thy name, he hath done evil to this people, neither hast thou delivered thy people at all. Then the Lord said unto Moses, Now shalt thou see what I will do to Pharaoh, for with a strong hand shall he let them go, and with a strong hand shall he drive them out of his land. And God spake unto Moses and said unto him, I am the Lord and I appeared unto Abraham, unto Isaac, and unto Jacob. I am the Lord God Almighty, the Lord JEHOVAH. And was not my name known unto them? Yea, and I have also established my covenant with them which I made with them, to give them the land of Canaan, the land of their pilgrimage wherein they were strangers. And I have also heard the groaning of the children of Israel whom the Egyptians keep in bondage, and I have remembered my covenant. Wherefore say unto the children of Israel, I am the Lord and I will bring you out from under the burdens of the Egyptians, and I will rid you out of their bondage, and I will redeem you with a stretched out arm, and with great judgments, and I will take you to me for a people, and I will be to you a God, and ye shall know that I am the Lord your God, which bringeth you out from under the burdens of the Egyptians. And I will bring you in unto the land concerning the which I did swear to give it to Abraham, to Isaac, and to Jacob, and I will give it you for a heritage, I the Lord will do it. And Moses spake so unto the children of Israel, but they hearkened not unto Moses for anguish of spirit, and for cruel bondage.

And the Lord spake unto Moses saying, Go in, speak unto Pharaoh king of Egypt, that he let the children of Israel go out of his land. And Moses spake before the Lord saying, Behold, the children of Israel have not hearkened unto me, how then shall Pharaoh hear me who is of uncircumcised lips? And the Lord spake unto Moses and unto Aaron, and gave them a charge unto the children of Israel and unto Pharaoh king of Egypt, to bring the children of Israel out of the land of Egypt.

These are the heads of their fathers' houses: The sons of Reuben the firstborn of Israel, Hanoch, and Pallu, Hezron, and Carmi, these are the families of Reuben. And the sons of Simeon, Jemuel, and Jamin, and Ohad, and Jachin, and Zohar, and Shaul the son of a Canaanitsh woman, these are the families of Simeon. And these are the names of the sons of Levi according to their generations: Gershon, and Kohath, and Merari, and the years of the life of Levi were a hundred thirty and seven years. The sons of Gershon: Libni, and Shimi, according to their families. And the sons of Kohath: Amram, and Izxhar, and Hebron, and Uzziel, and the years of the life of Kohath were a hundred thirty and three years. And the sons of Merari: Mahali and Mushi, these are the families of Levi according to their generations. And Amram took him Jochebed his father's sister to wife, and she bare him Aaron and Moses, and the years of the life of Amram were a hundred and thirty and seven years. And the sons of Izhar: Korah, and Nepheg, and Zichri. And the sons of Uzziel: Mishael, and Elzaphan, and Zithri. And Aaron took him Elisheba, daughter of Amminadab, sister of Naashon, to wife, and she bare him Nabad and Abihu, Eleazar and Ithamar. And the sons of Korah: Assir, and Elkanah, and Abiasaph, these are families of the Korhites. And Eleazar Aaron's son took him one of the daughters of Putiel to wife, and she bare him Phinehas; these are the heads of the fathers of the Levites according to their families. These are the sons of Aaron according to their families. And all these are the names of the children of Israel according to the heads of their families that the Lord said unto Aaron and Moses, they should bring up out of the land of Egypt according to their armies. These are they concerning whom the Lord spake to Pharaoh, king of Egypt, that he should let them go. And he sent Moses and Aaron to bring out the children of Israel from Egypt.

And it came to pass on the day the Lord spake unto Moses in the land of Egypt that the Lord commanded Moses that he should speak unto Pharaoh king of Egypt saying, I, the Lord, will do unto Pharaoh king of Egypt all that I say unto thee. And Moses said before the Lord, Behold, I am of stammering lips and slow of speech; how shall Pharaoh hearken unto me? And the Lord said unto Moses, See, I have made thee a prophet to Pharaoh, and Aaron thy brother shall be thy spokesman. Thou shalt speak unto thy brother all that I command thee, and Aaron thy brother shall speak unto Pharaoh that he send the children of Israel out of his land. And Pharaoh will harden his heart, as I said unto thee, and thou shalt multiply my signs and my wonders in the land of Egypt. But Pharaoh will not hearken unto you, therefore I will lay my hand upon Egypt and bring forth mine armies, my people, the children of Israel, out of the land of Egypt by great judgments. And the Egyptians shall know that I am the Lord when I stretch forth mine hand upon Egypt and bring out the children of Israel from among them. And Moses and Aaron did as the Lord commanded them, so did they. And Moses was fourscore years old and Aaron fourscore and three years old when they spake unto Pharaoh.

And the Lord spake unto Moses and unto Aaron saying, When Pharaoh shall speak unto you saying, Show a miracle that I may know you, then thou shalt say unto Aaron, Take thy rod and cast it before Pharaoh and it shall become a serpent. And Moses and Aaron went in unto Pharaoh and they did so as the Lord had commanded: and Aaron cast down his rod before Pharaoh, and before his servants, and it became a serpent. Then Pharaoh also called the wise men and the sorcerers, now the magicians of Egypt, they also did in like manner with their enchantments. For they cast down every man his rod and they became serpents, but Aaron's rod swallowed up their rods. And Pharaoh hardened his heart that he hearkened not unto them, as the Lord had said.

And the Lord said unto Moses, Pharaoh's heart is hardened, he refuseth to let the people go. Get thee unto Pharaoh in the morning, lo, he goeth out unto the water, and thou shalt stand by the river's brink against he come, and the rod which was turned to a serpent shalt thou take in thine hand. And thou shalt say unto him, The Lord God of the Hebrews hath sent me unto thee saying, Let my people go that they may serve me in the wilderness and behold, hitherto thou wouldest not hear. Thus saith the Lord, In this thou shalt know that I am the Lord: behold, I will smite with the rod that is in mine hand upon the waters which are in the river, and they shall be turned to blood. And the fish that is in the river shall die, and the river shall stink, and the Egyptians shall loathe to drink of the water of the river. And the Lord spake unto Moses, Say unto Aaron, Take thy rod and stretch out thine hand upon the waters of Egypt, upon their streams, upon their rivers, and upon their ponds, and upon all their pools of water, that they may become blood and that there may be blood throughout all the land of Egypt, both in vessels of wood, and in vessels of stone. And Moses and Aaron did so as the Lord commanded, and he lifted up the rod and smote the waters that were in the river, in the sight of Pharaoh and in the sight of his servants, and all the waters that were in the river were turned to blood. And the fish that was in the river died, and the river stank, and the Egyptians could not drink of the water of the river, and there was blood throughout all the land of Egypt. And the magicians of Egypt did so with their enchantments, and Pharaoh's heart was hardened, neither did he hearken unto them as the Lord had said. And Pharaoh turned and went into his house, neither did he set his heart to this also. And all the Egyptians digged round about the river for water to drink, for they could not drink of the water of the river.

And seven days were fulfilled after that the Lord had smitten the river. And the Lord spake unto Moses, Go unto Pharaoh and say unto him, Thus saith the Lord, Let my people go that they may serve me. And if thou refuse to let them go behold, I will smite all thy borders with frogs and the river shall bring forth frogs abundantly, which shall go up and come into thine house, and into thy bedchamber, and upon thy bed, and into the house of thy servants, and upon thy people, and into thine ovens, and into thy kneading troughs, and the frogs shall come up both on thee, and upon thy people, and upon all thy servants. And the Lord spake unto Moses, Say unto Aaron, Stretch forth thine hand with thy rod over the streams, over the rivers, and over the ponds, and cause frogs to come up upon the land of Egypt. And Aaron stretched out his hand over the waters of Egypt and the frogs came up and covered the land of Egypt. And the magicians did so with their enchantments and brought up frogs upon the land of Egypt. Then Pharaoh called for Moses and Aaron and said, Entreat the Lord that he may take away the frogs from me and from my people, and I will let the people go that they may do sacrifice unto the Lord. And Moses said unto Pharaoh, Glory over me, when shall I entreat for thee, and for thy servants, and for thy people, to destroy the frogs from thee and thy houses, that they may remain in the river only? And he said, Tomorrow. And he said, Be it according to thy word that thou mayest know that there is none like unto the Lord our God. And the frogs shall depart from thee, and from thy houses, and from thy servants, and from thy people, they shall remain in the river only. And Moses and Aaron went out from Pharaoh, and Moses cried unto the Lord because of the frogs which he had brought against Pharaoh. And the Lord did according to the word of Moses, and the frogs died out of the houses, out of the villages, and out of the fields. And they gathered them together upon heaps and the land stank. But when Pharaoh saw that there was respite, he hardened his heart and hearkened not unto them as the Lord had said.

And the Lord said unto Moses, Say unto Aaron, Stretch out thy rod and smite the dust of the land that it may become lice throughout all the land of Egypt. And they did so, for Aaron stretched out his hand with his rod, and smote the dust of the Earth, and it became lice in man, and in beast, all the dust of the land became lice throughout all the land of Egypt. And the magicians did so with their enchantments to bring forth lice, but they could not, so there were lice upon man and upon beast. Then the magicians said unto Pharaoh, This is the finger of God, and Pharaoh's heart was hardened and he hearkened not unto them as the Lord had said.

And the Lord said unto Moses, Rise up early in the morning and stand before Pharaoh, lo, he cometh forth to the water, and say unto him, Thus saith the Lord, Let my people go that they may serve me. Else if thou wilt not let my people go behold, I will send swarms of flies upon thee, and upon thy servants, and upon thy people, and into thy houses, and the houses of the Egyptians shall be full of swarms of flies, and also the ground whereon they are. And I will sever in that day the land of Goshen in which my people dwell, that no swarms of flies shall be there, to the end thou mayest know that I am the Lord in the midst of the Earth. And I will put a division between my people and thy people; tomorrow shall this sign be. And the Lord did so, and there came a grievous swarm of flies into the house of Pharaoh, and into his servants' houses, and into all the land of Egypt; the land was corrupted by reason of the swarm of flies. And Pharaoh called for Moses and for Aaron and said, Go ye, sacrifice to your God in the land. And Moses said, It is not meet so to do, for we shall sacrifice the abomination of the Egyptians to the Lord our God, lo, shall we sacrifice the abomination of the Egyptians before their eyes and will they not stone us? We will go three days' journey into the wilderness and sacrifice to the Lord our God as he shall command us. And Pharaoh said, I will let you go, that ye may sacrifice to the Lord your God in the wilderness, only ye shall not go very far away; entreat for me. And Moses said, Behold, I go out from thee and I will entreat the Lord that the swarms of flies may depart from Pharaoh, from his servants, and from his people, tomorrow, but let not Pharaoh deal deceitfully any more in not letting the people go to sacrifice to the Lord. And Moses went out from Pharaoh and entreated the Lord. And the Lord did according to the word of Moses and he removed the swarms of flies from Pharaoh, from his servants, and from his people; there remained not one. And Pharaoh hardened his heart at this time also, neither would he let the people go.

Then the Lord said unto Moses, Go in unto Pharaoh and tell him, Thus saith the Lord God of the Hebrews, Let my people go that they may serve me. For if thou refuse to let them go and wilt hold them still, behold, the hand of the Lord is upon thy cattle which is in the field, upon the horses, upon the asses, upon the camels, upon the oxen, and upon the sheep, there shall be a very grievous murrain. And the Lord shall sever between the cattle of Israel and the cattle of Egypt and there shall nothing die of all that is the children's of Israel. And the Lord appointed a set time, saying, Tomorrow the Lord shall do this thing in the land. And the Lord did that thing on the morrow, and all the cattle of Egypt died, but of the cattle of the children of Israel died not one. And Pharaoh sent and behold, there was not one of the cattle of the Israelites dead. And the heart of Pharaoh was hardened and he did not let the people go.

And the Lord said unto Moses and unto Aaron, Take to you handfuls of ashes of the furnace, and let Moses sprinkle it toward the Heaven in the sight of Pharaoh. And it shall become small dust in all the land of Egypt and shall be a boil breaking forth with blains upon man and upon beast throughout all the land of Egypt. And they took ashes of the furnace and stood before Pharaoh, and Moses sprinkled it up toward Heaven, and it became a boil breaking forth with blains upon man and upon beast. And the magicians could not stand before Moses because of the boils, for the boil was upon the magicians and upon all the Egyptians. And Pharaoh hardened his heart and he hearkened not unto them as the Lord had spoken unto Moses.

And the Lord said unto Moses, Rise up early in the morning and stand before Pharaoh and say unto him, Thus saith the Lord God of the Hebrews, Let my people go that they may serve me. For I will at this time send all my plagues upon thine heart, and upon thy servants, and upon thy people, that thou mayest know that there is none like me in all the Earth. For now I will stretch out my hand that I may smite thee and thy people with pestilence and thou shalt be cut off from the Earth. And in very deed for this cause have I raised thee up, for to show in thee my power, and that my name may be declared throughout all the Earth. Therefore speak unto Pharaoh the thing which I command thee, who as yet exalteth himself that he will not let them go. Behold, tomorrow about this time I will cause it to rain a very grievous hail, such as hath not been in Egypt since the foundation thereof even until now. Send therefore now and gather thy cattle and all that thou hast in the field, for upon every man and beast which shall be found in the field and shall not be brought home, the hail shall come down upon them and they shall die. He that feared the word of the Lord among the servants of Pharaoh made his servants and his cattle flee into the houses, And he that regarded not the word of the Lord left his servants and his cattle in the field. And the Lord said unto Moses, Stretch forth thine hand toward Heaven, that there may be hail in all the land of Egypt upon man, and upon beast, and upon every herb of the field throughout the land of Egypt. And Moses stretched forth his rod toward Heaven and the Lord sent thunder and hail, and the fire ran along upon the ground, and the Lord rained hail upon the land of Egypt.

So there was hail, and fire mingled with the hail, very grievous, such as there was none like it in all the land of Egypt since it became a nation. And the hail smote throughout all the land of Egypt all that was in the field, both man and beast, and the hail smote every herb of the field and brake every tree of the field. Only in the land of Goshen, where the children of Israel were, was there no hail. And Pharaoh sent and called for Moses and Aaron and said unto them, I have sinned this time, the Lord is righteous and I and my people are wicked. Entreat the Lord (for it is enough) that there be no more mighty thunderings and hail and I will let you go and ye shall stay no longer. And Moses said unto him, As soon as I am gone out of the city I will spread abroad my hands unto the Lord, and the thunder shall cease neither shall there be any more hail, that thou mayest know how that the Earth is the Lord's. But as for thee and thy servants I know that ye will not yet fear the Lord God. And the flax and the barley was smitten, for the barley was in the ear and the flax was bolled. But the wheat and the rye were not smitten for they were not grown up. And Moses went out of the city from Pharaoh and spread abroad his hands unto the Lord, and the thunders and hail ceased, and the rain was not poured upon the Earth. And when Pharaoh saw that the rain and the hail and the thunders were ceased, he sinned yet more and hardened his heart, he and his servants. And the heart of Pharaoh was hardened neither would he let the children of Israel go as the Lord had spoken by Moses.

And the Lord said unto Moses, Go in unto Pharaoh, for he hath hardened his heart and the hearts of his servants, therefore I will show these my signs before him, and that thou mayest tell in the ears of thy son, and of thy son's son what things I have wrought in Egypt and my signs which I have done among them, that ye may know how that I am the Lord. And Moses and Aaron came in unto Pharaoh and said unto him, Thus saith the Lord God of the Hebrews, How long wilt thou refuse to humble thyself before me? Let my people go that they may serve me. Else if thou refuse to let my people go, behold, tomorrow will I bring the locusts into thy coast and they shall cover the face of the Earth that one cannot be able to see the Earth, and they shall eat the residue of that which is escaped, which remaineth unto you from the hail, and shall eat every tree which groweth for you out of the field, and they shall fill thy houses, and the houses of all thy servants, and the houses of all the Egyptians, which neither thy fathers nor thy fathers' fathers have seen since the day that they were upon the Earth unto this day. And he turned himself and went out from Pharaoh.

And Pharaoh's servants said unto him, How long shall this man be a snare unto us? Let the men go that they may serve the Lord their God; knowest thou not yet that Egypt is destroyed? And Moses and Aaron were brought again unto Pharaoh, and he said unto them, Go serve the Lord your God, but who are they that shall go? And Moses said, We will go with our young and with our old, with our sons and with our daughters, with our flocks and with our herds will we go, for we must hold a feast unto the Lord. And he said unto them, Let the Lord be so with you, as I will let you go, and your little ones, look to it, for evil is before you. Not so, go now ye that are men, and serve the Lord, for that ye did desire. And they were driven out from Pharaoh's presence.

And the Lord said unto Moses, Stretch out thine hand over the land of Egypt for the locusts, that they may come up upon the land of Egypt and eat every herb of the land, even all that the hail hath left. And Moses stretched forth his rod over the land of Egypt and the Lord brought an east wind upon the land all that day and all that night, and when it was morning the east wind brought the locusts. And the locusts went up over all the land of Egypt and rested in all the coasts of Egypt, very grievous were they; before them there were no such locusts as they, neither after them shall be such. For they covered the face of the whole Earth so that the land was darkened, and they did eat every herb of the land and all the fruit of the trees which the hail had left, and there remained not any green thing in the trees, or in the herbs of the field, through all the land of Egypt. Then Pharaoh called for Moses and Aaron in haste and he said, I have sinned against the Lord your God and against you. Now therefore forgive, I pray thee, my sin only this once, and entreat the Lord your God that he may take away from me this death only. And he went out from Pharaoh and entreated the Lord. And the Lord turned a mighty strong west wind, which took away the locusts and cast them into the Red Sea; there remained not one locust in all the coasts of Egypt. But Pharaoh hardened his heart so that he would not let the children of Israel go.

And the Lord said unto Moses, Stretch out thine hand toward Heaven that there may be darkness over the land of Egypt, even darkness which may be felt. And Moses stretched forth his hand toward Heaven and there was a thick darkness in all the land of Egypt three days, they saw not one another, neither rose any from his place for three days, but all the children of Israel had light in their dwellings. And Pharaoh called unto Moses and said, Go ye, serve the Lord, only let your flocks and your herds be stayed, let your little ones also go with you. And Moses said, Thou must give us also sacrifices and burnt offerings that we may sacrifice unto the Lord our God. Our cattle also shall go with us, there shall not a hoof be left behind, for thereof must we take to serve the Lord our God, and we know not with what we must serve the Lord until we come thither. But Pharaoh hardened his heart and he would not let them go. And Pharaoh said unto him, Get thee from me, take heed to thyself, see my face no more, for in that day thou seest my face thou shalt die. And Moses said, Thou hast spoken well, I will see thy face again no more.

And the Lord said unto Moses, Yet will I bring one plague more upon Pharaoh and upon Egypt, afterwards he will let you go hence; when he shall let you go he shall surely thrust you out hence altogether. Speak now in the ears of the people and let every man borrow of his neighbor, and every woman of her neighbor jewels of silver and jewels of gold. And the Lord gave the people favor in the sight of the Egyptians. Moreover, the man Moses was very great in the land of Egypt, in the sight of Pharaoh's servants and in the sight of the people. And Moses said, Thus saith the Lord, About midnight will I go out into the midst of Egypt, and all the firstborn in the land of Egypt shall die, from the firstborn of Pharaoh that sitteth upon his throne even unto the firstborn of the maidservant that is behind the mill, and all the firstborn of beasts. And there shall be a great cry throughout all the land of Egypt such as there was none like it nor shall be like it any more. But against any of the children of Israel shall not a dog move his tongue, against man or beast, that ye may know how that the Lord doth put a difference between the Egyptians and Israel. And all these the servants of Pharaoh shall come down unto me and bow themselves down unto me saying, Get thee out, and all the people that follow thee, and after that I will go out. And the Lord said unto Moses, Pharaoh will not hearken unto you, therefore my wonders shall be multiplied in the land of Egypt. And Moses and Aaron did all these wonders before Pharaoh, and they went out from Pharaoh, and he was in a great anger. And Pharaoh hardened his heart so that he would not let the children of Israel go out of his land.

And the Lord spake unto Moses and Aaron in the land of Egypt saying, This month shall be unto you the beginning of months, it shall be the first month of the year to you. Speak ye unto all the congregation of Israel saying, In the tenth day of this month they shall take to them every man a lamb according to the house of their fathers, a lamb for a house, and if the household be too little for the lamb, let him and his neighbor next unto his house take it according to the number of the souls, every man according to his eating shall make your count for the lamb. Your lamb shall be without blemish, a male of the first year, ye shall take it out from the sheep or from the goats, and ye shall keep it up until the fourteenth day of the same month, and the whole assembly of the congregation of Israel shall kill it in the evening. And they shall take of the blood and strike it on the two side posts and on the upper doorpost of the houses wherein they shall eat it. And they shall eat the flesh in that night, roast with fire, and unleavened bread, and with bitter herbs they shall eat it. Eat not of it raw nor sodden at all with water, but roast with fire, his head with his legs and with the purtenance thereof. And ye shall let nothing of it remain until the morning, and that which remaineth of it until the morning ye shall burn with fire. And thus shall ye eat it, with your loins girded, your shoes on your feet, and your staff in your hand, and ye shall eat it in haste, it is the Lord's passover. For I will pass through the land of Egypt this night and will smite all the firstborn in the land of Egypt, both man and beast, and against all the gods of Egypt I will execute judgment, I am the Lord. And the blood shall be to you for a token upon the houses where ye are, and when I see the blood, I will pass over you, and the plague shall not be upon you to destroy you when I smite the land of Egypt. And this day shall be unto you for a memorial, and ye shall keep it a feast to the Lord throughout your generations, ye shall keep it a feast by an ordinance forever. Seven days shall ye eat unleavened bread, even the first day ye shall put away leaven out of your houses, for whosoever eateth leavened bread from the first day until the seventh day that soul shall be cut off from Israel. And in the first day there shall be a holy convocation and in the seventh day there shall be a holy convocation to you, no manner of work shall be done in them save that which every man must eat, that only may be done of you. And ye shall observe the feast of unleavened bread, for in this selfsame day have I brought your armies out of the land of Egypt, therefore shall ye observe this day in your generations by an ordinance forever. In the first month, on the fourteenth day of the month at even, ye shall eat unleavened bread, until the one and twentieth day of the month at even. Seven days shall there be no leaven found in your houses, for whosoever eateth that which is leavened, even that soul shall be cut off from the congregation of Israel, whether he be a stranger or born in the land. Ye shall eat nothing leavened, in all your habitations shall ye eat unleavened bread.

Then Moses called for all the elders of Israel and said unto them, Draw out and take you a lamb according to your families and kill the passover. And ye shall take a bunch of hyssop, and dip it in the blood that is in the basin, and strike the lintel and the two side posts with the blood that is in the basin, and none of you shall go out at the door of his house until the morning. For the Lord will pass through to smite the Egyptians, and when he seeth the blood upon the lintel and on the two side posts, the Lord will pass over the door and will not suffer the destroyer to come in unto your houses to smite you. And ye shall observe this thing for an ordinance to thee and to thy sons forever. And it shall come to pass when ye be come to the land which the Lord will give you according as he hath promised, that ye shall keep this service. And it shall come to pass when your children shall say unto you, What mean ye by this service?, that ye shall say, It is the sacrifice of the Lord's passover, who passed over the houses of the children of Israel in Egypt when he smote the Egyptians and delivered our houses. And the people bowed the head and worshiped. And the children of Israel went away and did as the Lord had commanded Moses and Aaron, so did they.

And it came to pass that at midnight the Lord smote all the firstborn in the land of Egypt, from the firstborn of Pharaoh that sat on his throne unto the firstborn of the captive that was in the dungeon, and all the firstborn of cattle. And Pharaoh rose up in the night, he and all his servants and all the Egyptians, and there was a great cry in Egypt, for there was not a house where there was not one dead. And he called for Moses and Aaron by night and said, Rise up and get you forth from among my people, both ye and the children of Israel, and go serve the Lord as ye have said. Also take your flocks and your herds as ye have said, and be gone and bless me also. And the Egyptians were urgent upon the people, that they might send them out of the land in haste, for they said, We have found our firstborn all dead, therefore get ye out of the land lest we die also. And the people took their dough before it was leavened, their kneading troughs being bound up in their clothes upon their shoulders. And the children of Israel did according to the word of Moses, and they borrowed of the Egyptians jewels of silver and jewels of gold, and raiment, and the Lord gave the people favor in the sight of the Egyptians so that they lent unto them such things as they required, and they spoiled the Egyptians.

And the children of Israel journeyed from Rameses to Succoth, about six hundred thousand men on foot, besides women and children. And a mixed multitude went up also with them, and flocks, and herds, even very much cattle. And they baked unleavened cakes of the dough which they brought forth out of Egypt, for it was not leavened because they were thrust out of Egypt and could not tarry, neither had they prepared for themselves any victuals. Now the sojourning of the children of Israel who dwelt in Egypt was four hundred and thirty years. And it came to pass at the end of the four hundred and thirty years, even the selfsame day it came to pass that all the hosts of the Lord went out from the land of Egypt. It is a night to be much observed unto the Lord for bringing them out from the land of Egypt, this is that night of the Lord to be observed of all the children of Israel in their generations.

And the Lord said unto Moses and Aaron, This is the ordinance of the passover, there shall no stranger eat thereof, but every man's servant that is bought for money, when thou hast circumcised him, then shall he eat thereof. A foreigner and a hired servant shall not eat thereof. In one house shall it be eaten, thou shalt not carry forth aught of the flesh abroad out of the house, neither shall ye break a bone thereof. All the congregation of Israel shall keep it. And when a stranger shall sojourn with thee and will keep the passover to the Lord, let all his males be circumcised, and then let him come near and keep it and he shall be as one that is born in the land, for no uncircumcised person shall eat thereof. One law shall be to him that is home-born and unto the stranger that sojourneth among you. Thus did all the children of Israel, as the Lord commanded Moses and Aaron so did they. And it came to pass the selfsame day that the Lord did bring the children of Israel out of the land of Egypt by their armies.

And the Lord spake unto Moses saying, Sanctify unto me all the firstborn, whatsoever openeth the womb among the children of Israel, both of man and of beast, it is mine. And Moses said unto the people, Remember this day in which ye came out from Egypt, out of the house of bondage, for by strength of hand the Lord brought you out from this place; there shall no leavened bread be eaten. This day came ye out in the month Abib. And it shall be when the Lord shall bring thee into the land of the Canaanites, and the Hittites, and the Amorites, and the Hivites, and the Jebusites, which he sware unto thy fathers to give thee, a land flowing with milk and honey, that thou shalt keep this service in this month. Seven days thou shalt eat unleavened bread, and in the seventh day shall be a feast to the Lord. Unleavened bread shall be eaten seven days, and there shall no leavened bread be seen with thee, neither shall there be leaven seen with thee in all thy quarters. And thou shalt show thy son in that day saying, This is done because of that which the Lord did unto me when I came forth out of Egypt. And it shall be for a sign unto thee upon thine hand and for a memorial between thine eyes, that the Lord's law may be in thy mouth, for with a strong hand hath the Lord brought thee out of Egypt. Thou shalt therefore keep this ordinance in his season from year to year. And it shall be when the Lord shall bring thee into the land of the Canaanites as he sware unto thee and thy fathers, and shall give it thee, that thou shalt set apart unto the Lord all that openeth the matrix, and every firstling that cometh of a beast which thou hast, the male shall be the Lord's. And every firstling of an ass thou shalt redeem with a lamb, and if thou wilt not redeem it, then thou shalt break his neck, and all the firstborn of man among thy children shalt thou redeem. And it shall be when thy son asketh thee in time to come, saying, What is this? that thou shalt say unto him, By strength of hand the Lord brought us out from Egypt, from the house of bondage, and it came to pass when Pharaoh would hardly let us go that the Lord slew all the firstborn in the land of Egypt, both the firstborn of man, and the firstborn of beast, therefore I sacrifice to the Lord all that openeth the matrix, being males, but all the firstborn of my children I redeem. And it shall be for a token upon thine hand and for frontlets between thine eyes, for by strength of hand the Lord brought us forth out of Egypt.

And it came to pass when Pharaoh had let the people go that God led them not through the way of the land of the Philistines, although that was near, for God said, Lest peradventure the people repent when they see war and they return to Egypt, but God led the people about through the way of the wilderness of the Red Sea, and the children of Israel went up harnessed out of the land of Egypt. And Moses took the bones of Joseph with him, for he had straitly sworn the children of Israel, saying, God will surely visit you, and ye shall carry up my bones away hence with you.

And they took their journey from Succoth and encamped in Etham in the edge of the wilderness. And the Lord went before them by day in a pillar of a cloud to lead them the way, and by night in a pillar of fire to give them light, to go by day and night. He took not away the pillar of the cloud by day nor the pillar of fire by night from before the people.

And the Lord spake unto Moses saying, Speak unto the children of Israel that they turn and encamp before Pi-hahiroth between Migdol and the sea, over against Baal-zephon, before it shall ye encamp by the sea. For Pharaoh will say of the children of Israel, They are entangled in the land, the wilderness hath shut them in. And Pharaoh will harden his heart and he shall follow after them, and I will be honored upon Pharaoh and upon all his host, that the Egyptians may know that I am the Lord. And they did so. And it was told the king of Egypt that the people fled, and the heart of Pharaoh and of his servants was turned against the people, and they said, Why have we done this, that we have let Israel go from serving us? And he made ready his chariot, and took his people with him, and he took six hundred chosen chariots, and all the chariots of Egypt, and captains over every one of them. And Pharaoh hardened his heart and he pursued after the children of Israel, and the children of Israel went out with a high hand. But the Egyptians pursued after them, all the horses and chariots of Pharaoh, and his horsemen, and his army, and overtook them encamping by the sea beside Pi-hahiroth, before Baal-zephon.

And when Pharaoh drew nigh, the children of Israel lifted up their eyes and behold, the Egyptians marched after them, and they were sore afraid, and the children of Israel cried out unto the Lord. And they said unto Moses, Because there were no graves in Egypt, hast thou taken us away to die in the wilderness? Wherefore hast thou dealt thus with us, to carry us forth out of Egypt? Is not this the word that we did tell thee in Egypt, saying, Let us alone, that we may serve the Egyptians? For it had been better for us to serve the Egyptians than that we should die in the wilderness. And Moses said unto the people, Fear ye not, stand still and see the salvation of the Lord which he will show to you today, for the Egyptians whom ye have seen today, ye shall see them again no more forever. The Lord shall fight for you and ye shall hold your peace.

And the Lord said unto Moses, Wherefore criest thou unto me? Speak unto the children of Israel that they go forward, but lift thou up thy rod, and stretch out thine hand over the sea, and divide it, and the children of Israel shall go on dry ground through the midst of the sea. And I say unto thee the hearts of the Egyptians shall be hardened and they shall follow them, and I will get me honor upon Pharaoh and upon all his host, upon his chariots and upon his horsemen. And the Egyptians shall know that I am the Lord, when I have gotten me honor upon Pharaoh, upon his chariots, and upon his horsemen. And the Angel of God, which went before the camp of Israel, removed and went behind them, and the pillar of the cloud went from before their face and stood behind them, and it came between the camp of the Egyptians and the camp of Israel, and it was a cloud and darkness to the Egyptians, but it gave light by night to the Israelites so that the one came not near the other all the night.

And Moses stretched out his hand over the sea, and the Lord caused the sea to go back by a strong east wind all that night and made the sea dry land, and the waters were divided. And the children of Israel went into the midst of the sea upon the dry ground, and the waters were a wall unto them on their right hand and on their left. And the Egyptians pursued and went in after them to the midst of the sea, even all Pharaoh's horses, his chariots, and his horsemen. And it came to pass that in the morning watch the Lord looked unto the host of the Egyptians through the pillar of fire and of the cloud, and troubled the host of the Egyptians. And took off their chariot wheels, that they drave them heavily, so that the Egyptians said, Let us flee from the face of Israel, for the Lord fighteth for them against the Egyptians. And the Lord said unto Moses, Stretch out thine hand over the sea that the waters may come again upon the Egyptians, upon their chariots, and upon their horsemen. And Moses stretched forth his hand over the sea, and the sea returned to his strength when the morning appeared, and the Egyptians fled against it, and the Lord overthrew the Egyptians in the midst of the sea. And the waters returned and covered the chariots, and the horsemen, and all the host of Pharaoh that came into the sea after them; there remained not so much as one of them. But the children of Israel walked upon dry land in the midst of the sea, and the waters were a wall unto them on their right hand and on their left. Thus the Lord saved Israel that day out of the hand of the Egyptians and Israel saw the Egyptians dead upon the seashore. And Israel saw that great work which the Lord did upon the Egyptians, and the people feared the Lord, and believed the Lord and his servant Moses.

Then sang Moses and the children of Israel this song unto the Lord, and spake saying, I will sing unto the Lord, for he hath triumphed gloriously, the horse and his rider hath he thrown into the sea. The Lord is my strength and song and he is become my salvation, he is my God and I will prepare him a habitation, my father's God and I will exalt him. The Lord is a man of war, the Lord is his name. Pharaoh's chariots and his host hath he cast into the sea, his chosen captains also are drowned in the Red Sea. The depths have covered them, they sank into the bottom as a stone. Thy right hand, O Lord, is become glorious in power, thy right hand, O Lord, hath dashed in pieces the enemy. And in the greatness of thine excellency thou hast overthrown them that rose up against thee, thou sentest forth thy wrath which consumed them as stubble. And with the blast of thy nostrils the waters were gathered together, the floods stood upright as a heap, and the depths were congealed in the heart of the sea. The enemy said, I will pursue, I will overtake, I will divide the spoil, my lust shall be satisfied upon them, I will draw my sword, my hand shall destroy them. Thou didst blow with thy wind, the sea covered them, they sank as lead in the mighty waters. Who is like unto thee, O Lord, among the gods? Who is like thee, glorious in holiness, fearful in praises, doing wonders? Thou stretchedst out thy right hand, the Earth swallowed them. Thou in thy mercy hast led forth the people which thou hast redeemed, thou hast guided them in thy strength unto thy holy habitation. The people shall hear and be afraid, sorrow shall take hold on the inhabitants of Palestina. Then the dukes of Edom shall be amazed, the mighty men of Moab, trembling shall take hold upon them, all the inhabitants of Canaan shall melt away. Fear and dread shall fall upon them, by the greatness of thine arm they shall be as still as a stone till the people pass over, O Lord, till the people pass over, which thou hast purchased. Thou shalt bring them in and plant them in the mountain of thine inheritance, in the place, O Lord, which thou hast made for thee to dwell in, in the sanctuary, O Lord, which thy hands have established. The Lord shall reign for ever and ever. For the horse of Pharaoh went in with his chariots and with his horsemen into the sea, and the Lord brought again the waters of the sea upon them, but the children of Israel went on dry land in the midst of the sea.

And Miriam the prophetess, the sister of Aaron, took a timbrel in her hand, and all the women went out after her with timbrels and with dances. And Miriam answered them, Sing ye to the Lord, for he hath triumphed gloriously, the horse and his rider hath he thrown into the sea.

3 SO Moses brought Israel from the Red Sea, and they went out into the wilderness of Shur, and they went three days in the wilderness and found no water. And when they came to Marah they could not drink of the waters of Marah for they were bitter, therefore the name of it was called Marah. And the people murmured against Moses saying, What shall we drink? And he cried unto the Lord and the Lord showed him a tree, which when he had cast into the waters, the waters were made sweet; there he made for them a statute and an ordinance, and there he proved them and said, If thou wilt diligently hearken to the voice of the Lord thy God, and wilt do that which is right in his sight, and wilt give ear to his commandments, and keep all his statutes, I will put none of these diseases upon thee which I have brought upon the Egyptians, for I am the Lord that healeth thee. And they came to Elim, where were twelve wells of water and threescore and ten palm trees, and they encamped there by the waters.

And they took their journey from Elim, and all the congregation of the children of Israel came unto the wilderness of Sin, which is between Elim and Sinai, on the fifteenth day of the second month after their departing out of the land of Egypt. And the whole congregation of the children of Israel murmured against Moses and Aaron in the wilderness, and the children of Israel said unto them, Would to God we had died by the hand of the Lord in the land of Egypt when we sat by the fleshpots and when we did eat bread to the full, for ye have brought us forth into this wilderness, to kill this whole assembly with hunger. Then said the Lord unto Moses, Behold, I will rain bread from Heaven for you and the people shall go out and gather a certain rate every day, that I may prove them whether they will walk in my law or no. And it shall come to pass that on the sixth day they shall prepare that which they bring in, and it shall be twice as much as they gather daily.

And Moses and Aaron said unto all the children of Israel, At even, then ye shall know that the Lord hath brought you out from the land of Egypt, and in the morning, then ye shall see the glory of the Lord, for that he heareth your murmurings against the Lord, and what are we that ye murmur against us? And Moses said, This shall be, when the Lord shall give you in the evening flesh to eat, and in the morning bread to the full, for that the Lord heareth your murmurings which ye murmur against him, and what are we? Your murmurings are not against us, but against the Lord. And Moses spake unto Aaron, Say unto all the congregation of the children of Israel, Come near before the Lord, for he hath heard your murmurings. And it came to pass, as Aaron spake unto the whole congregation of the children of Israel, that they looked toward the wilderness and behold, the glory of the Lord appeared in the cloud. And the Lord spake unto Moses saying, I have heard the murmurings of the children of Israel. Speak unto them saying, At even ye shall eat flesh, and in the morning ye shall be filled with bread, and ye shall know that I am the Lord your God.

And it came to pass that at even the quails came up and covered the camp, and in the morning the dew lay round about the host. And when the dew that lay was gone up, behold, upon the face of the wilderness there lay a small round thing, as small as the hoar frost on the ground. And when the children of Israel saw it they said one to another, It is manna, for they wist not what it was. And Moses said unto them, This is the bread which the Lord hath given you to eat. This is the thing which the Lord hath commanded, Gather of it every man according to his eating, an omer for every man, according to the number of your persons, take ye every man for them which are in his tents. And the children of Israel did so and gathered, some more, some less. And when they did mete it with an omer, he that gathered much had nothing over, and he that gathered little had no lack, they gathered every man according to his eating. And Moses said, Let no man leave of it till the morning. Notwithstanding they hearkened not unto Moses, but some of them left of it until the morning, and it bred worms and stank, and Moses was wroth with them. And they gathered it every morning, every man according to his eating, and when the sun waxed hot it melted. And it came to pass that on the sixth day they
gathered twice as much bread, two omers for one man, and all the rulers of the congregation came and told Moses. And he said unto them, This is that which the Lord hath said, Tomorrow is the rest of the holy sabbath unto the Lord. Bake that which ye will bake today, and seethe that ye will seethe, and that which remaineth over lay up for you to be kept until the morning. And they laid it up till the morning, as Moses bade, and it did not stink, neither was there any worm therein. And Moses said, Eat that today, for today is a sabbath unto the Lord, today ye shall not find it in the field. Six days ye shall gather it, but on the seventh day, which is the sabbath, in it there shall be none. And it came to pass that there went out some of the people on the seventh day for to gather and they found none.

And the Lord said unto Moses, How long refuse ye to keep my commandments and my laws? See, for that the Lord hath given you the sabbath, therefore he giveth you on the sixth day the bread of two days, abide ye every man in his place, let no man go out of his place on the seventh day. So the people rested on the seventh day. And the house of Israel called the name thereof Manna, and it was like coriander seed, white, and the taste of it was like wafers made with honey.

And Moses said, This is the thing which the Lord commandeth, Fill an omer of it to be kept for your generations, that they may see the bread wherewith I have fed you in the wilderness when I brought you forth from the land of Egypt. And Moses said unto Aaron, Take a pot, and put an omer full of manna therein, and lay it up before the Lord, to be kept for your generations. As the Lord commanded Moses, so Aaron laid it up before the Testimony, to be kept. And the children of Israel did eat manna forty years until they came to a land inhabited, they did eat manna until they came unto the borders of the land of Canaan. Now an omer is the tenth part of an ephah.

And all the congregation of the children of Israel journeyed from the wilderness of Sin after their journeys, according to the commandment of the Lord, and pitched in Rephidim, and there was no water for the people to drink. Wherefore the people did chide with Moses and said, Give us water that we may drink. And Moses said unto them, Why chide ye with me? Wherefore do ye tempt the Lord? And the people thirsted there for water, and the people murmured against Moses and said, Wherefore is this that thou hast brought us up out of Egypt, to kill us and our children and our cattle with thirst? And Moses cried unto the Lord, saying, What shall I do unto this people? They be almost ready to stone me. And the Lord said unto Moses, Go on before the people and take with thee of the elders of Israel, and thy rod wherewith thou smotest the river, take in thine hand and go. Behold, I will stand before thee there upon the rock in Horeb, and thou shalt smite the rock, and there shall come water out of it, that the people may drink. And Moses did so in the sight of the elders of Israel. And he called the name of the place Massah, and Meribah, because of the chiding of the children of Israel and because they tempted the Lord saying, Is the Lord among us, or not?

Then came Amalek and fought with Israel in Rephidim. And Moses said unto Joshua, Choose us out men and go out fight with Amalek; tomorrow I will stand on the top of the hill with the rod of God in mine hand. So Joshua did as Moses had said to him and fought with Amalek, and Moses, Aaron, and Hur went up to the top of the hill. And it came to pass when Moses held up his hand that Israel prevailed and when he let down his hand Amalek prevailed. But Moses' hands were heavy, and they took a stone, and put it under him, and he sat thereon, and Aaron and Hur stayed up his hands, the one on the one side and the other on the other side, and his hands were steady until the going down of the sun.

And Joshua discomfited Amalek and his people with the edge of the sword. And the Lord said unto Moses, Write this for a memorial in a book and rehearse it in the ears of Joshua, for I will utterly put out the remembrance of Amalek from under Heaven. And Moses built an altar and called the name of it Jehovah-nissi, for he said, Because the Lord hath sworn that the Lord will have war with Amalek from generation to generation.

When Jethro the high priest of Midian, Moses' father-in-law, heard of all that God had done for Moses and for Israel his people and that the Lord had brought Israel out of Egypt, then Jethro Moses' father-in-law took Zipporah, Moses' wife, after he had sent her back and her two sons, of which the name of the one was Gershom, for he said, I have been an alien in a strange land, and the name of the other was Eliezer, for the God of my father, said he, was mine help and delivered me from the sword of Pharaoh, and Jethro Moses' father-in-law came with his sons and his wife unto Moses into the wilderness where he encamped at the mount of God, and he said unto Moses, I, thy father-in-law Jethro, am come unto thee and thy wife and her two sons with her. And Moses went out to meet his father-in-law and did obeisance, and kissed him, and they asked each other of their welfare, and they came into the tent. And Moses told his father-in-law all that the Lord had done unto Pharaoh and to the Egyptians for Israel's sake, and all the travail that had come upon them by the way, and how the Lord delivered them. And Jethro rejoiced for all the goodness which the Lord had done to Israel, whom he had delivered out of the hand of the Egyptians. And Jethro said, Blessed be the Lord, who hath delivered you out of the hand of the Egyptians and out of the hand of Pharaoh, who hath delivered the people from under the hand of the Egyptians. Now I know that the Lord is greater than all gods, for in the thing wherein they dealt proudly he was above them. And Jethro Moses' father-in-law took a burnt offering and sacrifices for God, and Aaron came and all the elders of Israel to eat bread with Moses' father-in-law before God.

And it came to pass on the morrow that Moses sat to judge the people and the people stood by Moses from the morning unto the evening. And when Moses' father-in-law saw all that he did to the people he said, What is this thing that thou doest to the people? Why sittest thou thyself alone, and all the people stand by thee from morning unto even? And Moses said unto his father-in-law, Because the people come unto me to inquire of God when they have a matter, they come unto me, and I judge between one and another, and I do make them know the statutes of God and his laws. And Moses' father-in-law said unto him, The thing that thou doest is not good. Thou wilt surely wear away, both thou and this people that is with thee, for this thing is too heavy for thee, thou art not able to perform it thyself alone. Hearken now unto my voice, I will give thee counsel, and God shall be with thee. Be thou for the people to Godward, that thou mayest bring the causes unto God, and thou shalt teach them ordinances and laws, and shalt show them the way wherein they must walk, and the work that they must do. Moreover thou shalt provide out of all the people able men such as fear God, men of truth, hating covetousness, and place such over them to be rulers of thousands and rulers of hundreds, rulers of fifties and rulers of tens, and let them judge the people at all seasons, and it shall be that every great matter they shall bring unto thee, but every small matter they shall judge, so shall it be easier for thyself and they shall bear the burden with thee. If thou shalt do this thing and God command thee so, then thou shalt be able to endure and all this people shall also go to their place in peace. So Moses hearkened to the voice of his father-in-law and did all that he had said. And Moses chose able men out of all Israel, and made them heads over the people, rulers of thousands, rulers of hundreds, rulers of fifties, and rulers of tens. And they judged the people at all seasons: the hard causes they brought unto Moses, but every small matter they judged themselves. And Moses let his father-in-law depart and he went his way into his own land.

4 IN the third month, when the children of Israel were gone forth out of the land of Egypt, the same day came they into the wilderness of Sinai. For they were departed from Rephidim, and were come to the desert of Sinai, and had pitched in the wilderness, and there Israel camped before the mount. And Moses went up unto God, and the Lord called unto him out of the mountain saying, Thus shalt thou say to the house of Jacob, and tell the children of Israel, Ye have seen what I did unto the Egyptians, and how I bare you on eagles' wings and brought you unto myself. Now therefore, if ye will obey my voice indeed and keep my covenant, then ye shall be a peculiar treasure unto me above all people, for all the Earth is mine and ye shall be unto me a kingdom of priests and a holy nation. These are the words which thou shalt speak unto the children of Israel. And Moses came and called for the elders of the people and laid before their faces all these words which the Lord commanded him. And all the people answered together and said, All that the Lord hath spoken we will do. And Moses returned the words of the people unto the Lord.

And the Lord said unto Moses, Lo, I come unto thee in a thick cloud that the people may hear when I speak with thee, and believe thee forever. Moses told the words of the people unto the Lord. And the Lord said unto Moses, Go unto the people, and sanctify them today and tomorrow, and let them wash their clothes, And be ready against the third day, for the third day the Lord will come down in the sight of all the people upon mount Sinai. And thou shalt set bounds unto the people round about saying, Take heed to yourselves and that ye go not up into the mount, or touch the border of it; whosoever toucheth the mount shall be surely put to death. There shall not a hand touch it, but he shall surely be stoned or shot through, whether it be beast or man, it shall not live; when the trumpet soundeth long they shall come up to the mount. And Moses went down from the mount unto the people and sanctified the people and they washed their clothes. And he said unto the people, Be ready against the third day, come not at your wives.

And it came to pass on the third day in the morning that there were thunders and lightnings, and a thick cloud upon the mount, and the voice of the trumpet exceeding loud, so that all the people that was in the camp trembled. And Moses brought forth the people out of the camp to meet with God and they stood at the nether part of the mount. And mount Sinai was altogether on a smoke because the Lord descended upon it in fire, and the smoke thereof ascended as the smoke of a furnace, and the whole mount quaked greatly. And when the voice of the trumpet sounded long and waxed louder and louder, Moses spake and God answered him by a voice. And the Lord came down upon mount Sinai, on the top of the mount, and the Lord called Moses up to the top of the mount, and Moses went up. And the Lord said unto Moses, Go down, charge the people, lest they break through unto the Lord to gaze and many of them perish. And let the priests also which come near to the Lord sanctify themselves, lest the Lord break forth upon them. And Moses said unto the Lord, The people cannot come up to mount Sinai, for thou chargedst us saying, Set bounds about the mount and sanctify it. And the Lord said unto him, Away, get thee down, and thou shalt come up, thou and Aaron with thee, but let not the priests and the people break through to come up unto the Lord, lest he break forth upon them.

So Moses went down unto the people and spake unto them. And God spake all these words saying, I am the Lord thy God, which have brought thee out of the land of Egypt, out of the house of bondage. Thou shalt have no other gods before me. Thou shalt not make unto thee any graven image, or any likeness of anything that is in Heaven above, or that is in the Earth beneath, or that is in the water under the Earth, thou shalt not bow down thyself to them nor serve them, for I the Lord thy God am a jealous God, visiting the iniquity of the fathers upon the children unto the third and fourth generation of them that hate me, and showing mercy unto thousands of them that love me and keep my commandments. Thou shalt not take the name of the Lord thy God in vain, for the Lord will not hold him guiltless that taketh his name in vain. Remember the sabbath day, to keep it holy. Six days shalt thou labor and do all thy work, but the seventh day is the sabbath of the Lord thy God, in it thou shalt not do any work, thou, nor thy son, nor thy daughter, thy manservant, nor thy maidservant, nor thy cattle, nor thy stranger that is within thy gates, for in six days the Lord made Heaven and Earth, the sea and all that in them is, and rested the seventh day, wherefore the Lord blessed the sabbath day and hallowed it. Honor thy father and thy mother, that thy days may be long upon the land which the Lord thy God giveth thee. Thou shalt not kill. Thou shalt not commit adultery. Thou shalt not steal. Thou shalt not bear false witness against thy neighbor. Thou shalt not covet thy neighbor's house, thou shalt not covet thy neighbor's wife, nor his manservant, nor his maidservant, nor his ox, nor his ass, nor anything that is thy neighbor's.

And all the people saw the thunderings, and the lightnings, and the noise of the trumpet, and the mountain smoking, and when the people saw it they removed and stood afar off. And they said unto Moses, Speak thou with us and we will hear, but let not God speak with us lest we die. And Moses said unto the people, Fear not, for God is come to prove you, and that his fear may be before your faces, that ye sin not. And the people stood afar off, and Moses drew near unto the thick darkness where God was.

And the Lord said unto Moses, Thus thou shalt say unto the children of Israel, Ye have seen that I have talked with you from Heaven. Ye shall not make unto you gods of silver, neither shall ye make unto you gods of gold. An altar of earth thou shalt make unto me and shalt sacrifice thereon thy burnt offerings, and thy peace offerings, thy sheep, and thine oxen, in all places where I record my name I will come unto thee and I will bless thee. And if thou wilt make me an altar of stone, thou shalt not build it of hewn stone, for if thou lift up thy tool upon it, thou hast polluted it. Neither shalt thou go up by steps unto mine altar, that thy nakedness be not discovered thereon.

Now these are the judgments which thou shalt set before them: If thou buy a Hebrew servant, six years he shall serve and in the seventh he shall go out free for nothing. If he came in by himself, he shall go out by himself; if he were married, then his wife shall go out with him. If his master have given him a wife and she have borne him sons or daughters, the wife and her children shall be her master's and he shall go out by himself. And if the servant shall plainly say, I love my master, my wife, and my children, I will not go out free, then his master shall bring him unto the judges, he shall also bring him to his door, or unto the door post, and his master shall bore his ear through with an awl and he shall serve him forever. And if a man sell his daughter to be a maidservant, she shall not go out as the menservants do. If she please not her master, who hath betrothed her to himself, then shall he let her be redeemed, not to sell her unto a strange nation, he shall have no power to do this, seeing he hath dealt deceitfully with her. And if he have betrothed her unto his son, he shall deal with her after the manner of daughters. If he take him another wife, her food, her raiment, and her duty of marriage, shall he not diminish. And if he do not these three unto her, then shall she go out free without money.

He that smiteth a man so that he die shall be surely put to death. And if a man lie not in wait, but God deliver him into his hand, then I will appoint thee a place whither he shall flee. But if a man come presumptuously upon his neighbor to slay him with guile, thou shalt take him from mine altar that he may die. And he that smiteth his father or his mother shall be surely put to death. And he that stealeth a man and selleth him, or if he be found in his hand, he shall surely be put to death. And he that curseth his father or his mother shall surely be put to death. And if men strive together and one smite another with a stone or with his fist and he die not, but keepeth his bed, if he rise again and walk abroad upon his staff, then shall he that smote him be quit, only he shall pay for the loss of his time and shall cause him to be thoroughly healed. And if a man smite his servant or his maid with a rod and he die under his hand, he shall surely be put to death. Notwithstanding, if he continue a day or two and recover, he shall not be put to death, for he is his servant. If men strive and hurt a woman with child so that her fruit depart from her and yet no mischief follow, he shall be surely punished according as the woman's husband will lay upon him and he shall pay as the judges determine. And if any mischief follow, then thou shalt give life for life, eye for eye, tooth for tooth, hand for hand, foot for foot, burning for burning, wound for wound, stripe for stripe. And if a man smite the eye of his servant or the eye of his maid that it perish, he shall let him go free for his eye's sake. And if he smite out his manservant's tooth or his maidservant's tooth, he shall let him go free for his tooth's sake.

If an ox gore a man or a woman that they die, then the ox shall be surely stoned and his flesh shall not be eaten, but the owner of the ox shall be quit. But if the ox were wont to push with his horn in time past, and it hath been testified to his owner, and he hath not kept him in, but that he hath killed a man or a woman, the ox shall be stoned and his owner also shall be put to death. If there be laid on him a sum of money, then he shall give for the ransom of his life whatsoever is laid upon him. Whether he have gored a son or have gored a daughter, according to this judgment shall it be done unto him. If the ox shall push a manservant or a maidservant, he shall give unto their master thirty shekels of silver and the ox shall be stoned. And if a man shall open a pit or if a man shall dig a pit and not cover it, and an ox or an ass fall therein, the owner of the pit shall make it good and give money unto the owner of them and the dead beast shall be his. And if one man's ox hurt another's that he die, then they shall sell the live ox and divide the money of it, and the dead ox also they shall divide. Or if it be known that the ox hath used to push in time past and his owner hath not kept him in, he shall surely pay ox for ox and the dead shall be his own.

If a man shall steal an ox or a sheep and kill it or sell it, he shall restore five oxen for an ox and four sheep for a sheep. If a thief be found breaking up and be smitten that he die, there shall no blood be shed for him. If the sun be risen upon him, there shall be blood shed for him, for he should make full restitution; if he have nothing, then he shall be sold for his theft. If the theft be certainly found in his hand alive, whether it be ox, or ass, or sheep, he shall restore double. If a man shall cause a field or vineyard to be eaten, and shall put in his beast, and shall feed in another man's field, of the best of his own field and of the best of his own vineyard shall he make restitution. If fire break out and catch in thorns so that the stacks of corn, or the standing corn, or the field be consumed therewith, he that kindled the fire shall surely make restitution. If a man shall deliver unto his neighbor money or stuff to keep and it be stolen out of the man's house, if the thief be found, let him pay double. If the thief be not found, then the master of the house shall be brought unto the judges, to see whether he have put his hand unto his neighbor's goods. For all manner of trespass, whether it be for ox, for ass, for sheep, for raiment, or for any manner of lost thing which another challengeth to be his, the cause of both parties shall come before the judges and whom the judges shall condemn, he shall pay double unto his neighbor. If a man deliver unto his neighbor an ass, or an ox, or a sheep, or any beast to keep and it die, or be hurt, or driven away, no man seeing it, then shall an oath of the Lord be between them both that he hath not put his hand unto his neighbor's goods, and the owner of it shall accept thereof and he shall not make it good. And if it be stolen from him, he shall make restitution unto the owner thereof. If it be torn in pieces, then let him bring it for witness and he shall not make good that which was torn. And if a man borrow aught of his neighbor and it be hurt or die, the owner thereof being not with it, he shall surely make it good. But if the owner thereof be with it, he shall not make it good, if it be a hired thing, it came for his hire.

And if a man entice a maid that is not betrothed and lie with her, he shall surely endow her to be his wife. If her father utterly refuse to give her unto him, he shall pay money according to the dowry of virgins.

Thou shalt not suffer a murderer to live.

Whosoever lieth with a beast shall surely be put to death.

He that sacrificeth unto any god save unto the Lord only, he shall be utterly destroyed.

Thou shalt neither vex a stranger nor oppress him, for ye were strangers in the land of Egypt.

Ye shall not afflict any widow or fatherless child. If thou afflict them in any wise and they cry at all unto me, I will surely hear their cry, and my wrath shall wax hot, and I will kill you with the sword, and your wives shall be widows and your children fatherless.

If thou lend money to any of my people that is poor by thee, thou shalt not be to him as a usurer neither shalt thou lay upon him usury.

If thou at all take thy neighbor's raiment to pledge, thou shalt deliver it unto him by that the sun goeth down, for that is his covering only, it is his raiment for his skin, wherein shall he sleep? And it shall come to pass when he crieth unto me that I will hear, for I am gracious.

Thou shalt not revile against God nor curse the ruler of thy people.

Thou shalt not delay to offer the first of thy ripe fruits and of thy liquors, the firstborn of thy sons shalt thou give unto me. Likewise shalt thou do with thine oxen and with thy sheep, seven days it shall be with his dam, on the eighth day thou shalt give it me. And ye shall be holy men unto me, neither shall ye eat any flesh that is torn of beasts in the field, ye shall cast it to the dogs.

Thou shalt not raise a false report: put not thine hand with the wicked to be an unrighteous witness.

Thou shalt not follow a multitude to do evil, neither shalt thou speak in a cause to decline after many to wrest judgment, neither shalt thou countenance a wicked man in his cause.

If thou meet thine enemy's ox or his ass going astray, thou shalt surely bring it back to him again. If thou see the ass of him that hateth thee lying under his burden and wouldest forbear to help him, thou shalt surely help with him.

Thou shalt not wrest the judgment of thy poor in his cause. Keep thee far from a false matter, and the innocent and righteous slay thou not, for I will not justify the wicked. And thou shalt take no gift, for the gift blindeth the wise and perverteth the words of the righteous. Also thou shalt not oppress a stranger, for ye know the heart of a stranger, seeing ye were strangers in the land of Egypt.

And six years thou shalt sow thy land and shalt gather in the fruits thereof, but the seventh year thou shalt let it rest and lie still, that the poor of thy people may eat, and what they leave the beasts of the field shall eat. In like manner thou shalt deal with thy vineyard and with thy oliveyard. Six days thou shalt do thy work and on the seventh day thou shalt rest, that thine ox and thine ass may rest, and the son of thy handmaid, and the stranger may be refreshed. And in all things that I have said unto you be circumspect and make no mention of the name of other gods, neither let it be heard out of thy mouth.

Three times thou shalt keep a feast unto me in the year. Thou shalt keep the feast of unleavened bread (thou shalt eat unleavened bread seven days, as I commanded thee, in the time appointed of the month Abib, for in it thou camest out from Egypt and none shall appear before me empty), and the feast of harvest, the firstfruits of thy labors which thou hast sown in the field, and the feast of ingathering, which is in the end of the year when thou hast gathered in thy labors out of the field. Three times in the year all thy males shall appear before the Lord God. Thou shalt not offer the blood of my sacrifice with leavened bread, neither shall the fat of my sacrifice remain until the morning. The first of the firstfruits of thy land thou shalt bring into the house of the Lord thy God. Thou shalt not seeth a kid in his mother's milk.

Behold, I send an angel before thee, to keep thee in the way and to bring thee into the place which I have prepared. Beware of him and obey his voice, provoke him not, for he will not pardon your transgressions, for my name is in him. But if thou shalt indeed obey his voice and do all that I speak, then I will be an enemy unto thine enemies and an adversary unto thine adversaries. For mine angel shall go before thee, and bring thee in unto the Amorites, and the Hittites, and the Perizzites, and the Canaanites, the Hivites, and the Jebusites, and I will cut them off. Thou shalt not bow down to their gods, nor serve them, nor do after their works, but thou shalt utterly overthrow them and quite break down their images. And ye shall serve the Lord your God, and he shall bless thy bread and thy water, and I will take sickness away from the midst of thee. There shall nothing cast their young, nor be barren in thy land, the number of thy days I will fulfill.

I will send my fear before thee, and I will destroy all the people to whom thou shalt come, and I will make all thine enemies turn their backs unto thee. And I will send hornets before thee which shall drive out the Hivite, the Canaanite, and the Hittite from before thee. I will not drive them out from before thee in one year, lest the land become desolate, and the beast of the field multiply against thee. By little and little I will drive them out from before thee, until thou be increased and inherit the land. And I will set thy bounds from the Red Sea even unto the sea of the Philistines and from the desert unto the river, for I will deliver the inhabitants of the land into your hand and thou shalt drive them out before thee. Thou shalt make no covenant with them nor with their gods. They shall not dwell in thy land, lest they make thee sin against me, for if thou serve their gods, it will surely be a snare unto thee.

And he said unto Moses, Come up unto the Lord, thou and Aaron, Nadab and Abihu, and seventy of the elders of Israel, and worship ye afar off. And Moses alone shall come near the Lord, but they shall not come nigh, neither shall the people go up with him. And Moses came and told the people all the words of the Lord and all the judgments, and all the people answered with one voice and said, All the words which the Lord hath said will we do. And Moses wrote all the words of the Lord, and rose up early in the morning, and builded an altar under the hill, and twelve pillars according to the twelve tribes of Israel. And he sent young men of the children of Israel, which offered burnt offerings, and sacrificed peace offerings of oxen unto the Lord.

And Moses took half of the blood and put it in basins, and half of the blood he sprinkled on the altar. And he took the book of the covenant, and read in the audience of the people, and they said, All that the Lord hath said will we do and be obedient. And Moses took the blood and sprinkled it on the people and said, Behold the blood of the covenant which the Lord hath made with you concerning all these words. Then went up Moses and Aaron, Nadab and Abihu, and seventy of the elders of Israel and they saw the God of Israel, and there was under his feet as it were a paved work of a sapphire stone, and as it were the body of Heaven in his clearness. And upon the nobles of the children of Israel he laid not his hand, also they saw God and did eat and drink.

And the Lord said unto Moses, Come up to me into the mount and be there, and I will give thee tables of stone, and a law and commandments which I have written, that thou mayest teach them. And Moses rose up, and his minister Joshua, and Moses went up into the mount of God. And he said unto the elders, Tarry ye here for us until we come again unto you and behold, Aaron and Hur are with you, if any man have any matters to do, let him come unto them. And Moses went up into the mount and a cloud covered the mount. And the glory of the Lord abode upon mount Sinai, and the cloud covered it six days, and the seventh day he called unto Moses out of the midst of the cloud. And the sight of the glory of the Lord was like devouring fire on the top of the mount in the eyes of the children of Israel. And Moses went into the midst of the cloud and gat him up into the mount, and Moses was in the mount forty days and forty nights.

5 AND the Lord spake unto Moses saying, Speak unto the children of Israel, that they bring me an offering, of every man that giveth it willingly with his heart ye shall take my offering. And this is the offering which ye shall take of them, gold, and silver, and brass, and blue, and purple, and scarlet, and fine linen, and goats' hair, and rams' skins dyed red, and badgers' skins, and shittim wood, oil for the light, spices for anointing oil and for sweet incense, onyx stones, and stones to be set in the ephod and in the breastplate. And let them make me a sanctuary that I may dwell among them. According to all that I show thee, after

the pattern of the tabernacle and the pattern of all the instruments thereof, even so shall. And they shall make an ark of shittim wood, two cubits and a half shall be the length thereof, and a cubit and a half the breadth thereof, and a cubit and a half the height thereof. And thou shalt overlay it with pure gold, within and without shalt thou overlay it, and shalt make upon it a crown of gold round about. And thou shalt cast four rings of gold for it and put them in the four corners thereof, and two rings shall be in the one side of it and two rings in the other side of it. And thou shalt make staves of shittim wood and overlay them with gold. And thou shalt put the staves into the rings by the sides of the ark that the ark may be borne with them. The staves shall be in the rings of the ark, they shall not be taken from it. And thou shalt put into the ark the testimony which I shall give thee. And thou shalt make a mercy seat of pure gold, two cubits and a half shall be the length thereof and a cubit and a half the breadth thereof. And thou shalt make two cherubim of gold, of beaten work shalt thou make them, in the two ends of the mercy seat. And make one cherub on the one end and the other cherub on the other end, even of the mercy seat shall ye make the cherubim on the two ends thereof. And the cherubim shall stretch forth their wings on high, covering the mercy seat with their wings, and their faces shall look one to another, toward the mercy seat shall the faces of the cherubim be. And thou shalt put the mercy seat above upon the ark and in the ark thou shalt put the testimony that I shall give thee. And there I will meet with thee and I will commune with thee from above the mercy seat, from between the two cherubim which are upon the ark of the testimony, of all things which I will give thee in commandment unto the children of Israel.

 Thou shalt also make a table of shittim wood, two cubits shall be the length thereof, and a cubit the breadth thereof, and a cubit and a half the height thereof. And thou shalt overlay it with pure gold and make thereto a crown of gold round about. And thou shalt make unto it a border of a handbreadth round about, and thou shalt make a golden crown to the border thereof round about. And thou shalt make for it four rings of gold, and put the rings in the four corners that are on the four feet thereof. Over against the border shall the rings be for places of the staves to bear the table. And thou shalt make the staves of shittim wood and overlay them with gold, that the table may be borne with them. And thou shalt make the dishes thereof, and spoons thereof, and covers thereof, and bowls thereof, to cover withal, of pure gold shalt thou make them. And thou shalt set upon the table shewbread before me always.

 And thou shalt make a candlestick of pure gold, of beaten work shall the candlestick be made, his shaft, and his branches, his bowls, his knops, and his flowers shall be of the same. And six branches shall come out of the sides of it, three branches of the candlestick out of the one side, and three branches of the candlestick out of the other side, three bowls made like unto almonds, with a knop and a flower in one branch, and three bowls made like almonds in the other branch, with a knop and a flower, so in the six branches that come out of the candlestick. And in the candlestick shall be four bowls made like unto almonds, with their knops and their flowers. And there shall be a knop under two branches of the same, and a knop under two branches of the same, and a knop under two branches of the same, according to the six branches that proceed out of the candlestick. Their knops and their branches shall be of the same, all of it shall be one beaten work of pure gold. And thou shalt make the seven lamps thereof, and they shall light the lamps thereof, that they may give light over against it. And the tongs thereof and the snuff dishes thereof shall be of pure gold. Of a talent of pure gold shall he make it with all these vessels. And look that thou make them after their pattern, which was showed thee in the mount.

Moreover thou shalt make the tabernacle with ten curtains of fine twined linen, and blue, and purple, and scarlet, with cherubim of cunning work shalt thou make them. The length of one curtain shall be eight and twenty cubits, and the breadth of one curtain four cubits, and every one of the curtains shall have one measure. The five curtains shall be coupled together one to another, and other five curtains shall be coupled one to another. And thou shalt make loops of blue upon the edge of the one curtain from the selvage in the coupling, and likewise shalt thou make in the uttermost edge of another curtain, in the coupling of the second. Fifty loops shalt thou make in the one curtain, and fifty loops shalt thou make in the edge of the curtain that is in the coupling of the second, that the loops may take hold one of another. And thou shalt make fifty taches of gold, and couple the curtains together with the taches, and it shall be one tabernacle.

And thou shalt make curtains of to be a covering upon the tabernacle, eleven curtains shalt thou make. The length of one curtain shall be thirty cubits, and the breadth of one curtain four cubits, and the eleven curtains shall be all of one measure. And thou shalt couple five curtains by themselves, and six curtains by themselves, and shalt double the sixth curtain in the forefront of the tabernacle. And thou shalt make fifty loops on the edge of the one curtain that is outmost in the coupling, and fifty loops in the edge of the curtain which coupleth the second. And thou shalt make fifty taches of brass, and put the taches into the loops, and couple the tent together, that it may be one. And the remnant that remaineth of the curtains of the tent, the half curtain that remaineth, shall hang over the back side of the tabernacle. And a cubit on the one side, and a cubit on the other side of that which remaineth in the length of the curtains of the tent, it shall hang over the sides of the tabernacle, on this side and on that side, to cover it. And thou shalt make a covering for the tent of rams' skins dyed red and a covering above of badgers' skins.

And thou shalt make boards for the tabernacle of shittim wood standing up. Ten cubits shall be the length of a board, and a cubit and a half shall be the breadth of one board. Two tenons shall there be in one board, set in order one against another, thus shalt thou make for all the boards of the tabernacle. And thou shalt make the boards for the tabernacle twenty boards on the south side southward. And thou shalt make forty sockets of silver under the twenty boards, two sockets under one board for his two tenons and two sockets under another board for his two tenons. And for the second side of the tabernacle on the north side there shall be twenty boards. And their forty sockets of silver, two sockets under one board and two sockets under another board. And for the sides of the tabernacle westward thou shalt make six boards. And two boards shalt thou make for the corners of the tabernacle in the two sides. And they shall be coupled together beneath, and they shall be coupled together above the head of it unto one ring, thus shall it be for them both, they shall be for the two corners. And they shall be eight boards and their sockets of silver, sixteen sockets, two sockets under one board and two sockets under another board. And thou shalt make bars of shittim wood, five for the boards of the one side of the tabernacle, and five bars for the boards of the other side of the tabernacle, and five bars for the boards of the side of the tabernacle, for the two sides westward. And the middle bar in the midst of the boards shall reach from end to end. And thou shalt overlay the boards with gold, and make their rings of gold for places for the bars, and thou shalt overlay the bars with gold. And thou shalt rear up the tabernacle according to the fashion thereof which was showed thee in the mount.

And thou shalt make a veil of blue, and purple, and scarlet, and fine twined linen of cunning work, with cherubim shall it be made. And thou shalt hang it upon four pillars of shittim wood overlaid with gold, their hooks shall be of gold, upon the four sockets of silver. And thou shalt hang up the veil under the taches that thou mayest bring in thither within the veil the ark of the testimony, and the veil shall divide unto you between the holy place and the most holy. And thou shalt put the mercy seat upon the ark of the testimony in the most holy place. And thou shalt set the table without the veil, and the candlestick over against the table on the side of the tabernacle toward the south, and thou shalt put the table on the north side. And thou shalt make a hanging for the door of the tent of blue, and purple, and scarlet, and fine twined linen wrought with needlework. And thou shalt make for the hanging five pillars of shittim wood, and overlay them with gold, and their hooks shall be of gold, and thou shalt cast five sockets of brass for them.

And thou shalt make an altar of shittim wood, five cubits long and five cubits broad, the altar shall be foursquare and the height thereof shall be three cubits. And thou shalt make the horns of it upon the four corners thereof, his horns shall be of the same, and thou shalt overlay it with brass. And thou shalt make his pans to receive his ashes, and his shovels, and his basins, and his fleshhooks, and his firepans, and all the vessels thereof thou shalt make of brass. And thou shalt make for it a grate of network of brass, and upon the net shalt thou make four brazen rings in the four corners thereof. And thou shalt put it under the compass of the altar beneath that the net may be even to the midst of the altar. And thou shalt make staves for the altar, staves of shittim wood, and overlay them with brass. And the staves shall be put into the rings, and the staves shall be upon the two sides of the altar to bear it. Hollow with boards shalt thou make it, as it was showed thee in the mount, so shalt thou make it.

And thou shalt make the court of the tabernacle, for the south side southward there shall be hangings for the court of fine twined linen of a hundred cubits long for one side, and the twenty pillars thereof and their twenty sockets shall be of brass, the hooks of the pillars and their fillets shall be of silver. And likewise for the north side in length there shall be hangings of a hundred cubits long, and his twenty pillars and their twenty sockets of brass, the hooks of the pillars and their fillets of silver. And for the breadth of the court on the west side shall be hangings of fifty cubits, their pillars ten, and their sockets ten. And the breadth of the court on the east side eastward shall be fifty cubits. The hangings of one side of the gate shall be fifteen cubits, their pillars three, and their sockets three. And on the other side shall be hangings fifteen cubits, their pillars three, and their sockets three. And for the gate of the court shall be a hanging of twenty cubits, of blue, and purple, and scarlet, and fine twined linen wrought with needlework, and their pillars shall be four and their sockets four. All the pillars round about the court shall be filleted with silver, their hooks shall be of silver, and their sockets of brass. The length of the court shall be a hundred cubits, and the breadth fifty everywhere, and the height five cubits of fine twined linen, and their sockets of brass. All the vessels of the tabernacle in all the service thereof, and all the pins thereof, and all the pins of the court, shall be of brass.

And thou shalt command the children of Israel that they bring thee pure olive oil beaten for the light to cause the lamp to burn always. In the tabernacle of the congregation without the veil which is before the testimony, Aaron and his sons shall order it from evening to morning before the Lord; it shall be a statute for ever unto their generations on the behalf of the children of Israel. And take thou unto thee Aaron thy brother and his sons with him from among the children of Israel that he may minister unto me in the priest's office, even Aaron, Nadab and Abihu, Eleazar and Ithamar, Aaron's sons.

And thou shalt make holy garments for Aaron thy brother, for glory and for beauty. And thou shalt speak unto all that are wise-hearted whom I have filled with the spirit of wisdom, that they may make Aaron's garments to consecrate him that he may minister unto me in the priest's office. And these are the garments which they shall make: a breastplate, and an ephod, and a robe, and a broidered coat, a mitre, and a girdle, and they shall make holy garments for Aaron thy brother and his sons that he may minister unto me in the priest's office. And they shall take gold, and blue, and purple, and scarlet, and fine linen. And they shall make the ephod of gold, of blue, and of purple, of scarlet, and fine twined linen with cunning work. It shall have the two shoulderpieces thereof joined at the two edges thereof, and so it shall be joined together. And the curious girdle of the ephod which is upon it shall be of the same, according to the work thereof, even of gold, of blue, and purple, and scarlet, and fine twined linen. And thou shalt take two onyx stones and grave on them the names of the children of Israel, six of their names on one stone and the other six names of the rest on the other stone, according to their birth. With the work of an engraver in stone, like the engravings of a signet, shalt thou engrave the two stones with the names of the children of Israel, thou shalt make them to be set in ouches of gold. And thou shalt put the two stones upon the shoulders of the ephod for stones of memorial unto the children of Israel, and Aaron shall bear their names before the Lord upon his two shoulders for a memorial. And thou shalt make ouches of gold, And two chains of pure gold at the ends, of wreathen work shalt thou make them, and fasten the wreathen chains to the ouches.

And thou shalt make the breastplate of judgment with cunning work, after the work of the ephod thou shalt make it: of gold, of blue, and of purple, and of scarlet, and of fine twined linen shalt thou make it. Foursquare it shall be being doubled, a span shall be the length thereof, and a span shall be the breadth thereof. And thou shalt set in it settings of stones, even four rows of stones, the first row shall be a sardius, a topaz, and a carbuncle, this shall be the first row. And the second row shall be an emerald, a sapphire, and a diamond. And the third row, a ligure, and agate, and an amethyst. And the fourth row, a beryl, and an onyx, and a jasper, they shall be set in gold in their enclosings. And the stones shall be with the names of the children of Israel, twelve, according to their names, like the engravings of a signet, every one with his name shall they be according to the twelve tribes. And thou shalt make upon the breastplate chains at the ends of wreathen work of pure gold. And thou shalt make upon the breastplate two rings of gold, and shalt put the two rings on the two ends of the breastplate. And thou shalt put the two wreathen chains of gold in the two rings which are on the ends of the breastplate. And the other two ends of the two wreathen chains thou shalt fasten in the two ouches and put them on the shoulder pieces of the ephod before it. And thou shalt make two rings of gold and thou shalt put them upon the two ends of the breastplate in the border thereof which is in the side of the ephod inward. And two other rings of gold thou shalt make, and shalt put them on the two sides of the ephod underneath, toward the forepart thereof, over against the other coupling thereof, above the curious girdle of the ephod. And they shall bind the breastplate by the rings thereof unto the rings of the ephod with a lace of blue, that it may be above the curious girdle of the ephod and that the breastplate be not loosed from the ephod. And Aaron shall bear the names of the children of Israel in the breastplate of judgment upon his heart when he goeth in unto the holy place for a memorial before the Lord continually. And thou shalt put in the breastplate of judgment the Urim and the Thummim, and they shall be upon Aaron's heart when he goeth in before the Lord, and Aaron shall bear the judgment of the children of Israel upon his heart before the Lord continually.

And thou shalt make the robe of the ephod all of blue. And there shall be a hole in the top of it, in the midst thereof, it shall have a binding of woven work round about the hole of it, as it were the hole of an habergeon, that it be not rent. And beneath upon the hem of it thou shalt make pomegranates of blue, and of purple, and of scarlet, round about the hem thereof, and bells of gold between them round about, a golden bell and a pomegranate, a golden bell and a pomegranate, upon the hem of the robe round about. And it shall be upon Aaron to minister and his sound shall be heard when he goeth in unto the holy place before the Lord, and when he cometh out that he die not. And thou shalt make a plate of pure gold and grave upon it, like the engravings of a signet, HOLINESS TO THE LORD. And thou shalt put it on a blue lace that it may be upon the mitre, upon the forefront of the mitre it shall be. And it shall be upon Aaron's forehead that Aaron may bear the iniquity of the holy things which the children of Israel shall hallow in all their holy gifts, and it shall be always upon his forehead that they may be accepted before the Lord.

And thou shalt embroider the coat of fine linen, and thou shalt make the mitre of fine linen, and thou shalt make the girdle of needlework. And for Aaron's sons thou shalt make coats, and thou shalt make for them girdles, and bonnets shalt thou make for them, for glory and for beauty. And thou shalt put them upon Aaron thy brother and his sons with him and shalt anoint them, and consecrate them, and sanctify them that they may minister unto me in the priest's office. And thou shalt make them linen breeches to cover their nakedness, from the loins even unto the thighs they shall reach, and they shall be upon Aaron and upon his sons when they come in unto the tabernacle of the congregation or when they come near unto the altar to minister in the holy place that they bear not iniquity and die; it shall be a statute for ever unto him and his seed after him.

And this is the thing that thou shalt do unto them to hallow them, to minister unto me in the priest's office: take one young bullock, and two rams without blemish, and unleavened bread, and cakes unleavened tempered with oil, and wafers unleavened anointed with oil, of wheaten flour shalt thou make them. And thou shalt put them into one basket and bring them in the basket with the bullock and the two rams. And Aaron and his sons thou shalt bring unto the door of the tabernacle of the congregation and shalt wash them with water. And thou shalt take the garments and put upon Aaron the coat, and the robe of the ephod, and the ephod, and the breastplate, and gird him with the curious girdle of the ephod, and thou shalt put the mitre upon his head, and put the holy crown upon the mitre. Then shalt thou take the anointing oil, and pour it upon his head, and anoint him. And thou shalt bring his sons and put coats upon them. And thou shalt gird them with girdles, Aaron and his sons, and put the bonnets on them, and the priest's office shall be theirs for a perpetual statute, and thou shalt consecrate Aaron and his sons.

And thou shalt cause a bullock to be brought before the tabernacle of the congregation, and Aaron and his sons shall put their hands upon the head of the bullock. And thou shalt kill the bullock before the Lord by the door of the tabernacle of the congregation. And thou shalt take of the blood of the bullock and put it upon the horns of the altar with thy finger and pour all the blood beside the bottom of the altar. And thou shalt take all the fat that covereth the inwards, and the caul that is above the liver, and the two kidneys, and the fat that is upon them, and burn them upon the altar. But the flesh of the bullock, and his skin, and his dung shalt thou burn with fire without the camp; it is a sin offering.

Thou shalt also take one ram, and Aaron and his sons shall put their hands upon the head of the ram. And thou shalt slay the ram, and thou shalt take his blood, and sprinkle it round about upon the altar. And thou shalt cut the ram in pieces, and wash the inwards of him and his legs, and put them unto his pieces and unto his head. And thou shalt burn the whole ram upon the altar, it is a burnt offering unto the Lord, it is a sweet savor, an offering made by fire unto the Lord.

And thou shalt take the other ram and Aaron and his sons shall put their hands upon the head of the ram. Then shalt thou kill the ram and take of his blood, and put it upon the tip of the right ear of Aaron, and upon the tip of the right ear of his sons, and upon the thumb of their right hand, and upon the great toe of their right foot, and sprinkle the blood upon the altar round about. And thou shalt take of the blood that is upon the altar and of the anointing oil, and sprinkle it upon Aaron, and upon his garments, and upon his sons, and upon the garments of his sons with him, and he shall be hallowed, and his garments, and his sons, and his sons' garments with him.

Also thou shalt take of the ram the fat, and the rump, and the fat that covereth the inwards, and the caul above the liver, and the two kidneys, and the fat that is upon them, and the right shoulder, for it is a ram of consecration, and one loaf of bread, and one cake of oiled bread, and one wafer, out of the basket of the unleavened bread that is before the Lord, and thou shalt put all in the hands of Aaron and in the hands of his sons, and shalt wave them for a wave offering before the Lord. And thou shalt receive them of their hands, and burn them upon the altar for a burnt offering, for a sweet savor before the Lord; it is an offering made by fire unto the Lord.

And thou shalt take the breast of the ram of Aaron's consecration and wave it for a wave offering before the Lord, and it shall be thy part. And thou shalt sanctify the breast of the wave offering, and the shoulder of the heave offering which is waved, and which is heaved up, of the ram of the consecration, even of that which is for Aaron and of that which is for his sons, and it shall be Aaron's and his sons' by a statute for ever from the children of Israel, for it is a heave offering, and it shall be a heave offering from the children of Israel of the sacrifice of their peace offerings, even their heave offering unto the Lord.

And the holy garments of Aaron shall be his sons' after him, to be anointed therein and to be consecrated in them. And that son that is priest in his stead shall put them on seven days when he cometh into the tabernacle of the congregation to minister in the holy place.

And thou shalt take the ram of the consecration and seethe his flesh in the holy place. And Aaron and his sons shall eat the flesh of the ram and the bread that is in the basket by the door of the tabernacle of the congregation. And they shall eat those things wherewith the atonement was made, to consecrate and to sanctify them, but a stranger shall not eat thereof because they are holy. And if aught of the flesh of the consecrations or of the bread remain unto the morning, then thou shalt burn the remainder with fire; it shall not be eaten because it is holy.

And thus shalt thou do unto Aaron and to his sons according to all things which I have commanded thee; seven days shalt thou consecrate them. And thou shalt offer every day a bullock for a sin offering for atonement, and thou shalt cleanse the altar when thou hast made an atonement for it, and thou shalt anoint it to sanctify it. Seven days thou shalt make an atonement for the altar, and sanctify it, and it shall be an altar most holy; whatsoever toucheth the altar shall be holy.

Now this is that which thou shalt offer upon the altar: two lambs of the first year day by day continually. The one lamb thou shalt offer in the morning and the other lamb thou shalt offer at even, and with the one lamb a tenth deal of flour mingled with the fourth part of a hin of beaten oil, and the fourth part of a hin of wine for a drink offering. And the other lamb thou shalt offer at even, and shalt do thereto according to the meat offering of the morning, and according to the drink offering thereof, for a sweet savor, an offering made by fire unto the Lord. This shall be a continual burnt offering throughout your generations at the door of the tabernacle of the congregation before the Lord where I will meet you to speak there unto thee. And there I will meet with the children of Israel and the tabernacle shall be sanctified by my glory. And I will sanctify the tabernacle of the congregation and the altar; I will sanctify also both Aaron and his sons to minister to me in the priest's office. And I will dwell among the children of Israel and will be their God. And they shall know that I am the Lord their God that brought them forth out of the land of Egypt, that I may dwell among them I am the Lord their God.

And thou shalt make an altar to burn incense upon, of shittim wood shalt thou make it. A cubit shall be the length thereof, and a cubit the breadth thereof, foursquare shall it be, and two cubits shall be the height thereof, the horns thereof shall be of the same. And thou shalt overlay it with pure gold, the top thereof, and the sides thereof round about, and the horns thereof, and thou shalt make unto it a crown of gold round about. And two golden rings shalt thou make to it under the crown of it, by the two corners thereof, upon the two sides of it shalt thou make it, and they shall be for places for the staves to bear it withal. And thou shalt make the staves of shittim wood, and overlay them with gold. And thou shalt put it before the veil that is by the ark of the testimony, before the mercy seat that is over the testimony where I will meet with thee. And Aaron shall burn thereon sweet incense every morning, when he dresseth the lamps he shall burn incense upon it. And when Aaron lighteth the lamps at even he shall burn incense upon it, a perpetual incense before the Lord throughout your generations. Ye shall offer no strange incense thereon, nor burnt sacrifice, nor meat offering, neither shall ye pour drink offering thereon. And Aaron shall make an atonement upon the horns of it once in a year with the blood of the sin offering of atonements, once in the year shall he make atonement upon it throughout your generations, it is most holy unto the Lord.

And the Lord spake unto Moses saying, When thou takest the sum of the children of Israel after their number, then shall they give every man a ransom for his soul unto the Lord when thou numberest them, that there be no plague among them when thou numberest them. This they shall give: every one that passeth among them that are numbered, half a shekel after the shekel of the sanctuary (a shekel is twenty gerahs), a half shekel shall be the offering of the Lord. Every one that passeth among them that are numbered, from twenty years old and above, shall give an offering unto the Lord. The rich shall not give more, and the poor shall not give less than half a shekel when they give an offering unto the Lord to make an atonement for your souls. And thou shalt take the atonement money of the children of Israel and shalt appoint it for the service of the tabernacle of the congregation, that it may be a memorial unto the children of Israel before the Lord to make an atonement for your souls.

And the Lord spake unto Moses saying, Thou shalt also make a laver of brass, and his foot also of brass, to wash withal, and thou shalt put it between the tabernacle of the congregation and the altar, and thou shalt put water therein. For Aaron and his sons shall wash their hands and their feet thereat when they go into the tabernacle of the congregation, they shall wash with water, that they die not, or when they come near to the altar to minister, to burn offering made by fire unto the Lord, so they shall wash their hands and their feet, that they die not, and it shall be a statute for ever to them, even to him and to his seed throughout their generations.

Moreover the Lord spake unto Moses, saying, Take thou also unto thee principal spices, of pure myrrh five hundred shekels, and of sweet cinnamon half so much, even two hundred and fifty shekels, and of sweet calamus two hundred and fifty shekels, and of cassia five hundred shekels, after the shekel of the sanctuary, and of olive oil a hin, and thou shalt make it an oil of holy ointment, an ointment compound after the art of the apothecary, it shall be a holy anointing oil. And thou shalt anoint the tabernacle of the congregation therewith, and the ark of the testimony, and the table and all his vessels, and the candlestick and his vessels, and the altar of incense, and the altar of burnt offering with all his vessels, and the laver and his foot. And thou shalt sanctify them, that they may be most holy, whatsoever toucheth them shall be holy. And thou shalt anoint Aaron and his sons and consecrate them that they may minister unto me in the priest's office. And thou shalt speak unto the children of Israel saying, This shall be a holy anointing oil unto me throughout your generations. Upon man's flesh shall it not be poured, neither shall ye make any other like it after the composition of it, it is holy and it shall be holy unto you. Whosoever compoundeth any like it or whosoever putteth any of it upon a stranger shall even be cut off from his people.

And the Lord said unto Moses, Take unto thee sweet spices: stacte, and onycha, and galbanum, these sweet spices with pure frankincense, of each shall there be a like weight, and thou shalt make it a perfume, a confection after the art of the apothecary, tempered together, pure and holy, and thou shalt beat some of it very small and put of it before the testimony in the tabernacle of the congregation where I will meet with thee; it shall be unto you most holy. And as for the perfume which thou shalt make, ye shall not make to yourselves according to the composition thereof, it shall be unto thee holy for the Lord. Whosoever shall make like unto that, to smell thereto, shall even be cut off from his people.

And the Lord spake unto Moses saying, See, I have called by name Bezaleel the son of Uri the son of Hur of the tribe of Judah, and I have filled him with the Spirit of God, in wisdom, and in understanding, and in knowledge, and in all manner of workmanship, to devise cunning works, to work in gold, and in silver, and in brass, and in cutting of stones, to set them, and in carving of timber, to work in all manner of workmanship. And I, behold, I have given with him Aholiab the son of Ahisamach of the tribe of Dan, and in the hearts of all that are wise-hearted I have put wisdom that they may make all that I have commanded thee: the tabernacle of the congregation, and the ark of the testimony, and the mercy seat that is thereupon, and all the furniture of the tabernacle, and the table and his furniture, and the pure candlestick with all his furniture, and the altar of incense, and the altar of burnt offering with all his furniture, and the laver and his foot, and the clothes of service, and the holy garments of Aaron the priest, and the garments of his sons to minister in the priest's office, and the anointing oil, and sweet incense for the holy place according to all that I have commanded thee shall they do.

And the Lord spake unto Moses saying, Speak thou also unto the children of Israel saying, Verily my sabbaths ye shall keep, for it is a sign between me and you throughout your generations that ye may know that I am the Lord that doth sanctify you. Ye shall keep the sabbath therefore, for it is holy unto you. Everyone that defileth it shall surely be put to death, for whosoever doeth any work therein, that soul shall be cut off from among his people. Six days may work be done, but in the seventh is the sabbath of rest, holy to the Lord; whosoever doeth any work in the sabbath day, he shall surely be put to death. Wherefore the children of Israel shall keep the sabbath, to observe the sabbath throughout their generations, for a perpetual covenant. It is a sign between me and the children of Israel forever, for in six days the Lord made Heaven and Earth and on the seventh day he rested and was refreshed. And he gave unto Moses, when he had made an end of communing with him upon mount Sinai, two tables of testimony, tables of stone written with the finger of God.

And when the people saw that Moses delayed to come down out of the mount, the people gathered themselves together unto Aaron and said unto him, Up, make us gods which shall go before us, for as for this Moses, the man that brought us up out of the land of Egypt, we know not what is become of him. And Aaron said unto them, Break off the golden earrings which are in the ears of your wives, of your sons, and of your daughters, and bring them unto me. And all the people brake off the golden earrings which were in their ears and brought them unto Aaron. And he received them at their hand and fashioned it with a graving tool after he had made it a molten calf and they said, These be thy gods, O Israel, which brought thee up out of the land of Egypt. And when Aaron saw it he built an altar before it, and Aaron made proclamation and said, Tomorrow is a feast to the Lord. And they rose up early on the morrow, and offered burnt offerings, and brought peace offerings, and the people sat down to eat and to drink and rose up to play.

And the Lord said unto Moses, Go, get thee down, for thy people which thou broughtest out of the land of Egypt have corrupted themselves: they have turned aside quickly out of the way which I commanded them, they have made them a molten calf and have worshiped it, and have sacrificed thereunto and said, These be thy gods, O Israel, which have brought thee up out of the land of Egypt. And the Lord said unto Moses, I have seen this people and behold, it is a stiff-necked people, now therefore let me alone that my wrath may wax hot against them, and that I may consume them, and I will make of thee a great nation.

And Moses besought the Lord his God and said, Lord, why doth thy wrath wax hot against thy people which thou hast brought forth out of the land of Egypt with great power and with a mighty hand? Wherefore should the Egyptians speak and say, For mischief did he bring them out, to slay them in the mountains and to consume them from the face of the Earth? Turn from thy fierce wrath. Thy people will repent of this evil, therefore come thou not out against them. Remember Abraham, Isaac, and Israel thy servants, to whom thou swarest by thine own self and saidst unto them, I will multiply your seed as the stars of Heaven, and all this land that I have spoken of will I give unto your seed, and they shall inherit it forever. And the Lord said unto Moses, If they will repent of the evil which they have done, I will spare them and turn away my fierce wrath, but behold, thou shalt execute judgment upon all that will not repent of this evil this day. Therefore see thou do this thing that I have commanded thee or I will execute all that which I had thought to do unto my people.

And Moses turned and went down from the mount, and the two tables of the testimony were in his hand, the tables were written on both their sides, on the one side and on the other were they written. And the tables were the work of God and the writing was the writing of God graven upon the tables. And when Joshua heard the noise of the people as they shouted he said unto Moses, There is a noise of war in the camp. And he said, It is not the voice of them that shout for mastery, neither is it the voice of them that cry for being overcome, but the noise of them that sing do I hear.

And it came to pass as soon as he came nigh unto the camp, that he saw the calf, and the dancing, and Moses' anger waxed hot, and he cast the tables out of his hands, and brake them beneath the mount. And he took the calf which they had made, and burnt it in the fire, and ground it to powder, and strewed it upon the water, and made the children of Israel drink of it.

And Moses said unto Aaron, What did this people unto thee that thou hast brought so great a sin upon them? And Aaron said, Let not the anger of my lord wax hot; thou knowest the people that they are set on mischief. For they said unto me, Make us gods which shall go before us, for as for this Moses, the man that brought us up out of the land of Egypt, we know not what is become of him. And I said unto them, Whosoever hath any gold, let them break it off. So they gave it me, then I cast it into the fire, and there came out this calf.

And when Moses saw that the people were naked (for Aaron had made them naked unto their shame among their enemies), then Moses stood in the gate of the camp and said, Who is on the Lord's side? Let him come unto me. And all the sons of Levi gathered themselves together unto him. And he said unto them, Thus saith the Lord God of Israel, Put every man his sword by his side, and go in and out from gate to gate throughout the camp, and slay every man his brother, and every man his companion, and every man his neighbor. And the children of Levi did according to the word of Moses and there fell of the people that day about three thousand men. For Moses had said, Consecrate yourselves today to the Lord, even every man upon his son and upon his brother, that he may bestow upon you a blessing this day.

And it came to pass on the morrow that Moses said unto the people, Ye have sinned a great sin and now I will go up unto the Lord, peradventure I shall make an atonement for your sin.

And Moses returned unto the Lord and said, Oh, this people have sinned a great sin and have made them gods of gold. Yet now, if thou wilt, forgive their sin, and if not, blot me, I pray thee, out of thy book which thou hast written. And the Lord said unto Moses, Whosoever hath sinned against me, him will I blot out of my book. Therefore now go, lead the people unto the place of which I have spoken unto thee, Behold, mine angel shall go before thee, nevertheless, in the day when I visit, I will visit their sin upon them. And the Lord plagued the people because they worshiped the calf which Aaron made.

And the Lord said unto Moses, Depart and go up hence, thou and the people which thou hast brought up out of the land of Egypt, unto a land flowing with milk and honey, the land which I sware unto Abraham, to Isaac, and to Jacob saying, Unto thy seed will I give it, and I will send an angel before thee, and I will drive out the Canaanite, the Amorite and the Hittite, and the Perizzite, the Hivite and the Jebusite unto a land flowing with milk and honey, for I will not go up in the midst of thee, for thou art a stiff-necked people, lest I consume thee in the way. And when the people heard these evil tidings they mourned and no man did put on him his ornaments. For the Lord had said unto Moses, Say unto the children of Israel, Ye are a stiff-necked people, I will come up into the midst of thee in a moment and consume thee, therefore now put off thy ornaments from thee that I may know what to do unto thee. And the children of Israel stripped themselves of their ornaments by the mount Horeb.

6 AND Moses took the tabernacle and pitched it without the camp, afar off from the camp, and called it the Tabernacle of the congregation. And it came to pass that everyone which sought the Lord went out unto the tabernacle of the congregation which was without the camp. And it came to pass when Moses went out unto the tabernacle that all the people rose up, and stood every man at his tent door, and looked after Moses until he was gone into the tabernacle. And it came to pass as Moses entered into the tabernacle, the cloudy pillar descended, and stood at the door of the tabernacle, and the Lord talked with Moses. And all the people saw the cloudy pillar stand at the tabernacle door and all the people rose up and worshiped, every man in his tent door.

And the Lord spake unto Moses face to face as a man speaketh unto his friend. And he turned again into the camp, but his servant Joshua the son of Nun, a young man, departed not out of the tabernacle. And Moses said unto the Lord, See, thou sayest unto me, Bring up this people, and thou hast not let me know whom thou wilt send with me. Yet thou hast said, I know thee by name and thou hast also found grace in my sight. Now therefore, I pray thee, if I have found grace in thy sight, show me now thy way that I may know thee, that I may find grace in thy sight, and consider that this nation is thy people.

And he said, My presence shall go with thee and I will give thee rest. And he said unto him, If thy presence go not with me, carry us not up hence. For wherein shall it be known here that I and thy people have found grace in thy sight? Is it not in that thou goest with us? So shall we be separated, I and thy people, from all the people that are upon the face of the Earth.

And the Lord said unto Moses, I will do this thing also that thou hast spoken, for thou hast found grace in my sight and I know thee by name. And he said, I beseech thee, show me thy glory. And he said, I will make all my goodness pass before thee, and I will proclaim the name of the Lord before thee, and will be gracious to whom I will be gracious, and will show mercy on whom I will show mercy. And he said unto Moses, Thou canst not see my face at this time, lest mine anger be kindled against thee also and I destroy thee and thy people, for there shall no man among them see me at this time and live, for they are exceeding sinful. And no sinful man hath at any time, neither shall there be any sinful man at any time that shall see my face and live.

And the Lord said, Behold, thou shalt stand upon a rock and I will prepare a place by me for thee. And it shall come to pass while my glory passeth by that I will put thee in a cleft of a rock and cover thee with my hand while I pass by. And I will take away mine hand and thou shalt see my back parts, but my face shall not be seen as at other times, for I am angry with my people Israel.

And the Lord said unto Moses, Hew thee two other tables of stone like unto the first, and I will write upon them also the words of the law, according as they were written at the first on the tables which thou brakest, but it shall not be according to the first, for I will take away the priesthood out of their midst, therefore my holy order and the ordinances thereof shall not go before them, for my presence shall not go up in their midst lest I destroy them. But I will give unto them the law as at the first, but it shall be after the law of a carnal commandment, for I have sworn in my wrath that they shall not enter into my presence, into my rest, in the days of their pilgrimage. Therefore do as I have commanded thee, and be ready in the morning, and come up in the morning unto mount Sinai, and present thyself there to me in the top of the mount. And no man shall come up with thee, neither let any man be seen throughout all the mount, neither let the flocks nor herds feed before that mount.

And Moses hewed two tables of stone like unto the first, and he rose up early in the morning and went up unto mount Sinai, as the Lord had commanded him, and took in his hand the two tables of stone. And the Lord descended in the cloud, and stood with him there, and proclaimed the name of the Lord. And the Lord passed by before him and proclaimed, The Lord, The Lord God, merciful and gracious, long-suffering, and abundant in goodness and truth, keeping mercy for thousands, forgiving iniquity and transgression and sin, and that will by no means clear the rebellious, visiting the iniquity of the fathers upon the children and upon the children's children unto the third and to the fourth generation. And Moses made haste, and bowed his head toward the earth, and worshiped. And he said, If now I have found grace in thy sight, O Lord, let my Lord, I pray thee, go among us, for it is a stiff-necked people, and pardon our iniquity and our sin, and take us for thine inheritance.

And he said, Behold, I make a covenant, before all thy people I will do marvels, such as have not been done in all the Earth, nor in any nation, and all the people among which thou art shall see the work of the Lord, for it is a terrible thing that I will do with thee. Observe thou that which I command thee this day; behold, I drive out before thee the Amorite, and the Canaanite, and the Hittite, and the Perizzite, and the Hivite, and the Jebusite. Take heed to thyself lest thou make a covenant with the inhabitants of the land whither thou goest, lest it be for a snare in the midst of thee, but ye shall destroy their altars, break their images, and cut down their groves, for thou shalt worship no other god, for the Lord, whose name is Jehovah, is a jealous God. Lest thou make a covenant with the inhabitants of the land, and they go a whoring after their gods, and do sacrifice unto their gods, and one call thee, and thou eat of his sacrifice, and thou take of their daughters unto thy sons, and their daughters go a whoring after their gods and make thy sons go a whoring after their gods. Thou shalt make thee no molten gods.

The feast of unleavened bread shalt thou keep. Seven days thou shalt eat unleavened bread, as I commanded thee, in the time of the month Abib, for in the month Abib thou camest out from Egypt.

All that openeth the matrix is mine and every firstling among thy cattle, whether ox or sheep, that is male. But the firstling of an ass thou shalt redeem with a lamb, and if thou redeem him not, then shalt thou break his neck.

All the firstborn of thy sons thou shalt redeem. And none shall appear before me empty.

Six days thou shalt work, but on the seventh day thou shalt rest, in earing time and in harvest thou shalt rest.

And thou shalt observe the feast of weeks, of the firstfruits of wheat harvest, and the feast of ingathering at the year's end.

Thrice in the year shall all your men children appear before the Lord God, the God of Israel. For I will cast out the nations before thee and enlarge thy borders, neither shall any man desire thy land when thou shalt go up to appear before the Lord thy God thrice in the year.

Thou shalt not offer the blood of my sacrifice with leaven, neither shall the sacrifice of the feast of the passover be left unto the morning.

The first of the firstfruits of thy land thou shalt bring unto the house of the Lord thy God.

Thou shalt not seethe a kid in his mother's milk.

And the Lord said unto Moses, Write thou these words, for after the tenor of these words I have made a covenant with thee and with Israel. And he was there with the Lord forty days and forty nights, he did neither eat bread nor drink water. And he wrote upon the tables the words of the covenant, the ten commandments.

And it came to pass when Moses came down from mount Sinai with the two tables of testimony in Moses' hand, when he came down from the mount, that Moses wist not that the skin of his face shone while he talked with him. And when Aaron and all the children of Israel saw Moses, behold, the skin of his face shone and they were afraid to come nigh him. And Moses called unto them, and Aaron and all the rulers of the congregation returned unto him, and Moses talked with them. And afterward all the children of Israel came nigh and he gave them in commandment all that the Lord had spoken with him in mount Sinai. And till Moses had done speaking with them he put a veil on his face. But when Moses went in before the Lord to speak with him, he took the veil off until he came out. And he came out and spake unto the children of Israel that which he was commanded. And the children of Israel saw the face of Moses, that the skin of Moses' face shone, and Moses put the veil upon his face again until he went in to speak with the Lord.

And Moses gathered all the congregation of the children of Israel together and said unto them, These are the words which the Lord hath commanded that ye should do them. Six days shall work be done, but on the seventh day there shall be to you a holy day, a sabbath of rest to the Lord, whosoever doeth work therein shall be put to death. Ye shall kindle no fire throughout your habitations upon the sabbath day.

And Moses spake unto all the congregation of the children of Israel saying, This is the thing which the Lord commanded saying, Take ye from among you an offering unto the Lord, whosoever is of a willing heart let him bring it, an offering of the Lord, gold, and silver, and brass, and blue, and purple, and scarlet, and fine linen, and goats' hair, and rams' skins dyed red, and badgers' skins, and shittim wood, and oil for the light, and spices for anointing oil and for the sweet incense, and onyx stones, and stones to be set for the ephod, and for the breastplate. And every wise-hearted among you shall come and make all that the Lord hath commanded: the tabernacle, his tent and his covering, his taches and his boards, his bars, his pillars and his sockets, the ark and the staves thereof with the mercy seat, and the veil of the covering, the table and his staves, and all his vessels, and the shewbread, the candlestick also for the light, and his furniture, and his lamps with the oil for the light, and the incense altar and his staves, and the anointing oil, and the sweet incense, and the hanging for the door at the entering in of the tabernacle, the altar of burnt offering with his brazen grate, his staves and all his vessels, the laver and his foot, the hangings of the court, his pillars and their sockets, and the hanging for the door of the court, the pins of the tabernacle and the pins of the court and their cords, the clothes of service to do service in the holy place, the holy garments for Aaron the priest, and the garments of his sons to minister in the priest's office.

And all the congregation of the children of Israel departed from the presence of Moses. And they came, everyone whose heart stirred him up and everyone whom his spirit made willing, and they brought the Lord's offering to the work of the tabernacle of the congregation, and for all his service, and for the holy garments. And they came, both men and women, as many as were willing-hearted and brought bracelets, and earrings, and rings, and tablets, all jewels of gold, and every man that offered, offered an offering of gold unto the Lord. And every man with whom was found blue, and purple, and scarlet, and fine linen, and goats' hair, and red skins of rams, and badgers' skins brought them. Everyone that did offer an offering of silver and brass brought the Lord's offering, and every man with whom was found shittim wood for any work of the service brought it.

And all the women that were wise-hearted did spin with their hands and brought that which they had spun, both of blue, and of purple, and of scarlet, and of fine linen. And all the women whose heart stirred them up in wisdom spun goats' hair. And the rulers brought onyx stones, and stones to be set, for the ephod and for the breastplate, and spice and oil for the light, and for the anointing oil, and for the sweet incense. The children of Israel brought a willing offering unto the Lord, every man and woman whose heart made them willing to bring for all manner of work which the Lord had commanded to be made by the hand of Moses.

And Moses said unto the children of Israel, See, the Lord hath called by name Bezaleel the son of Uri the son of Hur of the tribe of Judah and he hath filled him with the Spirit of God, in wisdom, in understanding, and in knowledge, and in all manner of workmanship, and to devise curious works, to work in gold, and in silver, and in brass, and in the cutting of stones, to set them, and in carving of wood, to make any manner of cunning work. And he hath put in his heart that he may teach, both he and Aholiab the son of Ahisamach of the tribe of Dan. Them hath he filled with wisdom of heart, to work all manner of work, of the engraver, and of the cunning workman, and of the embroiderer, in blue and in purple, in scarlet and in fine linen, and of the weaver, even of them that do any work, and of those that devise cunning work.

Then wrought Bezaleel and Aholiab, and every wise-hearted man in whom the Lord put wisdom and understanding to know how to work all manner of work for the service of the sanctuary, according to all that the Lord had commanded.

And Moses called Bezaleel and Aholiab, and every wise-hearted man in whose heart the Lord had put wisdom, even every one whose heart stirred him up to come unto the work to do it, and they received of Moses all the offering which the children of Israel had brought for the work of the service of the sanctuary to make it withal. And they brought yet unto him free offerings every morning. And all the wise men that wrought all the work of the sanctuary came every man from his work which they made and they spake unto Moses saying, The people bring much more than enough for the service of the work which the Lord commanded to make. And Moses gave commandment, and they caused it to be proclaimed throughout the camp saying, Let neither man nor woman make any more work for the offering of the sanctuary. So the people were restrained from bringing. For the stuff they had was sufficient for all the work to make it and too much.

And every wise-hearted man among them that wrought the work of the tabernacle made ten curtains of fine twined linen, and blue, and purple, and scarlet, with cherubim of cunning work made he them. The length of one curtain was twenty and eight cubits, and the breadth of one curtain four cubits, the curtains were all of one size. And he coupled the five curtains one unto another and the other five curtains he coupled one unto another. And he made loops of blue on the edge of one curtain from the selvage in the coupling, likewise he made in the uttermost side of another curtain, in the coupling of the second. Fifty loops made he in one curtain and fifty loops made he in the edge of the curtain which was in the coupling of the second, the loops held one curtain to another. And he made fifty taches of gold and coupled the curtains one unto another with the taches,so it became one tabernacle.

And he made curtains of goats' hair for the tent over the tabernacle, eleven curtains he made them. The length of one curtain was thirty cubits, and four cubits was the breadth of one curtain, the eleven curtains were of one size. And he coupled five curtains by themselves and six curtains by themselves. And he made fifty loops upon the uttermost edge of the curtain in the coupling, and fifty loops made he upon the edge of the curtain which coupleth the second. And he made fifty taches of brass to couple the tent together,that it might be one. And he made a covering for the tent of rams' skins dyed red and a covering of badgers' skins above that.

And he made boards for the tabernacle of shittim wood standing up. The length of a board was ten cubits and the breadth of a board one cubit and a half. One board had two tenons equally distant one from another, thus did he make for all the boards of the tabernacle. And he made boards for the tabernacle, twenty boards for the south side southward, and forty sockets of silver he made under the twenty boards, two sockets under one board for his two tenons and two sockets under another board for his two tenons. And for the other side of the tabernacle which is toward the north corner he made twenty boards, and their forty sockets of silver, two sockets under one board and two sockets under another board. And for the sides of the tabernacle westward he made six boards. And two boards made he for the corners of the tabernacle in the two sides. And they were coupled beneath and coupled together at the head thereof to one ring, thus he did to both of them in both the corners. And there were eight boards, and their sockets were sixteen sockets of silver, under every board two sockets.

And he made bars of shittim wood, five for the boards of the one side of the tabernacle and five bars for the boards of the other side of the tabernacle, and five bars for the boards of the tabernacle, for the sides westward. And he made the middle bar to shoot through the boards from the one end to the other. And he overlaid the boards with gold, and made their rings of gold to be places for the bars, and overlaid the bars with gold.

And he made a veil of blue, and purple and scarlet, and fine twined linen, with cherubim made he it of cunning work. And he made thereunto four pillars of shittim wood and overlaid them with gold, their hooks were of gold and he cast for them four sockets of silver. And he made a hanging for the tabernacle door of blue, and purple, and scarlet, and fine twined linen, of needlework and the five pillars of it with their hooks, and he overlaid their chapiters and their fillets with gold, but their five sockets were of brass.

And Bezaleel made the ark of shittim wood, two cubits and a half was the length of it, and a cubit and a half the breadth of it, and a cubit and a half the height of it, and he overlaid it with pure gold within and without, and made a crown of gold to it round about. And he cast for it four rings of gold to be set by the four corners of it, even two rings upon the one side of it and two rings upon the other side of it. And he made staves of shittim wood and overlaid them with gold. And he put the staves into the rings by the sides of the ark to bear the ark. And he made the mercy seat of pure gold, two cubits and a half was the length thereof and one cubit and a half the breadth thereof. And he made two cherubim of gold, beaten out of one piece made he them, on the two ends of the mercy seat, one cherub on the end on this side, and another cherub on the other end on that side, out of the mercy seat made he the cherubim on the two ends thereof. And the cherubim spread out their wings on high, and covered with their wings over the mercy seat, with their faces one to another, even to the mercy seatward were the faces of the cherubim.

And he made the table of shittim wood, two cubits was the length thereof, and a cubit the breadth thereof, and a cubit and a half the height thereof, and he overlaid it with pure gold, and made thereunto a crown of gold round about. Also he made thereunto a border of a handbreadth round about, and made a crown of gold for the border thereof round about. And he cast for it four rings of gold and put the rings upon the four corners that were in the four feet thereof. Over against the border were the rings, the places for the staves to bear the table. And he made the staves of shittim wood and overlaid them with gold, to bear the table. And he made the vessels which were upon the table, his dishes, and his spoons, and his bowls, and his covers to cover withal, of pure gold.

And he made the candlestick of pure gold, of beaten work made he the candlestick, his shaft, and his branch, his bowls, his knops, and his flowers, were of the same, and six branches going out of the sides thereof, three branches of the candlestick out of the one side thereof and three branches of the candlestick out of the other side thereof, three bowls made after the fashion of almonds in one branch, a knop and a flower, and three bowls made like almonds in another branch, a knop and a flower, so throughout the six branches going out of the candlestick. And in the candlestick were four bowls made like almonds, his knops, and his flowers, and a knop under two branches of the same, and a knop under two branches of the same, and a knop under two branches of the same, according to the six branches going out of it. Their knops and their branches were of the same, all of it was one beaten work of pure gold. And he made his seven lamps, and his snuffers, and his snuff dishes, of pure gold. Of a talent of pure gold made he it, and all the vessels thereof.

And he made the incense altar of shittim wood, the length of it was a cubit and the breadth of it a cubit, it was foursquare and two cubits was the height of it, the horns thereof were of the same. And he overlaid it with pure gold, both the top of it, and the sides thereof round about, and the horns of it, also he made unto it a crown of gold round about. And he made two rings of gold for it under the crown thereof, by the two corners of it, upon the two sides thereof to be places for the staves to bear it withal. And he made the staves of shittim wood and overlaid them with gold.

And he made the holy anointing oil and the pure incense of sweet spices according to the work of the apothecary.

And he made the altar of burnt offering of shittim wood, five cubits was the length thereof and five cubits the breadth thereof, it was foursquare and three cubits the height thereof. And he made the horns thereof on the four corners of it, the horns thereof were of the same, and he overlaid it with brass.

And he made all the vessels of the altar, the pots, and the shovels, and the basins, and the fleshhooks, and the firepans, all the vessels thereof made he of brass. And he made for the altar a brazen grate of network under the compass thereof, beneath unto the midst of it. And he cast four rings for the four ends of the grate of brass to be places for the staves. And he made the staves of shittim wood, and overlaid them with brass. And he put the staves into the rings on the sides of the altar, to bear it withal, he made the altar hollow with boards. And he made the laver of brass, and the foot of it of brass, of the looking glasses of the women assembling which assembled at the door of the tabernacle of the congregation.

And he made the court, on the south side southward the hangings of the court were of fine twined linen, a hundred cubits, their pillars were twenty, and their brazen sockets twenty, the hooks of the pillars and their fillets were of silver. And for the north side the hangings were a hundred cubits, their pillars were twenty, and their sockets of brass twenty, the hooks of the pillars, and their fillets of silver. And for the west side were hangings of fifty cubits, their pillars ten, and their sockets ten, the hooks of the pillars and their fillets of silver. And for the east side eastward fifty cubits. The hangings of the one side of the gate were fifteen cubits, their pillars three and their sockets three. And for the other side of the court gate, on this hand and that hand, were hangings of fifteen cubits, their pillars three, and their sockets three. All the hangings of the court round about were of fine twined linen. And the sockets for the pillars were of brass, the hooks of the pillars and their fillets of silver, and the overlaying of their chapiters of silver, and all the pillars of the court were filleted with silver. And the hanging for the gate of the court was needlework, of blue, and purple, and scarlet, and fine twined linen, and twenty cubits was the length, and the height in the breadth was five cubits, answerable to the hangings of the court. And their pillars were four, and their sockets of brass four, their hooks of silver, and the overlaying of their chapiters and their fillets of silver. And all the pins of the tabernacle, and of the court round about, were of brass.

This is the sum of the tabernacle, even of the tabernacle of testimony, as it was counted according to the commandment of Moses, for the service of the Levites by the hand of Ithamar, son to Aaron the priest. And Bezaleel, the son of Uri the son of Hur of the tribe of Judah, made all that the Lord commanded Moses. And with him was Aholiab son of Ahisamach of the tribe of Dan, an engraver, and a cunning workman, and an embroiderer in blue, and in purple, and in scarlet, and fine linen.

All the gold that was occupied for the work in all the work of the holy place, even the gold of the offering, was twenty and nine talents and seven hundred and thirty shekels, after the shekel of the sanctuary. And the silver of them that were numbered of the congregation was a hundred talents and a thousand seven hundred and threescore and fifteen shekels after the shekel of the sanctuary, a bekah for every man, that is, half a shekel after the shekel of the sanctuary, for everyone that went to be numbered, from twenty years old and upward, for six hundred thousand and three thousand and five hundred and fifty men. And of the hundred talents of silver were cast the sockets of the sanctuary and the sockets of the veil, a hundred sockets of the hundred talents, a talent for a socket. And of the thousand seven hundred seventy and five shekels he made hooks for the pillars, and overlaid their chapiters and filleted them. And the brass of the offering was seventy talents, and two thousand and four hundred shekels. And therewith he made the sockets to the door of the tabernacle of the congregation, and the brazen altar, and the brazen grate for it, and all the vessels of the altar, and the sockets of the court round about, and the sockets of the court gate, and all the pins of the tabernacle, and all the pins of the court round about.

And of the blue, and purple, and scarlet they made clothes of service, to do service in the holy place, and made the holy garments for Aaron as the Lord commanded Moses. And he made the ephod of gold, blue, and purple, and scarlet, and fine twined linen. And they did beat the gold into thin plates and cut it into wires, to work it in the blue, and in the purple, and in the scarlet, and in the fine linen, with cunning work. They made shoulder pieces for it, to couple it together, by the two edges was it coupled together. And the curious girdle of his ephod that was upon it was of the same, according to the work thereof, of gold, blue, and purple, and scarlet, and fine twined linen as the Lord commanded Moses. And they wrought onyx stones enclosed in ouches of gold, graven, as signets are graven, with the names of the children of Israel. And he put them on the shoulders of the ephod, that they should be stones for a memorial to the children of Israel as the Lord commanded Moses.

And he made the breastplate of cunning work, like the work of the ephod, of gold, blue, and purple, and scarlet, and fine twined linen; it was foursquare. They made the breastplate double, a span was the length thereof, and a span the breadth thereof, being doubled. And they set in it four rows of stones, the first row was a sardius, a topaz, and a carbuncle, this was the first row. And the second row, an emerald, a sapphire, and a diamond. And the third row, a ligure, and agate, and an amethyst. And the fourth row, a beryl, and onyx, and a jasper; they were enclosed in ouches of gold in their enclosings. And the stones were according to the names of the children of Israel, twelve, according to their names, like the engravings of a signet, every one with his name according to the twelve tribes. And they made upon the breastplate chains at the ends of wreathen work of pure gold. And they made two ouches of gold, and two gold rings, and put the two rings in the two ends of the breastplate. And they put the two wreathen chains of gold in the two rings on the ends of the breastplate. And the two ends of the two wreathen chains they fastened in the two ouches, and put them on the shoulder pieces of the ephod before it. And they made two rings of gold and put them on the two ends of the breastplate, upon the border of it which was on the side of the ephod inward. And they made two other golden rings and put them on the two sides of the ephod underneath toward the forepart of it, over against the other coupling thereof, above the curious girdle of the ephod. And they did bind the breastplate by his rings unto the rings of the ephod with a lace of blue that it might be above the curious girdle of the ephod, and that the breastplate might not be loosed from the ephod as the Lord commanded Moses.

And he made the robe of the ephod of woven work, all of blue. And there was a hole in the midst of the robe, as the hole of an habergeon, with a band round about the hole that it should not rend. And they made upon the hems of the robe pomegranates of blue, and purple, and scarlet, and twined linen. And they made bells of pure gold, and put the bells between the pomegranates upon the hem of the robe, round about between the pomegranates, a bell and a pomegranate, a bell and a pomegranate, round about the hem of the robe to minister in as the Lord commanded Moses.

And they made coats of fine linen of woven work for Aaron and for his sons, and a mitre of fine linen, and goodly bonnets of fine linen, and linen breeches of fine twined linen, and a girdle of fine twined linen, and blue, and purple, and scarlet, of needlework as the Lord commanded Moses. And they made the plate of the holy crown of pure gold and wrote upon it a writing, like to the engravings of a signet, HOLINESS TO THE LORD. And they tied unto it a lace of blue, to fasten it on high upon the mitre as the Lord commanded Moses.

Thus was all the work of the tabernacle of the tent of the congregation finished, and the children of Israel did according to all that the Lord commanded Moses, so did they. And they brought the tabernacle unto Moses, the ten, and all his furniture, his taches, his boards, his bars, and his pillars, and his sockets, and the covering of rams' skins dyed red, and the covering of badgers' skins, and the veil of the covering, the ark of the testimony and the staves thereof, and the mercy seat, the table, and all the vessels thereof, and the shewbread, the pure candlestick with the lamps thereof, even with the lamps to be set in order, and all the vessels thereof, and the oil for light, and the golden altar, and the anointing oil, and the sweet incense, and the hanging for the tabernacle door, the brazen altar, and his grate of brass, his staves, and all his vessels, the laver and his foot, the hangings of the court, his pillars, and his sockets, and the hanging for the court gate, his cords, and his pins, and all the vessels of the service of the tabernacle, for the tent of the congregation, the clothes of service to do service in the holy place, and the holy garments for Aaron the priest, and his sons' garments, to minister in the priest's office. According to all that the Lord commanded Moses, so the children of Israel made all the work. And Moses did look upon all the work and behold, they had done it as the Lord had commanded, even so had they done it, and Moses blessed them.

And the Lord spake unto Moses saying, On the first day of the first month shalt thou set up the tabernacle of the tent of the congregation. And thou shalt put therein the ark of the testimony, and cover the ark with the veil. And thou shalt bring in the table, and set in order the things that are to be set in order upon it, and thou shalt bring in the candlestick and light the lamps thereof. And thou shalt set the altar of gold for the incense before the ark of the testimony and put the hanging of the door to the tabernacle. And thou shalt set the altar of the burnt offering before the door of the tabernacle of the tent of the congregation. And thou shalt set the laver between the tent of the congregation and the altar and shalt put water therein. And thou shalt set up the court round about and hang up the hanging at the court gate. And thou shalt take the anointing oil and anoint the tabernacle and all that is therein, and shalt hallow it and all the vessels thereof, and it shall be holy. And thou shalt anoint the altar of the burnt offering and all his vessels, and sanctify the altar, and it shall be an altar most holy. And thou shalt anoint the laver and his foot and sanctify it. And thou shalt bring Aaron and his sons unto the door of the tabernacle of the congregation and wash them with water. And thou shalt put upon Aaron the holy garments, and anoint him, and sanctify him that he may minister unto me in the priest's office. And thou shalt bring his sons and clothe them with coats, and thou shalt anoint them as thou didst anoint their father, that they may minister unto me in the priest's office, for their anointing shall surely be an everlasting priesthood throughout their generations. Thus did Moses, according to all that the Lord commanded him, so did he.

And it came to pass in the first month in the second year, on the first day of the month, that the tabernacle was reared up. And Moses reared up the tabernacle, and fastened his sockets, and set up the boards thereof, and put in the bars thereof, and reared up his pillars. And he spread abroad the tent over the tabernacle, and put the covering of the tent above upon it, as the Lord commanded Moses. And he took and put the testimony into the ark, and set the staves on the ark, and put the mercy seat above upon the ark, and he brought the ark into the tabernacle, and set up the veil of the covering, and covered the ark of the testimony, as the Lord commanded Moses. And he put the table in the tent of the congregation, upon the side of the tabernacle northward, without the veil. And he set the bread in order upon it before the Lord as the Lord had commanded Moses. And he put the candlestick in the tent of the congregation, over against the table, on the side of the tabernacle southward. And he lighted the lamps before the Lord as the Lord commanded Moses. And he put the golden altar in the tent of the congregation before the veil and he burnt sweet incense thereon as the Lord commanded Moses. And he set up the hanging at the door of the tabernacle. And he put the altar of burnt offering by the door of the tabernacle of the tent of the congregation and offered upon it the burnt offering and the meat offering as the Lord commanded Moses. And he set the laver between the tent of the congregation and the altar, and put water there to wash withal. And Moses and Aaron and his sons washed their hands and their feet thereat when they went into the tent of the congregation, and when they came near unto the altar they washed as the Lord commanded Moses. And he reared up the court round about the tabernacle and the altar, and set up the hanging of the court gate. So Moses finished the work.

Then a cloud covered the tent of the congregation, and the glory of the Lord filled the tabernacle. And Moses was not able to enter into the tent of the congregation because the cloud abode thereon, and the glory of the Lord filled the tabernacle. And when the cloud was taken up from over the tabernacle the children of Israel went onward in all their journeys, but if the cloud were not taken up, then they journeyed not till the day that it was taken up. For the cloud of the Lord was upon the tabernacle by day and fire was on it by night in the sight of all the house of Israel throughout all their journeys.

LEVITICUS

AND the Lord called unto Moses and spake unto him out of the tabernacle of the congregation saying, Speak unto the children of Israel and say unto them, If any man of you bring an offering unto the Lord, ye shall bring your offering of the cattle, even of the herd, and of the flock. If his offering be a burnt sacrifice of the herd, let him offer a male without blemish; he shall offer it of his own voluntary will at the door of the tabernacle of the congregation before the Lord. And he shall put his hand upon the head of the burnt offering and it shall be accepted for him to make atonement for him. And he shall kill the bullock before the Lord and the priests, Aaron's sons, shall bring the blood and sprinkle the blood round about upon the altar that is by the door of the tabernacle of the congregation. And he shall flay the burnt offering and cut it into his pieces. And the sons of Aaron the priest shall put fire upon the altar, and lay the wood in order upon the fire, and the priests, Aaron's sons, shall lay the parts, the head, and the fat in order upon the wood that is on the fire which is upon the altar, but his inwards and his legs shall he wash in water, and the priest shall burn all on the altar to be a burnt sacrifice, an offering made by fire, of a sweet savor unto the Lord.

And if his offering be of the flocks, namely of the sheep or of the goats, for a burnt sacrifice, he shall bring it a male without blemish. And he shall kill it on the side of the altar northward before the Lord, and the priests, Aaron's sons, shall sprinkle his blood round about upon the altar, and he shall cut it into his pieces with his head and his fat, and the priest shall lay them in order on the wood that is on the fire which is upon the altar. But he shall wash the inwards and the legs with water, and the priest shall bring it all and burn it upon the altar, it is a burnt sacrifice, an offering made by fire, of a sweet savor unto the Lord.

And if the burnt sacrifice for his offering to the Lord be of fowls, then he shall bring his offering of turtle doves or of young pigeons. And the priest shall bring it unto the altar, and wring off his head, and burn it on the altar, and the blood thereof shall be wrung out at the side of the altar, and he shall pluck away his crop with his feathers, and cast it beside the altar on the east part, by the place of the ashes. And he shall cleave it with the wings thereof, but shall not divide it asunder, and the priest shall burn it upon the altar, upon the wood that is upon the fire, it is a burnt sacrifice, an offering made by fire, of a sweet savor unto the Lord.

And when any will offer a meat offering unto the Lord, his offering shall be of fine flour, and he shall pour oil upon it, and put frankincense thereon. And he shall bring it to Aaron's sons the priests, and he shall take thereout his handful of the flour thereof, and of the oil thereof, with all the frankincense thereof, and the priest shall burn the memorial of it upon the altar, to be an offering made by fire, of a sweet savor unto the Lord, and the remnant of the meat offering shall be Aaron's and his sons', it is a thing most holy of the offerings of the Lord made by fire.

And if thou bring an oblation of a meat offering baken in the oven, it shall be unleavened cakes of fine flour mingled with oil or unleavened wafers anointed with oil. And if thy oblation be a meat offering baken in a pan, it shall be of fine flour unleavened, mingled with oil. Thou shalt part it in pieces and pour oil thereon, it is a meat offering. And if thy oblation be a meat offering baken in the frying pan, it shall be made of fine flour with oil. And thou shalt bring the meat offering that is made of these things unto the Lord and when it is presented unto the priest he shall bring it unto the altar. And the priest shall take from the meat offering a memorial thereof and shall burn it upon the altar, it is an offering made by fire, of a sweet savor unto the Lord. And that which is left of the meat offering shall be Aaron's and his sons', it is a thing most holy of the offerings of the Lord made by fire.

No meat offering which ye shall bring unto the Lord shall be made with leaven, for ye shall burn no leaven nor any honey in any offering of the Lord made by fire. As for the oblation of the firstfruits, ye shall offer them unto the Lord, but they shall not be burnt on the altar for a sweet savor. And every oblation of thy meat offering shalt thou season with salt, neither shalt thou suffer the salt of the covenant of thy God to be lacking from thy meat offering, with all thine offerings thou shalt offer salt.

And if thou offer a meat offering of thy firstfruits unto the Lord, thou shalt offer for the meat offering of thy firstfruits green ears of corn dried by the fire, even corn beaten out of full ears. And thou shalt put oil upon it and lay frankincense thereon, it is a meat offering. And the priest shall burn the memorial of it, part of the beaten corn thereof and part of the oil thereof with all the frankincense thereof, it is an offering made by fire unto the Lord.

And if his oblation be a sacrifice of peace offering, if he offer it of the herd, whether it be a male or female, he shall offer it without blemish before the Lord. And he shall lay his hand upon the head of his offering and kill it at the door of the tabernacle of the congregation and Aaron's sons the priests shall sprinkle the blood upon the altar round about. And he shall offer of the sacrifice of the peace offering an offering made by fire unto the Lord, the fat that covereth the inwards and all the fat that is upon the inwards. And the two kidneys and the fat that is on them which is by the flanks, and the caul above the liver with the kidneys, it shall he take away. And Aaron's sons shall burn it on the altar upon the burnt sacrifice which is upon the wood that is on the fire, it is an offering made by fire, of a sweet savor unto the Lord.

And if his offering for a sacrifice of peace offering unto the Lord be of the flock, male or female, he shall offer it without blemish. If he offer a lamb for his offering, then shall he offer it before the Lord. And he shall lay his hand upon the head of his offering and kill it before the tabernacle of the congregation and Aaron's sons shall sprinkle the blood thereof round about upon the altar. And he shall offer of the sacrifice of the peace offering an offering made by fire unto the Lord, the fat thereof and the whole rump, it shall he take off hard by the backbone, and the fat that covereth the inwards, and all the fat that is upon the inwards. And the two kidneys and the fat that is upon them which is by the flanks, and the caul above the liver with the kidneys, it shall he take away. And the priest shall burn it upon the altar, it is the food of the offering made by fire unto the Lord.

And if his offering be a goat, then he shall offer it before the Lord. And he shall lay his hand upon the head of it, and kill it before the tabernacle of the congregation, and the sons of Aaron shall sprinkle the blood thereof upon the altar round about. And he shall offer thereof his offering, even an offering made by fire unto the Lord, the fat that covereth the inwards and all the fat that is upon the inwards. And the two kidneys and the fat that is upon them which is by the flanks, and the caul above the liver with the kidneys, it shall he take away. And the priest shall burn them upon the altar, it is the food of the offering made by fire for a sweet savor, all the fat is the Lord's. It shall be a perpetual statute for your generations throughout all your dwellings that ye eat neither fat nor blood.

And the Lord spake unto Moses saying, Speak unto the children of Israel saying, If a soul shall sin through ignorance against any of the commandments of the Lord concerning things which ought not to be done and shall do against any of them, if the priest that is anointed do sin according to the sin of the people, then let him bring for his sin which he hath sinned a young bullock without blemish unto the Lord for a sin offering. And he shall bring the bullock unto the door of the tabernacle of the congregation before the Lord, and shall lay his hand upon the bullock's head, and kill the bullock before the Lord. And the priest that is anointed shall take of the bullock's blood and bring it to the tabernacle of the congregation, and the priest shall dip his finger in the blood and sprinkle of the blood seven times before the Lord before the veil of the sanctuary. And the priest shall put some of the blood upon the horns of the altar of sweet incense before the Lord which is in the tabernacle of the congregation, and shall pour all the blood of the bullock at the bottom of the altar of the burnt offering which is at the door of the tabernacle of the congregation. And he shall take off from it all the fat of the bullock for the sin offering, the fat that covereth the inwards, and all the fat that is upon the inwards, and the two kidneys and the fat that is upon them which is by the flanks, and the caul above the liver with the kidneys, it shall he take away as it was taken off from the bullock of the sacrifice of peace offerings, and the priest shall burn them upon the altar of the burnt offering. And the skin of the bullock and all his flesh, with his head, and with his legs, and his inwards, and his dung, even the whole bullock shall he carry forth without the camp unto a clean place where the ashes are poured out, and burn him on the wood with fire, where the ashes are poured out shall he be burnt.

And if the whole congregation of Israel sin through ignorance, and the thing be hid from the eyes of the assembly, and they have done somewhat against any of the commandments of the Lord concerning things which should not be done, and are guilty, when the sin which they have sinned against it is known, then the congregation shall offer a young bullock for the sin, and bring him before the tabernacle of the congregation. And the elders of the congregation shall lay their hands upon the head of the bullock before the Lord, and the bullock shall be killed before the Lord. And the priest that is anointed shall bring of the bullock's blood to the tabernacle of the congregation, and the priest shall dip his finger in some of the blood and sprinkle it seven times before the Lord, even before the veil. And he shall put some of the blood upon the horns of the altar which is before the Lord that is in the tabernacle of the congregation, and shall pour out all the blood at the bottom of the altar of the burnt offering which is at the door of the tabernacle of the congregation. And he shall take all his fat from him and burn it upon the altar. And he shall do with the bullock as he did with the bullock for a sin offering, so shall he do with this, and the priest shall make an atonement for them and it shall be forgiven them. And he shall carry forth the bullock without the camp and burn him as he burned the first bullock, it is a sin offering for the congregation.

When a ruler hath sinned, and done somewhat through ignorance against any of the commandments of the Lord his God concerning things which should not be done, and is guilty, or if his sin wherein he hath sinned come to his knowledge, he shall bring his offering, a kid of the goats, a male without blemish, and he shall lay his hand upon the head of the goat and kill it in the place where they kill the burnt offering before the Lord, it is a sin offering. And the priest shall take of the blood of the sin offering with his finger, and put it upon the horns of the altar of burnt offering, and shall pour out his blood at the bottom of the altar of burnt offering. And he shall burn all his fat upon the altar as the fat of the sacrifice of peace offerings, and the priest shall make an atonement for him as concerning his sin, and it shall be forgiven him.

And if any one of the common people sin through ignorance while he doeth somewhat against any of the commandments of the Lord concerning things which ought not to be done, and be guilty, or if his sin which he hath sinned come to his knowledge, then he shall bring his offering, a kid of the goats, a female without blemish, for his sin which he hath sinned. And he shall lay his hand upon the head of the sin offering and slay the sin offering in the place of the burnt offering. And the priest shall take of the blood thereof with his finger, and put it upon the horns of the altar of burnt offering, and shall pour out all the blood thereof at the bottom of the altar. And he shall take away all the fat thereof as the fat is taken away from off the sacrifice of peace offerings, and the priest shall burn it upon the altar for a sweet savour unto the Lord, and the priest shall make an atonement for him, and it shall be forgiven him.

And if he bring a lamb for a sin offering, he shall bring it a female without blemish. And he shall lay his hand upon the head of the sin offering and slay it for a sin offering in the place where they kill the burnt offering. And the priest shall take of the blood of the sin offering with his finger, and put it upon the horns of the altar of burnt offering, and shall pour out all the blood thereof at the bottom of the altar, and he shall take away all the fat thereof as the fat of the lamb is taken away from the sacrifice of the peace offerings, and the priest shall burn them upon the altar according to the offerings made by fire unto the Lord, and the priest shall make an atonement for his sin that he hath committed, and it shall be forgiven him.

And if a soul sin, and hear the voice of swearing and is a witness, whether he hath seen or known of it, if he do not utter it, then he shall bear his iniquity. Or if a soul touch any unclean thing, whether it be a carcass of an unclean beast, or a carcass of unclean cattle, or the carcass of unclean creeping things, and if it be hidden from him, he also shall be unclean and guilty. Or if he touch the uncleanness of man, whatsoever uncleanness it be that a man shall be defiled withal, and it be hid from him, when he knoweth of it, then he shall be guilty. Or if a soul swear, pronouncing with his lips to do evil or to do good, whatsoever it be that a man shall pronounce with an oath, and it be hid from him, when he knoweth of it, then he shall be guilty in one of these. And it shall be, when he shall be guilty in one of these things, that he shall confess that he hath sinned in that thing, and he shall bring his trespass offering unto the Lord for his sin which he hath sinned, a female from the flock, a lamb or a kid of the goats for a sin offering, and the priest shall make an atonement for him concerning his sin.

And if he be not able to bring a lamb, then he shall bring for his trespass which he hath committed two turtle doves or two young pigeons unto the Lord, one for a sin offering and the other for a burnt offering. And he shall bring them unto the priest, who shall offer that which is for the sin offering first, and wring off his head from his neck, but shall not divide it asunder, and he shall sprinkle of the blood of the sin offering upon the side of the altar and the rest of the blood shall be wrung out at the bottom of the altar, it is a sin offering. And he shall offer the second for a burnt offering according to the manner, and the priest shall make an atonement for him for his sin which he hath sinned and it shall be forgiven him.

But if he be not able to bring two turtle doves or two young pigeons, then he that sinned shall bring for his offering the tenth part of an ephah of fine flour for a sin offering, he shall put no oil upon it neither shall he put any frankincense thereon, for it is a sin offering. Then shall he bring it to the priest and the priest shall take his handful of it, even a memorial thereof, and burn it on the altar according to the offerings made by fire unto the Lord, it is a sin offering. And the priest shall make an atonement for him as touching his sin that he hath sinned in one of these and it shall be forgiven him, and the remnant shall be the priest's as a meat offering.

And the Lord spake unto Moses saying, If a soul commit a trespass and sin through ignorance in the holy things of the Lord, then he shall bring for his trespass unto the Lord a ram without blemish out of the flocks with thy estimation by shekels of silver after the shekel of the sanctuary, for a trespass offering, and he shall make amends for the harm that he hath done in the holy thing and shall add the fifth part thereto, and give it unto the priest, and the priest shall make an atonement for him with the ram of the trespass offering, and it shall be forgiven him.

And if a soul sin and commit any of these things which are forbidden to be done by the commandments of the Lord, though he wist it not, yet is he guilty and shall bear his iniquity. And he shall bring a ram without blemish out of the flock with thy estimation, for a trespass offering unto the priest, and the priest shall make an atonement for him concerning his ignorance wherein he erred and wist it not and it shall be forgiven him. It is a trespass offering, he hath certainly trespassed against the Lord.

And the Lord spake unto Moses saying, If a soul sin, and commit a trespass against the Lord, and lie unto his neighbor in that which was delivered him to keep, or in fellowship, or in a thing taken away by violence, or hath deceived his neighbor, or have found that which was lost and lieth concerning it, and sweareth falsely, in any of all these that a man doeth sinning therein, then it shall be because he hath sinned and is guilty, that he shall restore that which he took violently away, or the thing which he hath deceitfully gotten, or that which was delivered him to keep, or the lost thing which he found, or all that about which he hath sworn falsely he shall even restore it in the principal, and shall add the fifth part more thereto, and give it unto him to whom it appertaineth in the day of his trespass offering. And he shall bring his trespass offering unto the Lord, a ram without blemish out of the flock, with thy estimation, for a trespass offering unto the priest, and the priest shall make an atonement for him before the Lord, and it shall be forgiven him for any thing of all that he hath done in trespassing therein.

2 AND the Lord spake unto Moses saying, Command Aaron and his sons, saying, This is the law of the burnt offering, it is the burnt offering because of the burning upon the altar all night unto the morning, and the fire of the altar shall be burning in it. And the priest shall put on his linen garment and his linen breeches shall he put upon his flesh, and take up the ashes which the fire hath consumed with the burnt offering on the altar, and he shall put them beside the altar. And he shall put off his garments and put on other garments and carry forth the ashes without the camp unto a clean place. And the fire upon the altar shall be burning in it–it shall not be put out–and the priest shall burn wood on it every morning, and lay the burnt offering in order upon it, and he shall burn thereon the fat of the peace offerings. The fire shall ever be burning upon the altar; it shall never go out.

And this is the law of the meat offering, the sons of Aaron shall offer it before the Lord before the altar. And he shall take of it his handful, of the flour of the meat offering, and of the oil thereof, and all the frankincense which is upon the meat offering, and shall burn it upon the altar for a sweet savor, even the memorial of it unto the Lord. And the remainder thereof shall Aaron and his sons eat, with unleavened bread shall it be eaten in the holy place, in the court of the tabernacle of the congregation they shall eat it. It shall not be baken with leaven. I have given it unto them for their portion of my offerings made by fire, it is most holy as is the sin offering and as the trespass offering. All the males among the children of Aaron shall eat of it. It shall be a statute for ever in your generations concerning the offerings of the Lord made by fire, everyone that toucheth them shall be holy.

And the Lord spake unto Moses saying, This is the offering of Aaron and of his sons which they shall offer unto the Lord in the day when he is anointed: the tenth part of an ephah of fine flour for a meat offering perpetual, half of it in the morning and half thereof at night. In a pan it shall be made with oil, and when it is baken thou shalt bring it in, and the baken pieces of the meat offering shalt thou offer for a sweet savor unto the Lord. And the priest of his sons that is anointed in his stead shall offer it, it is a statute for ever unto the Lord, it shall be wholly burnt. For every meat offering for the priest shall be wholly burnt; it shall not be eaten.

And the Lord spake unto Moses, saying, Speak unto Aaron and to his sons saying, This is the law of the sin offering: in the place where the burnt offering is killed shall the sin offering be killed before the Lord, it is most holy. The priest that offereth it for sin shall eat it, in the holy place shall it be eaten, in the court of the tabernacle of the congregation. Whatsoever shall touch the flesh thereof shall be holy, and when there is sprinkled of the blood thereof upon any garment, thou shalt wash that whereon it was sprinkled in the holy place. But the earthen vessel wherein it is sodden shall be broken, and if it be sodden in a brazen pot, it shall be both scoured, and rinsed in water. All the males among the priests shall eat thereof, it is most holy. And no sin offering, whereof any of the blood is brought into the tabernacle of the congregation to reconcile withal in the holy place, shall be eaten, it shall be burnt in the fire.

Likewise this is the law of the trespass offering, it is most holy. In the place where they kill the burnt offering shall they kill the trespass offering and the blood thereof shall he sprinkle round about upon the altar. And he shall offer of it all the fat thereof, the rump, and the fat that covereth the inwards. And the two kidneys and the fat that is on them which is by the flanks, and the caul that is above the liver with the kidneys, it shall he take away, and the priest shall burn them upon the altar for an offering made by fire unto the Lord; it is a trespass offering. Every male among the priests shall eat thereof, it shall be eaten in the holy place, it is most holy. As the sin offering is, so is the trespass offering, there is one law for them, the priest that maketh atonement therewith shall have it. And the priest that offereth any man's burnt offering, even the priest shall have to himself the skin of the burnt offering which he hath offered. And all the meat offering that is baken in the oven, and all that is dressed in the frying pan, and in the pan, shall be the priest's that offereth it. And every meat offering, mingled with oil, and dry, shall all the sons of Aaron have, one as much as another.

And this is the law of the sacrifice of peace offerings, which he shall offer unto the Lord. If he offer it for a thanksgiving, then he shall offer with the sacrifice of thanksgiving unleavened cakes mingled with oil, and unleavened wafers anointed with oil, and cakes mingled with oil, of fine flour, fried. Besides the cakes, he shall offer for his offering leavened bread with the sacrifice of thanksgiving of his peace offerings. And of it he shall offer one out of the whole oblation for a heave offering unto the Lord, and it shall be the priest's that sprinkleth the blood of the peace offerings. And the flesh of the sacrifice of his peace offerings for thanksgiving shall be eaten the same day that it is offered, he shall not leave any of it until the morning. But if the sacrifice of his offering be a vow or a voluntary offering, it shall be eaten the same day that he offereth his sacrifice and on the morrow also the remainder of it shall be eaten, but the remainder of the flesh of the sacrifice on the third day shall be burnt with fire. And if any of the flesh of the sacrifice of his peace offerings be eaten at all on the third day, it shall not be accepted, neither shall it be imputed unto him that offereth it, it shall be an abomination and the soul that eateth of it shall bear his iniquity.

And the flesh that toucheth any unclean thing shall not be eaten, it shall be burnt with fire, and as for the flesh, all that be clean shall eat thereof. But the soul that eateth of the flesh of the sacrifice of peace offerings that pertain unto the Lord, having his uncleanness upon him, even that soul shall be cut off from his people. Moreover the soul that shall touch any unclean thing, as the uncleanness of man, or any unclean beast, or any abominable unclean thing, and eat of the flesh of the sacrifice of peace offerings which pertain unto the Lord, even that soul shall be cut off from his people.

And the Lord spake unto Moses saying, Speak unto the children of Israel saying, Ye shall eat no manner of fat, of ox, or of sheep, or of goat. And the fat of the beast that dieth of itself and the fat of that which is torn with beasts may be used in any other use, but ye shall in no wise eat of it. For whosoever eateth the fat of the beast of which men offer an offering made by fire unto the Lord, even the soul that eateth it shall be cut off from his people. Moreover ye shall eat no manner of blood, whether it be of fowl or of beast, in any of your dwellings. Whatsoever soul it be that eateth any manner of blood, even that soul shall be cut off from his people.

And the Lord spake unto Moses saying, Speak unto the children of Israel saying, He that offereth the sacrifice of his peace offerings unto the Lord shall bring his oblation unto the Lord of the sacrifice of his peace offerings. His own hands shall bring the offerings of the Lord made by fire, the fat with the breast, it shall he bring that the breast may be waved for a wave offering before the Lord. And the priest shall burn the fat upon the altar, but the breast shall be Aaron's and his sons'. And the right shoulder shall ye give unto the priest for a heave offering of the sacrifices of your peace offerings. He among the sons of Aaron that offereth the blood of the peace offerings and the fat shall have the right shoulder for his part. For the wave breast and the heave shoulder have I taken of the children of Israel from off the sacrifices of their peace offerings and have given them unto Aaron the priest and unto his sons, by a statute forever, from among the children of Israel. This is the portion of the anointing of Aaron and of the anointing of his sons out of the offerings of the Lord made by fire, in the day when he presented them to minister unto the Lord in the priest's office which the Lord commanded to be given them of the children of Israel, in the day that he anointed them by a statute for ever throughout their generations.

This is the law of the burnt offering, of the meat offering, and of the sin offering, and of the trespass offering, and of the consecrations, and of the sacrifice of the peace offerings which the Lord commanded Moses in mount Sinai in the day that he commanded the children of Israel to offer their oblations unto the Lord, in the wilderness of Sinai.

And the Lord spake unto Moses saying, Take Aaron and his sons with him, and the garments, and the anointing oil, and a bullock for the sin offering, and two rams, and a basket of unleavened bread, and gather thou all the congregation together unto the door of the tabernacle of the congregation. And Moses did as the Lord commanded him and the assembly was gathered together unto the door of the tabernacle of the congregation.

And Moses said unto the congregation, This is the thing which the Lord commanded to be done. And Moses brought Aaron and his sons, and washed them with water. And he put upon him the coat, and girded him with the girdle, and clothed him with the robe, and put the ephod upon him, and he girded him with the curious girdle of the ephod, and bound it unto him therewith. And he put the breastplate upon him, also he put in the breastplate the Urim and the Thummim. And he put the mitre upon his head, also upon the mitre, even upon his forefront, did he put the golden plate, the holy crown, as the Lord commanded Moses.

And Moses took the anointing oil and anointed the tabernacle and all that was therein and sanctified them. And he sprinkled thereof upon the altar seven times and anointed the altar and all his vessels, both the laver and his foot, to sanctify them. And he poured of the anointing oil upon Aaron's head and anointed him to sanctify him. And Moses brought Aaron's sons and put coats upon them, and girded them with girdles, and put bonnets upon them, as the Lord commanded Moses.

And he brought the bullock for the sin offering and Aaron and his sons laid their hands upon the head of the bullock for a sin offering. And he slew it and Moses took the blood and put it upon the horns of the altar round about with his finger, and purified the altar, and poured the blood at the bottom of the altar, and sanctified it to make reconciliation upon it. And he took all the fat that was upon the inwards, and the caul above the liver, and the two kidneys and their fat, and Moses burned it upon the altar. But the bullock and his hide, his flesh and his dung, he burnt with fire without the camp as the Lord commanded Moses.

And he brought the ram for the burnt offering and Aaron and his sons laid their hands upon the head of the ram. And he killed it and Moses sprinkled the blood upon the altar round about. And he cut the ram into pieces and Moses burnt the head, and the pieces, and the fat. And he washed the inwards and the legs in water and Moses burnt the whole ram upon the altar, it was a burnt sacrifice for a sweet savor and an offering made by fire unto the Lord as the Lord commanded Moses.

And he brought the other ram, the ram of consecration, and Aaron and his sons laid their hands upon the head of the ram. And he slew it and Moses took of the blood of it, and put it upon the tip of Aaron's right ear, and upon the thumb of his right hand, and upon the great toe of his right foot. And he brought Aaron's sons and Moses put of the blood upon the tip of their right ear, and upon the thumbs of their right hands, and upon the great toes of their right feet, and Moses sprinkled the blood upon the altar round about. And he took the fat, and the rump, and all the fat that was upon the inwards, and the caul above the liver, and the two kidneys and their fat, and the right shoulder, and out of the basket of unleavened bread that was before the Lord he took one unleavened cake, and a cake of oiled bread, and one wafer, and put them on the fat and upon the right shoulder, and he put all upon Aaron's hands and upon his sons' hands, and waved them for a wave offering before the Lord. And Moses took them from off their hands and burnt them on the altar upon the burnt offering, they were consecrations for a sweet savor, it is an offering made by fire unto the Lord. And Moses took the breast and waved it for a wave offering before the Lord, for of the ram of consecration it was Moses' part as the Lord commanded Moses.

And Moses took of the anointing oil and of the blood which was upon the altar, and sprinkled it upon Aaron, and upon his garments, and upon his sons, and upon his sons' garments with him, and sanctified Aaron, and his garments, and his sons, and his sons' garments with him.

And Moses said unto Aaron and to his sons, Boil the flesh at the door of the tabernacle of the congregation and there eat it with the bread that is in the basket of consecrations as I commanded saying, Aaron and his sons shall eat it. And that which remaineth of the flesh and of the bread shall ye burn with fire. And ye shall not go out of the door of the tabernacle of the congregation in seven days until the days of your consecration be at an end, for seven days shall he consecrate you. As he hath done this day, so the Lord hath commanded to do to make an atonement for you. Therefore shall ye abide at the door of the tabernacle of the congregation day and night seven days and keep the charge of the Lord that ye die not, for so I am commanded. So Aaron and his sons did all things which the Lord commanded by the hand of Moses.

And it came to pass on the eighth day that Moses called Aaron and his sons and the elders of Israel and he said unto Aaron, Take thee a young calf for a sin offering and a ram for a burnt offering, without blemish, and offer them before the Lord. And unto the children of Israel thou shalt speak saying, Take ye a kid of the goats for a sin offering, and a calf and a lamb, both of the first year, without blemish, for a burnt offering. Also a bullock and a ram for peace offerings to sacrifice before the Lord, and a meat offering mingled with oil, for today the Lord will appear unto you. And they brought that which Moses commanded before the tabernacle of the congregation and all the congregation drew near and stood before the Lord. And Moses said, This is the thing which the Lord commanded that ye should do and the glory of the Lord shall appear unto you. And Moses said unto Aaron, Go unto the altar, and offer thy sin offering, and thy burnt offering, and make an atonement for thyself and for the people, and offer the offering of the people and make an atonement for them as the Lord commanded.

Aaron therefore went unto the altar and slew the calf of the sin offering which was for himself. And the sons of Aaron brought the blood unto him, and he dipped his finger in the blood, and put it upon the horns of the altar, and poured out the blood at the bottom of the altar. But the fat, and the kidneys, and the caul above the liver of the sin offering he burnt upon the altar as the Lord commanded Moses. And the flesh and the hide he burnt with fire without the camp.

And he slew the burnt offering and Aaron's sons presented unto him the blood which he sprinkled round about upon the altar. And they presented the burnt offering unto him, with the pieces thereof and the head, and he burnt them upon the altar. And he did wash the inwards and the legs and burnt them upon the burnt offering on the altar.

And he brought the people's offering, and took the goat, which was the sin offering for the people, and slew it, and offered it for sin as the first. And he brought the burnt offering and offered it according to the manner. And he brought the meat offering, and took a handful thereof and burnt it upon the altar, besides the burnt sacrifice of the morning.

He slew also the bullock and the ram for a sacrifice of peace offerings which was for the people, and Aaron's sons presented unto him the blood, which he sprinkled upon the altar round about, and the fat of the bullock and of the ram, the rump, and that which covereth the inwards, and the kidneys, and the caul above the liver, and they put the fat upon the breasts, and he burnt the fat upon the altar, and the breasts and the right shoulder Aaron waved for a wave offering before the Lord as Moses commanded.

And Aaron lifted up his hand toward the people and blessed them and came down from offering of the sin offering, and the burnt offering, and peace offerings. And Moses and Aaron went into the tabernacle of the congregation, and came out and blessed the people, and the glory of the Lord appeared unto all the people. And there came a fire out from before the Lord and consumed upon the altar the burnt offering and the fat which when all the people saw, they shouted and fell on their faces.

And Nadab and Abihu, the sons of Aaron, took either of them his censer, and put fire therein, and put incense thereon, and offered strange fire before the Lord which he commanded them not. And there went out fire from the Lord and devoured them and they died before the Lord. Then Moses said unto Aaron, This is it that the Lord spake saying, I will be sanctified in them that come nigh me and before all the people I will be glorified. And Aaron held his peace.

And Moses called Mishael and Elzaphan, the sons of Uzziel the uncle of Aaron, and said unto them, Come near, carry your brethren from before the sanctuary out of the camp. So they went near and carried them in their coats out of the camp as Moses had said. And Moses said unto Aaron, and unto Eleazar, and unto Ithamar, his sons, Uncover not your heads, neither rend your clothes lest ye die and lest wrath come upon all the people, but let your brethren, the whole house of Israel, bewail the burning which the Lord hath kindled. And ye shall not go out from the door of the tabernacle of the congregation lest ye die, for the anointing oil of the Lord is upon you. And they did according to the word of Moses.

And the Lord spake unto Aaron, saying, Do not drink wine nor strong drink, thou, nor thy sons with thee, when ye go into the tabernacle of the congregation lest ye die, it shall be a statute for ever throughout your generations, and that ye may put difference between holy and unholy, and between unclean and clean, and that ye may teach the children of Israel all the statutes which the Lord hath spoken unto them by the hand of Moses.

And Moses spake unto Aaron, and unto Eleazar and unto Ithamar, his sons that were left, Take the meat offering that remaineth of the offerings of the Lord made by fire and eat it without leaven beside the altar, for it is most holy. And ye shall eat it in the holy place because it is thy due and thy sons' due of the sacrifices of the Lord made by fire, for so I am commanded. And the wave breast and heave shoulder shall ye eat in a clean place, thou and thy sons and thy daughters with thee, for they be thy due and thy sons' due which are given out of the sacrifices of peace offerings of the children of Israel. The heave shoulder and the wave breast shall they bring with the offerings made by fire of the fat to wave it for a wave offering before the Lord, and it shall be thine and thy sons' with thee by a statute forever, as the Lord hath commanded.

And Moses diligently sought the goat of the sin offering and behold, it was burnt, and he was angry with Eleazar and Ithamar, the sons of Aaron which were left alive saying, Wherefore have ye not eaten the sin offering in the holy place, seeing it is most holy, and God hath given it you to bear the iniquity of the congregation to make atonement for them before the Lord? Behold, the blood of it was not brought in within the holy place, ye should indeed have eaten it in the holy place as I commanded. And Aaron said unto Moses, Behold, this day have they offered their sin offering and their burnt offering before the Lord, and such things have befallen me, and if I had eaten the sin offering today, should it have been accepted in the sight of the Lord? And when Moses heard that he was content.

3 AND the Lord spake unto Moses and to Aaron, saying unto them, Speak unto the children of Israel saying, These are the beasts which ye shall eat among all the beasts that are on the Earth. Whatsoever parteth the hoof, and is cloven-footed, and cheweth the cud among the beasts, that shall ye eat. Nevertheless, these shall ye not eat of them that chew the cud, or of them that divide the hoof, as the camel because he cheweth the cud, but divideth not the hoof, he is unclean unto you. And the coney because he cheweth the cud, but divideth not the hoof, he is unclean unto you. And the hare because he cheweth the cud, but divideth not the hoof, he is unclean unto you. And the swine, though he divide the hoof, and be cloven-footed, yet he cheweth not the cud, he is unclean to you. Of their flesh shall ye not eat and their carcass shall ye not touch, they are unclean to you.

These shall ye eat of all that are in the waters, whatsoever hath fins and scales in the waters, in the seas, and in the rivers, them shall ye eat. And all that have not fins and scales in the seas, and in the rivers, of all that move in the waters, and of any living thing which is in the waters, they shall be an abomination unto you, they shall be even an abomination unto you, ye shall not eat of their flesh, but ye shall have their carcasses in abomination. Whatsoever hath no fins nor scales in the waters, that shall be an abomination unto you.

And these are they which ye shall have in abomination among the fowls, they shall not be eaten, they are an abomination: the eagle, and the ossifrage, and the ospray, and the vulture, and the kite after his kind, every raven after his kind, and the owl, and the nighthawk, and the cuckoo, and the hawk after his kind, and the little owl, and the cormorant, and the great owl, and the swan, and the pelican, and the gier eagle, and the stork, the heron after her kind, and the lapwing, and the bat.

All fowls that creep, going upon all four, shall be an abomination unto you. Yet these may ye eat of every flying creeping thing that goeth upon all four, which have legs above their feet, to leap withal upon the Earth, even these of them ye may eat: the locust after his kind, and the bald locust after his kind, and the beetle after his kind, and the grasshopper after his kind. But all other flying creeping things, which have four feet, shall be an abomination unto you.

And for these ye shall be unclean, whosoever toucheth the carcass of them shall be unclean until the even. And whosoever beareth aught of the carcass of them shall wash his clothes, and be unclean until the even. The carcasses of every beast which divideth the hoof, and is not cloven-footed nor cheweth the cud, are unclean unto you, everyone that toucheth them shall be unclean. And whatsoever goeth upon his paws, among all manner of beasts that go on all four, those are unclean unto you, whoso toucheth their carcass shall be unclean until the even. And he that beareth the carcass of them shall wash his clothes and be unclean until the even, they are unclean unto you.

These also shall be unclean unto you among the creeping things that creep upon the Earth, the weasel, and the mouse, and the tortoise after his kind, and the ferret, and the chameleon, and the lizard, and the snail, and the mole. These are unclean to you among all that creep, whosoever doth touch them when they be dead shall be unclean until the even. And upon whatsoever any of them when they are dead doth fall, it shall be unclean, whether it be any vessel of wood, or raiment, or skin, or sack, whatsoever vessel it be wherein any work is done, it must be put into water and it shall be unclean until the even, so it shall be cleansed. And every earthen vessel, whereinto any of them falleth, whatsoever is in it shall be unclean, and ye shall break it. Of all meat which may be eaten, that on which such water cometh shall be unclean, and all drink that may be drunk in every such vessel shall be unclean. And everything whereupon any part of their carcass falleth shall be unclean, whether it be oven, or ranges for pots, they shall be broken down, for they are unclean, and shall be unclean unto you. Nevertheless a fountain or pit wherein there is plenty of water shall be clean, but that which toucheth their carcass shall be unclean. And if any part of their carcass fall upon any sowing seed which is to be sown, it shall be clean. But if any water be put upon the seed, and any part of their carcass fall thereon, it shall be unclean unto you.

And if any beast of which ye may eat die, he that toucheth the carcass thereof shall be unclean until the even. And he that eateth of the carcass of it shall wash his clothes and be unclean until the even, he also that beareth the carcass of it shall wash his clothes and be unclean until the even

And every creeping thing that creepeth upon the Earth shall be an abomination, it shall not be eaten. Whatsoever goeth upon the belly, and whatsoever goeth upon all four, or whatsoever hath more feet among all creeping things that creep upon the Earth, them ye shall not eat for they are an abomination. Ye shall not make yourselves abominable with any creeping thing that creepeth, neither shall ye make yourselves unclean with them that ye should be defiled thereby. For I am the Lord your God, ye shall therefore sanctify yourselves and ye shall be holy, for I am holy, neither shall ye defile yourselves with any manner of creeping thing that creepeth upon the Earth. For I am the Lord that bringeth you up out of the land of Egypt, to be your God, ye shall therefore be holy, for I am holy.

This is the law of the beasts, and of the fowl, and of every living creature that moveth in the waters, and of every creature that creepeth upon the Earth, to make a difference between the unclean and the clean, and between the beast that may be eaten and the beast that may not be eaten.

4 AND the Lord spake unto Moses saying, Speak unto the children of Israel saying, If a woman have conceived seed and borne a man child, then she shall be unclean seven days, according to the days of the separation for her infirmity shall she be unclean. And in the eighth day the man child shall be circumcised. And she shall then continue in the time of her purifying which shall be three and thirty days, she shall touch no hallowed thing nor come into the sanctuary until the days of her purifying be fulfilled. But if she bear a maid child, she shall be unclean two weeks as in her separation, and she shall continue in the time of her purifying threescore and six days.

And when the days of her purifying are fulfilled, for a son or for a daughter, she shall bring a lamb of the first year for a burnt offering, and a young pigeon or a turtle dove for a sin offering, unto the door of the tabernacle of the congregation, unto the priest who shall offer it before the Lord, and make an atonement for her, and she shall be cleansed from the issue of her blood. This is the law for her that hath borne a male or a female. And if she be not able to bring a lamb, then she shall bring two turtles or two young pigeons, the one for the burnt offering and the other for a sin offering, and the priest shall make an atonement for her and she shall be clean.

And the Lord spake unto Moses and Aaron saying, When a man shall have in the skin of his flesh a rising, a scab, or bright spot, and it be in the skin of his flesh like the plague of leprosy, then he shall be brought unto Aaron the priest or unto one of his sons the priests, and the priest shall look on the plague in the skin of the flesh, and when the hair in the plague is turned white, and the plague in sight be deeper than the skin of his flesh, it is a plague of leprosy, and the priest shall look on him and pronounce him unclean. If the bright spot be white in the skin of his flesh, and in sight be not deeper than the skin, and the hair thereof be not turned white, then the priest shall shut up him that hath the plague seven days, and the priest shall look on him the seventh day and behold, if the plague in his sight be at a stay and the plague spread not in the skin, then the priest shall shut him up seven days more, and the priest shall look on him again the seventh day and behold, if the plague be somewhat dark and the plague spread not in the skin, the priest shall pronounce him clean, it is but a scab and he shall wash his clothes and be clean. But if the scab spread much abroad in the skin, after that he hath been seen of the priest for his cleansing, he shall be seen of the priest again, and if the priest see that, behold, the scab spreadeth in the skin, then the priest shall pronounce him unclean, it is a leprosy.

When the plague of leprosy is in a man, then he shall be brought unto the priest, and the priest shall see him and behold, if the rising be white in the skin, and it have turned the hair white, and there be quick raw flesh in the rising, it is an old leprosy in the skin of his flesh, and the priest shall pronounce him unclean, and shall not shut him up, for he is unclean. And if a leprosy break out abroad in the skin, and the leprosy cover all the skin of him that hath the plague from his head even to his foot wheresoever the priest looketh, then the priest shall consider and behold, if the leprosy have covered all his flesh, he shall pronounce him clean that hath the plague, it is all turned white, he is clean. But when raw flesh appeareth in him, he shall be unclean. And the priest shall see the raw flesh, and pronounce him to be unclean, for the raw flesh is unclean, it is a leprosy. Or if the raw flesh turn again, and be changed unto white, he shall come unto the priest, and the priest shall see him and behold, if the plague be turned into white, then the priest shall pronounce him clean that hath the plague, he is clean.

The flesh also in which, even in the skin thereof, was a boil and is healed, and in the place of the boil there be a white rising, or a bright spot, white and somewhat reddish, and it be showed to the priest, and if, when the priest seeth it, behold, it be in sight lower than the skin, and the hair thereof be turned white, the priest shall pronounce him unclean, it is a plague of leprosy broken out of the boil. But if the priest look on it and behold, there be no white hairs therein, and if it be not lower than the skin, but be somewhat dark, then the priest shall shut him up seven days, and if it spread much abroad in the skin, then the priest shall pronounce him unclean, it is a plague. But if the bright spot stay in his place and spread not, it is a burning boil, and the priest shall pronounce him clean.

Or if there be any flesh, in the skin whereof there is a hot burning, and the quick flesh that burneth have a white bright spot, somewhat reddish or white, then the priest shall look upon it and behold, if the hair in the bright spot be turned white, and it be in sight deeper than the skin, it is a leprosy broken out of the burning, wherefore the priest shall pronounce him unclean, it is the plague of leprosy. But if the priest look on it and behold, there be no white hair in the bright spot and it be no lower than the other skin, but be somewhat dark, then the priest shall shut him up seven days, and the priest shall look upon him the seventh day, and if it be spread much abroad in the skin, then the priest shall pronounce him unclean, it is the plague of leprosy. And if the bright spot stay in his place and spread not in the skin, but it be somewhat dark, it is a rising of the burning, and the priest shall pronounce him clean, for it is an inflammation of the burning.

If a man or woman have a plague upon the head or the beard, then the priest shall see the plague and behold, if it be in sight deeper than the skin, and there be in it a yellow thin hair, then the priest shall pronounce him unclean, it is a dry scall, even a leprosy upon the head or beard. And if the priest look on the plague of the scall and behold, it be not in sight deeper than the skin and that there is no black hair in it, then the priest shall shut up him that hath the plague of the scall seven days, and in the seventh day the priest shall look on the plague and behold, if the scall spread not, and there be in it no yellow hair, and the scall be not in sight deeper than the skin, he shall be shaven, but the scall shall he not shave, and the priest shall shut up him that hath the scall seven days more, and in the seventh day the priest shall look on the scall and behold, if the scall be not spread in the skin nor be in sight deeper than the skin, then the priest shall pronounce him clean, and he shall wash his clothes and be clean. But if the scall spread much in the skin after his cleansing, then the priest shall look on him and behold, if the scall be spread in the skin, the priest shall not seek for yellow hair, he is unclean. But if the scall be in his sight at a stay, and that there is black hair grown up therein, the scall is healed, he is clean and the priest shall pronounce him clean.

If a man also or a woman have in the skin of their flesh bright spots, even white bright spots, then the priest shall look and behold, if the bright spots in the skin of their flesh be darkish white, it is a freckled spot that groweth in the skin, he is clean.

And the man whose hair is fallen off his head, he is bald, yet is he clean. And he that hath his hair fallen off from the part of his head toward his face, he is forehead bald, yet is he clean. And if there be in the bald head or bald forehead a white reddish sore, it is a leprosy sprung up in his bald head, or his bald forehead. Then the priest shall look upon it and behold, if the rising of the sore be white reddish in his bald head or in his bald forehead as the leprosy appeareth in the skin of the flesh, he is a leprous man, he is unclean, the priest shall pronounce him utterly unclean, his plague is in his head.

And the leper in whom the plague is, his clothes shall be rent, and his head bare, and he shall put a covering upon his upper lip, and shall cry, Unclean, unclean. All the days wherein the plague shall be in him he shall be defiled, he is unclean, he shall dwell alone, without the camp shall his habitation be.

The garment also that the plague of leprosy is in, whether it be a woollen garment, or a linen garment, whether it be in the warp or woof of linen, or of woollen, whether in a skin, or in any thing made of skin, and if the plague be greenish or reddish in the garment, or in the skin, either in the warp, or in the woof, or in any thing of skin, it is a plague of leprosy, and shall be showed unto the priest, and the priest shall look upon the plague, and shut up it that hath the plague seven days, and he shall look on the plague on the seventh day, if the plague be spread in the garment, either in the warp, or in the woof, or in a skin, or in any work that is made of skin, the plague is a fretting leprosy, it is unclean. He shall therefore burn that garment, whether warp or woof, in woollen or in linen, or anything of skin, wherein the plague is, for it is a fretting leprosy, it shall be burnt in the fire.

And if the priest shall look and behold, the plague be not spread in the garment, either in the warp, or in the woof, or in anything of skin, then the priest shall command that they wash the thing wherein the plague is, and he shall shut it up seven days more, and the priest shall look on the plague, after that it is washed and behold, if the plague have not changed his color, and the plague be not spread, it is unclean, thou shalt burn it in the fire, it is fret inward, whether it be bare within or without.

And if the priest look and behold, the plague be somewhat dark after the washing of it, then he shall rend it out of the garment, or out of the skin, or out of the warp, or out of the woof, and if it appear still in the garment, either in the warp, or in the woof, or in any thing of skin, it is a spreading plague, thou shalt burn that wherein the plague is with fire. And the garment, either warp, or woof, or whatsoever thing of skin it be, which thou shalt wash, if the plague be departed from them, then it shall be washed the second time and shall be clean.

This is the law of the plague of leprosy in a garment of woollen or linen, either in the warp, or woof, or any thing of skins, to pronounce it clean, or to pronounce it unclean.

And the Lord spake unto Moses saying, This shall be the law of the leper in the day of his cleansing, he shall be brought unto the priest, and the priest shall go forth out of the camp, and the priest shall look and behold, if the plague of leprosy be healed in the leper, then shall the priest command to take for him that is to be cleansed two birds alive and clean, and cedar wood, and scarlet, and hyssop, and the priest shall command that one of the birds be killed in an earthen vessel over running water. As for the living bird, he shall take it, and the cedar wood, and the scarlet, and the hyssop, and shall dip them and the living bird in the blood of the bird that was killed over the running water, and he shall sprinkle upon him that is to be cleansed from the leprosy seven times, and shall pronounce him clean, and shall let the living bird loose into the open field. And he that is to be cleansed shall wash his clothes, and shave off all his hair, and wash himself in water that he may be clean, and after that he shall come into the camp and shall tarry abroad out of his tent seven days. But it shall be on the seventh day,that he shall shave all his hair off his head and his beard and his eyebrows, even all his hair he shall shave off, and he shall wash his clothes, also he shall wash his flesh in water, and he shall be clean.

And on the eighth day he shall take two he lambs without blemish, and one ewe lamb of the first year without blemish, and three tenth deals of fine flour for a meat offering, mingled with oil, and one log of oil, and the priest that maketh him clean shall present the man that is to be made clean, and those things, before the Lord, at the door of the tabernacle of the congregation. And the priest shall take one he lamb and offer him for a trespass offering, and the log of oil, and wave them for a wave offering before the Lord, and he shall slay the lamb in the place where he shall kill the sin offering and the burnt offering, in the holy place, for as the sin offering is the priest's, so is the trespass offering, it is most holy, and the priest shall take some of the blood of the trespass offering and the priest shall put it upon the tip of the right ear of him that is to be cleansed, and upon the thumb of his right hand, and upon the great toe of his right foot. And the priest shall take some of the log of oil, and pour it into the palm of his own left hand, and the priest shall dip his right finger in the oil that is in his left hand, and shall sprinkle of the oil with his finger seven times before the Lord, and of the rest of the oil that is in his hand shall the priest put upon the tip of the right ear of him that is to be cleansed, and upon the thumb of his right hand, and upon the great toe of his right foot, upon the blood of the trespass offering, and the remnant of the oil that is in the priest's hand he shall pour upon the head of him that is to be cleansed, and the priest shall make an atonement for him before the Lord. And the priest shall offer the sin offering and make an atonement for him that is to be cleansed from his uncleanness, and afterward he shall kill the burnt offering, and the priest shall offer the burnt offering and the meat offering upon the altar, and the priest shall make an atonement for him, and he shall be clean.

And if he be poor, and cannot get so much, then he shall take one lamb for a trespass offering to be waved, to make an atonement for him, and one tenth deal of fine flour mingled with oil for a meat offering, and a log of oil, and two turtle doves or two young pigeons, such as he is able to get, and the one shall be a sin offering, and the other a burnt offering. And he shall bring them on the eighth day for his cleansing unto the priest, unto the door of the tabernacle of the congregation, before the Lord. And the priest shall take the lamb of the trespass offering, and the log of oil, and the priest shall wave them for a wave offering before the Lord, and he shall kill the lamb of the trespass offering, and the priest shall take some of the blood of the trespass offering, and put it upon the tip of the right ear of him that is to be cleansed, and upon the thumb of his right hand, and upon the great toe of his right foot. And the priest shall pour of the oil into the palm of his own left hand, and the priest shall sprinkle with his right finger some of the oil that is in his left hand seven times before the Lord, and the priest shall put of the oil that is in his hand upon the tip of the right ear of him that is to be cleansed, and upon the thumb of his right hand, and upon the great toe of his right foot, upon the place of the blood of the trespass offering, and the rest of the oil that is in the priest's hand he shall put upon the head of him that is to be cleansed, to make an atonement for him before the Lord. And he shall offer the one of the turtle doves, or of the young pigeons, such as he can get, even such as he is able to get, the one for a sin offering, and the other for a burnt offering, with the meat offering, and the priest shall make an atonement for him that is to be cleansed before the Lord. This is the law of him in whom is the plague of leprosy, whose hand is not able to get that which pertaineth to his cleansing.

And the Lord spake unto Moses and unto Aaron saying, When ye be come into the land of Canaan, which I give to you for a possession, and I put the plague of leprosy in a house of the land of your possession, and he that owneth the house shall come and tell the priest, saying, It seemeth to me there is as it were a plague in the house, then the priest shall command that they empty the house, before the priest go into it to see the plague, that all that is in the house be not made unclean, and afterward the priest shall go in to see the house, and he shall look on the plague and behold, if the plague be in the walls of the house with hollow streaks, greenish or reddish, which in sight are lower than the wall, then the priest shall go out of the house to the door of the house, and shut up the house seven days, and the priest shall come again the seventh day, and shall look and behold, if the plague be spread in the walls of the house, then the priest shall command that they take away the stones in which the plague is, and they shall cast them into an unclean place without the city, and he shall cause the house to be scraped within round about, and they shall pour out the dust that they scrape off without the city into an unclean place, and they shall take other stones, and put them in the place of those stones, and he shall take other mortar, and shall plaster the house.

And if the plague come again, and break out in the house, after that he hath taken away the stones, and after he hath scraped the house, and after it is plastered, then the priest shall come and look and behold, if the plague be spread in the house, it is a fretting leprosy in the house, it is unclean. And he shall break down the house, the stones of it, and the timber thereof, and all the mortar of the house, and he shall carry them forth out of the city into an unclean place. Moreover, he that goeth into the house all the while that it is shut up shall be unclean until the even. And he that lieth in the house shall wash his clothes, and he that eateth in the house shall wash his clothes.

And if the priest shall come in, and look upon it and behold, the plague hath not spread in the house, after the house was plastered, then the priest shall pronounce the house clean, because the plague is healed. And he shall take to cleanse the house two birds, and cedar wood, and scarlet, and hyssop, and he shall kill the one of the birds in an earthen vessel over running water, and he shall take the cedar wood, and the hyssop, and the scarlet, and the living bird, and dip them in the blood of the slain bird, and in the running water, and sprinkle the house seven times, and he shall cleanse the house with the blood of the bird, and with the running water, and with the living bird, and with the cedar wood, and with the hyssop, and with the scarlet, but he shall let go the living bird out of the city into the open fields, and make an atonement for the house, and it shall be clean.

This is the law for all manner of plague of leprosy, and scall, and for the leprosy of a garment, and of a house, and for a rising, and for a scab, and for a bright spot, to teach when it is unclean, and when it is clean, this is the law of leprosy.

5 AND the Lord spake unto Moses and to Aaron saying, Speak unto the children of Israel, and say unto them, When any man hath a running issue out of his flesh, because of his issue he is unclean. And this shall be his uncleanness in his issue, whether his flesh run with his issue, or his flesh be stopped from his issue, it is his uncleanness. Every bed whereon he lieth that hath the issue, is unclean, and everything, whereon he sitteth, shall be unclean. And whosoever toucheth his bed shall wash his clothes, and bathe himself in water, and be unclean until the even. And he that sitteth on anything whereon he sat that hath the issue shall wash his clothes, and bathe himself in water, and be unclean until the even. And he that toucheth the flesh of him that hath the issue shall wash his clothes, and bathe himself in water, and be unclean until the even. And if he that hath the issue spit upon him that is clean, then he shall wash his clothes, and bathe himself in water, and be unclean until the even. And what saddle soever he rideth upon that hath the issue shall be unclean. And whosoever toucheth anything that was under him shall be unclean until the even, and he that beareth any of those things shall wash his clothes, and bathe himself in water, and be unclean until the even. And whomsoever he toucheth that hath the issue, and hath not rinsed his hands in water, he shall wash his clothes, and bathe himself in water, and be unclean until the even. And the vessel of earth that he toucheth which hath the issue, shall be broken, and every vessel of wood shall be rinsed in water.

And when he that hath an issue is cleansed of his issue, then he shall number to himself seven days for his cleansing, and wash his clothes, and bathe his flesh in running water, and shall be clean. And on the eighth day he shall take to him two turtle doves, or two young pigeons, and come before the Lord unto the door of the tabernacle of the congregation, and give them unto the priest, and the priest shall offer them, the one for a sin offering and the other for a burnt offering, and the priest shall make an atonement for him before the Lord for his issue.

And if any man's seed of copulation go out of him, then he shall wash all his flesh in water, and be unclean until the even. And every garment, and every skin, whereon is the seed of copulation, shall be washed with water, and be unclean until the even. The woman also with whom man shall lie with seed of copulation, they shall both bathe themselves in water and be unclean until the even.

And if a woman have an issue, and her issue in her flesh be blood, she shall be put apart seven days, and whosoever toucheth her shall be unclean until the even. And everything that she lieth upon in her separation shall be unclean, everything also that she sitteth upon shall be unclean. And whosoever toucheth her bed shall wash his clothes, and bathe himself in water, and be unclean until the even. And whosoever toucheth anything that she sat upon shall wash his clothes, and bathe himself in water, and be unclean until the even. And if it be on her bed, or on anything whereon she sitteth, when he toucheth it, he shall be unclean until the even. And if any man lie with her at all, and her flowers be upon him, he shall be unclean seven days, and all the bed whereon he lieth shall be unclean.

And if a woman have an issue of her blood many days out of the time of her separation, or if it run beyond the time of her separation, all the days of the issue of her uncleanness shall be as the days of her separation, she shall be unclean. Every bed whereon she lieth all the days of her issue shall be unto her as the bed of her separation, and whatsoever she sitteth upon shall be unclean, as the uncleanness of her separation. And whosoever toucheth those things shall be unclean, and shall wash his clothes, and bathe himself in water, and be unclean until the even. But if she be cleansed of her issue, then she shall number to herself seven days, and after that she shall be clean. And on the eighth day she shall take unto her two turtles, or two young pigeons, and bring them unto the priest, to the door of the tabernacle of the congregation. And the priest shall offer the one for a sin offering and the other for a burnt offering, and the priest shall make an atonement for her before the Lord for the issue of her uncleanness.

Thus shall ye separate the children of Israel from their uncleanness, that they die not in their uncleanness, when they defile my tabernacle that is among them. This is the law of him that hath an issue, and of him whose seed goeth from him and is defiled therewith, and of her that is sick of her flowers, and of him that hath an issue, of the man, and of the woman, and of him that lieth with her that is unclean.

6 AND the Lord spake unto Moses after the death of the two sons of Aaron, when they offered before the Lord and died, and the Lord said unto Moses, Speak unto Aaron thy brother, that he come not at all times into the holy place within the veil before the mercy seat which is upon the ark, that he die not, for I will appear in the cloud upon the mercy seat. Thus shall Aaron come into the holy place with a young bullock for a sin offering and a ram for a burnt offering. He shall put on the holy linen coat, and he shall have the linen breeches upon his flesh, and shall be girded with a linen girdle, and with the linen mitre shall he be attired, these are holy garments, therefore shall he wash his flesh in water and so put them on. And he shall take of the congregation of the children of Israel two kids of the goats for a sin offering and one ram for a burnt offering.

And Aaron shall offer his bullock of the sin offering which is for himself, and make an atonement for himself and for his house. And he shall take the two goats, and present them before the Lord at the door of the tabernacle of the congregation. And Aaron shall cast lots upon the two goats, one lot for the Lord and the other lot for the scapegoat. And Aaron shall bring the goat upon which the Lord's lot fell and offer him for a sin offering. But the goat on which the lot fell to be the scapegoat shall be presented alive before the Lord, to make an atonement with him and to let him go for a scapegoat into the wilderness.

And Aaron shall bring the bullock of the sin offering which is for himself, and shall make an atonement for himself and for his house, and shall kill the bullock of the sin offering which is for himself, and he shall take a censer full of burning coals of fire from off the altar before the Lord, and his hands full of sweet incense beaten small, and bring it within the veil, and he shall put the incense upon the fire before the Lord, that the cloud of the incense may cover the mercy seat that is upon the testimony that he die not, and he shall take of the blood of the bullock, and sprinkle it with his finger upon the mercy seat eastward, and before the mercy seat shall he sprinkle of the blood with his finger seven times.

Then shall he kill the goat of the sin offering, that is for the people, and bring his blood within the veil, and do with that blood as he did with the blood of the bullock, and sprinkle it upon the mercy seat, and before the mercy seat, and he shall make an atonement for the holy place, because of the uncleanness of the children of Israel, and because of their transgressions in all their sins, and so shall he do for the tabernacle of the congregation that remaineth among them in the midst of their uncleanness. And there shall be no man in the tabernacle of the congregation when he goeth in to make an atonement in the holy place until he come out, and have made an atonement for himself, and for his household, and for all the congregation of Israel. And he shall go out unto the altar that is before the Lord, and make an atonement for it, and shall take of the blood of the bullock and of the blood of the goat, and put it upon the horns of the altar round about. And he shall sprinkle of the blood upon it with his finger seven times, and cleanse it, and hallow it from the uncleanness of the children of Israel.

And when he hath made an end of reconciling the holy place, and the tabernacle of the congregation, and the altar, he shall bring the live goat, and Aaron shall lay both his hands upon the head of the live goat, and confess over him all the iniquities of the children of Israel, and all their transgressions in all their sins, putting them upon the head of the goat, and shall send him away by the hand of a fit man into the wilderness, and the goat shall bear upon him all their iniquities unto a land not inhabited, and he shall let go the goat in the wilderness.

And Aaron shall come into the tabernacle of the congregation, and shall put off the linen garments which he put on when he went into the holy place and shall leave them there, and he shall wash his flesh with water in the holy place, and put on his garments, and come forth, and offer his burnt offering, and the burnt offering of the people, and make an atonement for himself and for the people. And the fat of the sin offering shall he burn upon the altar. And he that let go the goat for the scapegoat shall wash his clothes, and bathe his flesh in water, and afterward come into the camp. And the bullock for the sin offering, and the goat for the sin offering, whose blood was brought in to make atonement in the holy place, shall one carry forth without the camp, and they shall burn in the fire their skins, and their flesh, and their dung. And he that burneth them shall wash his clothes, and bathe his flesh in water, and afterward he shall come into the camp.

And this shall be a statute for ever unto you, that in the seventh month on the tenth day of the month, ye shall afflict your souls and do no work at all, whether it be one of your own country or a stranger that sojourneth among you, for on that day shall the priest make an atonement for you, to cleanse you that ye may be clean from all your sins before the Lord, it shall be a sabbath of rest unto you, and ye shall afflict your souls, by a statute forever. And the priest, whom he shall anoint and whom he shall consecrate to minister in the priest's office in his father's stead, shall make the atonement and shall put on the linen clothes, even the holy garments, and he shall make an atonement for the holy sanctuary, and he shall make an atonement for the tabernacle of the congregation and for the altar, and he shall make an atonement for the priests and for all the people of the congregation. And this shall be an everlasting statute unto you, to make an atonement for the children of Israel for all their sins once a year. And he did as the Lord commanded Moses.

7 AND the Lord spake unto Moses saying, Speak unto Aaron, and unto his sons, and unto all the children of Israel, and say unto them, This is the thing which the Lord hath commanded saying, What man soever there be of the house of Israel, that killeth an ox, or lamb, or goat, in the camp, or that killeth it out of the camp, and bringeth it not into the door of the tabernacle of the congregation, to offer an offering unto the Lord before the tabernacle of the Lord, blood shall be imputed unto that man, he hath shed blood, and that man shall be cut off from among his people, to the end that the children of Israel may bring their sacrifices, which they offer in the open field, even that they may bring them unto the Lord, unto the door of the tabernacle of the congregation, unto the priest, and offer them for peace offering unto the Lord. And the priest shall sprinkle the blood upon the altar of the Lord at the door of the tabernacle of the congregation, and burn the fat for a sweet savor unto the Lord. And they shall no more offer their sacrifices unto devils after whom they have gone a whoring. This shall be a statute for ever unto them throughout their generations.

And thou shalt say unto them, Whatsoever man there be of the house of Israel or of the strangers which sojourn among you, that offereth a burnt offering or sacrifice and bringeth it not unto the door of the tabernacle of the congregation to offer it unto the Lord, even that man shall be cut off from among his people.

And whatsoever man there be of the house of Israel or of the strangers that sojourn among you that eateth any manner of blood, I will even set my face against that soul that eateth blood and will cut him off from among his people. For the life of the flesh is in the blood, and I have given it to you upon the altar to make an atonement for your souls, for it is the blood that maketh an atonement for the soul. Therefore I said unto the children of Israel, No soul of you shall eat blood, neither shall any stranger that sojourneth among you eat blood.

And whatsoever man there be of the children of Israel or of the strangers that sojourn among you which hunteth and catcheth any beast or fowl that may be eaten, he shall even pour out the blood thereof and cover it with dust. For it is the life of all flesh, the blood of it is for the life thereof, therefore I said unto the children of Israel, Ye shall eat the blood of no manner of flesh, for the life of all flesh is the blood thereof, whosoever eateth it shall be cut off. And every soul that eateth that which died of itself or that which was torn with beasts, whether it be one of your own country or a stranger, he shall both wash his clothes, and bathe himself in water, and be unclean until the even, then shall he be clean. But if he wash them not, nor bathe his flesh, then he shall bear his iniquity.

And the Lord spake unto Moses saying, Speak unto the children of Israel and say unto them, I am the Lord your God. After the doings of the land of Egypt wherein ye dwelt, shall ye not do, and after the doings of the land of Canaan whither I bring you, shall ye not do, neither shall ye walk in their ordinances. Ye shall do my judgments and keep mine ordinances, to walk therein, I am the Lord your God. Ye shall therefore keep my statutes and my judgments, which if a man do, he shall live in them, I am the Lord.

8 NONE of you shall approach to any that is near of kin to him to uncover their nakedness, I am the Lord. The nakedness of thy father or the nakedness of thy mother shalt thou not uncover, she is thy mother, thou shalt not uncover her nakedness. The nakedness of thy father's wife shalt thou not uncover, it is thy father's nakedness. The nakedness of thy sister, the daughter of thy father, or daughter of thy mother, whether she be born at home or born abroad, even their nakedness thou shalt not uncover. The nakedness of thy son's daughter, or of thy daughter's daughter, even their nakedness thou shalt not uncover, for theirs is thine own nakedness. The nakedness of thy father's wife's daughter, begotten of thy father, she is thy sister, thou shalt not uncover her nakedness. Thou shalt not uncover the nakedness of thy father's sister, she is thy father's near kinswoman. Thou shalt not uncover the nakedness of thy mother's sister, for she is thy mother's near kinswoman. Thou shalt not uncover the nakedness of thy father's brother, thou shalt not approach to his wife, she is thine aunt. Thou shalt not uncover the nakedness of thy daughter-in-law, she is thy son's wife, thou shalt not uncover her nakedness. Thou shalt not uncover the nakedness of thy brother's wife, it is thy brother's nakedness. Thou shalt not uncover the nakedness of a woman and her daughter, neither shalt thou take her son's daughter, or her daughter's daughter, to uncover her nakedness, for they are her near kinswomen, it is wickedness. Neither shalt thou take a wife to her sister, to vex her, to uncover her nakedness, besides the other in her lifetime.

Also thou shalt not approach unto a woman to uncover her nakedness, as long as she is put apart for her uncleanness, moreover thou shalt not lie carnally with thy neighbor's wife, to defile thyself with her. And thou shalt not let any of thy seed pass through the fire to Molech, neither shalt thou profane the name of thy God, I am the Lord. Thou shalt not lie with mankind, as with womankind, it is abomination. Neither shalt thou lie with any beast to defile thyself therewith, neither shall any woman stand before a beast to lie down thereto, it is confusion.

Defile not ye yourselves in any of these things, for in all these the nations are defiled which I cast out before you, and the land is defiled, therefore I do visit the iniquity thereof upon it, and the land itself vomiteth out her inhabitants. Ye shall therefore keep my statutes and my judgments, and shall not commit any of these abominations, neither any of your own nation, nor any stranger that sojourneth among you, (for all these abominations have the men of the land done, which were before you, and the land is defiled), that the land spew not you out also when ye defile it as it spewed out the nations that were before you. For whosoever shall commit any of these abominations, even the souls that commit them shall be cut off from among their people. Therefore shall ye keep mine ordinance, that ye commit not any one of these abominable customs which were committed before you, and that ye defile not yourselves therein, I am the Lord your God.

9 AND the Lord spake unto Moses saying, Speak unto all the congregation of the children of Israel and say unto them, Ye shall be holy, for I the Lord your God am holy. Ye shall fear every man his mother, and his father, and keep my sabbaths, I am the Lord your God. Turn ye not unto idols nor make to yourselves molten gods, I am the Lord your God.

And if ye offer a sacrifice of peace offerings unto the Lord ye shall offer it at your own will. It shall be eaten the same day ye offer it, and on the morrow, and if aught remain until the third day, it shall be burnt in the fire. And if it be eaten at all on the third day, it is abominable, it shall not be accepted. Therefore everyone that eateth it shall bear his iniquity because he hath profaned the hallowed thing of the Lord, and that soul shall be cut off from among his people.

And when ye reap the harvest of your land, thou shalt not wholly reap the corners of thy field, neither shalt thou gather the gleanings of thy harvest. And thou shalt not glean thy vineyard, neither shalt thou gather every grape of thy vineyard, thou shalt leave them for the poor and stranger, I am the Lord your God.

Ye shall not steal, neither deal falsely, neither lie one to another. And ye shall not swear by my name falsely, neither shalt thou profane the name of thy God, I am the Lord.

Thou shalt not defraud thy neighbor, neither rob him, the wages of him that is hired shall not abide with thee all night until the morning. Thou shalt not curse the deaf, nor put a stumbling block before the blind, but shall fear thy God, I am the Lord.

Ye shall do no unrighteousness in judgment, thou shalt not respect the person of the poor, nor honor the person of the mighty, but in righteousness shalt thou judge thy neighbor. Thou shalt not go up and down as a talebearer among thy people, neither shalt thou stand against the blood of thy neighbor, I am the Lord.

Thou shalt not hate thy brother in thine heart, thou shalt in any wise rebuke thy neighbor and not suffer sin upon him. Thou shalt not avenge nor bear any grudge against the children of thy people, but thou shalt love thy neighbor as thyself, I am the Lord.

Ye shall keep my statutes. Thou shalt not let thy cattle gender with a diverse kind, thou shalt not sow thy field with mingled seed, neither shall a garment mingled of linen and woollen come upon thee.

And whosoever lieth carnally with a woman that is a bondmaid betrothed to a husband, and not at all redeemed, nor freedom given her, she shall be scourged, they shall not be put to death, because she was not free. And he shall bring his trespass offering unto the Lord, unto the door of the tabernacle of the congregation, even a ram for a trespass offering. And the priest shall make an atonement for him with the ram of the trespass offering before the Lord for his sin which he hath done, and the sin which he hath done shall be forgiven him.

And when ye shall come into the land and shall have planted all manner of trees for food, then ye shall count the fruit thereof as uncircumcised, three years shall it be as uncircumcised unto you, it shall not be eaten of. But in the fourth year all the fruit thereof shall be holy to praise the Lord withal. And in the fifth year shall ye eat of the fruit thereof, that it may yield unto you the increase thereof, I am the Lord your God.

Ye shall not eat anything with the blood, neither shall ye use enchantment, nor observe times. Ye shall not round the corners of your heads, neither shalt thou mar the corners of thy beard. Ye shall not make any cuttings in your flesh for the dead, nor print any marks upon you, I am the Lord.

Do not prostitute thy daughter, to cause her to be a whore, lest the land fall to whoredom and the land become full of wickedness. Ye shall keep my sabbaths and reverence my sanctuary, I am the Lord.

Regard not them that have familiar spirits neither seek after wizards, to be defiled by them, I am the Lord your God.

Thou shalt rise up before the hoary head, and honor the face of the old man, and fear thy God, I am the Lord. And if a stranger sojourn with thee in your land, ye shall not vex him. But the stranger that dwelleth with you shall be unto you as one born among you, and thou shalt love him as thyself, for ye were strangers in the land of Egypt, I am the Lord your God.

Ye shall do no unrighteousness in judgment, in meteyard, in weight, or in measure. Just balances, just weights, a just ephah, and a just hin shall ye have, I am the Lord your God, which brought you out of the land of Egypt. Therefore shall ye observe all my statutes and all my judgments and do them, I am the Lord.

And the Lord spake unto Moses saying, Again, thou shalt say to the children of Israel, Whosoever he be of the children of Israel, or of the strangers that sojourn in Israel, that giveth any of his seed unto Molech, he shall surely be put to death: the people of the land shall stone him with stones. And I will set my face against that man and will cut him off from among his people because he hath given of his seed unto Molech, to defile my sanctuary and to profane my holy name. And if the people of the land do any ways hide their eyes from the man when he giveth of his seed unto Molech, and kill him not, then I will set my face against that man, and against his family, and will cut him off, and all that go a whoring after him to commit whoredom with Molech, from among their people.

And the soul that turneth after such as have familiar spirits and after wizards to go a whoring after them I will even set my face against that soul and will cut him off from among his people. Sanctify yourselves therefore and be ye holy, for I am the Lord your God. And ye shall keep my statutes and do them, I am the Lord which sanctify you. For every one that curseth his father or his mother shall be surely put to death, he hath cursed his father or his mother his blood shall be upon him.

And the man that committeth adultery with another man's wife, even he that committeth adultery with his neighbor's wife, the adulterer and the adulteress shall surely be put to death. And the man that lieth with his father's wife hath uncovered his father's nakedness, both of them shall surely be put to death, their blood shall be upon them. And if a man lie with his daughter-in-law, both of them shall surely be put to death, they have wrought confusion, their blood shall be upon them. If a man also lie with mankind, as he lieth with a woman, both of them have committed an abomination, they shall surely be put to death, their blood shall be upon them. And if a man take a wife and her mother, it is wickedness, they shall be burnt with fire, both he and they, that there be no wickedness among you. And if a man lie with a beast, he shall surely be put to death, and ye shall slay the beast. And if a woman approach unto any beast, and lie down thereto, thou shalt kill the woman and the beast, they shall surely be put to death, their blood shall be upon them.

And if a man shall take his sister, his father's daughter, or his mother's daughter, and see her nakedness, and she see his nakedness, it is a wicked thing, and they shall be cut off in the sight of their people, he hath uncovered his sister's nakedness, he shall bear his iniquity. And if a man shall lie with a woman having her sickness, and shall uncover her nakedness, he hath discovered her fountain, and she hath uncovered the fountain of her blood, and both of them shall be cut off from among their people. And thou shalt not uncover the nakedness of thy mother's sister, nor of thy father's sister, for he uncovereth his near kin, they shall bear their iniquity. And if a man shall lie with his uncle's wife, he hath uncovered his uncle's nakedness, they shall bear their sin, they shall die childless. And if a man shall take his brother's wife, it is an unclean thing, he hath uncovered his brother's nakedness, they shall be childless.

Ye shall therefore keep all my statutes, and all my judgments, and do them, that the land whither I bring you to dwell therein spew you not out. And ye shall not walk in the manners of the nation which I cast out before you, for they committed all these things, and therefore I abhorred them. But I have said unto you, Ye shall inherit their land and I will give it unto you to possess it, a land that floweth with milk and honey, I am the Lord your God which have separated you from other people. Ye shall therefore put difference between clean beasts and unclean, and between unclean fowls and clean, and ye shall not make your souls abominable by beast, or by fowl, or by any manner of living thing that creepeth on the ground, which I have separated from you as unclean. And ye shall be holy unto me, for I the Lord am holy, and have severed you from other people, that ye should be mine.

A man also or woman that hath a familiar spirit or that is a wizard shall surely be put to death, they shall stone them with stones, their blood shall be upon them.

And the Lord said unto Moses, Speak unto the priests the sons of Aaron and say unto them, There shall none be defiled with the dead among his people, but for his kin that is near unto him, that is, for his mother, and for his father, and for his son, and for his daughter, and for his brother, and for his sister a virgin that is nigh unto him, which hath had no husband, for her may he be defiled. But he shall not defile himself, being a chief man among his people, to profane himself. They shall not make baldness upon their head, neither shall they shave off the corner of their beard, nor make any cuttings in their flesh. They shall be holy unto their God and not profane the name of their God, for the offerings of the Lord made by fire, and the bread of their God they do offer, therefore they shall be holy. They shall not take a wife that is a whore or profane, neither shall they take a woman put away from her husband, for he is holy unto his God. Thou shalt sanctify him therefore, for he offereth the bread of thy God, he shall be holy unto thee, for I the Lord, which sanctify you, am holy. And the daughter of any priest, if she profane herself by playing the whore, she profaneth her father, she shall be burnt with fire.

10 AND he that is the high priest among his brethren, upon whose head the anointing oil was poured, and that is consecrated to put on the garments, shall not uncover his head nor rend his clothes, neither shall he go in to touch any dead body, nor defile himself for his father, or his mother, neither shall he go out of the sanctuary, nor profane the sanctuary of his God, for the crown of the anointing oil

of his God is upon him, I am the Lord. And he shall take a wife in her virginity. A widow, or a divorced woman, or profane, or a harlot, these shall he not take, but he shall take a virgin of his own people to wife. Neither shall he profane his seed among his people, for I the Lord do sanctify him.

And the Lord spake unto Moses saying, Speak unto Aaron saying, Whosoever he be of thy seed in their generations that hath any blemish, let him not approach to offer the bread of his God. For whatsoever man he be that hath a blemish, he shall not approach, a blind man, or a lame, or he that hath a flat nose, or anything superfluous, or a man that is broken-footed, or broken-handed, or crook-backed, or a dwarf, or that hath a blemish in his eye, or be scurvy, or scabbed, or hath his stones broken, no man that hath a blemish of the seed of Aaron the priest shall come nigh to offer the offerings of the Lord made by fire, he hath a blemish, he shall not come nigh to offer the bread of his God. He shall eat the bread of his God, both of the most holy, and of the holy. Only he shall not go in unto the veil, nor come nigh unto the altar, because he hath a blemish, that he profane not my sanctuaries, for I the Lord do sanctify them. And Moses told it unto Aaron, and to his sons, and unto all the children of Israel.

And the Lord spake unto Moses, saying, Speak unto Aaron and to his sons, that they separate themselves from the holy things of the children of Israel, and that they profane not my holy name in those things which they hallow unto me, I am the Lord. Say unto them, Whosoever he be of all your seed among your generations that goeth unto the holy things, which the children of Israel hallow unto the Lord, having his uncleanness upon him, that soul shall be cut off from my presence, I am the Lord. What man soever of the seed of Aaron is a leper, or hath a running issue, he shall not eat of the holy things, until he be clean. And whoso toucheth anything that is unclean by the dead, or a man whose seed goeth from him, or whosoever toucheth any creeping thing, whereby he may be made unclean, or a man of whom he may take uncleanness, whatsoever uncleanness he hath, the soul which hath touched any such shall be unclean until even, and shall not eat of the holy things, unless he wash his flesh with water. And when the sun is down he shall be clean, and shall afterward eat of the holy things because it is his food. That which dieth of itself, or is torn with beasts, he shall not eat to defile himself therewith, I am the Lord. They shall therefore keep mine ordinance, lest they bear sin for it, and die, therefore, if they profane not mine ordinances, I the Lord will sanctify them.

There shall no stranger eat of the holy thing, a sojourner of the priest, or a hired servant, shall not eat of the holy thing. But if the priest buy any soul with his money, he shall eat of it, and he that is born in his house, they shall eat of his meat. If the priest's daughter also be married unto a stranger, she may not eat of an offering of the holy things. But if the priest's daughter be a widow, or divorced, and have no child, and is returned unto her father's house, as in her youth, she shall eat of her father's meat, but there shall no stranger eat thereof. And if a man eat of the holy thing unwittingly, then he shall put the fifth part thereof unto it, and shall give it unto the priest with the holy thing. And they shall not profane the holy things of the children of Israel which they offer unto the Lord, or suffer them to bear the iniquity of trespass when they eat their holy things, for I the Lord do sanctify them.

And the Lord spake unto Moses saying, Speak unto Aaron, and to his sons, and unto all the children of Israel and say unto them, Whatsoever he be of the house of Israel, or of the strangers in Israel, that will offer his oblation for all his vows, and for all his free-will offerings, which they will offer unto the Lord for a burnt offering, ye shall offer at your own will a male without blemish, of the beeves, of the sheep, or of the goats. But whatsoever hath a blemish, that shall ye not offer, for it shall not be acceptable for you. And whosoever offereth a sacrifice of peace offerings unto the Lord to accomplish his vow or a free-will offering in beeves or sheep, it shall be perfect to be accepted, there shall be no blemish therein. Blind, or broken, or maimed, or having a wen, or scurvy, or scabbed, ye shall not offer these unto the Lord, nor make an offering by fire of them upon the altar unto the Lord. Either a bullock or a lamb that hath anything superfluous or lacking in his parts, that mayest thou offer for a free-will offering, but for a vow it shall not be accepted. Ye shall not offer unto the Lord that which is bruised, or crushed, or broken, or cut, neither shall ye make any offering thereof in your land. Neither from a stranger's hand shall ye offer the bread of your God of any of these, because their corruption is in them, and blemishes be in them, they shall not be accepted for you.

11 AND the Lord spake unto Moses saying, When a bullock, or a sheep, or a goat, is brought forth, then it shall be seven days under the dam, and from the eighth day and thenceforth it shall be accepted for an offering made by fire unto the Lord. And whether it be cow or ewe, ye shall not kill it and her young both in one day. And when ye will offer a sacrifice of thanksgiving unto the Lord, offer it at your own will. On the same day it shall be eaten up, ye shall leave none of it until the morrow, I am the Lord.

Therefore shall ye keep my commandments and do them, I am the Lord. Neither shall ye profane my holy name, but I will be hallowed among the children of Israel, I am the Lord which hallow you, that brought you out of the land of Egypt to be your God, I am the Lord.

And the Lord spake unto Moses saying, Speak unto the children of Israel and say unto them, Concerning the feasts of the Lord, which ye shall proclaim to be holy convocations, even these are my feasts.

Six days shall work be done, but the seventh day is the sabbath of rest, a holy convocation, ye shall do no work therein, it is the sabbath of the Lord in all your dwellings.

These are the feasts of the Lord, even holy convocations, which ye shall proclaim in their seasons: In the fourteenth day of the first month at even is the Lord's passover. And on the fifteenth day of the same month is the feast of unleavened bread unto the Lord, seven days ye must eat unleavened bread. In the first day ye shall have a holy convocation, ye shall do no servile work therein. But ye shall offer an offering made by fire unto the Lord seven days, in the seventh day is a holy convocation, ye shall do no servile work therein.

And the Lord spake unto Moses saying, Speak unto the children of Israel, and say unto them, When ye be come into the land which I give unto you, and shall reap the harvest thereof, then ye shall bring a sheaf of the firstfruits of your harvest unto the priest, and he shall wave the sheaf before the Lord, to be accepted for you, on the morrow after the sabbath the priest shall wave it. And ye shall offer that day when ye wave the sheaf a he lamb without blemish of the first year for a burnt offering unto the Lord. And the meat offering thereof shall be two tenth deals of fine flour mingled with oil, and offering made by fire unto the Lord for a sweet savor, and the drink offering thereof shall be of wine, the fourth part of a hin. And ye shall eat neither bread, nor parched corn, nor green ears, until the selfsame day that ye have brought an offering unto your God, it shall be a statute for ever throughout your generations in all your dwellings.

And ye shall count unto you from the morrow after the sabbath, from the day that ye brought the sheaf of the wave offering, seven sabbaths shall be complete, even unto the morrow after the seventh sabbath shall ye number fifty days, and ye shall offer a new meat offering unto the Lord. Ye shall bring out of your habitations two wave loaves of two tenth deals, they shall be of fine flour, they shall be baken with leaven, they are the firstfruits unto the Lord. And ye shall offer with the bread seven lambs without blemish of the first year, and one young bullock and two rams, they shall be for a burnt offering unto the Lord, with their meat offering and their drink offerings, even an offering made by fire, of sweet savor unto the Lord. Then ye shall sacrifice one kid of the goats for a sin offering, and two lambs of the first year for a sacrifice of peace offerings. And the priest shall wave them with the bread of the firstfruits for a wave offering before the Lord, with the two lambs, they shall be holy to the Lord for the priest. And ye shall proclaim on the selfsame day, that it may be a holy convocation unto you, ye shall do no servile work therein, it shall be a statute for ever in all your dwellings throughout your generations.

And when ye reap the harvest of your land, thou shalt not make clean riddance of the corners of thy field when thou reapest, neither shalt thou gather any gleaning of thy harvest, thou shalt leave them unto the poor and to the stranger, I am the Lord your God.

And the Lord spake unto Moses saying, Speak unto the children of Israel saying, In the seventh month, in the first day of the month, shall ye have a sabbath, a memorial of blowing of trumpets, a holy convocation. Ye shall do no servile work therein, but ye shall offer an offering made by fire unto the Lord.

And the Lord spake unto Moses saying, Also on the tenth day of this seventh month there shall be a day of atonement, it shall be a holy convocation unto you, and ye shall afflict your souls, and offer an offering made by fire unto the Lord. And ye shall do no work in that same day, for it is a day of atonement, to make an atonement for you before the Lord your God. For whatsoever soul it be that shall not be afflicted in that same day, he shall be cut off from among his people. And whatsoever soul it be that doeth any work in that same day, the same soul will I destroy from among his people. Ye shall do no manner of work, it shall be a statute for ever throughout your generations in all your dwellings. It shall be unto you a sabbath of rest, and ye shall afflict your souls, in the ninth day of the month at even, from even unto even, shall ye celebrate your sabbath.

And the Lord spake unto Moses saying, Speak unto the children of Israel saying, The fifteenth day of this seventh month shall be the feast of tabernacles for seven days unto the Lord. On the first day shall be a holy convocation, ye shall do no servile work therein. Seven days ye shall offer an offering made by fire unto the Lord, on the eighth day shall be a holy convocation unto you, and ye shall offer an offering made by fire unto the Lord, it is a solemn assembly and ye shall do no servile work therein.

These are the feasts of the Lord which ye shall proclaim to be holy convocations, to offer an offering made by fire unto the Lord, a burnt offering, and a meat offering, a sacrifice, and drink offerings, everything upon his day, beside the sabbaths of the Lord, and beside your gifts, and beside all your vows, and beside all your free-will offerings, which ye give unto the Lord.

Also in the fifteenth day of the seventh month, when ye have gathered in the fruit of the land, ye shall keep a feast unto the Lord seven days, on the first day shall be a sabbath, and on the eighth day shall be a sabbath. And ye shall take you on the first day the boughs of goodly trees, branches of palm trees, and the boughs of thick trees, and willows of the brook, and ye shall rejoice before the Lord your God seven days. And ye shall keep it a feast unto the Lord seven days in the year, it shall be a statute for ever in your generations, ye shall celebrate it in the seventh month. Ye shall dwell in booths seven days, all that are Israelites born shall dwell in booths, that your generations may know that I made the children of Israel to dwell in booths, when I brought them out of the land of Egypt, I am the Lord your God.

And Moses declared unto the children of Israel the feasts of the Lord.

And the Lord spake unto Moses saying, Command the children of Israel that they bring unto thee pure olive oil beaten for the light to cause the lamps to burn continually. Without the veil of the testimony, in the tabernacle of the congregation, shall Aaron order it from the evening unto the morning before the Lord continually; it shall be a statute for ever in your generations. He shall order the lamps upon the pure candlestick before the Lord continually.

And thou shalt take fine flour, and bake twelve cakes thereof, two tenth deals shall be in one cake. And thou shalt set them in two rows, six on a row, upon the pure table before the Lord. And thou shalt put pure frankincense upon each row, that it may be on the bread for a memorial, even an offering made by fire unto the Lord. Every Sabbath he shall set it in order before the Lord continually, being taken from the children of Israel by an everlasting covenant. And it shall be Aaron's and his sons', and they shall eat it in the holy place, for it is most holy unto him of the offerings of the Lord made by fire by a perpetual statute.

12 AND the son of an Israelitish woman, whose father was an Egyptian, went out among the children of Israel, and this son of the Israelitish woman and a man of Israel strove together in the camp, and the Israelitish woman's son blasphemed the name of the Lord and cursed. And they brought him unto Moses (and his mother's name was Shelomith, the daughter of Dibri, of the tribe of Dan), and they put him in ward, that the mind of the Lord might be showed them.

And the Lord spoke unto Moses saying, Bring forth him that hath cursed without the camp, and let all that heard him lay their hands upon his head, and let all the congregation stone him. And thou shalt speak unto the children of Israel saying, Whosoever curseth his God shall bear his sin. And he that blasphemeth the name of the Lord, he shall surely be put to death, and all the congregation shall certainly stone him, as well the stranger as he that is born in the land, when he blasphemeth the name of the Lord, shall be put to death.

And he that killeth any man shall surely be put to death. And he that killeth a beast shall make it good, beast for beast. And if a man cause a blemish in his neighbor, as he hath done, so shall it be done to him, breach for breach, eye for eye, tooth for tooth, as he hath caused a blemish in a man, so shall it be done to him again. And he that killeth a beast, he shall restore it, and he that killeth a man, he shall be put to death. Ye shall have one manner of law, as well for the stranger, as for one of your own country, for I am the Lord your God. And Moses spake to the children of Israel, that they should bring forth him that had cursed out of the camp, and stone him with stones, and the children of Israel did as the Lord commanded Moses.

13 AND the Lord spake unto Moses in mount Sinai saying, Speak unto the children of Israel, and say unto them, When ye come into the land which I give you, then shall the land keep a sabbath unto the Lord. Six years thou shalt sow thy field, and six years thou shalt prune thy vineyard, and gather in the fruit thereof, but in the seventh year shall be a sabbath of rest unto the land, a sabbath for the Lord, thou shalt neither sow thy field, nor prune thy vineyard. That which groweth of its own accord of thy harvest thou shalt not reap, neither gather the grapes of thy vine undressed, for it is a year of rest unto the land. And the sabbath of the land shall be meat for you, for thee, and for thy servant, and for thy maid, and for thy hired servant, and for thy stranger that sojourneth with thee, and for thy cattle, and for the beast that are in thy land, shall all the increase thereof be meat.

And thou shalt number seven sabbaths of years unto thee, seven times seven years, and the space of the seven sabbaths of years shall be unto thee forty and nine years. Then shalt thou cause the trumpet of the jubilee to sound on the tenth day of the seventh month, in the day of atonement shall ye make the trumpet sound throughout all your land. And ye shall hallow the fiftieth year, and proclaim liberty throughout all the land unto all the inhabitants thereof, it shall be a jubilee unto you, and ye shall return every man unto his possession, and ye shall return every man unto his family. A jubilee shall that fiftieth year be unto you, ye shall not sow, neither reap that which groweth of itself in it, nor gather the grapes in it of thy vine undressed. For it is the jubilee, it shall be holy unto you, ye shall eat the increase thereof out of the field.

In the year of this jubilee ye shall return every man unto his possession. And if thou sell aught unto thy neighbor, or buyest aught of thy neighbor's hand, ye shall not oppress one another. According to the number of years after the jubilee thou shalt buy of thy neighbor, and according unto the number of years of the fruits he shall sell unto thee, according to the multitude of years thou shalt increase the price thereof, and according to the fewness of years thou shalt diminish the price of it, for according to the number of the years of the fruits doth he sell unto thee. Ye shall not therefore oppress one another, but thou shalt fear thy God, for I am the Lord your God. Wherefore ye shall do my statutes, and keep my judgments and do them, and ye shall dwell in the land in safety. And the land shall yield her fruit, and ye shall eat your fill, and dwell therein in safety. And if ye shall say, What shall we eat the seventh year? behold, we shall not sow nor gather in our increase, then I will command my blessing upon you in the sixth year, and it shall bring forth fruit for three years. And ye shall sow the eighth year, and eat yet of old fruit until the ninth year, until her fruits come in ye shall eat of the old store.

The land shall not be sold forever, for the land is mine, for ye are strangers and sojourners with me. And in all the land of your possession ye shall grant a redemption for the land. If thy brother be waxen poor and hath sold away some of his possession, and if any of his kin come to redeem it, then shall he redeem that which his brother sold. And if the man have none to redeem it and himself be able to redeem it, then let him count the years of the sale thereof, and restore the overplus unto the man to whom he sold it, that he may return unto his possession. But if he be not able to restore it to him, then that which is sold shall remain in the hand of him that hath bought it until the year of jubilee, and in the jubilee it shall go out and he shall return unto his possession.

And if a man sell his dwelling-house in a walled city, then he may redeem it within a whole year after it is sold, within a full year may he redeem it. And if it be not redeemed within the space of a full year, then the house that is in the walled city shall be established for ever to him that bought it throughout his generations, it shall not go out in the jubilee. But the houses of the villages which have no wall round about them shall be counted as the fields of the country, they may be redeemed, and they shall go out in the jubilee. Notwithstanding the cities of the Levites, and the houses of the cities of their possession, may the Levites redeem at any time. And if a man purchase of the Levites, then the house that was sold and the city of his possession shall go out in the year of jubilee, for the houses of the cities of the Levites are their possession among the children of Israel. But the field of the suburbs of their cities may not be sold, for it is their perpetual possession.

And if thy brother be waxen poor and fallen in decay with thee, then thou shalt relieve him, yea, though he be a stranger or a sojourner, that he may live with thee. Take thou no usury of him, or increase, but fear thy God, that thy brother may live with thee. Thou shalt not give him thy money upon usury, nor lend him thy victuals for increase. I am the Lord your God, which brought you forth out of the land of Egypt, to give you the land of Canaan, and to be your God.

And if thy brother that dwelleth by thee be waxen poor, and be sold unto thee, thou shalt not compel him to serve as a bond-servant, but as a hired servant and as a sojourner, he shall be with thee, and shall serve thee unto the year of jubilee, and then shall he depart from thee, both he and his children with him, and shall return unto his own family, and unto the possession of his fathers shall he return. For they are my servants which I brought forth out of the land of Egypt, they shall not be sold as bond-men. Thou shalt not rule over him with rigor, but shalt fear thy God. Both thy bond-men and thy bond-maids which thou shalt have shall be of the heathen that are round about you, of them shall ye buy bond-men and bond-maids. Moreover, of the children of the strangers that do sojourn among you, of them shall ye buy, and of their families that are with you, which they begat in your land, and they shall be your possession. And ye shall take them as an inheritance for your children after you to inherit them for a possession, they shall be your bond-men forever, but over your brethren the children of Israel, ye shall not rule one over another with rigor.

And if a sojourner or stranger wax rich by thee, and thy brother that dwelleth by him wax poor and sell himself unto the stranger or sojourner by thee or to the stock of the stranger's family, after that he is sold he may be redeemed again, one of his brethren may redeem him, either his uncle, or his uncle's son, may redeem him, or any that is nigh of kin unto him of his family may redeem him, or if he be able, he may redeem himself. And he shall reckon with him that bought him from the year that he was sold to him unto the year of jubilee, and the price of his sale shall be according unto the number of years, according to the time of a hired servant shall it be with him. If there be yet many years behind, according unto them he shall give again the price of his redemption out of the money that he was bought for. And if there remain but few years unto the year of jubilee, then he shall count with him, and according unto his years shall he give him again the price of his redemption. And as a yearly hired servant shall he be with him, and the other shall not rule with rigor over him in thy sight. And if he be not redeemed in these years, then he shall go out in the year of jubilee, both he and his children with him. For unto me the children of Israel are servants, they are my servants whom I brought forth out of the land of Egypt, I am the Lord your God.

Ye shall make you no idols nor graven image, neither rear you up a standing image, neither shall ye set up any image of stone in your land, to bow down unto it, for I am the Lord your God. Ye shall keep my sabbaths, and reverence my sanctuary, I am the Lord.

If ye walk in my statutes, and keep my commandments, and do them, then I will give you rain in due season, and the land shall yield her increase, and the trees of the field shall yield their fruit. And your threshing shall reach unto the vintage, and the vintage shall reach unto the sowing time, and ye shall eat your bread to the full, and dwell in your land safely. And I will give peace in the land, and ye shall lie down, and none shall make you afraid, and I will rid evil beasts out of the land, neither shall the sword go through your land. And ye shall chase your enemies and they shall fall before you by the sword. And five of you shall chase a hundred, and a hundred of you shall put ten thousand to flight, and your enemies shall fall before you by the sword. For I will have respect unto you, and make you fruitful, and multiply you, and establish my covenant with you. And ye shall eat old store and bring forth the old because of the new. And I will set my tabernacle among you, and my soul shall not abhor you, and I will walk among you, and will be your God and ye shall be my people. I am the Lord your God, which brought you forth out of the land of Egypt, that ye should not be their bond-men, and I have broken the bands of your yoke, and made you go upright.

But if ye will not hearken unto me, and will not do all these commandments, and if ye shall despise my statutes, or if your soul abhor my judgments, so that ye will not do all my commandments, but that ye break my covenant, I also will do this unto you: I will even appoint over you terror, consumption, and the burning ague that shall consume the eyes, and cause sorrow of heart, and ye shall sow your seed in vain, for your enemies shall eat it. And I will set my face against you, and ye shall be slain before your enemies, they that hate you shall reign over you, and ye shall flee when none pursueth you. And if ye will not yet for all this hearken unto me, then I will punish you seven times more for your sins. And I will break the pride of your power, and I will make your Heaven as iron, and your Earth as brass, and your strength shall be spent in vain, for your land shall not yield her increase, neither shall the trees of the land yield their fruits.

And if ye walk contrary unto me and will not hearken unto me, I will bring seven times more plagues upon you according to your sins. I will also send wild beasts among you, which shall rob you of your children, and destroy your cattle, and make you few in number, and your highways shall be desolate.

And if ye will not be reformed by me by these things, but will walk contrary unto me, then will I also walk contrary unto you, and will punish you yet seven times for your sins. And I will bring a sword upon you, that shall avenge the quarrel of my covenant, and when ye are gathered together within your cities, I will send the pestilence among you, and ye shall be delivered into the hand of the enemy. And when I have broken the staff of your bread, ten women shall bake your bread in one oven, and they shall deliver you your bread again by weight, and ye shall eat, and not be satisfied.

And if ye will not for all this hearken unto me, but walk contrary unto me, then I will walk contrary unto you also in fury, and I, even I, will chastise you seven times for your sins. And ye shall eat the flesh of your sons and the flesh of your daughters shall ye eat. And I will destroy your high places, and cut down your images, and cast your carcasses upon the carcasses of your idols, and my soul shall abhor you. And I will make your cities waste, and bring your sanctuaries unto desolation, and I will not smell the savor of your sweet odors. And I will bring the land into desolation, and your enemies which dwell therein shall be astonished at it. And I will scatter you among the heathen, and will draw out a sword after you, and your land shall be desolate, and your cities waste.

Then shall the land enjoy her sabbaths, as long as it lieth desolate, and ye be in your enemies' land, even then shall the land rest and enjoy her sabbaths. As long as it lieth desolate it shall rest because it did not rest in your sabbaths when ye dwelt upon it. And upon them that are left alive of you I will send a faintness into their hearts in the lands of their enemies, and the sound of a shaken leaf shall chase them, and they shall flee as fleeing from a sword, and they shall fall when none pursueth. And they shall fall one upon another, as it were before a sword, when none pursueth, and ye shall have no power to stand before your enemies. And ye shall perish among the heathen and the land of your enemies shall eat you up. And they that are left of you shall pine away in their iniquity in your enemies' lands, and also in the iniquities of their fathers shall they pine away with them.

If they shall confess their iniquity, and the iniquity of their fathers, with their trespass which they trespassed against me, and that also they have walked contrary unto me, and that I also have walked contrary unto them, and have brought them into the land of their enemies, if then their uncircumcised hearts be humbled, and they then accept of the punishment of their iniquity, then will I remember my covenant with Jacob, and also my covenant with Isaac, and also my covenant with Abraham will I remember, and I will remember the land. The land also shall be left of them, and shall enjoy her sabbaths, while she lieth desolate without them, and they shall accept of the punishment of their iniquity because, even because they despised my judgments, and because their soul abhorred my statutes. And yet for all that, when they be in the land of their enemies, I will not cast them away, neither will I abhor them, to destroy them utterly, and to break my covenant with them, for I am the Lord their God. But I will for their sakes remember the covenant of their ancestors, whom I brought forth out of the land of Egypt in the sight of the heathen, that I might be their God, I am the Lord.

These are the statutes and judgments and laws, which the Lord made between him and the children of Israel in mount Sinai by the hand of Moses.

14 AND the Lord spake unto Moses saying, Speak unto the children of Israel, and say unto them, When a man shall make a singular vow, the persons shall be for the Lord by thy estimation. And thy estimation shall be of the male from twenty years old even unto sixty years old, even thy estimation shall be fifty shekels of silver, after the shekel of the sanctuary. And if it be a female, then thy estimation shall be thirty shekels. And if it be from five years old even unto twenty years old, then thy estimation shall be of the male twenty shekels, and for the female ten shekels. And if it be from a month old even unto five years old, then thy estimation shall be of the male five shekels of silver, and for the female thy estimation shall be three shekels of silver. And if it be from sixty years old and above, if it be a male, then thy estimation shall be fifteen shekels, and for the female ten shekels. But if he be poorer than thy estimation, then he shall present himself before the priest, and the priest shall value him, according to his ability that vowed shall the priest value him.

And if it be a beast, whereof men bring an offering unto the Lord, all that any man giveth of such unto the Lord shall be holy. He shall not alter it, nor change it, a good for a bad, or a bad for a good, and if he shall at all change beast for beast, then it and the exchange thereof shall be holy. And if it be any unclean beast of which they do not offer a sacrifice unto the Lord, then he shall present the beast before the priest, and the priest shall value it, whether it be good or bad, as thou valuest it, who art the priest, so shall it be. But if he will at all redeem it, then he shall add a fifth part thereof unto thy estimation.

And when a man shall sanctify his house to be holy unto the Lord, then the priest shall estimate it, whether it be good or bad, as the priest shall estimate it, so shall it stand. And if he that sanctified it will redeem his house, then he shall add the fifth part of the money of thy estimation unto it, and it shall be his.

And if a man shall sanctify unto the Lord some part of a field of his possession, then thy estimation shall be according to the seed thereof, a homer of barley seed shall be valued at fifty shekels of silver. If he sanctify his field from the year of jubilee, according to thy estimation it shall stand. But if he sanctify his field after the jubilee, then the priest shall reckon unto him the money according to the years that remain, even unto the year of the jubilee, and it shall be abated from thy estimation. And if he that sanctified the field will in any wise redeem it, then he shall add the fifth part of the money of thy estimation unto it, and it shall be assured to him. And if he will not redeem the field, or if he have sold the field to another man, it shall not be redeemed any more. But the field, when it goeth out in the jubilee, shall be holy unto the Lord, as a field devoted, the possession thereof shall be the priest's. And if a man sanctify unto the Lord a field which he hath bought, which is not of the fields of his possession, then the priest shall reckon unto him the worth of thy estimation, even unto the year of the jubilee, and he shall give thine estimation in that day as a holy thing unto the Lord. In the year of the jubilee the field shall return unto him of whom it was bought, even to him to whom the possession of the land did belong. And all thy estimation shall be according to the shekel of the sanctuary, twenty gerahs shall be the shekel.

Only the firstling of the beasts, which should be the Lord's firstling, no man shall sanctify it, whether it be ox, or sheep, it is the Lord's. And if it be of an unclean beast, then he shall redeem it according to thine estimation, and shall add a fifth part of it thereto, or if it be not redeemed, then it shall be sold according to thy estimation.

Notwithstanding, no devoted thing that a man shall devote unto the Lord of all that he hath, both of man and beast, and of the field of his possession, shall be sold or redeemed, every devoted thing is most holy unto the Lord. None devoted, which shall be devoted of men, shall be redeemed, but shall surely be put to death.

And all the tithe of the land, whether of the seed of the land or of the fruit of the tree, is the Lord's, it is holy unto the Lord. And if a man will at all redeem aught of his tithes, he shall add thereto the fifth part thereof. And concerning the tithe of the herd, or of the flock, even of whatsoever passeth under the rod, the tenth shall be holy unto the Lord. He shall not search whether it be good or bad, neither shall he change it, and if he change it at all, then both it and the change thereof shall be holy, it shall not be redeemed.

These are the commandments, which the Lord commanded Moses for the children of Israel in mount Sinai.

NUMBERS

AND the Lord spake unto Moses in the wilderness of Sinai, in the tabernacle of the congregation, on the first day of the second month, in the second year after they were come out of the land of Egypt saying, Take ye the sum of all the congregation of the children of Israel after their families, by the house of their fathers, with the number of their names every male by their polls, from twenty years old and upward, all that are able to go forth to war in Israel; thou and Aaron shall number them by their armies. And with you there shall be a man of every tribe, every one head of the house of his fathers. And these are the names of the men that shall stand with you: of the tribe of Reuben, Elizur the son of Shedeur. Of Simeon, Shelumiel the son of Zurishaddai. Of Judah, Nahshon the son of Amminadab. Of Issachar, Nethaneel the son of Zuar. Of Zebulun, Eliab the son of Helon. Of the children of Joseph, of Ephraim, Elishama the son of Ammihud, of Manasseh, Gamaliel the son of Pedahzur. Of Benjamin, Abidan the son of Gideoni. Of Dan, Ahiezer the son of Ammishaddai. Of Asher, Pagiel the son of Ocran. Of Gad, Eliasaph the son of Deuel. Of Naphtali, Ahira the son of Enan. These were the renowned of the congregation, princes of the tribes of their fathers, heads of thousands in Israel.

And Moses and Aaron took these men which are expressed by their names, and they assembled all the congregation together on the first day of the second month, and they declared their pedigrees after their families, by the house of their fathers, according to the number of the names, from twenty years old and upward, by their polls. As the Lord commanded Moses, so he numbered them in the wilderness of Sinai.

And the children of Reuben, Israel's eldest son, by their generations, after their families, by the house of their fathers, according to the number of the names, by their polls, every male from twenty years old and upward, all that were able to go forth to war, those that were numbered of them, even of the tribe of Reuben, were forty and six thousand and five hundred.

Of the children of Simeon, by their generations, after their families, by the house of their fathers, those that were numbered of them, according to the number of the names, by their polls, every male from twenty years old and upward, all that were able to go forth to war, those that were numbered of them, even of the tribe of Simeon, were fifty and nine thousand and three hundred. Of the children of Gad, by their generations, after their families, by the house of their fathers, according to the number of the names, from twenty years old and upward, all that were able to go forth to war, those that were numbered of them, even of the tribe of Gad, were forty and five thousand six hundred and fifty. Of the children of Judah, by their generations, after their families, by the house of their fathers, according to the number of the names, from twenty years old and upward, all that were able to go forth to war, those that were numbered of them, even of the tribe of Judah, were threescore and fourteen thousand and six hundred. Of the children of Issachar, by their generations, after their families, by the house of their fathers, according to the number of the names, from twenty years old and upward, all that were able to go forth to war, those that were numbered of them, even of the tribe of Issachar, were fifty and four thousand and four hundred. Of the children of Zebulun, by their generations, after their families, by the house of their fathers, according to the number of the names, from twenty years old and upward, all that were able to go forth to war, those that were numbered of them, even of the tribe of Zebulun, were fifty and seven thousand and four hundred. Of the children of Joseph, namely, of the children of Ephraim, by their generations, after their families, by the house of their fathers, according to the number of the names, from twenty years old and upward, all that were able to go forth to war, those that were numbered of them, even of the tribe of Ephraim, were forty thousand and five hundred. Of the children of Manasseh, by their generations, after their families, by the house of their fathers, according to the number of the names, from twenty years old and upward, all that were able to go forth to war, those that were numbered of them, even of the tribe of Manasseh, were thirty and two thousand and two hundred. Of the children of Benjamin, by their generations, after their families, by the house of their fathers, according to the number of the names, from twenty years old and upward, all that were able to go forth to war, those that were numbered of them, even of the tribe of Benjamin, were thirty and five thousand and four hundred. Of the children of Dan, by their generations, after their families, by the house of their fathers, according to the number of the names, from twenty years old and upward, all that were able to go forth to war, those that were numbered of them, even of the tribe of Dan, were threescore and two thousand and seven hundred. Of the children of Asher, by their generations, after their families, by the house of their fathers, according to the number of the names, from twenty years old and upward, all that were able to go forth to war, those that were numbered of them, even of the tribe of Asher, were forty and one thousand and five hundred. Of the children of Naphtali, throughout their generations, after their families, by the house of their fathers, according to the number of the names, from twenty years old and upward, all that were able to go forth to war, those that were numbered of them, even of the tribe of Naphtali, were fifty and three thousand and four hundred. These are those that were numbered, which Moses and Aaron numbered, and the princes of Israel, being twelve men, each one was for the house of his fathers. So were all those that were numbered of the children of Israel, by the house of their fathers, from twenty years old and upward, all that were able to go forth to war in Israel, even all they that were numbered were six hundred thousand and three thousand and five hundred and fifty.

But the Levites after the tribe of their fathers were not numbered among them. For the Lord had spoken unto Moses, saying, Only thou shalt not number the tribe of Levi, neither take the sum of them among the children of Israel, but thou shalt appoint the Levites over the tabernacle of testimony, and over all the vessels thereof, and over all things that belong to it, they shall bear the tabernacle and all the vessels thereof, and they shall minister unto it and shall encamp round about the tabernacle. And when the tabernacle setteth forward, the Levites shall take it down and when the tabernacle is to be pitched, the Levites shall set it up, and the stranger that cometh nigh shall be put to death. And the children of Israel shall pitch their tents, every man by his own camp and every man by his own standard, throughout their hosts. But the Levites shall pitch round about the tabernacle of testimony that there be no wrath upon the congregation of the children of Israel, and the Levites shall keep the charge of the tabernacle of testimony. And the children of Israel did according to all that the Lord commanded Moses, so did they.

And the Lord spake unto Moses and unto Aaron saying, Every man of the children of Israel shall pitch by his own standard, with the ensign of their father's house, far off about the tabernacle of the congregation shall they pitch. And on the east side toward the rising of the sun shall they of the standard of the camp of Judah pitch throughout their armies, and Nahshon the son of Amminadab shall be captain of the children of Judah. And his host, and those that were numbered of them, were threescore and fourteen thousand and six hundred. And those that do pitch next unto him shall be the tribe of Issachar, and Nethaneel the son of Zuar shall be captain of the children of Issachar. And his host, and those that were numbered thereof, were fifty and four thousand and four hundred. Then the tribe of Zebulun, and Eliab the son of Helon shall be captain of the children of Zebulun. And his host, and those that were numbered thereof, were fifty and seven thousand and four hundred. All that were numbered in the camp of Judah were a hundred thousand and fourscore thousand and six thousand and four hundred, throughout their armies, these shall first set forth.

On the south side shall be the standard of the camp of Reuben according to their armies, and the captain of the children of Reuben shall be Elizur the son of Shedeur. And his host, and those that were numbered thereof, were forty and six thousand and five hundred. And those which pitch by him shall be the tribe of Simeon, and the captain of the children of Simeon shall be Shelumiel the son of Zurishaddai. And his host, and those that were numbered of them, were fifty and nine thousand and three hundred. Then the tribe of Gad, and the captain of the sons of Gad shall be Eliasaph the son of Reuel. And his host, and those that were numbered of them, were forty and five thousand and six hundred and fifty. All that were numbered in the camp of Reuben were a hundred thousand and fifty and one thousand and four hundred and fifty, throughout their armies, and they shall set forth in the second rank.

Then the tabernacle of the congregation shall set forward with the camp of the Levites in the midst of the camp as they encamp, so shall they set forward every man in his place by their standards.

On the west side shall be the standard of the camp of Ephraim according to their armies, and the captain of the sons of Ephraim shall be Elishama the son of Ammihud. And his host, and those that were numbered of them, were forty thousand and five hundred. And by him shall be the tribe of Manasseh, and the captain of the children of Manasseh shall be Gamaliel the son of Pedahzur. And his host, and those that were numbered of them were thirty and two thousand and two hundred. Then the tribe of Benjamin, and the captain of the sons of Benjamin shall be Abidan the son of Gideoni. And his host, and those that were numbered of them, were thirty and five thousand and four hundred. All that were numbered of the camp of Ephraim were a hundred thousand and eight thousand and a hundred, throughout their armies, and they shall go forward in the third rank.

The standard of the camp of Dan shall be on the north side by their armies, and the captain of the children of Dan shall be Ahiezer the son of Ammishaddai. And his host, and those that were numbered of them, were threescore and two thousand and seven hundred. And those that encamp by him shall be the tribe of Asher, and the captain of the children of Asher shall be Pagiel the son of Ocran. And his host, and those that were numbered of them, were forty and one thousand and five hundred. Then the tribe of Naphtali, and the captain of the children of Naphtali shall be Ahira the son of Enan. And his host, and those that were numbered of them, were fifty and three thousand and four hundred. All they that were numbered in the camp of Dan were a hundred thousand and fifty and seven thousand and six hundred, they shall go hindmost with their standards.

These are those which were numbered of the children of Israel by the house of their fathers, all those that were numbered of the camps throughout their hosts were six hundred thousand and three thousand and five hundred and fifty. But the Levites were not numbered among the children of Israel, as the Lord commanded Moses. And the children of Israel did according to all that the Lord commanded Moses, so they pitched by their standards, and so they set forward, every one after their families, according to the house of their fathers.

These also are the generations of Aaron and Moses, in the days that the Lord spake with Moses in mount Sinai. And these are the names of the sons of Aaron: Nadab the firstborn, and Abihu, Eleazar, and Ithamar. These are the names of the sons of Aaron, the priests which were anointed, whom he consecrated to minister in the priest's office. And Nadab and Abihu died before the Lord when they offered strange fire before the Lord in the wilderness of Sinai, and they had no children, and Eleazar and Ithamar ministered in the priest's office in the sight of Aaron their father.

2 AND the Lord spake unto Moses saying, Bring the tribe of Levi near and present them before Aaron the priest that they may minister unto him. And they shall keep his charge, and the charge of the whole congregation before the tabernacle of the congregation, to do the service of the tabernacle. And they shall keep all the instruments of the tabernacle of the congregation, and the charge of the children of Israel, to do the service of the tabernacle. And thou shalt give the Levites unto Aaron and to his sons, they are wholly given to him out of the children of Israel. And thou shalt appoint Aaron and his sons, and they shall wait on their priest's office, and the stranger that cometh nigh shall be put to death.

And the Lord spake unto Moses saying, And I, behold, I have taken the Levites from among the children of Israel instead of all the firstborn that openeth the matrix among the children of Israel, therefore the Levites shall be mine because all the firstborn are mine, for on the day that I smote all the firstborn in the land of Egypt I hallowed unto me all the firstborn in Israel, both man and beast, mine they shall be, I am the Lord.

And the Lord spake unto Moses in the wilderness of Sinai saying, Number the children of Levi after the house of their fathers, by their families, every male from a month old and upward shalt thou number them. And Moses numbered them according to the word of the Lord as he was commanded. And these were the sons of Levi by their names: Gershon, and Kohath, and Merari. And these are the names of the sons of Gershon by their families: Libni and Shimei. And the sons of Kohath by their families: Amram and Izehar, Hebron and Uzziel. And the sons of Merari by their families: Mahli and Mushi. These are the families of the Levites according to the house of their fathers.

Of Gershon was the family of the Libnites, and the family of the Shimites, these are the families of the Gershonites. Those that were numbered of them, according to the number of all the males, from a month old and upward, even those that were numbered of them were seven thousand and five hundred. The families of the Gershonites shall pitch behind the tabernacle westward. And the chief of the house of the father of the Gershonites shall be Eliasaph the son of Lael. And the charge of the sons of Gershon in the tabernacle of the congregation shall be the tabernacle, and the tent, the covering thereof, and the hanging for the door of the tabernacle of the congregation, and the hangings of the court, and the curtain for the door of the court which is by the tabernacle, and by the altar round about, and the cords of it, for all the service thereof.

And of Kohath was the family of the Amramites, and the family of the Izeharites, and the family of the Hebronites, and the family of the Uzzielites, these are the families of the Kohathites. In the number of all the males, from a month old and upward, were eight thousand and six hundred, keeping the charge of the sanctuary. The families of the sons of Kohath shall pitch on the side of the tabernacle southward. And the chief of the house of the father of the families of the Kohathites shall be Elizaphan the son of Uzziel. And their charge shall be the ark, and the table, and the candlestick, and the altars, and the vessels of the sanctuary wherewith they minister, and the hanging, and all the service thereof. And Eleazar the son of Aaron the priest shall be chief over the chief of the Levites and have the oversight of them that keep the charge of the sanctuary.

Of Merari was the family of the Mahlites, and the family of the Mushites, these are the families of Merari. And those that were numbered of them, according to the number of all the males, from a month old and upward, were six thousand and two hundred. And the chief of the house of the father of the families of Merari was Zuriel the son of Abihail, these shall pitch on the side of the tabernacle northward. And under the custody and charge of the sons of Merari shall be the boards of the tabernacle, and the bars thereof, and the pillars thereof, and the sockets thereof, and all the vessels thereof, and all that serveth thereto, and the pillars of the court round about, and their sockets, and their pins, and their cords.

But those that encamp before the tabernacle toward the east, even before the tabernacle of the congregation eastward, shall be Moses and Aaron and his sons, keeping the charge of the sanctuary for the charge of the children of Israel, and the stranger that cometh nigh shall be put to death. All that were numbered of the Levites, which Moses and Aaron numbered at the commandment of the Lord, throughout their families, all the males from a month old and upward, were twenty and two thousand.

And the Lord said unto Moses, Number all the firstborn of the males of the children of Israel from a month old and upward, and take the number of their names. And thou shalt take the Levites for me (I am the Lord) instead of all the firstborn among the children of Israel, and the cattle of the Levites instead of all the firstlings among the cattle of the children of Israel. And Moses numbered, as the Lord commanded him, all the firstborn among the children of Israel. And all the firstborn males by the number of names, from a month old and upward, of those that were numbered of them, were twenty and two thousand two hundred and threescore and thirteen.

And the Lord spake unto Moses saying, Take the Levites instead of all the firstborn among the children of Israel, and the cattle of the Levites instead of their cattle, and the Levites shall be mine, I am the Lord. And for those that are to be redeemed of the two hundred and threescore and thirteen of the firstborn of the children of Israel, which are more than the Levites, thou shalt even take five shekels apiece by the poll, after the shekel of the sanctuary shalt thou take them (the shekel is twenty gerahs), and thou shalt give the money, wherewith the odd number of them is to be redeemed, unto Aaron and to his sons. And Moses took the redemption money of them that were over and above them that were redeemed by the Levites, of the firstborn of the children of Israel took he the money, a thousand three hundred and threescore and five shekels, after the shekel of the sanctuary, and Moses gave the money of them that were redeemed unto Aaron and to his sons, according to the word of the Lord, as the Lord commanded Moses.

And the Lord spake unto Moses, and unto Aaron, saying, Take the sum of the sons of Kohath from among the sons of Levi, after their families, by the house of their fathers, from thirty years old and upward even until fifty years old, all that enter into the host, to do the work in the tabernacle of the congregation. This shall be the service of the sons of Kohath in the tabernacle of the congregation: about the most holy things. And when the camp setteth forward, Aaron shall come, and his sons, and they shall take down the covering veil and cover the ark of testimony with it, and shall put thereon the covering of badgers' skins, and shall spread over it a cloth wholly of blue, and shall put in the staves thereof. And upon the table of shewbread they shall spread a cloth of blue, and put thereon the dishes, and the spoons, and the bowls, and covers to cover withal, and the continual bread shall be thereon, and they shall spread upon them a cloth of scarlet, and cover the same with a covering of badgers' skins, and shall put in the staves thereof. And they shall take a cloth of blue, and cover the candlestick of the light, and his lamps, and his tongs, and his snuff dishes, and all the oil vessels thereof wherewith they minister unto it, and they shall put it and all the vessels thereof within a covering of badgers' skins, and shall put it upon a bar. And upon the golden altar they shall spread a cloth of blue, and cover it with a covering of badgers' skins, and shall put to the staves thereof, and they shall take all the instruments of ministry wherewith they minister in the sanctuary, and put them in a cloth of blue, and cover them with a covering of badgers' skins, and shall put them on a bar. And they shall take away the ashes from the altar and spread a purple cloth thereon, and they shall put upon it all the vessels thereof wherewith they minister about it, even the censers, the flesh hooks, and the shovels, and the basins, all the vessels of the altar, and they shall spread upon it a covering of badgers' skins, and put to the staves of it. And when Aaron and his sons have made an end of covering the sanctuary, and all the vessels of the sanctuary, as the camp is to set forward, after that, the sons of Kohath shall come to bear it, but they shall not touch any holy thing lest they die. These things are the burden of the sons of Kohath in the tabernacle of the congregation.

And to the office of Eleazar the son of Aaron the Priest pertaineth the oil for the light, and the sweet incense, and the daily meat offering, and the anointing oil, and the oversight of all the tabernacle, and of all that therein is, in the sanctuary, and in the vessels thereof.

And the Lord spake unto Moses and unto Aaron saying, Cut ye not off the tribe of the families of the Kohathites from among the Levites, but thus do unto them, that they may live and not die when they approach unto the most holy things, Aaron and his sons shall go in, and appoint them every one to his service and to his burden, but they shall not go in to see when the holy things are covered lest they die.

And the Lord spake unto Moses saying, Take also the sum of the sons of Gershon, throughout the houses of their fathers, by their families, from thirty years old and upward until fifty years old shalt thou number them, all that enter in to perform the service, to do the work in the tabernacle of the congregation. This is the service of the families of the Gershonites, to serve and for burdens, and they shall bear the curtains of the tabernacle, and the tabernacle of the congregation, his covering and the covering of the badgers' skins that is above upon it, and the hanging for the door of the tabernacle of the congregation, and the hangings of the court, and the hanging for the door of the gate of the court which is by the tabernacle and by the altar round about, and their cords, and all the instruments of their service, and all that is made for them, so shall they serve. At the appointment of Aaron and his sons shall be all the service of the sons of the Gershonites, in all their burdens and in all their service, and ye shall appoint unto them in charge all their burdens. This is the service of the families of the sons of Gershon in the tabernacle of the congregation, and their charge shall be under the hand of Ithamar the son of Aaron the priest.

As for the sons of Merari, thou shalt number them after their families, by the house of their fathers, from thirty years old and upward even unto fifty years old shalt thou number them, everyone that entereth into the service to do the work of the tabernacle of the congregation. And this is the charge of their burden according to all their service in the tabernacle of the congregation: the boards of the tabernacle, and the bars thereof, and the pillars thereof, and sockets thereof, and the pillars of the court round about, and their sockets, and their pins, and their cords, with all their instruments, and with all their service, and by name ye shall reckon the instruments of the charge of their burden. This is the service of the families of the sons of Merari, according to all their service in the tabernacle of the congregation, under the hand of Ithamar the son of Aaron the priest.

And Moses and Aaron and the chief of the congregation numbered the sons of the Kohathites after their families and after the house of their fathers, from thirty years old and upward even unto fifty years old, everyone that entereth into the service for the work in the tabernacle of the congregation, and those that were numbered of them by their families were two thousand seven hundred and fifty. These were they that were numbered of the families of the Kohathites, all that might do service in the tabernacle of the congregation which Moses and Aaron did number according to the commandments of the Lord by the hand of Moses.

And those that were numbered of the sons of Gershon, throughout their families, and by the house of their fathers, from thirty years old and upward even unto fifty years old, everyone that entereth into the service for the work of the tabernacle of the congregation, even those that were numbered of them, throughout their families, by the house of their fathers, were two thousand and six hundred and thirty. These are they that were numbered of the families of the sons of Gershon, of all that might do service in the tabernacle of the congregation, whom Moses and Aaron did number according to the commandment of the Lord.

And those that were numbered of the families of the sons of Merari, throughout their families, by the house of their fathers, from thirty years old and upward even unto fifty years old, everyone that entereth into the service for the work of the tabernacle of the congregation, even those that were numbered of them after their families, were three thousand and two hundred. These be those that were numbered of the families of the sons of Merari, whom Moses and Aaron numbered according to the word of the Lord by the hand of Moses.

All those that were numbered of the Levites, whom Moses and Aaron and the chief of Israel numbered, after their families and after the house of their fathers, from thirty years old and upward even unto fifty years old, every one that came to do the service of the ministry, and the service of the burden in the tabernacle of the congregation, even those that were numbered of them, were eight thousand and five hundred and fourscore. According to the commandment of the Lord they were numbered by the hand of Moses, every one according to his service, and according to his burden, thus were they numbered of him as the Lord commanded Moses.

3 AND the Lord spake unto Moses saying, Command the children of Israel that they put out of the camp every leper, and everyone that hath an issue, and whosoever is defiled by the dead, both male and female shall ye put out, without the camp shall ye put them, that they defile not their camps, in the midst whereof I dwell. And the children of Israel did so, and put them out without the camp; as the Lord spake unto Moses, so did the children of Israel.

And the Lord spake unto Moses saying, Speak unto the children of Israel, When a man or woman shall commit any sin that men commit, to do a trespass against the Lord, and that person be guilty, then they shall confess their sin which they have done, and he shall recompense his trespass with the principal thereof, and add unto it the fifth part thereof, and give it unto him against whom he hath trespassed. But if the man have no kinsman to recompense the trespass unto, let the trespass be recompensed unto the Lord, even to the priest, beside the ram of the atonement, whereby an atonement shall be made for him. And every offering of all the holy things of the children of Israel, which they bring unto the Priest shall be his. And every man's hallowed things shall be his, whatsoever any man giveth the priest, it shall be his.

And the Lord spake unto Moses saying, Speak unto the children of Israel and say unto them, If any man's wife go aside and commit a trespass against him, and a man lie with her carnally, and it be hid from the eyes of her husband, and be kept close, and she be defiled, and there be no witnesses against her, neither she be taken with the manner, and the spirit of jealousy come upon him, and he be jealous of his wife, and she be defiled, or if the spirit of jealousy come upon him, and he be jealous of his wife, and she be not defiled, then shall the man bring his wife unto the priest, and he shall bring her offering for her, the tenth part of an ephah of barley meal; he shall pour no oil upon it, nor put frankincense thereon, for it is an offering of jealousy and offering of memorial, bringing iniquity to remembrance.

And the priest shall bring her near, and set her before the Lord, and the priest shall take holy water in an earthen vessel, and of the dust that is in the floor of the tabernacle the priest shall take and put it into the water, and the priest shall set the woman before the Lord, and uncover the woman's head, and put the offering of memorial in her hands, which is the jealousy offering, and the priest shall have in his hand the bitter water that causeth the curse. And the priest shall charge her by an oath, and say unto the woman, If no man have lain with thee, and if thou hast not gone aside to uncleanness with another instead of thy husband, be thou free from this bitter water that causeth the curse, but if thou hast gone aside to another instead of thy husband, and if thou be defiled, and some man have lain with thee beside thine husband, then the priest shall charge the woman with an oath of cursing, and the priest shall say unto the woman, The Lord make thee a curse and an oath among thy people, when the Lord doth make thy thigh to rot, and thy belly to swell, and this water that causeth the curse shall go into thy bowels, to make thy belly to swell, and thy thigh to rot. And the woman shall say, Amen, amen.

And the priest shall write these curses in a book, and he shall blot them out with the bitter water, and he shall cause the woman to drink the bitter water that causeth the curse, and the water that causeth the curse shall enter into her and become bitter. Then the priest shall take the jealousy offering out of the woman's hand and shall wave the offering before the Lord, and offer it upon the altar, and the priest shall take a handful of the offering, even the memorial thereof, and burn it upon the altar, and afterward shall cause the woman to drink the water. And when he hath made her to drink the water, then it shall come to pass that if she be defiled, and have done trespass against her husband, that the water that causeth the curse shall enter into her and become bitter, and her belly shall swell, and her thigh shall rot, and the woman shall be a curse among her people. And if the woman be not defiled, but be clean, then she shall be free, and shall conceive seed.

This is the law of jealousies, when a wife goeth aside to another instead of her husband, and is defiled, or when the spirit of jealousy cometh upon him, and he be jealous over his wife, and shall set the woman before the Lord, and the priest shall execute upon her all this law. Then shall the man be guiltless from iniquity, and this woman shall bear her iniquity.

4 AND the Lord spake unto Moses saying, Speak unto the children of Israel, and say unto them, When either man or woman shall separate themselves to vow a vow of a Nazarite, to separate themselves unto the Lord, he shall separate himself from wine and strong drink and shall drink no vinegar of wine, or vinegar of strong drink, neither shall he drink any liquor of grapes, nor eat moist grapes, or dried. All the days of his separation shall he eat nothing that is made of the vine tree, from the kernels even to the husk.

All the days of the vow of his separation there shall no razor come upon his head, until the days be fulfilled in the which he separateth himself unto the Lord, he shall be holy, and shall let the locks of the hair of his head grow.

All the days that he separateth himself unto the Lord, he shall come at no dead body. He shall not make himself unclean for his father, or for his mother, for his brother, or for his sister, when they die, because the consecration of his God is upon his head. All the days of his separation he is holy unto the Lord.

And if any man die very suddenly by him, and he hath defiled the head of his consecration, then he shall shave his head in the day of his cleansing, on the seventh day shall he shave it. And on the eighth day he shall bring two turtles, or two young pigeons, to the priest, to the door of the tabernacle of the congregation, and the priest shall offer the one for a sin offering, and the other for a burnt offering, and make an atonement for him, for that he sinned by the dead and shall hallow his head that same day. And he shall consecrate unto the Lord the days of his separation and shall bring a lamb of the first year for a trespass offering, but the days that were before shall be lost, because his separation was defiled.

And this is the law of the Nazarite when the days of his separation are fulfilled: he shall be brought unto the door of the tabernacle of the congregation, and he shall offer his offering unto the Lord, one he lamb of the first year without blemish for a burnt offering, and one ewe lamb of the first year without blemish for a sin offering, and one ram without blemish for peace offerings, and a basket of unleavened bread, cakes of fine flour mingled with oil, and wafers of unleavened bread anointed with oil, and their meat offering, and their drink offerings. And the priest shall bring them before the Lord, and shall offer his sin offering and his burnt offering, and he shall offer the ram for a sacrifice of peace offerings unto the Lord with the basket of unleavened bread, the priest shall offer also his meat offering and his drink offering. And the Nazarite shall shave the head of his separation at the door of the tabernacle of the congregation, and shall take the hair of the head of his separation and put it in the fire which is under the sacrifice of the peace offerings. And the priest shall take the sodden shoulder of the ram, and one unleavened cake out of the basket, and one unleavened wafer, and shall put them upon the hands of the Nazarite, after the hair of his separation is shaven, and the priest shall wave them for a wave offering before the Lord, this is holy for the priest, with the wave breast and heave shoulder, and after that the Nazarite may drink wine.

This is the law of the Nazarite who hath vowed, and of his offering unto the Lord for his separation, besides that that his hand shall get, according to the vow which he vowed, so he must do after the law of his separation.

And the Lord spake unto Moses saying, Speak unto Aaron and unto his sons saying, On this wise ye shall bless the children of Israel saying unto them,

> The Lord bless thee and keep thee,
> The Lord make his face shine upon thee and be gracious unto thee,
> The Lord lift up his countenance upon thee and give thee peace.

And they shall put my name upon the children of Israel and I will bless them.

5 AND it came to pass on the day that Moses had fully set up the tabernacle, and had anointed it, and sanctified it, and all the instruments thereof, both the altar and all the vessels thereof, and had anointed them, and sanctified them, that the princes of Israel, heads of the house of their fathers, who were the princes of the tribes and were over them that were numbered, offered, and they brought their offering before the Lord, six covered wagons, and twelve oxen, a wagon for two of the princes and for each one an ox, and they brought them before the tabernacle. And the Lord spake unto Moses saying, Take it of them, that they may be to do the service of the tabernacle of the congregation, and thou shalt give them unto the Levites, to every man according to his service. And Moses took the wagons and the oxen and gave them unto the Levites. Two wagons and four oxen he gave unto the sons of Gershon according to their service, and four wagons and eight oxen he gave unto the sons of Merari according unto their service, under the hand of Ithamar the son of Aaron the priest. But unto the sons of Kohath he gave none because the service of the sanctuary belonging unto them was that they should bear upon their shoulders. And the princes offered for dedicating of the altar in the day that it was anointed, even the princes offered their offering before the altar. And the Lord said unto Moses, They shall offer their offering, each prince on his day, for the dedicating of the altar.

And he that offered his offering the first day was Nahshon the son of Amminadab, of the tribe of Judah, and his offering was one silver charger, the weight whereof was a hundred and thirty shekels, one silver bowl of seventy shekels, after the shekel of the sanctuary, both of them were full of fine flour mingled with oil for a meat offering, one spoon of ten shekels of gold, full of incense, one young bullock, one ram, one lamb of the first year for a burnt offering, one kid of the goats for a sin offering, and for a sacrifice of peace offerings, two oxen, five rams, five he goats, five lambs of the first year, this was the offering of Nahshon the son of Amminadab.

On the second day Nethaneel the son of Zuar, prince of Issachar, did offer, he offered for his offering one silver charger, the weight whereof was a hundred and thirty shekels, one silver bowl of seventy shekels, after the shekel of the sanctuary, both of them full of fine flour mingled with oil for a meat offering, one spoon of gold of ten shekels, full of incense, one young bullock, one ram, one lamb of the first year for a burnt offering, one kid of the goats for a sin offering, and for a sacrifice of peace offerings, two oxen, five rams, five he goats, five lambs of the first year, this was the offering of Nethaneel the son of Zuar.

On the third day Eliab the son of Helon, prince of the children of Zebulun, did offer, his offering was one silver charger, the weight whereof was a hundred and thirty shekels, one silver bowl of seventy shekels, after the shekel of the sanctuary, both of them full of fine flour mingled with oil for a meat offering, one golden spoon of ten shekels, full of incense, one young bullock, one ram, one lamb of the first year for a burnt offering, one kid of the goats for a sin offering, and for a sacrifice of peace offerings, two oxen, five rams, five he goats, five lambs of the first year, this was the offering of Eliab the son of Helon.

On the fourth day Elizur the son of Shedeur, prince of the children of Reuben, did offer, his offering was one silver charger of the weight of a hundred and thirty shekels, one silver bowl of seventy shekels, after the shekel of the sanctuary, both of them full of fine flour mingled with oil for a meat offering, one golden spoon of ten shekels, full of incense, one young bullock, one ram, one lamb of the first year for a burnt offering, one kid of the goats for a sin offering, and for a sacrifice of peace offerings, two oxen, five rams, five he goats, five lambs of the first year, this was the offering of Elizur the son of Shedeur.

On the fifth day Shelumiel the son of Zurishaddai, prince of the children of Simeon, did offer, his offering was one silver charger, the weight whereof was a hundred and thirty shekels, one silver bowl of seventy shekels, after the shekel of the sanctuary, both of them full of fine flour mingled with oil for a meat offering, one golden spoon of ten shekels, full of incense, one young bullock, one ram, one lamb of the first year for a burnt offering, one kid of the goats for a sin offering, and for a sacrifice of peace offerings, two oxen, five rams, five he goats, five lambs of the first year, this was the offering of Shelumiel the son of Zurishaddai.

On the sixth day Eliasaph the son of Deuel, prince of the children of Gad, offered, his offering was one silver charger of the weight of a hundred and thirty shekels, a silver bowl of seventy shekels, after the shekel of the sanctuary, both of them full of fine flour mingled with oil for a meat offering, one golden spoon of ten shekels, full of incense, one young bullock, one ram, one lamb of the first year for a burnt offering, one kid of the goats for a sin offering, and for a sacrifice of peace offerings, two oxen, five rams, five he goats, five lambs of the first year, this was the offering of Eliasaph the son of Deuel.

On the seventh day Elishama the son of Ammihud, prince of the children of Ephraim, offered, his offering was one silver charger, the weight whereof was a hundred and thirty shekels, one silver bowl of seventy shekels, after the shekel of the sanctuary, both of them full of fine flour mingled with oil for a meat offering, one golden spoon of ten shekels, full of incense, one young bullock, one ram, one lamb of the first year for a burnt offering, one kid of the goats for a sin offering, and for a sacrifice of peace offerings, two oxen, five rams, five he goats, five lambs of the first year, this was the offering of Elishama the son of Ammihud.

On the eighth day offered Gamaliel the son of Pedahzur, prince of the children of Manasseh, his offering was one silver charger of the weight of a hundred and thirty shekels, one silver bowl of seventy shekels, after the shekel of the sanctuary, both of them full of fine flour mingled with oil for a meat offering, one golden spoon of ten shekels, full of incense, one young bullock, one ram, one lamb of the first year for a burnt offering, one kid of the goats for a sin offering, and for a sacrifice of peace offerings, two oxen, five rams, five he goats, five lambs of the first year, this was the offering of Gamaliel the son of Pedahzur.

One the ninth day Abidan the son of Gideoni, prince of the children of Benjamin, offered, his offering was one silver charger, the weight whereof was a hundred and thirty shekels, one silver bowl of seventy shekels, after the shekel of the sanctuary, both of them full of fine flour mingled with oil for a meat offering, one golden spoon of ten shekels, full of incense, one young bullock, one ram, one lamb of the first year for a burnt offering, one kid of the goats for a sin offering, and for a sacrifice of peace offerings, two oxen, five rams, five he goats, five lambs of the first year, this was the offering of Abidan the son of Gideoni.

On the tenth day Ahiezer the son of Ammishaddai, prince of the children of Dan, offered, his offering was one silver charger, the weight whereof was a hundred and thirty shekels, one silver bowl of seventy shekels, after the shekel of the sanctuary, both of them full of fine flour mingled with oil for a meat offering, one golden spoon of ten shekels, full of incense, one young bullock, one ram, one lamb of the first year for a burnt offering, one kid of the goats for a sin offering, and for a sacrifice of peace offerings, two oxen, five rams, five he goats, five lambs of the first year, this was the offering of Ahiezer the son of Ammishaddai.

On the eleventh day Pagiel the son of Ocran, prince of the children of Asher, offered, his offering was one silver charger, the weight whereof was a hundred and thirty shekels, one silver bowl of seventy shekels, after the shekel of the sanctuary, both of them full of fine flour mingled with oil for a meat offering, one golden spoon of ten shekels, full of incense, one young bullock, one ram, one lamb of the first year for a burnt offering, one kid of the goats for a sin offering, and for a sacrifice of peace offerings, two oxen, five rams, five he goats, five lambs of the first year, this was the offering of Pagiel the son of Ocran.

On the twelfth day Ahira the son of Enan, prince of the children of Naphtali, offered, his offering was one silver charger, the weight whereof was a hundred and thirty shekels, one silver bowl of seventy shekels, after the shekel of the sanctuary, both of them full of fine flour mingled with oil for a meat offering, one golden spoon of ten shekels, full of incense, one young bullock, one ram, one lamb of the first year for a burnt offering, one kid of the goats for a sin offering, and for a sacrifice of peace offerings, two oxen, five rams, five he goats, five lambs of the first year, this was the offering of Ahira the son of Enan.

This was the dedication of the altar, in the day when it was anointed, by the princes of Israel, twelve chargers of silver, twelve silver bowls, twelve spoons of gold, each charger of silver weighing a hundred and thirty shekels, each bowl seventy, all the silver vessels weighed two thousand and four hundred shekels, after the shekel of the sanctuary, the golden spoons were twelve, full of incense, weighing ten shekels apiece, after the shekel of the sanctuary, all the gold of the spoons was a hundred and twenty shekels. All the oxen for the burnt offering were twelve bullocks, the rams twelve, the lambs of the first year twelve, with their meat offering, and the kids of the goats for a sin offering twelve. And all the oxen for the sacrifice of the peace offerings were twenty and four bullocks, the rams sixty, the he goats sixty, the lambs of the first year sixty. This was the dedication of the altar, after that it was anointed.

6 AND when Moses was gone into the tabernacle of the congregation to speak with him, then he heard the voice of one speaking unto him from off the mercy seat that was upon the ark of the testimony, from between the two cherubim, and he spake unto him.

And the Lord spake unto Moses saying, Speak unto Aaron and say unto him, When thou lightest the lamps, the seven lamps shall give light over against the candlestick. And Aaron did so, he lighted the lamps thereof over against the candlestick as the Lord commanded Moses. And this work of the candlestick was of beaten gold unto the shaft thereof, unto the flowers thereof was beaten work according unto the pattern which the Lord had showed Moses, so he made the candlestick.

And the Lord spake unto Moses saying, Take the Levites from among the children of Israel, and cleanse them. And thus shalt thou do unto them to cleanse them, Sprinkle water of purifying upon them, and let them shave all their flesh, and let them wash their clothes, and so make themselves clean. Then let them take a young bullock with his meat offering, even fine flour mingled with oil, and another young bullock shalt thou take for a sin offering. And thou shalt bring the Levites before the tabernacle of the congregation, and thou shalt gather the whole assembly of the children of Israel together. And thou shalt bring the Levites before the Lord, and the children of Israel shall put their hands upon the Levites, and Aaron shall offer the Levites before the Lord for an offering of the children of Israel, that they may execute the service of the Lord. And the Levites shall lay their hands upon the heads of the bullocks, and thou shalt offer the one for a sin offering and the other for a burnt offering unto the Lord to make an atonement for the Levites. And thou shalt set the Levites before Aaron, and before his sons, and offer them for an offering unto the Lord.

Thus shalt thou separate the Levites from among the children of Israel and the Levites shall be mine. And after that shall the Levites go in to do the service of the tabernacle of the congregation and thou shalt cleanse them and offer them for an offering. For they are wholly given unto me from among the children of Israel, instead of such as open every womb, even instead of the firstborn of all the children of Israel have I taken them unto me. For all the firstborn of the children of Israel are mine, both man and beast, on the day that I smote every firstborn in the land of Egypt I sanctified them for myself. And I have taken the Levites for all the firstborn of the children of Israel. And I have given the Levites as a gift to Aaron and to his sons from among the children of Israel, to do the service of the children of Israel in the tabernacle of the congregation and to make an atonement for the children of Israel, that there be no plague among the children of Israel when the children of Israel come nigh unto the sanctuary.

And Moses, and Aaron, and all the congregation of the children of Israel, did to the Levites according unto all that the Lord commanded Moses concerning the Levites, so did the children of Israel unto them. And the Levites were purified, and they washed their clothes, and Aaron offered them as an offering before the Lord, and Aaron made an atonement for them to cleanse them. And after that went the Levites in to do their service in the tabernacle of the congregation before Aaron, and before his sons, as the Lord had commanded Moses concerning the Levites, so did they unto them.

And the Lord spake unto Moses saying, This is it that belongeth unto the Levites, from twenty and five years old and upward they shall go in to wait upon the service of the tabernacle of the congregation, and from the age of fifty years they shall cease waiting upon the service thereof and shall serve no more, but shall minister with their brethren in the tabernacle of the congregation to keep the charge and shall do no service. Thus shalt thou do unto the Levites touching their charge.

7 AND the Lord spake unto Moses in the wilderness of Sinai, in the first month of the second year after they were come out of the land of Egypt, saying, Let the children of Israel also keep the passover at his appointed season. In the fourteenth day of this month, at even, ye shall keep it in his appointed season, according to all the rites of it, and according to all the ceremonies thereof shall ye keep it. And Moses spake unto the children of Israel, that they should keep the passover. And they kept the passover on the fourteenth day of the first month at even in the wilderness of Sinai, according to all that the Lord commanded Moses, so did the children of Israel.

And there were certain men, who were defiled by the dead body of a man, that they could not keep the passover on that day, and they came before Moses and before Aaron on that day. And those men said unto him, We are defiled by the dead body of a man, wherefore are we kept back, that we may not offer an offering of the Lord in his appointed season among the children of Israel? And Moses said unto them, Stand still and I will hear what the Lord will command concerning you.

And the Lord spake unto Moses, saying, Speak unto the children of Israel saying, If any man of you or of your posterity shall be unclean by reason of a dead body or be in a journey afar off, yet he shall keep the passover unto the Lord. The fourteenth day of the second month at even they shall keep it and eat it with unleavened bread and bitter herbs. They shall leave none of it unto the morning, nor break any bone of it according to all the ordinances of the passover they shall keep it. But the man that is clean, and is not in a journey, and forbeareth to keep the passover, even the same soul shall be cut off from among his people because he brought not the offering of the Lord in his appointed season, that man shall bear his sin. And if a stranger shall sojourn among you and will keep the passover unto the Lord according to the ordinance of the passover, and according to the manner thereof so shall he do, ye shall have one ordinance, both for the stranger and for him that was born in the land.

And on the day that the tabernacle was reared up the cloud covered the tabernacle, namely, the tent of the testimony, and at even there was upon the tabernacle as it were the appearance of fire until the morning. So it was alway, the cloud covered it by day and the appearance of fire by night. And when the cloud was taken up from the tabernacle, then after that the children of Israel journeyed and in the place where the cloud abode, there the children of Israel pitched their tents. At the commandment of the Lord the children of Israel journeyed, and at the commandment of the Lord they pitched, as long as the cloud abode upon the tabernacle they rested in their tents. And when the cloud tarried long upon the tabernacle many days, then the children of Israel kept the charge of the Lord, and journeyed not. And so it was, when the cloud was a few days upon the tabernacle, according to the commandment of the Lord they abode in their tents, and according to the commandment of the Lord they journeyed. And so it was, when the cloud abode from even unto the morning, and that the cloud was taken up in the morning, then they journeyed, whether it was by day or by night that the cloud was taken up, they journeyed. Or whether it were two days, or a month, or a year, that the cloud tarried upon the tabernacle, remaining thereon, the children of Israel abode in their tents and journeyed not, but when it was taken up, they journeyed. At the commandment of the Lord they rested in their tents, and at the commandment of the Lord they journeyed, they kept the charge of the Lord, at the commandment of the Lord by the hand of Moses.

And the Lord spake unto Moses saying, Make thee two trumpets of silver, of a whole piece shalt thou make them, that thou mayest use them for the calling of the assembly and for the journeyings of the camps. And when they shall blow with them, all the assembly shall assemble themselves to thee at the door of the tabernacle of the congregation. And if they blow but with one trumpet, then the princes, which are heads of the thousands of Israel, shall gather themselves unto thee. When ye blow an alarm, then the camps that lie on the east parts shall go forward. When ye blow an alarm the second time, then the camps that lie on the south side shall take their journey, they shall blow an alarm for their journeys. But when the congregation is to be gathered together, ye shall blow, but ye shall not sound an alarm. And the sons of Aaron, the priests, shall blow with the trumpets, and they shall be to you for an ordinance for ever throughout your generations. And if ye go to war in your land against the enemy that oppresseth you, then ye shall blow an alarm with the trumpets, and ye shall be remembered before the Lord your God, and ye shall be saved from your enemies. Also in the day of your gladness, and in your solemn days, and in the beginnings of your months, ye shall blow with the trumpets over your burnt offerings and over the sacrifices of your peace offerings, that they may be to you for a memorial before your God; I am the Lord your God.

And it came to pass on the twentieth day of the second month, in the second year, that the cloud was taken up from off the tabernacle of the testimony. And the children of Israel took their journeys out of the wilderness of Sinai and the cloud rested in the wilderness of Paran. And they first took their journey according to the commandment of the Lord by the hand of Moses. In the first place went the standard of the camp of the children of Judah according to their armies and over his host was Nahshon the son of Amminadab. And over the host of the tribe of the children of Issachar was Nethaneel the son of Zuar. And over the host of the tribe of the children of Zebulun was Eliab the son of Helon. And the tabernacle was taken down and the sons of Gershon and the sons of Merari set forward, bearing the tabernacle.

And the standard of the camp of Reuben set forward according to their armies, and over his host was Elizur the son of Shedeur. And over the host of the tribe of the children of Simeon was Shelumiel the son of Zurishaddai. And over the host of the tribe of the children of Gad was Eliasaph the son of Deuel. And the Kohathites set forward, bearing the sanctuary, and the other did set up the tabernacle against they came.

And the standard of the camp of the children of Ephraim set forward according to their armies, and over his host was Elishama the son of Ammihud. And over the host of the tribe of the children of Manasseh was Gamaliel the son of Pedahzur. And over the host of the tribe of the children of Benjamin was Abidan the son of Gideoni.

And the standard of the camp of the children of Dan set forward, which was the rearward of all the camps throughout their hosts, and over his host was Ahiezer the son of Ammishaddai. And over the host of the tribe of the children of Asher was Pagiel the son of Ocran. And over the host of the tribe of the children of Naphtali was Ahira the son of Enan. Thus were the journeyings of the children of Israel according to their armies when they set forward.

And Moses said unto Hobab, the son of Raguel the Midianite Moses' father-in-law, We are journeying unto the place of which the Lord said, I will give it you; come thou with us and we will do thee good, for the Lord hath spoken good concerning Israel. And he said unto him, I will not go, but I will depart to mine own land and to my kindred. And he said, Leave us not, I pray thee, forasmuch as thou knowest how we are to encamp in the wilderness and thou mayest be to us instead of eyes. And it shall be, if thou go with us, yea, it shall be that what goodness the Lord shall do unto us, the same will we do unto thee.

And they departed from the mount of the Lord three days' journey, and the ark of the covenant of the Lord went before them in the three days' journey to search out a resting-place for them. And the cloud of the Lord was upon them by day when they went out of the camp. And it came to pass when the ark set forward, that Moses said, Rise up, Lord, and let thine enemies be scattered, and let them that hate thee flee before thee. And when it rested, he said, Return, O Lord, unto the many thousands of Israel.

And when the people complained, it displeased the Lord, and the Lord heard it, and his anger was kindled, and the fire of the Lord burnt among them and consumed them that were in the uttermost parts of the camp. And the people cried unto Moses, and when Moses prayed unto the Lord, the fire was quenched. And he called the name of the place Taberah, because the fire of the Lord burnt among them.

And the mixed multitude that was among them fell a lusting, and the children of Israel also wept again and said, Who shall give us flesh to eat? We remember the fish which we did eat in Egypt freely, the cucumbers, and the melons, and the leeks, and the onions, and the garlic, but now our soul is dried away, there is nothing at all besides this manna before our eyes.

And the manna was as coriander seed and the color thereof as the color of bdellium. And the people went about, and gathered it, and ground it in mills, or beat it in a mortar, and baked it in pans, and made cakes of it, and the taste of it was as the taste of fresh oil. And when the dew fell upon the camp in the night, the manna fell upon it.

Then Moses heard the people weep throughout their families, every man in the door of his tent, and the anger of the Lord was kindled greatly, Moses also was displeased. And Moses said unto the Lord, Wherefore hast thou afflicted thy servant? and wherefore have I not found favor in thy sight that thou layest the burden of all this people upon me? Have I conceived all this people? Have I begotten them that thou shouldest say unto me, Carry them in thy bosom as a nursing father beareth the sucking child, unto the land which thou swarest unto their fathers? Whence should I have flesh to give unto all this people? For they weep unto me saying, Give us flesh that we may eat. I am not able to bear all this people alone because it is too heavy for me. And if thou deal thus with me, kill me, I pray thee, out of hand, if I have found favor in thy sight, and let me not see my wretchedness.

And the Lord said unto Moses, Gather unto me seventy men of the elders of Israel, whom thou knowest to be the elders of the people and officers over them, and bring them unto the tabernacle of the congregation that they may stand there with thee. And I will come down and talk with thee there, and I will take of the Spirit which is upon thee and will put it upon them, and they shall bear the burden of the people with thee that thou bear it not thyself alone.

And say thou unto the people, Sanctify yourselves against tomorrow and ye shall eat flesh, for ye have wept in the ears of the Lord saying, Who shall give us flesh to eat? For it was well with us in Egypt, therefore the Lord will give you flesh and ye shall eat. Ye shall not eat one day, nor two days, nor five days, neither ten days, nor twenty days, but even a whole month, until it come out at your nostrils and it be loathsome unto you because that ye have despised the Lord which is among you and have wept before him saying, Why came we forth out of Egypt?

And Moses said, The people among whom I am are six hundred thousand footmen, and thou hast said, I will give them flesh that they may eat a whole month. Shall the flocks and the herds be slain for them to suffice them? Or shall all the fish of the sea be gathered together for them to suffice them? And the Lord said unto Moses, Is the Lord's hand waxed short? Thou shalt see now whether my word shall come to pass unto thee or not.

And Moses went out and told the people the words of the Lord, and gathered the seventy men of the elders of the people, and set them round about the tabernacle. And the Lord came down in a cloud and spake unto him, and took of the Spirit that was upon him and gave it unto the seventy elders; and it came to pass that when the Spirit rested upon them, they prophesied and did not cease.

But there remained two of the men in the camp, the name of the one was Eldad and the name of the other Medad, and the Spirit rested upon them and they were of them that were written, but went not out unto the tabernacle, and they prophesied in the camp. And there ran a young man and told Moses and said, Eldad and Medad do prophesy in the camp. And Joshua the son of Nun, the servant of Moses, one of his young men, answered and said, My lord Moses forbid them. And Moses said unto him, Enviest thou for my sake? Would God that all the Lord's people were prophets and that the Lord would put his Spirit upon them. And Moses gat him unto the camp, he and the elders of Israel.

And there went forth a wind from the Lord, and brought quails from the sea and let them fall by the camp, as it were a day's journey on this side and as it were a day's journey on the other side, round about the camp, and as it were two cubits high upon the face of the Earth. And the people stood up all that day, and all that night, and all the next day, and they gathered the quails, he that gathered least gathered ten homers, and they spread them all abroad for themselves round about the camp. And while the flesh was yet between their teeth, ere it was chewed, the wrath of the Lord was kindled against the people and the Lord smote the people with a very great plague. And he called the name of that place Kibroth-hattaavah because there they buried the people that lusted. And the people journeyed from Kibroth-hattaavah unto Hazeroth and abode at Hazeroth.

And Miriam and Aaron spake against Moses because of the Ethiopian woman whom he had married, for he had married an Ethiopian woman. And they said, Hath the Lord indeed spoken only by Moses? Hath he not spoken also by us?

And the Lord heard it (Now the man Moses was very meek, above all the men which were upon the face of the Earth.) And the Lord spake suddenly unto Moses and unto Aaron and unto Miriam, Come out ye three unto the tabernacle of the congregation. And they three came out. And the Lord came down in the pillar of the cloud, and stood in the door of the tabernacle, and called Aaron and Miriam, and they both came forth. And he said, Hear now my words, If there be a prophet among you, I the Lord will make myself known unto him in a vision and will speak unto him in a dream. My servant Moses is not so, who is faithful in all mine house. With him will I speak mouth to mouth, even apparently and not in dark speeches and the similitude of the Lord shall he behold, wherefore then were ye not afraid to speak against my servant Moses?

And the anger of the Lord was kindled against them and he departed. And the cloud departed from off the tabernacle and behold, Miriam became leprous, white as snow, and Aaron looked upon Miriam and behold, she was leprous. And Aaron said unto Moses, Alas, my lord, I beseech thee, lay not the sin upon us wherein we have done foolishly and wherein we have sinned. Let her not be as one dead of whom the flesh is half consumed when he cometh out of his mother's womb. And Moses cried unto the Lord, saying, Heal her now, O God, I beseech thee. And the Lord said unto Moses, If her father had but spit in her face, should she not be ashamed seven days? Let her be shut out from the camp seven days and after that let her be received in again. And Miriam was shut out from the camp seven days and the people journeyed not till Miriam was brought in again. And afterward the people removed from Hazeroth, and pitched in the wilderness of Paran.

8 AND the Lord spake unto Moses saying, Send thou men, that they may search the land of Canaan which I give unto the children of Israel, of every tribe of their fathers shall ye send a man, every one a ruler among them. And Moses by the commandment of the Lord sent them from the wilderness of Paran all those men were heads of the children of Israel. And these were their names: Of the tribe of Reuben, Shammua the son of Zaccur. Of the tribe of Simeon, Shaphat the son of Hori. Of the tribe of Judah, Caleb the son of Jephunneh. Of the tribe of Issachar, Igal the son of Joseph. Of the tribe of Ephraim, Oshea the son of Nun. Of the tribe of Benjamin, Palti the son of Raphu. Of the tribe of Zebulun, Gaddiel the son of Sodi. Of the tribe of Joseph, namely, of the tribe of Manasseh, Gaddi the son of Susi. Of the tribe of Dan, Ammiel the son of Gemalli. Of the tribe of Asher, Sethur the son of Michael. Of the tribe of Naphtali, Nahbi the son of Vophsi. Of the tribe of Gad, Geuel the son of Machi. These are the names of the men which Moses sent to spy out the land. And Moses called Oshea the son of Nun, Jehoshua.

And Moses sent them to spy out the land of Canaan and said unto them, Get you up this way southward, and go up into the mountain, and see the land, what it is and the people that dwelleth therein, whether they be strong or weak, few or many, and what the land is that they dwell in, whether it be good or bad, and what cities they be that they dwell in, whether in tents, or in strongholds, and what the land is, whether it be fat or lean, whether there be wood therein or not. And be of good courage and bring of the fruit of the land. Now the time was the time of the first ripe grapes.

So they went up, and searched the land from the wilderness of Zin unto Rehob, as men come to Hamath. And they ascended by the south and came unto Hebron, where Ahiman, Sheshai, and Talmai, the children of Anak, were (Now Hebron was built seven years before Zoan in Egypt). And they came unto the brook of Eshcol and cut down from thence a branch with one cluster of grapes, and they bare it between two upon a staff, and they brought of the pomegranates and of the figs. The place was called the brook Eshcol because of the cluster of grapes which the children of Israel cut down from thence.

And they returned from searching of the land after forty days. And they went and came to Moses, and to Aaron, and to all the congregation of the children of Israel, unto the wilderness of Paran to Kadesh, and brought back word unto them and unto all the congregation, and showed them the fruit of the land. And they told him and said, We came unto the land whither thou sentest us, and surely it floweth with milk and honey and this is the fruit of it. Nevertheless the people be strong that dwell in the land, and the cities are walled and very great, and moreover we saw the children of Anak there. The Amalekites dwell in the land of the south, and the Hittites, and the Jebusites, and the Amorites dwell in the mountains, and the Canaanites dwell by the sea and by the coast of Jordan.

And Caleb stilled the people before Moses and said, Let us go up at once and possess it, for we are well able to overcome it. But the men that went up with him said, We be not able to go up against the people for they are stronger than we. And they brought up an evil report of the land which they had searched unto the children of Israel saying, The land through which we have gone to search it is a land that eateth up the inhabitants thereof and all the people that we saw in it are men of a great stature. And there we saw the giants, the sons of Anak, which come of the giants, and we were in our own sight as grasshoppers, and so we were in their sight.

And all the congregation lifted up their voice, and cried, and the people wept that night. And all the children of Israel murmured against Moses and against Aaron, and the whole congregation said unto them, Would God that we had died in the land of Egypt. Or would God that we had died in this wilderness. And wherefore hath the Lord brought us unto this land, to fall by the sword, that our wives and our children should be a prey? Were it not better for us to return into Egypt? And they said one to another, Let us make a captain and let us return into Egypt.

Then Moses and Aaron fell on their faces before all the assembly of the congregation of the children of Israel. And Joshua the son of Nun and Caleb the son of Jephunneh, which were of them that searched the land, rent their clothes and they spake unto all the company of the children of Israel saying, The land which we passed through to search it is an exceeding good land. If the Lord delight in us, then he will bring us into this land and give it us, a land which floweth with milk and honey. Only rebel not ye against the Lord neither fear ye the people of the land, for they are bread for us, their defense is departed from them, and the Lord is with us, fear them not. And all the congregation bade stone them with stones. And the glory of the Lord appeared in the tabernacle of the congregation before all the children of Israel.

And the Lord said unto Moses, How long will this people provoke me? And how long will it be ere they believe me, for all the signs which I have showed among them? I will smite them with the pestilence and disinherit them, and will make of thee a greater nation and mightier than they.

And Moses said unto the Lord, Then the Egyptians shall hear it (for thou broughtest up this people in thy might from among them) and they will tell it to the inhabitants of this land, for they have heard that thou Lord art among this people, that thou Lord art seen face to face, and that thy cloud standeth over them, and that thou goest before them, by daytime in a pillar of a cloud and in a pillar of fire by night. Now if thou shalt kill all this people as one man, then the nations which have heard the fame of thee will speak saying, Because the Lord was not able to bring this people into the land which he sware unto them, therefore he hath slain them in the wilderness. And now, I beseech thee, let the power of my Lord be great according as thou hast spoken saying, The Lord is long-suffering and of great mercy, forgiving iniquity and transgression, and by no means clearing the guilty, visiting the iniquity of the fathers upon the children unto the third and fourth generation. Pardon, I beseech thee, the iniquity of this people according unto the greatness of thy mercy and as thou hast forgiven this people from Egypt even until now.

And the Lord said, I have pardoned according to thy word, but as truly as I live, all the Earth shall be filled with the glory of the Lord. Because all those men which have seen my glory and my miracles which I did in Egypt and in the wilderness, and have tempted me now these ten times and have not hearkened to my voice, surely they shall not see the land which I sware unto their fathers, neither shall any of them that provoked me see it, but my servant Caleb, because he had another spirit with him and hath followed me fully, him will I bring into the land whereinto he went and his seed shall possess it (Now the Amalekites and the Canaanites dwelt in the valley). Tomorrow turn you and get you into the wilderness by the way of the Red Sea.

And the Lord spake unto Moses and unto Aaron, saying, How long shall I bear with this evil congregation which murmur against me? I have heard the murmurings of the children of Israel which they murmur against me. Say unto them, As truly as I live, saith the Lord, as ye have spoken in mine ears, so will I do to you: your carcasses shall fall in this wilderness and all that were numbered of you, according to your whole number, from twenty years old and upward, which have murmured against me, doubtless ye shall not come into the land concerning which I sware to make you dwell therein, save Caleb the son of Jephunneh and Joshua the son of Nun. But your little ones which ye said should be a prey, them will I bring in and they shall know the land which ye have despised. But as for you, your carcasses, they shall fall in this wilderness. And your children shall wander in the wilderness forty years and bear your whoredoms, until your carcasses be wasted in the wilderness. After the number of the days in which he searched the land, even forty days, each day for a year shall ye bear your iniquities, even forty years, and ye shall know my breach of promise. I the Lord have said, I will surely do it unto all this evil congregation that are gathered together against me, in this wilderness they shall be consumed and there they shall die.

And the men which Moses sent to search the land, who returned and made all the congregation to murmur against him by bringing up a slander upon the land, even those men that did bring up the evil report upon the land, died by the plague before the Lord. But Joshua the son of Nun and Caleb the son of Jephunneh, which were of the men that went to search the land, lived still. And Moses told these sayings unto all the children of Israel, and the people mourned greatly.

And they rose up early in the morning and gat them up into the top of the mountain saying, Lo, we be here and will go up unto the place which the Lord hath promised, for we have sinned. And Moses said, Wherefore now do ye transgress the commandment of the Lord? But it shall not prosper. Go not up, for the Lord is not among you, that ye be not smitten before your enemies. For the Amalekites and the Canaanites are there before you, and ye shall fall by the sword because ye are turned away from the Lord, therefore the Lord will not be with you. But they presumed to go up unto the hilltop, nevertheless the ark of the covenant of the Lord and Moses departed not out of the camp. Then the Amalekites came down, and the Canaanites which dwelt in that hill, and smote them and discomfited them even unto Hormah.

And the Lord spake unto Moses, saying, Speak unto the children of Israel and say unto them, When ye be come into the land of your habitations which I give unto you, and will make an offering by fire unto the Lord, a burnt offering, or a sacrifice in performing a vow, or in a freewill offering, or in your solemn feasts, to make a sweet savor unto the Lord, of the herd or of the flock, then shall he that offereth his offering unto the Lord bring a meat offering of a tenth deal of flour mingled with the fourth part of a hin of oil. And the fourth part of a hin of wine for a drink offering shalt thou prepare with the burnt offering or sacrifice for one lamb. Or for a ram, thou shalt prepare for a meat offering two tenth deals of flour mingled with the third part of a hin of oil. And for a drink offering thou shalt offer the third part of a hin of wine, for a sweet savor unto the Lord. And when thou preparest a bullock for a burnt offering, or for a sacrifice in performing a vow, or peace offerings unto the Lord, then shall he bring with a bullock a meat offering of three tenth deals of flour mingled with half a hin of oil. And thou shalt bring for a drink offering half a hin of wine, for an offering made by fire, of a sweet savor unto the Lord. Thus shall it be done for one bullock, or for one ram, or for a lamb, or a kid. According to the number that ye shall prepare so shall ye do to every one according to their number.

All that are born of the country shall do these things after this manner in offering an offering made by fire, of a sweet savor unto the Lord. And if a stranger sojourn with you, or whosoever be among you in your generations, and will offer an offering made by fire, of a sweet savor unto the Lord, as ye do, so he shall do. One ordinance shall be both for you of the congregation and also for a stranger that sojourneth with you, an ordinance for ever in your generations; as ye are, so shall the stranger be before the Lord. One law and one manner shall be for you and for the stranger that sojourneth with you.

And the Lord spake unto Moses saying, Speak unto the children of Israel and say unto them, When ye come into the land whither I bring you, then it shall be that when ye eat of the bread of the land, ye shall offer up a heave offering unto the Lord. Ye shall offer up a cake of the first of your dough for a heave offering, as ye do the heave offering of the threshing floor so shall ye heave it. Of the first of your dough ye shall give unto the Lord a heave offering in your generations.

And if ye have erred and not observed all these commandments which the Lord hath spoken unto Moses, even all that the Lord hath commanded you by the hand of Moses from the day that the Lord commanded Moses and henceforward among your generations, then it shall be, if aught be committed by ignorance without the knowledge of the congregation, that all the congregation shall offer one young bullock for a burnt offering, for a sweet savor unto the Lord, with his meat offering, and his drink offering, according to the manner, and one kid of the goats for a sin offering. And the priest shall make an atonement for all the congregation of the children of Israel and it shall be forgiven them, for it is ignorance, and they shall bring their offering, a sacrifice made by fire unto the Lord, and their sin offering before the Lord for their ignorance, and it shall be forgiven all the congregation of the children of Israel and the stranger that sojourneth among them, seeing all the people were in ignorance.

And if any soul sin through ignorance, then he shall bring a she goat of the first year for a sin offering. And the priest shall make an atonement for the soul that sinneth ignorantly when he sinneth by ignorance before the Lord, to make an atonement for him, and it shall be forgiven him. Ye shall have one law for him that sinneth through ignorance, both for him that is born among the children of Israel and for the stranger that sojourneth among them. But the soul that doeth aught presumptuously, whether he be born in the land or a stranger, the same reproacheth the Lord, and that soul shall be cut off from among his people. Because he hath despised the word of the Lord and hath broken his commandment, that soul shall utterly be cut off; his iniquity shall be upon him.

And while the children of Israel were in the wilderness, they found a man that gathered sticks upon the sabbath day. And they that found him gathering sticks brought him unto Moses and Aaron and unto all the congregation. And they put him in ward because it was not declared what should be done to him. And the Lord said unto Moses, The man shall be surely put to death, all the congregation shall stone him with stones without the camp. And all the congregation brought him without the camp and stoned him with stones and he died, as the Lord commanded Moses.

9 AND the Lord spake unto Moses saying, Speak unto the children of Israel and bid them that they make them fringes in the borders of their garments, throughout their generations, and that they put upon the fringe of the borders a ribband of blue, and it shall be unto you for a fringe that ye may look upon it and remember all the commandments of the Lord, and do them, and that ye seek not after your own heart and your own eyes after which ye use to go a whoring, that ye may remember, and do all my commandments, and be holy unto your God. I am the Lord your God, which brought you out of the land of Egypt to be your god, I am the Lord your God.

Now Korah, the son of Izhar, the son of Kohath, the son of Levi, and Dathan and Abiram, the sons of Eliah, and On, the son of Peleth, sons of Reuben, took men, and they rose up before Moses with certain of the children of Israel, two hundred and fifty princes of the assembly, famous in the congregation, men of renown, and they gathered themselves together against Moses and against Aaron and said unto them, Ye take too much upon you, seeing all the congregation are holy, every one of them, and the Lord is among them, wherefore then lift ye up yourselves above the congregation of the Lord?

And when Moses heard it he fell upon his face and he spake unto Korah and unto all his company, saying, Even tomorrow the Lord will show who are his and who is holy and will cause him to come near unto him, even him whom he hath chosen will he cause to come near unto him. This do: Take you censers, Korah and all his company, and put fire therein, and put incense in them before the Lord tomorrow, and it shall be that the man whom the Lord doth choose, he shall be holy: ye take too much upon you, ye sons of Levi.

And Moses said unto Korah, Hear, I pray you, ye sons of Levi, seemeth it but a small thing unto you that the God of Israel hath separated you from the congregation of Israel, to bring you near to himself to do the service of the tabernacle of the Lord and to stand before the congregation to minister unto them? And he hath brought thee near to him, and all thy brethren the sons of Levi with thee, and seek ye the high priesthood also? For which cause both thou and all thy company are gathered together against the Lord, and what is Aaron that ye murmur against him?

And Moses sent to call Dathan and Abiram, the sons of Eliab, which said, We will not come up. Is it a small thing that thou hast brought us up out of a land that floweth with milk and honey to kill us in the wilderness, except thou make thyself altogether a prince over us? Moreover, thou hast not brought us into a land that floweth with milk and honey or given us inheritance of fields and vineyards; wilt thou put out the eyes of these men? We will not come up.

And Moses was very wroth and said unto the Lord, Respect not thou their offering: I have not taken one ass from them neither have I hurt one of them. And Moses said unto Korah, Be thou and all thy company before the Lord, thou and they and Aaron, tomorrow, and take every man his censer and put incense in them, and bring ye before the Lord every man his censer, two hundred and fifty censers, thou also and Aaron, each of you his censer. And they took every man his censer, and put fire in them, and laid incense thereon, and stood in the door of the tabernacle of the congregation with Moses and Aaron. And Korah gathered all the congregation against them unto the door of the tabernacle of the congregation, and the glory of the Lord appeared unto all the congregation.

And the Lord spake unto Moses and unto Aaron saying, Separate yourselves from among this congregation, that I may consume them in a moment. And they fell upon their faces and said, O God, the God of the spirits of all flesh, shall one man sin and wilt thou be wroth with all the congregation?

And the Lord spake unto Moses, saying, Speak unto the congregation saying, Get you up from about the tabernacle of Korah, Dathan, and Abiram. And Moses rose up and went unto Dathan and Abiram and the elders of Israel followed him. And he spake unto the congregation saying, Depart, I pray you, from the tents of these wicked men and touch nothing of theirs lest ye be consumed in all their sins. So they gat up from the tabernacle of Korah, Dathan, and Abiram, on every side, and Dathan and Abiram came out and stood in the door of their tents, and their wives, and their sons, and their little children. And Moses said, Hereby ye shall know that the Lord hath sent me to do all these works, for I have not done them of mine own mind. If these men die the common death of all men or if they be visited after the visitation of all men, then the Lord hath not sent me. But if the Lord make a new thing, and the Earth open her mouth and swallow them up with all that appertain unto them and they go down quick into the pit, then ye shall understand that these men have provoked the Lord.

And it came to pass, as he had made an end of speaking all these words, that the ground clave asunder that was under them and the Rarth opened her mouth and swallowed them up, and their houses, and all the men that appertained unto Korah, and all their goods. They, and all that appertained to them, went down alive into the pit and the Earth closed upon them, and they perished from among the congregation. And all Israel that were round about them fled at the cry of them, for they said, Lest the Earth swallow us up also. And there came out a fire from the Lord, and consumed the two hundred and fifty men that offered incense.

And the Lord spake unto Moses, saying, Speak unto Eleazar the son of Aaron the priest, that he take up the censers out of the burning and scatter thou the fire yonder, for they are hallowed, the censers of these sinners against their own souls, let them make them broad plates for a covering of the altar, for they offered them before the Lord, therefore they are hallowed, and they shall be a sign unto the children of Israel. And Eleazar the priest took the brazen censers wherewith they that were burnt had offered, and they were made broad plates for a covering of the altar, to be a memorial unto the children of Israel, that no stranger, which is not of the seed of Aaron, come near to offer incense before the Lord, that he be not as Korah, and as his company as the Lord said to him by the hand of Moses.

But on the morrow all the congregation of the children of Israel murmured against Moses and against Aaron saying, Ye have killed the people of the Lord. And it came to pass, when the congregation was gathered against Moses and against Aaron, that they looked toward the tabernacle of the congregation and behold, the cloud covered it, and the glory of the Lord appeared. And Moses and Aaron came before the tabernacle of the congregation. And the Lord spake unto Moses saying, Get you up from among this congregation that I may consume them as in a moment. And they fell upon their faces. And Moses said unto Aaron,

Take a censer and put fire therein from off the altar and put on incense, and go quickly into the congregation and make an atonement for them, for there is wrath gone out from the Lord, the plague is begun. And Aaron took as Moses commanded, and ran into the midst of the congregation and behold, the plague was begun among the people, and he put on incense and made an atonement for the people. And he stood between the dead and the living and the plague was stayed. Now they that died in the plague were fourteen thousand and seven hundred, besides them that died about the matter of Korah. And Aaron returned unto Moses unto the door of the tabernacle of the congregation and the plague was stayed.

And the Lord spake unto Moses saying, Speak unto the children of Israel and take of every one of them a rod according to the house of their fathers, of all their princes according to the house of their fathers, twelve rods: write thou every man's name upon his rod. And thou shalt write Aaron's name upon the rod of Levi, for one rod shall be for the head of the house of their fathers. And thou shalt lay them up in the tabernacle of the congregation before the testimony where I will meet with you. And it shall come to pass that the man's rod whom I shall choose shall blossom and I will make to cease from me the murmurings of the children of Israel whereby they murmur against you. And Moses spake unto the children of Israel, and every one of their princes gave him a rod apiece, for each prince one according to their fathers' houses, even twelve rods, and the rod of Aaron was among their rods. And Moses laid up the rods before the Lord in the tabernacle of witness.

And it came to pass that on the morrow Moses went into the tabernacle of witness and behold, the rod of Aaron for the house of Levi was budded, and brought forth buds, and bloomed blossoms and yielded almonds. And Moses brought out all the rods from before the Lord unto all the children of Israel and they looked and took every man his rod. And the Lord said unto Moses, Bring Aaron's rod again before the testimony to be kept for the token against the rebels, and thou shalt quite take away their murmurings from me that they die not. And Moses did so, as the Lord commanded him so did he.

And the children of Israel spake unto Moses, saying, Behold, we die, we perish, we all perish. Whosoever cometh anything near unto the tabernacle of the Lord shall die, shall we be consumed with dying?

And the Lord said unto Aaron, Thou and thy sons and thy father's house with thee shall bear the iniquity of the sanctuary, and thou and thy sons with thee shall bear the iniquity of your priesthood. And thy brethren also of the tribe of Levi, the tribe of thy father, bring thou with thee that they may be joined unto thee and minister unto thee, but thou and thy sons with thee shall minister before the tabernacle of witness. And they shall keep thy charge and the charge of all the tabernacle, only they shall not come nigh the vessels of the sanctuary and the altar, that neither they nor ye also die. And they shall be joined unto thee and keep the charge of the tabernacle of the congregation, for all the service of the tabernacle, and a stranger shall not come nigh unto you. And ye shall keep the charge of the sanctuary and the charge of the altar, that there be no wrath any more upon the children of Israel. And I, behold, I have taken your brethren the Levites from among the children of Israel, to you they are given as a gift for the Lord, to do the service of the tabernacle of the congregation. Therefore thou and thy sons with thee shall keep your priest's office for everything of the altar and within the veil, and ye shall serve, I have given your priest's office unto you as a service of gift, and the stranger that cometh nigh shall be put to death.

And the Lord spake unto Aaron, Behold, I also have given thee the charge of mine heave offerings of all the hallowed things of the children of Israel, unto thee have I given them by reason of the anointing, and to thy sons by an ordinance forever. This shall be thine of the most holy things: reserved from the fire every oblation of theirs, every meat offering of theirs, and every sin offering of theirs, and every trespass offering of theirs which they shall render unto me, shall be most holy for thee and for thy sons. In the most holy place shalt thou eat it, every male shall eat it, it shall be holy unto thee. And this is thine, the heave offering of their gift with all the wave offerings of the children of Israel, I have given them unto thee and to thy sons and to thy daughters with thee by a statute forever, every one that is clean in thy house shall eat of it. All the best of the oil, and all the best of the wine, and of the wheat, the firstfruits of them which they shall offer unto the Lord, them have I given thee. And whatsoever is first ripe in the land, which they shall bring unto the Lord, shall be thine, every one that is clean in thine house shall eat of it. Everything devoted in Israel shall be thine. Everything that openeth the matrix in all flesh which they bring unto the Lord, whether it be of men or beasts, shall be thine, nevertheless the firstborn of man shalt thou surely redeem and the firstling of unclean beasts shalt thou redeem. And those that are to be redeemed from a month old shalt thou redeem according to thine estimation, for the money of five shekels, after the shekel of the sanctuary, which is twenty gerahs. But the firstling of a cow, or the firstling of a sheep, or the firstling of a goat, thou shalt not redeem; they are holy, thou shalt sprinkle their blood upon the altar and shalt burn their fat for an offering made by fire, for a sweet savor unto the Lord. And the flesh of them shall be thine as the wave breast and as the right shoulder are thine. All the heave offerings of the holy things which the children of Israel offer unto the Lord have I given thee and thy sons and thy daughters with thee by a statute forever, it is a covenant of salt for ever before the Lord unto thee and to thy seed with thee. And the Lord spake unto Aaron, Thou shalt have no inheritance in their land, neither shalt thou have any part among them; I am thy part and thine inheritance among the children of Israel.

And, behold, I have given the children of Levi all the tenth in Israel for an inheritance, for their service which they serve, even the service of the tabernacle of the congregation. Neither must the children of Israel henceforth come nigh the tabernacle of the congregation, lest they bear sin and die. But the Levites shall do the service of the tabernacle of the congregation and they shall bear their iniquity, it shall be a statute for ever throughout your generations, that among the children of Israel they have no inheritance. But the tithes of the children of Israel which they offer as a heave offering unto the Lord I have given to the Levites to inherit, therefore I have said unto them, Among the children of Israel they shall have no inheritance.

And the Lord spake unto Moses saying, Thus speak unto the Levites and say unto them, When ye take of the children of Israel the tithes which I have given you from them for your inheritance, then ye shall offer up a heave offering of it for the Lord, even a tenth part of the tithe. And this your heave offering shall be reckoned unto you, as though it were the corn of the threshing floor and as the fullness of the winepress. Thus ye also shall offer a heave offering unto the Lord of all your tithes which ye receive of the children of Israel and ye shall give thereof the Lord's heave offering to Aaron the priest. Out of all your gifts ye shall offer every heave offering of the Lord, of all the best thereof, even the hallowed part thereof out of it. Therefore thou shalt say unto them, When ye have heaved the best thereof from it, then it shall be counted unto the Levites as the increase of the threshing floor and as the increase of the winepress. And ye shall eat it in every place, ye and your households, for it is your reward for your service in the tabernacle of the congregation. And ye shall bear no sin by reason of it when ye have heaved from it the best of it neither shall ye pollute the holy things of the children of Israel, lest ye die.

And the Lord spake unto Moses and unto Aaron saying, This is the ordinance of the law which the Lord hath commanded saying, Speak unto the children of Israel that they bring thee a red heifer without spot wherein is no blemish and upon which never came yoke. And ye shall give her unto Eleazar the priest that he may bring her forth without the camp, and one shall slay her before his face, and Eleazar the priest shall take of her blood with his finger and sprinkle of her blood directly before the tabernacle of the congregation seven times. And one shall burn the heifer in his sight, her skin, and her flesh, and her blood, with her dung shall he burn, and the priest shall take cedar wood, and hyssop, and scarlet, and cast it into the midst of the burning of the heifer. Then the priest shall wash his clothes, and he shall bathe his flesh in water, and afterward he shall come into the camp, and the priest shall be unclean until the even. And he that burneth her shall wash his clothes in water, and bathe his flesh in water, and shall be unclean until the even. And a man that is clean shall gather up the ashes of the heifer, and lay them up without the camp in a clean place, and it shall be kept for the congregation of the children of Israel for a water of separation, it is a purification for sin. And he that gathereth the ashes of the heifer shall wash his clothes, and be unclean until the even, and it shall be unto the children of Israel and unto the stranger that sojourneth among them for a statute forever.

He that toucheth the dead body of any man shall be unclean seven days. He shall purify himself with it on the third day, and on the seventh day he shall be clean, but if he purify not himself the third day, then the seventh day he shall not be clean. Whosoever toucheth the dead body of any man that is dead, and purifieth not himself, defileth the tabernacle of the Lord and that soul shall be cut off from Israel because the water of separation was not sprinkled upon him, he shall be unclean; his uncleanness is yet upon him.

This is the law: when a man dieth in a tent, all that come into the tent and all that is in the tent shall be unclean seven days. And every open vessel which hath no covering bound upon it is unclean. And whosoever toucheth one that is slain with a sword in the open fields, or a dead body, or a bone of a man, or a grave, shall be unclean seven days. And for an unclean person they shall take of the ashes of the burnt heifer of purification for sin, and running water shall be put thereto in a vessel, and a clean person shall take hyssop and dip it in the water, and sprinkle it upon the tent, and upon all the vessels, and upon the persons that were there, and upon him that touched a bone, or one slain, or one dead, or a grave. And the clean person shall sprinkle upon the unclean on the third day, and on the seventh day, and on the seventh day he shall purify himself, and wash his clothes, and bathe himself in water, and shall be clean at even.

But the man that shall be unclean and shall not purify himself, that soul shall be cut off from among the congregation because he hath defiled the sanctuary of the Lord, the water of separation hath not been sprinkled upon him, he is unclean. And it shall be a perpetual statute unto them, that he that sprinkleth the water of separation shall wash his clothes and he that toucheth the water of separation shall be unclean until even. And whatsoever the unclean person toucheth shall be unclean and the soul that toucheth it shall be unclean until even.

10 THEN came the children of Israel, even the whole congregation, into the desert of Zin in the first month, and the people abode in Kadesh, and Miriam died there and was buried there. And there was no water for the congregation, and they gathered themselves together against Moses and against Aaron. And the

people chided with Moses and spake saying, Would God that we had died when our brethren died before the Lord. And why have ye brought up the congregation of the Lord into this wilderness that we and our cattle should die there? And wherefore have ye made us to come up out of Egypt to bring us in unto this evil place? It is no place of seed, or of figs, or of vines, or of pomegranates, neither is there any water to drink. And Moses and Aaron went from the presence of the assembly unto the door of the tabernacle of the congregation, and they fell upon their faces, and the glory of the Lord appeared unto them. And the Lord spake unto Moses saying, Take the rod and gather thou the assembly together, thou and Aaron thy brother, and speak ye unto the rock before their eyes, and it shall give forth his water, and thou shalt bring forth to them water out of the rock, so thou shalt give the congregation and their beasts drink.

And Moses took the rod from before the Lord as he commanded him. And Moses and Aaron gathered the congregation together before the rock and he said unto them, Hear now, ye rebels, must we fetch you water out of this rock? And Moses lifted up his hand, and with his rod he smote the rock twice, and the water came out abundantly, and the congregation drank, and their beasts also. And the Lord spake unto Moses and Aaron, Because ye believed me not, to sanctify me in the eyes of the children of Israel, therefore ye shall not bring this congregation into the land which I have given them. This is the water of Meribah because the children of Israel strove with the Lord, and he was sanctified in them.

And Moses sent messengers from Kadesh unto the king of Edom, Thus saith thy brother Israel, Thou knowest all the travail that hath befallen us, how our fathers went down into Egypt, and we have dwelt in Egypt a long time, and the Egyptians vexed us and our fathers, and when we cried unto the Lord, he heard our voice, and sent an angel, and hath brought us forth out of Egypt and behold, we are in Kadesh, a city in the uttermost of thy border. Let us pass, I pray thee, through thy country: we will not pass through the fields, or through the vineyards, neither will we drink of the water of the wells, we will go by the king's highway, we will not turn to the right hand nor to the left until we have passed thy borders.

And Edom said unto him, Thou shalt not pass by me lest I come out against thee with the sword. And the children of Israel said unto him, We will go by the highway and if I and my cattle drink of thy water, then I will pay for it; I will only, without doing anything else, go through on my feet. And he said, Thou shalt not go through. And Edom came out against him with much people and with a strong hand. Thus Edom refused to give Israel passage through his border, wherefore Israel turned away from him.

And the children of Israel, even the whole congregation, journeyed from Kadesh, and came unto mount Hor. And the Lord spake unto Moses and Aaron in mount Hor by the coast of the land of Edom saying, Aaron shall be gathered unto his people, for he shall not enter into the land which I have given unto the children of Israel because ye rebelled against my word at the water of Meribah. Take Aaron and Eleazar his son and bring them up unto mount Hor, and strip Aaron of his garments and put them upon Eleazar his son, and Aaron shall be gathered unto his people and shall die there. And Moses did as the Lord commanded and they went up into mount Hor in the sight of all the congregation. And Moses stripped Aaron of his garments and put them upon Eleazar his son, and Aaron died there in the top of the mount, and Moses and Eleazar came down from the mount. And when all the congregation saw that Aaron was dead they mourned for Aaron thirty days, even all the house of Israel.

And when king Arad the Canaanite, which dwelt in the south, heard tell that Israel came by the way of the spies, then he fought against Israel and took some of them prisoners. And Israel vowed a vow unto the Lord and said, If thou wilt indeed deliver this people into my hand, then I will utterly destroy their cities.

And the Lord hearkened to the voice of Israel, and delivered up the Canaanites, and they utterly destroyed them and their cities, and he called the name of the place Hormah.

And they journeyed from mount Hor by the way of the Red Sea to compass the land of Edom and the soul of the people was much discouraged because of the way. And the people spake against God and against Moses, Wherefore have ye brought us up out of Egypt to die in the wilderness? For there is no bread neither is there any water and our soul loatheth this light bread.

And the Lord sent fiery serpents among the people and they bit the people and much people of Israel died. Therefore the people came to Moses and said, We have sinned, for we have spoken against the Lord and against thee; pray unto the Lord that he take away the serpents from us. And Moses prayed for the people. And the Lord said unto Moses, Make thee a fiery serpent and set it upon a pole and it shall come to pass that every one that is bitten, when he looketh upon it, shall live. And Moses made a serpent of brass and put it upon a pole and it came to pass that if a serpent had bitten any man, when he beheld the serpent of brass he lived.

And the children of Israel set forward, and pitched in Oboth. And they journeyed from Oboth, and pitched at Ijeabarim, in the wilderness which is before Moab toward the sunrising. From thence they removed and pitched in the valley of Zared. From thence they removed and pitched on the other side of Arnon which is in the wilderness that cometh out of the coasts of the Amorites, for Arnon is the border of Moab between Moab and the Amorites. Wherefore is it said in the book of the wars of the Lord:

> What he did in the Red Sea, and in the brooks of Arnon,
> And at the stream of the brooks that goeth down to the dwelling of Ar,
> and lieth upon the border of Moab.

And from thence they went to Beer, that is the well whereof the Lord spake unto Moses, Gather the people together and I will give them water. Then Israel sang this song:

> Spring up, O well, sing ye unto it,
> The princes digged the well, the nobles of the people digged it, by the
> direction of the lawgiver, with their staves.

And from the wilderness they went to Mattanah, and from Mattanah to Nahaliel, and from Nahaliel to Bamoth, and from Bamoth in the valley that is in the country of Moab to the top of Pisgah which looketh toward Jeshimon.

And Israel sent messengers unto Sihon king of the Amorites saying, Let me pass through thy land, we will not turn into the fields, or into the vineyards, we will not drink of the waters of the well, but we will go along by the king's highway, until we be past thy borders. And Sihon would not suffer Israel to pass through his border, but Sihon gathered all his people together and went out against Israel into the wilderness, and he came to Jahaz, and fought against Israel. And Israel smote him with the edge of the sword and possessed his land from Arnon unto Jabbok, even unto the children of Ammon, for the border of the children of Ammon was strong. And Israel took all these cities and Israel dwelt in all the cities of the Amorites, in Heshbon and in all the villages thereof. For Heshbon was the city of Sihon the king of the Amorites, who had fought against the former king of Moab and taken all his land out of his hand, even unto Arnon. Wherefore they that speak in proverbs say,

> Come unto Heshbon, let the city of Sihon be built and prepared,
> For there is a fire gone out of Heshbon, a flame from the city of Sihon,
> it hath consumed Ar of Moab and the lords of the high places of Arnon.
> Woe to thee, Moab. Thou art undone, O people of Chemosh: he hath

given his sons that escaped, and his daughters, into captivity unto Sihon king of the Amorites.

We have shot at them, Heshbon is perished even unto Dibon, and we have laid them waste even unto Nophah, which reacheth unto Medeba.

Thus Israel dwelt in the land of the Amorites. And Moses sent to spy out Jaazer and they took the villages thereof and drove out the Amorites that were there. And they turned and went up by the way of Bashan and Og the king of Bashan went out against them, he and all his people, to the battle at Edrei. And the Lord said unto Moses, Fear him not, for I have delivered him into thy hand, and all his people, and his land, and thou shalt do to him as thou didst unto Sihon king of the Amorites which dwelt at Heshbon. So they smote him, and his sons, and all his people, until there was none left him alive, and they possessed his land.

And the children of Israel set forward and pitched in the plains of Moab on this side Jordan by Jericho. And Balak the son of Zippor saw all that Israel had done to the Amorites. And Moab was sore afraid of the people because they were many and Moab was distressed because of the children of Israel. And Moab said unto the elders of Midian, Now shall this company lick up all that are round about us as the ox licketh up the grass of the field. And Balak the son of Zippor was king of the Moabites at that time. He sent messengers therefore unto Balaam the son of Beor to Pethor which is by the river of the land of the children of his people to call him saying, Behold, there is a people come out from Egypt, behold, they cover the face of the Earth, and they abide over against me. Come now therefore, I pray thee, curse me this people, for they are too mighty for me, peradventure I shall prevail, that we may smite them and that I may drive them out of the land, for I know that he whom thou blessest is blessed and he whom thou cursest is cursed.

And the elders of Moab and the elders of Midian departed with the rewards of divination in their hand and they came unto Balaam and spake unto him the words of Balak. And he said unto them, Lodge here this night and I will bring you word again as the Lord shall speak unto me, and the princes of Moab abode with Balaam. And God came unto Balaam and said, What men are these with thee? And Balaam said unto God, Balak the son of Zippor king of Moab hath sent unto me saying, Behold, there is a people come out of Egypt, which covereth the face of the Earth. Come now, curse me them, peradventure I shall be able to overcome them and drive them out. And God said unto Balaam, Thou shalt not go with them, thou shalt not curse the people, for they are blessed. And Balaam rose up in the morning and said unto the princes of Balak, Get you into your land, for the Lord refuseth to give me leave to go with you. And the princes of Moab rose up and they went unto Balak and said, Balaam refuseth to come with us.

And Balak sent yet again princes, more and more honorable than they. And they came to Balaam, and said to him, Thus saith Balak the son of Zippor, Let nothing, I pray thee, hinder thee from coming unto me, for I will promote thee unto very great honor and I will do whatsoever thou sayest unto me; come therefore, I pray thee, curse me this people. And Balaam answered and said unto the servants of Balak, If Balak would give me his house full of silver and gold, I cannot go beyond the word of the Lord my God, to do less or more. Now therefore, I pray you, tarry ye also here this night, that I may know what the Lord will say unto me more. And God came unto Balaam at night and said unto him, If the men come to call thee, rise up if thou wilt go with them, but yet the word which I shall say unto thee shalt thou speak.

And Balaam rose up in the morning and saddled his ass and went with the princes of Moab.

And God's anger was kindled because he went and the Angel of the Lord stood in the way for an adversary against him. Now he was riding upon his ass and his two servants were with him. And the ass saw the Angel of the Lord standing in the way, and his sword drawn in his hand, and the ass turned aside out of the way and went into the field, and Balaam smote the ass to turn her into the way. But the Angel of the Lord stood in a path of the vineyards, a wall being on this side and a wall on that side. And when the ass saw the Angel of the Lord, she thrust herself unto the wall, and crushed Balaam's foot against the wall, and he smote her again. And the Angel of the Lord went further and stood in a narrow place where was no way to turn either to the right hand or to the left. And when the ass saw the Angel of the Lord, she fell down under Balaam, and Balaam's anger was kindled, and he smote the ass with a staff. And the Lord opened the mouth of the ass and she said unto Balaam, What have I done unto thee that thou hast smitten me these three times? And Balaam said unto the ass, Because thou hast mocked me, I would there were a sword in mine hand, for now would I kill thee. And the ass said unto Balaam, Am not I thine ass, upon which thou hast ridden ever since I was thine unto this day? Was I ever wont to do so unto thee? And he said, Nay.

Then the Lord opened the eyes of Balaam, and he saw the Angel of the Lord standing in the way, and his sword drawn in his hand, and he bowed down his head, and fell flat on his face. And the Angel of the Lord said unto him, Wherefore hast thou smitten thine ass these three times? Behold, I went out to withstand thee, because thy way is perverse before me. And the ass saw me and turned from me these three times; unless she had turned from me, surely now also I had slain thee and saved her alive. And Balaam said unto the Angel of the Lord, I have sinned, for I knew not that thou stoodest in the way against me; now therefore, if it displease thee, I will get me back again. And the Angel of the Lord said unto Balaam, Go with the men, but only the word that I shall speak unto thee, that thou shalt speak. So Balaam went with the princes of Balak.

And when Balak heard that Balaam was come, he went out to meet him unto a city of Moab, which is in the border of Arnon which is in the utmost coast. And Balak said unto Balaam, Did I not earnestly send unto thee to call thee? Wherefore camest thou not unto me? Am I not able indeed to promote thee to honor? And Balaam said unto Balak, Lo, I am come unto thee; have I now any power at all to say anything? The word that God putteth in my mouth, that shall I speak. And Balaam went with Balak and they came unto Kirgath-huzoth. And Balak offered oxen and sheep and sent to Balaam and to the princes that were with him.

And it came to pass on the morrow that Balak took Balaam and brought him up into the high places of Baal, that thence he might see the utmost part of the people. And Balaam said unto Balak, Build me here seven altars, and prepare me here seven oxen and seven rams. And Balak did as Balaam had spoken, and Balak and Balaam offered on every altar a bullock and a ram. And Balaam said unto Balak, Stand by thy burnt offering and I will go, peradventure the Lord will come to meet me, and whatsoever he showeth me I will tell thee. And he went to a high place. And God met Balaam and he said unto him, I have prepared seven altars and I have offered upon every altar a bullock and a ram. And the Lord put a word in Balaam's mouth and said, Return unto Balak and thus thou shalt speak. And he returned unto him and lo, he stood by his burnt sacrifice, he and all the princes of Moab. And he took up his parable and said,

> Balak the king of Moab hath brought me from Aram out of the mountains of the east saying, Come, curse me Jacob, and come, defy Israel. How shall I curse whom God hath not cursed? Or how shall I defy whom the Lord hath not defied?

For from the top of the rocks I see him, and from the hills I behold him, lo, the people shall dwell alone, and shall not be reckoned among the nations. Who can count the dust of Jacob, and the number of the fourth part of Israel?

Let me die the death of the righteous, and let my last end be like his.

And Balak said unto Balaam, What hast thou done unto me? I took thee to curse mine enemies and behold, thou hast blessed them altogether. And he answered and said, Must I not take heed to speak that which the Lord hath put in my mouth? And Balak said unto him, Come, I pray thee, with me unto another place from whence thou mayest see them, thou shalt see but the utmost part of them and shalt not see them all and curse me them from thence. And he brought him into the field of Zophim, to the top of Pisgah, and built seven altars and offered a bullock and a ram on every altar. And he said unto Balak, Stand here by thy burnt offering while I meet the Lord yonder. And the Lord met Balaam and put a word in his mouth and said, Go again unto Balak and say thus. And when he came to him, behold, he stood by his burnt offering, and the princes of Moab with him. And Balak said unto him, What hath the Lord spoken?

And he took up his parable and said,

> Rise up, Balak, and hear, hearken unto me, thou son of Zippor,
>
> God is not a man that he should lie, neither the son of man that he should repent; hath he said and shall he not do it? Or hath he spoken and shall he not make it good?
>
> Behold, I have received commandment to bless and he hath blessed and I cannot reverse it.
>
> He hath not beheld iniquity in Jacob, neither hath he seen perverseness in Israel, the Lord his God is with him, and the shout of a king is among them.
>
> God brought them out of Egypt, he hath as it were the strength of a unicorn.
>
> Surely there is no enchantment against Jacob, neither is there any divination against Israel, according to this time it shall be said of Jacob and of Israel,
>
> What hath God wrought!
>
> Behold, the people shall rise up as a great lion, and lift up himself as a young lion, he shall not lie down until he eat of the prey, and drink the blood of the slain.

And Balak said unto Balaam, Neither curse them at all nor bless them at all. But Balaam answered and said unto Balak, Told not I thee saying, All that the Lord speaketh, that I must do? And Balak said unto Balaam, Come, I pray thee, I will bring thee unto another place, peradventure it will please God that thou mayest curse me them from thence. And Balak brought Balaam unto the top of Peor that looketh toward Jeshimon. And Balaam said unto Balak, Build me here seven altars and prepare me here seven bullocks and seven rams. And Balak did as Balaam had said and offered a bullock and a ram on every altar.

And when Balaam saw that it pleased the Lord to bless Israel, he went not, as at other times, to seek for enchantments, but he set his face toward the wilderness. And Balaam lifted up his eyes, and he saw Israel abiding in his tents according to their tribes, and the Spirit of God came upon him.

And he took up his parable, and said,

> Balaam the son of Beor hath said, and the man whose eyes are open hath said:
>
> He hath said, which heard the words of God, which saw the vision of the Almighty, falling into a trance, but having his eyes open,
>
> How goodly are thy tents, O Jacob, and thy tabernacles, O Israel!

As the valleys are they spread forth, as gardens by the river's side, as the trees of lign aloes which the Lord hath planted, and as cedar trees beside the waters.

He shall pour the water out of his buckets, and his seed shall be in many waters, and his king shall be higher than Agag, and his kingdom shall be exalted.

God brought him forth out of Egypt, he hath as it were the strength of a unicorn, he shall eat up the nations his enemies, and shall break their bones and pierce them through with his arrows.

He couched, he lay down as a lion, and as a great lion, who shall stir him up?

Blessed is he that blesseth thee, and cursed is he that curseth thee.

And Balak's anger was kindled against Balaam and he smote his hands together and Balak said unto Balaam, I called thee to curse mine enemies, and, behold, thou hast altogether blessed them these three times. Therefore now flee thou to thy place; I thought to promote thee unto great honor but lo, the Lord hath kept thee back from honor. And Balaam said unto Balak, Spake I not also to thy messengers which thou sentest unto me saying, If Balak would give me his house full of silver and gold, I cannot go beyond the commandment of the Lord to do either good or bad of mine own mind, but what the Lord saith, that will I speak? And now, behold, I go unto my people. Come therefore, and I will advertise thee what this people shall do to thy people in the latter days.

And he took up his parable and said,

Balaam the son of Beor hath said, and the man whose eyes are open hath said, He hath said, which heard the words of God, and knew the knowledge of the Most High, which saw the vision of the Almighty, falling into a trance, but having his eyes open,

I shall see him, but not now, I shall behold him, but not nigh, there shall come a Star out of Jacob, and a Scepter shall rise out of Israel, and shall smite the corners of Moab, and destroy all the children of Sheth. And Edom shall be a possession, Seir also shall be a possession for his enemies, and Israel shall do valiantly.

Out of Jacob shall come he that shall have dominion, and shall destroy him that remaineth of the city.

And when he looked on Amalek, he took up his parable and said,

Amalek was the first of the nations, but his latter end shall be that he perish forever.

And he looked on the Kenites, and took up his parable and said,

Strong is thy dwelling place, and thou puttest thy nest in a rock.

Nevertheless the Kenite shall be wasted, until Asshur shall carry thee away captive.

And he took up his parable and said,

Alas, who shall live when God doeth this! And ships shall come from the coast of Chittim, and shall afflict Asshur, and shall afflict Eber, and he also shall perish forever.

And Balaam rose up, and went and returned to his place, and Balak also went his way.

11 AND Israel abode in Shittim and the people began to commit whoredom with the daughters of Moab. And they called the people unto the sacrifices of their gods and the people did eat and bowed down to their gods. And Israel joined himself unto Baal-peor and the anger of the Lord was kindled against Israel. And the Lord said unto Moses, Take all the heads of the people and hang them

up before the Lord against the sun that the fierce anger of the Lord may be turned away from Israel. And Moses said unto the judges of Israel, Slay ye everyone his men that were joined unto Baal-peor. And behold, one of the children of Israel came and brought unto his brethren a Midianitish woman in the sight of Moses and in the sight of all the congregation of the children of Israel who were weeping before the door of the tabernacle of the congregation. And when Phinehas, the son of Eleazar the son of Aaron the priest saw it, he rose up from among the congregation, and took a javelin in his hand, and he went after the man of Israel into the tent, and thrust both of them through, the man of Israel, and the woman through her belly. So the plague was stayed from the children of Israel. And those that died in the plague were twenty and four thousand.

And the Lord spake unto Moses saying, Phinehas, the son of Eleazar the son of Aaron the priest hath turned my wrath away from the children of Israel while he was zealous for my sake among them, that I consumed not the children of Israel in my jealousy. Wherefore say, Behold, I give unto him my covenant of peace and he shall have it and his seed after him, even the covenant of an everlasting priesthood because he was zealous for his God and made an atonement for the children of Israel. Now the name of the Israelite that was slain, even that was slain with the Midianitish woman, was Zimri the son of Salu, a prince of a chief house among the Simeonites. And the name of the Midianitish woman that was slain was Cozbi the daughter of Zur, he was head over a people and of a chief house in Midian.

And the Lord spake unto Moses saying, Vex the Midianites and smite them, for they vex you with their wiles wherewith they have beguiled you in the matter of Peor, and in the matter of Cozbi, the daughter of a prince of Midian, their sister, which was slain in the day of the plague for Peor's sake.

And it came to pass after the plague that the Lord spake unto Moses and unto Eleazar the son of Aaron the priest saying, Take the sum of all the congregation of the children of Israel, from twenty years old and upward, throughout their fathers' house, all that are able to go to war in Israel. And Moses and Eleazar the priest spake with them in the plains of Moab by Jordan near Jericho saying, Take the sum of the people, from twenty years old and upward, as the Lord commanded Moses and the children of Israel which went forth out of the land of Egypt.

Reuben, the eldest son of Israel, the children of Reuben: Hanoch, of whom cometh the family of the Hanochites, of Pallu, the family of the Palluites, of Hezron, the family of the Hezronites, of Carmi, the family of the Carmites. These are the families of the Reubenites, and they that were numbered of them were forty and three thousand and seven hundred and thirty. And the sons of Pallu: Eliab. And the sons of Eliab: Nemuel, and Dathan, and Abiram. This is that Dathan and Abiram, which were famous in the congregation, who strove against Moses and against Aaron in the company of Korah when they strove against the Lord and the Earth opened her mouth and swallowed them up together with Korah, when that company died, what time the fire devoured two hundred and fifty men and they became a sign. Notwithstanding the children of Korah died not.

The sons of Simeon after their families, of Nemuel, the family of the Nemuelites, of Jamin, the family of the Jaminites, of Jachin, the family of the Jachinites, of Zerah, the family of the Zarhites, of Shaul, the family of the Shaulites. These are the families of the Simeonites, twenty and two thousand and two hundred.

The children of Gad after their families, of Zephon, the family of the Zephonites, of Haggi, the family of the Haggites, of Shuni, the family of the Shunites, of Ozni, the family of the Oznites, of Eri, the family of the Erites, of Arod, the family of the Arodites, of Areli, the family of the Arelites. These are the families of the children of Gad according to those that were numbered of them, forty thousand and five hundred.

The sons of Judah were Er and Onan, and Er and Onan died in the land of Canaan. And the sons of Judah after their families were, of Shelah, the family of the Shelanites, of Pharez, the family of the Pharzites, of Zerah, the family of the Zarhites. And the sons of Pharez were, of Hezron, the family of the Hezronites, of Hamul, the family of the Hamulites. These are the families of Judah according to those that were numbered of them, threescore and sixteen thousand and five hundred.

Of the sons of Issachar after their families, of Tola, the family of the Tolaites, of Pua, the family of the Punites, of Jashub, the family of the Jashubites, of Shimron, the family of the Shimronites. These are the families of Issachar according to those that were numbered of them, threescore and four thousand and three hundred.

Of the sons of Zebulun after their families, of Sered, the family of the Sardites, of Elon, the family of the Elonites, of Jahleel, the family of the Jahleelites. These are the families of the Zebulunites according to those that were numbered of them, threescore thousand and five hundred.

The sons of Joseph after their families were Manasseh and Ephraim. Of the sons of Manasseh, of Machir, the family of the Machirites, and Machir begat Gilead, of Gilead come the family of the Gileadites. These are the sons of Gilead, of Jeezer, the family of the Jeezerites, of Helek, the family of the Helekites, and of Asriel, the family of the Asrielites, and of Shechem, the family of the Shechemites, and of Shemida, the family of the Shemidaites, and of Hepher, the family of the Hepherites. And Zelophehad the son of Hepher had no sons, but daughters, and the names of the daughters of Zelophehad were Mahlah, and Noah, Hoglah, Milcah, and Tirzah. These are the families of Manasseh, and those that were numbered of them, fifty and two thousand and seven hundred. These are the sons of Ephraim after their families, of Shuthelah, the family of the Shuthalhites, of Becher, the family of the Bachrites, of Tahan, the family of the Tahanites. And these are the sons of Shuthelah, of Eran, the family of the Eranites. These are the families of the sons of Ephraim according to those that were numbered of them, thirty and two thousand and five hundred. These are the sons of Joseph after their families.

The sons of Benjamin after their families, of Bela, the family of the Belaites, of Ashbel, the family of the Ashbelites, of Ahiram, the family of the Ahiramites, of Shupham, the family of the Shuphamites, of Hupham, the family of the Huphamites. And the sons of Bela were Ard and Naaman, of Ard, the family of the Ardites, and of Naaman, the family of the Naamites. These are the sons of Benjamin after their families, and they that were numbered of them were forty and five thousand and six hundred.

These are the sons of Dan after their families, of Shuham, the family of the Shuhamites. These are the families of Dan after their families. All the families of the Shuhamites, according to those that were numbered of them, were threescore and four thousand and four hundred.

Of the children of Asher after their families, of Jimna, the family of the Jimnites, of Jesui, the family of the Jesuites, of Beriah, the family of the Beriites. Of the sons of Beriah, of Heber, the family of the Heberites, of Malchiel, the family of the Malchielites. And the name of the daughter of Asher was Sarah. These are the families of the sons of Asher according to those that were numbered of them, who were fifty and three thousand and four hundred.

Of the sons of Naphtali after their families, of Jahzeel, the family of the Jahzeelites, of Guni, the family of the Gunites, of Jezer, the family of the Jezerites, of Shillem, the family of the Shillemites. These are the families of Naphtali according to their families, and they that were numbered of them were forty and five thousand and four hundred. These were the numbered of the children of Israel, six hundred thousand and a thousand seven hundred and thirty.

And the Lord spake unto Moses, saying, Unto these the land shall be divided for an inheritance according to the number of names. To many thou shalt give the more inheritance, and to few thou shalt give the less inheritance, to everyone shall his inheritance be given according to those that were numbered of him. Notwithstanding the land shall be divided by lot, according to the names of the tribes of their fathers they shall inherit. According to the lot shall the possession thereof be divided between many and few.

And these are they that were numbered of the Levites after their families, of Gershon, the family of the Gershonites, of Kohath, the family of the Kohathites, of Merari, the family of the Merarites. These are the families of the Levites, the family of the Libnites, the family of the Hebronites, the family of the Mahlites, the family of the Mushites, the family of the Korathites. And Kohath begat Amaram. And the name of Amram's wife was Jochebed, the daughter of Levi, whom her mother bare to Levi in Egypt, and she bare unto Amram, Aaron and Moses, and Miriam their sister. And unto Aaron was born Nadab and Abihu, Eleazar and Ithamar. And Nadab and Abihu died when they offered strange fire before the Lord. And those that were numbered of them were twenty and three thousand, all males from a month old and upward, for they were not numbered among the children of Israel because there was no inheritance given them among the children of Israel. These are they that were numbered by Moses and Eleazar the priest, who numbered the children of Israel in the plains of Moab by Jordan near Jericho. But among these there was not a man of them whom Moses and Aaron the priest numbered, when they numbered the children of Israel in the wilderness of Sinai. For the Lord had said of them, They shall surely die in the wilderness. And there was not left a man of them, save Caleb the son of Jephunneh and Joshua the son of Nun.

Then came the daughters of Zelophehad, the son of Hepher, the son of Gilead, the son of Machir, the son of Manasseh, of the families of Manasseh the son of Joseph, and these are the names of his daughters, Mahlah, Noah, and Hoglah, and Milcah, and Tirzah. And they stood before Moses, and before Eleazar the priest, and before the princes and all the congregation, by the door of the tabernacle of the congregation saying, Our father died in the wilderness, and he was not in the company of them that gathered themselves together against the Lord in the company of Korah, but died in his own sin and had no sons. Why should the name of our father be done away from among his family because he hath no son? Give unto us therefore a possession among the brethren of our father. And Moses brought their cause before the Lord.

And the Lord spake unto Moses saying, The daughters of Zelophehad speak right, thou shalt surely give them a possession of an inheritance among their father's brethren, and thou shalt cause the inheritance of their father to pass unto them. And thou shalt speak unto the children of Israel saying, If a man die and have no son, then ye shall cause his inheritance to pass unto his daughter. And if he have no daughter, then ye shall give his inheritance unto his brethren. And if he have no brethren, then ye shall give his inheritance unto his father's brethren. And if his father have no brethren, then ye shall give his inheritance unto his kinsman that is next to him of his family and he shall possess it and it shall be unto the children of Israel a statute of judgment, as the Lord commanded Moses.

12 AND the Lord said unto Moses, Get thee up into this mount Abarim and see the land which I have given unto the children of Israel. And when thou hast seen it thou also shalt be gathered unto thy people as Aaron thy brother was gathered. For ye rebelled against my commandment in the desert of Zin, in the strife of the congregation, to sanctify me at the water before their eyes, that is the water of Meribah in Kadesh in the wilderness of Zin.

And Moses spake unto the Lord, saying, Let the Lord, the God of the spirits of all flesh, set a man over the congregation. Which may go out before them, and which may go in before them, and which may lead them out, and which may bring them in, that the congregation of the Lord be not as sheep which have no shepherd.

And the Lord said unto Moses, Take thee Joshua the son of Nun, a man in whom is the Spirit, and lay thine hand upon him, and set him before Eleazar the priest and before all the congregation, and give him a charge in their sight. And thou shalt put some of thine honor upon him, that all the congregation of the children of Israel may be obedient. And he shall stand before Eleazar the priest, who shall ask counsel for him after the judgment of Urim before the Lord, at his word shall they go out, and at his word they shall come in, both he and all the children of Israel with him, even all the congregation. And Moses did as the Lord commanded him, and he took Joshua, and set him before Eleazar the priest and before all the congregation, and he laid his hands upon him, and gave him a charge as the Lord commanded by the hand of Moses.

And the Lord spake unto Moses saying, Command the children of Israel and say unto them, My offering and my bread for my sacrifices made by fire, for a sweet savor unto me, shall ye observe to offer unto me in their due season. And thou shalt say unto them, This is the offering made by fire which ye shall offer unto the Lord: two lambs of the first year without spot day by day, for a continual burnt offering. The one lamb shalt thou offer in the morning and the other lamb shalt thou offer at even, and a tenth part of an ephah of flour for a meat offering mingled with the fourth part of a hin of beaten oil. It is a continual burn offering which was ordained in mount Sinai for a sweet savor, a sacrifice made by fire unto the Lord. And the drink offering thereof shall be the fourth part of a hin for the one lamb, in the holy place shalt thou cause the strong wine to be poured unto the Lord for a drink offering. And the other lamb shalt thou offer at even, as the meat offering of the morning and as the drink offering thereof thou shalt offer it, a sacrifice made by fire of a sweet savor unto the Lord.

And on the sabbath day two lambs of the first year without spot, and two tenth deals of flour for a meat offering mingled with oil, and the drink offering thereof, this is the burnt offering of every sabbath, beside the continual burnt offering and his drink offering. And in the beginnings of your months ye shall offer a burnt offering unto the Lord, two young bullocks, and one ram, seven lambs of the first year without spot, and three tenth deals of flour for a meat offering mingled with oil, for one bullock, and two tenth deals of flour for a meat offering mingled with oil, for one ram, and a several tenth deal of flour mingled with oil for a meat offering unto one lamb, for a burnt offering of a sweet savor, a sacrifice made by fire unto the Lord. And their drink offerings shall be half a hin of wine unto a bullock, and the third part of a hin unto a ram and a fourth part of a hin unto a lamb, this is the burnt offering of every month throughout the months of the year. And one kid of the goats for a sin offering unto the Lord shall be offered, beside the continual burnt offering and his drink offering.

And in the fourteenth day of the first month is the passover of the Lord. And in the fifteenth day of this month is the feast, seven days shall unleavened bread be eaten. In the first day shall be a holy convocation, ye shall do no manner of servile work therein, but ye shall offer a sacrifice made by fire for a burnt offering unto the Lord, two young bullocks, and one ram, and seven lambs of the first year, they shall be unto you without blemish. And their meat offering shall be of flour mingled with oil, three tenth deals shall ye offer for a bullock, and two tenth deals for a ram, a several tenth deal shalt thou offer for every lamb, throughout the seven lambs, and one goat for a sin offering, to make an atonement for you. Ye shall offer these beside the burnt offering in the morning which is for a continual burnt offering. After this manner ye shall offer daily, throughout the seven days, the meat of the sacrifice made by fire, of a sweet savor unto the Lord, it shall be offered beside the continual burnt offering and his drink offering. And on the seventh day ye shall have a holy convocation; ye shall do no servile work.

Also in the day of the firstfruits when ye bring a new meat offering unto the Lord, after your weeks be out ye shall have a holy convocation, ye shall do no servile work, but ye shall offer the burnt offering for a sweet savor unto the Lord, two young bullocks, one ram, seven lambs of the first year, and their meat offering of flour mingled with oil, three tenth deals unto one bullock, two tenth deals unto one ram, a several tenth deal unto one lamb, throughout the seven lambs, and one kid of the goats, to make an atonement for you. Ye shall offer them beside the continual burnt offering and his meat offering (they shall be unto you without blemish) and their drink offerings.

And in the seventh month, on the first day of the month, ye shall have a holy convocation, ye shall do no servile work, it is a day of blowing the trumpets unto you. And ye shall offer a burnt offering for a sweet savor unto the Lord, one young bullock, one ram, and seven lambs of the first year without blemish, and their meat offering shall be of flour mingled with oil, three tenth deals for a bullock, and two tenth deals for a ram, and one tenth deal for one lamb, throughout the seven lambs, and one kid of the goats for a sin offering, to make an atonement for you, beside the burnt offering of the month, and his meat offering, and the daily burnt offering, and his meat offering, and their drink offerings, according unto their manner, for a sweet savor, a sacrifice made by fire unto the Lord.

And ye shall have on the tenth day of this seventh month a holy convocation, and ye shall afflict your souls, ye shall not do any work therein, but ye shall offer a burnt offering unto the Lord for a sweet savor, one young bullock, one ram, and seven lambs of the first year, they shall be unto you without blemish. And their meat offering shall be of flour mingled with oil, three tenth deals to a bullock, and two tenth deals to one ram, a several tenth deal for one lamb, throughout the seven lambs, one kid of the goats for a sin offering, beside the sin offering of atonement, and the continual burnt offering, and the meat offering of it, and their drink offerings.

And on the fifteenth day of the seventh month ye shall have a holy convocation, ye shall do no servile work, and ye shall keep a feast unto the Lord seven days. And ye shall offer a burnt offering, a sacrifice made by fire, of a sweet savor unto the Lord, thirteen young bullocks, two rams, and fourteen lambs of the first year, they shall be without blemish, and their meat offering shall be of flour mingled with oil, three tenth deals unto every bullock of the thirteen bullocks, two tenth deals to each ram of the two rams, and a several tenth deal to each lamb of the fourteen lambs, and one kid of the goats for a sin offering, beside the continual burnt offering, his meat offering, and his drink offering.

And on the second day ye shall offer twelve young bullocks, two rams, fourteen lambs of the first year without spot, and their meat offering and their drink offerings for the bullocks, for the rams, and for the lambs, shall be according to their number, after the manner, and one kid of the goats for a sin offering, beside the continual burnt offering, and the meat offering thereof, and their drink offerings.

And on the third day eleven bullocks, two rams, fourteen lambs of the first year without blemish, and their meat offering and their drink offerings for the bullocks, for the rams, and for the lambs, shall be according to their number, after the manner, and one goat for a sin offering, beside the continual burnt offering, and his meat offering, and his drink offering.

And on the fourth day ten bullocks, two rams, and fourteen lambs of the first year without blemish, their meat offering and their drink offerings for the bullocks, for the rams, and for the lambs, shall be according to their number, after the manner, and one kid of the goats for a sin offering, beside the continual burnt offering, his meat offering, and his drink offering.

And on the fifth day nine bullocks, two rams, and fourteen lambs of the first year without spot, and their meat offering and their drink offerings for the bullocks, for the rams, and for the lambs, shall be according to their number, after the manner, and one goat for a sin offering, beside the continual burnt offering, and his meat offering, and his drink offering.

And on the sixth day eight bullocks, two rams, and fourteen lambs of the first year without blemish, and their meat offering and their drink offerings for the bullocks, for the rams, and for the lambs, shall be according to their number, after the manner, and one goat for a sin offering, beside the continual burnt offering, beside the continual burnt offering, his meat offering, and his drink offering.

And on the seventh day seven bullocks, two rams, and fourteen lambs of the first year without blemish, and their meat offering and their drink offerings for the bullocks, for the rams, and for the lambs, shall be according to their number, after the manner, and one goat for a sin offering, beside the continual burnt offering, his meat offering and his drink offering.

On the eighth day ye shall have a solemn assembly, ye shall do no servile work therein, but ye shall offer a burnt offering, a sacrifice made by fire, of a sweet savor unto the Lord, one bullock, one ram, seven lambs of the first year without blemish, their meat offering and their drink offerings for the bullock, for the ram, and for the lambs, shall be according to their number, after the manner, and one goat for a sin offering, beside the continual burnt offering, and his meat offering, and his drink offering.

These things ye shall do unto the Lord in your set feasts, beside your vows and your freewill offerings, for your burnt offerings, and for your meat offerings, and for your drink offerings, and for your peace offerings. And Moses told the children of Israel according to all that the Lord commanded Moses.

And Moses spake unto the heads of the tribes concerning the children of Israel, saying, This is the thing which the Lord hath commanded. If a man vow a vow unto the Lord or swear an oath to bind his soul with a bond, he shall not break his word, he shall do according to all that proceedeth out of his mouth.

If a woman also vow a vow unto the Lord, and bind herself by a bond, being in her father's house in her youth, and her father hear her vow, and her bond wherewith she hath bound her soul, and her father shall hold his peace at her, then all her vows shall stand, and every bond wherewith she hath bound her soul shall stand. But if her father disallow her in the day that he heareth, not any of her vows, or of her bonds wherewith she hath bound her soul, shall stand, and the Lord shall forgive her, because her father disallowed her.

And if she had at all a husband when she vowed, or uttered aught out of her lips wherewith she bound her soul, and her husband heard it and held his peace at her in the day that he heard it, then her vows shall stand, and her bonds wherewith she bound her soul shall stand. But if her husband disallowed her on the day that he heard it, then he shall make her vow which she vowed, and that which she uttered with her lips, wherewith she bound her soul, of none effect, and the Lord shall forgive her.

But every vow of a widow and of her that is divorced, wherewith they have bound their souls, shall stand against her. And if she vowed in her husband's house, or bound her soul by a bond with an oath, and her husband heard it and held his peace at her and disallowed her not, then all her vows shall stand, and every bond wherewith she bound her soul shall stand. But if her husband hath utterly made them void on the day he heard them, then whatsoever proceeded out of her lips concerning her vows or concerning the bond of her soul shall not stand, her husband hath made them void and the Lord shall forgive her.

Every vow and every binding oath to afflict the soul, her husband may establish it or her husband may make it void. But if her husband altogether hold his peace at her from day to day, then he establisheth all her vows, or all her bonds which are upon her, he confirmeth them because he held his peace at her in the day that he heard them. But if he shall anyways make them void after that he hath heard them, then he shall bear her iniquity. These are the statutes which the Lord commanded Moses, between a man and his wife, between the father and his daughter, being yet in her youth in her father's house.

13 AND the Lord spake unto Moses saying, Avenge the children of Israel of the Midianites, afterward shalt thou be gathered unto thy people. And Moses spake unto the people saying, Arm some of yourselves unto the war and let them go against the Midianites and avenge the Lord of Midian. Of every tribe a thousand, throughout all the tribes of Israel, shall ye send to the war. So there were delivered out of the thousands of Israel, a thousand of every tribe, twelve thousand armed for war. And Moses sent them to the war, a thousand of every tribe, them and Phinehas the son of Eleazar the priest, to the war, with the holy instruments and the trumpets to blow in his hand. And they warred against the Midianites as the Lord commanded Moses and they slew all the males. And they slew the kings of Midian, beside the rest of them that were slain, namely, Evi, and Rekem, and Zur, and Hur, and Reba, five kings of Midian, Balaam also the son of Beor they slew with the sword. And the children of Israel took all the women of Midian captives and their little ones, and took the spoil of all their cattle, and all their flocks, and all their goods. And they burnt all their cities wherein they dwelt, and all their goodly castles, with fire. And they took all the spoil, and all the prey, both of men and of beasts. And they brought the captives, and the prey, and the spoil, unto Moses and Eleazar the priest, and unto the congregation of the children of Israel, unto the camp at the plains of Moab which are by Jordan near Jericho.

And Moses, and Eleazar the priest, and all the princes of the congregation, went forth to meet them without the camp. And Moses was wroth with the officers of the host, with the captains over thousands, and captains over hundreds, which came from the battle. And Moses said unto them, Have ye saved all the women alive? Behold, these caused the children of Israel, through the counsel of Balaam, to commit trespass against the Lord in the matter of Peor, and there was a plague among the congregation of the Lord. Now therefore kill every male among the little ones and kill every woman that hath known man by lying with him. But all the women children that have not known a man by lying with him keep alive for yourselves. And do ye abide without the camp seven days, whosoever hath killed any person, and whosoever hath touched any slain, purify both yourselves and your captives on the third day, and on the seventh day. And purify all your raiment, and all that is made of skins, and all work of goats' hair, and all things made of wood.

And Eleazar the priest said unto the men of war which went to the battle, This is the ordinance of the law which the Lord commanded Moses: only the gold, and the silver, the brass, the iron, the tin, and the lead, everything that may abide the fire, ye shall make it go through the fire and it shall be clean, nevertheless it shall be purified with the water of separation, and all that abideth not the fire ye shall make go through the water. And ye shall wash your clothes on the seventh day, and ye shall be clean, and afterward ye shall come into the camp.

And the Lord spake unto Moses saying, Take the sum of the prey that was taken, both of man and of beast, thou, and Eleazar the priest, and the chief fathers of the congregation, and divide the prey into two parts, between them that took the war upon them, who went out to battle, and between all the congregation. And levy a tribute unto the Lord of the men of war which went out to battle, one soul of five hundred, both of the persons, and of the beeves, and of the asses, and of the sheep, take it of their half, and give it unto Eleazar the priest for a heave offering of the Lord. And of the children of Israel's half, thou shalt take one portion of fifty, of the persons, of the beeves, of the asses, and of the flocks, of all manner of beasts, and give them unto the Levites which keep the charge of the tabernacle of the Lord. And Moses and Eleazar the priest did as the Lord commanded Moses.

And the booty, being the rest of the prey which the men of war had caught, was six hundred thousand and seventy thousand and five thousand sheep, and threescore and twelve thousand beeves, and threescore and one thousand asses, and thirty and two thousand persons in all, of women that had not known man by lying with him.

And the half, which was the portion of them that went out to war, was in number three hundred thousand and seven and thirty thousand and five hundred sheep, and the Lord's tribute of the sheep was six hundred and threescore and fifteen. And the beeves were thirty and six thousand, of which the Lord's tribute was threescore and twelve. And the asses were thirty thousand and five hundred, of which the Lord's tribute was threescore and one. And the persons were sixteen thousand, of which the Lord's tribute was thirty and two persons. And Moses give the tribute, which was the Lord's heave offering, unto Eleazar the priest as the Lord commanded Moses.

And of the children of Israel's half, which Moses divided from the men that warred (now the half that pertained unto the congregation was three hundred thousand and thirty thousand and seven thousand and five hundred sheep, and thirty and six thousand beeves, and thirty thousand asses and five hundred, and sixteen thousand persons), even of the children of Israel's half, Moses took one portion of fifty, both of man and of beast, and gave them unto the Levites which kept the charge of the tabernacle of the Lord as the Lord commanded Moses.

And the officers which were over thousands of the host, the captains of thousands, and captains of hundreds, came near unto Moses, and they said unto Moses, Thy servants have taken the sum of the men of war which are under our charge, and there lacketh not one man of us. We have therefore brought an oblation for the Lord, what every man hath gotten, of jewels of gold, chains, and bracelets, rings, earrings and tablets, to make an atonement for our souls before the Lord. And Moses and Eleazar the priest took the gold of them, even all wrought jewels. And all the gold of the offering that they offered up to the Lord, of the captains of thousands, and of the captains of hundreds, was sixteen thousand seven hundred and fifty shekels (For the men of war had taken spoil, every man for himself). And Moses and Eleazar the priest took the gold of the captains of thousands and of hundreds, and brought it into the tabernacle of the congregation, for a memorial for the children of Israel before the Lord.

Now the children of Reuben and the children of Gad had a very great multitude of cattle, and when they saw the land of Jazer, and the land of Gilead, that, behold, the place was a place for cattle, the children of Gad and the children of Reuben came and spake unto Moses, and to Eleazar the priest, and unto the princes of the congregation, saying, Ataroth, and Dibon, and Jazer, and Nimrah, and Heshbon, and Elealeh, and Shebam, and Nebo, and Beon, even the country which the Lord smote before the congregation of Israel, is land for cattle, and thy servants have cattle, wherefore, said they, if we have found grace in thy sight, let this land be given unto thy servants for a possession and bring us not over Jordan.

And Moses said unto the children of Gad and to the children of Reuben, Shall your brethren go to war, and shall ye sit here? And wherefore discourage ye the heart of the children of Israel from going over into the land which the Lord hath given them? Thus did your fathers when I sent them from Kadesh-barnea to see the land. For when they went up into the valley of Eshcol and saw the land, they discouraged the heart of the children of Israel that they should not go into the land which the Lord had given them. And the Lord's anger was kindled the same time, and he sware saying, Surely none of the men that came up out of Egypt, from twenty years old and upward, shall see the land which I sware unto Abraham, unto Isaac, and unto Jacob because they have not wholly followed me, save Caleb the son of Jephunneh the Kenezite and Joshua the son of Nun, for they have wholly followed the Lord. And the Lord's anger was kindled against Israel, and he made them wander in the wilderness forty years, until all the generation that had done evil in the sight of the Lor, was consumed. And behold, ye are risen up in your fathers' stead, an increase of sinful men, to augment yet the fierce anger of the Lord toward Israel. For if ye turn away from after him, he will yet again leave them in the wilderness and ye shall destroy all this people.

And they came near unto him and said, We will build sheepfolds here for our cattle, and cities for our little ones, but we ourselves will go ready armed before the children of Israel, until we have brought them unto their place, and our little ones shall dwell in the fenced cities, because of the inhabitants of the land. We will not return unto our houses until the children of Israel have inherited every man his inheritance, for we will not inherit with them on yonder side Jordan or forward because our inheritance is fallen to us on this side Jordan eastward.

And Moses said unto them, If ye will do this thing, if ye will go armed before the Lord to war and will go all of you armed over Jordan before the Lord until he hath driven out his enemies from before him and the land be subdued before the Lord, then afterward ye shall return and be guiltless before the Lord and before Israel and this land shall be your possession before the Lord. But if ye will not do so, behold, ye have sinned against the Lord and be sure your sin will find you out. Build you cities for your little ones, and folds for your sheep, and do that which hath proceeded out of your mouth.

And the children of Gad and the children of Reuben spake unto Moses saying, Thy servants will do as my lord commandeth. Our little ones, our wives, our flocks, and all our cattle, shall be there in the cities of Gilead, but thy servants will pass over, every man armed for war, before the Lord to battle as my lord saith.

So concerning them Moses commanded Eleazar the priest and Joshua the son of Nun, and the chief fathers of the tribes of the children of Israel, and Moses said unto them, If the children of Gad and the children of Reuben will pass with you over Jordan, every man armed to battle before the Lord and the land shall be subdued before you, then ye shall give them the land of Gilead for a possession, but if they will not pass over with you armed, they shall have possessions among you in the land of Canaan. And the children of Gad and the children of Reuben answered saying, As the Lord hath said unto thy servants, so will we do. We will pass over armed before the Lord into the land of Canaan, that the possession of our inheritance on this side Jordan may be ours.

And Moses gave unto them, even to the children of Gad, and to the children of Reuben, and unto half the tribe of Manasseh, the son of Joseph, the kingdom of Sihon king of the Amorites, and the kingdom of Og king of Bashan, the land, with the cities thereof in the coasts, even the cities of the country round about. And the children of Gad built Dibon, and Ataroth, and Aroer, and Atroth, Shophan, and Jaazer, and Jogbehah, and Beth-nimrah, and Beth-haran, fenced cities and folds for sheep. And the children of Reuben built Heshbon, and Elealeh, and Kirjathaim, and Nebo, and Baal-meon (their names being changed), and Shibmah, and gave other names unto the cities which they builded. And the children of Machir the son of Manasseh went to Gilead, and took it, and dispossessed the Amorite which was in it. And Moses gave Gilead unto Machir the son of Manasseh and he dwelt therein. And Jair the son of Manasseh went and took the small towns thereof and called them Havoth-jair. And Nobah went and took Kenath, and the villages thereof, and called it Nobah after his own name.

These are the journeys of the children of Israel, which went forth out of the land of Egypt with their armies under the hand of Moses and Aaron. And Moses wrote their goings out according to their journeys by the commandment of the Lord and these are their journeys according to their goings out. And they departed from Rameses in the first month, on the fifteenth day of the first month, on the morrow after the passover the children of Israel went out with a high hand in the sight of all the Egyptians. For the Egyptians buried all their firstborn which the Lord had smitten among them, upon their gods also the Lord executed judgments.

And the children of Israel removed from Rameses, and pitched in Succoth. And they departed from Succoth, and pitched in Etham, which is in the edge of the wilderness. And they removed from Etham, and turned again unto Pi-hahiroth, which is before Baal-zephon, and they pitched before Migdol. And they departed from before Pi-hahiroth, and passed through the midst of the sea into the wilderness, and went three days' journey in the wilderness of Etham, and pitched in Marah. And they removed from Marah, and came unto Elim, and in Elim were twelve fountains of water, and threescore and ten palm trees, and they pitched there. And they removed from Elim and encamped by the Red Sea. And they removed from the Red Sea and encamped in the wilderness of Sin. And they took their journey out of the wilderness of Sin and encamped in Dophkah. And they departed from Dophkah and encamped in Alush. And they removed from Alush and encamped at Rephidim, where was no water for the people to drink. And they departed from Rephidim and pitched in the wilderness of Sinai. And they removed from the desert of Sinai and pitched at Kibroth-hattaavah. And they departed from Kibroth-hattaavah and encamped at Hazeroth. And they departed from Hazeroth and pitched in Rithmah. And they departed from Rithmah and pitched in Rimmon-parez. And they departed from Rimmon-parez and pitched in Libnah. And they removed from Libnah and pitched at Rissah. And they journeyed from Rissah and pitched in Kehelathah. And they went from Kehelathah and pitched in mount Shapher. And they removed from mount Shapher and encamped in Haradah. And they removed from Haradah and pitched in Makheloth. And they removed from Makheloth and encamped at Tahath. And they departed from Tahath and pitched at Tarah. And they removed from Tarah and pitched in Mithcah. And they went from Mithcah and pitched in Hashmonah. And they departed from Hashmonah and encamped at Moseroth. And they departed from Moseroth and pitched in Bene-jaakan. And they removed from Bene-jaakan and encamped at Hor-hagidgad. And they went from Hor-hagidgad and pitched in Jotbathah. And they removed from Jotbathah and encamped at Ebronah. And they departed from Ebronah and encamped at Ezion-gaber. And they removed from Ezion-gaber and pitched in the wilderness of Zin which is Kadesh. And they removed from Kadesh and pitched in mount Hor in the edge of the land of Edom.

And Aaron the priest went up into mount Hor at the commandment of the Lord and died there, in the fortieth year after the children of Israel were come out of the land of Egypt, in the first day of the fifth month. And Aaron was a hundred and twenty and three years old when he died in mount Hor.

And king Arad the Canaanite which dwelt in the south in the land of Canaan heard of the coming of the children of Israel.

And they departed from mount Hor and pitched in Zalmonah. And they departed from Zalmonah and pitched in Punon. And they departed from Punon and pitched in Oboth. And they departed from Oboth and pitched in Ijeabarim in the border of Moab. And they departed from Iim and pitched in Dibon-gad. And they removed from Dibongad and encamped in Almon-diblathaim. And they removed from Almon-diblathaim and pitched in the mountains of Abarim, before Nebo. And they departed from the mountains of Abarim and pitched in the plains of Moab by Jordan near Jericho. And they pitched by Jordan from Beth-jesimoth even unto Abel-shittim in the plains of Moab.

And the Lord spake unto Moses in the plains of Moab by Jordan near Jericho saying, Speak unto the children of Israel and say unto them, When ye are passed over Jordan into the land of Canaan, then ye shall drive out all the inhabitants of the land from before you, and destroy all their pictures, and destroy all their molten images, and quite pluck down all their high places, and ye shall dispossess the inhabitants of the land and dwell therein, for I have given you the land to possess it. And ye shall divide the land by lot for an inheritance among your families, and to the more ye shall give the more inheritance, and to the fewer ye shall give the less inheritance, every man's inheritance shall be in the place where his lot falleth, according to the tribes of your fathers ye shall inherit. But if ye will not drive out the inhabitants of the land from before you, then it shall come to pass that those which ye let remain of them shall be pricks in your eyes, and thorns in your sides, and shall vex you in the land wherein ye dwell. Moreover it shall come to pass that I shall do unto you as I thought to do unto them.

And the Lord spake unto Moses, saying, Command the children of Israel and say unto them, When ye come into the land of Canaan (this is the land that shall fall unto you for an inheritance, even the land of Canaan with the coasts thereof), then your south quarter shall be from the wilderness of Zin along by the coast of Edom, and your south border shall be the outmost coast of the salt sea eastward, and your border shall turn from the south to the ascent of Akrabbim and pass on to Zin, and the going forth thereof shall be from the south to Kadesh-barnea and shall go on to Hazar-addar and pass on to Azmon, and the border shall fetch a compass from Azmon unto the river of Egypt, and the goings out of it shall be at the sea.

And as for the western border, ye shall even have the great sea for a border, this shall be your west border.

And this shall be your north border, from the great sea ye shall point out for you mount Hor, from mount Hor ye shall point out your border unto the entrance of Hamath, and the goings forth of border shall be to Zedad, and the border shall go on to Ziphron, and the goings out of it shall be at Hazar-enan, this shall be your north border.

And ye shall point your east border from Hazar-enan to Shepham, and the coast shall go down from Shepham to Riblah, on the east side of Ain, and the border shall descend, and shall reach unto the side of the Sea of Chinnereth eastward, and the border shall go down to Jordan, and the goings out of it shall be at the salt sea, this shall be your land with the coasts thereof round about.

And Moses commanded the children of Israel saying, This is the land which ye shall inherit by lot, which the Lord commanded to give unto the nine tribes and to the half tribe, for the tribe of the children of Reuben according to the house of their fathers, and the tribe of the children of Gad according to the house of their fathers, have received their inheritance, and half the tribe of Manasseh have received their inheritance, the two tribes and the half tribe have received their inheritance on this side Jordan near Jericho eastward, toward the sunrising.

And the Lord spake unto Moses saying, These are the names of the men which shall divide the land unto you: Eleazar the priest and Joshua the son of Nun. And ye shall take one prince of every tribe to divide the land by inheritance. And the names of the men are these: Of the tribe of Judah, Caleb the son of Jephunneh. And of the tribe of the children of Simeon, Shemuel the son of Ammihud. Of the tribe of Benjamin, Elidad the son of Chislon. And the prince of the tribe of the children of Dan, Bukki the son of Jogli. The prince of the children of Joseph, for the tribe of the children of Manasseh, Hanniel the son of Ephod. And the prince of the tribe of the children of Ephraim, Kemuel the son of Shiphtan. And the prince of the tribe of the children of Zebulun, Elizaphan the son of Parnach. And the prince of the tribe of the children of Issachar, Paltiel the son of Azzan. And the prince of the tribe of the children of Asher, Ahihud the son of Shelomi. And the prince of the tribe of the children of Naphtali, Pedahel the son of Ammihud. These are they whom the Lord commanded to divide the inheritance unto the children of Israel in the land of Canaan.

And the Lord spake unto Moses in the plains of Moab by Jordan near Jericho saying, Command the children of Israel that they give unto the Levites of the inheritance of their possession cities to dwell in, and ye shall give also unto the Levites suburbs for the cities round about them. And the cities shall they have to dwell in, and the suburbs of them shall be for their cattle, and for their goods, and for all their beasts.

And the suburbs of the cities which ye shall give unto the Levites shall reach from the wall of the city and outward a thousand cubits round about. And ye shall measure from without the city on the east side two thousand cubits, and on the south side two thousand cubits, and on the west side two thousand cubits, and on the north side two thousand cubits, and the city shall be in the midst, this shall be to them the suburbs of the cities.

And among the cities which ye shall give unto the Levites there shall be six cities for refuge which ye shall appoint for the manslayer, that he may flee thither, and to them ye shall add forty and two cities. So all the cities which ye shall give to the Levites shall be forty and eight cities, them shall ye give with their suburbs. And the cities which ye shall give shall be of the possession of the children of Israel, from them that have many ye shall give many, but from them that have few ye shall give few, everyone shall give of his cities unto the Levites according to his inheritance which he inheriteth.

And the Lord spake unto Moses saying, Speak unto the children of Israel and say unto them, When ye be come over Jordan into the land of Canaan, then ye shall appoint you cities to be cities of refuge for you, that the slayer may flee thither which killeth any person at unawares. And they shall be unto you cities for refuge from the avenger, that the manslayer die not until he stand before the congregation in judgment. And of these cities which ye shall give, six cities shall ye have for refuge. Ye shall give three cities on this side Jordan, and three cities shall ye give in the land of Canaan, which shall be cities of refuge. These six cities shall be a refuge, both for the children of Israel and for the stranger and for the sojourner among them, that every one that killeth any person unawares may flee thither.

And if he smite him with an instrument of iron so that he die, he is a murderer; the murderer shall surely be put to death. And if he smite him with throwing a stone wherewith he may die and he die, he is a murderer, the murderer shall surely be put to death. Or if he smite him with a hand weapon of wood wherewith he may die and he die, he is a murderer, the murderer shall surely be put to death. The revenger of blood himself shall slay the murderer when he meeteth him, he shall slay him. But if he thrust him of hatred or hurl at him by laying of wait that he die, or in enmity smite him with his hand that he die, he that smote him shall surely be put to death, for he is a murderer; the revenger of blood shall slay the murderer when he meeteth him.

But if he thrust him suddenly without enmity or have cast upon him anything without laying of wait, or with any stone wherewith a man may die, seeing him not and cast it upon him that he die, and was not his enemy, neither sought his harm, then the congregation shall judge between the slayer and the revenger of blood according to these judgments, and the congregation shall deliver the slayer out of the hand of the revenger of blood, and the congregation shall restore him to the city of his refuge whither he was fled, and he shall abide in it unto the death of the high priest which was anointed with the holy oil. But if the slayer shall at any time come without the border of the city of his refuge, whither he was fled, and the revenger of blood find him without the borders of the city of his refuge, and the revenger of blood kill the slayer, he shall not be guilty of blood because he should have remained in the city of his refuge until the death of the high priest, but after the death of the high priest the slayer shall return into the land of his possession.

So these things shall be for a statute of judgment unto you throughout your generations in all your dwellings.

Whoso killeth any person, the murderer shall be put to death by the mouth of witnesses, but one witness shall not testify against any person to cause him to die. Moreover ye shall take no satisfaction for the life of a murderer which is guilty of death, but he shall be surely put to death. And ye shall take no satisfaction for him that is fled to the city of his refuge, that he should come again to dwell in the land until the death of the priest. So ye shall not pollute the land wherein ye are, for blood it defileth the land, and the land cannot be cleansed of the blood that is shed therein, but by the blood of him that shed it. Defile not therefore the land which ye shall inhabit, wherein I dwell, for I the Lord dwell among the children of Israel.

And the chief fathers of the families of the children of Gilead, the son of Machir, the son of Manasseh, of the families of the sons of Joseph, came near and spake before Moses, and before the princes, the chief fathers of the children of Israel and they said, The Lord commanded my lord to give the land for an inheritance by lot to the children of Israel, and my lord was commanded by the Lord to give the inheritance of Zelophehad our brother unto his daughters. And if they be married to any of the sons of the other tribes of the children of Israel, then shall their inheritance be taken from the inheritance of our fathers, and shall be put to the inheritance of the tribe whereunto they are received, so shall it be taken from the lot of our inheritance. And when the jubilee of the children of Israel shall be, then shall their inheritance be put unto the inheritance of the tribe whereunto they are received, so shall their inheritance be taken away from the inheritance of the tribe of our fathers.

And Moses commanded the children of Israel according to the word of the Lord, saying, The tribe of the sons of Joseph hath said well. This is the thing which the Lord doth command concerning the daughters of Zelophehad, saying, Let them marry to whom they think best, only to the family of the tribe of their fathers shall they marry. So shall not the inheritance of the children of Israel remove from tribe to tribe, for everyone of the children of Israel shall keep himself to the inheritance of the tribe of his fathers. And every daughter that possesseth an inheritance in any tribe of the children of Israel shall be wife unto one of the family of the tribe of her father, that the children of Israel may enjoy every man the inheritance of his fathers. Neither shall the inheritance remove from one tribe to another tribe, but every one of the tribes of the children of Israel shall keep himself to his own inheritance.

Even as the Lord commanded Moses, so did the daughters of Zelophehad, for Mahlah, Tirzah, and Hoglah, and Milcah, and Noah, the daughters of Zelophehad, were married unto their father's brothers' sons, and they were married into the families of the sons of Manasseh the son of Joseph, and their inheritance remained in the tribe of the family of their father.

These are the commandments and the judgments, which the Lord commanded, by the hand of Moses, unto the children of Israel in the plains of Moab by Jordan near Jericho.

DEUTERONOMY

THESE be the words which Moses spake unto all Israel on this side Jordan in the wilderness, in the plain over against the Red Sea between Paran, and Tophel, and Laban, and Hazeroth, and Dizahab (There are eleven days' journey from Horeb by the way of mount Seir unto Kadesh-barnea). And it came to pass in the fortieth year, in the eleventh month, on the first day of the month, that Moses spake unto the children of Israel, according unto all that the Lord had given him in commandment unto them, after he had slain Sihon the king of the Amorites which dwelt in Heshbon, and Og the king of Bashan which dwelt at Astaroth in Edrei. On this side Jordan in the land of Moab began Moses to declare this law saying:

The Lord our God spake unto us in Horeb saying, Ye have dwelt long enough in this mount, turn you and take your journey, and go to the mount of the Amorites, and unto all the places nigh thereunto, in the plain, in the hills, and in the vale, and in the south, and by the seaside, to the land of the Canaanites, and unto Lebanon, unto the great river, the river Euphrates. Behold, I have set the land before you, go in and possess the land which the Lord sware unto your fathers Abraham, Isaac, and Jacob, to give unto them and to their seed after them.

And I spake unto you at that time saying, I am not able to bear you myself alone; the Lord your God hath multiplied you and behold, ye are this day as the stars of Heaven for multitude. The Lord God of your fathers make you a thousand times so many more as ye are, and bless you as he hath promised you. How can I myself alone bear your cumbrance, and your burden, and your strife? Take you wise men, and understanding, and known among your tribes, and I will make them rulers over you. And ye answered me and said, The thing which thou hast spoken is good for us to do. So I took the chief of your tribes, wise men, and known, and made them heads over you, captains over thousands, and captains over hundreds, and captains over fifties, and captains over tens, and officers among your tribes. And I charged your judges at that time saying, Hear the causes between your brethren and judge righteously between every man and his brother and the stranger that is with him. Ye shall not respect persons in judgment, but ye shall hear the small as well as the great, ye shall not be afraid of the face of man, for the judgment is God's, and the cause that is too hard for you, bring it unto me and I will hear it. And I commanded you at that time all the things which ye should do.

And when we departed from Horeb, we went through all that great and terrible wilderness which ye saw by the way of the mountain of the Amorites as the Lord our God commanded us, and we came to Kadesh-barnea. And I said unto you, Ye are come unto the mountain of the Amorites which the Lord our God doth give unto us. Behold, the Lord thy God hath set the land before thee, go up and possess it as the Lord God of thy fathers hath said unto thee; fear not neither be discouraged. And ye came near unto me every one of you and said, We will send men before us, and they shall search us out the land, and bring us word again by what way we must go up, and into what cities we shall come. And the saying pleased me well and I took twelve men of you, one of a tribe, and they turned and went up into the mountain, and came unto the valley of Eschol, and searched it out. And they took of the fruit of the land in their hands, and brought it down unto us, and brought us word again and said, It is a good land which the Lord our God doth give us. Notwithstanding, ye would not go up, but rebelled against the commandment of the Lord your God, and ye murmured in your tents and said, Because the Lord hated us he hath brought us forth out of the land of Egypt to deliver us into the hand of the Amorites to destroy us. Whither shall we go up? Our brethren have discouraged our heart saying, The people is greater and taller than we, the cities are great and walled up to Heaven, and moreover we have seen the sons of the Anakim there. Then I said unto you, Dread not neither be afraid of them. The Lord your God which goeth before you, he shall fight for you according to all that he did for you in Egypt before your eyes and in the wilderness where thou hast seen how that the Lord thy God bare thee as a man doth bear his son, in all the way that ye went until ye came into this place. Yet in this thing ye did not believe the Lord your God, who went in the way before you to search you out a place to pitch your tents in, in fire by night to show you by what way ye should go and in a cloud by day. And the Lord heard the voice of your words and was wroth and sware saying, Surely there shall not one of these men of this evil generation see that good land which I sware to give unto your fathers, save Caleb the son of Jephunneh, he shall see it, and to him will I give the land that he hath trodden upon and to his children because he hath wholly followed the Lord. Also the Lord was angry with me for your sakes saying, Thou also shalt not go in thither. But Joshua the son of Nun which standeth before thee, he shall go in thither; encourage him, for he shall cause Israel to inherit it. Moreover your little ones which ye said should be a prey, and your children which in that day had no knowledge between good and evil, they shall go in thither, and unto them will I give it and they shall possess it. But as for you, turn you and take your journey into the wilderness by the way of the Red Sea. Then ye answered and said unto me, We have sinned against the Lord, we will go up and fight according to all that the Lord our God commanded us. And when ye had girded on every man his weapons of war ye were ready to go up into the hill. And the Lord said unto me, Say unto them, Go not up, neither fight, for I am not among you, lest ye be smitten before your enemies. So I spake unto you, and ye would not hear, but rebelled against the commandment of the Lord and went presumptuously up into the hill. And the Amorites, which dwell in that mountain, came out against you and chased you as bees do, and destroyed you in Seir, even unto Hormah. And ye returned and wept before the Lord, but the Lord would not hearken to your voice nor give ear unto you. So ye abode in Kadesh many days, according unto the days that ye abode there.

Then we turned and took our journey into the wilderness by the way of the Red Sea as the Lord spake unto me, and we compassed mount Seir many days. And the Lord spake unto me saying, Ye have compassed this mountain long enough, turn you northward. And command thou the people saying, Ye are to pass through the coast of your brethren the children of Esau which dwell in Seir, and they shall be afraid of you, take ye good heed unto yourselves therefore, meddle not with them, for I will not give you of their land, no, not so much as a foot breadth, because I have given mount Seir unto Esau for a possession. Ye shall buy meat of them for money that ye may eat and ye shall also buy water of them for money that ye may drink. For the Lord thy God hath blessed thee in all the works of thy hand, he knoweth thy walking through this great wilderness, these forty years the Lord thy God hath been with thee, thou hast lacked nothing. And when we passed by from our brethren the children of Esau which dwelt in Seir, through the way of the plain from Elath and from Ezion-gaber, we turned and passed by the way of the wilderness of Moab. And the Lord said unto me, Distress not the Moabites, neither contend with them in battle, for I will not give thee of their land for a possession because I have given Ar unto the children of Lot for a possession. The Emim dwelt therein in times past, a people great, and many, and tall as the Anakim, which also were accounted giants as the Anakim, but the Moabites call them Emim. The Horim also dwelt in Seir beforetime, but the children of Esau succeeded them when they had destroyed them from before them, and dwelt in their stead as Israel did unto the land of his possession which the Lord gave unto them. Now rise up, said I, and get you over the brook Zered. And we went over the brook Zered. And the space in which we came from Kadesh-barnea until we were come over the brook Zered was thirty and eight years, until all the generation of the men of war were wasted out from among the host as the Lord sware unto them. For indeed the hand of the Lord was against them, to destroy them from among the host until they were consumed.

So it came to pass, when all the men of war were consumed and dead from among the people, that the Lord spake unto me saying, Thou art to pass over through Ar, the coast of Moab, this day, and when thou comest nigh over against the children of Ammon, distress them not nor meddle with them, for I will not give thee of the land of the children of Ammon any possession because I have given it unto the children of Lot for a possession (that also was accounted a land of giants; giants dwelt therein in old time, and the Ammonites call them Zamzummim, a people great, and many, and tall as the Anakim, but the Lord destroyed them before them, and they succeeded them, and dwelt in their stead, as he did to the children of Esau, which dwelt in Seir when he destroyed the Horim from before them, and they succeeded them, and dwelt in their stead even unto this day, and the Avim which dwelt in Hazerim, even unto Azzah the Caphtorim, which came forth out of Caphtor, destroyed them, and dwelt in their stead). Rise ye up, take your journey, and pass over the river Arnon, behold, I have given into thine hand Sihon the Amorite, king of Heshbon, and his land, begin to possess it and contend with him in battle. This day will I begin to put the dread of thee and the fear of thee upon the nations that are under the whole Heaven who shall hear report of thee, and shall tremble, and be in anguish because of thee.

And I sent messengers out of the wilderness of Kedemoth unto Sihon king of Heshbon with words of peace saying, Let me pass through thy land: I will go along by the highway, I will neither turn unto the right hand nor to the left. Thou shalt sell me meat for money that I may eat, and give me water for money that I may drink, only I will pass through on my feet (as the children of Esau which dwell in Seir, and the Moabites which dwell in Ar, did unto me) until I shall pass over Jordan into the land which the Lord our God giveth us. But Sihon king of Heshbon would not let us pass by him, for he hardened his spirit and made his heart obstinate, that the Lord thy God might deliver him into thy hand as he hath done this day. And the Lord said unto me, Behold, I have begun to give Sihon and his land before thee; begin to possess that thou mayest inherit his land. Then Sihon came out against us, he and all his people, to fight at Jahaz. And the Lord our God delivered him before us, and we smote him, and his sons, and all his people. And we took all his cities at that time and utterly destroyed the men, and the women, and the little ones, of every city, we left none to remain, only the cattle we took for a prey unto ourselves and the spoil of the cities which we took. From Aroer, which is by the brink of the river of Arnon, and from the city that is by the river even unto Gilead, there was not one city too strong for us, the Lord our God delivered all unto us, only unto the land of the children of Ammon thou camest not, nor unto any place of the river Jabbok, nor unto the cities in the mountains, nor unto whatsoever the Lord our God forbade us.

Then we turned, and went up the way to Bashan, and Og the king of Bashan came out against us, he and all his people, to battle at Edrei. And the Lord said unto me, Fear him not, for I will deliver him, and all his people, and his land, into thy hand, and thou shalt do unto him as thou didst unto Sihon king of the Amorites which dwelt at Heshbon. So the Lord our God delivered into our hands Og also, the king of Bashan, and all his people, and we smote him until none was left to him remaining. And we took all his cities at that time, there was not a city which we took not from them, threescore cities, all the region of Argob, the kingdom of Og in Bashan. All these cities were fenced with high walls, gates, and bars, beside unwalled towns a great many. And we utterly destroyed them as we did unto Sihon king of Heshbon, utterly destroying the men, women, and children of every city. But all the cattle and the spoil of the cities we took for a prey to ourselves.

And we took at that time out of the hand of the two kings of the Amorites the land that was on this side Jordan, from the river of Arnon unto mount Hermon (which Hermon the Sidonians call Sirion and the Amorites call it Shenir), all the cities of the plain, and all Gilead, and all Bashan unto Salchah and Edrei, cities of the kingdom of Og in Bashan. For only Og king of Bashan remained of the remnant of giants; behold, his bedstead was a bedstead of iron; is it not in Rabbath of the children of Ammon? Nine cubits was the length thereof and four cubits the breadth of it, after the cubit of a man.

And this land, which we possessed at that time from Aroer, which is by the river Arnon, and half mount Gilead, and the cities thereof, gave I unto the Reubenites and to the Gadites. And the rest of Gilead, and all Bashan, being the kingdom of Og, gave I unto the half tribe of Manasseh, all the region of Argob with all Bashan, which was called the land of giants. Jair the son of Manasseh took all the country of Argob unto the coasts of Geshuri and Maachathi, and called them after his own name, Bashan-havoth-jair, unto this day. And I gave Gilead unto Machir. And unto the Reubenites and unto the Gadites I gave from Gilead even unto the river Arnon half the valley, and the border even unto the river Jabbok, which is the border of the children of Ammon, the plain also, and Jordan, and the coast thereof, from Chinnereth even unto the sea of the plain, even the salt sea under Ashdoth-pisgah eastward.

And I commanded you at that time saying, The Lord your God hath given you this land to possess it, ye shall pass over armed before your brethren the children of Israel, all that are meet for the war. But your wives, and your little ones, and your cattle (for I know that ye have much cattle) shall abide in your cities which I have given you, until the Lord have given rest unto your brethren as well as unto you, and until they also possess the land which the Lord your God hath given them beyond Jordan, and then shall ye return every man unto his possession which I have given you. And I commanded Joshua at that time saying, Thine eyes have seen all that the Lord your God hath done unto these two kings, so shall the Lord do unto all the kingdoms whither thou passest. Ye shall not fear them, for the Lord your God he shall fight for you.

And I besought the Lord at that time saying, O Lord God, thou hast begun to show thy servant thy greatness and the mighty hand, for what God is there in Heaven or in Earth that can do according to thy works and according to thy might? I pray thee, let me go over and see the good land that is beyond Jordan, that goodly mountain and Lebanon. But the Lord was wroth with me for your sakes, and would not hear me, and the Lord said unto me, Let it suffice thee, speak no more unto me of this matter. Get thee up into the top of Pisgah and lift up thine eyes westward, and northward, and southward, and eastward, and behold it with thine eyes, for thou shalt not go over this Jordan. But charge Joshua, and encourage him and strengthen him, for he shall go over before this people, and he shall cause them to inherit the land which thou shalt see. So we abode in the valley over against Beth-peor.

2 NOW therefore hearken, O Israel, unto the statutes and unto the judgments which I teach you for to do them, that ye may live, and go in and possess the land which the Lord God of your fathers giveth you. Ye shall not add unto the word which I command you, neither shall ye diminish aught from it, that ye may keep the commandments of the Lord your God which I command you. Your eyes have seen what the Lord did because of Baal-peor, for all the men that followed Baal-peor, the Lord thy God hath destroyed them from among you. But ye that did cleave unto the Lord your God are alive every one of you this day.

Behold, I have taught you statutes and judgments, even as the Lord my God commanded me, that ye should do so in the land whither ye go to possess it. Keep therefore and do them, for this is your wisdom and your understanding in the sight of the nations which shall hear all these statutes and say, Surely this great nation is a wise and understanding people. For what nation is there so great who hath God so nigh unto them, as the Lord our God is in all things that we call upon him for? And what nation is there so great that hath statutes and judgments so righteous as all this law which I set before you this day.

Only take heed to thyself, and keep thy soul diligently, lest thou forget the things which thine eyes have seen, and lest they depart from thy heart all the days of thy life, but teach them thy sons, and thy sons' sons. Specially the day that thou stoodest before the Lord thy God in Horeb, when the Lord said unto me, Gather me the people together, and I will make them hear my words, that they may learn to fear me all the days that they shall live upon the Earth, and that they may teach their children. And ye came near and stood under the mountain, and the mountain burned with fire unto the midst of Heaven, with darkness, clouds and thick darkness. And the Lord spake unto you out of the midst of the fire, ye heard the voice of the words, but saw no similitude, only ye heard a voice. And he declared unto you his covenant, which he commanded you to perform, even ten commandments, and he wrote them upon two tables of stone. And the Lord commanded me at that time to teach you statutes and judgments, that ye might do them in the land whither ye go over to possess it.

Take ye therefore good heed unto yourselves, for ye saw no manner of similitude on the day that the Lord spake unto you in Horeb out of the midst of the fire, lest ye corrupt yourselves, and make you a graven image, the similitude of any figure, the likeness of male or female, the likeness of any beast that is on the Earth, the likeness of any winged fowl that flieth in the air. The likeness of any thing that creepeth on the ground, the likeness of any fish that is in the waters beneath the Earth, and lest thou lift up thine eyes unto Heaven, and when thou seest the sun, and the moon, and the stars, even all the host of Heaven, shouldest be driven to worship them, and serve them, which the Lord thy God hath divided unto all nations under the whole Heaven. But the Lord hath taken you, and brought you forth out of the iron furnace, even out of Egypt, to be unto him a people of inheritance, as ye are this day.

Furthermore the Lord was angry with me for your sakes, and sware that I should not go over Jordan, and that I should not go in unto that good land, which the Lord thy God giveth thee for an inheritance, but I must die in this land, I must not go over Jordan, but ye shall go over, and possess that good land. Take heed unto yourselves, lest ye forget the covenant of the Lord your God, which he made with you, and make you a graven image, or the likeness of any thing, which the Lord thy God hath forbidden thee. For the Lord thy God is a consuming fire, even a jealous God.

When thou shalt beget children, and children's children, and ye shall have remained long in the land, and shall corrupt yourselves, and make a graven image, or the likeness of anything, and shall do evil in the sight of the Lord thy God, to provoke him to anger, I call Heaven and Earth to witness against you this day, that ye shall soon utterly perish from off the land whereunto ye go over Jordan to possess it, ye shall not prolong your days upon it, but shall utterly be destroyed. And the Lord shall scatter you among the nations, and ye shall be left few in number among the heathen, whither the Lord shall lead you. And there ye shall serve gods, the work of men's hands, wood and stone, which neither see, nor hear, nor eat, nor smell. But if from thence thou shalt seek the Lord thy God, thou shalt find him, if thou seek him with all thy heart and with all thy soul. When thou art in tribulation, and all these things are come upon thee, even in the latter days, if thou turn to the Lord thy God, and shalt be obedient unto his voice, (for the Lord thy God is a merciful God,) he will not forsake thee, neither destroy thee, nor forget the covenant of thy fathers, which he sware unto them.

For ask now of the days that are past, which were before thee, since the day that God created man upon the Earth, and ask from the one side of Heaven unto the other, whether there hath been any such thing as this great thing is, or hath been heard like it? Did ever people hear the voice of God speaking out of the midst of the fire, as thou hast heard, and live? Or hath God assayed to go and take him a nation from the midst of another nation, by temptations, by signs, and by wonders, and by war, and by a mighty hand, and by a stretched out arm, and by great terrors, according to all that the Lord your God did for you in Egypt before your eyes? Unto thee it was showed, that thou mightest know that the Lord he is God, there is none else beside him. Out of Heaven he made thee to hear his voice, that he might instruct thee, and upon Earth he showed thee his great fire, and thou heardest his words out of the midst of the fire. And because he loved thy fathers, therefore he chose their seed after them, and brought thee out in his sight with his mighty power out of Egypt, to drive out nations from before thee greater and mightier than thou art, to bring thee in, to give thee their land for an inheritance, as it is this day. Know therefore this day, and consider it in thine heart, that the Lord he is God in Heaven above, and upon the Earth beneath, there is none else. Thou shalt keep therefore his statutes, and his commandments, which I command thee this day, that it may go well with thee, and with thy children after thee, and that thou mayest prolong thy days upon the Earth, which the Lord thy God giveth thee, forever.

Then Moses severed three cities on this side Jordan toward the sunrising, that the slayer might flee thither, which should kill his neighbor unawares, and hated him not in times past, and that fleeing unto one of these cities he might live, namely, Bezer in the wilderness, in the plain country, of the Reubenites, and Ramoth in Gilead, of the Gadites, and Golan in Bashan, of the Manassites. And this is the law which Moses set before the children of Israel, these are the testimonies, and the statutes and the judgments, which Moses spake unto the children of Israel, after they came forth out of Egypt. On this side Jordan, in the valley over against Beth-peor, in the land of Sihon king of the Amorites, who dwelt at Heshbon, whom Moses and the children of Israel smote, after thy were come forth out of Egypt, and they possessed his land, and the land of Og king of Bashan, two kings of the Amorites, which were on this side Jordan toward the sunrising, from Aroer, which is by the bank of the river Arnon, even unto mount Sion, which is Hermon, and all the plain on this side Jordan eastward, even unto the sea of the plain, under the springs of Pisgah

And Moses called all Israel, and said unto them, Hear, O Israel, the statutes and judgments which I speak in your ears this day, that ye may learn them, and keep and do them. The Lord our God made a covenant with us in Horeb. The Lord made not this covenant with our fathers, but with us, even us, who are all of us here alive this day. The Lord talked with you face to face in the mount out of the midst of the fire, (I stood between the Lord and you at that time, to show you the word of the Lord, for ye were afraid by reason of the fire, and went not up into the mount,) saying,

I am the Lord thy God, which brought thee out of the land of Egypt, from the house of bondage. Thou shalt have none other gods before me. Thou shalt not make thee any graven image, or any likeness of anything that is in Heaven above, or that is in the Earth beneath, or that is in the waters beneath the Earth, thou shalt not bow down thyself unto them, nor serve them, for I the Lord thy God am a jealous God, visiting the iniquity of the fathers upon the children unto the third and fourth generation of them that hate me, and showing mercy unto thousands of them that love me and keep my commandments. Thou shalt not take the name of the Lord thy God in vain, for the Lord will not hold him guiltless that taketh his name in vain. Keep the sabbath day to sanctify it, as the Lord thy God hath commanded thee. Six days thou shalt labor, and do all thy work, but the seventh day is the sabbath of the Lord thy God, in it thou shalt not do any work, thou, nor thy son, nor thy daughter, nor thy manservant, nor thy maidservant, nor thine ox, nor thine ass, nor any of thy cattle, nor thy stranger that is within thy gates, that thy manservant and thy maidservant may rest as well as thou. And remember that thou wast a servant in the land of Egypt, and that the Lord thy God brought thee out thence through a mighty hand and by a stretched out arm, therefore the Lord thy God commanded thee to keep the sabbath day. Honor thy father and thy mother, as the Lord thy God hath commanded thee, that thy days may be prolonged, and that it may go well with thee, in the land which the Lord thy God giveth thee. Thou shalt not kill. Neither shalt thou commit adultery. Neither shalt thou steal. Neither shalt thou bear false witness against thy neighbor. Neither shalt thou desire thy neighbor's wife, neither shalt thou covet thy neighbor's house, his field, or his manservant, or his maidservant, his ox, or his ass, or anything that is thy neighbor's.

These words the Lord spake unto all your assembly in the mount out of the midst of the fire, of the cloud, and of the thick darkness, with a great voice, and he added no more. And he wrote them in two tables of stone, and delivered them unto me. And it came to pass, when ye heard the voice out of the midst of the darkness, (for the mountain did burn with fire,) that ye came near unto me, even all the heads of your tribes, and your elders, and ye said, Behold, the Lord our God hath showed us his glory and his greatness, and we have heard his voice out of the midst of the fire, we have seen this day that God doth talk with man, and he liveth. Now therefore why should we die? for this great fire will consume us; if we hear the voice of the Lord our God any more, then we shall die. For who is there of all flesh, that hath heard the voice of the living God speaking out of the midst of the fire, as we have, and lived? Go thou near, and hear all that the Lord our God shall say, and speak thou unto us all that the Lord our God shall speak unto thee, and we will hear it, and do it.

And the Lord heard the voice of your words, when ye spake unto me, and the Lord said unto me, I have heard the voice of the words of this people, which they have spoken unto thee, they have well said all that they have spoken. O that there were such a heart in them, that they would fear me, and keep all my commandments always, that it might be well with them, and with their children forever! Go say to them, Get you into your tents again. But as for thee, stand thou here by me, and I will speak unto thee all the commandments, and the statutes, and the judgments, which thou shalt teach them, that they may do them in the land which I give them to possess it. Ye shall observe to do therefore as the Lord your God hath commanded you, ye shall not turn aside to the right hand or to the left. Ye shall walk in all the ways which the Lord your God hath commanded you, that ye may live, and that it may be well with you, and that ye may prolong your days in the land which ye shall possess.

Now these are the commandments, the statutes, and the judgments, which the Lord your God commanded to teach you, that ye might do them in the land whither ye go to possess it, that thou mightest fear the Lord thy God, to keep all his statutes and his commandments, which I command thee, thou, and thy son, and thy son's son, all the days of thy life, and that thy days may be prolonged. Hear therefore, O Israel, and observe to do it, that it may be well with thee, and that ye may increase mightily, as the Lord God of thy fathers hath promised thee, in the land that floweth with milk and honey.

Hear, O Israel, The Lord our God is one Lord, and thou shalt love the Lord thy God with all thine heart, and with all thy soul, and with all thy might. And these words which I command thee this day, shall be in thine heart, and thou shalt teach them diligently unto thy children, and shalt talk of them when thou sittest in thine house, and when thou walkest by the way, and when thou liest down, and when thou risest up. And thou shalt bind them for a sign upon thine hand, and they shall be as frontlets between thine eyes. And thou shalt write them upon the posts of thy house, and on thy gates.

3 AND it shall be, when the Lord thy God shall have brought thee into the land which he sware unto thy fathers, to Abraham, to Isaac, and to Jacob, to give thee great and goodly cities, which thou buildedst not, and houses full of all good things, which thou filledst not, and wells digged, which thou diggedst not, vineyards and olive trees, which thou plantedst not, when thou shalt have eaten and be full, then beware lest thou forget the Lord, which brought thee forth out of the land of Egypt, from the house of bondage. Thou shalt fear the Lord thy God, and serve him, and shalt swear by his name. Ye shall not go after other gods, of the gods of the people which are round about you, (for the Lord thy God is a jealous God among you,) lest the anger of the Lord thy God be kindled against thee, and destroy thee from off the face of the Earth.

Ye shall not tempt the Lord your God, as ye tempted him in Massah. Ye shall diligently keep the commandments of the Lord your God, and his testimonies, and his statutes, which he hath commanded thee. And thou shalt do that which is right and good in the sight of the Lord, that it may be well with thee, and that thou mayest go in and possess the good land which the Lord sware unto thy fathers. To cast out all thine enemies from before thee, as the Lord hath spoken.

And when thy son asketh thee in time to come saying, What mean the testimonies, and the statutes, and the judgments, which the Lord our God hath commanded you? Then thou shalt say unto thy son, We were Pharaoh's bondmen in Egypt, and the Lord brought us out of Egypt with a mighty hand, and the Lord showed signs and wonders, great and sore, upon Egypt, upon Pharaoh, and upon all his household, before our eyes, and he brought us out from thence, that he might bring us in, to give us the land which he sware unto our fathers. And the Lord commanded us to do all these statutes, to fear the Lord our God, for our good always, that he might preserve us alive, as it is at this day. And it shall be our righteousness, if we observe to do all these commandments before the Lord our God, as he hath commanded us.

When the Lord thy God shall bring thee into the land whither thou goest to possess it, and hath cast out many nations before thee, the Hittites, and the Girgashites, and the Amorites, and the Canaanites, and the Perizzites, and the Hivites, and the Jebusites, seven nations greater and mightier than thou, and when the Lord thy God shall deliver them before thee, thou shalt smite them, and utterly destroy them, thou shalt make no covenant with them, nor show mercy unto them, neither shalt thou make marriages with them, thy daughter thou shalt not give unto his son, nor his daughter shalt thou take unto thy son. For they will turn away thy son from following me, that they may serve other gods, so will the anger of the Lord be kindled against you, and destroy thee suddenly. But thus shall ye deal with them, ye shall destroy their altars, and break down their images, and cut down their groves, and burn their graven images with fire. For thou art a holy people unto the Lord thy God, the Lord thy God hath chosen thee to be a special people unto himself, above all people that are upon the face of the Earth.

The Lord did not set his love upon you, nor choose you, because ye were more in number than any people, for ye were the fewest of all people, but because the Lord loved you, and because he would keep the oath which he had sworn unto your fathers, hath the Lord brought you out with a mighty hand, and redeemed you out of the house of bondmen, from the hand of Pharaoh king of Egypt. Know therefore that the Lord thy God, he is God, the faithful God, which keepeth covenant and mercy with them that love him and keep his commandments to a thousand generations, and repayeth them that hate him to their face, to destroy them, he will not be slack to him that hateth him, he will repay him to his face. Thou shalt therefore keep the commandments, and the statutes, and the judgments, which I command thee this day, to do them.

Wherefore it shall come to pass, if ye hearken to these judgments, and keep and do them, that the Lord thy God shall keep unto thee the covenant and the mercy which he sware unto thy fathers, and he will love thee, and bless thee, and multiply thee, he will also bless the fruit of thy womb, and the fruit of thy land, thy corn, and thy wine, and thine oil, the increase of thy kine, and the flocks of thy sheep, in the land which he sware unto thy fathers to give thee. Thou shalt be blessed above all people, there shall not be male or female barren among you, or among your cattle. And the Lord will take away from thee all sickness, and will put none of the evil diseases of Egypt, which thou knowest, upon thee, but will lay them upon all them that hate thee. And thou shalt consume all the people which the Lord thy God shall deliver thee, thine eye shall have no pity upon them, neither shalt thou serve their gods, for that will be a snare unto thee.

If thou shalt say in thine heart, These nations are more than I, how can I dispossess them? Thou shalt not be afraid of them, but shalt well remember what the Lord thy God did unto Pharaoh, and unto all Egypt, the great temptations which thine eyes saw, and the signs, and the wonders, and the mighty hand, and the stretched out arm, whereby the Lord thy God brought thee out, so shall the Lord thy God do unto all the people of whom thou art afraid. Moreover the Lord thy God will send the hornet among them, until they that are left, and hide themselves from thee, be destroyed. Thou shalt not be affrighted at them, for the Lord thy God is among you, a mighty God and terrible. And the Lord thy God will put out those nations before thee by little and little, thou mayest not consume them at once, lest the beasts of the field increase upon thee. But the Lord thy God shall deliver them unto thee, and shall destroy them with a mighty destruction, until they be destroyed. And he shall deliver their kings into thine hand, and thou shalt destroy their name from under Heaven, there shall no man be able to stand before thee, until thou have destroyed them. The graven images of their gods shall ye burn with fire, thou shalt not desire the silver or gold that is on them, nor take it unto thee, lest thou be snared therein, for it is an abomination to the Lord thy God. Neither shalt thou bring an abomination into thine house, lest thou be a cursed thing like it, but thou shalt utterly detest it, and thou shalt utterly abhor it, for it is a cursed thing.

All the commandments which I command thee this day shall ye observe to do, that ye may live, and multiply, and go in and possess the land which the Lord sware unto your fathers. And thou shalt remember all the way which the Lord thy God led thee these forty years in the wilderness, to humble thee, and to prove thee, to know what was in thine heart, whether thou wouldest keep his commandments, or not. And he humbled thee, and suffered thee to hunger, and fed thee with manna, which thou knewest not, neither did thy fathers know, that he might make thee know that man doth not live by bread only, but by every word that proceedeth out of the mouth of the Lord doth man live. Thy raiment waxed not old upon thee, neither did thy foot swell, these forty years. Thou shalt also consider in thine heart, that, as a man chasteneth his son, so the Lord thy God chasteneth thee. Therefore thou shalt keep the commandments of the Lord thy God, to walk in his ways, and to fear him. For the Lord thy God bringeth thee into a good land, a land of brooks of water, of fountains and depths that spring out of valleys and hills, a land of wheat, and barley, and vines, and fig trees, and pomegranates, a land of olive oil, and honey, a land wherein thou shalt eat bread without scarceness, thou shalt not lack anything in it, a land whose stones are iron, and out of whose hills thou mayest dig brass. When thou hast eaten and art full, then thou shalt bless the Lord thy God for the good land which he hath given thee.

Beware that thou forget not the Lord thy God, in not keeping his commandments, and his judgments, and his statutes, which I command thee this day, lest when thou hast eaten and art full, and hast built goodly houses and dwelt therein, and when thy herds and thy flocks multiply, and thy silver and thy gold is multiplied, and all that thou hast is multiplied, then thine heart be lifted up, and thou forget the Lord thy God which brought thee forth out of the land of Egypt, from the house of bondage, who led thee through that great and terrible wilderness wherein were fiery serpents, and scorpions, and drought, where there was no water, who brought thee forth water out of the rock of flint, who fed thee in the wilderness with manna, which thy fathers knew not, that he might humble thee and that he might prove thee, to do thee good at thy latter end and thou say in thine heart, My power and the might of mine hand hath gotten me this wealth. But thou shalt remember the Lord thy God, for it is he that giveth thee power to get wealth, that he may establish his covenant which he sware unto thy fathers, as it is this day. And it shall be, if thou do at all forget the Lord thy God and walk after other gods and serve them and worship them, I testify against you this day that ye shall surely perish. As the nations which the Lord destroyeth before your face, so shall ye perish because ye would not be obedient unto the voice of the Lord your God.

Hear, O Israel, Thou art to pass over Jordan this day to go in to possess nations greater and mightier than thyself, cities great and fenced up to Heaven, a people great and tall, the children of the Anakim whom thou knowest and of whom thou hast heard say, Who can stand before the children of Anak? Understand therefore this day that the Lord thy God is he which goeth over before thee, as a consuming fire he shall destroy them and he shall bring them down before thy face, so shalt thou drive them out and destroy them quickly as the Lord hath said unto thee.

Speak not thou in thine heart after that the Lord thy God hath cast them out from before thee saying, For my righteousness the Lord hath brought me in to possess this land, but for the wickedness of these nations the Lord doth drive them out from before thee. Not for thy righteousness or for the uprightness of thine heart dost thou go to possess their land, but for the wickedness of these nations the Lord thy God doth drive them out from before thee and that he may perform the word which the Lord sware unto thy fathers, Abraham, Isaac, and Jacob. Understand therefore that the Lord thy God giveth thee not this good land to possess it for thy righteousness, for thou art a stiff-necked people.

Remember, and forget not, how thou provokedst the Lord thy God to wrath in the wilderness; from the day that thou didst depart out of the land of Egypt until ye came unto this place ye have been rebellious against the Lord. Also in Horeb ye provoked the Lord to wrath so that the Lord was angry with you to have destroyed you. When I was gone up into the mount to receive the tables of stone, even the tables of the covenant which the Lord made with you, then I abode in the mount forty days and forty nights. I neither did eat bread nor drink water, and the Lord delivered unto me two tables of stone written with the finger of God, and on them was written according to all the words which the Lord spake with you in the mount out of the midst of the fire in the day of the assembly. And it came to pass at the end of forty days and forty nights that the Lord gave me the two tables of stone, even the tables of the covenant. And the Lord said unto me, Arise, get thee down quickly from hence for thy people which thou hast brought forth out of Egypt have corrupted themselves: they are quickly turned aside out of the way which I commanded them, they have made them a molten image. Furthermore the Lord spake unto me saying, I have seen this people and behold, it is a stiff-necked people. Let me alone, that I may destroy them and blot out their name from under Heaven, and I will make of thee a nation mightier and greater than they.

So I turned and came down from the mount, and the mount burned with fire, and the two tables of the covenant were in my two hands. And I looked and behold, ye had sinned against the Lord your God and had made you a molten calf, ye had turned aside quickly out of the way which the Lord had commanded you. And I took the two tables and cast them out of my two hands and brake them before your eyes. And I fell down before the Lord, as at the first: forty days and forty nights I did neither eat bread nor drink water because of all your sins which ye sinned in doing wickedly in the sight of the Lord to provoke him to anger. For I was afraid of the anger and hot displeasure wherewith the Lord was wroth against you to destroy you. But the Lord hearkened unto me at that time also. And the Lord was very angry with Aaron to have destroyed him and I prayed for Aaron also the same time. And I took your sin, the calf which ye had made, and burnt it with fire, and stamped it, and ground it very small, even until it was as small as dust, and I cast the dust thereof into the brook that descended out of the mount.

And at Taberah, and at Massah, and at Kibroth-hattaavah, ye provoked the Lord to wrath. Likewise when the Lord sent you from Kadesh-barnea saying, Go up and possess the land which I have given you, then ye rebelled against the commandment of the Lord your God, and ye believed him not, nor hearkened to his voice. Ye have been rebellious against the Lord from the day that I knew you.

Thus I fell down before the Lord forty days and forty nights, as I fell down at the first, because the Lord had said he would destroy you. I prayed therefore unto the Lord and said, O Lord God, destroy not thy people and thine inheritance which thou hast redeemed through thy greatness, which thou hast brought forth out of Egypt with a mighty hand. Remember thy servants Abraham, Isaac, and Jacob, look not unto the stubbornness of this people, nor to their wickedness, nor to their sin, lest the land whence thou broughtest us out say, Because the Lord was not able to bring them into the land which he promised them and because he hated them, he hath brought them out to slay them in the wilderness. Yet they are thy people and thine inheritance which thou broughtest out by thy mighty power and by thy stretched out arm.

At that time the Lord said unto me, Hew thee two other tables of stone like unto the first, and come up unto me upon the mount, and make thee an ark of wood. And I will write on the tables the words that were on the first tables which thou breakest, save the words of the everlasting covenant of the holy priesthood, and thou shalt put them in the ark. And I made an ark of shittim wood, and hewed two tables of stone like unto the first, and went up into the mount having the two tables in mine hand. And he wrote on the tables, according to the first writing, the ten commandments which the Lord spake unto you in the mount out of the midst of the fire in the day of the assembly, and the Lord gave them unto me. And I turned myself and came down from the mount, and put the tables in the ark which I had made, and there they be as the Lord commanded me.

And the children of Israel took their journey from Beeroth of the children of Jaakan to Mosera, there Aaron died and there he was buried, and Eleazar his son ministered in the priest's office in his stead. From thence they journeyed unto Gudgodah, and from Gudgodah to Jotbath, a land of rivers of waters. At that time the Lord separated the tribe of Levi, to bear the ark of the covenant of the Lord, to stand before the Lord to minister unto him, and to bless in his name unto this day. Wherefore Levi hath no part nor inheritance with his brethren, the Lord is his inheritance according as the Lord thy God promised him.

And I stayed in the mount, according to the first time, forty days and forty nights, and the Lord hearkened unto me at that time also, and the Lord would not destroy thee. And the Lord said unto me, Arise, take thy journey before the people, that they may go in and possess the land which I sware unto their fathers to give unto them.

And now, Israel, what doth the Lord thy God require of thee but to fear the Lord thy God, to walk in all his ways, and to love him, and to serve the Lord thy God with all thy heart and with all thy soul, to keep the commandments of the Lord and his statutes which I command thee this day for thy good? Behold, the Heaven and the Heaven of Heavens is the Lord's thy God, the Earth also, with all that therein is. Only the Lord had a delight in thy fathers to love them, and he chose their seed after them, even you above all people, as it is this day. Circumcise therefore the foreskin of your heart and be no more stiff-necked. For the Lord your God is God of gods, and Lord of lords, a great God, a mighty and a terrible, which regardeth not persons, nor taketh reward, he doth execute the judgment of the fatherless and widow, and loveth the stranger in giving him food and raiment. Love ye therefore the stranger for ye were strangers in the land of Egypt. Thou shalt fear the Lord thy God, him shalt thou serve, and to him shalt thou cleave, and swear by his name. He is thy praise, and he is thy God, that hath done for thee these great and terrible things which thine eyes have seen. Thy fathers went down into Egypt with threescore and ten persons and now the Lord thy God hath made thee as the stars of Heaven for multitude.

Therefore thou shalt love the Lord thy God, and keep his charge, and his statutes, and his judgments, and his commandments always. And know ye this day, for I speak not with your children which have not known, and which have not seen the chastisement of the Lord your God, his greatness, his mighty hand, and his stretched out arm, and his miracles, and his acts which he did in the midst of Egypt unto Pharaoh the king of Egypt, and unto all his land, and what he did unto the army of Egypt, unto their horses, and to their chariots, how he made the water of the Red Sea to overflow them as they pursued after you, and how the Lord hath destroyed them unto this day, and what he did unto you in the wilderness until ye came into this place, and what he did unto Dathan and Abiram, the sons of Eliab, the son of Reuben, how the Earth opened her mouth and swallowed them up, and their households, and their tents, and all the substance that was in their possession, in the midst of all Israel, but your eyes have seen all the great acts of the Lord which he did.

Therefore shall ye keep all the commandments which I command you this day, that ye may be strong, and go in and possess the land whither ye go to possess it, and that ye may prolong your days in the land which the Lord sware unto your fathers to give unto them and to their seed, a land that floweth with milk and honey. For the land whither thou goest in to possess it is not as the land of Egypt from whence ye came out, where thou sowedst thy seed and wateredst it with thy foot as a garden of herbs, but the land whither ye go to possess it is a land of hills and valleys, and drinketh water of the rain of Heaven, a land which the Lord thy God careth for: the eyes of the Lord thy God are always upon it, from the beginning of the year even unto the end of the year.

And it shall come to pass, if ye shall hearken diligently unto my commandments which I command you this day, to love the Lord your God, and to serve him with all your heart and with all your soul, that I will give you the rain of your land in his due season, the first rain and the latter rain, that thou mayest gather in thy corn, and thy wine, and thine oil. And I will send grass in thy fields for thy cattle that thou mayest eat and be full. Take heed to yourselves that your heart be not deceived, and ye turn aside and serve other gods and worship them, and then the Lord's wrath be kindled against you and he shut up the Heaven, that there be no rain, and that the land yield not her fruit, and lest ye perish quickly from off the good land which the Lord giveth you.

4 THEREFORE shall ye lay up these my words in your heart and in your soul, and bind them for a sign upon your hand, that they may be as frontlets between your eyes. And ye shall teach them your children, speaking of them when thou sittest in thine house, and when thou walkest by the way, when thou liest down, and when thou risest up. And thou shalt write them upon the doorposts of thine house, and upon thy gates, that your days may be multiplied, and the days of your children, in the land which the Lord sware unto your fathers to give them, as the days of Heaven upon the Earth. For if ye shall diligently keep all these commandments which I command you, to do them, to love the Lord your God, to walk in all his ways, and to cleave unto him, then will the Lord drive out all these nations from before you, and ye shall possess greater nations and mightier than yourselves. Every place whereon the soles of your feet shall tread shall be yours, from the wilderness and Lebanon, from the river, the river Euphrates, even unto the uttermost sea shall your coast be. There shall no man be able to stand before you, for the Lord your God shall lay the fear of you and the dread of you upon all the land that ye shall tread upon, as he hath said unto you.

Behold, I set before you this day a blessing and a curse, a blessing if ye obey the commandments of the Lord your God which I command you this day, and a curse if ye will not obey the commandments of the Lord your God, but turn aside out of the way which I command you this day to go after other gods which ye have not known. And it shall come to pass when the Lord thy God hath brought thee in unto the land whither thou goest to possess it, that thou shalt put the blessing upon mount Gerizim and the curse upon mount Ebal. Are they not on the other side Jordan by the way where the sun goeth down in the land of the Canaanites, which dwell in the champaign over against Gilgal beside the plains of Moreh? For ye shall pass over Jordan to go in to possess the land which the Lord your God giveth you, and ye shall possess it and dwell therein. And ye shall observe to do all the statutes and judgments which I set before you this day.

These are the statutes and judgments which ye shall observe to do in the land which the Lord God of thy fathers giveth thee to possess it, all the days that ye live upon the Earth. Ye shall utterly destroy all the places wherein the nations which ye shall possess served their gods, upon the high mountains, and upon the hills, and under every green tree, and ye shall overthrow their altars, and break their pillars, and burn their groves with fire, and ye shall hew down the graven images of their gods and destroy the names of them out of that place. Ye shall not do so unto the Lord your God. But unto the place which the Lord your God shall choose out of all your tribes to put his name there, even unto his habitation shall ye seek, and thither thou shalt come, and thither ye shall bring your burnt offerings, and your sacrifices, and your tithes, and heave offerings of your hand, and your vows, and your freewill offerings, and the firstlings of your herds and of your flocks, and there ye shall eat before the Lord your God, and ye shall rejoice in all that ye put your hand unto, ye and your households, wherein the Lord thy God hath blessed thee.

Ye shall not do after all the things that we do here this day, every man whatsoever is right in his own eyes. For ye are not as yet come to the rest and to the inheritance, which the Lord your God giveth you. But when ye go over Jordan and dwell in the land which the Lord your God giveth you to inherit, and when he giveth you rest from all your enemies round about so that ye dwell in safety, then there shall be a place which the Lord your God shall choose to cause his name to dwell there, thither shall ye bring all that I command you, your burnt offerings, and your sacrifices, your tithes, and the heave offering of your hand, and all your choice vows which ye vow unto the Lord, and ye shall rejoice before the Lord your God, ye, and your sons, and your daughters, and your menservants, and your maidservants, and the Levite that is within your gates, forasmuch as he hath no part nor inheritance with you.

Take heed to thyself that thou offer not thy burnt offerings in every place that thou seest, but in the place which the Lord shall choose in one of thy tribes, there thou shalt offer thy burnt offerings and there thou shalt do all that I command thee.

Notwithstanding, thou mayest kill and eat flesh in all thy gates, whatsoever thy soul lusteth after, according to the blessing of the Lord thy God which he hath given thee; the unclean and the clean may eat thereof, as of the roebuck, and as of the hart. Only ye shall not eat the blood, ye shall pour it upon the Earth as water. Thou mayest not eat within thy gates the tithe of thy corn, or of thy wine, or of thy oil, or the firstlings of thy herds or of thy flock, nor any of thy vows which thou vowest, nor thy freewill offerings, or heave offering of thine hand, but thou must eat them before the Lord thy God in the place which the Lord thy God shall choose, thou, and thy son, and thy daughter, and thy manservant, and thy maidservant, and the Levite that is within thy gates, and thou shalt rejoice before the Lord thy God in all that thou puttest thine hands unto. Take heed to thyself that thou forsake not the Levite as long as thou livest upon the Earth.

When the Lord thy God shall enlarge thy border as he hath promised thee, and thou shalt say, I will eat flesh, because thy soul longeth to eat flesh thou mayest eat flesh, whatsoever thy soul lusteth after. If the place which the Lord thy God hath chosen to put his name there be too far from thee, then thou shalt kill of thy herd and of thy flock which the Lord hath given thee, as I have commanded thee, and thou shalt eat in thy gates whatsoever thy soul lusteth after. Even as the roebuck and the hart is eaten, so thou shalt eat them, the unclean and the clean shall eat of them alike. Only be sure that thou eat not the blood, for the blood is the life, and thou mayest not eat the life with the flesh. Thou shalt not eat it, thou shalt pour it upon the Earth as water. Thou shalt not eat it, that it may go well with thee and with thy children after thee when thou shalt do that which is right in the sight of the Lord. Only thy holy things which thou hast and thy vows, thou shalt take and go unto the place which the Lord shall choose, and thou shalt offer thy burnt offerings, the flesh and the blood, upon the altar of the Lord thy God, and the blood of thy sacrifices shall be poured out upon the altar of the Lord thy God, and thou shalt eat the flesh.

Observe and hear all these words which I command thee, that it may go well with thee and with thy children after thee forever, when thou doest that which is good and right in the sight of the Lord thy God.

When the Lord thy God shall cut off the nations from before thee whither thou goest to possess them, and thou succeedest them and dwellest in their land, take heed to thyself that thou be not snared by following them after that they be destroyed from before thee, and that thou inquire not after their gods saying, How did these nations serve their gods? Even so will I do likewise. Thou shalt not do so unto the Lord thy God, for every abomination to the Lord which he hateth have they done unto their gods, for even their sons and their daughters they have burnt in the fire to their gods.

What thing soever I command you, observe to do it, thou shalt not add thereto nor diminish from it.

If there arise among you a prophet, or a dreamer of dreams, and giveth thee a sign or a wonder, and the sign or the wonder come to pass whereof he spake unto thee saying, Let us go after other gods which thou hast not known and let us serve them, thou shalt not hearken unto the words of that prophet, or that dreamer of dreams, for the Lord your God proveth you, to know whether ye love the Lord your God with all your heart and with all your soul. Ye shall walk after the Lord your God, and fear him, and keep his commandments, and obey his voice, and ye shall serve him and cleave unto him. And that prophet, or that dreamer of dreams, shall be put to death because he hath spoken to turn you away from the Lord your God, which brought you out of the land of Egypt and redeemed you out of the house of bondage, to thrust thee out of the way which the Lord thy God commanded thee to walk in. So shalt thou put the evil away from the midst of thee.

If thy brother, the son of thy mother, or thy son, or thy daughter, or the wife of thy bosom, or thy friend which is as thine own soul, entice thee secretly saying, Let us go and serve other gods which thou hast not known, thou, nor thy fathers, namely, of the gods of the people which are round about you, nigh unto thee or far off from thee, from the one end of the Earth even unto the other end of the Earth, thou shalt not consent unto him, nor hearken unto him, neither shall thine eye pity him, neither shalt thou spare, neither shalt thou conceal him, but thou shalt surely kill him; thine hand shall be first upon him to put him to death and afterwards the hand of all the people. And thou shalt stone him with stones that he die because he hath sought to thrust thee away from the Lord thy God which brought thee out of the land of Egypt from the house of bondage. And all Israel shall hear, and fear, and shall do no more any such wickedness as this is among you.

If thou shalt hear say in one of thy cities which the Lord thy God hath given thee to dwell there saying, Certain men, the children of Belial, are gone out from among you, and have withdrawn the inhabitants of their city saying, Let us go and serve other gods which ye have not known, then shalt thou inquire, and make search, and ask diligently and behold, if it be truth, and the thing certain that such abomination is wrought among you, thou shalt surely smite the inhabitants of that city with the edge of the sword, destroying it utterly, and all that is therein and the cattle thereof, with the edge of the sword. And thou shalt gather all the spoil of it into the midst of the street thereof, and shalt burn with fire the city, and all the spoil thereof every whit for the Lord thy God, and it shall be a heap forever, it shall not be built again. And there shall cleave naught of the cursed thing to thine hand, that the Lord may turn from the fierceness of his anger, and show thee mercy, and have compassion upon thee, and multiply thee, as he hath sworn unto thy fathers, when thou shalt hearken to the voice of the Lord thy God to keep all his commandments which I command thee this day, to do that which is right in the eyes of the Lord thy God.

5 YE are the children of the Lord your God. Ye shall not cut yourselves, nor make any baldness between your eyes for the dead. For thou art a holy people unto the Lord thy God, and the Lord hath chosen thee to be a peculiar people unto himself above all the nations that are upon the Earth.

Thou shalt not eat any abominable thing. These are the beasts which ye shall eat: the ox, the sheep and the goat, the hart and the roebuck, and the fallow deer, and the wild goat, and the pygarg, and the wild ox, and the chamois. And every beast that parteth the hoof, and cleaveth the cleft into two claws, and cheweth the cud among the beasts, that ye shall eat. Nevertheless these ye shall not eat, of them that chew the cud, or of them that divide the cloven hoof: as the camel, and the hare, and the coney, for they chew the cud, but divide not the hoof, therefore they are unclean unto you. And the swine, because it divideth the hoof, yet cheweth not the cud, it is unclean unto you, ye shall not eat of their flesh nor touch their dead carcass.

These ye shall eat of all that are in the waters: all that have fins and scales shall ye eat, and whatsoever hath not fins and scales ye may not eat, it is unclean unto you.

Of all clean birds ye shall eat. But these are they of which ye shall not eat: the eagle, and the ossifrage, and the ospray, and the glede, and the kite, and the vulture after his kind, and every raven after his kind, and the owl, and the night-hawk, and the cuckoo, and the hawk after his kind, the little owl and the great owl, and the swan, and the pelican, and the gier eagle, and the cormorant, and the stork, and the heron after her kind, and the lapwing, and the bat. And every creeping thing that flieth is unclean unto you, they shall not be eaten. But of all clean fowls ye may eat.

Ye shall not eat of anything that dieth of itself, thou shalt not give it unto the stranger that is in thy gates that he may eat it, or thou mayest not sell it unto an alien, for thou art a holy people unto the Lord thy God. Thou shalt not seethe a kid in his mother's milk. Thou shalt truly tithe all the increase of thy seed that the field bringeth forth year by year. And thou shalt eat before the Lord thy God, in the place which he shall choose to place his name there, the tithe of thy corn, of thy wine, and of thine oil, and the firstlings of thy herds and of thy flocks, that thou mayest learn to fear the Lord thy God always. And if the way be too long for thee so that thou art not able to carry it, or if the place be too far from thee which the Lord thy God shall choose to set his name there, when the Lord thy God hath blessed thee, then shalt thou turn it into money, and bind up the money in thine hand, and shalt go unto the place which the Lord thy God shall choose, and thou shalt bestow that money for whatsoever thy soul lusteth after, for oxen, or for sheep, or for wine, or for strong drink, or for whatsoever thy soul desireth, and thou shalt eat there before the Lord thy God, and thou shalt rejoice, thou, and thine household, and the Levite that is within thy gates, thou shalt not forsake him for he hath no part nor inheritance with thee. At the end of three years thou shalt bring forth all the tithe of thine increase the same year, and shalt lay it up within thy gates, and the Levite, (because he hath no part nor inheritance with thee,) and the stranger, and the fatherless, and the widow, which are within thy gates, shall come, and shall eat and be satisfied, that the Lord thy God may bless thee in all the work of thine hand which thou doest.

At the end of every seven years thou shalt make a release. And this is the manner of the release: every creditor that lendeth aught unto his neighbor shall release it, he shall not exact it of his neighbor, or of his brother because it is called the Lord's release. Of a foreigner thou mayest exact it again, but that which is thine with thy brother thine hand shall release, save when there shall be no poor among you, for the Lord shall greatly bless thee in the land which the Lord thy God giveth thee for an inheritance to possess it only if thou carefully hearken unto the voice of the Lord thy God to observe to do all these commandments which I command thee this day. For the Lord thy God blesseth thee as he promised thee, and thou shalt lend unto many nations, but thou shalt not borrow, and thou shalt reign over many nations, but they shall not reign over thee. If there be among you a poor man of one of thy brethren within any of thy gates in thy land which the Lord thy God giveth thee, thou shalt not harden thine heart, nor shut thine hand from thy poor brother, but thou shalt open thine hand wide unto him, and shalt surely lend him sufficient for his need in that which he wanteth. Beware that there be not a thought in thy wicked heart saying, The seventh year, the year of release, is at hand, and thine eye be evil against thy poor brother, and thou givest him naught, and he cry unto the Lord against thee, and it be sin unto thee. Thou shalt surely give him and thine heart shall not be grieved when thou givest unto him, because that for this thing the Lord thy God shall bless thee in all thy works and in all that thou puttest thine hand unto. For the poor shall never cease out of the land, therefore I command thee saying, Thou shalt open thine hand wide unto thy brother, to thy poor, and to thy needy in thy land.

And if thy brother, a Hebrew man or a Hebrew woman, be sold unto thee and serve thee six years, then in the seventh year thou shalt let him go free from thee. And when thou sendest him out free from thee thou shalt not let him go away empty; thou shalt furnish him liberally out of thy flock, and out of thy floor, and out of thy winepress, of that wherewith the Lord thy God hath blessed thee thou shalt give unto him. And thou shalt remember that thou wast a bondman in the land of Egypt and the Lord thy God redeemed thee, therefore I command thee this thing today. And it shall be, if he say unto thee, I will not go away from thee because he loveth thee and thine house, because he is well with thee, then thou shalt take an awl and thrust it through his ear unto the door and he shall be thy servant forever. And also unto thy maidservant thou shalt do likewise. It shall not seem hard unto thee, when thou sendest him away free from thee, for he hath been worth a double hired servant to thee in serving thee six years and the Lord thy God shall bless thee in all that thou doest.

All the firstling males that come of thy herd and of thy flock thou shalt sanctify unto the Lord thy God, thou shalt do no work with the firstling of thy bullock, nor shear the firstling of thy sheep. Thou shalt eat it before the Lord thy God year by year in the place which the Lord shall choose, thou and thy household. And if there be any blemish therein, as if it be lame, or blind, or have any ill blemish, thou shalt not sacrifice it unto the Lord thy God. Thou shalt eat it within thy gates, the unclean and the clean person shall eat it alike, as the roebuck and as the hart. Only thou shalt not eat the blood thereof, thou shalt pour it upon the ground as water.

Observe the month of Abib, and keep the passover unto the Lord thy God, for in the month of Abib the Lord thy God brought thee forth out of Egypt by night. Thou shalt therefore sacrifice the passover unto the Lord thy God of the flock and the herd in the place where the Lord shall choose to place his name there. Thou shalt eat no leavened bread with it; seven days shalt thou eat unleavened bread therewith, even the bread of affliction, for thou camest forth out of the land of Egypt in haste, that thou mayest remember the day when thou camest forth out of the land of Egypt all the days of thy life. And there shall be no leavened bread seen with thee in all thy coast seven days, neither shall there any thing of the flesh which thou sacrificedst the first day at even remain all night until morning. Thou mayest not sacrifice the passover within any of thy gates which the Lord thy God giveth thee, but at the place which the Lord thy God shall choose to place his name in, there thou shalt sacrifice the passover at even, at the going down of the sun, at the season that thou camest forth out of Egypt. And thou shalt roast and eat it in the place which the Lord thy God shall choose, and thou shalt turn in the morning and go unto thy tents. Six days thou shalt eat unleavened bread and on the seventh day shall be a solemn assembly to the Lord thy God, thou shalt do no work therein.

Seven weeks shalt thou number unto thee: begin to number the seven weeks from such time as thou beginnest to put the sickle to the corn. And thou shalt keep the feast of weeks unto the Lord thy God with a tribute of a freewill offering of thine hand which thou shalt give unto the Lord thy God according as the Lord thy God hath blessed thee, and thou shalt rejoice before the Lord thy God, thou, and thy son, and thy daughter, and thy manservant, and thy maidservant, and the Levite that is within thy gates, and the stranger, and the fatherless, and the widow, that are among you in the place which the Lord thy God hath chosen to place his name there. And thou shalt remember that thou wast a bondman in Egypt and thou shalt observe and do these statutes.

Thou shalt observe the feast of tabernacles seven days after that thou hast gathered in thy corn and thy wine, and thou shalt rejoice in thy feast, thou, and thy son, and thy daughter, and thy manservant, and thy maidservant, and the Levite, the stranger, and the fatherless, and the widow that are within thy gates. Seven days shalt thou keep a solemn feast unto the Lord thy God in the place which the Lord shall choose because the Lord thy God shall bless thee in all thine increase, and in all the works of thine hands, therefore thou shalt surely rejoice. Three times in a year shall all thy males appear before the Lord thy God in the place which he shall choose: in the feast of unleavened bread, and in the feast of weeks, and in the feast of tabernacles. And they shall not appear before the Lord empty: every man shall give as he is able according to the blessing of the Lord thy God which he hath given thee.

Judges and officers shalt thou make thee in all thy gates which the Lord thy God giveth thee, throughout thy tribes, and they shall judge the people with just judgment. Thou shalt not wrest judgment, thou shalt not respect persons, neither take a gift, for a gift doth blind the eyes of the wise and pervert the words of the righteous. That which is altogether just shalt thou follow that thou mayest live and inherit the land which the Lord thy God giveth thee.

Thou shalt not plant thee a grove of any trees near unto the altar of the Lord thy God which thou shalt make thee. Neither shalt thou set thee up any graven image which the Lord thy God hateth. Thou shalt not sacrifice unto the Lord thy God any bullock or sheep wherein is blemish or any evil-favoredness, for that is an abomination unto the Lord thy God.

If there be found among you within any of thy gates which the Lord thy God giveth thee, man or woman, that hath wrought wickedness in the sight of the Lord thy God in transgressing his covenant, and hath gone and served other gods, and worshiped them, either the sun, or moon, or any of the host of Heaven which I have not commanded, and it be told thee, and thou hast heard of it, and inquired diligently and behold, it be true and the thing certain that such abomination is wrought in Israel, then shalt thou bring forth that man or that woman which have committed that wicked thing unto thy gates, even that man or that woman, and shalt stone them with stones till they die, at the mouth of two witnesses or three witnesses shall he that is worthy of death be put to death, but at the mouth of one witness he shall not be put to death. The hands of the witnesses shall be first upon him to put him to death, and afterward the hands of all the people. So thou shalt put the evil away from among you.

If there arise a matter too hard for thee in judgment, between blood and blood, between plea and plea, and between stroke and stroke, being matters of controversy within thy gates, then shalt thou arise and get thee up into the place which the Lord thy God shall choose. And thou shalt come unto the priests, the Levites, and unto the judge that shall be in those days and inquire, and they shall show thee the sentence of judgment, and thou shalt do according to the sentence which they of that place which the Lord shall choose shall show thee. And thou shalt observe to do according to all that they inform thee, according to the sentence of the law which they shall teach thee, and according to the judgment which they shall tell thee thou shalt do. Thou shalt not decline from the sentence which they shall show thee, to the right hand nor to the left. And the man that will do presumptuously and will not hearken unto the priest that standeth to minister there before the Lord thy God or unto the judge, even that man shall die, and thou shalt put away the evil from Israel. And all the people shall hear and fear and do no more presumptuously.

6 WHEN thou art come unto the land which the Lord thy God giveth thee, and shalt possess it, and shalt dwell therein, and shalt say, I will set a king over me like as all the nations that are about me, thou shalt in any wise set him king over thee whom the Lord thy God shall choose, one from among thy brethren shalt thou set king over thee; thou mayest not set a stranger over thee which is not thy brother. But he shall not multiply horses to himself, nor cause the people to return to Egypt to the end that he should multiply horses, forasmuch as the Lord hath said unto you, Ye shall henceforth return no more that way. Neither shall he multiply wives to himself that his heart turn not away, neither shall he greatly multiply to himself silver and gold. And it shall be, when he sitteth upon the throne of his kingdom, that he shall write him a copy of this law in a book out of that which is before the priests the Levites, and it shall be with him, and he shall read therein all the days of his life that he may learn to fear the Lord his God, to keep all the words of this law and these statutes to do them, that his heart be not lifted up above his brethren, and that he turn not aside from the commandment, to the right hand or to the left, to the end that he may prolong his days in his kingdom, he and his children, in the midst of Israel.

The priests the Levites and all the tribe of Levi shall have no part nor inheritance with Israel, they shall eat the offerings of the Lord made by fire and his inheritance. Therefore shall they have no inheritance among their brethren; the Lord is their inheritance as he hath said unto them. And this shall be the priest's due from the people, from them that offer a sacrifice, whether it be ox or sheep, and they shall give unto the priest the shoulder, and the two cheeks, and the maw. The firstfruit also of thy corn, of thy wine, and of thine oil, and the first of the fleece of thy sheep shalt thou give him. For the Lord thy God hath chosen him out of all thy tribes, to stand to minister in the name of the Lord, him and his sons forever. And if a Levite come from any of thy gates out of all Israel where he sojourned, and come with all the desire of his mind unto the place which the Lord shall choose, then he shall minister in the name of the Lord his God, as all his brethren the Levites do, which stand there before the Lord. They shall have like portions to eat, besides that which cometh of the sale of his patrimony.

When thou art come into the land which the Lord thy God giveth thee, thou shalt not learn to do after the abominations of those nations. There shall not be found among you anyone that maketh his son or his daughter to pass through the fire, or that useth divination, or an observer of times, or an enchanter, or a witch, or a charmer, or a consulter with familiar spirits, or a wizard, or a necromancer. For all that do these things are an abomination unto the Lord, and because of these abominations the Lord thy God doth drive them out from before thee. Thou shalt be perfect with the Lord thy God. For these nations which thou shalt possess hearkened unto observers of times and unto diviners, but as for thee, the Lord thy God hath not suffered thee so to do.

The Lord thy God will raise up unto thee a Prophet from the midst of thee, of thy brethren, like unto me. Unto him ye shall hearken, according to all that thou desiredst of the Lord thy God in Horeb in the day of the assembly saying, Let me not hear again the voice of the Lord my God, neither let me see this great fire anymore, that I die not. And the Lord said unto me, They have well spoken that which they have spoken. I will raise them up a Prophet from among their brethren, like unto thee, and will put my words in his mouth, and he shall speak unto them all that I shall command him. And it shall come to pass that whosoever will not hearken unto my words which he shall speak in my name, I will require it of him. But the prophet which shall presume to speak a word in my name which I have not commanded him to speak, or that shall speak in the name of other gods, even that prophet shall die. And if thou say in thine heart, How shall we know the word which the Lord hath not spoken? When a prophet speaketh in the name of the Lord, if the thing follow not, nor come to pass, that is, the thing which the Lord hath not spoken, but the prophet hath spoken it presumptuously, thou shalt not be afraid of him.

When the Lord thy God hath cut off the nations whose land the Lord thy God giveth thee, and thou succeedest them, and dwellest in their cities, and in their houses, thou shalt separate three cities for thee in the midst of thy land which the Lord thy God giveth thee to possess it. Thou shalt prepare thee a way, and divide the coasts of thy land, which the Lord thy God giveth thee to inherit, into three parts, that every slayer may flee thither.

And this is the case of the slayer which shall flee thither that he may live: Whoso killeth his neighbor ignorantly whom he hated not in time past, as when a man goeth into the wood with his neighbor to hew wood, and his hand fetcheth a stroke with the axe to cut down the tree, and the head slippeth from the helve and lighteth upon his neighbor that he die, he shall flee unto one of those cities and live, lest the avenger of the blood pursue the slayer while his heart is hot, and overtake him because the way is long, and slay him, whereas he was not worthy of death inasmuch as he hated him not in time past. Wherefore I command thee saying, Thou shalt separate three cities for thee.

And if the Lord thy God enlarge thy coast as he hath sworn unto thy fathers and give thee all the land which he promised to give unto thy fathers, if thou shalt keep all these commandments to do them, which I command thee this day, to love the Lord thy God and to walk ever in his ways, then shalt thou add three cities more for thee, beside these three, that innocent blood be not shed in thy land which the Lord thy God giveth thee for an inheritance, and so blood be upon thee.

But if any man hate his neighbor, and lie in wait for him, and rise up against him, and smite him mortally that he die, and fleeth into one of these cities, then the elders of his city shall send and fetch him thence, and deliver him into the hand of the avenger of blood that he may die. Thine eye shall not pity him, but thou shalt put away the guilt of innocent blood from Israel that it may go well with thee.

Thou shalt not remove thy neighbor's landmark which they of old time have set in thine inheritance which thou shalt inherit in the land that the Lord thy God giveth thee to possess it. One witness shall not rise up against a man for any iniquity, or for any sin; in any sin that he sinneth, at the mouth of two witnesses or at the mouth of three witnesses shall the matter be established. If a false witness rise up against any man to testify against him that which is wrong, then both the men between whom the controversy is shall stand before the Lord, before the priests and the judges which shall be in those days, and the judges shall make diligent inquisition and behold, if the witness be a false witness and hath testified falsely against his brother, then shall ye do unto him as he had thought to have done unto his brother, so shalt thou put the evil away from among you. And those which remain shall hear, and fear, and shall henceforth commit no more any such evil among you. And thine eye shall not pity, but life shall go for life, eye for eye, tooth for tooth, hand for hand, foot for foot.

When thou goest out to battle against thine enemies and seest horses and chariots and a people more than thou, be not afraid of them, for the Lord thy God is with thee which brought thee up out of the land of Egypt. And it shall be, when ye are come nigh unto the battle, that the priest shall approach and speak unto the people and shall say unto them, Hear, O Israel, ye approach this day unto battle against your enemies, let not your hearts faint, fear not, and do not tremble, neither be ye terrified because of them, for the Lord your God is he that goeth with you to fight for you against your enemies, to save you.

And the officers shall speak unto the people saying, What man is there that hath built a new house and hath not dedicated it? Let him go and return to his house, lest he die in the battle and another man dedicate it. And what man is he that hath planted a vineyard, and hath not yet eaten of it? Let him also go and return unto his house, lest he die in the battle and another man eat of it. And what man is there that hath betrothed a wife and hath not taken her? Let him go and return unto his house, lest he die in the battle and another man take her. And the officers shall speak further unto the people and they shall say, What man is there that is fearful and faint-hearted? Let him go and return unto his house, lest his brethren's heart faint as well as his heart. And it shall be, when the officers have made an end of speaking unto the people, that they shall make captains of the armies to lead the people.

When thou comest nigh unto a city to fight against it, then proclaim peace unto it. And it shall be, if it make thee answer of peace and open unto thee, then it shall be that all the people that is found therein shall be tributaries unto thee and they shall serve thee. And if it will make no peace with thee, but will make war against thee, then thou shalt besiege it, and when the Lord thy God hath delivered it into thine hands, thou shalt smite every male thereof with the edge of the sword, but the women, and the little ones, and the cattle, and all that is in the city, even all the spoil thereof shalt thou take unto thyself and thou shalt eat the spoil of thine enemies which the Lord thy God hath given thee. Thus shalt thou do unto all the cities which are very far off from thee, which are not of the cities of these nations. But of the cities of these people which the Lord thy God doth give thee for an inheritance thou shalt save alive nothing that breatheth, but thou shalt utterly destroy them, namely, the Hittites, and the Amorites, the Canaanites, and the Perizzites, the Hivites, and the Jebusites, as the Lord thy God hath commanded thee, that they teach you not to do after all their abominations which they have done unto their gods, so should ye sin against the Lord your God.

When thou shalt besiege a city a long time in making war against it to take it, thou shalt not destroy the trees thereof by forcing an axe against them, for thou mayest eat of them and thou shalt not cut them down (for the tree of the field is man's life) to employ them in the siege, only the trees which thou knowest that they be not trees for meat thou shalt destroy and cut them down, and thou shalt build bulwarks against the city that maketh war with thee until it be subdued.

7 IF one be found slain in the land which the Lord thy God giveth thee to possess it, lying in the field, and it be not known who hath slain him, then thy elders and thy judges shall come forth and they shall measure unto the cities which are round about him that is slain, and it shall be that the city which is next unto the slain man, even the elders of that city shall take a heifer, which hath not been wrought with and which hath not drawn in the yoke, and the elders of that city shall bring down the heifer unto a rough valley which is neither eared nor sown and shall strike off the heifer's neck there in the valley. And the priests, the sons of Levi, shall come near, for them the Lord thy God hath chosen to minister unto him and to bless in the name of the Lord and by their word shall every controversy and every stroke be tried, and all the elders of that city that are next unto the slain man shall wash their hands over the heifer that is beheaded in the valley and they shall answer and say, Our hands have not shed this blood, neither have our eyes seen it. Be merciful, O Lord, unto thy people Israel whom thou hast redeemed and lay not innocent blood unto thy people of Israel's charge. And the blood shall be forgiven them. So shalt thou put away the guilt of innocent blood from among you when thou shalt do that which is right in the sight of the Lord.

When thou goest forth to war against thine enemies, and the Lord thy God hath delivered them into thine hands, and thou hast taken them captive, and seest among the captives a beautiful woman, and hast a desire unto her that thou wouldest have her to thy wife, then thou shalt bring her home to thine house, and she shall shave her head, and pare her nails, and she shall put the raiment of her captivity from off her, and shall remain in thine house, and bewail her father and her mother a full month, and after that thou shalt go in unto her and be her husband and she shall be thy wife. And it shall be, if thou have no delight in her, then thou shall let her go whither she will, but thou shalt not sell her at all for money, thou shalt not make merchandise of her because thou hast humbled her.

If a man have two wives, one beloved and another hated, and they have borne him children, both the beloved and the hated, and if the firstborn son be hers that was hated, then it shall be when he maketh his sons to inherit that which he hath that he may not make the son of the beloved firstborn before the son of the hated, which is indeed the firstborn, but he shall acknowledge the son of the hated for the firstborn by giving him a double portion of all that he hath, for he is the beginning of his strength, the right of the firstborn is his.

If a man have a stubborn and rebellious son, which will not obey the voice of his father or the voice of his mother and that, when they have chastened him, will not hearken unto them, then shall his father and his mother lay hold on him, and bring him out unto the elders of his city, and unto the gate of his place, and they shall say unto the elders of his city, This our son is stubborn and rebellious, he will not obey our voice, he is a glutton and a drunkard. And all the men of his city shall stone him with stones that he die, so shalt thou put evil away from among you, and all Israel shall hear and fear.

And if a man have committed a sin worthy of death, and he be to be put to death, and thou hang him on a tree, his body shall not remain all night upon the tree, but thou shalt in any wise bury him that day (for he that is hanged is accursed of God), that thy land be not defiled which the Lord thy God giveth thee for an inheritance.

Thou shalt not see thy brother's ox or his sheep go astray and hide thyself from them, thou shalt in any case bring them again unto thy brother. And if thy brother be not nigh unto thee, or if thou know him not, then thou shalt bring it unto thine own house and it shall be with thee until thy brother seek after it, and thou shalt restore it to him again. In like manner shalt thou do with his ass, and so shalt thou do with his raiment, and with all lost things of thy brother's which he hath lost and thou hast found shalt thou do likewise; thou mayest not hide thyself. Thou shalt not see thy brother's ass or his ox fall down by the way and hide thyself from them, thou shalt surely help him to lift them up again.

The woman shall not wear that which pertaineth unto a man, neither shall a man put on a woman's garment, for all that do so are abomination unto the Lord thy God. If a bird's nest chance to be before thee in the way in any tree or on the ground, whether they be young ones or eggs, and the dam sitting upon the young or upon the eggs, thou shalt not take the dam with the young, but thou shalt in any wise let the dam go and take the young to thee, that it may be well with thee and that thou mayest prolong thy days. When thou buildest a new house, then thou shalt make a battlement for thy roof, that thou bring not blood upon thine house if any man fall from thence. Thou shalt not sow thy vineyard with divers seeds, lest the fruit of thy seed which thou hast sown and the fruit of thy vineyard be defiled. Thou shalt not plough with an ox and an ass together. Thou shalt not wear a garment of divers sorts, as of woolen and linen together. Thou shalt make thee fringes upon the four quarters of thy vesture wherewith thou coverest thyself.

If any man take a wife, and go in unto her and hate her, and give occasions of speech against her, and bring up an evil name upon her and say, I took this woman, and when I came to her I found her not a maid, then shall the father of the damsel and her mother take and bring forth the tokens of the damsel's virginity unto the elders of the city in the gate, and the damsel's father shall say unto the elders, I gave my daughter unto this man to wife, and he hateth her and lo, he hath given occasions of speech against her saying, I found not thy daughter a maid and yet these are the tokens of my daughter's virginity. And they shall spread the cloth before the elders of the city. And the elders of that city shall take that man and chastise him, and they shall amerce him in a hundred shekels of silver and give them unto the father of the damsel, because he hath brought up an evil name upon a virgin of Israel, and she shall be his wife, he may not put her away all his days. But if this thing be true and the tokens of virginity be not found for the damsel, then they shall bring out the damsel to the door of her father's house, and the men of her city shall stone her with stones that she die because she hath wrought folly in Israel to play the whore in her father's house, so shalt thou put evil away from among you.

If a man be found lying with a woman married to a husband, then they shall both of them die, both the man that lay with the woman and the woman, so shalt thou put away evil from Israel. If a damsel that is a virgin be betrothed unto a husband, and a man find her in the city and lie with her, then ye shall bring them both out unto the gate of that city and ye shall stone them with stones that they die, the damsel because she cried not, being in the city, and the man because he hath humbled his neighbor's wife, so thou shalt put away evil from among you. But if a man find a betrothed damsel in the field, and the man force her and lie with her, then the man only that lay with her shall die, but unto the damsel thou shalt do nothing, there is in the damsel no sin worthy of death, for as when a man riseth against his neighbor and slayeth him, even so is this matter, for he found her in the field and the betrothed damsel cried and there was none to save her. If a man find a damsel that is a virgin which is not betrothed, and lay hold on her and lie with her and they be found, then the man that lay with her shall give unto the damsel's father fifty shekels of silver and she shall be his wife because he hath humbled her, he may not put her away all his days. A man shall not take his father's wife nor discover his father's skirt.

He that is wounded in the stones or hath his privy member cut off shall not enter into the congregation of the Lord. A bastard shall not enter into the congregation of the Lord even to his tenth generation shall he not enter into the congregation of the Lord. An Ammonite or Moabite shall not enter into the congregation of the Lord, even to their tenth generation shall they not enter into the congregation of the Lord forever, because they met you not with bread and with water in the way when ye came forth out of Egypt, and because they hired against thee Balaam the son of Beor of Pethor of Mesopotamia to curse thee. Nevertheless, the Lord thy God would not hearken unto Balaam, but the Lord thy God turned the curse into a blessing unto thee because the Lord thy God loved thee. Thou shalt not seek their peace nor their prosperity all thy days forever. Thou shalt not abhor an Edomite for he is thy brother, thou shalt not abhor an Egyptian because thou wast a stranger in his land. The children that are begotten of them shall enter into the congregation of the Lord in their third generation.

When the host goeth forth against thine enemies, then keep thee from every wicked thing. If there be among you any man that is not clean by reason of uncleanness that chanceth him by night, then shall he go abroad out of the camp, he shall not come within the camp, but it shall be, when evening cometh on he shall wash himself with water, and when the sun is down he shall come into the camp again. Thou shalt have a place also without the camp whither thou shalt go forth abroad, and thou shalt have a paddle upon thy weapon, and it shall be when thou wilt ease thyself abroad, thou shalt dig therewith and shalt turn back and cover that which cometh from thee, for the Lord thy God walketh in the midst of thy camp to deliver thee and to give up thine enemies before thee, therefore shall thy camp be holy, that he see no unclean thing in thee and turn away from thee.

Thou shalt not deliver unto his master the servant which is escaped from his master unto thee, he shall dwell with thee, even among you, in that place which he shall choose in one of thy gates where it liketh him best, thou shalt not oppress him. There shall be no whore of the daughters of Israel, nor a sodomite of the sons of Israel. Thou shalt not bring the hire of a whore, or the price of a dog, into the house of the Lord thy God for any vow, for even both these are abomination unto the Lord thy God. Thou shalt not lend upon usury to thy brother, usury of money, usury of victuals, usury of anything that is lent upon usury, unto a stranger thou mayest lend upon usury, but unto thy brother thou shalt not lend upon usury, that the Lord thy God may bless thee in all that thou settest thine hand to in the land whither thou goest to possess it. When thou shalt vow a vow unto the Lord thy God, thou shalt not slack to pay it, for the Lord thy God will surely require it of thee and it would be sin in thee. But if thou shalt forbear to vow, it shall be no sin in thee. That which is gone out of thy lips thou shalt keep and perform, even a freewill offering, according as thou hast vowed unto the Lord thy God which thou hast promised with thy mouth. When thou comest into thy neighbor's vineyard, then thou mayest eat grapes thy fill at thine own pleasure, but thou shalt not put any in thy vessel. When thou comest into the standing corn of thy neighbor, then thou mayest pluck the ears with thine hand, but thou shalt not move a sickle unto thy neighbor's standing corn.

When a man hath taken a wife and married her, and it come to pass that she find no favor in his eyes because he hath found some uncleanness in her, then let him write her a bill of divorcement and give it in her hand and send her out of his house. And when she is departed out of his house, she may go and be another man's wife. And if the latter husband hate her and write her a bill of divorcement, and giveth it in her hand, and sendeth her out of his house, or if the latter husband die, which took her to be his wife, her former husband which sent her away may not take her again to be his wife after that she is defiled, for that is abomination before the Lord and thou shalt not cause the land to sin which the Lord thy God giveth thee for an inheritance. When a man hath taken a new wife, he shall not go out to war neither shall he be charged with any business, but he shall be free at home one year and shall cheer up his wife which he hath taken.

No man shall take the nether or the upper millstone to pledge, for he taketh a man's life to pledge.

If a man be found stealing any of his brethren of the children of Israel and maketh merchandise of him or selleth him, then that thief shall die and thou shalt put evil away from among you.

Take heed in the plague of leprosy that thou observe diligently and do according to all that the priests the Levites shall teach you; as I commanded them so ye shall observe to do. Remember what the Lord thy God did unto Miriam by the way after that ye were come forth out of Egypt.

When thou dost lend thy brother anything thou shalt not go into his house to fetch his pledge. Thou shalt stand abroad and the man to whom thou dost lend shall bring out the pledge abroad unto thee. And if the man be poor thou shalt not sleep with his pledge, in any case thou shalt deliver him the pledge again when the sun goeth down that he may sleep in his own raiment and bless thee, and it shall be righteousness unto thee before the Lord thy God.

Thou shalt not oppress a hired servant that is poor and needy, whether he be of thy brethren or of thy strangers that are in thy land within thy gates, at his day thou shalt give him his hire, neither shall the sun go down upon it, for he is poor, and setteth his heart upon it, lest he cry against thee unto the Lord and it be sin unto thee.

The fathers shall not be put to death for the children neither shall the children be put to death for the fathers; every man shall be put to death for his own sin.

Thou shalt not pervert the judgment of the stranger, nor of the fatherless, nor take a widow's raiment to pledge, but thou shalt remember that thou wast a bondman in Egypt and the Lord thy God redeemed thee thence, therefore I command thee to do this thing.

When thou cuttest down thine harvest in thy field and hast forgot a sheaf in the field, thou shalt not go again to fetch it, it shall be for the stranger, for the fatherless, and for the widow, that the Lord thy God may bless thee in all the work of thine hands. When thou beatest thine olive tree, thou shalt not go over the boughs again, it shall be for the stranger, for the fatherless, and for the widow.

When thou gatherest the grapes of thy vineyard, thou shalt not glean it afterward, it shall be for the stranger, for the fatherless, and for the widow. And thou shalt remember that thou wast a bondman in the land of Egypt, therefore I command thee to do this thing.

If there be a controversy between men and they come unto judgmen that the judges may judge them, then they shall justify the righteous and condemn the wicked. And it shall be, if the wicked man be worthy to be beaten, that the judge shall cause him to lie down and to be beaten before his face according to his fault by a certain number. Forty stripes he may give him and not exceed, lest if he should exceed and beat him above these with many stripes, then thy brother should seem vile unto thee. Thou shalt not muzzle the ox when he treadeth out the corn.

If brethren dwell together and one of them die and have no child, the wife of the dead shall not marry without unto a stranger, her husband's brother shall go in unto her, and take her to him to wife, and perform the duty of a husband's brother unto her. And it shall be that the firstborn which she beareth shall succeed in the name of his brother which is dead that his name be not put out of Israel. And if the man like not to take his brother's wife, then let his brother's wife go up to the gate unto the elders and say, My husband's brother refuseth to raise up unto his brother a name in Israel, he will not perform the duty of my husband's brother. Then the elders of his city shall call him and speak unto him, and if he stand to it and say, I like not to take her, then shall his brother's wife come unto him in the presence of the elders and loose his shoe from off his foot, and spit in his face, and shall answer and say, So shall it be done unto that man that will not build up his brother's house. And his name shall be called in Israel, The house of him that hath his shoe loosed.

When men strive together one with another, and the wife of the one draweth near for to deliver her husband out of the hand of him that smiteth him, and putteth forth her hand and taketh him by the secrets, then thou shalt cut off her hand, thine eye shall not pity her. Thou shalt not have in thy bag divers weights, a great and a small, thou shalt not have in thine house divers measures, a great and a small, but thou shalt have a perfect and just weight, a perfect and just measure shalt thou have that thy days may be lengthened in the land which the Lord thy God giveth thee. For all that do such things and all that do unrighteously are an abomination unto the Lord thy God.

Remember what Amalek did unto thee by the way when ye were come forth out of Egypt, how he met thee by the way and smote the hindmost of thee, even all that were feeble behind thee, when thou wast faint and weary and he feared not God. Therefore it shall be when the Lord thy God hath given thee rest from all thine enemies round about in the land which the Lord thy God giveth thee for an inheritance to possess it, that thou shalt blot out the remembrance of Amalek from under Heaven, thou shalt not forget it.

And it shall be, when thou art come in unto the land which the Lord thy God giveth thee for an inheritance, and possessest it and dwellest therein, that thou shalt take of the first of all the fruit of the Earth which thou shalt bring of thy land that the Lord thy God giveth thee, and shalt put it in a basket and shalt go unto the place which the Lord thy God shall choose to place his name there. And thou shalt go unto the priest that shall be in those days and say unto him, I profess this day unto the Lord thy God that I am come unto the country which the Lord sware unto our fathers for to give us. And the priest shall take the basket out of thine hand and set it down before the altar of the Lord thy God. And thou shalt speak and say before the Lord thy God, A Syrian ready to perish was my father, and he went down into Egypt and sojourned there with a few, and became there a nation, great, mighty, and populous, and the Egyptians evil entreated us and afflicted us and laid upon us hard bondage. And when we cried unto the Lord God of our fathers, the Lord heard our voice and looked on our affliction, and our labor, and our oppression. And the Lord brought us forth out of Egypt with a mighty hand, and with an outstretched arm, and with great terribleness, and with signs, and with wonders, and he hath brought us into this place and hath given us this land, even a land that floweth with milk and honey. And now behold, I have brought the firstfruits of the land which thou, O Lord, hast given me. And thou shalt set it before the Lord thy God, and worship before the Lord thy God, and thou shalt rejoice in every good thing which the Lord thy God hath given unto thee, and unto thine house, thou, and the Levite, and the stranger that is among you.

When thou hast made an end of tithing all the tithes of thine increase the third year which is the year of tithing, and hast given it unto the Levite, the stranger, the fatherless, and the widow that they may eat within thy gates and be filled, then thou shalt say before the Lord thy God, I have brought away the hallowed things out of mine house, and also have given them unto the Levite, and unto the stranger, to the fatherless, and to the widow according to all thy commandments which thou hast commanded me; I have not transgressed thy commandments neither have I forgotten them, I have not eaten thereof in my mourning neither have I taken away aught thereof for any unclean use, nor given aught thereof for the dead, but I have hearkened to the voice of the Lord my God and have done according to all that thou hast commanded me. Look down from thy holy habitation, from Heaven, and bless thy people Israel and the land which thou hast given us as thou swarest unto our fathers, a land that floweth with milk and honey.

This day the Lord thy God hath commanded thee to do these statutes and judgments, thou shalt therefore keep and do them with all thine heart and with all thy soul. Thou hast avouched the Lord this day to be thy God and to walk in his ways, and keep his statutes, and his commandments, and his judgments, and to hearken unto his voice, and the Lord hath avouched thee this day to be his peculiar people as he hath promised thee, and that thou shouldest keep all his commandments, and to make thee high above all nations which he hath made, in praise, and in name, and in honor, and that thou mayest be a holy people unto the Lord thy God as he hath spoken.

8 AND Moses with the elders of Israel commanded the people saying, Keep all the commandments which I command you this day. And it shall be on the day when ye shall pass over Jordan unto the land which the Lord thy God giveth thee, that thou shalt set thee up great stones and plaster them with plaster, and thou shalt write upon them all the words of this law when thou art passed over, that thou mayest go in unto the land which the Lord thy God giveth thee, a land that floweth with milk and honey, as the Lord God of thy fathers hath promised thee. Therefore it shall be when ye be gone over Jordan, that ye shall set up these stones which I command you this day in mount Ebal, and thou shalt plaster them with plaster. And there shalt thou build an altar unto the Lord thy God, an altar of stones, thou shalt not lift up any iron tool upon them. Thou shalt build the altar of the Lord thy God of whole stones, and thou shalt offer burnt offerings thereon unto the Lord thy God, and thou shalt offer peace offerings, and shalt eat there and rejoice before the Lord thy God. And thou shalt write upon the stones all the words of this law very plainly.

And Moses and the priests the Levites spake unto all Israel saying, Take heed and hearken, O Israel, this day thou art become the people of the Lord thy God. Thou shalt therefore obey the voice of the Lord thy God and do his commandments and his statutes which I command thee this day.

And Moses charged the people the same day saying, These shall stand upon mount Gerizim to bless the people when ye are come over Jordan: Simeon, and Levi, and Judah, and Issachar, and Joseph, and Benjamin, and these shall stand upon mount Ebal to curse: Reuben, Gad, and Asher, and Zebulun, Dan, and Naphtali. And the Levites shall speak and say unto all the men of Israel with a loud voice, cursed be the man that maketh any graven or molten image, an abomination unto the Lord, the work of the hands of the craftsman, and putteth it in a secret place, and all the people shall answer and say, Amen. Cursed be he that setteth light by his father or his mother, and all the people shall say, Amen. Cursed be he that removeth his neighbor's landmark, and all the people shall say, Amen. Cursed be he that maketh the blind to wander out of the way, and all the people shall say, Amen. Cursed be he that perverteth the judgment of the stranger, fatherless, and widow, and all the people shall say, Amen. Cursed be he that lieth with his father's wife because he uncovereth his father's skirt, and all the people shall say, Amen. Cursed be he that lieth with any manner of beast, and all the people shall say, Amen. Cursed be he that lieth with his sister, the daughter of his father or the daughter of his mother, and all the people shall say, Amen. Cursed be he that lieth with his mother-in-law, and all the people shall say, Amen. Cursed be he that smiteth his neighbor secretly, and all the people shall say, Amen. Cursed be he that taketh reward to slay an innocent person, and all the people shall say, Amen. Cursed be he that confirmeth not all the words of this law to do them, and all the people shall say, Amen.

And it shall come to pass, if thou shalt hearken diligently unto the voice of the Lord thy God, to observe and to do all his commandments which I command thee this day, that the Lord thy God will set thee on high above all nations of the Earth, and all these blessings shall come on thee and overtake thee, if thou shalt hearken unto the voice of the Lord thy God. Blessed shalt thou be in the city, and blessed shalt thou be in the field. Blessed shall be the fruit of thy body, and the fruit of thy ground, and the fruit of thy cattle, the increase of thy kine, and the flocks of thy sheep. Blessed shall be thy basket and thy store. Blessed shalt thou be when thou comest in and blessed shalt thou be when thou goest out.

The Lord shall cause thine enemies that rise up against thee to be smitten before thy face, they shall come out against thee one way and flee before thee seven ways. The Lord shall command the blessing upon thee in thy storehouses, and in all that thou settest thine hand unto, and he shall bless thee in the land which the Lord thy God giveth thee. The Lord shall establish thee a holy people unto himself as he hath sworn unto thee, if thou shalt keep the commandments of the Lord thy God and walk in his ways. And all people of the Earth shall see that thou art called by the name of the Lord and they shall be afraid of thee. And the Lord shall make thee plenteous in goods, in the fruit of thy body, and in the fruit of thy cattle, and in the fruit of thy ground in the land which the Lord sware unto thy fathers to give thee. The Lord shall open unto thee his good treasure, the Heaven to give the rain unto thy land in his season, and to bless all the work of thine hand, and thou shalt lend unto many nations, and thou shalt not borrow. And the Lord shall make thee the head and not the tail, and thou shalt be above only and thou shalt not be beneath, if that thou hearken unto the commandments of the Lord thy God which I command thee this day to observe and to do them, and thou shalt not go aside from any of the words which I command thee this day, to the right hand or to the left, to go after other gods to serve them.

But it shall come to pass, if thou wilt not hearken unto the voice of the Lord thy God to observe to do all his commandments and his statutes which I command thee this day, that all these curses shall come upon thee and overtake thee, cursed shalt thou be in the city and cursed shalt thou be in the field. Cursed shall be thy basket and thy store. Cursed shall be the fruit of thy body and the fruit of thy land, the increase of thy kine and the flocks of thy sheep. Cursed shalt thou be when thou comest in and cursed shalt thou be when thou goest out, the Lord shall send upon thee cursing, vexation, and rebuke, in all that thou settest thine hand unto for to do, until thou be destroyed and until thou perish quickly because of the wickedness of thy doings whereby thou hast forsaken me. The Lord shall make the pestilence cleave unto thee until he have consumed thee from off the land whither thou goest to possess it. The Lord shall smite thee with a consumption, and with a fever, and with an inflammation, and with an extreme burning, and with the sword, and with blasting, and with mildew, and they shall pursue thee until thou perish. And thy Heaven that is over thy head shall be brass, and the Earth that is under thee shall be iron. The Lord shall make the rain of thy land powder and dust, from Heaven shall it come down upon thee until thou be destroyed.

The Lord shall cause thee to be smitten before thine enemies, thou shalt go out one way against them and flee seven ways before them, and shalt be removed into all the kingdoms of the Earth. And thy carcass shall be meat unto all fowls of the air and unto the beasts of the Earth, and no man shall fray them away.

The Lord will smite thee with the botch of Egypt, and with the emerods, and with the scab, and with the itch, whereof thou canst not be healed. The Lord shall smite thee with madness, and blindness, and astonishment of heart, and thou shalt grope at noonday as the blind gropeth in darkness, and thou shalt not prosper in thy ways, and thou shalt be only oppressed and spoiled evermore, and no man shall save thee. Thou shalt betroth a wife and another man shall lie with her, thou shalt build a house and thou shalt not dwell therein, thou shalt plant a vineyard and shalt not gather the grapes thereof. Thine ox shall be slain before thine eyes and thou shalt not eat thereof, thine ass shall be violently taken away from before thy face and shall not be restored to thee, thy sheep shall be given unto thine enemies and thou shalt have none to rescue them. Thy sons and thy daughters shall be given unto another people, and thine eyes shall look and fail with longing for them all the day long, and there shall be no might in thine hand. The fruit of thy land and all thy labors shall a nation which thou knowest not eat up, and thou shalt be only oppressed and crushed alway so that thou shalt be mad for the sight of thine eyes which thou shalt see. The Lord shall smite thee in the knees and in the legs with a sore botch that cannot be healed, from the sole of thy foot unto the top of thy head. The Lord shall bring thee, and thy king which thou shalt set over thee, unto a nation which neither thou nor thy fathers have known, and there shalt thou serve other gods, wood and stone. And thou shalt become an astonishment, a proverb, and a byword, among all nations whither the Lord shall lead thee.

Thou shalt carry much seed out into the field, and shalt gather but little in, for the locust shall consume it. Thou shalt plant vineyards, and dress them, but shalt neither drink of the wine, nor gather the grapes, for the worms shall eat them. Thou shalt have olive trees throughout all thy coasts, but thou shalt not anoint thyself with the oil, for thine olive shall cast his fruit. Thou shalt beget sons and daughters, but thou shalt not enjoy them, for they shall go into captivity. All thy trees and fruit of thy land shall the locust consume. The stranger that is within thee shall get up above thee very high, and thou shalt come down very low. He shall lend to thee, and thou shalt not lend to him, he shall be the head, and thou shalt be the tail.

Moreover, all these curses shall come upon thee, and shall pursue thee, and overtake thee till thou be destroyed because thou hearkenedst not unto the voice of the Lord thy God, to keep his commandments and his statutes which he commanded thee. And they shall be upon thee for a sign and for a wonder and upon thy seed for ever.

Because thou servedst not the Lord thy God with joyfulness and with gladness of heart for the abundance of all things, therefore shalt thou serve thine enemies which the Lord shall send against thee, in hunger, and in thirst, and in nakedness, and in want of all things, and he shall put a yoke of iron upon thy neck until he have destroyed thee.

The Lord shall bring a nation against thee from far, from the end of the Earth, as swift as the eagle flieth, a nation whose tongue thou shalt not understand, a nation of fierce countenance, which shall not regard the person of the old nor show favor to the young, and he shall eat the fruit of thy cattle and the fruit of thy land until thou be destroyed, which also shall not leave thee either corn, wine, or oil, or the increase of thy kine, or flocks of thy sheep until he have destroyed thee. And he shall besiege thee in all thy gates until thy high and fenced walls come down wherein thou trustedst throughout all thy land, and he shall besiege thee in all thy gates throughout all thy land which the Lord thy God hath given thee. And thou shalt eat the fruit of thine own body, the flesh of thy sons and of thy daughters which the Lord thy God hath given thee, in the siege, and in the straitness wherewith thine enemies shall distress thee so that the man that is tender among you and very delicate, his eye shall be evil toward his brother, and toward the wife of his bosom, and toward the remnant of his children which he shall leave, so that he will not give to any of them of the flesh of his children whom he shall eat because he hath nothing left him in the siege, and in the straitness wherewith thine enemies shall distress thee in all thy gates. The tender and delicate woman among you, which would not adventure to set the sole of her foot upon the ground for delicateness and tenderness, her eye shall be evil toward the husband of her bosom, and toward her son, and toward her daughter. And toward her young one that cometh out from between her feet, and toward her children which she shall bear, for she shall eat them for want of all things secretly in the siege and straitness wherewith thine enemy shall distress thee in thy gates.

If thou wilt not observe to do all the words of this law that are written in this book that thou mayest fear this glorious and fearful name: THE LORD THY GOD, then the Lord will make thy plagues wonderful, and the plagues of thy seed, even great plagues, and of long continuance, and sore sicknesses, and of long continuance. Moreover he will bring upon thee all the diseases of Egypt which thou wast afraid of and they shall cleave unto thee. Also every sickness and every plague which is not written in the book of this law, them will the Lord bring upon thee until thou be destroyed. And ye shall be left few in number, whereas ye were as the stars of Heaven for multitude, because thou wouldest not obey the voice of the Lord thy God. And it shall come to pass, that as the Lord rejoiced over you to do you good and to multiply you, so the Lord will rejoice over you to destroy you and to bring you to naught, and ye shall be plucked from off the land whither thou goest to possess it. And the Lord shall scatter thee among all people, from the one end of the Earth even unto the other, and there thou shalt serve other gods which neither thou nor thy fathers have known, even wood and stone. And among these nations shalt thou find no ease neither shall the sole of thy foot have rest, but the Lord shall give thee there a trembling heart, and failing of eyes, and sorrow of mind, and thy life shall hang in doubt before thee, and thou shalt fear day and night, and shalt have none assurance of thy life. In the morning thou shalt say, Would God it were even!, and at even thou shalt say, Would God it were morning!, for the fear of thine heart wherewith thou shalt fear, and for the sight of thine eyes which thou shalt see. And the Lord shall bring thee into Egypt again with ships by the way whereof I spake unto thee, Thou shalt see it no more again, and there ye shall be sold unto your enemies for bondmen and bondwomen, and no man shall buy you.

These are the words of the covenant, which the Lord commanded Moses to make with the children of Israel in the land of Moab, besides the covenant which he made with them in Horeb.

9 AND Moses called unto all Israel and said unto them, Ye have seen all that the Lord did before your eyes in the land of Egypt unto Pharaoh, and unto all his servants, and unto all his land, the great temptations which thine eyes have seen, the signs, and those great miracles, yet the Lord hath not given you a heart to perceive, and eyes to see, and ears to hear unto this day. And I have led you forty years in the wilderness, your clothes are not waxen old upon you, and thy shoe is not waxen old upon thy foot. Ye have not eaten bread, neither have ye drunk wine or strong drink, that ye might know that I am the Lord your God. And when ye came unto this place, Sihon the king of Heshbon and Og the king of Bashan came out against us unto battle, and we smote them, and we took their land, and gave it for an inheritance unto the Reubenites, and the Gadites, and to the half tribe of Manasseh. Keep therefore the words of this covenant and do them, that ye may prosper in all that ye do.

Ye stand this day all of you before the Lord your God, your captains of your tribes, your elders, and your officers, with all the men of Israel, your little ones, your wives, and thy stranger that is in thy camp, from the hewer of thy wood unto the drawer of thy water, that thou shouldest enter into covenant with the Lord thy God, and into his oath, which the Lord thy God maketh with thee this day, that he may establish thee today for a people unto himself, and that he may be unto thee a God, as he hath said unto thee and as he hath sworn unto thy fathers, to Abraham, to Isaac, and to Jacob.

Neither with you only do I make this covenant and this oath, but with him that standeth here with us this day before the Lord our God, and also with him that is not here with us this day (for ye know how we have dwelt in the land of Egypt, and how we came through the nations which ye passed by, and ye have seen their abominations, and their idols, wood and stone, silver and gold, which were among them), lest there should be among you man, or woman, or family, or tribe, whose heart turneth away this day from the Lord our God to go and serve the gods of these nations, lest there should be among you a root that beareth gall and wormwood, and it come to pass when he heareth the words of this curse that he bless himself in his heart saying, I shall have peace, though I walk in the imagination of mine heart, to add drunkenness to thirst, the Lord will not spare him, but then the anger of the Lord and his jealousy shall smoke against that man, and all the curses that are written in this book shall lie upon him, and the Lord shall blot out his name from under Heaven. And the Lord shall separate him unto evil out of all the tribes of Israel, according to all the curses of the covenant that are written in this book of the law, so that the generation to come of your children that shall rise up after you, and the stranger that shall come from a far land shall say when they see the plagues of that land, and the sicknesses which the Lord hath laid upon it, and that the whole land thereof is brimstone, and salt, and burning, that it is not sown, nor beareth, nor any grass groweth therein, like the overthrow of Sodom and Gomorrah, Admah and Zeboim, which the Lord overthrew in his anger and in his wrath, even all nations shall say, Wherefore hath the Lord done thus unto this land? What meaneth the heat of this great anger? Then men shall say, Because they have forsaken the covenant of the Lord God of their fathers which he made with them when he brought them forth out of the land of Egypt, for they went and served other gods and worshiped them, gods whom they knew not and whom he had not given unto them, and the anger of the Lord was kindled against this land to bring upon it all the curses that are written in this book, and the Lord rooted them out of their land in anger, and in wrath, and in great indignation, and cast them into another land as it is this day. The secret things belong unto the Lord our God, but those things which are revealed belong unto us and to our children forever, that we may do all the words of this law.

And it shall come to pass when all these things are come upon thee, the blessing and the curse which I have set before thee, and thou shalt call them to mind among all the nations, whither the Lord thy God hath driven thee, and shalt return unto the Lord thy God, and shalt obey his voice according to all that I command thee this day, thou and thy children, with all thine heart, and with all thy soul, that then the Lord thy God will turn thy captivity, and have compassion upon thee, and will return and gather thee from all the nations whither the Lord thy God hath scattered thee. If any of thine be driven out unto the outmost parts of Heaven, from thence will the Lord thy God gather thee and from thence will he fetch thee, and the Lord thy God will bring thee into the land which thy fathers possessed and thou shalt possess it, and he will do thee good and multiply thee above thy fathers.

And the Lord thy God will circumcise thine heart and the heart of thy seed, to love the Lord thy God with all thine heart, and with all thy soul, that thou mayest live. And the Lord thy God will put all these curses upon thine enemies and on them that hate thee, which persecuted thee. And thou shalt return and obey the voice of the Lord and do all his commandments which I command thee this day. And the Lord thy God will make thee plenteous in every work of thine hand, in the fruit of thy body, and in the fruit of thy cattle, and in the fruit of thy land for good, for the Lord will again rejoice over thee for good as he rejoiced over thy fathers, if thou shalt hearken unto the voice of the Lord thy God to keep his commandments and his statutes which are written in this book of the law, and if thou turn unto the Lord thy God with all thine heart and with all thy soul.

For this commandment which I command thee this day, it is not hidden from thee neither is it far off. It is not in Heaven that thou shouldest say, Who shall go up for us to Heaven and bring it unto us that we may hear it and do it? Neither is it beyond the sea that thou shouldest say, Who shall go over the sea for us and bring it unto us that we may hear it and do it? But the word is very nigh unto thee, in thy mouth, and in thy heart, that thou mayest do it.

See, I have set before thee this day life and good, and death and evil, in that I command thee this day to love the Lord thy God, to walk in his ways, and to keep his commandments, and his statutes, and his judgments, that thou mayest live and multiply, and the Lord thy God shall bless thee in the land whither thou goest to possess it. But if thine heart turn away so that thou wilt not hear, but shalt be drawn away and worship other gods and serve them, I denounce unto you this day that ye shall surely perish, and that ye shall not prolong your days upon the land whither thou passest over Jordan to go to possess it. I call Heaven and Earth to record this day against you that I have set before you life and death, blessing and cursing, therefore choose life, that both thou and thy seed may live, that thou mayest love the Lord thy God, and that thou mayest obey his voice, and that thou mayest cleave unto him, for he is thy life and the length of thy days, that thou mayest dwell in the land which the Lord sware unto thy fathers, to Abraham, to Isaac, and to Jacob, to give them.

And Moses went and spake these words unto all Israel. And he said unto them, I am a hundred and twenty years old this day, I can no more go out and come in; also the Lord hath said unto me, Thou shalt not go over this Jordan. The Lord thy God, he will go over before thee, and he will destroy these nations from before thee, and thou shalt possess them, and Joshua, he shall go over before thee as the Lord hath said. And the Lord shall do unto them as he did to Sihon and to Og, kings of the Amorites, and unto the land of them whom he destroyed. And the Lord shall give them up before your face, that ye may do unto them according unto all the commandments which I have commanded you. Be strong and of a good courage, fear not, nor be afraid of them, for the Lord thy God, he it is that doth go with thee, he will not fail thee nor forsake thee.

And Moses called unto Joshua and said unto him in the sight of all Israel, Be strong and of a good courage, for thou must go with this people unto the land which the Lord hath sworn unto their fathers to give them, and thou shalt cause them to inherit it. And the Lord, he it is that doth go before thee, he will be with thee, he will not fail thee, neither forsake thee, fear not, neither be dismayed.

And Moses wrote this law and delivered it unto the priests, the sons of Levi, which bare the ark of the covenant of the Lord, and unto all the elders of Israel. And Moses commanded them saying, At the end of every seven years, in the solemnity of the year of release, in the feast of tabernacles, when all Israel is come to appear before the Lord thy God in the place which he shall choose, thou shalt read this law before all Israel in their hearing. Gather the people together, men, and women, and children, and thy stranger that is within thy gates, that they may hear and that they may learn, and fear the Lord your God, and observe to do all the words of this law, and that their children which have not known anything may hear and learn to fear the Lord your God, as long as ye live in the land whither ye go over Jordan to possess it.

And the Lord said unto Moses, Behold, thy days approach that thou must die. Call Joshua and present yourselves in the tabernacle of the congregation that I may give him a charge. And Moses and Joshua went and presented themselves in the tabernacle of the congregation. And the Lord appeared in the tabernacle in a pillar of a cloud, and the pillar of the cloud stood over the door of the tabernacle. And the Lord said unto Moses, Behold, thou shalt sleep with thy fathers, and this people will rise up and go a whoring after the gods of the strangers of the land whither they go to be among them, and will forsake me and break my covenant which I have made with them. Then my anger shall be kindled against them in that day, and I will forsake them, and I will hide my face from them, and they shall be devoured, and many evils and troubles shall befall them so that they will say in that day, Are not these evils come upon us because our God is not among us? And I will surely hide my face in that day for all the evils which they shall have wrought, in that they are turned unto other gods.

Now therefore write ye this song for you, and teach it the children of Israel, put it in their mouths that this song may be a witness for me against the children of Israel. For when I shall have brought them into the land which I sware unto their fathers that floweth with milk and honey, and they shall have eaten and filled themselves and waxen fat, then will they turn unto other gods, and serve them, and provoke me, and break my covenant. And it shall come to pass when many evils and troubles are befallen them, that this song shall testify against them as a witness, for it shall not be forgotten out of the mouths of their seed, for I know their imagination which they go about, even now, before I have brought them into the land which I sware. Moses therefore wrote this song the same day, and taught it the children of Israel. And he gave Joshua the son of Nun a charge and said, Be strong and of a good courage, for thou shalt bring the children of Israel into the land which I sware unto them and I will be with thee.

And it came to pass when Moses had made an end of writing the words of this law in a book until they were finished, that Moses commanded the Levites, which bare the ark of the covenant of the Lord saying, Take this book of the law and put it in the side of the ark of the covenant of the Lord your God, that it may be there for a witness against thee. For I know thy rebellion, and thy stiff neck, behold, while I am yet alive with you this day, ye have been rebellious against the Lord, and how much more after my death? Gather unto me all the elders of your tribes and your officers, that I may speak these words in their ears and call Heaven and Earth to record against them. For I know that after my death ye will utterly corrupt yourselves and turn aside from the way which I have commanded you, and evil will befall you in the latter days because ye will do evil in the sight of the Lord to provoke him to anger through the work of your hands.

And Moses spake in the ears of all the congregation of Israel the words of this song, until they were ended: Give ear, O ye heavens, and I will speak, and hear, O Earth, the words of my mouth. My doctrine shall drop as the rain, my speech shall distill as the dew, as the small rain upon the tender herb and as the showers upon the grass, because I will publish the name of the Lord, ascribe ye greatness unto our God. He is the Rock, his work is perfect, for all his ways are judgment, a God of truth and without iniquity, just and right is he. They have corrupted themselves, their spot is not the spot of his children, they are a perverse and crooked generation. Do ye thus requite the Lord, O foolish people and unwise? Is not he thy father that hath bought thee? Hath he not made thee and established thee? Remember the days of old, consider the years of many generations, ask thy father and he will show thee, thy elders and they will tell thee. When the Most High divided to the nations their inheritance, when he separated the sons of Adam, he set the bounds of the people according to the number of the children of Israel. For the Lord's portion is his people, Jacob is the lot of his inheritance. He found him in a desert land, and in the waste howling wilderness he led him about, he instructed him, he kept him as the apple of his eye. As an eagle stirreth up her nest, fluttereth over her young, spreadeth abroad her wings, taketh them, beareth them on her wings so the Lord alone did lead him and there was no strange god with him. He made him ride on the high places of the Earth, that he might eat the increase of the fields, and he made him to suck honey out of the rock, and oil out of the flinty rock, butter of kine, and milk of sheep, with fat of lambs, and rams of the breed of Bashan, and goats, with the fat of kidneys of wheat, and thou didst drink the pure blood of the grape.

But Jeshurun waxed fat and kicked, thou art waxen fat, thou art grown thick, thou art covered with fatness, then he forsook God which made him, and lightly esteemed the Rock of his salvation. They provoked him to jealousy with strange gods, with abominations provoked they him to anger. They sacrificed unto devils, not to God, to gods whom they knew not, to new gods that came newly up whom your fathers feared not.

Of the Rock that begat thee thou art unmindful and hast forgotten God that formed thee. And when the Lord saw it, he abhorred them because of the provoking of his sons and of his daughters. And he said, I will hide my face from them, I will see what their end shall be, for they are a very forward generation, children in whom is no faith. They have moved me to jealousy with that which is not God, they have provoked me to anger with their vanities, and I will move them to jealousy with those which are not a people, I will provoke them to anger with a foolish nation. For a fire is kindled in mine anger, and shall burn unto the lowest hell, and shall consume the Earth with her increase, and set on fire the foundations of the mountains.

I will heap mischief upon them, I will spend mine arrows upon them. They shall be burnt with hunger and devoured with burning heat and with bitter destruction. I will also send the teeth of beasts upon them, with the poison of serpents of the dust. The sword without and terror within shall destroy both the young man and the virgin, the suckling also with the man of gray hairs. I said, I would scatter them into corners, I would make the remembrance of them to cease from among men were it not that I feared the wrath of the enemy, lest their adversaries should behave themselves strangely and lest they should say, Our hand is high and the Lord hath not done all this. For they are a nation void of counsel neither is there any understanding in them.

O that they were wise, that they understood this, that they would consider their latter end. How should one chase a thousand and two put ten thousand to flight, except their Rock had sold them and the Lord had shut them up? For their rock is not as our Rock, even our enemies themselves being judges. For their vine is of the vine of Sodom and of the fields of Gomorrah, their grapes are grapes of gall, their clusters are bitter, their wine is the poison of dragons, and the cruel venom of asps. Is not this laid up in store with me and sealed up among my treasures? To me belongeth vengeance and recompense, their foot shall slide in due time, for the day of their calamity is at hand and the things that shall come upon them make haste. For the Lord shall judge his people and repent himself for his servants when he seeth that their power is gone and there is none shut up or left. And he shall say, Where are their gods, their rock in whom they trusted, which did eat the fat of their sacrifices, and drank the wine of their drink offerings? Let them rise up and help you and be your protection. See now that I, even I am he and there is no god with me. I kill and I make alive, I wound and I heal, neither is there any that can deliver out of my hand. For I lift up my hand to Heaven and say, I live forever. If I whet my glittering sword and mine hand take hold on judgment, I will render vengeance to mine enemies and will reward them that hate me. I will make mine arrows drunk with blood, and my sword shall devour flesh, and that with the blood of the slain and of the captives, from the beginning of revenges upon the enemy.

Rejoice, O ye nations, with his people, for he will avenge the blood of his servants, and will render vengeance to his adversaries, and will be merciful unto his land and to his people.

And Moses came and spake all the words of this song in the ears of the people, he and Hoshea the son of Nun. And Moses made an end of speaking all these words to all Israel and he said unto them, Set your hearts unto all the words which I testify among you this day which ye shall command your children to observe to do, all the words of this law. For it is not a vain thing for you because it is your life, and through this thing ye shall prolong your days in the land whither ye go over Jordan to possess it.

And the Lord spake unto Moses that selfsame day saying, Get thee up into this mountain Abarim, unto mount Nebo which is in the land of Moab that is over against Jericho and behold the land of Canaan which I give unto the children of Israel for a possession, and die in the mount whither thou goest up, and be gathered unto thy people as Aaron thy brother died in mount Hor and was gathered unto his people, because ye trespassed against me among the children of Israel at the waters of Meribah-Kadesh in the wilderness of Zin, because ye sanctified me not in the midst of the children of Israel. Yet thou shalt see the land before thee, but thou shalt not go thither unto the land which I give the children of Israel.

And this is the blessing, wherewith Moses the man of God blessed the children of Israel before his death. And he said, The Lord came from Sinai and rose up from Seir unto them, he shined forth from mount Paran and he came with ten thousands of saints, from his right hand went a fiery law for them. Yea, he loved the people, all his saints are in thy hand, and they sat down at thy feet, every one shall receive of thy words. Moses commanded us a law, even the inheritance of the congregation of Jacob. And he was king in Jeshurun when the heads of the people and the tribes of Israel were gathered together.

Let Reuben live and not die, and let not his men be few. And this is the blessing of Judah and he said, Hear, Lord, the voice of Judah and bring him unto his people, let his hands be sufficient for him and be thou a help to him from his enemies. And of Levi he said, Let thy Thummim and thy Urim be with thy holy one whom thou didst prove at Massah and with whom thou didst strive at the waters of Meribah, who said unto his father and to his mother, I have not seen him, neither did he acknowledge his brethren, nor knew his own children, for they have observed thy word and kept thy covenant. They shall teach Jacob thy judgments and Israel thy law, they shall put incense before thee and whole burnt sacrifice upon thine altar. Bless, Lord, his substance and accept the work of his hands, smite through the loins of them that rise against him and of them that hate him, that they rise not again. And of Benjamin he said, The beloved of the Lord shall dwell in safety by him, and the Lord shall cover him all the day long, and he shall dwell between his shoulders. And of Joseph he said, Blessed of the Lord be his land, for the precious things of Heaven, for the dew, and for the deep that coucheth beneath, and for the precious fruits brought forth by the sun, and for the precious things put forth by the moon, and for the chief things of the ancient mountain, and for the precious things of the lasting hills, and for the precious things of the Earth and fullness thereof, and for the goodwill of him that dwelt in the bush, let the blessing come upon the head of Joseph and upon the top of the head of him that was separated from his brethren. His glory is like the firstling of his bullock, and his horns are like the horns of unicorns, with them he shall push the people together to the ends of the Earth, and they are the ten thousands of Ephraim, and they are the thousands of Manasseh. And of Zebulun he said, Rejoice, Zebulun, in thy going out, and Issachar, in thy tents. They shall call the people unto the mountain, there they shall offer sacrifices of righteousness, for they shall suck of the abundance of the seas and of treasures hid in the sand. And of Gad he said, Blessed be he that enlargeth Gad, he dwelleth as a lion and teareth the arm with the crown of the head. And he provided the first part for himself, because there, in a portion of the lawgiver, was he seated, and he came with the heads of the people, he executed the justice of the Lord, and his judgments with Israel. And of Dan he said, Dan is a lion's whelp, he shall leap from Bashan. And of Naphtali he said, O Naphtali, satisfied with favor and full with the blessing of the Lord, possess thou the west and the south. And of Asher he said, Let Asher be blessed with children, let him be acceptable to his brethren, and let him dip his foot in oil. Thy shoes shall be iron and brass and as thy days so shall thy strength be.

There is none like unto the God of Jeshurun, who rideth upon the Heaven in thy help and in his excellency on the sky. The Eternal God is thy refuge and underneath are the everlasting arms, and he shall thrust out the enemy from before thee and shall say, Destroy them. Israel then shall dwell in safety alone, the fountain of Jacob shall be upon a land of corn and wine, also his heavens shall drop down dew. Happy art thou, O Israel, who is like unto thee, O people saved by the Lord, the shield of thy help, and who is the sword of thy excellency? And thine enemies shall be found liars unto thee and thou shalt tread upon their high places.

And Moses went up from the plains of Moab unto the mountain of Nebo, to the top of Pisgah that is over against Jericho, and the Lord showed him all the land of Gilead unto Dan, and all Naphtali, and the land of Ephraim and Manasseh, and all the land of Judah unto the utmost sea, and the south, and the plain of the valley of Jericho, the city of palm trees unto Zoar. And the Lord said unto him, This is the land which I sware unto Abraham, unto Isaac, and unto Jacob saying, I will give it unto thy seed, I have caused thee to see it with thine eyes, but thou shalt not go over thither. So Moses the servant of the Lord died there in the land of Moab according to the word of the Lord. For the Lord took him unto his fathers in a valley in the land of Moab over against Beth-peor, therefore no man knoweth of his sepulcher unto this day. And Moses was a hundred and twenty years old when he died; his eye was not dim nor his natural force abated. And the children of Israel wept for Moses in the plains of Moab thirty days, so the days of weeping and mourning for Moses were ended.

And Joshua the son of Nun was full of the spirit of wisdom, for Moses had laid his hands upon him, and the children of Israel hearkened unto him, and did as the Lord commanded Moses. And there arose not a prophet since in Israel like unto Moses, whom the Lord knew face to face, in all the signs and the wonders which the Lord sent him to do in the land of Egypt, to Pharaoh and to all his servants, and to all his land, and in all that mighty hand, and in all the great terror which Moses showed in the sight of all Israel.

THE BOOK OF JOSHUA

NOW after the death of Moses the servant of the Lord, it came to pass that the Lord spake unto Joshua the son of Nun, Moses' minister, saying, Moses my servant is dead, now therefore arise, go over this Jordan, thou, and all this people, unto the land which I do give to them, even to the children of Israel. Every place that the sole of your foot shall tread upon, that have I given unto you, as I said unto Moses. From the wilderness and this Lebanon even unto the great river, the river Euphrates, all the land of the Hittites, and unto the great sea toward the going down of the sun, shall be your coast. There shall not any man be able to stand before thee all the days of thy life, as I was with Moses, so I will be with thee. I will not fail thee, nor forsake thee. Be strong and of a good courage, for unto this people shalt thou divide for an inheritance the land, which I sware unto their fathers to give them. Only be thou strong and very courageous, that thou mayest observe to do according to all the law, which Moses my servant commanded thee. Turn not from it to the right hand or to the left, that thou mayest prosper whithersoever thou goest. This book of the law shall not depart out of thy mouth, but thou shalt meditate therein day and night that thou mayest observe to do according to all that is written therein. For then thou shalt make thy way prosperous, and then thou shalt have good success. Have not I commanded thee? Be strong and of a good courage, be not afraid, neither be thou dismayed, for the Lord thy God is with thee whithersoever thou goest.

Then Joshua commanded the officers of the people, saying, Pass through the host, and command the people, saying, Prepare you victuals, for within three days ye shall pass over this Jordan to go in to possess the land, which the Lord your God giveth you to possess it. And to the Reubenites, and to the Gadites, and to half the tribe of Manasseh, spake Joshua, saying, Remember the word which Moses the servant of the Lord commanded you, saying, The Lord your God hath given you rest, and hath given you this land. Your wives, your little ones, and your cattle, shall remain in the land which Moses gave you on this side Jordan, but ye shall pass before your brethren armed, all the mighty men of valor, and help them, until the Lord have given your brethren rest, as he hath given you. And they also have possessed the land which the Lord your God giveth them. Then ye shall return unto the land of your possession, and enjoy it, which Moses the Lord's servant gave you on this side Jordan toward the sunrising. And they answered Joshua, saying, All that thou commandest us we will do, and whithersoever thou sendest us, we will go. According as we hearkened unto Moses in all things, so will we hearken unto thee; only the Lord thy God be with thee, as he was with Moses. Whosoever he be that doth rebel against thy commandment and will not hearken unto thy words in all that thou commandest him, he shall be put to death. Only be strong and of a good courage.

And Joshua the son of Nun sent out of Shittim two men to spy secretly, saying, Go view the land, even Jericho. And they went and came into a harlot's house, named Rahab, and lodged there. And it was told the king of Jericho, saying, Behold, there came men in hither tonight of the children of Israel to search out the country. And the king of Jericho sent unto Rahab, saying, Bring forth the men that are come to thee, which are entered into thine house, for they are come to search out all the country. And the woman took the two men, and hid them, and said thus, There came men unto me, but I wist not whence they were, and it came to pass about the time of shutting of the gate, when it was dark, that the men went out, whither the men went, I know not. Pursue after them quickly, for ye shall overtake them. But she had brought them up to the roof of the house, and hid them with the stalks of flax, which she had laid in order upon the roof. And the men pursued after them the way to Jordan unto the fords, and as soon as they which pursued after them were gone out, they shut the gate.

And before they were laid down, she came up unto them upon the roof, and she said unto the men, I know that the Lord hath given you the land and that your terror is fallen upon us and that all the inhabitants of the land faint because of you. For we have heard how the Lord dried up the water of the Red Sea for you when ye came out of Egypt, and what ye did unto the two kings of the Amorites, that were on the other side Jordan, Sihon and Og, whom ye utterly destroyed. And as soon as we had heard these things, our hearts did melt, neither did there remain any more courage in any man, because of you, for the Lord your God, he is God in Heaven above, and in Earth beneath. Now therefore, I pray you, swear unto me by the Lord, since I have showed you kindness, that ye will also show kindness unto my father's house, and give me a true token, and that you will save alive my father and my mother, and my brethren, and my sisters, and all that they have, and deliver our lives from death. And the men answered her, Our life for yours, if ye utter not this our business. And it shall be, when the Lord hath given us the land that we will deal kindly and truly with thee. Then she let them down by a cord through the window, for her house was upon the town wall, and she dwelt upon the wall. And she said unto them, Get you to the mountain lest the pursuers meet you, and hide yourselves there three days, until the pursuers be returned, and afterward may ye go your way. And the men said unto her, We will be blameless of this thine oath which thou hast made us swear. Behold, when we come into the land thou shalt bind this line of scarlet thread in the window which thou didst let us down by, and thou shalt bring thy father, and thy mother, and thy brethren, and all thy father's household, home unto thee. And it shall be that whosoever shall go out of the doors of thy house into the street, his blood shall be upon his head, and we will be guiltless. And whosoever shall be with thee in the house, his blood shall be on our head, if any hand be upon him. And if thou utter this our business, then we will be quit of thine oath which thou hast made us to swear. And she said, According unto your words, so be it. And she sent them away, and they departed, and she bound the scarlet line in the window. And they went, and came unto the mountain, and abode there three days until the pursuers were returned, and the pursuers sought them throughout all the way, but found them not. So the two men returned and descended from the mountain and passed over, and came to Joshua the son of Nun, and told him all things that befell them. And they said unto Joshua, Truly the Lord hath delivered into our hands all the land, for even all the inhabitants of the country do faint because of us.

And Joshua rose early in the morning, and they removed from Shittim, and came to Jordan, he and all the children of Israel, and lodged there before they passed over. And it came to pass after three days that the officers went through the host and they commanded the people, saying, When ye see the ark of the covenant of the Lord your God, and the priests the Levites bearing it, then ye shall remove from your place, and go after it. Yet there shall be a space between you and it, about two thousand cubits by measure. Come not near unto it, that ye may know the way by which ye must go, for ye have not passed this way heretofore. And Joshua said unto the people, Sanctify yourselves, for tomorrow the Lord will do wonders among you. And Joshua spake unto the priests, saying, Take up the ark of the covenant and pass over before the people. And they took up the ark of the covenant and went before the people.

And the Lord said unto Joshua, This day will I begin to magnify thee in the sight of all Israel that they may know that as I was with Moses, so I will be with thee. And thou shalt command the priests that bear the ark of the covenant, saying, When ye are come to the brink of the water of Jordan ye shall stand still in Jordan. And Joshua said unto the children of Israel, Come hither, and hear the words of the Lord your God. And Joshua said, Hereby ye shall know that the living God is among you, and that he will without fail drive out from before you the Canaanites, and the Hittites, and the Hivites, and the Perizzites, and the Girgashites, and the Amorites, and the Jebusites. Behold, the ark of the covenant of the Lord of all the Earth passeth over before you into Jordan. Now therefore take you twelve men out of the tribes of Israel, out of every tribe a man. And it shall come to pass as soon as the soles of the feet of the priests that bear the ark of the Lord, the Lord of all the Earth, shall rest in the waters of Jordan, that the waters of Jordan shall be cut off from the waters that come down from above, and they shall stand upon a heap.

And it came to pass when the people removed from their tents to pass over the Jordan, and the priests bearing the ark of the covenant before the people, and as they that bare the ark were come unto Jordan, and the feet of the priests that bare the ark were dipped in the brim of the water (for Jordan overfloweth all his banks all the time of harvest), that the waters which came down from above stood and rose up upon a heap very far from the city Adam, that is beside Zaretan, and those that came down toward the sea of the plain, even the salt sea, failed, and were cut off, and the people passed over right against Jericho. And the priests that bare the ark of the covenant of the Lord stood firm on dry ground in the midst of Jordan, and all the Israelites passed over on dry ground, until all the people were passed clean over Jordan.

And it came to pass when all the people were clean passed over Jordan, that the Lord spake unto Joshua, saying, Take you twelve men out of the people, out of every tribe a man, and command ye them, saying, Take you hence out of the midst of Jordan, out of the place where the priests' feet stood firm, twelve stones, and ye shall carry them over with you, and leave them in the lodging place, where ye shall lodge this night. Then Joshua called the twelve men whom he had prepared of the children of Israel, out of every tribe a man, and Joshua said unto them, Pass over before the ark of the Lord your God into the midst of Jordan, and take you up every man of you a stone upon his shoulder, according unto the number of the tribes of the children of Israel, that this may be a sign among you that when your children ask their fathers in time to come, saying, What mean ye by these stones? Then ye shall answer them, That the waters of Jordan were cut off before the ark of the covenant of the Lord, when it passed over Jordan, the waters of Jordan were cut off, and these stones shall be for a memorial unto the children of Israel forever.

And the children of Israel did so as Joshua commanded, and took up twelve stones out of the midst of Jordan, as the Lord spake unto Joshua, according to the number of the tribes of the children of Israel and carried them over with them unto the place where they lodged, and laid them down there. And Joshua set up twelve stones in the midst of Jordan, in the place where the feet of the priests which bare the ark of the covenant stood, and they are there unto this day. For the priests which bare the ark stood in the midst of Jordan, until everything was finished that the Lord commanded Joshua to speak unto the people, according to all that Moses commanded Joshua, and the people hasted and passed over. And it came to pass when all the people were clean passed over, that the ark of the Lord passed over, and the priests in the presence of the people. And the children of Reuben, and the children of Gad, and half the tribe of Manasseh, passed over armed before the children of Israel, as Moses spake unto them, about forty thousand prepared for war passed over before the Lord unto battle, to the plains of Jericho. On that day the Lord magnified Joshua in the sight of all Israel, and they feared him as they feared Moses all the days of his life.

And the Lord spake unto Joshua, saying, Command the priests that bear the ark of the testimony, that they come up out of Jordan. Joshua therefore commanded the priests saying, Come ye up out of Jordan. And it came to pass when the priests that bare the ark of the covenant of the Lord were come up out of the midst of Jordan, and the soles of the priests' feet were lifted up unto the dry land, that the waters of Jordan returned unto their place, and flowed over all his banks, as they did before. And the people came up out of Jordan on the tenth day of the first month, and encamped in Gilgal, in the east border of Jericho. And those twelve stones, which they took out of Jordan, did Joshua pitch in Gilgal. And he spake unto the children of Israel, saying, When your children shall ask their fathers in time to come, saying, What mean these stones? Then ye shall let your children know, saying, Israel came over this Jordan on dry land. For the Lord your God dried up the waters of Jordan from before you, until ye were passed over, as the Lord your God did to the Red Sea, which he dried up from before us, until we were gone over, that all the people of the Earth might know the hand of the Lord, that it is mighty, that ye might fear the Lord your God forever.

And it came to pass when all the kings of the Amorites, which were on the side of Jordan westward, and all the kings of the Canaanites, which were by the sea, heard that the Lord had dried up the waters of Jordan from before the children of Israel, until we were passed over, that their heart melted, neither was there spirit in them any more, because of the children of Israel.

At that time the Lord said unto Joshua, Make thee sharp knives, and circumcise again the children of Israel the second time. And Joshua made him sharp knives and circumcised the children of Israel at the hill of the foreskins. And this is the cause why Joshua did circumcise: All the people that came out of Egypt that were males, even all the men of war died in the wilderness by the way, after they came out of Egypt. Now all the people that came out were circumcised, but all the people that were born in the wilderness by the way as they came forth out of Egypt, them they had not circumcised. For the children of Israel walked forty years in the wilderness till all the people that were men of war, which came out of Egypt, were consumed, because they obeyed not the voice of the Lord, unto whom the Lord sware that he would not show them the land, which the Lord sware unto their fathers that he would give us, a land that floweth with milk and honey. And their children whom he raised up in their stead, them Joshua circumcised, for they were uncircumcised because they had not circumcised them by the way. And it came to pass when they had done circumcising all the people that they abode in their places in the camp till they were whole. And the Lord said unto Joshua, This day have I rolled away the reproach of Egypt from off you. Wherefore the name of the place is called Gilgal unto this day.

And the children of Israel encamped in Gilgal, and kept the passover on the fourteenth day of the month at even in the plains of Jericho. And they did eat of the old corn of the land on the morrow after the passover, unleavened cakes and parched corn in the selfsame day. And the manna ceased on the morrow after they had eaten of the old corn of the land. Neither had the children of Israel manna any more, but they did eat of the fruit of the land of Canaan that year.

And it came to pass when Joshua was by Jericho, that he lifted up his eyes and looked, and, behold, there stood a man over against him with his sword drawn in his hand, and Joshua went unto him, and said unto him, Art thou for us, or for our adversaries? And he said, Nay, but as captain of the host of the Lord am I now come. And Joshua fell on his face to the earth, and did worship and said unto him, What saith my lord unto his servant? And the captain of the Lord's host said unto Joshua, Loose thy shoe from off thy foot for the place whereon thou standest is holy. And Joshua did so.

2 NOW Jericho was straitly shut up because of the children of Israel. None went out, and none came in. And the Lord said unto Joshua, See, I have given into thine hand Jericho, and the king thereof, and the mighty men of valor. And ye shall compass the city, all ye men of war, and go round about the city once. Thus shalt thou do six days. And seven priests shall bear before the ark seven

trumpets of rams' horns, and the seventh day ye shall compass the city seven times, and the priests shall blow with the trumpets. And it shall come to pass, that when they make a long blast with the ram's horn, and when ye hear the sound of the trumpet, all the people shall shout with a great shout, and the wall of the city shall fall down flat, and the people shall ascend up every man straight before him.

And Joshua the son of Nun called the priests, and said unto them, Take up the ark of the covenant, and let seven priests bear seven trumpets of rams' horns before the ark of the Lord. And he said unto the people, Pass on, and compass the city, and let him that is armed pass on before the ark of the Lord. And it came to pass when Joshua had spoken unto the people, that the seven priests bearing the seven trumpets of rams' horns passed on before the Lord, and blew with the trumpets, and the ark of the covenant of the Lord followed them. And the armed men went before the priests that blew with the trumpets, and the rearward came after the ark, the priests going on, and blowing with the trumpets. And Joshua had commanded the people, saying, Ye shall not shout, nor make any noise with your voice, neither shall any word proceed out of your mouth, until the day I bid you shout, then shall ye shout. So the ark of the Lord compassed the city, going about it once, and they came into the camp and lodged in the camp.

And Joshua rose early in the morning, and the priests took up the ark of the Lord. And seven priests bearing seven trumpets of rams' horns before the ark of the Lord went on continually, and blew with the trumpets, and the armed men went before them, but the reward came after the ark of the Lord, the priests going on, and blowing with the trumpets. And the second day they compassed the city once and returned into the camp. So they did six days. And it came to pass on the seventh day that they rose early about the dawning of the day and compassed the city after the same manner seven times, only on that day they compassed the city seven times. And it came to pass the seventh time, when the priests blew with the trumpets, Joshua said unto the people, Shout, for the Lord hath given you the city. And the city shall be accursed, even it, and all that are therein to the Lord. Only Rahab the harlot shall live, she and all that are with her in the house because she hid the messengers that we sent. And ye, in any wise keep yourselves from the accursed thing, lest ye make yourselves accursed, when ye take of the accursed thing, and make the camp of Israel a curse, and trouble it. But all the silver, and gold, and vessels of brass and iron, are consecrated unto the Lord. They shall come into the treasury of the Lord. So the people shouted when the priests blew with the trumpets, and it came to pass when the people heard the sound of the trumpet, and the people shouted with a great shout, that the wall fell down flat, so that the people went up into the city, every man straight before him, and they took the city. And they utterly destroyed all that was in the city, both man and woman, young and old, and ox, and sheep, and ass, with the edge of the sword.

But Joshua had said unto the two men that had spied out the country, Go into the harlot's house, and bring out thence the woman, and all that she hath, as ye sware unto her. And the young men that were spies went in, and brought out Rahab, and her father, and her mother, and her brethren, and all that she had, and they brought out all her kindred, and left them without the camp of Israel. And they burnt the city with fire, and all that was therein, only the silver, and the gold, and the vessels of brass and of iron, they put into the treasury of the house of the Lord. And Joshua saved Rahab the harlot alive, and her father's household, and all that she had, and she dwelleth in Israel even unto this day because she hid the messengers which Joshua sent to spy out Jericho.

And Joshua adjured them at that time, saying, Cursed be the man before the Lord, that riseth up and buildeth this city Jericho, he shall lay the foundation thereof in his firstborn, and in his youngest son shall he set up the gates of it. So the Lord was with Joshua and his fame was noised throughout all the country.

But the children of Israel committed a trespass in the accursed thing, for Achan, the son of Carmi, the son of Zabdi, the son of Zerah of the tribe of Judah, took of the accursed thing, and the anger of the Lord was kindled against the children of Israel. And Joshua sent men from Jericho to Ai, which is beside Bethaven, on the east side of Beth-el, and spake unto them, saying, Go up and view the country. And the men went up and viewed Ai. And they returned to Joshua, and said unto him, Let not all the people go up, but let about two or three thousand men go up and smite Ai, and make not all the people to labor thither for they are but few. So there went up thither of the people about three thousand men, and they fled before the men of Ai. And the men of Ai smote of them about thirty and six men, for they chased them from before the gate even unto Shebarim, and smote them in the going down, wherefore the hearts of the people melted and became as water.

And Joshua rent his clothes and fell to the earth upon his face before the ark of the Lord until the eventide, he and the elders of Israel, and put dust upon their heads. And Joshua said, Alas, O Lord God, wherefore hast thou at all brought this people over Jordan to deliver us into the hand of the Amorites to destroy us? Would to God we had been content and dwelt on the other side Jordan! O Lord, what shall I say when Israel turneth their backs before their enemies! For the Canaanites and all the inhabitants of the land shall hear of it, and shall environ us round, and cut off our name from the Earth, and what wilt thou do unto thy great name? And the Lord said unto Joshua, Get thee up, wherefore liest thou thus upon thy face? Israel hath sinned and they have also transgressed my covenant which I commanded them, for they have even taken of the accursed thing, and have also stolen, and dissembled also and they have put it even among their own stuff. Therefore the children of Israel could not stand before their enemies, but turned their backs before their enemies because they were accursed. Neither will I be with you any more, except ye destroy the accursed from among you. Up, sanctify the people, and say, Sanctify yourselves against tomorrow, for thus saith the Lord God of Israel, There is an accursed thing in the midst of thee, O Israel. Thou canst not stand before thine enemies, until ye take away the accursed thing from among you. In the morning therefore ye shall be brought according to your tribes, and it shall be that the tribe which the Lord taketh shall come according to the families thereof, and the family which the Lord shall take shall come by households, and the household which the Lord shall take shall come man by man. And it shall be that he that is taken with the accursed thing shall be burnt with fire, he and all that he hath, because he hath transgressed the covenant of the Lord and because he hath wrought folly in Israel.

So Joshua rose up early in the morning, and brought Israel by their tribes, and the tribe of Judah was taken, and he brought the family of Judah, and he took the family of the Zarhites, and he brought the family of the Zarhites man by man, and Zabdi was taken, and he brought his household man by man, and Achan, the son of Carmi, the son of Zabdi, the son of Zerah, of the tribe of Judah, was taken. And Joshua said unto Achan, My son, give, I pray thee, glory to the Lord God of Israel and make confession unto him and tell me now what thou hast done. Hide it not from me. And Achan answered Joshua, and said, Indeed I have sinned against the Lord God of Israel, and thus and thus have I done. When I saw among the spoils a goodly Babylonish garment, and two hundred shekels of silver, and a wedge of gold of fifty shekels weight, then I coveted them and took them. And, behold, they are hid in the Earth in the midst of my tent, and the silver under it. So Joshua sent messengers and they ran unto the tent, and behold, it was hid in his tent and the silver under it. And they took them out of the midst of the tent and brought them unto Joshua and unto all the children of Israel, and laid them out before the Lord. And Joshua and all Israel with him took Achan the son of Zerah, and the silver, and the garment, and the wedge of gold, and his sons and his daughters, and his oxen, and his asses, and his sheep, and his tent, and all that he had, and they brought them unto the valley of Achor. And Joshua said, Why hast thou troubled us? The Lord shall trouble thee this day. And all Israel stoned him with stones, and burned them with fire after they had stoned them with stones. And they raised over him a great heap of stones unto this day. So the Lord turned from the fierceness of his anger. Wherefore the name of that place was called, The valley of Achor unto this day.

And the Lord said unto Joshua, Fear not, neither be thou dismayed. Take all the people of war with thee and arise, go up to Ai. See, I have given into thy hand the king of Ai, and his people, and his city, and his land. And thou shalt do to Ai and her king as thou didst unto Jericho and her king; only the spoil thereof, and the cattle thereof shall ye take for a prey unto yourselves. Lay thee an ambush for the city behind it. So Joshua arose, and all the people of war, to go up against Ai, and Joshua chose out thirty thousand mighty men of valor, and sent them away by night. And he commanded them, saying, Behold, ye shall lie in wait against the city, even behind the city. Go not very far from the city, but be ye all ready. And I and all the people that are with me will approach unto the city, and it shall come to pass when they come out against us, as at the first, that we will flee before them. (For they will come out after us,) till we have drawn them from the city. For they will say, They flee before us, as at the first. Therefore we will flee before them. Then ye shall rise up from the ambush and seize upon the city, for the Lord your God will deliver it into your hand. And it shall be when ye have taken the city, that ye shall set the city on fire, according to the commandment of the Lord shall ye do. See, I have commanded you. Joshua therefore sent them forth and they went to lie in ambush, and abode between Beth-el and Ai, on the west side of Ai, but Joshua lodged that night among the people.

And Joshua rose up early in the morning and numbered the people, and went up, he and the elders of Israel, before the people to Ai. And all the people, even the people of war that were with him, went up and drew nigh and came before the city and pitched on the north side of Ai. Now there was a valley between them and Ai. And he took about five thousand men and set them to lie in ambush between Beth-el and Ai, on the west side of the city. And when they had set the people, even all the host that was on the north of the city, and their liers in wait on the west of the city, Joshua went that night into the midst of the valley. And it came to pass when the king of Ai saw it, that they hasted and rose up early, and the men of the city went out against Israel to battle, he and all his people, at a time appointed, before the plain. But he wist not that there were liers in ambush against him behind the city. And Joshua and all Israel made as if they were beaten before them, and fled by the way of the wilderness. And all the people that were in Ai were called together to pursue after them and they pursued after Joshua, and were drawn away from the city. And there was not a man left in Ai or Beth-el that went not out after Israel, and they left the city open and pursued after Israel. And the Lord said unto Joshua, Stretch out the spear that is in thy hand toward Ai, for I will give it into thine hand. And Joshua stretched out the spear that he had in his hand toward the city. And the ambush arose quickly out of their place and they ran as soon as he had stretched out his hand, and they entered into the city and took it, and hasted and set the city on fire. And when the men of Ai looked behind them they saw, and behold, the smoke of the city ascended up to Heaven and they had no power to flee this way or that way, and the people that fled to the wilderness turned back upon the pursuers. And when Joshua and all Israel saw that the ambush had taken the city and that the smoke of the city ascended, then they turned again, and slew the men of Ai. And the other issued out of the city against them so they were in the midst of Israel, some on this side, and some on that side. And they smote them so that they let none of them remain or escape. And the king of Ai they took alive and brought him to Joshua.

And it came to pass when Israel had made an end of slaying all the inhabitants of Ai in the field, in the wilderness wherein they chased them, and when they were all fallen on the edge of the sword, until they were consumed, that all the Israelites returned unto Ai and smote it with the edge of the sword. And so it was that all that fell that day, both of men and women, were twelve thousand, even all the men of Ai. For Joshua drew not his hand back, wherewith he stretched out the spear until he had utterly destroyed all the inhabitants of Ai. Only the cattle and the spoil of that city Israel took for a prey unto themselves, according unto the word of the Lord which he commanded Joshua. And Joshua burnt Ai and made it a heap forever, even a desolation unto this day. And the king of Ai he hanged on a tree until eventide, and as soon as the sun was down Joshua commanded that they should take his carcass down from the tree and cast it at the entering of the gate of the city, and raise thereon a great heap of stones that remaineth unto this day.

Then Joshua built an altar unto the Lord God of Israel in mount Ebal, as Moses the servant of the Lord commanded the children of Israel, as it is written in the book of the law of Moses, an altar of whole stones over which no man hath lifted up any iron. And they offered thereon burnt offerings unto the Lord and sacrificed peace offerings. And he wrote there upon the stones a copy of the law of Moses, which he wrote in the presence of the children of Israel. And all Israel, and their elders, and officers, and their judges, stood on this side the ark and on that side before the priests the Levites, which bare the ark of the covenant of the Lord; as well the stranger, as he that was born among them, half of them over against mount Gerizim, and half of them over against mount Ebal, as Moses the servant of the Lord had commanded before, that they should bless the people of Israel. And afterward he read all the words of the law, the blessings and cursings, according to all that is written in the book of the law. There was not a word of all that Moses commanded, which Joshua read not before all the congregation of Israel, with the women, and the little ones, and the strangers that were conversant among them.

And it came to pass when all the kings which were on this side Jordan, in the hills, and in the valleys, and in all the coasts of the great sea over against Lebanon, the Hittite, and the Amorite, the Canaanite, the Perizzite, the Hivite, and the Jebusite, heard thereof, that they gathered themselves together to fight with Joshua and with Israel with one accord. And when the inhabitants of Gibeon heard what Joshua had done unto Jericho and to Ai, they did work wilily, and went and made as if they had been ambassadors, and took old sacks upon their asses, and wine bottles, old and rent and bound up, and old shoes and clouted upon their feet, and old garments upon them, and all the bread of their provision was dry and moldy. And they went to Joshua unto the camp at Gilgal, and said unto him and to the men of Israel, We be come from a far country, now therefore make ye a league with us. And the men of Israel said unto the Hivites, Peradventure ye dwell among us, and how shall we make a league with you? And they said unto Joshua, We are thy servants. And Joshua said unto them, Who are ye? And from whence come ye? And they said unto him, From a very far country thy servants are come, because of the name of the Lord thy God, for we have heard the fame of him and all that he did in Egypt. And all that he did to the two kings of the

Amorites that were beyond Jordan, to Sihon king of Heshbon, and to Og king of Bashan, which was at Ashtaroth. Wherefore our elders and all the inhabitants of our country spake to us, saying, Take victuals with you for the journey and go to meet them and say unto them, We are your servants, therefore now make ye a league with us. This our bread we took hot for our provision out of our houses on the day we came forth to go unto you, but now, behold, it is dry and it is moldy. And these bottles of wine which we filled were new, and behold, they be rent. And these our garments and our shoes are become old by reason of the very long journey. And the men took of their victuals and asked not counsel at the mouth of the Lord. And Joshua made peace with them and made a league with them to let them live, and the princes of the congregation sware unto them.

And it came to pass at the end of three days after they had made a league with them, that they heard that they were their neighbors, and that they dwelt among them. And the children of Israel journeyed and came unto their cities on the third day. Now their cities were Gibeon, and Chephirah, and Beeroth, and Kirjath-jearim. And the children of Israel smote them not because the princes of the congregation had sworn unto them by the Lord God of Israel. And all the congregation murmured against the princes. But all the princes said unto all the congregation, We have sworn unto them by the Lord God of Israel, now therefore we may not touch them. This we will do to them, we will even let them live lest wrath be upon us because of the oath which we sware unto them. And the princes said unto them, Let them live, but let them be hewers of wood and drawers of water unto all the congregation, as the princes had promised them. And Joshua called for them and he spake unto them saying, Wherefore have ye beguiled us saying, We are very far from you, when ye dwell among us? Now therefore ye are cursed and there shall none of you be freed from being bondmen and hewers of wood and drawers of water for the house of my God. And they answered Joshua and said, Because it was certainly told thy servants, how that the Lord thy God commanded his servant Moses to give you all the land and to destroy all the inhabitants of the land from before you, therefore we were sore afraid of our lives because of you and have done this thing. And now behold, we are in thine hand as it seemeth good and right unto thee to do unto us, do. And so did he unto them and delivered them out of the hand of the children of Israel that they slew them not. And Joshua made them that day hewers of wood and drawers of water for the congregation, and for the altar of the Lord, even unto this day, in the place which he should choose.

Now it came to pass, when Adoni-zedek king of Jerusalem had heard how Joshua had taken Ai and had utterly destroyed it as he had done to Jericho and her king, as he had done to Ai and her king, and how the inhabitants of Gibeon had made peace with Israel, and were among them, that they feared greatly because Gibeon was a great city, as one of the royal cities, and because it was greater than Ai, and all the men thereof were mighty. Wherefore Adoni-zedek king of Jerusalem sent unto Hoham king of Hebron, and unto Piram king of Jarmuth, and unto Japhia king of Lachish, and unto Debir king of Eglon, saying, Come up unto me and help me, that we may smite Gibeon, for it hath made peace with Joshua and with the children of Israel. Therefore the five kings of the Amorites, the king of Jerusalem, the king of Hebron, the king of Jarmuth, the king of Lachish, the king of Eglon, gathered themselves together and went up, they and all their hosts, and encamped before Gibeon and made war against it.

And the men of Gibeon sent unto Joshua to the camp to Gilgal saying, Slack not thy hand from thy servants, come up to us quickly, and save us and help us, for all the kings of the Amorites that dwell in the mountains are gathered together against us. So Joshua ascended from Gilgal, he and all the people of war with him, and all the mighty men of valor. And the Lord said unto Joshua, Fear them not, for I have delivered them into thine hand. There shall not a man of them stand before thee. Joshua therefore came unto them suddenly and went up from Gilgal all night. And the Lord discomfited them before Israel, and slew them with a great slaughter at Gibeon and chased them along the way that goeth up to Beth-horon, and smote them to Azekah, and unto Makkedah. And it came to pass as they fled from before Israel and were in the going down to Beth-horon, that the Lord cast down great stones from Heaven upon them unto Azekah and they died. They were more which died with hailstones than they whom the children of Israel slew with the sword.

Then spake Joshua to the Lord in the day when the Lord delivered up the Amorites before the children of Israel, and he said in the sight of Israel, Sun, stand thou still upon Gibeon, and thou, Moon, in the valley of Ajalon. And the sun stood still, and the moon stayed, until the people had avenged themselves upon their enemies. Is not this written in the book of Jasher? So the sun stood still in the midst of Heaven and hasted not to go down about a whole day. And there was no day like that before it or after it, that the Lord hearkened unto the voice of a man, for the Lord fought for Israel.

And Joshua returned, and all Israel with him, unto the camp to Gilgal. But these five kings fled and hid themselves in a cave at Makkedah. And it was told Joshua saying, The five kings are found hid in a cave at Makkedah. And Joshua said, Roll great stones upon the mouth of the cave and set men by it for to keep them, and stay ye not, but pursue after your enemies and smite the hindmost of them. Suffer them not to enter into their cities, for the Lord your God hath delivered them into your hand. And it came to pass when Joshua and the children of Israel had made an end of slaying them with a very great slaughter, till they were consumed, that the rest which remained of them entered into fenced cities. And all the people returned to the camp to Joshua at Makkedah in peace, none moved his tongue against any of the children of Israel. Then said Joshua, Open the mouth of the cave and bring out those five kings unto me out of the cave. And they did so and brought forth those five kings unto him out of the cave, the king of Jerusalem, the king of Hebron, the king of Jarmuth, the king of Lachish, and the king of Eglon. And it came to pass when they brought out those kings unto Joshua, that Joshua called for all the men of Israel, and said unto the captains of the men of war which went with him, Come near, put your feet upon the necks of these kings. And they came near, and put their feet upon the necks of them. And Joshua said unto them, Fear not nor be dismayed; be strong and of good courage, for thus shall the Lord do to all your enemies against whom ye fight. And afterward Joshua smote them and slew them, and hanged them on five trees, and they were hanging upon the trees until the evening. And it came to pass at the time of the going down of the sun, that Joshua commanded, and they took them down off the trees and cast them into the cave wherein they had been hid, and laid great stones in the cave's mouth which remain until this very day.

And that day Joshua took Makkedah and smote it with the edge of the sword, and the king thereof he utterly destroyed, them, and all the souls that were therein. He let none remain, and he did to the king of Makkedah as he did unto the king of Jericho. Then Joshua passed from Makkedah, and all Israel with him, unto Libnah and fought against Libnah. And the Lord delivered it also, and the king thereof into the hand of Israel, and he smote it with the edge of the sword, and all the souls that were therein. He let none remain in it, but did unto the king thereof as he did unto the king of Jericho. And Joshua passed from Libnah, and all Israel with him, unto Lachish, and encamped against it and fought against it. And the Lord delivered Lachish into the hand of Israel, which took it on the second day, and smote it with the edge of the sword, and all the souls that were therein according to all that he had done to Libnah. Then Horam king of Gezer came up to help Lachish, and Joshua smote him and his people until he had left him none remaining. And from Lachish Joshua passed unto Eglon, and all Israel with him, and they encamped against it and fought against it. And they took it on that day, and smote it with the edge of the sword, and all the souls that were therein he utterly destroyed that day according to all that he had done to Lachish. And Joshua went up from Eglon, and all Israel with him, unto Hebron and they fought against it. And they took it and smote it with the edge of the sword, and the king thereof, and all the cities thereof, and all the souls that were therein, he left none remaining according to all that he had done to Eglon, but destroyed it utterly, and all the souls that were therein. And Joshua returned, and all Israel with him, to Debir and fought against it. And he took it, and the king thereof, and all the cities thereof, and they smote them with the edge of the sword and utterly destroyed all the souls that were therein. He left none remaining as he had done to Hebron, so he did to Debir, and to the king thereof, as he had done also to Libnah, and to her king.

So Joshua smote all the country of the hills, and of the south, and of the vale, and of the springs, and all their kings, he left none remaining, but utterly destroyed all that breathed as the Lord God of Israel commanded. And Joshua smote them from Kadesh-barnea even unto Gaza, and all the country of Goshen, even unto Gibeon. And all these kings and their land did Joshua take at one time, because the Lord God of Israel fought for Israel. And Joshua returned and all Israel with him, unto the camp to Gilgal.

And it came to pass, when Jabin king of Hazor had heard those things, that he sent to Jobab king of Madon, and to the king of Shimron, and to the king of Achshaph, and to the kings that were on the north of the mountains, and of the plains south of Chinneroth, and in the valley, and in the borders of Dor on the west, and to the Canaanite on the east and on the west, and to the Amorite, and the Hittite, and the Perizzite, and the Jebusite in the mountains, and to the Hivite under Hermon in the land of Mizpeh. And they went out, they and all their hosts with them, much people, even as the sand that is upon the seashore in multitude, with horses and chariots very many. And when all these kings were met together they came and pitched together at the waters of Merom to fight against Israel. And the Lord said unto Joshua, Be not afraid because of them for tomorrow about this time will I deliver them up all slain before Israel, thou shalt hough their horses, and burn their chariots with fire. So Joshua came and all the people of war with him, against them by the waters of Merom suddenly, and they fell upon them. And the Lord delivered them into the hand of Israel, who smote them, and chased them unto great Zidon, and unto Misrephoth-maim, and unto the valley of Mizpeh eastward. And they smote them until they left them none remaining. And Joshua did unto them as the Lord bade him, he houghed their horses and burnt their chariots with fire.

And Joshua at that time turned back and took Hazor, and smote the king thereof with the sword, for Hazor beforetime was the head of all those kingdoms. And they smote all the souls that were therein with the edge of the sword, utterly destroying them. There was not any left to breathe, and he burnt Hazor with fire. And all the cities of those kings and all the kings of them did Joshua take, and smote them with the edge of the sword. And he utterly destroyed them as Moses the servant of the Lord commanded. But as for the cities that stood still in their strength, Israel burned none of them, save Hazor only, that did Joshua burn. And all the spoil of these cities and the cattle, the children of Israel took for a prey unto themselves, but every man they smote with the edge of the sword, until they had destroyed them, neither left they any to breathe.

As the Lord commanded Moses his servant, so did Moses command Joshua, and so did Joshua. He left nothing undone of all that the Lord commanded Moses.

So Joshua took all that land, the hills, and all the south country, and all the land of Goshen, and the valley, and the plain, and the mountain of Israel, and the valley of the same, even from the mount Halak, that goeth up to Seir, even unto Baal-gad in the valley of Lebanon under mount Hermon. And all their kings he took, and smote them and slew them. Joshua made war a long time with all those kings. There was not a city that made peace with the children of Israel, save the Hivites the inhabitants of Gibeon, all other they took in battle. For it was of the Lord to destroy them utterly, because they hardened their hearts that they should come against Israel in battle, that they might have no favor, that they might destroy them in battle, as the Lord commanded Moses. And at that time came Joshua, and cut off the Anakim from the mountains, from Hebron, from Debir, from Anab, and from all the mountains of Judah, and from all the mountains of Israel, Joshua destroyed them utterly with their cities. There was none of the Anakim left in the land of the children of Israel, only in Gaza, in Gath, and in Ashdod, there remained. So Joshua took the whole land according to all that the Lord said unto Moses, and Joshua gave it for an inheritance unto Israel according to their divisions by their tribes. And the land rested from war.

Now these are the kings of the land which the children of Israel smote and possessed their land on the other side Jordan toward the rising of the sun, from the river Arnon unto mount Hermon, and all the plain on the east: Sihon king of the Amorites, who dwelt in Heshbon, and ruled from Aroer, which is upon the bank of the river Arnon, and from the middle of the river, and from half Gilead, even unto the river Jabbok, which is the border of the children of Ammon, and from the plain to the sea of Chinneroth on the east, and unto the sea of the plain, even the salt sea on the east, the way to Beth-jeshimoth, and from the south, under Ashdoth-pisgah, and the coast of Og king of Bashan, which was of the remnant of the giants, that dwelt at Ashtaroth and at Edrei, and reigned in mount Hermon, and in Salcah, and in all Bashan, unto the border of the Geshurites and the Maachathites, and half Gilead, the border of Sihon king of Heshbon. Them did Moses the servant of the Lord and the children of Israel smite, and Moses the servant of the Lord gave it for a possession unto the Reubenites, and the Gadites, and the half tribe of Manasseh. And these are the kings of the country which Joshua and the children of Israel smote on this side Jordan on the west, from Baal-gad in the valley of Lebanon even unto the mount Halek, that goeth up to Seir, which Joshua gave unto the tribes of Israel for a possession according to their divisions: in the mountains, and in the valleys, and in the plains, and in the springs, and in the wilderness, and in the south country, the Hittites, the Amorites, and the Canaanites, the Perizzites, the Hivites, and the Jebusites, the king of Jericho, the king of Ai, which is beside Beth-el, the king of Jerusalem, the king of Hebron, the king of Jarmuth, the king of Lachish, the king of Eglon, the king of Gezer, the king of Debir, the king of Geder, the king of Hormah, the king of Arad, the king of Libnah, the king of Adullam, the king of Makkedah, the king of Beth-el, the king of Tappuah, the king of Hepher, the king of Aphek, the king of Lasharon, the king of Madon, the king of Hazor, the king of Shimron-meron, the king of Achshaph, the king of Taanach, the king of Megiddo, the king of Kedesh, the king of Jokneam of Carmel, the king of Dor in the coast of Dor, the king of the nations of Gilgal, the king of Tirzah; all the kings thirty and one.

3 NOW Joshua was old and stricken in years, and the Lord said unto him, Thou art old and stricken in years and there remaineth yet very much land to be possessed. This is the land that yet remaineth: all the borders of the Philistines, and all Geshuri, From Sihor, which is before Egypt, even unto the borders of Ekron

northward, which is counted to the Canaanites, five lords of the Philistines, the Gazathites, and the Ashdothites, the Eshkalonites, the Gitites, and the Ekronites, also the Avites, from the south, all the land of the Canaanites, and Mearah that is beside the Sidonians, unto Aphek, to the borders of the Amorites, and the land of the Giblites, and all Lebanon toward the sunrising, from Baal-gad under mount Hermon unto the entering into Hamath. All the inhabitants of the hill country from Lebanon unto Misrephoth-maim, and all the Sidonians, them will I drive out before the children of Israel, only divide thou it by lot unto the Israelites for an inheritance, as I have commanded thee. Now therefore divide this land for an inheritance unto the nine tribes, and the half tribe of Manasseh, with whom the Reubenites and the Gadites have received their inheritance, which Moses gave them, beyond Jordan eastward, even as Moses the servant of the Lord gave them, from Aroer, that is upon the bank of the river Arnon, and the city that is in the midst of the river, and all the plain of Medeba unto Dibon, and all the cities of Sihon king of the Amorites, which reigned in Heshbon, unto the border of the children of Ammon, and Gilead, and the border of the Geshurites and Maachathites, and all mount Hermon, and all Bashan unto Salcah, all the kingdom of Og in Bashan, which reigned in Ashtaroth and in Edrei, who remained of the remnant of the giants, for these did Moses smite, and cast them out. Nevertheless the children of Israel expelled not the Geshurites, nor the Maachathites, but the Geshurites and the Maachathites dwell among the Israelites until this day. Only unto the tribe of Levi he gave none inheritance, the sacrifices of the Lord God of Israel made by fire are their inheritance, as he said unto them.

And Moses gave unto the tribe of the children of Reuben inheritance according to their families. And their coast was from Aroer, that is on the bank of the river Arnon, and the city that is in the midst of the river, and all the plain by Medeba, Heshbon, and all her cities that are in the plain, Dibon, and Bamoth-baal, and Beth-baal-meon, and Jahaza, and Kedemoth, and Mephaath, and Kirjathaim, and Sibmah, and Zareth-shahar in the mount of the valley, and Beth-peor, and Ashdoth-pisgah, and Beth-jeshimoth, and all the cities of the plain, and all the kingdom of Sihon king of the Amorites, which reigned in Heshbon, whom Moses smote with the princes of Midian, Evi, and Rekem, and Zur, and Hur, and Reba, which were dukes of Sihon, dwelling in the country. Balaam also the son of Beor, the soothsayer, did the children of Israel slay with the sword among them that were slain by them. And the border of the children of Reuben was Jordan, and the border thereof. This was the inheritance of the children of Reuben after their families, the cities and the villages thereof.

And Moses gave inheritance unto the tribe of Gad, even unto the children of Gad, according to their families. And their coast was Jazer, and all the cities of Gilead, and half the land of the children of Ammon, unto Aroer that is before Rabbah, and from Heshbon unto Ramath-mispeh, and Betonim, and from Mahanaim unto the border of Debir, and in the valley, Betharam, and Beth-nimrah, and Succoth, and Zaphon, the rest of the kingdom of Sihon king of Heshbon, Jordan and his border, even unto the edge of the sea of Chinnereth on the other side Jordan eastward. This is the inheritance of the children of Gad after their families, the cities and their villages.

And Moses gave inheritance unto the half tribe of Manasseh, and this was the possession of the half tribe of the children of Manasseh by their families. And their coast was from Mahanaim, all Bashan, all the kingdom of Og king of Bashan, and all the towns of Jair, which are in Bashan, threescore cities, and half Gilead, and Ashtaroth, and Edrei, cities of the kingdom of Og in Bashan, were pertaining unto the children of Machir the son of Manasseh, even to the one half of the children of Machir by their families. These are the countries which Moses did distribute for inheritance in the plains of Moab, on the other side Jordan by Jericho eastward. But unto the tribe of Levi Moses gave not any inheritance, the Lord God of Israel was their inheritance, as he said unto them.

And these are the countries which the children of Israel inherited in the land of Canaan, which Eleazar the priest, and Joshua the son of Nun, and the heads of the fathers of the tribes of the children of Israel distributed for inheritance to them. By lot was their inheritance, as the Lord commanded by the hand of Moses, for the nine tribes, and for the half tribe. For Moses had given the inheritance of two tribes and a half tribe on the other side Jordan, but unto the Levites he gave none inheritance among them. For the children of Joseph were two tribes, Manasseh and Ephraim; therefore they gave no part unto the Levites in the land save cities to dwell in, with their suburbs for their cattle and for their substance. As the Lord commanded Moses, so the children of Israel did, and they divided the land.

Then the children of Judah came unto Joshua in Gilgal, and Caleb the son of Jephunneh the Kenezite said unto him, Thou knowest the thing that the Lord said unto Moses the man of God concerning me and thee in Kadesh-barnea. Forty years old was I when Moses the servant of the Lord sent me from Kadesh-barnea to espy out the land, and I brought him word again as it was in mine heart. Nevertheless my brethren that went up with me made the heart of the people melt, but I wholly followed the Lord my God. And Moses sware on that day, saying, Surely the land whereon thy feet have trodden shall be thine inheritance and thy children's for ever, because thou hast wholly followed the Lord my God. And now behold, the Lord hath kept me alive, as he said, these forty and five years, even since the Lord spake this word unto Moses while the children of Israel wandered in the wilderness, and now, lo, I am this day four-score and five years old. As yet I am as strong this day as I was in the day that Moses sent me, as my strength was then even so is my strength now for war, both to go out and to come in. Now therefore give me this mountain, whereof the Lord spake in that day, for thou heardest in that day how the Anakim were there and that the cities were great and fenced, if so be the Lord will be with me, then I shall be able to drive them out, as the Lord said. And Joshua blessed him, and gave unto Caleb, the son of Jephunneh, Hebron for an inheritance. Hebron therefore became the inheritance of Caleb the son of Jephunneh the Kenezite unto this day, because that he wholly followed the Lord God of Israel. And the name of Hebron before was Kirjath-arba, which Arba was a great man among the Anakim. And the land had rest from war.

This then was the lot of the tribe of the children of Judah by their families, even to the border of Edom the wilderness of Zin southward was the uttermost part of the south coast. And their south border was from the shore of the salt sea, from the bay that looketh southward, and it went out to the south side to Maaleh-acrabbim, and passed along to Zin, and ascended up on the south side unto Kadesh-barnea, and passed along to Hezron, and went up to Adar, and fetched a compass to Karkaa. From thence it passed toward Azmon, and went out unto the river of Egypt, and the goings out of that coast were at the sea, this shall be your south coast. And the east border was the salt sea, even unto the end of Jordan. And their border in the north quarter was from the bay of the sea at the uttermost part of Jordan. And the border went up to Bethhogla, and passed along by the north of Beth-arabah, and the border went up to the stone of Bohan the son of Reuben. And the border went up toward Debir from the valley of Achor, and so northward looking toward Gilgal, that is before the going up to Adummim, which is on the south side of the river, and the border passed toward the waters of En-shemesh, and the goings out thereof were at En-rogel. And the border went up by the valley of the son of Hinnom unto the south side of the Jebusite, the same is Jerusalem, and the border went up to the top of the mountain that lieth before the valley of Hinnom westward, which is at the end of the valley of the giants northward. And the border was drawn from the top of the hill unto the fountain of the water of Nephtoah, and went out to the cities of mount Ephron, and the border was drawn to Baalah, which is Kirjath-jearim. And the border compassed from Baalah westward unto mount Seir, and passed along unto the side of mount Jearim, which is Chesalon on the north side, and went down to Bethshemesh, and passed on to Timnah. And the border went out unto the side of Ekron northward, and the border was drawn to Shicron and passed along to mount Baalah and went out unto Jabneel, and the goings out of the border were at the sea. And the west border was to the great sea and the coast thereof. This is the coast of the children of Judah round about according to their families.

And unto Caleb the son of Jephunneh he gave a part among the children of Judah according to the commandment of the Lord to Joshua, even the city of Arba the father of Anak, which city is Hebron. And Caleb drove thence the three sons of Anak, Sheshai, and Ahiman, and Talmai, the children of Anak. And he went up thence to the inhabitants of Debir, and the name of Debir before was Kirjath-sepher. And Caleb said, He that smiteth Kirjath-sepher, and taketh it, to him will I give Achsah my daughter to wife. And Othniel the son of Kenaz, the brother of Caleb, took it and he gave him Achsah his daughter to wife. And it came to pass as she came unto him that she moved him to ask of her father a field, and she lighted off her ass, and Caleb said unto her, What wouldest thou? Who answered, Give me a blessing for thou hast given me a south land. Give me also springs of water. And he gave her the upper springs and the nether springs.

This is the inheritance of the tribe of the children of Judah according to their families. And the uttermost cities of the tribe of the children of Judah toward the coast of Edom southward were Kabzeel, and Eder, and Jagur, and Kinah, and Dimonah, and Adadah, and Kedesh, and Hazor, and Ithnan, Ziph, and Telem, and Bealoth, and Hazor, Hadattah, and Kerioth, and Hezron, which is Hazor, Amam, and Shema, and Moladah, and Hazar-gaddah, and Heshmon, and Beth-palet, and Hazar-shual, and Beer-sheba, and Bizjothjah, Baalah, and Iim, and Azem, and Eltolad, and Chesil, and Hormah, and Ziklag, and Madmannah and Sansannah, and Lebaoth, and Shilhim, and Ain, and Rimmon. All the cities are twenty and nine, with their villages. And in the valley, Eshtaol, and Zoreah, and Ashnah, and Zanoah, and En-gannim, Tappuah, and Enam, Jarmuth, and Adullam, Socoh, and Azehkah, and Sharaim, and Adithaim, and Gederah, and Gederothaim, fourteen cities with their villages; Zenan, and Hadashah, and Migdal-gad, and Dilean, and Mizpeh, and Joktheel, Lachish, and Bozkath, and Eglon, and Cabbon, and Lahmam, and Kithlish, and Gederoth, Beth-dagon, and Naamah, and Makkedah, sixteen cities with their villages; Libnah, and Ether, and Ashan, and Jiphtah, and Ashnah, and Nezib, and Keilah, and Achzib, and Mareshah, nine cities with their villages; Ekron, with her towns and her villages, from Ekron even unto the sea, all that lay near Ashdod, with their villages; Ashdod, with her towns and her villages; Gaza, with her towns and her villages, unto the river of Egypt, and the great sea, and the border thereof. And in the mountains, Shamir, and Jattir, and Socoh, and Dannah, and Kirjath-sannah, which is Debir, and Anab, and Eshtemoh, and Anim, and Goshen, and Holon, and Giloh, eleven cities with their villages; arab and Dumah, and Eshean, and Janum, and Beth-tappuah, and Aphekah, and Humtah, and Kirjatharba, which is Hebron and Zior, nine cities with their villages; Maon, Carmel, and Ziph, and Juttah, and Jezreel, and Jokdeam, and Zanoah, Cain, Gibeah, and Timnah, ten cities with their villages; Halhul, Beth-zur, and Gedor, and Maarath, and Bethanoth, and Eltekon, six cities with their villages; Kirjath-baal, which is Kirjath-jearim, and Rabbah, two cities with their villages; in the wilderness, Beth-arabah, Middin, and Secacah, and Nibshan, and the city of Salt, and En-gedi, six cities with their villages. As for the Jebusites the inhabitants of Jerusalem, the children of Judah could not drive them out, but the Jebusites dwell with the children of Judah at Jerusalem unto this day.

And the lot of the children of Joseph fell from Jordan by Jericho, unto the water of Jericho on the east, to the wilderness that goeth up from Jericho throughout mount Beth-el, and goeth out from Beth-el to Luz, and passeth along unto the borders of Archi to Ataroth, and goeth down westward to the coast of Japhleti, unto the coast of Beth-horon, the nether, and to Gezer, and the goings out thereof are at the sea. So the children of Joseph, Manasseh and Ephraim, took their inheritance. And the border of the children of Ephraim according to their families was thus, even the border of their inheritance on the east side was Ataroth-addar, unto Beth-horon the upper, and the border went out toward the sea to Michmethah on the north side, and the border went about eastward unto Taanath-shiloh, and passed by it on the east to Janohah, and it went down from Janohah to Ataroth, and to Naarath, and came to Jericho and went out at Jordan. The border went out from Tappuah westward unto the river Kanah, and the goings out thereof were at the sea. This is the inheritance of the tribe of the children of Ephraim by their families. And the separate cities for the children of Ephraim were among the inheritance of the children of Manasseh, all the cities with their villages. And they drave not out the Canaanites that dwelt in Gezer, but the Canaanites dwell among the Ephraimites unto this day and serve unto tribute.

There was also a lot for the tribe of Manasseh, for he was the firstborn of Joseph, to wit, for Machir the firstborn of Manasseh, the father of Gilead, because he was a man of war, therefore he had Gilead and Bashan. There was also a lot for the rest of the children of Manasseh by their families, for the children of Abiezer, and for the children of Helek, and for the children of Asriel, and for the children of Shechem, and for the children of Hepher, and for the children of Shemida, these were the male children of Manasseh the son of Joseph by their families. But Zelophehad, the son of Hepher, the son of Gilead, the son of Machir, the son of Manasseh, had no sons, but daughters, and these are the names of his daughters, Mahlah, and Noah, Hoglah, Milcah, and Tirzah. And they came near before Eleazar the priest, and before Joshua the son of Nun, and before the princes, saying, The Lord commanded Moses to give us an inheritance among our brethren. Therefore, according to the commandment of the Lord, he gave them an inheritance among the brethren of their father. And there fell ten portions to Manasseh, besides the land of Gilead and Bashan, which were on the other side of Jordan, because the daughters of Manasseh had an inheritance among his sons, and the rest of Manasseh's sons had the land of Gilead.

And the coast of Manasseh was from Asher to Michmethah, that lieth before Shechem, and the border went along on the right hand unto the inhabitants of En-tappuah. Now Manasseh had the land of Tappuah, but Tappuah on the border of Manasseh belonged to the children of Ephraim. And the coast descended unto the river Kanah, southward of the river. These cities of Ephraim are among the cities of Manasseh, the coast of Manasseh also was on the north side of the river, and the outgoings of it were at the sea. Southward it was Ephraim's, and northward it was Manasseh's, and the sea is his border, and they met together in Asher on the north, and in Issachar on the east. And Manasseh had in Issachar and in Asher Beth-shean and her towns, and Ibleam and her towns, and the inhabitants of Dor and her towns, and the inhabitants of Endor and her towns, and the inhabitants of Taanach and her towns, and the inhabitants of Megiddo and her towns, even three countries. Yet the children of Manasseh could not drive out the inhabitants of those cities, but the Canaanites would dwell in that land.

Yet it came to pass when the children of Israel were waxen strong, that they put the Canaanites to tribute, but did not utterly drive them out.

And the children of Joseph spake unto Joshua, saying, Why hast thou given me but one lot and one portion to inherit, seeing I am a great people, forasmuch as the Lord hath blessed me hitherto? And Joshua answered them, If thou be a great people, then get thee up to the wood country and cut down for thyself there in the land of the Perizzites and of the giants, if mount Ephraim be too narrow for thee. And the children of Joseph said, The hill is not enough for us, and all the Canaanites that dwell in the land of the valley have chariots of iron, both they who are of Bethshean and her towns, and they who are of the valley of Jezreel. And Joshua spake unto the house of Joseph, even to Ephraim and to Manasseh, saying, Thou art a great people, and hast great power. Thou shalt not have one lot only, but the mountain shall be thine, for it is a wood, and thou shalt cut it down, and the outgoings of it shall be thine, for thou shalt drive out the Canaanites, though they have iron chariots and though they be strong.

And the whole congregation of the children of Israel assembled together at Shiloh and set up the tabernacle of the congregation there, and the land was subdued before them. And there remained among the children of Israel seven tribes which had not yet received their inheritance. And Joshua said unto the children of Israel, How long are ye slack to go to possess the land which the Lord God of your fathers hath given you? Give out from among you three men for each tribe, and I will send them, and they shall rise and go through the land and describe it according to the inheritance of them, and they shall come again to me. And they shall divide it into seven parts, Judah shall abide in their coast on the south, and the house of Joseph shall abide in their coasts on the north. Ye shall therefore describe the land into seven parts and bring the description hither to me that I may cast lots for you here before the Lord our God. But the Levites have no part among you, for the priesthood of the Lord is their inheritance, and Gad, and Reuben, and half the tribe of Manasseh have received their inheritance beyond Jordan on the east, which Moses the servant of the Lord gave them. And the men arose and went away, and Joshua charged them that went to describe the land, saying, Go and walk through the land and describe it and come again to me that I may here cast lots for you before the Lord in Shiloh. And the men went and passed through the land and described it by cities into seven parts in a book, and came again to Joshua to the host at Shiloh. And Joshua cast lots for them in Shiloh before the Lord and there Joshua divided the land unto the children of Israel according to their divisions.

And the lot of the tribe of the children of Benjamin came up according to their families, and the coast of their lot came forth between the children of Judah and the children of Joseph. And their border on the north side was from Jordan, and the border went up to the side of Jericho on the north side and went up through the mountains westward, and the goings out thereof were at the wilderness of Beth-aven. And the border went over from thence toward Luz, to the side of Luz, which is Beth-el southward, and the border descended to Ataroth-adar, near the hill that lieth on the south side of the nether Beth-horon. And the border was drawn thence and compassed the corner of the sea southward from the hill that lieth before Beth-horon southward, and the goings out thereof were at Kirjah-baal, which is Kirjath-jearim, a city of the children of Judah. This was the west quarter. And the south quarter was from the end of Kirjath-jearim, and the border went out on the west and went out to the well of waters of Nephtoah. And the border came down to the end of the mountain that lieth before the valley of the son of Hinnom, and which is the valley of the giants on the north, and descended to the valley of Hinnom, to the side of Jebusi on the south, and descended to En-rogel, and was drawn from the north, and went forth to Enshemesh, and went forth toward Geliloth, which is over against the going up of Adummim, and descended to the stone of Bohan the son of Reuben, and passed along toward the side over against Arabah northward, and went down unto Arabah. And the border passed along to the side of Beth-hoglah northward, and the outgoings of the border were at the north bay of the salt sea at the south end of Jordan. This was the south coast. And Jordan was the border of it on the east side. This was the inheritance of the children of Benjamin, by the coasts thereof round about according to their families. Now the cities of the tribe of the children of Benjamin according to their families were Jericho, and Beth-hoglah, and the valley of Keziz, and Beth-arabah, and Zemaraim, and Beth-el, and Avim, and Parah, and Ophrah, and Chephar-haammonai, and Ophni, and Gaba, twelve cities with their villages; Gibeon, and Ramah, and Beeroth, and Mizpeh, and Chephirah, and Mozah, and Rekem, and Irpeel, and Taralah, and Zelah, Eleph, and Jebusi, which is Jerusalem, Gibeath, and Kirjath, fourteen cities with their villages. This is the inheritance of the children of Benjamin according to their families.

And the second lot came forth to Simeon, even for the tribe of the children of Simeon according to their families, and their inheritance was within the inheritance of the children of Judah. And they had in their inheritance Beer-sheba, or Sheba, and Moladah, and Hazar-shual, and Balah, and Azem, and Eltolad, and Beth-ul, and Hormah, and Ziklag, and Beth-marcaboth, and Hazar-susah, and Beth-lebaoth, and Sharuhen, thirteen cities and their villages; Ain, Remmon, and Ether, and Ashan, four cities and their villages; and all the villages that were round about these cities to Baalath-beer, Ramath of the south. This is the inheritance of the tribe of the children of Simeon according to their families. Out of the portion of the children of Judah was the inheritance of the children of Simeon, for the part of the children of Judah was too much for them, therefore the children of Simeon had their inheritance within the inheritance of them.

And the third lot came up for the children of Zebulun according to their families, and the border of their inheritance was unto Sarid, and their border went up toward the sea, and Maralah, and reached to Dabbasheth, and reached to the river that is before Jokneam, and turned from Sarid eastward toward the sunrising unto the border of Chisloth-tabor, and then goeth out to Daberath, and goeth up to Japhia, and from thence passeth on along the east to Gittah-hepher, to Ittah-kazin, and goeth out to Remmon-methoar to Neah, and the border compasseth it on the north side to Hannathon, and the outgoings thereof are in the valley of Jiphthah-el, and Kattath, and Nahallal, and Shimron, and Idalah, and Bethlehem, twelve cities with their villages. This is the inheritance of the children of Zebulun according to their families, these cities with their villages.

And the fourth lot came out to Issachar, for the children of Issachar according to their families. And their border was toward Jezreel, and Chesulloth, and Shunem, and Haphraim, and Shihon, and Anaharath, and Rabbith, and Kishion, and Abez, and Remeth, and En-gannim, and En-haddah, and Beth-pazzez, and the coast reacheth to Tabor, and Shahazimah, and Beth-shemesh, and the outgoings of their border were at Jordan, sixteen cities with their villages. This is the inheritance of the tribe of the children of Issachar according to their families, the cities and their villages.

And the fifth lot came out for the tribe of the children of Asher according to their families. And their border was Helkath, and Hali, and Beten, and Achshaph, and Alammelech, and Amad, and Misheal, and reacheth to Carmel westward, and to Shihor-libnath, and turneth toward the sunrising to Beth-dagon, and reacheth to Zebulun, and to the valley of Jiphthah-el toward the north side of Bethemek, and Neiel, and goeth out to Cabul on the left hand, and Hebron, and Rehob, and Hammon, and Kanah, even unto great Zidon, and then the coast turneth to Ramah, and to the strong city Tyre, and the coast turneth to Hosha, and the outgoings thereof are at the sea from the coast to Achzib, Ummah also, and Aphek, and Rehob, twenty and two cities with their villages. This is the inheritance of the tribe of the children of Asher according to their families, these cities with their villages.

The sixth lot came out to the children of Naphtali, even for the children of Naphtali according to their families. And their coast was from Heleph, from Allon to Zaanannim, and Adami, Nekeb, and Jabneel, unto Lakum, and the outgoings thereof were at Jordan, and then the coast turneth westward to Aznoth-tabor, and goeth out from thence to Hukkok, and reacheth to Zebulun on the south side, and reacheth to Asher on the west side, and to Judah upon Jordan toward the sun-rising. And the fenced cities are Ziddim, Zer, and Hammath, Rakkath, and Chinnereth, and Adamah, and Ramah, and Hazor, and Kedesh, and Edrei, and En-hazor, and Iron, and Migdal-el, Horem, and Beth-anath, and Beth-shemesh, nineteen cities with their villages. This is the inheritance of the tribe of the children of Naphtali according to their families, the cities and their villages.

And the seventh lot came out for the tribe of the children of Dan, according to their families. And the coast of their inheritance was Zorah, and Eshtaol, and Ir-shemesh, and Shaalabbin, and Ajalon, and Jethlah, and Elon, and Thimnathah, and Ekron, and Eltekeh, and Gibbethon, and Baalath, and Jehud, and Bene-berak, and Gath-rimmon, and Me-jarkon, and Rakkon, with the border before Japho. And the coast of the children of Dan went out too little for them, therefore the children of Dan went up to fight against Leshem and took it, and smote it with the edge of the sword, and possessed it, and dwelt therein, and called Leshem, Dan, after the name of Dan their father. This is the inheritance of the tribe of the children of Dan according to their families, these cities with their villages.

When they had made an end of dividing the land for inheritance by their coasts, the children of Israel gave an inheritance to Joshua the son of Nun among them. According to the word of the Lord they give him the city which he asked, even Timnath-serah in mount Ephraim, and he built the city and dwelt therein. These are the inheritances which Eleazar the priest, and Joshua the son of Nun, and the heads of the fathers of the tribes of the children of Israel divided for an inheritance by lot in Shiloh before the Lord, at the door of the tabernacle of the congregation. So they made an end of dividing the country.

The Lord also spake unto Joshua saying, Speak to the children of Israel, saying, Appoint out for you cities of refuge, whereof I spake unto you by the hand of Moses, that the slayer that killeth any person unawares and unwittingly may flee thither, and they shall be your refuge from the avenger of blood. And when he that doth flee unto one of those cities shall stand at the entering of the gate of the city, and shall declare his cause in the ears of the elders of that city, they shall take him into the city unto them and give him a place that he may dwell among them. And if the avenger of blood pursue after him, then they shall not deliver the slayer up into his hand, because he smote his neighbor unwittingly and hated him not beforetime. And he shall dwell in that city until he stand before the congregation for judgment and until the death of the high priest that shall be in those days, then shall the slayer return and come unto his own city and unto his own house unto the city from whence he fled. And they appointed Kedesh in Galilee in mount Naphtali, and Shechem in mount Ephraim, and Kirjath-arba, which is Hebron in the mountain of Judah. And on the other side Jordan by Jericho eastward, they assigned Bezer in the wilderness upon the plain out of the tribe of Reuben, and Ramoth in Gilead out of the tribe of Gad, and Golan in Bashan out of the tribe of Manasseh. These were the cities appointed for all the children of Israel, and for the stranger that sojourneth among them, that whosoever killeth any person at unawares might flee thither and not die by the hand of the avenger of blood, until he stood before the congregation.

Then came near the heads of the fathers of the Levites unto Eleazar the priest, and unto Joshua the son of Nun, and unto the heads of the fathers of the tribes of the children of Israel, and they spake unto them at Shiloh in the land of Canaan, saying, The Lord commanded by the hand of Moses to give us cities to dwell in with the suburbs thereof for our cattle. And the children of Israel gave unto the Levites out of their inheritance, at the commandment of the Lord, these cities and their suburbs. And the lot came out for the families of the Kohathites, and the children of Aaron the priest, which were of the Levites, had by lot out of the tribe of Judah, and out of the tribe of Simeon, and out of the tribe of Benjamin, thirteen cities. And the rest of the children of Kohath had by lot out of the families of the tribe of Ephraim, and out of the tribe of Dan, and out of the half tribe of Manasseh, ten cities. And the children of Gershon had by lot out of the families of the tribe of Issachar, and out of the tribe of Asher, and out of the tribe of Naphtali, and out of the half tribe of Manasseh in Bashan, thirteen cities. The children of Merari by their families had out of the tribe of Reuben, and out of the tribe of Gad, and out of the tribe of Zebulun, twelve cities. And the children of Israel gave by lot unto the Levites these cities with their suburbs, as the Lord commanded by the hand of Moses.

And they gave out of the tribe of the children of Judah, and out of the tribe of the children of Simeon, these cities which are here mentioned by name, which the children of Aaron, being of the families of the Kohathites, who were of the children of Levi, had, for theirs was the first lot. And they gave them the city of Arba the father of Anak, which city is Hebron, in the hill country of Judah, with the suburbs thereof round about it. But the fields of the city and the villages thereof, gave they to Caleb the son of Jephunneh for his possession. Thus they gave to the children of Aaron the priest Hebron with her suburbs, to be a city of refuge for the slayer, and Libnah with her suburbs, and Jattir with her suburbs, and Eshtemoa with her suburbs, and Holon with her suburbs, and Debir with her suburbs, and Ain with her suburbs, and Juttah with her suburbs, and Bethshemesh with her suburbs, nine cities out of those two tribes. And out of the tribe of Benjamin, Gibeon with her suburbs, Geba with her suburbs, Anathoth with her suburbs, and Almon with her suburbs, four cities. All the cities of the children of Aaron, the priest, were thirteen cities with their suburbs.

And the families of the children of Kohath, the Levites which remained of the children of Kohath, even they had the cities of their lot out of the tribe of Ephraim. For they gave them Shechem with her suburbs in mount Ephraim, to be a city of refuge for the slayer, and Gezer with her suburbs, and Kibzaim with her suburbs, and Beth-horon with her suburbs, four cities. And out of the tribe of Dan, Elteken with her suburbs, Gibethon with her suburbs, Aizalon with her suburbs, Gath-rimmon with her suburbs, four cities. And out of the half tribe of Manasseh, Tanach with her suburbs, and Gath-rimmon with her suburbs, two cities. All the cities were ten with their suburbs for the families of the children of Kohath that remained.

And unto the children of Gershon, of the families of the Levites, out of the other half tribe of Manasseh they gave Golan in Bashan with her suburbs, to be a city of refuge for the slayer, and Beeshterah with her suburbs, two cities. And out of the tribe of Issachar, Kishon with her suburbs, Dabareh with her suburbs, Jarmuth with her suburbs, Engannim with her suburbs, four cities. And out of the tribe of Asher, Mishal with her suburbs, Abdon with her suburbs, Helkath with her suburbs, and Rehob with her suburbs, four cities. And out of the tribe of Naphtali, Kedesh in Galilee with her suburbs, to be a city of refuge for the slayer, and Hammoth-dor with her suburbs, and Kartan with her suburbs, three cities. All the cities of the Gershonites according to their families were thirteen cities with their suburbs.

And unto the families of the children of Merari, the rest of the Levites, out of the tribe of Zebulun, Jokneam with her suburbs, and Kartah with her suburbs, Dimnah with her suburbs, Nahalal with her suburbs, four cities. And out of the tribe of Reuben, Bezer with her suburbs, and Jahazah with her suburbs, Kedemoth with her suburbs, and Mephaath with her suburbs, four cities. And out of the tribe of Gad, Ramoth in Gilead with her suburbs, to be a city of refuge for the slayer, and Mahanaim with her suburbs, Heshbon with her suburbs, Jazer with her suburbs, four cities in all. So all the cities for the children of Merari by their families, which were remaining of the families of the Levites, were by their lot twelve cities. All the cities of the Levites within the possession of the children of Israel were forty and eight cities with their suburbs. These cities were every one with their suburbs round about them, thus were all these cities.

And the Lord gave unto Israel all the land which he sware to give unto their fathers, and they possessed it and dwelt therein. And the Lord gave them rest round about, according to all that he sware unto their fathers, and there stood not a man of all their enemies before them, the Lord delivered all their enemies into their hand. There failed not aught of any good thing which the Lord had spoken unto the house of Israel, all came to pass.

4 THEN Joshua called the Reubenites, and the Gadites, and the half tribe of Manasseh and said unto them, Ye have kept all that Moses the servant of the Lord commanded you, and have obeyed my voice in all that I commanded you, ye have not left your brethren these many days unto this day, but have kept the charge of the commandment of the Lord your God. And now the Lord your God hath given rest unto your brethren, as he promised them, therefore now return ye and get you unto your tents and unto the land of your possession, which Moses the servant of the Lord gave you on the other side Jordan. But take diligent heed to do the commandment and the law which Moses the servant of the Lord charged you, to love the Lord your God, and to walk in all his ways, and to keep his commandments, and to cleave unto him, and to serve him with all your heart and with all your soul. So Joshua blessed them and sent them away and they went unto their tents. Now to the one half of the tribe of Manasseh Moses had given possession in Bashan, but unto the other half thereof gave Joshua among their brethren on this side Jordan westward. And when Joshua sent them away also unto their tents, then he blessed them and he spake unto them saying, Return with much riches unto your tents and with very much cattle, with silver, and with gold, and with brass, and with iron, and with very much raiment. Divide the spoil of your enemies with your brethren. And the children of Reuben and the children of Gad and the half tribe of Manasseh returned, and departed from the children of Israel out of Shiloh, which is in the land of Canaan, to go unto the country of Gilead, to the land of their possession, whereof they were possessed, according to the word of the Lord by the hand of Moses. And when they came unto the borders of Jordan that are in the land of Canaan, the children of Reuben and the children of Gad and the half tribe of Manasseh built there an altar by Jordan, a great altar to see to.

And the children of Israel heard say, Behold, the children of Reuben and the children of Gad and the half tribe of Manasseh have built an altar over against the land of Canaan, in the borders of Jordan, at the passage of the children of Israel. And when the children of Israel heard of it the whole congregation of the children of Israel gathered themselves together at Shiloh to go up to war against them. And the children of Israel sent unto the children of Reuben, and to the children of Gad, and to the half tribe of Manasseh, into the land of Gilead, Phinehas the son of Eleazar the priest, and with him ten princes, of each chief house a prince throughout all the tribes of Israel, and each one was a head of the house of their fathers among the thousands of Israel. And they came unto the children of Reuben, and to the children of Gad, and to the half tribe of Manasseh, unto the land of Gilead and they spake with them saying, Thus saith the whole congregation of the Lord, What trespass is this that ye have committed against the God of Israel, to turn away this day from following the Lord, in that ye have builded you an altar that ye might rebel this day against the Lord? Is the iniquity of Peor too little for us, from which we are not cleansed until this day, although there was a plague in the congregation of the Lord, but that ye must turn away this day from following the Lord? And it will be, seeing ye rebel today against the Lord, that tomorrow he will be wroth with the whole congregation of Israel. Notwithstanding, if the land of your possession be unclean, then pass ye over unto the land of the possession of the Lord, wherein the Lord's tabernacle dwelleth, and take possession among us, but rebel not against the Lord, nor rebel against us in building you an altar besides the altar of the Lord our God. Did not Achan the son of Zerah commit a trespass in the accursed thing, and wrath fell on all the congregation of Israel? And that man perished not alone in his iniquity.

Then the children of Reuben and the children of Gad and the half tribe of Manasseh answered and said unto the heads of the thousands of Israel, the Lord God of gods, the Lord God of gods, he knoweth, and Israel he shall know, if it be in rebellion, or if in transgression against the Lord, (save us not this day,) that we have built us an altar to turn from following the Lord, or if to offer thereon burnt offering or meat offering, or if to offer peace offerings thereon, let the Lord himself require it. And if we have not rather done it for fear of this thing, saying, In time to come your children might speak unto our children, saying, What have ye to do with the Lord God of Israel? For the Lord hath made Jordan a border between us and you, ye children of Reuben and children of Gad, ye have no part in the Lord, so shall your children make our children cease from fearing the Lord. Therefore we said, Let us now prepare to build us an altar, not for burnt offering nor for sacrifice, but that it may be a witness between us and you, and our generations after us, that we might do the service of the Lord before him with our burnt offerings, and with our sacrifices, and with our peace offerings, that your children may not say to our children in time to come, Ye have no part in the Lord. Therefore said we, that it shall be when they should so say to us or to our generations in time to come, that we may say again, Behold the pattern of the altar of the Lord, which our fathers made, not for burnt offerings, nor for sacrifices, but it is a witness between us and you. God forbid that we should rebel against the Lord and turn this day from following the Lord, to build an altar for burnt offerings, for meat offerings, or for sacrifices, besides the altar of the Lord our God that is before his tabernacle.

And when Phinehas the priest, and the princes of the congregation and heads of the thousands of Israel which were with him, heard the words that the children of Reuben and the children of Gad and the children of Manasseh spake, it pleased them. And Phinehas the son of Eleazar the priest said unto the children of Reuben, and to the children of Gad, and to the children of Manasseh, This day we perceive that the Lord is among us because we have not committed this trespass against the Lord. Now ye have delivered the children of Israel out of the hand of the Lord. And Phinehas the son of Eleazar the priest, and the princes, returned from the children of Reuben, and from the children of Gad, out of the land of Gilead, unto the land of Canaan, to the children of Israel, and brought them word again. And the thing pleased the children of Israel, and the children of Israel blessed God and did not intend to go up against them in battle to destroy the land wherein the children of Reuben and Gad dwelt. And the children of Reuben and the children of Gad called the altar Ed, for it shall be witness between us that the Lord is God.

And it came to pass a long time after that the Lord had given rest unto Israel from all their enemies round about, that Joshua waxed old and stricken in age. And Joshua called for all Israel, and for their elders, and for their heads, and for their judges, and for their officers, and said unto them, I am old and stricken in age, and ye have seen all that the Lord your God hath done unto all these nations because of you, for the Lord your God is he that hath fought for you. Behold, I have divided unto you by lot these nations that remain, to be an inheritance for your tribes, from Jordan, with all the nations that I have cut off, even unto the great sea westward. And the Lord your God, he shall expel them from before you and drive them from out of your sight, and ye shall possess their land as the Lord your God hath promised unto you. Be ye therefore very courageous to keep and to do all that is written in the book of the law of Moses, that ye turn not aside therefrom to the right hand or to the left, That ye come not among these nations, these that remain among you, neither make mention of the name of their gods, nor cause to swear by them, neither serve them, nor bow yourselves unto them, but cleave unto the Lord your God, as ye have done unto this day. For the Lord hath driven out from before you great nations and strong, but as for you, no man hath been able to stand before you unto this day. One man of you shall chase a thousand, for the Lord your God, he it is that fighteth for you, as he hath promised you. Take good heed therefore unto yourselves, that ye love the Lord your God. Else, if ye do in any wise go back and cleave unto the remnant of these nations, even these that remain among you, and shall make marriages with them, and go in unto them, and they to you, know for a certainty that the Lord your God will no more drive out any of these nations from before you, but they shall be snares and traps unto you, and scourges in your sides, and thorns in your eyes, until ye perish from off this good land which the Lord your God hath given you.

And, behold, this day I am going the way of all the Earth, and ye know in all your hearts and in all your souls, that not one thing hath failed of all the good things which the Lord your God spake concerning you, all are come to pass unto you, and not one thing hath failed thereof. Therefore it shall come to pass, that as all good things are come upon you which the Lord your God promised you, so shall the Lord bring upon you all evil things, until he have destroyed you from off this good land which the Lord your God hath given you. When ye have transgressed the covenant of the Lord your God, which he commanded you, and have gone and served other gods, and bowed yourselves to them, then shall the anger of the Lord be kindled against you, and ye shall perish quickly from off the good land which he hath given unto you.

And Joshua gathered all the tribes of Israel to Shechem, and called for the elders of Israel, and for their heads, and for their judges, and for their officers, and they presented themselves before God. And Joshua said unto all the people, Thus saith the Lord God of Israel, Your fathers dwelt on the other side of the flood in old time, even Terah, the father of Abraham, and the father of Nachor, and they served other gods. And I took your father Abraham from the other side of the flood and led him throughout all the land of Canaan and multiplied his seed, and gave him Isaac. And I gave unto Isaac Jacob and Esau, and I gave unto Esau mount Seir, to possess it, but Jacob and his children went down into Egypt. I sent Moses also and Aaron, and I plagued Egypt according to that which I did among them, and afterward I brought you out. And I brought your fathers out of Egypt, and ye came unto the sea, and the Egyptians pursued after your fathers with chariots and horsemen unto the Red Sea. And when they cried unto the Lord he put darkness between you and the Egyptians and brought the sea upon them and covered them. And your eyes have seen what I have done in Egypt, and ye dwelt in the wilderness a long season. And I brought you into the land of the Amorites, which dwelt on the other side Jordan, and they fought with you and I gave them into your hand that ye might possess their land. And I destroyed them from before you. Then Balak the son of Zipor, king of Moab, arose and warred against Israel, and sent and called Balaam the son of Beor to curse you, but I would not hearken unto Balaam, therefore he blessed you still, so I delivered you out of his hand. And ye went over Jordan and came unto Jericho and the men of Jericho fought against you, the Amorites, and the Perizzites, and the Canaanites, and the Hittites, and the Girgashites, the Hivites, and the Jebusites, and I delivered them into your hand. And I sent the hornet before you which drave them out from before you, even the two kings of the Amorites, but not with thy sword, nor with thy bow. And I have given you a land for which ye did not labor and cities which ye built not, and ye dwell in them, of the vineyards and oliveyards which ye planted not do ye eat.

Now therefore fear the Lord, and serve him in sincerity and in truth, and put away the gods which your fathers served on the other side of the flood, and in Egypt, and serve ye the Lord. And if it seem evil unto you to serve the Lord, choose you this day whom ye will serve, whether the gods which your fathers served that were on the other side of the flood, or the gods of the Amorites, in whose land ye dwell, but as for me and my house, we will serve the Lord.

And the people answered and said, God forbid that we should forsake the Lord, to serve other gods. For the Lord our God, he it is that brought us up and our fathers out of the land of Egypt, from the house of bondage, and which did those great signs in our sight, and preserved us in all the way wherein we went, and among all the people through whom we passed, and the Lord drave out from before us all the people, even the Amorites which dwelt in the land. Therefore will we also serve the Lord, for he is our God. And Joshua said unto the people, Ye cannot serve the Lord, for he is a holy God, he is a jealous God; he will not forgive your transgressions nor your sins. If ye forsake the Lord and serve strange gods, then he will turn and do you hurt and consume you, after that he hath done you good. And the people said unto Joshua, Nay, but we will serve the Lord. And Joshua said unto the people, Ye are witnesses against yourselves that ye have chosen you the Lord, to serve him. And they said, We are witnesses. Now therefore put away, said he, the strange gods which are among you and incline your heart unto the Lord God of Israel. And the people said unto Joshua, The Lord our God will we serve and his voice will we obey. So Joshua made a covenant with the people that day and set them a statute and an ordinance in Shechem.

And Joshua wrote these words in the book of the law of God, and took a great stone and set it up there under an oak that was by the sanctuary of the Lord. And Joshua said unto all the people, Behold, this stone shall be a witness unto us for it hath heard all the words of the Lord which he spake unto us. It shall be therefore a witness unto you, lest ye deny your God.

So Joshua let the people depart, every man unto his inheritance. And it came to pass after these things that Joshua the son of Nun, the servant of the Lord, died, being a hundred and ten years old. And they buried him in the border of his inheritance in Timnath-serah, which is in mount Ephraim, on the north side of the hill of Gaash. And Israel served the Lord all the days of Joshua, and all the days of the elders that overlived Joshua, and which had known all the works of the Lord that he had done for Israel. And the bones of Joseph, which the children of Israel brought up out of Egypt, buried they in Shechem, in a parcel of ground which Jacob bought of the sons of Hamor the father of Shechem for a hundred pieces of silver, and it became the inheritance of the children of Joseph. And Eleazar the son of Aaron died, and they buried him in a hill that pertained to Phinehas his son, which was given him in mount Ephraim.

THE BOOK OF JUDGES

NOW after the death of Joshua it came to pass, that the children of Israel asked the Lord saying, Who shall go up for us against the Canaanites first to fight against them? And the Lord said Judah shall go up, behold I have delivered the land into his hand. And Judah said unto Simeon his brother, Come up with me into my lot that we may fight against the Canaanites, and I likewise will go with thee into thy lot. So Simeon went with him. And Judah went up and the Lord delivered the Canaanites and the Perizzites into their hand and they slew of them in Bezek ten thousand men. And they found Adoni-bezek in Bezek and they fought against him, and they slew the Canaanites and the Perizzites, but Adoni-bezek fled, and they pursued after him and caught him and cut off his thumbs and his great toes. And Adoni-bezek said, Threescore and ten kings having their their thumbs and their great toes cut off, gathered their meat under my table as I have done, so God hath requited me. And they brought him to Jerusalem and there he died. Now the children of Judah had fought against Jerusalem and had taken it and smitten it with the edge of the sword and set the city on fire. And afterward the children of Judah went down to fight against the Canaanites that dwelt in the mountain and in the south and in the valley. And Judah went against the Canaanites that dwelt in Hebron. Now the name of Hebron before was Kirjath-arba, and they slew Sheshai, and Ahiman, and Talmai. And from thence he went against the inhabitants of Debir, and the name of Debir before was Kirjath-sepher. And Caleb said, He that smiteth Kirjath-sepher and taketh it, to him will I give Achsah my daughter to wife. And Othniel the son of Kenaz, Caleb's younger brother, took it and he gave him Achsah his daughter to wife. And it came to pass when she came to him that she moved him to ask of her father a field, and she lighted from off her ass, and Caleb said unto her, What wilt thou? And she said unto him, Give me a blessing for thou hast given me a south land. Give me also springs of water. And Caleb gave her the upper springs and the nether springs. And the children of the Kenite, Moses' father-in-law went up out of the city of palm trees with the children of Judah into the wilderness of Judah, which lieth in the south of Arad, and they went and dwelt among the people. And Judah went with Simeon his brother and they slew the Canaanites that inhabited Zephath and utterly destroyed it. And the name of the city was called Hormah. Also Judah took Gaza with the coast thereof, and Askelon with coast thereof, and Ekron with the coast thereof. And the Lord was with Judah and he drave out the inhabitants of the mountain, but could not drive out the inhabitants of the valley because they had chariots of iron. And they gave Hebron unto Caleb, as Moses said, and he expelled thence the three sons of Anak.

And the children of Benjamin did not drive out the Jebusites that inhabited Jerusalem, but the Jebusites dwell with the children of Benjamin in Jerusalem unto this day. And the house of Joseph, they also went up against Beth-el and the Lord was with them. And the house of Joseph sent to descry Beth-el. Now the name of the city before was Luz. And the spies saw a man come forth out of the city and they said unto him, Show us, we pray thee, the entrance into the city and we will show thee mercy. And when he showed them the entrance into the city they smote the city with the edge of the sword, but they let go the man and all his family. And the man went into the land of the Hittites and built a city and called the name thereof Luz, which is the name thereof unto this day. Neither did Manasseh drive out the inhabitants of Beth-shean and her towns, nor Taanach and her towns, nor the inhabitants of Dor and her towns, nor the inhabitants of Ibleam and her towns, nor the inhabitants of Megiddo and her towns, but the Canaanites would dwell in that land. And it came to pass when Israel was strong that they put the Canaanites to tribute and did not utterly drive them out. Neither did Ephraim drive out the Canaanites that dwelt in Gezer, but the Canaanites dwelt in Gezer among them. Neither did Zebulun drive out the inhabitants of Kitron, nor the inhabitants of Nahalol, but the Canaanites dwelt among them and became tributaries. Neither did Asher drive out the inhabitants of Accho, nor the inhabitants of Zidon, nor of Ahlab, nor of Achzib, nor of Helbah, nor of Aphik, nor of Rehob, but the Asherites dwelt among the Canaanites, the inhabitants of the land, for they did not drive them out. Neither did Naphtali drive out the inhabitants of Beth-shemesh, nor the inhabitants of Beth-anath, but he dwelt among the Canaanites, the inhabitants of the land. Nevertheless, the inhabitants of Beth-shemesh and of Beth-anath became tributaries unto them. And the Amorites forced the children of Dan into the mountain, for they would not suffer them to come down to the valley, but the Amorites would dwell in mount Heres in Aijalon, and in Shaalbim. Yet the hand of the house of Joseph prevailed so that they became tributaries. And the coast of the Amorites was from the going up to Akrabbim, from the rock, and upward.

And an Angel of the Lord came up from Gilgal to Bochim and said, I made you to go up out of Egypt and have brought you unto the land which I sware unto your fathers, and I said, I will never break my covenant with you. And ye shall make no league with the inhabitants of this land; ye shall throw down their altars. But ye have not obeyed my voice. Why have ye done this? Wherefore I also said, I will not drive them out from before you, but they shall be as thorns in your sides and their gods shall be a snare unto you. And it came to pass when the Angel of the Lord spake these words unto all the children of Israel, that the people lifted up their voice and wept. And they called the name of that place Bochim and they sacrificed there unto the Lord. And when Joshua had let the people go the children of Israel went every man unto his inheritance to possess the land. And the people served the Lord all the days of Joshua, and all the days of the elders that outlived Joshua, who had seen all the great works of the Lord, that he did for Israel. And Joshua the son of Nun, the servant of the Lord, died, being a hundred and ten years old. And they buried him in the border of his inheritance in Tim-nath-heres, in the mount of Ephraim, on the north side of the hill of Gaash.

And also all that generation were gathered unto their fathers, and there arose another generation after them, which knew not the Lord nor yet the works which he had done for Israel. And the children of Israel did evil in the sight of the Lord, and served Baalim. And they forsook the Lord God of their fathers which brought them out of the land of Egypt, and followed other gods, of the gods of the people that were round about them, and bowed themselves unto them, and provoked the Lord to anger. And they forsook the Lord and served Baal and Ashtaroth. And the anger of the Lord was hot against Israel and he delivered them into the hands of spoilers that spoiled them, and he sold them into the hands of their enemies round about so that they could not any longer stand before their enemies. Whithersoever they went out the hand of the Lord was against them for evil, as the Lord had said, and as the Lord had sworn unto them, and they were greatly distressed.

Nevertheless the Lord raised up judges which delivered them out of the hand of those that spoiled them. And yet they would not hearken unto their judges, but they went a whoring after other gods and bowed themselves unto them.

They turned quickly out of the way which their fathers walked in, obeying the commandments of the Lord; but they did not so. And when the Lord raised them up judges, then the Lord was with the judge, and delivered them out of the hand of their enemies all the days of the judge, for the Lord hearkened because of their groanings by reason of them that oppressed them and vexed them. And it came to pass when the judge was dead, that they returned and corrupted themselves more than their fathers, in following other gods to serve them, and to bow down unto them. They ceased not from their own doings nor from their stubborn way. And the anger of the Lord was hot against Israel and he said, Because that this people hath transgressed my covenant which I commanded their fathers and have not hearkened unto my voice, I also will not henceforth drive out any from before them of the nations which Joshua left when he died, that through them I may prove Israel, whether they will keep the way of the Lord to walk therein, as their fathers did keep it, or not. Therefore the Lord left those nations, without driving them out hastily. Neither delivered he them into the hand of Joshua.

Now these are the nations which the Lord left to prove Israel by them, even as many of Israel as had not known all the wars of Canaan, only that the generations of the children of Israel might know to teach them war, at the least such as before knew nothing thereof; namely, five lords of the Philistines, and all the Canaanites, and the Sidonians, and the Hivites that dwelt in mount Lebanon, from mount Baal-hermon unto the entering in of Hamath. And they were to prove Israel by them, to know whether they would hearken unto the commandments of the Lord which he commanded their fathers by the hand of Moses. And the children of Israel dwelt among the Canaanites, Hittites, and Amorites, and Perizzites, and Hivites, and Jebusites, and they took their daughters to be their wives, and gave their daughters to their sons, and served their gods.

2 AND the children of Israel did evil in the sight of the Lord and forgat the Lord their God and served Baalim and the groves. Therefore the anger of the Lord was hot against Israel and he sold them into the hand of Chushan-rishathaim king of Mesopotamia, and the children of Israel served Chushan-rishathaim eight years. And when the children of Israel cried unto the Lord, the Lord raised up a deliverer to the children of Israel, who delivered them, even Othniel the son of Kenaz, Caleb's younger brother. And the Spirit of the Lord came upon him, and he judged Israel, and went out to war, and the Lord delivered Chushan-rishathaim king of Mesopotamia into his hand, and his hand prevailed against Chushan-rishathaim. And the land had rest forty years and Othniel the son of Kenaz died.

And the children of Israel did evil again in the sight of the Lord and the Lord strengthened Eglon the king of Moab against Israel because they had done evil in the sight of the Lord. And he gathered unto him the children of Ammon and Amalek, and went and smote Israel, and possessed the city of palm trees. So the children of Israel served Eglon the king of Moab eighteen years. But when the children of Israel cried unto the Lord, the Lord raised them up a deliverer, Ehud the son of Gera, a Benjamite, a man left-handed, and by him the children of Israel sent a present unto Eglon the king of Moab. But Ehud made him a dagger which had two edges, of a cubit length, and he did gird it under his raiment upon his right thigh. And he brought the present unto Eglon king of Moab, and Eglon was a very fat man. And when he made an end to offer the present, he sent away the people that bare the present. But he himself turned again from the quarries that were by Gilgal and said, I have a secret errand unto thee, O king, who said, Keep silence. And all that stood by him went out from him. And Ehud came unto him, and he was sitting in a summer parlor which he had for himself alone. And Ehud said, I have a message from God unto thee. And he arose out of his seat. And Ehud put forth his left hand, and took the dagger from his right thigh, and thrust it into his belly and the haft also went in after the blade, and the fat closed upon the blade so that he could not draw the dagger out of his belly and the dirt came out. Then Ehud went forth through the porch and shut the doors of the parlor upon him and locked them. When he was gone out his servants came, and when they saw that, behold, the doors of the parlor were locked, they said, surely he covereth his feet in his summer chamber. And they tarried till they were ashamed and behold, he opened not the doors of the parlor, therefore they took a key, and opened them, and, behold, their lord was fallen down dead on the earth. And Ehud escaped while they tarried and passed beyond the quarries and escaped unto Seirath. And it came to pass when he was come that he blew a trumpet in the mountain of Ephraim and the children of Israel went down with him from the mount and he before them. And he said unto them, Follow after me for the Lord hath delivered your enemies the Moabites into your hand. And they went down after him and took the fords of Jordan toward Moab and suffered not a man to pass over. And they slew of Moab at that time about ten thousand men, all lusty and all men of valor, and there escaped not a man. So Moab was subdued that day under the hand of Israel. And the land had rest fourscore years. And after him was Shamgar the son of Anath, which slew of the Philistines six hundred men with an ox-goad, and he also delivered Israel. And the children of Israel again did evil in the sight of the Lord, when Ehud was dead. And the Lord sold them into the hand of Jabin king of Canaan, that reigned in Hazor, the captain of whose host was Sisera which dwelt in Harosheth of the Gentiles.

And the children of Israel cried unto the Lord, for he had nine hundred chariots of iron, and twenty years he mightily oppressed the children of Israel. And Deborah, a prophetess, the wife of Lapidoth, she judged Israel at that time. And she dwelt under the palm tree of Deborah, between Ramah and Beth-el in mount Ephraim, and the children of Israel came up to her for judgment. And she sent and called Barak the son of Abinoam out of Kedesh-naphtali, and said unto him, Hath not the Lord God of Israel commanded, saying, Go and draw toward mount Tabor and take with thee ten thousand men of the children of Naphtali and of the children of Zebulun? And I will draw unto thee, to the river Kishon, Sisera the captain of Jabin's army, with his chariots and his multitude, and I will deliver him into thine hand. And Barak said unto her, If thou wilt go with me, then I will go, but if thou wilt not go with me, then I will not go. And she said, I will surely go with thee, notwithstanding the journey that thou takest shall not be for thine honor, for the Lord shall sell Sisera into the hand of a woman. And Deborah arose and went with Barak to Kedesh. And Barak called Zebulun and Naphtali to Kedesh and he went up with ten thousand men at his feet, and Deborah went up with him.

Now Heber the Kenite, which was of the children of Hobab the father-in-law of Moses, had severed himself from the Kenites and pitched his tent unto the plain of Zaanaim which is by Kedesh.

And they showed Sisera that Barak the son of Abinoam was gone up to mount Tabor. And Sisera gathered together all his chariots, even nine hundred chariots of iron, and all the people that were with him, from Harosheth of the Gentiles unto the river of Kishon. And Deborah said unto Barak, Up, for this is the day in which the Lord hath delivered Sisera into thine hand. Is not the Lord gone out before thee? So Barak, went down from mount Tabor, and ten thousand men after him. And the Lord discomfited Sisera, and all his chariots, and all his hosts, with the edge of the sword before Barak, so that Sisera lighted down off his chariot and fled away on his feet. But Barak pursued after the chariots and after the host, unto Harosheth of the Gentiles, and all the host of Sisera fell upon the edge of the sword and there was not a man left.

Howbeit Sisera fled away on his feet to the tent of Jael the wife of Heber the Kenite, for there was peace between Jabin the king of Hazor and the house of Heber the Kenite. And Jael went out to meet Sisera and said unto him, Turn in, my lord, turn in to me. Fear not. And when he had turned in unto her into the tent, she covered him with a mantle. And he said unto her, Give me, I pray thee, a little water to drink for I am thirsty. And she opened a bottle of milk and gave him drink and covered him. Again he said unto her, Stand in the door of the tent, and it shall be, when any man doth come and inquire of thee, and say, Is there any man here? that thou shalt say, No. Then Jael Heber's wife took a nail of the tent, and took a hammer in her hand, and went softly unto him and smote the nail into his temples, and fastened it into the ground, for he was fast asleep and weary. So he died. And, behold, as Barak pursued Sisera, Jael came out to meet him and said unto him, Come, and I will show thee the man whom thou seekest. And when he came into her tent, behold, Sisera lay dead and the nail was in his temples. So God subdued on that day Jabin the king of Canaan before the children of Israel. And the hand of the children of Israel prospered and prevailed against Jabin the king of Canaan until they had destroyed Jabin king of Canaan.

Then sang Deborah and Barak the son of Abinoam on that day, saying:
>Praise ye the Lord for the avenging of Israel when the people willingly offered themselves.
>Hear, O ye kings, give ear, O ye princes, I even I, will sing unto the Lord, I will sing praise to the Lord God of Israel.
>Lord, when thou wentest out of Seir, when thou marchedst out of the field of Edom,
>the Earth trembled, and the heavens dropped, the clouds also dropped water.
>The mountains melted from before the Lord,
>even that Sinai from before the Lord God of Israel.
>In the days of Shamgar the son of Anath, in the days of Jael, the highways were unoccupied, and the travelers walked through byways.
>The inhabitants of the villages ceased, they ceased in Israel, until that I Deborah arose,
>that I arose a mother in Israel.
>They chose new gods, then was war in the gates.
>Was there a shield or spear seen among forty thousand in Israel?
>My heart is toward the governors of Israel,
>that offered themselves willingly among the people.
>Bless ye the Lord.
>Speak, ye that ride on white asses, ye that sit in judgment, and walk by the way.
>They that are delivered from the noise of archers in the places of drawing water,
>there shall they rehearse the righteous acts of the Lord, even the righteous acts toward the inhabitants of his villages in Israel.
>Then shall the people of the Lord go down to the gates.
>Awake, awake, Deborah, awake, awake, utter a song,
>Arise, Barak, and lead thy captivity captive, thou son of Abinoam.

Then he made him that remaineth have dominion over the nobles among the people,
the Lord made me have dominion over the mighty.
Out of Ephraim was there a root of them against Amalek, after thee, Benjamin, among thy people, out of Machir came down governors, and out of Zebulun they that handle the pen of the writer.
And the princes of Issachar were with Deborah, even Issachar, and also Barak, he was sent on foot into the valley.
For the divisions of Ruben there were great thoughts of heart.
Why abodest thou among the sheepfolds, to hear the bleatings of the flocks?
For the divisions of Ruben there were great searchings of heart.
Gilead abode beyond Jordan, and why did Dan remain in ships?
Asher continued on the seashore, and abode in his breaches.
Zebulun and Naphtali were a people that jeoparded their lives unto the death in the high places of the field.
The kings came and fought, then fought the kings of Canaan in Taanach by the waters of Megiddo, they took no gain of money.
They fought from Heaven, the stars in their courses fought against Sisera.
The river of Kishon swept them away, that ancient river, the river Kishon. O my soul, thou hast trodden down strength.
Then were the horsehoofs broken by the means of the prancings, the prancings of their mighty ones.
Curse ye Meroz, said the Angel of the Lord, curse ye bitterly the inhabitants thereof,
because they came not to the help of the Lord, to the help of the Lord against the mighty.
Blessed above women shall Jael the wife of Heber the Kenite be, blessed shall she be above women in the tent.
He asked water, and she gave him milk, she brought forth butter in a lordly dish.
She put her hand to the nail, and her right hand to the workmen's hammer,
and with the hammer she smote Sisera, she smote off his head, when she had pierced and stricken through his temples.
At her feet he bowed, he fell, he lay down, at her feet he bowed, he fell, where he bowed, there he fell down dead.
The mother of Sisera looked out at a window,
and cried through the lattice,
Why is his chariot so long in coming? why tarry the wheels of his chariots?
Her wise ladies answered her, yea, she returned answer to herself,
Have they not sped? have they not divided the prey, to every man a damsel or two,
to Sisera a prey of divers colors, a prey of divers colors of needlework, of divers colors of needlework on both sides, meet for the necks of them that take the spoil?
So let all thine enemies perish, O Lord, but let them that love him be as the sun when he goeth forth in his might.
 And the land had rest forty years.

And the children of Israel did evil in the sight of the Lord and the Lord delivered them into the hand of Midian seven years. And the hand of Midian prevailed against Israel and because of the Midianites the children of Israel made them the dens which are in the mountains, and caves, and strongholds. And so it was when Israel had sown, that the Midianites came up, and the Amalekites, and the children of the east, even they came up against them and they encamped against them and destroyed the increase of the earth, till thou came unto Gaza, and left no sustenance for Israel, neither sheep, nor ox, nor ass. For they came up with their cattle and their tents, and they came as grasshoppers for multitude, for both they and their camels were without number and they entered into the land to destroy it. And Israel was greatly impoverished because of the Midianites and the children of Israel cried unto the Lord. And it came to pass when the children of Israel cried unto the Lord because of the Midianites, that the Lord sent a prophet unto the children of Israel which said unto them, Thus saith the Lord God of Israel, I brought you up from Egypt and brought you forth out of the house of bondage and I delivered you out of the hand of the Egyptians and out of the hand of all that oppressed you, and drave them out from before you, and gave you their land. And I said unto you, I am the Lord your God, fear not the gods of the Amorites in whose land ye dwell, but ye have not obeyed my voice.

And there came an Angel of the Lord and sat under an oak which was in Ophrah, that pertained unto Joash the Abi-ezrite, and his son Gideon threshed wheat by the winepress, to hide it from the Midianites. And the Angel of the Lord appeared unto him and said unto him, The Lord is with thee, thou mighty man of valor. And Gideon said unto him, O my Lord, if the Lord be with us, why then is all this befallen us? And where be all his miracles which our fathers told us of, saying, Did not the Lord bring us up from Egypt? But now the Lord hath forsaken us and delivered us into the hands of the Midianites. And the Lord looked upon him and said, Go in this thy might, and thou shalt save Israel from the hand of the Midianites. Have not I sent thee? And he said unto him, O my Lord, wherewith shall I save Israel? Behold, my family is poor in Manasseh, and I am the least in my father's house. And the Lord said unto him, Surely I will be with thee, and thou shalt smite the Midianites as one man. And he said unto him, If now I have found grace in thy sight, then show me a sign that thou talkest with me. Depart not hence, I pray thee, until I come unto thee and bring forth my present and set it before thee. And he said, I will tarry until thou come again.

And Gideon went in and made ready a kid, and unleavened cakes of an ephah of flour. The flesh he put in a basket, and he put the broth in a pot, and brought it out unto him under the oak, and presented it. And the angel of God said unto him, Take the flesh and the unleavened cakes, and lay them upon this rock, and pour out the broth. And he did so. Then the Angel of the Lord put forth the end of the staff that was in his hand, and touched the flesh and the unleavened cakes, and there rose up fire out of the rock and consumed the flesh and the unleavened cakes. Then the Angel of the Lord departed out of his sight. And when Gideon perceived that he was an angel of the Lord, Gideon said, Alas, O Lord God! for because I have seen an angel of the Lord face to face. And the Lord said unto him, Peace be unto thee, fear not; thou shalt not die. Then Gideon built an altar there unto the Lord, and called it Jehovah-shalom. Unto this day it is yet in Ophrah of the Abi-ezrites.

And it came to pass the same night that the Lord said unto him, Take thy father's young bullock, even the second bullock of seven years old, and throw down the altar of Baal that thy father hath, and cut down the grove that is by it. And build an altar unto the Lord thy God upon the top of this rock, in the ordered place, and take the second bullock, and offer a burnt sacrifice with the wood of the grove which thou shalt cut down. Then Gideon took ten men of his servants and did as the Lord had said unto him, and so it was, because he feared his father's household, and the men of the city, that he could not do it by day, that he did it by night. And when the men of the city arose early in the morning, behold, the altar of Baal was cast down and the grove was cut down that was by it, and the second bullock was offered upon the altar that was built. And they said one to another, Who hath done this thing? And when they inquired and asked, they said, Gideon the son of Joash hath done this thing. Then the men of the city said unto Joash, Bring out thy son, that he may die because he hath cast down the altar of Baal, and because he hath cut down the grove that was by it. And Joash said unto all that stood against him, Will ye plead for Baal? Will ye save him? He that will plead for him, let him be put to death whilst it is yet morning. If he be a god, let him plead for himself, because one hath cast down his altar. Therefore on that day he called him Jerubbaal, saying, Let Baal plead against him because he hath thrown down his altar.

Then all the Midianites and the Amalekites and the children of the east were gathered together and went over and pitched in the valley of Jezreel. But the Spirit of the Lord came upon Gideon, and he blew a trumpet, and Abi-ezer was gathered after him. And he sent messengers throughout all Manasseh, who also was gathered after him, and he sent messengers unto Asher, and unto Zebulun, and unto Naphtali, and they came up to meet them. And Gideon said unto God, If thou wilt save Israel by mine hand as thou hast said, behold, I will put a fleece of wool in the floor, and if the dew be on the fleece only, and it be dry upon all the earth besides, then shall I know that thou wilt save Israel by mine hand as thou hast said. And it was so, for he rose up early on the morrow, and thrust the fleece together, and wringed the dew out of the fleece a bowl full of water. And Gideon said unto God, Let not thine anger be hot against me, and I will speak but this once, let me prove, I pray thee, but this once with the fleece, let it now be dry only upon the fleece, and upon all the ground let there be dew. And God did so that night, for it was dry upon the fleece only and there was dew on all the ground.

Then Jerubbaal, who is Gideon, and all the people that were with him, rose up early and pitched beside the well of Harod so that the host of the Midianites were on the north side of them, by the hill of Moreh, in the valley. And the Lord said unto Gideon, The people that are with thee are too many for me to give the Midianites into their hands, lest Israel vaunt themselves against me, saying, Mine own hand hath saved me. Now therefore go to, proclaim in the ears of the people, saying, Whosoever is fearful and afraid, let him return and depart early from mount Gilead. And there returned of the people twenty and two thousand, and there remained ten thousand. And the Lord said unto Gideon, The people are yet too many. Bring them down unto the water and I will try them for thee there. And it shall be that of whom I say unto thee, This shall go with thee, the same shall go with thee and of whomsoever I say unto thee, This shall not go with thee, the same shall not go. So he brought down the people unto the water and the Lord said unto Gideon, Every one that lappeth of the water with his tongue, as a dog lappeth, him shalt thou set by himself, likewise every one that boweth down upon his knees to drink. And the number of them that lapped, putting their hand to their mouth, were three hundred men, but all the rest of the people bowed down upon their knees to drink water. And the Lord said unto Gideon, By the three hundred men that lapped will I save you, and deliver the Midianites into thine hand, and let all the other people go every man unto his place. So the people took victuals in their hand, and their trumpets, and he sent all the rest of Israel every man unto his tent, and retained those three hundred men, and the host of Midian was beneath him in the valley.

And it came to pass the same night that the Lord said unto him, Arise, get thee down unto the host, for I have delivered it into thine hand. But if thou fear to go down, go thou with Phurah thy servant down to the host, and thou shalt hear what they say, and afterward shall thine hands be strengthened to go down unto the host. Then went he down with Phurah his servant unto the outside of the armed men that were in the host. And the Midianites and the Amalekites and all children of the east lay along in the valley like grasshoppers for multitude, and their camels were without number, as the sand by the seaside for multitude. And when Gideon was come, behold, there was a man that told a dream unto his fellow, and said, Behold, I dreamed a dream, and lo, a cake of barley bread tumbled into the host of Midian and came unto a tent, and smote it that it fell, and overturned it, that the tent lay along. And his fellow answered and said, This is nothing else save the sword of Gideon the son of Joash, a man of Israel, for into his hand hath God delivered Midian and all the host.

And it was so, when Gideon heard the telling of the dream, and the interpretation thereof, that he worshiped and returned into the host of Israel, and said, Arise, for the Lord hath delivered into your hand the host of Midian. And he divided the three hundred men into three companies, and he put a trumpet in every man's hand, with empty pitchers, and lamps within the pitchers. And he said unto them, Look on me, and do likewise, and behold, when I come to the outside of the camp, it shall be that, as I do, so shall ye do. When I blow with a trumpet, I and all that are with me, then blow ye the trumpets also on every side of all the camp, and say, The sword of the Lord, and of Gideon. So Gideon, and the hundred men that were with him, came unto the outside of the camp in the beginning of the middle watch, and they had but newly set the watch, and they blew the trumpets, and brake the pitchers that were in their hands. And the three companies blew the trumpets and brake the pitchers, and held the lamps in their left hands, and the trumpets in their right hands to blow withal, and they cried, The sword of the Lord, and of Gideon. And they stood every man in his place round about the camp, and all the host ran, and cried, and fled. And the three hundred blew the trumpets, and the Lord set every man's sword against his fellow, even throughout all the host, and the host fled to Beth-shittah in Zererath, and to the border of Abel-meholah, unto Tabbath. And the men of Israel gathered themselves together out of Naphtali, and out of Asher, and out of all Manasseh, and pursued after the Midianites. And Gideon sent messengers throughout all mount Ephraim, saying, Come down against the Midianites and take before them the waters unto Beth-barah and Jordan. Then all the men of Ephraim gathered themselves together and took the waters unto Beth-barah and Jordan. And they took two princes of the Midianites, Oreb and Zeeb, and they slew Oreb upon the rock Oreb, and Zeeb they slew at the winepress of Zeeb and pursued Midian, and brought the heads of Oreb and Zeeb to Gideon on the other side Jordan.

And the men of Ephraim said unto him, Why hast thou served us thus, that thou calledst not, when thou wentest to fight with the Midianites? And they did chide with him sharply. And he said unto them, What have I done now in comparison of you? Is not the gleaning of the grapes of Ephraim better than the vintage of Abi-ezer? God hath delivered into your hands the princes of Midian, Oreb and Zeeb, and what was I able to do in comparison of you? Then their anger was abated toward him when he had said that. And Gideon came to Jordan and passed over, he, and the three hundred men that were with him, faint, yet pursuing them. And he said unto the men of Succoth, Give, I pray you, loaves of bread unto the people that follow me, for they be faint, and I am pursuing after Zebah and Zalmunna, kings of Midian. And the princes of Succoth said, Are the hands of Zebah and Zalmunna now in thine hand, that we should give bread unto thine army? And Gideon said, Therefore when the Lord hath delivered Zebah and Zalmunna into mine hand, then I will tear your flesh with the thorns of the wilderness and with briers. And he went up thence to Penuel, and spake unto them likewise, and the men of Penuel answered him as the men of Succoth had answered him. And he spake also unto the men of Penuel, saying, When I come again in peace, I will break down this tower. Now Zebah and Zalmunna were in Karkor, and their hosts with them, about fifteen thousand men, all that were left of all the hosts of the children of the east, for there fell a hundred and twenty thousand men that drew sword. And Gideon went up by the way of them that dwelt in tents on the east of Nobah and Jogbehah, and smote the host, for the host was secure. And when Zebah and Zalmunna fled, he pursued after them and took the two kings of Midian, Zebah and Zalmunna, and discomfited all the host.

And Gideon the son of Joash returned from battle before the sun was up and caught a young man of the men of Succoth, and inquired of him, and he described unto him the princes of Succoth, and the elders thereof, even threescore and seventeen men. And he came unto the men of Succoth, and said, Behold Zebah and Zalmunna, with whom ye did upbraid me, saying, Are the hands of Zebah and Zalmunna now in thine hand, that we should give bread unto thy men that are weary? And he took the elders of the city, and thorns of the wilderness, and briers, and with them he taught the men of Succoth. And he beat down the tower of Penuel, and slew the men of the city. Then said he unto Zebah and Zalmunna, What manner of men were they whom ye slew at Tabor? And they answered, As thou art, so were they, each one resembled the children of a king. And he said, They were my brethren, even the sons of my mother. As the Lord liveth, if ye had saved them alive, I would not slay you. And he said unto Jether his firstborn, Up, and slay them. But the youth drew not his sword, for he feared, because he was yet a youth. Then Zebah and Zalmunna said, Rise thou, and fall upon us, for as the man is, so is his strength. And Gideon arose, and slew Zebah and Zalmunna, and took away the ornaments that were on their camels' necks.

Then the men of Israel said unto Gideon, Rule thou over us, both thou and thy son, and thy son's son, also, for thou hast delivered us from the hand of Midian. And Gideon said unto them, I will not rule over you neither shall my son rule over you; the Lord shall rule over you. And Gideon said unto them, I would desire a request of you, that ye would give me every man the earrings of his prey. (For they had golden earrings because they were Ishmaelites.) And they answered, We will willingly give them. And they spread a garment and did cast therein every man the earrings of his prey. And the weight of the golden earrings that he requested was a thousand and seven hundred shekels of gold, besides ornaments, and collars, and purple raiment that was on the kings of Midian, and besides the chains that were about their camels' necks. And Gideon made an ephod thereof and put it in his city, even in Ophrah, and all Israel went thither a whoring after it, which thing became a snare unto Gideon and to his house.

Thus was Midian subdued before the children of Israel so that they lifted up their heads no more. And the country was in quietness forty years in the days of Gideon. And Jerubbaal the son Joash went and dwelt in his own house. And Gideon had threescore and ten sons of his body begotten, for he had many wives. And his concubine that was in Shechem, she also bare him a son whose name he called Abimelech. And Gideon the son of Joash died in a good old age and was buried in the sepulcher of Joash his father, in Ophrah of the Abiezrites. And it came to pass as soon as Gideon was dead that the children of Israel turned again and went a whoring after Baalim, and made Baal-berith their god. And the children of Israel remembered not the Lord their God who had delivered them out of the hands of all their enemies on every side, neither showed they kindness to the house of Jerubbaal, namely, Gideon, according to all the goodness which he had showed unto Israel.

And Abimelech the son of Jerubbaal went to Shechem unto his mother's brethren and communed with them, and with all the family of the house of his mother's father, saying, Speak, I pray you, in the ears of all the men of Shechem, Whether is better for you, either that all the sons of Jerubbaal, which are threescore and ten persons, reign over you? Or that one reign over you? Remember also that I am your bone and your flesh. And his mother's brethren spake of him in the ears of all the men of Shechem all these words, and their hearts inclined to follow Abimelech, for they said, He is our brother. And they gave him threescore and ten pieces of silver out of the house of Baal-berith, wherewith Abimelech hired vain and light persons, which followed him. And he went unto his father's house at Ophrah, and slew his brethren the sons of Jerubbaal, being threescore and ten persons, upon one stone, notwithstanding, yet Jotham the youngest son of Jerubbaal was left, for he hid himself. And all the men of Shechem gathered together, and all the house of Millo, and went and made Abimelech king, by the plain of the pillar that was in Shechem.

And when they told it to Jotham, he went and stood in the top of mount Gerizim and lifted up his voice and cried, and said unto them, Hearken unto me ye men of Shechem, that God may hearken unto you. The trees went forth on a time to anoint a king over them, and they said unto the olive tree, Reign thou over us. But the olive tree said unto them, Should I leave my fatness, wherewith by me they honor God and man, and go to be promoted over the trees? And the trees said to the fig tree, Come thou and reign over us. But the fig tree said unto them, Should I forsake my sweetness, and my good fruit, and go to be promoted over the trees? Then said the trees unto the vine, Come thou and reign over us. And the vine said unto them, Should I leave my wine, which cheereth God and man, and go to be promoted over the trees? Then said all the trees unto the bramble, Come thou and reign over us. And the bramble said unto the trees, If in truth ye anoint me king over you, then come and put your trust in my shadow, and if not, let fire come out of the bramble, and devour the cedars of Lebanon. Now therefore, if ye have done truly and sincerely, in that ye have made Abimelech king, and if ye have dealt well with Jerubbaal and his house, and have done unto him according to the deserving of his hands, (for my father fought for you, and adventured his life far, and delivered you out of the hand of Midian, and ye are risen up against my father's house this day, and have slain his sons, threescore and ten persons, upon one stone, and have made Abimelech, the son of his maidservant, king over the men of Shechem, because he is your brother,) if ye then have dealt truly and sincerely with Jerubbaal and with his house this day, then rejoice ye in Abimelech, and let him also rejoice in you, but if not, let fire come out from Abimelech, and devour the men of Shechem, and the house of Millo, and let fire come out from the men of Shechem, and from the house of Millo, and devour Abimelech. And Jotham ran away, and fled, and went to Beer, and dwelt there for fear of Abimelech his brother.

When Abimelech had reigned three years over Israel, then God sent an evil spirit between Abimelech and the men of Shechem, and the men of Shechem dealt treacherously with Abimelech, that the cruelty done to the threescore and ten sons of Jerubbaal might come, and their blood be laid upon Abimelech their brother, which slew them, and upon the men of Shechem, which aided him in the killing of his brethren. And the men of Shechem set liers in wait for him in the top of the mountains, and they robbed all that came along that way by them, and it was told Abimelech. And Gaal the son of Ebed came with his brethren and went over to Shechem, and the men of Shechem put their confidence in him. And they went out into the fields, and gathered their vineyards, and trode the grapes, and made merry, and went into the house of their god, and did eat and drink, and cursed Abimelech. And Gaal the son of Ebed said, Who is Abimelech, and who is Shechem, that we should serve him? is not he the son of Jerubbaal? And Zebul his officer? Serve the men of Hamor the father of Shechem, for why should we serve him? And would to God these people were under my hand! Then would I remove Abimelech. And he said to Abimelech, Increase thine army, and come out. And when Zebul the ruler of the city heard the words of Gaal the son of Ebed, his anger was kindled. And he sent messengers unto Abimelech privily, saying, Behold, Gaal the son of Ebed and his brethren be come to Shechem, and, behold, they fortify the city against thee. Now therefore up by night, thou and the people that is with thee, and lie in wait in the field, and it shall be that in the morning, as soon as the sun is up, thou shalt rise early and set upon the city, and, behold, when he and the people that is with him come out against thee, then mayest thou do to them as thou shalt find occasion.

And Abimelech rose up, and all the people that were with him, by night, and they laid wait against Shechem in four companies. And Gaal the son of Ebed went out and stood in the entering of the gate of the city, and Abimelech rose up, and the people that were with him, from lying in wait. And when Gaal saw the people, he said to Zebul, Behold, there come people down from the top of the mountains. And Zebul said unto him, Thou seest the shadow of the mountains as if they were men. And Gaal spoke again and said, See, there come people down by the middle of the land, and another company come along by the plain of Meonenim. Then said Zebul unto him, Where is now thy mouth, wherewith thou saidst, Who is Abimelech, that we should serve him? is not this the people that thou hast despised? Go out, I pray now, and fight with them. And Gaal went out before the men of Shechem, and fought with Abimelech. And Abimelech chased him, and he fled before him, and many were overthrown and wounded even unto the entering of the gate. And Abimelech dwelt at Arumah, and Zebul thrust out Gaal and his brethren that they should not dwell in Shechem. And it came to pass on the morrow that the people went out into the field, and they told Abimelech. And he took the people and divided them into three companies, and laid wait in the field and looked, and behold, the people were come forth out of the city, and he rose up against them and smote them. And Abimelech and the company that was with him, rushed forward and stood in the entering of the gate of the city, and the two other companies ran upon all the people that were in the fields, and slew them. And Abimelech fought against the city all that day, and he took the city and slew the people that was therein, and beat down the city and sowed it with salt. And when all the men of the tower of Shechem heard that, they entered into a hold of the house of the god Berith. And it was told Abimelech, that all the men of the tower of Shechem were gathered together. And Abimelech gat him up to mount Zalmon, he and all the people that were with him, and Abimelech took an axe in his hand and cut down a bough from the trees, and took it, and laid it on his shoulder, and said unto the people that were with him, What ye have seen me do, make haste, and do as I have done. And all the people likewise cut down every man his bough, and followed Abimelech, and put them to the hold, and set the hold on fire upon them, so that all the men of the tower of Shechem died also, about a thousand men and women.

Then went Abimelech to Thebez and encamped against Thebez, and took it. But there was a strong tower within the cit, and thither fled all the men and women, and all they of the city, and shut it to them, and gat them up to the top of the tower. And Abimelech came unto the tower and fought against it, and went hard unto the door of the tower to burn it with fire. And a certain woman cast a piece of a millstone upon Abimelech's head, and all to brake his skull. Then he called hastily unto the young man his armor-bearer and said unto him, Draw thy sword, and slay me, that the men say not of me, A woman slew him. And his young man thrust him through and he died. And when the men of Israel saw that Abimelech was dead they departed every man unto his place. Thus God rendered the wickedness of Abimelech, which he did unto his father, in slaying his seventy brethren, and all the evil of the men of Shechem did God render upon their heads, and upon them came the curse of Jotham the son of Jerubbaal.

After Abimelech there arose to defend Israel Tola the son of Puah, the son of Dodo, a man of Issachar, and he dwelt in Shamir in mount Ephraim. And he judged Israel twenty and three years, and died and was buried in Shamir.

And after him arose Jair, a Gileadite, and judged Israel twenty and two years. And he had thirty sons that rode on thirty ass colts, and they had thirty cities, which are called Havoth-jair unto this day, which are in the land of Gilead. And Jair died and was buried in Camon.

And the children of Israel did evil again in the sight of the Lord, and served Baalim, and Ashtaroth, and the gods of Syria, and the gods of Zidon, and the gods of Moab, and the gods of the children of Ammon, and the gods of the Philistines, and forsook the Lord and served him not. And the anger of the Lord was hot against Israel, and he sold them into the hands of the Philistines and into the hands of the children of Ammon. And that year they vexed and oppressed the children of Israel, eighteen years, all the children of Israel that were on the other side Jordan in the land of the Amorites which is in Gilead. Moreover the children of Ammon passed over Jordan to fight also against Judah, and against Benjamin, and against the house of Ephraim, so that Israel was sore distressed.

And the children of Israel cried unto the Lord saying, We have sinned against thee, both because we have forsaken our God and also served Baalim. And the Lord said unto the children of Israel, Did not I deliver you from the Egyptians, and from the Amorites, from the children of Ammon, and from the Philistines? The Zidonians also, and the Amalekites, and the Maonites, did oppress you, and ye cried to me, and I delivered you out of their hand. Yet ye have forsaken me and served other gods. Wherefore I will deliver you no more. Go and cry unto the gods which ye have chosen; let them deliver you in the time of your tribulation. And the children of Israel said unto the Lord, We have sinned, do thou unto us whatsoever seemeth good unto thee. Deliver us only, we pray thee, this day. And they put away the strange gods from among them and served the Lord; and his soul was grieved for the misery of Israel. Then the children of Ammon were gathered together and encamped in Gilead. And the children of Israel assembled themselves together, and encamped in Mizpeh. And the people and princes of Gilead said to one another, What man is he that will begin to fight against the children of Ammon? He shall be head over all the inhabitants of Gilead.

Now Jephthah the Gileadite was a mighty man of valor, and he was the son of a harlot, and Gilead begat Jephthah. And Gilead's wife bare him sons, and his wife's sons grew up and they thrust out Jephthah and said unto him, Thou shalt not inherit in our father's house, for thou art the son of a strange woman. Then Jephthah fled from his brethren and dwelt in the land of Tob, and there were gathered vain men to Jephthah, and went out with him. And it came to pass in process of time that the children of Ammon made war against Israel. And it was so, that when the children of Ammon made war against Israel, the elders of Gilead went to fetch Jephthah out of the land of Tob, and they said unto Jephthah, Come and be our captain, that we may fight with the children of Ammon. And Jephthah said unto the elders of Gilead, Did not ye hate me and expel me out of my father's house? And why are ye come unto me now when ye are in distress? And the elders of Gilead said unto Jephthah, Therefore we turn again to thee now, that thou mayest go with us and fight against the children of Ammon, and be our head over all the inhabitants of Gilead. And Jephthah said unto the elders of Gilead, If ye bring me home again to fight against the children of Ammon, and the Lord deliver them before me, shall I be your head? And the elders of Gilead said unto Jephthah, The Lord be witness between us, if we do not so according to thy words. Then Jephthah went with the elders of Gilead, and the people made him head and captain over them, and Jephthah uttered all his words before the Lord in Mizpeh.

And Jephthah sent messengers unto the king of the children of Ammon, saying, What hast thou to do with me, that thou art come against me to fight in my land? And the king of the children of Ammon answered unto the messengers of Jephthah, Because Israel took away my land when they came up out of Egypt, from Arnon even unto Jabbok, and unto Jordan, now therefore restore those lands again peaceably. And Jephthah sent messengers again unto the king of the children of Ammon and said unto him, Thus saith Jephthah, Israel took not away the land of Moab nor the land of the children of Ammon, but when Israel came up from Egypt, and walked through the wilderness unto the Red Sea, and came to Kadesh, then Israel sent messengers unto the king of Edom, saying, Let me, I pray thee, pass through thy land, but the king of Edom would not hearken thereto. And in like manner they sent unto the king of Moab, but he would not consent, and Israel abode in Kadesh. Then they went along through the wilderness and compassed the land of Edom, and the land of Moab, and came by the east side of the land of Moab, and pitched on the other side of Arnon, but came not within the border of Moab, for Arnon was the border of Moab. And Israel sent messengers unto Sihon king of the Amorites, the king of Heshbon, and Israel said unto him, Let us pass, we pray thee, through thy land into my place. But Sihon trusted not Israel to pass through his coast, but Sihon gathered all his people together and pitched in Jahaz, and fought against Israel. And the Lord God of Israel delivered Sihon and all his people into the hand of Israel, and they smote them, so Israel possessed all the land of the Amorites, the inhabitants of that country. And they possessed all the coasts of the Amorites, from Arnon even unto Jabbok, and from the wilderness even unto Jordan. So now the Lord God of Israel hath dispossessed the Amorites from before his people Israel, and shouldest thou possess it? Wilt not thou possess that which Chemosh thy god giveth thee to possess? So whomsoever the Lord our God shall drive out from before us, them will we possess. And now art thou any thing better than Balak the son of Zippor, king of Moab? Did he ever strive against Israel or did he ever fight against them, while Israel dwelt in Heshbon and her towns, and in Aroer and her towns, and in all the cities that be along by the coasts of Arnon, three hundred years? Why therefore did ye not recover them within that time? Wherefore I have not sinned against thee, but thou doest me wrong to war against me; the Lord the Judge be judge this day between the children of Israel and the children of Ammon. Howbeit the king of the children of Ammon hearkened not unto the words of Jephthah which he sent him.

Then the Spirit of the Lord came upon Jephthah, and he passed over Gilead, and Manasseh, and passed over Mizpeh of Gilead, and from Mizpeh of Gilead he passed over unto the children of Ammon. And Jephthah vowed a vow unto the Lord and said, If thou shalt without fail deliver the children of Ammon into my hands, then it shall be, that whatsoever cometh forth of the doors of my house to meet me, when I return in peace from the children of Ammon, shall surely be the Lord's, and I will offer it up for a burnt offering. So Jephthah passed over unto the children of Ammon to fight against them, and the Lord delivered them into his hands. And he smote them from Aroer, even till thou come to Minnith, even twenty cities, and unto the plain of the vineyards, with a very great slaughter. Thus the children of Ammon were subdued before the children of Israel.

And Jephthah came to Mizpeh unto his house and behold, his daughter came out to meet him with timbrels and with dances, and she was his only child, beside her he had neither son nor daughter. And it came to pass when he saw her, that he rent his clothes, and said, Alas, my daughter! Thou hast brought me very low, and thou art one of them that trouble me, for I have opened my mouth unto the Lord and I cannot go back. And she said unto him, My father, if thou hast opened thy mouth unto the Lord, do to me according to that which hath proceeded out of thy mouth, forasmuch as the Lord hath taken vengeance for thee of thine enemies, even of the children of Ammon. And she said unto her father, Let this thing be done for me, let me alone two months, that I may go up and down upon the mountains, and bewail my virginity, I and my fellows. And he said, Go. And he sent her away for two months, and she went with her companions and bewailed her virginity upon the mountains. And it came to pass at the end of two months that she returned unto her father, who did with her according to his vow which he had vowed, and she knew no man. And it was a custom in Israel, that the daughters of Israel went yearly to lament the daughter of Jephthah the Gileadite four days in a year.

And the men of Ephraim gathered themselves together and went northward, and said unto Jephthah, Wherefore passedst thou over to fight against the children of Ammon, and didst not call us to go with thee? We will burn thine house upon thee with fire. And Jephthah said unto them, I and my people were at great strife with the children of Ammon, and when I called you, ye delivered me not out of their hands. And when I saw that ye delivered me not, I put my life in my hands, and passed over against the children of Ammon and the Lord delivered them into my hand, wherefore then are ye come up unto me this day, to fight against me? Then Jephthah gathered together all the men of Gilead, and fought with Ephraim, and the men of Gilead smote Ephraim, because they said, Ye Gileadites are fugitives of Ephraim among the Ephraimites, and among the Manassites. And the Gileadites took the passages of Jordan before the Ephraimites, and it was so, that when those Ephraimites which were escaped said, Let me go over, that the men of Gilead said unto him, Art thou an Ephraimite? If he said, Nay, then said they unto him, Say now Shibboleth, and he said Sibbolet, for he could not frame to pronounce it right. Then they took him and slew him at the passages of Jordan, and there fell at that time of the Ephraimites forty and two thousand. And Jephthah judged Israel six years. Then died Jephthah the Gileadite, and was buried in one of the cities of Gilead.

And after him Ibzan of Bethlehem judged Israel. And he had thirty sons, and thirty daughters, whom he sent abroad, and took in thirty daughters from abroad for his sons. And he judged Israel seven years. Then died Ibzan, and was buried at Bethlehem.

And after him Elon, a Zebulonite, judged Israel, and he judged Israel ten years. And Elon the Zebulonite died, and was buried in Aijalon in the country of Zebulun.

And after him Abdon the son of Hillel, a Pirathonite, judged Israel. And he had forty sons and thirty nephews, that rode on threescore and ten ass colts, and he judged Israel eight years. And Abdon the son of Hillel the Pirathonite died, and was buried in Pirathon in the land of Ephraim, in the mount of the Amalekites.

3 AND the children of Israel did evil again in the sight of the Lord, and the Lord delivered them into the hands of Philistines forty years. And there was a certain man of Zorah, of the family of the Danites, whose name was Manoah, and his wife was barren and bare not. And the Angel of the Lord appeared unto the woman and said unto her, Behold now, thou art barren and bearest not, but

thou shalt conceive and bear a son. Now therefore beware, I pray thee, and drink not wine nor strong drink and eat not any unclean thing, for lo, thou shalt conceive and bear a son, and no razor shall come on his head, for the child shall be a Nazarite unto God from the womb, and he shall begin to deliver Israel out of the hand of the Philistines. Then the woman came and told her husband, saying, A man of God came unto me, and his countenance was like the countenance of an angel of God, very terrible, but I asked him not whence he was, neither told he me his name, but he said unto me, behold, thou shalt conceive and bear a son, and now drink no wine nor strong drink, neither eat any unclean thing, for the child shall be a Nazarite to God from the womb to the day of his death.

Then Manoah entreated the Lord and said, O my Lord, let the man of God which thou didst send come again unto us and teach us what we shall do unto the child that shall be born. And God hearkened to the voice of Manoah and the angel of God came again unto the woman as she sat in the field, but Manoah her husband was not with her. And the woman made haste and ran, and showed her husband, and said unto him, Behold, the man hath appeared unto me that came unto me the other day. And Manoah arose and went after his wife, and came to the man and said unto him, Art thou the man that spakest unto the woman? And he said, I am. And Manoah said, Now let thy words come to pass. How shall we order the child and how shall we do unto him? And the Angel of the Lord said unto Manoah, Of all that I said unto the woman let her beware. She may not eat of any thing that cometh of the vine, neither let her drink wine or strong drink, nor eat any unclean thing; all that I commanded her let her observe. And Manoah said unto the Angel of the Lord, I pray thee, Let us detain thee until we shall have made ready a kid for thee. And the Angel of the Lord said unto Manoah, Though thou detain me, I will not eat of thy bread, and if thou wilt offer a burnt offering thou must offer it unto the Lord. For Manoah knew not that he was an angel of the Lord. And Manoah said unto the Angel of the Lord, What is thy name, that when thy sayings come to pass we may do thee honor? And the Angel of the Lord said unto him, Why askest thou thus after my name, seeing it is secret? So Manoah took a kid with a meat offerin, and offered it upon a rock unto the Lord, and the angel did wondrously, and Manoah and his wife looked on. For it came to pass when the flame went up toward Heaven from off the altar, that the Angel of the Lord ascended in the flame of the altar, and Manoah and his wife looked on it and fell on their faces to the ground. But the Angel of the Lord did no more appear to Manoah and to his wife. Then Manoah knew that he was an Angel of the Lord. And Manoah said unto his wife, We shall surely die because we have seen God. But his wife said unto him, If the Lord were pleased to kill us he would not have received a burnt offering and a meat offering at our hands, neither would he have showed us all these things, nor would as at this time have told us such things as these.

And the woman bare a son and called his name Samson, and the child grew and the Lord blessed him. And the Spirit of the Lord began to move him at times in the camp of Dan between Zorah and Eshtaol. And Samson went down to Timnath and saw a woman in Timnath of the daughters of the Philistines. And he came up and told his father and his mother and said, I have seen a woman in Timnath of the daughters of the Philistines, now therefore get her for me to wife. Then his father and his mother said unto him, Is there never a woman among the daughters of thy brethren, or among all my people, that thou goest to take a wife of the uncircumcised Philistines? And Samson said unto his father, Get her for me, for she pleaseth me well. But his father and his mother knew not that it was of the Lord, that he sought an occasion against the Philistines, for at that time the Philistines had dominion over Israel. Then went Samson down, and his father and his mother, to Timnath, and came to the vineyards of Timnath, and behold, a young lion roared against him. And the Spirit of the Lord came mightily upon him and he rent him as he would have rent a kid, and he had nothing in his hand, but he told not his father or his mother what he had done. And he went down and talked with the woman and she pleased Samson well. And after a time he returned to take her and he turned aside to see the carcass of the lion, and behold, there was a swarm of bees and honey in the carcass of the lion. And he took thereof in his hands, and went on eating, and came to his father and mother, and he gave them, and they did eat, but he told not them that he had taken the honey out of the carcass of the lion. So his father went down unto the woman, and Samson made there a feast for so used the young men to do. And it came to pass when they saw him, that they brought thirty companions to be with him. And Samson said unto them, I will now put forth a riddle unto you, if ye can certainly declare it me within the seven days of the feast, and find it out, then I will give you thirty sheets and thirty change of garments, but if ye cannot declare it me, then shall ye give me thirty sheets and thirty change of garments. And they said unto him, Put forth thy riddle that we may hear it. And he said unto them: Out of the eater came forth meat, and out of the strong came forth sweetness. And they could not in three days expound the riddle. And it came to pass on the seventh day that they said unto Samson's wife, Entice thy husband, that he may declare unto us the riddle, lest we burn thee and thy father's house with fire. Have ye called us to take that we have? is it not so? And Samson's wife wept before him and said, Thou dost but hate me, and lovest me not, thou hast put forth a riddle unto the children of my people, and hast not told it me. And he said unto her, Behold, I have not told it my father nor my mother, and shall I tell it thee? And she wept before him the seven days, while their feast lasted, and it came to pass on the seventh day that he told her, because she lay sore upon him, and she told the riddle to the children of her people. And the men of the city said unto him on the seventh day before the sun went down: What is sweeter than honey? And what is stronger than a lion? And he said unto them: If ye had not ploughed with my heifer, ye had not found out my riddle. And the Spirit of the Lord came upon him and he went down to Ashkelon, and slew thirty men of them, and took their spoil, and gave change of garments unto them which expounded the riddle. And his anger was kindled, and he went up to his father's house. But Samson's wife was given to his companion, whom he had used as his friend.

But it came to pass within a while after, in the time of wheat harvest, that Samson visited his wife with a kid, and he said, I will go in to my wife into the chamber. But her father would not suffer him to go in. And her father said, I verily thought that thou hadst utterly hated her, therefore I gave her to thy companion, is not her younger sister fairer than she? Take her, I pray thee, instead of her. And Samson said concerning them, Now shall I be more blameless than the Philistines, though I do them a displeasure. And Samson went and caught three hundred foxes, and took firebrands, and turned tail to tail, and put a firebrand in the midst between two tails. And when he had set the brands on fire, he let them go into the standing corn of the Philistines, and burnt up both the shocks, and also the standing corn, with the vineyards and olives. Then the Philistines said, Who hath done this? And they answered, Samson, the son-in-law of the Timnite, because he had taken his wife, and given her to his companion. And the Philistines came up and burnt her and her father with fire. And Samson said unto them, Though ye have done this, yet will I be avenged of you, and after that I will cease. And he smote them hip and thigh with a great slaughter, and he went down and dwelt in the top of the rock Etam.

Then the philistines went up and pitched in Judah and spread themselves in Lehi. And the men of Judah said, Why are ye come up against us? And they answered, To bind Samson are we come up, to do to him as he hath done to us. Then three thousand men of Judah went to the top of the rock Etam, and said to Samson, Knowest thou not that the Philistines are rulers over us? What is this that thou hast done unto us? And he said unto them, As they did unto me, so have I done unto them. And they said unto him, We are come down to bind thee that we may deliver thee into the hand of the Philistines. And Samson said unto them, Swear unto me, that ye will not fall upon me yourselves. And they spake unto him, saying, No, but we will bind thee fast and deliver thee into their hand, but surely we will not kill thee. And they bound him with two new cords, and brought him up from the rock. And when he came into Lehi, the Philistines shouted against him, and the Spirit of the Lord came mightily upon him, and the cords that were upon his arms became as flax that was burnt with fire, and his bands loosed from off his hands. And he found a new jawbone of an ass, and put forth his hand, and took it, and slew a thousand men therewith. And Samson said, With the jawbone of an ass, heaps upon heaps, with the jaw of an ass have I slain a thousand men. And it came to pass when he had made an end of speaking that he cast away the jawbone out of his hand, and called that place Ramathlehi. And he was sore athirst and called on the Lord and said, Thou hast given this great deliverance into the hand of thy servant, and now shall I die for thirst, and fall into the hand of the uncircumcised? But God clave a hollow place that was in the jaw, and there came water thereout, and when he had drunk, his spirit came again and he revived, wherefore he called the name thereof Enhakkore, which is in Lehi unto this day. And he judged Israel in the days of the Philistines twenty years.

Then went Samson to Gaza, and saw there a harlot, and went in unto her. And it was told the Gazites saying, Samson is come hither. And they compassed him in and laid wait for him all night in the gate of the city, and were quiet all the night saying, In the morning, when it is day we shall kill him. And Samson lay till midnight and arose at midnight and took the doors of the gate of the city, and the two posts, and went away with them, bar and all, and put them upon his shoulders, and carried them up to the top of a hill that is before Hebron.

And it came to pass afterward that he loved a woman in the valley of Sorek, whose name was Delilah. And the lords of the Philistines came up unto her and said unto her, Entice him and see wherein his great strength lieth, and by what means we may prevail against him, that we may bind him to afflict him. And we will give thee every one of us eleven hundred pieces of silver. And Delilah said to Samson, Tell me, I pray thee, wherein thy great strength lieth, and wherewith thou mightest be bound to afflict thee. And Samson said unto her, If they bind me with seven green withs that were never dried, then shall I be weak and be as another man. Then the lords of the Philistines brought up to her seven green withs which had not been dried, and she bound him with them. Now there were men lying in wait, abiding with her in the chamber. And she said unto him, The Philistines be upon thee, Samson. And he brake the withs as a thread of tow is broken when it toucheth the fire. So his strength was not known. And Delilah said unto Samson, Behold, thou hast mocked me and told me lies. Now tell me, I pray thee, wherewith thou mightest be bound. And he said unto her, If they bind me fast with new ropes that never were occupied, then shall I be weak and be as another man. Delilah therefore took new ropes and bound him therewith, and said unto him, The Philistines be upon thee, Samson. And there were liers in wait abiding in the chamber. And he brake them from off his arms like a thread. And Delilah said unto Samson, Hitherto thou has mocked me, and told me lies. Tell me wherewith thou mightest be bound. And he said unto her, If thou weavest the seven locks of my head with the web. And she fastened it with the pin, and said unto him, The Philistines be upon thee, Samson. And he awaked out of his sleep, and went away with the pin of the beam, and with the web. And she said unto him, How canst thou say I love thee, when thine heart is not with me? Thou has mocked me these three times. and hast not told me wherein thy great strength lieth. And it came to pass, when she pressed him daily with her words, and urged him, so that his soul was vexed unto death, that he told her all his heart and said unto her, There hath not come a razor upon mine head, for I have been a Nazarite unto God from my mother's womb. If I be shaven then my strength will go from me, and I shall become weak, and be like any other man. And when Delilah saw that he had told her all his heart, she sent and called for the lords of the Philistines, saying, Come up this once, for he hath showed me all his heart. Then the lords of the Philistines came up unto her and brought money in their hand. And she made him sleep upon her knees, and she called for a man, and she caused him to shave off the seven locks of his head, and she began to afflict him, and his strength went from him. And she said, The Philistines be upon thee, Samson. And he awoke out of his sleep, and said, I will go out as at other times before and shake myself. And he wist not that the Lord was departed from him. But the Philistines took him and put out his eyes, and brought him down to Gaza, and bound him with fetters of brass, and he did grind in the prison house. Howbeit the hair of his head began to grow again after he was shaven.

Then the lords of the Philistines gathered them together for to offer a great sacrifice unto Dagon their god, and to rejoice, for they said, Our god hath delivered Samson our enemy into our hand. And when the people saw him they praised their god, for they said, Our god hath delivered into our hands our enemy and the destroyer of our country, which slew many of us.

And it came to pass when their hearts were merry that they said, Call for Samson, that he may make us sport. And they called for Samson out of the prison house, and he made them sport, and they set him between the pillars. And Samson said unto the lad that held him by the hand, Suffer me that I may feel the pillars whereupon the house standeth, that I may lean upon them. Now the house was full of men and women, and all the lords of the Philistines were there, and there were upon the roof about three thousand men and women that beheld while Samson made sport.

And Samson called unto the Lord and said, O Lord God, remember me, I pray thee, and strengthen me, I pray thee, only this once, O God, that I may be at once avenged of the Philistines for my two eyes. And Samson took hold of the two middle pillars upon which the house stood and on which it was borne up, of the one with his right hand, and of the other with his left. And Samson said, Let me die with the Philistines. And he bowed himself with all his might, and the house fell upon the lords and upon all the people that were therein. So the dead which he slew at his death were more than they which he slew in his life. Then his brethren and all the house of his father came down and took him and brought him up, and buried him between Zorah and Eshtaol in the burying-place of Manoah his father. And he judged Israel twenty years.

4 AND there was a man of mount Ephraim whose name was Micah. And he said unto his mother, The eleven hundred shekels of silver that were taken from thee, about which thou cursedst, and spakest of also in mine ears, behold, the silver is with me, I took it. And his mother said, Blessed be thou of the Lord, my son. And when he had restored the eleven hundred shekels of silver to his mother, his mother said, I had wholly dedicated the silver unto the Lord from my hand for my son, to make a graven image and a molten image; now therefore I will restore it unto thee. Yet he restored the money unto his mother, and his mother took two hundred shekels of silver, and gave them to the founder who made

thereof a graven image and a molten image, and they were in the house of Micah. And the man Micah had a house of gods, and made an ephod, and teraphim, and consecrated one of his sons, who became his priest. In those days there was no king in Israel, but every man did that which was right in his own eyes.

And there was a young man out of Beth-lehem-judah of the family of Judah, who was a Levite, and he sojourned there. And the man departed out of the city from Beth-lehem-judah to sojourn where he could find a place, and he came to mount Ephraim to the house of Micah, as he journeyed. And Micah said unto him, Whence comest thou? And he said unto him, I am a Levite of Beth-lehem-judah and I go to sojourn where I may find a place. And Micah said unto him, Dwell with me and be unto me a father and a priest, and I will give thee ten shekels of silver by the year, and a suit of apparel, and thy victuals. So the Levite went in. And the Levite was content to dwell with the man, and the young man was unto him as one of his sons. And Micah consecrated the Levite and the young man became his priest and was in the house of Micah. Then said Micah, Now know I that the Lord will do me good, seeing I have a Levite to my priest.

In those days there was no king in Israel, and in those days the tribe of the Danites sought them an inheritance to dwell in, for unto that day all their inheritance had not fallen unto them among the tribes of Israel. And the children of Dan sent of their family five men from their coast, men of valor, from Zorah, and from Eshtaol, to spy out the land, and to search it, and they said unto them, Go, search the land, who when they came to mount Ephraim, to the house of Micah, they lodged there. When they were by the house of Micah they knew the voice of the young man the Levite, and they turned in thither, and said unto him, Who brought thee hither? And what makest thou in this place? And what hast thou here? And he said unto them, Thus and thus dealeth Micah with me, and hath hired me, and I am his priest. And they said unto him, Ask counsel, we pray thee, of God, that we may know whether our way which we go shall be prosperous. And the priest said unto them, Go in peace, before the Lord is your way wherein ye go.

Then the five men departed, and came to Laish, and saw the people that were therein, how they dwelt careless, after the manner of the Zidonians, quiet and secure, and there was no magistrate in the land that might put them to shame in anything, and they were far from the Zidonians, and had no business with any man. And they came unto their brethren to Zorah and Eshtaol, and their brethren said unto them, What say ye? And they said, Arise, that we may go up against them for we have seen the land, and behold, it is very good, and are ye still? Be not slothful to go and to enter to possess the land. When ye go ye shall come unto a people secure, and to a large land, for God hath given it into your hands, a place where there is no want of anything that is in the Earth.

And there went from thence of the family of the Danites, out of Zorah and out of Eshtaol, six hundred men appointed with weapons of war. And they went up, and pitched in Kirjath-jearim, in Judah, wherefore they called that place Mahaneh-dan unto this day. Behold, it is behind Kirjath-jearim. And they passed thence unto mount Ephraim and came unto the house of Micah. Then answered the five men that went to spy out the country of Laish, and said unto their brethren, Do ye know that there is in these houses an ephod, and teraphim, and a graven image, and a molten image? Now therefore consider what ye have to do. And they turned thitherward, and came to the house of the young man the Levite, even unto the house of Micah, and saluted him. And the six hundred men appointed with their weapons of war, which were of the children of Dan, stood by the entering of the gate. And the five men that went to spy out the land went up and came in thither, and took the graven image, and the ephod, and the teraphim, and the molten image, and the priest stood in the entering of the gate with the six hundred men that were appointed with weapons of war. And these went into Micah's house, and fetched the carved image, the ephod, and the teraphim, and the molten image. Then said the priest unto them, What do ye? And they said unto him, Hold thy peace, lay thine hand upon thy mouth, and go with us, and be to us a father and a priest. Is it better for thee to be a priest unto the house of one man, or that thou be a priest unto a tribe and a family in Israel? And the priest's heart was glad, and he took the ephod, and the teraphim, and the graven image, and went in the midst of the people.

So they turned and departed and put the little ones and the cattle and the carriage before them. And when they were a good way from the house of Micah, the men that were in the houses near to Micah's house were gathered together and overtook the children of Dan. And they cried unto the children of Dan. And they turned their faces, and said unto Micah, What aileth thee that thou comest with such a company? And he said, Ye have taken away my gods which I made, and the priest, and ye are gone away, and what have I more? And what is this that ye say unto me, What aileth thee? And the children of Dan said unto him, Let not thy voice be heard among us, lest angry fellows run upon thee, and thou lose thy life with the lives of thy household. And the children of Dan went their way, and when Micah saw that they were too strong for him he turned and went back unto his house.

And they took the things which Micah had made, and the priest which he had, and came unto Laish, unto a people that were at quiet and secure, and they smote them with the edge of the sword, and burnt the city with fire. And there was no deliverer because it was far from Zidon, and they had no business with any man, and it was in the valley that lieth by Beth-rehob. And they built a city and dwelt therein. And they called the name of the city Dan, after the name of Dan their father who was born unto Israel, howbeit the name of the city was Laish at the first. And the children of Dan set up the graven image, and Jonathan, the son of Gershom, the son of Manasseh, he and his sons were priests to the tribe of Dan until the day of the captivity of the land. And they set them up Micah's graven image, which he made, all the time that the house of God was in Shiloh.

And it came to pass in those days when there was no king in Israel that there was a certain Levite sojourning on the side of mount Ephraim, who took to him a concubine out of Beth-lehem-judah. And his concubine played the whore against him, and went away from him unto her father's house to Beth-lehem-judah, and was there four whole months. And her husband arose and went after her to speak friendly unto her and to bring her again, having his servant with him, and a couple of asses, and she brought him into her father's house. And when the father of the damsel saw him, he rejoiced to meet him. And his father-in-law, the damsel's father, retained him, and he abode with him three days, so they did eat and drink and lodged there. And it came to pass on the fourth day when they arose early in the morning, that he rose up to depart, and the damsel's father said unto his son-in-law, Comfort thine heart with a morsel of bread and afterward go your way. And they sat down and did eat and drink both of them together, for the damsel's father had said unto the man, Be content, I pray thee, and tarry all night, and let thine heart be merry. And when the man rose up to depart, his father-in-law urged him, therefore he lodged there again. And he arose early in the morning on the fifth day to depart, and the damsel's father said, Comfort thine heart, I pray thee. And they tarried until afternoon, and they did eat both of them. And when the man rose up to depart, he, and his concubine, and his servant, his father-in-law, the damsel's father, said unto him, Behold, now the day draweth toward evening, I pray you tarry all night, behold, the day groweth to an end. Lodge here, that thine heart may be merry, and tomorrow get you early on your way that thou mayest go home. But the man would not tarry that night, but he rose up and departed, and came over against Jebus, which is Jerusalem, and there were with him two asses saddled, his concubine also was with him. And when they were by Jebus, the day was far spent and the servant said unto his master, Come, I pray thee, and let us turn in into this city of the Jebusites and lodge in it. And his master said unto him, We will not turn aside hither into the city of a stranger, that is not of the children of Israel; we will pass over to Gibeah. And he said unto his servant, Come, and let us draw near to one of these places to lodge all night, in Gibeah, or in Ramah. And they passed on and went their way, and the sun went down upon them when they were by Gibeah, which belongeth to Benjamin. And they turned aside thither, to go in and to lodge in Gibeah, and when he went in he sat him down in a street of the city, for there was no man that took them into his house to lodging.

And, behold, there came an old man from his work out of the field at even, which was also of mount Ephraim, and he sojourned in Gibeah, but the men of the place were Benjamites. And when he had lifted up his eyes, he saw a wayfaring man in the street of the city and the old man said, Whither goest thou? And whence comest thou? And he said unto him, We are passing from Beth-lehem-judah toward the side of mount Ephraim, from thence am I, and I went to Beth-lehem-judah, but I am now going to the house of the Lord, and there is no man that receiveth me to house. Yet there is both straw and provender for our asses, and there is bread and wine also for me, and for thy hand-maid, and for the young man which is with thy servants, there is no want of any thing. And the old man said, Peace be with thee, howsoever, let all thy wants lie upon me, only lodge not in the street. So he brought him into his house, and gave provender unto the asses, and they washed their feet, and did eat and drink. Now as they were making their hearts merry, behold, the men of the city, certain sons of Belial, beset the house round about and beat at the door, and spake to the master of the house, the old man, saying, Bring forth the man that came into thine house, that we may know him. And the man, the master of the house, went out unto them and said unto them, Nay, my brethren, nay, I pray you, do not so wickedly, seeing that this man is come into mine house do not this folly. Behold, here is my daughter a maiden, and his concubine, them I will bring out now, and humble ye them, and do with them what seemeth good unto you, but unto this man do not so vile a thing. But the men would not hearken to him, so the man took his concubine, and brought her forth unto them, and they knew her, and abused her all the night until the morning, and when the day began to spring they let her go. Then came the woman in the dawning of the day, and fell down at the door of the man's house where her lord was, till it was light.

And her lord rose up in the morning, and opened the doors of the house and went out to go his way, and, behold, the woman, his concubine was fallen down at the door of the house, and her hands were upon the threshold. And he said unto her, Up, and let us be going. But none answered. Then the man took her up upon an ass, and the man rose up and gat him unto his place. And when he was come into his house, he took a knife, and laid hold on his concubine, and divided her, together with her bones, into twelve pieces, and sent her into all the coasts of Israel. And it was so, that all that saw it said, There was no such deed done nor seen from the day that the children of Israel came up out of the land of Egypt unto this day, consider of it, take advice, and speak your minds.

Then all the children of Israel went out, and the congregation was gathered together as one man, from Dan even to Beer-sheba, with the land of Gilead, unto the Lord in Mizpeh. And the chief of all the people, even of all the tribes of Israel, presented themselves in the assembly of the people of God, four hundred thousand footmen that drew sword. (Now the children of Benjamin heard that the children of Israel were gone up to Mizpeh.) Then said the children of Israel, Tell us, how was this wickedness? And the Levite, the husband of the woman that was slain answered, and said, I came into Gibeah that belongeth to Benjamin, I and my concubine, to lodge. And the men of Gibeah rose against me and beset the house round about upon me by night, and thought to have slain me, and my concubine have they forced, that she is dead. And I took my concubine and cut her in pieces and sent her throughout all the country of the inheritance of Israel, for they have committed lewdness and folly in Israel. Behold, ye are all children of Israel, give here your advice and counsel. And all the people arose as one man saying, We will not any of us go to his tent, neither will we any of us turn into his house. But now this shall be the thing which we will do to Gibeah. We will go up by lot against it, and we will take ten men of a hundred throughout all the tribes of Israel, and a hundred of a thousand, and a thousand out of ten thousand, to fetch victuals for the people, that they may do, when they come to Gibeah of Benjamin, according to all the folly that they have wrought in Israel. So all the men of Israel were gathered against the city, knit together as one man.

And the tribes of Israel sent men through all the tribe of Benjamin saying, What wickedness is this that is done among you? Now therefore deliver us the men, the children of Belial, which are in Gibeah, that we may put them to death, and put away evil from Israel. But the children of Benjamin would not hearken to the voice of their brethren the children of Israel, but the children of Benjamin gathered themselves together out of the cities unto Gibeah to go out to battle against the children of Israel. And the children of Benjamin were numbered at that time out of the cities twenty and six thousand men that drew sword, besides the inhabitants of Gibeah, which were numbered seven hundred chosen men. Among all this people there were seven hundred chosen men left-handed, every one could sling stones at a hair-breadth, and not miss. And the men of Israel, besides Benjamin, were numbered four hundred thousand men that drew sword, all these were men of war. And the children of Israel arose and went up to the house of God, and asked counsel of God, and said, Which of us shall go up first to the battle against the children of Benjamin? And the Lord said, Judah shall go up first.

And the children of Israel rose up in the morning and encamped against Gibeah. And the men of Israel went out to battle against Benjamin, and the men of Israel put themselves in array to fight against them at Gibeah. And the children of Benjamin came forth out of Gibeah and destroyed down to the ground of the Israelites that day twenty and two thousand men. And the people, the men of Israel, encouraged themselves, and set their battle again in array in the place where they put themselves in array the first day. (And the children of Israel went up and wept before the Lord until even, and asked counsel of the Lord saying, Shall I go up again to battle against the children of Benjamin my brother? And the Lord said, Go up against him.) And the children of Israel came near against the children of Benjamin the second day. And Benjamin went forth against them out of Gibeah the second day, and destroyed down the ground of the children of Israel again eighteen thousand men, all these drew the sword. Then all the children of Israel, and all the people, went up and came unto the house of God, and wept, and sat there before the Lord, and fasted that day until even, and offered burnt offerings and peace offerings before the Lord. And the children of Israel inquired of the Lord, (for the ark of the covenant of God was there in those days, and Phinehas, the son of Eleazar, the son of Aaron, stood before it in those days,) saying, Shall I yet again go out to battle against the children of Benjamin my brother, or shall I cease? And the Lord said, Go up, for tomorrow I will deliver them into thine hand.

And Israel set liers in wait round about Gibeah. And the children of Israel went up against the children of Benjamin on the third day, and put themselves in array against Gibeah, as at other times. And the children of Benjamin went out against the people and were drawn away from the city, and they began to smite of the people, and kill, as at other times, in the highways, of which one goeth up to the house of God, and the other to Gibeah in the field, about thirty men of Israel. And the children of Benjamin said, They are smitten down before us, as at the first. But the children of Israel said, Let us flee and draw them from the city unto the highways. And all the men of Israel rose up out of their place and put themselves in array at Baal-tamar, and the liers in wait of Israel came forth out of their places, even out of the meadows of Gibeah. And there came against Gibeah ten thousand chosen men out of all Israel, and the battle was sore, but they knew not that evil was near them. And the Lord smote Benjamin before Israel, and the children of Israel destroyed of the Benjamites that day twenty and five thousand and a hundred men, all these drew the sword.

So the children of Benjamin saw that they were smitten, for the men of Israel gave place to the Benjamites, because they trusted unto the liers in wait which they had set beside Gibeah. And the liers in wait hasted, and rushed upon Gibeah, and the liers in wait drew themselves along, and smote all the city with the edge of the sword. Now there was an appointed sign between the men of Israel and the liers in wait, that they should make a great flame with smoke rise up out of the city. And when the men of Israel retired in the battle, Benjamin began to smite and kill of the men of Israel about thirty persons, for they said, Surely they are smitten down before us, as in the first battle. But when the flame began to arise up out of the city with a pillar of smoke, the Benjamites looked behind them, and behold, the flame of the city ascended up to Heaven. And when the men of Israel turned again, the men of Benjamin were amazed for they saw that evil was come upon them. Therefore they turned their backs before the men of Israel unto the way of the wilderness, but the battle overtook them, and them which came out of the cities they destroyed in the midst of them. Thus they inclosed the Benjamites round about, and chased them, and trode them down with ease over against Gibeah, toward the sun-rising. And there fell of Benjamin eighteen thousand men, all these were men of valor. And they turned and fled toward the wilderness unto the rock of Rimmon, and they gleaned of them in the highways five thousand men, and pursued hard after them unto Gidom, and slew two thousand men of them. So that all which fell that day of Benjamin were twenty and five thousand men that drew the sword, all these were men of valor. But six hundred men turned and fled to the wilderness unto the rock of Rimmon and abode in the rock Rimmon four months. And the men of Israel turned again upon the children of Benjamin and smote them with the edge of the sword, as well the men of every city, as the beast, and all that came to hand, also they set on fire all the cities that they came to.

Now the men of Israel had sworn in Mizpeh, saying, There shall not any of us give his daughter unto Benjamin to wife. And the people came to the house of God, and abode there till even before God, and lifted up their voices, and wept sore, and said, O Lord God of Israel, why is this come to pass in Israel, that there should be today one tribe lacking in Israel? And it came to pass on the morrow that the people rose early, and built there an altar, and offered burnt offerings and peace offerings. And the children of Israel said, Who is there among all the tribes of Israel that came not up with the congregation unto the Lord? For they had made a great oath concerning him that came not up to the Lord to Mizpeh, saying, He shall surely be put to death. And the children of Israel repented them for Benjamin their brother and said, There is one tribe cut off from Israel this day. How shall we do for wives for them that remain, seeing we have sworn by the Lord that we will not give them of our daughters to wives? And they said, What one is there of the tribes of Israel that came not up to Mizpeh to the Lord? And, behold, there came none to the camp from Jabesh-gilead to the assembly. For the people were numbered, and, behold, there were none of the inhabitants of Jabesh-gilead there. And the congregation sent thither twelve thousand men of the valiantest, and commanded them, saying, Go and smite the inhabitants of Jabesh-gilead with the edge of the sword, with the women and the children. And this is the thing that ye shall do, Ye shall utterly destroy every male and every woman that hath lain by man. And they found among the inhabitants of Jabesh-gilead four hundred young virgins, that had known no man by lying with any male, and they brought them unto the camp to Shiloh, which is in the land of Canaan.

And the whole congregation sent some to speak to the children of Benjamin that were in the rock Rimmon, and to call peaceably unto them. And Benjamin came again at that time and they gave them wives which they had saved alive of the women of Jabesh-gilead, and yet so they sufficed them not. And the people repented them for Benjamin, because that the Lord had made a breach in the tribes of Israel. Then the elders of the congregation said, How shall we do for wives for them that remain, seeing the women are destroyed out of Benjamin? And they said, There must be an inheritance for them that be escaped of Benjamin, that a tribe be not destroyed out of Israel. Howbeit we may not give them wives of our daughters, for the children of Israel have sworn, saying, Cursed be he that giveth a wife to Benjamin. Then they said, Behold, there is a feast of the Lord in Shiloh yearly, in a place which is on the north side of Beth-el on the east side of the highway that goeth up from Beth-el to Shechem, and on the south of Lebonah. Therefore they commanded the children of Benjamin, saying, Go and lie in wait in the vineyards, and see and behold, if the daughters of Shiloh come out to dance in dances, then come ye out of the vineyards, and catch you every man his wife of the daughters of Shiloh, and go to the land of Benjamin. And it shall be when their fathers or their brethren come unto us to complain that we will say unto them, Be favorable unto them for our sakes, because we reserved not to each man his wife in the war, for ye did not give unto them at this time, that ye should be guilty. And the children of Benjamin did so and took them wives, according to their number, of them that danced, whom they caught, and they went and returned unto their inheritance, and repaired the cities and dwelt in them. And the children of Israel departed thence at that time, every man to his tribe and to his family, and they went out from thence every man to his inheritance.

In those days there was no king in Israel, every man did that which was right in his own eyes.

THE BOOK OF RUTH

NOW it came to pass in the days when the judges ruled that there was a famine in the land. And a certain man of Beth-lehem-judah went to sojourn in the country of Moab, he, and his wife, and his two sons. And the name of the man was Elimelech, and the name of his wife Naomi, and the name of his two sons Mahlon and Chilion, Ephrathites of Beth-lehem-judah. And they came into the country of Moab and continued there. And Elimelech Naomi's husband died. And she was left, and her two sons. And they took them wives of the women of Moab; the name of the one was Orpah, and the name of the other Ruth. And they dwelt there about ten years. And Mahlon and Chilion died also both of them, and the woman was left of her two sons and her husband.

Then she arose with her daughters-in-law, that she might return from the country of Moab, for she had heard in the country of Moab how that the Lord had visited his people in giving them bread. Wherefore she went forth out of the place where she was, and her two daughters-in-law with her, and they went on the way to return unto the land of Judah. And Naomi said unto her two daughters-in-law, Go, return each to her mother's house; the Lord deal kindly with you, as ye have dealt with the dead, and with me. The Lord grant you that ye may find rest, each of you in the house of her husband. Then she kissed them, and they lifted up their voice and wept. And they said unto her, Surely we will return with thee unto thy people. And Naomi said, Turn again, my daughters, why will ye go with me? Are there yet any more sons in my womb that they may be your husbands? Turn again, my daughters, go your way, for I am too old to have a husband. If I should say, I have hope, if I should have a husband also to-night, and should also bear sons, Would ye tarry for them till they were grown? Would ye stay for them from having husbands? Nay my daughters, for it grieveth me much for your sakes that the hand of the Lord is gone out against me. And they lifted up their voice and wept again, and Orpah kissed her mother-in-law, but Ruth clave unto her. And she said, Behold, thy sister-in-law is gone back unto her people, and unto her gods. Return thou after thy sister-in-law. And Ruth said, Entreat me not to leave thee or to return from following after thee, for whither thou goest, I will go; and where thou lodgest, I will lodge; thy people shall be my people, and thy God my God. Where thou diest, will I die, and there will I be buried; the Lord do so to me, and more also, if aught but death part thee and me. When she saw that she was steadfastly minded to go with her, then she left speaking unto her.

So they two went until they came to Beth-lehem. And it came to pass, when they were come to Beth-lehem, that all the city was moved about them, and they said, Is this Naomi? And she said unto them, Call me not Naomi, call me Mara, for the Almighty hath dealt very bitterly with me. I went out full, and the Lord hath brought me home again empty, why then call ye me Naomi, seeing the Lord hath testified against me, and the Almighty hath afflicted me? So Naomi returned, and Ruth the Moabitess, her daughter-in-law, with her, which returned out of the country of Moab, and they came to Beth-lehem in the beginning of barley harvest.

2 AND Naomi had a kinsman of her husband's, a mighty man of wealth, of the family of Elimelech, and his name was Boaz. And Ruth the Moabitess said unto Naomi, Let me now go to the field and glean ears of corn after him in whose sight I shall find grace. And she said unto her, Go, my daughter. And she went, and came, and gleaned in the field after the reapers and her hap was to light on a part of the field belonging unto Boaz, who was of the kindred of Elimelech. And, behold, Boaz came from Beth-lehem and said unto the reapers, The Lord be with you. And they answered him, The Lord bless thee. Then said Boaz unto his servant that was set over the reapers, Whose damsel is this? And the servant that was set over the reapers answered and said, It is the Moabitish damsel that came back with Naomi out of the country of Moab, And she said, I pray thee, let me glean and gather after the reapers among the sheaves. So she came and hath continued even from the morning until now, that she tarried a little in the house.

Then said Boaz unto Ruth, Hearest thou not, my daughter? Go not to glean in another field, neither go from hence, but abide here fast by my maidens. Let thine eyes be on the field that they do reap, and go thou after them. Have I not charged the young men that they shall not touch thee? And when thou art athirst, go unto the vessels and drink of that which the young men have drawn. Then she fell on her face and bowed herself to the ground, and said unto him, Why have I found grace in thine eyes that thou shouldest take knowledge of me, seeing I am a stranger? And Boaz answered and said unto her, It hath fully been showed me, all that thou hast done unto thy mother-in-law since the death of thine husband, and how thou hast left thy father and thy mother, and the land of thy nativity, and art come unto a people which thou knewest not heretofore. The Lord recompense thy work and a full reward be given thee of the Lord God of Israel, under whose wings thou art come to trust. Then she said, Let me find favor in thy sight, my Lord, for that thou hast comforted me and for that thou hast spoken friendly unto thine hand-maid, though I be not like unto one of thine hand-maidens.

And Boaz said unto her, At meal-time come thou hither, and eat of the bread, and dip thy morsel in the vinegar. And she sat beside the reapers and he reached her parched corn and she did eat, and was sufficed, and left. And when she was risen up to glean, Boaz commanded his young men saying, Let her glean even among the sheaves and reproach her not, And let fall also some of the handfuls of purpose for her, and leave them, that she may glean them, and rebuke her not.

So she gleaned in the field until even, and beat out that she had gleaned and it was about an ephah of barley. And she took it up and went into the city, and her mother-in-law saw what she had gleaned, and she brought forth, and gave to her that she had reserved after she was sufficed. And her mother-in-law said unto her, Where hast thou gleaned to-day? And where wroughtest thou? Blessed be he that did take knowledge of thee. And she showed her mother-in-law with whom she had wrought and said, The man's name with whom I wrought today is Boaz. And Naomi said unto her daughter-in-law, Blessed be he of the Lord who hath not left off his kindness to the living and to the dead. And Naomi said unto her, The man is near of kin unto us, one of our next kinsmen. And Ruth the Moabitess said, He said unto me also, Thou shalt keep fast by my young men until they have ended all my harvest. And Naomi said unto Ruth her daughter-in-law, It is good, my daughter, that thou go out with his maidens, that they meet thee not in any other field. So she kept fast by the maidens of Boaz to glean unto the end of barley harvest and of wheat harvest, and dwelt with her mother-in-law.

3 THEN Naomi her mother-in-law said unto her, My daughter, shall I not seek rest for thee, that it may be well with thee? And now is not Boaz of our kindred, with whose maidens thou wast? Behold, he winnoweth barley to-night in the threshing-floor. Wash thyself therefore, and anoint thee, and put thy raiment upon thee, and get thee down to the floor, but make not thyself known unto the man until he shall have done eating and drinking. And it shall be, when he lieth down that thou shalt mark the place where he shall lie, and thou shalt go in and uncover his feet, and lay thee down, and he will tell thee what thou shalt do. And she said unto her, All that thou sayest unto me I will do.

And she went down unto the floor and did according to all that her mother-in-law bade her. And when Boaz had eaten and drunk and his heart was merry, he went to lie down at the end of the heap of corn, and she came softly, and uncovered his feet, and laid her down. And it came to pass at midnight that the man was afraid, and turned himself, and, behold, a woman lay at his feet. And he said, Who art thou? And she answered, I am Ruth thine hand-maid. Spread therefore thy skirt over thine hand-maid, for thou art a near kinsman. And he said, Blessed be thou of the Lord, my daughter, for thou hast showed more kindness in the latter end than at the beginning, inasmuch as thou followedst not young men, whether poor or rich. And now, my daughter, fear not, I will do to thee all that thou requirest, for all the city of my people doth know that thou art a virtuous woman. And now it is true that I am thy near kinsman, howbeit there is a kinsman nearer than I. Tarry this night and it shall be in the morning, that if he will perform unto thee the part of a kinsman, well, let him do the kinsman's part, but if he will not do the part of a kinsman to thee, then will I do the part of a kinsman to thee. As the Lord liveth, lie down until the morning.

And she lay at his feet until the morning, and she rose up before one could know another. And he said, Let it not be known that a woman came into the floor. Also he said, Bring the veil that thou hast upon thee and hold it. And when she held it, he measured six measures of barley, and laid on her, and she went into the city. And when she came to her mother-in-law, she said, Who art thou, my daughter? And she told her all that the man had done to her. And she said, These six measures of barley gave he me, for he said to me, Go not empty unto thy mother-in-law. Then said she, Sit still, my daughter until thou know how the matter will fall, for the man will not be in rest until he have finished the thing this day.

Then went Boaz up to the gate and sat him down there, and behold, the kinsman of whom Boaz spake came by, unto whom he said, Ho, such a one! Turn aside, sit down here. And he turned aside and sat down. And he took ten men of the elders of the city and said, Sit ye down here. And they sat down. And he said unto the kinsman, Naomi, that is come again out of the country of Moab, selleth a parcel of land, which was our brother Elimelech's, And I thought to advertise thee, saying, Buy it before the inhabitants and before the elders of my people. If thou wilt redeem it, redeem it, but if thou wilt not redeem it, then tell me, that I may know, for there is none to redeem it besides thee, and I am after thee. And he said, I will redeem it. Then said Boaz, What day thou buyest the field of the hand of Naomi, thou must buy it also of Ruth the Moabitess, the wife of the dead, to raise up the name of the dead upon his inheritance. And the kinsman said, I cannot redeem it for myself, lest I mar mine own inheritance. Redeem thou my right to thyself, for I cannot redeem it.

Now this was the manner in former time in Israel concerning redeeming and concerning changing, for to confirm all things, a man plucked off his shoe and gave it to his neighbor, and this was a testimony in Israel. Therefore the kinsman said unto Boaz, Buy it for thee. So he drew off his shoe. And Boaz said unto the elders and unto all the people, Ye are witnesses this day that I have bought all that was Elimelech's, and all that was Chilion's and Mahlon's, of the hand of Naomi. Moreover Ruth the Moabitess, the wife of Mahlon, have I purchased to be my wife, to raise up the name of the dead upon his inheritance, that the name of the dead be not cut off from among his brethren, and from the gate of his place. Ye are witnesses this day. And all the people that were in the gate, and the elders said, We are witnesses. The Lord make the woman that is come into thine house like Rachel and like Leah, which two did build the house of Israel, and do thou worthily in Ephratah, and be famous in Beth-lehem, And let thy house be like the house of Pharez, whom Tamar bare unto Judah, of the seed which the Lord shall give thee of this young woman.

So Boaz took Ruth, and she was his wife. And when he went in unto her, the Lord gave her conception and she bare a son. And the woman said unto Naomi, Blessed be the Lord, which hath not left thee this day without a kinsman, that his name may be famous in Israel. And he shall be unto thee a restorer of thy life and a nourisher of thine old age, for thy daughter-in-law, which loveth thee, which is better to thee than seven sons, hath borne him. And Naomi took the child and laid it in her bosom, and became nurse unto it. And the women her neighbors gave it a name, saying, There is a son born to Naomi, and they called his name Obed, he is the father of Jesse, the father of David.

Now these are the generations of Pharez, Pharez begat Hezron, and Hezron begat Ram, and Ram begat Amminadab, and Amminadab begat Nahshon, and Nahshon begat Salmon, and Salmon begat Boaz, and Boaz begat Obed, and Obed begat Jesse, and Jesse begat David.

THE FIRST BOOK OF SAMUEL

NOW there was a certain man of Ramathaim-zophim, of mount Ephraim, and his name was Elkanah, the son of Jeroham, the son of Elihu, the son of Tohu, the son of Zuph, and Ephrathite; and he had two wives; the name of the one was Hannah, and the name of the other Peninnah; and Peninnah had children, but Hannah had no children. And this man went up out of his city yearly to worship and to sacrifice unto the Lord of hosts in Shiloh. And the two sons of Eli, Hophni and Phinehas, the priests of the Lord, were there. And when the time was that Elkanah offered, he gave to Peninnah his wife, and to all her sons and her daughters, portions; but unto Hannah he gave a worthy portion; for he loved Hannah; but the Lord had shut up her womb. And her adversary also provoked her sore, for to make her fret, because the Lord had shut up her womb. And as he did so year by year, when she went up to the house of the Lord, so she provoked her; therefore she wept, and did not eat. Then said Elkanah her husband to her, Hannah, why weepest thou? and why eatest thou not? and why is thy heart grieved? am not I better to thee than ten sons?

So Hannah rose up after they had eaten in Shiloh, and after they had drunk. Now Eli the priest sat upon a seat by a post of the temple of the Lord. And she was in bitterness of soul, and prayed unto the Lord, and wept sore. And she vowed a vow, and said, O Lord of hosts, if thou wilt indeed look on the affliction of thine handmaid, and remember me, and not forget thine handmaid, but wilt give unto thine handmaid a man-child, then I will give him unto the Lord all the days of his life, and there shall no razor come upon his head. And it came to pass as she continued praying before the Lord, that Eli marked her mouth. Now Hannah, she spake in her heart; only her lips moved, but her voice was not heard; therefore Eli thought she had been drunken. And Eli said unto her, How long wilt thou be drunken? put away thy wine from thee. And Hannah answered and said, No, my lord, I am a woman of a sorrowful spirit; I have drunk neither wine nor strong drink but have poured out my soul before the Lord. Count not thine handmaid for a daughter of Belial; for out of the abundance of my complaint and grief have I spoken hitherto. And Eli answered and said, Go in peace and the God of Israel grant thee thy petition that thou hast asked of him. And she said, Let thine handmaid find grace in thy sight. So the woman went her way and did eat, and her countenance was no more sad. And they rose up in the morning early and worshiped before the Lord, and returned and came to their house to Ramah; and Elkanah knew Hannah his wife; and the Lord remembered her. Wherefore it came to pass when the time was come about after Hannah had conceived that she bare a son and called his name Samuel, saying, Because I have asked him of the Lord.

And the man Elkanah and all his house, went up to offer unto the Lord the yearly sacrifice and his vow. But Hannah went not up; for she said unto her husband, I will not go up until the child be weaned, and then I will bring him that he may appear before the Lord and there abide forever. And Elkanah her husband said unto her, Do what seemeth thee good; tarry until thou have weaned him; only the Lord establish his word. So the woman abode, and gave her son suck until she weaned him. And when she had weaned him, she took him up with her, with three bullocks, and one ephah of flour, and a bottle of wine, and brought him unto the house of the Lord in Shiloh; and the child was young. And they slew a bullock, and brought the child to Eli. And she said, O my lord, as thy soul liveth, my Lord, I am the woman that stood by thee here praying unto the Lord. For this child I prayed; and the Lord hath given me my petition which I asked of him; therefore also I have lent him to the Lord; as long as he liveth he shall be lent to the Lord. And he worshiped the Lord there.

And Hannah prayed, and said, My heart rejoiceth in the Lord, mine horn is exalted in the Lord; my mouth is enlarged over mine enemies because I rejoiced in thy salvation. There is none holy as the Lord; for there is none besides thee; neither is there any rock like our God. Talk no more so exceeding proudly; let not arrogancy come out of your mouth; for the Lord is a God of knowledge and by him actions are weighed. The bows of the mighty men are broken and they that stumbled are girded with strength. They that were full have hired out themselves for bread; and they that were hungry ceased; so that the barren hath borne seven; and she that hath many children is waxed feeble. The Lord killeth and maketh alive; he bringeth down to the grave and bringeth up. The Lord maketh poor and maketh rich; he bringeth low and lifteth up. He raiseth up the poor out of the dust and lifteth up the beggar from the dunghill, to set them among princes and to make them inherit the throne of glory; for the pillars of the Earth are the Lord's, and he hath set the world upon them. He will keep the feet of his saints, and the wicked shall be silent in darkness; for by strength shall no man prevail. The adversaries of the Lord shall be broken to pieces; out of Heaven shall he thunder upon them; the Lord shall judge the ends of the Earth and he shall give strength unto his king, and exalt the horn of his anointed. And Elkanah went to Ramah to his house. And the child did minister unto the Lord before Eli the priest.

2 NOW the sons of Eli were sons of Belial; they knew not the Lord. And the priest's custom with the people was that when any man offered sacrifice, the priest's servant came while the flesh was in seething, with a fleshhook of three teeth in his hand; and he struck it into the pan, or kettle, or caldron, or pot; all that the fleshhook brought up the priest took for himself. So they did in Shiloh unto all the Israelites that came thither. Also before they burnt the fat, the priest's servant came and said to the man that sacrificed, Give flesh to roast for the priest; for he will not have sodden flesh of thee but raw. And if any man said unto him, Let them not fail to burn the fat presently and then take as much as thy soul desireth; then he would answer him, Nay; but thou shalt give it me now; and if not, I will take it by force. Wherefore the sin of the young men was very great before the Lord; for men abhorred the offering of the Lord.

But Samuel ministered before the Lord, being a child, girded with a linen ephod. Moreover his mother made him a little coat, and brought it to him from year to year when she came up with her husband to offer the yearly sacrifice. And Eli blessed Elkanah and his wife, and said, The Lord give thee seed of this woman for the loan which is lent to the Lord. And they went unto their own home. And the Lord visited Hannah, so that she conceived, and bare three sons and two daughters. And the child Samuel grew before the Lord.

Now Eli was very old, and heard all that his sons did unto all Israel; and how they lay with the women that assembled at the door of the tabernacle of the congregation. And he said unto them, Why do ye such things? for I hear of your evil dealings by all this people. Nay, my sons; for it is no good report that I hear ye make the Lord's people to transgress. If one man sin against another the judge shall judge him; but if a man sin against the Lord, who shall entreat for him? Notwithstanding, they hearkened not unto the voice of their father because the Lord would slay them. And the child Samuel grew on, and was in favor both with the Lord, and also with men.

And there came a man of God unto Eli, and said unto him, Thus saith the Lord, Did I plainly appear unto the house of thy father, when they were in Egypt in Pharaoh's house? And did I choose him out of all the tribes of Israel to be my priest, to offer upon mine altar, to burn incense, to wear an ephod before me?

and did I give unto the house of thy father all the offerings made by fire of the children of Israel? Wherefore kick ye at my sacrifice and at mine offering, which I have commanded in my habitation; and honorest thy sons above me, to make yourselves fat with the chiefest of all the offerings of Israel my people? Wherefore the Lord God of Israel saith, I said indeed that thy house, and the house of thy father, should walk before me forever. But now the Lord saith, Be it far from me; for them that honor me I will honor, and they that despise me shall be lightly esteemed. Behold, the days come that I will cut off thine arm and the arm of thy father's house, that there shall not be an old man in thine house. And thou shalt see an enemy in my habitation in all the wealth which God shall give Israel; and there shall not be an old man in thine house forever. And the man of thine whom I shall not cut off from mine altar, shall be to consume thine eyes and to grieve thine heart; and all the increase of thine house shall die in the flower of their age. And this shall be a sign unto thee, that shall come upon thy two sons, on Hophni and Phinehas; in one day they shall die both of them. And I will rise me up a faithful priest, that shall do according to that which is in mine heart and in my mind; and I will build him a sure house; and he shall walk before mine anointed forever. And it shall come to pass, that everyone that is left in thine house shall come and crouch to him for a piece of silver and a morsel of bread, and shall say, Put me, I pray thee, into one of the priests' offices, that I may eat a piece of bread.

And the child Samuel ministered unto the Lord before Eli. And the word of the Lord was precious in those days; there was no open vision. And it came to pass at that time when Eli was laid down in his place, and his eyes began to wax dim that he could not see; and ere the lamp of God went out in the temple of the Lord where the ark of God was, and Samuel was laid down to sleep. That the Lord called Samuel; and he answered, Here am I. And he ran unto Eli, and said, Here am I; for thou calledst me. And he said, I called not; lie down again. And he went and lay down. And the Lord called yet again, Samuel. And Samuel arose and went to Eli, and said, Here am I; for thou didst call me. And he answered, I called not, my son; lie down again. Now Samuel did not yet know the Lord, neither was the word of the Lord ye revealed unto him. And the Lord called Samuel again the third time. And he arose and went to Eli and said, Here am I; for thou didst call me. And Eli perceived that the Lord had called the child. Therefore Eli said unto Samuel, Go, lie down; and it shall be if he call thee that thou shalt say, Speak, Lord; for thy servant heareth. So Samuel went and lay down in his place.

And the Lord came and stood and called as at other times, Samuel, Samuel. Then Samuel answered, Speak; for thy servant heareth. And the Lord said to Samuel, Behold, I will do a thing in Israel, at which both the ears of everyone that heareth it shall tingle. In that day I will perform against Eli all things which I have spoken concerning his house; when I begin, I will also make an end. For I have told him that I will judge his house for ever for the iniquity which he knoweth; because his sons made themselves vile, and he restrained them not. And therefore I have sworn unto the house of Eli, that the iniquity of Eli's house shall not be purged with sacrifice nor offering forever.

And Samuel lay until the morning and opened the doors of the house of the Lord. And Samuel feared to show Eli the vision. Then Eli called Samuel and said, Samuel, my son. And he answered, Here am I. And he said, What is the thing that the Lord hath said unto thee? I pray thee hide it not from me. God do so to thee and more also, if thou hide anything from me of all the things that he said unto thee. And Samuel told him every whit and hid nothing from him. And he said, It is the Lord; let him do what seemeth him good.

And Samuel grew, and the Lord was with him, and did let none of his words fall to the ground. And all Israel from Dan even to Beer-sheba knew that Samuel was established to be a prophet of the Lord. And the Lord appeared again in Shiloh; for the Lord revealed himself to Samuel in Shiloh by the word of the Lord. And the word of Samuel came to all Israel.

3 NOW Israel went out against the Philistines to battle, and pitched beside Eben-ezer; and the Philistines pitched in Aphek. And the Philistines put themselves in array against Israel; and when they joined battle, Israel was smitten before the Philistines; and they slew of the army in the field about four thousand men.

And when the people were come into the camp, the elders of Israel said, Wherefore hath the Lord smitten us today before the Philistines? Let us fetch the ark of the covenant of the Lord out of Shiloh unto us that when it cometh among us it may save us out of the hand of our enemies. So the people sent to Shiloh that they might bring from thence the ark of the covenant of the Lord of hosts, which dwelleth between the cherubim, And the two sons of Eli, Hophni and Phinehas were there with the ark of the covenant of God. And when the ark of the covenant of the Lord came into the camp all Israel shouted with a great shout so that the Earth rang again.

And when the Philistines heard the noise of the shout they said, What meaneth the noise of this great shout in the camp of the Hebrews? And they understood that the ark of the Lord was come into the camp. And the Philistines were afraid; for they said, God is come into the camp. And they said, Wo unto us! for there hath not been such a thing heretofore. Wo unto us! who shall deliver us out of the hand of these mighty Gods? these are the Gods that smote the Egyptians with all the plagues in the wilderness. Be strong, and quit yourselves like men. O ye Philistines, that ye be not servants unto the Hebrews, as they have been to you; quit yourselves like men and fight.

And the Philistines fought, and Israel was smitten, and they fled every man into his tent. And there was very great slaughter; for there fell of Israel thirty thousand footmen. And the ark of God was taken; and the two sons of Eli, Hophni and Phinehas, were slain.

And there ran a man of Benjamin out of the army, and came to Shiloh the same day with his clothes rent, and with earth upon his head. And when he came, lo, Eli sat upon a seat by the wayside watching; for his heart trembled for the ark of God. And when the man came into the city and told it, all the city cried out. And when Eli heard the noise of the crying, he said, What meaneth the noise of this tumult? And the man came in hastily, and told Eli. Now Eli was ninety and eight years old; and his eyes were dim, that he could not see. And the man said unto Eli, I am he that came out of the army, and I fled today out of the army. And he said, What is there done, my son? And the messenger answered and said, Israel is fled before the Philistines, and there hath been also a great slaughter among the people, and thy two sons also, Hophni and Phinehas are dead, and the ark of God is taken. And it came to pass when he made mention of the ark of God, that he fell from off the seat backward by the side of the gate and his neck brake, and he died; for he was an old man, and heavy. And he had judged Israel forty years.

And his daughter-in-law, Phinehas' wife, was with child, near to be delivered; and when she heard the tidings that the ark of God was taken, and that her father-in-law and her husband were dead, she bowed herself and travailed; for her pains came upon her. And about the time of her death the women that stood by her said unto her, Fear not; for thou hast borne a son. But she answered not, neither did she regard it. And she named the child Ichabod, saying, The glory is departed from Israel; because the ark of God was taken and because of her father-in-law and her husband. And she said, The glory is departed from Israel; for the ark of God is taken.

And the Philistines took the ark of God and brought it from Eben-ezer unto Ashdod. When the Philistines took the ark of God they brought it into the house of Dagon, and set it by Dagon. And when they of Ashdod arose early on the morrow, behold, Dagon was fallen upon his face to the earth before the ark of the Lord. And they took Dagon and set him in his place again. And when they arose early on the morrow morning, behold, Dagon was fallen upon his face to the ground before the ark of the Lord; and the head of Dagon and both the palms of his hands were cut off upon the threshold; only the stump of Dagon was left to him. Therefore neither the priests of Dagon, nor any that come into Dagon's house, tread on the threshold of Dagon in Ashdod unto this day.

But the hand of the Lord was heavy upon them of Ashdod, and he destroyed them, and smote them with emerods, even Ashdod and the coasts thereof. And when the men of Ashdod saw that it was so, they said, The ark of the God of Israel shall not abide with us; for his hand is sore upon us, and upon Dagon our god. They sent therefore and gathered all the lords of the Philistines unto them, and said, What shall we do with the ark of the God of Israel? And they answered, Let the ark of the God of Israel be carried about unto Gath.

And they carried the ark of the God of Israel about thither. And it was so, that after they had carried it about, the hand of the Lord was against the city with a very great destruction; and he smote the men of the city, both small and great, and they had emerods in their secret parts. Therefore they sent the ark of God to Ekron. And it came to pass, as the ark of God came to Ekron, that the Ekronites cried out, saying, They have brought about the ark of the God of Israel to us, to slay us and our people. So they sent and gathered together all the lords of the Philistines and said, Send away the ark of the God of Israel, and let it go again to his own place that it slay us not, and our people; for there was a deadly destruction throughout all the city; the hand of God was very heavy there. And the men that died not were smitten with the emerods; and the cry of the city went up to Heaven.

And the ark of the Lord was in the country of the Philistines seven months. And the Philistines called for the priests and the diviners, saying, What shall we do to the ark of the Lord? tell us wherewith we shall send it to his place. And they said, If ye send away the ark of the God of Israel, send it not empty; but in any wise return him a trespass offering; then ye shall be healed, and it shall be known to you why his hand is not removed from you. Then said they, What shall be the trespass offering which we shall return to him? They answered, Five golden emerods, and five golden mice, according to the number of the lords of the Philistines; for one plague was on you all, and on your lords. Wherefore ye shall make images of your emerods, and images of your mice that mar the land; and ye shall give glory unto the God of Israel; peradventure he will lighten his hand from off you, and from off your gods, and from off your land. Wherefore then do ye harden your hearts, as the Egyptians and Pharaoh hardened their hearts? when he had wrought wonderfully among them, did they not let the people go, and they departed? Now therefore make a new cart, and take two milch kine, on which there hath come no yoke, and tie the kine to the cart, and bring their calves home from them; and take the ark of the Lord, and lay it upon the cart; and put the jewels of gold, which ye return him for a trespass offering in a coffer by the side thereof; and send it away that it may go. And see if it goeth up by the way of his own coast to Beth-shemesh, then he hath done us this great evil; but if not, then we shall know that it is not his hand that smote us; it was a chance that happened to us.

And the men did so; and took two milch kine, and tied them to the cart, and shut up their calves at home. And they laid the ark of the Lord upon the cart and the coffer with the mice of gold and the images of their emerods. And the kine took the straight way to the way of Beth-shemesh, and went along the highway, lowing as they went, and turned not aside to the right hand or to the left; and the lords of the Philistines went after them unto the border of Beth-shemesh. And they of Beth-shemesh were reaping their wheat harvest in the valley; and they lifted up their eyes and saw the ark, and rejoiced to see it. And the cart came into the field of Joshua, a Beth-shemite, and stood there where there was a great stone; and they clave the wood of the cart and offered the kine a burnt offering unto the Lord. And the Levites took down the ark of the Lord, and the coffer that was with it, wherein the jewels of gold were, and put them on the great stone; and the men of Beth-shemesh offered burnt offerings and sacrificed sacrifices the same day unto the Lord. And when the five lords of the Philistines had seen it, they returned to Ekron the same day. And these are the golden emerods which the Philistines returned for a trespass offering unto the Lord; for Ashdod one, for Gaza one, for Askelon one, for Gath one, for Ekron one; and the golden mice, according to the number of all the cities of the Philistines belonging to the five lords, both of fenced cities, and of country villages, even unto the great stone of Abel, whereon they set down the ark of the Lord; which stone remaineth unto this day in the field of Joshua, the Beth-shemite.

And he smote the men of Beth-shemesh, because they had looked into the ark of the Lord, even he smote of the people fifty thousand and threescore and ten men; and the people lamented because the Lord had smitten many of the people with a great slaughter. And the men of Beth-shemesh said, Who is able to stand before this holy Lord God? and to whom shall he go up from us? And they sent messengers to the inhabitants of Kirjath-jearim, saying, The Philistines have brought again the ark of the Lord; come ye down and fetch it up to you. And the men of Kirjath-jearim came, and fetched up the ark of the Lord, and brought it into the house of Abinadab in the hill, and sanctified Eleazar his son to keep the ark of the Lord.

And it came to pass, while the ark abode in Kirjath-jearim, that the time was long; for it was twenty years; and all the house of Israel lamented after the Lord. And Samuel spake unto all the house of Israel, saying, If ye do return unto the Lord with all your hearts, then put away the strange gods and Ashtaroth from among you, and prepare your hearts unto the Lord, and serve him only; and he will deliver you out of the hand of the Philistines. Then the children of Israel did put away Baalim and Ashtaroth, and served the Lord only.

And Samuel said, Gather all Israel to Mizpeh and I will pray for you unto the Lord. And they gathered together to Mizpeh, and drew water and poured it out before the Lord, and fasted on that day, and said there, We have sinned against the Lord. And Samuel judged the children of Israel in Mizpeh.

And when the Philistines heard that the children of Israel were gathered together to Mizpeh, the lords of the Philistines went up against Israel. And when the children of Israel heard it they were afraid of the Philistines. And the Children of Israel said to Samuel, Cease not to cry unto the Lord our God for us that he will save us out of the hand of the Philistines. And Samuel took a suckling lamb, and offered it for a burnt offering wholly unto the Lord; and Samuel cried unto the Lord for Israel; and the Lord heard him. And as Samuel was offering up the burnt offering, the Philistines drew near to battle against Israel; but the Lord thundered with a great thunder on that day upon the Philistines and discomfited them; and they were smitten before Israel. And the men of Israel went out of Mizpeh, and pursued the Philistines, and smote them until they came under Beth-car.

Then Samuel took a stone and set it between Mizpeh and Shen, and called the name of it Eben-ezer, saying, Hitherto hath the Lord helped us. So the Philistines were subdued and they came no more into the coast of Israel; and the hand of the Lord was against the Philistines all the days of Samuel. And the cities which the Philistines had taken from Israel were restored to Israel, from Ekron even unto Gath; and the coasts thereof did Israel deliver out of the hands of the Philistines. And there was peace between Israel and the Amorites.

And Samuel judged Israel all the days of his life. And he went from year to year in circuit to Beth-el, and Gilgal, and Mizpeh, and judged Israel in all those places. And his return was to Ramah; for there was his house; and there he judged Israel; and there he built an altar unto the Lord.

4 AND it came to pass, when Samuel was old that he made his sons judges over Israel. Now the name of his firstborn was Joel; and the name of his second, Abiah; they were judges in Beer-sheba. And his sons walked not in his ways, but turned aside after lucre and took bribes, and perverted judgment. Then all the elders of Israel gathered themselves together and came to Samuel unto Ramah and said unto him, Behold, thou art old, and thy sons walk not in thy ways; now make us a king to judge us like all the nations. But the thing displeased Samuel when they said, Give us a king to judge us. And Samuel prayed unto the Lord. And the Lord said unto Samuel, Hearken unto the voice of the people in all that they say unto thee; for they have not rejected thee but they have rejected me, that I should not reign over them. According to all the works which they have done since the day that I brought them up out of Egypt even unto this day, wherewith they have forsaken me and served other gods, so do they also unto thee. Now therefore hearken unto their voice; howbeit yet protest solemnly unto them and show them the manner of the king that shall reign over them.

And Samuel told all the words of the Lord unto the people that asked of him a king. And he said, This will be the manner of the king that shall reign over you: He will take your sons, and appoint them for himself, for his chariots, and to be his horsemen; and some shall run before his chariots. And he will appoint him captains over thousands, and captains over fifties; and will set them to ear his ground, and to reap his harvest and to make his instruments of war, and instruments of his chariots. And he will take your daughters to be confectioneries, and to be cooks, and to be bakers. And he will take your fields and your vineyards and your olive yards, even the best of them, and give them to his servants. And he will take the tenth of your seed and of your vineyards, and give to his officers and to his servants. And he will take your menservants and your maidservants and your goodliest young men and your asses, and put them to his work. He will take the tenth of your sheep; and ye shall be his servants. And ye shall cry out in that day because of your king which ye shall have chosen you; and the Lord will not hear you in that day.

Nevertheless the people refused to obey the voice of Samuel; and they said, Nay; but we will have a king over us; that we also may be like all the nations; and that our king may judge us and go out before us, and fight our battles. And Samuel heard all the words of the people, and he rehearsed them in the ears of the Lord. And the Lord said to Samuel, Hearken unto their voice, and make them a king. And Samuel said unto the men of Israel, Go ye every man unto his city.

Now there was a man of Benjamin, whose name was Kish, the son of Abiel, the son of Zeror, the son of Bechorath, the son of Aphiah, a Benjamite, a mighty man of power. And he had a son whose name was Saul, a choice young man and a goodly; and there was not among the children of Israel a goodlier person than he; from his shoulders and upward he was higher than any of the people. And the asses of Kish Saul's father were lost. And Kish said to Saul his son, Take now one of the servants with thee, and arise, go seek the asses. And he passed through mount Ephraim and passed through the land of Shalisha but they found them not; then they passed through the land of Shalim and there they were not; and he passed through the land of the Benjamites but they found them not. And when they were come to the land of Zuph, Saul said to his servant that was with him, Come and let us return lest my father leave caring for the asses and take thought for us. And he said unto him, Behold now, there is in this city a man of God, and he is an honorable man; all that he saith cometh surely to pass; now let us go thither; peradventure he can show us our way that we should go.

Then said Saul to his servant, But, behold, if we go, what shall we bring the man? for the bread is spent in our vessels, and there is not a present to bring to the man of God; what have we? And the servant answered Saul again, and said, Behold, I have here at hand the fourth part of a shekel of silver; that will I give to the man of God to tell us our way. (Beforetime in Israel, when a man went to inquire of God, thus he spake, Come, and let us go to the seer; for he that is now called a Prophet was beforetime called a Seer.) Then said Saul to his servant, Well said; come, let us go. So they went unto the city where the man of God was. And as they went up the hill to the city, they found young maidens going out to draw water, and said unto them, Is the seer here? And they answered them and said, He is; behold, he is before you; make haste now, for he came today to the city; for there is a sacrifice of the people today in the high place; as soon as ye be come into the city, ye shall straightway find him before he go up to the high place to eat; for the people will not eat until he come, because he doth bless the sacrifice; and afterwards they eat that be bidden. Now therefore get you up; for about this time ye shall find him. And they went up into the city; and when they were come into the city, behold, Samuel came out against them, for to go up to the high place.

Now the Lord had told Samuel in his ear a day before Saul came, saying, Tomorrow about this time I will send thee a man out of the land of Benjamin, and thou shalt anoint him to be a captain over my people Israel, that he may save my people out of the hand of the Philistines; for I have looked upon my people because their cry is come unto me. And when Samuel saw Saul, the Lord said unto him, Behold the man whom I spake to thee of! this same shall reign over my people.

Then Saul drew near to Samuel in the gate and said, Tell me I pray thee, where the seer's house is. And Samuel answered Saul and said, I am the seer; go up before me unto the high place; for ye shall eat with me today, and tomorrow I will let thee go and will tell thee all that is in thine heart. And as for thine asses that were lost three days ago set not thy mind on them; for they are found. And on whom is all the desire of Israel? Is it not on thee and on all thy father's house? And Saul answered and said, Am not I a Benjamite, of the smallest of the tribes of Israel? and my family the least of all the families of the tribe of Benjamin? wherefore then speakest thou so to me? And Samuel took Saul and his servant and brought them into the parlor and made them sit in the chiefest place among them that were bidden, which were about thirty persons. And Samuel said unto the cook, Bring the portion which I gave thee, of which I said unto thee, Set it by thee. And the cook took up the shoulder, and that which was upon it, and set it before Saul. And Samuel said, Behold that which is left! set it before thee and eat; for unto this time hath it been kept for thee since I said, I have invited the people. So Saul did eat with Samuel that day.

And when they were come down from the high place into the city, Samuel communed with Saul upon the top of the house. And they arose early; and it came to pass about the spring of the day that Samuel called Saul to the top of the house, saying, Up, that I may send thee away. And Saul arose, and they went out both of them, he and Samuel abroad. And as they were going down to the end of the city, Samuel said to Saul, Bid the servant pass on before us (and he passed on,) but stand thou still a while that I may show thee the word of God.

Then Samuel took a vial of oil and poured it upon his head and kissed him and said, Is it not because the Lord hath anointed thee to be captain over his inheritance? When thou art departed from me today, then thou shalt find two men by Rachel's sepulcher in the border of Benjamin at Zelzah; and they will say unto thee, The asses which thou wentest to seek are found; and lo, thy father hath left the care of the asses, and sorroweth for you, saying, What shall I do for my son? Then shalt thou go on forward from thence, and thou shalt come to the plain of Tabor, and there shall meet thee three men going up to God to Beth-el, one carrying three kids, and another carrying three loaves of bread, and another carrying a bottle of wine; and they will salute thee, and give thee two loaves of bread; which thou shalt receive of their hands. After that thou shalt come to the hill of God, where is the garrison of the Philistines; and it shall come to pass, when thou art come thither to the city, that thou shalt meet a company of prophets coming down from the high place with a psaltery, and a tabret, and a pipe, and a harp, before them; and they shall prophesy; and the Spirit of the Lord will come upon thee, and thou shalt prophesy with them, and shalt be turned into another man. And let it be, when these signs are come unto thee, that thou do as occasion serve thee; for God is with thee. And thou shalt go down before me to Gilgal; and, behold, I will come down unto thee, to offer burnt offerings, and to sacrifice sacrifices of peace offerings; seven days shalt thou tarry, till I come to thee, and show thee what thou shalt do.

And it was so, that when he had turned his back to go from Samuel, God gave him another heart; and all those signs came to pass that day. And when they came thither to the hill, behold, a company of prophets met him and the Spirit of God came upon him and he prophesied among them. And it came to pass when all that knew him beforetime saw that, behold, he prophesied among the prophets, then the people said one to another, What is this that is come unto the son of Kish? Is Saul also among the prophets? And one of the same place answered and said, But who is their father? Therefore it became a proverb, Is Saul also among the prophets? And when he had made an end of prophesying he came to the high place. And Saul's uncle said unto him and to his servant, Whither went ye? And he said, To seek the asses; and when we saw that they were nowhere, we came to Samuel. And Saul's uncle said, Tell me, I pray thee, what Samuel said unto you. And Saul said unto his uncle, He told us plainly that the asses were found. But of the matter of the kingdom, whereof Samuel spake, he told him not.

And Samuel called the people together unto the Lord to Mizpeh; and said unto the children of Israel, Thus saith the Lord God of Israel, I brought up Israel out of Egypt and delivered you out of the hand of the Egyptians, and out of the hand of all kingdoms, and of them that oppressed you; and ye have this day rejected your God, who himself saved you out of all your adversities and your tribulations; and ye have said unto him, Nay, but set a king over us. Now therefore present yourselves before the Lord by your tribes, and by your thousands.

And when Samuel had caused all the tribes of Israel to come near, the tribe of Benjamin was taken. When he had caused the tribe of Benjamin to come near by their families, the family of Matri was taken, and Saul the son of Kish was taken; and when they sought him, he could not be found. Therefore they inquired of the Lord further, if the man should yet come thither. And the Lord answered, Behold, he hath hid himself among the stuff. And they ran and fetched him thence; and when he stood among the people, he was higher than any of the people from his shoulders and upward. And Samuel said to all the people, See ye him whom the Lord hath chosen, that there is none like him among all the people? And all the people shouted, and said, God save the king. Then Samuel told the people the manner of the kingdom, and wrote it in a book, and laid it up before the Lord. And Samuel sent all the people away, every man to his house. And Saul also went home to Gibeah; and there went with him a band of men, whose hearts God had touched. But the children of Belial said, How shall this man save us? And they despised him, and brought him no presents. But he held his peace.

5 THEN Nahash the Ammonite came up, and encamped against Jabesh-gilead; and all the men of Jabesh said unto Nahash, Make a covenant with us, and we will serve thee. And Nahash the Ammonite answered them, On this condition will I make a covenant with you, that I may thrust out all your right eyes, and lay it for a reproach in all Israel. And the elders of Jabesh said unto him, Give us seven days' respite that we may send messengers unto all the coasts of Israel; and then, if there be no man to save us, we will come out unto thee. Then came the messengers to Gibeah of Saul, and told the tidings in the ears of the people; and all the people lifted up their voices, and wept.

And, behold, Saul came after the herd out of the field; and Saul said, What aileth the people that they weep? And they told him the tidings of the men of Jabesh. And the Spirit of God came upon Saul when he heard those tidings, and his anger was kindled greatly. And he took a yoke of oxen, and hewed them in pieces, and sent them throughout all the coasts of Israel by the hands of messengers, saying, Whosoever cometh not forth after Saul and after Samuel, so shall it be done unto his oxen. And the fear of the Lord fell on the people, and they came out with one consent. And when he numbered them in Bezek, the children of Israel were three hundred thousand, and the men of Judah thirty thousand. And they said unto the messengers that came, Thus shall ye say unto the men of Jabesh-gilead, Tomorrow, by that time the sun be hot, ye shall have help. And the messengers came and showed it to the men of Jabesh; and they were glad. Therefore the men of Jabesh said, Tomorrow we will come out unto you, and ye shall do with us all that seemeth good unto you. And it was so on the morrow that Saul put the people in three companies; and they came into the midst of the host in the morning watch and slew the Ammonites until the heat of the day; and it came to pass, that they which remained were scattered, so that two of them were not left together.

And the people said unto Samuel, Who is he that said, Shall Saul reign over us? bring the men that we may put them to death. And Saul said, There shall not a man be put to death this day; for today the Lord hath wrought salvation in Israel. Then said Samuel to the people, Come and let us go to Gilgal and renew the kingdom there. And all the people went to Gilgal; and there they made Saul king before the Lord in Gilgal; and there they sacrificed sacrifices of peace offerings before the Lord; and there Saul and all the men of Israel rejoiced greatly.

And Samuel said unto all Israel, Behold, I have hearkened unto your voice in all that ye said unto me, and have made a king over you. And now, behold, the king walketh before you; and I am old and grayheaded; and behold, my sons are with you; and I have walked before you from my childhood unto this day. Behold, here I am; witness against me before the Lord, and before his anointed; whose ox have I taken? or whose ass have I taken? or whom have I defrauded? whom have I oppressed? or of whose hand have I received any bribe to blind mine eyes therewith? and I will restore it you. And they said, Thou hast not defrauded us nor oppressed us, neither hast thou taken aught of any man's hand. And he said unto them, The Lord is witness against you and his anointed is witness this day that ye have not found aught in my hand. And they answered, He is witness.

And Samuel said unto the people, It is the Lord that advanced Moses and Aaron, and that brought your fathers up out of the land of Egypt. Now therefore stand still, that I may reason with you before the Lord of all the righteous acts of the Lord, which he did to you and to your fathers. When Jacob was come into Egypt, and your fathers cried unto the Lord, then the Lord sent Moses and Aaron, which brought forth your fathers out of Egypt, and made them dwell in this place. And when they forgat the Lord their God, he sold them into the hand of Sisera, captain of the host of Hazor, and into the hand of the Philistines, and into the hand of the king of Moab, and they fought against them. And they cried unto the Lord, and said, We have sinned, because we have forsaken the Lord, and have served Baalim and Ashtaroth; but now deliver us out of the hand of our enemies, and we will serve thee. And the Lord sent Jerubbaal, and Bedan, and Jephthah, and Samuel, and delivered you out of the hand of your enemies on every side, and ye dwelt safe.

And when ye saw that Nahash the king of the children of Ammon came against you, ye said unto me, Nay; but a king shall reign over us; when the Lord your God was your king. Now therefore behold the king whom ye have chosen, and whom ye have desired! and, behold, the Lord hath set a king over you. If ye will fear the Lord, and serve him, and obey his voice and not rebel against the commandment of the Lord; then shall both ye and also the king that reigneth over you continue following the Lord your God; but if ye will not obey the voice of the Lord, but rebel against the commandment of the Lord; then shall the hand of the Lord be against you, as it was against your fathers. Now therefore stand and see this great thing, which the Lord will do before your eyes. Is it not wheat harvest today? I will call unto the Lord, and he shall send thunder and rain; that ye may perceive and see that your wickedness is great, which ye have done in the sight of the Lord in asking you a king. So Samuel called unto the Lord; and the Lord sent thunder and rain that day; and all the people greatly feared the Lord and Samuel.

And all the people said unto Samuel, Pray for thy servants unto the Lord thy God, that we die not; for we have added unto all our sins this evil, to ask us a king. And Samuel said unto the people, Fear not; ye have done all this wickedness; yet turn not aside from following the Lord but serve the Lord with all your heart; and turn ye not aside; for then should ye go after vain things, which cannot profit nor deliver; for they are vain. For the Lord will not forsake his people for his great name's sake; because it hath pleased the Lord to make you his people. Moreover as for me, God forbid that I should sin against the Lord in ceasing to pray for you; but I will teach you the good and the right way; only fear the Lord and serve him in truth with all your heart; for consider how great things he hath done for you. But if ye shall still do wickedly, ye shall be consumed, both ye and your king.

6 SAUL reigned one year; and when he had reigned two years over Israel Saul chose him three thousand men of Israel; whereof two thousand were with Saul in Michmash and in mount Beth-el, and a thousand were with Jonathan in Gibeah of Benjamin; and the rest of the people he sent every man to his tent. And Jonathan smote the garrison of the Philistines that was in Geba, and the Philistines heard of it. And Saul blew the trumpet throughout all the land, saying, Let the Hebrews hear. And all Israel heard say that Saul had smitten a garrison of the Philistines and that Israel also was had in abomination with the Philistines. And the people were called together after Saul to Gilgal.

And the Philistines gathered themselves together to fight with Israel, thirty thousand chariots and six thousand horsemen, and people as the sand which is on the seashore in multitude; and they came up, and pitched in Michmash eastward from Beth-aven. When the men of Israel saw that they were in a strait (for the people were distressed,) then the people did hide themselves in caves and in thickets and in rocks and in high places and in pits. And some of the Hebrews went over Jordan to the land of Gad and Gilead. As for Saul, he was yet in Gilgal and all the people followed him trembling.

And he tarried seven days, according to the set time that Samuel had appointed; but Samuel came not to Gilgal; and the people were scattered from him. And Saul said, Bring hither a burnt offering to me, and peace offerings. And he offered the burnt offering.

And it came to pass, that as soon as he had made an end of offering the burnt offering, behold, Samuel came; and Saul went out to meet him that he might salute him. And Samuel said, What hast thou done? And Saul said, Because I saw that the people were scattered from me, and that thou camest not within the days appointed, and that the Philistines gathered themselves together at Michmash; therefore said I, The Philistines will come down now upon me to Gilgal, and I have not made supplication unto the Lord; I forced myself therefore, and offered a burnt offering. And Samuel said to Saul, Thou hast done foolishly; thou hast not kept the commandment of the Lord thy God, which he commanded thee; for now would the Lord have established thy kingdom upon Israel forever. But now thy kingdom shall not continue; the Lord hath sought him a man after his own heart, and the Lord hath commanded him to be captain over his people, because thou hast not kept that which the Lord commanded thee.

And Samuel arose, and gat him up from Gilgal unto Gibeah of Benjamin. And Saul numbered the people that were present with him, about six hundred men. And Saul, and Jonathan his son, and the people that were present with them, abode in Gibeah of Benjamin; but the Philistines encamped in Michmash. And the spoilers came out of the camp of the Philistines in three companies; one company turned unto the way that leadeth to Ophrah, unto the land of Shual; and another company turned the way to Beth-horon; and another company turned to the way of the border that looketh to the valley of Zeboim toward the wilderness.

Now there was no smith found throughout all the land of Israel; for the Philistines said, Lest the Hebrews make them swords or spears; but all the Israelites went down to the Philistines to sharpen every man his share, and his coulter, and his axe, and his mattock. Yet they had a file for the mattocks, and for the coulters, and for the forks, and for the axes, and to sharpen the goads. So it came to pass in the day of battle, that there was neither sword nor spear found in the hand of any of the people that were with Saul and Jonathan; but with Saul and with Jonathan his son was there found. And the garrison of the Philistines went out to the passage of Michmash.

Now it came to pass upon a day, that Jonathan the son of Saul said unto the young man that bare his armor, Come, and let us go over to the Philistines' garrison, that is on the other side. But he told not his father. And Saul tarried in the uttermost part of Gibeah under a pomegranate tree which is in Migron; and the people that were with him were about six hundred men; and Ahiah, the son of Ahitub, Ichabod's brother, the son of Phinehas, the son of Eli, the Lord's priest in Shiloh, wearing an ephod. And the people knew not that Jonathan was gone. And between the passages, by which Jonathan sought to go over unto the Philistines' garrison, there was a sharp rock on the one side, and a sharp rock on the other side; and the name of the one was Bozez, and the name of the other Seneh. The forefront of the one was situate northward over against Michmash, and the other southward over against Gibeah.

And Jonathan said to the young man that bare his armor, Come, and let us go over unto the garrison of these uncircumcised; it may be that the Lord will work for us; for there is no restraint to the Lord to save by many or by few. And his armor-bearer said unto him, Do all that is in thy heart; turn thee; behold, I am with thee according to thy heart. Then said Jonathan, Behold, we will pass over unto these men, and we will discover ourselves unto them. If they say thus unto us, Tarry until we come to you; then we will stand still in our place, and will not go up unto them. But if they say thus, Come up unto us; then we will go up; for the Lord hath delivered them into our hand; and this shall be a sign unto us. And both of them discovered themselves unto the garrison of the Philistines; and the Philistines said, Behold, the Hebrews come forth out of the holes where they had hid themselves. And the men of the garrison answered Jonathan and his armor-bearer, and said, Come up to us, and we will show you a thing. And Jonathan said unto his armor-bearer, Come up after me; for the Lord hath delivered them into the hand of Israel. And Jonathan climbed up upon his hands and upon his feet, and his armor-bearer after him; and they fell before Jonathan; and his armor-bearer slew after him. And that first slaughter, which Jonathan and his armor-bearer made, was about twenty men, within as it were a half acre of land, which a yoke of oxen might plough.

And there was trembling in the host, in the field, and among all the people; the garrison, and the spoilers, they also trembled, and the Earth quaked; so it was a very great trembling. And the watchmen of Saul in Gibeah of Benjamin looked; and, behold, the multitude melted away, and they went on beating down one another. Then said Saul unto the people that were with him, Number now and see who is gone from us. And when they had numbered, behold, Jonathan and his armor-bearer were not there. And Saul said unto Ahiah, Bring hither the ark of God. For the ark of God was at that time with the children of Israel. And it came to pass while Saul talked unto the priest, that the noise that was in the host of the Philistines went on and increased; and Saul said unto the priest, Withdraw thine hand. And Saul and all the people that were with him assembled themselves, and they came to the battle; and behold, every man's sword was against his fellow and there was a very great discomfiture. Moreover, the Hebrews that were with the Philistines before that time, which went up with them into the camp from the country round about, even they also turned to be with the Israelites that were with Saul and Jonathan. Likewise all the men of Israel which had hid themselves in mount Ephraim, when they heard that the Philistines fled, even they also followed hard after them in the battle. So the Lord saved Israel that day and the battle passed over unto Beth-aven.

And the men of Israel were distressed that day; for Saul had adjured the people, saying, Cursed be the man that eateth any food until evening, that I may be avenged on mine enemies. So none of the people tasted any food. And all they of the land came to a wood and there was honey upon the ground. And when the people were come into the wood, behold, the honey dropped; but no man put his hand to his mouth; for the people feared the oath. But Jonathan heard not when his father charged the people with the oath; wherefore he put forth the end of the rod that was in his hand, and dipped it in a honeycomb, and put his hand to his mouth; and his eyes were enlightened. Then answered one of the people, and said, Thy father straitly charged the people with an oath, saying, Cursed be the man that eateth any food this day. And the people were faint. Then said Jonathan, My father hath troubled the land; see, I pray you, how mine eyes have been enlightened, because I tasted a little of this honey. How much more if haply the people had eaten freely today of the spoil of their enemies which they found? for had their not been now a much greater slaughter among the Philistines?

And they smote the Philistines that day from Michmash to Aijalon; and the people were very faint. And the people flew upon the spoil, and took sheep, and oxen, and calves, and slew them on the ground; and the people did eat them with the blood. Then they told Saul, saying, Behold, the people sin against the Lord in that they eat with the blood. And he said, Ye have transgressed; roll a great stone unto me this day. And Saul said, Disperse yourselves among the people, and say unto them, Bring me hither every man his ox, and every man his sheep, and slay them here, and eat; and sin not against the Lord in eating with the blood. And all the people brought every man his ox with him that night, and slew them there. And Saul built an altar unto the Lord; the same was the first altar that he built unto the Lord.

And Saul said, Let us go down after the Philistines by night, and spoil them until the morning light, and let us not leave a man of them. And they said, Do whatsoever seemeth good unto thee. Then said the priest, Let us draw near hither unto God. And Saul asked counsel of God, Shall I go down after the Philistines? wilt thou deliver them into the hand of Israel? But he answered him not that day. And Saul said, Draw ye near hither, all the chief of the people; and know and see wherein this sin hath been this day. For, as the Lord liveth, which saveth Israel, though it be in Jonathan my son, he shall surely die. But there was not a man among all the people that answered him. Then said he unto all Israel, Be ye on one side, and I and Jonathan my son will be on the other side. And the people said unto Saul, Do what seemeth good unto thee. Therefore Saul said unto the Lord God of Israel, Give a perfect lot. And Saul and Jonathan were taken; but the people escaped. And Saul said, Cast lots between me and Jonathan my son. And Jonathan was taken.

Then Saul said to Jonathan, Tell me what thou hast done. And Jonathan told him, and said, I did but taste a little honey with the end of the rod that was in mine hand, and lo, I must die. And Saul answered, God do so and more also for thou shalt surely die, Jonathan. And the people said unto Saul, Shall Jonathan die, who hath wrought this great salvation in Israel? God forbid; as the Lord liveth, there shall not one hair of his head fall to the ground; for he hath wrought with God this day. So the people rescued Jonathan that he died not. Then Saul went up from following the Philistines; and the Philistines went to their own place.

So Saul took the kingdom over Israel and fought against all his enemies on every side, against Moab, and against the children of Ammon, and against Edom, and against the kings of Zobah, and against the Philistines; and whithersoever he turned himself, he vexed them. And he gathered a host, and smote the Amalekites, and delivered Israel out of the hands of them that spoiled them.

7 NOW the sons of Saul were Jonathan, and Ishui, and Melchishua; and the names of his two daughters were these; the name of the firstborn Merab, and the name of the younger Michal; and the name of Saul's wife was Ahinoam, the daughter of Ahimaaz; and the name of the captain of his host was Abner, the son of Ner, Saul's uncle. And Kish was the father of Saul; and Ner the father of Abner was the son of Abiel.

And there was sore war against the Philistines all the days of Saul; and when Saul saw any strong man or any valiant man, he took him unto him. Samuel also said unto Saul, The Lord sent me to anoint thee to be king over his people, over Israel; now therefore hearken thou unto the voice of the words of the Lord. Thus saith the Lord of hosts, I remember that which Amalek did to Israel, how he laid wait for him in the way when he came up from Egypt. Now go and smite Amalek and utterly destroy all that they have, and spare them not; but slay both man and woman, infant and suckling, ox and sheep, camel and ass.

And Saul gathered the people together and numbered them in Telaim, two hundred thousand footmen, and ten thousand men of Judah. And Saul came to a city of Amalek and laid wait in the valley. And Saul said unto the Kenites, Go, depart, get you down from among the Amalekites, lest I destroy you with them;

for ye showed kindness to all the children of Israel when they came up out of Egypt. So the Kenites departed from among the Amalekites. And Saul smote the Amalekites from Havilah until thou comest to Shur that is over against Egypt. And he took Agag the king of the Amalekites alive, and utterly destroyed all the people with the edge of the sword. But Saul and the people spared Agag, and the best of the sheep, and of the oxen, and of the fatlings, and the lambs, and all that was good, and would not utterly destroy them; but everything that was vile and refuse, that they destroyed utterly.

Then came the word of the Lord unto Samuel, saying, I have set up Saul to be a king, and he repenteth not that he hath sinned, for he is turned back from following me, and hath not performed my commandments. And it grieved Samuel; and he cried unto the Lord all night. And when Samuel rose early to meet Saul in the morning, it was told Samuel, saying, Saul came to Carmel, and behold, he set him up a place, and is gone about, and passed on and gone down to Gilgal. And Samuel came to Saul; and Saul said unto him, Blessed be thou of the Lord; I have performed the commandment of the Lord. And Samuel said, What meaneth then this bleating of the sheep in mine ears, and the lowing of the oxen which I hear? And Saul said, They have brought them from the Amalekites; for the people spared the best of the sheep and of the oxen, to sacrifice unto the Lord thy God; and the rest we have utterly destroyed. Then Samuel said unto Saul, Stay, and I will tell thee what the Lord hath said to me this night. And he said unto him, Say on.

And Samuel said, When thou wast little in thine own sight, wast thou not made the head of the tribes of Israel and the Lord anointed thee king over Israel? And the Lord sent thee on a journey, and said, Go and utterly destroy the sinners the Amalekites, and fight against them until they be consumed. Wherefore then didst thou not obey the voice of the Lord, but didst fly upon the spoil, and didst evil in the sight of the Lord?

And Saul said unto Samuel, Yea, I have obeyed the voice of the Lord, and have gone the way which the Lord sent me, and have brought Agag the king of Amalek, and have utterly destroyed the Amalekites. But the people took of the spoil, sheep and oxen, the chief of the things which should have been utterly destroyed, to sacrifice unto the Lord thy God in Gilgal.

And Samuel said, Hath the Lord as great delight in burnt offering and sacrifices, as in obeying the voice of the Lord? Behold, to obey is better than sacrifice, and to hearken than the fat of rams. For rebellion is as the sin of witchcraft, and stubbornness is as iniquity and idolatry. Because thou hast rejected the word of the Lord, he hath also rejected thee from being king.

And Saul said unto Samuel, I have sinned; for I have transgressed the commandment of the Lord, and thy words; because I feared the people, and obeyed their voice. Now therefore, I pray thee, pardon my sin, and turn again with me, that I may worship the Lord. And Samuel said unto Saul, I will not return with thee; for thou hast rejected the word of the Lord, and the Lord hath rejected thee from being king over Israel. And as Samuel turned about to go away, he laid hold upon the skirt of his mantle, and it rent. And Samuel said unto him, The Lord hath rent the kingdom of Israel from thee this day, and hath given it to a neighbor of thine, that is better than thou. And also the Strength of Israel will not lie nor repent; for he is not a man that he should repent. Then he said, I have sinned; yet honor me now, I pray thee before the elders of my people and before Israel, and turn again with me that I may worship the Lord thy God. So Samuel turned again after Saul; and Saul worshiped the Lord.

Then said Samuel, Bring ye hither to me Agag the king of the Amalekites. And Agag came unto him delicately. And Agag said, Surely the bitterness of death is past. And Samuel said, As thy sword hath made women childless, so shall thy mother be childless among women. And Samuel hewed Agag in pieces before the Lord in Gilgal.

Then Samuel went to Ramah; and Saul went up to his house to Gibeah of Saul. And Samuel came no more to see Saul until the day of his death; nevertheless, Samuel mourned for Saul; and the Lord rent the kingdom from Saul whom he had made king over Israel.

And the Lord said unto Samuel, How long wilt thou mourn for Saul, seeing I have rejected him from reigning over Israel? fill thine horn with oil, and go, I will send thee to Jesse the Bethlehemite; for I have provided me a king among his sons. And Samuel said, How can I go? if Saul hear it, he will kill me. And the Lord said, Take a heifer with thee, and say, I am come to sacrifice to the Lord. And call Jesse to the sacrifice, and I will show thee what thou shalt do; and thou shalt anoint unto me him whom I name unto thee. And Samuel did that which the Lord spake, and came to Bethlehem. And the elders of the town trembled at his coming, and said, Comest thou peaceably? And he said, Peaceably; I am come to sacrifice unto the Lord; sanctify yourselves, and come with me to the sacrifice. And he sanctified Jesse and his sons, and called them to the sacrifice.

And it came to pass, when they were come, that he looked on Eliab, and said, Surely the Lord's anointed is before him. But the Lord said unto Samuel, Look not on his countenance or on the height of his stature; because I have refused him; for the Lord seeth not as man seeth; for man looketh on the outward appearance, but the Lord looketh on the heart. Then Jesse called Abinadab, and made him pass before Samuel. And he said, Neither hath the Lord chosen this. Then Jesse made Shammah to pass by. And he said, Neither hath the Lord chosen this. Again Jesse made seven of his sons to pass before Samuel. And Samuel said unto Jesse, The Lord hath not chosen these. And Samuel said unto Jesse, Are here all thy children? And he said, There remaineth yet the youngest, and, behold, he keepeth the sheep. And Samuel said unto Jesse, Send and fetch him; for we will not sit down till he come hither.

And he sent, and brought him in. Now he was ruddy, and withal of a beautiful countenance, and goodly to look to. And the Lord said, Arise, anoint him; for this is he. Then Samuel took the horn of oil, and anointed him in the midst of his brethren; and the Spirit of the Lord came upon David from that day forward. So Samuel rose up, and went to Ramah.

But the Spirit of the Lord departed from Saul, and an evil spirit which was not of the Lord troubled him. And Saul's servants said unto him, Behold now, an evil spirit which is not of God troubleth thee. Let our lord now command thy servants, which are before thee, to seek out a man, who is a cunning player on a harp; and it shall come to pass, when the evil spirit, which is not of God, is upon thee, that he shall play with his hand, and thou shalt be well. And Saul said unto his servants, Provide me now a man that can play well, and bring him to me. Then answered one of the servants, and said, Behold, I have seen a son of Jesse the Bethlehemite, that is cunning in playing, and a mighty valiant man, and a man of war, and prudent in matters, and a comely person, and the Lord is with him. Wherefore Saul sent messengers unto Jesse, and said, Send me David thy son, which is with the sheep. And Jesse took an ass laden with bread, and a bottle of wine, and a kid, and sent them by David his son unto Saul. And David came to Saul, and stood before him; and he loved him greatly; and he became his armor-bearer. And Saul sent to Jesse, saying, Let David, I pray thee, stand before me; for he hath found favor in my sight. And it came to pass when the evil spirit, which was not of God, was upon Saul, that David took a harp and played with his hand; so Saul was refreshed, and was well, and the evil spirit departed from him.

8 NOW the Philistines gathered together their armies to battle, and were gathered together at Shochoh, which belongeth to Judah, and pitched between Shochoh and Azekhah, in Ephes-dammim. And Saul and the men of Israel were gathered together, and pitched by the valley of Elah, and set the battle in array against the Philistines. And the Philistines stood on a mountain on the one side, and Israel stood on a mountain on the other side; and there was a valley between them. And there went out a champion out of the camp of the Philistines named Goliath of Gath, whose height was six cubits and a span. And he had a helmet of brass upon his head and he was armed with a coat of mail; and the weight of the coat was five thousand shekels of brass. And he had greaves of brass upon his legs and a target of brass between his shoulders. And the staff of his spear was like a weaver's beam; and his spear's head weighed six hundred shekels of iron; and one bearing a shield went before him. And he stood and cried unto the armies of Israel and said unto them, Why are ye come out to set your battle in array? am not I a Philistine, and ye servants to Saul? choose you a man for you, and let him come down to me. If he be able to fight with me, and to kill me, then will we be your servants; but if I prevail against him, and kill him, then shall ye be our servants, and serve us. And the Philistine said, I defy the armies of Israel this day; give me a man, that we may fight together. When Saul and all Israel heard those words of the Philistine they were dismayed and greatly afraid.

Now David was the son of that Ephrathite of Bethlehem-Judah, whose name was Jesse; and he had eight sons; and the man went among men for an old man in the days of Saul. And the three eldest sons of Jesse went and followed Saul to the battle; and the names of his three sons that went to the battle were Eliab the firstborn, and next unto him Abinadab, and the third Shammah. And David was the youngest; and the three eldest followed Saul. But David went and returned from Saul to feed his father's sheep at Bethlehem. And the Philistine drew near morning and evening, and presented himself forty days.

And Jesse said unto David his son, Take now for thy brethren an ephah of this parched corn, and these ten loaves, and run to the camp to thy brethren; and carry these ten cheeses unto the captain of their thousand, and look how thy brethren fare, and take their pledge. Now Saul and they, and all the men of Israel were in the valley of Elah, fighting with the Philistines.

And David rose up early in the morning, and left the sheep with a keeper, and took and went as Jesse had commanded him; and he came to the trench, as the host was going forth to the fight and shouted for the battle. For Israel and the Philistines had put the battle in array, army against army. And David left his carriage in the hand of the keeper of the carriage and ran into the army and came and saluted his brethren. And as he talked with them behold, there came up the champion, the Philistine of Gath, Goliath by name, out of the armies of the Philistines and spake according to the same words; and David heard them.

And all the men of Israel, when they saw the man, fled from him, and were sore afraid. And the men of Israel said, Have ye seen this man that is come up? surely to defy Israel is he come up; and it shall be that the man who killeth him, the king will enrich him with great riches, and will give him his daughter, and make his father's house free in Israel.

And David spake to the men that stood by him, saying, What shall be done to the man that killeth this Philistine, and taketh away the reproach from Israel? for who is this uncircumcised Philistine that he should defy the armies of the living God? And the people answered him after this manner, saying, So shall it be done to the man that killeth him.

And Eliab his eldest brother heard when he spake unto the men; and Eliab's anger was kindled against David, and he said, Why camest thou down hither?

and with whom hast thou left those few sheep in the wilderness? I know thy pride and the naughtiness of thine heart; for thou art come down that thou mightest see the battle. And David said, What have I now done? Is there not a cause? And he turned from him toward another, and spake after the same manner; and the people answered him again after the former manner.

And when the words were heard which David spake, they rehearsed them before Saul; and he sent for him. And David said to Saul, Let no man's heart fail because of him; thy servant will go and fight with this Philistine. And Saul said to David, Thou art not able to go against this Philistine to fight with him; for thou art but a youth, and he a man of war from his youth. And David said unto Saul, Thy servant kept his father's sheep, and there came a lion, and a bear, and took a lamb out of the flock; and I went out after him, and smote him and delivered it out of his mouth; and when he arose against me, I caught him by his beard, and smote him, and slew him. Thy servant slew both the lion and the bear; and this uncircumcised Philistine shall be as one of them seeing he hath defied the armies of the living God. David said moreover, The Lord that delivered me out of the paw of the lion and out of the paw of the bear, he will deliver me out of the hand of this Philistine. And Saul said unto David, Go and the Lord be with thee. And Saul armed David with his armor and he put a helmet of brass upon his head; also he armed him with a coat of mail. And David girded his sword upon his armor, and he assayed to go; for he had not proved it. And David said unto Saul, I cannot go with these; for I have not proved them. And David put them off him. And he took his staff in his hand, and chose him five smooth stones out of the brook, and put them in a shepherd's bag which he had, even in a scrip; and his sling was in his hand; and he drew near to the Philistine.

And the Philistine came on and drew near unto David; and the man that bare the shield went before him. And when the Philistine looked about and saw David, he disdained him; for he was but a youth, and ruddy, and of a fair countenance. And the Philistine said unto David, Am I a dog, that thou comest to me with staves? And the Philistine cursed David by his gods. And the Philistine said to David, Come to me, and I will give thy flesh unto the fowls of the air, and to the beasts of the field. Then said David to the Philistine, Thou comest to me with a sword, and with a spear, and with a shield; but I come to thee in the name of the Lord of hosts, the God of the armies of Israel, whom thou hast defied. This day will the Lord deliver thee into mine hand; and I will smite thee, and take thine head from thee and I will give the carcasses of the host of the Philistines this day unto the fowls of the air and to the wild beasts of the Earth; that all the earth may know that there is a God in Israel. And all this assembly shall know that the Lord saveth not with sword and spear; for the battle is the Lord's, and he will give you into our hands.

And it came to pass, when the Philistine arose, and came and drew nigh to meet David, that David hasted, and ran toward the army to meet the Philistine. And David put his hand in his bag, and took thence a stone, and slang it, and smote the Philistine in his forehead, that the stone sunk into his forehead; and he fell upon his face to the earth.

So David prevailed over the Philistines with a sling and with a stone, and smote the Philistine, and slew him; but there was no sword in the hand of David. Therefore David ran, and stood upon the Philistine, and took his sword and drew it out of the sheath thereof, and slew him, and cut off his head therewith. And when the Philistines saw their champion was dead, they fled. And the men of Israel and of Judah arose and shouted, and pursued the Philistines until thou come to the valley, and to the gates of Ekron. And the wounded of the Philistines fell down by the way to Shaaraim, even unto Gath, and unto Ekron. And the children of Israel returned from chasing after the Philistines, and they spoiled their tents. And David took the head of the Philistine and brought it to Jerusalem; but he put his armor in his tent.

And when Saul saw David go forth against the Philistine he said unto Abner, the captain of the host, Abner, whose son is this youth? And Abner said, As thy soul liveth, O king, I cannot tell. And the king said, Inquire thou whose son the stripling is. And as David returned from the slaughter of the Philistine, Abner took him, and brought him before Saul with the head of the Philistine in his hand. And Saul said to him, Whose son art thou, thou young man? And David answered, I am the son of thy servant Jesse the Bethlehemite.

And it came to pass, when he had made an end of speaking unto Saul, that the soul of Jonathan was knit with the soul of David and Jonathan loved him as his own soul. And Saul took him that day and would let him go no more home to his father's house. Then Jonathan and David made a covenant because he loved him as his own soul. And Jonathan stripped himself of the robe that was upon him and gave it to David, and his garments, even to his sword, and to his bow, and to his girdle. And David went out whithersoever Saul sent him and behaved himself wisely; and Saul set him over the men of war, and he was accepted in the sight of all the people, and also in the sight of Saul's servants. And it came to pass as they came, when David was returned from the slaughter of the Philistine, that the women came out of all cities of Israel, singing and dancing, to meet king Saul with tabrets, with joy, and with instruments of music. And the women answered one another as they played, and said, Saul hath slain his thousands, and David his ten thousands.

And Saul was very wroth and the saying displeased him; and he said, They have ascribed unto David ten thousands and to me they have ascribed but thousands; and what can he have more but the kingdom? And Saul eyed David from that day and forward.

And it came to pass on the morrow, that the evil spirit which was not of God came upon Saul, and he prophesied in the midst of the house; and David played with his hand as at other times; and there was a javelin in Saul's hand. And Saul cast the javelin; for he said, I will smite David even to the wall with it. And David avoided out of his presence twice. And Saul was afraid of David because the Lord was with him and was departed from Saul. Therefore Saul removed him from him and made him his captain over a thousand; and he went out and came in before the people. And David behaved himself wisely in all his ways and the Lord was with him. Wherefore when Saul saw that he behaved himself very wisely he was afraid of him. But all Israel and Judah loved David because he went out and came in before them.

And Saul said to David, Behold my elder daughter Merab, her will I give thee to wife; only be thou valiant for me and fight the Lord's battles. For Saul said, Let not mine hand be upon him, but let the hand of the Philistines be upon him. And David said unto Saul, Who am I? and what is my life, or my father's family in Israel, that I should be son-in-law to the king? But it came to pass at the time when Merab Saul's daughter should have been given to David, that she was given unto Adriel the Meholathite to wife.

And Michal Saul's daughter loved David; and they told Saul, and the thing pleased him. And Saul said, I will give him her that she may be a snare to him, and that the hand of the Philistines may be against him. Wherefore Saul said to David, Thou shalt this day be my son-in-law in the one of the twain. And Saul commanded his servants, saying, Commune with David secretly and say, Behold, the king hath delight in thee and all his servants love thee; now therefore be the king's son-in-law. And Saul's servants spake those words in the ears of David. And David said, Seemeth it to you a light thing to be a king's son-in-law, seeing that I am a poor man, and lightly esteemed? And the servants of Saul told him, saying, On this manner spake David. And Saul said, Thus shall ye say to David, The king desireth not any dowry but a hundred foreskins of the Philistines to be avenged of the king's enemies. But Saul thought to make David fall by the hand of the Philistines. And when his servants told David these words it pleased David well to be the king's son-in-law; and the days were not expired. Wherefore David arose and went, he and his men, and slew of the Philistines two hundred men; and David brought their foreskins, and they gave them in full tale to the king, that he might be the king's son-in-law. And Saul gave him Michal his daughter to wife. And Saul saw and knew that the Lord was with David and that Michal Saul's daughter loved him. And Saul was yet the more afraid of David; and Saul became David's enemy continually.

Then the princes of the Philistines went forth; and it came to pass after they went forth, that David behaved himself more wisely than all the servants of Saul; so that his name was much set by. And Saul spake to Jonathan his son and to all his servants, that they should kill David. But Jonathan Saul's son delighted much in David; and Jonathan told David, saying, Saul my father seeketh to kill thee; now therefore, I pray thee, take heed to thyself until the morning, and abide in a secret place, and hide thyself; and I will go out and stand beside my father in the field where thou art, and I will commune with my father of thee; and what I see, that I will tell thee.

And Jonathan spake good of David unto Saul his father, and said unto him, Let not the king sin against his servant, against David; because he hath not sinned against thee, and because his works have been to thee-ward very good; for he did put his life in his hand, and slew the Philistine, and the Lord wrought a great salvation for all Israel; thou sawest it, and didst rejoice; wherefore then wilt thou sin against innocent blood, to slay David without a cause? And Saul hearkened unto the voice of Jonathan; and Saul sware, As the Lord liveth, he shall not be slain. And Jonathan called David, and Jonathan showed him all those things. And Jonathan brought David to Saul, and he was in his presence, as in times past.

9 AND there was war again; and David went out, and fought with the Philistines, and slew them with a great slaughter; and they fled from him. And the evil spirit which was not of the Lord was upon Saul as he sat in his house with his javelin in his hand; and David played with his hand. And Saul sought to smite David even to the wall with the javelin; but he slipped away out of Saul's presence, and he smote the javelin into the wall; and David fled and escaped that night. Saul also sent messengers unto David's house to watch him and to slay him in the morning; and Michal David's wife told him, saying, If thou save not thy life tonight, tomorrow thou shalt be slain.

So Michal let David down through a window; and he went and fled and escaped. And Michal took an image and laid it in the bed and put a pillow of goats' hair for his bolster, and covered it with a cloth. And when Saul sent messengers to take David, she said, He is sick. And Saul sent the messengers again to see David, saying, Bring him up to me in the bed, that I may slay him. And when the messengers were come in, behold, there was an image in the bed, with a pillow of goats' hair for his bolster. And Saul said unto Michal, Why hast thou deceived me so, and sent away mine enemy that he is escaped? And Michal answered Saul, He said unto me, Let me go; why should I kill thee?

So David fled, and escaped and came to Samuel to Ramah, and told him all that Saul had done to him. And he and Samuel went and dwelt in Naioth. And it was told Saul, saying, Behold, David is at Naioth in Ramah. And Saul sent messengers to take David; and when they saw the company of the prophets prophesying and Samuel standing as appointed over them, the Spirit of God was upon the messengers of Saul, and they also prophesied. And when it was told Saul, he sent other messengers and they prophesied likewise. And Saul sent messengers again the third time, and they prophesied also. Then went he also to Ramah, and came to a great well that is in Sechu; and he asked and said, Where are Samuel and David? And one said, Behold, they be at Naioth in Ramah. And he went thither to Naioth in Ramah; and the Spirit of God was upon him also, and he went on, and prophesied, until he came to Naioth in Ramah. And he stripped off his clothes also, and prophesied before Samuel in like manner, and lay down naked all that day and all that night. Wherefore they say, Is Saul also among the prophets?

And David fled from Naioth in Ramah, and came and said before Jonathan, What have I done? what is mine iniquity? and what is my sin before thy father, that he seeketh my life? And he said unto him, God forbid; thou shalt not die; behold, my father will do nothing either great or small but that he will show it me; and why should my father hide this thing from me? it is not so. And David sware moreover, and said, Thy father certainly knoweth that I have found grace in thine eyes; and he saith, Let not Jonathan know this, lest he be grieved; but truly, as the Lord liveth, and as thy soul liveth, there is but a step between me and death.

Then said Jonathan unto David, Whatsoever thy soul desireth, I will even do it for thee. And David said unto Jonathan, Behold, tomorrow is the new moon, and I should not fail to sit with the king at meat; but let me go that I may hide myself in the field unto the third day at even. If thy father at all miss me, then say, David earnestly asked leave of me that he might run to Bethlehem his city; for there is a yearly sacrifice there for all the family. If he say thus, It is well; thy servant shall have peace; but if he be very wroth, then be sure that evil is determined by him. Therefore thou shalt deal kindly with thy servant; for thou hast brought thy servant into a covenant of the Lord with thee; notwithstanding, if there be in me iniquity, slay me thyself; for why shouldest thou bring me to thy father? And Jonathan said, Far be it from thee; for if I knew certainly that evil were determined by my father to come upon thee, then would not I tell it thee? Then said David to Jonathan, Who shall tell me? or what if thy father answer thee roughly?

And Jonathan said unto David, Come, and let us go out into the field. And they went out both of them into the field. And Jonathan said unto David, O Lord God of Israel, when I have sounded my father about tomorrow any time, or the third day, and behold, if there be good toward David, and I then send not unto thee, and show it thee; the Lord do so and much more to Jonathan; but if it please my father to do thee evil, then I will show it thee, and send thee away, that thou mayest go in peace; and the Lord be with thee, as he hath been with my father. And thou shalt not only while yet I live show me the kindness of the Lord, that I die not; but also thou shalt not cut off thy kindness from my house forever; no, not when the Lord hath cut off the enemies of David every one from the face of the Earth. So Jonathan made a covenant with the house of David, saying, Let the Lord even require it at the hand of David's enemies. And Jonathan caused David to swear again, because he loved him; for he loved him as he loved his own soul.

Then Jonathan said to David, Tomorrow is the new moon; and thou shalt be missed, because thy seat will be empty. And when thou hast stayed three days, then thou shalt go down quickly and come to the place where thou didst hide thyself when the business was in hand, and shalt remain by the stone Ezel. And I will shoot three arrows on the side thereof, as though I shot at a mark. And, behold, I will send a lad, saying, Go, find out the arrows. If I expressly say unto the lad, Behold, the arrows are on this side of thee, take them; then come thou; for there is peace to the and no hurt; as the Lord liveth. But if I say thus unto the young man, Behold, the arrows are beyond thee; go thy way; for the Lord hath sent thee away. And as touching the matter which thou and I have spoken of, behold, the Lord be between thee and me forever.

So David hid himself in the field; and when the new moon was come, the king sat him down to eat meat. And the king sat upon his seat as at other times, even upon a seat by the wall; and Jonathan arose, and Abner sat by Saul's side, and David's place was empty. Nevertheless Saul spake not anything that day; for he thought, Something hath befallen him, he is not clean; surely he is not clean. And it came to pass on the morrow, which was the second day of the month, that David's place was empty; and Saul said unto Jonathan his son, Wherefore cometh not the son of Jesse to meat, neither yesterday, nor today? And Jonathan answered Saul, David earnestly asked leave of me to go to Bethlehem; and he said, Let me go, I pray thee; for our family hath a sacrifice in the city and my brother, he hath commanded me to be there; and now, if I have found favor in thine eyes, let me get away, I pray thee, and see my brethren. Therefore he cometh not unto the king's table.

Then Saul's anger was kindled against Jonathan, and he said unto him, Thou son of the perverse rebellious woman, do not I know that thou hast chosen the son of Jesse to thine own confusion, and unto the confusion of thy mother's nakedness? For as long as the son of Jesse liveth upon the ground, thou shalt not be established, nor thy kingdom. Wherefore now send and fetch him unto me, for he shall surely die. And Jonathan answered Saul his father, and said unto him, Wherefore shall he be slain? what hath he done? And Saul cast a javelin at him to smite him; whereby Jonathan knew that it was determined of his father to slay David. So Jonathan arose from the table in fierce anger and did eat no meat the second day of the month; for he was grieved for David, because his father had done him shame.

And it came to pass in the morning, that Jonathan went out into the field at the time appointed with David, and a little lad with him. And he said unto his lad, Run, find out now the arrows which I shoot. And as the lad ran, he shot an arrow beyond him. And when the lad was come to the place of the arrow which Jonathan had shot, Jonathan cried after the lad, and said, Is not the arrow beyond thee? And Jonathan cried after the lad, Make speed, haste, stay not. And Jonathan's lad gathered up the arrows, and came to his master. But the lad knew not anything; only Jonathan and David knew the matter. And Jonathan gave his artillery unto his lad, and said unto him, Go, carry them to the city. And as soon as the lad was gone, David arose out of a place toward the south and fell on his face to the ground, and bowed himself three times; and they kissed one another, and wept one with another, until David exceeded. And Jonathan said to David, Go in peace, forasmuch as we have sworn both of us in the name of the Lord, saying, The Lord be between me and thee, and between my seed and thy seed forever. And he arose and departed; and Jonathan went into the city.

Then came David to Nob to Ahimelech the priest; and Ahimelech was afraid at the meeting of David, and said unto him, Why art thou alone, and no man with thee? And David said unto Ahimelech the priest, The king hath commanded me a business, and hath said unto me, Let no man know anything of the business whereabout I send thee, and what I have commanded thee; and I have appointed my servants to such and such a place. Now therefore what is under thine hand? give me five loaves of bread in mine hand, or what there is present. And the priest answered David, and said, There is no common bread under mine hand, but there is hallowed bread; if the young men have kept themselves at least from women.

And David answered the priest, and said unto him, Of a truth women have been kept from us about these three days, since I came out, and the vessels of the young men are holy and the bread is in a manner common, yea, though it were sanctified this day in the vessel. So the priest gave him hallowed bread; for there was no bread there but the shewbread, that was taken from before the Lord, to put hot bread in the day when it was taken away. Now a certain man of the servants of Saul was there that day, detained before the Lord; and his name was Doeg, an Edomite, the chiefest of the herdmen that belonged to Saul. And David said unto Ahimelech, And is there not here under thine hand spear or sword? for I have neither brought my sword nor my weapons with me, because the king's business required haste. And the priest said, The sword of Goliath the Philistine, whom thou slewest in the valley of Elah, behold, it is here wrapped in a cloth behind the ephod; if thou wilt take that, take it; for there is no other save that here. And David said, There is none like that; give it me.

And David arose, and fled that day for fear of Saul, and went to Achish the king of Gath. And the servants of Achish said unto him, Is not this David the king of the land? did they not sing one to another of him in dances, saying, Saul hath slain his thousands, and David his ten thousands? And David laid up these words in his heart, and was sore afraid of Achish the king of Gath. And he changed his behavior before them, and feigned himself mad in their hands; and scrabbled on the doors of the gate, and let his spittle fall down upon his beard. Then said Achish unto his servants, Lo, ye see the man is mad; wherefore then have ye brought him to me? Have I need of madmen, that ye have brought this fellow to play the madman in my presence? shall this fellow come into my house?

David therefore departed thence, and escaped to the cave Adullam; and when his brethren and all his father's house heard it, they went down thither to him. And everyone that was in distress, and everyone that was in debt, and everyone that was discontented, gathered themselves unto him; and he became a captain over them; and there were with him about four hundred men. And David went thence to Mizpeh of Moab; and he said unto the king of Moab, Let my father and my mother, I pray thee, come forth and be with you, till I know what God will do for me. And he brought them before the king of Moab; and they dwelt with him all the while that David was in the hold. And the prophet Gad said unto David, Abide not in the hold; depart and get thee into the land of Judah. Then David departed, and came into the forest of Hareth.

When Saul heard that David was discovered, and the men that were with him, (now Saul abode in Gibeah under a tree in Ramah, having his spear in his hand, and all his servants were standing about him;) then Saul said unto his servants that stood about him, Hear now ye Benjamites; will the son of Jesse give every one of you fields and vineyards and make you all captains of thousands, and captains of hundreds; that all of you have conspired against me and there is none that showeth me that my son hath made a league with the son of Jesse, and there is none of you that is sorry for me, or showeth unto me that my son hath stirred up my servant against me, to lie in wait, as at this day? Then answered Doeg the Edomite, which was set over the servants of Saul, and said, I saw the son of Jesse coming to Nob, to Ahimelech the son of Ahitub. And he inquired of the Lord for him, and gave him victuals and gave him the sword of Goliath the Philistine. Then the king sent to call Ahimelech the priest, the son of Ahitub, and all his father's house, the priests that were in Nob; and they came all of them to the king. And Saul said, Hear now, thou son of Ahitub. And he answered, Here I am, my lord. And Saul said unto him, Why have ye conspired against me, thou and the son of Jesse, in that thou hast given him bread and a sword, and hast inquired of God for him, that he should rise against me to lie in wait, as at this day?

Then Ahimelech answered the king, and said, And who is so faithful among all thy servants as David, which is the king's son-in-law, and goeth at thy bidding, and is honorable in thine house? Did I then begin to inquire of God for him? be it far from me; let not the king impute anything unto his servant nor to all the house of my father; for thy servant knew nothing of all this, less or more. And the king said, Thou shalt surely die, Ahimelech, thou, and all thy father's house. And the king said unto the footmen that stood about him, Turn, and slay the priests of the Lord; because their hand also is with David, and because they knew when he fled, and did not show it to me. But the servants of the king would not put forth their hand to fall upon the priests of the Lord. And the king said to Doeg, Turn thou, and fall upon the priests. And Doeg the Edomite turned, and he fell upon the priests, and slew on that day fourscore and five persons that did wear a linen ephod. And Nob, the city of the priests, smote he with the edge of the sword, both men and women, children and sucklings, and oxen, and asses, and sheep, with the edge of the sword.

And one of the sons of Ahimelech the son of Ahitub, named Abiathar, escaped, and fled after David. And Abiathar showed David that Saul had slain the Lord's priests. And David said unto Abiathar, I knew it that day, when Doeg the Edomite was there, that he would surely tell Saul; I have occasioned the death of all the persons of thy father's house. Abide thou with me, fear not; for he that seeketh my life seeketh thy life; but with me thou shalt be in safeguard.

Then they told David, saying, Behold, the Philistines fight against Keilah, and they rob the threshing floors. Therefore David inquired of the Lord, saying, Shall I go and smite these Philistines? And the Lord said unto David, Go, and smite the Philistines, and save Keilah. And David's men said unto him, Behold, we be afraid here in Judah; how much more then if we come to Keilah against the armies of the Philistines? Then David inquired of the Lord yet again. And the Lord answered him and said, Arise, go down to Keilah; for I will deliver the Philistines into thine hand. So David and his men went to Keilah, and fought with the Philistines, and brought away their cattle, and smote them with a great slaughter. So David saved the inhabitants of Keilah. And it came to pass, when Abiathar the son of Ahimelech fled to David to Keilah, that he came down with an ephod in his hand.

And it was told Saul that David was come to Keilah. And Saul said, God hath delivered him into mine hand; for he is shut in, by entering into a town that hath gates and bars. And Saul called all the people together to war, to go down to Keilah, to besiege David and his men. And David knew that Saul secretly practiced mischief against him; and he said to Abiathar the priest, Bring hither the ephod. Then said David, O Lord God of Israel, thy servant hath certainly heard that Saul seeketh to come to Keilah, to destroy the city for my sake. Will the men of Keilah deliver me up into his hand? will Saul come down, as thy servant hath heard? O Lord God of Israel, I beseech thee, tell thy servant. And the Lord said, He will come down. Then said David, Will the men of Keilah deliver me and my men into the hand of Saul? And the Lord said, They will deliver thee up. Then David and his men, which were about six hundred, arose and departed out of Keilah, and sent whithersoever they could go. And it was told Saul that David was escaped from Keilah; and he forbear to go forth. And David abode in the wilderness in strongholds, and remained in a mountain in the wilderness of Ziph. And Saul sought him every day, but God delivered him not into his hand. And David saw that Saul was come out to seek his life; and David was in the wilderness of Ziph in a wood.

And Jonathan Saul's son arose, and went to David into the wood, and strengthened his hand in God. And he said unto him, Fear not; for the hand of Saul my father shall not find thee; and thou shalt be king over Israel, and I shall be next unto thee; and that also Saul my father knoweth. And they two made a covenant before the Lord; and David abode in the wood, and Jonathan went to his house.

Then came up the Ziphites to Saul to Gibeah, saying, Doth not David hide himself with us in strongholds in the wood, in the hill of Hachilah, which is on the south of Jeshimon? Now therefore, O king, come down according to all the desire of thy soul to come down; and our part shall be to deliver him into the king's hand. And Saul said, Blessed be ye of the Lord; for ye have compassion on me. Go, I pray you, prepare yet, and know and see his place where his haunt is, and who hath seen him there; for it is told me that he dealeth very subtilely. See therefore, and take knowledge of all the lurking places where he hideth himself, and come ye again to me with the certainty, and I will go with you; and it shall come to pass, if he be in the land, that I will search him out throughout all the thousands of Judah. And they arose, and went to Ziph before Saul; but David and his men were in the wilderness of Maon, in the plain on the south of Jeshimon. Saul also and his men went to seek him. And they told David; wherefore he came down into a rock, and abode in the wilderness of Maon. And when Saul heard that, he pursued after David in the wilderness of Maon. And Saul went on this side of the mountain, and David and his men on that side of the mountain; and David made haste to get away for fear of Saul; for Saul and his men compassed David and his men round about to take them. But there came a messenger unto Saul, saying, Haste thee, and come; for the Philistines have invaded the land. Wherefore Saul returned from pursuing after David, and went against the Philistines; therefore they called that place Sela-ham-mahlekoth.

And David went up from thence, and dwelt in strongholds at En-gedi.

And it came to pass, when Saul was returning from following the Philistines, that it was told him, saying, Behold, David is in the wilderness of En-gedi. Then Saul took three thousand chosen men out of all Israel, and went to seek David and his men upon the rocks of the wild goats. And he came to the sheepcotes by the way, where was a cave; and Saul went in to cover his feet; and David and his men remained in the sides of the cave. And the men of David said unto him, Behold the day of which the Lord said unto thee, Behold, I will deliver thine enemy into thine hand that thou mayest do to him as it shall seem good unto thee. Then David arose, and cut off the skirt of Saul's robe privily. And it came to pass afterward that David's heart smote him because he had cut off Saul's skirt. And he said unto his men, The Lord forbid that I should do this thing unto my master, the Lord's anointed, to stretch forth mine hand against him, seeing he is the anointed of the Lord. So David stayed his servants with these words and suffered them not to rise against Saul. But Saul rose up out of his cave and went on his way. David also arose afterward and went out of the cave and cried after Saul, saying, My Lord the king. And when Saul looked behind him, David stooped with his face to the earth, and bowed himself.

And David said to Saul, Wherefore hearest thou men's words, saying, Behold, David seeketh thy hurt? Behold, this day thine eyes have seen how that the Lord had delivered thee today into mine hand in the cave; and some bade me kill thee; but mine eye spared thee; and I said, I will not put forth mine hand against my lord; for he is the Lord's anointed. Moreover my father, see, yea, see the skirt of thy robe in my hand; for in that I cut off the skirt of thy robe, and killed thee not, know thou and see that there is neither evil nor transgression in mine hand, and I have not sinned against thee; yet thou huntest my soul to take it. The Lord judge between me and thee, and the Lord avenge me of thee; but mine hand shall not be upon thee. As saith the proverb of the ancients, Wickedness proceedeth from the wicked; but mine hand shall not be upon thee. After whom is the king of Israel come out? after whom dost thou pursue? after a dead dog, after a flea. The Lord therefore be judge, and judge between me and thee, and see, and plead my cause, and deliver me out of thine hand.

And it came to pass, when David had made an end of speaking these words unto Saul, that Saul said, Is this thy voice, my son David? And Saul lifted up his voice, and wept. And he said to David, Thou art more righteous than I; for thou hast rewarded me good, whereas I have rewarded thee evil. And thou hast showed this day how that thou hast dealt well with me; forasmuch as when the Lord had delivered me into thy hand, thou killedst me not. For if a man find his enemy, will he let him go well away? wherefore the Lord reward thee good for that thou hast done unto me this day. And now, behold, I know well that thou shalt surely be king, and that the kingdom of Israel shall be established in thine hand. Swear now therefore unto me by the Lord, that thou wilt not cut off my seed after me, and that thou wilt not destroy my name out of my father's house. And David sware unto Saul. And Saul went home; but David and his men gat them up unto the hold.

10 AND Samuel died; and all the Israelites were gathered together, and lamented him, and buried him in his house at Ramah. And David arose, and went down to the wilderness of Paran. And there was a man in Maon, whose possessions were in Carmel; and the man was very great, and he had three thousand sheep and a thousand goats; and he was shearing his sheep in Carmel. Now the name of the man was Nabal, and the name of his wife Abigail; and she was a woman of good understanding, and of a beautiful countenance; but the man was churlish and evil in his doings; and he was of the hose of Caleb. And David heard in the wilderness that Nabal did shear his sheep. And David sent out ten young men, and David said unto the young men, Get you up to Carmel, and go to Nabal, and greet him in my name; and thus shall ye say to him that liveth in prosperity, Peace be both to thee, and peace be to thine house, and peace be unto all that thou hast. And now I have heard that thou hast shearers; now thy shepherds which were with us, we hurt them not, neither was there aught missing unto them, all the while they were in Carmel. Ask thy young men, and they will show thee. Wherefore let the young men find favor in thine eyes; for we come in a good day; give, I pray thee, whatsoever cometh to thine hand unto thy servants, and to thy son David.

And when David's young men came, they spake to Nabal according to all those words in the name of David, and ceased. And Nabal answered David's servants, and said, Who is David? and who is the son of Jesse? there be many servants nowadays that break away every man from his master. Shall I then take my bread and my water, and my flesh that I have killed for my shearers, and give it unto men whom I know not whence they be? So David's young men turned their way, and went again, and came and told him all those sayings. And David said unto his men, Gird ye on every man his sword. And they girded on every man his sword; and David also girded on his sword; and there went up after David about four hundred men; and two hundred abode by the stuff.

But one of the young men told Abigail, Nabal's wife, saying, Behold, David sent messengers out of the wilderness to salute our master and he railed on them. But the men were very good unto us and we were not hurt neither missed we anything as long as we were conversant with them when we were in the fields. They were a wall unto us both by night and day, all the while we were with them keeping the sheep. Now therefore know and consider what thou wilt do; for evil is determined against our master, and against all his household; for he is such a son of Belial, that a man cannot speak to him.

Then Abigail made haste, and took two hundred loaves and two bottles of wine, and five sheep ready dressed, and five measures of parched corn, and a hundred clusters of raisins, and two hundred cakes of figs, and laid them on asses. And she said unto her servants, Go on before me; behold, I come after you. But she told not her husband Nabal. And it was so, as she rode on the ass, that she came down by the covert of the hill, and, behold, David and his men came down against her; and she met them. Now David had said, Surely in vain have I kept all that this fellow hath in the wilderness, so that nothing was missed of all that pertained unto him; and he hath requited me evil for good. So and more also do God unto the enemies of David, if I leave of all that pertain to him by the morning light any that pisseth against the wall.

And when Abigail saw David, she hasted, and lighted off the ass, and fell before David on her face, and bowed herself to the ground. And fell at his feet, and said, Upon me, my lord, upon me let this iniquity be; and let thine handmaid, I pray thee, speak in thine audience, and hear the words of thine handmaid. Let not my lord, I pray thee, regard this man of Belial, even Nabal; for as his name is, so is he; Nabal is his name, and folly is with him; but I thine handmaid saw not the young men of my lord, whom thou didst send.

Now therefore, my lord, as the Lord liveth, and as thy soul liveth, seeing the Lord hath withholden thee from coming to shed blood and from avenging thyself with thine own hand, now let thine enemies, and they that seek evil to my lord, be as Nabal. And now this blessing which thine handmaid hath brought unto my lord, let it even be given unto the young men that follow my lord. I pray thee, forgive the trespass of thine handmaid; for the Lord will certainly make my lord a sure house; because my lord fighteth the battles of the Lord, and evil hath not been found in thee all thy days. Yet a man is risen to pursue thee, and to seek thy soul; but the soul of my lord shall be bound in the bundle of life with the Lord thy God; and the souls of thine enemies, them shall he sling out, as out of the middle of a sling. And it shall come to pass, when the Lord shall have done to my lord according to all the good that he hath spoken concerning thee, and shall have appointed thee ruler over Israel; that this shall be no grief unto thee, nor offense of heart unto my lord, either that thou hast shed blood causeless, or that my lord hath avenged himself; but when the Lord shall have dealt well with my lord, then remember thine handmaid.

And David said to Abigail, Blessed be the Lord God of Israel, which sent thee this day to meet me; and blessed be thy advice, and blessed be thou, which hast kept me this day from coming to shed blood, and from avenging myself with mine own hand. For in very deed, as the Lord God of Israel liveth, which hath kept me back from hurting thee, except thou hadst hasted and come to meet me, surely there had not been left unto Nabal by the morning light any that pisseth against the wall. So David received of her hand that which she had brought him, and said unto her, Go up in peace to thine house; see, I have hearkened to thy voice, and have accepted thy person.

And Abigail came to Nabal; and, behold, he held a feast in his house, like the feast of a king; and Nabal's heart was merry within him, for he was very drunken; wherefore she told him nothing, less or more, until the morning light. But it came to pass in the morning when the wine was gone out of Nabal, and his wife had told him these things, that his heart died within him, and he became as a stone; and it came to pass about ten days after, that the Lord smote Nabal, that he died.

And when David heard that Nabal was dead, he said, Blessed be the Lord that hath pleaded the cause of my reproach from the hand of Nabal, and hath kept his servant from evil; for the Lord hath returned the wickedness of Nabal upon his own head. And David sent and communed with Abigail, to take her to him to wife. And when the servants of David were come to Abigail to Carmel, they spake unto her, saying, David sent us unto thee, to take thee to him to wife. And she arose, and bowed herself on her face to the earth, and said, Behold, let thine handmaid be a servant to wash the feet of the servants of my lord. And Abigail hasted, and arose, and rode upon an ass, with five damsels of hers that went after her; and she went after the messengers of David, and became his wife. David also took Ahinoam of Jezreel; and they were also both of them his wives. But Saul had given Michal his daughter, David's wife, to Phalti, the son of Laish, which was of Gallim.

And the Ziphites came unto Saul to Gibeah, saying, Doth not David hide himself in the hill of Hachilah, which is before Jeshimon? Then Saul arose, and went down to the wilderness of Ziph, having three thousand chosen men of Israel with him to seek David in the wilderness of Ziph. And Saul pitched in the hill of Hachilah, which is before Jeshimon, by the way. But David abode in the wilderness and he saw that Saul came after him into the wilderness. David therefore sent out spies and understood that Saul was come in very deed. And David arose and came to the place where Saul had pitched; and David beheld the place where Saul lay, and Abner the son of Ner, the captain of his host; and Saul lay in the trench, and the people pitched round about him.

Then answered David and said to Ahimelech the Hittite, and to Abishai the son of Zeruiah, brother to Joab, saying, Who will go down with me to Saul to the camp? And Abishai said, I will go down with thee. So David and Abishai came to the people by night; and, behold, Saul lay sleeping within the trench and his spear stuck in the ground at his bolster; but Abner and the people lay round about him. Then said Abishai to David, God hath delivered thine enemy into thine hand this day; now therefore let me smite him, I pray thee, with the spear even to the earth at once, and I will not smite him the second time. And David said to Abishai, Destroy him not; for who can stretch forth his hand against the Lord's anointed and be guiltless? David said furthermore, As the Lord liveth, the Lord shall smite him; or his day shall come to die; or he shall descend into battle, and perish. The Lord forbid that I should stretch forth mine hand against the Lord's anointed; but, I pray thee, take thou now the spear that is at his bolster, and the cruse of water, and let us go. So David took the spear and the cruse of water from Saul's bolster; and they gat them away, and no man saw it, nor knew it, neither awaked; for they were all asleep; because a deep sleep from the Lord was fallen upon them.

Then David went over to the other side, and stood on the top of a hill afar off; a great space being between them; and David cried to the people, and to Abner the son of Ner, saying, Answerest thou not, Abner? Then Abner answered and said, Who art thou that criest to the king? And David said to Abner, Art not thou a valiant man? and who is like to thee in Israel? wherefore then hast thou not kept thy lord the king? for there came one of the people in to destroy the king thy lord. This thing is not good that thou hast done. As the Lord liveth, ye are worthy to die, because ye have not kept your master, the Lord's anointed. And now see where the king's spear is, and the cruse of water that was at his bolster.

And Saul knew David's voice, and said, Is this thy voice, my son David? And David said, It is my voice, my lord, O king. And he said, Wherefore doth my lord thus pursue after his servant? for what have I done? or what evil is in mine hand? Now therefore, I pray thee, let my lord the king hear the words of his servant. If the Lord have stirred thee up against me, let him accept an offering; but if they be the children of men, cursed be they before the Lord; for they have driven me out this day from abiding in the inheritance of the Lord, saying, Go, serve other gods. Now therefore, let not my blood fall to the earth before the face of the Lord; for the king of Israel is come out to seek a flea, as when one doth hunt a partridge in the mountains.

Then said Saul, I have sinned; return, my son David; for I will no more do thee harm, because my soul was precious in thine eyes this day; behold, I have played the fool, and have erred exceedingly. And David answered and said, Behold the king's spear! and let one of the young men come over and fetch it. The

Lord render to every man his righteousness and his faithfulness; for the Lord delivered thee into my hand today, but I would not stretch forth mine hand against the Lord's anointed. And, behold, as thy life was much set by this day in mine eyes, so let my life be much set by in the eyes of the Lord, and let him deliver me out of all tribulation. Then Saul said to David, Blessed be thou, my son David; thou shalt both do great things and also shalt still prevail. So David went on his way, and Saul returned to his place.

And David said in his heart, I shall now perish one day by the hand of Saul; there is nothing better for me than that I should speedily escape into the land of the Philistines; and Saul shall despair of me, to seek me anymore in any coast of Israel; so shall I escape out of his hand. And David arose, and he passed over with the six hundred men that were with him unto Achish, the son of Maoch, king of Gath. And David dwelt with Achish at Gath, he and his men, every man with his household, even David with his two wives, Ahinoam the Jezreelitess, and Abigail the Carmelitess, Nabal's wife. And it was told Saul that David was fled to Gath; and he sought no more again for him. And David said unto Achish, If I have now found grace in thine eyes, let them give me a place in some town in the country, that I may dwell there; for why should thy servant dwell in the royal city with thee? Then Achish gave him Ziklag that day; wherefore Ziklag pertaineth unto the kings of Judah unto this day. And the time that David dwelt in the country of the Philistines was a full year and four months.

11 AND David and his men went up and invaded the Geshurites, and the Gezrites, and the Amalekites; for those nations were of old the inhabitants of the land, as thou goest to Shur, even unto the land of Egypt. And David smote the land, and left neither man nor woman alive, and took away the sheep, and the oxen, and the asses, and the camels, and the apparel, and returned, and came to Achish. And Achish said, Whither have ye made a road today? And David said, Against the south of Judah, and against the south of the Jerahmeelites, and against the south of the Kenites. And David saved neither man nor woman alive to bring tidings to Gath, saying, Lest they should tell on us, saying, So did David, and so will be his manner all the while he dwelleth in the country of the Philistines. And Achish believed David, saying, He hath made his people Israel utterly to abhor him; therefore he shall be my servant forever.

And it came to pass in those days, that the Philistines gathered their armies together for warfare, to fight with Israel. And Achish said unto David, Know thou assuredly, that thou shalt go out with me to battle, thou and thy men. And David said to Achish, Surely thou shalt know what thy servant can do. And Achish said to David, Therefore will I make thee keeper of mine head forever.

Now Samuel was dead, and all Israel had lamented him and buried him in Ramah, even in his own city. And Saul had put away those that had familiar spirits, and the wizards, out of the land. And the Philistines gathered themselves together and came and pitched in Shunem; and Saul gathered all Israel together, and they pitched in Gilboa. And when Saul saw the host of the Philistines, he was afraid, and his heart greatly trembled. And when Saul inquired of the Lord, the Lord answered him not, neither by dreams, nor by Urim, nor by prophets. Then said Saul unto his servants, Seek me a woman that hath a familiar spirit that I may go to her and inquire of her. And his servants said to him, Behold, there is a woman that hath a familiar spirit at En-dor. And Saul disguised himself and put on other raiment, and he went and two men with him, and they came to the woman by night; and he said, I pray thee, divine unto me by the familiar spirit, and bring me him up, whom I shall name unto thee. And the woman said unto him, Behold, thou knowest what Saul hath done, how he hath cut off those that have familiar spirits, and the wizards, out of the land; wherefore then layest thou a snare for my life, to cause me to die also, who hath not a familiar spirit? And Saul sware to her by the Lord, saying, As the Lord liveth, there shall no punishment happen to thee for this thing. Then said the woman, The word of whom shall I bring up unto thee? And he said, Bring me up the word of Samuel. And when the woman saw the words of Samuel, she cried with a loud voice; and the woman spake to Saul, saying, Why hast thou deceived me? for thou art Saul. And the king said unto her, Be not afraid; for what sawest thou? And the woman said unto Saul, I saw the words of Samuel ascending out of the earth. And she said, I saw Samuel also. And he said unto her, What form is he of? And she said, I saw an old man coming up, covered with a mantle. And Saul perceived that it was Samuel, and he stooped his face to the ground and bowed himself.

And these are the words of Samuel unto Saul, Why hast thou disquieted me, to bring me up? And Saul answered, I am sore distressed; for the Philistines make war against me and God is departed from me, and answereth me no more, neither by prophets, nor by dreams; therefore I have called thee, that thou mayest make known unto me what I shall do. Then said Samuel, Wherefore then dost thou ask of me, seeing the Lord is departed from thee, and is become thine enemy? And the Lord hath done to him, as he spake by me; for the Lord hath rent the kingdom out of thine hand, and given it to thy neighbor, even to David; because thou obeyedst not the voice of the Lord, nor executedst his fierce wrath upon Amalek, therefore hath the Lord done this thing unto thee this day. Moreover the Lord will also deliver Israel with thee into the hand of the Philistines; and tomorrow shalt thou and thy sons be with me; the Lord also shall deliver the host of Israel into the hand of the Philistines.

Then Saul fell straightway all along on the earth, and was sore afraid because of the words of Samuel; and there was no strength in him; for he had eaten no bread all the day, nor all the night. And the woman came unto Saul and saw that he was sore troubled, and said unto him, Behold, thine handmaid hath obeyed thy voice, and I have put my life in my hand, and have hearkened unto thy words which thou spakest unto me. Now therefore, I pray thee, hearken thou also unto the voice of thine handmaid and let me set a morsel of bread before thee; and eat, that thou mayest have strength when thou goest on thy way. But he refused and said, I will not eat. But his servants, together with the woman, compelled him; and he hearkened unto their voice. So he rose from the earth and sat upon the bed. And the woman had a fat calf in the house; and she hasted, and killed it, and took flour, and kneaded it, and did bake unleavened bread thereof; and she brought it before Saul, and before his servants; and they did eat. Then they rose up, and went away that night.

12 NOW the Philistines gathered together all their armies to Aphek; and the Israelites pitched by a fountain which is in Jezreel. And the lords of the Philistines passed on by hundreds, and by thousands; but David and his men passed on in the rearward with Achish. Then said the princes of the Philistines, What do these Hebrews here? And Achish said unto the princes of the Philistines, Is not this David the servant of Saul the king of Israel, which hath been with me these days, or these years, and I have found no fault in him since he fell unto me unto this day? And the princes of the Philistines were wroth with him; and the princes of the Philistines said unto him, Make this fellow return that he may go again to his place which thou hast appointed him; and let him not go down with us to battle, lest in the battle he be an adversary to us; for wherewith should he reconcile himself unto his master? should it not be with the heads of these men? Is not this David, of whom they sang one to another in dances, saying, Saul slew his thousands, and David his ten thousands?

Then Achish called David, and said unto him, Surely, as the Lord liveth, thou hast been upright and thy going out and thy coming in with me in the host is good in my sight; for I have not found evil in thee since the day of thy coming unto me unto this day; nevertheless the lords favor thee not. Wherefore now return, and go in peace that thou displease not the lords of the Philistines. And David said unto Achish, But what have I done? and what hast thou found in thy servant so long as I have been with thee unto this day, that I may not go fight against the enemies of my lord the king? And Achish answered and said to David, I know that thou art good in my sight, as an angel of God; notwithstanding, the princes of the Philistines have said, He shall not go up with us to the battle. Wherefore now rise up early in the morning with thy master's servants that are come with thee; and as soon as ye be up early in the morning, and have light, depart. So David and his men rose up early to depart in the morning, to return into the land of the Philistines. And the Philistines went up to Jezreel.

And it came to pass, when David and his men were come to Ziklag on the third day, that the Amalekites had invaded the south, and Ziklag, and smitten Ziklag, and burned it with fire; and had taken the women captives, that were therein; they slew not any, either great or small, but carried them away, and went on their way. So David and his men came to the city, and behold, it was burned with fire; and their wives and their sons and their daughters were taken captives. Then David and the people that were with him lifted up their voices and wept until they had not more power to weep. And David's two wives were taken captives, Ahinoam the Jezreelitess, and Abigail the wife of Nabal the Carmelite. And David was greatly distressed; for the people spake of stoning him because the soul of all the people was grieved, every man for his sons and for his daughters; but David encouraged himself in the Lord his God.

And David said to Abiathar the priest, Ahimelech's son, I pray thee, bring me hither the ephod. And Abiathar brought thither the ephod to David. And David inquired at the Lord, saying, Shall I pursue after this troop? shall I overtake them? And he answered him, Pursue; for thou shalt surely overtake them, and without fail recover all. So David went, he and the six hundred men that were with him, and came to the brook Besor, where those that were left behind stayed. But David pursued, he and four hundred men; for two hundred abode behind, which were so faint that they could not go over the brook Besor.

And they found an Egyptian in the field, and brought him to David, and gave him bread, and he did eat; and they made him drink water; and they gave him a piece of a cake of figs and two clusters of raisins; and when he had eaten, his spirit came again to him for he had eaten no bread, nor drank any water, three days and three nights. And David said unto him, To whom belongest thou? and whence art thou? And he said, I am a young man of Egypt, servant to an Amalekite; and my master left me, because three days agone I fell sick. We made an invasion upon the south of the Cherethites, and upon the coast which belongeth to Judah, and upon the south of Caleb; and we burned Ziklag with fire. And David said to him, Canst thou bring me down to this company? And he said, Swear unto me by God, that thou wilt neither kill me nor deliver me into the hands of my master, and I will bring thee down to this company. And when he had brought him down, behold, they were spread abroad upon all the earth, eating and drinking, and dancing, because of all the great spoil that they had taken out of the land of the Philistines, and out of the land of Judah.

And David smote them from the twilight even unto the evening of the next day; and there escaped not a man of them, save four hundred young men, which rode upon camels and fled. And David recovered all that the Amalekites had carried away; and David rescued his two wives. And there was nothing lacking to them, neither small nor great, neither sons nor daughters, neither spoil, nor anything that they had taken to them; David recovered all. And David took all the flocks and the herds, which they drave before those other cattle, and said, This is David's spoil.

And David came to the two hundred men, which were so faint that they could not follow David, whom they had made also to abide at the brook Besor; and they went forth to meet David, and to meet the people that were with him; and when David came near to the people, he saluted them. Then answered all the wicked men and men of Belial, of those that went with David, and said, Because they went not with us, we will not give them aught of the spoil that we have recovered, save to every man his wife and his children, that they may lead them away, and depart. Then said David, Ye shall not do so, my brethren, with that which the Lord hath given us, who hath preserved us, and delivered the company that came against us into our hand. For who will hearken unto you in this matter? but as his part is that goeth down to the battle, so shall his part be that tarrieth by the stuff; they shall part alike. And it was so from that day forward, that he made it a statute and an ordinance for Israel unto this day.

And when David came to Ziklag, he sent of the spoil unto the elders of Judah, even to his friends, saying, Behold a present for you of the spoil of the enemies of the Lord; to them which were in Beth-el, and to them which were in south Ramoth, and to them which were in Jattir. And to them which were in Aroer, and to them which were in Siphmoth, and to them which were in Eshtemoa, and to them which were in Rachal, and to them which were in the cities of the Jerahmeelites, and to them which were in the cities of the Kenites, and to them which were in Hormah, and to them which were in Chor-ashan, and to them which were in Athach, and to them which were in Hebron, and to all the places where David himself and his men were wont to haunt.

Now the Philistines fought against Israel; and the men of Israel fled from before the Philistines, and fell down slain in mount Gilboa. And the Philistines followed hard upon Saul and upon his sons; and the Philistines slew Jonathan, and Abinadab, and Melchi-shua, Saul's sons. And the battle went sore against Saul, and the archers hit him; and he was sore wounded of the archers. Then said Saul unto his armor-bearer, Draw thy sword, and thrust me through therewith; lest these uncircumcised come and thrust me through and abuse me. But his armor-bearer would not; for he was sore afraid. Therefore Saul took a sword, and fell upon it. And when his armor-bearer saw that Saul was dead, he fell likewise upon his sword and died with him. So Saul died, and his three sons, and his armor-bearer, and all his men, that same day together.

And when the men of Israel that were on the other side of the valley, and they that were on the other side Jordan, saw that the men of Israel fled, and that Saul and his sons were dead, they forsook the cities and fled; and the Philistines came and dwelt in them. And it came to pass on the morrow, when the Philistines came to strip the slain, that they found Saul and his three sons fallen in mount Gilboa. And they cut off his head, and stripped off his armor, and sent into the land of the Philistines round about to publish it in the house of their idols, and among the people. And they put his armor in the house of Ashtaroth; and they fastened his body to the wall of Beth-shan. And when the inhabitants of Jabesh-gilead heard of that which the Philistines had done to Saul, all the valiant men arose, and went all night, and took the body of Saul and the bodies of his sons from the wall of Beth-shan, and came to Jabesh, and burnt them there. And they took their bones, and buried them under a tree at Jabesh, and fasted seven days.

THE SECOND BOOK OF SAMUEL

NOW it came to pass after the death of Saul when David was returned from the slaughter of the Amalekites and David had abode two days in Ziklag. It came even to pass on the third day that behold a man came out of the camp from Saul with his clothes rent and earth upon his head and so it was when he came to David that he fell to the earth and did obeisance. And David said unto him, From whence comest thou? And he said unto him, Out of the camp of Israel am I escaped. And David said unto him, How went the matter? I pray thee, tell me. And he answered, That the people are fled from the battle, and many of the people also are fallen and dead and Saul and Jonathan his son are dead also. And David said unto the young man that told him, How knowest thou that Saul and Jonathan his son be dead? And the young man that told him said, As I happened by chance upon mount Gilboa, behold Saul leaned upon his spear; and lo the chariots and horsemen followed hard after him. And when he looked behind him he saw me and called unto me. And I answered, Here am I. And he said unto me, Who art thou? And I answered him, I am an Amalekite. He said unto me again, Stand I pray thee upon me and slay me, for anguish is come upon me because my life is yet whole in me. So I stood upon him and slew him because I was sure that he could not live after that he was fallen, and I took the crown that was upon his head and the bracelet that was on his arm and have brought them hither unto my lord. Then David took hold on his clothes and rent them, and likewise all the men that were with him? And they mourned and wept and fasted until even for Saul and for Jonathan his son and for the people of the Lord and for the house of Israel, because they were fallen by the sword. And David said unto the young man that told him, Whence art thou? And he answered, I am the son of a stranger, an Amalekite. And David said unto him, How wast thou not afraid to stretch forth thine hand to destroy the Lord's anointed? And David called one of the young men and said, Go near and fall upon him. And he smote him that he died. And David said unto him, Thy blood be upon thy head for thy mouth hath testified against thee, saying, I have slain the Lord's anointed.

And David lamented with this lamentation over Saul and over Jonathan his son (also he bade them teach the children of Judah the use of the bow, behold it is written in the book of Jasher). The beauty of Israel is slain upon thy high places, how are the mighty fallen! Tell it not in Gath, publish it not in the streets of Askelon lest the daughters of the Philistines rejoice, lest the daughters of the uncircumcised triumph. Ye mountains of Gilboa let there be no dew neither let there be rain upon you nor fields of offerings, for there the shield of the mighty is vilely cast away, the shield of Saul as though he had not been anointed with oil. From the blood of the slain, from the fat of the mighty, the bow of Jonathan turned not back and the sword of Saul returned not empty. Saul and Jonathan were lovely and pleasant in their lives and in their death they were not divided. They were swifter than eagles, they were stronger than lions. Ye daughters of Israel, weep over Saul who clothed you in scarlet with other delights, who put on ornaments of gold upon your apparel. How are the mighty fallen in the midst of the battle! O Jonathan thou wast slain in thine high places. I am distressed for thee my brother Jonathan, very pleasant hast thou been unto me, thy love to me was wonderful, passing the love of women. How are the mighty fallen and the weapons of war perished!

And it came to pass after this that David inquired of the Lord saying, Shall I go up into any of the cities of Judah? And the Lord said unto him, Go up. And David said, Whither shall I go up? And he said, Unto Hebron. So David went up thither and his two wives also, Ahinoam the Jezreelitess, and Abigail Nabal's wife the Carmelite. And his men that were with him did David bring up, every man with his household and they dwelt in the cities of Hebron. And the men of Judah came and there they anointed David king over the house of Judah. And they told David saying, That the men of Jabesh-gilead were they that buried Saul. And David sent messengers unto the men of Jabesh-gilead, and said unto them, Blessed be ye of the Lord, that ye have showed this kindness unto your lord, even unto Saul and have buried him. And now the Lord show kindness and truth unto you, and I also will requite you this kindness because ye have done this thing. Therefore now let your hands be strengthened and be ye valiant for your master Saul is dead and also the house of Judah have anointed me king over them.

But Abner the son of Ner, captain of Saul's host, took Ishbosheth the son of Saul and brought him over to Mahanaim and made him king over Gilead and over the Ashurites and over Jezreel and over Ephraim and over Benjamin and over all Israel. Ishbosheth, Saul's son, was forty years old when he began to reign over Israel and reigned two years. But the house of Judah followed David. And the time that David was king in Hebron over the house of Judah was seven years and six months.

2 AND Abner the son of Ner and the servants of Ishbosheth the son of Saul, went out from Mahanaim to Gibeon. And Joab the son of Zeruiah and the servants of David, went out and met together by the pool of Gibeon, and they sat down, the one on the one side of the pool, and the other on the other side of the pool. And Abner said to Joab, Let the young men now arise, and play before us. And Joab said, Let them arise. Then there arose and went over by number twelve of Benjamin, which pertained to Ishbosheth the son of Saul, and twelve of the servants of David. And they caught every one his fellow by the head and thrust his sword in his fellow's side so they fell down together, wherefore that place was called Helkath-hazzurim which is in Gibeon. And there was a very sore battle that day, and Abner was beaten and the men of Israel before the servants of David.

And there were three sons of Zeruiah there, Joab and Abishai and Asahel. And Asahel was as light of foot as a wild roe. And Asahel pursued after Abner, and in going he turned not to the right hand nor to the left from following Abner. Then Abner looked behind him and said, Art thou Asahel? And he answered, I am. And Abner said to him, Turn thee aside to thy right hand or to thy left, and lay thee hold on one of the young men and take thee his armor. But Asahel would not turn aside from following of him. And Abner said again to Asahel, Turn thee aside from following me, wherefore should I smite thee to the ground? How then should I hold up my face to Joab thy brother? Howbeit he refused to turn aside. Wherefore Abner with the hinder end of the spear smote him under the fifth rib that the spear came out behind him, and he fell down there and died in the same place. And it came to pass, that as many as came to the place where Asahel fell down and died stood still. Joab also and Abishai pursued after Abner. And the sun went down when they were come to the hill of Ammah that lieth before Giah by the way of the wilderness of Gibeon. And the children of Benjamin gathered themselves together after Abner and became one troop and stood on the top of a hill. Then Abner called to Joab and said, Shall the sword devour forever? Knowest thou not that it will be a bitterness in the latter end? How long shall it be then ere thou bid the people return from following their brethren? And Joab said, As God liveth, unless thou hadst spoken surely then in the morning the people had gone up every one from following his brother. So

Joab blew a trumpet, and all the people stood still, and pursued after Israel no more, neither fought they anymore.

And Abner and his men walked all that night through the plain and passed over Jordan and went through all Bithron and they came to Mahanaim. And Joab returned from following Abner and when he had gathered all the people together, there lacked of David's servants nineteen men and Asahel. But the servants of David had smitten of Benjamin and of Abner's men, so that three hundred and threescore men died. And they took up Asahel and buried him in the sepulcher of his father which was in Bethlehem. And Joab and his men went all night and they came to Hebron at break of day.

3 NOW there was long war between the house of Saul and the house of David, but David waxed stronger and stronger and the house of Saul waxed weaker and weaker. And unto David were sons born in Hebron, and his firstborn was Amnon of Ahinoam the Jezreelitess, and his second, Chileab of Abigail the wife of Nabal the Carmelite, and the third, Absalom the son of Maacah the daughter of Talmai king of Geshur, and the fourth, Adonijah the son of Haggith, and the fifth, Shephatiah the son of Abital, and the sixth, Ithream by Eglah David's wife. These were born to David in Hebron.

And it came to pass while there was war between the house of Saul and the house of David, that Abner made himself strong for the house of Saul. And Saul had a concubine whose name was Rizpah, the daughter of Aiah. And Ishbosheth said to Abner, Wherefore hast thou gone in unto my father's concubine? Then was Abner very wroth for the words of Ishbosheth and said, Am I a dog's head, which against Judah do show kindness this day unto the house of Saul thy father, to his brethren and to his friends and have not delivered thee into the hand of David, that thou chargest me today with a fault concerning this woman? So do God to Abner and more also, except as the Lord hath sworn to David, even so I do to him, to translate the kingdom from the house of Saul and to set up the throne of David over Israel and over Judah, from Dan even to Beer-sheba. And he could not answer Abner a word again because he feared him.

And Abner sent messengers to David on his behalf, saying, Whose is the land? saying also, Make thy league with me and behold my hand shall be with thee to bring about all Israel unto thee. And he said, Well, I will make a league with thee, but one thing I require of thee, that is, Thou shalt not see my face except thou first bring Michal, Saul's daughter, when thou comest to see my face. And David sent messengers to Ishbosheth, Saul's son, saying, Deliver me my wife Michal which I espoused to me for a hundred foreskins of the Philistines. And Ishbosheth sent and took her from her husband even from Phaltiel the son of Laish. And her husband went with her along weeping behind her to Bahurim. Then said Abner unto him, Go, return. And he returned.

And Abner had communication with the elders of Israel, saying, Ye sought for David in times past to be king over you, now then do it. For the Lord hath spoken of David, saying, By the hand of my servant David I will save my people Israel out of the hand of the Philistines, and out of the hand of all their enemies. And Abner also spake in the ears of Benjamin, and Abner went also to speak in the ears of David in Hebron all that seemed good to Israel and that seemed good to the whole house of Benjamin. So Abner came to David to Hebron and twenty men with him. And David made Abner and his men that were with him a feast. And Abner said unto David, I will arise and go and will gather all Israel unto my lord the king that they may make a league with thee and that thou mayest reign over all that thine heart desireth. And David sent Abner away, and he went in peace

4 AND behold the servants of David and Joab came from pursuing a troop and brought in a great spoil with them but Abner was not with David in Hebron, for he had sent him away and he was gone in peace. When Joab and all the host that was with him were come they told Joab, saying, Abner the son of Ner came to the king and he hath sent him away and he is gone in peace. Then Joab came to the king and said, What hast thou done? Behold, Abner came unto thee, why is it that thou hast sent him away and he is quite gone? Thou knowest Abner the son of Ner that he came to deceive thee and to know thy going out and thy coming in and to know all that thou doest. And when Joab was come out from David he sent messengers after Abner which brought him again from the well of Sirah, but David knew it not. And when Abner was returned to Hebron, Joab took him aside in the gate to speak with him quietly and smote him there under the fifth rib that he died for the blood of Asahel his brother.

And afterward when David heard it he said, I and my kingdom are guiltless before the Lord for ever from the blood of Abner the son of Ner. Let it rest on the head of Joab and on all his father's house, and let there not fail from the house of Joab one that hath an issue or that is a leper or that leaneth on a staff or that falleth on the sword or that lacketh bread. So Joab and Abishai his brother slew Abner because he had slain their brother Asahel at Gibeon in the battle.

And David said to Joab and to all the people that were with him, Rend your clothes and gird you with sackcloth and mourn before Abner. And king David himself followed the bier. And they buried Abner in Hebron and the king lifted up his voice, and wept at the grave of Abner and all the people wept. And the king lamented over Abner and said, Died Abner as a fool dieth? Thy hands were not bound nor thy feet put into fetters, as a man falleth before wicked men so fellest thou.

And all the people wept again over him. And when all the people came to cause David to eat meat while it was yet day, David sware saying, So do God to me and more also if I taste bread or aught else till the sun be down. And all the people took notice of it and it pleased them, as whatsoever the king did pleased all the people. For all the people and all Israel understood that day that it was not of the king to slay Abner the son of Ner. And the king said unto his servants, Know ye not that there is a prince and a great man fallen this day in Israel? And I am this day weak though anointed king, and these men the sons of Zeruiah be too hard for me, the Lord shall reward the doer of evil according to his wickedness.

5 AND when Saul's son heard that Abner was dead in Hebron, his hands were feeble and all the Israelites were troubled. And Saul's son had two men that were captains of bands, the name of the one was Baanah and the name of the other Rechab, the sons of Rimmon a Beerothite of the children of Benjamin (for Beeroth also was reckoned to Benjamin; and the Beerothites fled to Gittaim, and were sojourners there until this day).

And Jonathan, Saul's son, had a son that was lame of his feet. He was five years old when the tidings came of Saul and Jonathan out of Jezreel, and his nurse took him up and fled and it came to pass as she made haste to flee that he fell and became lame. And his name was Mephibosheth.

And the sons of Rimmon the Beerothite, Rechab and Baanah, went and came about the heat of the day to the house of Ishbosheth who lay on a bed at noon. And they came thither into the midst of the house as though they would have fetched wheat and they smote him under the fifth rib and Rechab and Baanah his brother escaped. For when they came into the house he lay on his bed in his bedchamber and they smote him and slew him and beheaded him and took his head and gat them away through the plain all night. And they brought the head of Ishbosheth unto David to Hebron and said to the king, Behold the head of

Ishbosheth the son of Saul thine enemy which sought thy life, and the Lord hath avenged my lord the king this day of Saul and of his seed.

And David answered Rechab and Baanah his brother the sons of Rimmon the Beerothite and said unto them, As the Lord liveth who hath redeemed my soul out of all adversity, when one told me saying, Behold, Saul is dead, thinking to have brought good tidings, I took hold of him and slew him in Ziklag, who thought that I would have given him a reward for his tidings. How much more when wicked men have slain a righteous person in his own house upon his bed? Shall I not therefore now require his blood of your hand and take you away from the Earth? And David commanded his young men and they slew them and cut off their hands and their feet and hanged them up over the pool in Hebron. But they took the head of Ishbosheth, and buried it in the sepulcher of Abner in Hebron.

Then came all the tribes of Israel to David unto Hebron and spake saying, Behold, we are thy bone and thy flesh. Also in time past when Saul was king over us thou wast he that leddest out and broughtest in Israel. And the Lord said to thee, Thou shalt feed my people Israel and thou shalt be a captain over Israel. So all the elders of Israel came to the king to Hebron and king David made a league with them in Hebron before the Lord. And they anointed David king over Israel. David was thirty years old when he began to reign and he reigned forty years. InHebron he reigned over Judah seven years and six months and in Jerusalem he reigned thirty and three years over all Israel and Judah.

And the king and his men went to Jerusalem unto the Jebusites, the inhabitants of the land, which spake unto David saying, Except thou take away the blind and the lame, thou shalt not come in hither. thinking David cannot come in hither. Nevertheless David took the stronghold of Zion, the same is the city of David. And David said on that day, Whosoever getteth up to the gutter and smiteth the Jebusites and the lame and the blind that are hated of David's soul, he shall be chief and captain. Wherefore they said, The blind and the lame shall not come into the house. So David dwelt in the fort, and called it the city of David. And David built round about from Millo and inward. And David went on and grew great and the Lord God of hosts was with him. And Hiram king of Tyre sent messengers to David, and cedar trees and carpenters and masons and they built David a house. And David perceived that the Lord had established him king over Israel, and that he had exalted his kingdom for his people Israel's sake.

And David took him more concubines and wives out of Jerusalem after he was come from Hebron. And there were yet sons and daughters born to David. And these be the names of those that were born unto him in Jerusalem; Shammuah, and Shobab, and Nathan, and Solomon, Ibhar also, and Elishua, and Nepheg, and Japhia, and Elishama, and Eliada, and Eliphalet.

But when the Philistines heard that they had anointed David king over Israel, all the Philistines came up to seek David, and David heard of it and went down to the hold. The Philistines also came and spread themselves in the valley of Rephaim. And David inquired of the Lord, saying, Shall I go up to the Philistines? Wilt thou deliver them into mine hand? And the Lord said unto David, Go up; for I will doubtless deliver the Philistines into thine hand. And David came to Baal-perazim and David smote them there and said, The Lord hath broken forth upon mine enemies before me as the breach of waters. Therefore he called the name of that place Baal-perazim. And there they left their images and David and his men burned them. And the Philistines came up yet again and spread themselves in the valley of Rephaim. And when David inquired of the Lord, he said, Thou shalt not go up but fetch a compass behind them and come upon them over against the mulberry trees. And let it be when thou hearest the sound of a going in the tops of the mulberry trees that then thou shalt bestir thyself, for then shall the Lord go out before thee to smite the host of the Philistines. And David did so as the Lord had commanded him and smote the Philistines from Geba until thou come to Gazer.

6 AGAIN David gathered together all the chosen men of Israel, thirty thousand. And David arose and went with all the people that were with him from Baale of Judah to bring up from thence the ark of God whose name is called by the name of the Lord of hosts that dwelleth between the cherubim. And they set the ark of God upon a new cart and brought it out of the house of Abinadab that was in Gibeah. And Uzzah and Ahio, the sons of Abinadab drave the new cart. And they brought it out of the house of Abinadab which was at Gibeah, accompanying the ark of God and Ahio went before the ark. And David and all the house of Israel played before the Lord on all manner of instruments made of fir wood, even on harps and on psalteries and on timbrels and on cornets and on cymbals.

And when they came to Nachon's threshing floor Uzzah put forth his hand to the ark of God, and took hold of it, for the oxen shook it. And the anger of the Lord was kindled against Uzzah and God smote him there for his error, and there he died by the ark of God. And David was displeased because the Lord had made a breach upon Uzzah and he called the name of the place Perez-uzzah to this day. And David was afraid of the Lord that day and said, How shall the ark of the Lord come to me? So David would not remove the ark of the Lord unto him into the city of David but David carried it aside into the house of Obed-edom the Gittite. And the ark of the Lord continued in the house of Obed-edom the Gittite three months and the Lord blessed Obed-edom, and all his household.

And it was told king David saying, The Lord hath blessed the house of Obed-edom and all that pertaineth unto him because of the ark of God. So David went and brought up the ark of God from the house of Obed-edom into the city of David with gladness. And it was so that when they that bare the ark of the Lord had gone six paces he sacrificed oxen and fatlings. And David danced before the Lord with all his might, and David was girded with a linen ephod. So David and all the house of Israel brought up the ark of the Lord with shouting and with the sound of the trumpet.

And as the ark of the Lord came into the city of David, Michal Saul's daughter looked through a window, and saw king David leaping and dancing before the Lord and she despised him in her heart.

And they brought in the ark of the Lord and set it in his place in the midst of the tabernacle that David had pitched for it and David offered burnt offerings and peace offerings before the Lord. And as soon as David had made an end of offering burnt offering and peace offerings he blessed the people in the name of the Lord of hosts. And he dealt among all the people even among the whole multitude of Israel as well to the women as men, to everyone a cake of bread and a good piece of flesh and a flagon of wine. So all the people departed everyone to his house.

Then David returned to bless his household. And Michal the daughter of Saul came out to meet David and said, How glorious was the king of Israel today who uncovered himself today in the eyes of the handmaids of his servants as one of the vain fellows shamelessly uncovereth himself! And David said unto Michal, It was before the Lord, which chose me before thy father and before all his house to appoint me ruler over the people of the Lord, over Israel. Therefore will I play before the Lord and I will yet be more vile than thus, and will be base in mine own sight, and of the maidservants which thou has spoken of, of them shall I be had in honor. Therefore Michal the daughter of Saul had no child unto the day of her death.

And it came to pass when the king sat in his house and the Lord had given him rest round about from all his enemies that the king said unto Nathan the prophet, See, now, I dwell in a house of cedar but the ark of God dwelleth within curtains. And Nathan said to the king, Go, do all that is in thine heart for the Lord is with thee.

And it came to pass that night that the word of the Lord came unto Nathan saying, Go and tell my servant David, Thus said the Lord, Shalt thou build me a house for me to dwell in? Whereas I have not dwelt in any house since the time that I brought up the children of Israel out of Egypt even to this day but have walked in a tent and in a tabernacle. In all the places wherein I have walked with all the children of Israel spake I a word with any of the tribes of Israel whom I commanded to feed my people Israel, saying, Why build ye not me a house of cedar?

Now therefore so shalt thou say unto my servant David, Thus saith the Lord of hosts, I took thee from the sheepcote from following the sheep to be ruler over my people over Israel and I was with thee whithersoever thou wentest and have cut off all thine enemies out of thy sight and have made thee a great name like unto the name of the great men that are in the Earth. Moreover I will appoint a place for my people Israel and will plant them that they may dwell in a place of their own and move no more, neither shall the children of wickedness afflict them anymore as before time and as since the time that I commanded judges to be over my people Israel and have caused thee to rest from all thine enemies. Also the Lord telleth thee that he will make thee a house. And when thy days be fulfilled and thou shalt sleep with thy fathers I will set up thy seed after thee which shall proceed out of thy bowels and I will establish his kingdom. He shall build a house for my name and I will establish the throne of his kingdom forever. I will be his father and he shall be my son. If he commit iniquity I will chasten him with the rod of men and with the stripes of the children of men. But my mercy shall not depart away from him as I took it from Saul, whom I put away before thee. And thine house and thy kingdom shall be established for ever before thee, thy throne shall be established forever. According to all these words and according to all this vision so did Nathan speak unto David.

Then went king David in and sat before the Lord and he said, Who am I, O Lord God? And what is my house that thou hast brought me hitherto? And this was yet a small thing in thy sight, O Lord God, but thou hast spoken also of thy servant's house for a great while to come. And is this the manner of man, O Lord God? And what can David say more unto thee? For thou Lord God knowest thy servant. For thy word's sake and according to thine own heart hast thou done all these great things to make thy servant know them. Wherefore thou art great O Lord God, for there is none like thee neither is there any God besides thee according to all that we have heard with our ears. And what one nation in the Earth is like thy people even like Israel whom God went to redeem for a people to himself and to make him a name and to do for you great things and terrible for thy land before thy people which thou redeemedst to thee from Egypt from the nations and their gods? For thou hast confirmed to thyself thy people Israel to be a people unto thee for ever and thou Lord art become their God. And now O Lord God the word that thou hast spoken concerning thy servant and concerning his house establish it for ever and do as thou hast said. And let thy name be magnified for ever saying, The Lord of hosts is the God over Israel and let the house of thy servant David be established before thee. For thou O Lord of hosts God of Israel hast revealed to thy servant saying, I will build thee a house therefore hath thy servant found in his heart to pray this prayer unto thee. And now O Lord God, thou art that God, and thy words be true and thou hast promised this goodness unto thy servant. Therefore now let it please thee to bless the house of thy servant that it may continue for ever before thee, for thou O Lord God hast spoken it and with thy blessing let the house of thy servant be blessed forever.

7 AND after this it came to pass that David smote the Philistines and subdued them, and David took Metheg-ammah out of the hand of the Philistines. And he smote Moab and measured them with a line, casting them down to the ground even with two lines measured he to put to death and one full line to keep alive. And so the Moabites became David's servants and brought gifts.

David smote also Hadadezer the son of Rehob, king of Zobah, as he went to recover his border at the river Euphrates. And David took from him a thousand chariots and seven hundred horsemen and twenty thousand footmen and David hocked all the chariot horses but reserved of them for a hundred chariots. And when the Syrians of Damascus came to succor Hadadezer king of Zobah, David slew of the Syrians two and twenty thousand men. Then David put garrisons in Syria of Damascus and the Syrians became servants to David and brought gifts. And the Lord preserved David whithersoever he went. And David took the shields of gold that were on the servants of Hadadezer and brought them to Jerusalem. And from Betah and from Berothai, cities of Hadadezer, king David took exceeding much brass.

When Toi king of Hamath heard that David had smitten all the hosts of Hadadezer, then Toi sent Joram his son unto king David to salute him and to bless him because he had fought against Hadadezer and smitten him, for Hadadezer had wars with Toi. And Joram brought with him vessels of silver and vessels of gold and vessels of brass, which also king David did dedicate unto the Lord with the silver and gold that he had dedicated of all nations which he subdued, of Syria and of Moab and of the children of Ammon and of the Philistines and of Amalek and of the spoil of Hadadezer, son of Rehob king of Zobah.

And David gat him a name when he returned from smiting of the Syrians in the valley of salt, being eighteen thousand men. And he put garrisons in Edom, throughout all Edom put he garrisons and all they of Edom became David's servants. And the Lord preserved David whithersoever he went.

And David reigned over all Israel and David executed judgment and justice unto all his people. And Joab the son of Zeruiah was over the host, and Jehoshaphat the son of Ahilud was recorder, and Zadok the son of Ahitub and Ahimelech the son of Abiathar were the priests, and Seraiah was the scribe, and Benaiah the son of Jehoiada was over both the Cherethites and the Pelethites, and David's sons were chief rulers.

8 AND David said, Is there yet any that is left of the house of Saul that I may show him kindness for Jonathan's sake? And there was of the house of Saul a servant whose name was Ziba. And when they had called him unto David the king said unto him, Art thou Ziba? And he said, Thy servant is he. And the king said, Is there not yet any of the house of Saul that I may show the kindness of God unto him? And Ziba said unto the king, Jonathan hath yet a son which is lame on his feet. And the king said unto him, Where is he? And Ziba said unto the king, Behold he is in the house of Machir, the son of Ammiel in Lo-debar. Then king David sent and fetched him out of the house of Machir the son of Ammiel from Lo-debar. Now when Mephibosheth the son of Jonathan the son of Saul was come unto David, he fell on his face and did reverence. And David said, Mephibosheth. And he answered, Behold thy servant! And David said unto him, Fear not for I will surely show thee kindness for Jonathan thy father's sake and will restore thee

all the land of Saul thy father and thou shalt eat bread at my table continually. And he bowed himself and said, What is thy servant that thou shouldest look upon such a dead dog as I am?

Then the king called to Ziba Saul's servant and said unto him, I have given unto thy master's son all that pertained to Saul and to all his house. Thou therefore and thy sons and thy servants shall till the land for him and thou shalt bring in the fruits that thy master's son may have food to eat, but Mephibosheth thy master's son shall eat bread always at my table. Now Ziba had fifteen sons and twenty servants. Then said Ziba unto the king, According to all that my lord the king hath commanded his servant so shall thy servant do. As for Mephibosheth, said the king, he shall eat at my table as one of the king's sons. And Mephibosheth had a young son whose name was Micha. And all that dwelt in the house of Ziba were servants unto Mephibosheth. So Mephibosheth dwelt in Jerusalem for he did eat continually at the king's table and was lame on both his feet.

9 AND it came to pass after this that the king of the children of Ammon died and Hanun his son reigned in his stead. Then said David, I will show kindness unto Hanun the son of Nahash as his father showed kindness unto me. And David sent to comfort him by the hand of his servants for his father. And David's servants came into the land of the children of Ammon. And the princes of the children of Ammon said unto Hanun their lord, Thinkest thou that David doth honor thy father that he hath sent comforters unto thee? Hath not David rather sent his servants unto thee to search the city and to spy it out and to overthrow it? Wherefore Hanun took David's servants and shaved off the one half of their beards and cut off their garments in the middle even to their buttocks, and sent them away. When they told it unto David he sent to meet them because the men were greatly ashamed and the king said, Tarry at Jericho until your beards be grown and then return.

And when the children of Ammon saw that they stank before David, the children of Ammon sent and hired the Syrians of Beth-rehob and the Syrians of Zoba twenty thousand footmen and of king Maacah a thousand men and of Ish-tob twelve thousand men. And when David heard of it he sent Joab and all the host of the mighty men. And the children of Ammon came out and put the battle in array at the entering in of the gate and the Syrians of Zoba and of Rehob and Ish-tob and Maacah were by themselves in the field.

When Joab saw that the front of the battle was against him before and behind, he chose of all the choice men of Israel and put them in array against the Syrians, and the rest of the people he delivered into the hand of Abishai his brother that he might put them in array against the children of Ammon. And he said, If the Syrians be too strong for me then thou shalt help me, but if the children of Ammon be too strong for thee then I will come and help thee. Be of good courage and let us play the men for our people and for the cities of our God and the Lord do that which seemeth him good. And Joab drew nigh and the people that were with him unto the battle against the Syrians and they fled before him. And when the children of Ammon saw that the Syrians were fled then fled they also before Abishai and entered into the city. So Joab returned from the children of Ammon and came to Jerusalem.

And when the Syrians saw that they were smitten before Israel they gathered themselves together. And Hadarezer sent and brought out the Syrians that were beyond the river, and they came to Helam and Shobach the captain of the host of Hadarezer went before them. And when it was told David he gathered all Israel together and passed over Jordan and came to Helam. And the Syrians set themselves in array against David and fought with him. And the Syrians fled before Israel and David slew the men of seven hundred chariots of the Syrians and forty thousand horsemen and smote Shobach the captain of their host who died there. And when all the kings that were servants to Hadarezer saw that they were smitten before Israel they made peace with Israel and served them. So the Syrians feared to help the children of Ammon anymore.

10 AND it came to pass after the year was expired at the time when kings go forth to battle that David sent Joab and his servants with him and all Israel and they destroyed the children of Ammon and besieged Rabbah. But David tarried still at Jerusalem.

And it came to pass in an evening-tide that David arose from off his bed and walked upon the roof of the king's house, and from the roof he saw a woman washing herself and the woman was very beautiful to look upon. And David sent and inquired after the woman. And one said, Is not this Bath-sheba, the daughter of Eliam the wife of Uriah the Hittite? And David sent messengers and took her, and she came in unto him and he lay with her for she was purified from her uncleanness and she returned unto her house. And the woman conceived and sent and told David and said, I am with child.

And David sent to Joab, saying, Send me Uriah the Hittite. And Joab sent Uriah to David. And when Uriah was come unto him David demanded of him how Joab did and how the people did and how the war prospered. And David said to Uriah, Go down to thy house and wash thy feet. And Uriah departed out of the king's house and there followed him a mess of meat from the king. But Uriah slept at the door of the king's house with all the servants of his lord and went not down to his house. And when they had told David saying, Uriah went not down unto his house, David said unto Uriah, Camest thou not from thy journey? Why then didst thou not go down unto thine house? And Uriah said unto David, The ark and Israel and Judah abide in tents and my lord Joab and the servants of my lord are encamped in the open fields, shall I then go into mine house to eat and drink and to lie with my wife? As thou livest and as thy soul liveth I will not do this thing. And David said to Uriah, Tarry here today also and tomorrow I will let thee depart. So Uriah abode in Jerusalem that day and the morrow. And when David had called him he did eat and drink before him and he made him drunk, and at even he went out to lie on his bed with the servants of his lord but went not down to his house.

And it came to pass in the morning that David wrote a letter to Joab and sent it by the hand of Uriah. And he wrote in the letter saying, Set ye Uriah in the forefront of the hottest battle, and retire ye from him that he may be smitten and die. And it came to pass when Joab observed the city, that he assigned Uriah unto a place where he knew that valiant men were. And the men of the city went out and fought with Joab and there fell some of the people of the servants of David and Uriah the Hittite died also. Then Joab sent and told David all the things concerning the war and charged the messenger saying, When thou hast made an end of telling the matters of the war unto the king and if so be that the king's wrath arise and he say unto thee, Wherefore approached ye so nigh unto the city when ye did fight? Knew ye not that they would shoot from the wall? Who smote Abimelech the son of Jerubbesheth? Did not a woman cast a piece of a millstone upon him from the wall that he died in Thebez? Why went ye nigh the wall? then say thou, Thy servant Uriah the Hittite is dead also.

So the messenger went, and came and showed David all that Joab had sent him for. And the messenger said unto David, Surely the men prevailed against us and came out unto us into the field and we were upon them even unto the entering of the gate. And the shooters shot from off the wall upon thy servants and some of the king's servants be dead and thy servant Uriah the Hittite is dead also. Then

David said unto the messenger, Thus shalt thou say unto Joab, Let not this thing displease thee for the sword devoureth one as well as another make thy battle more strong against the city and overthrow it and encourage thou him.

And when the wife of Uriah heard that Uriah her husband was dead, she mourned for her husband. And when the mourning was past David sent and fetched her to his house and she became his wife and bare him a son. But the thing that David had done displeased the Lord.

And the Lord sent Nathan unto David. And he came unto him and said unto him, There were two men in one city, the one rich and the other poor. The rich man had exceeding many flocks and herds but the poor man had nothing save one little ewe lamb which he had bought and nourished up, and it grew up together with him and with his children, it did eat of his own meat and drank of his own cup and lay in his bosom and was unto him as a daughter. And there came a traveler unto the rich man and he spared to take of his own flock and of his own herd to dress for the wayfaring man that was come unto him, but took the poor man's lamb and dressed it for the man that was come to him.

And David's anger was greatly kindled against the man and he said to Nathan, As the Lord liveth, the man that hath done this thing shall surely die, and he shall restore the lamb fourfold because he did this thing, and because he had no pity.

And Nathan said to David, Thou art the man. Thus saith the Lord God of Israel I anointed thee king over Israel and I delivered thee out of the hand of Saul and I gave thee thy master's house and thy master's wives into thy bosom and gave thee the house of Israel and of Judah and if that had been too little, I would moreover have given unto thee such and such things. Wherefore hast thou despised the commandment of the Lord to do evil in his sight? Thou hast killed Uriah the Hittite with the sword and hast taken his wife to be thy wife and hast slain him with the sword of the children of Ammon. Now therefore the sword shall never depart from thine house because thou hast despised me and hast taken the wife of Uriah the Hittite to be thy wife. Thus saith the Lord, Behold, I will raise up evil against thee out of thine own house and I will take thy wives before thine eyes and give them unto thy neighbor and he shall lie with thy wives in the sight of this sun. For thou didst it secretly but I will do this thing before all Israel and before the sun.

And David said unto Nathan, I have sinned against the Lord. And Nathan said unto David, The Lord also hath not put away thy sin that thou shalt not die. Howbeit because by this deed thou hast given great occasion to the enemies of the Lord to blaspheme the child also that is born unto thee shall surely die. And Nathan departed unto his house. And the Lord struck the child that Uriah's wife bare unto David and it was very sick. David therefore besought God for the child and David fasted and went in and lay all night upon the earth. And the elders of his house arose and went to him to raise him up from the earth but he would not, neither did he eat bread with them. And it came to pass on the seventh day that the child died. And the servants of David feared to tell him that the child was dead for they said, Behold, while the child was yet alive we spake unto him and he would not hearken unto our voice how will he then vex himself if we tell him that the child is dead? But when David saw that his servants whispered David perceived that the child was dead, therefore David said unto his servants, Is the child dead? And they said, He is dead. Then David arose from the earth, and washed and anointed himself and changed his apparel and came into the house of the Lord and worshiped, then he came to his own house and when he required they set bread before him and he did eat.

Then said his servants unto him, What thing is this that thou hast done? Thou didst fast and weep for the child while it was alive but when the child was dead thou didst rise and eat bread. And he said, While the child was yet alive I fasted and wept, for I said, Who can tell whether God will be gracious to me that the child may live? But now he is dead wherefore should I fast? Can I bring him back again? I shall go to him but he shall not return to me.

And David comforted Bath-sheba his wife and went in unto her and lay with her, and she bare a son and he called his name Solomon and the Lord loved him. And he sent by the hand of Nathan the prophet and he called his name Jedidiah because of the Lord.

And Joab fought against Rabbah of the children of Ammon and took the royal city. And Joab sent messengers to David and said, I have fought against Rabbah, and have taken the city of waters. Now therefore gather the rest of the people together and encamp against the city and take it lest I take the city and it be called after my name. And David gathered all the people together, and went to Rabbah, and fought against it and took it. And he took their king's crown from off his head, the weight whereof was a talent of gold with the precious stones, and it was set on David's head. And he brought forth the spoil of the city in great abundance. And he brought forth the people that were therein, and put them under saws and under harrows of iron and under axes of iron and made them pass through the brick kiln, and thus did he unto all the cities of the children of Ammon. So David and all the people returned unto Jerusalem.

11 AND it came to pass after this that Absalom the son of David had a fair sister whose name was Tamar, and Amnon the son of David loved her. And Amnon was so vexed that he fell sick for his sister Tamar for she was a virgin and Amnon thought it hard for him to do anything to her. But Amnon had a friend whose name was Jonadab the son of Shimeah David's brother, and Jonadab was a very subtile man. And he said unto him, Why art thou, being the king's son, lean from day to day? Wilt thou not tell me? And Amnon said unto him I love Tamar my brother Absalom's sister. And Jonadab said unto him, Lay thee down on thy bed, and make thyself sick and when thy father cometh to see thee say unto him, I pray thee, let my sister Tamar come and give me meat and dress the meat in my sight that I may see it and eat it at her hand. So Amnon lay down and made himself sick and when the king was come to see him Amnon said unto the king, I pray thee, let Tamar my sister come and make me a couple of cakes in my sight that I may eat at her hand.

Then David sent home to Tamar, saying, Go now to thy brother Amnon's house and dress him meat. So Tamar went to her brother Amnon's house, and he was laid down. And she took flour and kneaded it and made cakes in his sight and did bake the cakes. And she took a pan and poured them out before him, but he refused to eat. And Amnon said, Have out all men from me. And they went out every man from him. And Amnon said unto Tamar, Bring the meat into the chamber, that I may eat of thine hand. And Tamar took the cakes which she had made and brought them into the chamber to Amnon her brother. And when she had brought them unto him to eat he took hold of her and said unto her, Come lie with me, my sister. And she answered him, Nay, my brother, do not force me, for no such thing ought to be done in Israel, do not thou this folly. And I, whither shall I cause my shame to go? And as for thee, thou shalt be as one of the fools in Israel. Now therefore I pray thee, speak unto the king, for he will not withhold me from thee. Howbeit he would not hearken unto her voice but being stronger than she, forced her and lay with her.

Then Amnon hated her exceedingly, so that the hatred wherewith he hated her was greater than the love wherewith he had loved her. And Amnon said to her, Arise, be gone. And she said unto him, There is no cause, this evil in sending me away is greater than the other that thou didst unto me. But he would not hearken unto her. Then he called his servant that ministered unto him and said, Put now this woman out from me and bolt the door after her. And she had a garment of divers colors upon her, for with such robes were the king's daughters that were virgins appareled. Then his servant brought her out and bolted the door after her. And Tamar put ashes on her head and rent her garment of divers colors that was on her, and laid her hand on her head and went on crying.

And Absalom her brother said unto her, Hath Amnon thy brother been with thee? But hold now thy peace my sister, he is thy brother, regard not this thing. So Tamar remained desolate in her brother Absalom's house. But when king David heard of all these things he was very wroth. And Absalom spake unto his brother Amnon neither good nor bad, for Absalom hated Amnon because he had forced his sister Tamar.

And it came to pass after two full years that Absalom had sheep shearers in Baal-hazor which is beside Ephraim, and Absalom invited all the king's sons. And Absalom came to the king and said, Behold now, thy servant hath sheep shearers let the king I beseech thee and his servants go with thy servant. And the king said to Absalom, Nay my son, let us not all now go lest we be chargeable unto thee. And he pressed him, howbeit he would not go, but blessed him. Then said Absalom, If not I pray thee, let my brother Amnon go with us. And the king said unto him, Why should he go with thee? But Absalom pressed him that he let Amnon and all the king's sons go with him.

Now Absalom had commanded his servants saying, Mark ye now when Amnon's heart is merry with wine, and when I say unto you, Smite Amnon, then kill him, Fear not, have I not commanded you? be courageous, and be valiant. And the servants of Absalom did unto Amnon as Absalom had commanded. Then all the king's sons arose and every man gat him up upon his mule and fled.

And it came to pass, while they were in the way that tidings came to David saying, Absalom hath slain all the king's sons and there is not one of them left. Then the king arose and tare his garments and lay on the earth, and all his servants stood by with their clothes rent. And Jonadab, the son of Shimeah David's brother, answered and said, Let not my lord suppose that they have slain all the young men the king's sons; for Amnon only is dead; for by the appointment of Absalom this hath been determined from the day that he forced his sister Tamar. Now therefore let not my Lord the king take the thing to his heart to think that all the king's sons are dead, for Amnon only is dead.

But Absalom fled. And the young man that kept the watch lifted up his eyes and looked, and behold, there came much people by the way of the hillside behind him. And Jonadab said unto the king, Behold, the king's sons come as thy servant said so it is. And it came to pass, as soon as he had made an end of speaking that behold the king's sons came and lifted up their voice and wept; and the king also and all his servants wept very sore.

But Absalom fled and went to Talmai the son of Ammihud king of Geshur. And David mourned for his son every day. So Absalom fled and went to Geshur, and was there three years. And the soul of king David longed to go forth unto Absalom for he was comforted concerning Amnon, seeing he was dead.

12 NOW Joab the son of Zeruiah perceived that the king's heart was toward Absalom. And Joab sent to Tekoah and fetched thence a wise woman and said unto her, I pray thee feign thyself to be a mourner and put on now mourning apparel and anoint not thyself with oil but be as a woman that had a long time mourned for the dead, and come to the king and speak on this manner unto him. So Joab put the words in her mouth.

And when the woman of Tekoah spake to the king she fell on her face to the ground and did obeisance and said, Help, O king. And the king said unto her, What aileth thee? And she answered, I am indeed a widow woman and mine husband is dead. And thy handmaid had two sons and they two strove together in the field and there was none to part them but the one smote the other and slew him. And behold the whole family is risen against thine handmaid and they said, Deliver him that smote his brother that we may kill him for the life of his brother whom he slew, and we will destroy the heir also, and so they will quench my coal which is left and shalt not leave to my husband neither name nor remainder upon the earth.

And the king said unto the woman, Go to thine house and I will give charge concerning thee. And the woman of Tekoah said unto the king, My lord O king, the iniquity be on me and on my father's house and the king and his throne be guiltless. And the king said, Whosoever saith aught unto thee bring him to me and he shall not touch thee anymore. Then said she, I pray thee, let the king remember the Lord thy God that thou wouldest not suffer the revengers of blood to destroy anymore lest they destroy my son. And he said, As the Lord liveth there shall not one hair of thy son fall to the earth.

Then the woman said, Let thine handmaid, I pray thee, speak one word unto my lord the king. And he said, Say on. And the woman said, Wherefore then hast thou thought such a thing against the people of God? For the king doth speak this thing as one which is faulty in that the king doth not fetch home again his banished. For we must needs die and are as water spilt on the ground which cannot be gathered up again, neither doth God respect any person yet doth he devise means that his banished be not expelled from him. Now therefore that I am come to speak of this thing unto my lord the king it is because the people have made me afraid and thy handmaid said, I will now speak unto the king, it may be that the king will perform the request of his handmaid. For the king will hear to deliver his handmaid out of the hand of the man that would destroy me and my son together out of the inheritance of God. Then thine handmaid said, The word of my lord the king shall now be comfortable, for as an angel of God so is my lord the king to discern good and bad therefore the Lord thy God will be with thee.

Then the king answered and said unto the woman, Hide not from me I pray thee the thing that I shall ask thee. And the woman said, Let my lord the king now speak. And the king said, Is not the hand of Joab with thee in all this? And the woman answered and said, As thy soul liveth, my lord the king, none can turn to the right hand or to the left from aught that my lord the king hath spoken. For thy servant Joab, he bade me and he put all these words in the mouth of thine handmaid, to fetch about this form of speech hath thy servant Joab done this thing and my lord is wise according to the wisdom of an angel of God to know all things that are in the Earth.

And the king said unto Joab, Behold now, I have done this thing. Go therefore, bring the young man Absalom again. And Joab fell to the ground on his face and bowed himself and thanked the king, and Joab said, Today thy servant knoweth that I have found grace in thy sight my lord O king, in that the king hath fulfilled the request of his servant. So Joab arose and went to Geshur and brought Absalom to Jerusalem. And the king said, Let him turn to his own house and let him not see my face. So Absalom returned to his own house and saw not the king's face.

But in all Israel there was none to be so much praised as Absalom for his beauty, from the sole of his foot even to the crown of his head there was no blemish in him. And when he polled his head, (for it was at every year's end that he polled it, because the hair was heavy on him, therefore he polled it) he weighed the hair of his head at two hundred shekels after the king's weight. And unto Absalom there were born three sons and one daughter whose name was Tamar. She was a woman of a fair countenance.

So Absalom dwelt two full years in Jerusalem and saw not the king's face. Therefore Absalom sent for Joab to have sent him to the king, but he would not come to him, and when he sent again the second time he would not come. Therefore he said unto his servants, See, Joab's field is near mine and he hath barley there, go and set it on fire. And Absalom's servants set the field on fire. Then Joab arose and came to Absalom unto his house and said unto him, Wherefore have thy servants set my field on fire? And Absalom answered Joab, Behold I sent unto thee saying, Come hither that I may send thee to the king to say, Wherefore am I come from Geshur? It had been good for me to have been there still. Now therefore let me see the king's face and if there be any iniquity in me let him kill me. So Joab came to the king and told him. And when he had called for Absalom, he came to the king and bowed himself on his face to the ground before the king and the king kissed Absalom.

13 AND it came to pass after this, that Absalom prepared him chariots and horses and fifty men to run before him. And Absalom rose up early and stood beside the way of the gate. And it was so that when any man that had a controversy came to the king for judgment then Absalom called unto him and said, Of what city art thou? And he said, Thy servant is of one of the tribes of Israel. And Absalom said unto him, See, thy matters are good and right, but there is no man deputed of the king to hear thee. Absalom said moreover, O that I were made judge in the land that every man which hath any suit or cause might come unto me and I would do him justice! And it was so that when any man came nigh to him to do him obeisance he put forth his hand and took him and kissed him. And on this manner did Absalom to all Israel that came to the king for judgment. So Absalom stole the hearts of the men of Israel.

And it came to pass after forty years, that Absalom said unto the king, I pray thee let me go and pay my vow which I have vowed unto the Lord in Hebron. For thy servant vowed a vow while I abode at Geshur in Syria saying, If the Lord shall bring me again indeed to Jerusalem then I will serve the Lord. And the king said unto him, Go in peace. So he arose and went to Hebron. But Absalom sent spies throughout all the tribes of Israel saying, As soon as ye hear the sound of the trumpet, then ye shall say, Absalom reigneth in Hebron. And with Absalom went two hundred men out of Jerusalem that were called, and they went in their simplicity and they knew not anything. And Absalom sent for Ahithophel the Gilonite, David's counselor, from his city even from Giloh while he offered sacrifices. And the conspiracy was strong, for the people increased continually with Absalom.

And there came a messenger to David saying, The hearts of the men of Israel are after Absalom. And David said unto all his servants that were with him at Jerusalem, Arise and let us flee for we shall not else escape from Absalom, make speed to depart lest he overtake us suddenly and bring evil upon us and smite the city with the edge of the sword. And the king's servants said unto the king, Behold, thy servants are ready to do whatsoever my lord the king shall appoint. And the king went forth and all his household after him. And the king left ten women which were concubines to keep the house. And the king went forth and all the people after him and tarried in a place that was far off. And all his servants passed on beside him and all the Cherethites and all the Pelethites and all the Gittites six hundred men which came after him from Gath, passed on before the king.

Then said the king to Ittai the Gittite, Wherefore goest thou also with us? Return to thy place and abide with the king for thou art a stranger and also an exile. Whereas thou camest but yesterday should I this day make thee go up and down with us? Seeing I go whither I may, return thou and take back thy brethren, mercy and truth be with thee. And Ittai answered the king and said, As the Lord liveth and as my lord the king liveth surely in what place my lord the king shall be whether in death or life even there also will thy servant be. And David said to Ittai, Go and pass over. And Ittai the Gittite passed over and all his men and all the little ones that were with him. And all the country wept with a loud voice and all the people passed over. The king also himself passed over the brook Kidron and all the people passed over toward the way of the wilderness.

And lo Zadok also and all the Levites were with him bearing the ark of the covenant of God, and they set down the ark of God and Abiathar went up until all the people had done passing out of the city. And the king said unto Zadok, Carry back the ark of God into the city. If I shall find favor in the eyes of the Lord he will bring me again and show me both it and his habitation. But if he thus say I have no delight in thee behold here am I let him do to me as seemeth good unto him. The king said also unto Zadok the priest, Art not thou a seer? Return into the city in peace and your two sons with you, Ahimaaz thy son and Jonathan the son of Abiathar. See, I will tarry in the plain of the wilderness until there come word from you to certify me. Zadok therefore and Abiathar carried the ark of God again to Jerusalem and they tarried there.

And David went up by the ascent of mount Olivet and wept as he went up and had his head covered and he went barefoot and all the people that was with him covered every man his head and they went up weeping as they went up. And one told David saying, Ahithophel is among the conspirators with Absalom. And David said, O Lord I pray thee turn the counsel of Ahithophel into foolishness.

And it came to pass, that when David was come to the top of the mount where he worshiped God behold Hushai the Archite came to meet him with his coat rent and earth upon his head unto whom David said, If thou passest on with me then thou shalt be a burden unto me, but if thou return to the city and say unto Absalom I will be thy servant O king as I have been thy father's servant hitherto so will I now also be thy servant, then mayest thou for me defeat the counsel of Ahithophel. And hast thou not there with thee Zadok and Abiathar the priests? Therefore it shall be that what thing soever thou shalt hear out of the king's house thou shalt tell it to Zadok and Abiathar the priests. Behold, they have there with them their two sons, Ahimaaz Zadok's son and Jonathan Abiathar's son, and by them ye shall send unto me everything that ye can hear. So Hushai David's friend came into the city and Absalom came into Jerusalem.

And when David was a little past the top of the hill behold, Ziba the servant of Mephibosheth met him with a couple of asses saddled and upon them two hundred loaves of bread and a hundred bunches of raisins and a hundred of summer fruits and a bottle of wine. And the king said unto Ziba, What meanest thou by these? And Ziba said, The asses be for the king's household to ride on; and the bread and summer fruit for the young men to eat and the wine, that such as be faint in the wilderness may drink. And the king said, And where is thy master's son? And Ziba said unto the king, Behold, he abideth at Jerusalem for he said, Today shall the house of Israel restore me the kingdom of my father. Then said the king to Ziba, Behold thine are all that pertained unto Mephibosheth. And Ziba said, I humbly beseech thee that I may find grace in thy sight my lord O king.

And when king David came to Bahurim, behold, thence came out a man of the family of the house of Saul whose name was Shimei, the son of Gera, he came forth and cursed still as he came. And he cast stones at David and at all the servants of king David and all the people and all the mighty men were on his right hand and on his left. And thus said Shimei when he cursed, Come out come out thou bloody man and thou man of Belial the Lord hath returned upon thee all the blood of the house of Saul in whose stead thou hast reigned and the Lord hath delivered the kingdom into the hand of Absalom thy son and behold thou art taken in thy mischief because thou art a bloody man.

Then said Abishai the son of Zeruiah unto the king, Why should this dead dog curse my lord the king? Let me go over I pray thee and take off his head. And the king said, What have I to do with you ye sons of Zeruiah? So let him curse because the Lord hath said unto him, Curse David. Who shall then say, Wherefore hast thou done so? And David said to Abishai and to all his servants, Behold my son which came forth of my bowels seeketh my life how much more now may this Benjamite do it? Let him alone and let him curse for the Lord hath bidden him. It may be that the Lord will look on mine affliction and that the Lord will requite me good for his cursing this day. And as David and his men went by the way Shimei went along on the hill's side over against him and cursed as he went and threw stones at him and cast dust. And the king and all the people that were with him came weary and refreshed themselves there.

14 AND Absalom and all the people the men of Israel came to Jerusalem and Ahithophel with him. And it came to pass when Hushai the Archite, David's friend was come unto Absalom that Hushai said unto Absalom, God save the king, God save the king. And Absalom said to Hushai, Is this thy kindness to thy friend? Why wentest thou not with thy friend? And Hushai said unto Absalom, Nay, but whom the Lord and this people and all the men of Israel choose, his will I be and with him will I abide. And again whom should I serve? Should I not serve in the presence of his son? As I have served in thy father's presence so will I be in thy presence.

Then said Absalom to Ahithophel, Give counsel among you what we shall do. And Ahithophel said unto Absalom, Go in unto thy father's concubines which he hath left to keep the house and all Israel shall hear that thou art abhorred of thy father then shall the hands of all that are with thee be strong. So they spread Absalom a tent upon the top of the house and Absalom went in unto his father's concubines in the sight of all Israel. And the counsel of Ahithophel, which he counseled in those days was as if a man had inquired at the oracle of God. So was all the counsel of Ahithophel both with David and with Absalom.

Moreover Ahithophel said unto Absalom, Let me now choose out twelve thousand men and I will arise and pursue after David this night and I will come upon him while he is weary and weakhanded and will make him afraid and all the people that are with him shall flee and I will smite the king only. And I will bring back all the people unto thee, the man whom thou seekest is as if all returned so all the people shall be in peace. And the saying pleased Absalom well and all the elders of Israel.

Then said Absalom, Call now Hushai the Archite also and let us hear likewise what he saith. And when Hushai was come to Absalom, Absalom spake unto him saying, Ahithophel hath spoken after this manner, shall we do after his saying? If not speak thou. And Hushai said unto Absalom, The counsel that Ahithophel hath given is not good at this time. For, said Hushai, thou knowest thy father and his men that they be mighty men and they be chafed in their minds as a bear robbed of her whelps in the field and thy father is a man of war and will not lodge with the people. Behold, he is hid now in some pit or in some other place and it will come to pass, when some of them be overthrown at the first that whosoever heareth it will say, There is a slaughter among the people that follow Absalom. And he also that is valiant whose heart is as the heart of a lion shall utterly melt, for all Israel knoweth that thy father is a mighty man and they which be with him are valiant men. Therefore I counsel that all Israel be generally gathered unto thee, from Dan even to Beer-sheba, as the sand that is by the sea for multitude and that thou go to battle in thine own person. So shall we come upon him in some place where he shall be found and we will light upon him as the dew falleth on the ground and of him and of all the men that are with him there shall not be left so much as one. Moreover if he be gotten into a city then shall all Israel bring ropes to that city, and we will draw it into the river until there be not one small stone found there. And Absalom and all the men of Israel said, The counsel of Hushai the Archite is better than the counsel of Ahithophel. For the Lord had appointed to defeat the good counsel of Ahithophel to the intent that the Lord might bring evil upon Absalom.

Then said Hushai unto Zadok and to Abiathar the priests, Thus and thus did Ahithophel counsel Absalom and the elders of Israel, and thus and thus have I counseled. Now therefore send quickly and tell David saying, Lodge not this night in the plains of the wilderness but speedily pass over lest the king be swallowed up and all the people that are with him. Now Jonathan and Ahimaaz stayed by En-rogel; for they might not be seen to come into the city, and a wench went and told them, and they went and told king David. Nevertheless, a lad saw them and told Absalom, but they went both of them away quickly and came to a man's house in Bahurim which had a well in his court whither they went down. And the woman took and spread a covering over the well's mouth, and spread ground corn thereon; and the thing was not known. And when Absalom's servants came to the woman to the house, they said, Where is Ahimaaz and Jonathan? And the woman said unto them, They be gone over the brook of water. And when they had sought and could not find them, they returned to Jerusalem.

And it came to pass after they were departed that they came up out of the well and went and told king David and said unto David, Arise and pass quickly over the water for thus hath Ahithophel counseled against you. Then David arose and all the people that were with him, and they passed over Jordan by the morning light there lacked not one of them that was not gone over Jordan.

And when Ahithophel saw that his counsel was not followed he saddled his ass and arose and gat him home to his house, to his city and put his household in order and hanged himself and died and was buried in the sepulcher of his father.

15 THEN David came to Mahanaim. And Absalom passed over Jordan he and all the men of Israel with him. And Absalom made Amasa captain of the hosts instead of Joab. Which Amasa was a man's son whose name was Ithra an Israelite that went in to Abigail the daughter of Nahash sister to Zeruiah Joab's mother. So Israel and Absalom pitched in the land of Gilead.

And it came to pass, when David was come to Mahanaim, that Shobi the son of Nahash of Rabbah of the children of Ammon, and Machir the son of Ammiel of Lo-debar and Barzillai the Gileadite of Rogelim, brought beds and basins and earthen vessels and wheat and barley and flour and parched corn and beans and lentiles and parched pulse and honey and butter and sheep and cheese of kine for David and for the people that were with him to eat. For they said, The people is hungry and weary and thirsty in the wilderness.

And David numbered the people that were with him and set captains of thousands and captains of hundreds over them. And David sent forth a third part of the people under the hand of Joab, and a third part under the hand of Abishai the son of Zeruiah Joab's brother, and the third part under the hand of Ittai the Gittite. And the king said unto the people, I will surely go forth with you myself also. But the people answered, Thou shalt not go forth for if we flee away they will not care for us neither if half of us die will they care for us but now thou art worth ten thousand of us therefore now it is better that thou succor us out of the city. And the king said unto them, What seemeth you best I will do. And the king stood by the gate side, and all the people came out by hundreds and by thousands. And the king commanded Joab and Abishai and Ittai, saying, Deal gently for my sake with the young man, even with Absalom. And all the people heard when the king gave all the captains charge concerning Absalom.

So the people went out into the field against Israel and the battle was in the wood of Ephraim where the people of Israel were slain before the servants of David and there was there a great slaughter that day of twenty thousand men. For the battle was there scattered over the face of all the country and the wood devoured more people that day than the sword devoured.

And Absalom met the servants of David. And Absalom rode upon a mule and the mule went under the thick boughs of a great oak and his head caught hold of the oak and he was taken up between the Heaven and the Earth and the mule that was under him went away. And a certain man saw it and told Joab and said, Behold, I saw Absalom hanged in an oak. And Joab said unto the man that told him, And behold thou sawest him and why didst thou not smite him there to the ground? And I would have given thee ten shekels of silver and a girdle. And the man said unto Joab, Though I should receive a thousand shekels of silver in mine hand yet would I not put forth mine hand against the king's son; for in our hearing the king charged thee and Abishai and Ittai, saying, Beware that none touch the young man Absalom. Otherwise I should have wrought falsehood against mine own life for there is no matter hid from the king and thou thyself wouldest have set thyself against me. Then said Joab, I may not tarry thus with thee. And he took three darts in his hand, and thrust them through the heart of Absalom while he was yet alive in the midst of the oak. And ten young men that bare Joab's armor compassed about and smote Absalom, and slew him.

And Joab blew the trumpet, and the people returned from pursuing after Israel for Joab held back the people. And they took Absalom and cast him into a great pit in the wood and laid a very great heap of stones upon him and all Israel fled everyone to his tent. Now Absalom in his lifetime had taken and reared up for himself a pillar, which is in the king's dale, for he said, I have no son to keep my name in remembrance. And he called the pillar after his own name and it is called unto this day, Absalom's place.

16 THEN said Ahimaaz the son of Zadok, Let me now run and bear the king tidings how that the Lord hath avenged him of his enemies. And Joab said unto him, Thou shalt not bear tidings this day but thou shalt bear tidings another day but this day thou shalt bear no tidings because the king's son is dead. Then said Joab to Cushi, Go tell the king what thou hast seen. And Cushi bowed himself unto Joab and ran. Then said Ahimaaz the son of Zadok yet again to Joab, But howsoever let me I pray thee also run after Cushi. And Joab said, Wherefore wilt thou run my son seeing that thou hast no tidings ready? But howsoever said he, Let me run. And he said unto him, Run. Then Ahimaaz ran by the way of the plain and overran Cushi.

And David sat between the two gates and the watchman went up to the roof over the gate unto the wall and lifted up his eyes and looked and behold a man running alone. And the watchman cried and told the king. And the king said, If he be alone there is tidings in his mouth. And he came apace and drew near. And the watchman saw another man running and the watchman called unto the porter and said, Behold another man running alone. And the king said, He also bringeth tidings. And the watchman said, Me thinketh the running of the foremost is like the running of Ahimaaz the son of Zadok. And the king said, He is a good man, and cometh with good tidings.

And Ahimaaz called and said unto the king, All is well. And he fell down to the earth upon his face before the king and said, Blessed be the Lord thy God which hath delivered up the men that lifted up their hand against my lord the king. And the king said, Is the young man Absalom safe? And Ahimaaz answered, When Joab sent the king's servant and me thy servant I saw a great tumult but I knew not what it was. And the king said unto him, Turn aside and stand here. And he turned aside and stood still. And behold Cushi came and Cushi said, Tidings my lord the king for the Lord hath avenged thee this day of all them that rose up against thee. And the king said unto Cushi, Is the young man Absalom safe? And Cushi answered, The enemies of my lord the king and all that rise against thee to do thee hurt be as that young man is. And the king was much moved and went up to the chamber over the gate and wept and as he went thus he said, O my son Absalom! My son, my son Absalom! Would God I had died for thee, O Absalom my son my son!

And it was told Joab, Behold, the king weepeth and mourneth for Absalom. And the victory that day was turned into mourning unto all the people for the people heard say that day how the king was grieved for his son. And the people gat them by stealth that day into the city as people being ashamed steal away when they flee in battle. But the king covered his face and the king cried with a loud voice, O my son Absalom! O Absalom, my son, my son!

And Joab came into the house to the king and said, Thou hast shamed this day the faces of all thy servants which this day have saved thy life and the lives of thy sons and of thy daughters and the lives of thy wives and the lives of thy concubines, in that thou lovest thine enemies and hatest thy friends. For thou hast declared this day that thou regardest neither princes nor servants for this day I perceive that if Absalom had lived and all we had died this day then it had pleased thee well. Now therefore arise go forth and speak comfortably unto thy servants for I swear by the Lord if thou go not forth there will not tarry one with thee this night and that will be worse unto thee than all the evil that befell thee from thy youth until now.

Then the king arose, and sat in the gate. And they told unto all the people saying Behold, the king doth sit in the gate. And all the people came before the king for Israel had fled every man to his tent. And all the people were at strife throughout all the tribes of Israel saying, The king saved us out of the hand of our enemies and he delivered us out of the hand of the Philistines and now he is fled out of the land for Absalom. And Absalom whom we anointed over us is dead in battle. Now therefore why speak ye not a word of bringing the king back?

17 AND king David sent to Zadok and to Abiathar the priests saying, Speak unto the elders of Judah saying, Why are ye the last to bring the king back to his house? Seeing the speech of all Israel is come to the king even to his house. Ye are my brethren ye are my bones and my flesh wherefore then are ye the last to bring back the king? And say ye to Amasa, Art thou not of my bone, and of my flesh? God do so to me and more also if thou be not captain of the host before me continually in the room of Joab. And he bowed the heart of all the men of Judah even as the heart of one man so that they sent this word unto the king, Return thou and all thy servants. So the king returned and came to Jordan. And Judah came to Gilgal to go to meet the king to conduct the king over Jordan.

And Shimei the son of Gera, a Benjamite which was of Bahurim hasted and came down with the men of Judah to meet king David. And there were a thousand men of Benjamin with him, and Ziba the servant of the house of Saul and his fifteen sons and his twenty servants with him and they went over Jordan before the king.

And there went over a ferry boat to carry over the king's household and to do what he thought good. And Shimei the son of Gera fell down before the king as he was come over Jordan. And said unto the king, Let not my lord impute iniquity unto me neither do thou remember that which thy servant did perversely the day that my lord the king went out of Jerusalem that the king should take it to his heart. For thy servant doth know that I have sinned therefore behold I am come the first this day of all the house of Joseph to go down to meet my lord the king. But Abishai the son of Zeruiah answered and said, Shall not Shimei be put to death for this because he cursed the Lord's anointed? And David said, What have I to do with you ye sons of Zeruiah that ye should this day be adversaries unto me? Shall there any man be put to death this day in Israel? For do not I know that I am this day king over Israel? Therefore the king said unto Shimei, Thou shalt not die. And the king sware unto him.

And Mephibosheth the son of Saul came down to meet the king and had neither dressed his feet nor trimmed his beard nor washed his clothes from the day the king departed until the day he came again in peace. And it came to pass when he was come to Jerusalem to meet the king that the king said unto him, Wherefore wentest not thou with me, Mephibosheth? And he answered, My lord O king my servant deceived me, for thy servant said, I will saddle me an ass that I may ride thereon and go to the king because thy servant is lame. And he hath slandered thy servant unto my lord the king, but my lord the king is as an angel of God, do therefore what is good in thine eyes. For all of my father's house were but dead men before my lord the king yet didst thou set thy servant among them that did eat at thine own table. What right therefore have I yet to cry anymore unto the king? And the king said unto him, Why speakest thou any more of thy matters? I have said, Thou and Ziba divide the land. And Mephibosheth said unto the king, Yea, let him take all, forasmuch as my lord the king is come again in peace unto his own house.

And Barzillai the Gileadite came down from Rogelim and went over Jordan with the king to conduct him over Jordan. Now Barzillai was a very aged man even fourscore years old and he had provided the king of sustenance while he lay at Mahanaim for he was a very great man. And the king said unto Barzillai Come thou over with me and I will feed thee with me in Jerusalem. And Barzillai said unto the king, How long have I to live that I should go up with the king unto Jerusalem? I am this day fourscore years old and can I discern between good and evil? Can thy servant taste what I eat or what I drink? Can I hear anymore the voice of singing men and singing women. Wherefore then should thy servant be yet a burden unto my lord the king? Thy servant will go a little way over Jordan with the king and why should the king recompense it me with such a reward? Let thy servant I pray thee turn back again that I may die in mine own city and be buried by the grave of my father and of my mother. But behold thy servant Chimham, let him go over with my lord the king and do to him what shall seem good unto thee. And the king answered, Chimham shall go over with me and I will do to him that which shall seem good unto thee and whatsoever thou shalt require of me that will I do for thee. And all the people went over Jordan. And when the king was come over the king kissed Barzillai, and blessed him and he returned unto his own place. Then the king went on to Gilgal and Chimham went on with him and all the people of Judah conducted the king and also half the people of Israel.

And behold all the men of Israel came to the king and said unto the king, Why have our brethren the men of Judah stolen thee away and have brought the king and his household and all David's men with him over Jordan? And all the men of Judah answered the men of Israel, Because the king is near of kin to us wherefore then be ye angry for this matter? Have we eaten at all of the king's cost? Or hath he given us any gift? And the men of Israel answered the men of Judah and said, We have ten parts in the king, and we have also more right in David than ye why then did ye despise us that our advice should not be first had in bringing back our king? And the words of the men of Judah were fiercer than the words of the men of Israel.

And there happened to be there a man of Belial, whose name was Sheba, the son of Bichri a Benjamite and he blew a trumpet and said, We have no part in David neither have we inheritance in the son of Jesse every man to his tents O Israel. So every man of Israel went up from after David and followed Sheba the son of Bichri, but the men of Judah clave unto their king from Jordan even to Jerusalem. And David came to his house at Jerusalem and the king took the ten women his concubines whom he had left to keep the house and put them in ward and fed them, but went not in unto them. So they were shut up unto the day of their death living in widowhood.

18 THEN said the king to Amasa, Assemble me the men of Judah within three days and be thou here present. So Amasa went to assemble the men of Judah but he tarried longer than the set time which he had appointed him. And David said to Abishai, Now shall Sheba the son of Bichri do us more harm than did Absalom, take thou thy lord's servants and pursue after him lest he get him fenced cities and escape us. And there went out after him Joab's men and the Cherethites and the Pelethites and all the mighty men and they went out of Jerusalem to pursue after Sheba the son of Bichri. When they were at the great stone which is in Gibeon Amasa went before them. And Joab's garment that he had put on was girded unto him and upon it a girdle with a sword fastened upon his loins in the sheath thereof; and as he went forth it fell out. And Joab said to Amasa, Art thou in health my brother? And Joab took Amasa by the beard with the right hand to kiss him.

But Amasa took no heed to the sword that was in Joab's hand so he smote him therewith in the fifth rib, and shed out his bowels to the ground and struck him not again and he died. So Joab and Abishai his brother pursued after Sheba the son of Bichri. And one of Joab's men stood by him and said, He that favoreth Joab, and he that is for David let him go after Joab. And Amasa wallowed in blood in the midst of the highway. And when the man saw that all the people stood still, he removed Amasa out of the highway into the field and cast a cloth upon him when he saw that everyone that came by him stood still. When he was removed out of the highway all the people went on after Joab to pursue after Sheba the son of Bichri.

And he went through all the tribes of Israel unto Abel and to Beth-maachah and all the Berites, and they were gathered together and went also after him. And they came and besieged him in Abel of Beth-maachah, and they cast up a bank against the city and it stood in the trench; and all the people that were with Joab battered the wall to throw it down. Then cried a wise woman out of the city, Hear, hear, say I pray you unto Joab, Come near hither, that I may speak with thee. And when he was come near unto her the woman said, Art thou Joab? And he answered, I am he. Then she said unto him, Hear the words of thine handmaid. And he answered, I do hear. Then she spake saying, They are wont to speak in old time saying, They shall surely ask counsel at Abel and so they ended the matter. I am one of them that are peaceable and faithful in Israel thou seekest to destroy a city and a mother in Israel. Why wilt thou swallow up the inheritance of the Lord? And Joab answered and said, Far be it far be it from me that I should swallow up or destroy. The matter is not so but a man of mount Ephraim Sheba the son of Bichri by name hath lifted up his hand against the king even against David. Deliver him only and I will depart from the city. And the woman said unto Joab, Behold his head shall be thrown to thee over the wall. Then the woman went unto all the people in her wisdom and they cut off the head of Sheba the son of

Bichri and cast it out to Joab. And he blew a trumpet, and they retired from the city every man to his tent. And Joab returned to Jerusalem unto the king.

Now Joab was over all the host of Israel and Benaiah the son of Jehoiada was over the Cherethites and over the Pelethites and Adoram was over the tribute and Jehoshaphat the son of Ahilud was recorder and Sheva was scribe and Zadok and Abiathar were the priests and Ira also the Jairite was a chief ruler about David.

19 THEN there was a famine in the days of David three years, year after year. And David inquired of the Lord. And the Lord answered, It is for Saul and for his bloody house because he slew the Gibeonites. And the king called the Gibeonites, and said unto them (now the Gibeonites were not of the children of Israel, but of the remnant of the Amorites and the children of Israel had sworn unto them and Saul sought to slay them in his zeal to the children of Israel and Judah), Wherefore David said unto the Gibeonites, What shall I do for you? And wherewith shall I make the atonement that ye may bless the inheritance of the Lord? And the Gibeonites said unto him, We will have no silver nor gold of Saul nor of his house neither for us shalt thou kill any man in Israel. And he said, What ye shall say that will I do for you. And they answered the king, The man that consumed us and that devised against us that we should be destroyed from remaining in any of the coasts of Israel, let seven men of his sons be delivered unto us and we will hang them up unto the Lord in Gibeah of Saul, whom the Lord did choose. And the king said, I will give them.

But the king spared Mephibosheth, the son of Jonathan the son of Saul, because of the Lord's oath that was between them between David and Jonathan the son of Saul. But the king took the two sons of Rizpah the daughter of Aiah whom she bare unto Saul, Armoni and Mephibosheth and the five sons of Michal the daughter of Saul, whom she brought up for Adriel the son of Barzillai the Meholathite. And he delivered them into the hands of the Gibeonites and they hanged them in the hill before the Lord, and they fell all seven together and were put to death in the days of harvest, in the first days in the beginning of barley harvest.

And Rizpah the daughter of Aiah took sackcloth and spread it for her upon the rock from the beginning of harvest until water dropped upon them out of Heaven and suffered neither the birds of the air to rest on them by day nor the beasts of the field by night. And it was told David what Rizpah the daughter of Aiah, the concubine of Saul, had done. And David went and took the bones of Saul and the bones of Jonathan his son from the men of Jabesh-gilead, which had stolen them from the street of Beth-shan where the Philistines had hanged them when the Philistines had slain Saul in Gilboa. And he brought up from thence the bones of Saul and the bones of Jonathan his son and they gathered the bones of them that were hanged. And the bones of Saul and Jonathan his son buried they in the country of Benjamin in Zelah in the sepulcher of Kish his father and they performed all that the king commanded. And after that God was entreated for the land.

Moreover the Philistines had yet war again with Israel and David went down and his servants with him and fought against the Philistines and David waxed faint. And Ishbi-benob which was of the sons of the giant, the weight of whose spear weighed three hundred shekels of brass in weight, he being girded with a new sword thought to have slain David. But Abishai the son of Zeruiah succored him and smote the Philistine and killed him. Then the men of David sware unto him, saying, Thou shalt go no more out with us to battle that thou quench not the light of Israel.

And it came to pass after this that there was again a battle with the Philistines at Gob, then Sibbechai the Hushathite slew Saph which was of the sons of the giant. And there was again a battle in Gob with the Philistines where Elhanan the son of Jaare-oregim a Bethlehemite slew the brother of Goliath the Gittite, the staff of whose spear was like a weaver's beam. And there was yet a battle in Gath where was a man of great stature that had on every hand six fingers, and on every foot six toes, four and twenty in number; and he also was born to the giant. And when he defied Israel, Jonathan the son of Shimeah the brother of David slew him. These four were born to the giant in Gath, and fell by the hand of David and by the hand of his servants.

20 AND David spake unto the Lord the words of this song, in the day that the Lord had delivered him out of the hand of all his enemies and out of the hand of Saul, and he said,

> The Lord is my rock and my fortress and my deliverer.
> The God of my rock in him will I trust, he is my shield and the horn of my salvation.
> My high tower and my refuge, my savior, thou savest me from violence.
> I will call on the Lord who is worthy to be praised, so shall I be saved from mine enemies.
>
> When the waves of death compassed me, the floods of ungodly men made me afraid.
> The sorrows of hell compassed me about, the snares of death prevented me.
> In my distress I called upon the Lord, and cried to my God.
> And he did hear my voice out of his temple, and my cry did enter into his ears.
>
> Then the Earth shook and trembled, the foundations of Heaven moved and shook because he was wroth.
> There went up a smoke out of his nostrils, and fire out of his mouth devoured, coals were kindled by it.
> He bowed the heavens also, and came down and darkness was under his feet.
> And he rode upon a cherub and did fly, and he was seen upon the wings of the wind.
> And he made darkness pavilions round about him, dark waters and thick clouds of the skies.
> Through the brightness before him were coals of fire kindled.
> The Lord thundered from Heaven, and the Most High uttered his voice.
> And he sent out arrows and scattered them, lightning and discomfited them.
> And the channels of the sea appeared, the foundations of the world were discovered
> At the rebuking of the Lord, at the blast of the breath of his nostrils.
> He sent from above, he took me, he drew me out of many waters.

He delivered me from my strong enemy, and from them that hated me, for they were too strong for me.

They prevented me in the day of my calamity, but the Lord was my stay.

He brought me forth also into a large place, he delivered me because he delighted in me.

The Lord rewarded me according to my righteousness;

According to the cleanness of my hands hath he recompensed me.

For I have kept the ways of the Lord, and have not wickedly departed from my God.

For all his judgments were before me, and as for his statutes, I did not depart from them.

I was also upright before him, and have kept myself from mine iniquity.

Therefore the Lord hath recompensed me according to my righteousness,

According to my cleanness in his eyesight.

With the merciful thou wilt show thyself merciful, and with the upright man thou wilt show thyself upright.

With the pure thou wilt show thyself pure, and with the froward thou wilt show thyself unsavory.

And the afflicted people thou wilt save, but thine eyes are upon the haughty that thou mayest bring them down.

For thou art my lamp O Lord, and the Lord will lighten my darkness.

For by thee I have run through a troop, by my God have I leaped over a wall.

As for God, his way is perfect.

The word of the Lord is tried, he is a buckler to all them that trust in him.

For who is God, save the Lord? And who is a rock, save our God?

God is my strength and power, and he maketh my way perfect.

He maketh my feet like hinds' feet, and setteth me upon my high places.

He teacheth my hands to war, so that a bow of steel is broken by mine arms.

Thou hast also given me the shield of thy salvation, and thy gentleness hath made me great.

Thou hast enlarged my steps under me, so that my feet did not slip.

I have pursued mine enemies and destroyed them, and turned not again until I had consumed them.

And I have consumed them and wounded them that they could not arise, yea they are fallen under my feet.

For thou hast girded me with strength to battle, them that rose up against me hast thou subdued under me.

Thou hast also given me the necks of mine enemies, that I might destroy them that hate me.

They looked, but there was none to save, even unto the Lord, but he answered them not.

Then did I beat them as small as the dust of the earth.

I did stamp them as the mire of the street, and did spread them abroad.

Thou also hast delivered me from the strivings of my people,
Thou hast kept me to be head of the heathen, a people which I knew not shall serve me.
Strangers shall submit themselves unto me, as soon as they hear they shall be obedient unto me.
Strangers shall fade away, and they shall be afraid out of their close places.

The Lord liveth and blessed be my rock, and exalted be the God of the rock of my salvation.
It is God that avengeth me and that bringeth down the people unto me,
And that bringeth me forth from mine enemies.
Thou also hast lifted me up on high above them that rose up against me.
Thou hast delivered me from the violent man.
Therefore I will give thanks unto thee O Lord, among the heathen and I will sing praises unto thy name.
He is the tower of salvation for his king, and showeth mercy to his anointed,
unto David, and to his seed for evermore.

21 NOW these be the last words of David. David the son of Jesse said, and the man who was raised up on high, the anointed of the God of Jacob, and the sweet psalmist of Israel, said,

The Spirit of the Lord spake by me, and his word was in my tongue.
The God of Israel said, the Rock of Israel spake to me,
'He that ruleth over men must be just, ruling in the fear of God.
And he shall be as the light of the morning, when the sun riseth,
even a morning without clouds, as the tender grass springing out of the earth by clear shining after rain.'

Although my house be not so with God, yet he hath made with me an everlasting covenant,
ordered in all things and sure, for this is all my salvation and all my desire although he make it not to grow.
But the sons of Belial shall be all of them as thorns thrust away, because they cannot be taken with hands,
but the man that shall touch them must be fenced with iron and the staff of a spear,
and they shall be utterly burned with fire in the same place.

These be the names of the mighty men whom David had: The Tachmonite that sat in the seat chief among the captains, the same was Adino the Eznite, he lifted up his spear against eight hundred whom he slew at one time. And after him was Eleazar the son of Dodo the Ahohite, one of the three mighty men with David, when they defied the Philistines that were there gathered together to battle and the men of Israel were gone away. He arose and smote the Philistines until his hand was weary and his hand clave unto the sword, and the Lord wrought a great victory that day and the people returned after him only to spoil.

And after him was Shammah the son of Agee the Hararite. And the Philistines were gathered together into a troop where was a piece of ground full of lentiles and the people fled from the Philistines. But he stood in the midst of the ground and defended it and slew the Philistines, and the Lord wrought a great victory.

And three of the thirty chief went down and came to David in the harvest-time unto the cave of Adullam and the troop of the Philistines pitched in the valley of Rephaim. And David was then in a hold, and the garrison of the Philistines was then in Bethlehem. And David longed and said, O that one would give me drink of the water of the well of Bethlehem which is by the gate! And the three mighty men brake through the host of the Philistines and drew water out of the well of Bethlehem that was by the gate and took it and brought it to David, nevertheless he would not drink thereof but poured it out unto the Lord. And he said, Be it far from me, O Lord, that I should do this, is not this the blood of the men that went in jeopardy of their lives? Therefore he would not drink it. These things did these three mighty men.

And Abishai the brother of Joab the son of Zeruiah was chief among three. And he lifted up his spear against three hundred and slew them and had the name among three. Was he not most honorable of three? Therefore he was their captain, howbeit he attained not unto the first three.

And Benaiah the son of Jehoiada the son of a valiant man of Kabzeel who had done many acts, he slew two lion-like men of Moab. He went down also and slew a lion in the midst of a pit in time of snow. And he slew an Egyptian a goodly man, and the Egyptian had a spear in his hand, but he went down to him with a staff and plucked the spear out of the Egyptian's hand and slew him with his own spear. These things did Benaiah the son of Jehoiada and had the name among three mighty men. He was more honorable than the thirty but he attained not to the first three. And David set him over his guard.

Asahel the brother of Joab was one of the thirty, Elhanan the son of Dodo of Bethlehem, Shammah the Harodite, Elika the Harodite, Helez the Paltite, Ira the son of Ikkesh the Tekoite, Abiezer the Anethothite, Mebunnai the Hushathite, Zalmon the Ahohite, Maharal the Netophathite, Heleb the son of Maanah, a Netophathite, Ittai the son of Ribai out of Gibeah of the children of Benjamin, Benaiah the Pirathonite, Hiddai of the brooks of Gaash, Abi-albon the Arbathite, Azmaveth the Barhumite, Eliahba the Shaalbonite, of the sons of Jashen, Jonathan, Shammah the Hararite, Ahiam the son of Sharar the Hararite, Eliphelet the son of Ahasbai, the son of the Maachathite, Eliam the son of Ahithophel the Gilonite, Hezrai the Carmelite, Paarai the Arbite, Igal the son of Nathan of Zobah, Bani the Gadite, Zelek the Ammonite, Nahari the Beerothite, armor-bearer to Joab the son of Zeruiah, Ira an Ithrite, Bareb an Ithrite, Uriah the Hittite; thirty and seven in all.

22 AND again the anger of the Lord was kindled against Israel and he moved David against them to say, Go, number Israel and Judah. For the king said to Joab the captain of the host which was with him, Go now through all the tribes of Israel from Dan even to Beer-sheba and number ye the people that I may know the number of the people. And Joab said unto the king, Now the Lord thy God add unto the people, how many soever they be, a hundredfold, and that the eyes of my lord the king may see it but why doth my lord the king delight in this thing? Notwithstanding the king's word prevailed against Joab, and against the captains of the host. And Joab and the captains of the host went out from the presence of the king to number the people of Israel. And they passed over Jordan and pitched in Aroer on the right side of the city that lieth in the midst of the river of Gad and toward Jazer, then they came to Gilead and to the land of Tahtim-hodshi and they came to Dan-jaan and about to Zidon and came to the stronghold of Tyre and to all the cities of the Hivites and of the Canaanites and they went out to the south of Judah even to Beer-sheba. So when they had

gone through all the land they came to Jerusalem at the end of nine months and twenty days. And Joab gave up the sum of the number of the people unto the king, and there were in Israel eight hundred thousand valiant men that drew the sword; and the men of Judah were five hundred thousand men.

And David's heart smote him after that he had numbered the people. And David said unto the Lord, I have sinned greatly in that I have done and now I beseech thee O Lord, take away the iniquity of thy servant, for I have done very foolishly. For when David was up in the morning the word of the Lord came unto the prophet Gad, David's seer, saying, Go and say unto David, Thus saith the Lord, I offer thee three things, choose thee one of them, that I may do it unto thee. So Gad came to David and told him and said unto him, Shall seven years of famine come unto thee in thy land? Or wilt thou flee three months before thine enemies while they pursue thee? Or that there be three days' pestilence in thy land? Now advise and see what answer I shall return to him that sent me. And David said unto Gad, I am in a great strait, let us fall now into the hand of the Lord for his mercies are great and let me not fall into the hand of man.

So the Lord sent a pestilence upon Israel from the morning even to the time appointed; and there died of the people from Dan even to Beer-sheba seventy thousand men. And when the angel stretched out his hand upon Jerusalem to destroy it the Lord said unto him, Stay now thine hand it is enough for the people repented and the Lord stayed the hand of the angel, that he destroyed not the people. And the Angel of the Lord was by the threshing floor of Araunah the Jebusite. For David spake unto the Lord when he saw the angel that smote the people and said, Lo I have sinned and I have done wickedly, but these sheep, what have they done? Let thine hand I pray thee be against me and against my father's house.

And Gad came that day to David, and said unto him, Go up rear an altar unto the Lord in the threshing floor of Araunah the Jebusite. And David, according to the saying of Gad went up as the Lord commanded. And Arunah looked and saw the king and his servants coming on toward him and Arunah went out and bowed himself before the king on his face upon the ground. And Arunah said, Wherefore is my Lord the king come to his servant? And David said, To buy the threshing floor of thee to build an altar unto the Lord that the plague may be stayed from the people. And Araunah said unto David, Let my lord the king take and offer up what seemeth good unto him, behold here be oxen for burnt sacrifice and threshing instruments and other instruments of the oxen for wood. All these things did Arunah, as a king give unto

the king. And Araunah said unto the king, The Lord thy God accept thee. And the king said unto Arunah, Nay; but I will surely buy it of thee at a price, neither will I offer burnt offerings unto the Lord my God of that which doth cost me nothing. So David bought the threshing floor and the oxen for fifty shekels of silver. And David built there an altar unto the Lord and offered burnt offerings and peace offerings. So the Lord was entreated for the land and the plague was stayed from Israel.

THE FIRST BOOK OF THE KINGS

NOW king David was old and stricken in years; and they covered him with clothes, but he gat no heat. Wherefore his servants said unto him, Let there be sought for my lord the king a young virgin; and let her stand before the king, and let her cherish him, and let her lie in thy bosom, that my lord the king may get heat. So they sought for a fair damsel throughout all the coasts of Israel, and found Abishag a Shunammite, and brought her to the king. And the damsel was very fair, and cherished the king, and ministered to him; but the king knew her not.

Then Adonijah the son of Haggith exalted himself, saying, I will be king; and he prepared him chariots and horsemen, and fifty men to run before him. And his father had not displeased him at any time in saying, Why hast thou done so? and he also was a very goodly man; and his mother bare him after Absalom. And he conferred with Joab the son of Zeruiah, and with Abiathar the priest; and they following Adonijah helped him. But Zadok the priest, and Benaiah the son of Jehoiada, and Nathan the prophet, and Shimei, and Rei, and the mighty men which belonged to David, were not with Adonijah. And Adonijah slew sheep and oxen and fat cattle by the stone of Zoheleth, which is by En-rogel, and called all his brethren the king's sons, and all the men of Judah the king's servants; but Nathan the prophet, and Benaiah, and the mighty men, and Solomon his brother, he called not.

Wherefore Nathan spake unto Bath-sheba the mother of Solomon, saying, Hast thou not heard that Adonijah the son of Haggith doth reign, and David our lord knoweth it not? Now therefore come, let me, I pray thee, give thee counsel, that thou mayest save thine own life, and the life of thy son Solomon. Go and get thee in unto king David, and say unto him, Didst not thou, my lord O king, swear unto thine handmaid, saying, Assuredly Solomon thy son shall reign after me, and he shall sit upon my throne? why then doth Adonijah reign? Behold, while thou yet talkest there with the king, I also will come in after thee, and confirm thy words.

And Bath-sheba went in unto the king into the chamber; and the king was very old; and Abishag the Shunammite ministered unto the king. And Bath-sheba bowed, and did obeisance unto the king. And the king said, What wouldest thou? And she said unto him, My lord, thou swarest by the Lord thy God unto thine handmaid, saying, Assuredly Solomon thy son shall reign after me, and he shall sit upon my throne. And now, behold, Adonijah reigneth; and now, my lord the king, thou knowest it not; and he hath slain oxen and fat cattle and sheep in abundance, and hath called all the sons of the king, and Abiathar the priest, and Joab the captain of the host; but Solomon thy servant hath he not called. And thou, my lord, O king, the eyes of all Israel are upon thee, that thou shouldest tell them who shall sit on the throne of my lord the king after him. Otherwise it shall come to pass, when my lord the king shall sleep with his father, that I and my son Solomon shall be counted offenders.

And, lo, while she yet talked with the king, Nathan the prophet also came in. And they told the king, saying, Behold Nathan the prophet. And when he was come in before the king, he bowed himself before the king with his face to the ground. And Nathan said, My lord, O king, hast thou said, Adonijah shall reign after me, and he shall sit upon my throne? For he is gone down this day, and hath slain oxen and fat cattle and sheep in abundance, and hath called all the king's sons, and the captains of the host, and Abiathar the priest; and, behold, they eat and drink before him, and say, God save king Adonijah. But me, even me thy servant, and Zadok the priest, and Benaiah the son of Jehoiada, and thy servant Solomon, hath he not called. Is this thing done by my lord the king, and thou hast not showed it unto thy servant, who should sit on the throne of my lord the king after him?

Then king David answered and said, Call me Bath-sheba. And she came into the king's presence, and stood before the king. And the king sware, and said, As the Lord liveth, that hath redeemed my soul out of all distress, even as I sware unto thee by the Lord God of Israel, saying, Assuredly Solomon thy son shall reign after me, and he shall sit upon my throne in my stead; even so will I certainly do this day. Then Bath-sheba bowed with her face to the earth, and did reverence to the king, and said, Let my lord king David live forever.

And king David said, Call me Zadok the priest, and Nathan the prophet, and Benaiah the son of Jehoiada. And they came before the king. The king also said unto them, Take with you the servants of your lord, and cause Solomon my son to ride upon mine own mule, and bring him down to Gihon; and let Zadok the priest and Nathan the prophet anoint him there king over Israel; and blow ye with the trumpet, and say, God save king Solomon. Then ye shall come up after him, that he may come and sit upon my throne; for he shall be king in my stead; and I have appointed him to be ruler over Israel and over Judah. And Benaiah the son of Jehoiada answered the king, and said, Amen; the Lord God of my lord the king say so too. As the Lord hath been with my lord the king, even so be he with Solomon, and make his throne greater than the throne of my lord king David.

So Zadok the priest, and Nathan the prophet, and Benaiah the son of Jehoiada, and the Cherethites, and the Pelethites, went down, and caused Solomon to ride upon king David's mule, and brought him to Gihon. And Zadok the priest took a horn of oil out of the tabernacle, and anointed Solomon. And they blew the trumpet; and all the people said, God save king Solomon. And all the people came up after him, and the people piped with pipes, and rejoiced with great joy, so that the Earth rent with the sound of them.

And Adonijah and all the guests that were with him heard it as they had made an end of eating. And when Joab heard the sound of the trumpet, he said, Wherefore is this noise of the city being in an uproar? And while he yet spake, behold Jonathan the son of Abiathar the priest came; and Adonijah said unto him, Come in; for thou art a valiant man, and bringest good tidings. And Jonathan answered and said to Adonijah, Verily our lord king David hath made Solomon king. And the king hath sent with him Zadok the priest, and Nathan the prophet, and Benaiah the son of Jehoiada, and the Cherethites, and the Pelethites, and they have caused him to ride upon the king's mule; and Zadok the priest and Nathan the prophet have anointed him king in Gihon; and they are come up from thence rejoicing, so that the city rang again. This is the noise that ye have heard. And also Solomon sitteth on the throne of the kingdom. And moreover the king's servants came to bless our lord king David, saying, God make the name of Solomon better than thy name, and make his throne greater than thy throne. And the king bowed himself upon the bed. And also thus said the king, Blessed be the Lord God of Israel, which hath given one to sit on my throne this day, mine eyes even seeing it.

And all the guests that were with Adonijah were afraid, and rose up, and went every man his way. And Adonijah feared because of Solomon, and arose, and went, and caught hold on the horns of the altar. And it was told Solomon, saying, Behold, Adonijah feareth king Solomon; for, lo, he hath caught hold on the horns of the altar, saying, Let king Solomon swear unto me today that he will not slay his servant with the sword. And Solomon said, If he will show himself a worthy man, there shall not a hair of him fall to the earth; but if wickedness shall be found in him, he shall die. So king Solomon sent, and they brought him down from the altar. And he came and bowed himself to king Solomon; and Solomon said unto him, Go to thine house.

2 NOW the days of David drew nigh that he should die; and he charged Solomon his son, saying, I go the way of all the Earth; be thou strong therefore, and show thyself a man; and keep the charge of the Lord thy God, to walk in his ways, to keep his statutes, and his commandments, and his judgments, and his testimonies, as it is written in the law of Moses, that thou mayest prosper in all that thou doest, and whithersoever thou turnest thyself; that the Lord may continue his word

which he spake concerning me, saying, If thy children take heed to their way, to walk before me in truth with all their heart and with all their soul, there shall not fail thee (said he) a man on the throne of Israel.

Moreover thou knowest also what Joab the son of Zeruiah did to me, and what he did to the two captains of the hosts of Israel, unto Abner the son of Ner, and unto Amasa the son of Jether, whom he slew, and shed the blood of war in peace, and put the blood of war upon his girdle that was about his loins, and in his shoes that were on his feet. Do therefore according to thy wisdom, and let not his hoar head go down to the grave in peace. But show kindness unto the sons of Barzillai the Gileadite, and let them be of those that eat at thy table; for so they came to me when I fled because of Absalom thy brother. And, behold, thou hast with thee Shimei the son of Gera, a Benjamite of Bahurim, which cursed me with a grievous curse in the day when I went to Mahanaim; but he came down to meet me at Jordan, and I sware to him by the Lord, saying, I will not put thee to death with the sword. Now therefore hold him not guiltless; for thou art a wise man, and knowest what thou oughtest to do unto him; but his hoar head bring thou down to the grave with blood.

So David slept with his fathers, and was buried in the city of David. And the days that David reigned over Israel were forty years; seven years reigned he in Hebron, and thirty and three years reigned he in Jerusalem. Then sat Solomon upon the throne of David his father; and his kingdom was established greatly.

And Adonijah the son of Haggith came to Bath-sheba the mother of Solomon. And she said, Comest thou peaceably? And he said, Peaceably. He said moreover, I have somewhat to say unto thee. And she said, Say on. And he said, Thou knowest that the kingdom was mine, and that all Israel set their faces on me, that I should reign; howbeit the kingdom is turned about, and is become my brother's; for it was his from the Lord. And now I ask one petition of thee, deny me not. And she said unto him, Say on. And he said, Speak, I pray thee, unto Solomon the king, (for he will not say thee nay,) that he give me Abishag the Shunammite to wife. And Bath-sheba said, Well; I will speak for thee unto the king.

Bath-sheba therefore went unto king Solomon, to speak unto him for Adonijah. And the king rose up to meet her, and bowed himself unto her, and sat down on his throne, and caused a seat to be set for the king's mother; and she sat on his right hand. Then she said, I desire one small petition of thee; I pray thee, say me not nay. And the king said unto her, Ask on, my mother; for I will not say thee nay. And she said, Let Abishag the Shunammite be given to Adonijah thy brother to wife. And king Solomon answered and said unto his mother, And why dost thou ask Abishag the Shunammite for Adonijah? ask for him the kingdom also; for he is mine elder brother; even for him, and for Abiathar the priest, and for Joab the son of Zeruiah. Then king Solomon sware by the Lord, saying, God do so to me, and more also, if Adonijah have not spoken this word against his own life. Now therefore, as the Lord liveth, which hath established me, and set me on the throne of David my father, and who hath made me a house, as he promised, Adonijah shall be put to death this day. And king Solomon sent by the hand of Benaiah the son of Jehoiada; and he fell upon him that he died.

And unto Abiathar the priest said the king, Get thee to Anathoth, unto thine own fields; for thou art worthy of death; but I will not at this time put thee to death, because thou barest the ark of the Lord God before David my father, and because thou hast been afflicted in all wherein my father was afflicted. So Solomon thrust out Abiathar from being priest unto the Lord; that he might fulfill the word of the Lord, which he spake concerning the house of Eli in Shiloh.

Then tidings came to Joab; for Joab had turned after Adonijah, though he turned not after Absalom. And Joab fled unto the tabernacle of the Lord, and caught hold on the horns of the altar. And it was told king Solomon that Joab was fled unto the tabernacle of the Lord; and, behold, he is by the altar. Then Solomon sent Benaiah the son of Jehoiada, saying, Go, fall upon him. And Benaiah came to the tabernacle of the Lord, and said unto him, Thus saith the king, Come forth. And he said, Nay; but I will die here. And Benaiah brought the king word again, saying, Thus said Joab, and thus he answered me. And the king said unto him, Do as he hath said, and fall upon him, and bury him; that thou mayest take away the innocent blood, which Joab shed, from me, and from the house of my father. And the Lord shall return his blood upon his own head, who fell upon two men more righteous and better than he, and slew them with the sword, my father David not knowing thereof, to wit, Abner the son of Ner, captain of the host of Israel, and Amasa the son of Jether, captain of the host of Judah. Their blood shall therefore return upon the head of Joab, and upon the head of his seed forever; but upon David, and upon his seed, and upon his house, and upon his throne, shall there be peace for ever from the Lord. So Benaiah the son of Jehoiada went up, and fell upon him, and slew him; and he was buried in his own house in the wilderness. And the king put Benaiah the son of Jehoiada in his room over the host; and Zadok the priest did the king put in the room of Abiathar.

And the king sent and called for Shimei, and said unto him, Build thee a house in Jerusalem, and dwell there, and go not forth thence any whither. For it shall be, that on the day thou goest out, and passest over the brook Kidron, thou shalt know for certain that thou shalt surely die; thy blood shall be upon thine own head. And Shimei said unto the king, The saying is good; as my lord the king hath said, so will thy servant do. And Shimei dwelt in Jerusalem many days.

And it came to pass at the end of three years, that two of the servants of Shimei ran away unto Achish son of Maachah king of Gath. And they told Shimei, saying, Behold, thy servants be in Gath. And Shimei arose, and saddled his ass, and went to Gath to Achish to seek his servants; and Shimei went, and brought his servants from Gath. And it was told Solomon that Shimei had gone from Jerusalem to Gath, and was come again. And the king sent and called for Shimei, and said unto him, Did I not make thee to swear by the Lord, and protested unto thee, saying, Know for a certain, on the day thou goest out, and walkest abroad any whither, that thou shalt surely die? and thou saidst unto me, The word that I have heard is good. Why then hast thou not kept the oath of the Lord, and the commandment that I have charged thee with? The king said moreover to Shimei, Thou knowest all the wickedness which thine heart is privy to, that thou didst to David my father; therefore the Lord shall return thy wickedness upon thine own head; and king Solomon shall be blessed, and the throne of David shall be established before the Lord forever. So the king commanded Benaiah the son of Jehoiada; which went out, and fell upon him, that he died. And the kingdom was established in the hand of Solomon.

And the Lord was not pleased with Solomon, for he made affinity with Pharaoh, king of Egypt, and took Pharaoh's daughter to wife, and brought her into the house of David until he had made an end of building his own house, and the house of the Lord, and the wall of Jerusalem round about. And the Lord blessed Solomon for the people's sake only. And the people sacrificed in high places, because there was no house built unto the name of the Lord, until those days. And because the Lord blessed Solomon as he was walking in the statutes of David, his father, he began to love the Lord, and he sacrificed and burnt incense in high places, and he called on the name of the Lord. And the king went to Gibeon to sacrifice there, for Gibeon was in a great high place; and Solomon offered upon that altar, in Gibeon, a thousand burnt offerings.

And the Lord God hearkened unto Solomon, and appeared unto him in a dream by night, and said, Ask what I shall give thee. And Solomon said, Thou hast showed unto thy servant David, my father, great things according to thy mercy when he walked before thee in truth, and in righteousness, and in uprightness of heart with thee; and thou hast kept for him this great kindness, that thou hast given him a son to sit on his throne this day. And now, O Lord my God, thou hast made thy servant king, instead of David, my father, over thy people. And I know not how to lead them, to go out, or come in before them, and I, thy servant, am as a little child, in the midst of thy people whom thou hast chosen, a great people that cannot be numbered, nor counted for multitude. Give therefore thy servant an understanding heart to judge thy people, that I may discern between good and bad; for who is able to judge this thy people, so great a people? And the speech pleased the Lord, that Solomon had asked this thing. And God said unto him, Because thou hast asked this thing, and hast not asked for thyself long life; neither hast asked riches for thyself, nor hast asked the life of thine enemies; but hast asked for thyself understanding to discern judgment; behold, I have done according to thy word; lo, I have given thee a wise and an understanding heart; so that there was none made king over Israel like unto thee before thee, neither after thee shall any arise like unto thee. And I have also given thee that which thou hast not asked, both riches, and honor; so that there shall not be any among the kings like unto thee all thy days. And if thou wilt walk in my ways to keep my statutes, and my commandments, then I will lengthen thy days, and thou shalt not walk in unrighteousness, as did thy father David. And Solomon awoke; and, behold, it was a dream. And he came to Jerusalem, and stood before the ark of the covenant of the Lord, and offered up burnt offerings, and offered peace offerings, and made a feast to all his servants.

Then came there two women, that were harlots, unto the king, and stood before him. And the one woman said, O my lord, I and this woman dwell in one house; and I was delivered of a child with her in the house. And it came to pass the third day after that I was delivered, that this woman was delivered also; and we were together; there was no stranger with us in the house, save we two in the house. And this woman's child died in the night, because she overlaid it. And she arose at midnight, and took my son from beside me, while thine handmaid slept, and laid it in her bosom, and laid her dead child in my bosom. And when I rose in the morning to give my child suck, behold, it was dead; but when I had considered it in the morning, behold, it was not my son, which I did bear. And the other woman said, Nay; but the living is my son, and the dead is thy son. And this said, No; but the dead is thy son, and the living is my son. Thus they spake before the king.

Then said the king, The one saith, This is my son that liveth, and thy son is the dead; and the other saith, Nay; but thy son is the dead, and my son is the living. And the king said, Bring me a sword. And they brought a sword before the king. And the king said, Divide the living child in two, and give half to the one, and half to the other. Then spake the woman whose the living child was unto the king, for her bowels yearned upon her son, and she said, O my lord, give her the living child, and in no wise slay it. But the other said, Let it be neither mine nor thine, but divide it. Then the king answered and said, Give her the living child, and in no wise slay it; she is the mother thereof. And all Israel heard of the judgment which the king had judged; and they feared the king; for they saw that the wisdom of God was in him to do judgment.

So king Solomon was king over all Israel. And these were the princes which he had; Azariah the son of Zadok the priest, Elihoreph and Ahiah, the sons of Shisha, scribes; Jehoshaphat the son of Ahilud, the recorder. And Benaiah the son of Jehoiada was over the host; and Zadok and Abiathar were the priests;

and Azariah the son of Nathan was over the officers; and Zabud the son of Nathan was principal officer, and the king's friend; and Ahishar was over the household; and Adoniram the son of Abda was over the tribute.

And Solomon had twelve officers over all Israel, which provided victuals for the king and his household; each man his month in a year made provision. And these are their names; The son of Hur, in mount Ephraim; the son of Dekar, in Makaz, and in Shaalbim, and Beth-shemesh, and Elon-beth-hanan; the son of Hesed, in Aruboth; to him pertained Sochoh, and all the land of Hepher; the son of Abinadab, in all the region of Dor; which had Taphath the daughter of Solomon to wife; Baana the son of Ahilud; to him pertained Taanach and Megiddo, and all Beth-shean, which is by Zartanah beneath Jezreel, from Beth-shean to Abel-meholah, even unto the place that is beyond Jokneam; the son of Geber, in Ramothgilead; to him pertained the towns of Jair the son of Manasseh, which are in Gilead; to him also pertained the region of Argob, which is in Bashan, threescore great cities with walls and brazen bars; Ahinadab the son of Iddo had Mahanaim; Ahimaaz was in Naphtali; he also took Basmath the daughter of Solomon to wife; Baanah the son of Hushai was in Asher and in Aloth; Jehoshaphat the son of Paruah, in Issachar; Shimei the son of Elah, in Benjamin; Geber the son of Uri was in the country of Gilead, in the country of Sihon king of the Amorites, and of Og king of Bashan; and he was the only officer which was in the land.

Judah and Israel were many, as the sand which is by the sea in multitude, eating and drinking, and making merry.

And Solomon reigned over all kingdoms from the river unto the land of the Philistines, and unto the border of Egypt, they brought presents, and served Solomon all the days of his life.

And Solomon's provision for one day was thirty measures of fine flour, and threescore measures of meal. Ten fat oxen, and twenty oxen out of the pastures, and a hundred sheep, besides harts, and roebucks, and fallow deer, and fatted fowl. For he had dominion over all the region on this side the river, from Tiphsah even to Azzah, over all the kings on this side the river; and he had peace on all sides round about him. And Judah and Israel dwelt safely, every man under his vine and under his fig tree, from Dan even to Beer-sheba, all the days of Solomon. And Solomon had forty thousand stalls of horses for his chariots, and twelve thousand horsemen. And those officers provided victuals for king Solomon, and for all that came unto king Solomon's table, every man in his month; they lacked nothing. Barley also and straw for the horses and dromedaries brought they unto the place where the officers were, every man according to his charge.

And God gave Solomon wisdom and understanding exceeding much, and largeness of heart, even as the sand that is on the seashore. And Solomon's wisdom excelled the wisdom of all the children of the east country, and all the wisdom of Egypt. For he was wiser than all men, than Ethan the Ezrahite, and Heman, and Chalcol, and Darda, the sons of Mahol; and his fame was in all nations round about. And he spake three thousand proverbs; and his songs were a thousand and five. And he spake of trees, from the cedar tree that is in Lebanon even unto the hyssop that springeth out of the wall; he spake also of beasts, and of fowl, and of creeping things, and of fishes. And there came of all people to hear the wisdom of Solomon, from all kings of the Earth, which had heard of his wisdom.

And Hiram king of Tyre sent his servants unto Solomon; for he had heard that they had anointed him king in the room of his father; for Hiram was ever a lover of David. And Solomon sent to Hiram, saying, Thou knowest how that David my father could not build a house unto the name of the Lord his God, for the wars which were about him on every side, until the Lord put them under the soles of his feet. But now the Lord my God hath given me rest on every side, so that there is neither adversary nor evil occurrent. And, behold, I purpose to build a house unto the name of the Lord my God, as the Lord spake unto David my father, saying, Thy son, whom I will set upon thy throne in thy room, he shall build a house unto my name. Now therefore command thou that they hew me cedar trees out of Lebanon; and my servants shall be with thy servants; and unto thee will I give hire for thy servants according to all that thou shalt appoint; for thou knowest that there is not among us any that can skill to hew timber like unto the Sidonians.

And it came to pass, when Hiram heard the words of Solomon, that he rejoiced greatly, and said, Blessed be the Lord this day, which hath given unto David a wise son over this great people. And Hiram sent to Solomon, saying, I have considered the things which thou sentest to me for; and I will do all thy desire concerning timber of cedar, and concerning timber of fir. My servants shall bring them down from Lebanon unto the sea; and I will convey them by sea in floats unto the place that thou shalt appoint me, and will cause them to be discharged there, and thou shalt receive them; and thou shalt accomplish my desire, in giving food for my household. So Hiram gave Solomon cedar trees and fir trees according to all his desire. And Solomon gave Hiram twenty thousand measures of wheat for food to his household, and twenty measures of pure oil; thus gave Solomon to Hiram year by year. And the Lord gave Solomon wisdom, as he promised him; and there was peace between Hiram and Solomon; and they two made a league together.

And king Solomon raised a levy out of all Israel; and the levy was thirty thousand men. And he sent them to Lebanon, ten thousand a month by courses; a month they were in Lebanon, and two months at home; and Adoniram was over the levy. And Solomon had threescore and ten thousand that bare burdens, and fourscore thousand hewers in the mountains; besides the chief of Solomon's officers which were over the work, three thousand and three hundred, which ruled over the people that wrought in the work. And the king commanded, and they brought great stones, costly stones, and hewed stones, to lay the foundation of the house. And Solomon's builders and Hiram's builders did hew them, and the stone-squarers; so they prepared timber and stones to build the house.

And it came to pass in the four hundred and eightieth year after the children of Israel were come out of the land of Egypt, in the fourth year of Solomon's reign over Israel, in the month of Zif, which is the second month, that he began to build the house of the Lord. And the house which king Solomon built for the Lord, the length thereof was threescore cubits, and the breadth thereof twenty cubits, the height thereof thirty cubits. And the porch before the temple of the house, twenty cubits was the length thereof, according to the breadth of the house; and ten cubits was the breadth thereof before the house. And for the house he made windows of narrow lights.

And against the wall of the house he built chambers round about, against the walls of the house round about, both of the temple and of the oracle; and he made chambers round about. The nethermost chamber was five cubits broad, and the middle was six cubits broad, and the third was seven cubits broad; for without in the wall of the house he made narrowed rests round about, that the beams should not be fastened in the walls of the house. And the house, when it was in building, was built of stone made ready before it was brought thither; so that there was neither hammer nor axe nor any tool of iron heard in the house, while it was in building. The door for the middle chamber was in the right side of the house; and they went up with winding stairs into the middle chamber, and out of the middle into the third. So he built the house, and finished it; and covered the house with beams and boards of cedar. And then he built chambers against all the house, five cubits high; and they rested on the house with timber of cedar.

And the word of the Lord came to Solomon, saying, Concerning this house which thou art in building, if thou wilt walk in my statutes, and execute my judgments, and keep all my commandments to walk in them; then will I perform my word with thee which I spake unto David thy father; and I will dwell among the children of Israel, and will not forsake my people Israel.

So Solomon built the house, and finished it. And he built the walls of the house within with boards of cedar, both the floor of the house, and the walls of the ceiling; and he covered them on the inside with wood, and covered the floor of the house with planks of fir. And he built twenty cubits on the sides of the house, both the floor and the walls with boards of cedar; he even built them for it within, even for the oracle, even for the most holy place. And the house, that is, the temple before it, was forty cubits long. And the cedar of the house within was carved with knops and open flowers; all was cedar; there was no stone seen. And the oracle he prepared in the house within, to set there the ark of the covenant of the Lord. And the oracle in the forepart was twenty cubits in length, and twenty cubits in breadth, and twenty cubits in the height thereof; and he overlaid it with pure gold; and so covered the altar which was of cedar. So Solomon overlaid the house within with pure gold; and he made a partition by the chains of gold before the oracle; and he overlaid it with gold. And the whole house he overlaid with gold, until he had finished all the house; also the whole altar that was by the oracle he overlaid with gold.

And within the oracle he made two cherubim of olive tree, each ten cubits high. And five cubits was the one wing of the cherub, and five cubits the other wing of the cherub; from the uttermost part of the one wing unto the uttermost part of the other were ten cubits. And the other cherub was ten cubits; both the cherubim were of one measure and one size. The height of one cherub was ten cubits, and so was it of the other cherub. And he set the cherubim within the inner house; and they stretched forth the wings of the cherubim, so that the wing of the one touched the one wall, and the wing of the other cherub touched the other wall; and their wings touched one another in the midst of the house. And he overlaid the cherubim with gold. And he carved all the walls of the house round about with carved figures of cherubim and palm trees and open flowers, within and without. And the floor of the house he overlaid with gold, within and without.

And for the entering of the oracle he made doors of olive tree; the lintel and side posts were a fifth part of the wall. The two doors also were of olive tree; and he carved upon them carvings of cherubim and palm trees and open flowers, and overlaid them with gold, and spread gold upon the cherubim, and upon the palm trees. So also made he for the door of the temple posts of olive tree, a fourth part of the wall. And the two doors were of fir tree; the two leaves of the one door were folding, and the two leaves of the other door were folding. And he carved thereon cherubim and palm trees and open flowers; and covered them with gold fitted upon the carved work.

And he built the inner court with three rows of hewed stone, and a row of cedar beams. In the fourth year was the foundation of the house of the Lord laid, in the month Zif; and in the eleventh year, in the month Bul, which is the eighth month, was the house finished throughout all the parts thereof, and according to all the fashion of it. So was he seven years in building it.

But Solomon was building his own house thirteen years, and he finished all his house. He built also the house of the forest of Lebanon; the length thereof was a hundred cubits, and the breadth thereof fifty cubits, and the height thereof thirty cubits, upon four rows of cedar pillars, with cedar beams upon the pillars. And it was covered with cedar above upon the beams, that lay on forty-five pillars, fifteen in a row. And there were windows in three rows, and light was against light in three ranks. And all the doors and posts were square, with the windows;

and light was against light in three ranks. And he made a porch of pillars; the length thereof was fifty cubits, and the breadth thereof thirty cubits; and the porch was before them; and the other pillars and the thick beam were before them. Then he made a porch for the throne where he might judge, even the porch of judgment; and it was covered with cedar from one side of the floor to the other. And his house where he dwelt had another court within the porch, which was of the like work. Solomon made also a house for Pharaoh's daughter, whom he had taken to wife, like unto his porch. All these were of costly stones, according to the measure of hewed stones, sawed with saws, within and without, even from the foundation unto the coping, and so on the outside toward the great court. And the foundation was of costly stones, even great stones, stones of ten cubits, and stones of eight cubits. And above were costly stones, after the measures of hewed stones, and cedars. And the great court round about was with three rows of hewed stones, and a row of cedar beams, both for the inner court of the house of the Lord, and for the porch of the house.

And king Solomon sent and fetched Hiram out of Tyre. He was a widow's son of the tribe of Naphtali, and his father was a man of Tyre, a worker in brass; and he was filled with wisdom, and understanding, and cunning to work all works in brass. And he came to king Solomon, and wrought all his work. For he cast two pillars of brass of eighteen cubits high apiece; and a line of twelve cubits did compass either of them about. And he made two chapiters of molten brass, to set upon the tops of the pillars; the height of the one chapiter was five cubits, and the height of the other chapiter was five cubits; and nets of checker work, and wreaths of chain work, for the chapiters which were upon the top of the pillars; seven for the one chapiter, and seven for the other chapiter. And he made the pillars, and two rows round about upon the one network, to cover the chapiters that were upon the top, with pomegranates; and so did he for the other chapiter. And the chapiters that were upon the top of the pillars were of lily work in the porch, four cubits. And the chapiters upon the two pillars had pomegranates also above, over against the belly which was by the network; and the pomegranates were two hundred in rows round about upon the other chapiter. And he set up the pillars in the porch of the temple; and he set up the right pillar, and called the name thereof Jachin; and he set up the left pillar, and called the name thereof Boaz. And upon the top of the pillars was lily work; so was the work of the pillars finished.

And he made a molten sea, ten cubits from the one brim to the other; it was round all about, and his height was five cubits; and a line of thirty cubits did compass it round about. And under the brim of it round about there were knops compassing it, ten in a cubit, compassing the sea round about; the knops were cast in two rows, when it was cast. It stood upon twelve oxen, three looking toward the north, and three looking toward the west, and three looking toward the south, and three looking toward the east; and the sea was set above upon them, and all their hinder parts were inward. And it was a handbreadth thick, and the brim thereof was wrought like the brim of a cup, with flowers of lilies; it contained two thousand baths.

And he made ten bases of brass; four cubits was the length of one base, and four cubits the breadth thereof, and three cubits the height of it. And the work of the bases was on this manner; they had borders, and the borders were between the ledges; and on the borders that were between the ledges were lions, oxen, and cherubim; and upon the ledges there was a base above; and beneath the lions and oxen were certain additions made of thin work. And every base had four brazen wheels, and plates of brass; and the four corners thereof had undersetters; under the laver were undersetters molten, at the side of every addition. And the mouth of it within the chapiter and above was a cubit; but the mouth thereof was round after the work of the base, a cubit and a half; and also upon the mouth of it were gravings with their borders, foursquare, not round. And under the borders were four wheels; and the axletrees of the wheels were joined to the base; and the height of a wheel was a cubit and half a cubit. And the work of the wheels was like the work of a chariot wheel; their axletrees, and their naves, and their felloes, and their spokes, were all molten. And there were four undersetters to the four corners of one base; and the undersetters were of the very base itself. And in the top of the base was there a round compass of half a cubit high; and on the top of the base the ledges thereof and the border thereof were of the same. For on the plates of the ledges thereof, and on the borders thereof, he graved cherubim, lions, and palm trees, according to the proportion of every one, and additions round about. After this manner he made the ten bases; all of them had one casting, one measure, and one size.

Then made he ten lavers of brass; one laver contained forty baths; and every laver was four cubits; and upon every one of the ten bases one laver. And he put five bases on the right side of the house, and five on the left side of the house; and he set the sea on the right side of the house eastward, over against the south.

And Hiram made the lavers, and the shovels, and the basins. So Hiram made an end of doing all the work that he made king Solomon for the house of the Lord. The two pillars, and the two bowls of the chapiters that were on the top of the two pillars; and the two networks, to cover the two bowls of the chapiters which were upon the top of the pillars; and four hundred pomegranates for the two networks, even two rows of pomegranates for one network, to cover the two bowls of the chapiters that were upon the pillars; and the ten bases, and ten lavers on the bases; and one sea, and twelve oxen under the sea; and the pots, and the shovels, and the basins; and all these vessels, which Hiram made to king Solomon for the house of the Lord, were of bright brass. In the plain of Jordan did the king cast them, in the clay ground between Succoth and Zarthan. And Solomon left all the vessels unweighed, because they were exceeding many; neither was the weight of the brass found out.

And Solomon made all the vessels that pertained unto the house of the Lord; the altar of gold, and the table of gold, whereupon the shewbread was. And the candlesticks of pure gold, five on the right side, and five on the left, before the oracle, with the flowers, and the lamps, and the tongs of gold. And the bowls, and the snuffers, and the basins, and the spoons, and the censers of pure gold; and the hinges of gold, both for the doors of the inner house, the most holy place, and for the doors of the house, to wit, of the temple.

So was ended all the work that king Solomon made for the house of the Lord. And Solomon brought in the things which David his father had dedicated; even the silver, and the gold, and the vessels, did he put among the treasures of the house of the Lord.

Then Solomon assembled the elders of Israel, and all the heads of the tribes, the chief of the fathers of the children of Israel, unto king Solomon in Jerusalem, that they might bring up the ark of the covenant of the Lord out of the city of David, which is Zion. And all the men of Israel assembled themselves unto king Solomon at the feast in the month Ethanim, which is the seventh month. And all the elders of Israel came, and the priests took up the ark. And they brought up the ark of the Lord, and the tabernacle of the congregation, and all the holy vessels that were in the tabernacle, even those did the priests and the Levites bring up. And king Solomon, and all the congregation of Israel, that were assembled unto him, where with him before the ark, sacrificing sheep and oxen that could not be told nor numbered for multitude. And the priests brought in the ark of the covenant of the Lord unto his place, into the oracle of the house, to the most holy place, even under the wings of the cherubim. For the cherubim spread forth their two wings over the place of the ark, and the cherubim covered the ark and the staves thereof above. And they drew out the staves, that the ends of the staves were seen out in the holy place before the oracle, and they were not seen without; and there they are unto this day. There was nothing in the ark save the two tables of stone, which Moses put there at Horeb, when the Lord made a covenant with the children of Israel, when they came out of the land of Egypt.

And it came to pass, when the priests were come out of the holy place, that the cloud filled the house of the Lord. So that the priests could not stand to minister because of the cloud; for the glory of the Lord had filled the house of the Lord. Then spake Solomon, The Lord said that he would dwell in the thick darkness. I have surely built thee a house to dwell in, a settled place for thee to abide in forever. And the king turned his face about, and blessed all the congregation of Israel; and all the congregation of Israel stood; and he said, Blessed be the Lord God of Israel, which spake with his mouth unto David my father, and hath with his hand fulfilled it, saying, Since the day that I brought forth my people Israel out of Egypt, I chose no city out of all the tribes of Israel to build a house, that my name might be therein; but I chose David to be over my people Israel. And it was in the heart of David my father to build a house for the name of the Lord God of Israel. And the Lord said unto David my father, Whereas it was in thine heart to build a house unto my name, thou didst well that it was in thine heart. Nevertheless thou shalt not build the house; but thy son that shall come forth out of thy loins, he shall build the house unto my name. And the Lord hath performed his word that he spake, and I am risen up in the room of David my father, and sit on the throne of Israel, as the Lord promised, and have built a house for the name of the Lord God of Israel. And I have set there a place for the ark, wherein is the covenant of the Lord, which he made with our fathers, when he brought them out of the land of Egypt.

And Solomon stood before the altar of the Lord in the presence of all the congregation of Israel, and spread forth his hands toward Heaven; and he said, Lord God of Israel, there is no God like thee, in Heaven above, or on Earth beneath, who keepest covenant and mercy with thy servants that walk before thee with all their heart; who hast kept with thy servant David my father that thou promisedst him; thou spakest also with thy mouth, and hast fulfilled it with thine hand, as it is this day. Therefore now, Lord God of Israel, keep with thy servant David my father that thou promisedst him, saying, There shall not fail thee a man in my sight to sit on the throne of Israel; so that thy children take heed to their way, that they walk before me as thou hast walked before me. And now, O God of Israel, let thy word, I pray thee, be verified, which thou spakest unto thy servant David my father.

But will God indeed dwell on the Earth? behold, the Heaven and Heaven of heavens cannot contain thee; how much less this house that I have builded? Yet have thou respect unto the prayer of thy servant, and to his supplication, O Lord my God, to hearken unto the cry and to the prayer, which thy servant prayeth before thee today; that thine eyes may be open toward this house night and day, even toward the place of which thou hast said, My name shall be there; that thou mayest hearken unto the prayer which thy servant shall make toward this place. And hearken thou to the supplication of thy servant, and of thy people Israel, when they shall pray toward this place; and hear thou in Heaven thy dwelling place; and when thou hearest, forgive.

If any man trespass against his neighbor, and an oath be laid upon him to cause him to swear, and the oath come before thine altar in this house; then hear thou in Heaven, and do, and judge thy servants, condemning the wicked, to bring his way upon his head; and justifying the righteous, to give him according to his righteousness.

When thy people Israel be smitten down before the enemy, because they have sinned against thee, and shall turn again to thee, and confess thy name, and pray, and make supplication unto thee in this house; then hear thou in Heaven, and forgive the sin of thy people Israel, and bring them again unto the land which thou gavest unto their fathers.

When Heaven is shut up, and there is no rain, because they have sinned against thee; if they pray toward this place, and confess thy name, and turn from their sin, when thou afflictest them; then hear thou in Heaven, and forgive the sin of thy servants, and of thy people Israel, that thou teach them the good way wherein they should walk, and give rain upon thy land, which thou hast given to thy people for an inheritance.

If there be in the land famine, if there be pestilence, blasting, mildew, locust, or if there be caterpillar; if their enemy besiege them in the land of their cities; whatsoever plague, whatsoever sickness there be; what prayer and supplication soever be made by any man, or by all thy people Israel, which shall know every man the plague of his own heart, and spread forth his hands toward this house; then hear thou in Heaven thy dwelling place, and forgive, and do, and give to every man according to his ways, whose heart thou knowest; (for thou, even thou only, knowest the hearts of all the children of men;) that they may fear thee all the days that they live in the land which thou gavest unto our fathers.

Moreover concerning a stranger, that is not of thy people Israel, but cometh out of a far country for thy name's sake; (for they shall hear of thy great name and of thy strong hand, and of thy stretched out arm;) when he shall come and pray toward this house; hear thou in Heaven thy dwelling place, and do according to all that the stranger calleth to thee for; that all people of the Earth may know thy name, to fear thee, as do thy people Israel; and that they may know that this house, which I have builded, is called by thy name.

If thy people go out to battle against their enemy, whithersoever thou shalt send them, and shall pray unto the Lord toward the city which thou hast chosen, and toward the house that I have built for thy name; then hear thou in Heaven their prayer and their supplication, and maintain their cause. If they sin against thee, (for there is no man that sinneth not,) and thou be angry with them, and deliver them to the enemy, so that they carry them away captives unto the land of the enemy, far or near; yet if they shall bethink themselves in the land whither they were carried captives, and repent, and make supplication unto thee in the land of them that carried them captives, saying, We have sinned, and have done perversely, we have committed wickedness; and so return unto thee with all their heart, and with all their soul, in the land of their enemies, which led them away captive, and pray unto thee toward their land, which thou gavest unto their fathers, the city which thou hast chosen, and the house which I have built for thy name; then hear thou their prayer and their supplication in Heaven thy dwelling place, and maintain their cause, and forgive thy people that have sinned against thee, and all their transgressions wherein they have transgressed against thee, and give them compassion before them who carried them captive, that they may have compassion on them; for they be thy people, and thine inheritance, which thou broughtest forth out of Egypt, from the midst of the furnace of iron; that thine eyes may be open unto the supplication of thy servant, and unto the supplication of thy people Israel, to hearken unto them in all that they call for unto thee. For thou didst separate them from among all the people of the Earth, to be thine inheritance, as thou spakest by the hand of Moses thy servant, when thou broughtest our fathers out of Egypt, O Lord God.

And it was so, that when Solomon had made an end of praying all this prayer and supplication unto the Lord, he arose from before the altar of the Lord, from kneeling on his knees with his hands spread up to Heaven. And he stood, and blessed all the congregation of Israel with a loud voice, saying, Blessed be the Lord, that hath given rest unto his people Israel, according to all that he promised; there hath not failed one word of all his good promise, which he promised by the hand of Moses his servant. The Lord our God be with us, as he was with our fathers; let him not leave us, nor forsake us; that he may incline our hearts unto him, to walk in all his ways, and to keep his commandments, and his statutes, and his judgments, which he commanded our fathers. And let these my words, wherewith I have made supplication before the Lord, be nigh unto the Lord our God day and night, that he maintain the cause of his servant, and the cause of his people Israel at all times, as the matter shall require; that all the people of the Earth may know that the Lord is God, and that there is none else. Let your heart therefore be perfect with the Lord our God, to walk in his statutes, and to keep his commandments, as at this day.

And the king, and all Israel with him, offered sacrifice before the Lord. And Solomon offered a sacrifice of peace offerings which he offered unto the Lord, two and twenty thousand oxen, and a hundred and twenty thousand sheep. So the king and all the children of Israel dedicated the house of the Lord. The same day did the king hallow the middle of the court that was before the house of the Lord; for there he offered burnt offerings, and meat offering, and the fat of the peace offerings; because the brazen altar that was before the Lord was too little to receive the burnt offerings, and meat offerings, and the fat of the peace offerings. And at that time Solomon held a feast, and all Israel with him, a great congregation, from the entering in of Hamath unto the river of Egypt, before the Lord our God, seven days and seven days, even fourteen days. On the eighth day he sent the people away; and they blessed the king, and went unto their tents joyful and glad of heart for all the goodness that the Lord had done for David his servant, and for Israel his people.

And it came to pass, when Solomon had finished the building of the house of the Lord, and the king's house, and all Solomon's desire which he was pleased to do, that the Lord appeared to Solomon the second time, as he had appeared unto him at Gibeon. And the Lord said unto him, I have heard thy prayer and thy supplication, that thou hast made before me; I have hallowed this house, which thou hast built, to put my name there forever; and mine eyes and mine heart shall be there perpetually. And if thou wilt walk before me, as David thy father walked, in integrity of heart, and in uprightness, to do according to all that I have commanded thee, and wilt keep my statutes and my judgments; then I will establish the throne of thy kingdom upon Israel forever, as I promised to David thy father, saying, There shall not fail thee a man upon the throne of Israel. But if ye shall at all turn from following me, ye or your children, and will not keep my commandments and statutes which I have set before you, but go and serve other gods, and worship them; then will I cut off Israel out of the land which I have given them, and this house, which I have hallowed for my name, will I cast out of my sight; and Israel shall be a proverb and a byword among all people; and at this house, which is high, every one that passeth by it shall be astonished, and shall hiss; and they shall say, Why hath the Lord done thus unto this land, and to this house? And they shall answer, Because they forsook the Lord their God, who brought forth their fathers out of the land of Egypt, and have taken hold upon other gods, and have worshiped them, and served them; therefore hath the Lord brought upon them all this evil.

And it came to pass at the end of twenty years, when Solomon had built the two houses, the house of the Lord, and the king's house, (now Hiram the king of Tyre had furnished Solomon with cedar trees and fir trees, and with gold, according to all his desire,) that then king Solomon gave Hiram twenty cities in the land of Galilee. And Hiram came out from Tyre to see the cities which Solomon had given him; and they pleased him not. And he said, What cities are these which thou hast given me, my brother? And he called them the land of Cabul unto this day. And Hiram sent to the king sixscore talents of gold.

And this is the reason of the levy which king Solomon raised; for to build the house of the Lord, and his own house, and Millo, and the wall of Jerusalem, and Hazor, and Megiddo, and Gezer. For Pharaoh king of Egypt had gone up, and taken Gezer, and burnt it with fire, and slain the Canaanites that dwelt in the city, and given it for a present unto his daughter, Solomon's wife. And Solomon built Gezer, and Beth-horon the nether, and Baalath, and Tadmor in the wilderness, in the land, and all the cities of store that Solomon had, and cities for his chariots, and cities for his horsemen, and that which Solomon desired to build in Jerusalem, and in Lebanon, and in all the land of his dominion. And all the people that were left of the Amorites, Hittites, Perizzites, Hivites, and Jebusites, which were not of the children of Israel, their children that were left after them in the land, whom the children of Israel also were not able utterly to destroy, upon those did Solomon levy a tribute of bondservice unto this day. But of the children of Israel did Solomon make no bondmen; but they were men of war, and his servants, and his princes, and his captains, and rulers of his chariots, and his horsemen. These were the chief of the officers that were over Solomon's work, five hundred and fifty, which bare rule over the people that wrought in the work. But Pharaoh's daughter came up out of the city of David unto her house which Solomon had built for her; then did he build Millo. And three times in a year did Solomon offer burnt offerings and peace offerings upon the altar which he built unto the Lord, and he burnt incense upon the altar that was before the Lord. So he finished the house.

And king Solomon made a navy of ships in Ezion-geber, which is beside Eloth, on the shore of the Red Sea, in the land of Edom. And Hiram sent in the navy his servants, shipmen that had knowledge of the sea, with the servants of Solomon. And they came to Ophir, and fetched from thence gold, four hundred and twenty talents, and brought it to king Solomon.

And when the queen of Sheba heard of the fame of Solomon concerning the name of the Lord, she came to prove him with hard questions. And she came to Jerusalem with a very great train, with camels that bare spices, and very much gold, and precious stones; and when she was come to Solomon, she communed with him of all that was in her heart. And Solomon told her all her questions; there was not anything hid from the king, which he told her not. And when the queen of Sheba had seen all Solomon's wisdom, and the house that he had built, and the meat of his table, and the sitting of his servants, and the attendance of his ministers, and their apparel, and his cup-bearers, and his ascent by which he went up unto the house of the Lord; there was no more spirit in her. And she said to the king, It was a true report that I heard in mine own land of thy acts and of thy wisdom. Howbeit I believed not the words, until I came, and mine eyes had seen it; and, behold, the half was not told me; thy wisdom and prosperity exceedeth the fame which I heard. Happy are thy men, happy are these thy servants, which stand continually before thee, and that hear thy wisdom. Blessed be the Lord thy God, which delighted in thee, to set thee on the throne of Israel; because the Lord loved Israel forever, therefore made he thee king, to do judgment and justice. And she gave the king a hundred and twenty talents of gold, and of spices very great store, and precious stones; there came no more such abundance of spices as these which the queen of Sheba gave to king Solomon.

And the navy also of Hiram, that brought gold from Ophir, brought in from Ophir great plenty of almug trees, and precious stones. And the king made of the almug trees pillars for the house of the Lord, and for the king's house, harps also and psalteries for singers; there came no such almug trees, nor were seen unto this day.

And king Solomon gave unto the queen of Sheba all her desire, whatsoever she asked, besides that which Solomon gave her of his royal bounty. So she turned and went to her own country, she and her servants.

Now the weight of gold that came to Solomon in one year was six hundred threescore and six talents of gold. Besides that he had of the merchantmen, and of the traffic of the spice merchants, and of all the kings of Arabia, and of the governors of the country. And king Solomon made two hundred targets of beaten gold; six hundred shekels of gold went to one target. And he made three hundred shields of beaten gold; three pounds of gold went to one shield; and the king put them in the house of the forest of Lebanon. Moreover, the king made a great throne of ivory, and overlaid it with the best gold. The throne had six steps, and the top of the throne was round behind; and there were stays on either side on the place of the seat, and two lions stood beside the stays. And twelve lions stood there on the one side and on the other upon the six steps; there was not the like made in any kingdom. And all king Solomon's drinking vessels were of gold, and all the vessels of the house of the forest of Lebanon were of pure gold; none were of silver; it was nothing accounted of in the days of Solomon. For the king had at sea a navy of Tharshish with the navy of Hiram; once in three years came the navy of Tharshish, bringing gold, and silver, ivory, and apes, and peacocks.

So king Solomon exceeded all the kings of the Earth for riches and for wisdom. And all the earth sought to Solomon, to hear his wisdom, which God had put in his heart. And they brought every man his present, vessels of silver, and vessels of gold, and garments, and armor, and spices, horses, and mules, a rate year by year.

And Solomon gathered together chariots and horsemen; and he had a thousand and four hundred chariots, and twelve thousand horsemen, whom he bestowed in the cities for chariots, and with the king at Jerusalem. And the king made silver to be in Jerusalem as stones, and cedars made he to be as the sycamore trees that are in the vale, for abundance. And Solomon had horses brought out of Egypt, and linen yarn; the king's merchants received the linen yarn at a price. And a chariot came up and went out of Egypt for six hundred shekels of silver, and a horse for a hundred and fifty; and so for all the kings of the Hittites, and for the kings of Syria, did they bring them out by their means.

But king Solomon loved many strange women, together with the daughter of Pharaoh, women of the Moabites, Ammonites, Edomites, Zidonians, and Hittites; of the nations concerning which the Lord said unto the children of Israel, Ye shall not go in to them, neither shall they come in unto you; for surely they will turn away your heart after their gods; Solomon clave unto these in love. And he had seven hundred wives, princesses, and three hundred concubines; and his wives turned away his heart. For it came to pass, when Solomon was old, his wives turned away his heart after other gods; and his heart was not perfect with the Lord his God, and it became as the heart of David his father. For Solomon went after Ashtoreth the goddess of the Zidonians, and after Milcom the abomination of the Ammonites. And Solomon did evil in the sight of the Lord, as David his father, and went not fully after the Lord. Then did Solomon build a high place for Chemosh, the abomination of Moab, in the hill that is before Jerusalem, and for Molech, the abomination of the children of Ammon. And likewise did he for all his strange wives, which burnt incense and sacrificed unto their gods.

And the Lord was angry with Solomon, because his heart was turned from the Lord God of Israel, which had appeared unto him twice, and had commanded him concerning this thing, that he should not go after other gods; but he kept not that which the Lord commanded. Wherefore the Lord said unto Solomon, Forasmuch as this is done of thee, and thou hast not kept my covenant and my statutes, which I have commanded thee, I will surely rend the kingdom from thee, and will give it to thy servant. Notwithstanding, in thy days I will not do it for David thy father's sake; but I will rend it out of the hand of thy son. Howbeit I will not rend away all the kingdom; but will give one tribe to thy son for David my servant's sake, and for Jerusalem's sake which I have chosen.

And the Lord stirred up an adversary unto Solomon, Hadad the Edomite; he was of the king's seed in Edom. For it came to pass, when David was in Edom, and Joab the captain of the host was gone up to bury the slain, after he had smitten every male in Edom; (for six months did Joab remain there with all Israel, until he had cut off every male in Edom;) that Hadad fled, he and certain Edomites of his father's servants with him, to go into Egypt; Hadad being yet a little child. And they arose out of Midian, and came to Paran; and they took men with them out of Paran, and they came to Egypt, unto Pharaoh king of Egypt; which gave him a house, and appointed him victuals, and gave him land. And Hadad found great favor in the sight of Pharaoh, so that he gave him to wife, the sister of his own wife, the sister of Tahpenes the queen. And the sister of Tahpenes bare him Genubath his son, whom Tahpenes weaned in Pharaoh's house; and Genubath was in Pharaoh's household among the sons of Pharaoh. And when Hadad heard in Egypt that David slept with his fathers, and that Joab the captain of the host was dead, Hadad said to Pharaoh, Let me depart, that I may go to mine own country. Then Pharaoh said unto him, But what hast thou lacked with me, that, behold, thou seekest to go to thine own country? And he answered, Nothing; howbeit let me go in any wise.

And God stirred him up another adversary, Rezon the son of Eliadah, which fled from his lord Hadadezer king of Zobah; and he gathered men unto him, and became captain over a band, when David slew them of Zobah; and they went to Damascus, and dwelt therein, and reigned in Damascus. And he was an adversary to Israel all the days of Solomon, besides the mischief that Hadad did; and he abhorred Israel, and reigned over Syria.

And Jeroboam, the son of Nebat, an Ephrathite of Zereda, Solomon's servant, whose mother's name was Zeruah, a widow woman, even he lifted up his hand against the king. And this was the cause that he lifted up his hand against the king; Solomon built Millo, and repaired the breaches of the city of David his father. And the man Jeroboam was a mighty man of valor; and Solomon seeing the young man that he was industrious, he made him ruler over all the charge of the house of Joseph. And it came to pass at that time when Jeroboam went out of Jerusalem, that the prophet Ahijah the Shilonite found him in the way; and he had clad himself with a new garment; and they two were alone in the field; and Ahijah caught the new garment that was on him, and rent it in twelve pieces; and he said to Jeroboam, Take thee ten pieces; for thus saith the Lord, the God of Israel, Behold, I will rend the kingdom out of the hand of Solomon, and will give ten tribes to thee; (but he shall have one tribe for my servant David's sake, and for Jerusalem's sake, the city which I have chosen out of all the tribes of Israel;) because that they have forsaken me, and have worshiped Ashtoreth the goddess of the Zidonians, Chemosh the god of the Moabites, and Milcom the god of the children of Ammon, and have not walked in my ways, to do that which is right in mine eyes, and my statutes, and my judgments, and his heart is become as David his father; and he repenteth not as did David his father, that I may forgive him. Howbeit, I will not take the whole kingdom out of his hand, but I will make him prince all the days of his life, for David my servant's sake, whom I chose, because he kept my commandments and my statutes in that day.

But I will take the kingdom out of his son's hand, and will give unto thee ten tribes. And unto his son will I give one tribe. That David my servant may have a light always before me in Jerusalem, the city which I have chosen me to put my name there. And I will take thee, and thou shalt reign according to all that thy soul desireth, and shall be king over Israel. And it shall be, if thou wilt hearken unto all that I command thee, and wilt walk in my ways, and do right in my sight, to keep my statutes and my commandments, as David my servant did in the day that I blessed him; I will be with thee, and build thee a sure house as I built for David, and gave Israel unto thee. And for the transgression of David, and also for the people, I have rent the kingdom, and for this I will afflict the seed of David, but not forever. Solomon sought therefore to kill Jeroboam. And Jeroboam arose, and fled into Egypt, unto Shishak king of Egypt, and was in Egypt until the death of Solomon.

And the rest of the acts of Solomon, and all that he did, and his wisdom, are they not written in the book of the acts of Solomon? And the time that Solomon reigned in Jerusalem over all Israel was forty years. And Solomon slept with his fathers, and was buried in the city of David his father; and Rehoboam his son reigned in his stead.

3 AND Rehoboam went to Shechem; for all Israel were come to Shechem to make him king. And it came to pass, when Jeroboam the son of Nebat, who was yet in Egypt, heard it, (for he was fled from the presence of king Solomon, and Jeroboam dwelt in Egypt,) that they sent and called him. And Jeroboam and all the congregation of Israel came, and spake unto Rehoboam, saying, Thy father made our yoke grievous; now therefore make thou the grievous service of thy father, and his heavy yoke which he put upon us, lighter, and we will serve thee. And he said unto them, Depart yet for three days, then come again to me. And the people departed.

And king Rehoboam consulted with the old men, that stood before Solomon his father while he yet lived, and said, How do ye advise that I may answer this people? And they spake unto him, saying, If thou wilt be a servant unto this people this day, and wilt serve them, and answer them, and speak good words to them, then they will be thy servants forever. But he forsook the counsel of the old men, which they had given him, and consulted with the young men that were grown up with him, and which stood before him; and he said unto them, What counsel give ye that we may answer this people, who have spoken to me, saying, Make the yoke which thy father did put upon us lighter? And the young men that were grown up with him spake unto him, saying, Thus shalt thou speak unto this people that spake unto thee, saying, Thy father made our yoke heavy, but make thou it lighter unto us; thus shalt thou say unto them, My little finger shall be thicker than my father's loins. And now whereas my father did lade you with a heavy yoke, I will add to your yoke; my father hath chastised you with whips, but I will chastise you with scorpions.

So Jeroboam and all the people came to Rehoboam the third day, as the king had appointed, saying, Come to me again the third day. And the king answered the people roughly, and forsook the old men's counsel that they gave him; and spake to them after the counsel of the young men, saying, My father made your yoke heavy, and I will add to your yoke; my father also chastised you with whips, but I will chastise you with scorpions. Wherefore the king hearkened not unto the people; for the cause was from the Lord, that he might perform his saying, which the Lord spake by Ahijah the Shilonite unto Jeroboam the son of Nebat.

So when all Israel saw that the king hearkened not unto them, the people answered the king, saying, What portion have we in David? neither have we inheritance in the son of Jesse; to your tents, O Israel; now see to thine own house, David.

So Israel departed into their tents. But as for the children of Israel which dwelt in the cities of Judah, Rehoboam reigned over them. Then king Rehoboam sent Adoram, who was over the tribute; and all Israel stoned him with stones, that he died. Therefore king Rehoboam made speed to get him up to his chariot, to flee to Jerusalem. So Israel rebelled against the house of David unto this day. And it came to pass, when all Israel heard that Jeroboam was come again, that they sent and called him unto the congregation, and made him king over all Israel; there was none that followed the house of David, but the tribe of Judah only.

And when Rehoboam was come to Jerusalem, he assembled all the house of Judah, with the tribe of Benjamin, a hundred and fourscore thousand chosen men, which were warriors, to fight against the house of Israel, to bring the kingdom again to Rehoboam the son of Solomon. But the word of God came unto Shemaiah the man of God, saying, Speak unto Rehoboam, the son of Solomon, king of Judah, and unto all the house of Judah and Benjamin, and to the remnant of the people, saying, Thus saith the Lord, Ye shall not go up, nor fight against your brethren the children of Israel; return every man to his house; for this thing is from me. They hearkened therefore to the word of the Lord, and returned to depart, according to the word of the Lord.

Then Jeroboam built Shechem in mount Ephraim, and dwelt therein; and went out from thence, and built Penuel. And Jeroboam said in his heart, Now shall the kingdom return to the house of David. If this people go up to do sacrifice in the house of the Lord at Jerusalem, then shall the heart of this people turn again unto their lord, even unto Rehoboam king of Judah, and they shall kill me, and go again to Rehoboam king of Judah. Whereupon the king took counsel, and made two calves of gold, and said unto them, It is too much for you to go up to Jerusalem; behold thy gods, O Israel, which brought thee up out of the land of Egypt. And he set the one in Beth-el, and the other put he in Dan. And this thing became a sin; for the people went to worship before the one, even unto Dan. And he made a house of high places, and made priests of the lowest of people, which were not of the sons of Levi. And Jeroboam ordained a feast in the eighth month, on the fifteenth day of the month, like unto the feast that is in Judah, and he offered upon the altar. So did he in Beth-el, sacrificing unto the calves that he had made; and he placed in Beth-el the priests of the high places which he had made. So he offered upon the altar which he had made in Beth-el the fifteenth day of the eighth month, even in the month which he had devised of his own heart; and ordained a feast unto the children of Israel; and he offered upon the altar, and burnt incense.

And, behold, there came a man of God out of Judah by the word of the Lord unto Beth-el; and Jeroboam stood by the altar to burn incense. And he cried against the altar in the word of the Lord, and said, O altar, altar, thus saith the Lord; Behold, a child shall be born unto the house of David, Josiah by name; and upon thee shall he offer the priests of the high places that burn incense upon thee, and men's bones shall be burnt upon thee. And he gave a sign the same day, saying, This is the sign which the Lord hath spoken; Behold the altar shall be rent, and the ashes that are upon it shall be poured out. And it came to pass, when king Jeroboam heard the saying of the man of God, which had cried against the altar in Beth-el, that he put forth his hand from the altar, saying, Lay hold on him. And his hand, which he put forth against him, dried up, so that he could not pull it in again to him. The altar also was rent, and the ashes poured out from the altar, according to the sign which the man of God had given by the word of the Lord. And the king answered and said unto the man of God, Entreat now the face of the Lord thy God, and pray for me, that my hand may be restored me again. And the man of God besought the Lord, and the king's hand was restored him again, and became as it was before. And the king said unto the man of God, Come home with me, and refresh thyself, and I will give thee a reward, and the man of God said unto the king, If thou wilt give me half thine house, I will not go in with thee, neither will I eat bread nor drink water in this place; for so was it charged me by the word of the Lord, saying, Eat no bread, nor drink water, nor turn again by the same way that thou camest. So he went another way, and returned not by the way that he came to Beth-el.

Now there dwelt an old prophet in Beth-el; and his sons came and told him all the works that the man of God had done that day in Beth-el; the words which he had spoken unto the king, them they told also to their father. And their father said unto them, What way went he? For his sons had seen what way the man of God went, which came from Judah. And he said unto his sons, Saddle me the ass. So they saddled him the ass; and he rode thereon, and went after the man of God, and found him sitting under an oak; and he said unto him, Art thou the man of God that camest from Judah? And he said, I am. Then he said unto him, Come home with me, and eat bread. And he said, I may not return with thee, nor go in with thee; neither will I eat bread nor drink water with thee in this place; for it was said to me by the word of the Lord, Thou shalt eat no bread nor drink water there, nor turn again to go by the way that thou camest. He said unto him, I am a prophet also, even as thou, and an angel spake unto me by the word of the Lord, saying, Bring him back with thee into thine house, that he may eat bread and drink water, that I may prove him; and he lied not unto him. So he went back with him, and did eat bread in his house, and drank water.

And it came to pass, as they sat at the table, that the word of the Lord came unto the prophet that brought him back; and he cried unto the man of God that came from Judah, saying, Thus saith the Lord, Forasmuch as thou hast disobeyed the mouth of the Lord, and hast not kept the commandment which the Lord thy God commanded thee, but camest back, and hast eaten bread and drunk water in the place, of the which the Lord did say to thee, Eat no bread, and drink no water; thy carcass shall not come unto the sepulcher of thy fathers.

And it came to pass, after he had eaten bread, and after he had drunk, that he saddled for him the ass, to wit, for the prophet whom he had brought back. And when he was gone, a lion met him by the way, and slew him; and his carcass was cast in the way, and the ass stood by it, the lion also stood by the carcass. And, behold, men passed by, and saw the carcass cast in the way, and the lion standing by the carcass; and they came and told it in the city where the old prophet dwelt.

And when the prophet that brought him back from the way heard thereof, he said, It is the man of God, who was disobedient unto the word of the Lord; therefore the Lord hath delivered him unto the lion, which hath torn him, and slain him, according to the word of the Lord, which he spake unto me. And he spake to his sons, saying, Saddle me the ass. And they saddled him. And he went and found his carcass cast in the way, and the ass and the lion standing by the carcass; the lion had not eaten the carcass, nor torn the ass. And the prophet took up the carcass of the man of God, and laid it upon the ass, and brought it back; and the old prophet came to the city, to mourn and to bury him. And he laid his carcass in his own grave; and they mourned over him, saying, Alas, my brother! And it came to pass, after he had buried him, that he spake to his sons, saying, When I am dead, then bury me in the sepulcher wherein the man of God is buried; lay my bones beside his bones; for the saying which he cried by the word of the Lord against the altar in Beth-el, and against all the houses of the high places which are in the cities of Samaria, shall surely come to pass.

After this thing Jeroboam returned not from his evil way, but made again of the lowest of the people priests of the high places; whosoever would, he consecrated him, and he became one of the priests of the high places. And this thing became sin unto the house of Jeroboam, even to cut it off, and to destroy it from off the face of the Earth.

At that time Abijah the son of Jeroboam fell sick. And Jeroboam said to his wife, Arise, I pray thee, and disguise thyself, that thou be not known to be the wife of Jeroboam; and get thee to Shiloh; behold, there is Ahijah the prophet, which told me that I should be king over this people. And take with thee ten loaves, and cracknels, and a cruse of honey, and go to him; he shall tell thee what shall become of the child.

And Jeroboam's wife did so, and arose, and went to Shiloh, and came to the house of Ahijah. But Ahijah could not see; for his eyes were set by reason of his age. And the Lord said unto Ahijah, Behold, the wife of Jeroboam cometh to ask a thing of thee for her son; for he is sick; thus and thus shalt thou say unto her; for it shall be, when she cometh in, that she shall feign herself to be another woman.

And it was so, when Ahijah heard the sound of her feet, as she came in at the door, that he said, Come in, thou wife of Jeroboam; why feignest thou thyself to be another? for I am sent to thee with heavy tidings. Go, tell Jeroboam, Thus saith the Lord God of Israel, Forasmuch as I exalted thee from among the people, and made thee prince over my people Israel, and rent the kingdom away from the house of David and gave it thee, because he kept not my commandments. But thou hast not been as my servant David, when he followed me with all his heart only to do right in mine eyes. But hast done evil above all that were before thee; for thou hast gone and made thee other gods, and molten images, to provoke me to anger, and hast cast me behind thy back; therefore, behold, I will bring evil upon the house of Jeroboam, and will cut off from Jeroboam him that pisseth against the wall, and him that is shut up and left in Israel, and will take away the remnant of the house of Jeroboam, as a man taketh away dung, till it be all gone. Him that dieth of Jeroboam in the city shall the dogs eat; and him that dieth in the field shall the fowls of the air eat; for the Lord hath spoken it. Arise thou therefore, get thee to thine own house; and when thy feet inter into the city, the child shall die. And all Israel shall mourn for him, and bury him; for he only of Jeroboam shall come to the grave, because in him there is found some good thing toward the Lord God of Israel in the house of Jeroboam. Moreover the Lord shall raise him up a king over Israel, who shall cut off the house of Jeroboam that day; but what? even now.

For the Lord shall smite Israel, as a reed is shaken in the water, and he shall root up Israel out of this good land, which he gave to their fathers, and shall scatter them beyond the river, because they have made their groves, provoking the Lord to anger. And he shall gave Israel up because of the sins of Jeroboam, who did sin, and who made Israel to sin.

And Jeroboam's wife arose, and departed, and came to Tirzah; and when she came to the threshold of the door, the child died; and they buried him; and all Israel mourned for him, according to the word of the Lord, which he spake by the hand of his servant Ahijah the prophet.

And the rest of the acts of Jeroboam, how he warred, and how he reigned, behold, they are written in the book of the Chronicles of the kings of Israel. And the days which Jeroboam reigned were two and twenty years; and he slept with his fathers, and Nadab his son reigned in his stead.

And Rehoboam the son of Solomon reigned in Judah. Rehoboam was forty and one years old when he began to reign, and he reigned seventeen years in Jerusalem, the city which the Lord did choose out of all the tribes of Israel, to put his name there. And his mother's name was Naamah an Ammonitess. And Judah did evil in the sight of the Lord, and they provoked him to jealousy with their sins which they had committed, above all that their fathers had done. For they also built them high places, and images, and groves, on every high hill, and under every green tree. And there were also sodomites in the land; and they did according to all the abominations of the nations which the Lord cast out before the children of Israel.

And it came to pass in the fifth year of king Rehoboam, that Shishak king of Egypt came up against Jerusalem; and he took away the treasures of the house of the Lord, and the treasures of the king's house; he even took away all; and he took away all the shields of gold which Solomon had made. And king Rehoboam made in their stead brazen shields, and committed them unto the hands of the chief of the guard, which kept the door of the king's house. And it was so, when the king went into the house of the Lord, that the guard bare them, and brought them back into the guard chamber.

Now the rest of the acts of Rehoboam, and all that he did, are they not written in the book of the chronicles of the kings of Judah? And there was war between Rehoboam and Jeroboam all their days. And Rehoboam slept with his fathers, and was buried with his fathers in the city of David. And his mother's name was Naamah an Ammonitess. And Abijam his son reigned in his stead.

Now in the eighteenth year of king Jeroboam the son of Nebat reigned Abijam over Judah. Three years reigned he in Jerusalem. And his mother's name was Maachah, the daughter of Abishalom. And he walked in all the sins of his father, which he had done before him; and his heart was not perfect with the Lord his God, as the Lord commanded David his father. Nevertheless for David's sake did the Lord his God give him a lamp in Jerusalem, to set up his son after him, and to establish Jerusalem; because David did right in the eyes of the Lord, and turned not aside from all that he commanded him, to sin against the Lord; but repented of the evil all the days of his life, save only in the matter of Uriah the Hittite, wherein the Lord cursed him. And there was war between Rehoboam and Jeroboam all the days of his life.

Now the rest of the acts of Abijam, and all that he did, are they not written in the book of the Chronicles of the kings of Judah? And there was war between Abijam and Jeroboam.

And Abijam slept with his fathers; and they buried him in the city of David; and Asa his son reigned in his stead.

And in the twentieth year of Jeroboam king of Israel reigned Asa over Judah. And forty and one years reigned he in Jerusalem. And his mother's name was Maachah, the daughter of Abishalom. And Asa did right in the eyes of the Lord, as he commanded David his father. And he took away the sodomites out of the land, and removed all the idols that his fathers had made; and it pleased the Lord. And also Maachah his mother, even her he removed from being queen, because she had made an idol in a grove; and Asa destroyed her idol, and burnt it by the brook Kidron. But the high places were not removed; nevertheless Asa's heart was perfect with the Lord all his days. And he brought in the things which his father had dedicated, and the things which himself had dedicated, into the house of the Lord, silver, and gold, and vessels.

And there was war between Asa and Baasha king of Israel all their days. And Baasha king of Israel went up against Judah, and built Ramah, that he might not suffer any to go out or come in to Asa king of Judah. Then Asa took all the silver and the gold that were left in the treasures of the house of the Lord, and the treasures of the king's house, and delivered them into the hand of his servants; and king Asa sent them to Ben-hadad, the son of Tabrimon, the son of Hezion, king of Syria, that dwelt at Damascus, saying, There is a league between me and thee, and between my father and thy father; behold, I have sent unto thee a present of silver and gold; come and break thy league with Baasha king of Israel, that he may depart from me. So Ben-hadad hearkened unto king Asa, and sent the captains of the hosts which he had against the cities of Israel, and smote Ijon, and Dan, and Abel-beth-maachah, and all Cinneroth, with all the land of Naphtali. And it came to pass, when Baasha heard thereof, that he left off building of Ramah, and dwelt in Tirzah. Then king Asa made a proclamation throughout all Judah; none was exempted; and they took away the stones of Ramah, and the timber thereof, wherewith Baasha had builded; and king Asa built with them Geba of Benjamin, and Mizpah.

The rest of all the acts of Asa, and all his might, and all that he did, and the cities which he built, are they not written in the book of the chronicles of the kings of Judah? Nevertheless in the time of his old age he was diseased in his feet. And Asa slept with his fathers, and was buried with his fathers in the city of David his father; and Jehoshaphat his son reigned in his stead.

And Nadab the son of Jeroboam began to reign over Israel in the second year of Asa king of Judah, and reigned over Israel two years. And he did evil in the sight of the Lord, and walked in the way of his father, and in his sin wherewith he made Israel to sin. And Baasha the son of Ahijah, of the house of Issachar, conspired against him; and Baasha smote him at Gibbethon, which belonged to the Philistines; for Nadab and all Israel laid siege to Gibbethon.

Even in the third year of Asa king of Judah did Baasha slay him, and reigned in his stead. And it came to pass, when he reigned, that he smote all the house of Jeroboam; he left not to Jeroboam any that breathed, until he had destroyed him, according unto the saying of the Lord, which he spake by his servant Ahijah the Shilonite; because of the sins of Jeroboam which he sinned, and which he made Israel sin, by his provocation wherewith he provoked the Lord God of Israel to anger.

Now the rest of the acts of Nadab, and all that he did, are they not written in the book of the Chronicles of the kings of Israel?

And there was war between Asa and Baasha king of Israel all their days.

In the third year of Asa king of Judah began Baasha the son of Ahijah to reign over all Israel in Tirzah, twenty and four years. And he did evil in the sight of the Lord, and walked in the way of Jeroboam, and in his sin wherewith he made Israel to sin.

Then the word of the Lord came to Jehu the son of Hanani against Baasha, saying, Forasmuch as I exalted thee out of the dust, and made thee prince over my people Israel; and thou hast walked in the way of Jeroboam, and hast made my people Israel to sin, to provoke me to anger with their sins; behold, I will take away the posterity of Baasha, and the posterity of his house; and will make thy house like the house of Jeroboam the son of Nebat. Him that dieth of Baasha in the city shall the dogs eat; and him that dieth of his in the fields shall the fowls of the air eat. Now the rest of the acts of Baasha, and what he did, and his might, are they not written in the book of the Chronicles of the kings of Israel? So Baasha slept with his fathers, and was buried in Tirzah; and Elah his son reigned in his stead. And also by the hand of the prophet Jehu the son of Hanani came the word of the Lord against Baasha, and against his house, even for all the evil that he did in the sight of the Lord, in provoking him to anger with the work of his hands, in being like the house of Jeroboam; and because he killed him.

In the twenty and sixth year of Asa king of Judah began Elah the son of Baasha to reign over Israel in Tirzah, two years. And his servant Zimri, captain of half his chariots, conspired against him, as he was in Tirzah, drinking himself drunk in the house of Arza steward of his house in Tirzah. And Zimri went in and smote him, and killed him, in the twenty and seventh year of Asa king of Judah, and reigned in his stead. And it came to pass, when he began to reign, as soon as he sat on his throne, that he slew all the house of Baasha; he left him not one that pisseth against a wall, neither of his kinsfolks, nor of his friends. Thus did Zimri destroy all the house of Baasha, according to the word of the Lord, which he spake against Baasha by Jehu the prophet. For all the sins of Baasha, and the sins of Elah his son, by which they sinned, and by which they made Israel to sin, in provoking the Lord God of Israel to anger with their vanities. Now the rest of the acts of Elah, and all that he did, are they not written in the book of the Chronicles of the kings of Israel?

In the twenty and seventh year of Asa king of Judah did Zimri reign seven days in Tirzah. And the people were encamped against Gibbethon, which belonged to the Philistines. And the people that were encamped heard say, Zimri hath conspired, and hath also slain the king; wherefore all Israel made Omri, the captain of the host, king over Israel that day in the camp. And Omri went up from Gibbethon, and all Israel with him, and they besieged Tirzah. And it came to pass, when Zimri saw that the city was taken, that he went into the palace of the king's house, and burnt the king's house over him with fire, and died, for his sins which he sinned in doing evil in the sight of the Lord, in walking in the way of Jeroboam, and in his sin which he did, to make Israel to sin. Now the rest of the acts of Zimri, and his treason that he wrought, are they not written in the book of the Chronicles of the kings of Israel?

Then were the people of Israel divided into two parts; half of the people followed Tibni the son of Ginath, to make him king; and half followed Omri. But the people that followed Omri prevailed against the people that followed Tibni the son of Ginath; so Tibni died, and Omri reigned. In the thirty and first year of Asa king of Judah began Omri to reign over Israel, twelve years; six years reigned he in Tirzah. And he bought the hill Samaria of Shemer for two talents of silver, and built on the hill, and called the name of the city which he built, after the name of Shemer, owner of the hill, Samaria. But Omri wrought evil in the eyes of the Lord, and did worse than all that were before him. For he walked in all the way of Jeroboam, the son of Nebat, and in his sin wherewith he made Israel to sin, to provoke the Lord God of Israel to anger with their vanities. Now the rest of the acts of Omri which he did, and his might that he showed, are they not written in the book of the Chronicles of the kings of Israel? So Omri slept with his fathers, and was buried in Samaria; and Ahab his son reigned in his stead.

And in the thirty and eighth year of Asa king of Judah began Ahab the son of Omri to reign over Israel; and Ahab the son of Omri reigned over Israel in Samaria twenty and two years. And Ahab the son of Omri did evil in the sight of the Lord above all that were before him. And it came to pass, as if it had been a light thing for him to walk in the sins of Jeroboam the son of Nebat, that he took to wife Jezebel, the daughter of Ethbaal king of the Zidonians, and went and served Baal, and worshiped him. And he reared up an altar for Baal in the hose of Baal, which he had built in Samaria. And Ahab made a grove; and Ahab did more to provoke the Lord God of Israel to anger than all the kings of Israel that were before him.

In his days did Hiel the Bethelite build Jericho; he laid the foundation thereof in Abiram his firstborn, and set up the gates thereof in his youngest son Segub, according to the word of the Lord, which he spake by Joshua the son of Nun.

4 AND Elijah the Tishbite, who was of the inhabitants of Gilead, said unto Ahab, As the Lord God of Israel liveth, before whom I stand, there shall not be dew nor rain these years, but according to my word. And the word of the Lord came unto him, saying, Get thee hence, and turn thee eastward, and hide thyself by

the brook Cherith, that is before Jordan. And it shall be, that thou shalt drink of the brook; and I have commanded the ravens to feed thee there. So he went and did according unto the word of the Lord; for he went and dwelt by the brook Cherith, that is before Jordan. And the ravens brought him bread and flesh in the morning, and bread and flesh in the evening; and he drank of the brook. And it came to pass after a while, that the brook dried up, because there had been no rain in the land.

And the word of the Lord came unto him, saying, Arise, get thee to Zarephath, which belongeth to Zidon, and dwell there; behold, I have commanded a widow woman there to sustain thee. So he arose and went to Zarephath. And when he came to the gate of the city, behold, the widow woman was there gathering of sticks; and he called to her, and said, Fetch me, I pray thee, a little water in a vessel, that I may drink. And as she was going to fetch it, he called to her, and said, Bring me, I pray thee, a morsel of bread in thine hand. And she said, As the Lord thy God liveth, I have not a cake, but a handful of meal in a barrel, and a little oil in a cruse; and, behold, I am gathering two sticks, that I may go in and dress it for me and my son, that we may eat it, and die. And Elijah said unto her, Fear not; go and do as thou hast said; but make me thereof a little cake first, and bring it unto me, and after make for thee and for thy son. For thus saith the Lord God of Israel, The barrel of meal shall not waste, neither shall the cruse of oil fail, until the day that the Lord sendeth rain upon the Earth. And she went and did according to the saying of Elijah; and she, and he, and her house, did eat many days. And the barrel of meal wasted not, neither did the cruse of oil fail, according to the word of the Lord, which he spake by Elijah.

And it came to pass after these things, that the son of the woman, the mistress of the house, fell sick; and his sickness was so sore, that there was no breath left in him. And she said unto Elijah, What have I to do with thee, O thou man of God? art thou come unto me to call my sin to remembrance, and to slay my son? And he said unto her, Give me thy son. And he took him out of her bosom, and carried him up into a loft, where he abode, and laid him upon his own bed. And he cried unto the Lord, and said, O Lord my God, hast thou also brought evil upon the widow with whom I sojourn, by slaying her son? And he stretched himself upon the child three times, and cried unto the Lord, and said, O Lord my God, I pray thee, let this child's soul come into him again. And the Lord heard the voice of Elijah; and the soul of the child came into him again, and he revived. And Elijah took the child, and brought him down out of the chamber into the house, and delivered him unto his mother; and Elijah said, See, thy son liveth. And the woman said to Elijah, Now by this I know that thou art a man of God, and that the word of the Lord in thy mouth is truth.

And it came to pass after many days, that the word of the Lord came to Elijah in the third year, saying, Go, show thyself unto Ahab; and I will send rain upon the Earth. And Elijah went to show himself unto Ahab. And there was a sore famine in Samaria. And Ahab called Obadiah, which was the governor of his house. (Now Obadiah feared the Lord greatly; for it was so, when Jezebel cut off the prophets of the Lord, that Obadiah took a hundred prophets, and hid them by fifty in a cave, and fed them with bread and water.) And Ahab said unto Obadiah, Go into the land, unto all fountains of water, and unto all brooks; peradventure we may find grass to save the horses and mules alive, that we lose not all the beasts. So they divided the land between them to pass throughout it; Ahab went one way by himself, and Obadiah went another way by himself.

And as Obadiah was in the way, behold, Elijah met him; and he knew him, and fell on his face, and said, Art thou that my Lord Elijah? And he answered him, I am; go, tell thy lord, Behold, Elijah is here. And he said, What have I sinned, that thou wouldest deliver thy servant into the hand of Ahab, to slay me? As the

Lord thy God liveth, there is no nation or kingdom, whither my lord hath not sent to seek thee; and when they said, He is not there; he took an oath of the kingdom and nation, that they found thee not. And now thou sayest, Go, tell thy lord, Behold, Elijah is here. And it shall come to pass, as soon as I am gone from thee, that the Spirit of the Lord shall carry thee whither I know not; and so when I come and tell Ahab, and he cannot find thee, he shall slay me; but I thy servant fear the Lord from my youth. Was it not told my lord what I did when Jezebel slew the prophets of the Lord, how I hid a hundred men of the Lord's prophets by fifty in a cave, and fed them with bread and water? And now thou sayest, Go, tell thy lord, Behold, Elijah is here; and he shall slay me. And Elijah said, As the Lord of hosts liveth, before whom I stand, I will surely show myself unto him today.

So Obadiah went to meet Ahab, and told him; and Ahab went to meet Elijah. And it came to pass, when Ahab saw Elijah, that Ahab said unto him, Art thou he that troubleth Israel? And he answered, I have not troubled Israel; but thou, and thy father's house, in that ye have forsaken the commandments of the Lord, and thou hast followed Baalim. Now therefore send, and gather to me all Israel unto mount Carmel, and the prophets of Baal four hundred and fifty, and the prophets of the groves four hundred, which eat at Jezebel's table.

So Ahab sent unto all the children of Israel, and gathered the prophets together unto mount Carmel. And Elijah came unto all the people, and said, How long halt ye between two opinions? if the Lord be God, follow him; but if Baal, then follow him. And the people answered him not a word. Then said Elijah unto the people, I, even I only, remain a prophet of the Lord; but Baal's prophets are four hundred and fifty men. Let them therefore give us two bullocks; and let them choose one bullock for themselves, and cut it in pieces, and lay it on wood, and put no fire under; and I will dress the other bullock, and lay it on wood, and put no fire under; and call ye on the name of your gods, and I will call on the name of the Lord; and the God that answereth by fire, let him be God. And all the people answered and said, It is well spoken.

And Elijah said unto the prophets of Baal, Choose you one bullock for yourselves, and dress it first; for ye are many; and call on the name of your gods, but put no fire under. And they took the bullock which was given them, and they dressed it, and called on the name of Baal from morning even until noon, saying, O Baal, hear us. But there was no voice, nor any that answered. And they leaped upon the altar which was made. And it came to pass at noon, that Elijah mocked them, and said, Cry aloud; for he is a god; either he is talking, or he is pursuing, or he is in a journey, or peradventure he sleepeth, and must be awaked. And they cried aloud, and cut themselves after their manner with knives and lancets, till the blood gushed out upon them. And it came to pass, when midday was past, and they prophesied until the time of the offering of the evening sacrifice, that there was neither voice, nor any to answer, nor any that regarded.

And Elijah said unto all the people, Come near unto me. And all the people came near unto him. And he repaired the altar of the Lord that was broken down. And Elijah took twelve stones, according to the number of the tribes of the sons of Jacob, unto whom the word of the Lord came, saying, Israel shall be thy name; and with the stones he built an altar in the name of the Lord; and he made a trench about the altar, as great as would contain two measures of seed. And he put the wood in order, and cut the bullock in pieces, and laid him on the wood, and said, Fill four barrels with water, and pour it on the burnt sacrifice, and on the wood. And he said, Do it the second time. And they did it the second time. And he said, Do it the third time. And they did it the third time. And the water ran round about the altar; and he filled the trench also with water.

And it came to pass at the time of the offering of the evening sacrifice, that Elijah the prophet came near, and said, Lord God of Abraham, Isaac, and of Israel, let it be known this day that thou art God in Israel, and that I am thy servant, and that I have done all these things at thy word. Hear me, O Lord, hear me, that this people may know that thou art the Lord God, and thou mayest turn their heart back again. Then the fire of the Lord fell, and consumed the burnt sacrifice, and the wood, and the stones, and the dust, and licked up the water that was in the trench. And when all the people saw it, they fell on their faces; and they said, the Lord, he is the God; the Lord, he is the God. And Elijah said unto them, Take the prophets of Baal; let not one of them escape. And they took them; and Elijah brought them down to the brook Kishon, and slew them there.

And Elijah said unto Ahab, Get thee up, eat and drink; for there is a sound of abundance of rain. So Ahab went up to eat and to drink. And Elijah went up to the top of Carmel; and he cast himself down upon the earth, and put his face between his knees, and said to his servant, Go up now, look toward the sea. And he went up, and looked, and said, There is nothing. And he said, Go again seven times. And it came to pass at the seventh time, that he said, Behold, there ariseth a little cloud out of the sea, like a man's hand. And he said, Go up, say unto Ahab, Prepare thy chariot, and get thee down, that the rain stop thee not. And it came to pass in the meanwhile, that the Heaven was black with clouds and wind, and there was a great rain. And Ahab rode, and went to Jezreel. And the hand of the Lord was on Elijah; and he girded up his loins, and ran before Ahab to the entrance of Jezreel.

And Ahab told Jezebel all that Elijah had done, and withal how he had slain all the prophets with the sword. Then Jezebel sent a messenger unto Elijah, saying, So let the gods do to me, and more also, if I make not thy life as the life of one of them by tomorrow about this time. And when he saw that, he arose, and went for his life, and came to Beer-sheba, which belongeth to Judah, and left his servant there. But he himself went a day's journey into the wilderness, and came and sat down under a juniper tree; and he requested for himself that he might die; and said, It is enough; now, O Lord, take away my life; for I am not better than my fathers. And as he lay and slept under a juniper tree, behold, then an angel touched him, and said unto him, Arise and eat. And he looked, and, behold, there was a cake baken on the coals, and a cruse of water at his head. And he did eat and drink, and laid him down again. And the Angel of the Lord came again the second time, and touched him, and said, Arise and eat; because the journey is too great for thee. And he arose, and did eat and drink, and went in the strength of that meat forty days and forty nights unto Horeb the mount of God.

And he came thither unto a cave, and lodged there; and, behold, the word of the Lord came to him, and he said unto him, What doest thou here Elijah? And he said, I have been very jealous for the Lord God of hosts; for the children of Israel have forsaken thy covenant, thrown down thine altars, and slain thy prophets with the sword; and I, even I only, am left; and they seek my life, to take it away.

And he said, Go forth, and stand upon the mount before the Lord. And, behold, the Lord passed by, and a great and strong wind rent the mountains, and brake in pieces the rocks before the Lord; but the Lord was not in the wind; and after the wind an earthquake; but the Lord was not in the earthquake; and after the earthquake a fire, but the Lord was not in the fire; and after the fire a still small voice. And it was so, when Elijah heard it, that he wrapped his face in his mantle, and went out, and stood in the entering in of the cave. And, behold, there came a voice unto him, and said, What doest thou here, Elijah? And he said, I have been very jealous for the Lord God of hosts; because the children of Israel have forsaken thy covenant, thrown down thine altars, and slain thy prophets with the sword, and I, even I only, am left; and they seek my life, to take it away.

And the Lord said unto him, Go, return on thy way to the wilderness of Damascus; and when thou comest, anoint Hazael to be king over Syria; and Jehu the son of Nimshi shalt thou anoint to be king over Israel; and Elisha the son of Shaphat of Abel-meholah shalt thou anoint to be prophet in thy room. And it shall come to pass, that him that escapeth the sword of Hazael shall Jehu slay; and him that escapeth from the sword of Jehu shall Elisha slay. Yet I have left me seven thousand in Israel, all the knees which have not bowed unto Baal, and every mouth which hath not kissed him.

So he departed thence, and found Elisha the son of Shaphat, who was ploughing with twelve yoke of oxen before him, and he with the twelfth; and Elijah passed by him, and cast his mantle upon him. And he left the oxen, and ran after Elijah, and said, Let me, I pray thee, kiss my father and my mother, and then I will follow thee. And he said unto him, Go back again; for what have I done to thee? And he returned back from him and took a yoke of oxen, and slew them, and boiled their flesh with the instruments of the oxen, and gave unto the people, and they did eat. Then he arose, and went after Elijah, and ministered unto him.

And Ben-hadad the king of Syria gathered all his host together; and there were thirty and two kings with him, and horses and chariots; and he went up and besieged Samaria, and warred against it. And he sent messengers to Ahab king of Israel into the city, and said unto him, Thus saith Ben-hadad, thy silver and thy gold is mine; thy wives also and thy children, even the goodliest, are mine. And the king of Israel answered and said, My lord, O king, according to thy saying, I am thine, and all that I have. And the messengers came again, and said, thus speaketh Ben-hadad, saying, Although I have sent unto thee, saying, Thou shalt deliver me thy silver and thy gold, and thy wives, and thy children; yet I will send my servants unto thee tomorrow about this time, and they shall search thine house, and the houses of thy servants; and it shall be, that whatsoever is pleasant in thine eyes, they shall put it in their hand and take it away.

Then the king of Israel called all the elders of the land, and said, Mark, I pray you, and see how this man seeketh mischief; for he sent unto me for my wives, and for my children, and for my silver, and for my gold, and I denied him not. And all the elders and all the people said unto him, Hearken not unto him, nor consent. Wherefore he said unto the messengers of Ben-hadad, Tell my lord the king, All that thou didst send for to thy servant at the first I will do; but this thing I may not do. And the messengers departed, and brought him word again. And Ben-hadad sent unto him, and said, The gods do so unto me, and more also, if the dust of Samaria shall suffice for handfuls for all the people that follow me. And the king of Israel answered and said, Tell him, Let not him that girdeth on his harness boast himself as he that putteth it off. And it came to pass, when Ben-hadad heard this message, as he was drinking, he and the kings in the pavilions, that he said unto his servants, Set yourselves in array. And they set themselves in array against the city.

And behold, there came a prophet unto Ahab king of Israel, saying, Thus saith the Lord, Hast thou seen all this great multitude? behold, I will deliver it into thine hand this day; and thou shalt know that I am the Lord. And Ahab said, By whom? And he said, Thus saith the Lord, Even by the young men of the princes of the provinces. Then he said, Who shall order the battle? And he answered, Thou. Then he numbered the young men of the princes of the provinces, and they were two hundred and thirty-two; and after them he numbered all the people, even all the children of Israel, being seven thousand.

And they went out at noon. But Ben-hadad was drinking himself drunk in the pavilions, he and the kings, the thirty and two kings that helped him. And the young men of the princes of the provinces went out first; and Ben-hadad sent out, and they told him, saying, There are men come out of Samaria. And he said, Whether they be come out for peace, take them alive; or whether they be come out for war, take them alive.

So these young men of the princes of the provinces came out of the city, and the army which followed them. And they slew every one his man; and the Syrians fled; and Israel pursued them; and Ben-hadad the king of Syria escaped on a horse with the horsemen. And the king of Israel went out, and smote the horses and chariots, and slew the Syrians with a great slaughter.

And the prophet came to the king of Israel, and said unto him, Go strengthen thyself, and mark, and see what thou doest; for at the return of the year the king of Syria will come up against thee. And the servants of the king of Syria said unto him, Their gods are gods of the hills; therefore they were stronger than we; but let us fight against them in the plain, and surely we shall be stronger than they. And do this thing, Take the kings away, every man out of his place, and put captains in their rooms; and number thee an army, like the army that thou hast lost, horse for horse, and chariot for chariot; and we will fight against them in the plain, and surely we shall be stronger than they. And he hearkened unto their voice, and did so.

And it came to pass at the return of the year that Ben-hadad numbered the Syrians, and went up to Aphek, to fight against Israel. And the children of Israel were numbered, and were all present, and went against them; and the children of Israel pitched before them like two little flocks of kids; but the Syrians filled the country. And there came a man of God, and spake unto the king of Israel, and said, Thus saith the Lord, Because the Syrians have said, The Lord is God of the hills, but he is not God of the valleys, therefore will I deliver all this great multitude into thine hand, and ye shall know that I am the Lord. And they pitched one over against the other seven days. And so it was, that in the seventh day the battle was joined; and the children of Israel slew of the Syrians a hundred thousand footmen in one day. But the rest fled to Aphek, into the city; and there a wall fell upon twenty and seven thousand of the men that were left. And Ben-hadad fled, and came into the city, into an inner chamber.

And his servants said unto him, Behold now, we have heard that the kings of the house of Israel are merciful kings; let us, I pray thee, put sackcloth on our loins, and ropes upon our heads, and go out to the king of Israel; peradventure he will save thy life. So they girded sackcloth on their loins, and put ropes on their heads, and came to the king of Israel, and said, Thy servant Ben-hadad saith, I pray thee, let me live. And he said, Is he yet alive? he is my brother. Now the men did diligently observe whether anything would come from him, and did hastily catch it; and they said, Thy brother Ben-hadad. Then he said, Go ye, bring him. Then Ben-hadad came forth to him; and he caused him to come up into the chariot. And Beh-hadad said unto him, The cities, which my father took from thy father, I will restore; and thou shalt make streets for thee in Damascus, as my father made in Samaria. Then said Ahab, I will send three away with this covenant. So he made a covenant with him, and sent him away.

And a certain man of the sons of the prophets said unto his neighbor in the word of the Lord, Smite me, I pray thee. And the man refused to smite him. Then said he unto him, Because thou hast not obeyed the voice of the Lord, Behold, as soon as thou art departed from me, a lion shall slay thee. And as soon as he was departed from him, a lion found him, and slew him. Then he found another man, and said, Smite me, I pray thee. And the man smote him, so that in smiting he wounded him. So the prophet departed, and waited for the king by the way, and disguised himself with ashes upon his face. And as the king passed by, he cried unto the king; and he said, Thy servant went out into the midst of the battle; and, behold, a man turned aside, and brought a man unto me, and said, Keep this man; if by any means he be missing, then shall thy life be for his life, or else thou shalt pay a talent of silver. And as thy servant was busy here and there, he was gone. And the king of Israel said unto him, So shall thy judgment be; thyself hast decided it. And he hasted, and took the ashes away from his face; and the king of Israel discerned him that he was of the prophets. And he said unto him, Thus saith the Lord, Because thou hast let go out of thy hand a man whom I appointed to utter destruction, therefore thy life shall go for his life, and thy people for his people. And the king of Israel went to his house heavy and displeased, and came to Samaria.

And it came to pass after these things, that Naboth the Jezreelite had a vineyard, which was in Jezreel, hard by the palace of Ahab king of Samaria. And Ahab spake unto Naboth, saying, Give me thy vineyard, that I may have it for a garden of herbs, because it is near unto my house; and I will give thee for it a better vineyard than it; or, if it seem good to thee, I will give thee the worth of it in money. And Naboth said to Ahab, The Lord forbid it me, that I should give the inheritance of my fathers unto thee. And Ahab came into his house heavy and displeased because of the word which Naboth the Jezreelite had spoken to him; for he had said, I will not give thee the inheritance of my fathers. And he laid him down upon his bed, and turned away his face, and would eat no bread.

But Jezebel his wife came to him, and said unto him, Why is thy spirit so sad, that thou eatest no bread? And he said unto her, Because I spake unto Naboth the Jezreelite, and said unto him, Give me thy vineyard for money; or else, if it please thee, I will give thee another vineyard for it; and he answered, I will not give thee my vineyard. And Jezebel his wife said unto him, Dost thou now govern the kingdom of Israel? arise, and eat bread, and let thine heart be merry; I will give thee the vineyard of Naboth the Jezreelite.

So she wrote letters in Ahab's name, and sealed them with his seal, and sent the letters unto the elders and to the nobles that were in his city, dwelling with Naboth. And she wrote in the letters, saying, Proclaim a fast, and set Naboth on high among the people; and set two men, sons of Belial, before him, to bear witness against him, saying, Thou didst blaspheme God and the king. And then carry him out, and stone him, that he may die.

And the men of his city, even the elders and the nobles who were the inhabitants in his city, did as Jezebel had sent unto them, and as it was written in the letters which she had sent unto them. They proclaimed a fast, and set Naboth on high among the people. And there came in two men, children of Belial, and sat before him; and the men of Belial witnessed against him, even against Naboth, in the presence of the people, saying, Naboth did blaspheme God and the king. Then they carried him forth out of the city, and stoned him with stones, that he died. Then they sent to Jezebel, saying, Naboth is stoned, and is dead.

And it came to pass, when Jezebel heard that Naboth was stoned, and was dead, that Jezebel said to Ahab, Arise, take possession of the vineyard of Naboth the Jezreelite, which he refused to give thee for money; for Naboth is not alive, but dead. And it came to pass, when Ahab heard that Naboth was dead, that Ahab rose up to go down to the vineyard of Naboth the Jezreelite, to take possession of it.

And the word of the Lord came to Elijah the Tishbite, saying, Arise, go down to meet Ahab, king of Israel, which is in Samaria; behold he is in the vineyard of Naboth, whither he is gone down to possess it. And thou shalt speak unto him, saying, Thus saith the Lord, Hast thou killed, and also taken possession? And thou shalt speak unto him, saying, Thus saith the Lord, In the place where dogs licked the blood of Naboth shall dogs lick thy blood, even thine.

And Ahab said to Elijah, Hast thou found me, O mine enemy? And he answered, I have found thee; because thou hast sold thyself to work evil in the sight of the Lord. Behold, I will bring evil upon thee, and will take away thy posterity, and will cut off from Ahab him that pisseth against the wall, and him that is shut up and left in Israel. And will make thine house like the house of Jeroboam the son of Nebat, and like the house of Baasha the son of Ahijah, for the provocation wherewith thou hast provoked me to anger, and made Israel to sin. And of Jezebel also spake the Lord, saying, The dogs shall eat Jezebel by the wall of Jezreel. Him that dieth of Ahab in the city the dogs shall eat; and him that dieth in the field shall the fowls of the air eat.

But there was none like unto Ahab, which did sell himself to work wickedness in the sight of the Lord whom Jezebel his wife stirred up. And he did very abominably in following idols, according to all things as did the Amorites, whom the Lord cast out before the children of Israel.

And it came to pass, when Ahab heard those words, that he rent his clothes, and put sackcloth upon his flesh, and fasted, and lay in sackcloth, and went softly. And the word of the Lord came to Elijah the Tishbite, saying, Seest thou how Ahab humbleth himself before me? because he humbleth himself before me, I will not bring the evil in his days; but in his son's days will I bring the evil upon his house.

5 AND they continued three years without war between Syria and Israel. And it came to pass in the third year, that Jehoshaphat the king of Judah came down to the king of Israel. And the king of Israel said unto his servants, Know ye that Ramoth in Gilead is ours, and we be still, and take it not out of the hand of the king of Syria? And he said unto Jehoshaphat, Wilt thou go with me to battle to Ramoth-gilead? And Jehoshaphat said to the king of Israel, I am as thou art, my people as thy people, my horses as thy horses.

And Jehoshaphat said unto the king of Israel, Inquire, I pray thee, at the word of the Lord today. Then the king of Israel gathered the prophets together, about four hundred men, and said unto them, Shall I go against Ramoth-gilead to battle, or shall I forbear? And they said, Go up; for the Lord shall deliver it into the hand of the king. And Jehoshaphat said, Is there not here a prophet of the Lord besides, that we might inquire of him? And the king of Israel said unto Jehoshaphat, There is yet one man, Micaiah the son of Imlah, by whom we may inquire of the Lord; but I hate him; for he doth not prophesy good concerning me, but evil. And Jehoshaphat said, Let not the king say so. Then the king of Israel called an officer, and said, Hasten hither Micaiah the son of Imlah. And the king of Israel and Jehoshaphat the king of Judah sat each on his throne, having put on their robes, in a void place in the entrance of the gate of Samaria; and all the prophets prophesied before them. And Zedekiah the son of Chenaanah made him horns of iron; and he said, Thus saith the Lord, With these shalt thou push the Syrians, until thou have consumed them. And all the prophets prophesied so, saying, Go up to Ramoth-gilead, and prosper; for the Lord shall deliver it into the king's hand.

And the messenger that was gone to call Micaiah spake unto him, saying, Behold now, the words of the prophets declare good unto the king with one mouth; let thy word, I pray thee, be like the word of one of them, and speak that which is good. And Micaiah said, As the Lord liveth, what the Lord saith unto me, that will I speak.

So he came to the king. And the king said unto him, Micaiah, shall we go against Ramoth-gilead to battle, or shall we forbear? And he answered him, Go, and prosper; for the Lord shall deliver it into the hand of the king. And the king said unto him, How many times shall I adjure thee that thou tell me nothing but that which is true in the name of the Lord? And he said, I saw all Israel scattered upon the hills, as sheep that have not a shepherd; and the Lord said, These have no master; let them return every man to his house in peace. And the king of Israel said unto Jehoshaphat, Did I not tell that he would prophesy no good concerning me, but evil? And he said, Hear thou therefore the word of the Lord; I saw the Lord sitting on his throne, and all the host of Heaven standing by him on his right hand and on his left. And the Lord said, Who shall persuade Ahab, that he may go up and fall at Ramoth-gilead? And one said on this manner, and another said on that manner. And there came forth a spirit, and stood before the Lord, and said, I will persuade him. And the Lord said unto him, Wherewith? And he said, I will go forth, and I will be a lying spirit in the mouth of all his prophets. And he said, Thou shalt persuade him, and prevail also; go forth, and do so. Now therefore, behold, the Lord hath put a lying spirit in the mouth of all these thy prophets, and the Lord hath spoken evil concerning thee. But Zedekiah the son of Chenaanah went near, and smote Micaiah on the cheek and said, Which way went the Spirit of the Lord from me to speak unto thee? And Micaiah said, Behold, thou shalt see in that day, when thou shalt go into an inner chamber to hide thyself. And the king of Israel said, Take Micaiah, and carry him back unto Amon the governor of the city, and to Joash the king's son; and say, Thus saith the king, Put this fellow in the prison, and feed him with bread of affliction and with water of affliction, until I come in peace. And Micaiah said, If thou return at all in peace, the Lord hath not spoken by me. And he said, Hearken, O people, every one of you.

So the king of Israel and Jehoshaphat the king of Judah went up to Ramoth-gilead. And the king of Israel said unto Jehoshaphat, I will disguise myself, and enter into the battle; but put thou on thy robes. And the king of Israel disguised himself, and went into the battle. But the king of Syria commanded his thirty and two captains that had rule over his chariots, saying, Fight neither with small nor great, save only with the king of Israel. And it came to pass, when the captains of the chariots saw Jehoshaphat, that they said, Surely it is the king of Israel. And they turned aside to fight against him; and Jehoshaphat cried out. And it came to pass, when the captains of the chariots perceived that it was not the king of Israel, that they turned back from pursuing him.

And a certain man drew a bow at a venture, and smote the king of Israel between the joints of the harness; wherefore he said unto the driver of his chariot, Turn thine hand, and carry me out of the host; for I am wounded. And the battle increased that day; and the king was stayed up in his chariot against the Syrians, and died at even: and the blood ran out of the wound into the midst of the chariot. And there went a proclamation throughout the host about the going down of the sun, saying, Every man to his city, and every man to his own country.

So the king died, and was brought to Samaria; and they buried the king in Samaria. And one washed the chariot in the pool of Samaria; and the dogs licked up his blood; and they washed his armor; according unto the word of the Lord which he spake. Now the rest of the acts of Ahab, and all that he did, and the ivory house which he made, and all the cities that he built, are they not written in the book of the Chronicles of the kings of Israel? So Ahab slept with his fathers; and Ahaziah his son reigned in his stead.

And Jehoshaphat the son of Asa began to reign over Judah in the fourth year of Ahab king of Israel. Jehoshaphat was thirty and five years old when he began to reign; and he reigned twenty and five years in Jerusalem. And his mother's name was Azubah the daughter of Shilhi. And he walked in all the ways of Asa his father; he turned not aside from it, doing that which was right in the eyes of the Lord; nevertheless the high places were not taken away; for the people offered and burnt incense yet in the high places. And Jehoshaphat made peace with the king of Israel.

Now the rest of the acts of Jehoshaphat, and his might that he showed, and how he warred, are they not written in the book of the Chronicles of the kings of Judah? And the remnant of the sodomites, which remained in the days of his father Asa, he took out of the land.

There was then no king in Edom; a deputy was king. Jehoshaphat made ships of Tharshish to go to Ophir for gold; but they went not; for the ships were broken at Ezion-geber. Then said Ahaziah the son of Ahab unto Jehoshaphat, Let my servants go with thy servants in the ships. But Jehoshaphat would not. And Jehoshaphat slept with his fathers, and was buried with his fathers in the city of David his father; and Jehoram his son reigned in his stead.

Ahaziah the son of Ahab began to reign over Israel in Samaria the seventeenth year of Jehoshaphat king of Judah, and reigned two years over Israel. And he did evil in the sight of the Lord, and walked in the way of his father, and in the way of his mother, and in the way of Jeroboam the son of Nebat, who made Israel to sin; for he served Baal, and worshiped him, and provoked to anger the Lord God of Israel, according to all that his father had done.

THE SECOND BOOK OF THE KINGS

THEN Moab rebelled against Israel after the death of Ahab. And Ahaziah fell down through a lattice in his upper chamber that was in Samaria, and was sick; and he sent messengers, and said unto them, Go, inquire of Baalzebub the god of Ekron whether I shall recover of this disease. But the Angel of the Lord said to Elijah the Tishbite, Arise, go up to meet the messengers of the king of Samaria, and say unto them, Is it not because there is not a God in Israel, that ye go to inquire of Baalzebub the god of Ekron? Now therefore thus saith the Lord, Thou shalt not come down from that bed on which thou art gone up, but shalt surely die. And Elijah departed.

And when the messengers turned back unto him, he said unto them, Why are ye now turned back? And they said unto him, There came a man up to meet us, and said unto us, Go, turn again unto the king that sent you, and say unto him, Thus saith the Lord, Is it not because there is not a God in Israel, that thou sendest to inquire of Baalzebub the god of Ekron? therefore thou shalt not come down from that bed on which thou art gone up, but shalt surely die. And he said unto them, What manner of man was he which came up to meet you, and told you these words? And they answered him, He was a hairy man, and girt with a girdle of leather about his loins. And he said, It is Elijah the Tishbite.

Then the king sent unto him a captain of fifty with his fifty. And he went up to him; and, behold, he sat on the top of a hill. And he spake unto him, Thou man of God, the king hath said, Come down. And Elijah answered and said to the captain of fifty, If I be a man of God, then let fire come down out of Heaven and consume thee and thy fifty. And there came down fire out of Heaven, and consumed him and his fifty.

Again also he sent unto him another captain of fifty with his fifty. And he answered and said unto him, O man of God, thus hath the king said, Come down quickly. And Elijah answered and said unto them, If I be a man of God, let fire come down out of Heaven, and consume thee and thy fifty. And the fire of God came down out of Heaven, and consumed him and his fifty.

And he sent again a captain of the third fifty with his fifty. And the third captain of fifty went up, and came and fell on his knees before Elijah, and besought him, and said unto him, O man of God, I pray thee, let my life, and the life of these fifty thy servants, be precious in thy sight. Behold, there came fire down out of Heaven, and burnt up the two captains of the former fifties with their fifties; therefore let my life now be precious in thy sight. And the Angel of the Lord said unto Elijah, Go down with him; be not afraid of him. And he arose, and went down with him unto the king. And he said unto him, Thus saith the Lord, Forasmuch as thou hast sent messengers to inquire of Baalzebub the god of Ekron, is it not because there is no God in Israel to inquire of his word? therefore thou shalt not come down off that bed on which thou art gone up, but shalt surely die.

So he died according to the word of the Lord which Elijah had spoken. And Jehoram reigned in his stead, in the second year of Jehoram the son of Jehoshaphat king of Judah; because he had no son. Now the rest of the acts of Ahaziah which he did, are they not written in the book of the chronicles of the kings of Israel?

And it came to pass, when the Lord would take up Elijah into Heaven by a whirlwind, that Elijah went with Elisha from Gilgal. And Elijah said unto Elisha, Tarry here, I pray thee; for the Lord hath sent me to Beth-el. And Elisha said unto him, As the Lord liveth, and as thy soul liveth, I will not leave thee. So they went down to Beth-el. And the sons of the prophets that were at Beth-el came forth to Elisha, and said unto him, Knowest thou that the Lord will take away thy master from thy head today? And he said, Yea, I know it; hold ye your peace.

And Elijah said unto him, Elisha, tarry here, I pray thee; for the Lord hath sent me to Jericho. And he said, As the lord liveth, and as thy soul liveth, I will not leave thee. So they came to Jericho. And the sons of the prophets that were at Jericho came to Elisha, and said unto him, Knowest thou that the Lord will take away thy master from thy head today? And he answered, Yea, I know it; hold ye your peace. And Elijah said unto him, Tarry, I pray thee, here; for the Lord hath sent me to Jordan. And he said, As the Lord liveth, and as thy soul liveth, I will not leave thee. And they two went on.

And fifty men of the sons of the prophets went, and stood to view afar off; and they two stood by Jordan. And Elijah took his mantle, and wrapped it together, and smote the waters, and they were divided hither and thither, so that they two went over on dry ground.

And it came to pass, when they were gone over, that Elijah said unto Elisha, Ask what I shall do for thee, before I be taken away from thee. And Elisha said, I pray thee, let a double portion of thy spirit be upon me. And he said, Thou hast asked a hard thing; nevertheless, if thou see me when I am taken from thee, it shall be so unto thee; but if not, it shall not be so.

And it came to pass, as they still went on, and talked, that, behold, there appeared a chariot of fire, and horses of fire, and parted them both asunder; and Elijah went up by a whirlwind into Heaven. And Elisha saw it, and he cried, My father, my father, the chariot of Israel, and the horsemen thereof! And he saw him no more; and he took hold of his own clothes, and rent them in two pieces. He took up also the mantle of Elijah that fell from him, and went back, and stood by the bank of Jordan. And he took the mantle of Elijah that fell from him, and smote the waters, and said, Where is the Lord God of Elijah? And when he also had smitten the waters, they parted hither and thither; and Elisha went over.

And when the sons of the prophets which were to view at Jericho saw him, they said, The spirit of Elijah doth rest on Elisha. And they came to meet him, and bowed themselves to the ground before him. And they said unto him, Behold now, there be with thy servants fifty strong men; let them go, we pray thee, and seek thy master; lest peradventure the Spirit of the Lord hath taken him up, and cast him upon some mountain, or into some valley. And he said,

Ye shall not send. And when they urged him till he was ashamed, he said, Send. They sent therefore fifty men; and they sought three days, but found him not. And when they came again to him, (for he tarried at Jericho,) he said unto them, Did I not say unto you, Go not?

And the men of the city said unto Elisha, Behold, I pray thee, the situation of this city is pleasant, as my lord seeth; but the water is naught, and the ground barren. And he said, Bring me a new cruse, and put salt therein. And they brought it to him. And he went forth unto the spring of the waters, and cast the salt in there, and said, Thus saith the Lord, I have healed these waters; there shall not be from thence anymore death or barren land. So the waters were healed unto this day, according to the saying of Elisha which he spake.

And he went up from thence unto Beth-el; and as he was going up by the way, there came forth little children out of the city, and mocked him, and said unto him, Go up, thou bald head; go up, thou bald head. And he turned back, and looked on them and cursed them in the name of the Lord. And there came forth two she bears out of the wood, and tare forty and two children of them. And he went from thence to mount Carmel, and from thence he returned to Samaria.

2 NOW Jehoram the son of Ahab began to reign over Israel in Samaria in the eighteenth year of Jehoshaphat king of Judah, and reigned twelve years. And he wrought evil in the sight of the Lord; but not like his father, and like his mother; for he put away the image of Baal that his father had made. Nevertheless he cleaved unto the sins of Jeroboam the son of Nebat, which made Israel to sin; he departed not therefrom.

And Mesha king of Moab was a sheepmaster, and rendered unto the king of Israel a hundred thousand lambs, and a hundred thousand rams, with the wool. But it came to pass, when Ahab was dead, that the king of Moab rebelled against the king of Israel. And king Jehoram went out of Samaria the same time, and numbered all Israel. And he went and sent to Jehoshaphat the king of Judah, saying, The king of Moab hath rebelled against me; wilt thou go with me against Moab to battle? And he said, I will go up; I am as thou art, my people as thy people, and my horses as thy horses. And he said, Which way shall we go up? And he answered, The way through the wilderness of Edom.

So the king of Israel went, and the king of Judah, and the king of Edom; and they fetched a compass of seven days' journey; and there was no water for the host, and for the cattle that followed them. And the king of Israel said, Alas! that the Lord hath called these three kings together, to deliver them into the hand of Moab! But Jehoshaphat said, Is there not here a prophet of the Lord, that we may inquire of the Lord by him? And one of the king of Israel's servants answered and said, Here is Elisha the son of Shaphat, which poured water on the hands of Elijah. And Jehoshaphat said, The word of the Lord is with him. So the king of Israel and Jehoshaphat and the king of Edom went down to him.

And Elisha said unto the king of Israel, What have I to do with thee? get thee to the prophets of thy father, and to the prophets of thy mother. And the king of Israel said unto him, Nay; for the Lord hath called these three kings together, to deliver them into the hand of Moab. And Elisha said, As the Lord of hosts liveth, before whom I stand, surely, were it not that I regard the presence of Jehoshaphat the king of Judah, I would not look toward thee, nor see thee. But now bring me a minstrel. And it came to pass, when the minstrel played, that the hand of the Lord came upon him. And he said, Thus saith the Lord, Make this valley full of ditches. For thus saith the Lord, Ye shall not see wind, neither shall ye see rain; yet that valley shall be filled with water, that ye may drink, both ye, and your cattle, and your beasts. And this is but a light thing in the sight of the Lord; he will deliver the Moabites also into your hand. And ye shall smite every fenced city, and every choice city, and shall fell every good tree, and stop all wells of water, and mar every good piece of land with stones. And it came to pass in the morning, when the meat offering was offered, that, behold, there came water by the way of Edom, and the country was filled with water.

And when all the Moabites heard that the kings were come up to fight against them, they gathered all that were able to put on armor, and upward, and stood in the border. And they rose up early in the morning, and the sun shone upon the water, and the Moabites saw the water on the other side as red as blood; and they said, This is blood; the kings are surely slain, and they have smitten one another; now therefore, Moab, to the spoil. And when they came to the camp of Israel, the Israelites rose up and smote the Moabites, so that they fled before them; but they went forward smiting the Moabites, even in their country. And they beat down the cities, and on every good piece of land cast every man his stone, and filled it; and they stopped all the wells of water, and felled all the good trees; only in Kir-haraseth left they the stones thereof; howbeit the slingers went about it, and smote it. And when the king of Moab saw that the battle was too sore for him, he took with him seven hundred men that drew swords, to break through even unto the king of Edom; but they could not. Then he took his eldest son that should have reigned in his stead, and offered him for a burnt offering upon the wall. And there was great indignation against Israel; and they departed from him, and returned to their own land.

Now there cried a certain woman of the wives of the sons of the prophets unto Elisha, saying, Thy servant my husband is dead; and thou knowest that thy servant did fear the Lord; and the creditor is come to take unto him my two sons to be bondmen. And Elisha said unto her, What shall I do for thee? tell me, what hast thou in the house? And she said, Thine handmaid hath not anything in the house, save a pot of oil. Then he said, Go, borrow thee vessels abroad of all thy neighbors, even empty vessels; borrow not a few. And when thou art come in, thou shalt shut the door upon thee and upon thy sons, and shalt pour out into all those vessels, and thou shalt set aside that which is full. So she went from him, and shut the door upon her and upon her sons, who brought the vessels to her; and she poured out. And it came to pass, when the vessels were full, that she said unto her son, Bring me yet a vessel. And he said unto her. There is not a vessel more. And the oil stayed. Then she came and told the man of God. And he said, Go, sell the oil, and pay thy dept, and live thou and thy children of the rest.

And it fell on a day, that Elisha passed to Shunem, where was a great woman; and she constrained him to eat bread. And so it was, that, as oft as he passed by, he turned in thither to eat bread. And she said unto her husband, Behold now, I perceive that this is a holy man of God, which passeth by us continually. Let us make a little chamber, I pray thee, on the wall; and let us set for him there a bed, and a table, and a stool, and a candlestick; and it shall be, when he cometh to us, that he shall turn in thither. And it fell on a day, that he came thither, and he turned into the chamber, and lay there. And he said to Gehazi his servant, Call this Shunammite. And when he had called her, she stood before him. And he said unto him, Say now unto her, Behold, thou hast been careful for us with all this care; what is to be done for thee; wouldest thou be spoken for to the king, or the captain of the host? And she answered, I dwell among mine own people. And he said, What then is to be done for her? And Gehazi answered, Verily she hath no child, and her husband is old. And he said, Call her. And when he had called her, she stood in the door. And he said, About this season, according to the time of life, thou shalt embrace a son. And she said, Nay, my lord, thou man of God, do not lie unto thine handmaid. And the woman conceived, and bare a son at that season that Elisha had said unto her, according to the time of life.

And when the child was grown, it fell on a day, that he went out to his father to the reapers. And he said unto his father, My head, my head! And he said to a lad, Carry him to his mother. And when he had taken him, and brought him to his mother, he sat on her knees till noon, and then died. And she went up, and laid him on the bed of the man of God, and shut the door upon him, and went out. And she called unto her husband, and said, Send me, I pray thee, one of the young men, and one of the asses, that I may run to the man of God, and come again. And he said, Wherefore wilt thou go to him today? it is neither new moon, nor sabbath. And she said, It shall be well. Then she saddled an ass, and said to her servant, Drive, and go forward, slack not thy riding for me, except I bid thee. So she went and came unto the man of God to mount Carmel. And it came to pass, when the man of God saw her afar off, that he said to Gehazi his servant, Behold, yonder is that Shunammite; run now, I pray thee, to meet her, and say unto her, Is it well with thee? is it well with thy husband? is it well with the child? and she answered, It is well. And when she came to the man of God to the hill, she caught him by the feet; but Gehazi came near to thrust her away. And the man of God said, Let her alone; for her soul is vexed within her; and the Lord hath hid it from me, and hath not told me. Then she said, Did I desire a son of my lord? did I not say, Do not deceive me?

Then he said to Gehazi, Gird up thy loins, and take my staff in thine hand, and go thy way; if thou meet any man, salute him not; and if any salute thee, answer him not again; and lay my staff upon the face of the child. And the mother of the child said, As the Lord liveth, and as thy soul liveth, I will not leave thee. And he arose, and followed her. And Gehazi passed on before them, and laid the staff upon the face of the child; but there was neither voice, nor hearing. Wherefore he went again to meet him, and told him, saying, The child is not awaked.

And when Elisha was come into the house, behold, the child was dead, and laid upon his bed. He went in therefore, and shut the door upon them twain, and prayed unto the Lord. And he went up, and lay upon the child, and put his mouth upon his mouth, and his eyes upon his eyes, and his hands upon his hands; and he stretched himself upon the child; and the flesh of the child waxed warm. Then he returned and walked in the house to and fro; and went up, and stretched himself upon him; and the child sneezed seven times, and the child opened his eyes. And he called Gehazi, and said, Call this Shunammite. So he called her. And when she was come in unto him, he said, Take up thy son. Then she went in, and fell at his feet, and bowed herself to the ground, and took up her son, and went out.

And Elisha came again to Gilgal; and there was a dearth in the land; and the sons of the prophets were sitting before him; and he said unto his servant, Set on the great pot, and seethe pottage for the sons of the prophets. And one went out into the field to gather herbs, and found a wild vine, and gathered thereof wild gourds his lap full, and came and shred them into the pot of pottage, for they knew them not. So they poured out for the men to eat. And it came to pass, as they were eating of the pottage, that they cried out, and said, O thou man of God, there is death in the pot. And they could not eat thereof. But he said, Then bring meal. And he cast it into the pot; and he said, Pour out for the people, that they may eat. And there was no harm in the pot.

And there came a man from Baal-shalisha, and brought the man of God bread of the firstfruits, twenty loaves of barley, and full ears of corn in the husk thereof. And he said, Give unto the people, that they may eat. And his servitor said, What, should I set this before a hundred men? He said again, Give the people, that they may eat; for thus saith the Lord, They shall eat, and shall leave thereof. So he set it before them, and they did eat, and left thereof, according to the word of the Lord.

Now Naaman, captain of the host of the king of Syria, was a great man with his master, and honorable, because by him the Lord had given deliverance unto Syria; he was also a mighty man in valor, but he was a leper. And the Syrians had gone out by companies, and had brought away captive out of the land of Israel a little maid; and she waited on Naaman's wife. And she said unto her mistress, Would God my lord were with the prophet that is in Samaria! for he would recover him of his leprosy. And one went in, and told his lord, saying, Thus and thus said the maid that is of the land of Israel. And the king of Syria said, Go to, go, and I will send a letter unto the king of Israel. And he departed, and took with him ten talents of silver, and six thousand pieces of gold, and ten changes of raiment.

And he brought the letter to the king of Israel, saying, Now when this letter is come unto thee, behold, I have therewith sent Naaman my servant to thee, that thou mayest recover him of his leprosy. And it came to pass, when the king of Israel had read the letter, that he rent his clothes, and said, Am I God, to kill and to make alive, that this man doth send unto me to recover a man of his leprosy? Wherefore consider, I pray you, and see how he seeketh a quarrel against me.

And it was so, when Elisha the man of God had heard that the king of Israel had rent his clothes, that he sent to the king, saying, Wherefore hast thou rent thy clothes? let him come now to me, and he shall know that there is a prophet in Israel. So Naaman came with his horses and with his chariot, and stood at the door of the house of Elisha. And Elisha sent a messenger unto him, saying, Go and wash in Jordan seven times, and thy flesh shall come again to thee, and thou shalt be clean. But Naaman was wroth, and went away, and said, Behold, I thought, He will surely come out to me, and stand, and call on the name of the Lord his God, and strike his hand over the place, and recover the leper. Are not Abana and Pharpar, rivers of Damascus, better than all the waters of Israel? may I not wash in them, and be clean? So he turned and went away in a rage. And his servants came near, and spake unto him, and said, My father if the prophet had bid thee do some great thing, wouldest thou not have done it? how much rather then, when he saith to thee, Wash, and be clean? Then went he down, and dipped himself seven times in Jordan, according to the saying of the man of God; and his flesh came again like unto the flesh of a little child, and he was clean.

And he returned to the man of God, he and all his company, and came, and stood before him; and he said, Behold, now I know that there is no God in all the Earth, but in Israel; now therefore, I pray thee, take a blessing of thy servant. But he said, As the Lord liveth, before whom I stand, I will receive none. And he urged him to take it; but he refused. And Naaman said, Shall there not then, I pray thee, be given to thy servant two mules' burden of earth? for thy servant will henceforth offer neither burnt offering nor sacrifice unto other gods, but unto the Lord. In this thing the Lord pardon thy servant, that when my master goeth into the house of Rimmon to worship there, and he leaneth on my hand, and I bow myself in the house of Rimmon; when I bow down myself in the house of Rimmon, the Lord pardon thy servant in this thing. And he said unto him, Go in peace. So he departed from him a little way.

But Gehazi, the servant of Elisha the man of God, said, Behold, my master hath spared Naaman this Syrian, in not receiving at his hands that which he brought; but, as the Lord liveth, I will run after him, and take somewhat of him. So Gehazi followed after Naaman. And when Naaman saw him running after him, he lighted down from the chariot to meet him, and said, Is all well? And he said, All is well. My master hath sent me, saying, Behold, even now there be come to me from mount Ephraim two young men of the sons of the prophets; give them, I pray thee, a talent of silver, and two changes of garments. And Naaman said, Be content, take two talents. And he urged him, and bound two talents of silver in two bags, with two changes of garments, and laid them upon two of his servants; and they bare them before them.

And when he came to the tower, he took them from their hand, and bestowed them in the house; and he let the men go, and they departed. But he went in, and stood before his master. And Elisha said unto him, Whence comest thou, Gehazi? And he said, Thy servant went no whither. And he said unto him, Went not mine heart with thee, when the man turned again from his chariot to meet thee? Is it a time to receive money, and to receive garments, and olive yards, and vineyards, and sheep, and oxen, and menservants, and maidservants? The leprosy therefore of Naaman shall cleave unto thee, and unto thy seed forever. And he went out from his presence a leper as white as snow.

And the sons of the prophets said unto Elisha, Behold now, the place where we dwell with thee is too strait for us. Let us go, we pray thee, unto Jordan, and take thence every man a beam, and let us make us a place there, where we may dwell. And he answered, Go ye. And one said, Be content, I pray thee, and go with thy servants. And he answered, I will go. So he went with them. And when they came to Jordan, they cut down wood. But as one was felling a beam, the axhead fell into the water; and he cried, and said, Alas, master! for it was borrowed. And the man of God said, Where fell it? And he showed him the place. And he cut down a stick, and cast it in thither; and the iron did swim. Therefore said he, Take it up to thee. And he put out his hand, and took it.

Then the king of Syria warred against Israel, and took counsel with his servants, saying, In such and such a place shall be my camp. And the man of God sent unto the king of Israel, saying, Beware that thou pass not such a place; for thither the Syrians are come down. And the king of Israel sent to the place which the man of God told him and warned him of, and saved himself there, not once nor twice.

Therefore the heart of the king of Syria was sore troubled for this thing; and he called his servants, and said unto them, Will ye not show me which of us is for the king of Israel? And one of his servants said, None, my lord, O king; but Elisha, the prophet that is in Israel, telleth the king of Israel the words that thou speakest in thy bedchamber. And he said, Go and spy where he is, that I may send and fetch him. And it was told him, saying, Behold, he is in Dothan. Therefore sent he thither horses, and chariots, and a great host; and they came by night, and compassed the city about.

And when the servant of the man of God was risen early, and gone forth, behold, a host compassed the city both with horses and chariots. And his servant said unto him, Alas, my master! how shall we do? And he answered, Fear not; for they that be with us are more than they that be with them. And Elisha prayed, and said, Lord, I pray thee, open his eyes, that he may see. And the Lord opened the eyes of the young man; and he saw; and, behold, the mountain was full of horses and chariots of fire round about Elisha. And when they came down to him, Elisha prayed unto the Lord, and said, Smite this people, I pray thee, with blindness. And he smote them with blindness according to the word of Elisha. And Elisha said unto them, This is not the way, neither is this the city; follow me; and I will bring you to the man whom ye seek. But he led them to Samaria.

And it came to pass, when they were come into Samaria, that Elisha said, Lord, open the eyes of these men that they may see. And the Lord opened their eyes, and they saw; and, behold, they were in the midst of Samaria. And the king of Israel said unto Elisha, when he saw them, My father, shall I smite them? shall I smite them? And he answered, Thou shalt not smite them; wouldest thou smite those whom thou hast taken captive with thy sword and with thy bow? set bread and water before them, that they may eat and drink, and go to their master. And he prepared great provision for them; and when they had eaten and drunk, he sent them away, and they went to their master. So the bands of Syria came no more into the land of Israel.

And it came to pass after this, that Ben-hadad king of Syria gathered all his host, and went up, and besieged Samaria. And there was a great famine in Samaria; and, behold, they besieged it, until an ass's head was sold for fourscore pieces of silver, and the fourth part of a cab of dove's dung for five pieces of silver. And as the king of Israel was passing by upon the wall, there cried a woman unto him, saying, Help, my lord, O king. And he said, If the Lord do not help thee, whence shall I help thee? out of the barn floor, or out of the winepress? And the king said unto her, What aileth thee? And she answered, This woman said unto me, Give thy son, that we may eat him today, and we will eat my son tomorrow. So we boiled my son, and did eat him; and I said unto her on the next day, Give thy son, that we may eat him; and she hath hid her son. And it came to pass, when the king heard the words of the woman, that he rent his clothes; and he passed by upon the wall, and the people looked, and, behold, he had sackcloth within upon his flesh. Then he said, God do so and more also to me, if the head of Elisha the son of Shaphat shall stand on him this day.

But Elisha sat in his house, and the elders sat with him; and the king sent a man from before him; but ere the messenger came to him, he said to the elders, See ye how this son of a murderer hath sent to take away mine head? look, when the messenger cometh, shut the door, and hold him fast at the door; is not the sound of his master's feet behind him? And while he yet talked with them, behold, the messenger came down unto him; and he said, Behold, this evil is of the Lord; what should I wait for the Lord any longer?

Then Elisha said, Hear ye the word of the Lord; Thus saith the Lord, Tomorrow about this time shall a measure of fine flour be sold for a shekel, and two measures of barley for a shekel, in the gate of Samaria. Then a lord on whose hand the king leaned answered the man of God, and said, Behold, if the Lord would make windows in Heaven, might this thing be? And he said, Behold, thou shalt see it with thine eyes, but shall not eat thereof.

And there were four leprous men at the entering in of the gate; and they said one to another, Why sit we here until we die? If we say, We will enter into the city, then the famine is in the city, and we shall die there; and if we sit still here, we die also. Now therefore come, and let us fall unto the host of the Syrians; if they save us alive, we shall live; and if they kill us, we shall but die.

And they rose up in the twilight, to go unto the camp of the Syrians; and when they were come to the uttermost part of the camp of Syria, behold, there was no man there. For the Lord had made the host of the Syrians to hear a noise of chariots, and a noise of horses, even the noise of a great host; and they said one to another, Lo, the king of Israel hath hired against us the kings of the Hittites, and the kings of the Egyptians, to come upon us. Wherefore they arose and fled in the twilight, and left their tents, and their horses, and their asses, even the camp as it was, and fled for their life.

And when these lepers came to the uttermost part of the camp, they went into one tent, and did eat and drink, and carried thence silver, and gold, and raiment, and went and hid it; and came again, and entered into another tent, and carried thence also, and went and hid it. Then they said one to another, We do not well; this day is a day of good tidings; and we hold our peace; if we tarry till the morning light, some mischief will come upon us; now therefore come, that we may go and tell the king's household. So they came and called unto the porter of the city; and they told them, saying, We came to the camp of the Syrians, and, behold, there was no man there, neither voice of man, but horses tied, and asses tied, and the tents as they were. And he called the porters; and they told it to the king's house within.

And the king arose in the night, and said unto his servants, I will now show you what the Syrians have done to us. They know that we be hungry; therefore are they gone out of the camp to hide themselves in the field, saying, When they come out of the city, we shall catch them alive, and get into the city. And one of his servants answered and said, Let some take, I pray thee, five of the horses that remain, which are left in the city, (behold, they are as all the multitude of Israel that are left in it; behold, I say, they are even as all the multitude of the Israelites that are consumed;) and let us send and see.

They took therefore two chariot horses; and the king sent after the host of the Syrians, saying, Go and see. And they went after them unto Jordan; and, lo, all the way was full of garments and vessels, which the Syrians had cast away in their haste. And the messengers returned, and told the king. And the people went out, and spoiled the tents of the Syrians. So a measure of fine flour was sold for a shekel, and two measures of barley for a shekel, according to the word of the Lord.

And the king appointed the lord on whose hand he leaned to have the charge of the gate; and the people trode upon him in the gate, and he died, as the man of God had said, who spake when the king came down to him. And it came to pass as the man of God had spoken to the king, saying, Two measures of barley for a shekel, and a measure of fine flour for a shekel, shall be tomorrow about this time in the gate of Samaria; and that lord answered the man of God, and said, Now, behold, if the Lord should make windows in Heaven, might such a thing be? And he said, Behold, thou shalt see it with thine eyes, but shalt not eat thereof. And so it fell out unto him; for the people trode upon him in the gate, and he died.

Then spake Elisha unto the woman, whose son he had restored to life, saying, Arise, and go thou and thine household, and sojourn wheresoever thou canst sojourn; for the Lord hath called for a famine; and it shall also come upon the land seven years. And the woman arose, and did after the saying of the man of God; and she went with her household, and sojourned in the land of the Philistines seven years. And it came to pass at the seven years' end, that the woman returned out of the land of the Philistines; and she went forth to cry unto the king for her house and for her land. And the king talked with Gehazi the servant of the man of God, saying, Tell me, I pray thee, all the great things that Elisha hath done. And it came to pass, as he was telling the king how he had restored a dead body to life, that, behold, the woman, whose son he had restored to life, cried to the king for her house and for her land. And Gehazi said, My lord, O, king, this is the woman, and this is her son, whom Elisha restored to life. And when the king asked the woman, she told him. So the king appointed unto her a certain officer, saying, Restore all that was hers, and all the fruits of the field since the day that she left the land, even until now.

And Elisha came to Damascus; and Ben-hadad the king of Syria was sick; and it was told him, saying, The man of God is come hither. And the king said unto Hazael, Take a present in thine hand, and go, meet the man of God, and inquire of the Lord by him, saying, Shall I recover of this disease? So Hazael went to meet him, and took a present with him, even of every good thing of Damascus, forty camels' burden, and came and stood before him, and said, Thy son Ben-hadad king of Syria hath sent me to thee, saying, Shall I recover of this disease? And Elisha said unto him, Thou wilt go, and say unto him, Thou mayest certainly recover; howbeit, the Lord hath showed me that he shall surely die. And he settled his countenance steadfastly, until he was ashamed; and the man of God wept. And Hazael said, Why weepeth my lord? And he answered, Because I know the evil that thou wilt do unto the children of Israel; their strongholds wilt thou set on fire, and their young men wilt thou slay with the sword, and wilt dash their children, and rip up their women with child. And Hazael said, But what, is thy servant a dog, that he should do this great thing? And Elisha answered, The Lord hath showed me that thou shalt be king over Syria.

So he departed from Elisha, and came to his master; who said to him, What said Elisha to thee? And he answered, He told me that thou shouldest surely recover. And it came to pass on the morrow, that he took a thick cloth, and dipped it in water, and spread it on his face, so that he died; and Hazael reigned in his stead.

And in the fifth year of Joram the son of Ahab king of Israel, Jehoshaphat being then king of Judah, Jehoram the son of Jehoshaphat king of Judah began to reign. Thirty and two years old was he when he began to reign; and he reigned eight years in Jerusalem.

And he walked in the way of the kings of Israel, as did the house of Ahab; for the daughter of Ahab was his wife; and he did evil in the sight of the Lord. Yet the Lord would not destroy Judah for David his servant's sake, as he promised him to give him always a light, and to his children.

In his days Edom revolted from under the hand of Judah, and made a king over themselves. So Joram went over to Zair, and all the chariots with him; and he rose by night, and smote the Edomites which compassed him about, and the captains of the chariots; and the people fled into their tents. Yet Edom revolted from under the hand of Judah unto this day. Then Libnah revolted at the same time. And the rest of the acts of Joram, and all that he did, are they not written in the book of the Chronicles of the kings of Judah? And Joram slept with his fathers, and was buried with his fathers in the city of David; and Ahaziah his son reigned in his stead.

In the twelfth year of Joram the son of Ahab king of Israel did Ahaziah the son of Jehoram king of Judah begin to reign. Two and twenty years old was Ahaziah when he began to reign; and he reigned one year in Jerusalem. And his mother's name was Athaliah, the daughter of Omri king of Israel. And he walked in the way of the house of Ahab, and did evil in the sight of the Lord, as did the house of Ahab; for he was the son-in-law of the house of Ahab.

And he went with Joram the son of Ahab to the war against Hazael king of Syria in Ramoth-gilead; and the Syrians wounded Joram. And king Joram went back to be healed in Jezreel of the wounds which the Syrians had given him at Ramah, when he fought against Hazael king of Syria. And Ahaziah the son of Jehoram king of Judah went down to see Joram the son of Ahab in Jezreel, because he was sick.

And Elisha the prophet called one of the children of the prophets, and said unto him, Gird up thy loins, and take this box of oil in thine hand, and go to Ramoth-gilead; and when thou comest thither, look out there Jehu the son of Jehoshaphat the son of Nimshi, and go in, and make him arise up from among his brethren, and carry him to an inner chamber; then take the box of oil, and pour it on his head, and say, Thus saith the Lord, I have anointed thee king over Israel. Then open the door, and flee, and tarry not.

So the young man, even the young man the prophet, went to Ramoth-gilead. And when he came, behold, the captains of the host were sitting; and he said, I have an errand to thee, O captain. And Jehu said, Unto which of all us? And he said, To thee, O captain. And he arose, and went into the house; and he poured the oil on his head, and said unto him, Thus saith the Lord God of Israel, I have anointed thee king over the people of the Lord, even over Israel. And thou shalt smite the house of Ahab thy master, that I may avenge the blood of my servants the prophets, and the blood of all the servants of the Lord, at the hand of Jezebel. For the whole house of Ahab shall perish; and I will cut off from Ahab him that pisseth against the wall, and him that is shut up and left in Israel; and I will make the house of Ahab like the house of Jeroboam the son of Nebat, and like the house of Baasha the son of Ahijah; and the dogs shall eat Jezebel in the portion of Jezreel, and there shall be none to bury her. And he opened the door, and fled.

Then Jehu came forth to the servants of his lord; and one said unto him, Is all well? wherefore came this mad fellow to thee? And he said unto them, Ye know the man, and his communication. And they said, It is false; tell us now. And he said, Thus and thus spake he to me, saying, Thus saith the Lord, I have anointed thee king over Israel. Then they hasted, and took every man his garment, and put it under him on the top of the stairs, and blew with trumpets, saying, Jehu is king.

So Jehu the son of Jehoshaphat the son of Nimshi conspired against Joram. (Now Joram had kept Ramoth-gilead, he and all Israel, because of Hazael king of Syria; but king Joram was returned to be healed in Jezreel of the wounds which the Syrians had given him, when he fought with Hazael king of Syria.) And Jehu said, If it be your minds, then let none go forth nor escape out of the city to go to tell it in Jezreel. So Jehu rode in a chariot, and went to Jezreel; for Joram lay there. And Ahaziah king of Judah was come down to see Joram.

And there stood a watchman on the tower of Jezreel, and he spied the company of Jehu as he came, and said, I see a company. And Joram said, Take a horseman, and send to meet them, and let him say, Is it peace? So there went one on horseback to meet him, and said, Thus saith the king, Is it peace? And Jehu said, What hast thou to do with peace? turn thee behind me. And the watchman told, saying, The messenger came to them, but he cometh not again. Then he sent out a second on horseback, which came to them, and said, Thus saith the king, Is it peace? And Jehu answered, What hast thou to do with peace? turn thee behind me. And the watchman told, saying, He came even unto them, and cometh not again; and the driving is like the driving of Jehu the son of Nimshi; for he driveth furiously.

And Joram said, Make ready. And his chariot was made ready. And Joram king of Israel and Ahaziah king of Judah went out, each in his chariot, and they went out against Jehu, and met him in the portion of Naboth the Jezreelite. And it came to pass, when Joram saw Jehu, that he said, Is it peace, Jehu? And he answered, What peace, so long as the whoredoms of thy mother Jezebel and her witchcrafts are so many? And Joram turned his hands, and fled, and said to Ahaziah, There is treachery, O Ahaziah. And Jehu drew And the land had rest forty years. a bow with his full strength, and smote Jehoram between his arms, and the arrow went out at his heart, and he sunk down in his chariot. Then said Jehu to Bidkar his captain, Take up, and cast him in the portion of the field of Naboth the Jezreelite; for remember how that, when I and thou rode together after Ahab his father, the Lord laid this burden upon him; surely I have seen yesterday the blood of Naboth, and the blood of his sons, saith the Lord; and I will requite thee in this plat, saith the Lord. Now therefore take and cast him into the plat of ground, according to the word of the Lord.

But when Ahaziah the king of Judah saw this, he fled by the way of the garden house. And Jehu followed after him, and said, Smite him also in the chariot. And they did so at the going up to Gur, which is by Ibleam. And he fled to Megiddo, and died there. And his servants carried him in a chariot to Jerusalem, and buried him in his sepulcher with his fathers in the city of David. And in the eleventh year of Joram the son of Ahab began Ahaziah to reign over Judah.

And when Jehu was come to Jezreel, Jezebel heard of it; and she painted her face, and tired her head, and looked out at a window. And as Jehu entered in at the gate, she said, Had Zimri peace, who slew his master? And he lifted up his face to the window, and said, Who is on my side? who? And there looked out to him two or three eunuchs. And he said, Throw her down. So they threw her down; and some of her blood was sprinkled on the wall, and on the horses; and he trode her underfoot. And when he was come in, he did eat and drink, and said, Go, see now this cursed woman, and bury her; for she is a king's daughter. And they went to bury her; but they found no more of her than the skull, and the feet, and the palms of her hands. Wherefore they came again, and told him. And he said, This is the word of the Lord, which he spake by his servant Elijah the Tishbite, saying, In the portion of Jezreel shall dogs eat the flesh of Jezebel; and the carcass of Jezebel shall be as dung upon the face of the field in the portion of Jezreel; so that they shall not say, This is Jezebel.

3 AND Ahab had seventy sons in Samaria. And Jehu wrote letters, and sent to Samaria, unto the rulers of Jezreel, to the elders, and to them that brought up Ahab's children, saying, Now as soon as this letter cometh to you, seeing your master's sons are with you, and there are with you chariots and horses, a fenced city also, and armor; look even out the best and meetest of your master's sons, and set him on his father's throne, and fight for your master's house.

But they were exceedingly afraid, and said, Behold, two kings stood not before him; how then shall we stand? And he that was over the house, and he that was over the city, the elders also, and the bringers up of the children, sent to Jehu, saying, We are thy servants, and will do all that thou shalt bid us; we will not make any king; do thou that which is good in thine eyes.

Then he wrote a letter the second time to them, saying, If ye be mine, and if ye will hearken unto my voice, take ye the heads of the men your master's sons, and come to me to Jezreel by tomorrow this time. Now the king's sons, being seventy persons, were with the great men of the city, which brought them up.

And it came to pass, when the letter came to them, that they took the king's sons, and slew seventy persons, and put their heads in baskets, and sent him them to Jezreel. And there came a messenger, and told him, saying, They have brought the heads of the king's sons. And he said, Lay ye them in two heaps at the entering in of the gate until the morning.

And it came to pass in the morning, that he went out, and stood, and said to all the people, Ye be righteous; behold, I conspired against my master, and slew him; but who slew all these? Know now that there shall fall unto the earth nothing of the word of the Lord, which the Lord spake concerning the house of Ahab; for the Lord hath done that which he spake by his servant Elijah. So Jehu slew all that remained of the house of Ahab in Jezreel, and all his great men, and his kinsfolks, and his priests, until he left him none remaining.

And he arose and departed, and came to Samaria. And as he was at the shearing house in the way, Jehu met with the brethren of Ahaziah king of Judah, and said, Who are ye? And they answered, We are the brethren of Ahaziah; and we go down to salute the children of the king and the children of the queen. And he said, Take them alive. And they took them alive, and slew them at the pit of the shearing house, even two and forty men; neither left he any of them.

And when he was departed thence, he lighted on Jehonadab the son of Rechab coming to meet him; and he saluted him, and said to him, Is thine heart right, as my heart is with thy heart? And Jehonadab answered, It is. If it be, give me thine hand. And he gave him his hand; and he took him up to him into the chariot. And he said, Come with me, and see my zeal for the Lord. So they made him ride in his chariot. And when he came to Samaria, he slew all that remained unto Ahab in Samaria, till he had destroyed him, according to the saying of the Lord, which he spake to Elijah.

And Jehu gathered all the people together, and said unto them, Ahab served Baal a little; but Jehu shall serve him much. Now therefore call unto me all the prophets of Baal, all his servants, and all his priests; let none be wanting; for I have a great sacrifice to do to Baal; whosoever shall be wanting, he shall not live.

But Jehu did it in subtilty, to the intent that he might destroy the worshipers of Baal. And Jehu said, Proclaim a solemn assembly for Baal. And they proclaimed it. And Jehu sent through all Israel; and all the worshipers of Baal came, so that there was not a man left that come not. And they came into the house of Baal; and the house of Baal was full from one end to another. And he said unto him that was over the vestry, Bring forth vestments for all the worshipers of Baal. And he brought them forth vestments. And Jehu went, and Jehonadab the son of Rechab, into the house of Baal, and said unto the worshipers of Baal, Search, and look that there be here with you none of the servants of the Lord, but the worshipers of Baal only. And when they went in to offer sacrifices and burnt offerings, Jehu appointed fourscore men without, and said, If any of the men whom I have brought into your hands escape, he that letteth him go, his life shall be for the life of him.

And it came to pass, as soon as he had made an end of offering the burnt offering, that Jehu said to the guard and to the captains, Go in, and slay them; let none come forth. And they smote them with the edge of the sword; and the guard and the captains cast them out, and went to the city of the house of Baal. And they brought forth the images out of the house of Baal, and burned them. And they brake down the image of Baal, and brake down the house of Baal, and made it a draught house unto this day. Thus Jehu destroyed Baal out of Israel.

Howbeit, from the sins of Jeroboam the son of Nebat, who made Israel to sin, Jehu departed not from after them, to wit, the golden calves that were in Beth-el, and that were in Dan. And the Lord said unto Jehu, Because thou hast done well in executing that which is right in mine eyes, and hast done unto the house of Ahab according to all that was in mine heart, thy children of the fourth generation shall sit on the throne of Israel. But Jehu took no heed to walk in the law of the Lord God of Israel with all his heart; for he departed not from the sins of Jeroboam, which made Israel to sin.

In those days the Lord began to cut Israel short; and Hazael smote them in all the coasts of Israel; from Jordan eastward, all the land of Gilead, the Gadites, and the Reubenites, and the Manassites, from Aroer, which is by the river Arnon, even Gilead and Bashan.

Now the rest of the acts of Jehu, and all that he did, and all his might, are they not written in the book of the Chronicles of the kings of Israel? And Jehu slept with his fathers; and they buried him in Samaria. And Jehoahaz his son reigned in his stead. And the time that Jehu reigned over Israel in Samaria was twenty and eight years.

4 AND when Athaliah the mother of Ahaziah saw that her son was dead, she arose and destroyed all the seed royal. But Jehosheba, the daughter of king Joram, sister of Ahaziah, took Joash the son of Ahaziah, and stole him from among the king's sons which were slain; and they hid him, even him and his nurse, in the bedchamber from Athaliah, so that he was not slain. And he was with her hid in the house of the Lord six years. And Athaliah did reign over the land.

And the seventh year Jehoiada sent and fetched the rulers over hundreds, with the captains and the guard, and brought them to him into the house of the Lord, and made a covenant with them, and took an oath of them in the house of the Lord, and showed them the king's son. And he commanded them, saying, This is the thing that ye shall do; A third part of you that enter in on the sabbath shall even be keepers of the watch of the king's house; and a third part shall be at the gate of Sur; and a third part at the gate behind the guard; so shall ye keep the watch of the house, that it be not broken down. And two parts of all you that go forth on the sabbath, even they shall keep the watch of the house of the Lord about the king. And ye shall compass the king round about, every man with his weapons in his hand; and he that cometh within the ranges, let him be slain; and be ye with the king as he goeth out and as he cometh in.

And the captains over the hundreds did according to all things that Jehoiada the priest commanded; and they took every man his men that were to come in on the sabbath, with them that should go out on the sabbath, and came to Jehoiada the priest. And to the captains over hundreds did the priest give king David's spears and shields, that were in the temple of the Lord. And the guard stood, every man with his weapons in his hand, round about the king, from the right corner of the temple to the left corner of the temple, along by the altar and the temple. And he brought forth the king's son, and put the crown upon him, and gave him the testimony; and they made him king, and anointed him; and they clapped their hands, and said, God save the king.

And when Athaliah heard the noise of the guard and of the people, she came to the people into the temple of the Lord. And when she looked, behold, the king stood by a pillar, as the manner was, and the princes and the trumpeters by the king, and all the people of the land rejoiced, and blew with trumpets; and Athaliah rent her clothes, and cried, Treason, treason. But Jehoiada the priest commanded the captains of the hundreds, the officers of the host, and said unto them, Have her forth without the ranges; and him that followeth her kill with the sword. For the priest had said, Let her not be slain in the house of the Lord. And they laid hands on her; and she went by the way by the which the horses came into the king's house; and there was she slain.

And Jehoiada made a covenant between the Lord and the king and the people, that they should be the Lord's people; between the king also and the people. And all the people of the land went into the house of Baal, and brake it down; his altars and his images brake they in pieces thoroughly, and slew Mattan the priest of Baal before the altars. And the priest appointed officers over the house of the Lord. And he took the rulers over hundreds, and the captains, and the guard, and all the people of the land; and they brought down the king from the house of the Lord, and came by the way of the gate of the guard to the king's house. And he sat on the throne of the kings. And all the people of the land rejoiced, and the city was in quiet; and they slew Athaliah with the sword beside the king's house. Seven years old was Jehoash when he began to reign.

In the seventh year of Jehu, Jehoash began to reign; and forty years reigned he in Jerusalem. And his mother's name was Zibiah of Beer-sheba. And Jehoash did that which was right in the sight of the Lord all his days wherein Jehoiada the priest instructed him. But the high places were not taken away; the people still sacrificed and burnt incense in the high places.

And Jehoash said to the priests, All the money of the dedicated things that is brought into the house of the Lord, even the money of everyone that passeth the account, the money that every man is set at, and all the money that cometh into any man's heart to bring into the house of the Lord, let the priests take it to them, every man of his acquaintance; and let them repair the breaches of the house, wheresoever any breach shall be found.

But it was so, that in the three and twentieth year of king Jehoash the priests had not repaired the breaches of the house. Then king Jehoash called for Jehoiada the priest, and the other priests, and said unto them, Why repair ye not the breaches of the house? now therefore receive no more money of your acquaintance, but deliver it for the breaches of the house. And the priests consented to receive no more money of the people, neither to repair the breaches of the house.

But Jehoiada the priest took a chest, and bored a hole in the lid of it, and set it beside the altar, on the right side as one cometh into the house of the Lord; and the priests that kept the door put therein all the money that was brought into the house of the Lord. And it was so, when they saw that there was much money in the chest, that the king's scribe and the high priest came up, and they put up in bags, and told the money that was found in the house of the Lord. And they gave the money, being told, into the hands of them that did the work, that had the oversight of the house of the Lord; and they laid it out to the carpenters and builders, that wrought upon the house of the Lord. And to masons, and hewers of stone, and to buy timber and hewed stone to repair the breaches of the house of the Lord, and for all that was laid out for the house to repair it.

Howbeit there were not made for the house of the Lord bowls of silver, snuffers, basins, trumpets, any vessels of gold, or vessels of silver, of the money that was brought into the house of the Lord; but they gave that to the workmen, and repaired therewith the house of the Lord. Moreover they reckoned not with the men, into whose hand they delivered the money to be bestowed on workmen; for they dealt faithfully. The trespass money and sin money was not brought into the house of the Lord; it was the priests'.

Then Hazael king of Syria went up and fought against Gath, and took it; and Hazael set his face to go up to Jerusalem. And Jehoash king of Judah took all the hallowed things that Jehoshaphat, and Jehoram, and Ahaziah, his fathers, kings of Judah, had dedicated, and his ownhallowed things, and all the gold that was found in the treasures of the house of the Lord, and in the king's house, and sent it to Hazael king of Syria; and he went away from Jerusalem.

And the rest of the acts of Joash, and all that he did, are they not written in the book of the Chronicles of the kings of Judah? And his servants arose, and made a conspiracy, and slew Joash in the house of Millo, which goeth down to Silla. For Jozachar the son of Shimeath and Jehozabad the son of Shomer, his servants, smote him, and he died; and they buried him with his fathers in the city of David; and Amaziah his son reigned in his stead.

In the three and twentieth year of Joash the son of Ahaziah king of Judah, Jehoahaz the son of Jehu began to reign over Israel in Samaria, and reigned seventeen years. And he did that which was evil in the sight of the Lord, and followed the sins of Jeroboam the son of Nebat, which made Israel to sin; he departed not therefrom. And the anger of the Lord was kindled against Israel, and he delivered them into the hand of Hazael king of Syria, and into the hand of Ben-hadad the son of Hazael, all their days.

And Jehoahaz besought the Lord, and the Lord hearkened unto him; for he saw the oppression of Israel, because the king of Syria oppressed them. (And the Lord gave Israel a savior, so that they went out from under the hand of the Syrians; and the children of Israel dwelt in their tents, as beforetime. Nevertheless they departed not from the sins of the house of Jeroboam, who made Israel sin, but walked therein; and there remained the grove also in Samaria.) Neither did he leave of the people to Jehoahaz but fifty horsemen, and ten chariots, and ten thousand footmen; for the king of Syria had destroyed them, and had made them like the dust by threshing. Now the rest of the acts of Jehoahaz, and all that he did, and his might, are they not written in the book of the chronicles of the kings of Israel? And Jehoahaz slept with his fathers; and they buried him in Samaria; and Joash his son reigned in his stead.

In the thirty and seventh year of Joash king of Judah began Jehoash the son of Jehoahaz to reign over Israel in Samaria, and reigned sixteen years. And he did that which was evil in the sight of the Lord; he departed not from all the sins of Jeroboam the son of Nebat, who made Israel sin; but he walked therein. And the rest of the acts of Joash, and all that he did, and his might wherewith he fought against Amaziah king of Judah, are they not written in the book of the Chronicles of the kings of Israel? And Joash slept with his fathers; and Jeroboam sat upon his throne; and Joash was buried in Samaria with the kings of Israel.

Now Elisha was fallen sick of his sickness whereof he died. And Joash the king of Israel came down unto him, and wept over his face, and said, O my father, my father! the chariot of Israel, and the horsemen thereof. And Elisha said unto him, Take bow and arrows. And he took unto him bow and arrows. And he said to the king of Israel, Put thine hand upon the bow. And he put his hand upon it; and Elisha put his hands upon the king's hands. And he said, Open the window eastward. And he opened it. Then Elisha said, Shoot. And he shot. And he said, The arrow of the Lord's deliverance, and the arrow of deliverance from Syria; for thou shalt smite the Syrians in Aphek, till thou have consumed them. And he said, Take the arrows. And he took them. And he said unto the king of Israel, Smite upon the ground. And he smote thrice and stayed. And the man of God was wroth with him, and said, Thou shouldest have smitten five or six times; then hadst thou smitten Syria till thou hadst consumed it; whereas now thou shalt smite Syria but thrice.

And Elisha died, and they buried him. And the bands of the Moabites invaded the land at the coming in of the year. And it came to pass, as they were burying a man, that, behold, they spied a band of men; and they cast the man into the sepulcher of Elisha; and when the man was let down, and touched the bones of Elisha, he revived, and stood up on his feet.

But Hazael king of Syria oppressed Israel all the days of Jehoahaz. And the Lord was gracious unto them, and had compassion on them, and had respect unto them, because of his covenant with Abraham, Isaac, and Jacob, and would not destroy them, neither cast he them from his presence as yet. So Hazael king of Syria died; and Ben-hadad his son reigned in his stead. And Jehoash the son of Jehoahaz took again out of the hand of Ben-hadad the son of Hazael the cities, which he had taken out of the hand of Jehoahaz his father by war. Three times did Joash beat him, and recovered the cities of Israel.

5 IN the second year of Joash son of Jehoahaz king of Israel reigned Amaziah the son of Joash king of Judah. He was twenty and five years old when he began to reign, and reigned twenty and nine years in Jerusalem. And his mother's name was Jehoaddan of Jerusalem. And he did that which was right in the sight of the Lord, yet not like David his father; he did according to all things as Joash his father did. Howbeit the high places were not taken away; as yet the people did sacrifice and burnt incense on the high places.

And it came to pass, as soon as the kingdom was confirmed in his hand, that he slew his servants which had slain the king his father. But the children of the murderers he slew not; according unto that which is written in the book of the law of Moses, wherein the Lord commanded, saying, The fathers shall not be put to death for the children, nor the children be put to death for the fathers; but every man shall be put to death for his own sin. He slew of Edom in the valley of salt ten thousand, and took Selah by war, and called the name of it Joktheel unto this day.

Then Amaziah sent messengers to Jehoash, the son of Jehoahaz son of Jehu, king of Israel, saying, Come, let us look one another in the face. And Jehoash the king of Israel sent to Amaziah king of Judah, saying, The thistle that was in Lebanon sent to the cedar that was in Lebanon, saying, Give thy daughter to my son to wife; and there passed by a wild beast that was in Lebanon, and trode down the thistle. Thou hast indeed smitten Edom, and thine heart hath lifted thee up; glory of this, and tarry at home; for why shouldest thou meddle to thy hurt, that thou shouldest fall, even thou, and Judah with thee? But Amaziah would not hear. Therefore Jehoash king of Israel went up; and he and Amaziah king of Judah looked one another in the face at Beth-shemesh, which belongeth to Judah. And Judah was put to the worse before Israel; and they fled every man to their tents. And Jehoash king of Israel took Amaziah king of Judah, the son of Jehoash the son of Ahaziah at Beth-shemesh, and came to Jerusalem, and brake down the wall of Jerusalem from the gate of Ephraim unto the corner gate, four hundred cubits. And he took all the gold and silver, and all the vessels that were found in the house of the Lord, and in the treasures of the king's house, and hostages, and returned to Samaria. Now the rest of the acts of Jehoash which he did, and his might, and how he fought with Amaziah king of Judah, are they not written in the book of the Chronicles of the kings of Israel? And Jehoash slept with his fathers, and was buried in Samaria with the kings of Israel; and Jeroboam his son reigned in his stead.

And Amaziah the son of Joash king of Judah lived after the death of Jehoash son of Jehoahaz king of Israel fifteen years. And the rest of the acts of Amaziah, are they not written in the book of the Chronicles of the kings of Judah? Now they made a conspiracy against him in Jerusalem; and he fled to Lachish; but they sent after him to Lachish, and slew him there. And they brought him on horses; and he was buried at Jerusalem with his fathers in the city of David. And all the people of Judah took Azariah, which was sixteen years old, and made him king instead of his father Amaziah. He built Elath, and restored it to Judah, after that the king slept with his fathers.

In the fifteenth year of Amaziah the son of Joash king of Judah, Jeroboam the son of Joash king of Israel began to reign in Samaria, and reigned forty and one years. And he did that which was evil in the sight of the Lord; he departed not from all the sins of Jeroboam the son of Nebat, who made Israel to sin. He restored the coast of Israel from the entering of Hamath unto the sea of the plain, according to the word of the Lord God of Israel, which he spake by the hand of his servant Jonah, the son of Amittai, the prophet, which was of Gath-hepher. For the Lord saw the affliction of Israel, that it was very bitter; for there was not any shut up, nor any left, nor any helper for Israel.

And the Lord said not that he would blot out the name of Israel from under Heaven; but he saved them by the hand of Jeroboam the son of Joash. Now the rest of the acts of Jeroboam, and all that he did, and his might, how he warred, and how he recovered Damascus, and Hamath, which belonged to Judah, for Israel, are they not written in the book of the Chronicles of the kings of Israel? And Jeroboam slept with his fathers, even with the kings of Israel; and Zachariah his son reigned in his stead.

In the twenty and seventh year of Jeroboam king of Israel began Azariah son of Amaziah king of Judah to reign. Sixteen years old was he when he began to reign, and he reigned two and fifty years in Jerusalem. And his mother's name was Jecholiah of Jerusalem. And he did that which was right in the sight of the Lord, according to all that his father Amaziah had done; save that the high places were not removed; the people sacrificed and burnt incense still on the high places. And the Lord smote the king, so that he was a leper unto the day of his death, and dwelt in a several house. And Jotham the king's son was over the house, judging the people of the land. And the rest of the acts of Azariah, and all that he did, are they not written in the book of the Chronicles of the kings of Judah? So Azariah slept with his fathers; and they buried him with his fathers in the city of David, and Jotham his son reigned in his stead.

In the thirty and eighth year of Azariah king of Judah did Zachariah the son of Jeroboam reign over Israel in Samaria six months. And he did that which was evil in the sight of the Lord, as his fathers had done; he departed not from the sins of Jeroboam the son of Nebat, who made Israel to sin. And Shallum the son of Jabesh conspired against him, and smote him before the people, and slew him, and reigned in his stead. And the rest of the acts of Zachariah, behold, they are written in the book of the Chronicles of the kings of Israel. This was the word of the Lord which he spake unto Jehu, saying, Thy sons shall sit on the throne of Israel unto the fourth generation. And so it came to pass.

Shallum the son of Jabesh began to reign in the nine and thirtieth year of Uzziah king of Judah; and he reigned a full month in Samaria. For Menahem the son of Gadi went up from Tirzah, and came to Samaria, and smote Shallum the son of Jabesh in Samaria, and slew him, and reigned in his stead. And the rest of the acts of Shallum, and his conspiracy which he made, behold, they are written in the book of the Chronicles of the kings of Israel.

Then Menahem smote Tiphsah, and all that were therein, and the coasts thereof from Tirzah; because they opened not to him, therefore he smote it; and all the women therein that were with child he ripped up. In the nine and thirtieth year of Azariah king of Judah began Menahem the son of Gadi to reign over Israel, and reigned ten years in Samaria. And he did that which was evil in the sight of the Lord; he departed not all his days from the sins of Jeroboam the son of Nebat, who made Israel to sin. And Pul the king of Assyria came against the land; and Menahem gave Pul a thousand talents of silver, that his hand might be with him to confirm the kingdom in his hand. And Menahem exacted the money of Israel, even of all the mighty men of wealth, of each man fifty shekels of silver, to give to the king of Assyria. So the king of Assyria turned back, and stayed not there in the land. And the rest of the acts of Menahem, and all that he did, are they not written in the book of the Chronicles of the kings of Israel? And Menahem slept with his fathers; and Pekahiah his son reigned in his stead.

In the fiftieth year of Azariah king of Judah, Pekahiah the son of Menahem began to reign over Israel in Samaria, and reigned two years. And he did that which was evil in the sight of the Lord; he departed not from the sins of Jeroboam the son of Nebat, who made Israel to sin. But Pekah the son of Remaliah, a captain of his, conspired against him, and smote him in Samaria, in the palace of the king's house, with Argob and Arieh, and with him fifty men of the Gileadites; and he killed him, and reigned in his room. And the rest of the acts of Pekahiah, and all that he did, behold, they are written in the book of the Chronicles of the kings of Israel.

In the two and fiftieth year of Azariah king of Judah, Pekah the son of Remaliah began to reign over Israel in Samaria, and reigned twenty years. And he did that which was evil in the sight of the Lord; he departed not from the sins of Jeroboam the son of Nebat, who made Israel to sin. In the days of Pekah king of Israel came Tiglath-pileser king of Assyria, and took Ijon, and Abel-beth-maachah, and Janoah, and Kedesh, and Hazor, and Gilead, and Galilee, all the land of Naphtali, and carried them captive to Assyria. And Hoshea the son of Elah made a conspiracy against Pekah the son of Remaliah, and smote him, and slew him, and reigned in his stead, in the twentieth year of Jotham the son of Uzziah. And the rest of the acts of Pekah, and all that he did, behold, they are written in the book of the Chronicles of the kings of Israel.

In the second year of Pekah the son of Remaliah king of Israel began Jotham the son of Uzziah king of Judah to reign. Five and twenty years old was he when he began to reign, and he reigned sixteen years in Jerusalem. And his mother's name was Jerusha, the daughter of Zadok. And he did that which was right in the sight of the Lord; he did according to all that his father Uzziah had done. Howbeit the high places were not removed; the people sacrificed and burned incense still in the high places. He built the higher gate of the house of the Lord. Now the rest of the acts of Jotham, and all that he did, are they not written in the book of the Chronicles of the kings of Judah? In those days the Lord began to send against Judah Rezin the king of Syria, and Pekah the son of Remaliah.

And Jotham slept with his fathers, and was buried with his fathers in the city of David his father and Ahaz his son reigned in his stead.

In the seventeenth year of Pekah the son of Remaliah, Ahaz the son of Jotham king of Judah began to reign. Twenty years old was Ahaz when he began to reign, and reigned sixteen years in Jerusalem, and did not that which was right in the sight of the Lord his God, like David his father. But he walked in the way of the kings of Israel, yea, and made his son to pass through the fire, according to the abominations of the heathen, whom the Lord cast out from before the children of Israel. And he sacrificed and burnt incense in the high places, and on the hills, and under every green tree.

Then Rezin king of Syria, and Pekah son of Remaliah king of Israel, came up to Jerusalem to war; and they besieged Ahaz, but could not overcome him. At that time Rezin king of Syria recovered Elath to Syria, and drave the Jews from Elath; and the Syrians came to Elath, and dwelt there unto this day. So Ahaz sent messengers to Tiglath-pileser king of Assyria, saying, I am thy servant and thy son; come up, and save me out of the hand of the king of Syria, and out of the hand of the king of Israel, which rise up against me. And Ahaz took the silver and gold that was found in the house of the Lord, and in the treasures of the king's house, and sent it for a present to the king of Assyria. And the king of Assyria hearkened unto him; for the king of Assyria went up against Damascus, and took it, and carried the people of it captive to Kir, and slew Rezin.

And king Ahaz went to Damascus to meet Tiglath-pileser king of Assyria, and saw an altar that was at Damascus; and king Ahaz sent to Urijah the priest the fashion of the altar, and the pattern of it, according to all the workmanship thereof. And Urijah the priest built an altar according to all that king Ahaz had sent from Damascus; so Urijah the priest made it against king Ahaz came from Damascus. And when the king was come from Damascus, the king saw the altar; and the king approached to the altar, and offered thereon. And he burnt his burnt offering and his meat offering, and poured his drink offering, and sprinkled the blood of his peace offerings, upon the altar. And he brought also the brazen altar, which was before the Lord from the forefront of the house, from between the altar and the house of the Lord, and put it on the north side of the altar.

And king Ahaz commanded Urijah the priest, saying, Upon the great altar burn the morning burnt offering, and the evening meat offering, and the king's burnt sacrifice, and his meat offering, with the burnt offering of all the people of the land, and their meat offering, and their drink offerings; and sprinkle upon it all the blood of the burnt offering, and all the blood of the sacrifice; and the brazen altar shall be for me to inquire by. Thus did Urijah the priest, according to all that king Ahaz commanded. And king Ahaz cut off the borders of the bases, and removed the laver from off them; and took down the sea from off the brazen oxen that were under it, and put it upon a pavement of stones. And the covert for the sabbath that they had built in the house, and the king's entry without, turned he from the house of the Lord for the king of Assyria.

Now the rest of the acts of Ahaz which he did, are they not written in the book of Chronicles of the kings of Judah? And Ahaz slept with his fathers, and was buried with his fathers in the city of David; and Hezekiah his son reigned in his stead.

In the twelfth year of Ahaz king of Judah began Hoshea the son of Elah to reign in Samaria over Israel nine years. And he did that which was evil in the sight of the Lord, but not as the kings of Israel that were before him. Against him came up Shalmaneser king of Assyria; and Hoshea became his servant, and gave him presents. And the king of Assyria found conspiracy in Hoshea; for he had sent messengers to So king of Egypt, and brought no present to the king of Assyria, as he had done year by year; therefore the king of Assyria shut him up, and bound him in prison. Then the king of Assyria came up throughout all the land, and went up to Samaria, and besieged it three years. In the ninth year of Hoshea the king of Assyria took Samaria, and carried Israel away into Assyria, and placed them in Halah and in Habor by the river of Gozan, and in the cities of the Medes.

For so it was, that the children of Israel had sinned against the Lord their God, which had brought them up out of the land of Egypt, from under the hand of Pharaoh king of Egypt, and had feared other gods, and walked in the statutes of the heathen, whom the Lord cast out from before the children of Israel, and of the kings of Israel, which they had made.

And the children of Israel did secretly those things that were not right against the Lord their God, and they built them high places in all their cities, from the tower of the watchmen to the fenced city. And they set them up images and groves in every high hill, and under every green tree; and there they burnt incense in all the high places, as did the heathen whom the Lord carried away before them; and wrought wicked things to provoke the Lord to anger; for they served idols, whereof the Lord had said unto them, Ye shall not do this thing. Yet the Lord testified against Israel, and against Judah, by all the prophets, and by all the seers, saying, Turn ye from your evil ways, and keep my commandments and my statutes, according to all the law which I commanded your fathers, and which I sent to you by my servants the prophets.

Notwithstanding, they would not hear, but hardened their necks, like to the neck of their fathers, that did not believe in the Lord their God. And they rejected his statutes, and his covenant that he made with their fathers, and his testimonies which he testified against them; and they followed vanity, and became vain, and went after the heathen that were round about them, concerning whom the Lord had charged them, that they should not do like them. And they left all the commandments of the Lord their God, and made them molten images, even two calves, and made a grove, and worshiped all the host of Heaven, and served Baal. And they caused their sons and their daughters to pass through the fire, and used divination and enchantments, and sold themselves to do evil in the sight of the Lord, to provoke him to anger. Therefore the Lord was very angry with Israel, and removed them out of his sight; there was none left but the tribe of Judah only.

Also Judah kept not the commandments of the Lord their God, but walked in the statutes of Israel which they made. And the Lord rejected all the seed of Israel, and afflicted them, and delivered them into the hand of spoilers, until he had cast them out of his sight.

For he rent Israel from the house of David; and they made Jeroboam the son of Nebat king; and Jeroboam drave Israel from following the Lord, and made them sin a great sin. For the children of Israel walked in all the sins of Jeroboam which he did; they departed not from them; until the Lord removed Israel out of his sight, as he had said by all his servants the prophets. So was Israel carried away out of their own land to Assyria unto this day.

And the king of Assyria brought men from Babylon, and from Cuthah, and from Ava, and from Hamath, and from Sepharvaim, and placed them in the cities of Samaria instead of the children of Israel; and they possessed Samaria, and dwelt in the cities thereof. And so it was at the beginning of their dwelling there, that they feared not the Lord; therefore the Lord sent lions among them, which slew some of them. Wherefore they spake to the king of Assyria, saying, The nations which thou hast removed, and placed in the cities of Samaria, know not the manner of the God of the land; therefore he hath sent lions among them, and, behold, they slay them, because they know not the manner of the God of the land.

Then the king of Assyria commanded, saying, Carry thither one of the priests whom ye brought from thence; and let them go and dwell there, and let him teach them the manner of the God of the land. Then one of the priests whom they had carried away from Samaria came and dwelt in Beth-el, and taught them how they should fear the Lord.

Howbeit every nation made gods of their own, and put them in the houses of the high places which the Samaritans had made, every nation in their cities wherein they dwelt. And the men of Babylon made Succoth-benoth, and the men of Cuth made Nergal, and the men of Hamath made Ashima, and the Avites made Nibhaz and Tartak, and the Sepharvites burnt their children in fire to Adrammelech and Anammelech, the gods of Sepharvaim. So they feared the Lord, and made unto themselves of the lowest of them priests of the high places, which sacrificed for them in the houses of the high places. They feared the Lord and served their own gods, after the manner of the nations whom they carried away from thence.

Unto this day they do after the former manners; they fear not the Lord, neither do they after their statutes, or after their ordinances, or after the law and commandment which the Lord commanded the children of Jacob, whom he named Israel; with whom the Lord had made a covenant, and charged them, saying, Ye shall not fear other gods, nor bow yourselves to them, nor serve them, nor sacrifice to them; but the Lord, who brought you up out of the land of Egypt with great power and a stretched out arm, him shall ye fear, and him shall ye worship, and to him shall ye do sacrifice. And the statutes, and the ordinances, and the law, and the commandment, which he wrote for you, ye shall observe to do for evermore; and ye shall not fear other gods. And the covenant that I have made with you ye shall not forget; neither shall ye fear other gods. But the Lord your God ye shall fear; and he shall deliver you out of the hand of all your enemies. Howbeit they did not hearken, but they did after their former manner. So these nations feared the Lord, and served their graven images, both their children, and their children's children; as did their fathers, so do they unto this day.

6 NOW it came to pass in the third year of Hoshea son of Elah king of Israel, that Hezekiah the son of Ahaz king of Judah began to reign. Twenty and five years old was he when he began to reign; and he reigned twenty and nine years in Jerusalem. His mother's name also was Abi, the daughter of Zachariah. And he did that which was right in the sight of the Lord, according to all that David his father did. He removed the high places, and brake the images, and cut down the groves, and brake in pieces the brazen serpent that Moses had made; for unto those days the children of Israel did burn incense to it; and he called it Nehushtan. He trusted in the Lord God of Israel; so that after him was none like him among all the kings of Judah, nor any that were before him. For he clave to the Lord, and departed not from following him, but kept his commandments, which the Lord commanded Moses. And the Lord was with him; and he prospered whithersoever he went forth; and he rebelled against the king of Assyria, and served him not. He smote the Philistines, even unto Gaza, and the borders thereof, from the tower of the watchmen to the fenced city.

And it came to pass in the fourth year of king Hezekiah, which was the seventh year of Hoshea son of Elah king of Israel, that Shalmaneser king of Assyria came up against Samaria, and besieged it. And at the end of three years they took it; even in the sixth year of Hezekiah, that is the ninth year of Hoshea king of Israel, Samaria was taken. And the king of Assyria did carry away Israel unto Assyria, and put them in Halah and in Habor by the river of Gozan, and in the cities of the Medes; because they obeyed not the voice of the Lord their God, but transgressed his covenant, and all that Moses the servant of the Lord commanded, and would not hear them, nor do them.

Now in the fourteenth year of king Hezekiah did Sennacherib king of Assyria come up against all the fenced cities of Judah, and took them. And Hezekiah king of Judah sent to the king of Assyria to Lachish, saying, I have offended; return from me; that which thou puttest on me will I bear. And the king of Assyria appointed unto Hezekiah king of Judah three hundred talents of silver and thirty talents of gold. And Hezekiah gave him all the silver that was found in the house of the Lord, and in the treasures of the king's house. At that time did Hezekiah cut off the gold from the doors of the temple of the Lord, and from the pillars which Hezekiah king of Judah had overlaid, and gave it to the king of Assyria.

And the king of Assyria sent Tartan and Rabsaris and Rab-shakeh from Lachish to king Hezekiah with a great host against Jerusalem; and they went up and came to Jerusalem. And when they were come up, they came and stood by the conduit of the upper pool, which is in the highway of the fuller's field. And when they had called to the king, there came out to them Eliakim the son of Hilkiah, which was over the household, and Shebna the scribe, and Joah the son of Asaph the recorder. And Rab-shakeh said unto them, Speak ye now to Hezekiah, Thus saith the great king, the king of Assyria, What confidence is this wherein thou trustest? Thou sayest, (but they are but vain words,) I have counsel and strength for the war. Now on whom dost thou trust, that thou rebellest against me? Now, behold, thou trustest upon the staff of this bruised reed, even upon Egypt, on which if a man lean, it will go into his hand, and pierce it; so is Pharaoh king of Egypt unto all that trust on him. But if ye say unto me, We trust in the Lord our God; is not that he, whose high places and whose altars Hezekiah hath taken away, and hath said to Judah and Jerusalem, Ye shall worship before this altar in Jerusalem? Now therefore, I pray thee, give pledges to my lord the king of Assyria, and I will deliver thee two thousand horses, if thou be able on thy part to set riders upon them. How then wilt thou turn away the face of one captain of the least of my master's servants, and put thy trust on Egypt for chariots and for horsemen? Am I now come up without the Lord against this place to destroy it? The Lord said to me, Go up against this land, and destroy it.

Then said Eliakim the son of Hilkiah, and Shebna, and Joah, unto Rab-shakeh, Speak, I pray thee, to thy servants in the Syrian language; for we understand it; and talk not with us in the Jews' language in the ears of the people that are on the wall. But Rab-shakeh said unto them, Hath my master sent me to thy master, and to thee, to speak these words? hath he not sent me to the men which sit on the wall, that they may eat their own dung, and drink their own piss with you? Then Rab-shakeh stood and cried with a loud voice in the Jews' language, and spake, saying, Hear the word of the great king, the king of Assyria; thus saith the king, Let not Hezekiah deceive you; for he shall not be able to deliver you out of his hand; neither let Hezekiah make you trust in the Lord, saying, The Lord will surely deliver us, and this city shall not be delivered into the hand of the king of Assyria. Hearken not to Hezekiah; for thus saith the king of Assyria, Make an agreement with me by a present, and come out to me, and then eat ye every man of his own vine, and everyone of his fig tree, and drink ye everyone the waters of his cistern; until I come and take you away to a land like your own land, a land of corn and wine, a land of bread and vineyards, a land of olive oil and of honey, that ye may live, and not die; and hearken not unto Hezekiah, when he persuadeth you, saying, the Lord will deliver us. Hath any of the gods of the nations delivered at all this land out of the hand of the king of Assyria? Where are the gods of Hamath, and of Arpad?

where are the gods of Sepharvaim, Hena, and Ivah? have they delivered Samaria out of mine hand? Who are they among all the gods of the countries, that have delivered their country out of mine hand, that the Lord should deliver Jerusalem out of mine hand? But the people held their peace, and answered him not a word; for the king's commandment was, saying, Answer him not. Then came Eliakim the son of Hilkiah, which was over the household, and Shebna the scribe, and Joah the son of Asaph the recorder, to Hezekiah with their clothes rent, and told him the word of Rab-shakeh.

And it came to pass, when king Hezekiah heard it, that he rent his clothes, and covered himself with sackcloth, and went into the house of the Lord. And he sent Eliakim, which was over the household, and Shebna the scribe, and the elders of the priests, covered with sackcloth, to Isaiah the prophet the son of Amoz. And they said unto him, Thus saith Hezekiah, This day is a day of trouble, and of rebuke, and blasphemy; for the children are come to the birth, and there is not strength to bring forth. It may be the Lord thy God will hear all the words of Rab-shakeh, whom the king of Assyria his master hath sent to reproach the living God; and will reprove the words which the Lord thy God hath heard; wherefore lift up thy prayer for the remnant that are left.

So the servants of king Hezekiah came to Isaiah. And Isaiah said unto them, Thus shall ye say to your master, Thus saith the Lord, Be not afraid of the words which thou hast heard, with which the servants of the king of Assyria have blasphemed me. Behold I will send a blast upon him, and he shall hear a rumor, and shall return to his own land; and I will cause him to fall by the sword in his own land.

So Rab-shakeh returned, and found the king of Assyria warring against Libnah; for he had heard that he was departed from Lachish. And when he heard say of Tirhakah king of Ethiopia, Behold, he is come out to fight against thee; he sent messengers again unto Hezekiah, saying, Thus shall ye speak to Hezekiah king of Judah, saying, Let not thy God in whom thou trustest deceive thee, saying, Jerusalem shall not be delivered into the hand of the king of Assyria. Behold, thou hast heard what the kings of Assyria have done to all lands, by destroying them utterly; and shalt thou be delivered? Have the gods of the nations delivered them which my fathers have destroyed; as Gozan, and Haran, and Rezeph, and the children of Eden which were in Thelasar? Where is the king of Hamath, and the king of Arpad, and the king of the city of Sepharvaim, of Hena, and Ivah?

And Hezekiah received the letter of the hand of the messengers, and read it; and Hezekiah went up into the house of the Lord, and spread it before the Lord. And Hezekiah prayed before the Lord, and said, O Lord God of Israel, which dwellest between the cherubim, thou art the God, even thou alone, of all the kingdoms of the Earth; thou hast made Heaven and Earth. Lord, bow down thine ear, and hear; open, Lord, thine eyes, and see; and hear the words of Sennacherib, which hath sent him to reproach the living God. Of a truth, Lord, the kings of Assyria have destroyed the nations and their lands. And have cast their gods into the fire; for they were no gods, but the work of men's hands, wood and stone; therefore they have destroyed them. Now therefore, O Lord our God, I beseech thee, save thou us out of his hand, that all the kingdoms of the Earth may know that thou art the Lord God, even thou only.

Then Isaiah the son of Amoz sent to Hezekiah, saying, Thus saith the Lord God of Israel, That which thou hast prayed to me against Sennacherib king of Assyria I have heard. This is the word that the Lord hath spoken concerning him; The virgin the daughter of Zion hath despised thee, and laughed thee to scorn; the daughter of Jerusalem hath shaken her head at thee. Whom hast thou reproached and blasphemed? and against whom hast thou exalted thy voice, and lifted up thine eyes on high? even against the Holy One of Israel. By thy messengers thou hast reproached the Lord, and hast said, With the multitude of my chariots I am come up to the height of the mountains, to the sides of Lebanon, and will cut down the tall cedar trees thereof, and the choice fir trees thereof; and I will enter into the lodgings of his borders, and into the forest of his Carmel. I have digged and drunk strange waters, and with the sole of my feet have I dried up all the rivers of besieged places. Hast thou not heard long ago how I have done it, and of ancient times that I have formed it? now have I brought it to pass, that thou shouldest be to lay waste fenced cities into ruinous heaps. Therefore their inhabitants were of small power, they were dismayed and confounded; they were as the grass of the field, and as the green herb, as the grass on the housetops, and as corn blasted before it be grown up. But I know thy abode, and thy going out, and thy coming in, and thy rage against me. Because thy rage against me and thy tumult is come up into mine ears, therefore I will put my hook in thy nose, and my bridle in thy lips, and I will turn thee back by the way by which thou camest. And this shall be a sign unto thee. Ye shall eat this year such things as grow of themselves, and in the second year that which springeth of the same; and in the third year sow ye, and reap, and plant vineyards, and eat the fruits thereof. And the remnant that is escaped of the house of Judah shall yet again take root downward, and bear fruit upward. For out of Jerusalem shall go forth a remnant, and they that escape out of mount Zion; the zeal of the Lord of hosts shall do this. Therefore thus saith the Lord concerning the king of Assyria, He shall not come into this city, nor shoot an arrow there, nor come before it with shield, nor cast a bank against it. By the way that he came, by the same shall he return, and shall not come into this city, saith the Lord. For I will defend this city to save it, for mine own sake, and for my servant David's sake.

And it came to pass that night, that the Angel of the Lord went out, and smote in the camp of the Assyrians a hundred fourscore and five thousand; and when they who were left arose early in the morning, behold, they were all dead corpses. So Sennacherib king of Assyria, departed, and went and returned, and dwelt at Nineveh. And it came to pass, as he was worshiping in the house of Nisroch his god, that Adrammelech and Sharezer his sons smote him with the sword; and they escaped into the land of Armenia. And Essar-haddon his son reigned in his stead.

In those days was Hezekiah sick unto death. And the prophet Isaiah the son of Amoz came to him, and said unto him, Thus saith the Lord, Set thine house in order; for thou shalt die, and not live. Then he turned his face to the wall, and prayed unto the Lord, saying, I beseech thee, O Lord, remember now how I have walked before thee in truth and with a perfect heart, and have done that which is good in thy sight. And Hezekiah wept sore.

And it came to pass, afore Isaiah was gone out into the middle court, that the word of the Lord came to him, saying, Turn again, and tell Hezekiah the captain of my people, Thus saith the Lord, the God of David thy father, I have heard thy prayer, I have seen thy tears; behold, I will heal thee; on the third day thou shalt go up unto the house of the Lord. And I will add unto thy days fifteen years; and I will deliver thee and this city out of the hand of the king of Assyria; and I will defend this city for mine own sake, and for my servant David's sake. And Isaiah said, Take a lump of figs. And they took and laid it on the boil, and he recovered. And Hezekiah said unto Isaiah, What shall be the sign that the Lord will heal me, and that I shall go up into the house of the Lord the third day? And Isaiah said, This sign shalt thou have of the Lord, that the Lord will do the thing that he hath spoken; shall the shadow go forward ten degrees, or go back ten degrees? And Hezekiah answered, It is a light thing for the shadow to go down ten degrees; nay, but let the shadow return backward ten degrees. And Isaiah the prophet cried unto the Lord; and he brought the shadow ten degrees backward, by which it had gone down in the dial of Ahaz.

At that time Berodach-baladan, the son of Baladan, king of Babylon, sent letters and a present unto Hezekiah; for he had heard that Hezekiah had been sick. And Hezekiah hearkened unto them, and showed them all the house of his precious things, the silver, and the gold, and the spices, and the precious ointment, and all the house of his armor, and all that was found in his treasures; there was nothing in his house, nor in all his dominion, that Hezekiah showed them not.

Then came Isaiah the prophet unto king Hezekiah, and said unto him, What said these men? and from whence came they unto thee? And Hezekiah said, They are come from a far country, even from Babylon. And he said, What have they seen in thy house? And Hezekiah answered, All the things that are in mine house have they seen; there is nothing among my treasures that I have not showed them. And Isaiah said unto Hezekiah, Hear the word of the Lord. Behold, the days come, that all that is in thine house, and that which thy fathers have laid up in store unto this day, shall be carried unto Babylon; nothing shall be left, saith the Lord. And of thy sons that shall issue from thee, which thou shalt beget, shall they take away; and they shall be eunuchs in the palace of the king of Babylon.

Then said Hezekiah unto Isaiah, Good is the word of the Lord which thou hast spoken. And he said, Is it not good, if peace and truth be in my days? And the rest of the acts of Hezekiah, and all his might, and how he made a pool, and a conduit, and brought water into the city, are they not written in the book of the Chronicles of the kings of Judah? And Hezekiah slept with his fathers; and Manasseh his son reigned in his stead.

7 MANASSEH was twelve years old when he began to reign, and reigned fifty and five years in Jerusalem. And his mother's name was Hephzibah. And he did that which was evil in the sight of the Lord, after the abominations of the heathen, whom the Lord cast out before the children of Israel. For he built up again the high places which Hezekiah his father had destroyed; and he reared up altars for Baal, and made a grove, as did Ahab king of Israel; and worshiped all the host of Heaven, and served them. And he built altars in the house of the Lord, of which the Lord said, In Jerusalem will I put my name. And he built altars for all the host of Heaven in the two courts of the house of the Lord. And he made his son pass through the fire, and observed times, and used enchantments, and dealt with familiar spirits and wizards; he wrought much wickedness in the sight of the Lord, to provoke him to anger. And he set a graven image of the grove that he had made in the house, of which the Lord said to David, and to Solomon his son, In this house, and in Jerusalem, which I have chosen out of all the tribes of Israel, will I put my name forever. Neither will I make the feet of Israel move anymore out of the land which I gave their fathers; only if they will observe to do according to all that I have commanded them, and according to all the law that my servant Moses commanded them. But they hearkened not; and Manasseh seduced them to do more evil than did the nations whom the Lord destroyed before the children of Israel.

And the Lord spake by his servants the prophets, saying, Because Manasseh king of Judah hath done these abominations, and hath done wickedly above all that the Amorites did, which were before him, and hath made Judah also to sin with his idols; therefore thus saith the Lord God of Israel, Behold, I am bringing such evil upon Jerusalem and Judah, that whosoever heareth of it, both his ears shall tingle. And I will stretch over Jerusalem the line of Samaria, and the plummet of the house of Ahab; and I will wipe Jerusalem as a man wipeth a dish, wiping it, and turning it upside down. And I will forsake the remnant of mine inheritance, and deliver them into the hand of their enemies; and they shall become a prey and a spoil to all their enemies; because they have done that which was evil in my sight, and have provoked me to anger, since the day their fathers came forth out of Egypt, even unto this day.

Moreover Manasseh shed innocent blood very much, till he had filled Jerusalem from one end to another; beside his sin wherewith he made Judah to sin, in doing that which was evil in the sight of the Lord. Now the rest of the acts of Manasseh, and all that he did, and his sin that he sinned, are they not written in the book of the Chronicles of the kings of Judah? And Manasseh slept with his fathers, and was buried in the garden of his own house, in the garden of Uzza; and Amon his son reigned in his stead.

Amon was twenty and two years old when he began to reign, and he reigned two years in Jerusalem. And his mother's name was Meshullemeth, the daughter of Haruz of Jotbah. And he did that which was evil in the sight of the Lord, as his father Manasseh did. And he walked in all the way that his father walked in, and served the idols that his father served, and worshiped them; and he forsook the Lord God of his fathers, and walked not in the way of the Lord. And the servants of Amon conspired against him, and slew the king in his own house. And the people of the land slew all them that had conspired against king Amon; and the people of the land made Josiah his son king in his stead. Now the rest of the acts of Amon which he did, are they not written in the book of the Chronicles of the kings of Judah? And he was buried in his sepulcher in the garden of Uzza; and Josiah his son reigned in his stead.

Josiah was eight years old when he began to reign, and he reigned thirty and one years in Jerusalem. And his mother's name was Jedidah, the daughter of Adaiah of Boscath. And he did that which was right in the sight of the Lord, and walked in all the way of David his father, and turned not aside to the right hand or to the left. And it came to pass in the eighteenth year of king Josiah, that the king sent Shaphan the son of Azaliah, the son of Meshullam, the scribe, to the house of the Lord, saying, Go up to Hilkiah the high priest, that he may sum the silver which is brought into the house of the Lord, which the keepers of the door have gathered of the people; and let them deliver it into the hand of the doers of the work, that have the oversight of the house of the Lord; and let them give it to the doers of the work, which is in the house of the Lord, to repair the breaches of the house. Unto carpenters, and builders, and masons, and to buy timber and hewn stone to repair the house. Howbeit, there was no reckoning made with them of the money that was delivered into their hand, because they dealt faithfully.

And Hilkiah the high priest said unto Shaphan the scribe, I have found the book of the law in the house of the Lord. And Hilkiah gave the book to Shaphan, and he read it. And Shaphan the scribe came to the king, and brought the king word again, and said, Thy servants have gathered the money that was found in the house, and have delivered it into the hand of them that do the work, that have the oversight of the house of the Lord. And Shaphan the scribe showed the king, saying, Hilkiah the priest hath delivered me a book. And Shaphan read it before the king.

And it came to pass, when the king had heard the words of the book of the law, that he rent his clothes. And the king commanded Hilkiah the priest, and Ahikam the son of Shaphan, and Achbor the son of Michaiah, and Shaphan the scribe, and Asahiah a servant of the king's, saying, Go ye, inquire of the Lord for me, and for the people, and for all Judah, concerning the words of this book that is found; for great is the wrath of the Lord that is kindled against us, because our fathers have not hearkened unto the words of this book, to do according unto all that is written concerning us.

So Hilkiah the priest, and Ahikam, and Achbor, and Shaphan, and Asahiah, went unto Huldah, the prophetess, the wife of Shallum the son of Tikvah, the son of Harhas, keeper of the wardrobe; (now she dwelt in Jerusalem in the college;) and they communed with her. And she said unto them, Thus saith the Lord God of Israel, Tell the man that sent you to me, Thus saith the Lord, Behold, I will bring evil upon this place, and upon the inhabitants thereof, even all the words of the book which the king of Judah hath read; because they have forsaken me, and have burned incense unto other gods, that they might provoke me to anger with all the works of their hands; therefore my wrath shall be kindled against this place, and shall not be quenched. But to the king of Judah which sent you to inquire of the Lord, thus shall ye say to him, Thus saith the Lord God of Israel, As touching the words which thou hast heard; because thine heart was tender, and thou hast humbled thyself before the Lord, when thou heardest what I spake against this place, and against the inhabitants thereof, that they should become a desolation and a curse, and hast rent thy clothes, and wept before me; I also have heard thee, saith the Lord. Behold therefore, I will gather thee unto thy fathers, and thou shalt be gathered into thy grave in peace; and thine eyes shall not see all the evil which I will bring upon this place. And they brought the king word again.

And the king sent, and they gathered unto him all the elders of Judah and of Jerusalem. And the king went up into the house of the Lord, and all the men of Judah and all the inhabitants of Jerusalem with him, and the priests, and the prophets, and all the people, both small and great; and he read in their ears all the words of the book of the covenant which was found in the house of the Lord. And the king stood by a pillar, and made a covenant before the Lord, to walk after the Lord, and to keep his commandments and his testimonies and his statutes with all their heart and all their soul, to perform the words of this covenant that were written in this book. And all the people stood to the covenant.

And the king commanded Hilkiah the high priest, and the priests of the second order, and the keepers of the door, to bring forth out of the temple of the Lord all the vessels that were made for Baal, and for the grove, and for all the host of Heaven; and he burned them without Jerusalem in the fields of Kidron, and carried the ashes of them unto Beth-el. And he put down the idolatrous priests, whom the kings of Judah had ordained to burn incense in the high places in the cities of Judah, and in the places round about Jerusalem; them also that burned incense unto Baal, to the sun, and to the moon, and to the planets, and to all the host of Heaven. And he brought out the grove from the house of the Lord, without Jerusalem, unto the brook Kidron, and burned it at the brook Kidron, and stamped it small to powder, and cast the powder thereof upon the graves of the children of the people. And he brake down the houses of the sodomites, that were by the house of the Lord, where the women wove hangings for the grove. And he brought all the priests out of the cities of Judah, and defiled the high places where the priests had burned incense, from Geba to Beer-sheba, and brake down the high places of the gates that were in the entering in of the gate of Joshua the governor of the city, which were on a man's left hand at the gate of the city.

Nevertheless the priests of the high places came not up to the altar of the Lord in Jerusalem, but they did eat of the unleavened bread among their brethren. And he defiled Tophet, which is in the valley of the children of Hinnom, that no man might make his son or his daughter to pass through the fire to Molech. And he took away the horses that the kings of Judah had given to the sun, at the entering in of the house of the Lord, by the chamber of Nathan-melech the chamberlain, which was in the suburbs, and burned the chariots of the sun with fire. And the altars that were on the top of the upper chamber of Ahaz, which the kings of Judah had made, and the altars which Manasseh had made in the two courts of the house of the Lord, did the king beat down, and brake them down from thence, and cast the dust of them into the brook Kidron. And the high places that were before Jerusalem, which were on the right hand of the mount of corruption, which Solomon the king of Israel had builded for Ashtoreth the abomination of the Zidonians, and for Chemosh the abomination of the Moabites, and for Milcom the abomination of the children of Ammon, did the king defile. And he brake in pieces the images, and cut down the groves, and filled their places with the bones of men.

Moreover the altar that was at Beth-el, and the high place which Jeroboam the son of Nebat, who made Israel to sin, had made, both that altar and the high place he brake down, and burned the high place, and stamped it small to powder, and burned the grove. And As Josiah turned himself, he spied the sepulchers that were there in the mount, and sent, and took the bones out of the sepulchers, and burned them upon the altar, and polluted it, according to the word of the Lord which the man of God proclaimed, who proclaimed these words. Then he said, What title is that that I see? And the men of the city told him, It is the sepulcher of the man of God, which came from Judah, and proclaimed these things that thou hast done against the altar of Beth-el. And he said, Let him alone; let no man move his bones. So they let his bones alone, with the bones of the prophet that came out of Samaria.

And all the houses also of the high places that were in the cities of Samaria, which the kings of Israel had made to provoke the Lord to anger, Josiah took away, and did to them according to all the acts that he had done in Beth-el. And he slew all the priests of the high places that were there upon the altars, and burned men's bones upon them, and returned to Jerusalem.

And the king commanded all the people, saying, Keep the passover unto the Lord your God, as it is written in the book of this covenant. Surely there was not holden such a passover from the days of the judges that judged Israel, nor in all the days of the kings of Israel, nor of the kings of Judah; but in the eighteenth year of king Josiah, wherein this passover was holden to the Lord in Jerusalem. Moreover the workers with familiar spirits, and the wizards, and the images, and the idols, and all the abominations that were spied in the land of Judah and in Jerusalem, did Josiah put away, that he might perform the words of the law, which were written in the book that Hilkiah the priest found in the house of the Lord. And like unto him was there no king before him, that turned to the Lord with all his heart, and with all his soul, and with all his might, according to all the law of Moses; neither after him arose there any like him.

Notwithstanding, the Lord turned not from the fierceness of his great wrath, wherewith his anger was kindled against Judah, because of all the provocations that Manasseh had provoked him withal. And the Lord said, I will remove Judah also out of my sight, as I have removed Israel, and will cast off this city Jerusalem which I have chosen, and the house of which I said, My name shall be there. Now the rest of the acts of Josiah, and all that he did, are thy not written in the book of the Chronicles of the kings of Judah? In his days Pharaoh-nechoh king of Egypt went up against the king of Assyria to the river Euphrates; and king Josiah went against him; and he slew him at Megiddo, when he had seen him. And his servants carried him in a chariot dead from Megiddo, and brought him to Jerusalem, and buried him in his own sepulcher. And the people of the land took Jehoahaz the son of Josiah, and anointed him, and made him king in his father's stead.

Jehoahaz was twenty and three years old when he began to reign, and he reigned three months in Jerusalem. And his mother's name was Hamutal, the daughter of Jeremiah of Libnah. And he did that which was evil in the sight of the Lord, according to all that his fathers had done. And Pharaoh-nechoh put him in bands at Riblah in the land of Hamath, that he might not reign in Jerusalem; and put the land to a tribute of a hundred talents of silver, and a talent of gold. And Pharaoh-nechoh made Eliakim the son of Josiah king in the room of Josiah his father, and turned his name to Jehoiakim, and took Jehoahaz away; and he came to Egypt, and died there. And Jehoiakim gave the silver and the gold to Pharaoh; but he taxed the land to give the money according to the commandment of Pharaoh; he exacted the silver and the gold of the people of the land, of everyone according to his taxation, to give it unto Pharaoh-nechoh.

Jehoiakim was twenty and five years old when he began to reign; and he reigned eleven years in Jerusalem. And his mother's name was Zebudah, the daughter of Pedaiah of Rumah. And he did that which was evil in the sight of the Lord, according to all that his fathers had done.

8 IN his days Nebuchadnezzar king of Babylon came up, and Jehoiakim became his servant three years; then he turned and rebelled against him. And the Lord sent against him bands of the Chaldees, and bands of the Syrians, and bands of the Moabites, and bands of the children of Ammon, and sent them against Judah to destroy it, according to the word of the Lord, which he spake by his servants the prophets. Surely at the commandment of the Lord came this upon Judah, to remove them out of his sight, for the sins of Manasseh, according to all that he did; and also for the innocent blood that he shed; for he filled Jerusalem with innocent blood; which the Lord would not pardon. Now the rest of the acts of Jehoiakim, and all that he did, are they not written in the book of the Chronicles of the kings of Judah? So Jehoiakim slept with his fathers; and Jehoiachin his son reigned in his stead. And the king of Egypt came not again anymore out of his land; for the king of Babylon had taken from the river of Egypt unto the river Euphrates all that pertained to the king of Egypt.

Jehoiachin was eighteen years old when he began to reign, and he reigned in Jerusalem three months. And his mother's name was Nehushta, the daughter of Elnathan of Jerusalem. And he did that which was evil in the sight of the Lord, according to all that his father had done.

At that time the servants of Nebuchadnezzar king of Babylon came up against Jerusalem, and the city was besieged. And Nebuchadnezzar king of Babylon came against the city, and his servants did besiege it. And Jehoiachin the king of Judah went out to the king of Babylon, he, and his mother, and his servants, and his princes, and his officers; and the king of Babylon took him in the eighth year of his reign. And he carried out thence all the treasures of the house of the Lord, and the treasures of the king's house, and cut in pieces all the vessels of gold which Solomon king of Israel had made in the temple of the Lord, as the Lord had said. And he carried away all Jerusalem, and all the princes, and all the mighty men of valor, even ten thousand captives, and all the craftsmen and smiths; none remained, save the poorest sort of the people of the land.

And he carried away Jehoiachin to Babylon, and the king's mother, and the king's wives, and his officers, and the mighty of the land, those carried he into captivity from Jerusalem to Babylon. And all the men of might, even seven thousand, and craftsmen and smiths a thousand, all that were strong and apt for war, even them the king of Babylon brought captive to Babylon. And the king of Babylon made Mattaniah his father's brother king in his stead, and changed his name to Zedekiah.

Zedekiah was twenty and one years old when he began to reign, and he reigned eleven years in Jerusalem. And his mother's name was Hamutal, the daughter of Jeremiah of Libnah. And he did that which was evil in the sight of the Lord, according to all that Jehoiakim had done. For through the anger of the Lord it came to pass in Jerusalem and Judah, until he had cast them out from his presence, that Zedekiah rebelled against the king of Babylon.

And it came to pass in the ninth year of his reign, in the tenth month, in the tenth day of the month, that Nebuchadnezzar king of Babylon came, he, and all his host, against Jerusalem, and pitched against it; and they built forts against it round about. And the city was besieged unto the eleventh year of king Zedekiah. And on the ninth day of the fourth month the famine prevailed in the city, and there was no bread for the people of the land. And the city was broken up, and all the men of war fled by night by the way of the gate between two walls, which is by the king's garden; (now the Chaldees were against the city round about;) and the king went the way toward the plain. And the army of the Chaldees pursued after the king, and overtook him in the plains of Jericho; and all his army was scattered from him. So they took the king, and brought him up to the king of Babylon to Riblah; and they gave judgment upon him. And they slew the sons of Zedekiah before his eyes, and put out the eyes of Zedekiah, and bound him with fetters of brass, and carried him to Babylon.

And in the fifth month, on the seventh day of the month, which is the nineteenth year of king Nebuchadnezzar king of Babylon, came Nebuzar-adan, captain of the guard, a servant of the king of Babylon, unto Jerusalem; and he burnt the house of the Lord, and the king's house, and all the houses of Jerusalem, and every great man's house burnt he with fire. And all the army of the Chaldees, that were with the captain of the guard, brake down the walls of Jerusalem round about. Now the rest of the people that were left in the city, and the fugitives that fell away to the king of Babylon, with the remnant of the multitude, did Nebuzar-adan the captain of the guard carry away. But the captain of the guard left of the poor of the land to be vinedressers and husbandmen.

And the pillars of brass that were in the house of the Lord, and the bases, and the brazen sea that was in the house of the Lord, did the Chaldees break in pieces, and carried the brass of them to Babylon. And the pots, and the shovels, and the snuffers, and the spoons, and all the vessels of brass wherewith they ministered, took they away. And the fire-pans, and the bowls, and such things as were of gold, in gold, and of silver, in silver, the captain of the guard took away. The two pillars, one sea, and the bases which Solomon had made for the house of the Lord; the brass of all these vessels was without weight. The height of the one pillar was eighteen cubits, and the chapiter upon it was brass; and the height of the chapiter three cubits; and the wreathen work and pomegranates upon the chapiter round about, all of brass; and like unto these had the second pillar with wreathen work.

And the captain of the guard took Seraiah the chief priest, and Zephaniah the second priest, and the three keepers of the door; and out of the city he took an officer that was set over the men of war, and five men of them that were in the king's presence, which were found in the city, and the principal scribe of the host, which mustered the people of the land, and threescore men of the people of the land that were found in the city; and Nebuzar-adan captain of the guard took these, and brought them to the king of Babylon to Riblah; and the king of Babylon smote them, and slew them at Riblah in the land of Hamath. So Judah was carried away out of their land.

And as for the people that remained in the land of Judah, whom Nebuchadnezzar king of Babylon had left, even over them he made Gedaliah the son of Ahikam, the son of Shaphan, ruler. And when all the captains of the armies, they and their men, heard that the king of Babylon had made Gedaliah governor, there came to Gedaliah to Mizpah, even Ishmael the son of Nethaniah, and Johanan the son of Careah, and Seraiah the son of Tanhumeth the Netophathite, and Jaazaniah the son of a Maachathite, they and their men. And Gedaliah sware to them, and to their men, and said unto them, Fear not to be the servants of the Chaldees; dwell in the land, and serve the king of Babylon; and it shall be well with you. But it came to pass in the seventh month that Ishmael, the son of Nethaniah, the son of Elishama, of the seed royal, came, and ten men with him, and smote Gedaliah, that he died, and the Jews and the Chaldees that were with him at Mizpah. And all the people, both small and great, and the captains of the armies, arose and came to Egypt; for they were afraid of the Chaldees.

And it came to pass in the seven and thirtieth year of the captivity of Jehoiachin king of Judah, in the twelfth month, on the seven and twentieth day of the month, that Evilmerodach king of Babylon in the year that he began to reign did lift up the head of Jehoiachin king of Judah out of prison; and he spake kindly to him, and set his throne above the throne of the kings that were with him in Babylon; and changed his prison garments; and he did eat bread continually before him all the days of his life. And his allowance was a continual allowance given him of the king, a daily rate for every day, all the days of his life.

THE FIRST BOOK OF THE CHRONICLES

ADAM, Seth, Enos, Cainan, Mahalaleel, Jared, Enoch, Methuselah, Lamech, Noah, Shem, Ham, and Japheth.

The sons of Japheth: Gomer, and Magog, and Madai, and Javan, and Tubal, and Meshech, and Tiras. And the sons of Gomer: Ashchenaz, and Riphath, and Togarmah. And the sons of Javan: Elishah, and Tarshish, Kittim, and Dodanim.

The sons of Ham: Cush, and Mizraim, Put, and Canaan. And the sons of Cush: Seba, and Havilah, and Sabta, and Raamah, and Sabtecha. And the sons of Raamah: Sheba, and Dedan. And Cush begat Nimrod, he began to be mighty upon the Earth. And Mizraim begat Ludim, and Anamim, and Lehabim, and Napthtuhim. And Parhrusim, and Casluhim (of whom came the Philistines), and Caphtorim. And Canaan begat Zidon his firstborn, and Heth, the Jebusite also, and the Amorite, and the Girgashite, and the Hivite, and the Arkite, and the Sinite, and the Arvadite, and the Zemarite, and the Hamathite.

The sons of Shem: Elam, and Asshur, and Arphaxad, and Lud, and Aram, and Uz, and Hul, and Gether, and Meshech. And Arphaxad begat Shelah, and Shelah begat Eber. And unto Eber were born two sons, the name of the one was Peleg because in his days the Earth was divided and his brother's name was Joktan. And Joktan begat Almodad, and Sheleph, and Hazarmaveth, and Jerah, Hadoram also, and Uzal, and Diklah, and Ebal, and Abimael, and Sheba, and Ophir, and Havilah, and Jobab. All these were the sons of Joktan.

Shem, Arphaxad, Shelah, Eber, Peleg, Reu, Serug, Nahor, Terah, Abram, the same is Abraham. The sons of Abraham: Isaac, and Ishmael.

These are their generations: The firstborn of Ishmael: Nebaioth, then Kedar, and Adbeel, and Mibsam, Misma, and Dumah, Massa, Hadad, and Tema, Jetur, Naphish, and Kedemah. There are the sons of Ishmael.

Now the sons of Keturah, Abraham's concubine, she bare Zimran, and Jokshan, and Medan, and Midian, and Ishbak, and Shuah. And the sons of Jokshan: Sheba, and Dedan. And the sons of Midian: Ephah, and Epher, and Enoch, and Abida, and Eldaah. All these are the sons of Keturah.

And Abraham begat Isaac. The sons of Isaac: Esau and Israel.

The sons of Esau: Eliphaz, Reuel, and Jeush, and Jaalam, and Korah. The sons of Eliphaz: Teman, and Omar, Zephi, and Gatam, Kenaz, and Timna, and Amalek. The sons of Reuel: Nahath, Zerah, Shammah, and Mizzah.

And the sons of Seir: Lotan, and Shobal, and Zibeon, and Anah, and Dishon, and Ezar, and Dishan. And the sons of Lotan: Hori, and Homan, and Timna was

Lotan's sister. The sons of Shobal: Alian, and Manahath, and Ebal, Shephi, and Onam. And the sons of Zibeon: Aiah, and Anah. The sons of Anah: Dishon. And the sons of Dishon: Amram, and Eshban, and Ithran, and Cheran. The sons of Ezer: Bilhan, and Zavan, and Jakan. The sons of Dishan: Uz, and Aran.

Now these are the kings that reigned in the land of Edom before any king reigned over the children of Israel: Bela the son of Beor, and the name of his city was Dinhabah. And when Bela was dead, Jobab the son of Zerah of Bozrah reigned in his stead. And when Jobab was dead, Husham of the land of the Temanites reigned in his stead. And when Husham was dead, Hadad the son of Bedad, which smote Midian in the field of Moab, reigned in his stead, and the name of his city was Avith. And when Hadad was dead, Samlah of Masrekah reigned in his stead. And when Samalah was dead, Shaul of Rehoboth by the river reigned in his stead. And when Shaul was dead, Baal-hanan the son of Achbor reigned in his stead. And when Baal-hanan was dead, Hadad reigned in his stead, and the name of his city was Pai, and his wife's name was Mehetabel, the daughter of Matred, the daughter of Mezahab. Hadad died also. And the dukes of Edom were duke Timnah, duke Aliah, duke Jetheth, Duke Aholibamah, duke Elah, duke Pinon, Duke Kenaz, duke Teman, duke Mibzar, Duke Magdiel, duke Iram. These are the dukes of Edom.

These are the sons of Israel: Reuben, Simeon, Levi, and Judah, Issachar, and Zebulun, Dan, Joseph, and Benjamin, Naphtali, Gad, and Asher.

The sons of Judah: Er, and Onan, and Shelah, which three were born unto him of the daughter of Shua the Canaanitess. And Er, the firstborn of Judah, was evil in the sight of the Lord and he slew him. And Tamar his daughter-in-law bare him Pharez and Zerah. All the sons of Judah were five. The sons of Phrez: Hezron, and Hamul.

And the sons of Zerah: Zimri, and Ethan, and Heman, and Calcol, and Dara, five of them in all. And the sons of Carmi: Achar, the troubler of Israel who transgressed in the thing accursed. And the sons of Ethan: Azariah.

The sons also of Hezron that were born unto him: Jerahmeel, and Ram, and Chelubai. And Ram begat Amminadab, and Amminadab begat Nahshon, prince of the children of Judah, and Nahshon begat Salma, and Salma begat Boaz, and Boaz begat Obed, and Obed begat Jesse. And Jesse begat his firstborn Eliab, and Abinadab the second, and Shimma the third, Nethaneel the fourth, Raddai the fifth, Ozem the sixth, David the seventh, whose sisters were Zeruiah, and Abigail. And the sons of Zeruiah: Abishai, and Joab, and Asahel, three. And Abigail bare Amasa, and the father of Amasa was Jether the Ishmaelite.

And Caleb the son of Hezron begat children of Azubah his wife, and of Jerioth, her sons are these: Jesher, and Shobab, and Ardon. And when Azubah was dead, Caleb took unto him Ephrath, which bare him Hur. And Hur begat Uri, and Uri begat Bezaleel.

And afterward Hezron went in to the daughter of Machir the father of Gilead whom he married when he was threescore years old and she bare him Segub. And Segub begat Jair, who had three and twenty cities in the land of Gilead. And he took Geshur and Aram, with the towns of Jair, from them with Kenath, and the towns thereof, even threescore cities. All these belonged to the sons of Machir the father of Gilead. And after that Hezron was dead in Caleb-ephratah, then Abiah Hezron's wife bare him Ashur the father of Tekoa.

And the sons of Jerahmeel the firstborn of Hezron were Ram the firstborn, and Bunah, and Oren, and Ozem, and Ahijah. Jerahmeel had also another wife, whose name was Atarah, she was the mother of Onam. And the sons of Ram the firstborn of Jerahmeel were Maaz, and Jamin, and Eker. And the sons of Onam were Shammai, and Jada. And the sons of Shammai: Nadab, and Abishur. And the name of the wife of Abishur was Abihail, and she bare him Ahban, and Molid. And the sons of Nadab: Seled, and Appaim, but Seled died without children. And the sons of Appaim: Ishi. And the sons of Ishi: Sheshan. And the children of Sheshan: Ahlai. And the sons of Jada the brother of Shammai: Jether, and Jonathan, and Jether died without children. And the sons of Jonathan: Peleth, and Zaza. These were the sons of Jerahmeel. Now Sheshan had no sons, but daughters. And Sheshan had a servant, an Egyptian whose name was Jarha. And Sheshan gave his daughter to Jarha his servant to wife and she bare him Attai. And Attai begat Nathan, and Nathan begat Zabad, and Zabad begat Ephial, and Ephial begat Obed, and Obed begat Jehu, and Jehu begat Azariah, and Azariah begat Helez, and Helez begat Eleasah, and Eleasah begat Sisamai, and Sisamai begat Shallum, and Shallum begat Jekamiah, and Jekamiah begat Elishama.

Now the sons of Caleb the brother of Jerahmeel were Mesha his firstborn which was the father of Ziph, and the sons of Mareshah the father of Hebron. And the sons of Hebron: Korah, and Tappuah, and Rekem, and Shema. And Shema begat Raham, the father of Jorkoam, and Rekem begat Shammai. And the son of Shammai was Maon, and Maon was the father of Beth-zur. And Ephah, Caleb's concubine, bare Haran, and Moza, and Gazez, and Haran begat Gazez. And the sons of Jahdai: Regem, and Jotham, and Gesham, and Pelet, and Ephah, and Shaaph. Maachah, Caleb's concubine, bare Sheber, and Tirhanah. She bare also Shaaph the father of Madmannah, Sheva the father of Machbenah, and the father of Gibea, and the daughter of Caleb was Achssa.

These were the sons of Caleb the son of Hur: the firstborn of Ephratah, Shobal the father of Kirjath-jearim. Salma the father of Bethlehem, Hareph the father of Beth-gader. And Shobal the father of Kirjath-jearim had sons, Haroeh, and half the Manahethites. And the families of Kirjath-jearim, the Ithrites, and the Puhites, and the Shumathites, and the Mishraites, of them came the Zareathites, and the Eshtaulites. The sons of Salma: Bethlehem, and the Netophathites, Ataroth, the house of Joab, and half of the Manahethites, the Zorites. And the families of the scribes which dwelt at Jabez: the Tirathites, the Shimeathites, and Suchathites. These are the Kenites that came of Hemath, the father of the house of Rechab.

Now these were the sons of David, which were born unto him in Hebron: the firstborn Amnon, of Ahinoam the Jezreelitess, the second, Daniel, of Abigail the Carmelitess, the third, Absalom the son of Maachah the daughter of Talmai king of Geshur, the fourth, Adonijah the son of Haggith, the fifth Shephatiah of Abital, the sixth, Ithream by Eglah his wife. These six were born unto him in Hebron, and there he reigned seven years and six months, and in Jerusalem he reigned thirty and three years. And these were born unto him in Jerusalem: Shimea, and Shobab, and Nathan, and Solomon, four, of Bath-shua the daughter of Ammiel, Ibhar also, and Elishama, and Eliphelet, and Nogah, and Nepheg, and Japhia, and Elishama, and Eliada, and Eliphelet, nine. These were all the sons of David, besides the sons of the concubines, and Tamar their sister.

And Solomon's son was Rehoboam, Abia his son, Asa his son, Jehoshaphat his son, Joram his son, Ahaziah his son, Joash his son, Amaziah his son, Azariah his son, Jotham his son, Ahaz his son, Hezekiah his son, Manasseh his son, Amon his son, Josiah his son. And the sons of Josiah were the firstborn Johanan, the second Jehoiakim, the third Zedekiah, the fourth Shallum. And the sons of Jehoiakim: Jeconiah his son, Zedekiah his son.

And the sons of Jeconiah: Assir, Salathiel his son, Malchiram also, and Pedaiah, and Shenazar, Jecamiah, Hoshama, and Nedabiah. And the sons of Pedaiah were Zerubbabel, and Shimei, and the sons of Zerubbabel, Meshullam, and Hananiah, and Shelomith their sister, and Hashubah, and Ohel, and Berechiah, and Hasadiah, Jushabhesed, five. And the sons of Hananiah: Pelatiah, and Jesaiah, the sons of Rephaiah, the sons of Arnan, the sons of Obadiah, the sons of Shechaniah. And the sons of Shechaniah: Shemaiah, and the sons of Shemaiah: Hattush, and Igeal, and Bariah, and Neariah, and Shaphat, six. And the sons of Neariah: Elioenai, and Hezekiah, and Azrikam, three. And the sons of Elioenai were Hodaiah, and Eliashib, and Pelaiah, and Akkub, and Johanan, and Daliaiah, and Anani, seven.

The sons of Judah: Pharez, Hezron, and Carmi, and Hur, and Shobal. And Reaiah the son of Shobal begat Jahath, and Jahath begat Ahumai, and Lahad. These are the families of the Zorathites. And these were of the father of Etam, Jezreel, and Ishma, and Idbash, and the name of their sister was Hazelelponi, and Penuel the father of Gedor, and Ezer the father of Hushah. These are the sons of Hur, the firstborn of Ephratah, the father of Bethlehem.

And Ashur the father of Tekoa had two wives, Helah and Naarah. And Naarah bare him Ahuzam, and Hepher, and Temeni, and Haahashtari. These were the sons of Naarah. And the sons of Helah were Zereth, and Jezoar, and Ethnan. And Coz begat Anub, and Zobebah, and the families of Aharhel the son of Harum.

And Jabez was more honorable than his brethren, and his mother called his name Jabez, saying, Because I bare him with sorrow. And Jabez called on the God of Israel, saying, O that thou wouldest bless me indeed, and enlarge my coast, and that thine hand might be with me, and that thou wouldest keep me from evil, that it may not grieve me. And God granted him that which he requested.

And Chelub the brother of Shuah begat Mehir, which was the father of Eshton. And Eshton begat Beth-rapha, and Paseah, and Tehinnah the father of Irnahash. These are the men of Rechah. And the sons of Kenaz: Othniel, and Seraiah, and the sons of Othniel: Hathath. And Meonothai begat Ophrah, and Seraiah begat Joab, the father of the valley of Charashim, for they were craftsmen. And the sons of Caleb the son of Jephunneh: Iru, Elah, and Naam, and the sons of Elah, even Kenaz. And the sons of Jehaleleel: Ziph, and Ziphah, Tiria, and Asareel. And the sons of Ezra were Jether, and Mered, and Epher, and Jalon, and she bare Miriam, and Shammai, and Ishbah the father of Eshtemoa. And his wife Jehudijah bare Jered the father of Gedor, and Heber the father of Socho, and Jekuthiel the father of Zanoah. And these are the sons of Bithiah the daughter of Pharaoh which Mered took. And the sons of his wife Hodiah the sister of Naham, the father of Keilah the Garmite, and Eshtemoa the Maachathite. And the sons of Shimon were Amnon, and Rinnah, Benhanan, and Tilon. And the sons of Ishi were Zoheth, and Ben-zoheth.

The sons of Shelah the son of Judah were Er the father of Lecah, and Laadah the father of Mareshah, and the families of the house of them that wrought fine linen, of the house of Ashbea. And Jokim, and the men of Chozeba, and Joash, and Saraph, who had the dominion in Moab, and Jashubi-lehem. And these are ancient things. These were the potters, and those that dwelt among plants and hedges, there they dwelt with the king for his work.

The sons of Simeon were Nemuel, and Jamin, Jarib, Zerah, and Shaul, Shallum his son, Mibsam his son, Mishma his son. And the sons of Mishma: Hamuel his son, Zacchur his son, Shimei his son. And Shimei had sixteen sons and six daughters, but his brethren had not many children, neither did all their family multiply, like to the children of Judah. And they dwelt at Beer-sheba, and Moladah, and Hazarshual, and at Bilhah, and at Ezem, and at Tolad, and at Bethuel, and at Hormak, and at Ziklag, and at Beth-marcaboth, and Hazar-susim, and at Beth-birei and at Shaaraim. These were their cities unto the reign of David. And their villages were, Etam, and Ain, Rimmon, and Tochen, and Ashan, five cities, and all their villages that were round about the same cities, unto Baal. These were their habitations and their genealogy.

And Meshobab, and Jamlech, and Joshah the son of Amaziah, and Joel, and Jehu the son of Josibiah, the son of Seraiah, the son of Asiel, and Elioenai, and Jaakobah, and Seshohaiah, and Asaiah, and Adiel, and Jesimiel, and Benaiah. And Ziza the son of Shiphi, the son of Allon, the son of Jedaiah, the son of

Shimri, the son of Shemaiah, these mentioned by their names were princes in their families, and the house of their fathers increased greatly. And they went to the entrance of Gedor, even unto the east side of the valley, to seek pasture for their flocks. And they found fat pasture and good, and the land was wide, and quiet, and peaceable, for they of Ham had dwelt there of old. And these written by name came in the days of Hezekiah king of Judah, and smote their tents and the habitations that were found there, and destroyed them utterly unto this day, and dwelt in their rooms because there was pasture there for their flocks. And some of them, even of the sons of Simeon, five hundred men, went to mount Seir, having for their captains Pelatiah, and Neariah, and Rephaiah, and Uzziel, the sons of Ishi. And they smote the rest of the Amalekites that were escaped and dwelt there unto this day.

Now the sons of Reuben the firstborn of Israel (for he was the firstborn, but, forasmuch as he defiled his father's bed, his birthright was given unto the sons of Joseph the son of Israel and the genealogy is not to be reckoned after the birthright. For Judah prevailed above his brethren and of him came the chief ruler, but the birthright was Joseph's), The sons, I say, of Reuben the firstborn of Israel were Hanoch, and Pallu, Hezron, and Carmi. The sons of Joel: Shemnaiah his son, Gog his son, Shimei his son, Micah his son, Reaia, his son, Baal his son, Beerah his son, whom Tilgathpilneser king of Assyria carried away captive, he was prince of the Reubenites. And his brethren by their families, when the genealogy of their generations were reckoned, were the chief: Jeiel, and Zechariah, and Bela the son of Azaz, the son of Shema, the son of Joel, who dwelt in Aroer, even unto Nebo and Baal-meon, and eastward he inhabited unto the entering in of the wilderness from the river Euphrates because their cattle were multiplied in the land of Gilead. And in the days of Saul they made war with the Hagarites who fell by their hand and they dwelt in their tents throughout all the east land of Gilead.

And the children of Gad dwelt over against them in the land of Bashan unto Salcah, Joel the chief, and Shapham the next, and Jaanai, and Shaphat in Bashan. And their brethren of the house of their fathers were Michael, and Meshullam, and Sheba, and Jorai, and Jachan, and Zia, and Heber, seven. These are the children of Abihail the son of Huri, the son of Jaroah, the son of Gilead, the son of Michael, the son of Jeshishai, the son of Jahdo, the son of Buz, Ahi the son of Abdiel, the son of Guni, chief of the house of their fathers. And they dwelt in Gilead in Bashan, and in her towns, and in all the suburbs of Sharon upon their borders. All these were reckoned by genealogies in the days of Jotham king of Judah and in the days of Jeroboam king of Israel.

The sons of Reuben, and the Gadites, and half the tribe of Manasseh, of valiant men, men able to bear buckler and sword, and to shoot with bow, and skillful in war, were four and forty thousand seven hundred and threescore that went out to the war. And they made war with the Hagarites, with Jetur, and Nephish, and Nodab. And they were helped against them, and the Hagarites were delivered into their hand and all that were with them, for they cried to God in the battle and he was entreated of them because they put their trust in him. And they took away their cattle, of their camels fifty thousand, and of sheep two hundred and fifty thousand, and of asses two thousand, and of men a hundred thousand. For there fell down many slain because the war was of God. And they dwelt in their steads until the captivity. And the children of the half tribe of Manasseh dwelt in the land, they increased from Bashan unto Baal-hermon and Senir and unto mount Hermon. And these were the heads of the house of their fathers, even Epher, and Ishi, and Eliel, and Azriel, and Jeremiah, and Hodaviah, and Jahdiel, mighty men of valor, famous men, and heads of the house of their fathers. And they transgressed against the God of their fathers and went a whoring after the gods of the people of the land whom God destroyed before them. And the God of Israel stirred up the spirit of Pul king of Assyria and the spirit of Tilgath-pilneser king of Assyria and he carried them away, even the Reubenites, and the Gadites, and the half tribe of Manasseh, and brought them unto Halah, and Habor, and Hara, and to the river Gozan unto this day.

The sons of Levi: Gershon, Kohath, and Merari. And the sons of Kohath: Amram, Izhar, and Hebron, and Uzziel. And the children of Amram: Aaron, and Moses, and Miriam. The sons also of Aaron: Nadab and Abihu, Eleazar and Ithamar.

Eleazar begat Phinehas, Phinehas begat Abishua. And Abishua begat Bukki, and Bukki begat Uzzi. And Uzzi begat Zerahiah, and Zerahiah begat Meraioth. Meraioth begat Amariah, and Amariah begat Ahitub, and Ahitub begat Zadok, and Zadok begat Ahimaaz, and Ahimaaz begat Azariah, and Azariah begat Johanan, and Johanan begat Azariah (he it is that executed the priest's office in the temple that Solomon built in Jerusalem). And Azariah begat Amariah, and Amariah begat Ahitub, and Ahitub begat Zadok, and Zadok begat Shallum, and Shallum begat Hilkiah, and Hilkiah begat Azariah, and Azariah begat Seraiah, and Seraiah begat Jehozadak, and Jehozadak went into captivity when the Lord carried away Judah and Jerusalem by the hand of Nebuchadnezzar.

The sons of Levi: Gershom, Kohath, and Merari. And these be the names of the sons of Gershom, Libni, and Shimei. And the sons of Kohath were: Amram, and Izhar, and Hebron, and Uzziel. The sons of Merari, Mahli, and Mushi. And these are the families of the Levites according to their fathers.

Of Gershom: Libni his son, Jahath his son, Zimmah his son, Joah his son, Iddo his son, Zerah his son, Jeaterai his son.

The sons of Kohath: Amminadab his son, Korah his son, Assir his son. Elkanah his son, and Ebiasaph his son, and Assir his son, Tahath his son, Uriel his son, Uzziah his son, and Shaul his son. And the sons of Elkanah: Amasai, and Ahimoth. As for Elkanah, the sons of Elkanah: Zophai his son, and Nahath his son, Eliab his son, Jeroham his son, Elkanah his son. And the sons of Samuel: the firstborn Vashni, and Abiah.

The sons of Merari: Mahli, Libni his son, Shimei his son, Uzza his son, Shimea his son, Haggiah his son, Asaiah his son. And these are they whom David set over the service of song in the house of the Lord, after that the ark had rest. And they ministered before the dwelling place of the tabernacle of the congregation with singing until Solomon had built the house of the Lord in Jerusalem and then they waited on their office according to their order. And these are they that waited with their children.

Of the sons of the Kohathites: Heman a singer, the son of Joel, the son of Shemuel, the son of Elkanah, the son of Jeroham, the son of Eliel, the son of Toah, the son of Zuph, the son of Elkanah, the son of Mahath, the son of Amasai, the son of Elkanah, the son of Joel, the son of Azariah, the son of Zephaniah, the son of Tahath, the son of Assir, the son of Ebiasaph, the son of Korah, the son of Izhar, the son of Kohath, the son of Levi, the son of Israel.

And his brother Asaph who stood on his right hand, even Asaph the son of Berachiah, the son of Shimeah, the son of Michael, the son of Baaseiah, the son of Malchiah, the son of Ethni, the son of Zerah, the son of Adaiah, the son of Ethan, the son of Zimmah, the son of Shimei, the son of Jahath, the son of Gershom, the son of Levi.

And their brethren the sons of Merari stood on the left hand: Ethan the son of Kishi, the son of Abdi, the son of Malluch, the son of Hashabiah, the son of Amaziah, the son of Hilkiah, the son of Amzi, the son of Bani, the son of Shamer, the son of Mahli, the son of Mushi, the son of Merari, the son of Levi.

Their brethren also the Levites were appointed unto all manner of service of the tabernacle of the house of God. But Aaron and his sons offered upon the altar of the burnt offering and on the altar of incense, and were appointed for all the work of the place most holy, and to make an atonement for Israel according to all that Moses the servant of God had commanded. And these are the sons of Aaron: Eleazar his son, Phinehas his son, Abishua his son, Bukki his son, Uzzi his son, Zerahiah his son, Meraioth his son, Amariah his son, Ahitub his son, Zadok his son, Ahimaaz his son.

2 NOW these are their dwelling places throughout their castles in their coasts, of the sons of Aaron, of the families of the Kohathites, for theirs was the lot. And they gave them Hebron in the land of Judah and the suburbs thereof round about it. But the fields of the city, and the villages thereof, they gave to Caleb the son of Jephunneh. And to the sons of Aaron they gave the cities of Judah, namely, Hebron, the city of refuge, and Libnah with her suburbs, and Jattir, and Eshtemoa, with their suburbs, and Hilen with her suburbs, Debir with her suburbs, and Ashan with her suburbs, and Beth-shemesh with her suburbs, and out of the tribe of Benjamin, Geba with her suburbs, and Alemeth with her suburbs, and Anathoth with her suburbs. All their cities throughout their families were thirteen cities.

And unto the sons of Kohath, which were left of the family of that tribe, were cities given out of the half tribe, namely, out of the half tribe of Manasseh, by lot, ten cities. And to the sons of Gershom throughout their families out of the tribe of Issachar, and out of the tribe of Asher, and out of the tribe of Naphtali, and out of the tribe of Manasseh in Bashan, thirteen cities. Unto the sons of Merari were given by lot, throughout their families, out of the tribe of Reuben, and out of the tribe of Gad, and out of the tribe of Zebulun, twelve cities. And the children of Israel gave to the Levites these cities with their suburbs. And they gave by lot out of the tribe of the children of Judah, and out of the tribe of the children of Simeon, and out of the tribe of the children of Benjamin, these cities, which are called by their names. And the residue of the families of the sons of Kohath had cities of their coasts out of the tribe of Ephraim. And they gave unto them, of the cities of refuge, Shechem in mount Ephraim with her suburbs, they gave also Gezer with her suburbs, and Jokmeam with her suburbs, and Beth-horon with her suburbs, and Ajalon with her suburbs, and Gath-rimmon with her suburbs, and out of the half tribe of Manasseh, Aner with her suburbs, and Bileam with her suburbs, for the family of the remnant of the sons of Kohath.

Unto the sons of Gershom were given, out of the family of the half tribe of Manasseh, Golan in Bashan with her suburbs, and Ashtaroth with her suburbs, and out of the tribe of Issachar, Kedesh with her suburbs, Daberath with her suburbs, and Ramoth with her suburbs, and Anem with her suburbs, and out of the tribe of Asher, Mashal with her suburbs, and Abdon with her suburbs, and Hukok with her suburbs, and Rehob with her suburbs, and out of the tribe of Naphtali, Kedesh in Galilee with her suburbs, and Hammon with her suburbs, and Kirjathaim with her suburbs.

Unto the rest of the children of Merari were given, out of the tribe of Zebulun, Rimmon with her suburbs, Tabor with her suburbs, and on the other side Jordan by Jericho, on the east side of Jordan, were given them, out of the tribe of Reuben, Bezer in the wilderness with her suburbs, and Jahzah with her suburbs, Kedemoth also with her suburbs, and Mephaath with her suburbs, and out of the tribe of Gad, Ramoth in Gilead with her suburbs, and Mahanaim with her suburbs, and Heshbon with her suburbs, and Jazer with her suburbs.

Now the sons of Issachar were Tola, and Puah, Jashup, and Shimrom, four. And the sons of Tola: Uzzi, and Rephaiah, and Jeriel, and Jahmai, and Jibsam, and Shemuel, heads of their father's house, to wit, of Tola, they were valiant men of might in their generations whose number was in the days of David two and twenty thousand and six hundred. And the sons of Uzzi: Izrahiah, and the sons of Izrahiah, Michael, and Obadiah, and Joel, Ishiah, five, all of them chief men. And with them, by their generations, after the house of their fathers, were bands of soldiers for war, six and thirty thousand men, for they had many wives and sons. And their brethren among all the families of Issachar were valiant men of might, reckoned in all by their genealogies fourscore and seven thousand.

The sons of Benjamin: Bela, and Becher, and Jediael, three. And the sons of Bela: Ezbon, and Uzzi, and Uzziel, and Jerimoth, and Iri, five, heads of the house of their fathers mighty men of valor, and were reckoned by their genealogies twenty and two thousand and thirty and four. And the sons of Becher: Zemira, and Joash, and Eliezer, and Elioenai, and Omri, and Jerimoth, and Abiah, and Anathoth, and Alameth. All these are the sons of Becher. And the number of them, after their genealogy by their generations, heads of the house of their fathers, mighty men of valor, was twenty thousand and two hundred. The sons also of Jediael: Bilhan, and the sons of Bilhan: Jeush, and Benjamin, and Ehud, and Chenaanah, and Zethan, and Tharshish and Ahishahar. All these the sons of Jediael, by the heads of their fathers, mighty men of valor, were seventeen thousand and two hundred soldiers, fit to go out for war and battle. Shuppim also, and Huppim, the children of Ir, and Hushim, the sons of Aher.

The sons of Naphtali: Jahziel, and Guni, and Jezer, and Shallum, the sons of Bilhah.

The sons of Manasseh: Ashriel, whom she bare (but his concubine the Aramitess bare Machir the father of Gilead, and Machir took to wife the sister of Huppim and Shuppim, whose sister's name was Maachah), and the name of the second was Zelophehad, and Zelophehad had daughters. And Maachah the wife of Machir bare a son, and she called his name Peresh, and the name of his brother was Sheresh, and his sons were Ulam and Rakem. And the sons of Ulam: Badan. These were the sons of Gilead, the son of Machir, the son of Manasseh. And his sister Hammoleketh bare Ishod, and Abiezer, and Mahalah. And the sons of Shemidah were Ahian, and Shechem, and Likhi, and Aniam.

And the sons of Ephraim: Shuthelah, and Bered his son, and Tahath his son, and Eladah his son, and Tahath his son, and Zabad his son, and Shuthelah his son, and Ezer, and Elead, whom the men of Gath that were born in that land slew because they came down to take away their cattle. And Ephraim their father mourned many days and his brethren came to comfort him. And when he went in to his wife she conceived and bare a son, and he called his name Beriah because it went evil with his house. (And his daughter was Sherah, who built Beth-horon the nether, and the upper, and Uzzen-sherah). And Rephah was his son, also Resheph, and Telah his son, and Tahan his son, Laadan his son, Ammihud his son, Elishama his son, Non his son, Jehoshuah his son.

And their possessions and habitations were Beth-el and the towns thereof, and eastward Naaran, and westward Gezer, with the towns thereof, Shechem also and the towns thereof, unto Gaza and the towns thereof, and by the borders of the children of Manasseh, Beth-shean and her towns, Taanach and her towns, Megiddo and her towns, Dor and her towns. In these dwelt the children of Joseph the son of Israel.

The sons of Asher: Imnah, and Isuah, and Ishuai, and Beriah, and Serah their sister. And the sons of Beriah: Heber, and Malchiel, who is the father of Birzavith. And Heber begat Japhlet, and Shomer, and Hotham, and Shua their sister. And the sons of Japhlet: Pasach, and Bimhal, and Ashvath. These are the children of Japhlet. And the sons of Shamer: Ahi, and Rohgah, Jehubbah, and Aram. And the sons of his brother Helem: Zophah, and Imna, and Shelesh, and Amal. The sons of Zophah: Suah, and Harnepher, and Shual, and Beri, and Imrah, Bezer, and Hod, and Shamma, and Shilshah, and Ithran, and Beera. And the sons of Jether: Jephunneh, and Pispah, and Ara. And the sons of Ulla: Arah, and Haniel, and Rezia. All these were the children of Asher, heads of their father's house, choice and mighty men of valor, chief of the princes. And the number throughout the genealogy of them that were apt to the war and to battle was twenty and six thousand men.

Now Benjamin begat Bela his firstborn, Ashbel the second, and Aharah the third, Nohah the fourth, and Rapha the fifth. And the sons of Bela were, Addar, and Gera, and Abihud, and Abishua, and Naaman, and Ahoah, and Gera, and Shephuphan, and Huram. And these are the sons of Ehud, these are the heads of the fathers of the inhabitants of Geba, and they removed them to Manahath, and Naaman, and Ahiah, and Gera, he removed them, and begat Uzza, and Ahihud. And Shaharaim begat children in the country of Moab after he had sent them away; Hushim and Baara were his wives. And he begat of Hodesh his wife: Jobab, and Zibia, and Mesha, and Malcham, and Jeuz and Shachia, and Mirma. These were his sons, heads of the fathers. And of Hushim he begat Abitub, and Elpaal. The sons of Elpaal: Eber, and Misham, and Shamed, who built Ono, and Lod, with the towns thereof, Beriah also, and Shema, who were heads of the fathers of the inhabitants of Ajalon, who drove away the inhabitants of Gath, and Ahio, Shashak, and Jeremoth, and Zebadiah, and Arad, and Ader, and Michael, and Ispah, and Joha, the sons of Beriah, and Zebadiah, and Meshullam, and Hezeki, and Heber, Ishmerai also, and Jezliah, and Jobab, the sons of Elpaal, and Jakim, and Zichri, and Zabdi, and Elienai, and Zilthai, and Eliel, and Adaiah, and Beraiah, and Shimrath, the sons of Shimhi, and Ishpan, and Heber, and Eliel, and Abdon, and Zichri, and Hanan, and Hananiah, and Elam, and Antothijah, and Iphediah, and Penuel, the sons of Shashak, and Shamsherai, and Shehariah, and Athaliah, and Jaresiah, and Eliah, and Zichri, the sons of Jeroham. These were heads of the fathers, by their generations, chief men. These dwelt in Jerusalem.

And at Gibeon dwelt the father of Gibeon, whose wife's name was Maachah, and his firstborn son Abdon, and Zur, and Kish, and Baal, and Nadab, and Gedor, and Ahio, and Zacher. And Mikloth begat Shimeah. And these also dwelt with their brethren in Jerusalem over against them.

And Ner begat Kish, and Kish begat Saul, and Saul begat Jonathan, and Malchi-shua, and Abinadab, and Esh-baal. And the son of Jonathan was Merib-baal, and Merib-baal begat Micah. And the sons of Micah were Pithon, and Melech, and Tarea, and Ahaz. And Ahaz begat Jehoadah, and Jehoadah begat Alemeth, and Azmaveth, and Zimri, and Zimri begat Moza, and Moza begat Binea, Rapha was his son, Eleasah his son, Azel his son. And Azel had six sons, whose names are these: Azrikam, Bocheru, and Ishmael, and Sheariah, and Obadiah, and Hanan. All these were the sons of Azel. And the sons of Eshek his brother were Ulam, his firstborn, Jehush the second, and Eliphelet the third. And the sons of Ulam were mighty men of valor, archers, and had many sons, and sons' sons a hundred and fifty. All these are of the sons of Benjamin.

So all Israel were reckoned by genealogies, and, behold, they were written in the book of the kings of Israel and Judah who were carried away to Babylon for their transgression.

Now the first inhabitants that dwelt in their possessions in their cities were, the Israelites, the priests, Levites, and the Nethinim. And in Jerusalem dwelt of the children of Judah, and of the children of Benjamin, and of the children of Ephraim, and Manasseh, Uthai the son of Ammihud, the son of Omri, the son of Imri, the son of Bani, of the children of Pharez the son of Judah. And of the Shilonites: Asaiah the firstborn, and his sons. And of the sons of Zerah: Jeuel, and their brethren, six hundred and ninety. And of the sons of Benjamin: Sallu the son of Meshullam, the son of Hodaviah, the son of Hasenuah, and Ibneiah the son of Jeroha, and Elam the son of Uzzi, the son of Michri, and Meshullam the son of Shephathiah, the son of Reuel, the son of Ibnijah, and their brethren, according to their generations, nine hundred and fifty and six. All these men were chief of the fathers in the house of their fathers.

And of the priests: Jedaiah, and Jehoiarib, and Jachin, and Azariah, the son of Hilkiah, the son of Meshullam, the son of Zadok, the son of Meraioth, the son of Ahitub, the ruler of the house of God, and Adaiah the son of Jeroham, the son of Pashur, the son of Malchijah, and Maasiai the son of Adiel, the son of Jazerab, the son of Meshullam, the son of Meshillemith, the son of Immer, and their brethren, heads of the house of their fathers, a thousand and seven hundred and threescore, very able men for the work of the service of the house of God.

And of the Levites: Shemaiah the son of Hasshub, the son of Azrikam, the son of Hashabiah, of the sons of Merari, and Bakbakkar, Heresh, and Galal, and Mattaniah, the son of Micah, the son of Zichri, the son of Asaph, and Obadiah the son of Shemaiah, the son of Galal, the son of Jeduthun, and Berechiah, the son of Asa, the son of Elkanah, that dwelt in the villages of the Netophathites.

And the porters were Shallum, and Akkub, and Talmon, and Ahiman, and their brethren, Shallum was the chief, who hitherto waited in the king's gate eastward, they were porters in the companies of the children of Levi. And Shallum the son of Kore, the son of Ebiasaph, the son of Korah, and his brethren, of the house of his father, the Korahites, were over the work of the service, keepers of the gates of the tabernacle, and their fathers, being over the host of the Lord, were keepers of the entry. And Phinehas the son of Eleazar was the ruler over them in time past and the Lord was with him. And Zechariah the son of Meshelemiah was porter of the door of the tabernacle of the congregation. All these which were chosen to be porters in the gates were two hundred and twelve. These were reckoned by their genealogy in their villages whom David and Samuel the seer did ordain in their set office. So they and their children had the oversight of the gates of the house of the Lord, namely, the house of the tabernacle, by wards. In four quarters were the porters, toward the east, west, north, and south. And their brethren, which were in their villages, were to come after seven days from time to time with them. For these Levites, the four chief porters, were in their set office and were over the chambers and treasuries of the house of God. And they lodged round about the house of God because the charge was upon them and the opening thereof every morning pertained to them.

And certain of them had the charge of the ministering vessels, that they should bring them in and out by tale. Some of them also were appointed to oversee the vessels and all the instruments of the sanctuary, and the fine flour, and the wine, and the oil, and the frankincense, and the spices. And some of the sons of the priests made the ointment of the spices. And Mattithiah, one of the Levites who was the firstborn of Shallum the Korahite, had the set office over the things that were made in the pans. And other of their brethren of the sons of the Kohathites were over the shewbread to prepare it every sabbath.

And these are the singers, chief of the fathers of the Levites, who remaining in the chambers were free, for they were employed in that work day and night. These chief fathers of the Levites were chief throughout their generations, these dwelt at Jerusalem.

And in Gibeon dwelt the father of Gibeon, Jehiel, whose wife's name was Maachah, and his firstborn son Abdon, then Zur, and Kish, and Baal, and Ner, and Nadab, and Gedor, and Ahio, and Zechariah, and Mikloth. And Mikloth begat Shimeam. And they also dwelt with their brethren at Jerusalem over against their brethren. And Ner begat Kish, and Kish begat Saul, and Saul begat Jonathan, and Malchi-shua, and Abinadab, and Esh-baal. And the son of Jonathan was Merib-baal, and Merib-baal begat Micah. And the sons of Micah were, Pithon, and Melech, and Tahrea, and Ahaz. And Ahaz begat Jarah, and

Jarah begat Alemeth, and Azmaveth, and Zimri, and Zmiri begat Moza, and Moza begat Binea, and Rephaiah his son, Eleasah his son, Azel his son. And Azel had six sons, whose names are these, Azrikam, Bocheru, and Ishmael, and Sheariah, and Obadiah, and Hanan. These were the son of Azel.

3 NOW the Philistines fought against Israel and the men of Israel fled from before the Philistines and fell down slain in mount Gilboa. And the Philistines followed hard after Saul and after his sons, and the Philistines slew Jonathan, and Abinadab, and Malchi-shua, the sons of Saul. And the battle went sore against Saul and the archers hit him and he was wounded of the archers. Then said Saul to his armor-bearer, Draw thy sword and thrust me through therewith lest these uncircumcised come and abuse me. But his armor-bearer would not, for he was sore afraid. So Saul took a sword and fell upon it. And when his armor-bearer saw that Saul was dead he fell likewise on the sword and died. So Saul died, and his three sons, and all his house died together.

And when all the men of Israel that were in the valley saw that they fled and that Saul and his sons were dead, then they forsook their cities and fled, and the Philistines came and dwelt in them. And it came to pass on the morrow when the Philistines came to strip the slain that they found Saul and his sons fallen in mount Gilboa. And when they had stripped him, they took his head, and his armor, and sent into the land of the Philistines round about, to carry tidings unto their idols and to the people. And they put his armor in the house of their gods and fastened his head in the temple of Dagon. And when all Jabesh-gilead heard all that the Philistines had done to Saul, they arose, all the valiant men, and took away the body of Saul, and the bodies of his sons, and brought them to Jabesh, and buried their bones under the oak in Jabesh, and fasted seven days. So Saul died for his transgression which he committed against the Lord, or against the word of the Lord, which he kept not, and also for asking for counsel of one that had a familiar spirit, to inquire of it and inquired not of the Lord, therefore he slew him and turned the kingdom unto David the son of Jesse.

Then all Israel gathered themselves to David unto Hebron, saying, Behold, we are thy bone and thy flesh. And moreover in time past, even when Saul was king, thou wast he that leddest out and broughtest in Israel and the Lord thy God said unto thee, Thou shalt feed my people Israel and thou shalt be ruler over my people Israel. Therefore came all the elders of Israel to the king to Hebron, and David made a covenant with them in Hebron before the Lord, and they anointed David king over Israel according to the word of the Lord by Samuel.

And David and all Israel went to Jerusalem, which is Jebus where the Jebusites were, the inhabitants of the land. And the inhabitants of Jebus said to David, Thou shalt not come hither. Nevertheless David took the castle of Zion which is the city of David. And David said, Whosoever smiteth the Jebusites first shall be chief and captain. So Joab the son of Zeruiah went first up and was chief. And David dwelt in the castle therefore they called it the city of David. And he built the city round about, even from Millo round about, and Joab repaired the rest of the city. So David waxed greater and greater, for the Lord of hosts was with him.

These also are the chief of the mighty men whom David had, who strengthened themselves with him in his kingdom and with all Israel, to make him king according to the word of the Lord concerning Israel. And this is the number of the mighty men whom David had, Jashobeam, a Hachmonite, the chief of the captains, he lifted up his spear against three hundred slain by him at one time.

And after him was Eleazar the son of Dodo, the Ahohite, who was one of the three mighties. He was with David at Pasdammim and there the Philistines were gathered together to battle, where was a parcel of ground full of barley, and the people fled from before the Philistines. And they set themselves in the midst of that parcel and delivered it, and slew the Philistines, and the Lord saved them by a great deliverance.

Now three of the thirty captains went down to the rock to David into the cave of Adullam and the host of the Philistines encamped in the valley of Rephaim. And David was then in the hold and the Philistines' garrison was then at Bethlehem. And David longed and said, O that one would give me drink of the water of the well of Bethlehem that is at the gate. And the three brake through the host of the Philistines, and drew water out of the well of Bethlehem that was by the gate, and took it and brought it to David, but David would not drink of it, but poured it out to the Lord. And said, My God forbid it me that I should do this thing; shall I drink the blood of these men that have put their lives in jeopardy? for with the jeopardy of their lives they brought it, therefore he would not drink it. These things did these three mightiest.

And Abishai the brother of Joab, he was chief of the three for lifting up his spear against three hundred, he slew them and had a name among the three. Of the three, he was more honorable than the two, for he was their captain howbeit he attained not to the first three.

Benaiah the son of Jehoiada, the son of a valiant man of Kabzeel who had done many acts, he slew two lion-like men of Moab, also he went down and slew a lion in a pit in a snowy day. And he slew an Egyptian, a man of great stature, five cubits high, and in the Egyptian's hand was a spear like a weaver's beam, and he went down to him with a staff, and plucked the spear out of the Egyptian's hand, and slew him with his own spear. These things did Benaiah the son of Jehoiada and had a name among the three mighties. Behold, he was honorable among the thirty, but attained not to the first three, and David set him over his guard.

Also the valiant men of the armies were Asahel the brother of Joab, Elhanan the son of Dodo of Bethlehem, Shammoth the Harorite, Helez the Pelonite, Ira the son of Ikkesh the Tekoite, Abi-ezer the Anthothite, Sibbecai the Hushathite, Ilai the Ahohite, Maharai the Netophathite, Heled the son of Baanah the Netophathite, Ithai the son of Ribai of Gibeah, that pertained to the children of Benjamin, Benaiah the Pirathonite, Hurai of the brooks of Gaash, Abiel the Arbathite, Azmaveth the Baharumite, Eliahba the Shaalbonite, the sons of Hashem the Gizonite, Jonathan the son of Shage the Hararite, Ahiam the son of Sacar the Hararite, Eliphal the son of Ur. Hepher the Mecherathite, Ahijah the Pelonite, Hezro the Carmelite, Naarai the son of Ezbai, Joel the brother of Nathan, Mibhar the son of Haggeri, Zelek the Ammonite, Naharai the Berothite, the armor-bearer of Joab the son of Zeruiah, Ira the Ithrite, Gareb the Ithrite, Uriah the Hittite, Zabad the son of Ahlai, Adina the son of Shiza the Reubenite, a captain of the Reubenites and thirty with him, Hanan the son of Maachah, and Joshaphat the Mithnite, Uzzia the Ashterathite, Shama and Jehiel the sons of Hothan the Aroerite, Jediael the son of Shimri, and Joha his brother, the Tizite, Eliel the Mahavite, and Jeribai and Joshaviah the sons of Elnaam, and Ithmah the Moabite, Eliel, and Obed, and Jasiel the Mesobaite.

Now these are they that came to David to Ziklag while he yet kept himself close because of Saul the son of Kish, and they were among the mighty men, helpers of the war. They were armed with bows and could use both the right hand and the left in hurling stones and shooting arrows out of a bow, even of Saul's brethren of Benjamin. The chief was Ahiezer, then Joash, the sons of Shemaah the Gibeathite, and Jeziel, and Pelet, the sons of Azmaveth, and Berachah, and Jehu the Antothite, and Ismaiah the Gibeonite, a mighty man among the thirty, and over the thirty, and Jeremiah, and Jahaziel, and Johanan, and Josabad the Gederathite, Eluzai, and Jerimoth, and Bealiah, and Shemariah, and Shephatiah the Haruphite, Elkanah, and Jesiah, and Azareel, and Joezer, and Jashobeam, the Korhites, and Joelah, and Zebadiah, the sons of Jeroham of Gedor.

And of the Gadites there separated themselves unto David into the hold to the wilderness men of might, and men of war fit for the battle that could handle shield and buckler, whose faces were like the faces of lions and were as swift as the roes upon the mountains: Ezer the first, Obadiah the second, Eliab the third, Mishmannah the fourth, Jeremiah the fifth, Attai the sixth, Eliel the seventh, Johanan the eighth, Elzabad the ninth, Jeremiah the tenth, Machbanai the eleventh. These were of the sons of Gad, captains of the host, one of the least was over a hundred, and the greatest over a thousand. These are they that went over Jordan in the first month when it had overflown all his banks and they put to flight all them of the valleys, both toward the east, and toward the west.

And there came of the children of Benjamin and Judah to the hold unto David. And David went out to meet them and answered and said unto them, If ye be come peaceably unto me to help me, mine heart shall be knit unto you, but if ye be come to betray me to mine enemies, seeing there is no wrong in mine hands, the God of our fathers look thereon and rebuke it.

Then the Spirit came upon Amasai who was chief of the captains and he said, Thine are we, David, and on thy side, thou son of Jesse, peace, peace be unto thee, and peace be to thine helpers for thy God helpeth thee. Then David received them and made them captains of the band.

And there fell some of Manasseh to David, when he came with the Philistines against Saul to battle, but they helped them not, for the lords of the Philistines upon advisement sent him away saying, He will fall to his master Saul to the jeopardy of our heads. As he went to Ziklag, there fell to him of Manasseh: Adnah, and Jozabad, and Jediael, and Michael, and Jozabad, and Elihu, and Zilthai, captains of the thousands that were of Manasseh. And they helped David against the band of the rovers, for they were all mighty men of valor and were captains in the host. For at that time day by day there came to David to help him, until it was a great host like the host of God. And these are the numbers of the bands that were ready armed to the war and came to David to Hebron, to turn the kingdom of Saul to him according to the word of the Lord. The children of Judah that bare shield and spear were six thousand and eight hundred, ready armed to the war. Of the children of Simeon, mighty men of valor for the war, seven thousand one hundred. Of the children of Levi, four thousand and six hundred. And Jehoiada was the leader of the Aaronites, and with him were three thousand and seven hundred. And Zadok, a young man mighty of valor, and of his father's house twenty and two captains. And of the children of Benjamin, the kindred of Saul, three thousand, for hitherto the greatest part of them had kept the ward of the house of Saul. And of the children of Ephraim twenty thousand and eight hundred, mighty men of valor, famous throughout the house of their fathers. And of the half tribe of Manasseh eighteen thousand, which were expressed by name, to come and make David king. And of the children of Issachar, which were men that had understanding of the times, to know what Israel ought to do, the heads of them were two hundred, and all their brethren were at their commandment. Of Zebulun, such as went forth to battle, expert in war, with all instruments of war, fifty thousand, which could keep rank, they were not of double heart. And of Naphtali a thousand captains, and with them with shield and spear, thirty and seven thousand. And of the Danites expert in war twenty and eight thousand and six hundred. And of Asher, such as went forth to battle, expert in war, forty thousand. And on the other side of Jordan, of the Reubenites, and the Gadites, and of the half tribe of Manasseh, with all manner of instruments of war for the battle, a hundred and twenty thousand.

All these men of war that could keep rank, came with a perfect heart to Hebron to make David king over all Israel, and all the rest also of Israel were of one heart to make David king. And there they were with David three days, eating and drinking, for their brethren had prepared for them. Moreover they that were with them, even unto Issachar and Zebulun and Naphtali, brought bread on asses, and on camels, and on mules, and on oxen, and meat, meal, cakes of figs, and bunches of raisins, and wine, and oil, and oxen, and sheep abundantly, for there was joy in Israel.

4 AND David consulted with the captains of thousands and hundreds and with every leader. And David said unto all the congregation of Israel, If it seem good unto you, and that it be of the Lord our God, let us send abroad unto our brethren everywhere that are left in all the land of Israel and with them also to the priests and Levites which are in their cities and suburbs, that they may gather themselves unto us and let us bring again the ark of our God to us, for we inquired not at it in the days of Saul. And all the congregation said that they would do so, for the thing was right in the eyes of all the people.

So David gathered all Israel together, from Shihor of Egypt even unto the entering of Hemath, to bring the ark of God from Kirjath-jearim. And David went up, and all Israel, to Baalah, that is to Kirjath-jearim which belonged to Judah, to bring up thence the ark of God the Lord that dwelleth between the cherubim, whose name is called on it. And they carried the ark of God in a new cart out of the house of Abinadab, and Uzza and Ahio drave the cart. And David and all Israel played before God with all their might, and with singing, and with harps, and with psalteries, and with timbrels, and with cymbals, and with trumpets.

And when they came unto the threshing floor of Chidon, Uzza put forth his hand to hold the ark, for the oxen stumbled. And the anger of the Lord was kindled against Uzza, and he smote him because he put his hand to the ark, and there he died before God. And David was displeased because the Lord had made a breach upon Uzza, wherefore that place is called Perez-uzza to this day. And David was afraid of God that day, saying, How shall I bring the ark of God home to me? So David brought not the ark home to himself to the city of David, but carried it aside into the house of Obed-edom the Gittite. And the ark of God remained with the family of Obed-edom in his house three months. And the Lord blessed the house of Obed-edom and all that he had.

Now Hiram king of Tyre sent messengers to David, and timber of cedars, with masons and carpenters to build him a house. And David perceived that the Lord had confirmed him king over Israel, for his kingdom was lifted up on high because of his people Israel.

And David took more wives at Jerusalem and David begat more sons and daughters. Now these are the names of his children which he had in Jerusalem: Shammua, and Shobab, Nathan, and Solomon, and Ibhar, and Elishua, and Elpalet, and Nogah, and Nephag, and Japhia, and Elishama, and Beeliada, and Eliphalet.

And when the Philistines heard that David was anointed king over all Israel, all the Philistines went up to seek David. And David heard of it and went out against them. And the Philistines came and spread themselves in the valley of Rephaim. And David inquired of God saying, Shall I go up against the Philistines? And wilt thou deliver them into mine hand? And the Lord said unto him, Go up, for I will deliver them into thine hand. So they came up to Baal-perazim and David smote them there. Then David said, God hath broken in upon mine enemies by mine hand like the breaking forth of waters, therefore they called the name of that place Baal-perazim. And when they had left their gods there, David gave a commandment and they were burned with fire.

And the Philistines yet again spread themselves abroad in the valley. Therefore David inquired again of God and God said unto him, Go not up after them, turn away from them and come upon them over against the mulberry trees. And it shall be when thou shalt hear a sound of going in the tops of the mulberry trees that then thou shalt go out to battle, for God is gone forth before thee to smite the host of the Philistines. David therefore did as God commanded him and they smote the host of the Philistines from Gibeon even to Gazer. And the fame of David went out into all lands and the Lord brought the fear of him upon all nations.

And David made him houses in the city of David, and prepared a place for the ark of God, and pitched for it a tent. Then David said, None ought to carry the ark of God but the Levites, for them hath the Lord chosen to carry the ark of God and to minister unto him forever. And David gathered all Israel together to Jerusalem, to bring up the ark of the Lord unto his place which he had prepared for it. And David assembled the children of Aaron, and the Levites, of the sons of Kohath, Uriel the chief, and his brethren a hundred and twenty, of the sons of Merari, Asaiah the chief, and his brethren two hundred and twenty, of the sons of Gershom, Joel the chief, and his brethren a hundred and thirty, of the sons of Elizaphan, Shemaiah the chief, and his brethren two hundred, of the sons of Hebron, Eliel the chief, and his brethren fourscore, of the sons of Uzziel, Amminadab the chief, and his brethren a hundred and twelve.

And David called for Zadok and Abiathar the priests, and for the Levites, for Uriel, Asaiah, and Joel, Shemaiah, and Eliel, and Amminadab. And said unto them, Ye are the chief of the fathers of the Levites, sanctify yourselves, both ye and your brethren, that ye may bring up the ark of the Lord God of Israel unto the place that I have prepared for it. For because ye did it not at the first the Lord our God made a breach upon us, for that we sought him not after the due order. So the priests and the Levites sanctified themselves to bring up the ark of the Lord God of Israel. And the children of the Levites bare the ark of God upon their shoulders with the staves thereon, as Moses commanded, according to the word of the Lord. And David spake to the chief of the Levites to appoint their brethren to be the singers with instruments of music, psalteries and harps and cymbals, sounding, by lifting up the voice with joy. So the Levites appointed Heman the son of Joel, and of his brethren, Asaph the son of Berechiah, and of the sons of Merari their brethren, Ethan the son of Kushaiah, and with them their brethren of the second degree, Zechariah, Ben, and Jaaziel, and Shemiramoth, and Jehiel, and Unni, Eliab, and Benaiah, and Maaseiah, and Mattithiah, and Elipheleh, and Mikneiah, and Obededom, and Jeiel, the porters. So the singers, Heman, Asaph, and Ethan, were appointed to sound with cymbals of brass, and Zechariah, and Aziel, and Shemiramoth, and Jehiel, and Unni, and Eliab, and Maaseiah, and Benaiah, with psalteries on Alamoth, and Mattithiah, and Elipheleh, and Mikneiah, and Obed-edom, and Jeiel, and Azaziah, with harps on the Sheminith to excel. And Chenaniah, chief of the Levites, was for song, he instructed about the song, because he was skillful. And Berechiah and Elkanah were doorkeepers for the ark. And Shebaniah, and Jehoshaphat, and Nethaneel, and Amasai, and Zechariah, and Benaiah, and Eliezer, the priests, did blow with the trumpets before the ark of God, and Obed-edom and Jehiah were doorkeepers for the ark.

So David, and the elders of Israel, and the captains over thousands went to bring up the ark of the covenant of the Lord out of the house of Obed-edom with joy, and it came to pass when God helped the Levites that bare the ark of the covenant of the Lord that they offered seven bullocks and seven rams. And David was clothed with a robe of fine linen, and all the Levites that bare the ark, and the singers, and Chenaniah the master of the song with the singers, David also had upon him an ephod of linen. Thus all Israel brought up the ark of the covenant of the Lord with shouting, and with sound of the cornet, and with trumpets, and with cymbals, making a noise with psalteries and harps. And it came to pass as the ark of the covenant of the Lord came to the city of David that Michal the daughter of Saul looking out at a window saw king David dancing and playing and she despised him in her heart.

So they brought the ark of God, and set it in the midst of the tent that David had pitched for it and they offered burnt sacrifices and peace offerings before God. And when David had made an end of offering the burnt offerings and the peace offerings he blessed the people in the name of the Lord. And he dealt to every one of Israel, both man and woman, to every one a loaf of bread, and a good piece of flesh, and a flagon of wine. And he appointed certain of the Levites to minister before the ark of the Lord, and to record, and to thank and praise the Lord God of Israel: Asaph the chief, and next to him Zachariah, Jeiel, and Shemiramoth, and Jehiel, and Mattithiah, and Eliab, and Benaiah, and Obed-edom, and Jeiel with psalteries and with harps, but Asaph made a sound with cymbals, Benaiah also and Jahaziel the priests with trumpets continually before the ark of the covenant of God.

Then on that day David delivered first this psalm to thank the Lord into the hand of Asaph and his brethren: Give thanks unto the Lord, call upon his name, make known his deeds among the people. Sing unto him, sing psalms unto him, talk ye of all his wondrous works. Glory ye in his holy name, let the heart of them rejoice that seek the Lord. Seek the Lord and his strength, seek his face continually. Remember his marvelous works that he hath done, his wonders and the judgments of his mouth, O ye seed of Israel his servant, ye children of Jacob, his chosen ones. He is the Lord our God, his judgments are in all the Earth. Be ye mindful always of his covenant, the word which he commanded to a thousand generations, even of the covenant which he made with Abraham and of his oath unto Isaac, and hath confirmed the same to Jacob for a law, and to Israel for an everlasting covenant, saying, Unto thee will I give the land of Canaan, the lot of your inheritance, when ye were but few, even a few and strangers in it. And when they went from nation to nation and from one kingdom to another people, he suffered no man to do them wrong, yea, he reproved kings for their sakes saying, Touch not mine anointed and do my prophets no harm. Sing unto the Lord, all the Earth, show forth from day to day his salvation. Declare his glory among the heathen, his marvelous works among all nations. For great is the Lord and greatly to be praised, he also is to be feared above all gods. For all the gods of the people are idols, but the Lord made the Heavens. Glory and honor are in his presence, strength and gladness are in his place. Give unto the Lord, ye kindreds of the people, give unto the Lord glory and strength. Give unto the Lord the glory due unto his name, bring an offering and come before him, worship the Lord in the beauty of holiness. Fear before him, all the Earth, the world also shall be stable that it be not moved. Let the heavens be glad, and let the Earth rejoice, and let men say among the nations, The Lord reigneth. Let the sea roar and the fullness thereof, let the fields rejoice and all that is therein. Then shall the trees of the wood sing out at the presence of the Lord because he cometh to judge the earth. O give thanks unto the Lord for he is good, for his mercy endureth forever. And say ye, Save us, O God of our salvation, and gather us together, and deliver us from the heathen that we may give thanks to thy holy name and glory in thy praise. Blessed be the Lord God of Israel for ever and ever. And all the people said, Amen, and praised the Lord.

So he left there before the ark of the covenant of the Lord, Asaph and his brethren, to minister before the ark continually as every day's work required, and Obed-edom with their brethren, threescore and eight, Obed-edom also the son of Jeduthun and Hosah to be porters, and Zadok the priest, and his brethren the priests, before the tabernacle of the Lord in the high place that was at Gibeon, to offer burnt offerings unto the Lord upon the altar of the burnt offering continually morning and evening and to do according to all that is written in the law of the Lord which he commanded Israel, and with them Heman and Jeduthun and the rest that were chosen, who were expressed by name, to give thanks to the Lord because his mercy endureth forever, and with them Heman and Jeduthun with trumpets and cymbals for those that should make a sound and with musical instruments of God. And the sons of Jeduthun were porters. And all the people departed every man to his house and David returned to bless his house.

5 NOW it came to pass as David sat in his house, that David said to Nathan the prophet, Lo, I dwell in a house of cedars, but the ark of the covenant of the Lord remaineth under curtains. Then Nathan said unto David, Do all that is in thine heart, for God is with thee.

And it came to pass the same night, that the word of God came to Nathan saying, Go and tell David my servant, Thus saith the Lord, Thou shalt not build me a house to dwell in, for I have not dwelt in a house since the day that I brought up Israel unto this day, but have gone from tent to tent and from one tabernacle to another. Wheresoever I have walked with all Israel, spake I a word to any of the judges of Israel whom I commanded to feed my people saying, Why have ye not built me a house of cedars? Now therefore thus shalt thou say unto my servant David, Thus saith the Lord of hosts, I took thee from the sheepcote, even from following the sheep, that thou shouldest be ruler over my people Israel. And I have been with thee whithersoever thou hast walked, and have cut off all thine enemies from before thee, and have made thee a name like the name of the great men that are in the Earth. Also I will ordain a place for my people Israel and will plant them, and they shall dwell in their place, and shall be moved no more, neither shall the children of wickedness waste them anymore as at the beginning, and since the time that I commanded judges to be over my people Israel. Moreover I will subdue all thine enemies. Furthermore I tell thee that the Lord will build thee a house. And it shall come to pass when thy days be expired that thou must go to be with thy fathers, that I will raise up thy seed after thee which shall be of thy sons and I will establish his kingdom. He shall build me a house and I will establish his throne forever. I will be his father and he shall be my son, and I will not take my mercy away from him as I took it from him that was before thee, but I will settle him in mine house and in my kingdom for ever and his throne shall be established for evermore. According to all these words and according to all this vision, so did Nathan speak unto David.

And David the king came and sat before the Lord and said, Who am I, O Lord God, and what is mine house that thou hast brought me hitherto? And yet this was a small thing in thine eyes, O God, for thou hast also spoken of thy servant's house for a great while to come and hast regarded me according to the estate of a man of high degree, O Lord God. What can David speak more to thee for the honor of thy servant? For thou knowest thy servant. O Lord, for thy servant's sake, and according to thine own heart hast thou done all this greatness in making known all these great things. O Lord, there is none like thee, neither is there any God besides thee according to all that we have heard with our ears. And what one nation in the Earth is like thy people Israe, whom God went to redeem to be his own people, to make thee a name of greatness and terribleness by driving out nations from before thy people whom thou hast redeemed out of Egypt? For thy people Israel didst thou make thine own people forever, and thou, Lord, becamest their God.

Therefore now, Lord, let the thing that thou hast spoken concerning thy servant and concerning his house be established forever, and do as thou hast said. Let it even be established that thy name may be magnified for ever saying, The Lord of hosts is the God of Israel, even a God to Israel, and let the house of David thy servant be established before thee. For thou, O my God, hast told thy servant that thou wilt build him a house, therefore thy servant hath found in his heart to pray before thee. And now, Lord, thou art God and hast promised this goodness unto thy servant, now therefore let it please thee to bless the house of thy servant that it may be before thee forever, for thou blessest, O Lord, and it shall be blessed forever.

Now after this it came to pass that David smote the Philistines, and subdued them, and took Gath and her towns out of the hand of the Philistines. And he smote Moab, and the Moabites became David's servants and brought gifts. And David smote Hadarezer king of Zobah unto Hamath as he went to establish his dominion by the river Euphrates. And David took from him a thousand chariots, and seven thousand horsemen, and twenty thousand footmen; David also houghed all the chariot horses, but reserved of them a hundred chariots. And when the Syrians of Damascus came to help Hadarezer king of Zobah, David slew of the Syrians two and twenty thousand men. Then David put garrisons in Syria-damascus and the Syrians became David's servants and brought gifts. Thus the Lord preserved David whithersoever he went. And David took the shields of gold that were on the servants of Hadarezer and brought them to Jerusalem. Likewise from Tibhath and from Chun, cities of Hadarezer, brought David very much brass wherewith Solomon made the brazen sea, and the pillars, and the vessels of brass. Now when Tou king of Hamath heard how David had smitten all the host of Hadarezer king of Zobah, he sent Hadoram his son to king David to inquire of his welfare and to congratulate him, because he had fought against Hadarezer and smitten him (for Hadarezer had war with Tou), and with him all manner of vessels of gold and silver and brass. Them also king David dedicated unto the Lord with the silver and the gold that he brought from all these nations, from Edom, and from Moab, and from the children of Ammon, and from the Philistines, and from Amalek. Moreover, Abishai the son of Zeruiah slew of the Edomites in the valley of salt eighteen thousand. And he put garrisons in Edom, and all the Edomites became David's servants. Thus the Lord preserved David whithersoever he went.

So David reigned over all Israel and executed judgment and justice among all his people. And Joab the son of Zeruiah was over the host, and Jehoshaphat the son of Ahilud, recorder, and Zadok the son of Ahitub, and Abimelech the son of Abiathar, were the priests, and Shavsha was scribe, and Benaiah the son of Jehoiada was over the Cherethites and the Pelethites, and the sons of David were chief about the king.

Now it came to pass after this that Nahash the king of the children of Ammon died and his son reigned in his stead. And David said, I will show kindness unto Hanun the son of Nahash because his father showed kindness to me. And David sent messengers to comfort him concerning his father. So the servants of David came into the land of the children of Ammon to Hanun to comfort him. But the princes of the children of Ammon said to Hanun, Thinkest thou that David doth honor thy father that he hath sent comforters unto thee? Are not his servants come unto thee for to search, and to overthrow, and to spy out the land? Wherefore Hanun took David's servants, and shaved them, and cut off their garments in the midst hard by their buttocks, and sent them away. Then there went certain and told David how the men were served, and he sent to meet them for the men were greatly ashamed. And the king said, Tarry at Jericho until your beards be grown and then return.

And when the children of Ammon saw that they had made themselves odious to David, Hanun and the children of Ammon sent a thousand talents of silver to hire them chariots and horsemen out of Mesopotamia, and out of Syriamaachah, and out of Zobah. So they hired thirty and two thousand chariots, and the king of Maachah and his people, who came and pitched before Medeba. And the children of Ammon gathered themselves together from their cities and came to battle. And when David heard of it he sent Joab and all the host of the mighty men. And the children of Ammon came out, and put the battle in array before the gate of the city, and the kings that were come were by themselves in the field.

Now when Joab saw that the battle was set against him before and behind he chose out of all the choice of Israel and put them in array against the Syrians. And the rest of the people he delivered unto the hand of Abishai his brother and they set themselves in array against the children of Ammon. And he said, If the Syrians be too strong for me, then thou shalt help me, but if the children of Ammon be too strong for thee, then I will help thee. Be of good courage, and let us behave ourselves valiantly for our people and for the cities of our God, and let the Lord do that which is good in his sight. So Joab and the people that were with him drew nigh before the Syrians unto the battle and they fled before him. And when the children of Ammon saw that the Syrians were fled, they likewise fled before Abishai his brother and entered into the city. Then Joab came to Jerusalem.

And when the Syrians saw that they were put to the worse before Israel, they sent messengers and drew forth the Syrians that were beyond the river, and Shophach the captain of the host of Hadarezer went before them. And it was told David and he gathered all Israel, and passed over Jordan, and came upon them, and set the battle in array against them. So when David had put the battle in array against the Syrians they fought with him. But the Syrians fled before Israel and David slew of the Syrians seven thousand men which fought in chariots, and forty thousand footmen, and killed Shophach the captain of the host. And when the servants of Hadarezer saw that they were put to the worse before Israel they made peace with David and became his servants, neither would the Syrians help the children of Ammon anymore.

And it came to pass that after the year was expired, at the time that kings go out to battle Joab led forth the power of the army and wasted the country of the children of Ammon and came and besieged Rabbah. But David tarried at Jerusalem. And Joab smote Rabbah and destroyed it. And David took the crown of their king from off his head and found it to weigh a talent of gold, and there were precious stones in it, and it was set upon David's head, and he brought also exceeding much spoil out of the city. And he brought out the people that were in it, and cut them with saws, and with harrows of iron, and with axes. Even so dealt David with all the cities of the children of Ammon. And David and all the people returned to Jerusalem.

And it came to pass after this that there arose war at Gezer with the Philistines, at which time Sibbechai the Hushathite slew Sippai that was of the children of the giant and they were subdued. And there was war again with the Philistines and Elhanan the son of Jair slew Lahmi the brother of Goliath the Gittite whose spear staff was like a weaver's beam. And yet again there was war at Gath where was a man of great stature, whose fingers and toes were four and twenty, six on each hand, and six on each foot, and he also was the son of the giant. But when he defied Israel Jonathan the son of Shimea David's brother slew him. These were born unto the giant in Gath and they fell by the hand of David and by the hand of his servants.

And Satan stood up against Israel, and provoked David to number Israel. And David said to Joab and to the rulers of the people, Go, number Israel from Beer-sheba even to Dan and bring the number of them to me that I may know it.

And Joab answered, The Lord make his people a hundred times so many more as they be, but, my lord the king, are they not all my lord's servants? Why then doth my lord require this thing? Why will he be a cause of trespass to Israel? Nevertheless the king's word prevailed against Joab. Wherefore Joab departed and went throughout all Israel and came to Jerusalem. And Joab gave the sum of the number of the people unto David. And all they of Israel were a thousand thousand and a hundred thousand men that drew sword, and Judah was four hundred threescore and ten thousand men that drew sword. But Levi and Benjamin counted he not among them, for the king's word was abominable to Joab.

And God was displeased with this thing, therefore he smote Israel. And David said unto God, I have sinned greatly because I have done this thing, but now I beseech thee, do away the iniquity of thy servant, for I have done very foolishly. And the Lord spake unto Gad, David's seer, saying, Go and tell David, saying, Thus saith the Lord, I offer thee three things, choose thee one of them, that I may do it unto thee. So Gad came to David, and said unto him, Thus saith the Lord, Choose thee, either three years' famine, or three months to be destroyed before thy foes while that the sword of thine enemies overtaketh thee, or else three days the sword of the Lord, even the pestilence in the land and the Angel of the Lord destroying throughout all the coasts of Israel. Now therefore advise thyself what word I shall bring again to him that sent me. And David said unto Gad, I am in a great strait, let me fall now into the hand of the Lord, for very great are his mercies, but let me not fall into the hand of man. So the Lord sent pestilence upon Israel and there fell of Israel seventy thousand men.

And God sent an angel unto Jerusalem to destroy it. And the angel stretched forth his hand unto Jerusalem to destroy it and God said to the angel, Stay now thine hand, it is enough, for as he was destroying, the Lord beheld Israel, that he repented him of the evil, therefore the Lord stayed the angel that destroyed as he stood by the threshing floor of Ornan, the Jebusite. And David lifted up his eyes, and saw the Angel of the Lord stand between the Earth and the Heaven, having a drawn sword in his hand stretched out over Jerusalem. Then David and the elders of Israel who were clothed in sackcloth, fell upon their faces. And David said unto God, Is it not I that commanded the people to be numbered? Even I it is that have sinned and done evil indeed, but as for these sheep, what have they done? Let thine hand I pray thee, O Lord my God, be on me and on my father's house, but not on thy people, that they should be plagued.

Then the Angel of the Lord commanded Gad to say to David that David should go up and set up an altar unto the Lord in the threshing floor of Ornan the Jebusite. And David went up at the saying of Gad which he spake in the name of the Lord. Now Ornan was threshing wheat and his four sons with him, and Ornan turned back and saw the angel and they hid themselves. And as David came to Ornan, Ornan looked and saw David, and went out of the threshing floor, and bowed himself to David with his face to the ground. Then David said to Ornan, Grant me the place of this threshing floor that I may build an altar therein unto the Lord; thou shalt grant it me for the full price that the plague may be stayed from the people. And Ornan said unto David, Take it to thee and let my lord the king do that which is good in his eyes, lo, I give thee the oxen also for burnt offerings, and the threshing instruments for wood, and the wheat for the meat offering, I give it all. And king David said to Ornan, Nay, but I will verily buy it for the full price, for I will not take that which is thine for the Lord, nor offer burnt offerings without cost. So David gave to Ornan for the place six hundred shekels of gold by weight. And David built there an altar unto the Lord, and offered burnt offerings and peace offerings, and called upon the Lord, and he answered him from Heaven by fire upon the altar of burnt offering. And the Lord commanded the angel and he put up his sword again into the sheath thereof.

At that time when David saw that the Lord had answered him in the threshing floor of Ornan the Jebusite, then he sacrificed there. For the tabernacle of the Lord, which Moses made in the wilderness and the altar of the burnt offering were at that season in the high place at Gibeon. But David could not go before it to inquire of God, for he was afraid because of the sword of the Angel of the Lord.

Then David said, This is the house of the Lord God and this is the altar of the burnt offering for Israel. And David commanded to gather together the strangers that were in the land of Israel and he set masons to hew wrought stones to build the house of God. And David prepared iron in abundance for the nails for the doors of the gates, and for the joinings, and brass in abundance without weight, also cedar trees in abundance, for the Zidonians and they of Tyre brought much cedar wood to David. And David said, Solomon my son is young and tender, and the house that is to be builded for the Lord must be exceeding magnifical, of fame and of glory throughout all countries, I will therefore now make preparation for it. So David prepared abundantly before his death.

Then he called for Solomon his son and charged him to build a house for the Lord God of Israel. And David said to Solomon, My son, as for me, it was in my mind to build a house unto the name of the Lord my God. But the word of the Lord came to me, saying, Thou hast shed blood abundantly and hast made great wars, thou shalt not build a house unto my name because thou hast shed much blood upon the Earth in my sight. Behold, a son shall be born to thee who shall be a man of rest and I will give him rest from all his enemies round about, for his name shall be Solomon and I will give peace and quietness unto Israel in his days. He shall build a house for my name, and he shall be my son and I will be his father, and I will establish the throne of his kingdom over Israel forever. Now, my son, the Lord be with thee, and prosper thou, and build the house of the Lord thy God as he hath said of thee. Only the Lord give thee wisdom and understanding, and give thee charge concerning Israel that thou mayest keep the law of the Lord thy God. Then shalt thou prosper, if thou takest heed to fulfill the statutes and judgments which the Lord charged Moses with concerning Israel; be strong, and of good courage, dread not, nor be dismayed. Now, behold, in my trouble I have prepared for the house of the Lord a hundred thousand talents of gold, and a thousand thousand talents of silver, and of brass and iron without weight, for it is in abundance, timber also and stone have I prepared, and thou mayest add thereto. Moreover, there are workmen with thee in abundance, hewers and workers of stone and timber, and all manner of cunning men for every manner of work. Of the gold, the silver, and the brass, and the iron, there is no number. Arise therefore, and be doing, and the Lord be with thee.

David also commanded all the princes of Israel to help Solomon his son saying, Is not the Lord your God with you? And hath he not given you rest on every side? For he hath given the inhabitants of the land into mine hand and the land is subdued before the Lord and before his people. Now set your heart and your soul to seek the Lord your God, arise therefore, and build ye the sanctuary of the Lord God to bring the ark of the covenant of the Lord and the holy vessels of God into the house that is to be built to the name of the Lord.

6 SO when David was old and full of days he made Solomon his son king over Israel. And he gathered together all the princes of Israel, with the priests and the Levites. Now the Levites were numbered from the age of thirty years and upward, and their number by their polls, man by man, was thirty and eight thousand. Of which, twenty and four thousand were to set forward the work of the house of the Lord, and six thousand were officers and judges, moreover four thousand

were porters, and four thousand praised the Lord with the instruments which I made, said David, to praise therewith. And David divided them into courses among the sons of Levi, namely, Gershon, Kohath, and Merari.

Of the Gershonites were Laadan, and Shimei. The sons of Laadan: the chief was Jehiel, and Zetham, and Joel, three. The sons of Shimei: Shelomith, and Haziel, and Haran, three. These were the chief of the fathers of Laadan. And the sons of Shimei were Jahath, Zina, and Jeush, and Beriah. These four were the sons of Shimei. And Jahath was the chief, and Zizah the second, but Jeush and Beriah had not many sons, therefore they were in one reckoning, according to their father's house.

The sons of Kohath: Amram, Izhar, Hebron, and Uzziel, four. The sons of Amram: Aaron and Moses, and Aaron was separated that he should sanctify the most holy things, he and his sons forever, to burn incense before the Lord, to minister unto him, and to bless in his name forever. Now concerning Moses the man of God, his sons were named of the tribe of Levi. The sons of Moses were Gershom and Eliezer. Of the sons of Gershom, Shebuel was the chief. And the sons of Eliezer were Rehabiah the chief. And Eliezer had none other sons, but the sons of Rehabiah were very many. Of the sons of Izhar: Shelomith the chief. Of the sons of Hebron: Jeriah the first, Amariah the second, Jahaziel the third, and Jekameam the fourth. Of the sons of Uzziel: Micah the first, and Jesiah the second.

The sons of Merari: Mahli, and Mushi. The sons of Mahli: Eleazar, and Kish. And Eleazar died, and had no sons, but daughters, and their brethren the sons of Kish took them. The sons of Mushi: Mahli, and Eder, and Jeremoth, three.

These were the sons of Levi after the house of their fathers, even the chief of the fathers, as they were counted by number of names by their polls, that did the work for the service of the house of the Lord, from the age of twenty years and upward. For David said, The Lord God of Israel hath given rest unto his people, that they may dwell in Jerusalem forever, and also unto the Levites, they shall no more carry the tabernacle, nor any vessels of it for the service thereof. For by the last words of David the Levites were numbered from twenty years old and above, because their office was to wait on the sons of Aaron for the service of the house of the Lord, in the courts, and in the chambers, and in the purifying of all holy things, and the work of the service of the house of God, both for the shewbread, and for the fine flour for meat offering, and for the unleavened cakes, and for that which is baked in the pan, and for that which is fried, and for all manner of measure and size, and to stand every morning to thank and praise the Lord, and likewise at even, and to offer all burnt sacrifices unto the Lord in the sabbaths, in the new moons, and on the set feasts, by number, according to the order commanded unto them continually before the Lord, and that they should keep the charge of the tabernacle of the congregation, and the charge of the holy place, and the charge of the sons of Aaron their brethren, in the service of the house of the Lord.

Now these are the divisions of the sons of Aaron. The sons of Aaron: Nadab and Abihu, Eleazar and Ithamar. But Nadab and Abihu died before their father, and had no children, therefore Eleazar and Ithamar executed the priest's office. And David distributed them, both Zadok of the sons of Eleazar, and Ahimelch of the sons of Ithamar, according to their offices in their service. And there were more chief men found of the sons of Eleazar than of the sons of Ithamar, and thus were they divided. Among the sons of Eleazar there were sixteen chief men of the house of their fathers, and eight among the sons of Ithamar according to the house of their fathers. Thus were they divided by lot, one sort with another, for the governors of the sanctuary and governors of the house of God were of the sons of Eleazar and of the sons of Ithamar. And Shemaiah the son of Nethaneel the scribe, one of the Levites, wrote them before the king, and the princes, and Zadok the priest, and Ahimelech the son of Abiathar, and before the chief of the fathers of the priests and Levites, one principal household being taken for Eleazar and one taken for Ithamar.

Now the first lot came forth to Jehoiarib, the second to Jedaiah, the third to Harim, the fourth to Seorim, the fifth to Malchijah, the sixth to Mijamin, the seventh to Hakkoz, the eighth to Abijah, the ninth to Jeshuah, the tenth to Shecaniah, the eleventh to Eliashib, the twelfth to Jakim, the thirteenth to Huppah, the fourteenth to Jeshebeab, the fifteenth to Bilgah, the sixteenth to Immer, the seventeenth to Hezir, the eighteenth to Aphses, the nineteenth to Pethahiah, the twentieth to Jehezekel, the one and twentieth to Jachin, the two and twentieth to Gamul, the three and twentieth to Delaiah, the four and twentieth to Maaziah. These were the orderings of them in their service to come into the house of the Lord according to their manner, under Aaron their father, as the Lord God of Israel had commanded him.

And the rest of the sons of Levi were these: Of the sons of Amram: Shubael, of the sons of Shubael: Jehdeiah. Concerning Rehabiah, of the sons of Rehabiah: the first was Isshiah. Of the Izharites, Shelomoth, of the sons of Shelomoth: Jahath. And the sons of Hebron: Jeriah the first, Amariah the second, Jahaziel the third, Jekameam the fourth. Of the sons of Uzziel: Michah, of the sons of Michah: Shamir. The brother of Michah was Isshiah, of the sons of Isshiah: Zechariah. The sons of Merari were Mahli and Mushi, the sons of Jaaziah: Beno. The sons of Merari by Jaaziah: Beno, and Shoham, and Zaccur, and Ibri. Of Mahli came Eleazar, who had no sons. Concerning Kish, the son of Kish was Jerahmeel. The sons also of Mushi: Mahli, and Eder, and Jerimoth. These were the sons of the Levites after the house of their fathers. These likewise cast lots over against their brethren the sons of Aaron in the presence of David the king, and Zadok, and Ahimelech, and the chief of the fathers of the priests and Levites, even the principal fathers over against their younger brethren.

Moreover David and the captains of the host separated to the service of the sons of Asaph, and of Heman, and of Jeduthun, who should prophesy with harps, with psalteries, and with cymbals, and the number of the workmen according to their service was, of the sons of Asaph: Zaccur, and Joseph, and Nethaniah, and Asarelah, the sons of Asaph under the hands of Asaph, which prophesied according to the order of the king. Of Jeduthun, the sons of Jeduthun: Gedaliah, and Zeri, and Jeshaiah, Hashabiah, and Mattithiah, six, under the hands of their father Jeduthun who prophesied with a harp to give thanks and to praise the Lord. Of Heman, the sons of Heman: Bukkiah, Mattaniah, Uzziel, Shebuel, and Jerimoth, Hananiah, Hanani, Eliathah, Giddalti, and Romamti-ezer, Joshbekashah, Mallothi, Hothir, and Mahazioth, all these were the son of Heman the king's seer in the words of God to lift up the horn. And God gave to Heman fourteen sons and three daughters. All these were under the hands of their father for song in the house of the Lord, with cymbals, psalteries, and harps, for the service of the house of God according to the king's order to Asaph, Jeduthun, and Heman. So the number of them, with their brethren that were instructed in the songs of the Lord, even all that were cunning, was two hundred fourscore and eight.

And they cast lots, ward against ward, as well the small as the great, the teacher as the scholar. Now the first lot came forth for Asaph to Joseph, the second to Gedaliah, who with his brethren and sons were twelve, the third to Zaccur, he, his sons, and his brethren were twelve, the fourth to Izri, he, his sons, and his brethren were twelve, the fifth to Nethaniah, he, his sons and his brethren were twelve, the sixth to Bukkiah, he, his sons, and his brethren were twelve, the seventh to Jesharelah, he, his sons, and his brethren were twelve, the eighth to Jeshaiah, he, his sons, and his brethren were twelve, the ninth to Mattaniah, he, his sons, and his brethren were twelve, the tenth to Shimei, he, his sons, and his brethren were twelve, the eleventh to Azareel, he, his sons, and his brethren were twelve, the twelfth to Hashabiah, he, his sons, and his brethren were twelve, the thirteenth to Shubael, he, his sons, and his brethren were twelve, the fourteenth to Mattithiah, he, his sons, and his brethren were twelve, the fifteenth to Jeremoth, he, his sons, and his brethren were twelve, the sixteenth to Hanahiah, he, his sons, and his brethren were twelve, the seventeenth to Joshbekasha, he, his sons, and his brethren were twelve, the eighteenth to Hanani, he, his sons, and his brethren were twelve, the nineteenth to Mallothi, he, his sons, and his brethren were twelve, the twentieth to Eliathah, he, his sons, and his brethren were twelve, the one and twentieth to Hothir, he, his sons, and his brethren were twelve, the two and twentieth to Giddalti, he, his sons, and his brethren were twelve, the three and twentieth to Mahazioth, he, his sons, and his brethren were twelve, the four and twentieth to Romamti-ezer, his sons, and his brethren were twelve.

Concerning the divisions of the porters, Of the Korhites was Meshelemiah the son of Kore, of the sons of Asaph. And the sons of Meshelemiah were Zechariah the firstborn, Jediael the second, Zebadiah the third, Jathniel the fourth, Elam the fifth, Jehohanan the sixth, Elioenai the seventh. Moreover the sons of Obed-edom were Shemaiah the firstborn, Jehozabad the second, Joah the third, and Sacar the fourth, and Nethaneel the fifth, Ammiel the sixth, Issachar the seventh, Peulthai the eighth, for God blessed him. Also unto Shemaiah his son were sons born, that ruled throughout the house of their father, for they were mighty men of valor. The sons of Shemaiah: Othni, and Rephael, and Obed, Elzabad, whose brethren were strong men, Elihu, and Semachiah. All these of the sons of Obed-edom, they and their sons and their brethren, able men for strength for the service, were threescore and two of Obed-edom. And Meshelemiah had sons and brethren, strong men, eighteen. Also Hosah, of the children of Merari had sons: Simri the chief (for though he was not the firstborn, yet his father made him the chief), Hilkiah the second, Tebaliah the third, Zechariah the fourth, all the sons and brethren of Hosah were thirteen. Among these were the divisions of the porters, even among the chief men, having wards one against another, to minister in the house of the Lord.

And they cast lots, as well the small as the great, according to the house of their fathers, for every gate. And the lot eastward fell to Shelemiah. Then for Zechariah his son, a wise counselor, they cast lots and his lot came out northward. To Obed-edom southward and to his sons the house of Asuppim. To Shuppim and Hosah the lot came forth westward with the gate Shallecheth by the causeway of the going up, ward against ward. Eastward were six Levites, northward four a day, southward four a day, and toward Asuppim two and two. At Parbar westward, four at the causeway and two at Parbar. These are the divisions of the porters among the sons of Kore, and among the sons of Merari.

And of the Levites, Ahijah was over the treasures of the house of God and over the treasures of the dedicated things. As concerning the sons of Laadan, the sons of the Gershanite Laadan, chief fathers, even of Laadan the Gershonite, were Jehieli.

The sons of Jehieli: Zetham, and Joel his brother, which were over the treasures of the house of the Lord. Of the Amramites, and the Izharites, the Hebronites, and the Uzzielites, and Shebuel the son of Gershom, the son of Moses, was ruler of the treasures. And his brethren by Eliezer, Rehabiah his son, and Jeshaiah his son, and Joram his son, and Zichri his son, and Shelomith his son, which Shelomith and his brethren were over all the treasures of the dedicated things which David the king, and the chief fathers, the captains over thousands and hundreds, and the captains of the host, had dedicated. Out of the spoils won in battles did they dedicate to maintain the house of the Lord. And all that Samuel the seer, and Saul the son of Kish, and Abner the son of Ner, and Joab the son of Zeruiah, had dedicated, and whosoever had dedicated anything, it was under the hand of Shelomith and of his brethren.

Of the Izharies, Chenaniah and his sons were for the outward business over Israel, for officers and judges. And of the Hebronite, Hashabiah and his brethren, men of valor, a thousand and seven hundred, were officers among them of Israel on this side Jordan westward in all the business of the Lord and in the service of the king. Among the Hebronites was Jerijah the chief, even among the Hebronites, according to the generations of his fathers. In the fortieth year of the reign of David they were sought for, and there were found among them mighty men of valor at Jazer of Gilead. And his brethren, men of valor, were two thousand and seven hundred chief fathers, whom king David made rulers over the Reubenites, the Gadites, and the half tribe of Manasseh, for every matter pertaining to God and affairs of the king.

Now the children of Israel after their number, to wit, the chief fathers and captains of thousands and hundreds, and their officers that served the king in any matter of the courses, which came in and went out month by month throughout all the months of the year, of every course were twenty and four thousand.

Over the first course for the first month was Jashobeam the son of Zabdiel, and in his course were twenty and four thousand. Of the children of Perez was the chief of all the captains of the host for the first month. And over the course of the second month was Dodai an Ahohite, and of his course was Mikloth also the ruler, in his course likewise were twenty and four thousand. The third captain of the host for the third month was Benaiah the son of Jehoiada, a chief priest, and in his course were twenty and four thousand. This is that Benaiah, who was mighty among the thirty, and above the thirty, and in his course was Ammizabad his son. The fourth captain for the fourth month was Asahel the brother of Joab, and Zebadiah his son after him, and in his course were twenty and four thousand. The fifth captain for the fifth month was Shamhuth the Izrahite, and in his course were twenty and four thousand. The sixth captain for the sixth month was Ira the son of Ikkesh the Tekoite, and in his course were twenty and four thousand. The seventh captain for the seventh month was Helez the Pelonite, of the children of Ephraim, and in his course were twenty and four thousand. The eighth captain for the eighth month was Sibbecai the Hushathite, of the Zarhites, and in his course were twenty and four thousand. The ninth captain for the ninth month was Abiezer the Anehothite, of the Benjamites, and in his course were twenty and four thousand. The tenth captain for the tenth month was Maharai the Netophathite, of the Zarhites, and in his course were twenty and four thousand. The eleventh captain for the eleventh month was Benaiah the Pirathonite, of the children of Ephraim, and in his course were twenty and four thousand. The twelfth captain for the twelfth month was Heldai the Netophathite, of Othniel, and in his course were twenty and four thousand.

Furthermore over the tribes of Israel, the ruler of the Reubenites was Eliezer the son of Zichri, of the Simeonites, Shephatiah the son of Maachah, of the Levites, Hashabiah the son of Kemuel, of the Aaronites, Zadok, of Judah, Elihu, one of the brethren of David, of Issachar, Omri the son of Michael, of Zebulun, Ishmaiah the son of Obadiah, of Naphtali, Jerimoth the son of Azriel, of the children of Ephraim, Hosea, the son of Azaziah, of the half tribe of Manasseh, Joel the son of Pedaiah, of the half tribe of Manasseh in Gilead, Iddo the son of Zechariah, of Benjamin, Jaasiel the son of Abner. Of Dan, Azareel the son of Jeroham. These were the princes of the tribes of Israel. But David took not the number of them from twenty years old and under because the Lord had said he would increase Israel like to the stars of the heavens. Joab the son of Zeruiah began to number, but he finished not because there fell wrath for it against Israel, neither was the number put in the account of the chronicles of king David.

And over the king's treasures was Azmaveth the son of Adiel, and over the storehouses in the fields, in the cities, and in the villages, and in the castles, was Jehonathan the son of Uzziah, and over them that did the work of the field for tillage of the ground was Ezri the son of Chelub, and over the vineyards was Shimei the Remathite, over the increase of the vineyards for the wine cellars was Zabdi the Shiphmite, and over the olive trees and the sycamore trees that were in the low plains was Baal-hanan the Gederite, and over the cellars of oil was Joash, and over the herds that fed in Sharon was Shitrai the Sharonite, and over the herds that were in the valleys was Shaphat the son of Adlai, over the camels also was Obil the Ishmaelite, and over the asses was Jedeiah the Meronothite, and over the flocks was Jaziz the Hagarite. All these were the rulers of the substance which was king David's.

Also Jonathan David's uncle was a counselor, a wise man, and a scribe, and Jehiel the son of Hachmoni was with the king's sons, and Ahithophel was the king's counsellor, and Hushai the Archite was the king's companion, and after Ahithophel was Jehoiada the son of Benaiah, and Abiathar, and the general of the king's army was Joab.

And David assembled all the princes of Israel, the princes of the tribes, and the captains of the companies that ministered to the king by course, and the captains over the thousands, and captains over the hundreds, and the stewards over all the substance and possession of the king, and of his sons, with the officers, and with the mighty men, and with all the valiant men, unto Jerusalem. Then David the king stood up upon his feet, and said, Hear me, my brethren, and my people, As for me, I had in mine heart to build a house of rest for the ark of the covenant of the Lord, and for the footstool of our God, and had made ready for the building, but God said unto me, Thou shalt not build a house for my name because thou hast been a man of war and hast shed blood. Howbeit the Lord God of Israel chose me before all the house of my father to be king over Israel forever, for he hath chosen Judah to be the ruler, and of the house of Judah, the house of my father, and among the sons of my father he liked me to make me king over all Israel, and of all my sons (for the Lord hath given me many sons), he hath chosen Solomon my son to sit upon the throne of the kingdom of the Lord over Israel. And he said unto me, Solomon thy son, he shall build my house and my courts, for I have chosen him to be my son and I will be his father. Moreover I will establish his kingdom forever, if he be constant to do my commandments and my judgments as at this day. Now therefore, in the sight of all Israel the congregation of the Lord and in the audience of our God, keep and seek for all the commandments of the Lord your God that ye may possess this good land and leave it for an inheritance for your children after you forever.

And thou, Solomon my son, know thou the God of thy father and serve him with a perfect heart and with a willing mind, for the Lord searcheth all hearts and understandeth all the imaginations of the thoughts, if thou seek him, he will be found of thee, but if thou forsake him, he will cast thee off forever. Take heed now, for the Lord hath chosen thee to build a house for the sanctuary; be strong, and do it.

Then David gave to Solomon his son the pattern of the porch, and of the houses thereof, and of the treasuries thereof, and of the upper chambers thereof, and of the inner parlors thereof, and of the place of the mercy seat. And the pattern of all that he had by the Spirit, of the courts of the house of the Lord, and of all the chambers round about, of the treasuries of the house of God, and of the treasuries of the dedicated things, also for the courses of the priests and the Levites, and for all the work of the service of the house of the Lord, and for all the vessels of service in the house of the Lord. He gave of gold by weight for things of gold, for all instruments of all manner of service, silver also for all instruments of silver by weight, for all instruments of every kind of service, even the weight for the candlesticks of gold, and for their lamps of gold, by weight for every candlestick and for the lamps thereof, and for the candlesticks of silver by weight, both for the candlestick and also for the lamps thereof, according to the use of every candlestick. And by weight he gave gold for the tables of shewbread, for every table and likewise silver for the tables of silver, also pure gold for the fleshhooks, and the bowls, and the cups, and for the golden basins he gave gold by weight for every basin, and likewise silver by weight for every basin of silver, and for the altar of incense refined gold by weight, and gold for the pattern of the chariot of the cherubim that spread out their wings and covered the ark of the covenant of the Lord.

All this, said David, the Lord made me understand in writing by his hand upon me, even all the works of this pattern.

And David said to Solomon his son, Be strong and of good courage, and do it, fear not, nor be dismayed, for the Lord God, even my God, will be with thee, he will not fail thee, nor forsake thee, until thou hast finished all the work for the service of the house of the Lord. And, behold, the courses of the priests and the Levites, even they shall be with thee for all the service of the house of God, and there shall be with thee for all manner of workmanship every willing skillful man, for any manner of service, also the princes and all the people will be wholly at thy commandment.

Furthermore David the king said unto all the congregation, Solomon my son, whom alone God hath chosen, is yet young and tender and the work is great, for the palace is not for man, but for the Lord God. Now I have prepared with all my might for the house of my God the gold for things to be made of gold, and the silver for things of silver, and the brass for things of brass, the iron for things of iron, and wood for things of wood, onyx stones, and stones to be set, glistering stones, and of divers colors, and all manner of precious stones and marble stones in abundance. Moreover, because I have set my affection to the house of my God, I have of mine own proper good, of gold and silver, which I have given to the house of my God, over and above all that I have prepared for the holy house, even three thousand talents of gold, of the gold of Ophir, and seven thousand talents of refined silver to overlay the walls of the houses withal, the gold for things of gold, and the silver for things of silver, and for all manner of work to be made by the hands of artificers. And who then is willing to consecrate his service this day unto the Lord?

Then the chief of the fathers and princes of the tribes of Israel, and the captains of thousands and of hundreds, with the rulers of the king's work, offered willingly and gave, for the service of the house of God, of gold five thousand talents and ten thousand drams, and of silver ten thousand talents, and of brass eighteen thousand talents, and one hundred thousand talents of iron. And they with whom precious stones were found gave them to the treasure of the house of the Lord by the hand of Jehiel the Gershonite. Then the people rejoiced, for that they offered willingly because with perfect heart they offered willingly to the Lord and David the king also rejoiced with great joy.

Wherefore David blessed the Lord before all the congregation and David said, Blessed be thou, Lord God of Israel our father, for ever and ever. Thine, O Lord, is the greatness, and the power, and the glory, and the victory, and the majesty, for all that is in the Heaven and in the Earth is thine, thine is the kingdom, O Lord, and thou art exalted as head above all. Both riches and honor come of thee, and thou reignest over all, and in thine hand is power and might, and in thine hand it is to make great, and to give strength unto all. Now therefore, our God, we thank thee, and praise thy glorious name. But who am I, and what is my people, that we should be able to offer so willingly after this sort? For all things come of thee and of thine own have we given thee. For we are strangers before thee and sojourners, as were all our fathers, our days on the Earth are as a shadow, and there is none abiding. O Lord our God, all this store that we have prepared to build thee a house for thine holy name cometh of thine hand and is all thine own. I know also, my God, that thou triest the heart and hast pleasure in uprightness. As for me, in the uprightness of mine heart I have willingly offered all these things, and now have I seen with joy thy people which are present here, to offer willingly unto thee. O Lord God of Abraham, Isaac, and of Israel, our fathers, keep this for ever in the imagination of the thoughts of the heart of thy people, and prepare their heart unto thee, and give unto Solomon my son a perfect heart, to keep thy commandments, thy testimonies, and thy statutes, and to do all these things, and to build the palace for the which I have made provision.

And David said to all the congregation, Now bless the Lord your God. And all the congregation blessed the Lord God of their fathers and bowed down their heads and worshiped the Lord and the king. And they sacrificed sacrifices unto the Lord, and offered burnt offerings unto the Lord on the morrow after that day, even a thousand bullocks, a thousand rams, and a thousand lambs, with their drink offerings and sacrifices in abundance for all Israel, and did eat and drink before the Lord on that day with great gladness. And they made Solomon the son of David king the second time, and anointed him unto the Lord to be the chief governor and Zadok to be priest. Then Solomon sat on the throne of the Lord as king instead of David his father and prospered and all Israel obeyed him. And all the princes, and the mighty men, and all the sons likewise of king David submitted themselves unto Solomon the king. And the Lord magnified Solomon exceedingly in the sight of all Israel and bestowed upon him such royal majesty as had not been on any king before him in Israel.

Thus David the son of Jesse reigned over all Israel. And the time that he reigned over Israel was forty years; seven years reigned he in Hebron, and thirty and three years reigned he in Jerusalem. And he died in a good old age, full of days, riches, and honor, and Solomon his son reigned in his stead. Now the acts of David the king, first and last, behold, they are written in the book of Samuel the seer, and in the book of Nathan the prophet, and in the book of Gad the seer, with all his reign and his might, and the times that went over him, and over Israel, and over all the kingdoms of the countries.

THE SECOND BOOK OF THE CHRONICLES

AND Solomon the son of David was strengthened in his kingdom and the Lord his God was with him and magnified him exceedingly. Then Solomon spake unto all Israel, to the captains of thousands and of hundreds, and to the judges, and to every governor in all Israel, the chief of the fathers. So Solomon and all the congregation with him went to the high place that was at Gibeon, for there was the tabernacle of the congregation of God which Moses the servant of the Lord had made in the wilderness. But the ark of God had David brought up from Kirjath-jearim to the place which David had prepared for it, for he had pitched a tent for it at Jerusalem. Moreover the brazen altar that Bezaleel the son of Uri the son of Hur had made, he put before the tabernacle of the Lord and Solomon and the congregation sought unto it. And Solomon went up thither to the brazen altar before the Lord which was at the tabernacle of the congregation and offered a thousand burnt offerings upon it.

In that night did God appear unto Solomon and said unto him, Ask what I shall give thee. And Solomon said unto God, Thou hast showed great mercy unto David my father and hast made me to reign in his stead. Now, O Lord God, let thy promise unto David my father be established, for thou hast made me king over a people like the dust of the Earth in multitude. Give me now wisdom and knowledge that I may go out and come in before this people, for who can judge this thy people that is so great? And God said to Solomon, Because this was in thine heart and thou hast not asked riches, wealth, or honor, nor the life of thine enemies, neither yet hast asked long life, but hast asked wisdom and knowledge for thyself that thou mayest judge my people over whom I have made thee king, wisdom and knowledge is granted unto thee and I will give thee riches, and wealth, and honor such as none of the kings have had that have been before thee, neither shall there any after thee have the like.

Then Solomon came from his journey to the high place that was at Gibeon to Jerusalem, from before the tabernacle of the congregation, and reigned over Israel. And Solomon gathered chariots and horsemen, and he had a thousand and four hundred chariots and twelve thousand horsemen, which he placed in the chariot cities and with the king at Jerusalem. And the king made silver and gold at Jerusalem as plenteous as stones, and cedar trees made he as the sycamore trees that are in the vale for abundance. And Solomon had horses brought out of Egypt, and linen yarn; the king's merchants received the linen yarn at a price. And they fetched up and brought forth out of Egypt a chariot for six hundred shekels of silver and a horse for a hundred and fifty, and so brought they out horses for all the kings of the Hittites and for the kings of Syria by their means

And Solomon determined to build a house for the name of the Lord and a house for his kingdom. And Solomon told out threescore and ten thousand men to bear burdens, and fourscore thousand to hew in the mountain, and three thousand and six hundred to oversee them.

And Solomon sent to Huram the king of Tyre saying, As thou didst deal with David my father and didst send him cedars to build him a house to dwell therein, therefore, even so deal with me. Behold, I build a house to the name of the Lord my God, to dedicate it to him, and to burn before him sweet incense, and for the continual shewbread, and for the burnt offerings morning and evening on the sabbaths, and on the new moons, and on the solemn feasts of the Lord our God. And this ordinance shall be kept in Israel forever. And the house which I build shall be a great house, for great is the Lord our God above all gods. But who is able to build him a house, seeing the Heaven and Heaven of Heavens cannot contain him? Who am I then, that I should build him a house, save only to burn sacrifice before him? Send me now therefore a man cunning to work in gold, and in silver, and in brass, and in iron, and in purple, and crimson, and blue, and that has skill to grave with the cunning men that are with me in Judah and in Jerusalem whom David my father did provide. Send me also cedar trees, fir trees, and algum trees out of Lebanon, for I know that thy servants have skill to cut timber in Lebanon and behold, I will send my servants with thy servants, even to prepare me timber in abundance, for the house which I am about to build shall be wonderful great. And, behold, I will give to thy servants, the hewers that cut timber, twenty thousand measures of beaten wheat, and twenty thousand measures of barley, and twenty thousand baths of wine, and twenty thousand baths of oil.

Then Huram the king of Tyre answered in writing which he sent to Solomon, Because the Lord hath loved his people, he hath made thee king over them. Huram said moreover, Blessed be the Lord God of Israel that made Heaven and Earth, who hath given to David the king a wise son, endued with prudence and understanding, that might build a house for the Lord and a house for his kingdom. And now I have sent a cunning man, endued with understanding, of Huram my father's, the son of a woman of the daughters of Dan, and his father was a man of Tyre, skillful to work in gold, and in silver, in brass, in iron, in stone, and in timber, in purple, in blue, and in fine linen, and in crimson, also to grave any manner of graving, and to find out every device which shall be put to him, with thy cunning men and with the cunning men of my lord David thy father. Now therefore the wheat, and the barley, the oil, and the wine, which my lord hath spoken of, let him send unto his servants, and we will cut wood out of Lebanon, as much as thou shalt need, and we will bring it to thee in floats by sea to Joppa, and thou shalt carry it up to Jerusalem.

And Solomon numbered all the strangers that were in the land of Israel, after the numbering wherewith David his father had numbered them, and they were found a hundred and fifty thousand and three thousand and six hundred. And he set threescore and ten thousand of them to be bearers of burdens, and fourscore thousand to be hewers in the mountain, and three thousand and six hundred overseers to set the people at work.

Then Solomon began to build the house of the Lord at Jerusalem in mount Moriah where the Lord appeared unto David his father in the place that David had prepared in the threshing floor of Ornan the Jebusite. And he began to build in the second day of the second month in the fourth year of his reign.

Now these are the things wherein Solomon was instructed for the building of the house of God: The length by cubits after the first measure was threescore cubits, and the breadth twenty cubits. And the porch that was in the front of the house, the length of it was according to the breadth of the house, twenty cubits, and the height was a hundred and twenty, and he overlaid it within with pure gold. And the greater house he ceiled with fir tree, which he overlaid with fine gold, and set thereon palm trees and chains. And he garnished the house with precious stones for beauty, and the gold was gold of Parvaim. He overlaid also the house, the beams, the posts, and the walls thereof, and the doors thereof, with gold, and graved cherubim on the walls. And he made the most holy house, the length whereof was according to the breadth of the house, twenty cubits, and the breadth thereof twenty cubits, and he overlaid it with fine gold, amounting to six hundred talents. And the weight of the nails was fifty shekels of gold. And he overlaid the upper chambers with gold.

And in the most holy house he made two cherubim of image work, and overlaid them with gold. And the wings of the cherubim were twenty cubits long, one wing of the one cherub was five cubits, reaching to the wall of the house, and the other wing was likewise five cubits, reaching to the wing of the other cherub. And one wing of the other cherub was five cubits, reaching to the wall of the house, and the other wing was five cubits also, joining to the wing of the other cherub. The wings of these cherubim spread themselves forth twenty cubits, and they stood on their feet, and their faces were inward.

And he made the veil of blue, and purple, and crimson, and fine linen, and wrought cherubim thereon. Also he made before the house two pillars of thirty and five cubits high, and the chapiter that was on the top of each of them was five cubits. And he made chains, as in the oracle, and put them on the heads of the pillars, and made a hundred pomegranates, and put them on the chains. And he reared up the pillars before the temple, one on the right hand and the other on the left, and called the name of that on the right hand Jachin and the name of that on the left Boaz.

Moreover he made an altar of brass, twenty cubits the length thereof, and twenty cubits the breadth thereof, and ten cubits the height thereof.

Also he made a molten sea of ten cubits from brim to brim, round in compass, and five cubits the height thereof, and a line of thirty cubits did compass it round about. And under it was the similitude of oxen, which did compass it round about, ten in a cubit, compassing the sea round about. Two rows of oxen were cast when it was cast. It stood upon twelve oxen, three looking toward the north and three looking toward the west, and three looking toward the south, and three looking toward the east, and the sea was set above upon them and all their hinder parts were inward. And the thickness of it was a handbreadth, and the brim of it like the work of the brim of a cup, with flowers of lilies, and it received and held three thousand baths.

He made also ten lavers, and put five on the right hand and five on the left, to wash in them such things as they offered for the burnt offering they washed in them, but the sea was for the priests to wash in. And he made ten candlesticks of gold according to their form, and set them in the temple, five on the right hand and five on the left. He made also ten tables, and placed them in the temple, five on the right side and five on the left. And he made a hundred basins of gold. Furthermore he made the court of the priests, and the great court, and doors for the court, and overlaid the doors of them with brass. And he set the sea on the right side of the east end, over against the south.

And Huram made the pots, and the shovels, and the basins. And Huram finished the work that he was to make for king Solomon for the house of God, to wit, the two pillars, and the pommels, and the chapiters which were on the top of the two pillars, and the two wreaths to cover the two pommels of the chapiters which were on the top of the pillars, and four hundred pomegranates on the two wreaths, two rows of pomegranates on each wreath, to cover the two pommels of the chapiters which were upon the pillars. He made also bases, and lavers made he upon the bases, one sea, and twelve oxen under it. The pots also, and the shovels, and the fleshhooks, and all their instruments, did Huram his father make to king Solomon for the house of the Lord, of bright brass. In the plain of Jordan did the king cast them, in the clay ground between Succoth and Zeredathah. Thus Solomon made all these vessels in great abundance, for the weight of the brass could not be found out. And Solomon made all the vessels that were for the house of God, the golden altar also, and the tables whereon the shewbread was set, moreover the candlesticks with their lamps, that they should burn after the manner before the oracle, of pure gold, and the flowers, and the lamps, and the tongs, made he of gold, and that perfect gold. And the snuffers, and the basins, and the spoons, and the censers, of pure gold, and the entry of the house, the inner doors thereof for the most holy place, and the doors of the house of the temple were of gold.

Thus all the work that Solomon made for the house of the Lord was finished, and Solomon brought in all the things that David his father had dedicated, and the silver, and the gold, and all the instruments, put he among the treasures of the house of God.

Then Solomon assembled the elders of Israel and all the heads of the tribes, the chief of the fathers of the children of Israel, unto Jerusalem, to bring up the ark of the covenant of the Lord out of the city of David which is Zion. Wherefore all the men of Israel assembled themselves unto the king in the feast which was in the seventh month. And all the elders of Israel came and the Levites took up the ark. And they brought up the ark, and the tabernacle of the congregation, and all the holy vessels that were in the tabernacle, these did the priests and the Levites bring up. Also king Solomon and all the congregation of Israel that were assembled unto him before the ark sacrificed sheep and oxen, which could not be told nor numbered for multitude. And the priests brought in the ark of the covenant of the Lord unto his place, to the oracle of the house, into the most holy place, even under the wings of the cherubim, for the cherubim spread forth their wings over the place of the ark and the cherubim covered the ark and the staves thereof above. And they drew out the staves of the ark, that the ends of the staves were seen from the ark before the oracle, but they were not seen without. And there it is unto this day. There was nothing in the ark save the two tables which Moses put therein at Horeb when the Lord made a covenant with the children of Israel when they came out of Egypt. And it came to pass when the priests were come out of the holy place (for all the priests that were present were sanctified and did not then wait by course, also the Levites which were the singers, all of them of Asaph, of Heman, of Jeduthun, with their sons and their brethren, being arrayed in white linen, having cymbals and psalteries and harps, stood at the east end of the altar, and with them a hundred and twenty priests sounding with trumpets), it came even to pass as the trumpeters and singers were as one to make one sound to be heard in praising and thanking the Lord and when they lifted up their voice with the trumpets and cymbals and instruments of music and praised the Lord saying, For he is good, for his mercy endureth forever, that then the house was filled with a cloud, even the house of the Lord, so that the priests could not stand to minister by reason of the cloud, for the glory of the Lord had filled the house of God.

Then said Solomon, The Lord hath said that he would dwell in the thick darkness. But I have built a house of habitation for thee and a place for thy dwelling forever. And the king turned his face and blessed the whole congregation of Israel and all the congregation of Israel stood. And he said, Blessed be the Lord God of Israel who hath with his hands fulfilled that which he spake with his mouth to my father David saying, Since the day that I brought forth my people out of the land of Egypt I chose no city among all the tribes of Israel to build a house in that my name might be there, neither chose I any man to be a ruler over my people Israel, but I have chosen Jerusalem that my name might be there and have chosen David to be over my people Israel. Now it was in the heart of David my father to build a house for the name of the Lord God of Israel. But the Lord said to David my father, Forasmuch as it was in thine heart to build a house for my name, thou didst well in that it was in thine heart, notwithstanding thou shalt not build the house, but thy son which shall come forth out of thy loins, he shall build the house for my name. The Lord therefore hath performed his word that he hath spoken, for I am risen up in the room of David my father, and am set on the throne of Israel as the Lord promised, and have built the house for the name of the Lord God of Israel. And in it have I put the ark wherein is the covenant of the Lord that he made with the children of Israel.

And he stood before the altar of the Lord in the presence of all the congregation of Israel and spread forth his hands, for Solomon had made a brazen scaffold of five cubits long, and five cubits broad, and three cubits high, and had set it in the midst of the court, and upon it he stood, and kneeled down upon his knees before all the congregation of Israel, and spread forth his hands toward Heaven and said, O Lord God of Israel, there is no God like thee in the Heaven nor in the Earth, which keepest covenant and showest mercy unto thy servants that walk before thee with all their hearts, thou which hast kept with thy servant David my father that which thou hast promised him, and spakest with thy mouth, and hast fulfilled it with thine hand as it is this day. Now therefore, O Lord God of Israel, keep with thy servant David my father that which thou hast promised him saying, There shall not fail thee a man in my sight to sit upon the throne of Israel, yet so that thy children take heed to their way to walk in my law as thou hast walked before me. Now then, O Lord God of Israel, let the word be verified which thou hast spoken unto thy servant David.

But will God in very deed dwell with men on the Earth? Behold, Heaven and the Heaven of Heavens cannot contain thee, how much less this house which I have built! Have respect therefore to the prayer of thy servant and to his supplication, O Lord my God, to hearken unto the cry and the prayer which thy servant prayeth before thee, that thine eyes may be open upon this house day and night, upon the place whereof thou hast said that thou wouldest put thy name there to hearken unto the prayer which thy servant prayeth toward this place. Hearken therefore unto the supplications of thy servant and of thy people Israel which they shall make toward this place, hear thou from thy dwelling place, even from Heaven, and when thou hearest, forgive.

If a man sin against his neighbor, and an oath be laid upon him to make him swear, and the oath come before thine altar in this house, then hear thou from Heaven and do and judge thy servants by requiting the wicked by recompensing his way upon his own head, and by justifying the righteous by giving him according to his righteousness.

And if thy people Israel be put to the worse before the enemy because they have sinned against thee, and shall return and confess thy name, and pray and make supplication before thee in this house, then hear thou from the heavens, and forgive the sin of thy people Israel, and bring them again unto the land which thou gavest to them and to their fathers.

When the Heaven is shut up and there is no rain because they have sinned against thee, yet if they pray toward this place, and confess thy name, and turn from their sin when thou dost afflict them, then hear thou from Heaven, and forgive the sin of thy servants, and of thy people Israel, when thou hast taught them the good way wherein they should walk, and send rain upon thy land which thou hast given unto thy people for an inheritance.

If there be dearth in the land, if there be pestilence, if there be blasting or mildew, locusts or caterpillars, if their enemies besiege them in the cities of their land, whatsoever sore or whatsoever sickness there be, then what prayer or what supplication soever shall be made of any man or of all thy people Israel, when everyone shall know his own sore and his own grief, and shall spread forth his hands in this house, then hear thou from Heaven thy dwelling place and forgive, and render unto every man according unto all his ways whose heart thou knowest (for thou only knowest the hearts of the children of men), that they may fear thee, to walk in thy ways so long as they live in the land which thou gavest unto our fathers.

Moreover concerning the stranger which is not of thy people Israel, but is come from a far country for thy great name's sake and thy mighty hand and thy stretched out arm, if they come and pray in this house, then hear thou from the heavens, even from thy dwelling place, and do according to all that the stranger calleth to thee for that all people of the Earth may know thy name and fear thee as doth thy people Israel, and may know that this house which I have built is called by thy name.

If thy people go out to war against their enemies by the way that thou shalt send them, and they pray unto thee toward this city which thou hast chosen and the house which I have built for thy name, then hear thou from the heavens their prayer and their supplication and maintain their cause. If they sin against thee (for there is no man which sinneth not), and thou be angry with them, and deliver them over before their enemies, and they carry them away captives unto a land far off or near, yet if they bethink themselves in the land whither they are carried captive, and turn and pray unto thee in the land of their captivity saying, We have sinned, we have done amiss, and have dealt wickedly, if they return to thee with all their heart and with all their soul in the land of their captivity whither they have carried them captives, and pray toward their land which thou gavest unto their fathers, and toward the city which thou hast chosen, and toward the house which I have built for thy name, then hear thou from the heavens, even from thy dwelling place, their prayer and their supplications, and maintain their cause, and forgive thy people which have sinned against thee.

Now, my God, let, I beseech thee, thine eyes be open, and let thine ears be attent unto the prayer that is made in this place. Now therefore arise, O Lord God, into thy resting place, thou and the ark of thy strength, let thy priests, O Lord God, be clothed with salvation, and let thy saints rejoice in goodness. O Lord God, turn not away the face of thine anointed, remember the mercies of David thy servant.

Now when Solomon had made an end of praying, the fire came down from Heaven and consumed the burnt offering and the sacrifices, and the glory of the Lord filled the house. And the priests could not enter into the house of the Lord because the glory of the Lord had filled the Lord's house. And when all the children of Israel saw how the fire came down and the glory of the Lord upon the house, they bowed themselves with their faces to the ground upon the pavement, and worshiped and praised the Lord saying, For he is good, for his mercy endureth forever.

Then the king and all the people offered sacrifices before the Lord. And king Solomon offered a sacrifice of twenty and two thousand oxen, and a hundred and twenty thousand sheep. So the king and all the people dedicated the house of God. And the priests waited on their offices, the Levites also with instruments of music of the Lord which David the king had made to praise the Lord because his mercy endureth for ever when David praised by their ministry, and the priests sounded trumpets before them, and all Israel stood. Moreover Solomon hallowed the middle of the court that was before the house of the Lord, for there he offered burnt offerings, and the fat of the peace offerings, because the brazen altar which Solomon had made was not able to receive the burnt offerings, and the meat offerings, and the fat. Also at the same time Solomon kept the feast seven days, and all Israel with him, a very great congregation, from the entering in of Hamath unto the river of Egypt. And in the eighth day they made a solemn assembly, for they kept the dedication of the altar seven days, and the feast seven days. And on the three and twentieth day of the seventh month he sent the people away into their tents, glad and merry in heart for the goodness that the Lord had showed unto David, and to Solomon, and to Israel his people.

Thus Solomon finished the house of the Lord and the king's house, and all that came into Solomon's heart to make in the house of the Lord and in his own house, he prosperously effected. And the Lord appeared to Solomon by night and said unto him, I have heard thy prayer and have chosen this place to myself for a house of sacrifice. If I shut up Heaven that there be no rain, or if I command the locusts to devour the land, or if I send pestilence among my people, if my people which are called by my name shall humble themselves, and pray and seek my face, and turn from their wicked ways, then will I hear from Heaven, and will forgive their sin, and will heal their land. Now mine eyes shall be open and mine ears attent unto the prayer that is made in this place. For now have I chosen and sanctified this house, that my name may be there forever, and mine eyes and mine heart shall be there perpetually. And as for thee, if thou wilt walk before me as David thy father walked, and do according to all that I have commanded thee, and shalt observe my statutes and my judgments, then will I establish the throne of thy kingdom according as I have covenanted with David thy father saying, There shall not fail thee a man to be ruler in Israel. But if ye turn away and forsake my statutes and my commandments which I have set before you, and shall go and serve other gods and worship them, then will I pluck them up by the roots out of my land which I have given them, and this house which I have sanctified for my name will I cast out of my sight and will make it to be a proverb and a byword among all nations. And this house which is high shall be an astonishment to every one that passeth by it, so that he shall say, Why hath the Lord done thus unto this land and unto this house? And it shall be answered, Because they forsook the Lord God of their fathers, which brought them forth out of the land of Egypt, and laid hold on other gods and worshiped them and served them, therefore hath he brought evil upon them

2 AND it came to pass at the end of twenty years, wherein Solomon had built the house of the Lord and his own house, that the cities which Huram had restored to Solomon, Solomon built them and caused the children of Israel to dwell there. And Solomon went to Hamath-zobah, and prevailed against it. And he built Tadmor in the wilderness and all the store cities which he built in Hamath. Also he built Beth-horon the upper, and Beth-horon the nether, fenced cities with walls, gates, and bars, and Baalath, and all the store cities that Solomon had, and all the chariot cities, and the cities of the horsemen, and all that Solomon desired to build in Jerusalem, and in Lebanon, and throughout all the land of his dominion. As for all the people that were left of the Hittites, and the Amorites, and the Perizzites, and the Hivites, and the Jebusites which were not of Israel, but of their children who were left after them in the land whom the children of Israel consumed not, them did Solomon make to pay tribute until this day. But of the children of Israel did Solomon make no servants for his work, but they were men of war, and chief of his captains, and captains of his chariots and horsemen. And these were the chief of king Solomon's officers, even two hundred and fifty, that bare rule over the people. And Solomon brought up the daughter of Pharaoh out of the city of David unto the house that he had built for her, for he said, My wife shall not dwell in the house of David king of Israel because the places are holy whereunto the ark of the Lord hath come.

Then Solomon offered burnt offerings unto the Lord on the altar of the Lord which he had built before the porch. Even after a certain rate every day offering according to the commandment of Moses on the sabbaths, and on the new moons, and on the solemn feasts, three times in the year, even in the feast of unleavened bread, and in the feast of weeks, and in the feast of tabernacles. And he appointed, according to the order of David his father, the courses of the priests to their service and the Levites to their charges, to praise and minister before the priests as the duty of every day required, the porters also by their courses at every gate, for so had David the man of God commanded. And they departed not from the commandment of the king unto the priests and Levites concerning any matter or concerning the treasures. Now all the work of Solomon was prepared unto the day of the foundation of the house of the Lord and until it was finished. So the house of the Lord was perfected.

Then went Solomon to Ezion-geber and to Eloth, at the seaside in the land of Edom. And Huram sent him by the hands of his servants, ships, and servants that had knowledge of the sea, and they went with the servants of Solomon to Ophir, and took thence four hundred and fifty talents of gold, and brought them to king Solomon.

And when the queen of Sheba heard of the fame of Solomon, she came to prove Solomon with hard questions at Jerusalem with a very great company, and camels that bare spices, and gold in abundance, and precious stones, and when she was come to Solomon she communed with him of all that was in her heart. And Solomon told her all her questions and there was nothing hid from Solomon which he told her not. And when the queen of Sheba had seen the wisdom of

Solomon, and the house that he had built, and the meat of his table, and the sitting of his servants, and the attendance of his ministers, and their apparel, his cupbearers also and their apparel, and his ascent by which he went up into the house of the Lord, there was no more spirit in her. And she said to the king, It was a true report which I heard in mine own land of thine acts and of thy wisdom, howbeit I believed not their words until I came and mine eyes had seen it and behold, the one-half of the greatness of thy wisdom was not told me, for thou exceedest the fame that I heard. Happy are thy men and happy are these thy servants which stand continually before thee and hear thy wisdom. Blessed be the Lord thy God, which delighted in thee to set thee on his throne, to be king for the Lord thy God because thy God loved Israel, to establish them forever, therefore made he thee king over them, to do judgment and justice. And she gave the king a hundred and twenty talents of gold, and of spices great abundance, and precious stones, neither was there any such spice as the queen of Sheba gave king Solomon. And the servants also of Huram, and the servants of Solomon, which brought gold from Ophir, brought algum trees and precious stones. And the king made of the algum trees terraces to the house of the Lord and to the king's palace, and harps and psalteries for singers, and there were none such seen before in the land of Judah. And king Solomon gave to the queen of Sheba all her desire, whatsoever she asked, besides that which she had brought unto the king. So she turned, and went away to her own land, she and her servants.

Now the weight of gold that came to Solomon in one year was six hundred and threescore and six talents of gold, besides that which chapmen and merchants brought. And all the kings of Arabia and governors of the country brought gold and silver to Solomon. And king Solomon made two hundred targets of beaten gold, six hundred shekels of beaten gold went to one target. And three hundred shields made he of beaten gold, three hundred shekels of gold went to one shield. And the king put them in the house of the forest of Lebanon. Moreover the king made a great throne of ivory, and overlaid it with pure gold. And there were six steps to the throne, with a footstool of gold, which were fastened to the throne, and stays on each side of the sitting place, and two lions standing by the stays, and twelve lions stood there on the one side and on the other upon the six steps. There was not the like made in any kingdom. And all the drinking vessels of king Solomon were of gold, and all the vessels of the house of the forest of Lebanon were of pure gold, none were of silver, it was not anything accounted of in the days of Solomon. For the king's ships went to Tarshish with the servants of Huram, every three years once came the ships of Tarshish bringing gold, and silver, ivory, and apes, and peacocks. And king Solomon passed all the kings of the Earth in riches and wisdom. And all the kings of the Earth sought the presence of Solomon, to hear his wisdom that God had put in his heart. And they brought every man his present: vessels of silver, and vessels of gold, and raiment, harness, and spices, horses, and mules, a rate year by year. And Solomon had four thousand stalls for houses and chariots, and twelve thousand horsemen, whom he bestowed in the chariot cities, and with the king at Jerusalem. And he reigned over all the kings from the river even unto the land of the Philistines and to the border of Egypt. And the king made silver in Jerusalem as stones, and cedar trees made he as the sycamore trees that are in the low plains in abundance. And they brought unto Solomon horses out of Egypt and out of all lands.

Now the rest of the acts of Solomon, first and last, are they not written in the book of Nathan the prophet, and in the prophecy of Ahijah the Shilonite, and in the visions of Iddo the seer against Jeroboam the son of Nebat? And Solomon reigned in Jerusalem over all Israel forty years. And Solomon slept with his fathers, and he was buried in the city of David his father, and Rehoboam his son reigned in his stead.

3 AND Rehoboam went to Shechem, for to Shechem were all Israel come to make him king. And it came to pass when Jeroboam the son of Nebat, who was in Egypt whither he had fled from the presence of Solomon the king, heard it, that Jeroboam returned out of Egypt. And they sent and called him. So Jeroboam and all Israel came and spake to Rehoboam, saying, Thy father made our yoke grievous, now therefore ease thou somewhat the grievous servitude of thy father, and his heavy yoke that he put upon us, and we will serve thee. And he said unto them, Come again unto me after three days. And the people departed.

And king Rehoboam took counsel with the old men that had stood before Solomon his father while he yet lived saying, What counsel give ye me to return answer to this people? And they spake unto him saying, If thou be kind to this people, and please them, and speak good words to them, they will be thy servants forever. But he forsook the counsel which the old men gave him, and took counsel with the young men that were brought up with him, that stood before him. And he said unto them, What advice give ye that we may return answer to this people, which have spoken to me, saying, Ease somewhat the yoke that thy father did put upon us? And the young men that were brought up with him spake unto him, saying, Thus shalt thou answer the people that spake unto thee, saying, Thy father made our yoke heavy, but make thou it somewhat lighter for us, thus shalt thou say unto them, My little finger shall be thicker than my father's loins. For whereas my father put a heavy yoke upon you, I will put more to your yoke, my father chastised you with whips, but I will chastise you with scorpions.

So Jeroboam and all the people came to Rehoboam on the third day, as the king bade saying, Come again to me on the third day. And the king answered them roughly, and king Rehoboam forsook the counsel of the old men, and answered them after the advice of the young men saying, My father made your yoke heavy, but I will add thereto, my father chastised you with whips, but I will chastise you with scorpions. So the king hearkened not unto the people, for the cause was of God, that the Lord might perform his word which he spake by the hand of Ahijah the Shilonite to Jeroboam the son of Nebat.

And when all Israel saw that the king would not hearken unto them, the people answered the king, saying, What portion have we in David? And we have none inheritance in the son of Jesse; every man to your tents, O Israel, and now David, see to thine own house. So all Israel went to their tents.

But as for the children of Israel that dwelt in the cities of Judah, Rehoboam reigned over them. Then king Rehoboam sent Hadoram that was over the tribute, and the children of Israel stoned him with stones that he died. But king Rehoboam made speed to get him up to his chariot to flee to Jerusalem. And Israel rebelled against the house of David unto this day.

And when Rehoboam was come to Jerusalem, he gathered of the house of Judah and Benjamin a hundred and fourscore thousand chosen men which were warriors to fight against Israel, that he might bring the kingdom again to Rehoboam. But the word of the Lord came to Shemaiah the man of God saying, Speak unto Rehoboam the son of Solomon king of Judah and to all Israel in Judah and Benjamin saying, Thus saith the Lord, Ye shall not go up, nor fight against your brethren, return every man to his house, for this thing is done of me. And they obeyed the words of the Lord and returned from going against Jeroboam.

And Rehoboam dwelt in Jerusalem and built cities for defense in Judah. He built even Bethlehem, and Etam, and Tekoa, and Beth-zur, and Shoco, and Adullam, and Gath, and Mareshah, and Ziph, and Adoraim, and Lachish, and Azekah, and Zorah, and Ajaion, and Hebron which are in Judah and in Benjamin fenced cities. And he fortified the strongholds and put captains in them, and store of victuals, and of oil and wine. And in every several city he put shields and spears and made them exceeding strong having Judah and Benjamin on his side. And the priests and the Levites that were in all Israel resorted to him out of all their coasts. For the Levites left their suburbs and their possession and came to Judah and Jerusalem, for Jeroboam and his sons had cast them off from executing the priest's office unto the Lord. And he ordained him priests for the high places, and for the devils, and for the calves which he had made. And after them out of all the tribes of Israel, such as set their hearts to seek the Lord God of Israel came to Jerusalem to sacrifice unto the Lord God of their fathers. So they strengthened the kingdom of Judah and made Rehoboam the son of Solomon strong three years, for three years they walked in the way of David and Solomon.

And Rehoboam took him Mahalath the daughter of Jerimoth the son of David to wife, and Abihail the daughter of Eliab the son of Jesse, which bare him children: Jeush, and Shamariah, and Zaham. And after her he took Maachah the daughter of Absalom which bare him Abijah, and Attai, and Ziza, and Shelomith. And Rehoboam loved Maachah the daughter of Absalom above all his wives and his concubines (for he took eighteen wives, and threescore concubines, and begat twenty and eight sons, and threescore daughters). And Rehoboam made Abijah the son of Maachah the chief to be ruler among his brethren, for he thought to make him king. And he dealt wisely and dispersed of all his children throughout all the countries of Judah and Benjamin, unto every fenced city, and he gave them victuals in abundance. And he desired many wives.

And it came to pass when Rehoboam had established the kingdom and had strengthened himself, he forsook the law of the Lord and all Israel with him. And it came to pass that in the fifth year of king Rehoboam, Shishak king of Egypt came up against Jerusalem because they had transgressed against the Lord. With twelve hundred chariots, and threescore thousand horsemen, and the people were without number that came with him out of Egypt, the Lubim, the Sukkim, and the Ethiopians. And he took the fenced cities which pertained to Judah and came to Jerusalem. Then came Shemaiah the prophet to Rehoboam and to the princes of Judah that were gathered together to Jerusalem because of Shishak and said unto them, Thus saith the Lord, Ye have forsaken me and therefore have I also left you in the hand of Shishak. Whereupon the princes of Israel and the king humbled themselves and they said, The Lord is righteous. And when the Lord saw that they humbled themselves the word of the Lord came to Shemaiah saying, They have humbled themselves, therefore I will not destroy them, but I will grant them some deliverance and my wrath shall not be poured out upon Jerusalem by the hand of Shishak. Nevertheless they shall be his servants that they may know my service and the service of the kingdoms of the countries. So Shishak king of Egypt came up against Jerusalem and took away the treasures of the house of the Lord and the treasures of the king's house, he took all. He carried away also the shields of gold which Solomon had made. Instead of which king Rehoboam made shields of brass and committed them to the hands of the chief of the guard that kept the entrance of the king's house. And when the king entered into the house of the Lord, the guard came and fetched them and brought them again into the guard chamber. And when he humbled himself the wrath of the Lord turned from him that he would not destroy him altogether and also in Judah things went well.

So king Rehoboam strengthened himself in Jerusalem and reigned, for Rehoboam was one and forty years old when he began to reign, and he reigned seventeen years in Jerusalem, the city which the Lord had chosen out of all the tribes of Israel to put his name there. And his mother's name was Naamah an

Ammonitess. And he did evil because he prepared not his heart to seek the Lord. Now the acts of Rehoboam, first and last, are they not written in the book of Shemaiah the prophet, and of Iddo the seer concerning genealogies? And there were wars between Rehoboam and Jeroboam continually. And Rehoboam slept with his fathers and was buried in the city of David and Abijah his son reigned in his stead.

4 NOW in the eighteenth year of king Jeroboam began Abijah to reign over Judah. He reigned three years in Jerusalem. His mother's name also was Michaiah the daughter of Uriel of Gibeah. And there was war between Abijah and Jeroboam. And Abijah set the battle in array with an army of valiant men of war, even four hundred thousand chosen men, Jeroboam also set the battle in array against him with eight hundred thousand men being mighty men of valor.

And Abijah stood up upon mount Zemaraim which is in Mount Ephraim and said, Hear me, thou Jeroboam and all Israel, ought ye not to know that the Lord God of Israel gave the kingdom over Israel to David forever, even to him and to his sons by a covenant of salt? Yet Jeroboam the son of Nebat the servant of Solomon the son of David is risen up and hath rebelled against his lord. And there are gathered unto him vain men the children of Belial, and have strengthened themselves against Rehoboam the son of Solomon when Rehoboam was young and tenderhearted and could not withstand them. And now ye think to withstand the kingdom of the Lord in the hand of the sons of David, and ye be a multitude, and there are with you golden calves which Jeroboam made you for gods. Have ye not cast out the priests of the Lord, the sons of Aaron and the Levites, and have made you priests after the manner of the nations of other lands? So that whosoever cometh to consecrate himself with a young bullock and seven rams the same may be a priest of them that are no gods. But as for us, the Lord is our God and we have not forsaken him and the priests which minister unto the Lord are the sons of Aaron, and the Levites wait upon their business and they burn unto the Lord every morning and every evening burnt sacrifices and sweet incense, the shewbread also set they in order upon the pure table and the candlestick of gold with the lamps thereof to burn every evening, for we keep the charge of the Lord our God, but ye have forsaken him. And behold, God himself is with us for our captain, and his priests with sounding trumpets to cry alarm against you. O children of Israel, fight ye not against the Lord God of your fathers, for ye shall not prosper.

But Jeroboam caused an ambushment to come about behind them, so they were before Judah and the ambushment was behind them. And when Judah looked back, behold, the battle was before and behind and they cried unto the Lord and the priests sounded with the trumpets. Then the men of Judah gave a shout, and as the men of Judah shouted it came to pass that God smote Jeroboam and all Israel before Abijah and Judah. And the children of Israel fled before Judah and God delivered them into their hand. And Abijah and his people slew them with a great slaughter so there fell down slain of Israel five hundred thousand chosen men. Thus the children of Israel were brought under at that time and the children of Judah prevailed because they relied upon the Lord God of their fathers. And Abijah pursued after Jeroboam and took cities from him, Beth-el with the towns thereof, and Jeshanah with the towns thereof, and Ephraim with the towns thereof. Neither did Jeroboam recover strength again in the days of Abijah, and the Lord struck him and he died. But Abijah waxed mighty, and married fourteen wives, and begat twenty and two sons, and sixteen daughters. And the rest of the acts of Abijah, and his ways, and his sayings are written in the story of the prophet Iddo.

So Abijah slept with his fathers, and they buried him in the city of David, and Asa his son reigned in his stead. In his days the land was quiet ten years.

And Asa did that which was good and right in the eyes of the Lord his God, for he took away the altars of the strange gods and the high places, and brake down the images, and cut down the groves, and commanded Judah to seek the Lord God of their fathers and to do the law and the commandment. Also he took away out of all the cities of Judah the high places and the images and the kingdom was quiet before him. And he built fenced cities in Judah, for the land had rest and he had no war in those years because the Lord had given him rest. Therefore he said unto Judah, Let us build these cities and make about them walls and towers, gates and bars, while the land is yet before us because we have sought the Lord our God, we have sought him and he hath given us rest on every side. So they built and prospered. And Asa had an army of men that bare targets and spears out of Judah three hundred thousand, and out of Benjamin that bare shields and drew bows two hundred and fourscore thousand, all these were mighty men of valor.

And there came out against them Zerah the Ethiopian with a host of a thousand thousand, and three hundred chariots, and came unto Mareshah. Then Asa went out against him and they set the battle in array in the valley of Zephathah at Mareshah. And Asa cried unto the Lord his God and said, Lord, it is nothing with thee to help, whether with many or with them that have no power; help us, O Lord our God, for we rest on thee and in thy name we go against this multitude. O Lord, thou art our God, let not man prevail against thee. So the Lord smote the Ethiopians before Asa and before Judah and the Ethiopians fled. And Asa and the people that were with him pursued them unto Gerar and the Ethiopians were overthrown that they could not recover themselves, for they were destroyed before the Lord and before his host and they carried away very much spoil. And they smote all the cities round about Gerar, for the fear of the Lord came upon them and they spoiled all the cities, for there was exceeding much spoil in them. They smote also the tents of cattle and carried away sheep and camels in abundance and returned to Jerusalem.

And the Spirit of God came upon Azariah the son of Oded and he went out to meet Asa and said unto him, Hear ye me, Asa and all Judah and Benjamin, The Lord is with you while ye be with him, and if ye seek him, he will be found of you, but if ye forsake him, he will forsake you. Now for a long season Israel hath been without the true God, and without a teaching priest, and without law. But when they in their trouble did turn unto the Lord God of Israel and sought him, he was found of them. And in those times there was no peace to him that went out nor to him that came in, but great vexations were upon all the inhabitants of the countries. And nation was destroyed of nation and city of city, for God did vex them with all adversity. Be ye strong therefore and let not your hands be weak, for your work shall be rewarded.

And when Asa heard these words and the prophecy of Oded the prophet, he took courage and put away the abominable idols out of all the land of Judah and Benjamin and out of the cities which he had taken from mount Ephraim, and renewed the altar of the Lord that was before

the porch of the Lord. And he gathered all Judah and Benjamin and the strangers with them out of Ephraim and Manasseh and out of Simeon, for they fell to him out of Israel in abundance when they saw that the Lord his God was with him. So they gathered themselves together at Jerusalem in the third month, in the fifteenth year of the reign of Asa. And they offered unto the Lord the same time of the spoil which they had brought seven hundred oxen and seven thousand sheep. And they entered into a covenant to seek the Lord God of their fathers with all their heart and with all their soul, that whosoever would not seek the Lord God of Israel should be put to death, whether small or great, whether man or woman. And they sware unto the Lord with a loud voice, and with shouting, and with trumpets, and with cornets. And all Judah rejoiced at the oath, for they had sworn with all their heart, and sought him with their whole desire, and he was found of them, and the Lord gave them rest round about.

And also concerning Maachah the mother of Asa the king, he removed her from being queen because she had made an idol in a grove, and Asa cut down her idol, and stamped it, and burnt it at the brook Kidron. But the high places were not taken away out of Israel, nevertheless the heart of Asa was perfect all his days. And he brought into the house of God the things that his father had dedicated and that he himself had dedicated: silver, and gold, and vessels. And there was no more war unto the five and thirtieth year of the reign of Asa.

In the six and thirtieth year of the reign of Asa, Baasha king of Israel came up against Judah, and built Ramah, to the intent that he might let none go out or come into Asa king of Judah. Then Asa brought out silver and gold out of the treasures of the house of the Lord and of the king's house and sent to Ben-hadad king of Syria that dwelt in Damascus saying, There is a league between me and thee as there was between my father and thy father, behold, I have sent thee silver and gold, go, break thy league with Baasha king of Israel that he may depart from me. And Ben-hadad hearkened unto king Asa and sent the captains of his armies against the cities of Israel, and they smote Ijon, and Dan, and Abel-maim, and all the store cities of Naphtali. And it came to pass when Baasha heard it that he left off building of Ramah and let his work cease. Then Asa the king took all Judah and they carried away the stones of Ramah and the timber thereof wherewith Baasha was building, and he built therewith Geba and Mizpah.

And at that time Hanani the seer came to Asa king of Judah, and said unto him, Because thou hast relied on the king of Syria and not relied on the Lord thy God, therefore is the host of the king of Syria escaped out of thine hand. Were not the Ethiopians and the Lubim a huge host with very many chariots and horsemen? Yet, because thou didst rely on the Lord, he delivered them into thine hand. For the eyes of the Lord run to and fro throughout the whole Earth to show himself strong in the behalf of them whose heart is perfect toward him. Herein thou hast done foolishly, therefore from henceforth thou shalt have wars. Then Asa was wroth with the seer and put him in a prison house, for he was in a rage with him because of this thing. And Asa oppressed some of the people the same time.

And, behold, the acts of Asa first and last, lo, they are written in the book of the kings of Judah and Israel. And Asa in the thirty and ninth year of his reign was diseased in his feet until his disease was exceeding great, yet in his disease he sought not to the Lord, but to the physicians. And Asa slept with his fathers, and died in the one and fortieth year of his reign. And they buried him in his own sepulchers which he had made for himself in the city of David, and laid him in the bed which was filled with sweet odors and divers kinds of spices prepared by the apothecaries' art and they made a very great burning for him

5 AND Jehoshaphat his son reigned in his stead, and strengthened himself against Israel. And he placed forces in all the fenced cities of Judah, and set garrisons in the land of Judah, and in the cities of Ephraim which Asa his father had taken.

And the Lord was with Jehoshaphat, because he walked in the first ways of his father David and sought not unto Baalim, but sought to the Lord God of his father and walked in his commandments and not after the doings of Israel. Therefore the Lord established the kingdom in his hand and all Judah brought to Jehoshaphat presents and he had riches and honor in abundance. And his heart was lifted up in the ways of the Lord, moreover he took away the high places and groves out of Judah.

Also in the third year of his reign he sent to his princes, even to Ben-hail, and to Obadiah, and to Zechariah, and to Nethaneel, and to Michaiah to teach in the cities of Judah. And with them he sent Levites, even Shemaiah, and Nethaniah, and Zebadiah, and Asahel, and Shemiramoth, and Jehonathan, and Adonijah, and Tobijah, and Tobadonijah, Levites, and with them Elishama and Jehoram, priests. And they taught in Judah and had the book of the law of the Lord with them, and went about throughout all the cities of Judah and taught the people.

And the fear of the Lord fell upon all the kingdoms of the lands that were round about Judah so that they made no war against Jehoshaphat. Also some of the Philistines brought Jehoshaphat presents and tribute silver, and the Arabians brought him flocks, seven thousand and seven hundred rams, and seven thousand and seven hundred he goats. And Jehoshaphat waxed great exceedingly and he built in Judah castles and cities of store. And he had much business in the cities of Judah, and the men of war, mighty men of valor, were in Jerusalem. And these are the numbers of them according to the house of their fathers: Of Judah, the captains of thousands, Adnah the chief, and with him mighty men of valor three hundred thousand. And next to him was Jehohanan the captain, and with him two hundred and fourscore thousand. And next to him was Amasiah the son of Zichri, who willingly offered himself unto the Lord, and with him two hundred thousand mighty men of valor. And of Benjamin, Eliada a mighty man of valor, and with him armed men with bow and shield two hundred thousand. And next to him was Jehozabad, and with him a hundred and fourscore thousand ready prepared for the war. These waited on the king besides those whom the king put in the fenced cities throughout all Judah

Now Jehoshaphat had riches and honor in abundance and joined affinity with Ahab. And after certain years he went down to Ahab to Samaria. And Ahab killed sheep and oxen for him in abundance and for the people that he had with him and persuaded him to go up with him to Ramoth-gilead. And Ahab king of Israel said unto Jehoshaphat king of Judah, Wilt thou go with me to Ramoth-gilead? And he answered him, I am as thou art and my people as thy people and we will be with thee in the war.

And Jehoshaphat said unto the king of Israel, Inquire, I pray thee, at the word of the Lord today. Therefore the king of Israel gathered together of prophets four hundred men and said unto them, Shall we go to Ramoth-gilead to battle or shall I forbear? And they said, Go up, for God will deliver it into the king's hand. But Jehoshaphat said, Is their not here a prophet of the Lord besides, that we might inquire of him? And the king of Israel said unto Jehoshaphat, There is yet one man by whom we may inquire of the Lord, but I hate him, for he never prophesied good unto me, but always evil, the same is Micaiah the son of Imla. And Jehoshaphat said, Let not the king say so.

And the king of Israel called for one of his officers and said, Fetch quickly Micaiah the son of Imla. And the king of Israel and Jehoshaphat king of Judah sat either of them on his throne, clothed in their robes, and they sat in a void place at the entering in of the gate of Samaria and all the prophets prophesied before them. And Zedekiah the son of Chenaanah had made him horns of iron and said, Thus saith the Lord, With these thou shalt push Syria until they be consumed. And all the prophets prophesied so saying, Go up to Ramoth-gilead and prosper, for the Lord shall deliver it into the hand of the king.

And the messenger that went to call Micaiah spake to him, saying, Behold, the words of the prophets declare good to the king with one assent, let thy word therefore, I pray thee, be like one of theirs and speak thou good. And Micaiah said, As the Lord liveth, even what my God saith, that will I speak.

And when he was come to the king, the king said unto him, Micaiah, shall we go to Ramoth-gilead to battle or shall I forbear? And he said, Go ye up and prosper, and they shall be delivered into your hand. And the king said to him,

How many times shall I adjure thee that thou say nothing but the truth to me in the name of the Lord?

Then he said, I did see all Israel scattered upon the mountains as sheep that have no shepherd and the Lord said, These have no master, let them return therefore every man to his house in peace.

And the king of Israel said to Jehoshaphat, Did I not tell thee that he would not prophesy good unto me, but evil? Again he said, Therefore hear the word of the Lord, I saw the Lord sitting upon his throne and all the host of Heaven standing on his right hand and on his left. And the Lord said, Who shall entice Ahab king of Israel that he may go up and fall at Ramoth-gilead? And one spake saying after this manner, and another saying after that manner. Then there came out of them a lying spirit and stood before the Lord and said, I will entice him. And the Lord said unto him, Wherewith? And he said, I will go out and be a lying spirit in the mouth of all his prophets. And the Lord said, Thou shalt entice him and thou shalt also prevail, go out and do even so, for all these have sinned against me. Now therefore, behold, the Lord hath found a lying spirit in the mouth of these thy prophets and the Lord hath spoken evil against thee.

Then Zedekiah the son of Chenaanah came near and smote Micaiah upon the cheek and said, Which way went the Spirit of the Lord from me to speak unto thee? And Micaiah said, Behold, thou shalt see on that day when thou shalt go into an inner chamber to hide thyself. Then the king of Israel said, Take ye Micaiah and carry him back to Amon the governor of the city and to Joash the king's son and say, Thus saith the king, Put this fellow in the prison and feed him with bread of affliction and with water of affliction until I return in peace. And Micaiah said, If thou certainly return in peace, then hath not the Lord spoken by me. And he said, Hearken, all ye people.

So the king of Israel and Jehoshaphat the king of Judah went up to Ramoth-gilead. And the king of Israel said unto Jehoshaphat, I will disguise myself and will go to the battle, but put thou on thy robes. So the king of Israel disguised himself and they went to the battle. Now the king of Syria had commanded the captains of the chariots that were with him saying, Fight ye not with small or great, save only with the king of Israel. And it came to pass when the captains of the chariots saw Jehoshaphat that they said, It is the king of Israel. Therefore they compassed about him to fight, but Jehoshaphat cried out and the Lord helped him and God moved them to depart from him. For it came to pass that when the captains of the chariots perceived that it was not the king of Israel they turned back again from pursuing him. And a certain man drew a bow at a venture and smote the king of Israel between the joints of the harness, therefore he said to his chariot man, Turn thine hand that thou mayest carry me out of the host for I am wounded. And the battle increased that day, howbeit the king of Israel stayed himself up in his chariot against the Syrians until the even, and about the time of the sun going down he died.

And Jehoshaphat the king of Judah returned to his house in peace to Jerusalem. And Jehu the son of Hanani the seer went out to meet him and said to king Jehoshaphat, Shouldest thou help the ungodly and love them that hate the Lord? Therefore is wrath upon thee from before the Lord. Nevertheless, there are good things found in thee, in that thou hast taken away the groves out of the land and hast prepared thine heart to seek God.

And Jehoshaphat dwelt at Jerusalem, and he went out again through the people from Beer-sheba to mount Ephraim and brought them back unto the Lord God of their fathers. And he set judges in the land throughout all the fenced cities of Judah, city by city, and said to the judges, Take heed what ye do, for ye judge not for man, but for the Lord who is with you in the judgment. Wherefore now let the fear of the Lord be upon you, take heed and do it, for there is no iniquity with the Lord our God, nor respect of persons, nor taking of gifts. Moreover in Jerusalem did Jehoshaphat set of the Levites, and of the priests, and of the chief of the fathers of Israel, for the judgment of the Lord, and for controversies, when they returned to Jerusalem. And he charged them, saying, Thus shall ye do in the fear of the Lord, faithfully and with a perfect heart. And what cause soever shall come to you of your brethren that dwell in their cities, between blood and blood, between law and commandment, statutes and judgments, ye shall even warn them that they trespass not against the Lord, and so wrath come upon you and upon your brethren, this do and ye shall not trespass. And, behold, Amariah the chief priest is over you in all matters of the Lord, and Zebadiah the son of Ishmael, the ruler of the house of Judah, for all the king's matters, also the Levites shall be officers before you. Deal courageously and the Lord shall be with the good.

It came to pass after this also that the children of Moab, and the children of Ammon, and with them other besides the Ammonites, came against Jehoshaphat to battle. Then there came some that told Jehoshaphat saying, There cometh a great multitude against thee from beyond the sea on this side Syria and behold, they are in Hazazon-tamar, which was called En-gedi. And Jehoshaphat feared and set himself to seek the Lord and proclaimed a fast throughout all Judah. And Judah gathered themselves together to ask help of the Lord, even out of all the cities of Judah they came to seek the Lord.

And Jehoshaphat stood in the congregation of Judah and Jerusalem in the house of the Lord before the new court and said, O Lord God of our fathers, thou God who art in Heaven and rulest over all the kingdoms of the heathen, and in thy hand thou hast power and might so that none is able to withstand thee, thou our God didst drive out the inhabitants of this land before thy people Israel, and gavest it to the seed of Abraham thy friend forever. And they dwelt therein and have built thee a sanctuary therein for thy name saying, If, when evil cometh upon us, as the sword, judgment, or pestilence, or famine, we stand before this house and in thy presence (for thy name is in this house) and cry unto thee in our affliction, then thou wilt hear and help. And now, behold, the children of Ammon, and Moab, and mount Seir, whom thou wouldest not let Israel invade when they came out of the land of Egypt, but they turned from them and destroyed them not, behold, they reward us not, but have come to cast us out of thy possession which thou hast given us to inherit. O our God, wilt thou not judge them? For we have no might against this great company that cometh against us, neither know we what to do, but our eyes are upon thee.

And all Judah stood before the Lord, with their little ones, their wives, and their children.

Then upon Jahaziel the son of Zechariah, the son of Benaiah, the son of Jeiel, the son of Mattaniah, a Levite of the sons of Asaph, came the Spirit of the Lord in the midst of the congregation and he said, Hearken ye, all Judah, and ye inhabitants of Jerusalem, and thou king Jehoshaphat, Thus saith the Lord unto you, Be not afraid nor dismayed by reason of this great multitude, for the battle is not yours, but God's. Tomorrow go ye down against them, behold, they come up by the cliff of Ziz, and ye shall find them at the end of the brook before the wilderness of Jeruel. Ye shall not go to fight in this day, set yourselves, stand ye still, and see the salvation of the Lord with you, O Judah and Jerusalem, fear not, nor be dismayed, tomorrow go out against them for the Lord will be with you.

And Jehoshaphat bowed his head with his face to the ground, and all Judah and the inhabitants of Jerusalem fell before the Lord worshiping the Lord. And the Levites, of the children of the Kohathites, and of the children of the Korhites, stood up to praise the Lord God of Israel with a loud voice on high.

And they rose early in the morning and went forth into the wilderness of Tekoa, and as they went forth Jehoshaphat stood and said, Hear me, O Judah, and ye inhabitants of Jerusalem, Believe in the Lord your God, so shall ye be established, believe his prophets, so shall ye prosper. And when he had consulted with the people he appointed singers unto the Lord and that should praise the beauty of holiness, as they went out before the army and to say, Praise the Lord, for his mercy endureth forever. And when they began to sing and to praise, the Lord set ambushments against the children of Ammon, Moab, and mount Seir, which were come against Judah and they were smitten. For the children of Ammon and Moab stood up against the inhabitants of mount Seir, utterly to slay and destroy them, and when they had made an end of the inhabitants of Seir, everyone helped to destroy another.

And when Judah came toward the watchtower in the wilderness, they looked unto the multitude and behold, they were dead bodies fallen to the Earth and none escaped. And when Jehoshaphat and his people came to take away the spoil of them, they found among them in abundance both riches with the dead bodies and precious jewels, which they stripped off for themselves, more than they could carry away, and they were three days in gathering of the spoil it was so much.

And on the fourth day they assembled themselves in the valley of Berachah, for there they blessed the Lord, therefore the name of the same place was called, The valley of Berachah, unto this day. Then they returned, every man of Judah and Jerusalem and Jehoshaphat in the forefront of them, to go again to Jerusalem with joy, for the Lord had made them to rejoice over their enemies. And they came to Jerusalem with psalteries and harps and trumpets unto the house of the Lord. And the fear of God was on all the kingdoms of those countries when they had heard that the Lord had fought against the enemies of Israel. So the realm of Jehoshaphat was quiet, for his God gave him rest round about.

And Jehoshaphat reigned over Judah, he was thirty and five years old when he began to reign, and he reigned twenty and five years in Jerusalem. And his mother's name was Azubah, the daughter of Shilhi. And he walked in the way of Asa his father and departed not from it, doing that which was right in the sight of the Lord. Howbeit the high places were not taken away, for as yet the people had not prepared their hearts unto the God of their fathers.

Now the rest of the acts of Jehoshaphat, first and last, behold, they are written in the book of Jehu the son of Hanani, who is mentioned in the book of the kings of Israel.

6 AND after this did Jehoshaphat king of Judah join himself with Ahaziah king of Israel who did very wickedly, and he joined himself with him to make ships to go to Tarshish and they made the ships in Ezion-geber. Then Eliezer the son of Dodavah of Mareshah prophesied against Jehoshaphat saying, Because thou hast joined thyself with Ahaziah, the Lord hath broken thy works. And the ships were broken that they were not able to go to Tarshish.

Now Jehoshaphat slept with his fathers, and was buried with his fathers in the city of David. And Jehoram his son reigned in his stead. And he had brethren the sons of Jehoshaphat: Azariah, and Jehiel, and Zechariah, and Azariah, and Michael, and Shephatiah, all these were the sons of Jehoshaphat king of Israel. And their father gave them great gifts of silver, and of gold, and of precious things, with fenced cities in Judah, but the kingdom gave he to Jehoram because he was the firstborn. Now when Jehoram was risen up to the kingdom of his father, he strengthened himself and slew all his brethren with the sword and divers also of the princes of Israel.

Jehoram was thirty and two years old when he began to reign and he reigned eight years in Jerusalem. And he walked in the way of the kings of Israel like as did the house of Ahab, for he had the daughter of Ahab to wife, and he wrought that which was evil in the eyes of the Lord. Howbeit the Lord would not destroy the house of David because of the covenant that he had made with David and as he promised to give a light to him and to his sons forever. In his days the Edomites revolted from under the dominion of Judah and made themselves a king. Then Jehoram went forth with his princes and all his chariots with him and he rose up by night and smote the Edomites which compassed him in and the captains of the chariots. So the Edomites revolted from under the hand of Judah unto this day. The same time also did Libnah revolt from under his hand because he had forsaken the Lord God of his fathers. Moreover he made high places in the mountains of Judah and caused the inhabitants of Jerusalem to commit fornication and compelled Judah thereto.

And there came a writing to him from Elijah the prophet, saying, Thus saith the Lord God of David thy father, Because thou hast not walked in the ways of Jehoshaphat thy father nor in the ways of Asa king of Judah, but hast walked in the way of the kings of Israel, and hast made Judah and the inhabitants of Jerusalem to go a whoring like to the whoredoms of the house of Ahab, and also hast slain thy brethren of thy father's house which were better than thyself, behold, with a great plague will the Lord smite thy people, and thy children, and thy wives, and all thy goods. And thou shalt have great sickness by disease of thy bowels, until thy bowels fall out by reason of the sickness day by day.

Moreover the Lord stirred up against Jehoram the spirit of the Philistines, and of the Arabians that were near the Ethiopians, and they came up into Judah and brake into it and carried away all the substance that was found in the king's house, and his sons also and his wives, so that there was never a son left him, save Jehoahaz, the youngest of his sons.

And after all this the Lord smote him in his bowels with an incurable disease. And it came to pass that in process of time, after the end of two years his bowels fell out by reason of his sickness, so he died of sore diseases. And his people made no burning for him like the burning of his fathers. Thirty and two years old was he when he began to reign and he reigned in Jerusalem eight years and departed without being desired. Howbeit they buried him in the city of David, but not in the sepulchers of the kings.

And the inhabitants of Jerusalem made Ahaziah his youngest son king in his stead, for the band of men that came with the Arabians to the camp had slain all the eldest. So Ahaziah the son of Jehoram king of Judah reigned. Two and twenty years old was Ahaziah when he began to reign and he reigned one year in Jerusalem. His mother's name also was Athaliah the daughter of Omri. He also walked in the ways of the house of Ahab, for his mother was his counselor to do wickedly. Wherefore he did evil in the sight of the Lord like the house of Ahab, for they were his counselors after the death of his father to his destruction.

He walked also after their counsel and went with Jehoram the son Ahab king of Israel to war against Hazael king of Syria at Ramoth-gilead, and the Syrians smote Joram. And he returned to be healed in Jezreel because of the wounds which were given him at Ramah when he fought with Hazael king of Syria. And Azariah the son of Jehoram king of Judah went down to see Jehoram the son of Ahab at Jezreel because he was sick.

And the destruction of Ahaziah was of God by coming to Joram, for when he was come, he went out with Jehoram against Jehu the son of Nimshi, whom the Lord had anointed to cut off the house of Ahab.

And it came to pass that, when Jehu was executing judgment upon the house of Ahab, and found the princes of Judah, and the sons of the brethren of Ahaziah that ministered to Ahaziah, he slew them. And he sought Ahaziah, and they caught him (for he was hid in Samaria) and brought him to Jehu, and when they had slain him they buried him, Because, said they, he is the son of Jehoshaphat who sought the Lord with all his heart. So the house of Ahaziah had no power to keep still the kingdom.

But when Athaliah the mother of Ahaziah saw that her son was dead, she arose and destroyed all the seed royal of the house of Judah. But Jehoshabeath, the daughter of the king took Joash the son of Ahaziah and stole him from among the king's sons that were slain, and put him and his nurse in a bedchamber. So Jehoshabeath the daughter of king Jehoram, the wife of Jehoiada the priest (for she was the sister of Ahaziah), hid him from Athaliah so that she slew him not. And he was with them hid in the house of God six years and Athaliah reigned over the land.

And in the seventh year Jehoiada strengthened himself and took the captains of hundreds, Azariah the son of Jeroham, and Ishmael the son of Jehohanan, and Azariah the son of Obed, and Maaseiah the son of Adaiah, and Elishaphat the son of Zichri into covenant with him. And they went about in Judah and gathered the Levites out of all the cities of Judah, and the chief of the fathers of Israel, and they came to Jerusalem. And all the congregation made a covenant with the king in the house of God. And he said unto them, Behold, the king's son shall reign as the Lord hath said of the sons of David. This is the thing that ye shall do, A third part of you entering on the sabbath, of the priests and of the Levites, shall be porters of the doors, and a third part shall be at the king's house, and a third part at the gate of the foundation, and all the people shall be in the courts of the house of the Lord. But let none come into the house of the Lord save the priests, and they that minister of the Levites, they shall go in, for they are holy, but all the people shall keep the watch of the Lord. And the Levites shall compass the king round about, every man, with his weapons in his hand, and whosoever else cometh into the house he shall be put to death, but be ye with the king when he cometh in and when he goeth out.

So the Levites and all Judah did according to all things that Jehoiada the priest had commanded and took every man his men that were to come in on the sabbath with them that were to go out on the sabbath, for Jehoiada the priest dismissed not the courses. Moreover Jehoiada the priest delivered to the captains of hundreds spears, and bucklers, and shields that had been king David's which were in the house of God. And he set all the people, every man having his weapon in his hand, from the right side of the temple to the left side of the temple, along by the altar and the temple by the king round about. Then they brought out the king's son, and put upon him the crown, and gave him the testimony, and made him king. And Jehoiada and his sons anointed him and said, God save the king.

Now when Athaliah heard the noise of the people running and praising the king, she came to the people into the house of the Lord. And she looked and behold, the king stood at his pillar at the entering in, and the princes and the trumpets by the king, and all the people of the land rejoiced and sounded with trumpets, also the singers with instruments of music, and such as taught to sing praise. Then Athaliah rent her clothes and said, Treason, treason. Then Jehoiada the priest brought out the captains of hundreds that were set over the host and said unto them, Have her forth of the ranges and whoso followeth her, let him be slain with the sword. For the priest said, Slay her not in the house of the Lord. So they laid hands on her and when she was come to the entering of the horse gate by the king's house, they slew her there.

And Jehoiada made a covenant between him, and between all the people, and between the king, that they should be the Lord's people. Then all the people went to the house of Baal and brake it down, and brake his altars and his images in pieces, and slew Mattan the priest of Baal before the altars. Also Jehoiada appointed the offices of the house of the Lord by the hand of the priests the Levites whom

David had distributed in the house of the Lord to offer the burnt offerings of the Lord, as it is written in the law of Moses, with rejoicing and with singing as it was ordained by David. And he set the porters at the gates of the house of the Lord, that none which was unclean in anything should enter in. And he took the captains of hundreds, and the nobles, and the governors of the people, and all the people of the land, and brought down the king from the house of the Lord, and they came through the high gate into the king's house, and set the king upon the throne of the kingdom. And all the people of the land rejoiced, and the city was quiet after that they had slain Athaliah with the sword.

Joash was seven years old when he began to reign, and he reigned forty years in Jerusalem. His mother's name also was Zibiah of Beer-sheba. And Joash did that which was right in the sight of the Lord all the days of Jehoiada the priest. And Jehoiada took for him two wives and he begat sons and daughters.

And it came to pass after this, that Joash was minded to repair the house of the Lord. And he gathered together the priest and the Levites, and said to them, Go out unto the cities of Judah and gather of all Israel money to repair the house of your God from year to year and see that ye hasten the matter. Howbeit the Levites hastened it not. And the king called for Jehoiada the chief and said unto him, Why hast thou not required of the Levites to bring in out of Judah and out of Jerusalem the collection, according to the commandment of Moses the servant of the Lord and of the congregation of Israel, for the tabernacle of witness? For the sons of Athaliah, that wicked woman, had broken up the house of God and also all the dedicated things of the house of the Lord did they bestow upon Baalim.

And at the king's commandment they made a chest, and set it without at the gate of the house of the Lord. And they made a proclamation through Judah and Jerusalem to bring in to the Lord the collection Moses the servant of God laid upon Israel in the wilderness. And all the princes and all the people rejoiced, and brought in and cast into the chest until they had made an end. Now it came to pass that at what time the chest was brought unto the king's office by the hand of the Levites, and when they saw that there was much money, the king's scribe and the high priest's officer came and emptied the chest and took it and carried it to his place again. Thus they did day by day and gathered money in abundance. And the king and Jehoiada gave it to such as did the work of the service of the house of the Lord, and hired masons and carpenters to repair the house of the Lord, and also such as wrought iron and brass to mend the house of the Lord. So the workmen wrought and the work was perfected by them, and they set the house of God in his state and strengthened it. And when they had finished it, they brought the rest of the money before the king and Jehoiada whereof were made vessels for the house of the Lord, even vessels to minister, and to offer withal, and spoons, and vessels of gold and silver. And they offered burnt offerings in the house of the Lord continually all the days of Jehoiada.

But Jehoiada waxed old, and was full of days when he died, a hundred and thirty years old was he when he died. And they buried him in the city of David among the kings, because he had done good in Israel, both toward God, and toward his house.

Now after the death of Jehoiada came the princes of Judah and made obeisance to the king. Then the king hearkened unto them. And they left the house of the Lord God of their fathers, and served groves and idols, and wrath came upon Judah and Jerusalem for this their trespass. Yet he sent prophets to them to bring them again unto the Lord and they testified against them, but they would not give ear.

And the Spirit of God came upon Zechariah the son of Jehoiada the priest, which stood above the people and said unto them, Thus saith God, Why transgress ye the commandments of the Lord that ye cannot prosper? Because ye have forsaken the Lord, he hath also forsaken you. And they conspired against him and stoned him with stones at the commandment of the king in the court of the house of the Lord. Thus Joash the king remembered not the kindness which Jehoiada his father had done to him, but slew his son. And when he died he said, The Lord look upon me and require me.

And it came to pass at the end of the year that the host of Syria came up against him, and they came to Judah and Jerusalem and destroyed all the princes of the people from among the people and sent all the spoil of them unto the king of Damascus. For the army of the Syrians came with a small company of men and the Lord delivered a very great host into their hand because they had forsaken the Lord God of their fathers. So they executed judgment against Joash.

And when they were departed from him (for they left him in great diseases), his own servants conspired against him for the blood of the sons of Jehoiada the priest and slew him on his bed and he died and they buried him in the city of David, but they buried him not in the sepulchers of the kings. And these are they that conspired against him: Zabad the son of Shimeath an Ammonitess, and Jehozabad the son of Shimrith a Moabitess. Now concerning his sons, and the greatness of the burdens laid upon him, and the repairing of the house of God, behold, they are written in the story of the book of the kings. And Amaziah his son reigned in his stead.

7 AMAZIAH was twenty and five years old when he began to reign, and he reigned twenty and nine years in Jerusalem. And his mother's name was Jehoaddan of Jerusalem. And he did that which was right in the sight of the Lord, but not with a perfect heart. Now it came to pass when the kingdom was established to him that he slew his servants that had killed the king his father. But he slew not their children, but did as it is written in the law in the book of Moses where the Lord commanded saying, The fathers shall not die for the children, neither shall the children die for the fathers, but every man shall die for his own sin.

Moreover Amaziah gathered Judah together and made them captains over thousands, and captains over hundreds, according to the houses of their fathers throughout all Judah and Benjamin, and he numbered them from twenty years old and above and found them three hundred thousand choice men able to go forth to war that could handle spear and shield. He hired also a hundred thousand mighty men of valor out of Israel for a hundred talents of silver. But there came a man of God to him saying, O king, let not the army of Israel go with thee, for the Lord is not with Israel, to wit, with all the children of Ephraim. But if thou wilt go, do it, be strong for the battle, God shall make thee fall before the enemy, for God hath power to help and to cast down. And Amaziah said to the man of God, But what shall we do for the hundred talents which I have given to the army of Israel? And the man of God answered, The Lord is able to give thee much more than this. Then Amaziah separated them, to wit, the army that was come to him out of Ephraim to go home again, wherefore their anger was greatly kindled against Judah and they returned home in great anger. And Amaziah strengthened himself, and led forth his people, and went to the valley of salt, and smote of the children of Seir ten thousand. And other ten thousand left alive did the children of Judah carry away captive, and brought them unto the top of the rock, and cast them down from the top of the rock that they all were broken in pieces. But the soldiers of the army which Amaziah sent back that they should not go with him to battle fell upon the cities of Judah, from Samaria even unto Beth-horon, and smote three thousand of them and took much spoil.

Now it came to pass after that Amaziah was come from the slaughter of the Edomites, that he brought the gods of the children of Seir and set them up to be his gods, and bowed down himself before them, and burned incense unto them. Wherefore the anger of the Lord was kindled against Amaziah and he sent unto him a prophet which said unto him, Why hast thou sought after the gods of the people which could not deliver their own people out of thine hand? And it came to pass as he talked with him, that the king said unto him, Art thou made of the king's counsel? Forbear; why shouldest thou be smitten? Then the prophet forbare and said, I know that God hath determined to destroy thee because thou hast done this and hast not hearkened unto my counsel.

Then Amaziah king of Judah took advice and sent to Joash the son of Jehoahaz the son of Jehu, king of Israel saying, Come, let us see one another in the face. And Joash king of Israel sent to Amaziah king of Judah saying, The thistle that grew in Lebanon sent to the cedar that grew in Lebanon saying, Give thy daughter to my son to wife, and there passed by a wild beast that was in Lebanon and trode down the thistle. Thou sayest, Lo, thou hast smitten the Edomites and thine heart lifteth thee up to boast; abide now at home, why shouldest thou meddle to thine hurt that thou shouldest fall, even thou and Judah with thee?

But Amaziah would not hear, for it came of God that he might deliver them into the hand of their enemies because they sought after the gods of Edom. So Joash the king of Israel went up and they saw one another in the face, both he and Amaziah king of Judah, at Beth-shemesh which belongeth to Judah. And Judah was put to the worse before Israel and they fled every man to his tent. And Joash the king of Israel took Amaziah king of Judah, the son of Joash, the son of Jehoahaz, at Beth-shemesh, and brought him to Jerusalem and brake down the wall of Jerusalem from the gate of Ephraim to the corner gate, four hundred cubits. And he took all the gold and the silver, and all the vessels that were found in the house of God with Obed-edom, and the treasures of the king's house, the hostages also, and returned to Samaria.

And Amaziah the son of Joash king of Judah lived after the death of Joash son of Jehoahaz king of Israel fifteen years. Now the rest of the acts of Amaziah, first and last, behold, are they not written in the book of the kings of Judah and Israel? Now after the time that Amaziah did turn away from following the Lord they made a conspiracy against him in Jerusalem and he fled to Lachish, but they sent to Lachish after him and slew him there. And they brought him upon horses and buried him with his fathers in the city of Judah.

8 THEN all the people of Judah took Uzziah, who was sixteen years old, and made him king in the room of his father Amaziah. He built Eloth and restored it to Judah after that the king slept with his fathers. Sixteen years old was Uzziah when he began to reign and he reigned fifty and two years in Jerusalem. His mother's name also was Jecoliah of Jerusalem. And he did that which was right in the sight of the Lord according to all that his father Amaziah did. And he sought God in the days of Zechariah who had understanding in the visions of God, and as long as he sought the Lord God made him to prosper.

And he went forth and warred against the Philistines, and brake down the wall of Gath, and the wall of Jabneh, and the wall of Ashdod, and built cities about Ashdod, and among the Philistines. And God helped him against the Philistines, and against the Arabians that dwelt in Gurbaal, and the Mehunim. And the Ammonites gave gifts to Uzziah and his name spread abroad even to the entering in of Egypt, for he strengthened himself exceedingly. Moreover Uzziah built towers in Jerusalem at the corner gate, and at the valley gate, and at the turning of the wall, and fortified them. Also he built towers in the desert, and digged many wells, for he had much cattle, both in the low country and in the plains, husbandmen also, and vinedressers in the mountains and in Carmel, for he loved husbandry. Moreover Uzziah had a host of fighting men that went out to war by bands, according to the number of their account by the hand of Jeiel the scribe and Maaseiah the ruler under the hand of Hananiah one of the king's captains. The whole number of the chief of the fathers of the mighty men of valor were two thousand and six hundred. And under their hand was an army, three hundred thousand and seven thousand and five hundred that made war with mighty power to help the king against the enemy. And Uzziah prepared for them throughout all the host shields, and spears, and helmets, and habergeons, and bows, and slings to cast stones. And he made in Jerusalem engines, invented by cunning men, to be on the towers and upon the bulwarks to shoot arrows and great stones withal. And his name spread far abroad, for he was marvelously helped till he was strong.

But when he was strong, his heart was lifted up to his destruction, for he transgressed against the Lord his God and went into the temple of the Lord to burn incense upon the altar of incense. And Azariah the priest went in after him and with him fourscore priests of the Lord that were valiant men, and they withstood Uzziah the king and said unto him, It appertaineth not unto thee, Uzziah, to burn incense unto the Lord, but to the priests, the sons of Aaron that are consecrated to burn incense. Go out of the sanctuary, for thou hast trespassed, neither shall it be for thine honor from the Lord God. Then Uzziah was wroth, and had a censer in his hand to burn incense, and while he was wroth with the priests, the leprosy even rose up in his forehead before the priests in the house of the Lord from beside the incense altar. And Azariah the chief priest and all the priests looked upon him and behold, he was leprous in his forehead and they thrust him out from thence, yea, himself hasted also to go out because the Lord had smitten him. And Uzziah the king was a leper unto the day of his death and dwelt in a several house, being a leper, for he was cut off from the house of the Lord, and Jotham his son was over the king's house judging the people of the land.

Now the rest of the acts of Uzziah, first and last, did Isaiah the prophet, the son of Amoz, write. So Uzziah slept with his fathers and they buried him with his fathers in the field of the burial which belonged to the kings, for they said, He is a leper, and Jotham his son reigned in his stead.

Jotham was twenty and five years old when he began to reign, and he reigned sixteen years in Jerusalem. His mother's name also was Jerushah, the daughter of Zadok. And he did that which was right in the sight of the Lord, according to all that his father Uzziah did, howbeit he entered not into the temple of the Lord. And the people did yet corruptly. He built the high gate of the house of the Lord and on the wall of Ophel he built much. Moreover he built cities in the mountains of Judah and in the forests he built castles and towers. He fought also with the king of the Ammonites and prevailed against them. And the children of Ammon gave him the same year a hundred talents of silver, and ten thousand measures of wheat, and ten thousand of barley. So much did the children of Ammon pay unto him, both the second year, and the third. So Jotham became mighty because he prepared his ways before the Lord his God. Now the rest of the acts of Jotham, and all his wars, and his ways, lo, they are written in the book of the kings of Israel and Judah. He was five and twenty years old when he began to reign and reigned sixteen years in Jerusalem. And Jotham slept with his fathers, and they buried him in the city of David, and Ahaz his son reigned in his stead.

Ahaz was twenty years old when he began to reign, and he reigned sixteen years in Jerusalem, but he did not that which was right in the sight of the Lord like David his father, for he walked in the ways of the kings of Israel and made also molten images for Baalam. Moreover he burnt incense in the valley of the son of Hinnom and burnt his children in the fire after the abominations of the heathen whom the Lord had cast out before the children of Israel. He sacrificed also and burnt incense in the high places, and on the hills, and under every green tree.

Wherefore the Lord his God delivered him into the hand of the king of Syria, and they smote him and carried away a great multitude of them captives and brought them to Damascus. And he was also delivered into the hand of the king of Israel who smote him with a great slaughter. For Pekah the son of Remaliah slew in Judah a hundred and twenty thousand in one day, which were all valiant men, because they had forsaken the Lord God of their fathers. And Zichri, a mighty man of Ephraim, slew Maaseiah the king's son, and Azrikam the governor of the house, and Elkanah that was next to the king.

And the children of Israel carried away captive of their brethren two hundred thousand, women, sons, and daughters, and took also away much spoil from them, and brought the spoil to Samaria. But a prophet of the Lord was there, whose name was Oded, and he went out before the host that came to Samaria and said unto them, Behold, because the Lord God of your fathers was wroth with Judah, he hath delivered them into your hand, and ye have slain them in a rage that reacheth up into Heaven. And now ye purpose to keep under the children of Judah and Jerusalem for bondmen and bondwomen unto you, but are there not with you, even with you, sins against the Lord your God? Now hear me therefore, and deliver the captives again which ye have taken captive of your brethren, for the fierce wrath of the Lord is upon you. Then certain of the heads of the children of Ephraim, Azariah the son of Johanan, Berechiah the son of Meshillemoth, and Jehizkiah the son of Shallum, and Amasa the son of Hadlai, stood up against them that came from the war. And said unto them, Ye shall not bring in the captives hither, for whereas we have offended against the Lord already, ye intend to add more to our sins and to our trespass, for our trespass is great and there is fierce wrath against Israel. So the armed men left the captives and the spoil before the princes and all the congregation. And the men which were expressed by name rose up and took the captives, and with the spoil clothed all that were naked among them, and arrayed them, and shod them, and gave them to eat and to drink, and anointed them, and carried all the feeble of them upon asses, and brought them to Jericho, the city of palm trees, to their brethren, then they returned to Samaria.

At that time did king Ahaz send unto the kings of Assyria to help him. For again the Edomites had come and smitten Judah and carried away captives. The Philistines also had invaded the cities of the low country and of the south of Judah, and had taken Beth-shemesh, and Ajalon, and Gederoth, and Shoco with the villages thereof, and Timnah with the villages thereof, Gimzo also and the villages thereof, and they dwelt there. For the Lord brought Judah low because of Ahaz king of Israel, for he made Judah naked and transgressed sore against the Lord. And Tilgath-pilneser king of Assyria came unto him and distressed him, but strengthened him not. For Ahaz took away a portion out of the house of the Lord, and out of the house of the king, and of the princes, and gave it unto the king of Assyria, but he helped him not.

And in the time of his distress did he trespass yet more against the Lord, this is that king Ahaz. For he sacrificed unto the gods of Damascus which smote him and he said, Because the gods of the kings of Syria help them, therefore will I sacrifice to them that they may help me. But they were the ruin of him and of all Israel. And Ahaz gathered together the vessels of the house of God, and cut in pieces the vessels of the house of God, and shut up the doors of the house of the Lord, and he made him altars in every corner of Jerusalem. And in every several city of Judah he made high places to burn incense unto other gods and provoked to anger the Lord God of his fathers.

Now the rest of his acts and of all his ways, first and last, behold, they are written in the book of the kings of Judah and Israel. And Ahaz slept with his fathers, and they buried him in the city, even in Jerusalem, but they brought him not into the sepulchers of the kings of Israel, and Hezekiah his son reigned in his stead.

9

HEZEKIAH began to reign when he was five and twenty years old, and he reigned nine and twenty years in Jerusalem. And his mother's name was Abijah, the daughter of Zechariah. And he did that which was right in the sight of the Lord according to all that David his father had done.

He in the first year of his reign, in the first month, opened the doors of the house of the Lord and repaired them. And he brought in the priests and the Levites and gathered them together into the east street and said unto them, Hear me, ye Levites, sanctify now yourselves, and sanctify the house of the Lord God of your fathers, and carry forth the filthiness out of the holy place. For our fathers have trespassed and done that which was evil in the eyes of the Lord our God, and have forsaken him, and have turned away their faces from the habitation of the Lord, and turned their backs. Also they have shut up the doors of the porch, and put out the lamps, and have not burned incense nor offered burnt offerings in the holy place unto the God of Israel. Wherefore the wrath of the Lord was upon Judah and Jerusalem, and he hath delivered them to trouble, to astonishment, and to hissing as ye see with your eyes. For lo, our fathers have fallen by the sword and our sons and our daughters and our wives are in captivity for this. Now it is in mine heart to make a covenant with the Lord God of Israel that his fierce wrath may turn away from us. My sons, be not now negligent, for the Lord hath chosen you to stand before him, to serve him and that ye should minister unto him and burn incense.

Then the Levites arose: Mahath the son of Amasai, and Joel the son of Azariah, of the sons of the Kohathites, and of the sons of Merari, Kish the son of Abdi, and Azariah the son of Jehalelel, and of the Gershonites, Joah the son of Zimmah, and Eden the son of Joah, and of the sons of Elizaphan, Shimri, and Jeiel, and of the sons of Asaph, Zechariah, and Mattaniah, and of the sons of Heman, Jehiel, and Shimei, and of the sons of Jeduthun, Shemaiah, and Uzziel. And they gathered their brethren, and sanctified themselves, and came according to the commandment of the king, by the words of the Lord to cleanse the house of the Lord. And the priests went into the inner part of the house of the Lord to cleanse it and brought out all the uncleanness that they found in the temple of the Lord into the court of the house of the Lord. And the Levites took it, to carry it out abroad into the brook Kidron. Now they began on the first day of the first month to sanctify and on the eighty day of the month came they to the porch of the Lord, so they sanctified the house of the Lord in eight days and in the sixteenth day of the first month they made an end. Then they went in to Hezekiah the king and said, We have cleansed all the house of the Lord, and the altar of burnt offering with all the vessels thereof, and the shewbread table with all the vessels thereof. Moreover all the vessels which king Ahaz in his reign did cast away in his transgression have we prepared and sanctified and behold, they are before the altar of the Lord.

Then Hezekiah the king rose early, and gathered the rulers of the city, and went up to the house of the Lord. And they brought seven bullocks, and seven rams, and seven lambs, and seven he goats, for a sin offering for the kingdom, and for the sanctuary, and for Judah. And he commanded the priests the sons of Aaron to offer them on the altar of the Lord. So they killed the bullocks, and the priests received the blood and sprinkled it on the altar, likewise when they had killed the rams, they sprinkled the blood upon the altar, they killed also the lambs and they sprinkled the blood upon the altar. And they brought forth the he goats for the sin offering before the king and the congregation, and they laid their hands upon them, and the priests killed them, and they made reconciliation with their blood upon the altar to make an atonement for all Israel, for the king commanded that the burnt offering and the sin offering should be made for all Israel.

And he set the Levites in the house of the Lord with cymbals, with psalteries, and with harps, according to the commandment of David, and of Gad the king's seer, and Nathan the prophet, for so was the commandment of the Lord by his prophets. And the Levites stood with the instruments of David and the priests with the trumpets. And Hezekiah commanded to offer the burnt offering upon the altar. And when the burnt offering began, the song of the Lord began also with the trumpets and with the instruments ordained by David king of Israel. And all the congregation worshiped, and the singers sang, and the trumpeters sounded, and all this continued until the burnt offering was finished.

And when they had made an end of offering, the king and all that were present with him bowed themselves and worshiped. Moreover Hezekiah the king and the princes commanded the Levites to sing praise unto the Lord with the words of David and of Asaph the seer. And they sang praises with gladness and they bowed their heads and worshiped.

Then Hezekiah answered and said, Now ye have consecrated yourselves unto the Lord, come near and bring sacrifices and thank offerings into the house of the Lord. And the congregation brought in sacrifices and thank offerings and, as many as were of a free heart, burnt offerings. And the number of the burnt offerings which the congregation brought was threescore and ten bullocks, a hundred rams, and two hundred lambs, all these were for a burnt offering to the Lord. And the consecrated things were six hundred oxen and three thousand sheep. But the priests were too few, so that they could not flay all the burnt offerings, wherefore their brethren the Levites did help them till the work was ended and until the other priests had sanctified themselves, for the Levites were more upright in heart to sanctify themselves than the priests. And also the burnt offerings were in abundance, with the fat of the peace offerings and the drink offerings for every burnt offering. So the service of the house of the Lord was set in order. And Hezekiah rejoiced and all the people that God had prepared the people, for the thing was done suddenly.

And Hezekiah sent to all Israel and Judah and wrote letters also to Ephraim and Manasseh that they should come to the house of the Lord at Jerusalem to keep the passover unto the Lord God of Israel. For the king had taken counsel, and his princes, and all the congregation in Jerusalem to keep the passover in the second month. For they could not keep it at that time because the priests had not sanctified themselves sufficiently, neither had the people gathered themselves together to Jerusalem. And the thing pleased the king and all the congregation. So they established a decree to make proclamation throughout all Israel, from Beer-sheba even to Dan, that they should come to keep the passover unto the Lord God of Israel at Jerusalem, for they had not done it of a long time in such sort as it was written. So the posts went with the letters from the king and his princes throughout all Israel and Judah and according to the commandment of the king saying, Ye children of Israel, turn again unto the Lord God of Abraham, Isaac, and Israel, and he will return to the remnant of you that are escaped out of the hand of the kings of Assyria. And be not ye like your fathers, and like your brethren, which trespassed against the Lord God of their fathers, who therefore gave them up to desolation as ye see. Now be ye not stiff-necked as your fathers were, but yield yourselves unto the Lord, and enter into his sanctuary which he hath sanctified forever, and serve the

Lord your God that the fierceness of his wrath may turn away from you. For if ye turn again unto the Lord, your brethren and your children shall find compassion before them that lead them captive so that they shall come again into this land, for the Lord your God is gracious and merciful and will not turn away his face from you if ye return unto him.

So the posts passed from city to city, through the country of Ephraim and Manasseh, even unto Zebulun, but they laughed them to scorn and mocked them. Nevertheless, divers of Asher and Manasseh and of Zebulun humbled themselves and came to Jerusalem. Also in Judah the hand of God was to give them one heart to do the commandment of the king and of the princes by the word of the Lord.

And there assembled at Jerusalem much people to keep the feast of unleavened bread in the second month, a very great congregation. And they arose and took away the altars that were in Jerusalem and all the altars for incense took they away and cast them into the brook Kidron. Then they killed the passover on the fourteenth day of the second month, and the priests and the Levites were ashamed and sanctified themselves and brought in the burnt offerings into the house of the Lord. And they stood in their places after their manner according to the law of Moses the man of God; the priests sprinkled the blood which they received of the hand of the Levites. For there were many in the congregation that were not sanctified, therefore the Levites had the charge of the killing of the passovers for everyone that was not clean, to sanctify them unto the Lord. For a multitude of the people, even many of Ephraim and Manasseh, Issachar and Zebulun, had not cleansed themselves, yet did they eat the passover otherwise than it was written. But Hezekiah prayed for them saying, The good Lord pardon everyone that prepareth his heart to seek God, the Lord God of his fathers, though he be not cleansed according to the purification of the sanctuary. And the Lord hearkened to Hezekiah and healed the people. And the children of Israel that were present at Jerusalem kept the feast of unleavened bread seven days with great gladness, and the Levites and the priests praised the Lord day by day, singing with loud instruments unto the Lord. And Hezekiah spake comfortably unto all the Levites that taught the good knowledge of the Lord, and they did eat throughout the feast seven days, offering peace offerings and making confession to the Lord God of their fathers.

And the whole assembly took counsel to keep other seven days and they kept other seven days with gladness. For Hezekiah king of Judah did give to the congregation a thousand bullocks and seven thousand sheep and the princes gave to the congregation a thousand bullocks and ten thousand sheep, and a great number of priests sanctified themselves. And all the congregation of Judah, with the priests and the Levites, and all the congregation that came out of Israel, and the strangers that came out of the land of Israel and that dwelt in Judah rejoiced. So there was great joy in Jerusalem, for since the time of Solomon the son of David king of Israel there was not the like in Jerusalem. Then the priests the Levites arose and blessed the people and their voice was heard and their prayer came up to his holy dwelling place, even unto Heaven.

Now when all this was finished, all Israel that were present went out to the cities of Judah and brake the images in pieces, and cut down the groves, and threw down the high places and the altars out of all Judah and Benjamin, in Ephraim also and Manasseh, until they had utterly destroyed them all. Then all the children of Israel returned, every man to his possession, into their own cities.

And Hezekiah appointed the courses of the priests and the Levites after their courses, every man according to his service, the priests and Levites for burnt offerings and for peace offerings, to minister, and to give thanks, and to praise in the gates of the tents of the Lord.

He appointed also the king's portion of his substance for the burnt offerings, to wit, for the morning and evening burnt offerings, and the burnt offerings for the sabbaths, and for the new moons, and for the set feasts as it is written in the law of the Lord. Moreover he commanded the people that dwelt in Jerusalem to give the portion of the priests and the Levites, that they might be encouraged in the law of the Lord. And as soon as the commandment came abroad, the children of Israel brought in abundance the firstfruits of corn, wine, and oil, and honey, and of all the increase of the field, and the tithe of all things brought they in abundantly. And concerning the children of Israel and Judah that dwelt in the cities of Judah, they also brought in the tithe of oxen and sheep and the tithe of holy things which were consecrated unto the Lord their God and laid them by heaps. In the third month they began to lay the foundation of the heaps and finished them in the seventh month. And when Hezekiah and the princes came and saw the heaps, they blessed the Lord and his people Israel. Then Hezekiah questioned with the priests and the Levites concerning the heaps. And Azariah the chief priest of the house of Zadok answered him and said, Since the people began to bring the offerings into the house of the Lord, we have had enough to eat and have left plenty, for the Lord hath blessed his people and that which is left is this great store.

Then Hezekiah commanded to prepare chambers in the house of the Lord, and they prepared them, and brought in the offerings and the tithes and the dedicated things faithfully, over which Cononiah the Levite was ruler, and Shimei his brother was the next. And Jehiel, and Azaziah, and Nahath, and Asahel, and Jerimoth, and Jozabad, and Eliel, and Ismachiah, and Mahath, and Benaiah were overseers under the hand of Cononiah and Shimei his brother at the commandment of Hezekiah the king and Azariah the ruler of the house of God. And Kore the son of Imnah the Levite, the porter toward the east, was over the freewill offerings of God, to distribute the oblations of the Lord and the most holy things. And next to him were Eden, and Miniamin, and Jeshua, and Shemaiah, Amariah, and Shecaniah, in the cities of the priests, in their set office, to give to their brethren by courses, as well to the great as to the small, besides their genealogy of males, from three years old and upward, even unto everyone that entereth into the house of the Lord, his daily portion for their service in their charges according to their courses, both to the genealogy of the priests by the house of their fathers and the Levites from twenty years old and upward, in their charges by their courses, and to the genealogy of all their little ones, their wives, and their sons, and their daughters, through all the congregation, for in their set office they sanctified themselves in holiness. Also of the sons of Aaron the priests which were in the fields of the suburbs of their cities, in every several city, the men that were expressed by name, to give portions to all the males among the priests and to all that were reckoned by genealogies among the Levites.

And thus did Hezekiah throughout all Judah and wrought that which was good and right and truth before the Lord his God. And in every work that he began in the service of the house of God, and in the law, and in the commandments to seek his God, he did it with all his heart and prospered.

After these things and the establishment thereof, Sennacherib king of Assyria came, and entered into Judah, and encamped against the fenced cities, and thought to win them for himself. And when Hezekiah saw that Sennacherib was come and that he was purposed to fight against Jerusalem, he took counsel with his princes and his mighty men to stop the waters of the fountains which were without the city, and they did help him. So there was gathered much people together who stopped all the fountains, and the brook that ran through the midst of the land saying, Why should the kings of Assyria come and find much water? Also he strengthened himself, and built up all the wall that was broken and raised it up to the towers, and another wall without, and repaired Millo in the city of David, and made darts and shields in abundance. And he set captains of war over the people and gathered them together to him in the street of the gate of the city, and spake comfortably to them saying, Be strong and courageous, be not afraid nor dismayed for the king of Assyria, nor for all the multitude that is with him, for there be more with us than with him. With him is an arm of flesh, but with us is the Lord our God to help us and to fight our battles. And the people rested themselves upon the words of Hezekiah king of Judah.

After this did Sennacherib king of Assyria send his servants to Jerusalem (but he himself laid siege against Lachish and all his power with him) unto Hezekiah king of Judah and unto all Judah that were at Jerusalem saying, Thus saith Sennacherib king of Assyria, Whereon do ye trust that ye abide in the siege in Jerusalem? Doth not Hezekiah persuade you to give over yourselves to die by famine and by thirst saying, The Lord our God shall deliver us out of the hand of the king of Assyria? Hath not the same Hezekiah taken away his high places and his altars and commanded Judah and Jerusalem saying, Ye shall worship before one altar and burn incense upon it? Know ye not what I and my fathers have done unto all the people of other lands? Were the gods of the nations of those lands any ways able to deliver their lands out of mine hand? Who was there among all the gods of those nations that my fathers utterly destroyed that could deliver his people out of mine hand that your God should be able to deliver you out of mine hand? Now therefore let not Hezekiah deceive you, nor persuade you on this manner, neither yet believe him, for no god of any nation or kingdom was able to deliver his people out of mine hand and out of the hand of my fathers; how much less shall your God deliver you out of mine hand?

And his servants spake yet more against the Lord God and against his servant Hezekiah. He wrote also letters to rail on the Lord God of Israel and to speak against him saying, As the gods of the nations of other lands have not delivered their people out of mine hand, so shall not the God of Hezekiah deliver his people out of mine hand. Then they cried with a loud voice in the Jews' speech unto the people of Jerusalem that were on the wall, to affright them, and to trouble them that they might take the city. And they spake against the God of Jerusalem as against the gods of the people of the Earth which were the work of the hands of man.

And for this cause Hezekiah the king, and the prophet Isaiah the son of Amoz, prayed and cried to Heaven. And the Lord sent an angel which cut off all the mighty men of valor and the leaders and captains in the camp of the king Assyria. So he returned with shame of face to his own land. And when he was come into the house of his god they that came forth of his own bowels slew him there with the sword. Thus the Lord saved Hezekiah and the inhabitants of Jerusalem from the hand of Sennacherib the king of Assyria and from the hand of all other and guided them on every side. And many brought gifts unto the Lord to Jerusalem and presents to Hezekiah king of Judah, so that he was magnified in the sight of all nations from thenceforth.

In those days Hezekiah was sick to the death and prayed unto the Lord, and he spake unto him and he gave him a sign. But Hezekiah rendered not again according to the benefit done unto him, for his heart was lifted up, therefore there was wrath upon him and upon Judah and Jerusalem. Notwithstanding, Hezekiah humbled himself for the pride of his heart, both he and the inhabitants of Jerusalem, so that the wrath of the Lord came not upon them in the days of Hezekiah.

And Hezekiah had exceeding much riches and honor and he made himself treasuries for silver, and for gold, and for precious stones, and for spices, and for shields, and for all manner of pleasant jewels, storehouses also for the increase of corn, and wine, and oil, and stalls for all manner of beasts, and cotes for flocks. Moreover he provided him cities and possessions of flocks and herds in abundance, for God had given him substance very much. This same Hezekiah also stopped the upper watercourse of Gihon and brought it straight down to the west side of the city of David. And Hezekiah prospered in all his works. Howbeit, in the business of the ambassadors of the princes of Babylon who sent unto him to inquire of the wonder that was done in the land, God left him, to try him, that he might know all that was in his heart.

Now the rest of the acts of Hezekiah, and his goodness, behold, they are written in the vision of Isaiah the prophet, the son of Amoz, and in the book of the kings of Judah and Israel. And Hezekiah slept with his fathers, and they buried him in the chiefest of the sepulchers of the sons of David and all Judah and the inhabitants of Jerusalem did him honor at his death. And Manasseh his son reigned in his stead

10 MANASSEH was twelve years old when he began to reign and he reigned fifty and five years in Jerusalem, but did that which was evil in the sight of the Lord like unto the abominations of the heathen whom the Lord had cast out before the children of Israel. For he built again the high places which Hezekiah his father had broken down, and he reared up altars for Baalim, and made groves, and worshiped all the host of Heaven and served them. Also he built altars in the house of the Lord whereof the Lord had said, In Jerusalem shall my name be forever. And he built altars for all the host of Heaven in the two courts of the house of the Lord. And he caused his children to pass through the fire in the valley of the son of Hinnom, also he observed times, and used enchantments, and used witchcraft, and dealt with a familiar spirit, and with wizards: he wrought much evil in the sight of the Lord to provoke him to anger. And he set a carved image, the idol which he had made, in the house of God of which God had said to David and to Solomon his son, In this house and in Jerusalem, which I have chosen before all the tribes of Israel, will I put my name forever. Neither will I anymore remove the foot of Israel from out of the land which I have appointed for your fathers, so that they will take heed to do all that I have commanded them according to the whole law and the statutes and the ordinances by the hand of Moses. So Manasseh made Judah and the inhabitants of Jerusalem to err and to do worse than the heathen whom the Lord had destroyed before the children of Israel.

And the Lord spake to Manasseh and to the people, but they would not hearken. Wherefore the Lord brought upon them the captains of the host of the king of Assyria which took Manasseh among the thorns, and bound him with fetters, and carried him to Babylon. And when he was in affliction, he besought the Lord his God and humbled himself greatly before the God of his fathers, and prayed unto him, and he was entreated of him, and heard his supplication, and brought him again to Jerusalem into his kingdom. Then Manasseh knew that the Lord he was God.

Now after this he built a wall without the city of David, on the west side of Gihon in the valley, even to the entering in at the fish gate, and compassed about Ophel, and raised it up a very great height, and put captains of war in all the fenced cities of Judah. And he took away the strange gods, and the idol out of the house of the Lord, and all the altars that he had built in the mount of the house of the Lord and in Jerusalem and cast them out of the city.

And he repaired the altar of the Lord, and sacrificed thereon peace offerings and thank offerings and commanded Judah to serve the Lord God of Israel. Nevertheless the people did sacrifice still in the high places, yet unto the Lord their God only. Now the rest of the acts of Manasseh, and his prayer unto his

God, and the words of the seers that spake to him in the name of the Lord God of Israel, behold, they are written in the book of the kings of Israel. His prayer also, and how God was entreated of him, and all his sins, and his trespass, and the places wherein he built high places, and set up groves and graven images before he was humbled, behold, they are written among the sayings of the seers. So Manasseh slept with his fathers, and they buried him in his own house, and Amon his son reigned in his stead.

Amon was two and twenty years old when he began to reign, and reigned two years in Jerusalem. But he did that which was evil in the sight of the Lord as did Manasseh his father, for Amon sacrificed unto all the carved images which Manasseh his father had made, and served them, and humbled not himself before the Lord as Manasseh his father had humbled himself, but Amon trespassed more and more. And his servants conspired against him and slew him in his own house. But the people of the land slew all them that had conspired against king Amon, and the people of the land made Josiah his son king in his stead.

11 JOSIAH was eight years old when he began to reign and he reigned in Jerusalem one and thirty years. And he did that which was right in the sight of the Lord, and walked in the ways of David his father, and declined neither to the right hand nor to the left. For in the eighth year of his reign, while he was yet young, he began to seek after the God of David his father, and in the twelfth year he began to purge Judah and Jerusalem from the high places, and the groves, and the carved images, and the molten images. And they brake down the altars of Baalim in his presence, and the images that were on high above them he cut down, and the groves, and the carved images, and the molten images he brake in pieces and made dust of them, and strewed it upon the graves of them that had sacrificed unto them. And he burnt the bones of the priests upon their altars and cleansed Judah and Jerusalem. And so did he in the cities of Manasseh, and Ephraim, and Simeon, even unto Naphtali, with their mattocks round about. And when he had broken down the altars and the groves, and had beaten the graven images into powder, and cut down all the idols throughout all the land of Israel, he returned to Jerusalem.

Now in the eighteenth year of his reign, when he had purged the land and the house, he sent Shaphan the son of Azaliah, and Maaseiah the governor of the city, and Joah the son of Joahaz the recorder, to repair the house of the Lord his God. And when they came to Hilkiah the high priest, they delivered the money that was brought into the house of God, which the Levites that kept the doors had gathered of the hand of Manasseh and Ephraim, and of all the remnant of Israel, and of all Judah and Benjamin, and they returned to Jerusalem. And they put it in the hand of the workmen that had the oversight of the house of the Lord, and they gave it to the workmen that wrought in the house of the Lord, to repair and amend the house, even to the artificers and builders gave they it, to buy hewn stone and timber for couplings, and to floor the houses which the king of Judah had destroyed. And the men did the work faithfully, and the overseers of them were Jahath and Obadiah, the Levites, of the sons of Merari, and Zechariah and Meshullam, of the sons of the Kohathites, to set it forward, and other of the Levites, all that could skill of instruments of music. Also they were over the bearers of burdens, and were overseers of all that wrought the work in any manner of service, and of the Levites there were scribes, and officers, and porters.

And when they brought out the money that was brought into the house of the Lord, Hilkiah the priest found a book of the law of the Lord given by Moses. And Hilkiah answered and said to Shaphan the scribe, I have found the book of the law in the house of the Lord. And Hilkiah delivered the book to Shaphan. And Shaphan carried the book to the king, and brought the word of the king back again, saying, All that was committed to thy servants, they do. And they have gathered together the money that was found in the house of the Lord, and have delivered it into the hand of the overseers, and to the hand of the workmen. Then Shaphan the scribe told the king, saying, Hilkiah the priest hath given me a book. And Shaphan read it before the king.

And it came to pass when the king had heard the words of the law that he rent his clothes. And the king commanded Hilkiah, and Ahikam the son of Shaphan, and Abdon the son of Micah, and Shaphan the scribe, and Asaiah a servant of the king's saying, Go inquire of the Lord for me, and for them that are left in Israel and in Judah, concerning the words of the book that is found, for great is the wrath of the Lord that is poured out upon us because our fathers have not kept the word of the Lord to do after all that is written in this book.

And Hilkiah and they that the king had appointed went to Huldah the prophetess, the wife of Shallum the son of Tikvah, the son of Hasrah, keeper of the wardrobe (now she dwelt in Jerusalem in the college) and they spake to her to that effect. And she answered them, Thus saith the Lord God of Israel, Tell ye the man that sent you to me, Thus saith the Lord, Behold, I will bring evil upon this place and upon the inhabitants thereof, even all the curses that are written in the book which they have read before the king of Judah, because they have forsaken me and have burned incense unto other gods that they might provoke me to anger with all the works of their hands, therefore my wrath shall be poured out upon this place and shall not be quenched. And as for the king of Judah, who sent you to inquire of the Lord, so shall ye say unto him, Thus saith the Lord God of Israel concerning the words which thou hast heard, because thine heart was tender and thou didst humble thyself before God when thou heardest his words against this place and against the inhabitants thereof, and humbledst thyself before me, and didst rend thy clothes, and weep before me, I have even heard thee also, saith the Lord. Behold, I will gather thee to thy fathers, and thou shalt be gathered to thy grave in peace, neither shall thine eyes see all the evil that I will bring upon this place and upon the inhabitants of the same. So they brought the king word again.

Then the king sent and gathered together all the elders of Judah and Jerusalem. And the king went up into the house of the Lord, and all the men of Judah, and the inhabitants of Jerusalem, and the priests, and the Levites, and all the people, great and small, and he read in their ears all the words of the book of the covenant that was found in the house of the Lord.

And the king stood in his place and made a covenant before the Lord, to walk after the Lord, and to keep his commandments, and his testimonies, and his statutes with all his heart and with all his soul to perform the words of the covenant which are written in this book. And he caused all that were present in Jerusalem and Benjamin to stand to it. And the inhabitants of Jerusalem did according to the covenant of God, the God of their fathers. And Josiah took away all the abominations out of all the countries that pertained to the children of Israel and made all that were present in Israel to serve, even to serve the Lord their God. And all his days they departed not from following the Lord, the God of their fathers.

Moreover, Josiah kept a passover unto the Lord in Jerusalem and they killed the passover on the fourteenth day of the first month. And he set the priests in their charges and encouraged them to the service of the house of the Lord. And said unto the Levites that taught all Israel which were holy unto the Lord, Put the holy ark in the house which Solomon the son of David king of Israel did build; it shall not be a burden upon your shoulders. Serve now the Lord your God and his people Israel, and prepare yourselves by the houses of your fathers after your courses, according to the writing of David king of Israel and according to the writing of Solomon his son, and stand in the holy place according to the divisions of the families of the fathers of your brethren the people and after the division of the families of the Levites. So kill the passover, and sanctify yourselves, and prepare your brethren that they may do according to the word of the Lord by the hand of Moses.

And Josiah gave to the people of the flock, lambs and kids, all for the passover offerings, for all that were present, to the number of thirty thousand, and three thousand bullocks, these were of the king's substance. And his princes gave willingly unto the people, to the priests and to the Levites, Hilkiah and Zechariah and Jehiel, rulers of the house of God, gave unto the priests for the passover offerings two thousand and six hundred small cattle, and three hundred oxen. Conaniah also, and Shemaiah and Nethaneel, his brethren, and Hashabiah and Jeiel and Jozabad, chief of the Levites, gave unto the Levites for passover offerings five thousand small cattle and five hundred oxen.

So the service was prepared, and the priests stood in their place, and the Levites in their courses according to the king's commandment. And they killed the passover, and the priests sprinkled the blood from their hands, and the Levites flayed them. And they removed the burnt offerings, that they might give according to the divisions of the families of the people to offer unto the Lord as it is written in the book of Moses. And so did they with the oxen. And they roasted the passover with fire according to the ordinance, but the other holy offerings sod they in pots, and in caldrons, and in pans, and divided them speedily among all the people. And afterward they made ready for themselves and for the priests because the priests the sons of Aaron were busied in offering of burnt offerings and the fat until night, therefore the Levites prepared for themselves and for the priests the sons of Aaron. And the singers the sons of Asaph were in their place according to the commandment of David, and Asaph, and Heman, and Jeduthun the king's seer, and the porters waited at every gate; they might not depart from their service, for their brethren the Levites prepared for them.

So all the service of the Lord was prepared the same day to keep the passover and to offer burnt offerings upon the altar of the Lord according to the commandment of king Josiah. And the children of Israel that were present kept the passover at that time, and the feast of unleavened bread seven days. And there was no passover like to that kept in Israel from the days of Samuel the prophet, neither did all the kings of Israel keep such a passover as Josiah kept, and the priests, and the Levites, and all Judah and Israel that were present, and the inhabitants of Jerusalem. In the eighteenth year of the reign of Josiah was this passover kept.

After all this when Josiah had prepared the temple, Necho king of Egypt came up to fight against Charchemish by Euphrates and Josiah went out against him. But he sent ambassadors to him saying, What have I to do with thee, thou king of Judah? I come not against thee this day, but against the house wherewith I have war, for God commanded me to make haste; forbear thee from meddling with God who is with me that he destroy thee not. Nevertheless Josiah would not turn his face from him, but disguised himself that he might fight with him, and hearkened not unto the words of Necho from the mouth of God, and came to fight in the valley of Megiddo. And the archers shot at king Josiah and the king said to his servants, Have me away for I am sore wounded. His servants therefore took him out of that chariot, and put him in the second chariot that he had, and they brought him to Jerusalem, and he died, and was buried in one of the sepulchers of his fathers. And all Judah and Jerusalem mourned for Josiah.

And Jeremiah lamented for Josiah, and all the singing men and the singing women spake of Josiah in their lamentations to this day, and made them an ordinance in Israel and behold, they are written in the lamentations. Now the rest of the acts of Josiah, and his goodness according to that which was written in the law of the Lord, and his deeds, first and last, behold, they are written in the book of the kings of Israel and Judah.

12 THEN the people of the land took Jehoahaz the son of Josiah, and made him king in his father's stead in Jerusalem. Jehoahaz was twenty and three years old when he began to reign and he reigned three months in Jerusalem. And the king of Egypt put him down at Jerusalem and condemned the land in a hundred talents of silver and a talent of gold. And the king of Egypt made Eliakim his brother king over Judah and Jerusalem and turned his name to Jehoiakim. And Necho took Jehoahaz his brother and carried him to Egypt.

Jehoiakim was twenty and five years old when he began to reign, and he reigned eleven years in Jerusalem, and he did that which was evil in the sight of the Lord his God. Against him came up Nebuchadnezzar king of Babylon and bound him in fetters to carry him to Babylon. Nebuchadnezzar also carried of the vessels of the house of the Lord to Babylon and put them in his temple at Babylon. Now the rest of the acts of Jehoiakim, and his abominations which he did and that which was found in him, behold, they are written in the book of the kings of Israel and Judah, and Jehoiachin his son reigned in his stead.

Jehoiachin was eight years old when he began to reign, and he reigned three months and ten days in Jerusalem, and he did that which was evil in the sight of the Lord.

And when the year was expired, king Nebuchadnezzar sent and brought him to Babylon with the goodly vessels of the house of the Lord and made Zedekiah his brother king over Judah and Jerusalem.

Zedekiah was one and twenty years old when he began to reign, and reigned eleven years in Jerusalem. And he did that which was evil in the sight of the Lord his God and humbled not himself before Jeremiah the prophet speaking from the mouth of the Lord. And he also rebelled against king Nebuchadnezzar who had made him swear by God, but he stiffened his neck and hardened his heart from turning unto the Lord God of Israel. Moreover all the chief of the priests and the people transgressed very much after all the abominations of the heathen and polluted the house of the Lord which he had hallowed in Jerusalem.

And the Lord God of their fathers sent to them by his messengers, rising up betimes and sending, because he had compassion on his people and on his dwelling place, but they mocked the messengers of God, and despised his words, and misused his prophets until the wrath of the Lord arose against his people, till there was no remedy. Therefore he brought upon them the king of the Chaldees who slew their young men with the sword in the house of their sanctuary and had no compassion upon young man or maiden, old man, or him that stooped for age, he gave them all into his hand. And all the vessels of the house of God, great and small, and the treasures of the house of the Lord, and the treasures of the king, and of his princes, all these he brought to Babylon. And they burnt the house of God and brake down the wall of Jerusalem, and burnt all the palaces thereof with fire, and destroyed all the goodly vessels thereof. And them that had escaped from the sword carried he away to Babylon where they were servants to him and his sons until the reign of the kingdom of Persia, to fulfill the word of the Lord by the mouth of Jeremiah until the land had enjoyed her sabbaths, for as long as she lay desolate she kept sabbath, to fulfill threescore and ten years.

Now in the first year of Cyrus king of Persia that the word of the Lord spoken by the mouth of Jeremiah might be accomplished, the Lord stirred up the spirit of Cyrus king of Persia that he made a proclamation throughout all his kingdom and put it also in writing saying, Thus saith Cyrus king of Persia, All the kingdoms of the Earth hath the Lord God of Heaven given me and he hath charged me to build him a house in Jerusalem which is in Judah. Who is there among you of all his people? The Lord his God be with him and let him go up.

EZRA

NOW in the first year of Cyrus king of Persia, that the word of the Lord by the mouth of Jeremiah might be fulfilled, the Lord stirred up the spirit of Cyrus king of Persia that he made a proclamation throughout all his kingdom and put it also in writing saying, Thus saith Cyrus king of Persia, The Lord God of Heaven hath given me all the kingdoms of the Earth and he hath charged me to build him a house at Jerusalem which is in Judah. Who is there among you of all his people? His God be with him and let him go up to Jerusalem, which is Judah, and build the house of the Lord God of Israel (he is the God) which is in Jerusalem. And whosoever remaineth in any place where he sojourneth, let the men of his place help him with silver, and with gold, and with goods, and with beasts, besides the freewill offering for the house of God that is in Jerusalem.

Then rose up the chief of the fathers of Judah and Benjamin, and the priests, and the Levites, with all them whose spirit God had raised, to go up to build the house of the Lord which is in Jerusalem. And all they that were about them strengthened their hands with vessels of silver, with gold, with goods, and with beasts, and with precious things, besides all that was willingly offered. Also Cyrus the king brought forth the vessels of the house of the Lord which Nebuchadnezzar had brought forth out of Jerusalem and had put them in the house of his gods, even those did Cyrus king of Persia bring forth by the hand of Mithredath the treasurer, and numbered them unto Sheshbazzar the prince of Judah. And this is the number of them: thirty chargers of gold, a thousand chargers of silver, nine and twenty knives, thirty basins of gold, silver basins of a second sort four hundred and ten, and other vessels a thousand. All the vessels of gold and of silver were five thousand and four hundred. All these did Sheshbazzar bring up with them of the captivity that were brought up from Babylon unto Jerusalem

Now these are the children of the province that went up out of the captivity of those which had been carried away whom Nebuchadnezzar the king of Babylon had carried away unto Babylon and came again unto Jerusalem and Judah, everyone unto his city, which came with Zerubbabel, Jeshua, Nehemiah, Seraiah, Reelaiah, Mordecai, Bilshan, Mizpar, Bigvai, Rehum, Baanah.

The number of the men of the people of Israel, the children of Parosh, two thousand a hundred seventy and two. The children of Shephatiah, three hundred seventy and two. The children of Arah, seven hundred seventy and five. The children of Pahath-moab, of the children of Jeshua and Joab, two thousand eight hundred and twelve. The children of Elam, a thousand two hundred fifty and four. The children of Zattu, nine hundred forty and five. The children of Zaccai, seven hundred and threescore. The children of Bani, six hundred forty and two. The children of Bebai, six hundred twenty and three. The children of Azgad, a thousand two hundred and twenty and two. The children of Adonikam, six hundred sixty and six. The children of Bigvai, two thousand fifty and six. The children of Adin, four hundred fifty and four. The children of Ater of Hezekiah, ninety and eight. The children of Bezai, three hundred twenty and three. The children of Jorah, a hundred and twelve. The children of Hashum, two hundred twenty and three. The children of Gibbar, ninety and five. The children of Bethlehem, a hundred twenty and three. The men of Netophah, fifty and six. The men of Anathoth, a hundred twenty and eight. The children of Azmaveth, forty and two. The children of Kirjath-arim, Chephirah, and Beeroth, seven hundred and forty and three. The children of Ramah and Gaba, six hundred twenty and one. The men of Michmas, a hundred twenty and two. The men of Beth-el and Ai, two hundred twenty and three. The children of Nebo, fifty and two. The children of Magbish, a hundred fifty and six. The children of the other Elam, a thousand two hundred fifty and four. The children of Harim, three hundred and twenty. The children of Lod, Hadid, and Ono, seven hundred twenty and five. The children of Jericho, three hundred forty and five. The children of Senaah, three thousand and six hundred and thirty.

The priests, the children of Jediah, of the house of Jeshua, nine hundred seventy and three. The children of Immer, a thousand fifty and two. The children of Pashur, a thousand two hundred forty and seven. The children of Harim, a thousand and seventeen.

The Levites, the children of Jeshua and Kadmiel, of the children of Hodaviah, seventy and four. The singers, the children of Asaph, a hundred twenty and eight. The children of the porters, the children of Shallum, the children of Ater, the children of Talmon, the children of Akkub, the children of Hatita, the children of Shobai, in all a hundred thirty and nine.

The Nethinim, the children of Ziha, the children of Hasupha, the children of Tabbaoth, the children of Keros, the children of Siaha, the children of Padon, the children of Lebanah, the children of Hagabah, the children of Akkub, the children of Hagab, the children of Shalmai, the children of Hanan. The children of Giddel, the children of Gahar, the children of Reaiah, the children of Rezin, the children of Nekoda, the children of Gazzam. The children of Uaaz, the children of Paseah, the children of Besai, the children of Asnah, the children of Mehunim, the children of Nephusim. The children of Bakbauk, the children of Hakupha, the children of Harhur. The children of Bazluth, the children of Mehida, the children of Harsha, the children of Barkos, the children of Sisera, the children of Thamah, the children of Neziah, the children of Hatipha.

The children of Solomon's servants, the children of Sotai, the children of Sophereth, the children of Peruda, the children of Jaaiah, the children of Darkon, the children of Giddel, the children of Shephatiah, the children of Hattil, the children of Pochereth of Zebaim, the children of Ami. All the Nethinim and the children of Solomon's servants were three hundred ninety and two.

And these were they which went up from Tel-mela: Tel-harsa, Cherub, Addan, and Immer, but they could not show their father's house and their seed, whether they were of Israel, the children of Delaiah, the children of Tobiah, the children of Nekodah, six hundred fifty and two. And of the children of the priests, the children of Habaiah, the children of Koz, the children of Barzillai which took a wife of the daughters of Barzillai the Gileadite and was called after their name, these sought their register among those that were reckoned by genealogy, but they were not found, therefore were they as polluted put from the priesthood. And the Tirshatha said unto them that they should not eat of the most holy things till there stood up a priest with Urim and with Thummim.

The whole congregation together was forty and two thousand three hundred and threescore, besides their servants and their maids, of whom there were seven thousand three hundred thirty and seven, and there were among them two hundred singing men and singing women. Their horses were seven hundred thirty and six, their mules, two hundred forty and five, their camels, four hundred thirty and five, their asses, six thousand seven hundred and twenty.

And some of the chief of the fathers, when they came to the house of the Lord which is at Jerusalem, offered freely for the house of God to set it up in his place, they gave after their ability unto the treasure of the work threescore and one thousand drams of gold, and five thousand pounds of silver, and one hundred priests' garments. So the priests, and the Levites, and some of the people, and the singers, and the porters, and the Nethinim dwelt in their cities and all Israel in their cities

And when the seventh month was come and the children of Israel were in the cities, the people gathered themselves together as one man to Jerusalem. Then stood up Jeshua the son of Jozadak and his brethren the priests, and Zerubbabel the son of Shealtiel and his brethren, and built the altar of the God of Israel to offer burnt offerings thereon as it is written in the law of Moses the man of God. And they set the altar upon his bases, for fear was upon them because of the people of those countries, and they offered burnt offerings thereon unto the Lord, even burnt offerings morning and evening. They kept also the feast of tabernacles as it is written and offered the daily burnt offerings by number according to the custom as the duty of every day required, and afterward offered the continual burnt offering, both of the new moons and of all the set feasts of the Lord that were consecrated and of everyone that willingly offered a freewill offering unto the Lord. From the first day of the seventh month began they to offer burnt offerings unto the Lord. But the foundation of the temple of the Lord was not yet laid. They gave money also unto the masons, and to the carpenters, and meat, and drink, and oil, unto them of Zidon and to them of Tyre, to bring cedar trees from Lebanon to the Sea of Joppa according to the grant that they had of Cyrus king of Persia.

Now in the second year of their coming unto the house of God at Jerusalem, in the second month, began Zerubbabel the son of Shealtiel, and Jeshua the son of Jozadak, and the remnant of their brethren the priests and the Levites, and all they that were come out of the captivity unto Jerusalem, and appointed the Levites from twenty years old and upward to set forward the work of the house of the Lord. Then stood Jeshua with his sons and his brethren, Kadmiel and his sons, the sons of Judah, together to set forward the workmen in the house of God, the sons of Henadad with their sons and their brethren the Levites.

And when the builders laid the foundation of the temple of the Lord they set the priests in their apparel with trumpets, and the Levites the sons of Asaph with cymbals, to praise the Lord after the ordinance of David king of Israel. And they sang together by course in praising and giving thanks unto the Lord because he is good, for his mercy endureth for ever toward Israel. And all the people shouted with a great shout when they praised the Lord because the foundation of the house of the Lord was laid. But many of the priests and Levites and chief of the fathers, who were ancient men, that had seen the first house, when the foundation of this house was laid before their eyes wept with a loud voice and many shouted aloud for joy so that the people could not discern the noise of the shout of joy from the noise of the weeping of the people, for the people shouted with a loud shout and the noise was heard afar off

Now when the adversaries of Judah and Benjamin heard that the children of the captivity builded the temple unto the Lord God of Israel, then they came to Zerubbabel and to the chief of the fathers and said unto them, Let us build with you, for we seek your God as ye do and we do sacrifice unto him since the days of Esar-haddon king of Assur, which brought us up hither. But Zerubbabel, and Jeshua, and the rest of the chief of the fathers of Israel said unto them, Ye have nothing to do with us to build a house unto our God, but we ourselves together will build unto the Lord God of Israel, as king Cyrus the king of Persia hath commanded us. Then the people of the land weakened the hands of the people of Judah, and troubled them in building, and hired counselors against them to frustrate their purpose all the days of Cyrus king of Persia, even until the reign of Darius king of Persia. And in the reign of Ahasuerus, in the beginning of his reign, wrote they unto him an accusation against the inhabitants of Judah and Jerusalem. And in the days of Artaxerxes wrote Bishlam, Mithredath, Tabeel, and the rest of their companions unto Artaxerxes king of Persia, and the writing of the letter was written in the Syrian tongue and interpreted in the Syrian tongue.

Rehum the chancellor and Shimshai the scribe wrote a letter against Jerusalem to Artaxerxes the king in this sort; then wrote Rehum the chancellor, and Shimshai the scribe, and the rest of their companions, the Dinaites, the Apharsathchites, the Tarpelites, the Apharsites, the Archevites, the Babylonians, the Susanchites, the Dehavites, and the Elamites, and the rest of the nations whom the great and noble Asnapper brought over and set in the cities of Samaria, and the rest that are on this side the river, and at such a time. This is the copy of the letter that they sent unto him, even unto Artaxerxes the king:

Thy servants the men on this side the river and at such a time. Be it known unto the king, that the Jews which came up from thee to us are come unto Jerusalem, building the rebellious and the bad city, and have set up the walls thereof and joined the foundations. Be it known now unto the king, that, if this city be builded and the walls set up again, then will they not pay toll, tribute, and custom, and so thou shalt endamage the revenue of the kings. Now because we have maintenance from the king's palace, and it was not meet for us to see the king's dishonor, therefore have we sent and certified the king that search may be made in the book of the records of thy fathers, so shalt thou find in the book of the records and know that this city is a rebellious city, and hurtful unto kings and provinces, and that they have moved sedition within the same of old time, for which cause was this city destroyed. We certify the king that, if this city be builded again and the walls thereof set up, by this means thou shalt have no portion on this side the river.

Then sent the king an answer unto Rehum the chancellor, and to Shimshai the scribe, and to the rest of their companions that dwell in Samaria, and unto the rest beyond the river:

Peace, and at such a time. The letter which ye sent unto us hath been plainly read before me. And I commanded, and search hath been made, and it is found that this city of old time hath made insurrection against kings and that rebellion and sedition have been made therein. There have been mighty kings also over Jerusalem which have ruled over all countries beyond the river, and toll, tribute, and custom was paid unto them. Give ye now commandment to cause these men to cease and that this city be not builded until another commandment shall be given from me. Take heed now that ye fail not to do this; why should damage grow to the hurt of the kings?

Now when the copy of king Artaxerxes' letter was read before Rehum, and Shimshai the scribe, and their companions, they went up in haste to Jerusalem unto the Jews and made them to cease by force and power. Then ceased the work of the house of God which is at Jerusalem. So it ceased unto the second year of the reign of Darius king of Persia.

Then the prophets, Haggai the prophet and Zechariah the son of Iddo, prophesied unto the Jews that were in Judah and Jerusalem in the name of the God of Israel, even unto them. Then rose up Zerubbabel the son of Shealtiel and Jeshua the son of Jozadak and began to build the house of God which is at Jerusalem and with them were the prophets of God helping them.

At the same time came to them Tatnai, governor on this side the river, and Shethar-boznai and their companions and said thus unto them, Who hath commanded you to build this house and to make up this wall? Then said we unto them after this manner, What are the names of the men that make this building? But the eye of their God was upon the elders of the Jews, that they could not cause them to cease till the matter came to Darius and then they returned answer by letter concerning this matter. The copy of the letter that Tatnai, governor on this side the river, and Shethar-boznai and his companions the Apharsachites, which were on this side the river, sent unto Darius the king; they sent a letter unto him, wherein was written thus:

Unto Darius the king, all peace. Be it known unto the king that we went into the province of Judea, to the house of the great God which is builded with great stones and timber is laid in the walls, and his work goeth fast on and prospereth in their hands. Then asked we those elders and said unto them thus, Who commanded you to build this house and to make up these walls? We asked their names also to certify thee that we might write the names of the men that were the chief of them. And thus they returned us answer saying, We are the servants of the God of Heaven and Earth and build the house that was builded these many years ago which a great king of Israel builded and set up. But after that our fathers had provoked the God of Heaven unto wrath he gave them into the hand of Nebuchadnezzar the king of Babylon, the Chaldean, who destroyed this house and carried the people away into Babylon. But in the first year of Cyrus the king of Babylon, the same king Cyrus made a decree to build this house of God. And the vessels also of gold and silver of the house of God, which Nebuchadnezzar took out of the temple that was in Jerusalem, and brought them into the temple of Babylon, those did Cyrus the king take out of the temple of Babylon and they were delivered unto one whose name was Sheshbazzar, whom he had made governor, and said unto him, Take these vessels, go, carry them into the temple that is in Jerusalem and let the house of God be builded in his place. Then came the same Sheshbazzar and laid the foundation of the house of God which is in Jerusalem, and since that time even until now hath it been in building and yet it is not finished. Now therefore, if it seem good to the king, let there be search made in the king's treasure house which is there at Babylon, whether it be so that a decree was made of Cyrus the king to build this house of God at Jerusalem and let the king send his pleasure to us concerning this matter.

Then Darius the king made a decree, and search was made in the house of the rolls, where the treasures were laid up in Babylon. And there was found at Achmetha, in the palace that is in the province of the Medes, a roll, and therein was a record thus written:

In the first year of Cyrus the king, the same Cyrus the king made a decree concerning the house of God at Jerusalem: Let the house be builded, the place where they offered sacrifices, and let the foundations thereof be strongly laid, the height thereof threescore cubits, and the breadth thereof threescore cubits, with three rows of great stones and a row of new timber and let the expenses be given out of the king's house, and also let the golden and silver vessels of the house of God, which Nebuchadnezzar took forth out of the temple which is at Jerusalem and brought unto Babylon, be restored and brought again unto the temple which is at Jerusalem, every one to his place, and place them in the house of God. Now therefore, Tatnai, governor beyond the river, Shethat-boznai, and your companions the Apharsachites which are beyond the river, be ye far from thence, let the work of this house of God alone, let the governor of the Jews and the elders of the Jews build this house of God in his place. Moreover I make a decree what ye shall do to the elders of these Jews for the building of this house of God, that of the king's goods, even of the tribute beyond the river, forthwith expenses be given unto these men that they be not hindered. And that which they have need of, both young bullocks, and rams, and lambs, for the burnt offerings of the God of Heaven, wheat, salt, wine, and oil, according to the appointment of the priests which are at Jerusalem, let it be given them day by day without fail that they may offer sacrifices of sweet savors unto the God of Heaven and pray for the life of the king and of his sons. Also I have made a decree that whosoever shall alter this word, let timber be pulled down from his house and being set up, let him be hanged thereon and let his house be made a dunghill for this. And the God that hath caused his name to dwell there destroy all kings and people that shall put to their hand to alter and to destroy this house of God which is at Jerusalem. I Darius have made a decree, let it be done with speed.

Then Tatnai, governor on this side the river, Shethar-boznai and their companions, according to that which Darius the king had sent, so they did speedily. And the elders of the Jews builded, and they prospered through the prophesying of Haggai the prophet and Zechariah the son of Iddo. And they builded and finished it according to the commandment of the God of Israel and according to the commandment of Cyrus, and Darius, and Artaxerxes king of Persia. And this house was finished on the third day of the month Adar, which was in the sixth year of the reign of Darius the king. And the children of Israel, the priests, and the Levites, and the rest of the children of the captivity, kept the dedication of this house of God with joy and offered at the dedication of this house of God a hundred bullocks, two hundred rams, four hundred lambs, and for a sin offering for all Israel, twelve he goats according to the number of the tribes of Israel. And they set the priests in their divisions and the Levites in their courses, for the service of God which is at Jerusalem as it is written in the book of Moses.

And the children of the captivity kept the passover upon the fourteenth day of the first month. For the priests and the Levites were purified together, all of them were pure and killed the passover for all the children of the captivity, and for their brethren the priests, and for themselves. And the children of Israel which were come again out of captivity, and all such as had separated themselves unto them from the filthiness of the heathen of the land to seek the Lord God of Israel, did eat and kept the feast of unleavened bread seven days with joy, for the Lord had made them joyful and turned the heart of the king of Assyria unto them to strengthen their hands in the work of the house of God, the God of Israel.

2 NOW after these things, in the reign of Artaxerxes king of Persia, Ezra the son of Seraiah, the son of Azariah, the son of Hilkiah, the son of Shallum, the son of Zadok, the son of Ahitub, the son of Amariah, the son of Azariah, the son of Meraioth, the son of Zerahiah, the son of Uzzi, the son of Bukki, the son of Abishua, the son of Phinehas, the son of Eleazar, the son of Aaron the chief priest, this Ezra went up from Babylon and he was a ready scribe in the law of Moses which the Lord God of Israel had given and the king granted him all his request according to the hand of the Lord his God upon him. And there went up some of the children of Israel, and of the priests, and the Levites, and the singers, and the porters, and the Nethinim, unto Jerusalem, in the seventh year of Artaxerxes the king. And he came to Jerusalem in the fifth month, which was in the seventh year of the king. For upon the first day of the first month began he to go up from Babylon, and on the first day of the fifth month came he to Jerusalem according to the good hand of his God upon him. For Ezra had prepared his heart to seek the law of the Lord and to do it and to teach in Israel statutes and judgments. Now this is the copy of the letter that the king Artaxerxes gave unto Ezra the priest, the scribe, even a scribe of the words of the commandments of the Lord and of his statutes to Israel:

Artaxerxes, king of kings, unto Ezra the priest, a scribe of the law of the God of Heaven, perfect peace, and at such a time. I make a decree, that all they of the people of Israel, and of his priests and Levites in my realm, which are minded of their own freewill to go up to Jerusalem, go with thee. Forasmuch as thou art sent of the king and of his seven counselors to inquire concerning Judah and Jerusalem according to the law of thy God which is in thine hand, and to carry the silver and gold which the king and his counselors have freely offered unto the God of Israel whose habitation is in Jerusalem, and all the silver and gold that thou canst find in all the province of Babylon, with the freewill offering of the people and of the priests, offering willingly for the house of their God which is in Jerusalem, that thou mayest buy speedily with this money bullocks, rams, lambs, with their meat offerings and their drink offerings, and offer them upon the altar of the house of your God which is in Jerusalem. And whatsoever shall seem good to thee and to thy brethren to do with the rest of the silver and the gold, that do after the will of your God. The vessels also that are given thee for the service of the house of thy God, those deliver thou before the God of Jerusalem. And whatsoever more shall be needful for the house of thy God which thou shalt have occasion to bestow, bestow it out of the king's treasure house.

And I, even I Artaxerxes the king, do make a decree to all the treasurers which are beyond the river that whatsoever Ezra the priest, the scribe of the law of the God of Heaven, shall require of you, it be done speedily unto a hundred talents of silver, and to a hundred measures of wheat, and to a hundred baths of wine, and to a hundred baths of oil, and salt without prescribing how much. Whatsoever is commanded by the God of Heaven, let it be diligently done for the house of the God of Heaven, for why should there be wrath against the realm of the king and his sons? Also we certify you, that, touching any of the priests and Levites, singers, porters, Nethinim, or ministers of this house of God, it shall not be lawful to impose toll, tribute, or custom, upon them.

And thou, Ezra, after the wisdom of thy God that is in thine hand, set magistrates and judges which may judge all the people that are beyond the river, all such as know the laws of thy God, and teach ye them that know them not. And whosoever will not do the law of thy God and the law of the king, let judgment be executed speedily upon him, whether it be unto death, or to banishment, or to confiscation of goods, or to imprisonment.

Blessed be the Lord God of our fathers, which hath put such a thing as this in the king's heart, to beautify the house of the Lord which is in Jerusalem, and hath extended mercy unto me before the king and his counselors, and before all the king's mighty princes. And I was strengthened as the hand of the Lord my God was upon me and I gathered together out of Israel chief men to go up with me.

These are now the chief of their fathers, and this is the genealogy of them that went up with me from Babylon, in the reign of Artaxerxes the king: Of the sons of Phinehas, Gershom, of the sons of Ithamar, Daniel, of the sons of David, Hattush. Of the sons of Shechaniah, of the sons of Pharosh, Zechariah, and with him were reckoned by genealogy of the males a hundred and fifty. Of the sons of Pahath-moab, Elihoenai the son of Zerahiah, and with him two hundred males. Of the sons of Shechaniah, the son of Jonathan, and with him three hundred males. Of the sons also of Adin, Ebed the son of Jonathan, and with him fifty males. And of the sons of Elam, Jeshaiah the son of Athaliah, and with him seventy males. And of the sons of Shephatiah, Zebadiah the son of Michael, and with him fourscore males. Of the sons of Joab, Obadiah the son of Jehiel, and with him two hundred and eighteen males. And of the sons of Shelomith, the son of Josiphiah, and with him a hundred and threescore males. And of the sons of Bebai, Zechariah the son of Bebai, and with him twenty and eight males. And of the sons of Azgad, Johanan the son of Hakkatan, and with him a hundred and ten males. And of the last sons of Adonikam, whose names are these, Eliphelet, Jeiel, and Shemaiah, and with them threescore males. Of the sons also of Bigvai, Uthai, and Zabbud, and with them seventy males.

And I gathered them together to the river that runneth to Ahava and there abode we in tents three days and I viewed the people, and the priests, and found there none of the sons of Levi. Then sent I for Eliezer, for Ariel, for Shemaiah, and for Elnathan, and for Jarib, and for Elnatnan, and for Nathan, and for Zechariah, and for Meshullam, chief men, also for Joiarib, and for Elnathan, men of understanding. And I sent them with commandment unto Iddo the chief at the place Casiphia and I told them what they should say unto Iddo, and to his brethren the Nethinim at the place Casiphia, that they should bring unto us ministers for the house of our God. And by the good hand of our God upon us they brought us a man of understanding, of the sons of Mahili, the son of Levi, the son of Israel, and Sherebiah, with his sons and his brethren, eighteen, and Hashabiah, and with him Jeshaiah of the sons of Merari, his brethren and their sons, twenty, also of the Nethinim, whom David and the princes had appointed for the service of the Levites, two hundred and twenty Nethinim, all of them were expressed by name.

Then I proclaimed a fast there at the river of Ahava that we might afflict ourselves before our God, to seek of him a right way for us, and for our little ones, and for all our substance, for I was ashamed to require of the king a band of soldiers and horsemen to help us against the enemy in the way, because we had spoken unto the king saying, The hand of our God is upon all them for good that seek him, but his power and his wrath is against all them that forsake him. So we fasted and besought our God for this, and he was entreated of us.

Then I separated twelve of the chief of the priests, Sherebiah, Hashabiah, and ten of their brethren with them, and weighed unto them the silver, and the gold, and the vessels, even the offering of the house of our God, which the king, and his counselors, and his lords, and all Israel there present, had offered. I even weighed unto their hand six hundred and fifty talents of silver, and silver vessels a hundred talents, and of gold a hundred talents, also twenty basins of gold, of a thousand drams, and two vessels of fine copper, precious as gold. And I said unto them, Ye are holy unto the Lord, the vessels are holy also, and the silver and the gold are a freewill offering unto the Lord God of your fathers. Watch ye, and keep them, until ye weigh them before the chief of the priests and the Levites, and chief of the fathers of Israel, at Jerusalem, in the chambers of the house of the Lord. So took the priests and the Levites the weight of the silver, and the gold, and the vessels, to bring them to Jerusalem unto the house of our God.

Then we departed from the river of Ahava on the twelfth day of the first month to go unto Jerusalem, and the hand of our God was upon us, and he delivered us from the hand of the enemy, and of such as lay in wait by the way. And we came to Jerusalem and abode there three days.

Now on the fourth day was the silver and the gold and the vessels weighed in the house of our God by the hand of Meremoth the son of Uriah the priest, and with him was Eleazar the son of Phinehas, and with them was Jozabad the son of Jeshua, and Noadiah the son of Binnui, Levites, by number and by weight of everyone, and all the weight was written at that time.

Also the children of those that had been carried away, which were come out of the captivity, offered burnt offerings unto the God of Israel, twelve bullocks for all Israel, ninety and six rams, seventy and seven lambs, twelve he goats for a sin offering, all this was a burnt offering unto the Lord. And they delivered the king's commissions unto the king's lieutenants and to the governors on this side the river and they furthered the people and the house of God.

Now when these things were done, the princes came to me saying, The people of Israel, and the priests, and the Levites, have not separated themselves from the people of the lands, doing according to their abominations, even of the Canaanites, the Hittites, the Perizzites, the Jebusites, the Ammonites, the Moabites, the Egyptians, and the Amorites. For they have taken of their daughters for themselves and for their sons, so that the holy seed have mingled themselves with the people of those lands, yea, the hand of the princes and rulers hath been chief in this trespass. And when I heard this thing I rent my garment and my mantle, and plucked off the hair of my head and of my beard, and sat down astonished. Then were assembled unto me everyone that trembled at the words of the God of Israel because of the transgression of those that had been carried away and I sat astonished until the evening sacrifice. And at the evening sacrifice I arose up from my heaviness and having rent my garment and my mantle, I fell upon my knees and spread out my hands unto the Lord my God, and said,

O my God, I am ashamed and blush to lift up my face to thee, my God, for our iniquities are increased over our head and our trespass is grown up unto the heavens. Since the days of our fathers have we been in a great trespass unto this day and for our iniquities have we, our kings and our priests, been delivered into the hand of the kings of the lands, to the sword, to captivity, and to a spoil, and to confusion of face as it is this day. And now for a little space grace hath been showed from the Lord our God, to leave us a remnant to escape and to give us a nail in his holy place, that our God may lighten our eyes and give us a little reviving in our bondage. For we were bondmen, yet our God hath not forsaken us in our bondage, but hath extended mercy unto us in the sight of the kings of Persia, to give us a reviving, to set up the house of our God, and to repair the desolations thereof, and to give us a wall in Judah and in Jerusalem.

And now, O our God, what shall we say after this? For we have forsaken thy commandments which thou hast commanded by thy servants the prophets saying, The land, unto which ye go to possess it, is an unclean land with the filthiness of the people of the lands, with their abominations which have filled it from one end to another with their uncleanness. Now therefore give not your daughters unto their sons, neither take their daughters unto your sons, nor seek their peace or their wealth forever, that ye may be strong, and eat the good of the land, and leave it for an inheritance to your children forever. And after all that is come upon us for our evil deeds and for our great trespass, seeing that thou our God hast punished us less than our iniquities deserve and hast given us such deliverance as this, should we again break thy commandments and join in affinity with the people of these abominations? Wouldest not thou be angry with us till thou hadst consumed us so that there should be no remnant nor escaping? O Lord God of Israel, thou art righteous, for we remain yet escaped as it is this day, behold, we are before thee in our trespasses, for we cannot stand before thee because of this.

Now when Ezra had prayed and when he had confessed, weeping and casting himself down before the house of God, there assembled unto him out of Israel a very great congregation of men and women and children, for the people wept very sore. And Shechaniah the son of Jehiel, one of the sons of Elam, answered and said unto Ezra, We have trespassed against our God and have taken strange wives of the people of the land, yet now there is hope in Israel concerning this thing. Now therefore let us make a covenant with our God to put away all the wives and such as are born of them, according to the counsel of my lord and of those that tremble at the commandment of our God and let it be done according to the law. Arise, for this matter belongeth unto thee, we also will be with thee, be of good courage, and do it.

Then arose Ezra, and made the chief priests, the Levites, and all Israel to swear that they should do according to this word. And they sware.

Then Ezra rose up from before the house of God and went into the chamber of Johanan the son of Eliashib and when he came thither he did eat no bread, nor drink water, for he mourned because of the transgression of them that had been carried away. And they made proclamation throughout Judah and Jerusalem unto all the children of the captivity that they should gather themselves together unto Jerusalem and that whosoever would not come within three days, according to the counsel of the princes and the elders, all his substance should be forfeited and himself separated from the congregation of those that had been carried away.

Then all the men of Judah and Benjamin gathered themselves together unto Jerusalem within three days. It was the ninth month, on the twentieth day of the month and all the people sat in the street of the house of God trembling because of this matter and for the great rain. And Ezra the priest stood up, and said unto them, Ye have transgressed and have taken strange wives to increase the trespass of Israel. Now therefore make confession unto the Lord God of your fathers and do his pleasure and separate yourselves from the people of the land and from the strange wives. Then all the congregation answered and said with a loud voice, As thou hast said, so must we do. But the people are many and it is a time of much rain and we are not able to stand without, neither is this a work of one day or two, for we are many that have transgressed in this thing. Let now our rulers of all the congregation stand and let all them which have taken strange wives in our cities come at appointed times and with them the elders of every city and the judges thereof, until the fierce wrath of our God for this matter be turned from us. Only Jonathan the son of Asahel and Jahaziah the son of Tikvah were employed about this matter, and Meshullam and Shabbethai the Levite helped them.

And the children of the captivity did so. And Ezra the priest with certain chief of the fathers, after the house of their fathers and all of them by their names, were separated and sat down in the first day of the tenth month to examine the matter. And they made an end with all the men that had taken strange wives by the first day of the first month.

And among the sons of the priests there were found that had taken strange wives, namely, of the sons of Jeshua the son of Jozadak, and his brethren, Maaseiah, and Eliezer, and Jarib, and Gedaliah. And they gave their hands that they would put away their wives, and being guilty they offered a ram of the flock for their trespass. And of the sons of Immer, Hanani, and Zebadiah. And of the sons of Harim, Maaseiah, and Elijah, and Shemaiah, and Jehiel, and Uzziah. And of the sons of Pashur, Elioenai, Maaseiah, Ishamael, Nethaneel, Jozabad, and Elasah.

Also of the Levites, Jozabad, and Shimei, and Kelaiah, (the same is Kelita,) Pethahiah, Judah, and Eliezer.

Of the singers also, Eliashib, and of the porters, Shallum, and Telem, and Uri.

Moreover of Israel, of the sons of Parosh, Ramiah, and Jeziah, and Malchiah, and Miamin, and Eleazar, and Malchijah, and Benaiah. And of the sons of Elam, Mattaniah, Zechariah, and Jehiel, and Abdi, and Jeremoth, and Eliah. And of the sons of Zattu, Elioenai, Eliashib, Mattaniah, and Jeremoth, and Zabad, and Aziza. Of the sons also of Bebai, Jehohanan, Hananiah, Zabbai, and Athlai. And of the sons of Bani, Meshullam, Malluch, and Adaiah, Jashub, and Sheal, and Ramoth. And of the sons of Pahath-moab, Adna, and Chelal, Benaiah, Maaseiah, Mattaniah, Bezaleel, and Binnui, and Manasseh. And of the sons of Harim, Eliezer, Ishijah, Malchiah, Semaiah, Shimeon, Benjamin, Malluch, and Shemariah. Of the sons of Hashum, Mattenai, Mattathah, Zabad, Eliphelet, Jeremai, Manasseh, and Shimei. Of the sons of Bani, Maadai, Amram, and Uel, Benaiah, Bedeiah, Chelluh, Vaniah, Meremoth, Eliashib, Mattaniah, Mattenai, and Jaasau, and Bani, and Binnui, Shimei, and Shelemiah, and Nathan, and Adaiah, Machnadebai, Shashai, Sharai, Azareel, and Shelemiah, Shemariah, Shallum, Amariah, and Joseph. Of the sons of Nebo, Jeiel, Mattithiah, Zabad, Zebina, Jadau, and Joel, Benaiah. All these had taken strange wives and some of them had wives by whom they had children.

THE BOOK OF NEHEMIAH

THE words of Nehemiah the son of Hachaliah. And it came to pass in the month Chisleu, in the twentieth year, as I was in Shushan the palace, that Hanani, one of my brethren, came, he and certain men of Judah, and I asked them concerning the Jews that had escaped which were left of the captivity and concerning Jerusalem. And they said unto me, The remnant that are left of the captivity there in the province are in great affliction and reproach, the wall of Jerusalem also is broken down and the gates thereof are burned with fire.

And it came to pass when I heard these words that I sat down and wept and mourned certain days, and fasted and prayed before the God of Heaven, and said, I beseech thee, O Lord God of Heaven, the great and terrible God, that keepeth covenant and mercy for them that love him and observe his commandments, let thine ear now be attentive, and thine eyes open that thou mayest hear the prayer of thy servant which I pray before thee now, day and night, for the children of Israel thy servants and confess the sins of the children of Israel which we have sinned against thee, both I and my father's house have sinned. We have dealt very corruptly against thee and have not kept the commandments, nor the statutes, nor the judgments, which thou commandedst thy servant Moses. Remember, I beseech thee, the word that thou commandedst thy servant Moses saying, If ye transgress, I will scatter you abroad among the nations, but if ye turn unto me and keep my commandments and do them, though there were of you cast out unto the uttermost part of the Heaven, yet will I gather them from thence and will bring them unto the place that I have chosen to set my name there. Now these are thy servants and thy people whom thou hast redeemed by thy great power and by thy strong hand. O Lord, I beseech thee, let now thine ear be attentive to the prayer of thy servant and to the prayer of thy servants who desire to fear thy name, and prosper, I pray thee, thy servant this day and grant him mercy in the sight of this man. For I was the king's cupbearer

And it came to pass in the month Nisan, in the twentieth year of Artaxerxes the king, that wine was before him and I took up the wine and gave it unto the king. Now I had not been beforetime sad in his presence. Wherefore the king said unto me, Why is thy countenance sad, seeing thou art not sick? This is nothing else but sorrow of heart. Then I was very sore afraid and said unto the king, Let the king live forever; why should not my countenance be sad when the city, the place of my fathers' sepulchers, lieth waste and the gates thereof are consumed with fire? Then the king said unto me, For what dost thou make request? So I prayed to the God of Heaven. And I said unto the king, If it please the king, and if thy servant have found favor in thy sight, that thou wouldest send me unto Judah, unto the city of my fathers' sepulchers, that I may build it. And the king said unto me (the queen also sitting by him), For how long shall thy journey be? And when wilt thou return? So it pleased the king to send me and I set him a time. Moreover I said unto the king, If it please the king, let letters be given me to the governors beyond the river, that they may convey me over till I come into Judah and a letter unto Asaph the keeper of the king's forest, that he may gave me timber to make beams for the gates of the palace which appertained to the house, and for the wall of the city, and for the house that I shall enter into. And the king granted me according to the good hand of my God upon me.

2 THEN I came to the governors beyond the river and gave them the king's letters. Now the king had sent captains of the army and horsemen with me. When Sanballat the Horonite and Tobiah the servant the Ammonite heard of it, it grieved them exceedingly that there was come a man to seek the welfare of the children

of Israel. So I came to Jerusalem and was there three days. And I arose in the night I and some few men with me, neither told I any man what my God had put in my heart to do at Jerusalem, neither was there any beast with me save the beast that I rode upon. And I went out by night by the gate of the valley, even before the dragon well and to the dung port and viewed the walls of Jerusalem which were broken down and the gates thereof were consumed with fire. Then I went on to the gate of the fountain and to the king's pool, but there was no place for the beast that was under me to pass. Then went I up in the night by the brook and viewed the wall, and turned back and entered by the gate of the valley, and so returned. And the rulers knew not whither I went, or what I did, neither had I as yet told it to the Jews, nor to the priests, nor to the nobles, nor to the rulers, nor to the rest that did the work.

Then said I unto them, Ye see the distress that we are in, how Jerusalem lieth waste and the gates thereof are burned with fire; come and let us build up the wall of Jerusalem, that we be no more a reproach. Then I told them of the hand of my God which was good upon me as also the king's words that he had spoken unto me. And they said, Let us rise up and build. So they strengthened their hands for this good work. But when Sanballat the Horonite, and Tobiah the servant the Ammonite, and Geshem the Arabian heard it, they laughed us to scorn and despised us and said, What is this thing that ye do? Will ye rebel against the king? Then answered I them and said unto them, The God of Heaven, he will prosper us, therefore we his servants will arise and build, but ye have no portion, nor right, nor memorial, in Jerusalem.

Then Eliashib the high priest rose up with his brethren the priests and they builded the sheep gate, they sanctified it and set up the doors of it, even unto the tower of Meah they sanctified it, unto the tower of Hananeel. And next unto him builded the men of Jericho. And next to them builded Zaccur the son of Imri.

But the fish gate did the sons of Hassenaah build, who also laid the beams thereof, and set up the doors thereof, the locks thereof, and the bars thereof. And next unto them repaired Meremoth the son of Urijah, the son of Koz. And next unto them repaired Meshullam the son of Berechiah, the son of Meshezabeel. And next unto them repaired Zadok the son of Baana. And next unto them the Tekoites repaired, but their nobles put not their necks to the work of their Lord.

Moreover the old gate repaired Jehoiada the son of Paseah and Meshullam the son of Besodeiah, they laid the beams thereof, and set up the doors thereof, and the locks thereof, and the bars thereof. And next unto them repaired Melatiah the Gibeonite, and Jadon the Meronothite, the men of Gibeon and of Mizpah unto the throne of the governor on this side the river. Next unto him repaired Uzziel the son of Harhaiah, of the goldsmiths. Next unto him also repaired Hananiah the son of one of the apothecaries and they fortified Jerusalem unto the broad wall. And next unto them repaired Rephaiah the son of Hur, the ruler of the half part of Jerusalem. And next unto them repaired Jedaiah the son of Harumaph, even over against his house. And next unto him repaired Hattush the son of Hashabniah. Malchijah the son of Harim and Hashub the son of Pahath-moab repaired the other piece and the tower of the furnaces. And the next unto him repaired Shallum the son of Halohesh, the ruler of the half part of Jerusalem, he and his daughters.

The valley gate repaired Hanun and the inhabitants of Zanoah, they built it, and set up the doors thereof, the locks thereof, and the bars thereof, and a thousand cubits on the wall unto the dung gate.

But the dung gate repaired Malchiah the son of Rechab, the ruler of part of Beth-haccerem; he built it and set up the doors thereof, the locks thereof, and the bars thereof.

But the gate of the fountain repaired Shallum the son of Colhozeh, the ruler of part of Mizpah; he built it, and covered it, and set up the doors thereof, the locks thereof, and the bars thereof, and the wall of the pool of Siloah by the king's garden and unto the stairs that go down from the city of David. After him repaired Nehemiah the son of Azbuk, the ruler of the half part of Beth-zur, unto the place over against the sepulchers of David, and to the pool that was made, and unto the house of the mighty. After him repaired the Levites, Rehum the son of Bani. Next unto him repaired Hashabiah, the ruler of the half part of Keilah, in his part. After him repaired their brethren, Bavai the son of Henadad, the ruler of the half part of Kielah. And next to him repaired Ezer the son of Jeshua, the ruler of Mizpah, another piece over against the going up to the armory at the turning of the wall. After him Baruch the son of Zabbai earnestly repaired the other piece, from the turning of the wall unto the door of the house of Eliashib the high priest. After him repaired Meremoth the son of Urijah the son of Koz another piece, from the door of the house of Eliashib even to the end of the house of Eliashib. And after him repaired the priests, the men of the plain. After him repaired Benjamin and Hashub over against their house. After him repaired Azariah the son of Maaseiah the son of Ananiah by his house. After him repaired Binnui the son of Henadad another piece, from the house of Azariah unto the turning of the wall, even unto the corner. Palal the son of Uzai, over against the turning of the wall, and the tower which lieth out from the king's high house, that was by court of the prison. After him Pedaiah the son of Parosh. Moreover the Nethinim dwelt in Ophel unto the place over against the water gate toward the east and the tower that lieth out. After them the Tekoites repaired another piece over against the great tower that lieth out, even unto the wall of Ophel.

From above the horse gate repaired the priests, everyone over against his house. After them repaired Zadok the son of Immer over against his house. After him repaired also Shemaiah the son of Shechaniah, the keeper of the east gate. After him repaired Hananiah the son of Shelemiah and Hanun the sixth son of Zalaph another piece. After him repaired Meshullam the son of Berechiah over against his chamber. After him repaired Malchiah the goldsmith's son unto the place of the Nethinim and of the merchants, over against the gate Miphkad, and to the going up of the corner. And between the going up of the corner unto the sheep gate repaired the goldsmiths and the merchants.

But it came to pass that when Sanballat heard that we builded the wall, he was wroth, and took great indignation, and mocked the Jews. And he spake before his brethren and the army of Samaria and said, What do these feeble Jews? Will they fortify themselves? Will they sacrifice? Will they make an end in a day? Will they revive the stones out of the heaps of the rubbish which are burned? Now Tobiah the Ammonite was by him and he said, Even that which they build, if a fox go up, he shall even break down their stone wall.

Hear, O our God, for we are despised, and turn their reproach upon their own head, and give them for a prey in the land of captivity, and cover not their iniquity, and let not their sin be blotted out from before thee, for they have provoked thee to anger before the builders. So built we the wall, and all the wall was joined together unto the half thereof, for the people had a mind to work.

But it came to pass, that when Sanballat, and Tobiah, and the Arabians, and the Ammonites, and the Ashdodites heard that the walls of Jerusalem were made up and that the breaches began to be stopped, then they were very wroth and conspired all of them together to come and fight against Jerusalem and to hinder it. Nevertheless we made our prayer unto our God and set a watch against them day and night because of them. And Judah said, The strength of the bearers of burdens is decayed and there is much rubbish so that we are not able to build the wall. And our adversaries said, They shall not know, neither see till we come in the midst among them, and slay them, and cause the work to cease. And it came to pass that when the Jews which dwelt by them came, they said unto us ten times, From all places whence ye shall return unto us they will be upon you. Therefore set I in the lower places behind the wall and on the higher places, I even set the people after their families with their swords, their spears, and their bows. And I looked and rose up and said unto the nobles, and to the rulers, and to the rest of the people, Be not ye afraid of them, remember the Lord which is great and terrible, and fight for your brethren, your sons, and your daughters, your wives and your houses.

And it came to pass when our enemies heard that it was known unto us and God had brought their counsel to naught that we returned all of us to the wall, everyone unto his work. And it came to pass from that time forth that the half of my servants wrought in the work and the other half of them held both the spears, the shields, and the bows, and the habergeons, and the rulers were behind all the houses of Judah. They which builded on the wall and they that bare burdens with those that laded, everyone with one of his hands wrought in the work and with the other hand held a weapon. For the builders, everyone had his sword girded by his side and so builded. And he that sounded the trumpet was by me. And I said unto the nobles, and to the rulers, and to the rest of the people, The work is great and large and we are separated upon the wall, one far from another. In what place therefore ye hear the sound of the trumpet, resort ye thither unto us, our God shall fight for us.

So we labored in the work and half of them held the spears from the rising of the morning till the stars appeared. Likewise at the same time said I unto the people, Let everyone with his servant lodge within Jerusalem that in the night they may be a guard to us and labor on the day. So neither I, nor my brethren, nor my servants, nor the men of the guard which followed me, none of us put off our clothes saving that everyone put them off for washing.

And there was a great cry of the people and of their wives against their brethren the Jews. For there were that said, We, our sons, and our daughters are many, therefore we take up corn for them that we may eat and live. Some also there were that said, We have mortgaged our lands, vineyards, and houses that we might buy corn because of the dearth. There were also that said, We have borrowed money for the king's tribute, and that upon our lands and vineyards. Yet now our flesh is as the flesh of our brethren, our children as their children and lo, we bring into bondage our sons and our daughters to be servants, and some of our daughters are brought into bondage already, neither is it in our power to redeem them, for other men have our lands and vineyards.

And I was very angry when I heard their cry and these words. Then I consulted with myself and I rebuked the nobles and the rulers and said unto them, Ye exact usury, every one of his brother. And I set a great assembly against them. And I said unto them, We after our ability have redeemed our brethren the Jews which were sold unto the heathen, and will ye even sell your brethren? Or shall they be sold unto us? Then held they their peace and found nothing to answer. Also I said, It is not good that ye do, ought ye not to walk in the fear of our God because of the reproach of the heathen our enemies? I likewise, and my brethren, and my servants might exact of them money and corn, I pray you, let us leave off this usury. Restore, I pray you, to them, even this day their lands, their vineyards, their olive yards, and their houses, also the hundredth part of the money, and of the corn, the wine, and the oi, that ye exact of them. Then said they, We will restore them and will require nothing of them, so will we do as thou sayest. Then I called the priests and took an oath of them that they should do according to this promise. Also I shook my lap and said, So God shake out every man from his house and from his labor that performeth not this promise, even thus be he shaken out and emptied. And all the congregation said, Amen, and praised the Lord. And the people did according to this promise.

Moreover from the time that I was appointed to be their governor in the land of Judah, from the twentieth year even unto the two and thirtieth year of Artaxerxes the king, that is, twelve years, I and my brethren have not eaten the bread of the governor. But the former governors that had been before me were chargeable unto the people and had taken of them bread and wine besides forty shekels of silver, yea, even their servants bare rule over the people, but so did not I because of the fear of God. Yea, also I continued in the work of this wall, neither bought we any land and all my servants were gathered thither unto the work. Moreover there were at my table a hundred and fifty of the Jews and rulers besides those that came unto us from among the heathen that are about us. Now that which was prepared for me daily was one ox and six choice sheep, also fowls were prepared for me, and once in ten days store of all sorts of wine, yet for all this required not I the bread of the governor because the bondage was heavy upon this people. Think upon me, my God, for good according to all that I have done for this people.

Now it came to pass when Sanballat, and Tobiah, and Geshem the Arabian, and the rest of our enemies heard that I had builded the wall and that there was no breach left therein (though at that time I had not set up the doors upon the gates), that Sanballat and Geshem sent unto me saying, Come, let us meet together in some one of the villages in the plain of Ono. But they thought to do me mischief. And I sent messengers unto them saying, I am doing a great work so that I cannot come down; why should the work cease whilst I leave it and come down to you? Yet they sent unto me four times after this sort and I answered them after the same manner. Then sent Sanballat his servant unto me in like manner the fifth time with an open letter in his hand wherein was written, It is reported among the heathen and Gashmu saith it, that thou and the Jews think to rebel, for which cause thou buildest the wall, that thou mayest be their king according to these words. And thou hast also appointed prophets to preach of thee at Jerusalem saying, There is a king in Judah and now shall it be reported to the king according to these words. Come now therefore, and let us take counsel together. Then I sent unto him saying, There are no such things done as thou sayest, but thou feignest them out of thine own heart. For they all made us afraid saying, Their hands shall be weakened from the work that it be not done. Now therefore, O God, strengthen my hands.

Afterward I came unto the house of Shemaiah the son of Delaiah the son of Mehetabeel, who was shut up, and he said, Let us meet together in the house of God, within the temple, and let us shut the doors of the temple, for they will come to slay thee, yea, in the night will they come to slay thee. And I said, Should such a man as I flee? And who is mine enemy, that such a man as I would go into the temple to save his life? I will not go in. And, lo, I perceived that God had not sent him, but that he pronounced this prophecy against me, for Tobiah and Sanballat had hired him. Therefore should I be afraid of him he hired, and do so as he said, and sin, and that they might have me for an evil report, that they might reproach me? My God think thou upon Tobiah and Sanballat according to these their works, and on the prophetess Noadiah, and the rest of the prophets that would have put me in fear.

So the wall was finished in the twenty and fifth day of the month Elul, in fifty and two days. And it came to pass that when all our enemies heard thereof and all the heathen that were about us saw these things, they were much cast down in their own eyes, for they perceived that this work was wrought of our God. Moreover in those days the nobles of Judah sent many letters unto Tobiah and the letters of Tobiah came unto them. For there were many in Judah sworn unto him because he was the son-in-law of Shechaniah the son of Arah, and his son Johanan had taken the daughter of Meshullam the son of Berechiah. Also they reported his good deeds before me and uttered my words to him. And Tobiah sent letters to put me in fear.

Now it came to pass when the wall was built and I had set up the doors, and the porters and the singers and the Levites were appointed that I gave my brother Hanani and Hananiah the ruler of the palace charge over Jerusalem, for he was a faithful man and feared God above many. And I said unto them, Let not the gates of Jerusalem be opened until the sun be hot and while they stand by let them shut the doors, and bar them, and appoint watches of the inhabitants of Jerusalem, everyone in his watch and everyone to be over against his house. Now the city was large and great, but the people were few therein and the houses were not builded.

And my God put into mine heart to gather together the nobles, and the rulers, and the people, that they might be reckoned by genealogy. And I found a register of the genealogy of them which came up at the first and found written therein.

These are the children of the province that went up out of the captivity of those that had been carried away whom Nebuchadnezzar the king of Babylon had carried away and came again to Jerusalem and to Judah, everyone unto his city, who came with Zerubbabel, Jeshua, Nehemiah, Azariah, Raamaiah, Nahamani, Mordecai, Bilshan, Mispereth, Bigvai, Nehum, Baanah. The number, I say, of the men of the people of Israel was this:

The children of Parosh, two thousand a hundred seventy and two. The children of Shephatiah, three hundred seventy and two. The children of Arah, seven hundred seventy and five. The children of Pahath-moab, of the children of Jeshua and Joab, two thousand and eight hundred and twelve. The children of Elam, a thousand two hundred fifty and four. The children of Zattu, nine hundred forty and five. The children of Zaccai, seven hundred and threescore. The children of Bani, six hundred forty and two. The children of Bebai, six hundred twenty and three. The children of Azgad, a thousand two hundred twenty and two. The children of Adonikam, six hundred sixty and six. The children of Bigvai, two thousand fifty and six. The children of Adin, four hundred fifty and four. The children of Ater of Hezekiah, ninety and eight. The children of Hashum, two hundred twenty and three. The children of Bezai, three hundred twenty and three. The children of Jorah, a hundred and twelve. The children of Gibeon, ninety and five. The men of Bethlehem and Netophah, a hundred fourscore and eight. The men of Anthoth, a hundred twenty and eight. The men of Beth-azmaveth, forty and two. The men of Kirjath-jearim, Chephirah, and Beeroth, seven hundred forty and three. The men of Ramah and Gaba, six hundred twenty and one. The men of Michmas, a hundred and twenty and two. The men of Beth-el and Ai, two hundred twenty and three. The men of the other Nebo, fifty and two. The children of the other Elam, a thousand two hundred fifty and four. The children of Harim, three hundred and twenty. The children of Jericho, three hundred forty and five. The children of Lod, Hadid, and Ono, seven hundred twenty and five. The children of Senaah, three thousand six hundred and thirty.

The priests, the children of Jedaiah, of the house of Jeshua, nine hundred seventy and three. The children of Immer, a thousand fifty and two, the children of Pshur, a thousand two hundred forty and seven. The children of Harim, a thousand and seventeen.

The Levites, the children of Jeshua, of Kadmiel, and of the children of Hodevah, seventy and four. The singers of the children of Asaph, a hundred twenty and eight. The porters, the children of Shallum, the children of Ater, the children of Talmon, the children of Akkub, the children of Hatita, the children of Shobai, a hundred thirty and nine.

The Nethinim, the children of Ziha, the children of Hashupha, the children of Tabbaoth, the children of Keros, the children of Sia, the children of Padon, the children of Lebana, the children of Hagaba, the children of Shalmai, the children of Hanan, the children of Giddel, the children of Gahar, the children of Reaiah, the children of Rezin, the children of Nekoda, the children of Gazzam, the children of Uzza, the children of Phaseah, the children of Besai, the children of Meunim, the children of Nephishesim, the children of Bakbuk, the children of Hakupha, the children of Harhur, the children of Bazlith, the children of Mehida, the children of Harsha, the children of Barkos, the children of Sisera, the children of Tamah, the children of Neziah, the children of Hatipha.

The children of Solomon's servants, the children of Sotai, the children of Sophereth, the children of Perida, the children of Jaala, the children of Darkon, the children of Giddel, the children of Shephatiah, the children of Hattil, the children of Pochereth of Zebaim, the children of Amon. All the Nethinim, and the children of Solomon's servants were three hundred ninety and two.

And these were they which went up also from Tel-melah, Tel-haresha, Cherub, Addon, and Immer, but they could not show their father's house, nor their seed, whether they were of Israel. The children of Delaiah, the children of Tobiah, the children of Nekoda, six hundred fifty and two. And of the priests, the children of Habaiah, the children of Koz, the children of Barzillai, which took one of the daughters of Barzillai the Gileadite to wife and was called after their name. These sought their register among those that were reckoned by genealogy, but it was not found, therefore were they as polluted put from the priesthood. And the Tirshatha said unto them, that they should not eat of the most holy things till there stood up a priest with Urim and Thummim.

The whole congregation together was forty and two thousand three hundred and threescore, besides their manservants and their maidservants, of whom there were seven thousand three hundred thirty and seven and they had two hundred forty and five singing men and singing women. Their horses, seven hundred thirty and six, their mules, two hundred forty and five, their camels, four hundred thirty and five, six thousand seven hundred and twenty asses.

And some of the chief of the fathers gave unto the work. The Tirshatha gave to the treasure a thousand drams of gold, fifty basins, five hundred and thirty priests' garments. And some of the chief of the fathers gave to the treasure of the work twenty thousand drams of gold and two thousand and two hundred pounds of silver. And that which the rest of the people gave was twenty thousand drams of gold, and two thousand pounds of silver, and threescore and seven priests' garments. So the priests, and the Levites, and the porters, and the singers, and some of the people, and the Nethinim, and all Israel dwelt in their cities and when the seventh month came the children of Israel were in their cities.

And all the people gathered themselves together as one man into the street that was before the water gate and they spake unto Ezra the scribe to bring the book of the law of Moses which the Lord had commanded to Israel. And Ezra the priest brought the law before the congregation both of men and women and all that could hear with understanding, upon the first day of the seventh month. And he read therein before the street that was before the water gate from the morning until midday, before the men and the women and those that could understand, and the ears of all the people were attentive unto the book of the law. And Ezra the scribe stood upon a pulpit of wood which they had made for the purpose and beside him stood Mattithiah, and Shema, and Anaiah, and Urijah, and Hilkiah, and Maaseiah, on his right hand and on his left hand, Pedaiah, and Mishael, and Malchiah, and Hashum, and Hashbadana, Zechariah, and Meshullam. And Ezra opened the book in the sight of all the people (for he was above all the people), and when he opened it all the people stood up and Ezra blessed the Lord, the great God. And all the people answered, Amen, Amen, with lifting up their hands, and they bowed their heads and worshiped the Lord with their faces to the ground. Also Jeshua, and Bani, and Sherebiah, Jamin, Akkub, Shabbethai, Hodijah, Maaseiah, Kelita, Azariah, Jozabad, Hanan, Pelaiah, and the Levites caused the people to understand the law and the people stood in their place. So they read in the book in the law of God distinctly and gave the sense and caused them to understand the reading.

And Nehemiah, which is the Tirshatha, and Ezra the priest the scribe, and the Levites that taught the people, said unto all the people, This day is holy unto the Lord your God; mourn not, nor weep. For all the people wept when they heard the words of the law. Then he said unto them, Go your way, eat the fat, and drink the sweet, and send portions unto them for whom nothing is prepared, for this day is holy unto our Lord, neither be ye sorry, for the joy of the Lord is your strength. So the Levites stilled all the people saying, Hold your peace, for the day is holy, neither be ye grieved. And all the people went their way to eat, and to drink, and to send portions, and to make great mirth, because they had understood the words that were declared unto them.

And on the second day were gathered together the chief of the fathers of all the people, the priests and the Levites, unto Ezra the scribe, even to understand the words of the law. And they found written in the law which the Lord had commanded by Moses that the children of Israel should dwell in booths in the feast of the seventh month and that they should publish and proclaim in all their cities and in Jerusalem saying, Go forth unto the mount, and fetch olive branches, and pine branches, and myrtle branches, and palm branches, and branches of thick trees to make booths as it is written. So the people went forth, and brought them, and made themselves booths, everyone upon the roof of his house, and in their courts, and in the courts of the house of God, and in the street of the water gate, and in the street of the gate of Ephraim. And all the congregation of them that were come again out of the captivity made booths and sat under the booths, for since the days of Jeshua the son of Nun unto that day had not the children of Israel done so. And there was very great gladness. Also day by day, from the first day unto the last day, he read in the book of the law of God. And they kept the feast seven days, and on the eighth day was a solemn assembly according unto the manner.

Now in the twenty and fourth day of this month the children of Israel were assembled with fasting, and with sackclothes, and earth upon them. And the seed of Israel separated themselves from all strangers, and stood and confessed their sins, and the iniquities of their fathers. And they stood up in their place, and read in the book of the law of the Lord their God one fourth part of the day, and another fourth part they confessed and worshiped the Lord their God. Then stood up upon the stairs, of the Levites, Jeshua, and Bani, Kadmiel, Shebaniah, Bunni, Sherebiah, Bani, and Chenani, and cried with a loud voice unto the Lord their God.

Then the Levites, Jeshua, and Kadmiel, Bani, Hashabniah, Sherebiah, Hodijah, Shebaniah, and Pethahiah said, Stand up and bless the Lord your God for ever and ever, and blessed be thy glorious name which is exalted above all blessing and praise. Thou, even thou, art Lord alone, thou hast made Heaven, the Heaven of Heavens with all their host, the Earth and all things that are therein, the seas and all that is therein, and thou preservest them all and the host of Heaven worshipeth thee. Thou art the Lord the God who didst choose Abram, and broughtest him forth out of Ur of the Chaldees, and gavest him the name of Abraham, and foundest his heart faithful before thee, and madest a covenant with him to give the land of the Canaanites, the Hittites, the Amorites, and the Perizzites, and the Jebusites, and the Girgashites, to give it, I say, to his seed, and hast performed thy words, for thou art righteous and didst see the affliction of our fathers in Egypt, and heardest their cry by the Red Sea, and showedst signs and wonders upon Pharaoh, and on all his servants, and on all the people of his land, for thou knewest that they dealt proudly against them. So didst thou get thee a name, as it is this day. And thou didst divide the sea before them so that they went through the midst of the sea on the dry land, and their persecutors thou threwest into the deeps as a stone into the mighty waters. Moreover thou leddest them in the day by a cloudy pillar and in the night by a pillar of fire to give them light in the way wherein they should go. Thou camest down also upon mount Sinai, and spakest with them from Heaven, and gavest them right judgments, and true laws, good statutes and commandments, and madest known unto them thy holy sabbath, and commandedst them precepts, statutes, and laws by the hand of Moses thy servant, and gavest them bread from Heaven for their hunger, and broughtest forth water for them out of the rock for their thirst, and promisedst them that they should go in to possess the land which thou hadst sworn to give them. But they and our fathers dealt proudly, and hardened their necks, and hearkened not to thy commandments, and refused to obey, neither were mindful of thy wonders that thou didst among them, but hardened their necks and in their rebellion appointed a captain to return to their bondage, but thou art a God ready to pardon, gracious and merciful, slow to anger and of great kindness, and forsookest them not. Yea, when they had made them a molten calf and said, This is thy God that brought thee up out of Egypt and had wrought great provocations, yet thou in thy manifold mercies forsookest them not in the wilderness, the pillar of the cloud departed not from them by day to lead them in the way, neither the pillar of fire by night to show them light and the way wherein they should go. Thou gavest also thy good Spirit to instruct them and withheldest not thy manna from their mouth and gavest them water for their thirst. Yea, forty years didst thou sustain them in the wilderness so that they lacked nothing, their clothes waxed not old, and their feet swelled not. Moreover thou gavest them kingdoms and nations and didst divide them into corners so they possessed the land of Sihon, and the land of the king of Heshbon, and the land of Og king of Bashan. Their children also multipliedst thou as the stars of Heaven and broughtest them into the land concerning which thou hadst promised to their fathers that they should go in to possess it. So the children went in and possessed the land and thou subduedst before them the inhabitants of the land, the Canaanites, and gavest them into their hands, with their kings and the people of the land, that they might do with them as they would. And they took strong cities and a fat land and possessed houses full of all goods, wells digged, vineyards, and olive yards, and fruit trees in abundance, so they did eat, and were filled, and became fat, and delighted themselves in thy great goodness. Nevertheless they were disobedient, and rebelled against thee, and cast thy law behind their backs, and slew thy prophets which testified against them to turn them to thee, and they wrought great provocations. Therefore thou deliveredst them into the hand of their enemies who vexed them, and in the time of their trouble when they cried unto thee thou heardest them from Heaven, and according to thy manifold mercies thou gavest them saviors who saved them out of the hand of their enemies. But after they had rest they did evil again before thee, therefore leftest thou them in the hand of their enemies so that they had the dominion over them, yet when they returned and cried unto thee, thou heardest them from Heaven and many times didst thou deliver them according to thy mercies, and testifiedst against them that thou mightest bring them again unto thy law. Yet they dealt proudly and hearkened not unto thy commandments, but sinned against thy judgments (which if a man do, he shall live in them), and withdrew the shoulder, and hardened their neck, and would not hear. Yet many years didst thou forbear them and testifiedst against them by thy Spirit in thy prophets, yet would they not give ear, therefore gavest thou them into the hand of the people of the lands. Nevertheless for thy great mercies' sake thou didst not utterly consume them nor forsake them, for thou art a gracious and merciful God. Now therefore, our God, the great, the mighty, and the terrible God who keepest covenant and mercy, let not all the trouble seem little before thee that hath come upon us, on our kings, on our princes, and on our priests, and on our prophets, and on our fathers, and on all thy people, since the time of the kings of Assyria unto this day. Howbeit thou art just in all that is brought upon us, for thou hast done right, but we have done wickedly, neither have our kings, our princes, our priests, nor our fathers kept thy law, nor hearkened unto thy commandments and thy testimonies wherewith thou didst testify against them. For they have not served thee in their kingdom, and in thy great goodness that thou gavest them, and in the large and fat land which thou gavest before them, neither turned they from their wicked works. Behold, we are servants this day and for the land that thou gavest unto our fathers to eat the fruit thereof and the good thereof, behold, we are servants in it, and it yieldeth much increase unto the kings whom thou hast set over us because of our sins, also they have dominion over our bodies, and over our cattle at their pleasure, and we are in great distress. And because of all this we make a sure covenant and write it, and our princes, Levites, and priests, seal unto it.

Now those that sealed were, Nehemiah, the Tirshatha, the son of Hachaliah, and Zidkijah, Seraiah, Azariah, Jeremiah, Pashur, Amariah, Malchijah, Hattush, Shebaniah, Malluch, Harim, Meremoth, Obadiah, Daniel, Ginnethon, Baruch, Meshullam, Abijah, Mijamin, Maaziah, Bilgai, Shemaiah, these were the priests. And the Levites, both Jeshua the son of Azaniah, Binnui of the sons of Henadad, Kadmiel, and their brethren, Shebaniah, Hodijah, Kelita, Pelaiah, Hanan, Micha, Rehob, Hashabiah, Zaccur, Sherebiah, Shebaniah, Hodijah, Bani, Beninu. The chief of the people, Parosh, Pahath-moab, Elam, Zatthu, Bani, Bunni, Azgad, Behai, Adonijah, Bigvai, Adin, Ater, Hizkijah, Azzur, Aodijah, Hashum, Bezai, Aariph, Anathoth, Nebai, Magpiash, Meshullam, Hezir, Meshezabeel, Zadok, Jaddua, Pelatiah, Hanan, Anaiah, Hoshea, Hananiah, Hashub, Hallohesh, Pileha, Shobek, Rehum, Hashabnah, Maaseiah. And Ahijah, Hanan, Anan, Malluch, Harim, Baanah.

And the rest of the people, the priests, the Levites, the porters, the singers, the Nethinim, and all they that had separated themselves from the people of the lands unto the law of God, their wives, their sons, and their daughters, everyone having knowledge and having understanding, they clave to their brethren their nobles, and entered into an oath that a curse should come upon them if they did not walk in God's law which was given by Moses the servant of God, and to observe and do all the commandments of the Lord their God, and his judgments and statutes and that they would not give their daughters unto the people of the land, nor take the daughters of the people for their sons. And if the people of the land bring ware or any victuals on the sabbath day to sell, that we would not buy it of them on the sabbath, or on the holy day, and that we would leave the seventh year and the exaction of every debt.

Also we made ordinances for us, to charge ourselves yearly with the third part of a shekel for the service of the house of our God, for the shewbread, and for the continual meat offering, and for the continual burnt offering, of the sabbaths, of the new moons, for the set feasts, and for the holy things, and for the sin offerings to make an atonement for Israel, and for all the work of the house of our God.

And we cast the lots among the priests, the Levites, and the people for the wood offering, to bring it into the house of our God, after the houses of our fathers, at times appointed year by year to burn upon the altar of the Lord our God as it is written in the law, and to bring the firstfruits of our ground and the firstfruits of all fruit of all trees, year by year, unto the house of the Lord, also the firstborn of our sons and of our cattle as it is written in the law, and the firstlings of our herds and of our flocks, to bring to the house of our God unto the priests that minister in the house of our God, and that we should bring the firstfruits of our dough, and our offerings, and the fruit of all manner of trees, of wine, and of oil unto the priests, to the chambers of the house of our God, and the tithes of our ground unto the Levites that the same Levites might have the tithes in all the cities of our tillage. And the priest the son of Aaron shall be with the Levites when the Levites take tithes, and the Levites shall bring up the tithe of the tithes unto the house of our God, to the chambers, into the treasure house. For the children of Israel and the children of Levi shall bring the offering of the corn, of the new wine, and the oil, unto the chambers where are the vessels of the sanctuary, and the priests that minister, and the porters, and the singers, and we will not forsake the house of our God.

And the rulers of the people dwelt at Jerusalem; the rest of the people also cast lots to bring one of ten to dwell in Jerusalem the holy city and nine parts to dwell in other cities. And the people blessed all the men that willingly offered themselves to dwell at Jerusalem. Now these are the chief of the province that dwelt in Jerusalem, but in the cities of Judah dwelt everyone in his possession in their cities, to wit, Israel, the priests, and the Levites, and the Nethinim, and the children of Solomon's servants. And at Jerusalem dwelt certain of the children of Judah, and of the children of Benjamin. Of the children of Judah, Athaiah the son of Uzziah, the son of Zechariah, the son of Amariah, the son of Shephatiah, the son of Mahalaleel, of the children of Perez, and Maaseiah the son of Baruch, the son of Col-hozeh, the son of Hazaiah, the son of Adaiah, the son of Joiarib, the son of Zechariah, the son of Shiloni. All the sons of Perez that dwelt at Jerusalem were four hundred threescore and eight valiant men. And these are the sons of Benjamin, Sallu the son of Meshullam, the son of Joed, the son of Pedaiah, the son of Kolaiah, the son of Maaseiah, the son of Ithiel, the son of Jesaiah. And after him Gabbai, Sallai, nine hundred twenty and eight. And Joel the son of Zichri was their overseer and Judah the son of Senuah was second over the city.

Of the priests, Jedaiah the son of Joiarib, Jachin. Seraiah the son of Hilkiah, the son of Meshullam, the son of Zadok, the son of Meraioth, the son of Ahitub, was the ruler of the house of God. And their brethren that did the work of the house were eight hundred twenty and two, and Adaiah the son of Jeroham, the son of Pelaliah, the son of Amnzi, the son of Zechariah, the son of Pashur, the son of Malchiah, and his brethren, chief of the fathers, two hundred forty and two, and Amashai the son of Azareel, the son of Ahasai, the son of Meshillemoth, the son of Immer, and their brethren, mighty men of valor, a hundred twenty and eight, and their overseer was Zabdiel, the son of one of the great men.

Also of the Levites, Shemaiah the son of Hashub, the son of Azrikam, the son of Hashabiah, the son of Bunni, and Shabbethai and Jozabad, of the chief of the Levites, had the oversight of the outward business of the house of God. And Mattaniah the son of Micha, the son of Zabdi, the son of Asaph, was the principal to begin the thanksgiving in prayer, and Bakbukiah the second among his brethren, and Abda the son of Shammua, the son of Galal, the son of Jeduthun. All the Levites in the holy city were two hundred fourscore and four. Moreover the porters, Akkub, Talmon, and their brethren that kept the gates, were a hundred seventy and two.

And the residue of Israel, of the priests, and the Levites, were in all the cities of Judah, everyone in his inheritance. But the Nethinim dwelt in Ophel and Ziha and Gispa were over the Nethinim. The overseer also of the Levites at Jerusalem was Uzzi the son of Bani, the son of Hashabiah, the son of Mattaniah, the son of Micha. Of the sons of Asaph, the singers were over the business of the house of God. For it was the king's commandment concerning them that a certain portion should be for the singers, due for every day. And Pethahiah the son of Meshezabeel, of the children of Zerah the son of Judah, was at the king's hand in all matters concerning the people.

And for the villages with their fields, some of the children of Judah dwelt at Kirjath-arba and in the villages thereof, and at Dibon and in the villages thereof, and at Jekabzeel and in the villages thereof, and at Jeshua, and at Moladah, and at Beth-phelet, and at Hazar-shual, and at Beer-sheba and in the villages thereof, and at Ziklag, and at Mekonah and in the villages thereof, and at En-rimmon, and at Zareah, and at Jarmuth, Zanoah, Adullam and in their villages, at Lachish and the fields thereof, at Azekah and in the villages thereof. And they dwelt from Beer-sheba unto the valley of Hinnom. The children also of Benjamin from Geba dwelt at Michmash, and Aija, and Beth-el and in their villages, and at Anathoth, Nob, Ananiah, Hazor, Ramah, Gittaim, Hadid, Zeboim, Neballat, Lod, and Ono, the valley of craftsmen. And of the Levites were divisions in Judah, and in Benjamin.

Now these are the priests and the Levites that went up with Zerubbabel the son of Shealtiel, and Jeshua: Seraiah, Jeremiah, Ezra, Amariah, Malluch, Hattush, Shechaniah, Rehum, Meremoth, Iddo, Ginnetho, Abijah, Miamin, Maadiah, Bigah, Shemaiah, and Joiarib, Jedaiah, Sallu, Amok, Hilkiah, Jedaiah. These were the chief of the priests and of their brethren in the days of Jeshua. Moreover the Levites, Jeshua, Binnui, Kadmiel, Sherebiah, Judah, and Mattaniah, which was over the thanksgiving, he and his brethren. Also Bakbukiah and Unni, their brethren, were over against them in the watches.

And Jeshua begat Joiakim, Joiakim also begat Eliashib, and Eliashib begat Joiada. And Joiada begat Jonathan, and Jonathan begat Jaddua.

And in the days of Joiakim were priests, the chief of the fathers, of Seraiah, Meraiah, of Jeremiah, Hananiah, of Ezra, Meshullam, of Amariah, Jehohanan, of Melicu, Jonathan, of Shebaniah, Joseph, of Harim, Adna, of Meraioth, Helkai, of Iddo, Zechariah, of Ginnethon, Meshullam, of Abijah, Zichri, of Miniamin, of Moadiah, Piltai, of Bilgah, Shammua, of Shemaiah, Jehonathan, and of Joiarib, Mattenai, of Jedaiah, Uzzi, of Sallai, Kallai, of Amok, Eber, of Hilkiah, Hashabiah, of Jedaiah, Nethaneel.

The Levites in the days of Eliashib, Joiada, and Johanan, and Jaddua were recorded chief of the fathers, also the priests, to the reign of Darius the Persian. The sons of Levi, the chief of the fathers, were written in the book of the Chronicles, even until the days of Johanan the son of Eliashib. And the chief of the Levites, Hashabiah, Sherebiah, and Jeshua the son of Kadmiel, with their brethren over against them, to praise and to give thanks according to the commandment of David the man of God, ward over against ward. Mattaniah, and Bakbukiah, Obadiah, Meshullam, Talmon, Akkub, were porters keeping the ward at the thresholds of the gates. These were in the days of Joiakim the son of Jeshua, the son of Jozadak, and in the days of Nehemiah the governor, and of Ezra the priest, the scribe.

And at the dedication of the wall of Jerusalem they sought the Levites out of all their places, to bring them to Jerusalem, to keep the dedication with gladness, both with thanksgivings and with singing, with cymbals, psalteries, and with harps. And the sons of the singers gathered themselves together, both out of the plain country round about Jerusalem and from the villages of Netophathi, also from the house of Gilgal and out of the fields of Geba and Azmaveth, for the singers had builded them villages round about Jerusalem, and the priests and the Levites purified themselves and purified the people, and the gates, and the wall.

Then I brought up the princes of Judah upon the wall and appointed two great companies of them that gave thanks, whereof one went on the right hand upon the wall toward the dung gate and after them went Hoshaiah, and half of the princes of Judah, and Azariah, Ezra, and Meshullam, Judah, and Benjamin, and Shemaiah, and Jeremiah, and certain of the priests' sons with trumpets, namely, Zechariah, the son of Jonathan, the son of Shemaiah, the son of Mattaniah, the son of Michaiah, the son of Zaccur, the son of Asaph, and his brethren, Shemaiah, and Azarael, Milalai, Gilalai, Maai, Nethaneel, and Judah, Hanani, with the musical instruments of David the man of God, and Ezra the scribe before them. And at the fountain gate which was over against them they went up by the stairs of the city of David, at the going up of the wall, above the house of David, even unto the water gate eastward.

And the other company of them that gave thanks went over against them, and I after them, and the half of the people upon the wall from beyond the tower of the furnaces even unto the broad wall, and from above the gate of Ephraim, and above the old gate, and above the fish gate, and the tower of Hananeel, and the tower of Meah, even unto the sheep gate, and they stood still in the prison gate. So stood the two companies of them that gave thanks in the house of God, and I, and the half of the rulers with me, and the priests, Eliakim, Maaseiah, Miniamin, Michaiah, Elioenai, Zechariah, and Hananiah, with trumpets, and Maaseiah, and Shemaiah, and Eleazar, and Uzzi, and Jehohanan, and Malchijah, and Elam, and Ezer. And the singers sang loud with Jezrahiah their overseer. Also that day they offered great sacrifices and rejoiced, for God had made them rejoice with great joy, the wives also and the children rejoiced so that the joy of Jerusalem was heard even afar off.

And at that time were some appointed over the chambers for the treasures, for the offerings, for the firstfruits and for the tithes, to gather into them out of the fields of the cities the portions of the law for the priests and Levites, for Judah rejoiced for the priests and for the Levites that waited. And both the singers and the porters kept the ward of their God and the ward of the purification according to the commandment of David and of Solomon his son. For in the days of David and Asaph of old there were chief of the singers and songs of praise and thanksgiving unto God. And all Israel in the days of Zerubbabel and in the days of Nehemiah gave the portions of the singers and the porters every day his portion, and they sanctified holy things unto the Levites, and the Levites sanctified them unto the children of Aaron.

On that day they read in the book of Moses in the audience of the people and therein was found written that the Ammonite and the Moabite should not come into the congregation of God for ever because they met not the children of Israel with bread and with water, but hired Baalam against them that he should curse them, howbeit our God turned the curse into a blessing. Now it came to pass when they had heard the law that they separated from Israel all the mixed multitude.

And before this, Eliashib the priest, having the oversight of the chamber of the house of our God, was allied unto Tobiah and he had prepared for him a great chamber where aforetime they laid the meat offerings, the frankincense, and the vessels, and the tithes of the corn, the new wine, and the oil which was commanded to be given to the Levites, and the singers, and the porters, and the offerings of the priests. But in all this time was not I at Jerusalem, for in the two and thirtieth year of Artaxerxes king of Babylon came I unto the king, and after certain days obtained I leave of the king and I came to Jerusalem and understood of the evil that Eliashib did for Tobiah in preparing him a chamber in the courts of the house of God. And it grieved me sore, therefore I cast forth all the household stuff of Tobiah out of the chamber. Then I commanded and they cleansed the chambers, and thither brought I again the vessels of the house of God with the meat offering and the frankincense.

And I perceived that the portions of the Levites had not been given them, for the Levites and the singers that did the work were fled everyone to his field. Then contended I with the rulers and said, Why is the house of God forsaken? And I gathered them together and set them in their place. Then brought all Judah the tithe of the corn and the new wine and the oil unto the treasuries. And I made treasurers over the treasuries Shelemiah the priest, and Zadok the scribe, and of the Levites, Pedaiah, and next to them was Hanan the son of Zaccur, the son of Mattaniah, for they were counted faithful and their office was to distribute unto their brethren. Remember me, O my God, concerning this and wipe not out my good deeds that I have done for the house of my God and for the offices thereof.

In those days saw I in Judah some treading wine-presses on the sabbath, and bringing in sheaves, and lading asses, as also wine, grapes, and figs, and all manner of burdens, which they brought into Jerusalem on the sabbath day, and I testified against them in the day wherein they sold victuals. There dwelt men of Tyre also therein, which brought fish, and all manner of ware, and sold on the sabbath unto the children of Judah, and in Jerusalem. Then I contended with the nobles of Judah and said unto them, What evil thing is this that ye do and profane the sabbath day? Did not your fathers thus and did not our God bring all this evil upon us and upon this city, yet ye bring more wrath upon Israel by profaning the sabbath.

And it came to pass, that when the gates of Jerusalem began to be dark before the sabbath, I commanded that the gates should be shut and charged that they should not be opened till after the sabbath and some of my servants set I at the gates that there should no burden be brought in on the sabbath day. So the merchants and sellers of all kind of ware lodged without Jerusalem once or twice. Then I testified against them and said unto them, Why lodge ye about the wall? If ye do so again, I will lay hands on you. From that time forth came they no more on the sabbath. And I commanded the Levites that they should cleanse themselves and that they should come and keep the gates to sanctify the sabbath day. Remember me, O my God, concerning this also and spare me according to the greatness of thy mercy.

In those days also saw I Jews that had married wives of Ashdod, of Ammon, and of Moab, and their children spake half in the speech of Ashdod and could not speak in the Jews' language, but according to the language of each people. And I contended with them. and cursed them, and smote certain of them, and plucked off their hair, and made them swear by God saying, Ye shall not give your daughters unto their sons, nor take their daughters unto your sons or for yourselves. Did not Solomon king of Israel sin by these things? Yet among many nations was there no king like him who was beloved of his God and God made him king over all Israel, nevertheless even him did outlandish women cause to sin. Shall we then hearken unto you to do all this great evil, to transgress against our God in marrying strange wives? And one of the sons of Joiada, the son of Eliashib the high priest, was son-in-law to Sanballat the Horonite, therefore I chased him from me. Remember then, O my God, because they have defiled the priesthood and the covenant of the priesthood and of the Levites.

Thus cleansed I them from all strangers and appointed the wards of the priests and the Levites, everyone in his business and for the wood offering, at times appointed, and for the firstfruits. Remember me, O my God, for good.

THE BOOK OF ESTHER

NOW it came to pass in the days of Ahasuerus (this is Ahasuerus which reigned from India even unto Ethiopia, over a hundred and seven and twenty provinces), that in those days when the king Ahasuerus sat on the throne of his kingdom which was in Shushan the palace, in the third year of his reign he made a feast unto all his princes and his servants: the power of Persia and Media, the nobles and princes of the provinces being before him, when he showed the riches of his glorious kingdom and the honor of his excellent majesty many days, even a hundred and fourscore days. And when these days were expired the king made a feast unto all the people that were present in Shushan the palace, both unto great and small, seven days, in the court of the garden of the king's palace, where were white, green, and blue hangings, fastened with cords of fine linen and purple to silver rings and pillars of marble; the beds were of gold and silver upon a pavement of red, and blue, and white, and black marble. And they gave them drink in vessels of gold (the vessels being diverse one from another) and royal wine in abundance according to the state of the king. And the drinking was according to the law; none did compel for so the king had appointed to all the officers of his house, that they should do according to every man's pleasure. Also Vashti the queen made a feast for the women in the royal house which belonged to king Ahasuerus.

On the seventh day, when the heart of the king was merry with wine, he commanded Mehuman, Biztha, Harbona, Bigtha, and Abagtha, Zethar, and Carcas, the seven chamberlains that served in the presence of Ahasuerus the king, to bring Vashti the queen before the king with the crown royal, to show the people and the princes her beauty, for she was fair to look on. But the queen Vashti refused to come at the king's commandment by his chamberlains, therefore was the king very wroth and his anger burned in him.

Then the king said to the wise men which knew the times (for so was the king's manner toward all that knew law and judgment; and the next unto him was Carshena, Shethar, Admatha, Tarshish, Meres, Marsena, and Memucan, the seven princes of Persia and Media, which saw the king's face and which sat the first in the kingdom), What shall we do unto the queen Vashti according to law because she hath not performed the commandment of the king Ahasuerus by the chamberlains? And Memucan answered before the king and the princes, Vashti the queen hath not done wrong to the king only, but also to all the princes and to all the people that are in all the provinces of the king Ahasuerus. For this deed of the queen shall come abroad unto all women so that they shall despise their husbands in their eyes when it shall be reported. The king Ahasuerus commanded Vashti the queen to be brought in before him, but she came not. Likewise shall the ladies of Persia and Media say this day unto all the king's princes which have heard of the deed of the queen. Thus shall there arise too much contempt and wrath. If it please the king, let there go a royal commandment from him, and let it be written among the laws of the Persians and the Medes that it be not altered, that Vashti come no more before king Ahasuerus and let the king give her royal estate unto another that is better than she. And when the king's decree, which he shall make, shall be published throughout all his empire (for it is great), all the wives shall give to their husbands honor, both to great and small.

And the saying pleased the king and the princes and the king did according to the word of Memucan, for he sent letters into all the king's provinces, into every province according to the writing thereof and to every people after their language, that every man should bear rule in his own house and that it should be published according to the language of every people.

After these things, when the wrath of king Ahasuerus was appeased, he remembered Vashti, and what she had done, and what was decreed against her. Then said the king's servants that ministered unto him, Let there be fair young virgins sought for the king and let the king appoint officers in all the provinces of his kingdom that they may gather together all the fair young virgins unto Shushan the palace, to the house of the women, unto the custody of Hegai the king's chamberlain, keeper of the women; and let their things for purification be given them; and let the maiden which pleaseth the king be queen instead of Vashti. And the thing pleased the king and he did so.

Now in Shushan the palace there was a certain Jew whose name was Mordecai the son of Jair the son of Shimei the son of Kish, a Benjamite, who had been carried away from Jerusalem with the captivity which had been carried away with Jeconiah king of Judah, whom Nebuchadnezzar the king of Babylon had carried away. And he brought up Hadassah, that is, Esther, his uncle's daughter, for she had neither father nor mother and the maid was fair and beautiful, whom Mordecai, when her father and mother were dead, took for his own daughter.

So it came to pass, when the king's commandment and his decree was heard and when many maidens were gathered together unto Shushan the palace to the custody of Hegai, that Esther was brought also unto the king's house to the custody of Hegai, keeper of the women. And the maiden pleased him and she obtained kindness of him, and he speedily gave her her things for purification with such things as belonged to her, and seven maidens which were meet to be given her out of the king's house, and he preferred her and her maids unto the best place of the house of the women. Esther had not showed her people nor her kindred, for Mordecai had charged her that she should not show it. And Mordecai walked every day before the court of the women's house, to know how Esther did and what should become of her.

Now when every maid's turn was come to go in to king Ahasuerus after that she had been twelve months according to the manner of the women,(for so were the days of their purifications accomplished: to wit, six months with oil of myrrh, and six months with sweet odors, and with other things for the purifying of the women), then thus came every maiden unto the king; whatsoever she desired was given her to go with her out of the house of the women unto the king's house. In the evening she went and on the morrow she returned into the second house of the women to the custody of Shaashgaz, the king's chamberlain, which kept the concubines; she came in unto the king no more, except the king delighted in her and that she were called by name.

Now when the turn of Esther, the daughter of Abihail the uncle of Mordecai, who had taken her for his daughter, was come to go in unto the king, she required nothing but what Hegai the king's chamberlain, the keeper of the women, appointed. And Esther obtained favor in the sight of all them that looked upon her. So Esther was taken unto king Ahasuerus into his house royal in the tenth month, which is the month Tebeth, in the seventh year of his reign.

And the king loved Esther above all the women and she obtained grace and favor in his sight more than all the virgins so that he set the royal crown upon her head and made her queen instead of Vashti. Then the king made a great feast unto all his princes and his servants, even Esther's feast, and he made a release to the provinces and gave gifts according to the state of the king.

And when the virgins were gathered together the second time, then Mordecai sat in the king's gate. Esther had not yet showed her kindred nor her people, as Mordecai had charged her, for Esther did the commandment of Mordecai, like as when she was brought up with him.

In those days, while Mordecai sat in the king's gate, two of the king's chamberlains, Bigthan and Teresh, of those which kept the door, were wroth and sought to lay hand on the king Ahasuerus. And the thing was known to Mordecai, who told it unto Esther the queen, and Esther certified the king thereof in Mordecai's name. And when inquisition was made of the matter it was found out, therefore they were both hanged on a tree; and it was written in the book of the chronicles before the king.

After these things did king Ahasuerus promote Haman the son of Hammedatha the Agagite, and advanced him and set his seat above all the princes that were with him. And all the king's servants that were in the king's gate, bowed and reverenced Haman, for the king had so commanded concerning him. But Mordecai bowed not, nor did him reverence. Then the king's servants which were in the king's gate said unto Mordecai, Why transgressest thou the king's commandment? Now it came to pass, when they spake daily unto him, and he hearkened not unto them, that they told Haman, to see whether Mordecai's matters would stand, for he had told them that he was a Jew. And when Haman saw that Mordecai bowed not nor did him reverence, then was Haman full of wrath. And he thought scorn to lay hands on Mordecai alone, for they had showed him the people of Mordecai; wherefore Haman sought to destroy all the Jews that were throughout the whole kingdom of Ahasuerus, even the people of Mordecai.

In the first month, that is, the month Nisan, in the twelfth year of king Ahasuerus, they cast Pur, that is, the lot, before Haman from day to day and from month to month, to the twelfth month, that is, the month Adar. And Haman said unto king Ahasuerus, There is a certain people scattered abroad and dispersed among the people in all the provinces of thy kingdom, and their laws are diverse from all people, neither keep they the king's laws, therefore it is not for the king's profit to suffer them. If it please the king, let it be written that they may be destroyed and I will pay ten thousand talents of silver to the hands of those that have the charge of the business, to bring it into the king's treasuries. And the king took his ring from his hand and gave it unto Haman the son of Hammedatha the Agagite, the Jews' enemy. And the king said unto Haman, The silver is given to thee, the people also, to do with them as it seemeth good to thee.

Then were the king's scribes called on the thirteenth day of the first month and there was written according to all that Haman had commanded unto the king's lieutenants, and to the governors that were over every province, and to the rulers of every people of every province according to the writing thereof, and to every people after their language; in the name of king Ahasuerus was it written and sealed with the king's ring. And the letters were sent by posts into all the king's provinces, to destroy, to kill, and to cause to perish, all Jews, both young and old, little children and women, in one day, even upon the thirteenth day of the twelfth month, which is the month Adar, and to take the spoil of them for a prey. The copy of the writing for a commandment to be given in every province was published unto all people that they should be ready against that day. The posts went out, being hastened by the king's commandment, and the decree was given in Shushan the palace. And the king and Haman sat down to drink, but the city Shushan was perplexed.

When Mordecai perceived all that was done, Mordecai rent his clothes and put on sackcloth with ashes, and went out into the midst of the city, and cried with a loud and a bitter cry, and came even before the king's gate, for none might enter into the king's gate clothed with sackcloth. And in every province, whithersoever the king's commandment and his decree came, there was great mourning among the Jews, and fasting, and weeping, and wailing, and many lay in sackcloth and ashes.

So Esther's maids and her chamberlains came and told it her. Then was the queen exceedingly grieved and she sent raiment to clothe Mordecai and to take away his sackcloth from him, but he received it not. Then called Esther for Hatach, one of the king's chamberlains whom he had appointed to attend upon her, and gave him a commandment to Mordecai, to know what it was and why it was. So Hatach went forth to Mordecai unto the street of the city which was before the king's gate. And Mordecai told him of all that had happened unto him and of the sum of the money that Haman had promised to pay to the king's treasuries for the Jews to destroy them. Also he gave him a copy of the writing of the decree that was given at Shushan to destroy them, to show it unto Esther, and to declare it unto her, and to charge her that she should go in unto the king, to make supplication unto him and to make request before him for her people.

And Hatach came and told Esther the words of Mordecai. Again Esther spake unto Hatach and gave him commandment unto Mordecai: All the king's servants and the people of the king's provinces do know that whosoever, whether man or woman, shall come unto the king into the inner court who is not called, there is one law of his to put him to death, except such to whom the king shall hold out the golden scepter that he may live, but I have not been called to come in unto the king these thirty days. And they told to Mordecai Esther's words.

Then Mordecai commanded to answer Esther, Think not with thyself that thou shalt escape in the king's house more than all the Jews. For if thou altogether holdest thy peace at this time, then shall there enlargement and deliverance arise to the Jews from another place, but thou and thy father's house shall be destroyed and who knoweth whether thou art come to the kingdom for such a time as this?

Then Esther bade them return Mordecai this answer, Go gather together all the Jews that are present in Shushan and fast ye for me, and neither eat nor drink three days, night or day; I also and my maidens will fast likewise; and so will I go in unto the king, which is not according to the law, and if I perish, I perish. So Mordecai went his way and did according to all that Esther had commanded him.

Now it came to pass on the third day that Esther put on her royal apparel and stood in the inner court of the king's house over against the king's house, and the king sat upon his royal throne in the royal house over against the gate of the house. And it was so when the king saw Esther the queen standing in the court that she obtained favor in his sight, and the king held out to Esther the golden scepter that was in his hand. So Esther drew near and touched the top of the scepter. Then said the king unto her, What wilt thou, queen Esther? And what is thy request? It shall be even given thee to the half of the kingdom. And Esther answered, If it seem good unto the king, let the king and Haman come this day unto the banquet that I have prepared for him. Then the king said, Cause Haman to make haste that he may do as Esther hath said. So the king and Haman came to the banquet that Esther had prepared. And the king said unto Esther at the banquet of wine, What is thy petition? And it shall be granted thee; and what is thy request? Even to the half of the kingdom it shall be performed. Then answered Esther and said, My petition and my request is: If I have found favor in the sight of the king and if it please the king to grant my petition, and to perform my request, let the king and Haman come to the banquet that I shall prepare for them and I will do tomorrow as the king hath said.

Then went Haman forth that day joyful and with a glad heart, but when Haman saw Mordecai in the king's gate, that he stood not up, nor moved for him, he was full of indignation against Mordecai. Nevertheless Haman refrained himself, and when he came home he sent and called for his friends and Zeresh his wife. And Haman told them of the glory of his riches, and the multitude of his children, and all the things wherein the king had promoted him, and how he had advanced him above the princes and servants of the king. Haman said moreover, Yea, Esther the queen did let no man come in with the king unto the banquet that she had prepared but myself, and tomorrow am I invited unto her also with the king. Yet all this availeth me nothing so long as I see Mordecai the Jew sitting at the king's gate. Then said Zeresh his wife and all his friends unto him, Let a gallows be made of fifty cubits high and tomorrow speak thou unto the king that Mordecai may be hanged thereon; then go thou in merrily with the king unto the banquet. And the thing pleased Haman and he caused the gallows to be made.

On that night could not the king sleep and he commanded to bring the book of records of the chronicles and they were read before the king. And it was found written that Mordecai had told of Bigthana and Teresh, two of the king's chamberlains, the keepers of the door, who sought to lay hand on the king Ahasuerus. And the king said, What honor and dignity hath been done to Mordecai for this? Then said the king's servants that ministered unto him, There is nothing done for him. And the king said, Who is in the court? Now Haman was come into the outward court of the king's house to speak unto the king to hang Mordecai on the gallows that he had prepared for him. And the king's servants said unto him, Behold, Haman standeth in the court. And the king said, Let him come in. So Haman came in. And the king said unto him, What shall be done unto the man whom the king delighteth to honor? Now, Haman thought in his heart, To whom would the king delight to do honor more than to myself? And Haman answered the king, For the man whom the king delighteth to honor, let the royal apparel be brought which the king useth to wear, and the horse that the king rideth upon, and the crown royal which is set upon his head, and let this apparel and horse be delivered to the hand of one of the king's most noble princes, that they may array the man withal whom the king delighteth to honor, and bring him on horseback through the street of the city, and proclaim before him, Thus shall it be done to the man whom the king delighteth to honor.

Then the king said to Haman, make haste, and take the apparel and the horse, as thou hast said, and do even so to Mordecai the Jew that sitteth at the king's gate; let nothing fail of all that thou hast spoken. Then took Haman the apparel and the horse and arrayed Mordecai, and brought him on horseback through the street of the city, and proclaimed before him, Thus shall it be done unto the man whom the king delighteth to honor.

And Mordecai came again to the king's gate. But Haman hasted to his house mourning and having his head covered. And Haman told Zeresh his wife and all his friends everything that had befallen him. Then said his wise men and Zeresh his wife unto him, If Mordecai be of the seed of the Jews, before whom thou hast begun to fall, thou shalt not prevail against him but shalt surely fall before him.

And while they were yet talking with him, came the king's chamberlains and hasted to bring Haman unto the banquet that Esther had prepared.

So the king and Haman came to banquet with Esther the queen. And the king said again unto Esther on the second day at the banquet of wine, What is thy petition, queen Esther? And it shall be granted thee; And what is thy request? And it shall be performed, even to the half of the kingdom. Then Esther the queen answered and said, If I have found favor in thy sight, O king, and if it please the king, let my life be given me at my petition and my people at my request; for we are sold, I and my people, to be destroyed, to be slain, and to perish. But if we had been sold for bondmen and bondwomen, I had held my tongue, although the enemy could not countervail the king's damage. Then the king Ahasuerus answered and said unto Esther the queen, Who is he and where is he that durst presume in his heart to do so? And Esther said, The adversary and enemy is this wicked Haman. Then Haman was afraid before the king and the queen.

And the king arising from the banquet of wine in his wrath went into the palace garden and Haman stood up to make request for his life to Esther the queen, for he saw that there was evil determined against him by the king. Then the king returned out of the palace garden into the place of the banquet of wine and Haman was fallen upon the bed whereon Esther was. Then said the king, Will he force the queen also before me in the house? As the word went out of the king's mouth, they covered Haman's face. And Harbonah, one of the chamberlains, said before the king, Behold also the gallows fifty cubits high, which Haman had made for Mordecai, who had spoken good for the king, standeth in the house of Haman. Then the king said, Hang him thereon. So they hanged Haman on the gallows that he had prepared for Mordecai. Then was the king's wrath pacified.

On that day did the king Ahasuerus give the house of Haman the Jews' enemy unto Esther the queen. And Mordecai came before the king, for Esther had told what he was unto her. And the king took off his ring which he had taken from Haman and gave it unto Mordecai. And Esther set Mordecai over the house of Haman.

And Esther spake yet again before the king, and fell down at his feet, and besought him with tears to put away the mischief of Haman the Agagite and his device that he had devised against the Jews. Then the king held out the golden scepter toward Esther. So Esther arose and stood before the king and said, If it please the king, and if I have found favor in his sight, and the thing seem right before the king, and I be pleasing in his eyes, let it be written to reverse the letters devised by Haman the son of Hammedatha the Agagite which he wrote to destroy the Jews which are in all the king's provinces; for how can I endure to see the evil that shall come unto my people? Or how can I endure to see the destruction of my kindred?

Then the king Ahasuerus said unto Esther the queen and to Mordecai the Jew, Behold, I have given Esther the house of Haman, and him they have hanged upon the gallows because he laid his hands upon the Jews. Write ye also for the Jews as it liketh you, in the king's name and seal it with the king's ring, for the writing which is written in the king's name and sealed with the king's ring may no man reverse.

Then were the king's scribes called at that time in the third month, that is, the month Sivan, on the three and twentieth day thereof, and it was written according to all that Mordecai commanded unto the Jews, and to the lieutenants, and the deputies and rulers of the provinces which are from India unto Ethiopia, a hundred twenty and seven provinces, unto every province according to the writing thereof, and unto every people after their language, and to the Jews according to their writing and according to their language. And he wrote in the king Ahasuerus' name and sealed it with the king's ring and sent letters by posts on horseback, and riders on mules, camels, and young dromedaries, wherein the king granted the Jews which were in every city to gather themselves together and to stand for their life, to destroy, to slay, and to cause to perish, all the power of the people and province that would assault them, both little ones and women, and to take the spoil of them for a prey. Upon one day in all the provinces of king Ahasuerus, namely, upon the thirteenth day of the twelfth month, which is the month Adar. The copy of the writing for a commandment to be given in every province was published unto all people and that the Jews should be ready against that day to avenge themselves on their enemies. So the posts that rode upon mules and camels went out, being hastened and pressed on by the king's commandment. And the decree was given at Shushan the palace.

And Mordecai went out from the presence of the king in royal apparel of blue and white, and with a great crown of gold, and with a garment of fine linen and purple, and the city of Shushan rejoiced and was glad. The Jews had light, and gladness, and joy, and honor. And in every province and in every city whithersoever the king's commandment and his decree came, the Jews had joy and gladness, a feast and a good day. And many of the people of the land became Jews, for the fear of the Jews fell upon them.

Now in the twelfth month, that is, the month Adar, on the thirteenth day of the same, when the king's commandment and his decree drew near to be put in execution, in the day that the enemies of the Jews hoped to have power over them (though it was turned to the contrary, that the Jews had rule over them that hated them), the Jews gathered themselves together in their cities throughout all the provinces of the king Ashasuerus to lay hand on such as sought their hurt, and no man could withstand them for the fear of them fell upon all people. And all the rulers of the provinces, and the lieutenants, and the deputies, and officers of the king, helped the Jews because the fear of Mordecai fell upon them. For Mordecai was great in the king's house and his fame went out throughout all the provinces, for this man Mordecai waxed greater and greater. Thus the Jews smote all their enemies with the stroke of the sword, and slaughter, and destruction, and did what they would unto those that hated them. And in Shushan the palace the Jews slew and destroyed five hundred men. And Parshandatha, and Dalphon, and Aspatha, and Poratha, and Adalia, and Aridatha, and Parmashta, and Arisai, and Aridai, and Vajezatha, the ten sons of Haman the son of Hammedatha, the enemy of the Jews, slew they, but on the spoil laid they not their hand. On that day the number of those that were slain in Shushan the palace was brought before the king.

And the king said unto Esther the queen, The Jews have slain and destroyed five hundred men in Shushan the palace, and the ten sons of Haman; what have they done in the rest of the king's provinces? Now what is thy petition and it shall be granted thee? Or what is thy request further and it shall be done? Then said Esther, If it please the king, let it be granted to the Jews which are in Shushan to do tomorrow also according unto this day's decree and let Haman's ten sons be hanged upon the gallows. And the king commanded it so to be done and the decree was given at Shushan, and they hanged Haman's ten sons. For the Jews that were in Shushan gathered themselves together on the fourteenth day also of the month Adar and slew three hundred men at Shushan, but on the prey they laid not their hand.

But the other Jews that were in the king's provinces gathered themselves together and stood for their lives, and had rest from their enemies, and slew of their foes seventy and five thousand, but they laid not their hands on the prey, on the thirteenth day of the month Adar; and on the fourteenth day of the same rested they and made it a day of feasting and gladness.

But the Jews that were at Shushan assembled together on the thirteenth day thereof, and on the fourteenth thereof, and on the fifteenth day of the same they rested and made it a day of feasting and gladness. Therefore the Jews of the villages that dwelt in the unwalled towns made the fourteenth day of the month Adar a day of gladness and feasting, and a good day, and of sending portions one to another.

And Mordecai wrote these things, and sent letters unto all the Jews that were in all the provinces of the king Ahasuerus, both nigh and far, to establish this among them, that they should keep the fourteenth day of the month Adar and the fifteenth day of the same, yearly. As the days wherein the Jews rested from their enemies, and the month which was turned unto them from sorrow to joy, and from mourning into a good day, that they should make them days of feasting and joy, and of sending portions one to another, and gifts to the poor.

And the Jews undertook to do as they had begun and as Mordecai had written unto them, because Haman the son of Hammedatha the Agagite, the enemy of all the Jews, had devised against the Jews to destroy them and had cast Pur, that is, the lot, to consume them and to destroy them, but when Esther came before the king, he commanded by letters that his wicked device which he devised against the Jews should return upon his own head and that he and his sons should be hanged on the gallows. Wherefore they called these days Purim after the name of Pur. Therefore for all the words of this letter, and of that which they had seen concerning this matter, and which had come unto them, the Jews ordained and took upon them, and upon their seed, and upon all such as joined themselves unto them so as it should not fail, that they would keep these two days according to their writing and according to their appointed time every year, and that these days should be remembered and kept throughout every generation, every family, every province, and every city, and that these days of Purim should not fail from among the Jews, nor the memorial of them perish from their seed.

Then Esther the queen the daughter of Abihail, and Mordecai the Jew wrote with all authority to confirm this second letter of Purim. And he sent the letters unto all the Jews, to the hundred twenty and seven provinces of the kingdom of Ahasuerus, with words of peace and truth to confirm these days of Purim in their times appointed according as Mordecai the Jew and Esther the queen had enjoined them and as they had decreed for themselves and for their seed, the matters of the fastings and their cry. And the decree of Esther confirmed these matters of Purim, and it was written in the book.

And the king Ahasuerus laid a tribute upon the land and upon the isles of the sea. And all the acts of his power and of his might, and the declaration of the greatness of Mordecai whereunto the king advanced him, are they not written in the book of the chronicles of the kings of Media and Persia? For Mordecai the Jew was next unto king Ahasuerus, and great among the Jews, and accepted of the multitude of his brethren, seeking the wealth of his people and speaking peace to all his seed.

THE BOOK OF JOB

THERE was a man in the land of Uz whose name was Job, and that man was perfect and upright, and one that feared God and eschewed evil. And there were born unto him seven sons and three daughters. His substance also was seven thousand sheep, and three thousand camels, and five hundred yoke of oxen, and five hundred she asses, and a very great household, so that this man was the greatest of all the men of the east. And his sons went and feasted in their houses, every one his day, and sent and called for their three sisters to eat and to drink with them. And it was so, when the days of their feasting were gone about, that Job sent and sanctified them, and rose up early in the morning, and offered burnt offerings according to the number of them all, for Job said, It may be that my sons have sinned, and cursed God in their hearts. Thus did Job continually.

Now there was a day when the children of God came to present themselves before the Lord, and Satan came also among them. And the Lord said unto Satan, Whence comest thou? Then Satan answered the Lord, and said, From going to and fro in the Earth, and from walking up and down in it. And the Lord said unto Satan, Hast thou considered my servant Job, that there is none like him in the Earth, a perfect and an upright man, one that feareth God, and escheweth evil? Then Satan answered the Lord, and said, Doth Job fear God for naught? Hast not thou made a hedge about him, and about his house, and about all that he hath on every side? thou hast blessed the work of his hands, and his substance is increased in the land. But put forth thine hand now, and touch all that he hath, and he will curse thee to thy face. And the Lord said unto Satan, Behold, all that he hath is in thy power, only upon himself put not forth thine hand. So Satan went forth from the presence of the Lord.

And there was a day when his sons and his daughters were eating and drinking wine in their eldest brother's house, and there came a messenger unto Job, and said, The oxen were ploughing, and the asses feeding beside them, and the Sabeans fell upon them, and took them away, yea, they have slain the servants with the edge of the sword, and I only am escaped alone to tell thee. While he was yet speaking, there came also another, and said, The fire of God is fallen from Heaven, and hath burned up the sheep, and the servants, and consumed them, and I only am escaped alone to tell thee. While he was yet speaking, there came also another, and said, The Chaldeans made out three bands, and fell upon the camels, and have carried them away, yea, and slain the servants with the edge of the sword, and I only am escaped alone to tell thee. While he was yet speaking, there came also another, and said, Thy sons and thy daughters were eating and drinking wine in their eldest brother's house, and, behold, there came a great wind from the wilderness, and smote the four corners of the house, and it fell upon the young men, and they are dead, and I only am escaped alone to tell thee. Then Job arose and rent his mantle, and shaved his head, and fell down upon the ground and worshiped, and said, Naked came I out of my mother's womb, and naked shall I return thither, the Lord gave, and the Lord hath taken away, blessed be the name of the Lord.

In all this Job sinned not, nor charged God foolishly.

2 AGAIN there was a day when the children of God came to present themselves before the Lord, and Satan came also among them to present himself before the Lord. And the Lord said unto Satan, From whence comest thou? And Satan answered the Lord, and said, From going to and fro in the Earth, and from walking up and down in it. And the Lord said unto Satan, Hast thou considered my servant Job, that there is none like him in the Earth, a perfect and an upright man, one that feareth God and escheweth evil? And still he holdeth fast his integrity, although thou movedst me against him, to destroy him without cause. And Satan answered the Lord, and said, Skin for skin, yea, all that man hath will he give for his life. But put forth thine hand now, and touch his bone and his flesh, and he will curse thee to thy face. And the Lord said unto Satan, Behold, he is in thine hand, but save his life. So went Satan forth from the presence of the Lord, and smote Job with sore boils from the sole of his foot unto his crown. And he took him a potsherd to scrape himself withal, and he sat down among the ashes. Then said his wife unto him, Dost thou still retain thine integrity? Curse God, and die. But he said unto her, Thou speakest as one of the foolish women speaketh. What? shall we receive good at the hand of God, and shall we not receive evil? In all this did not Job sin with his lips.

Now when Job's three friends heard of all this evil that was come upon him, they came every one from his own place, Eliphaz the Temanite, and Bildad the Shuhite, and Zophar the Naamathite, for they had made an appointment together to come to mourn with him, and to comfort him. And when they lifted up their eyes afar off, and knew him not, they lifted up their voice and wept, and they rent everyone his mantle, and sprinkled dust upon their heads toward Heaven. So they sat down with him upon the ground seven days and seven nights, and none spake a word unto him, for they saw that his grief was very great.

After this opened Job his mouth, and cursed his day. And Job spake, and said, Let the day perish wherein I was born, and the night in which it was said, There is a man-child conceived. Let that day be darkness, let not God regard it from above, neither let the light shine upon it. Let darkness and the shadow of death stain it, let a cloud dwell upon it, let the blackness of the day terrify it. As for that night, let darkness seize upon it, let it not be joined unto the days of the year, let it not come into the number of the months. Lo, let that night be solitary, let no joyful voice come therein. Let them curse it that curse the day, who are ready to raise up their mourning. Let the stars of the twilight thereof be dark, let it look for light, but have none, neither let it see the dawning of the day, Because it shut not up the doors of my mother's womb, nor hid sorrow from mine eyes. Why died I not from the womb? why did I not give up the ghost when I came out of the belly? Why did the knees prevent me? or why the breasts that I should suck? For now should I have lain still and been quiet, I should have slept, then had I been at rest, with kings and counselors of the Earth, which built desolate places for themselves, or with princes that had gold, who filled their houses with silver, or as a hidden untimely birth I had not been, as infants which never saw light. There the wicked cease from troubling, and there the weary be at rest. There the prisoners rest together, they hear not the voice of the oppressor. The small and great are there, and the servant is free from his master.

Wherefore is light given to him that is in misery, and life unto the bitter in soul, which long for death, but it cometh not, and dig for it more than for hid treasures, which rejoice exceedingly, and are glad, when they can find the grave? Why is light given to a man whose way is hid, and whom God hath hedged in? For my sighing cometh before I eat, and my roarings are poured out like the waters. For the thing which I greatly feared is come upon me, and that which I was afraid of is come unto me. I was not in safety, neither had I rest, neither was I quiet, yet trouble came.

Then Eliphaz the Temanite answered and said, If we assay to commune with thee, wilt thou be grieved? but who can withhold himself from speaking? Behold, thou hast instructed many, and thou hast strengthened the weak hands. Thy words have upholden him that was falling, and thou hast strengthened the feeble knees. But now it is come upon thee, and thou faintest, it toucheth thee, and thou art troubled. Is not this thy fear, thy confidence, thy hope, and the uprightness of thy ways? Remember, I pray thee, whoever perished, being innocent, or where were the righteous cut off? Even as I have seen, they that plough iniquity, and sow wickedness, and reap the same. By the blast of God they perish, and by the breath of his nostrils are they consumed. The roaring of the lion, and the voice of the fierce lion, and the teeth of the young lions, are broken. The old lion perisheth for lack of prey, and the stout lion's whelps are scattered abroad. Now a thing was secretly brought to me, and mine ear received a little thereof. In thoughts from the visions of the night, when deep sleep falleth on men, fear came upon me, and trembling, which made all my bones to shake. Then a spirit passed before my face, the hair of my flesh stood up, it stood still, but I could not discern the form thereof, an image was before mine eyes, there was silence, and I heard a voice, saying, Shall mortal man be more just than God? shall a man be more pure than his Maker? Behold, he put no trust in his servants, and his angels he charged with folly, how much less in them that dwell in houses of clay, whose foundation is in the dust, which are crushed before the moth? They are destroyed from morning to evening, they perish for ever without any regarding it. Doth not their excellency which is in them go away? they die, even without. Call now, if there be any that will answer thee, and to which of the saints wilt thou turn? For wrath killeth the foolish man, and envy slayeth the silly one. I have seen the foolish taking root, but suddenly I cursed his habitation. His children are far from safety, and they are crushed in the gate, neither is there any to deliver them. Whose harvest the hungry eateth up, and taketh it even out of the thorns, and the robber swalloweth up their substance. Although affliction cometh not forth of the dust, neither doth trouble spring out of the ground. Yet man is born unto trouble, as the sparks fly upward. I would seek unto God, and unto God would I commit my cause, which doeth great things and unsearchable, marvelous things without number, who giveth rain upon the Earth, and sendeth waters upon the fields, to set up on high those that be low, that those which mourn may be exalted to safety. He disappointeth the devices of the crafty, so that their hands cannot perform their enterprise. He taketh the wise in their own craftiness, and the counsel of the froward is carried headlong. They meet with darkness in the daytime, and grope in the noonday as in the night. But he saveth the poor from the sword, from their mouth, and from the hand of the mighty. So the poor hath hope, and iniquity stoppeth her mouth. Behold, happy is the man whom God correcteth, therefore despise not thou the chastening of the Almighty, for he maketh sore, and bindeth up, he woundeth, and his hands make whole. He shall deliver thee in six troubles, yea in seven there shall no evil touch thee. In famine he shall redeem thee from death, and in war from the power of the sword. Thou shalt be hid from the scourge of the tongue, neither shalt thou be afraid of destruction when it cometh. At destruction and famine thou shalt laugh, neither shalt thou be afraid of the beasts of the Earth. For thou shalt be in league with the stones of the field, and the beasts of the field shall be at peace with thee. And thou shalt know that thy tabernacle shall be in peace, and thou shalt visit thy habitation, and shalt not sin. Thou shalt know also that thy seed shall be great, and thine offspring as the grass of the Earth. Thou shalt come to thy grave in a full age, like as a shock of corn cometh in in his season. Lo this, we have searched it, so it is, hear it, and know thou it for thy good.

But Job answered and said, O that my grief were thoroughly weighed, and my calamity laid in the balances together! For now it would be heavier than the sand of the sea, therefore my words are swallowed up. For the arrows of the Almighty are within me, the poison whereof drinketh up my spirit, the terrors of God do set themselves in array against me. Doth the wild ass bray when he hath grass? or loweth the ox over his fodder? Can that which is unsavory be eaten without salt? or is there any taste in the white of an egg? The things that my soul refused to touch are as my sorrowful meat. O that I might have my request, and that God would grant me the thing that I long for! Even that it would please God to destroy me, that he would let loose his hand, and cut me off! Then should I yet have comfort, yea, I would harden myself in sorrow, let him not spare, for I have not concealed the words of the Holy One.

What is my strength, that I should hope? and what is mine end, that I should prolong my life? Is my strength the strength of stones? or is my flesh of brass? Is not my help in me? and is wisdom driven quite from me? To him that is afflicted pity should be showed from his friend, but he forsaketh the fear of the Almighty. My brethren have dealt deceitfully as a brook, and as the stream of brooks they pass away, which are blackish by reason of the ice, and wherein the snow is hid, what time they wax warm, they vanish, when it is hot, they are consumed out of their place. The paths of their way are turned aside, they go to nothing, and perish. The troops of Tema looked, the companies of Sheba waited for them. They were confounded because they had hoped, they came thither, and were ashamed.

For now ye are nothing, ye see my casting down, and are afraid. Did I say, Bring unto me? or, Give me a reward for me of your substance? Or, Deliver me from the enemy's hand? or, Redeem me from the hand of the mighty? Teach me, and I will hold my tongue, and cause me to understand wherein I have erred. How forcible are right words! but what doth your arguing reprove? Do ye imagine to reprove words, and the speeches of one that is desperate, which are as wind? Yea, ye overwhelm the fatherless, and ye dig a pit for your friend. Now therefore be content, look upon me, for it is evident unto you if I lie. Return, I pray you, let it not be iniquity, yea, return again, my righteousness is in it. Is there iniquity in my tongue? cannot my taste discern perverse things? Is there not an appointed time to man upon Earth? are not his days also like the days of a hireling? As a servant earnestly desireth the shadow, and as a hireling looketh for the reward of his work, so am I made to possess months of vanity, and wearisome nights are appointed to me. When I lie down, I say, When shall I arise, and the night be gone? and I am full of tossings to and fro unto the dawning of the day. My flesh is clothed with worms and clods of dust, my skin is broken, and become loathsome. My days are swifter than a weaver's shuttle, and are spent without hope. O remember that my life is wind, mine eyes shall no more see good. The eye of him that hath seen me shall see me no more, thine eyes are upon me, and I am not. As the cloud is consumed and vanisheth away, so he that goeth down to the grave shall come up no more. He shall return no more to his house, neither shall his place know him anymore. Therefore I will not refrain my mouth, I will speak in the anguish of my spirit, I will complain in the bitterness of my soul. Am I a sea, or a whale, that thou settest a watch over me? When I say, My bed shall comfort me, my couch shall ease my complaint, then thou scarest me with dreams, and terrifiest me through visions, so that my soul chooseth strangling, and death rather than my life. I loath it, I would not live alway, let me alone, for my days are vanity. What is man, that thou shouldest magnify him? and that thou shouldest set thine heart upon him? And that thou shouldest visit him every morning, and try him every moment? How long wilt thou not depart from me, nor let me alone till I swallow down my spittle? I have sinned, what shall I do unto thee, O thou preserver of men? why hast thou set me as a mark against thee, so that I am a burden to myself? And why dost thou not pardon my transgression, and take away mine iniquity? for now shall I sleep in the dust, and thou shalt seek me in the morning, but I shall not be.

Then answered Bildad the Shuhite, and said, How long wilt thou speak these things? and how long shall the words of thy mouth be like a strong wind? Doth God pervert judgment? or doth the Almighty pervert justice? If thy children have sinned against him, and he have cast them away for their transgression, if thou wouldest seek unto God betimes, and make thy supplication to the Almighty, if thou wert pure and upright, surely now he would awake for thee, and make the habitation of thy righteousness prosperous. Though thy beginning was small, yet thy latter end should greatly increase. For inquire, I pray thee, of the former age, and prepare thyself to the search of their fathers. (For we are but of yesterday, and know nothing, because our days upon Earth are a shadow,) shall not they teach thee, and tell thee, and utter words out of their heart? Can the rush grow up without mire? can the flag grow without water? Whilst it is yet in his greenness, and not cut down, it withereth before any other herb. So are the paths of all that forget God, and the hypocrite's hope shall perish, whose hope shall be cut off, and whose trust shall be a spider's web. He shall lean upon his house, but it shall not stand, he shall hold it fast, but it shall not endure. He is green before the sun, and his branch shooteth forth in his garden. His roots are wrapped about the heap, and seeth the place of stones. If he destroy him from his place, then it shall deny him, saying, I have not seen thee. Behold, this is the joy of his way, and out of the Earth shall others grow. Behold, God will not cast away a perfect man, neither will he help the evildoers, till he fill thy mouth with laughing, and thy lips with rejoicing. They that hate thee shall be clothed with shame, and the dwelling place of the wicked shall come to naught.

Then Job answered and said, I know it is so of a truth, but how should man be just with God? If he will contend with him, he cannot answer him one of a thousand. He is wise in heart, and mighty in strength, who hath hardened himself against him, and hath prospered?

Which removeth the mountains, and they know not, which overturneth them in his anger, which shaketh the Earth out of her place, and the pillars thereof tremble, which commandeth the sun, and it riseth not, and sealeth up the stars, which alone spreadeth out the heavens, and treadeth upon the waves of the sea, which maketh Arcturus, Orion, and Pleiades, and the chambers of the south, which doeth great things past finding out, yea, and wonders without number. Lo, he goeth by me, and I see him not, he passeth on also, but I perceive him not. Behold, he taketh away, who can hinder him? who will say unto him, What doest thou? If God will not withdraw his anger, the proud helpers do stoop under him. How much less shall I answer him, and choose out my words to reason with him? Whom, though I were righteous, yet would I not answer, but I would make supplication to my judge. If I had called, and he had answered me, yet would I not believe that he had hearkened unto my voice. For he breaketh me with a tempest, and multiplieth my wounds without cause. He will not suffer me to take my breath, but filleth me with bitterness. If I speak of strength, lo, he is strong, and if of judgment, who shall set me a time to plead? If I justify myself, mine own mouth shall condemn me, if I say, I am perfect, it shall also prove me perverse. Though I were perfect, yet would I not know my soul, I would despise my life. This is one thing, therefore I said it, He destroyeth the perfect and the wicked. If the scourge slay suddenly, he will laugh at the trial of the innocent. The Earth is given into the hand of the wicked, he covereth the faces of the judges thereof, if not, where, and who is he? Now my days are swifter than a post, they flee away, they see no good. They are passed away as the swift ships, as the eagle that hasteth to the prey. If I say, I will forget my complaint, I will leave off my heaviness, and comfort myself, I am afraid of all my sorrows, I know that thou wilt not hold me innocent. If I be wicked, why then labor I in vain? If I wash myself with snow water, and make my hands never so clean, yet shalt thou plunge me in the ditch, and mine own clothes shall abhor me. For he is not a man, as I am, that I should answer him, and we should come together in judgment. Neither is there any daysman betwixt us, that might lay his hand upon us both. Let him take his rod away from me, and let not his fear terrify me, then would I speak, and not fear him, but it is not so with me. My soul is weary of my life, I will leave my complaint upon myself, I will speak in the bitterness of my soul. I will say unto God, Do not condemn me, show me wherefore thou contendest with me. Is it good unto thee that thou shouldest oppress, that thou shouldest despise the work of thine hands, and shine upon the counsel of the wicked? Hast thou eyes of flesh? or seest thou as man seeth? Are thy days as the days of man? are thy years as man's days, that thou inquirest after mine iniquity, and searchest after my sin? Thou knowest that I am not wicked, and there is none that can deliver out of thine hand. Thine hands have made me and fashioned me together round about, yet thou dost destroy me. Remember, I beseech thee, that thou hast made me as the clay, and wilt thou bring me into dust again? Hast thou not poured me out as milk, and curdled me like cheese? Thou hast clothed me with skin and flesh, and hast fenced me with bones and sinews. Thou hast granted me life and favor, and thy visitation hath preserved my spirit. And these things hast thou hid in thine heart, I know that this is with thee. If I sin, then thou markest me, and thou wilt not acquit me from mine iniquity. If I be wicked, wo unto me, and if I be righteous, yet will I not lift up my head. I am full of confusion, therefore see thou mine affliction, for it increaseth. Thou huntest me as a fierce lion, and again thou showest thyself marvelous upon me. Thou renewest thy witnesses against me, and increasest thine indignation upon me, changes and war are against me. Wherefore then hast thou brought me forth out of the womb? O that I had given up the ghost, and no eye had seen me! I should have been as though I had not been, I should have been carried from the womb to the grave. Are not my days few? cease then, and let me alone, that I may take comfort a little, before I go whence I shall not return, even to the land of darkness and the shadow of death, a land of darkness, as darkness itself, and of the shadow of death, without any order, and where the light is as darkness.

Then answered Zophar the Naamathite, and said, Should not the multitude of words be answered? and should a man full of talk be justified? Should thy lies make men hold their peace? and when thou mockest, shall no man make thee ashamed? For thou hast said, My doctrine is pure, and I am clean in thine eyes. But O that God would speak, and open his lips against thee, and that he would show thee the secrets of wisdom, that they are double to that which is! Know therefore that God exacteth of thee less than thine iniquity deserveth.

Canst thou by searching find out God? canst thou find out the Almighty unto perfection? It is as high as Heaven, what canst thou do? deeper than hell, what canst thou know? The measure thereof is longer than the Earth, and broader than the sea. If he cut off, and shut up, or gather together, then who can hinder him? For he knoweth vain men, he seeth wickedness also, will he not then consider it? For vain man would be wise, thou man be born like a wild ass's colt.

If thou prepare thine heart, and stretch out thine hands toward him, if iniquity be in thine hand, put it far away, and let not wickedness dwell in thy tabernacles. For then shalt thou lift up thy face without spot, yea, thou shalt be steadfast, and shalt not fear, Because thou shalt forget thy misery, and remember it as waters that pass away, and thine age shall be clearer than the noonday, thou shalt shine forth, thou shalt be as the morning, and thou shalt be secure, because there is hope, yea, thou shalt dig about thee, and thou shalt take thy rest in safety. Also thou shalt lie down, and none shall make thee afraid, yea, many shall make suit unto thee. But the eyes of the wicked shall fail, and they shall not escape, and their hope shall be as the giving up of the ghost.

And Job answered and said, No doubt but ye are the people, and wisdom shall die with you. But I have understanding as well as you, I am not inferior to you, yea, who knoweth not such things as these? I am as one mocked of his neighbor, who calleth upon God, and he answereth him, the just upright man is laughed to scorn. He that is ready to slip with his feet is as a lamp despised in the thought of him that is at ease. The tabernacles of robbers prosper, and they that provoke God are secure, into whose hand God bringeth abundantly. But ask now the beasts, and they shall teach thee, and the fowls of the air, and they shall tell thee, or speak to the Earth, and it shall teach thee, and the fishes of the sea shall declare unto thee. Who knoweth not in all these that the hand of the Lord hath wrought this? In whose hand is the soul of every living thing, and the breath of all mankind. Doth not the ear try words? and the mouth taste his meat? With the ancient is wisdom, and in length of days understanding. With him is wisdom and strength, he hath counsel and understanding. Behold, he breaketh down, and it cannot be built again, he shutteth up a man, and there can be no opening. Behold, he withholdeth the waters, and they dry up, also he sendeth them out, and they overturn the Earth. With him is strength and wisdom, the deceived and the deceiver are his. He leadeth counselors away spoiled, and maketh the judges fools. He looseth the bond of kings, and girdeth their loins with a girdle. He leadeth princes away spoiled, and overthroweth the mighty. He removeth away the speech of the trusty, and taketh away the understanding of the aged. He poureth contempt upon princes, and weakeneth the strength of the mighty. He discovereth deep things out of darkness, and bringeth out to light the shadow of death. He increaseth the nations, and destroyeth them, he enlargeth the nations, and straiteneth them again. He taketh away the heart of the chief of the people of the Earth, and causeth them to wander in a wilderness where there is no way. They grope in the dark without light, and he maketh them to stagger like a drunken man. Lo, mine eye hath seen all this, mine ear hath heard and understood it. What ye know, the same do I know also, I am not inferior unto you.

Surely I would speak to the Almighty, and I desire to reason with God. But ye are forgers of lies, ye are all physicians of no value. O that ye would altogether hold your peace! and it should be your wisdom. Hear now my reasoning, and hearken to the pleadings of my lips.

Will ye speak wickedly for God? and talk deceitfully for him? Will ye accept his person? will ye contend for God? Is it good that he should search you out? or as one man mocketh another, do ye so mock him? He will surely reprove you, if ye do secretly accept persons. Shall not his excellency make you afraid? and his dread fall upon you? Your remembrances are like unto ashes, your bodies to bodies of clay. Hold your peace, let me alone, that I may speak, and let come on me what will. Wherefore do I take my flesh in my teeth, and put my life in mine hand? Though he slay me, yet will I trust in him, but I will maintain mine own ways before him. He also shall be my salvation, for a hypocrite shall not come before him. Hear diligently my speech, and my declaration with your ears. Behold now, I have ordered my cause, I know that I shall be justified. Who is he that will plead with me? for now, if I hold my tongue, I shall give up the ghost. Only do not two things unto me, then will I not hide myself from thee. Withdraw thine hand far from me, and let not thy dread make me afraid. Then call thou, and I will answer, or let me speak, and answer thou me. How many are mine iniquities and sins? make me to know my transgression and my sin. Wherefore hidest thou thy face, and holdest me for thine enemy? Wilt thou break a leaf driven to and fro? and wilt thou pursue the dry stubble? For thou writest bitter things against me, and makest me to possess the iniquities of my youth. Thou puttest my feet also in the stocks, and lookest narrowly unto all my paths, thou settest a print upon the heels of my feet. And he, as a rotten thing, consumeth, as a garment that is moth-eaten. Man that is born of a woman is of few days, and full of trouble. He cometh forth like a flower, and is cut down, he fleeth also as a shadow, and continueth not. And dost thou open thine eyes upon such a one, and bringest me into judgment with thee?

Who can bring a clean thing out of an unclean? not one. Seeing his days are determined, the number of his months are with thee, thou hast appointed his bounds that he cannot pass, turn from him, that he may rest, till he shall accomplish, as a hireling, his day. For there is hope of a tree, if it be cut down, that it will sprout again, and that the tender branch thereof will not cease. Though the root thereof wax old in the Earth, and the stock thereof die in the ground, yet through the scent of water it will bud, and bring forth boughs like a plant. But man dieth, and wasteth away, yea, man giveth up the ghost, and where is he? As the waters fail from the sea, and the flood decayeth and drieth up, so man lieth down, and riseth not, till the heavens be no more, they shall not awake, nor be raised out of their sleep. O that thou wouldest hide me in the grave, that thou wouldest keep me secret, until thy wrath be past, that thou wouldest appoint me a set time, and remember me! If a man die, shall he live again? all the days of my appointed time will I wait, till my change come. Thou shalt call, and I will answer thee, thou wilt have a desire to the work of thine hands. For now thou numberest my steps, dost thou not watch over my sin? My transgression is sealed up in a bag, and thou sewest up mine iniquity. And surely the mountain falling cometh to naught, and the rock is removed out of his place. The waters wear the stones, thou washest away the things which grow out of the dust of the Earth, and thou destroyest the hope of man. Thou prevailest for ever against him, and he passeth, thou changest his countenance, and sendest him away. His sons come to honor, and he knoweth it not, and they are brought low, but he perceiveth it not of them. But his flesh upon him shall have pain, and his soul within him shall mourn.

3   THEN answered Eliphaz the Temanite, and said, Should a wise man utter vain knowledge, and fill his belly with the east wind? Should he reason with unprofitable talk? or with speeches wherewith he can do no good? Yea, thou castest off fear, and restrainest prayer before God. For thy mouth uttereth thine iniquity, and thou choosest the tongue of the crafty. Thine own mouth condemneth thee, and not I, yea, thine own lips testify against thee.

Art thou the first man that was born? or wast thou made before the hills? Hast thou heard the secret of God? and dost thou restrain wisdom to thyself? What knowest thou, that we know not? what understandest thou, which is not in us? With us are both the grayheaded and very aged men, much elder than thy father. Are the consolations of God small with thee? is there any secret thing with thee? Why doth thine heart carry thee away? and what do thy eyes wink at, that thou turnest thy spirit against God, and lettest such words go out of thy mouth? What is man, that he should be clean? and he which is born of a woman, that he should be righteous? Behold, he putteth no trust in his saints, yea, the heavens are not clean in his sight. How much more abominable and filthy is man, which drinketh iniquity like water? I will show thee, hear me, and that which I have seen I will declare, which wise men have told from their fathers, and have not hid it, unto whom alone the Earth was given, and no stranger passed among them. The wicked man travaileth with pain all his days, and the number of years is hidden to the oppressor. A dreadful sound is in his ears, in prosperity the destroyer shall come upon him. He believeth not that he shall return out of darkness, and he is waited for of the sword. He wandereth abroad for bread, saying, Where is it? he knoweth that the day of darkness is ready at his hand. Trouble and anguish shall make him afraid, they shall prevail against him, as a king ready to the battle. For he stretcheth out his hand against God, and strengtheneth himself against the Almighty. He runneth upon him, even on his neck, upon the thick bosses of his bucklers, because he covereth his face with his fatness, and maketh collops of fat on his flanks. And he dwelleth in desolate cities, and in houses which no man inhabiteth, which are ready to become heaps. He shall not be rich, neither shall his substance continue, neither shall he prolong the perfection thereof upon the Earth. He shall not depart out of darkness, the flame shall dry up his branches, and by the breath of his mouth shall he go away.

Let not him that is deceived trust in vanity, for vanity shall be his recompense. It shall be accomplished before his time, and his branch shall not be green. He shall shake off his unripe grape as the vine, and shall cast off his flower as the olive. For the congregation of hypocrites shall be desolate, and fire shall consume the tabernacles of bribery. They conceive mischief, and bring forth vanity, and their belly prepareth deceit.

Then Job answered and said, I have heard many such things, miserable comforters are ye all. Shall vain words have an end? or what emboldeneth thee that thou answerest? I also could speak as ye do, if your soul were in my soul's stead, I could heap up words against you, and shake mine head at you. But I would strengthen you with my mouth, and the moving of my lips should assuage your grief. Though I speak, my grief is not assuaged, and though I forbear, what am I eased? But now he hath made me weary, thou hast made desolate all my company. And thou hast filled me with wrinkles, which is a witness against me, and my leanness rising up in me beareth witness to my face. He teareth me in his wrath, who hateth me, he gnasheth upon me with his teeth, mine enemy sharpeneth his eyes upon me. They have gaped upon me with their mouth, they have smitten me upon the cheek reproachfully, they have gathered themselves together against me. God hath delivered me to the ungodly, and turned me over into the hands of the wicked. I was at ease, but he hath broken me asunder, he hath also taken me by the neck, and shaken me to pieces, and set me up for his mark. His archers compass me round about, he cleaveth my reins asunder, and doth not spare, he poureth out my gall upon the ground. He breaketh me with breach upon breach, he runneth upon me like a giant. I have sewed sackcloth upon my skin, and defiled my horn in the dust. My face is foul with weeping, and on my eyelids is the shadow of death, not for any injustice in mine hands, also my prayer is pure. O Earth, cover not thou my blood, and let my cry have no place. Also now, behold, my witness is in Heaven, and my record is on high. My friends scorn me, but mine eye poureth out tears unto God. O that one might plead for a man with God, as a man pleadeth for his neighbor! When a few years are come, then I shall go the way whence I shall not return. My breath is corrupt, my days are extinct, the graves are ready for me. Are there not mockers with me? and doth not mine eye continue in their provocation? Lay down now, put me in a surety with thee, who is he that will strike hands with me? For thou hast hid their heart from understanding, therefore shalt thou not exalt them. He that speaketh flattery to his friends, even the eyes of his children shall fail. He hath made me also a byword of the people, and aforetime I was as a tabret. Mine eye also is dim by reason of sorrow, and all my members are as a shadow. Upright men shall be astonished at this, and the innocent shall stir up himself against the hypocrite. The righteous also shall hold on his way, and he that hath clean hands shall be stronger and stronger. But as for you all, do ye return, and come now, for I cannot find one wise man among you. My days are past, my purposes are broken off, even the thoughts of my heart. They change the night into day, the light is short because of darkness. If I wait, the grave is mine house, I have made my bed in the darkness. I have said to corruption, Thou art my father, to the worm, Thou art my mother, and my sister. And where is now my hope? as for my hope, who shall see it? They shall go down to the bars of the pit, when our rest together is in the dust.

Then answered Bildad the Shuhite, and said, How long will it be ere ye make an end of words? mark, and afterwards we will speak. Wherefore are we counted as beasts, and reputed vile in your sight? He teareth himself in his anger, shall the Earth be forsaken for thee? and shall the rock be removed out of his place? Yea, the light of the wicked shall be put out, and the spark of his fire shall not shine. The light shall be dark in his tabernacle, and his candle shall be put out with him. The steps of his strength shall be straitened, and his own counsel shall cast him down. For he is cast into a net by his own feet, and he walketh upon a snare. The gin shall take him by the heel, and the robber shall prevail against him. The snare is laid for him in the ground, and a trap for him in the way. Terrors shall make him afraid on every side, and shall drive him to his feet. His strength shall be hunger-bitten, and destruction shall be ready at his side. It shall devour the strength of his skin, even the firstborn of death shall devour his strength. His confidence shall be rooted out of his tabernacle, and it shall bring him to the king of terrors. It shall dwell in his tabernacle, because it is none of his, brimstone shall be scattered upon his habitation. His roots shall be dried up beneath, and above shall his branch be cut off. His remembrance shall perish from the Earth, and he shall have no name in the street. He shall be driven from light into darkness, and chased out of the world. He shall neither have son nor nephew among his people, nor any remaining in his dwellings. They that come after him shall be astonished at his day, as they that went before were affrighted. Surely such are the dwellings of the wicked, and this is the place of him that knoweth not God.

Then Job answered and said, How long will ye vex my soul and break me in pieces with words? These ten times have ye reproached me, ye are not ashamed that ye make yourselves strange to me. And be it indeed that I have erred, mine error remaineth with myself. If indeed ye will magnify yourselves against me, and plead against me my reproach, know now that God hath overthrown me, and hath compassed me with his net. Behold, I cry out of wrong, but I am not heard, I cry aloud, but there is no judgment. He hath fenced up my way that I cannot pass, and he hath set darkness in my paths. He hath stripped me of my glory, and taken the crown from my head. He hath destroyed me on every side, and I am gone, and mine hope hath he removed like a tree. He hath also kindled his wrath against me, and he counteth me unto him as one of his enemies. His troops come together, and raise up their way against me, and encamp round about my tabernacle. He hath put my brethren far from me, and mine acquaintance are verily estranged from me. My kinsfolk have failed, and my familiar friends have forgotten me. They that dwell in mine house, and my maids, count me for a stranger, I am an alien in their sight. I called my servant, and he gave me no answer, I entreated him with my mouth. My breath is strange to my wife, though I entreated for the children's sake of mine own body. Yea, young children despised me, I arose, and they spake against me. All my inward friends abhorred me, and they whom I loved are turned against me. My bone cleaveth to my skin and to my flesh, and I am escaped with the skin of my teeth. Have pity upon me, have pity upon me, O ye my friends, for the hand of God hath touched me. Why do ye persecute me as God, and are not satisfied with my flesh? O that my words were now written! O that they were printed in a book! That they were graven with an iron pen and lead in the rock forever! For I know that my Redeemer liveth, and that he shall stand at the latter day upon the Earth, and though after my skin worms destroy this body, yet in my flesh shall I see God, whom I shall see for myself, and mine eyes shall behold, and not another, though my reins be consumed within me. But ye should say, Why persecute we him, seeing the root of the matter is found in me? Be ye afraid of the sword, for wrath bringeth the punishments of the sword, that ye may know there is a judgment.

Then answered Zophar the Naamathite, and said, Therefore do my thoughts cause me to answer, and for this I make haste. I have heard the check of my reproach, and the spirit of my understanding causeth me to answer. Knowest thou not this of old, since man was placed upon Earth, that the triumphing of the wicked is short, and the joy of the hypocrite but for a moment? Though his excellency mount up to the heavens, and his head reach unto the clouds, yet he shall perish for ever like his own dung, they which have seen him shall say, Where is he? He shall fly away as a dream, and shall not be found, yea, he shall be chased away as a vision of the night, the eye also which saw him shall see him no more, neither shall his place anymore behold him. His children shall seek to please the poor, and his hands shall restore their goods. His bones are full of the sin of his youth, which shall lie down with him in the dust. Though wickedness be sweet in his mouth, though he hide it under his tongue, though he spare it, and forsake it not, but keep it still within his mouth, yet his meat in his bowels is turned, it is the gall of asps within him. He hath swallowed down riches, and he shall vomit them up again, God shall cast them out of his belly. He shall suck the poison of asps, the viper's tongue shall slay him. He shall not see the rivers, the floods, the brooks of honey and butter. That which he labored for shall he restore, and shall not swallow it down, according to his substance shall the restitution be, and he shall not rejoice therein. Because he hath oppressed and hath forsaken the poor, because he hath violently taken away a house which he builded not, surely he shall not feel quietness in his belly, he shall not save of that which he desired. There shall none of his meat be left, therefore shall no man look for his goods. In the fullness of his sufficiency he shall be in straits, every hand of the wicked shall come upon him. When he is about to fill his belly, God shall cast the fury of his wrath upon him, and shall rain it upon him while he is eating. He shall flee from the iron weapon, and the bow of steel shall strike him through. It is drawn, and cometh out of the body, yea, the glittering sword cometh out of his gall, terrors are upon him. All darkness shall be hid in his secret places, a fire not blown shall consume him, it shall go ill with him that is left in his tabernacle. The Heaven shall reveal his iniquity, and the Earth shall rise up against him. The increase of his house shall depart, and his goods shall flow away in the day of his wrath. This is the portion of a wicked man from God, and the heritage appointed unto him by God.

But Job answered and said, Hear diligently my speech, and let this be your consolations. Suffer me that I may speak, and after that I have spoken, mock on. As for me, is my complaint to man? and if it were so, why should not my spirit be troubled? Mark me, and be astonished, and lay your hand upon your mouth. Even when I remember I am afraid, and trembling taketh hold on my flesh. Wherefore do the wicked live, become old, yea, are mighty in power? Their seed is established in their sight with them, and their offspring before their eyes. Their houses are safe from fear, neither is the rod of God upon them. Their bull gendereth, and faileth not, their cow calveth, and casteth not her calf. They send forth their little ones like a flock, and their children dance. They take the timbrel and harp, and rejoice at the sound of the organ. They spend their days in wealth, and in a moment go down to the grave. Therefore they say unto God, Depart from us, for we desire not the knowledge of thy ways. What is the Almighty, that we should serve him, and what profit should we have, if we pray unto him? Lo, their good is not in their hand, the counsel of the wicked is far from me. How oft is the candle of the wicked put out! and how oft cometh their destruction upon them! God distributeth sorrows in his anger. They are as stubble before the wind, and as chaff that the storm carrieth away. God layeth up his iniquity for his children, he rewardeth him, and he shall know it. His eyes shall see his destruction, and he shall drink of the wrath of the Almighty. For what pleasure hath he in his house after him, when the number of his months is cut off in the midst? Shall any teach God knowledge? seeing he judgeth those that are high. One dieth in his full strength, being wholly at ease and quiet. His breasts are full of milk, and his bones are moistened with marrow. And another dieth in the bitterness of his soul, and never eateth with pleasure. They shall lie down alike in the dust, and the worms shall cover them. Behold, I know your thoughts, and the devices which ye wrongfully imagine against me. For ye say, Where is the house of the prince? and where are the dwelling places of the wicked? Have ye not asked them that go by the way? and do ye not know their tokens, that the wicked is reserved to the day of destruction? they shall be brought forth to the day of wrath. Who shall declare his way to his face? and who shall repay him what he hath done? Yet shall he be brought to the grave, and shall remain in the tomb. The clods of the valley shall be sweet unto him, and every man shall draw after him, as there are innumerable before him. How then comfort ye me in vain, seeing in your answers there remaineth falsehood.

Then Eliphaz the Temanite answered and said, Can a man be profitable unto God, as he that is wise may be profitable unto himself? Is it any pleasure to the Almighty, that thou art righteous? or is it gain to him, that thou makest thy ways perfect? Will he reprove thee for fear of thee? will he enter with thee into judgment? Is not thy wickedness great? and thine iniquities infinite? For thou hast taken a pledge from thy brother for naught, and stripped the naked of their clothing. Thou hast not given water to the weary to drink, and thou hast withholden bread from the hungry. But as for the mighty man, he had the Earth, and the honorable man dwelt in it. Thou hast sent widows away empty, and the arms of the fatherless have been broken. Therefore snares are round about thee, and sudden fear troubleth thee, or darkness, that thou canst not see? and abundance of waters cover thee. Is not God in the height of Heaven? and behold the height of the stars, how high they are! And thou sayest, How doth God know? can he judge through the dark cloud? Thick clouds are a covering to him, that he seeth not, and he walketh in the circuit of Heaven. Hast thou marked the old way which wicked men have trodden? Which were cut down out of time, whose foundation was overflown with a flood, which said unto God, Depart from us, and what can the Almighty do for them? Yet he filled their houses with good things, but the counsel of the wicked is far from me. The righteous see it, and are glad, and the innocent laugh them to scorn. Whereas our substance is not cut down, but the remnant of them the fire consumeth. Acquaint now thyself with him, and be at peace, thereby good shall come unto thee. Receive, I pray thee, the law from his mouth, and lay up his words in thine heart. If thou return to the Almighty, thou shalt be built up, thou shalt put away iniquity far from thy tabernacles. Then shalt thou lay up gold as dust, and the gold of Ophir as the stones of the brooks. Yea, the Almighty shall be thy defense, and thou shalt have plenty of silver. For then shalt thou have thy delight in the Almighty, and shalt lift up thy face unto God. Thou shalt make thy prayer unto him, and he shall hear thee, and thou shalt pay thy vows. Thou shalt also decree a thing, and it shall be established unto thee, and the light shall shine upon thy ways. When men are cast down, then thou shalt say, There is lifting up, and he shall save the humble person. He shall deliver the island of the innocent, and it is delivered by the pureness of thine hands.

Then Job answered and said, Even today is my complaint bitter, my stroke is heavier than my groaning. O that I knew where I might find him! that I might come even to his seat! I would order my cause before him, and fill my mouth with arguments. I would know the words which he would answer me, and understand what he would say unto me.

Will he plead against me with his great power? No, but he would put strength in me. There the righteous might dispute with him, so should I be delivered for ever from my judge. Behold, I go forward, but he is not there, and backward, but I cannot perceive him, on the left hand, where he doth work, but I cannot behold him, he hideth himself on the right hand, that I cannot see him: But he knoweth the way that I take, when he hath tried me, I shall come forth as gold. My foot hath held his steps, his way have I kept, and not declined. Neither have I gone back from the commandment of his lips, I have esteemed the words of his mouth more than my necessary food. But he is in one mind, and who can turn him? and what his soul desireth, even that he doeth. For he performeth the thing that is appointed for me, and many such things are with him. Therefore am I troubled at his presence, when I consider, I am afraid of him. For God maketh my heart soft, and the Almighty troubleth me, because I was not cut off before the darkness, neither hath he covered the darkness from my face. Why, seeing times are not hidden from the Almighty, do they that know him not see his days? Some remove the landmarks, they violently take away flocks, and feed thereof. They drive away the ass of the fatherless, they take the widow's ox for a pledge. They turn the needy out of the way, the poor of the Earth hide themselves together. Behold, as wild asses in the desert, go they forth to their work, rising betimes for a prey, the wilderness yieldeth food for them and for their children. They reap every one his corn in the field, and they gather the vintage of the wicked. They cause the naked to lodge without clothing, that they have no covering in the cold. They are wet with the showers of the mountains, and embrace the rock for want of a shelter. They pluck the fatherless from the breast, and take a pledge of the poor. They cause him to go naked without clothing, and they take away the sheaf from the hungry, which make oil within their walls, and tread their winepresses, and suffer thirst. Men groan from out of the city, and the soul of the wounded crieth out, yet God layeth not folly to them. They are of those that rebel against the light, they know not the ways thereof, nor abide in the paths thereof. The murderer rising with the light killeth the poor and needy, and in the night is as a thief. The eye also of the adulterer waiteth for the twilight, saying, No eye shall see me, and disguiseth his face. In the dark they dig through houses, which they had marked for themselves in the daytime, they know not the light. For the morning is to them even as the shadow of death, if one know them, they are in the terrors of the shadow of death. He is swift as the waters, their portion is cursed in the Earth, he beholdeth not the way of the vineyards. Drought and heat consume the snow waters, so doth the grave those which have sinned. The womb shall forget him, the worm shall feed sweetly on him, he shall be no more remembered, and wickedness shall be broken as a tree. He evil entreateth the barren that beareth not, and doeth not good to the widow. He draweth also the mighty with his power, he riseth up, and no man is sure of life. Though it be given him to be in safety, whereon he resteth, yet his eyes are upon their ways. They are exalted for a little while, but are gone and brought low, they are taken out of the way as all other, and cut off as the tops of the ears of corn. And if it be not so now, who will make me a liar, and make my speech nothing worth?

4 THEN answered Bildad the Shuhite, and said, Dominion and fear are with him, he maketh peace in his high places. Is there any number of his armies? and upon whom doth not his light arise? How then can man be justified with God? or how can he be clean that is born of a woman? Behold even to the moon, and it shineth not, yea, the stars are not pure in his sight. How much less man, that is a worm? and the son of man, which is a worm?

But Job answered and said, How hast thou helped him that is without power? how savest thou the arm that hath no strength? How hast thou counseled him that hath no wisdom? and how hast thou plentifully declared the thing as it is? To whom hast thou uttered words? and whose spirit came from thee? Dead things are formed from under the waters, and the inhabitants thereof. Hell is naked before him, and destruction hath no covering. He stretcheth out the north over the empty place, and hangeth the earth upon nothing. He bindeth up the waters in his thick clouds, and the cloud is not rent under them. He holdeth back the face of his throne, and spreadeth his cloud upon it. He hath compassed the waters with bounds, until the day and night come to an end. The pillars of Heaven tremble, and are astonished at his reproof. He divideth the sea with his power, and by his understanding he smiteth through the proud. By his Spirit he hath garnished the heavens, his hand hath formed the crooked serpent.

Lo, these are parts of his ways, but how little a portion is heard of him? but the thunder of his power who can understand?

Moreover Job continued his parable, and said, As God liveth, who hath taken away my judgment, and the Almighty, who hath vexed my soul, all the while my breath is in me, and the Spirit of God is in my nostrils, my lips shall not speak wickedness, nor my tongue utter deceit. God forbid that I should justify you, till I die I will not remove mine integrity from me. My righteousness I hold fast, and will not let it go, my heart shall not reproach me so long as I live. Let mine enemy be as the wicked, and he that riseth up against me as the unrighteous. For what is the hope of the hypocrite, though he hath gained, when God taketh away his soul? Will God hear his cry when trouble cometh upon him? Will he delight himself in the Almighty? will he always call upon God? I will teach you by the hand of God, that which is with the Almighty will I not conceal. Behold, all ye yourselves have seen it, why then are ye thus altogether vain?

This is the portion of a wicked man with God, and the heritage of oppressors, which they shall receive of the Almighty. If his children be multiplied, it is for the sword, and his offspring shall not be satisfied with bread. Those that remain of him shall be buried in death, and his widows shall not weep. Though he heap up silver as the dust, and prepare raiment as the clay, he may prepare it, but the just shall put it on, and the innocent shall divide the silver. He buildeth his house as a moth, and as a booth that the keeper maketh. The rich man shall lie down, but he shall not be gathered, he openeth his eyes, and he is not. Terrors take hold on him as waters, a tempest stealeth him away in the night. The east wind carrieth him away, and he departeth, and as a storm hurleth him out of his place. For God shall cast upon him, and not spare, he would fain flee out of his hand. Men shall clap their hands at him, and shall hiss him out of his place. Surely there is a vein for the silver, and a place for gold where they find it. Iron is taken out of the Earth, and brass is molten out of the stone. He setteth an end to darkness, and searcheth out all perfection, the stones of darkness, and the shadow of death. The flood breaketh out from the inhabitant, even the waters forgotten of the foot, they are dried up, they are gone away from men. As for the Earth, out of it cometh bread, and under it is turned up as it were fire. The stones of it are the place of sapphires, and it hath dust of gold. There is a path which no fowl knoweth, and which the vulture's eye hath not seen, the lion's whelps have not trodden it, nor the fierce lion passed by it. He putteth forth his hand upon the rock, he overturneth the mountains by the roots. He cutteth out rivers among the rocks, and his eye seeth every precious thing. He bindeth the floods from overflowing, and the thing that is hid bringeth he forth to light. But where shall wisdom be found? and where is the place of understanding? Man knoweth not the price thereof, neither is it found in the land of the living. The depth saith, It is not in me, and the sea saith, It is not with me. It cannot be gotten for gold, neither shall silver be weighed for the price thereof. It cannot be valued with the gold of Ophir, with the precious onyx, or the sapphire. The gold and the crystal cannot equal it, and the exchange of it shall not be for jewels of fine gold. No mention shall be made of coral, or of pearls, for the price of wisdom is above rubies. The topaz of Ethiopia shall not equal it, neither shall it be valued with pure gold. Whence then cometh wisdom? and where is the place of understanding? Seeing it is hid from the eyes of all living, and kept close from the fowls of the air. Destruction and death say, We have heard the fame thereof with our ears. God understandeth the way thereof, and he knoweth the place thereof. For he looketh to the ends of the Earth, and seeth under the whole Heaven, To make the weight for the winds, and he weigheth the waters by measure. When he made a decree for the rain, and a way for the lightning of the thunder, then did he see it, and declare it, he prepared it, yea, and searched it out. And unto man he said, Behold, the fear of the Lord, that is wisdom, and to depart from evil is understanding.

Moreover Job continued his parable, and said, O that I were as in months past, as in the days when God preserved me, when his candle shined upon my head, and when by his light I walked through darkness, as I was in the days of my youth, when the secret of God was upon my tabernacle, when the Almighty was yet with me, when my children were about me, when I washed my steps with butter, and the rock poured me out rivers of oil, When I went out to the gate through the city, when I prepared my seat in the street! The young men saw me, and hid themselves, and the aged arose, and stood up. The princes refrained talking, and laid their hand on their mouth. The nobles held their peace, and their tongue cleaved to the roof of their mouth. When the ear heard me, then it blessed me, and when the eye saw me, it gave witness to me, because I delivered the poor that cried, and the fatherless, and him that had none to help him. The blessing of him that was ready to perish came upon me, and I caused the widow's heart to sing for joy. I put on righteousness, and it clothed me, my judgment was as a robe and a diadem. I was eyes to the blind, and feet was I to the lame. I was a father to the poor, and the cause which I knew not I searched out. And I brake the jaws of the wicked, and plucked the spoil out of his teeth. Then I said, I shall die in my nest, and I shall multiply my days as the sand. My root was spread out by the waters, and the dew lay all night upon my branch. My glory was fresh in me, and my bow was renewed in my hand. Unto me men gave ear, and waited, and kept silence at my counsel. After my words they spake not again, and my speech dropped upon them. And they waited for me as for the rain, and they opened their mouth wide as for the latter rain. If I laughed on them, they believed it not, and the light of my countenance they cast not down. I chose out their way, and sat chief, and dwelt as a king in the army, as one that comforteth the mourners. But now they that are younger than I have me in derision, whose fathers I would have disdained to have set with the dogs of my flock. Yea, whereto might the strength of their hands profit me, in whom old age was perished? For want and famine they were solitary, fleeing into the wilderness in former time desolate and waste, who cut up mallows by the bushes, and juniper roots for their meat. They were driven forth from among men, (they cried after them as after a thief,) to dwell in the cliffs of the valleys, in caves of the earth, and in the rocks. Among the bushes they brayed, under the nettles they were gathered together. They were children of fools, yea, children of base men, they were viler than the earth. And now am I their song, yea, I am their byword. They abhor me, they flee far from me, and spare not to spit in my face. Because he hath loosed my cord, and afflicted me, they have also let loose the bridle before me. Upon my right hand rise the youth, they push away my feet, and they raise up against me the ways of their destruction. They mar my path, they set forward my calamity, they have no helper. They came upon me as a wide breaking in of waters, in the desolation they rolled themselves upon me. Terrors are turned upon me, they pursue my soul as the wind, and my welfare passeth away as a cloud. And now my soul is poured out upon me, the days of affliction have taken hold upon me. My bones are pierced in me in the night season, and my sinews take no rest. By the great force of my disease is my garment changed, it bindeth me about as the collar of my coat. He hath cast me into the mire, and I am become like dust and ashes. I cry unto thee, and thou dost not hear me, I stand up, and thou regardest me not. Thou art become cruel to me, with thy strong hand thou opposest thyself against me. Thou liftest me up to the wind, thou causest me to ride upon it, and dissolvest my substance. For I know that thou wilt bring me to death, and to the house appointed for all living. Howbeit he will not stretch out his hand to the grave, though they cry in his destruction.

 Did not I weep for him that was in trouble? was not my soul grieved for the poor? When I looked for good, then evil came unto me, and when I waited for light, there came darkness. My bowels boiled, and rested not, the days of affliction prevented me. I went mourning without the sun, I stood up, and I cried in the congregation. I am a brother to dragons, and a companion to owls. My skin is black upon me, and my bones are burned with heat. My harp also is turned to mourning, and my organ into the voice of them that weep. I made a covenant with mine eyes, why then should I think upon a maid? For what portion of God is there from above? and what inheritance of the Almighty from on high? Is not destruction to the wicked? and a strange punishment to the workers of iniquity? Doth not he see my ways, and count all my steps? If I have walked with vanity, or if my foot hath hasted to deceit, let me be weighed in an even balance, that God may know mine integrity. If my step hath turned out of the way, and mine heart walked after mine eyes, and if any blot hath cleaved to mine hands, then let me sow, and let another eat, yea, let my offspring be rooted out. If mine heart have been deceived by a woman, or if I have laid wait at my neighbor's door, then let my wife grind unto another, and let others bow down upon her. For this is a heinous crime, yea, it is an iniquity to be punished by the judges. For it is a fire that consumeth to destruction, and would root out all mine increase. If I did despise the cause of my manservant or of my maidservant, when they contended with me, what then shall I do when God riseth up? and when he visiteth, what shall I answer him? Did not he that made me in the womb make him? and did not one fashion us in the womb? If I have withheld the poor from their desire, or have caused the eyes of the widow to fail, or have eaten my morsel myself alone, and the fatherless hath not eaten thereof, (for from my youth he was brought up with me, as with a father, and I have guided her from my mother's womb,) if I have seen any perish for want of clothing, or any poor without covering, if his loins have not blessed me, and if he were not warmed with the fleece of my sheep, if I have lifted up my hand against the fatherless, when I saw my help in the gate, then let mine arm fall from my shoulder blade, and mine arm be broken from the bone. For destruction from God was a terror to me, and by reason of his highness I could not endure. If I have made gold my hope, or have said to the fine gold, Thou art my confidence, if I rejoiced because my wealth was great, and because mine hand had gotten much, if I beheld the sun when it shined, or the moon walking in brightness, and my heart hath been secretly enticed, or my mouth hath kissed my hand, this also were an iniquity to be punished by the judge, for I should have denied the God that is above. If I rejoiced at the destruction of him that hated me, or lifted up myself when evil found him, (neither have I suffered my mouth to sin by wishing a curse to his soul.) If the men of my tabernacle said not, O that we had of his flesh! we cannot be satisfied. The stranger did not lodge in the street, but I opened my doors to the traveler. If I covered my transgressions as Adam, by hiding mine iniquity in my bosom, did I fear a great multitude, or did the contempt of families terrify me, that I kept silence, and went not out of the door? O that one would hear me! behold, my desire is, that the Almighty would answer me, and that mine adversary had written a book. Surely I would take it upon my shoulder, and bind it as a crown to me. I would declare unto him the number of my steps, as a prince would I go near unto him. If my land cry against me, or that the furrows likewise thereof complain, if I have eaten the fruits thereof without money, or have caused the owners thereof to lose their life, let thistles grow instead of wheat, and cockle instead of barley. The words of Job are ended.

5 SO these three men ceased to answer Job, because he was righteous in his own eyes. Then was kindled the wrath of Elihu the son of Barachel the Buzite, of the kindred of Ram, against Job was his wrath kindled, because he justified

himself rather than God. Also against his three friends was his wrath kindled, because they had found no answer, and yet had condemned Job. Now Elihu had waited till Job had spoken, because they were elder than he. When Elihu saw that there was no answer in the mouth of these three men, then his wrath was kindled.

And Elihu the son of Barachel the Buzite answered and said, I am young, and ye are very old, wherefore I was afraid, and durst not show you mine opinion. I said, Days should speak, and multitude of years should teach wisdom. But there is a spirit in man, and the inspiration of the Almighty giveth them understanding. Great men are not always wise, neither do the aged understand judgment. Therefore I said, Hearken to me, I also will show mine opinion. Behold, I waited for your words, I gave ear to your reasons, whilst ye searched out what to say. Yea, I attended unto you, and behold, there was none of you that convinced Job, or that answered his words, lest ye should say, We have found out wisdom, God thrusteth him down, not man. Now he hath not directed his words against me, neither will I answer him with your speeches.

They were amazed, they answered no more, they left off speaking. When I had waited, (for they spake not, but stood still, and answered no more,) I said, I will answer also my part, I also will show mine opinion. For I am full of matter, the spirit within me constraineth me. Behold, my belly is as wine which hath no vent, it is ready to burst like new bottles. I will speak, that I may be refreshed, I will open my lips and answer. Let me not, I pray you, accept any man's person, neither let me give flattering titles unto man. For I know not to give flattering titles, in so doing my Maker would soon take me away.

Wherefore, Job, I pray thee, hear my speeches, and hearken to all my words. Behold, now I have opened my mouth, my tongue hath spoken in my mouth. My words shall be of the uprightness of my heart, and my lips shall utter knowledge clearly. The Spirit of God hath made me, and the breath of the Almighty hath given me life. If thou canst answer me, set thy words in order before me, stand up. Behold, I am according to thy wish in God's stead, I also am formed out of the clay. Behold, my terror shall not make thee afraid, neither shall my hand be heavy upon thee. Surely thou hast spoken in mine hearing, and I have heard the voice of thy words, saying, I am clean without transgression, I am innocent, neither is there iniquity in me. Behold, he findeth occasions against me, he counteth me for his enemy, he putteth my feet in the stocks, he marketh all my paths. Behold, in this thou art not just, I will answer thee, that God is greater than man. Why dost thou strive against him? for he giveth not account of any of his matters. For God speaketh once, yea twice, yet man perceiveth it not. In a dream, in a vision of the night, when deep sleep falleth upon men, in slumberings upon the bed, then he openeth the ears of men, and sealeth their instruction, that he may withdraw man from his purpose, and hide pride from man. He keepeth back his soul from the pit, and his life from perishing by the sword. He is chastened also with pain upon his bed, and the multitude of his bones with strong pain, so that his life abhorreth bread, and his soul dainty meat. His flesh is consumed away, that it cannot be seen, and his bones that were not seen stick out. Yea, his soul draweth near unto the grave, and his life to the destroyers. If there be a messenger with him, an interpreter, one among a thousand, to show unto man his uprightness, then he is gracious unto him, and saith, Deliver him from going down to the pit, I have found a ransom. His flesh shall be fresher than a child's, he shall return to the days of his youth, he shall pray unto God, and he will be favorable unto him, and he shall see his face with joy, for he will render unto man his righteousness. He looketh upon men, and if any say, I have sinned, and perverted that which was right, and it profited me not, he will deliver his soul from going into the pit, and his life shall see the light. Lo, all these things worketh God oftentimes with man. To bring back his soul from the pit, to be enlightened with the light of the living. Mark well, O Job, hearken unto me, hold thy peace, and I will speak. If thou hast anything to say, answer me, speak, for I desire to justify thee. If not, hearken unto me, hold thy peace, and I shall teach thee wisdom.

Furthermore Elihu answered and said, Hear my words, O ye wise men, and give ear unto me, ye that have knowledge. For the ear trieth words, as the mouth tasteth meat. Let us choose to us judgment, let us know among ourselves what is good. For Job hath said, I am righteous, and God hath taken away my judgment. Should I lie against my right? my wound is incurable without transgression. What man is like Job, who drinketh up scorning like water? Which goeth in company with the workers of iniquity, and walketh with wicked men. For he hath said, It profiteth a man nothing that he should delight himself with God. Therefore hearken unto me, ye men of understanding, far be it from God, that he should do wickedness, and from the Almighty, that he should commit iniquity. For the work of a man shall he render unto him, and cause every man to find according to his ways. Yea, surely God will not do wickedly, neither will the Almighty pervert judgment. Who hath given him a charge over the Earth? or who hath disposed the whole world? If he set his heart upon man, if he gather unto himself his spirit and his breath, all flesh shall perish together, and man shall turn again unto dust. If now thou hast understanding, hear this, hearken to the voice of my words. Shall even he that hateth right govern? and wilt thou condemn him that is most just? Is it fit to say to a king, Thou art wicked? and to princes, Ye are ungodly? How much less to him that accepteth not the persons of princes, nor regardeth the rich more than the poor? for they all are the work of his hands. In a moment shall they die, and the people shall be troubled at midnight, and pass away, and the mighty shall be taken away without hand. For his eyes are upon the ways of man, and he seeth all his goings. There is no darkness, nor shadow of death, where the workers of iniquity may hide themselves. For he will not lay upon man more than right, that he should enter into judgment with God. He shall break in pieces mighty men without number, and set others in their stead. Therefore he knoweth their works, and he overturneth them in the night, so that they are destroyed. He striketh them as wicked men in the open sight of others, because they turned back from him, and would not consider any of his ways, so that they cause the cry of the poor to come unto him, and he heareth the cry of the afflicted.

When he giveth quietness, who then can make trouble? and when he hideth his face, who then can behold him? whether it be done against a nation, or against a man only, that the hypocrite reign not, lest the people be ensnared. Surely it is meet to be said unto God, I have borne chastisement, I will not offend anymore. That which I see not teach thou me, if I have done iniquity, I will do no more. Should it be according to thy mind? he will recompense it, whether thou refuse, or whether thou choose, and not I, therefore speak what thou knowest. Let men of understanding tell me, and let a wise man hearken unto me. Job hath spoken without knowledge, and his words were without wisdom. My desire is that Job may be tried unto the end, because of his answers for wicked men. For he addeth rebellion unto his sin, he clappeth his hands among us, and multiplieth his words against God.

Elihu spake moreover, and said, Thinkest thou this to be right, that thou saidst, My righteousness is more than God's? For thou saidst, What advantage will it be unto thee? and, What profit shall I have, if I be cleansed from my sin? I will answer thee, and thy companions with thee. Look unto the heavens, and see, and behold the clouds which are higher than thou. If thou sinnest, what doest thou against him? or if thy transgressions be multiplied, what doest thou unto him? If thou be righteous, what givest thou him? or what receiveth he of thine hand? Thy wickedness may hurt a man as thou art, and thy righteousness may profit the son of man. By reason of the multitude of oppressions they make the oppressed to cry, they cry out by reason of the arm of the mighty. But none saith, Where is God my maker, who giveth songs in the night, who teacheth us more than the beasts of the Earth, and maketh us wiser than the fowls of Heaven? There they cry, but none giveth answer, because of the pride of evil men. Surely God will not hear vanity, neither will the Almighty regard it. Although thou sayest thou shalt not see him, yet judgment is before him, therefore trust thou in him. But now, because it is not so, he hath visited in his anger, yet he knoweth it not in great extremity, therefore doth Job open his mouth in vain, he multiplieth words without knowledge.

Elihu also proceeded, and said, Suffer me a little, and I will show thee that I have yet to speak on God's behalf. I will fetch my knowledge from afar, and will ascribe righteousness to my Maker. For truly my words shall not be false, he that is perfect in knowledge is with thee. Behold, God is mighty, and despiseth not any, he is mighty in strength and wisdom. He preserveth not the life of the wicked, but giveth right to the poor. He withdraweth not his eyes from the righteous, but with kings are they on the throne, yea, he doth establish them forever, and they are exalted. And if they be bound in fetters, and be holden in cords of affliction, then he showeth them their work, and their transgressions that they have exceeded. He openeth also their ear to discipline, and commandeth that they return from iniquity.

If they obey and serve him, they shall spend their days in prosperity, and their years in pleasures. But if they obey not, they shall perish by the sword, and they shall die without knowledge. But the hypocrites in heart heap up wrath, they cry not when he bindeth them. They die in youth, and their life is among the unclean. He delivereth the poor in his affliction, and openeth their ears in oppression. Even so would he have removed thee out of the strait into a broad place, where there is no straitness, and that which should be set on thy table should be full of fatness. But thou hast fulfilled the judgment of the wicked, judgment and justice take hold on thee. Because there is wrath, beware lest he take thee away with his stroke, then a great ransom cannot deliver thee. Will he esteem thy riches, no, not gold, nor all the forces of strength. Desire not the night, when people are cut off in their place. Take heed, regard not iniquity, for this hast thou chosen rather than affliction. Behold, God exalteth by his power, who teacheth like him? Who hath enjoined him his way? or who can say, Thou hast wrought iniquity? Remember that thou magnify his work, which men behold. Every man may see it, man may behold it afar off. Behold, God is great, and we know him not, neither can the number of his years be searched out. For he maketh small the drops of water, they pour down rain according to the vapor thereof, which the clouds do drop and distil upon man abundantly. Also can any understand the spreadings of the clouds, or the noise of his tabernacle?

Behold, he spreadeth his light upon it, and covereth the bottom of the sea. For by them judgeth he the people, he giveth meat in abundance. With clouds he covereth the light, and commandeth it not to shine by the cloud that cometh betwixt. The noise thereof showeth concerning it, the cattle also concerning the vapor. At this also my heart trembleth, and is moved out of his place. Hear attentively the noise of his voice, and the sound that goeth out of his mouth. He directeth it under the whole Heaven, and his lightning unto the ends of the Earth. After it a voice roareth, he thundereth with the voice of his excellency, and he will not stay them when his voice is heard. God thundereth marvelously with his voice, great things doeth he, which we cannot comprehend. For he saith to the snow, Be thou on the Earth, likewise to the small rain, and to the great rain of his strength. He sealeth up the hand of every man, that all men may know his work. Then the beasts go into dens, and remain in their places. Out of the south cometh the whirlwind, and cold out of the north. By the breath of God frost is given, and the breadth of the waters is straitened. Also by watering he wearieth the thick cloud, he scattereth his bright cloud, and it is turned round about by his counsels, that they may do whatsoever he commandeth them upon the face of the world in the Earth. He causeth it to come, whether for correction, or for his land, or for mercy. Hearken unto this, O Job, stand still, and consider the wondrous works of God. Dost thou know when God disposed them, and caused the light of his cloud to shine? Dost thou know the balancings of the clouds, the wondrous works of him which is perfect in knowledge? How thy garments are warm, when he quieteth the Earth by the south wind? Hast thou with him spread out the sky, which is strong, and as a molten looking glass? Teach us what we shall say unto him, for we cannot order our speech by reason of darkness. Shall it be told him that I speak? if a man speak, surely he shall be swallowed up. And now men see not the bright light which is in the clouds, but the wind passeth, and cleanseth them. Fair weather cometh out of the north, with God is terrible majesty. Touching the Almighty, we cannot find him out, he is excellent in power, and in judgment, and in plenty of justice, he will not afflict. Men do therefore fear him, he respecteth not any that are wise of heart.

6 THEN the Lord answered Job out of the whirlwind, and said, Who is this that darkeneth counsel by words without knowledge? Gird up now thy loins like a man, for I will demand of thee, and answer thou me.

Where wast thou when I laid the foundations of the Earth? declare, if thou hast understanding. Who hath laid the measures thereof, if thou knowest? or who hath stretched the line upon it? Whereupon are the foundations thereof fastened? or who laid the cornerstone thereof, when the morning stars sang together, and all the sons of God shouted for joy?

Or who shut up the sea with doors, when it brake forth, as if it had issued out of the womb? When I made the cloud the garment thereof, and thick darkness a swaddling band for it, and brake up for it my decreed place, and set bars and doors, and said, Hitherto shalt thou come, but no further, and here shall thy proud waves be stayed?

Hast thou commanded the morning since thy days, and caused the dayspring to know his place, that it might take hold of the ends of the Earth, that the wicked might be shaken out of it? It is turned as clay to the seal, and they stand as a garment. And from the wicked their light is withholden, and the high arm shall be broken.

Hast thou entered into the springs of the sea? or hast thou walked in the search of the depth? Have the gates of death been opened unto thee? or hast thou seen the doors of the shadow of death? Hast thou perceived the breadth of the Earth? declare if thou knowest it all. Where is the way where light dwelleth? and as for darkness, where is the place thereof, that thou shouldest take it to the bound thereof, and that thou shouldest know the paths to the house thereof? Knowest thou it, because thou wast then born? or because the number of thy days is great?

Hast thou entered into the treasures of the snow? or hast thou seen the treasures of the hail, which I have reserved against the time of trouble, against the day of battle and war? By what way is the light parted, which scattereth the east wind upon the Earth? Who hath divided a water course for the overflowing of waters, or a way for the lightning of thunder, to cause it to rain on the Earth where no man is, on the wilderness wherein there is no man, to satisfy the desolate and waste ground, and to cause the bud of the tender herb to spring forth?

Hath the rain a father? or who hath begotten the drops of dew? Out of whose womb came the ice? and the hoary frost of Heaven, who hath gendered it? The waters are hid as with a stone, and the face of the deep is frozen.

Canst thou bind the sweet influences of Pleiades, or loose the bands of Orion? Canst thou bring forth Mazzaroth in his season? or canst thou guide Arcturus with his sons? Knowest thou the ordinances of Heaven? cast thou set the dominion thereof in the Earth?

Canst thou lift up thy voice to the clouds, that abundance of waters may cover thee? Canst thou send lightnings, that they may go, and say unto thee, Here we are? Who hath put wisdom in the inward parts? or who hath given understanding to the heart? Who can number the clouds in wisdom? or who can stay the bottles of Heaven. When the dust groweth into hardness, and the clods cleave fast together?

Wilt thou hunt the prey for the lion? or fill the appetite of the young lions. When they couch in their dens, and abide in the covert to lie in wait? Who provideth for the raven his food? when his young ones cry unto God, they wander for lack of meat.

Knowest thou the time when the wild goats of the rock bring forth? or canst thou mark when the hinds do calve? Canst thou number the months that they fulfill? or knowest thou the time when they bring forth? They bow themselves, they bring forth their young ones, they cast out their sorrows. Their young ones are in good liking, they grow up with corn, they go forth, and return not unto them.

Who hath sent out the wild ass free? or who hath loosed the bands of the wild ass? Whose house I have made the wilderness, and the barren land his dwellings. He scorneth the multitude of the city, neither regardeth he the crying of the driver. The range of the mountains is his pasture, and he searcheth after every green thing.

Will the unicorn be willing to serve thee, or abide by thy crib? Canst thou bind the unicorn with his band in the furrow? or will he harrow the valleys after thee? Wilt thou trust him, because his strength is great? or wilt thou leave thy labor to him? Wilt thou believe him, that he will bring home thy seed, and gather it into thy barn?

Gavest thou the goodly wings unto the peacocks? or wings and feathers unto the ostrich? Which leaveth her eggs in the earth, and warmeth them in the dust, and forgetteth that the foot may crush them, or that the wild beast may break them. She is hardened against her young ones, as though they were not hers, her labor is in vain without fear, because God hath deprived her of wisdom, neither hath he imparted to her understanding. What time she lifteth up herself on high, she scorneth the horse and his rider.

Hast thou given the horse strength? hast thou clothed his neck with thunder? Canst thou make him afraid as a grasshopper? the glory of his nostrils is terrible. He paweth in the valley, and rejoiceth in his strength, he goeth on to meet the armed men. He mocketh at fear, and is not affrighted, neither turneth he back from the sword, the quiver rattleth against him, the glittering spear and the shield. He swalloweth the ground with fierceness and rage, neither believeth he that it is the sound of the trumpet. He saith among the trumpets, Ha, Ha! and he smelleth the battle afar off, the thunder of the captains, and the shouting.

Doth the hawk fly by thy wisdom, and stretch her wings toward the south? Doth the eagle mount up at thy command, and make her nest on high? She dwelleth and abideth on the rock, upon the crag of the rock, and the strong place. From thence she seeketh the prey, and her eyes behold afar off. Her young ones also suck up blood, and where the slain are, there is she.

Moreover the Lord answered Job, and said, Shall he that contendeth with the Almighty instruct him? he that reproveth God, let him answer it.

7 THEN Job answered the Lord, and said, Behold, I am vile, what shall I answer thee? I will lay mine hand upon my mouth. Once have I spoken, but I will not answer, yea, twice, but I will proceed no further.

Then answered the Lord unto Job out of the whirlwind, and said, Gird up thy loins now like a man, I will demand of thee, and declare thou unto me. Wilt thou also disannul my judgment? wilt thou condemn me, that thou mayest be righteous? Hast thou an arm like God? or canst thou thunder with a voice like him?

Deck thyself now with majesty and excellency, and array thyself with glory and beauty. Cast abroad the rage of thy wrath, and behold everyone that is proud, and abase him. Look on everyone that is proud, and bring him low, and tread down the wicked in their place. Hide them in the dust together, and bind their faces in secret. Then will I also confess unto thee that thine own right hand can save thee.

Behold now behemoth, which I made with thee? he eateth grass as an ox. Lo now, his strength is in his loins, and his force is in the navel of his belly. He moveth his tail like a cedar, the sinews of his stones are wrapped together. His bones are as strong pieces of brass, his bones are like bars of iron.

He is the chief of the ways of God, he that made him can make his sword to approach unto him. Surely the mountains bring him forth food, where all the beasts of the field play. He lieth under the shady trees, in the covert of the reed, and fens. The shady trees cover him with their shadow, the willows of the brook compass him about. Behold, he drinketh up a river, and hasteth not, he trusteth that he can draw up Jordan into his mouth. He taketh it with his eyes, his nose pierceth through snares.

Canst thou draw out leviathan with a hook, or his tongue with a cord which thou lettest down? Canst thou put a hook into his nose? or bore his jaw through with a thorn? Will he make many supplications unto thee? will he speak soft words unto thee? Will he make a covenant with thee? wilt thou take him for a servant forever? Wilt thou play with him as with a bird? or wilt thou bind him for thy maidens? Shall the companions make a banquet of him? shall they part him among the merchants? Canst thou fill his skin with barbed irons? or his head with fish spears? Lay thine hand upon him, remember the battle, do no more. Behold, the hope of him is in vain, shall not one be cast down even at the sight of him?

None is so fierce that dare stir him up, who then is able to stand before me? Who hath prevented me, that I should repay him? whatsoever is under the whole Heaven is mine.

I will not conceal his parts, nor his power, nor his comely proportion. Who can discover the face of his garment? or who can come to him with his double bridle? Who can open the doors of his face? his teeth are terrible round about. His scales are his pride, shut up together as with a close seal. One is so near to another, that no air can come between them. They are joined one to another, they stick together, that they cannot be sundered. By his neesings a light doth shine, and his eyes are like the eyelids of the morning. Out of his mouth go burning lamps, and sparks of fire leap out. Out of his nostrils goeth smoke, as out of a seething pot or caldron. His breath kindleth coals, and a flame goeth out of his mouth. In his neck remaineth strength, and sorrow is turned into joy before him. The flakes of his flesh are joined together, they are firm in themselves, they cannot be moved. His heart is as firm as a stone, yea, as hard as a piece of the nether millstone. When he raiseth up himself, the mighty are afraid, by reason of breakings they purify themselves. The sword of him that layeth at him cannot hold, the spear, the dart, nor the habergeon. He esteemeth iron as straw, and brass as rotten wood. The arrow cannot make him flee, sling-stones are turned with him into stubble. Darts are counted as stubble, he laugheth at the shaking of a spear. Sharp stones are under him, he spreadeth sharp pointed things upon the mire. He maketh the deep to boil like a pot, he maketh the sea like a pot of ointment. He maketh a path to shine after him, one would think the deep to be hoary. Upon Earth there is not his like, who is made without fear. He beholdeth all high things, he is a king over all the children of pride.

Then Job answered the Lord, and said, I know that thou canst do everything, and that no thought can be withholden from thee. Who is he that hideth counsel without knowledge? therefore have I uttered that I understood not, things too wonderful for me, which I knew not.

Hear, I beseech thee, and I will speak, I will demand of thee, and declare thou unto me. I have heard of thee by the hearing of the ear, but now mine eye seeth thee, wherefore I abhor myself, and repent in dust and ashes.

8 AND it was so, that after the Lord had spoken these words unto Job, the Lord said to Eliphaz the Temanite, My wrath is kindled against thee, and against thy two friends, for ye have not spoken of me the thing that is right, as my servant Job hath. Therefore take unto you now seven bullocks and seven rams, and go to my servant Job, and offer up for yourselves a burnt offering, and my servant Job shall pray for you, for him will I accept, lest I deal with you after your folly, in that ye have not spoken of me the things which is right, like my servant Job.

So Eliphaz the Temanite and Bildad the Shuhite and Zophar the Naamathite went, and did according as the Lord commanded them, the Lord also accepted Job. And the Lord turned the captivity of Job, when he prayed for his friends, also the Lord gave Job twice as much as he had before. Then came there unto him all his brethren, and all his sisters, and all they that had been of his acquaintance before, and did eat bread with him in his house, and they bemoaned him, and comforted him over all the evil that the Lord had brought upon him, every man also gave him a piece of money, and everyone an earring of gold.

So the Lord blessed the latter end of Job more than his beginning, for he had fourteen thousand sheep, and six thousand camels, and a thousand yoke of oxen, and a thousand she asses. He had also seven sons and three daughters. And he called the name of the first Jemima, and the name of the second, Kezia, and the name of the third Keren-happuch. And in all the land were no women found so fair as the daughters of Job, and their father gave them inheritance among their brethren. After this lived Job a hundred and forty years, and saw his sons, and his sons' sons, even four generations. So Job died, being old and full of days.

THE BOOK OF PSALMS

PSALM 1

Blessed is the man that walketh not in the counsel of the ungodly, nor standeth in the way of sinners, nor sitteth in the seat of the scornful. But his delight is in the law of the Lord and in his law doth he meditate day and night. And he shall be like a tree planted by the rivers of water that bringeth forth his fruit in his season, his leaf also shall not wither, and whatsoever he doeth shall prosper. The ungodly are not so, but are like the chaff which the wind driveth away. Therefore the ungodly shall not stand in the judgment, nor sinners in the congregation of the righteous. For the Lord knoweth the way of the righteous, but the way of the ungodly shall perish.

PSALM 2

Why do the heathen rage, and the people imagine a vain thing? The kings of the Earth set themselves, and the rulers take counsel together against the Lord and against his Anointed saying, Let us break their bands asunder and cast away their cords from us. He that sitteth in the heavens shall laugh, the Lord shall have them in derision. Then shall he speak unto them in his wrath and vex them in his sore displeasure. Yet have I set my King upon my holy hill of Zion. I will declare the decree, the Lord hath said unto me, Thou art my Son, this day have I begotten thee. Ask of me and I shall give thee the heathen for thine inheritance and the uttermost parts of the Earth for thy possession. Thou shalt break them with a rod of iron, thou shalt dash them in pieces like a potter's vessel. Be wise now therefore, O ye kings, be instructed, ye judges of the Earth. Serve the Lord with fear and rejoice with trembling. Kiss the Son, lest he be angry and ye perish from the way when his wrath is kindled but a little. Blessed are all they that put their trust in him.

PSALM 3

A Psalm of David, when he fled from Absalom his son.

Lord, how are they increased that trouble me! Many are they that rise up against me. Many there be which say of my soul, There is no help for him in God. Selah. But thou, O Lord, art a shield for me, my glory and the lifter up of mine head. I cried unto the Lord with my voice and he heard me out of his holy hill. Selah. I laid me down and slept, I awaked, for the Lord sustained me. I will not be afraid of ten thousands of people that have set themselves against me round about. Arise, O Lord, save me, O my God, for thou hast smitten all mine enemies upon the cheekbone, thou hast broken the teeth of the ungodly. Salvation belongeth unto the Lord, thy blessing is upon thy people. Selah.

PSALM 4

To the chief Musician on Neginoth, A Psalm of David

Hear me when I call, O God of my righteousness, thou hast enlarged me when I was in distress; have mercy upon me and hear my prayer. O ye sons of men, how long will ye turn my glory into shame? How long will ye love vanity and seek after leasing? Selah. But know that the Lord hath set apart him that is godly for himself, the Lord will hear when I call unto him. Stand in awe and sin not, commune with your own heart upon your bed and be still. Selah. Offer the sacrifices of righteousness and put your trust in the Lord. There be many that say, Who will show us any good? Lord, lift thou up the light of thy countenance upon us. Thou hast put gladness in my heart, more than in the time that their corn and their wine increased. I will both lay me down in peace and sleep, for thou, Lord, only makest me dwell in safety.

PSALM 5

To the chief Musician upon Nehiloth, A Psalm of David.

Give ear to my words, O Lord, consider my meditation. Hearken unto the voice of my cry, my King and my God, for unto thee will I pray. My voice shalt thou hear in the morning, O Lord, in the morning will I direct my prayer unto thee and will look up. For thou art not a God that hath pleasure in wickedness, neither shall evil dwell with thee. The foolish shall not stand in thy sight; thou hatest all workers of iniquity. Thou shalt destroy them that speak leasing, the Lord will abhor the bloody and deceitful man. But as for me, I will come into thy house in the multitude of thy mercy and in thy fear will I worship toward thy holy temple. Lead me, O Lord, in thy righteousness because of mine enemies, make thy way straight before my face. For there is no faithfulness in their mouth, their inward part is very wickedness, their throat is an open sepulcher, they flatter with their tongue. Destroy thou them, O God, let them fall by their own counsels, cast them out in the multitude of their transgressions, for they have rebelled against thee. But let all those that put their trust in thee rejoice, let them ever shout for joy because thou defendest them, let them also that love thy name be joyful in thee. For thou, Lord, wilt bless the righteous, with favor wilt thou compass him as with a shield.

PSALM 6
To the chief Musician on Neginoth upon Sheminith, A Psalm of David.

Lord, rebuke me not in thine anger, neither chasten me in thy hot displeasure. Have mercy upon me, O Lord, for I am weak; O Lord, heal me, for my bones are vexed. My soul is also sore vexed, but thou, O Lord, how long? Return, O Lord, deliver my soul, O save me for thy mercies' sake. For in death there is no remembrance of thee; in the grave, who shall give thee thanks? I am weary with my groaning, all the night make I my bed to swim, I water my couch with my tears. Mine eye is consumed because of grief, it waxeth old because of all mine enemies. Depart from me, all ye workers of iniquity, for the Lord hath heard the voice of my weeping. The Lord hath heard my supplication, the Lord will receive my prayer. Let all mine enemies be ashamed and sore vexed, let them return and be ashamed suddenly.

PSALM 7
*Shiggaion of David, which he sang unto the Lord
concerning the words of Cush the Benjamite.*

O Lord my God, in thee do I put my trust, save me from all them that persecute me, and deliver me lest he tear my soul like a lion, rending it in pieces, while there is none to deliver. O Lord my God, if I have done this, if there be iniquity in my hands, if I have rewarded evil unto him that was at peace with me (yea, I have delivered him that without cause is mine enemy), let the enemy persecute my soul and take it, yea, let him tread down my life upon the earth and lay mine honor in the dust. Selah. Arise, O Lord, in thine anger, lift up thyself because of the rage of mine enemies and awake for me to the judgment that thou hast commanded. So shall the congregation of the people compass thee about, for their sakes therefore return thou on high. The Lord shall judge the people, judge me, O Lord, according to my righteousness and according to mine integrity that is in me. O let the wickedness of the wicked come to an end, but establish the just, for the righteous God trieth the hearts and reins. My defense is of God, which saveth the upright in heart. God judgeth the righteous and God is angry with the wicked every day. If he turn not, he will whet his sword, he hath bent his bow and made it ready. He hath also prepared for him the instruments of death, he ordaineth his arrows against the persecutors. Behold, he travaileth with iniquity, and hath conceived mischief, and brought forth falsehood. He made a pit and digged it and is fallen into the ditch which he made. His mischief shall return upon his own head and his violent dealing shall come down upon his own pate. I will praise the Lord according to his righteousness and will sing praise to the name of the Lord most high.

PSALM 8
To the chief Musician upon Gittith, A Psalm of David.

O Lord our Lord, how excellent is thy name in all the Earth who hast set thy glory above the heavens! Out of the mouth of babes and sucklings hast thou ordained strength because of thine enemies that thou mightest still the enemy and the avenger. When I consider thy heavens, the work of thy fingers, the moon and the stars which thou hast ordained, what is man that thou art mindful of him? And the son of man that thou visitest him? For thou hast made him a little lower than the angels and hast crowned him with glory and honor. Thou madest him to have dominion over the works of thy hands, thou hast put all things under his feet, all sheep and oxen, yea, and the beasts of the field, the fowl of the air, and the fish of the sea, and whatsoever passeth through the paths of the seas. O Lord our Lord, how excellent is thy name in all the Earth!

PSALM 9
To the chief Musician upon Muthlabben, A Psalm of David.

I will praise thee, O Lord, with my whole heart, I will show forth all thy marvelous works. I will be glad and rejoice in thee, I will sing praise to thy name, O thou Most High. When mine enemies are turned back they shall fall and perish at thy presence. For thou hast maintained my right and my cause, thou satest in the throne judging right. Thou hast rebuked the heathen, thou hast destroyed the wicked, thou hast put out their name for ever and ever. O thou enemy, destructions are come to a perpetual end, and thou hast destroyed cities, their memorial is perished with them. But the Lord shall endure forever, he hath prepared his throne for judgment. And he shall judge the world in righteousness, he shall minister judgment to the people in uprightness. The Lord also will be a refuge for the oppressed, a refuge in times of trouble. And they that know thy name will put their trust in thee, for thou, Lord, hast not forsaken them that seek thee. Sing praises to the Lord which dwelleth in Zion, declare among the people his doings. When he maketh inquisition for blood, he remembereth them, he forgetteth not the cry of the humble. Have mercy upon me, O Lord, consider my trouble which I suffer of them that hate me, thou that liftest me up from the gates of death, that I may show forth all thy praise in the gates of the daughter of Zion, I will rejoice in thy salvation. The heathen are sunk down in the pit that they made, in the net which they hid is their own foot taken. The Lord is known by the judgment which he executeth, the wicked is snared in the work of his own hands. Higgaion. Selah. The wicked shall be turned into hell and all the nations that forget God. For the needy shall not always be forgotten, the expectation of the poor shall not perish forever. Arise, O Lord, let not man prevail, let the heathen be judged in thy sight. Put them in fear, O Lord, that the nations may know themselves to be but men. Selah.

PSALM 10
A psalm of David.

Why standest thou afar off, O Lord? Why hidest thou thyself in times of trouble? The wicked in his pride doth persecute the poor, let them be taken in the devices that they have imagined. For the wicked boasteth of his heart's desire and blesseth the covetous whom the Lord abhorreth. The wicked, through the pride of his countenance, will not seek after God, God is not in all his thoughts. His ways are always grievous, thy judgments are far above out of his sight, as for all his enemies, he puffeth at them. For he hath said in his heart, I shall not be moved, never in adversity. His mouth is full of cursing and deceit, and his heart is full of fraud, and under his tongue is mischief and vanity. He sitteth in the lurking places of the villages, in the secret places doth he murder the innocent, his eyes are privily set against the poor. He lieth in wait secretly as a lion in his den, he lieth in wait to catch the poor, he doth catch the poor when he draweth him into his net. He croucheth to the strong ones and humbleth himself, that the poor may fall by his devices. He hath said in his heart, God hath forgotten, he hideth his face, he will never see it. Arise, O Lord, O God, lift up thine hand, forget not the humble. The wicked condemn God, wherefore he doth say in his heart, Thou wilt not require iniquity at my hand. O Lord, thou hast seen all this, for thou beholdest mischief and spite, to requite it with thy hand. The poor committeth himself unto thee, thou art the helper of the fatherless. O Lord, thou wilt break the arm of the wicked and of the evil, and seek out his wickedness until thou find none that remain. And the Lord shall be king for ever and ever over his people, for the wicked shall perish out of his land. Lord, thou hast heard the desire of the humble, thou wilt prepare their heart, thou wilt cause thine ear to hear, to judge the fatherless and the oppressed, that the man of the Earth may no more oppress.

PSALM 11
To the chief Musician, A Psalm of David

In that day thou shalt come, O Lord, and I will put my trust in thee. Thou shalt say unto thy people, for mine ear hath heard thy voice, thou shalt say unto every soul, Flee unto my mountain, and the righteous shall flee like a bird that is let go from the snare of the fowler. For the wicked bend their bow, lo, they make ready their arrow upon the string, that they may privily shoot at the upright in heart to destroy their foundation. But the foundations of the wicked shall be destroyed and what can they do? For the Lord, when he shall come into his holy temple, sitting upon God's throne in Heaven, his eyes shall pierce the wicked. Behold his eyelids shall try the children of men, and he shall redeem the righteous, and they shall be tried. The Lord loveth the righteous, but the wicked and him that loveth violence, his soul hateth. Upon the wicked he shall rain snares, fire, and brimstone, and a horrible tempest, the portion of their cup. For the righteous Lord loveth righteousness, his countenance doth behold the upright.

PSALM 12
A psalm of David.

In that day thou shalt help, O Lord, the poor and the meek of the Earth. For the godly man shall cease to be found and the faithful fail from among the children of men. They shall speak vanity every one with his neighbor, with flattering lips, with a double heart do they speak. But the Lord shall cut off all flattering lips, the tongue that speaketh proud things, who have said, With our tongue will we prevail, our lips are our own; who shall be Lord over us? Therefore, thus saith the Lord, I will arise in that day, I will stand upon the Earth, and I will judge the earth for the oppression of the poor, for the sighing of the needy, and their cry hath entered into mine ear. Therefore the Lord shall sit in judgment upon all those who say in their hearts, We all sit in safety, and puffeth at him. These are the words of the Lord, yea, pure words like silver tried in a furnace of earth, purified seven times. Thou shalt save thy people, O Lord, thou shalt keep them, thou shalt preserve them from the wickedness of their generations forever. The wicked walk on every side and the vilest men are exalted, but in the day of their pride thou shalt visit them.

PSALM 13
The grace and mercy of God.

How long, O Lord, wilt thou withdraw thyself from me? How long wilt thou hide thy face from me, that I may not see thee? Wilt thou forget me and cast me off from thy presence forever? How long shall I take counsel in my soul, sorrowing in my heart daily? How long shall mine enemy be exalted over me? Consider me, O Lord, and hear my cry, O my God, and lighten mine eyes, lest I sleep the death of the ungodly, lest mine enemy say, I have prevailed against him. Those that trouble me rejoice when I am moved, but I have trusted in thy mercy, my heart shall rejoice in thy salvation. I will sing unto the Lord because he hath dealt bountifully with me.

PSALM 14
To the chief Musician, A Psalm of David.

The fool hath said in his heart, There is no man that hath seen God. Because he showeth himself not unto us, therefore there is no God. Behold, they are corrupt, thy have done abominable works, and none of them doeth good. For the Lord looked down from Heaven upon the children of men, and by his voice said unto his servant, Seek ye among the children of men to see if there are any that do understand God. And he opened his mouth unto the Lord and said, Behold, all these who say they are thine. The Lord answered and said, They are all gone aside, they are together become filthy, thou canst behold none of them that are doing good, no, not one. All they have for their teachers are workers of iniquity and there is no knowledge in them. They are they who eat up my people. They eat bread and call not upon the Lord. They are in great fear, for God dwells in the generation of the righteous. He is the counsel of the poor because they are ashamed of the wicked and flee unto the Lord for their refuge. They are ashamed of the counsel of the poor because the Lord is his refuge. O that Zion were established out of Heaven, the salvation of Israel. O Lord, when wilt thou establish Zion? When the Lord bringeth back the captivity of his people, Jacob shall rejoice, Israel shall be glad.

PSALM 15
A Psalm of David.

Lord, who shall abide in thy tabernacle? Who shall dwell in thy holy hill of Zion? He that walketh uprightly, and worketh righteousness, and speaketh the truth in his heart. He that backbiteth not with his tongue, nor doeth evil to his neighbor, nor taketh up a reproach against his neighbor. In whose eyes a vile person is condemned, but he honoreth them that fear the Lord, sweareth not falsely to hurt any man, and changeth not. He that putteth not out his money to usury, nor taketh reward against the innocent. He that doeth these things shall never be moved.

PSALM 16
Michtam of David.

Preserve me, O God, for in thee do I put my trust. Thou hast said unto me that thou art the Lord my God, and, My goodness is extended unto thee, and to all the saints that dwell in the earth, and the excellent in whom is all my delight. And the wicked, there is no delight in them, their sorrows shall be multiplied upon all those who hasten for to seek another god, their drink offerings of blood will I not accept, nor take up their names into my lips. Therefore thou, Lord, art the portion of mine inheritance,and of my cup, thou maintainest my lot. The lines are fallen unto me in pleasant places, yea I have a goodly heritage. I will bless the Lord, who hath given me counsel, my reins also instruct me in the night seasons. I have set the Lord always before me, because he is at my right hand, I shall not be moved. Therefore my heart is glad and my glory rejoiceth, my flesh also shall rest in hope. For thou wilt not leave my soul in hell, neither wilt thou suffer thine Holy One to see corruption. Thou wilt show me the path of life, in thy presence is fullness of joy, at thy right hand there are pleasures for evermore.

PSALM 17
A Prayer of David.

Give me right words, O Lord, speak and thy servant shall hear thee, attend unto my cry and give ear unto my prayer. I come not unto thee out of feigned lips. Let my sentence come forth from thy presence, let thine eyes behold the things that are equal. Thou hast proved my heart, thou hast visited me in the night, thou hast tried me, thou shalt find nothing evil in me, for I am purposed my mouth shall not transgress concerning the works of men. By the word of thy lips I have kept out of the paths of the destroyer. Hold up my goings in thy paths, that my footsteps slip not. I have called upon thee, for thou wilt hear, O God, my speech and incline thine ear unto me. Show thy marvelous lovingkindness, O thou that savest them which put their trust in thee, by thy right hand from those that rise up. Keep me as the apple of the eye. Hide me under the shadow of thy wings from the wicked that oppress me. My deadly enemies compass me about, they are enclosed in their own fat, with their mouth they speak proudly. They have now compassed us in our steps, they have set their eyes, bowing down to the earth like as a lion that is greedy of his prey, and as it were a young lion lurking in secret places. Arise, O Lord, disappoint him, cast him down. Deliver my soul from the wicked by thy sword, from men by thy strong hand. Yea, O Lord, from men of the world, for their portion is in their life and whose belly thou fillest with thy good things, they are full of children, and they die and leave the rest of their inheritance to their babes. As for me, I will behold thy face in righteousness, I shall be satisfied, when I awake, with thy likeness.

PSALM 18
To the chief Musician, A Psalm of David, the servant of the Lord, who spake unto the Lord the words of this song in the day that the Lord delivered him from the hand of all his enemies and from the hand of Saul. And he said,

I will love thee, O Lord, my strength. The Lord is my rock, and my fortress, and my deliverer, my God, my strength in whom I will trust, my buckler, and the horn of my salvation, and my high tower. I will call upon the Lord, for he is worthy to be praised, so shall I be saved from mine enemies. The sorrows of death compassed me, and the floods of ungodly men made me afraid. The sorrows of hell compassed me about, the snares of death prevented me. In my distress I called upon the Lord and cried unto my God, he heard my voice out of his temple and my cry came before him, even into his ears. Then the earth shook and trembled, the foundations also of the hills moved and were shaken because he was wroth. There went up a smoke out of his nostrils, and fire out of his mouth devoured, coals were kindled by it. He bowed the heavens also, and came down, and darkness was under his feet. And he rode upon a cherub and did fly, yea, he did fly upon the wings of the wind. He made darkness his secret place, his pavilion round about him were dark waters and thick clouds of the skies. At the brightness that was before him his thick clouds passed, hailstones and coals of fire. The Lord also thundered in the heavens and the Highest gave his voice, hailstones and coals of fire. Yea, he sent out his arrows and scattered them, and he shot out lightnings and discomfited them. Then the channels of waters were seen and the foundations of the world were discovered at thy rebuke, O Lord, at the blast of the breath of thy nostrils. He sent from above, he took me, he drew me out of many waters. He delivered me from my strong enemy and from them which hated me, for they were too strong for me. They prevented me in the day of my calamity, but the Lord was my stay. He brought me forth also into a large place, he delivered me because he delighted in me. The Lord rewarded me according to my righteousness, according to the cleanness of my hands hath he recompensed me. For I have kept the ways of the Lord and have not wickedly departed from my God. For all his judgments were before me and I did not put away his statutes from me. I was also upright before him and I kept myself from mine iniquity. Therefore hath the Lord recompensed me according to my righteousness, according to the cleanness of my hands in his eyesight. With the merciful thou wilt show thyself merciful, with an upright man thou wilt show thyself upright, with the pure thou wilt show thyself pure, and with the froward thou wilt show thyself froward. For thou wilt save the afflicted people, but wilt bring down high looks. For thou wilt light my candle, the Lord my God will enlighten my darkness. For by thee I have run through a troop and by my God have I leaped over a wall. O God, thy ways are perfect, the word of the Lord is tried, he is a buckler to all those who trust in him. For who is God save the Lord? Or who is a rock save our God, our God that girdeth me with strength and maketh my way perfect? He maketh my feet like hinds' feet and setteth me upon my high places. He teacheth my hands to war so that a bow of steel is broken by mine arms. Thou hast also given me the shield of thy salvation, and thy right hand hath holden me up, and thy gentleness hath made me great. Thou hast enlarged my steps under me that my feet did not slip. I have pursued mine enemies and overtaken them, neither did I turn again till they were consumed. I have wounded them that they were not able to rise, they are fallen under my feet. For thou hast girded me with strength unto the battle, thou hast subdued under me those that rose up against me. Thou hast also given me the necks of mine enemies that I might destroy them that hate me. They cried, but found none to save, unto the Lord, but he answered them not. Then did I beat them small as the dust before the wind, I did cast them out as the dirt in the streets. Thou hast delivered me from the strivings of the people, and thou hast made me the head of the heathen, a people whom I have not known shall serve me. As soon as they hear of me they shall obey me, the strangers shall submit themselves unto me. The strangers shall fade away and be afraid out of their close places. The Lord liveth, and blessed be my Rock, and let the God of my salvation be exalted. It is God that avengeth me and subdueth the people under me. He delivereth me from mine enemies, yea, thou liftest me up above those that rise up against me, thou hast delivered me from the violent man. Therefore will I give thanks unto thee, O Lord, among the heathen, and sing praises unto thy name. Great deliverance giveth he to his king, and showeth mercy to his anointed, to David, and to his seed for evermore.

PSALM 19
To the chief Musician, A Psalm of David.

The heavens declare the glory of God, and the firmament showeth his handiwork. Day unto day uttereth speech, and night unto night showeth knowledge. No speech nor language can be, if their voice is not heard. Their line is gone out through all the Earth, and their words to the end of the world. In them hath he set a tabernacle for the sun, which is as a bridegroom coming out of his chamber, and rejoiceth as a strong man to run a race. His going forth is from the end of the Heaven, and his circuit unto the ends of it, and there is nothing hid from the heat thereof. The law of the Lord is perfect, converting the soul, the testimony of the Lord is sure, making wise the simple. The statutes of the Lord are right, rejoicing the heart, the commandment of the Lord is pure, enlightening the eyes. The fear of the Lord is clean, enduring forever, the judgments of the Lord are true and righteous altogether. More to be desired are they than gold, yea, than much fine gold, sweeter also than honey and the honeycomb. Moreover by them is thy servant warned, and in keeping of them there is great reward. Who can understand his errors? Cleanse thou me from secret faults. Keep back thy servant also from presumptuous acts, let them not have dominion over me, then shall I be upright and I shall be innocent from the great transgression. Let the words of my mouth, and the meditation of my heart be acceptable in thy sight, O Lord, my strength and my redeemer.

PSALM 20
To the chief Musician, A Psalm of David.

The Lord hear thee in the day of trouble, the name of the God of Jacob defend thee, send thee help from the sanctuary, and strengthen thee out of Zion, remember all thy offerings, and accept thy burnt sacrifice, Selah. Grant thee according to thine own heart and fulfill all thy counsel. We will rejoice in thy salvation, and in the name of our God we will set up our banners, the Lord fulfill all thy petitions. Now know I that the Lord saveth his anointed, he will hear him from his holy Heaven with the saving strength of his right hand. Some trust in chariots, and some in horses, but we will remember the name of the Lord our God. They are brought down and fallen, but we are risen, and stand upright. Save, Lord, let the king hear us when we call.

PSALM 21
To the chief Musician, A Psalm of David.

The king shall joy in thy strength, O Lord, and in thy salvation how greatly shall he rejoice! Thou hast given him his heart's desire and hast not withholden the request of his lips. Selah. For thou preventest him with the blessings of goodness, thou settest a crown of pure gold on his head. He asked life of thee and thou gavest it him, even length of days for ever and ever. His glory is great in thy salvation, honor and majesty hast thou laid upon him. For thou hast made him most blessed forever, thou hast made him exceeding glad with thy countenance. For the king trusteth in the Lord, and through the mercy of the Most High he shall not be moved. Thine hand shall find out all thine enemies, thy right hand shall find out those that hate thee. Thou shalt make them as a fiery oven in the time of thine anger, the Lord shall swallow them up in his wrath, and the fire shall devour them. Their fruit shalt thou destroy from the earth and their seed from among the children of men. For they intended evil against thee, they imagined a mischievous device which they are not able to perform. Therefore shalt thou make them turn their back when thou shalt make ready thine arrows upon thy strings against the face of them. Be thou exalted, Lord, in thine own strength, so will we sing and praise thy power.

PSALM 22
To the chief Musician upon Aijeleth Shahar, A Psalm of David.

My God, why hast thou forsaken me? My God, hear the words of my roaring, thou art far from helping me. O my God, I cry in the daytime, but thou answerest not, and in the night season, and am not silent. But thou art holy that inhabitest the heavens, thou art worthy of the praises of Israel. Our fathers trusted in thee, they trusted and thou didst deliver them. They cried unto thee and were delivered, they trusted in thee and were not confounded. But I, a worm, am loved of no man, a reproach of men and despised of the people. All they that see me laugh me to scorn, they shoot out the lip, they shake the head saying, He trusted on the Lord that he would deliver him, let him deliver him, seeing he delighted in him. But thou art he that took me out of the womb, thou didst make me hope when I was upon my mother's breasts. I was cast upon thee from the womb, thou wast my God from my mother's breasts. Be not far from me, for trouble is near, for there is none to help. Many armies have compassed me, strong armies of Bashan have beset me around. They gaped upon me with their mouths, like a ravening and a roaring lion. I am poured out like water and all my bones are out of joint, my heart is like wax, it is melted in the midst of my bowels. My strength is dried up like a potsherd, and my tongue cleaveth to my jaws, and thou hast brought me into the dust of death. For dogs have compassed me, the assembly of the wicked have enclosed me, they pierced my hands and my feet. I may tell all my bones, they look and stare upon me. They part my garments among them and cast lots upon my vesture. But be not thou far from me, O Lord, O my strength, haste thee to help me. Deliver my soul from the sword, my darling from the power of the dog. Save me from the lion's mouth, for thou hast heard me speak from the secret places of the wilderness, through the horns of the unicorns. I will declare thy name unto my brethren, in the midst of the congregation will I praise thee. Ye that fear the Lord, praise him, all ye the seed of Jacob, glorify him, and fear him all ye the seed of Israel. For he hath not despised nor abhorred the affliction of the afflicted, neither hath he hid his face from him, but when he cried unto him, he heard. My praise shall be of thee in the great congregation, I will pay my vows before them that fear him. The meek shall eat and be satisfied, they shall praise the Lord that seek him, your heart shall live forever. All the ends of the world shall remember and turn unto the Lord, and all the kindreds of the nations shall worship before thee. For the kingdom is the Lord's, and he is the governor among the nations. All they that be fat upon earth shall eat and worship, all they that go down to the dust shall bow before him and none can keep alive his own soul. A seed shall serve him, it shall be accounted to the Lord for a generation. They shall come and shall declare his righteousness unto a people that shall be born, what he hath done.

PSALM 23
A Psalm of David.

The Lord is my shepherd, I shall not want. He maketh me to lie down in green pastures, he leadeth me beside the still waters. He restoreth my soul, he leadeth me in the paths of righteousness for his name's sake. Yea, though I walk through the valley of the shadow of death I will fear no evil, for thou art with me, thy rod and thy staff they comfort me. Thou preparest a table before me in the presence of mine enemies, thou anointest my head with oil, my cup runneth over. Surely goodness and mercy shall follow me all the days of my life and I will dwell in the house of the Lord forever.

PSALM 24
A Psalm of David.

The earth is the Lord's and the fullness thereof, the world and they that dwell therein. For he hath founded it upon the seas and established it upon the floods. Who shall ascend into the hill of the Lord? Or who shall stand in his holy place? He that hath clean hands and a pure heart, who hath not lifted up his soul unto vanity nor sworn deceitfully. He shall receive the blessing from the Lord and righteousness from the God of his salvation. This is the generation of them that seek him, that seek thy face, O Jacob. Selah. Lift up your heads, O ye generations of Jacob, and be ye lifted up, and the Lord strong and mighty, the Lord mighty in battle, who is the king of glory shall establish you forever. And he will roll away the heavens, and will come down to redeem him people, to make you an everlasting name, to establish you upon his everlasting rock. Lift up your heads, O ye generations of Jacob, lift up your heads, ye everlasting generations, and the Lord of hosts, the king of kings, even the king of glory shall come unto you, and shall redeem his people, and shall establish them in righteousness. Selah.

PSALM 25
A Psalm of David.

Unto thee, O Lord, do I lift up my soul. O my God, I trust in thee, let me not be ashamed, let not mine enemies triumph over me. Yea, let none that wait on thee be ashamed, let them be ashamed which transgress without cause. Show me thy ways, O Lord, teach me thy paths. Lead me in thy truth, and teach me, for thou art the God of my salvation, on thee do I wait all the day. Remember, O Lord, thy tender mercies and thy lovingkindnesses, for they have been ever of old. Remember not the sins of my youth nor my transgressions, according to thy mercy remember thou me for thy goodness' sake, O Lord. Good and upright is the Lord, therefore will he teach sinners in the way. The meek will he guide in judgment and the meek will he teach his way. All the paths of the Lord are mercy and truth unto such as keep his covenant and his testimonies. For thy name's sake, O Lord, pardon mine iniquity, for it is great. What man is he that feareth the Lord? Him shall he teach in the way that he shall choose. His soul shall dwell at ease, and his seed shall inherit the earth. The secret of the Lord is with them that fear him and he will show them his covenant. Mine eyes are ever toward the Lord, for he shall pluck my feet out of the net. Turn thee unto me and have mercy upon me, for I am desolate and afflicted. The troubles of my heart are enlarged, O bring thou me out of my distresses. Look upon mine affliction and my pain, and forgive all my sins. Consider mine enemies, for they are many, and they hate me with cruel hatred. O keep my soul and deliver me, let me not be ashamed, for I put my trust in thee. Let integrity and uprightness preserve me, for I wait on thee. Redeem Israel, O God, out of all his troubles.

PSALM 26
A Psalm of David.

Judge me, O Lord, for I have walked in mine integrity, I have trusted also in the Lord, therefore I shall not slide. Examine me, O Lord, and prove me, try my reins and my heart. For thy lovingkindness is before mine eyes and I have walked in thy truth. I have not sat with vain persons, neither will I go in with dissemblers. I have hated the congregation of evildoers and will not sit with the wicked. I will wash mine hands in innocency, so will I compass thine altar, O Lord, that I may publish with the voice of thanksgiving and tell of all thy wondrous works. Lord, I have loved the habitation of thy house and the place where thine honor dwelleth. Gather not my soul with sinners, nor my life with bloody men, in whose hands is mischief and their right hand is full of bribes. But as for me, I will walk in mine integrity, redeem me and be merciful unto me. My foot standeth in an even place, in the congregations will I bless the Lord.

PSALM 27
A Psalm of David.

The Lord is my light and my salvation, whom shall I fear? The Lord is the strength of my life, of whom shall I be afraid? When the wicked, even mine enemies and my foes, came upon me to eat up my flesh, they stumbled and fell. Though a host should encamp against me, my heart shall not fear, though war should rise against me, in this I am confident. One thing have I desired of the Lord, that will I seek after, that I may dwell in the house of the Lord all the days of my life, to behold the beauty of the Lord and to inquire in his temple. For in the time of trouble he shall hide me in his pavilion, in the secret of his tabernacle shall he hide me, he shall set me up upon a rock. And now shall mine head be lifted up above mine enemies round about me, therefore will I offer in his tabernacle sacrifices of joy; I will sing, yea, I will sign praises unto the Lord. Hear, O Lord, when I cry with my voice, have mercy also upon me and answer me. When thou saidst, Seek ye my face, my heart said unto thee, Thy face, Lord, will I seek. Hide not thy face far from me, put not thy servant away in anger, thou hast been my help, leave me not, neither forsake me, O God of my salvation. When my father and my mother forsake me, then the Lord will take me up. Teach me thy way, O Lord, and lead me in a plain path because of mine enemies. Deliver me not over unto the will of mine enemies, for false witnesses are risen up against me and such as breathe out cruelty. Unless I had believed to see the goodness of the Lord in the land of the living, thou wouldst deliver my soul into hell. Thou didst say unto me, Wait on the Lord, be of good courage, and he shall strengthen thy heart. Wait, I say, on the Lord.

PSALM 28
A Psalm of David.

Unto thee will I cry, O Lord, my rock, be not silent to me, lest, if thou be silent to me, I become like them that go down into the pit. Hear the voice of my supplications, when I cry unto thee, when I lift up my hands towards thy holy oracle. Draw me not away with the wicked, and with the workers of iniquity, which speak peace to their neighbors, but mischief is in their hearts. Give them according to their deeds and according to the wickedness of their endeavors, give them after the work of their hands, render to them their desert. Because they regard not the works of the Lord, nor the operation of his hands, he shall destroy them and not build them up. Blessed be the Lord because he hath heard the voice of my supplications. The Lord is my strength and my shield, my heart trusted in him and I am helped, therefore my heart greatly rejoiceth and with my song will I praise him. The Lord is their strength and he is the saving strength of his anointed. Save thy people and bless thine inheritance, feed them also, and lift them up forever.

PSALM 29
A Psalm of David.

Give unto the Lord, O ye mighty, give unto the Lord glory and strength. Give unto the Lord the glory due unto his name, worship the Lord in the beauty of holiness. The voice of the Lord is upon the waters, the God of glory thundereth, the Lord is upon many waters. The voice of the Lord is powerful, the voice of the Lord is full of majesty. The voice of the Lord breaketh the cedars, yea, the Lord breaketh the cedars of Lebanon. He maketh them also to skip like a calf, Lebanon and Sirion like a young unicorn. The voice of the Lord divideth the flames of fire. The voice of the Lord shaketh the wilderness, the Lord shaketh the wilderness of Kadesh. The voice of the Lord maketh the hinds to calve, and discovereth the forests, and in his temple doth everyone speak of his glory. The Lord sitteth upon the flood, yea, the Lord sitteth King forever. The Lord will give strength unto his people, the Lord will bless his people with peace.

PSALM 30
A Psalm and Song at the dedication of the house of David.

I will extol thee, O Lord, for thou hast lifted me up and hast not made my foes to rejoice over me. O Lord my God, I cried unto thee and thou hast healed me. O Lord, thou hast brought up my soul from the grave, thou hast kept me alive that I should not go down to the pit. Sing unto the Lord, O ye saints of his, and give thanks at the remembrance of his holiness. For his anger kindleth against the wicked, they repent and in a moment it is turned away, and they are in his favor, and he giveth them life, therefore, weeping may endure for a night, but joy cometh in the morning. And in my prosperity I said, I shall never be moved.

Lord, by thy favor thou hast made my mountain to stand strong, thou didst hide thy face and I was troubled. I cried to thee, O Lord, and unto the Lord I made supplication. When I go down to the pit, my blood shall return to the dust. I will praise thee, my soul shall declare thy truth, for what profit am I if I do it not? Hear, O Lord, and have mercy upon me, Lord, be thou my helper. Thou hast turned for me my mourning into dancing, thou hast put off my sackcloth and girded me with gladness to the end that my soul may give glory to thy name, and sing praise to thee, and not be silent. O Lord my God, I will give thanks unto thee forever.

PSALM 31

To the chief Musician, A Psalm of David.

In thee, O Lord, do I put my trust, let me never be ashamed, deliver me in thy righteousness. Bow down thine ears to me, deliver me speedily, be thou my strong rock, for a house of defense to save me. For thou art my rock and my fortress, therefore for thy name's sake lead me and guide me. Pull me out of the net that they have laid privily for me, for thou art my strength. Into thine hand I commit my spirit, thou hast redeemed me, O Lord God of truth. I have hated them that regard lying vanities, but I trust in the Lord. I will be glad and rejoice in thy mercy, for thou hast considered my trouble, thou hast known my soul in adversities, and hast not shut me up into the hand of the enemy, thou hast set my feet in a large room. Have mercy upon me, O Lord, for I am in trouble, mine eye is consumed with grief, yea, my soul and my belly. For my life is spent with grief, and my years with sighing, my strength faileth because of mine iniquity and my bones are consumed. I was a reproach among all mine enemies, but especially among my neighbors, and a fear to mine acquaintance, they that did see me without fled from me. I am forgotten as a dead man out of mind, I am like a broken vessel. For I have heard the slander of many, fear was on every side, while they took counsel together against me, they devised to take away my life. But I trusted in thee, O Lord, I said, Thou art my God. My times are in thy hand, deliver me from the hand of mine enemies and from them that persecute me. Make thy face to shine upon thy servant, save me for thy mercies' sake. Let me not be ashamed, O Lord, for I have called upon thee, let the wicked be ashamed and let them be silent in the grave. Let the lying lips be put to silence, which speak grievous things proudly and contemptuously against the righteous. O how great is thy goodness which thou hast laid up for them that fear thee, which thou hast wrought for them that trust in thee before the sons of men! Thou shalt hide them in the secret of thy presence from the pride of man, thou shalt keep them secretly in a pavilion from the strife of tongues. Blessed be the Lord, for he hath showed me his marvelous kindness in a strong city. For I said in my haste, I am cut off from before thine eyes, nevertheless thou heardest the voice of my supplications when I cried unto thee. O love the Lord, all ye his saints, for the Lord preserveth the faithful, and plentifully rewardeth the proud doer. Be of good courage, and he shall strengthen your heart, all ye that hope in the Lord.

PSALM 32

A Psalm of David, Maschil.

Blessed are they whose transgressions are forgiven and who have no sins to be covered. Blessed is the man unto whom the Lord imputeth not iniquity and in whose spirit there is no guile. When I kept silence my spirit failed within me, when I opened my mouth my bones waxed old through my speaking all the day long. For day and night thy Spirit was heavy upon me, my moisture is turned into the drought of summer. Selah. I acknowledged my sin unto thee and mine iniquity have I not hid. I said, I will confess my transgressions unto the Lord and thou forgavest the iniquity of my sin. Selah. For this shall every one that is godly pray unto thee in a time when thou mayest be found, surely in the floods of great waters they shall not come nigh unto him. Thou art my hiding place, thou shalt preserve me from trouble, thou shalt compass me about with songs of deliverance. Selah. Thou hast said, I will instruct thee and teach thee in the way which thou shalt go, I will guide thee with mine eye. Be ye not as the horse or as the mule which have no understanding, whose mouth must be held in with bit and bridle, lest they come near unto thee. Many sorrows shall be to the wicked, but he that trusteth in the Lord, mercy shall compass him about. Be glad in the Lord, and rejoice, ye righteous, and shout for joy, all ye that are upright in heart.

PSALM 33

Rejoice in the Lord, O ye righteous, to praise the Lord is comely for the upright in heart. Praise the Lord with thy voice, sing unto him with the psaltery and harp, an instrument with ten strings. Sing unto him a new song, play skillfully with a loud noise. For the word of the Lord is given to the upright and all his works are done in truth. He loveth righteousness and judgment, the earth is full of the goodness of the Lord. By the word of the Lord were the heavens made and all the host of them by the breath of his mouth. He gathereth the waters of the sea together as a heap, he layeth up the depth in storehouses. Let all the earth fear the Lord, let all the inhabitants of the world stand in awe of him. For he spake and it was finished, he commanded and it stood fast. The Lord bringeth the counsel of the heathen to naught, he maketh the devices of the people of none effect. The counsel of the Lord standeth forever, the thoughts of his heart to all generations. Blessed are the nations and the people whom the Lord God hath chosen for his own inheritance. The Lord looketh from Heaven, he beholdeth all the sons of men. From the place of his habitation he looketh upon all the inhabitants of the earth. He fashioneth their hearts alike, he considereth all their works. There is no king saved by the multitude of host, a mighty man is not delivered by much strength. A horse is a vain thing for safety, neither shall he deliver any by his great strength. Behold, the eye of the Lord is upon them that fear him, upon them that hope in his mercy to deliver their soul from death and to keep them alive in a time of famine. Our soul waiteth for the Lord, he is our help and our shield. For our heart shall rejoice in him because we have trusted in his holy name. Let thy mercy, O Lord, be upon us according as we hope in thee.

PSALM 34

A Psalm of David when he changed his behavior before Abimelech, who drove him away and he departed.

I will bless the Lord at all times, his praise shall continually be in my mouth. My soul shall make her boast in the Lord, the humble shall hear thereof and be glad. O magnify the Lord with me and let us exalt his name together. I sought the Lord and he heard me and delivered me from all my fears. They looked unto him and were lightened and their faces were not ashamed. This poor man cried and the Lord heard him and saved him out of all his troubles. The Angel of the Lord encampeth round about them that fear him and delivereth them. O taste and see that the Lord is good, blessed is the man that trusteth in him. O fear the Lord, ye his saints, for there is no want to them that fear him. The young lions do lac, and suffer hunger, but they that seek the Lord shall not want any good thing. Come, ye children, hearken unto me, I will teach you the fear of the Lord. What man is he that desireth life and loveth many days that he may see good. Keep thy tongue from evil and thy lips from speaking guile. Depart from evil, and do good, seek peace and pursue it. The eyes of the

Lord are upon the righteous and his ears are open unto their cry. The face of the Lord is against them that do evil, to cut off the remembrance of them from the earth. The righteous cry and the Lord heareth and delivereth them out of all their troubles. The Lord is nigh unto them that are of a broken heart and saveth such as be of a contrite spirit. Many are the afflictions of the righteous, but the Lord delivereth him out of them all. He keepeth all his bones, not one of them is broken. Evil shall slay the wicked and they that hate the righteous shall be desolate. The Lord redeemeth the soul of his servants and none of them that trust in him shall be desolate.

PSALM 35

A Psalm of David.

Plead my cause, O Lord, with them that strive with me, fight against them that fight against me. Take hold of shield and buckler and stand up for mine help. Draw out also the spear, and stop the way against them that persecute me, say unto my soul, I am thy salvation. Let them be confounded and put to shame that seek after my soul, let them be turned back and brought to confusion that devise my hurt. Let them be as chaff before the wind and let the Angel of the Lord chase them. Let their way be dark and slippery and let the Angel of the Lord persecute them. For without cause have they hid for me their net in a pit, which without cause they have digged for my soul. Let destruction come upon him at unawares and let his net that he hath hid catch himself, into that very destruction let him fall. And my soul shall be joyful in the Lord, it shall rejoice in his salvation. All my bones shall say, Lord, who is like unto thee, which deliverest the poor from him that is too strong for him, yea, the poor and the needy from him that spoileth him? False witnesses did rise up, they laid to my charge things that I knew not. They rewarded me evil for good, for the purpose of the spoiling of my soul. But as for me, when they were sick, my clothing was sackcloth, I humbled my soul with fasting, and my prayer returned into mine own bosom. I behaved myself as though he had been my friend or brother, I bowed down heavily as one that mourneth for his mother. But in mine adversity they rejoiced, and gathered themselves together, yea, the abjects gathered themselves together against me and I knew it not, they did tear me and ceased not with hypocritical mockers in feasts, they gnashed upon me with their teeth. Lord, how long wilt thou look on? Rescue my soul from their destructions, my darling from the lions. I will give thee thanks in the great congregation, I will praise thee among much people. Let not them that are mine enemies wrongfully rejoice over me, neither let them wink with the eye that hate me without a cause. For they speak not peace, but they devise deceitful matters against them that are quiet in the land. Yea, they opened their mouth wide against me and said, Aha, aha, our eye hath seen it. This thou hast seen, O Lord, keep not silence, O Lord, be not far from me. Stir up thyself, and awake to my judgment, even unto my cause, my God and my Lord. Judge me, O Lord my God, according to thy righteousness and let them not rejoice over me. Let them not say in their hearts, Ah, so would we have it, let them not say, We have swallowed him up. Let them be ashamed and brought to confusion together that rejoice at mine hurt, let them be clothed with shame and dishonor that magnify themselves against me. Let them shout for joy and be glad, that favor my righteous cause, yea, let them say continually, Let the Lord be magnified which hath pleasure in the prosperity of his servant. And my tongue shall speak of thy righteousness and of thy praise all the day long.

PSALM 36
To the chief Musician, A Psalm of David the servant of the Lord.

The wicked, who live in transgression, saith in their hearts, There is no condemnation, for there is no fear of God before their eyes, for they flatter themselves in their own eyes until their iniquities are found to be hateful. The words of their mouth are full of iniquity and deceit. The wicked man hath left off to be wise, and to do good he deviseth mischief upon his bed, he setteth himself in a way that is not good. O Lord, thou art in the heavens, they are full of thy mercy. And the thoughts of a righteous man ascendeth up unto thee whose throne is far above the clouds. He is filled with thy righteousness like the great mountains, and with thy judgments like a great deep. O Lord, thou preservest man and beast. How excellent is thy lovingkindness, O God! Therefore the children of men put their trust under the shadow of thy wings. They shall be abundantly satisfied with the fatness of thy house and thou shalt make them drink of the river of thy pleasures. For with thee is the fountain of life, in thy light shall we see light. O continue thy lovingkindness unto them that know thee and thy righteousness to the upright in heart. Let not the foot of pride come against me and let not the hand of the wicked remove me. They are the workers of iniquity and shall fall, they shall be cast down and shall not be able to rise.

PSALM 37
A Psalm of David.

Fret not thyself because of evildoers, neither be thou envious against the workers of iniquity. For they shall soon be cut down like the grass and wither as the green herb. Trust in the Lord and do good, so shalt thou dwell in the land, and verily thou shalt be fed. Delight thyself also in the Lord and he shall give thee the desires of thine heart. Commit thy way unto the Lord, trust also in him and he shall bring it to pass. And he shall bring forth thy righteousness as the light and thy judgment as the noonday. Rest in the Lord and wait patiently for him, fret not thyself because of him who prospereth in his way, because of the man who bringeth wicked devices to pass. Cease from anger and forsake wrath, fret not thyself in any wise to do evil. For evildoers shall be cut off, but those that wait upon the Lord, they shall inherit the Earth. For yet a little while and the wicked shall not be, yea, thou shalt diligently consider his place and it shall not be. But the meek shall inherit the Earth and shall delight themselves in the abundance of peace. The wicked plotteth against the just and gnasheth upon him with his teeth. The Lord shall laugh at him, for he seeth that his day is coming. The wicked have drawn out the sword and have bent their bow to cast down the poor and needy and to slay such as be of upright conversation. Their sword shall enter into their own heart and their bows shall be broken. A little that a righteous man hath is better than the riches of many wicked. For the arms of the wicked shall be broken, but the Lord upholdeth the righteous. The Lord knoweth the days of the upright and their inheritance shall be forever. They shall not be ashamed in the evil time and in the days of famine they shall be satisfied. But the wicked shall perish and the enemies of the Lord shall be as the fat of lambs, they shall consume, into smoke shall they consume away. The wicked borroweth and payeth not again, but the righteous showeth mercy and giveth. For such as be blessed of him shall inherit the earth and they that be cursed of him shall be cut off. The steps of a good man are ordered by the Lord and he delighteth in his way. Though he fall, he shall not be utterly cast down, for the Lord upholdeth him with his hand. I have been young and now am old, yet have I not seen the righteous forsaken, nor his seed begging bread. He is ever merciful and lendeth and his seed is blessed. Depart from evil and do good and dwell for evermore. For the Lord loveth judgment and forsaketh not his saints, they are preserved forever, but the seed of the wicked shall be cut off. The righteous shall inherit the land and dwell therein forever. The mouth of the righteous speaketh wisdom and his tongue talketh of judgment. The law of his God is in his heart, none of his steps shall slide. The wicked watcheth the righteous and seeketh to slay him. The Lord will not leave him in his hand nor condemn him when he is judged. Wait on the Lord and keep his way and he shall exalt thee to inherit the land when the wicked are cut off, thou shalt see it. I have seen the wicked in great power and spreading himself like a green bay tree. Yet he passed away and lo, he was not, yea, I sought him, but he could not be found. Mark the perfect man and behold the upright, for the end of that man is peace. But the transgressors shall be destroyed together, the end of the wicked shall come and they shall be cut off. But the salvation of the righteous is of the Lord, he is their strength in the time of trouble. And the Lord shall help them and deliver them, he shall deliver them from the wicked and save them because they trust in him.

PSALM 38

A Psalm of David, to bring to remembrance.

O Lord, rebuke me not in thy wrath neither chasten me in thy hot displeasure. For thine arrows stick fast in me and thy hand presseth me sore. There is no soundness in my flesh because of thine anger neither is there any rest in my bones because of my sin. For mine iniquities are gone over mine head, as a heavy burden they are too heavy for me. My wounds stink and are corrupt because of my foolishness. I am troubled, I am bowed down greatly, I go mourning all the day long. For my loins are filled with a loathsome distress and no soundness is found in my flesh. I am feeble and broken and very sore. I have wept by reason of the disquietness of my heart. Lord, all my desire is before thee and my groaning is not hid from thee. My heart panteth, my strength faileth me, as for the light of mine eyes, it also is gone from me. My lovers and my friends stand aloof because of my sore and my kinsmen stand afar off. They also that seek after my life lay snares for me and they that seek my hurt speak mischievous things and imagine deceits all the day long. But I, as a deaf man, heard not, and I was as a dumb man that openeth not his mouth. Thus I was as a man that heareth not and in whose mouth are no reproofs. For in thee, O Lord, do I hope, thou wilt hear, O Lord my God. For I said, Hear me, lest otherwise they should rejoice over me when my foot slippeth, they magnify themselves against me. For I am ready to halt, and my sorrow is continually before me. For I will declare mine iniquity, I will be sorry for my sin. But mine enemies are lively and they are strong and they that hate me wrongfully are multiplied. They also that render evil for good are mine adversaries because I follow the thing that good is. Forsake me not, O Lord, O my God, be not far from me. Make haste to help me, O Lord my salvation.

PSALM 39

To the chief Musician, even to Jeduthun, A Psalm of David.

I said, I will take heed to my ways that I sin not with my tongue, I will keep my mouth with a bridle while the wicked is before me. I was dumb with silence, I held my peace even from good and my sorrow was stirred. My heart was hot within me while I was musing, the fire burned, then spake I with my tongue. Lord, make me to know mine end and the measure of my days, what it is, that I may know how frail I am. Behold, thou hast made my days as a handbreadth and mine age is as nothing before thee, verily every man at his best state is altogether vanity. Selah. Surely every man walketh in a vain show, surely they are disquieted in vain, he heapeth up riches and knoweth not who shall gather them. And now, Lord, what wait I for? My hope is in thee. Deliver me from all my transgressions, make me not the reproach of the foolish. I was dumb and opened not my mouth because thou didst chasten me. Remove thy stroke away from me or I shall be consumed by the blow of thy hand. When thou with rebukes dost correct man for iniquity, thou makest his beauty to consume away like a moth, surely every man is vanity. Selah. Hear my prayer, O Lord, and give ear unto my cry, hold not thy peace at my tears, for I am a stranger with thee, and a sojourner as all my fathers were. O spare me, that I may recover strength before I go hence and be no more.

PSALM 40
To the chief Musician, A Psalm of David.

I waited patiently for the Lord, and he inclined unto me and heard my cry. He brought me up also out of a horrible pit, out of the miry clay, and set my feet upon a rock and established my doings. And he hath put a new song in my mouth, even praise unto our God; many shall see it and fear and shall trust in the Lord. Blessed is that man that maketh the Lord his trust and respecteth not the proud, nor such as turn aside to lies. Many, O Lord my God, are thy wonderful works which thou hast don, and thy thoughts which are to usward, they cannot be reckoned up in order unto thee, if I would declare and speak of them, they are more than can be numbered. Sacrifice and offering thou didst not desire, mine ears hast thou opened, burnt offering and sin offering hast thou not required. Then said I, Lo, I come, in the volume of the book it is written of me. I delight to do thy will, O my God, yea, thy law is within my heart. I have preached righteousness in the great congregation, lo, I have not refrained my lips, O Lord, thou knowest. I have not hid thy righteousness within my heart, I have declared thy faithfulness and thy salvation, I have not concealed thy lovingkindness and thy truth from the great congregation. Withhold not thou thy tender mercies from me, O Lord, let thy lovingkindness and thy truth continually preserve me. For innumerable evils have compassed me about, mine iniquities have taken hold upon me so that I am not able to look up, they are more than the hairs of mine head, therefore my heart faileth me. Be pleased, O Lord, to deliver me, O Lord, make haste to help me. Let them be ashamed and confounded together that seek after my soul to destroy it, let them be driven backward and put to shame that wish me evil. Let them be desolate for a reward of their shame that say unto me, Aha, aha. Let all those that seek thee rejoice and be glad in thee, let such as love thy salvation say continually, The Lord be magnified. But I am poor and needy, yet the Lord thinketh upon me, thou art my help and my deliverer, make no tarrying, O my God.

PSALM 41
To the chief Musician, A Psalm of David.

Blessed is he that considereth the poor, the Lord will deliver him in time of trouble. The Lord will preserve him and keep him alive, and he shall be blessed upon the earth and thou wilt not deliver him unto the will of his enemies. The Lord will strengthen him upon the bed of languishing, thou wilt make all his pains to cease when he is laid in his bed of sickness. I said, Lord, be merciful unto me, heal my soul for I have sinned against thee. Mine enemies speak evil of me, When shall he die and his name perish? And if he come to see me, he speaketh vanity, his heart gathereth iniquity to itself, when he goeth abroad he telleth it. All that hate me whisper together against me, against me do they devise my hurt. An evil disease, say they, cleaveth fast unto him and now that he lieth he shall rise up no more. Yea, mine own familiar friend in whom I trusted, which did eat of my bread, hath lifted up his heel against me. But thou, O Lord, be merciful unto me and raise me up that I may requite them. By this I know that thou favorest me, because mine enemy doth not triumph over me. And as for me, thou upholdest me in mine integrity and settest me before thy face forever. Blessed be the Lord God of Israel from everlasting and to everlasting. Amen and Amen.

PSALM 42
To the chief Musician, Maschil, for the sons of Korah.
As the hart panteth after the water brooks, so panteth my soul after thee, O God. My soul thirsteth for to see God, for to see the living God, when shall I come and appear before thee, O God? My tears have been poured out unto thee day and night, while mine enemies continually say unto me, Where is thy God? When I remember these mine enemies, I pour out my soul unto thee, for I had gone with the multitude, I also went with them to the house of God, with the voice of joy and praise, with the multitude that kept holyday. Why art thou cast down, O my soul? And why art thou disquieted in me? Hope thou in God, for I shall yet praise him for the help of his countenance. O my God, my soul is cast down within me, therefore will I remember thee from the land of Jordan and of the Hermonites, from the hill Mizar. Deep calleth unto deep at the noise of thy waterspouts, all thy waves and thy billows are gone over me. Yet the Lord will command his lovingkindness in the daytime and in the night his song shall be with me and my prayer unto the God of my life. I will say unto God my Rock, Why hast thou forgotten me? Why go I mourning because of the oppression of the enemy? As with a sword in my bones mine enemies reproach me, while they say daily unto me, Where is thy God? Why art thou cast down, O my soul? And why art thou disquieted within me? Hope thou in God, for I shall yet praise him who is the health of my countenance, and my God.

PSALM 43
A psalm of David.
Judge me, O God, and plead my cause against an ungodly nation, O deliver me from the deceitful and unjust man. For thou art the God of my strength, why dost thou cast me off? Why go I mourning because of the oppression of the enemy? O send out thy light and thy truth, let them lead me, let them bring me unto thy holy hill and to thy tabernacles. Then will I go unto the altar of God, unto God my exceeding joy, yea, upon the harp will I praise thee, O God my God. Why art thou cast down, O my soul? And why art thou disquieted within me? Hope in God, for I shall yet praise him who is the health of my countenance and my God.

PSALM 44
To the chief Musicians, for the sons of Korah, Maschil.
We have heard with our ears, O God, our fathers have told us what work thou didst in their days, in the times of old. How thou didst drive out the heathen with thy hand and plantedst them, how thou didst afflict the people and cast them out. For they got not the land in possession by their own sword, neither did their own arm save them, but thy right hand, and thine arm, and the light of thy countenance, because thou hadst a favor unto them. Thou art my King, O God, command deliverances for Jacob. Through thee will we push down our enemies, through thy name will we tread them under that rise up against us. For I will not trust in my bow, neither shall my sword save me. But thou hast saved us from our enemies, and hast put them to shame that hated us. In God we boast all the day long and praise thy name forever. Selah. But thou hast cast off and put us to shame and goest not forth with our armies. Thou makest us to turn back from the enemy and they which hate us spoil for themselves. Thou hast given us

like sheep appointed for meat and hast scattered us among the heathen. Thou sellest thy people for naught and dost not increase thy wealth by their price. Thou makest us a reproach to our neighbors, a scorn and a derision to them that are round about us. Thou makest us a byword among the heathen, a shaking of the head among the people. My confusion is continually before me and the shame of my face hath covered me, for the voice of him that reproacheth and blasphemeth, by reason of the enemy and avenger. All this is come upon us, yet have we not forgotten thee neither have we dealt falsely in thy covenant. Our heart is not turned back neither have our steps declined from thy way, though thou hast sore broken us in the place of dragons and covered us with the shadow of death. If we have forgotten the name of our God, or stretched out our hands to a strange god, shall not God search this out? For he knoweth the secrets of the heart. Yea, for thy sake are we killed all the day long, we are counted as sheep for the slaughter. Awake, why sleepest thou, O Lord? Arise, cast us not off forever. Wherefore hidest thou thy face and forgettest our affliction and our oppression? For our soul is bowed down to the dust, our belly cleaveth unto the earth. Arise for our help and redeem us for thy mercies' sake.

PSALM 45

To the chief Musician upon Shoshannim, for the son of Korah, Maschil, A Song of loves.
My heart is inditing a good matter, I speak of the things which I have made touching the King, my tongue is the pen of a ready writer. Thou art fairer than the children of men, grace is poured into thy lips, therefore God hath blessed thee forever. Gird thy sword upon thy thigh, O most Mighty, with thy glory and thy majesty. And in thy majesty ride prosperously because of truth and meekness and righteousness, and thy right hand shall teach thee terrible things. Thine arrows are sharp in the heart of the King's enemies, whereby the people fall under thee. Thy throne, O God, is for ever and ever, the scepter of thy kingdom is a right scepter. Thou lovest righteousness and hatest wickedness, therefore God, thy God, hath anointed thee with the oil of gladness above thy fellows. All thy garments smell of myrrh, and aloes, and cassia, out of the ivory palaces whereby they have made thee glad. Kings' daughters were among thy honorable women, upon thy right hand did stand the queen in gold of Ophir. Hearken, O daughter, and consider and incline thine ear, forget also thine own people and thy father's house, so shall the King greatly desire thy beauty, for he is thy Lord and worship thou him. And the daughter of Tyre shall be there with a gift, even the rich among the people shall entreat thy favor. The King's daughter is all glorious within, her clothing is of wrought gold. She shall be brought unto the King in raiment of needlework, the virgins her companions that follow her shall be brought unto thee. With gladness and rejoicing shall they be brought, they shall enter into the King's palace. Instead of thy fathers shall be thy children, whom thou mayest make princes in all the earth. I will make thy name to be remembered in all generations, therefore shall the people praise thee for ever and ever.

PSALM 46

To the chief Musician for the sons of Korah, A Song upon Alamoth.
God is our refuge and strength, a present help in trouble. Therefore we will not fear, though the Earth shall be removed, and though the mountains shall be carried into the midst of the sea, and the waters thereof roar, being troubled, and the mountains shake with the swelling thereof. Yet there shall be a river, the streams whereof shall make glad the city of God, the holy place of the tabernacle of the Most High. For Zion shall come and God shall be in the midst of her, she shall not be moved, God shall help her right early. The heathen shall

be enraged and their kingdoms shall be moved, and the Lord shall utter his voice and the Earth shall be melted. The Lord of hosts who shall be with us, the God of Jacob our refuge. Selah. Come, behold the works of the Lord, what desolations he shall make in the earth in the latter days. He maketh wars to cease unto the end of the earth, he breaketh the bow and cutteth the spear in sunder, he burneth the chariot in the fire and saith unto the nations, Be still and know that I am God, I will be exalted among the heathen, I will be exalted in the earth. The Lord of hosts shall be with us, the God of Jacob our refuge. Selah.

PSALM 47
To the chief Musician, A Psalm for the sons of Korah.
O clap your hands, all ye people, shout unto God with the voice of triumph. For the Lord most high is terrible, he is a great King over all the earth. He shall subdue the people under us and the nations under our feet. He shall choose our inheritance for us, the excellency of Jacob whom he loved. Selah. God is gone up with a shout, the Lord with the sound of a trumpet. Sing praises to God, sing praises, sing praises unto our King, sing praises. For God is the King of all the earth, sing ye praises with understanding. God reigneth over the heathen, God sitteth upon the throne of his holiness. The princes of the people are gathered together, even the people of the God of Abraham, for the shields of the earth belong unto God, he is greatly exalted.

PSALM 48
A Song and Psalm for the sons of Korah.
Great is the Lord and greatly to be praised in the city of our God in the mountain of his holiness. Beautiful for situation, the joy of the whole earth, is mount Zion, on the sides of the north, the city of the great King. God is known in her palaces for a refuge. For lo, the kings were assembled, they passed by together. They saw it and so they marveled, they were troubled and hasted away. Fear took hold upon them there, and pain as of a woman in travail. Thou breakest the ships of Tarshish with an east wind. As we have heard, so have we seen in the city of the Lord of hosts, in the city of our God, God will establish it forever. Selah. We have thought of thy lovingkindness, O God, in the midst of thy temple. According to thy name, O God, so is thy praise unto the ends of the earth, thy right hand is full of righteousness. Let mount Zion rejoice, let the daughters of Judah be glad because of thy judgments. Walk about Zion and go round about her, tell the towers thereof. Mark ye well her bulwarks, consider her palaces that ye may tell it to the generation following. For this God is our God for ever and ever, he will be our guide even unto death.

PSALM 49
To the chief Musician, A Psalm for the sons of Korah.
Hear this, all ye people, give ear, all ye inhabitants of the world, both low and high, rich and poor together. My mouth shall speak of wisdom and the meditation of my heart shall be of understanding. I will incline mine ear to a parable, I will open my dark saying upon the harp. Wherefore should I fear in the days of evil when the iniquity of my heels shall compass me about? They that trust in their wealth and boast themselves in the multitude of their riches, none can by any means redeem his brother, nor give to God a ransom for him that he should still live forever, that it ceaseth not for ever to see corruption. For the redemption of their souls is through God and precious. For he seeth wise men die, likewise the fool and the brutish person perish, and leave their wealth to others, their inward thought of their houses forever, their dwelling places to all generations. Lands they called after their own names and they are honorable. Nevertheless,

man in honor abideth not, he is also like the beasts that perish. This I speak of them who walk in their way and forsaketh the Almighty in their folly, yet their posterity approve their sayings. Selah. Like sheep they are laid in the grave, death shall feed on them and the upright shall have dominion over them in the morning, and their beauty shall consume in the grave from their dwelling. But God will redeem my soul from the power of the grave, for he shall receive me. Selah. Be not thou afraid when one is made rich, when the glory of his house is increased, for when he dieth he shall carry nothing away, his glory shall not descend after him. Though while he lived he blessed his soul (and men will praise thee, when thou doest well to thyself), he shall go to the generation of his fathers, they shall never see light. Man that is in honor, and understandeth not, is like the beasts that perish.

PSALM 50
A Psalm of Asaph.

The mighty God, even the Lord, hath spoken and called the earth from the rising of the sun unto the going down thereof. Out of Zion, the perfection of beauty, God hath shined. Our God shall come and shall not keep silence, a fire shall devour before him and it shall be very tempestuous round about him. He shall call to the heavens from above and to the earth that he may judge his people. Gather my saints together unto me, those that have made a covenant with me by sacrifice. And the heavens shall declare his righteousness, for God is judge himself. Selah. Hear, O my people, and I will speak, O Israel, and I will testify against thee, I am God, even thy God. I will not reprove thee for thy sacrifices or thy burnt offerings to have been continually before me. I will take no bullock out of thy house, nor he goats out of thy folds, for every beast of the forest is mine and the cattle upon a thousand hills. I know all the fowls of the mountains and the wild beasts of the field are mine. If I were hungry, I would not tell thee, for the world is mine and the fullness thereof. Will I eat the flesh of bulls or drink the blood of goats? Offer unto God thanksgiving, and pay thy vows unto the Most High, and call upon me in the day of trouble, I will deliver thee and thou shalt glorify me. But unto the wicked God saith, What hast thou to do to declare my statutes or that thou shouldest take my covenant in thy mouth? Seeing thou hatest instruction and castest my words behind thee. When thou sawest a thief, then thou consentedst with him and hast been partaker with adulterers. Thou givest thy mouth to evil and thy tongue frameth deceit. Thou sittest and speakest against thy brother, thou slanderest thine own mother's son. These things hast thou done and I kept silence, thou thoughtest that I was altogether such a one as thyself, but I will reprove thee, and set covenants in order before thine eyes. Now consider this, ye that forget God, lest I tear you in pieces and there be none can deliver. Whoso offereth praise glorifieth me and to him that ordereth his conversation aright will I show the salvation of God.

PSALM 51
To the chief Musician, A Psalm of David
when Nathan the prophet came unto him after he had gone into Bath-sheba.

Have mercy upon me, O God, according to thy lovingkindness, according unto the multitude of thy tender mercies blot out my transgressions. Wash me thoroughly from mine iniquity and cleanse me from my sin. For I acknowledge my transgressions and my sin is ever before me. Against thee, thee only, have I sinned and done this evil in thy sight, that thou mightest be justified when thou speakest and be clear when thou judgest. Behold, I was shapen in iniquity and in sin did my mother conceive me. Behold, thou desirest truth in the inward parts and in the hidden part thou shalt make me to know wisdom. Purge me with hyssop and I shall be clean, wash me and I shall be whiter than snow. Make me to hear joy and gladness, that the bones which thou hast broken may rejoice. Hide thy face from my sins and blot out all mine iniquities. Create in me a clean heart, O God, and renew a right spirit within me. Cast me not away from thy presence and take not thy Holy Spirit from me. Restore unto me the joy of thy salvation and uphold me with thy free Spirit. Then will I teach transgressors thy ways and sinners shall be converted unto thee. Deliver me from bloodguiltiness, O God, thou God of my salvation, and my tongue shall sing aloud of thy righteousness. O Lord, open thou my lips and my mouth shall show forth thy praise. For thou desirest not sacrifice, else would I give it, thou delightest not in burnt offering. The sacrifices of God are a broken spirit, a broken and a contrite heart, O God, thou wilt not despise. Do good in thy good pleasure unto Zion, build thou the walls of Jerusalem. Then shalt thou be pleased with the sacrifices of righteousness, with burnt offering and whole burnt offering, then shall they offer bullocks upon thine altar.

PSALM 52
To the chief Musician, Maschil, A Psalm of David when Doeg the Edomite came and told Saul and said unto him, David is come to the house of Ahimelech.
Why boastest thou thyself in mischief, O mighty man? The goodness of God endureth continually. Thy tongue deviseth mischiefs, like a sharp razor working deceitfully. Thou lovest evil more than good and lying rather than to speak righteousness. Selah. Thou lovest all devouring words, O thou deceitful tongue. God shall likewise destroy thee forever, he shall take thee away, and pluck thee out of thy dwelling place, and root thee out of the land of the living. Selah. The righteous also shall see, and fear, and shall laugh at him. Lo, the man who made not God his strength, but trusted in the abundance of his riches and strengthened himself in his wickedness. But I am like a green olive tree in the house of God, I trust in the mercy of God for ever and ever. I will praise thee forever, because thou hast done wonderful works I will wait on thy name, for thou art good before thy saints.

PSALM 53
To the chief Musician upon Mahalath, Maschil, A Psalm of David.
The fool hath said in his heart, There is no God. Such are corrupt and they have done abominable iniquity. There is none that doeth good. God looked down from Heaven upon the children of men to see if there were any that did understand, that did seek God. Every one of them is gone back, they are altogether become filthy. The workers of iniquity have no knowledge, they eat up my people as they eat bread, they have not called upon God. There is none that doeth good, no not one. They were in great fear, for God hath scattered the bones of him that encampeth against him. O Lord, thou hast put to shame those who have said in their hearts there was no fear because thou hast despised them. O that Zion were come, the salvation of Israel, for out of Zion shall they be judged when God bringeth back the captivity of his people. And Jacob shall rejoice, Israel shall be glad.

PSALM 54
To the chief Musician on Neginoth, Maschil, A Psalm of David when the Ziphim came and said to Saul, Doth not David hide himself with us?
Save me, O God, by thy name and judge me by thy strength. Hear my prayer, O God, give ear to the words of my mouth. For strangers are risen up against me and oppressors seek after my soul, they have not set God before them. Selah. Behold, God is mine helper, the Lord is with them that uphold my soul. He shall

reward evil unto mine enemies, cut them off in thy truth. I will freely sacrifice unto thee, I will praise thy name, O Lord, for it is good. For he hath delivered me out of all trouble, and mine eye hath seen his desire upon mine enemies.

PSALM 55
To the chief Musician on Neginoth, Maschil, A Psalm of David.
Give ear to my prayer, O God, and hide not thyself from my supplication. Attend unto me and hear me, I mourn in my complaint, and make a noise because of the voice of the enemy, because of the oppression of the wicked, for they cast iniquity upon me and in wrath they hate me. My heart is sore pained within me and the terrors of death are fallen upon me. Fearfulness and trembling are come upon me and horror hath overwhelmed me. And I said, O that I had wings like a dove! For then would I fly away and be at rest. Lo, then would I wander far off and remain in the wilderness. Selah. I would hasten my escape from the windy storm and tempest. Destroy, O Lord, and divide their tongues, for I have seen violence and strife in the city. Day and night they go about it upon the walls thereof, mischief also and sorrow are in the midst of it. Wickedness is in the midst thereof, deceit and guile depart not from her streets. For it was not an enemy that reproached me, neither he that hated me that did magnify himself against me; if so, then I could have borne it, I would have hid myself from him. But it was a man mine equal, my guide, and mine acquaintance. We took sweet counsel together and walked unto the house of God in company. Let death seize upon them and let them go down quick into hell, for wickedness is in their dwellings and among them. As for me, I will call upon God and the Lord shall save me. Evening, and morning, and at noon will I pray and cry aloud and he shall hear my voice. He hath delivered my soul in peace from the battle that was against me, for there were many with me. God shall hear and afflict them, even he that abideth of old. Selah. Because they have no changes, therefore they fear not God. They have put forth their hands against such as be at peace with them, they have broken the Lord's covenant. The words of their mouth were smoother than butter, but war was in their heart. Their words were softer than oil, yet they have drawn swords. Cast thy burden upon the Lord and he shall sustain thee, he shall never suffer the righteous to be moved. But thou, O God, shalt bring them down into the pit of destruction, bloody and deceitful men shall not live out half their days, but I will trust in thee.

PSALM 56
To the chief Musician upon Jonathelemrechokim, Michtam of David, when the Philistines took him in Gath.
Be merciful unto me, O God, for man would swallow me up, he fighting daily oppresseth me. Mine enemies would daily swallow me up, for they be many that fight against me, O thou Most High. What, am I afraid? I will trust in thee. In God I will praise his word, in God I have put my trust, I will not fear what flesh can do unto me. Every day they wrest my words, all their thoughts are against me for evil. They gather themselves together, they hide themselves, they mark my steps when they wait for my soul. Shall they escape by iniquity? In thine anger cast down the people, O God. Thou tellest my wanderings, put thou my tears into thy bottle, are they not in thy book? When I cry unto thee, then shall mine enemies turn back, this I know, for God is for me. In God will I praise his word, in the Lord will I praise his word. In God have I put my trust, I will not be afraid what man can do unto me. Thy vows are upon me, O God, I will render praises unto thee. For thou hast delivered my soul from death, wilt not thou deliver my feet from falling that I may walk before God in the light of the living?

PSALM 57
To the chief Musician, Al-taschith,
Michtam of David when he fled from Saul in the cave.

Be merciful unto me, O God, be merciful unto me, for my soul trusteth in thee, yea, in the shadow of thy wings will I make my refuge until these calamities be overpast. I will cry unto God most high, unto God that performeth all things for me. He shall send from Heaven and save me from the reproach of him that would swallow me up. Selah. God shall send forth his mercy and his truth. My soul is among lions and I lie even among them that are set on fire, even the sons of men, whose teeth are spears and arrows and their tongue a sharp sword. Be thou exalted, O God, above the heavens, let thy glory be above all the earth. They have prepared a net for my steps, my soul is bowed down, they have digged a pit before me into the midst whereof they are fallen themselves. Selah. My heart is fixed, O God, my heart is fixed, I will sing and give praise. Awake up, my glory, awake, psaltery and harp, I myself will awake early. I will praise thee, O Lord, among the people, I will sing unto thee among the nations. For thy mercy is great unto the heavens and thy truth unto the clouds. Be thou exalted, O God, above the heavens, let thy glory be above all the earth.

PSALM 58
To the chief Musician, Al-taschith, Michtam of David.

Do ye indeed speak righteousness, O congregation? Do ye judge uprightly, O ye sons of men? Yea, in heart ye work wickedness, ye weigh the violence of your hands in the earth. The wicked are estranged from the womb, they go astray as soon as they be born, speaking lies. Their poison is like the poison of a serpent, they are like the deaf adder that stoppeth her ear, which will not hearken to the voice of charmers, charming never so wisely. Break their teeth, O God, in their mouth, break out the great teeth of the young lions, O Lord. Let them melt away as waters which run continually, when he bendeth his bow to shoot his arrows let them be as cut in pieces. As a snail which melteth, let every one of them pass away like the untimely birth of a woman that they may not see the sun. Before your pots can feel the thorns, he shall take them away as with a whirlwind, both living, and in his wrath. The righteous shall rejoice when he seeth the vengeance, he will wash his feet in the blood of the wicked. So that a man shall say, Verily there is a reward for the righteous, verily he is a God that judgeth in the earth.

PSALM 59
To the chief Musician, Al-taschith, Michtam of David
when Saul sent and they watched the house to kill him.

Deliver me from mine enemies, O my God, defend me from them that rise up against me. Deliver me from the workers of iniquity and save me from bloody men. For lo, they lie in wait for my soul, the mighty are gathered against me, not for my transgression nor for my sin, O Lord. They run and prepare themselves without my fault, awake to help me and behold. Thou therefore, O Lord God of hosts, the God of Israel, awake to visit all the heathen, be not merciful to any wicked transgressors. Selah. They return at evening, they make a noise like a dog and go round about the city. Behold, they belch out with their mouth, swords are in their lips, for who, say they, doth hear? But thou, O Lord, shalt laugh at them, thou shalt have all the heathen in derision. Because of his strength will I wait upon thee, for God is my defense. The God of my mercy shall prevent me, God shall let me see my desire upon mine enemies. Slay them not, lest my people forget, scatter them by thy power and bring them down, O Lord, our shield. For the sin of their mouth and the words of their lips let them even be taken in their pride and for cursing and lying which they speak. Consume them in wrath, consume them, that they may not be, and let them know that God ruleth in Jacob unto the ends of the earth. Selah. And at evening let them return, and let them make a noise like a dog and go round about the city. Let them wander up and down for meat, and grudge if they be not satisfied. But I will sing of thy power, yea, I will sing aloud of thy mercy in the morning, for thou hast been my defense and refuge in the day of my trouble. Unto thee, O my strength, will I sing, for God is my defense and the God of my mercy.

PSALM 60
*To the chief Musician upon Sushane-duth, Michtam of David,
to teach when he strove with Aram-naharaim and with Aram-zobah when Joab
returned and smote of Edom in the valley of salt twelve thousand.*

O God, thou hast cast us off, thou hast scattered us, thou hast been displeased, O turn thyself to us again. Thou hast made the Earth to tremble, thou hast broken it, heal the breaches thereof for it shaketh. Thou hast showed thy people hard things, thou hast made us to drink the wine of astonishment. Thou hast given a banner to them that fear thee that it may be displayed because of the truth. Selah. That thy beloved may be delivered, save with thy right hand and hear me. God hath spoken in his holiness, I will rejoice, I will divide Shechem and mete out the valley of Succoth. Gilead is mine, and Manasseh is mine, Ephraim also is the strength of mine head, Judah is my lawgiver, Moab is my washpot, over Edom will I cast out my shoe, Philistia, triumph thou because of me. Who will bring me into the strong city? Who will lead me into Edom? Wilt not thou, O God, which hadst cast us off? And thou, O God, which didst not go out with our armies? Give us help from trouble, for vain is the help of man. Through God we shall do valiantly, for he it is that shall tread down our enemies.

PSALM 61
To the chief Musician upon Neginah, a Psalm of David.

Hear my cry, O God, attend unto my prayer. From the end of the Earth will I cry unto thee, when my heart is overwhelmed, lead me to the Rock that is higher than I. For thou hast been a shelter for me and a strong tower from the enemy. I will abide in thy tabernacle forever, I will trust in the covert of thy wings. Selah. For thou, O God, hast heard my vows, thou hast given me the heritage of those that fear thy name. Thou wilt prolong the king's life and his years as many generations. He shall abide before God forever, O prepare mercy and truth which may preserve him. So will I sing praise unto thy name for ever that I may daily perform my vows.

PSALM 62
To the chief Musician, to Jeduthun, A Psalm of David.

Truly my soul waiteth upon God, from him cometh my salvation. He only is my rock and my salvation, he is my defense, I shall not be greatly moved. How long will he imagine mischief against a man? Ye shall be slain all of you, as a bowing wall shall ye be and as a tottering fence. They only consult to cast him down from his excellency, they delight in lies, they bless with their mouth, but they curse inwardly. Selah. My soul, wait thou only upon God, for my expectation is from him. He only is my rock and my salvation, he is my defense, I shall not be moved. In God is my salvation and my glory, the rock of my strength, and my refuge is in God. Trust in him at all times, ye people, pour out your heart before him, God is a refuge for us. Selah. Surely men of low degree are vanity, and men of high degree are a lie, to be laid in the balance they are altogether lighter than vanity. Trust not in oppression and become not vain in robbery, if riches increase, set not your heart upon them. God hath spoken once, twice have I heard this, that power belongeth unto God. Also unto thee, O Lord, belongeth mercy, for thou renderest to every man according to his work.

PSALM 63
David's Psalm in the wilderness of Judah.
O God, thou art my God, early will I seek thee, my soul thirsteth for thee, my flesh longeth for thee in a dry and thirsty land where no water is, to see thy power and thy glory so as I have seen thee in the sanctuary. Because thy lovingkindness is better than life, my lips shall praise thee. Thus will I bless thee while I live, I will lift up my hands in thy name. My soul shall be satisfied as with marrow and fatness, and my mouth shall praise thee with joyful lips when I remember thee upon my bed and meditate on thee in the night watches. Because thou hast been my help, therefore in the shadow of thy wings will I rejoice. My soul followeth hard after thee, thy right hand upholdeth me. But those that seek my soul to destroy it shall go into the lower parts of the Earth. They shall fall by the sword, they shall be a portion for foxes. But the king shall rejoice in God, everyone that sweareth by him shall glory, but the mouth of them that speak lies shall be stopped.

PSALM 64
To the chief Musician, A Psalm of David.
Hear my voice, O God, in my prayer, preserve my life from fear of the enemy. Hide me from the secret counsel of the wicked, from the insurrection of the workers of iniquity who whet their tongue like a sword and bend their bows to shoot their arrows, even bitter words, that they may shoot in secret at the perfect, suddenly do they shoot at him and fear not. They encourage themselves in an evil matter, they commune of laying snares privily, they say, Who shall see them? They search out iniquities, they accomplish a diligent search, both the inward thought of every one of them and the heart is deep. But God shall shoot at them with an arrow, suddenly shall they be wounded. So they shall make their own tongue to fall upon themselves, all that see them shall flee away. And all men shall fear and shall declare the work of God, for they shall wisely consider of his doing. The righteous shall be glad in the Lord and shall trust in him and all the upright in heart shall glory.

PSALM 65
To the chief Musician, A Psalm and Song of David.
Praise waiteth for thee, O God, in Zion and unto thee shall the vow be performed. O thou that hearest prayer unto thee shall all flesh come. Iniquities prevail against me, as for our transgressions thou shalt purge them away. Blessed is the man whom thou choosest and causest to approach unto thee that he may dwell in thy courts, we shall be satisfied with the goodness of thy house, even of thy holy temple. By terrible things in righteousness wilt thou answer us, O God of our salvation, who art the confidence of all the ends of the Earth, and of them that are afar off upon the sea, which by his strength setteth fast the mountains, being girded with power, which stilleth the noise of the seas, the noise of their waves, and the tumult of the people. They also that dwell in the uttermost parts are afraid at thy tokens, thou makest the outgoings of the morning and evening to rejoice. Thou visitest the Earth and waterest it, thou greatly enrichest it with the river of God which is full of water, thou preparest them corn when thou hast so provided for it. Thou waterest the ridges thereof abundantly, thou settlest the furrows thereof, thou makest it soft with showers, thou blessest the springing thereof. Thou crownest the year with thy goodness and thy paths drop fatness. They drop upon the pastures of the wilderness and the little hills rejoice on every

side. The pastures are clothed with flocks, the valleys also are covered over with corn, they shout for joy, they also sing.

PSALM 66
To the chief Musician, A Song or Psalm.
Make a joyful noise unto God, all ye lands, sing forth the honor of his name, make his praise glorious. Say unto God, How terrible art thou in thy works! Through the greatness of thy power shall thine enemies submit themselves unto thee. All the earth shall worship thee, and shall sing unto thee, they shall sing to thy name. Selah. Come and see the works of God, he is terrible in his doing toward the children of men. He turned the sea into dry land, they went through the flood on foot, there did we rejoice in him. He ruleth by his power forever, his eyes behold the nations, let not the rebellious exalt themselves. Selah. O bless our God, ye people, and make the voice of his praise to be heard, which holdeth our soul in life and suffereth not our feet to be moved. For thou, O God, hast proved us, thou hast tried us as silver is tried. Thou broughtest us into the net, thou laidest affliction upon our loins. Thou hast caused men to ride over our heads, we went through fire and through water, but thou broughtest us out into a wealthy place. I will go into thy house with burnt offerings, I will pay thee my vows, which my lips have uttered and my mouth hath spoken when I was in trouble. Come and hear, all ye that fear God, and I will declare what he hath done for my soul. I cried unto him with my mouth and he was extolled with my tongue. If I regard iniquity in my heart, the Lord will not hear me, but verily God hath heard me, he hath attended to the voice of my prayer. Blessed be God, which hath not turned away my prayer nor his mercy from me.

PSALM 67
To the chief Musician on Neginoth, A Psalm or Song.
God be merciful unto us, and bless us, and cause his face to shine upon us, Selah, that thy way may be known upon earth, thy saving health among all nations. Let the people praise thee, O God, let all the people praise thee. O let the nations be glad and sing for joy, for thou shalt judge the people righteously and govern the nations upon earth. Selah. Let the people praise thee, O God, let all the people praise thee. Then shall the earth yield her increase, and God, even our own God, shall bless us. God shall bless us and all the ends of the earth shall fear him.

PSALM 68
To the chief Musician, A Psalm or Song of David.
Let God arise, let his enemies be scattered, let them also that hate him flee before him. As smoke is driven away so drive them away, as wax melteth before the fire so let the wicked perish at the presence of God. But let the righteous be glad, let them rejoice before God, yea, let them exceedingly rejoice. Sing unto God, sing praises to his name, extol him that rideth upon the heavens by his name JAH, and rejoice before him. A father of the fatherless and a judge of the widows is God in his holy habitation. God setteth the solitary in families, he bringeth out those which are bound with chains, but the rebellious dwell in a dry land. O God, when thou wentest forth before thy people, when thou didst march through the wilderness, Selah, the Earth shook, the heavens also dropped at the presence of God, even Sinai itself was moved at the presence of God, the God of Israel. Thou, O God, didst send a plentiful rain, whereby thou didst confirm thine inheritance when it was weary. Thy congregation hath dwelt therein, thou, O God, hast prepared of thy goodness for the poor. The Lord gave the word, great was the company of those that published it. Kings

of armies did flee apace and she that tarried at home divided the spoil. Though ye have lain among the pots, yet shall ye be as the wings of a dove covered with silver and her feathers with yellow gold. When the Almighty scattered kings in it, it was white as snow in Salmon. The hill of God is as the hill of Bashan, a high hill as the hill of Bashan. Why leap ye, ye high hills? This is the hill which God desireth to dwell in, yea, the Lord will dwell in it forever. The chariots of God are twenty thousand, even thousands of angels, the Lord is among them as in Sinai in the holy place. Thou hast ascended on high, thou hast led captivity captive, thou hast received gifts for men, yea, for the rebellious also, that the Lord God might dwell among them. Blessed be the Lord, who daily loadeth us with benefits, even the God of our salvation. Selah. He that is our God is the God of salvation and unto God the Lord belong the issues from death. But God shall wound the head of his enemies and the hairy scalp of such a one as goeth on still in his trespasses. The Lord said, I will bring again from Bashan, I will bring my people again from the depths of the sea that thy foot may be dipped in the blood of thine enemies and the tongue of thy dogs in the same. They have seen thy goings, O God, even the goings of my God, my King, in the sanctuary. The singers went before, the players on instruments followed after, among them were the damsels playing with timbrels. Bless ye God in the congregations, even the Lord, from the fountain of Israel. There is little Benjamin with their ruler, the princes of Judah and their council, the princes of Zebulun, and the princes of Naphtali. Thy God hath commanded thy strength; strengthen, O God, that which thou hast wrought for us. Because of thy temple at Jerusalem shall kings bring presents unto thee. Rebuke the company of spearmen, the multitude of the bulls, with the calves of the people, till everyone submit himself with pieces of silver; scatter thou the people that delight in war. Princes shall come out of Egypt, Ethiopia shall soon stretch out her hands unto God. Sing unto God, ye kingdoms of the earth, O sing praises unto the Lord, Selah. To him that rideth upon the Heavens of Heavens which were of old, lo, he doth send out his voice and that a mighty voice. Ascribe ye strength unto God, his excellency is over Israel, and his strength is in the clouds. O God, thou art terrible out of thy holy places, the God of Israel is he that giveth strength and power unto his people. Blessed be God.

PSALM 69

To the chief Musician upon Shoshannim, A Psalm of David.

Save me, O God, for the waters are come in unto my soul. I sink in deep mire where there is no standing, I am come into deep waters where the floods overflow me. I am weary of my crying, my throat is dried, mine eyes fail while I wait for my God. They that hate me without a cause are more than the hairs of mine head, they that would destroy me, being mine enemies wrongfully, are mighty, then I restored that which I took not away. O God, thou knowest my foolishness and my sins are not hid from thee. Let not them that wait on thee, O Lord God of hosts, be ashamed for my sake, let not those that seek thee be confounded for my sake, O God of Israel. Because for thy sake I have borne reproach, shame hath covered my face. I am become a stranger unto my brethren and an alien unto my mother's children. For the zeal of thine house hath eaten me up and the reproaches of them that reproached thee are fallen upon me. When I wept and chastened my soul with fasting, that was to my reproach. I made sackcloth also my garment and I became a proverb to them. They that sit in the gate speak against me and I was the song of the drunkards. But as for me, my prayer is unto thee, O Lord, in an acceptable time, O God, in the multitude of thy mercy hear me, in the truth of thy salvation deliver me out of the mire and let me not sink, let me be delivered from them that hate me and out of the deep waters. Let not the waterflood overflow me, neither let the deep swallow me up, and let not the pit shut her mouth upon me. Hear me, O Lord, for thy lovingkindness is good, turn unto me according to the multitude of thy tender mercies. And hide not thy face from thy servant, for I am in trouble, hear me speedily. Draw nigh unto my soul and redeem it, deliver me because of mine enemies. Thou hast known my reproach, and my shame, and my dishonor, mine adversaries are all before thee. Reproach hath broken my heart and I am full of heaviness, and I looked for some to take pity, but there was none, and for comforters, but I found none. They gave me also gall for my meat and in my thirst they gave me vinegar to drink. Let their table become a snare before them and that which should have been for their welfare let it become a trap. Let their eyes be darkened that they see not and make their loins continually to shake. Pour out thine indignation upon them and let thy wrathful anger take hold of them. Let their habitation be desolate and let none dwell in their tents. For they persecute him whom thou hast smitten and they talk to the grief of those whom thou hast wounded. Add iniquity unto their iniquity and let them not come into thy righteousness. Let them be blotted out of the book of the living and not be written with the righteous. But I am poor and sorrowful, let thy salvation, O God, set me up on high. I will praise the name of God with a song and will magnify him with thanksgiving. This also shall please the Lord better than an ox or bullock that hath horns and hooves. The humble shall see this and be glad and your heart shall live that seek God. For the Lord heareth the poor and despiseth not his prisoners. Let the Heaven and Earth praise him, the seas and everything that moveth therein. For God will save Zion and will build the cities of Judah, that they may dwell there and have it in possession. The seed also of his servants shall inherit it and they that love his name shall dwell therein.

PSALM 70
To the chief Musician, A Psalm of David, to bring to remembrance.
Make haste, O God, to deliver me, make haste to help me, O Lord. Let them be ashamed and confounded that seek after my soul, let them be turned backward and put to confusion that desire my hurt. Let them be turned back for a reward of their shame that say, Aha, aha. Let all those that seek thee rejoice and be glad in thee and let such as love thy salvation say continually, Let God be magnified. But I am poor and needy, make haste unto me, O God, thou art my help and my deliverer, O Lord, make no tarrying.

PSALM 71
A psalm of David.
In thee, O Lord, do I put my trust, let me never be put to confusion. Deliver me in thy righteousness and cause me to escape, incline thine ear unto me and save me. Be thou my strong habitation whereunto I may continually resort, thou hast given commandment to save me, for thou art my rock and my fortress. Deliver me, O my God, out of the hand of the wicked, out of the hand of the unrighteous and cruel man. For thou art my hope, O Lord God, thou art my trust from my youth. By thee have I been holden up from the womb, thou art he that took me out of my mother's bowels, my praise shall be continually of thee. I am as a wonder unto many, but thou art my strong refuge. Let my mouth be filled with thy praise and with thy honor all the day. Cast me not off in the time of old age, forsake me not when my strength faileth. For mine enemies speak against me, and they that lay wait for my soul take counsel together saying, God hath forsaken him, persecute and take him, for there is none to deliver him. O God, be not far from me, O my God, make haste for my help. Let them be confounded and consumed that are adversaries to my soul, let them be covered with reproach and dishonor that seek my hurt. But I will

hope continually and will yet praise thee more and more. My mouth shall show forth thy righteousness and thy salvation all the day, for I know not the numbers thereof. I will go in the strength of the Lord God, I will make mention of thy righteousness, even of thine only. O God, thou hast taught me from my youth and hitherto have I declared thy wondrous works. Now also when I am old and gray-headed, O God, forsake me not until I have showed thy strength unto this generation and thy power to everyone that is to come. Thy righteousness also, O God, is very high, who hast done great things, O God, who is like unto thee? Thou, which hast showed me great and sore troubles shalt quicken me again and shalt bring me up again from the depths of the Earth. Thou shalt increase my greatness and comfort me on every side. I will also praise thee with the psaltery, even thy truth, O my God, unto thee will I sing with the harp, O thou Holy One of Israel. My lips shall greatly rejoice when I sing unto thee, and my soul, which thou hast redeemed. My tongue also shall talk of thy righteousness all the day long, for they are confounded, for they are brought unto shame that seek my hurt.

PSALM 72
A Psalm for Solomon.

Give the king thy judgments, O God and thy righteousness unto the king's son. He shall judge thy people with righteousness and thy poor with judgment. The mountains shall bring peace to the people and the little hills by righteousness. He shall judge the poor of the people, he shall save the children of the needy, and shall break in pieces the oppressor. They shall fear thee as long as the sun and moon endure throughout all generations. He shall come down like rain upon the mown grass, as showers that water the earth. In his days shall the righteous flourish and abundance of peace so long as the moon endureth. He shall have dominion also from sea to sea and from the river unto the ends of the Earth. They that dwell in the wilderness shall bow before him and his enemies shall lick the dust. The kings of Tarshish and of the isles shall bring presents, the kings of Sheba and Seba shall offer gifts. Yea, all kings shall fall down before him, all nations shall serve him. For he shall deliver the needy when he crieth, the poor also and him that hath no helper. He shall spare the poor and needy and shall save the souls of the needy. He shall redeem their soul from deceit and violence, and precious shall their blood be in his sight. And he shall live, and to him shall be given of the gold of Sheba, prayer also shall be made for him continually and daily shall he be praised. There shall be a handful of corn in the earth upon the top of the mountains, the fruit thereof shall shake like Lebanon, and they of the city shall flourish like grass of the earth. His name shall endure forever, his name shall be continued as long as the sun, and men shall be blessed in him, all nations shall call him blessed. Blessed be the Lord God, the God of Israel, who only doeth wondrous things. And blessed be his glorious name forever, and let the whole earth be filled with his glory. Amen, and Amen. The prayers of David the son of Jesse are ended.

PSALM 73
A Psalm of Asaph.

Truly God is good to Israel, even to such as are of a clean heart. But as for me, my feet were almost gone, my steps had well-nigh slipped. For I was envious at the foolis, when I saw the prosperity of the wicked. For there are no bands in their death, but their strength is firm. They are not in trouble as other men, neither are they plagued like other men. Therefore pride compasseth them about as a chain, violence covereth them as a garment. Their eyes stand out with fatness, they have more than heart could wish. They are corrupt, and speak wickedly concerning oppression, they speak loftily. They set their mouth against the heavens and their tongue walketh through the earth. Therefore his people return hither and waters of a full cup are wrung out to them. And they say, How doth God know? And is there knowledge in the Most High? Behold, these are the ungodly who prosper in the world, they increase in riches. Verily I have cleansed my heart in vain and washed my hands in innocency. For all the day long have I been plagued and chastened every morning. If I say, I will speak thus, behold, I should offend against the generation of thy children. When I thought to know this, it was too painful for me until I went into the sanctuary of God, then understood I their end. Surely thou didst set them in slippery places, thou castedst them down into destruction. How are they brought into desolation, as in a moment! They are utterly consumed with terrors. As a dream when one awaketh, so, O Lord, when thou awakest thou shalt despise their image. Thus my heart was grieved and I was pricked in my reins. So foolish was I and ignorant, I was as a beast before thee. Nevertheless I am continually with thee, thou hast holden me by my right hand. Thou shalt guide me with thy counsel and afterward receive me to glory. Whom have I in Heaven but thee? And there is none upon earth that I desire besides thee. My flesh and my heart faileth, but God is the strength of my heart and my portion forever. For lo, they that are far from thee shall perish, thou hast destroyed all them that go a whoring from thee. But it is good for me to draw near to God, I have put my trust in the Lord God that I may declare all thy works.

PSALM 74
Maschil of Asaph.

O God, why hast thou cast us off forever? Why doth thine anger smoke against the sheep of thy pasture? Remember thy congregation which thou hast purchased of old, the rod of thine inheritance which thou hast redeemed, this mount Zion wherein thou hast dwelt. Lift up thy feet unto the perpetual desolations, even all that the enemy hath done wickedly in the sanctuary. Thine enemies roar in the midst of thy congregations, they set up their ensigns for signs. A man was famous according as he had lifted up axes upon the thick trees. But now they break down the carved work thereof at once with axes and hammers. They have cast fire into thy sanctuary, they have defiled by casting down the dwelling place of thy name to the ground. They said in their hearts, Let us destroy them together, they have burned up all the synagogues of God in the land. We see not our signs, there is no more any prophet, neither is there among us any that knoweth how long. O God, how long shall the adversary reproach, shall the enemy blaspheme thy name forever? Why withdrawest thou thy hand, even thy right hand? Pluck it out of thy bosom. For God is my King of old, working salvation in the midst of the earth. Thou didst divide the sea by thy strength, thou brakest the heads of the dragons in the waters. Thou brakest the heads of leviathan in pieces and gavest him to be meat to the people inhabiting the wilderness. Thou didst cleave the fountain and the flood, thou driedst up mighty rivers. The day is thine, the night also is thine, thou hast prepared the light and the sun. Thou hast set all the borders of the Earth, thou hast made summer and winter. Remember this, that the enemy hath reproached, O Lord, and that the foolish people have blasphemed thy name. O deliver not the soul of thy turtledove unto the multitude of the wicked, forget not the congregation of thy poor forever. Have respect unto the covenant, for the dark places of the earth are full of the habitations of cruelty. O let not the oppressed return ashamed, let the poor and needy praise thy name. Arise, O God, plead thine own cause, remember how the foolish man reproacheth thee daily. Forget not the voice of thine enemies, the tumult of those that rise up against thee increaseth continually.

PSALM 75
To the Chief Musician, Al-taschith, A Psalm or Song of Asaph.
Unto thee, O God, do we give thanks, unto thee do we give thanks, for that thy name is near thy wondrous works declare. When I shall receive the congregation I will judge uprightly. The Earth and all the inhabitants thereof are dissolved, I bear up the pillars of it. Selah. I said unto the fools, Deal not foolishly, and to the wicked, Lift not up the horn. Lift not up your horn on high, speak not with a stiff neck. For promotion cometh neither from the east, nor from the west, nor from the south. But God is the judge, he putteth down one and setteth up another. For in the hand of the Lord there is a cup and the wine is red, it is full of mixture and he poureth out of the same, but the dregs thereof, all the wicked of the earth shall wring them out and drink them. But I will declare forever, I will sing praises to the God of Jacob. All the horns of the wicked also will I cut off, but the horns of the righteous shall be exalted.

PSALM 76
To the chief Musician on Neginoth, A Psalm or Song of Asaph.
In Judah is God known, his name is great in Israel. In Salem also is his tabernacle and his dwelling place in Zion. There brake he the arrows of the bow, the shield, and the sword, and the battle. Selah. Thou art more glorious and excellent than the mountains of prey. The stouthearted are spoiled, they have slept their sleep, and none of the men of might have found their hands. At thy rebuke, O God of Jacob, both the chariot and horse are cast into a dead sleep. Thou, even thou, art to be feared, and who may stand in thy sight when once thou art angry? Thou didst cause judgment to be heard from Heaven, the earth feared and was still when God arose to judgment to save all the meek of the earth. Selah. Surely the wrath of man shall praise thee, the remainder of wrath shalt thou restrain. Vow and pay unto the Lord your God, let all that be round about him bring presents unto him that ought to be feared. He shall cut off the spirit of princes, he is terrible to the kings of the earth.

PSALM 77
To the chief Musician, to Jeduthun, A Psalm of Asaph.
I cried unto God with my voice, even unto God with my voice, and he gave ear unto me. In the day of my trouble I sought the Lord, my sore ran in the night and ceased not, my soul refused to be comforted. I remembered God and was troubled, I complained and my spirit was overwhelmed. Selah. Thou holdest mine eyes waking, I am so troubled that I cannot speak. I have considered the days of old, the years of ancient times. I call to remembrance my song in the night, I commune with mine own heart and my spirit made diligent search. Will the Lord cast off forever? And will he be favorable no more? Is his mercy clean gone forever? Doth his promise fail for evermore? Hath God forgotten to be gracious? Hath he in anger shut up his tender mercies? Selah. And I said, This is my infirmity, but I will remember the years of the right hand of the Most High. I will remember the works of the Lord, surely I will remember thy wonders of old. I will meditate also of all thy work and talk of thy doings. Thy way, O God, is in the sanctuary; who is so great a God as our God? Thou art the God that doest wonders, thou hast declared thy strength among the people. Thou hast with thine arm redeemed thy people, the sons of Jacob and Joseph. Selah. The waters saw thee, O God, the waters saw thee, they were afraid, the depths also were troubled. The clouds poured out water, the skies sent out a sound, thine arrows also went abroad. The voice of thy thunder was in the Heaven, the lightnings lightened the world, the Earth trembled and shook. Thy way is in the sea and thy path in

the great waters and thy footsteps are not known. Thou ledst thy people like a flock by the hand of Moses and Aaron.

PSALM 78
Maschil of Asaph.

Give ear, O my people, to my law, incline your ears to the words of my mouth. I will open my mouth in a parable, I will utter dark sayings of old which we have heard and known and our fathers have told us. We will not hide them from their children, showing to the generation to come the praises of the Lord, and his strength, and his wonderful works that he hath done. For he established a testimony in Jacob and appointed a law in Israel, which he commanded our fathers that they should make them known to their children, that the generation to come might know them, even the children which should be born who should arise and declare them to their children, that they might set their hope in God and not forget the works of God, but keep his commandments and might not be as their fathers a stubborn and rebellious generation, a generation that set not their heart aright and whose spirit was not steadfast with God. The children of Ephraim, being armed and carrying bows, turned back in the day of battle. They kept not the covenant of God and refused to walk in his law and forgat his works and his wonders that he had showed them. Marvelous things did he in the sight of their fathers in the land of Egypt, in the field of Zoan. He divided the sea and caused them to pass through and he made the waters to stand as a heap. In the daytime also he led them with a cloud and all the night with a light of fire. He clave the rocks in the wilderness and gave them drink as out of the great depths. He brought streams also out of the rock and caused waters to run down like rivers. And they sinned yet more against him by provoking the Most High in the wilderness. And they tempted God in their heart by asking meat for their lust. Yea, they spake against God, they said, Can God furnish a table in the wilderness? Behold, he smote the rock that the waters gushed out and the streams overflowed; can he give bread also? Can he provide flesh for his people? Therefore the Lord heard this and was wroth, so a fire was kindled against Jacob and anger also came up against Israel, because they believed not in God and trusted not in his salvation, though he had commanded the clouds from above, and opened the doors of Heaven, and had rained down manna upon them to eat, and had given them of the corn of Heaven. Man did eat angels' food, he sent them meat to the full. He caused an east wind to blow in the Heaven, and by his power he brought in the south wind. He rained flesh also upon them as dust, and feathered fowls like as the sand of the sea, and he let it fall in the midst of their camp, round about their habitations. So they did eat and were well filled, for he gave them their own desire, they were not estranged from their lust, but while their meat was yet in their mouths, the wrath of God came upon them and slew the fattest of them and smote down the chosen men of Israel. For all this they sinned still and believed not for his wondrous works. Therefore their days did he consume in vanity and their years in trouble. When he slew them, then they sought him and they returned and inquired early after God. And they remembered that God was their Rock, and the high God their Redeemer. Nevertheless they did flatter him with their mouth and they lied unto him with their tongues. For their heart was not right with him, neither were they steadfast in his covenant. But he, being full of compassion, forgave their iniquity and destroyed them not, yea, many a time turned he his anger away and did not stir up all his wrath. For he remembered that they were but flesh, a wind that passeth away and cometh not again. How oft did they provoke him in the wilderness and grieve him in the desert! Yea, they turned back and tempted God and limited the Holy One of Israel. They remembered not his hand nor the day when he delivered them from the enemy, how he had wrought his signs in Egypt and his wonders in the field of Zoan, and had turned their rivers into blood, and their floods that they could not drink. He sent divers sorts of flies among them which devoured them and frogs which destroyed them. He gave also their increase unto the caterpillar and their labor unto the locust. He destroyed their vines with hail and their sycamore trees with frost. He gave up their cattle also to the hail and their flocks to hot thunderbolts. He cast upon them the fierceness of his anger, wrath, and indignation, and trouble by sending evil angels among them. He made a way to his anger, he spared not their soul from death, but gave their life over to the pestilence, and smote all the firstborn in Egypt, the chief of their strength in the tabernacles of Ham, but made his own people to go forth like sheep and guided them in the wilderness like a flock. And he led them on safely so that they feared not, but the sea overwhelmed their enemies. And he brought them to the border of his sanctuary, even to this mountain which his right hand had purchased. He cast out the heathen also before them, and divided them an inheritance by line, and made the tribes of Israel to dwell in their tents. Yet they tempted and provoked the Most High God and kept not his testimonies, but turned back and dealt unfaithfully like their fathers, they were turned aside like a deceitful bow. For they provoked him to anger with their high places and moved him to jealousy with their graven images. When God heard this, he was wroth and greatly abhorred Israel. So that he forsook the tabernacle of Shiloh, the tent which he placed among men, and delivered his strength into captivity and his glory into the enemy's hand. He gave his people over also unto the sword and was wroth with his inheritance, the fire consumed their young men and their maidens were not given to marriage. Their priests fell by the sword and their widows made no lamentation. Then the Lord awaked as one out of sleep and like a mighty man that shouteth by reason of wine. And he smote his enemies in the hinder parts, he put them to a perpetual reproach. Moreover he refused the tabernacle of Joseph and chose not the tribe of Ephraim, but chose the tribe of Judah, the mount Zion which he loved. And he built his sanctuary like high palaces, like the earth which he hath established forever. He chose David also his servant and took him from the sheepfolds, from following the ewes great with young he brought him to feed Jacob his people and Israel his inheritance. So he fed them according to the integrity of his heart and guided them by the skillfulness of his hands.

PSALM 79
A Psalm of Asaph.

O God, the heathen are come into thine inheritance, thy holy temple have they defiled, they have laid Jerusalem on heaps. The dead bodies of thy servants have they given to be meat unto the fowls of the Heaven, the flesh of thy saints unto the beasts of the earth. Their blood have they shed like water round about Jerusalem and there was none to bury them. We are become a reproach to our neighbors, a scorn and derision to them that are round about us. How long, Lord? Wilt thou be angry forever? Shall thy jealousy burn like fire? Pour out thy wrath upon the heathen that have not known thee and upon the kingdoms that have not called upon thy name. For they have devoured Jacob and laid waste his dwelling place. O remember not against us former iniquities, let thy tender mercies speedily prevent us, for we are brought very low. Help us, O God of our salvation, for the glory of thy name, and deliver us and purge away our sins for thy name's sake. Wherefore should the heathen say, Where is their God? Let him be known among the heathen in our sight by the revenging of the blood of thy servants which is shed. Let the sighing of the prisoner come before thee, according to the greatness of thy power preserve thou those that are appointed to die, and render unto our neighbors sevenfold into their bosom their reproach wherewith they have reproached thee, O Lord. So we thy people and sheep of thy pasture will give thee thanks forever, we will show forth thy praise to all generations.

PSALM 80

To the chief Musician upon Shoshannim-Eduth, A Psalm of Asaph.

Give ear, O Shepherd of Israel, thou that leadest Joseph like a flock, thou that dwellest between the cherubim, shine forth. Before Ephraim and Benjamin and Manasseh stir up thy strength and come and save us. Turn us again, O God, and cause thy face to shine, and we shall be saved. O Lord God of hosts, how long wilt thou be angry against the prayer of thy people? Thou feedest them with the bread of tears and givest them tears to drink in great measure. Thou makest us a strife unto our neighbors, and our enemies laugh among themselves. Turn us again, O God of hosts, and cause thy face to shine, and we shall be saved. Thou hast brought a vine out of Egypt, thou hast cast out the heathen and planted it. Thou preparest room before it, and didst cause it to take deep root, and it filled the land. The hills were covered with the shadow of it and the boughs thereof were like the goodly cedars. She sent out her boughs unto the sea and her branches unto the river. Why hast thou then broken down her hedges so that all they which pass by the way do pluck her? The boar out of the wood doth waste it and the wild beast of the field doth devour it. Return, we beseech thee, O God of hosts, look down from Heaven and behold, and visit this vine and the vineyard which thy right hand hath planted, and the branch that thou madest strong for thyself. It is burned with fire, it is cut down, they perish at the rebuke of thy countenance. Let thy hand be upon the man of thy right hand, upon the son of man whom thou madest strong for thyself. So will not we go back from thee, quicken us and we will call upon thy name. Turn us again, O Lord God of hosts, cause thy face to shine and we shall be saved.

PSALM 81

To the chief Musician upon Gittith, A Psalm of Asaph.

Sing aloud unto God our strength, make a joyful noise unto the God of Jacob. Take a psalm, and bring hither the timbrel, the pleasant harp with the psaltery. Blow up the trumpet in the new moon, in the time appointed, on our solemn feast day. For this was a statute for Israel and a law of the God of Jacob. This he ordained in Joseph for a testimony when he went out through the land of Egypt, where I heard a language that I understood not. I removed his shoulder from the burden, his hands were delivered from the pots. Thou calledst in trouble and I delivered thee, I answered thee in the secret place of thunder, I proved thee at the waters of Merribah. Selah. Hear, O my people, and I will testify unto thee, O Israel, if thou wilt hearken unto me, there shall no strange god be in thee, neither shalt thou worship any strange god. I am the Lord thy God, which brought thee out of the land of Egypt, open thy mouth wide and I will fill it. But my people would not hearken to my voice and Israel would none of me. So I gave them up unto their own hearts' lust and they walked in their own counsels. O that my people had hearkened unto me and Israel had walked in my ways! I should soon have subdued their enemies and turned my hand against their adversaries. The haters of the Lord should have submitted themselves unto him, but their time should have endured forever. He should have fed them also with the finest of the wheat and with honey out of the rock should I have satisfied thee.

PSALM 82
A Psalm of Asaph.

God standeth in the congregation of the mighty, he judgeth among the gods. How long will ye suffer them to judge unjustly and accept the persons of the wicked? Selah. Defend the poor and fatherless, do justice to the afflicted and needy. Deliver the poor and needy, rid them out of the hand of the wicked. They know not, neither will they understand, they walk on in darkness, all the foundations of the earth are out of course. I have said, Ye are gods and all of you are children of the Most High. But ye shall die like men and fall like one of the princes. Arise, O God, judge the earth, for thou shalt inherit all nations.

PSALM 83
A Song or Psalm of Asaph.

Keep not thou silence, O God, hold not thy peace, and be not still, O God. For lo, thine enemies make a tumult, and they that hate thee have lifted up the head. They have taken crafty counsel against thy people and consulted against thy hidden ones. They have said, Come and let us cut them off from being a nation, that the name of Israel may be no more in remembrance. For they have consulted together with one consent, they are confederate against thee, the tabernacles of Edom and the Ishmaelites, of Moab and the Hagarenes, Gebal and Ammon and Amalek, the Philistines with the inhabitants of Tyre. Assur also is joined with them, they have holpen the children of Lot. Selah. Do unto them as unto the Midianites, as to Sisera, as to Jabin at the brook of Kishon, which perished at En-dor, they became as dung for the Earth. Make their nobles like Oreb and like Zeeb, yea, all their princes as Zebah and as Zalmunna, who said, Let us take to ourselves the houses of God in possession. O my God, make them like a wheel, as the stubble before the wind. As the fire burneth a wood and as the flame setteth the mountains on fire, so persecute them with thy tempest and make them afraid with thy storm. Fill their faces with shame that they may seek thy name, O Lord. Let them be confounded and troubled forever, yea, let them be put to shame and perish. That men may know that thou, whose name alone is JEHOVAH, art the Most High over all the earth.

PSALM 84
To the chief Musician upon Gittith, A Psalm for the sons of Korah.

How amiable are thy tabernacles, O Lord of hosts! My soul longeth, yea, even fainteth for the courts of the Lord, my heart and my flesh crieth out for the living God. Yea, the sparrow hath found a house and the swallow a nest for herself where she may lay her young, even thine altars, O Lord of hosts, my King, and my God. Blessed are they that dwell in thy house, they will be still praising thee. Selah. Blessed is the man whose strength is in thee, in whose heart are the ways of them, who passing through the valley of Baca make it a well, the rain also filleth the pools. They go from strength to strength, every one of them in Zion appeareth before God. O Lord God of hosts, hear my prayer, give ear, O God of Jacob. Selah. Behold, O God our shield, and look upon the face of thine anointed. For a day in thy courts is better than a thousand. I had rather be a doorkeeper in the house of my God than to dwell in the tents of wickedness. For the Lord God is a sun and shield, the Lord will give grace and glory, no good thing will he withhold from them that walk uprightly. O Lord of hosts, blessed is the man that trusteth in thee.

PSALM 85
To the chief Musician, A Psalm for the sons of Korah.
Lord, thou hast been favorable unto thy land, thou hast brought back the captivity of Jacob. Thou hast forgiven the iniquity of thy people, thou hast covered all their sin. Selah. Thou hast taken away all thy wrath, thou hast turned thyself from the fierceness of thine anger. Turn us, O God of our salvation, and cause thine anger toward us to cease. Wilt thou be angry with us forever? Wilt thou draw out thine anger to all generations? Wilt thou not revive us again, that thy people may rejoice in thee? Show us thy mercy, O Lord, and grant us thy salvation. I will hear what God the Lord will speak, for he will speak peace unto his people and to his saints, but let them not turn again to folly. Surely his salvation is nigh them that fear him that glory may dwell in our land. Mercy and truth are met together, righteousness and peace have kissed each other. Truth shall spring out of the earth and righteousness shall look down from Heaven. Yea, the Lord shall give that which is good and our land shall yield her increase. Righteousness shall go before him and shall set us in the way of his steps.

PSALM 86
A Prayer of David.
Bow down thine ear, O Lord, hear me, for I am poor and needy. Preserve my soul, for I am holy, O thou my God, save thy servant that trusteth in thee. Be merciful unto me, O Lord, for I cry unto thee daily. Rejoice the soul of thy servant, for unto thee, O Lord, do I lift up my soul. For thou, Lord, art good and ready to forgive and plenteous in mercy unto all them that call upon thee. Give ear, O Lord, unto my prayer and attend to the voice of my supplications. In the day of my trouble I will call upon thee, for thou wilt answer me. Among the gods there is none like unto thee, O Lord, neither are there any works like unto thy works. All nations whom thou hast made shall come and worship before thee, O Lord, and shall glorify thy name. For thou art great and doest wondrous things, thou art God alone. Teach me thy way, O Lord, I will walk in thy truth, unite my heart to fear thy name. I will praise thee, O Lord my God, with all my heart, and I will glorify thy name for evermore. For great is thy mercy toward me and thou hast delivered my soul from the lowest hell. O God, the proud are risen against me, and the assemblies of violent men have sought after my soul, and have not set thee before them. But thou, O Lord, art a God full of compassion and gracious, long-suffering and plenteous in mercy and truth. O turn unto me and have mercy upon me, give thy strength unto thy servant and save the son of thine handmaid. Show me a token for good, that they which hate me may see it and be ashamed, because thou, Lord, hast holpen me and comforted me.

PSALM 87
A Psalm or Song for the sons of Korah.
His foundation is in the holy mountains. The Lord loveth the gates of Zion more than all the dwellings of Jacob. Glorious things are spoken of thee, O city of God. Selah. I will make mention of Rahab and Babylon to them that know me, behold Philistia and Tyre with Ethiopia, this man was born there. And of Zion it shall be said, This and that man was born in her and the Highest himself shall establish her. The Lord shall count, when he writeth up the people, that this man was born there. Selah. As well the singers as the players on instruments shall be there, all my springs are in thee.

PSALM 88
A Song or Psalm for the sons of Korah, to the chief Musician
upon Mahalath Leannoth, Maschil of Heman the Ezrahite.

O Lord God of my salvation, I have cried day and night before thee, let my prayer come before thee, incline thine ear unto my cry, for my soul is full of troubles, and my life draweth nigh unto the grave. I am counted with them that go down into the pit, I am as a man that hath no strength, free among the dead, like the slain that lie in the grave whom thou rememberest no more and they are cut off from thy hand. Thou hast laid me in the lowest pit, in darkness, in the deeps. Thy wrath lieth hard upon me and thou hast afflicted me with all thy waves. Selah. Thou hast put away mine acquaintance far from me, thou hast made me an abomination unto them, I am shut up and I cannot come forth. Mine eye mourneth by reason of affliction, Lord, I have called daily upon thee, I have stretched out my hands unto thee. Wilt thou show wonders to the dead? Shall the dead arise and praise thee? Selah. Shall thy lovingkindness be declared in the grave? Or thy faithfulness in destruction? Shall thy wonders be known in the dark? And thy righteousness in the land of forgetfulness? But unto thee have I cried, O Lord, and in the morning shall my prayer prevent thee. Lord, why castest thou off my soul? Why hidest thou thy face from me? I am afflicted and ready to die from my youth up; while I suffer thy terrors I am distracted. Thy fierce wrath goeth over me, thy terrors have cut me off. They came round about me daily like water, they compassed me about together. Lover and friend hast thou put far from me and mine acquaintance into darkness.

PSALM 89
Maschil of Ethan the Ezrahite.

I will sing of the mercies of the Lord forever, with my mouth will I make known thy faithfulness to all generations. For I have said, Mercy shall be built up forever, thy faithfulness shalt thou establish in the very heavens. I have made a covenant with my chosen, I have sworn unto David my servant. Thy seed will I establish for ever and build up thy throne to all generations. Selah. And the heavens shall praise thy wonders, O Lord, thy faithfulness also in the congregation of the saints. For who in the Heaven can be compared unto the Lord? Who among the sons of the mighty can be likened unto the Lord? God is greatly to be feared in the assembly of the saints and to be had in reverence of all them that are about him. O Lord God of hosts, who is a strong Lord like unto thee? Or to thy faithfulness round about thee? Thou rulest the raging of the sea, when the waves thereof arise thou stillest them. Thou hast broken Rahab in pieces as one that is slain, thou hast scattered thine enemies with thy strong arm. The heavens are thine the Earth also is thine, as for the world and the fullness thereof, thou hast founded them. The north and the south thou hast created them, Tabor and Hermon shall rejoice in thy name. Thou hast a mighty arm, strong is thy hand, and high is thy right hand. Justice and judgment are the habitation of thy throne, mercy and truth shall go before thy face. Blessed is the people that know the joyful sound, they shall walk, O Lord, in the light of thy countenance. In thy name shall they rejoice all the day and in thy righteousness shall they be exalted. For thou art the glory of their strength and in thy favor our horn shall be exalted. For the Lord is our defense and the Holy One of Israel is our King. Then thou spakest in vision to thy Holy One and saidst, I have laid help upon one that is mighty, I have exalted one chosen out of the people. I have found David my servant, with my holy oil have I anointed him with whom my hand shall be established, mine arm also shall strengthen him. The enemy shall not exact upon him, nor the son of wickedness afflict him. And I will beat down his foes before his face and plague them that hate him. But my faithfulness and my mercy shall be with him, and in my name shall his horn be exalted. I will set his hand also in the sea and his right hand in the rivers. He shall cry unto me, Thou art my Father, my God, and the Rock of my salvation. Also I will make him my firstborn, higher than the kings of the earth. My mercy will I keep for him for evermore and my covenant shall stand fast with him. His seed also will I make to endure for ever and his throne as the days of Heaven. If his children forsake my law and walk not in my judgments, if they break my statutes and keep not my commandments, then will I visit their transgression with the rod and their iniquity with stripes. Nevertheless my lovingkindness will I not utterly take from him nor suffer my faithfulness to fail. My covenant will I not break, nor alter the thing that is gone out of my lips. Once have I sworn by my holiness that I will not lie unto David. His seed shall endure for ever and his throne as the sun before me. It shall be established for ever as the moon and as a faithful witness in Heaven. Selah. But thou hast cast off and abhorred, thou hast been wroth with thine anointed. Thou hast made void the covenant of thy servant, thou hast profaned his crown by casting it to the ground. Thou hast broken down all his hedges, thou hast brought his strongholds to ruin. All that pass by the way spoil him, he is a reproach to his neighbors. Thou hast set up the right hand of his adversaries, thou hast made all his enemies to rejoice. Thou hast also turned the edge of his sword and hast not made him to stand in the battle. Thou hast made his glory to cease and cast his throne down to the ground. The days of his youth hast thou shortened, thou hast covered him with shame. Selah. How long, Lord? Wilt thou hide thyself forever? Shall thy wrath burn like fire? Remember how short my time is, wherefore hast thou made all men in vain? What man is he that liveth and shall not see death? Shall he deliver his soul from the hand of the grave? Selah. Lord, where are thy former lovingkindnesses which thou swarest unto David in thy truth? Remember, Lord, the reproach of thy servants, how I do bear in my bosom the reproach of all the mighty people wherewith thine enemies have reproached, O Lord, wherewith they have reproached the footsteps of thine anointed. Blessed be the Lord for evermore. Amen and Amen.

PSALM 90
A Prayer of Moses, the man of God.

Lord, thou hast been our dwelling place in all generations. Before the mountains were brought forth, or ever thou hadst formed the Earth and the world, even from everlasting to everlasting thou art God. Thou turnest man to destruction and sayest, Return, ye children of men. For a thousand years in thy sight are but as yesterday when it is past and as a watch in the night. Thou carriest them away as with a flood, they are as a sleep, in the morning they are like grass which groweth up. In the morning it flourisheth and groweth up, in the evening it is cut down and withereth. For we are consumed by thine anger and by thy wrath are we troubled. Thou hast set our iniquities before thee, our secret sins in the light of thy countenance. For all our days are passed away in thy wrath, we spend our years as a tale that is told. The days of our years are threescore years and ten, and if by reason of strength they be fourscore years, yet is their strength labor and sorrow, for it is soon cut off, and we fly away. Who knoweth the power of thine anger? Even according to thy fear, so is thy wrath. So teach us to number our days that we may apply our hearts unto wisdom. Return us, O Lord. How long wilt thou hide thy face from thy servants? And let them repent of all their hard speeches they have spoken concerning thee. O satisfy us early with thy mercy, that we may rejoice and be glad all our days. Make us glad according to the days wherein thou hast afflicted us and the years wherein we have seen evil. Let thy work appear unto thy servants and thy glory unto their children. And let the beauty of the Lord our God be upon us and establish thou the work of our hands upon us, yea, the work of our hands establish thou it.

PSALM 91

He that dwelleth in the secret place of the Most High shall abide under the shadow of the Almighty. I will say of the Lord, He is my refuge and my fortress, my God, in him will I trust. Surely he shall deliver thee from the snare of the fowler and from the noisome pestilence. He shall cover thee with his feathers and under his wings shalt thou trust, his truth shall be thy shield and buckler. Thou shalt not be afraid for the terror by night, nor for the arrow that flieth by day, nor for the pestilence that walketh in darkness, nor for the destruction that wasteth at noonday. A thousand shall fall at thy side and ten thousand at thy right hand, but it shall not come nigh thee. Only with thine eyes shalt thou behold and see the reward of the wicked. Because thou hast made the Lord, which is my refuge, even the Most High, thy habitation, there shall no evil befall thee neither shall any plague come nigh thy dwelling. For he shall give his angels charge over thee to keep thee in all thy ways. They shall bear thee up in their hands, lest thou dash thy foot against a stone. Thou shalt tread upon the lion and adder, the young lion and the dragon shalt thou trample under feet. Because he hath set his love upon me, therefore will I deliver him, I will set him on high because he hath known my name. He shall call upon me and I will answer him, I will be with him in trouble, I will deliver him and honor him. With long life will I satisfy him and show him my salvation.

PSALM 92

It is a good thing to give thanks unto the Lord and to sing praises unto thy name, O Most High, to show forth thy lovingkindness in the morning and thy faithfulness every night upon an instrument of ten strings, and upon the psaltery, upon the harp with a solemn sound. For thou, Lord, hast made me glad through thy work, I will triumph in the works of thy hands. O Lord, how great are thy works and thy thoughts are very deep. A brutish man knoweth not, neither doth a fool understand this. When the wicked spring as the grass and when all the workers of iniquity do flourish, it is that they shall be destroyed forever, but thou, Lord, art most high for evermore. For lo, thine enemies, O Lord, for lo, thine enemies shall perish, all the workers of iniquity shall be scattered. But my horn shalt thou exalt like the horn of a unicorn I shall be anointed with fresh oil. Mine eye also shall see my desire on mine enemies and mine ears shall hear my desire of the wicked that rise up against me. The righteous shall flourish like the palm tree, he shall grow like a cedar in Lebanon. Those that he planted in the house of the Lord shall flourish in the courts of our God. They shall still bring forth fruit in old age, they shall be fat and flourishing, to show that the Lord is upright, he is my rock and there is no unrighteousness in him.

PSALM 93

The Lord reigneth, he is clothed with majesty, the Lord is clothed with strength wherewith he hath girded himself, the world also is established that it cannot be moved. Thy throne is established of old, thou art from everlasting. The floods have lifted up, O Lord, the floods have lifted up their voice, the floods lift up their waves. The Lord on high is mightier than the noise of many waters, yea, than the mighty waves of the sea. Thy testimonies are very sure, holiness becometh thine house, O Lord, forever.

PSALM 94

O Lord God, to whom vengeance belongeth, O God, to whom vengeance belongeth, show thyself. Lift up thyself, thou Judge of the earth, render a reward to the proud. Lord, how long shall the wicked, how long shall the wicked triumph? How long shall they utter and speak hard things? And all the workers of iniquity boast themselves? They break in pieces thy people, O Lord, and afflict thine heritage. They slay the widow and the stranger and murder the fatherless. Yet they say, the Lord shall not see, neither shall the God of Jacob regard it. Understand, ye brutish among the people, and ye fools, when will ye be wise? He that planteth the ear, shall he not hear? He that formed the eye, shall he not see? He that chastiseth the heathen, shall not he correct? He that teacheth man knowledge, shall not he know? The Lord knoweth the thoughts of man, that they are vanity. Blessed is the man whom thou chastenest, O Lord, and teachest him out of thy law, that thou mayest give him rest from the days of adversity until the pit be digged for the wicked. For the Lord will not cast off his people, neither will he forsake his inheritance. But judgment shall return unto righteousness, and all the upright in heart shall follow it. Who will rise up for me against the evildoers? Or who will stand up for me against the workers of iniquity? Unless the Lord had been my help, my soul had almost dwelt in silence. When I said, My foot slippeth, thy mercy, O Lord, held me up. In the multitude of my thoughts within me thy comforts delight my soul. Shall the throne of iniquity have fellowship with thee, which frameth mischief by a law? They gather themselves together against the soul of the righteous and condemn the innocent blood. But the Lord is my defense and my God is the Rock of my refuge. And he shall bring upon them their own iniquity and shall cut them off in their own wickedness, yea, the Lord our God shall cut them off.

PSALM 95

O come let us sing unto the Lord, let us make a joyful noise to the Rock of our salvation. Let us come before his presence with thanksgiving and make a joyful noise unto him with psalms. For the Lord is a great God and a great King above all gods. In his hand are the deep places of the Earth, the strength of the hills is his also. The sea is his and he made it, and his hand formed the dry land. O come let us worship and bow down, let us kneel before the Lord our maker. For he is our God and we are the people of his pasture and the sheep of his hand. Today if ye will hear his voice, harden not your heart as in the provocation and as in the day of temptation in the wilderness when your fathers tempted me, proved me, and saw my work. Forty years long was I grieved with this generation and said, It is a people that do err in their heart and they have not known my ways, unto whom I sware in my wrath that they should not enter into my rest.

PSALM 96

O sing unto the Lord a new song, sing unto the Lord all the earth. Sing unto the Lord, bless his name, show forth his salvation from day to day. Declare his glory among the heathen, his wonders among all people. For the Lord is great and greatly to be praised, he is to be feared above all gods. For all the gods of the nations are idols, but the Lord made the heavens. Honor and majesty are before him, strength and beauty are in his sanctuary. Give unto the Lord, O ye kindreds of the people, give unto the Lord glory and strength. Give unto the Lord the glory due unto his name, bring an offering and come into his courts. O worship the Lord in the beauty of holiness, fear before him, all the earth. Say among the heathen that the Lord reigneth, the world also shall be established that it shall not be moved, he shall judge the people righteously. Let the heavens rejoice and let the Earth be glad, let the sea roar and the fullness thereof. Let the field be joyful and all that is therein, then shall all the trees of the wood rejoice. Before the Lord, for he cometh, for he cometh to judge the earth, he shall judge the world with righteousness and the people with his truth.

PSALM 97

The Lord reigneth, let the Earth rejoice, let the multitude of isles be glad thereof. Clouds and darkness are round about him, righteousness and judgment are the habitation of his throne. A fire goeth before him and burneth up his enemies round about. His lightnings enlightened the world, the Earth saw and trembled. The hills melted like wax at the presence of the Lord, at the presence of the Lord of the whole earth. The heavens declare his righteousness and all the people see his glory. Confounded be all they that serve graven images, that boast themselves of idols; worship him all ye gods. Zion heard and was glad and the daughters of Judah rejoiced because of thy judgments, O Lord. For thou, Lord, art high above all the earth, thou art exalted far above all gods. Ye that love the Lord, hate evil, he preserveth the souls of his saints, he delivereth them out of the hand of the wicked. Light is sown for the righteous and gladness for the upright in heart. Rejoice in the Lord, ye righteous, and give thanks at the remembrance of his holiness.

PSALM 98
A Psalm.

O sing unto the Lord a new song, for he hath done marvelous things, his right hand and his holy arm hath gotten him the victory. The Lord hath made known his salvation, his righteousness hath he openly showed in the sight of the heathen. He hath remembered his mercy and his truth toward the house of Israel, all the ends of the earth have seen the salvation of our God. Make a joyful noise unto the Lord all the earth make a loud noise, and rejoice, and sing praise. Sing unto the Lord with the harp, with the harp, and the voice of a psalm. With trumpets and sound of cornet make a joyful noise before the Lord, the King. Let the sea roar, and the fullness thereof, the world and they that dwell therein. Let the floods clap their hands, let the hills be joyful together before the Lord, for he cometh to judge the earth, with righteousness shall he judge the world and the people with equity.

PSALM 99

The Lord reigneth, let the people tremble, he sitteth between the cherubim, let the earth be moved. The Lord is great in Zion and he is high above all the people. Let them praise thy great and terrible name, for it is holy. The king's strength also loveth judgment, thou dost establish equity, thou executest judgment and righteousness in Jacob. Exalt ye the Lord our God and worship at his footstool, for he is holy. Moses and Aaron among his priests, and Samuel among them that call upon his name, they called upon the Lord and he answered them. He spake unto them in the cloudy pillar, they kept his testimonies and the ordinance that he gave them. Thou answeredst them, O Lord our God, thou wast a God that forgavest them, though thou tookest vengeance of their inventions. Exalt the Lord our God and worship at his holy hill, for the Lord our God is holy.

PSALM 100
A Psalm of praise.

Make a joyful noise unto the Lord, all ye lands. Serve the Lord with gladness, come before his presence with singing. Know ye that the Lord he is God, it is he that hath made us and not we ourselves, we are his people and the sheep of his pasture. Enter into his gates with thanksgiving and into his courts with praise, be thankful unto him, and bless his name. For the Lord is good, his mercy is everlasting, and his truth endureth to all generations.

PSALM 101
A Psalm of David.

I will sing of mercy and judgment unto thee, O Lord, will I sing. I will behave myself wisely in a perfect way. O when wilt thou come unto me? I will walk within my house with a perfect heart. I will set no wicked thing before mine eyes, I hate the work of them that turn aside, it shall not cleave to me. A froward heart shall depart from me, I will not know a wicked person. Whoso privily slandereth his neighbor, him will I cut off, him that hath a high look and a proud heart will not I suffer. Mine eyes shall be upon the faithful of the land, that they may dwell with me, he that walketh in a perfect way, he shall serve me. He that worketh deceit shall not dwell within my house, he that telleth lies shall not tarry in my sight. I will early destroy all the wicked of the land that I may cut off all wicked doers from the city of the Lord.

PSALM 102
A prayer of the afflicted when he is overwhelmed and poureth out his complaint before the Lord.

Hear my prayer, O Lord, and let my cry come unto thee. Hide not thy face from me in the day when I am in trouble, incline thine ear unto me in the day when I call answer me speedily. For my days are consumed like smoke and my bones are burned as a hearth. My heart is smitten and withered like grass so that I forget to eat my bread. By reason of the voice of my groaning my bones cleave to my skin. I am like a pelican of the wilderness, I am like an owl of the desert. I watch and am as a sparrow alone upon the housetop. Mine enemies reproach me all the day and they that are mad against me are sworn against me. For I have eaten ashes like bread and mingled my drink with weeping because of thine indignation and thy wrath, for thou hast lifted me up and cast me down. My days are like a shadow that declineth and I am withered like grass. But thou, O Lord, shalt endure for ever and thy remembrance unto all generations. Thou shalt arise and have mercy upon Zion, for the time to favor her, yea, the set time is come. For thy servants take pleasure in her stones and favor the dust thereof. So the heathen shall fear the name of the Lord and all the kings of the earth thy glory. When the Lord shall build up Zion, he shall appear in his glory. He will regard the prayer of the destitute and not despise their prayer. This shall be written for the generation to come and the people which shall be gathered shall praise the Lord. For he hath looked down from the height of his sanctuary, from Heaven did the Lord behold the earth, to hear the groaning of the prisoner, to loose those that are appointed to death, to declare the name of the Lord in Zion and his praise in Jerusalem when the people are gathered together and the kingdoms to serve the Lord. He weakened my strength in the way he shortened my days. I said, O my God, take me not away in the midst of my days, thy years are throughout all generations. Of old hast thou laid the foundation of the Earth and the heavens are the work of thy hands. They shall perish, but thou shalt endure, yea, all of them shall wax old like a garment, as a vesture shalt thou change them and they shall be changed, but thou art the same and thy years shall have no end. The children of thy servants shall continue and their seed shall be established before thee.

PSALM 103
A Psalm of David.

Bless the Lord, O my soul, and all that is within me, bless his holy name. Bless the Lord, O my soul, and forget not all his benefits, who forgiveth all thine iniquities, who healeth all thy diseases, who redeemeth thy life from destruction, who crowneth thee with lovingkindness and tender mercies, who satisfieth thy mouth with good things so that thy youth is renewed like the eagle's. The Lord executeth righteousness and judgment for all that are oppressed. He made known his ways unto Moses, his acts unto the children of Israel. The Lord is merciful and gracious, slow to anger and plenteous in mercy. He will not always chide, neither will he keep his anger forever. He hath not dealt with us after our sins, nor rewarded us according to our iniquities. For as the Heaven is high above the Earth, so great is his mercy toward them that fear him. As far as the east is from the west, so far hath he removed our transgressions from us. Like as a father pitieth his children, so the Lord pitieth them that fear him. For he knoweth our frame, he remembereth that we are dust. As for man, his days are as grass, as a flower of the field, so he flourisheth. For the wind passeth over it and it is gone and the place thereof shall know it no more. But the mercy of the Lord is from everlasting to everlasting upon them that fear him and his righteousness unto children's children to such as keep his covenant and to those that remember his commandments to do them. The Lord hath prepared his throne in the heavens and his kingdom ruleth over all. Bless the Lord, ye his angels, that excel in strength, that do his commandments, hearkening unto the voice of his word. Bless ye the Lord all ye his hosts, ye ministers of his that do his pleasure. Bless the Lord, all his works in all places of his dominion, bless the Lord, O my soul.

PSALM 104

Bless the Lord, O my soul. O Lord my God, thou art very great, thou art clothed with power and majesty, who coverest thyself with light as with a garment, who stretchest out the heavens like a curtain, who layeth the beams of his chambers in the waters, who maketh the clouds his chariot, who walketh upon the wings of the wind, who maketh his angels spirits, his ministers a flaming fire, who laid the foundations of the Earth, that it should not be removed forever. Thou coveredst it with the deep as with a garment, the waters stood above the mountains. At thy rebuke they fled, at the voice of thy thunder they hasted away. They go up by the mountains, they go down by the valleys unto the place which thou hast founded for them. Thou hast set a bound that they may not pass over, that they turn not again to cover the Earth. He sendeth the springs into the valleys which run among the hills. They give drink to every beast of the field, the wild asses quench their thirst. By them shall the fowls of the Heaven have their habitation, which sing among the branches. He watereth the hills from his chambers, the earth is satisfied with the fruit of thy works. He causeth the grass to grow for the cattle and herb for the service of man that he may bring forth food out of the Earth, and wine that maketh glad the heart of man and oil to make his face to shine and bread which strengtheneth man's heart. The trees of the Lord are full of sap, the cedars of Lebanon which he hath planted, where the birds make their nests, as for the stork, the fir trees are her house. The high hills are a refuge for the wild goats and the rocks for the conies. He appointed the moon for seasons, the sun knoweth his going down. Thou makest darkness and it is night wherein all the beasts of the forest do creep forth. The young lions roar after their prey and seek their meat from God. The sun ariseth, they gather themselves together and lay them down in their dens. Man goeth forth unto his work and to his labor until the evening. O Lord, how manifold are thy works. In wisdom hast thou made them all, the earth is full of thy riches. So is this great and wide sea wherein are things creeping innumerable, both small and great beasts. There go the ships and thou hast made leviathan to play therein. These wait all upon thee that thou mayest give them their meat in due season. That thou givest them they gather, thou openest thine hand, they are filled with good. Thou hidest thy face, they are troubled, thou takest away their breath, they die and return to their dust. Thou sendest forth thy Spirit, they are created and thou renewest the face of the Earth. The glory of the Lord shall endure forever, the Lord shall rejoice in his works. He looketh on the Earth and it trembleth, he toucheth the hills and they smoke. I will sing unto the Lord as long as I live, I will sing praise to my God while I have my being. My meditation of him shall be sweet, I will be glad in the Lord. Let the sinners be consumed out of the earth and let the wicked be no more. Bless thou the Lord, O my soul. Praise ye the Lord.

PSALM 105

O give thanks unto the Lord, call upon his name, make known his deeds among the people. Sing unto him, sing psalms unto him, talk ye of all his wondrous works. Glory ye in his holy name, let the heart of them rejoice that seek the Lord. Seek the Lord, and his strength, seek his face evermore. Remember his marvelous works that he hath done, his wonders and the judgments of his mouth, O ye seed of Abraham his servant, ye children of Jacob his chosen. He is the Lord our God, his judgments are in all the earth. He hath remembered his covenant forever, the word which he commanded to a thousand generations. Which covenant he made with Abraham and his oath unto Isaac and confirmed the same unto Jacob for a law and to Israel for an everlasting covenant, saying, Unto thee will I give the land of Canaan, the lot of your inheritance when they were but a few men in number, yea, very few and strangers in it. When they went from one nation to another, from one kingdom to another people, he suffered no man to do them wrong, yea, he reproved kings for their sakes saying, Touch not mine anointed and do my prophets no harm. Moreover he called for a famine upon the land, he brake the whole staff of bread. He sent a man before them, even Joseph, who was sold for a servant, whose feet they hurt with fetters, he was laid in iron until the time that his word came, the word of the Lord tried him. The king sent and loosed him, even the ruler of the people and let him go free. He made him lord of his house and ruler of all his substance, to bind his princes at his pleasure and teach his senators wisdom. Israel also came into Egypt, and Jacob sojourned in the land of Ham. And he increased his people greatly and made them stronger than their enemies. He turned their heart to hate his people, to deal subtlely with his servants. He sent Moses his servant and Aaron whom he had chosen. They showed his signs among them and wonders in the land of Ham. He sent darkness and made it dark and they rebelled not against his word. He turned their waters into blood and slew their fish. Their land brought forth frogs in abundance in the chambers of their kings. He spake and there came divers sorts of flies and lice in all their coasts. He gave them hail for rain and flaming fire in their land. He smote their vines also and their fig trees and brake the trees of their coasts. He spake and the locusts came and caterpillars, and that without number and did eat up all the herbs in their land and devoured the fruit of their ground. He smote also all the firstborn in their land, the chief of all their strength. He brought them forth also with silver and gold and there was not one feeble person among their tribes. Egypt was glad when they departed, for the fear of them fell upon them. He spread a cloud for a covering and fire to give light in the night. The people asked and he brought quails and satisfied them with the bread of Heaven. He opened the rock and the waters gushed out, they ran in the dry places like a river. For he remembered his holy promise unto Abraham his servant. And he brought forth his people with joy and his chosen with gladness and gave them the lands of the heathen, and they inherited the labor of the people that they might observe his statutes and keep his laws. Praise ye the Lord.

PSALM 106

Praise ye the Lord. O give thanks unto the Lord, for he is good, for his mercy endureth forever. Who can utter the mighty acts of the Lord? Who can show forth all his praise? Blessed are they that keep judgment and he that doeth righteousness at all times. Remember me, O Lord, with the favor of thy people, O visit me with thy salvation that I may see the good of thy chosen, that I may rejoice in the gladness of thy nation, that I may glory with thine inheritance. We have sinned with our fathers, we have committed iniquity, we have done wickedly. Our fathers understood not thy wonders in Egypt, they remembered not the multitude of thy mercies, but provoked thee at the sea, at the Red Sea. Nevertheless he saved them for his name's sake that he might make his mighty power to be known. He rebuked the Red Sea also and it was dried up, so he led them through the depths as through the wilderness. And he saved them from the hand of him that hated them and redeemed them from the hand of the enemy. And the waters covered their enemies, there was not one of them left. Then believed they his words, they sang his praise. They soon forgat his works, they waited not for his counsel, but lusted exceedingly in the wilderness and tempted God in the desert. And he gave them their request, but sent leanness into their soul. They envied Moses also in the camp and Aaron the saint of the Lord. The Earth opened and swallowed up Dathan and covered the company of Abiram. And a fire was kindled in their company, the flame burned up the wicked. They made a calf in Horeb and worshiped the molten image. Thus they changed their glory into the similitude of an ox that eateth grass. They forgat God their savior which had done great things in Egypt, wondrous works in the land of Ham and terrible things by the Red Sea. Therefore he said that he would destroy them, had not Moses his chosen stood before him in the breach to turn away his wrath lest he should destroy them. Yea, they despised the pleasant land, they believed not his word, but murmured in their tents and hearkened not unto the voice of the Lord. Therefore he lifted up his hand against them to overthrow them in the wilderness, to overthrow their seed also among the nations and to scatter them in the lands. They joined themselves also unto Baal-peor, and ate the sacrifices of the dead. Thus they provoked him to anger with their inventions and the plague brake in upon them. Then stood up Phinehas and executed judgment and so the plague was stayed. And that was counted unto him for righteousness unto all generations for evermore. They angered him also at the waters of strife so that it went ill with Moses for their sakes because they provoked his spirit so that he spake unadvisedly with his lips. They did not destroy the nations, concerning whom the Lord commanded them, but were mingled among the heathen and learned their works. And they served their idols which were a snare unto them. Yea, they sacrificed their sons and their daughters unto devils and shed innocent blood, even the blood of their sons and of their daughters whom they sacrificed unto the idols of Canaan, and the land was polluted with blood. Thus were they defiled with their own works and went a whoring with their own inventions. Therefore was the wrath of the Lord kindled against his people insomuch that he abhorred his own inheritance. And he gave them into the hand of the heathen and they that hated them ruled over them. Their enemies also oppressed them and they were brought into subjection under their hand. Many times did he deliver them, but they provoked him with their counsel and were brought low for their iniquity. Nevertheless he regarded their affliction when he heard their cry, and he remembered for them his covenant, and spared his people according to the multitude of his mercies. He made them also to be pitied of all those that carried them captive. Save us, O Lord our God, and gather us from among the heathen to give thanks unto thy holy name and to triumph in thy praise. Blessed be the Lord God of Israel from everlasting to everlasting and let all the people say, Amen. Praise ye the Lord.

PSALM 107

O give thanks unto the Lord, for he is good, for his mercy endureth forever. Let the redeemed of the Lord say so, whom he hath redeemed from the hand of the enemy and gathered them out of the lands, from the east, and from the west, from the north, and from the south. They wandered in the wilderness in a solitary way, they found no city to dwell in. Hungry and thirsty, their soul fainted in them. Then they cried unto the Lord in their trouble and he delivered them out of their distresses. And he led them forth by the right way that they might go to a city of habitation. O that men would praise the Lord for his goodness and for his wonderful works to the children of men. For he satisfieth the longing soul and filleth the hungry soul with goodness. Such as sit in darkness and in the shadow of death, being bound in affliction and iron because they rebelled against the works of God and contemned the counsel of the Most High, therefore he brought down their heart with labor, they fell down and there was none to help. Then they cried unto the Lord in their trouble and he saved them out of their distresses. He brought them out of darkness and the shadow of death and brake their bands in sunder. O that men would praise the Lord for his goodness, and for his wonderful works to the children of men. For he hath broken the gates of brass, and cut the bars of iron in sunder. Fools, because of their transgression and because of their iniquities, are afflicted. Their soul abhorreth all manner of meat and they draw near unto the gates of death. Then they cry unto the Lord in their trouble and he saveth them out of their distresses. He sent his word and healed them and delivered them from their destructions. O that men would praise the Lord for his goodness and for his wonderful works to the children of men. And let them sacrifice the sacrifices of thanksgiving and declare his works with rejoicing. They that go down to the sea in ships, that do business in great waters, these see the works of the Lord and his wonders in the deep. For he commandeth and raiseth the stormy wind which lifteth up the waves thereof. They mount up to the Heaven, they go down again to the depths, their soul is melted because of trouble. They reel to and fro and stagger like a drunken man and are at their wit's end. Then they cry unto the Lord in their trouble and he bringeth them out of their distresses. He maketh the storm a calm so that the waves thereof are still. Then are they glad because they be quiet, so he bringeth them unto their desired haven. On that men would praise the Lord for his goodness and for his wonderful works to the children of men. Let them exalt him also in the congregation of the people and praise him in the assembly of the elders. He turneth rivers into a wilderness and the watersprings into dry ground, a fruitful land into barrenness for the wickedness of them that dwell therein. He turneth the wilderness into a standing water and dry ground into watersprings. And there he maketh the hungry to dwell that they may prepare a city for habitation, and sow the fields, and plant vineyards which may yield fruits of increase. He blesseth them also so that they are multiplied greatly and suffereth not their cattle to decrease. Again, they are minished and brought low through oppression, affliction, and sorrow. He poureth contempt upon princes and causeth them to wander in the wilderness where there is no way. Yet setteth he the poor on high from affliction and maketh him families like a flock. The righteous shall see it and rejoice and all iniquity shall stop her mouth. Whoso is wise and will observe these things, even they shall understand the lovingkindness of the Lord.

PSALM 108
A Song or Psalm of David.

O God, my heart is fixed, I will sing and give praise, even with my glory. Awake, psaltery and harp, I myself will awake early. I will praise thee, O Lord, among the people and I will sing praises unto thee among the nations. For thy mercy is great above the heavens and thy truth reacheth unto the clouds. Be thou exalted, O God, above the heavens and thy glory above all the earth, that thy beloved may be delivered save with thy right hand and answer me. God hath spoken in his holiness, I will rejoice, I will divide Shechem and mete out the valley of Succoth. Gilead is mine, Manasseh is mine, Ephraim also is the strength of mine head, Judah is my lawgiver, Moab is my washpot, over Edom will I cast out my shoe, over Philistia will I triumph. Who will bring me into the strong city? Who will lead me into Edom? Wilt not thou, O God, who hast cast us off? And wilt not thou, O God, go forth with our hosts? Give us help from trouble, for vain is the help of man. Through God we shall do valiantly, for he it is that shall tread down our enemies.

PSALM 109
To the chief Musician, A Psalm of David.

Hold not thy peace, O God of my praise, for the mouth of the wicked and the mouth of the deceitful are opened against me, they have spoken against me with a lying tongue. They compassed me about, they spake against me also with words of hatred and fought against me without a cause. And notwithstanding my love they are my adversaries, yet I will continue in prayer for them. And they have rewarded me evil for good and hatred for my love. Set thou a wicked man over them and let Satan stand at his right hand. When they shall be judged, let them be condemned and let their prayer become sin. Let their days be few, let another take their office. Let their children be fatherless and their wives widows. Let their children be continually vagabonds and beg, let them seek also out of their desolate places. Let the extortioner catch all that they have and let the stranger spoil their labor. Let there be none to extend mercy unto them, neither let there be any to favor their fatherless children. Let their posterity be cut off in the generation following, let their names be blotted out. Let the iniquity of their fathers be remembered before the Lord and let not the sin of their mothers be blotted out. Let them be before the Lord continually that he may cut off the memory of them from the earth. Because they remembered not to show mercy, but persecuted the poor and needy man that they might even slay the broken in heart. As they loved cursing, so let it come upon them, as they delighted not in blessing, so let it be far from them. As they clothed themselves with cursing like as with their garments, so let it come into their bowels like water and like oil into their bones. Let it be unto them as a garment which covereth them and for a girdle wherewith they are girded continually. This shall be the reward of mine adversaries from the Lord and of them who speak evil against my soul. But do thou deliver me, O Lord my God, for thy name's sake because thy mercy is good, therefore deliver thou me. For I am poor and needy and my heart is wounded within me. I am gone like the shadow when it declineth, I am tossed up and down as the locust. My knees are weak through fasting and my flesh faileth of fatness. I became also a reproach unto them, when they looked upon me they shaked their heads. Help me, O Lord my God, O save me according to thy mercy that they may know that this is thy hand, that thou, Lord, hast done it. Let them curse, but bless thou, when they arise let them be ashamed, but let thy servant rejoice. Let mine adversaries be clothed with shame and let them cover themselves with their own confusion as with a mantle. I will greatly praise the Lord with my mouth, yea, I will praise him among the multitude. For he shall stand at the right hand of the poor to save him from those that condemn his soul.

PSALM 110
A Psalm of David.

The Lord said unto my Lord, Sit thou at my right hand until I make thine enemies thy footstool. The Lord shall send the rod of thy strength out of Zion, rule thou in the midst of thine enemies. Thy people shall be willing in the day of thy power, in the beauties of holiness from the womb of the morning, thou hast the dew of thy youth. The Lord hath sworn, and will not repent, Thou art a priest for ever after the order of Melchizedek. The Lord at thy right hand shall strike through kings in the day of his wrath. He shall judge among the heathen, he shall fill their streets with their dead bodies, he shall wound the heads over many countries. He shall drink of the brook in the way, therefore shall he lift up the head.

PSALM 111

Praise ye the Lord. I will praise the Lord with my whole heart in the assembly of the upright and in the congregation. The works of the Lord are great, sought out of all them that have pleasure therein. His work is honorable and glorious and his righteousness endureth forever. He hath made his wonderful works to be remembered, the Lord is gracious and full of compassion. He hath given meat unto them that fear him, he will ever be mindful of his covenant. He hath showed his people the power of his works that he may give them the heritage of the heathen. The works of his hands are verity and judgment, all his commandments are sure. They stand fast for ever and ever, and are done in truth and uprightness. He sent redemption unto his people, he hath commanded his covenant forever, holy and reverend is his name. The fear of the Lord is the beginning of wisdom, a good understanding have all they that do his commandments, his praise endureth forever.

PSALM 112

Praise ye the Lord. Blessed is the man who feareth the Lord and delighteth greatly in his commandments. His seed shall be mighty upon earth, the generation of the upright shall be blessed. Wealth and riches shall be in his house and his righteousness endureth forever. Unto the upright there ariseth light in the darkness, he is gracious, and full of compassion, and righteous. A good man showeth favor and lendeth, he will guide his affairs with discretion. Surely he shall not be moved forever, the righteous shall be in everlasting remembrance. He shall not be afraid of evil tidings, his heart is fixed, trusting in the Lord. His heart is established, he shall not be afraid, until he see judgment executed upon his enemies. He hath dispersed, he hath given to the poor, his righteousness endureth forever, his horn shall be exalted with honor. The wicked shall see it and be grieved, he shall gnash with his teeth and melt away, the desire of the wicked shall perish.

PSALM 113

Praise ye the Lord. Praise, O ye servants of the Lord, praise the name of the Lord. Blessed be the name of the Lord from this time forth and for evermore. From the rising of the sun unto the going down of the same the Lord's name is to be praised. The Lord is high above all nations and his glory above the heavens. Who is like unto the Lord our God, who dwelleth on high, who humbleth himself to behold the things that are in Heaven and in the earth? He raiseth up the poor out of the dust and lifteth the needy out of the dunghill that he may set him with princes, even with the princes of his people. He maketh the barren woman to keep house and to be a joyful mother of children. Praise ye the Lord.

PSALM 114

When Israel went out of Egypt, the house of Jacob from a people of strange language, Judah was his sanctuary and Israel his dominion. The sea saw it and fled, Jordan was driven back. The mountains skipped like rams and the little hills like lambs. What ailed thee, O thou sea, that thou fleddest? Thou Jordan, that thou wast driven back? Ye mountains, that ye skipped like rams and ye little hills, like lambs? Tremble, thou Earth, at the presence of the Lord, at the presence of the God of Jacob, which turned the rock into a standing water, the flint into a fountain of waters.

PSALM 115

Not unto us, O Lord, not unto us, but unto thy name be glory, for thy mercy and for thy truth's sake. Wherefore should the heathen say, Where is now their God? But our God is in the Heavens, he hath done whatsoever he hath pleased. Their idols are silver and gold, the work of men's hands. They have mouths, but they speak not, eyes have they, but they see not, they have ears, but they hear not, noses have they, but they smell not, they have hands, but they handle not, feet have they, but they walk not, neither speak they through their throat. They that make them are like unto them so is everyone that trusteth in them. O Israel, trust thou in the Lord, he is thy help and thy shield. O house of Aaron, trust in the Lord, he is thy help and thy shield. Ye that fear the Lord, trust in the Lord, he is your help and your shield. The Lord hath been mindful of us, he will bless us, he will bless the house of Israel, he will bless the house of Aaron. He will bless them that fear the Lord, both small and great. The Lord shall increase you more and more, you and your children. Ye are blessed of the Lord which made Heaven and Earth. The Heaven, even the heavens, are the Lord's, but the Earth hath he given to the children of men. The dead praise not the Lord, neither any that go down into silence. But we will bless the Lord from this time forth and for evermore. Praise the Lord.

PSALM 116

I love the Lord because he hath heard my voice and my supplications. Because he hath inclined his ear unto me, therefore will I call upon him as long as I live. The sorrows of death compassed me and the pains of hell gat hold upon me, I found trouble and sorrow. Then called I upon the name of the Lord, O Lord, I beseech thee, deliver my soul. Gracious is the Lord and righteous, yea, our God is merciful. The Lord preserveth the simple, I was brought low and he helped me. Return unto thy rest, O my soul, for the Lord hath dealt bountifully with thee. For thou hast delivered my soul from death, mine eyes from tears, and my feet from falling. I will walk before the Lord in the land of the living. I believed, therefore have I spoken, I was greatly afflicted, I said in my haste, All men are liars. What shall I render unto the Lord for all his benefits toward me? I will take the cup of salvation and call upon the name of the Lord. I will pay my vows unto the Lord now in the presence of all his people. Precious in the sight of the Lord is the death of his saints. O Lord, truly I am thy servant, I am thy servant and the son of thine handmaid, thou hast loosed my bonds. I will offer to thee the sacrifice of thanksgiving and will call upon the name of the Lord. I will pay my vows unto the Lord now in the presence of all his people, in the courts of the Lord's house, in the midst of thee, O Jerusalem. Praise ye the Lord.

PSALM 117

O praise the Lord, all ye nations, praise him all ye people. For his merciful kindness is great toward us and the truth of the Lord endureth forever. Praise ye the Lord.

PSALM 118

O give thanks unto the Lord, for he is good, because his mercy endureth forever. Let Israel now say that his mercy endureth forever. Let the house of Aaron now say that his mercy endureth forever. Let them now that fear the Lord say that his mercy endureth forever. I called upon the Lord in distress, the Lord answered me, and set me in a large place. The Lord is on my side, I will not fear; what can man do unto me? The Lord taketh my part with them that help me, therefore shall I see my desire upon them that hate me. It is better to trust in the Lord than to put confidence in man. It is better to trust in the Lord than to put confidence in princes. All nations compassed me about, but in the name of the Lord will I destroy them. They compassed me about, yea, they compassed me about, but in the name of the Lord I will destroy them. They compassed me about like bees, they are quenched as the fire of thorns, for in the name of the Lord I will destroy them. Thou hast thrust sore at me that I might fall, but the Lord helped me. The Lord is my strength and song and is become my salvation. The voice of rejoicing and salvation is in the tabernacles of the righteous, the right hand of the Lord doeth valiantly. The right hand of the Lord is exalted, the right hand of the Lord doeth valiantly. I shall not die, but live and declare the works of the Lord. The Lord hath chastened me sore, but he hath not given me over unto death. Open to me the gates of righteousness, I will go into them and I will praise the Lord, this gate of the Lord into which the righteous shall enter. I will praise thee, for thou hast heard me and art become my salvation. The stone which the builders refused has become the headstone of the corner. This is the Lord's doing, it is marvelous in our eyes. This is the day which the Lord hath made, we will rejoice and be glad in it. Save now, I beseech thee, O Lord, O Lord, I beseech thee, send now prosperity. Blessed be he that cometh in the name of the Lord, we have blessed you out of the house of the Lord. God is the Lord which hath showed us light, bind the sacrifice with cords, even unto the horns of the altar. Thou art my God and I will praise thee, thou art my God, I will exalt thee. O give thanks unto the Lord for he is good, for his mercy endureth forever.

PSALM 119

ALEPH

Blessed are the undefiled in the way, who walk in the law of the Lord. Blessed are they that keep his testimonies and that seek him with the whole heart. They also do no iniquity, they walk in his ways. Thou hast commanded us to keep thy precepts diligently. O that my ways were directed to keep thy statutes. Then shall I not be ashamed when I have respect unto all thy commandments. I will praise thee with uprightness of heart, when I shall have learned thy righteous judgments. I will keep thy statutes, O forsake me not utterly.

BETH

Wherewithal shall a young man cleanse his way? By taking heed thereto according to thy word. With my whole heart have I sought thee, O let me not wander from thy commandments. Thy word have I hid in mine heart that I might not sin against thee. Blessed art thou, O Lord, teach me thy statutes. With my lips have I declared all the judgments of thy mouth. I have rejoiced in the way of thy testimonies as much as in all riches. I will meditate upon thy precepts and have respect unto thy ways. I will delight myself in thy statutes, I will not forget thy word.

GIMEL

Deal bountifully with thy servant that I may live and keep thy word. Open thou mine eyes that I may behold wondrous things out of thy law. I am a stranger in the earth, hide not thy commandments from me. My heart breaketh, for my soul longeth after thy judgments at all times. Thou hast rebuked the proud, they are cursed who do err from thy commandments. Remove from me reproach and contempt, for I have kept thy testimonies. Princes also did sit and speak against me, but thy servant did meditate in thy statutes. Thy testimonies also are my delight, and my counselors.

DALETH

My soul cleaveth unto the dust, quicken thou me according to thy word. I have declared my ways and thou heardest me, teach me thy statutes. Make me to understand the way of thy precepts, so shall I talk of thy wondrous works. My soul melteth for heaviness, strengthen thou me according unto thy word. Remove from me the way of lying and grant me thy law graciously. I have chosen the way of truth, thy judgments have I laid before me. I have stuck unto thy testimonies, O Lord, put me not to shame. I will run the way of thy commandments when thou shalt enlarge my heart.

HE

Teach me, O Lord, the way of thy statutes, and I shall keep it to the end. Give me understanding, and I shall keep thy law, yea, I shall observe it with my whole heart. Make me to go in the path of thy commandments for therein do I delight. Incline my heart unto thy testimonies and not to covetousness. Turn away mine eyes from beholding vanity and quicken thou me in thy way. Establish thy word unto thy servant who is devoted to thy fear. Turn away my reproach which I fear, for thy judgments are good. Behold, I have longed after thy precepts, quicken me in thy righteousness.

VAU

Let thy mercies come also unto me, O Lord, even thy salvation according to thy word. So shall I have wherewith to answer him that reproacheth me, for I trust in thy word. And take not the word of truth utterly out of my mouth, for I have hoped in thy judgments. So shall I keep thy law continually for ever and ever. And I will walk at liberty, for I seek thy precepts. I will speak of thy testimonies also before kings and will not be ashamed. And I will delight myself in thy commandments which I have loved. My hands also will I lift up unto thy commandments which I have loved and I will meditate upon thy statutes.

ZAIN

Remember the word unto thy servant upon which thou hast caused me to hope. This is my comfort in my affliction, for thy word hath quickened me. The proud have had me greatly in derision, yet have I not declined from thy law. I remembered thy judgments of old, O Lord, and have comforted myself. Horror hath taken hold upon me because of the wicked that forsake thy law. Thy statutes have been my songs in the house of my pilgrimage. I have remembered thy name, O Lord, in the night and have kept thy law. This I had because I kept thy precepts.

CHETH

Thou art my portion, O Lord, I have said that I would keep thy words. I entreated thy favor with my whole heart, be merciful unto me according to thy word. I thought on my ways and turned my feet unto thy testimonies. I made haste and delayed not to keep thy commandments. The bands of the wicked have robbed me, but I have not forgotten thy law. At midnight I will rise to give thanks unto thee because of thy righteous judgments. I am a companion of all them that fear thee and of them that keep thy precepts. The earth, O Lord, is full of thy mercy, teach me thy statutes.

TETH

Thou hast dealt well with thy servant, O Lord, according unto thy word. Teach me good judgment and knowledge, for I have believed thy commandments. Before I was afflicted I went astray, but now have I kept thy word. Thou art good and doest good, teach me thy statutes. The proud have forged a lie against me, but I will keep thy precepts with my whole heart. Their heart is as fat as grease, but I delight in thy law. It is good for me that I have been afflicted, that I might learn thy statutes. The law of thy mouth is better unto me than thousands of gold and silver.

JOD

Thy hands have made me and fashioned me, give me understanding that I may learn thy commandments. They that fear thee will be glad when they see me because I have hoped in thy word. I know, O Lord, that thy judgments are right and that thou in faithfulness hast afflicted me. Let, I pray thee, thy merciful kindness be for my comfort according to thy word unto thy servant. Let thy tender mercies come unto me, that I may live, for thy law is my delight. Let the proud be ashamed, for they dealt perversely with me without a cause, but I will meditate upon thy precepts. Let those that fear thee turn unto me and those that have known thy testimonies. Let my heart be sound in thy statutes that I be not ashamed.

CAPH

My soul fainteth for thy salvation, but I hope in thy word. Mine eyes fail for thy word, saying, When wilt thou comfort me? For I am become like a bottle in the smoke, yet do I not forget thy statutes. How many are the days of thy servant? When wilt thou execute judgment on them that persecute me? The proud have digged pits for me which are not after thy law. All thy commandments are faithful, they persecute me wrongfully, help thou me. They had almost consumed me upon earth, but I forsook not thy precepts. Quicken me after thy lovingkindness, so shall I keep the testimony of thy mouth.

LAMED

Forever, O Lord, thy word is settled in Heaven. Thy faithfulness is unto all generations, thou hast established the earth and it abideth. They continue this day according to thine ordinances, for all are thy servants. Unless thy law had been my delight, I should then have perished in mine affliction. I will never forget thy precepts, for with them thou hast quickened me. I am thine, save me, for I have sought thy precepts. The wicked have waited for me to destroy me, but I will consider thy testimonies. I have seen an end of all perfection, but thy commandment is exceeding broad.

MEM

O how love I thy law. it is my meditation all the day. Thou through thy commandments hast made me wiser than mine enemies, for they are ever with me. I have more understanding than all my teachers, for thy testimonies are my meditation. I understand more than the ancients, because I keep thy precepts. I have refrained my feet from every evil way, that I might keep thy word. I have not departed from thy judgments, for thou hast taught me. How sweet are thy words unto my taste! Yea, sweeter than honey to my mouth. Through thy precepts I get understanding, therefore I hate every false way.

NUN

Thy word is a lamp unto my feet and a light unto my path. I have sworn and I will perform it, that I will keep thy righteous judgments. I am afflicted very much, quicken me, O Lord, according unto thy word. Accept, I beseech thee, the freewill offerings of my mouth, O Lord, and teach me thy judgments. My soul is continually in thy hand and I do not forget thy law. The wicked have laid a snare for me, yet I erred not from thy precepts. Thy testimonies have I taken as a heritage forever, for they are the rejoicing of my heart. I have inclined mine heart to perform thy statutes always, even unto the end.

SAMECH

I hate vain thoughts, but thy law do I love. Thou art my hiding place and my shield, I hope in thy word. Depart from me, ye evildoers, for I will keep the commandments of my God. Uphold me according unto thy word that I may live, and let me not be ashamed of my hope. Hold thou me up and I shall be safe and I will have respect unto thy statutes continually. Thou hast trodden down all them that err from thy statutes, for their deceit is falsehood. Thou puttest away all the wicked of the earth like dross, therefore I love thy testimonies. My flesh trembleth for fear of thee and I am afraid of thy judgments.

AIN

I have done judgment and justice, leave me not to mine oppressors. Be surety for thy servant for good, let not the proud oppress me. Mine eyes fail for thy salvation and for the word of thy righteousness. Deal with thy servant according unto thy mercy and teach me thy statutes. I am thy servant, give me understanding that I may know thy testimonies and the time, O Lord, for me to work, for they have made void thy law. Therefore I love thy commandments above gold, yea, above fine gold. Therefore I esteem all thy precepts concerning all things to be thy right and I hate every false way.

PE

Thy testimonies are wonderful, therefore doth my soul keep them. The entrance of thy words giveth light, they give understanding unto the simple. I opened my mouth and panted, for I longed for thy commandments. Look thou upon me and be merciful unto me as thou usest to do unto those that love thy name. Order my steps in thy word and let not any iniquity have dominion over me. Deliver me from the oppression of man, so will I keep thy precepts. Make thy face to shine upon thy servant and teach me thy statutes. Rivers of water run down mine eyes because they keep not thy law.

TZADDI

Righteous art thou, O Lord, and upright are thy judgments. Thy testimonies that thou hast commanded are righteous and very faithful. My zeal hath consumed me because mine enemies have forgotten thy words. Thy word is very pure, therefore thy servant loveth it. I am small and despised, yet do not I forget thy precepts. Thy righteousness is an everlasting righteousness and thy law is the truth. Trouble and anguish have taken hold on me, yet thy commandments are my delights. The righteousness of thy testimonies is everlasting, give me understanding and I shall live.

KOPH

I cried with my whole heart, Hear me, O Lord, I will keep thy statutes. I cried unto thee, Save me and I shall keep thy testimonies. I prevented the dawning of the morning and cried, I hoped in thy word. Mine eyes prevent the night watches that I might meditate in thy word. Hear my voice according unto thy lovingkindness, O Lord, quicken me according to thy judgment. They draw nigh that follow after mischief, they are far from thy law. Thou art near, O Lord, and all thy commandments are truth. Concerning thy testimonies, I have known of old that thou hast founded them forever.

RESH

Consider mine affliction, and deliver me, for I do not forget thy law. Plead my cause and deliver me, quicken me according to thy word. Salvation is far from the wicked, for they seek not thy statutes. Great are thy tender mercies, O Lord, quicken me according to thy judgments. Many are my persecutors and mine enemies, yet do I not decline from thy testimonies. I beheld the transgressors and was grieved because they kept not thy word. Consider how I love thy precepts, quicken me, O Lord, according to thy lovingkindness. Thy word is true from the beginning and every one of thy righteous judgments endureth forever.

SCHIN

Princes have persecuted me without a cause, but my heart standeth in awe of thy word. I rejoice at thy word, as one that findeth great spoil. I hate and abhor lying, but thy law do I love. Seven times a day do I praise thee because of thy righteous judgments. Great peace have they which love thy law and nothing shall offend them. Lord, I have hoped for thy salvation and done thy commandments. My soul hath kept thy testimonies and I love them exceedingly. I have kept thy precepts and thy testimonies for all my ways are before thee.

TAU

Let my cry come near before thee, O Lord, give me understanding according to thy word. Let my supplication come before thee, deliver me according to thy word. My lips shall utter praise when thou hast taught me thy statutes. My tongue shall speak of thy word, for all thy commandments are righteousness. Let thine hand help me, for I have chosen thy precepts. I have longed for thy salvation, O Lord, and thy law is my delight. Let my soul live and it shall praise thee and let thy judgments help me. I have gone astray like a lost sheep, seek thy servant, for I do not forget thy commandments.

PSALM 120
A Song of degrees.

In my distress I cried unto the Lord, and he heard me. Deliver my soul, O Lord, from lying lips and from a deceitful tongue. What shall be given unto thee? Or what shall be done unto thee, thou false tongue? Sharp arrows of the mighty, with coals of juniper. Wo is me, that I sojourn in Mesech, that I dwell in the tents of Kedar. My soul hath long dwelt with him that hateth peace. I am for peace, but when I speak, they are for war.

PSALM 121
A Song of degrees.

I will lift up mine eyes unto the hills from whence cometh my help. My help cometh from the Lord, which made Heaven and Earth. Behold, he that keepeth Israel shall neither slumber nor sleep. He will not suffer thy foot to be moved, he that keepeth thee will not slumber. The Lord is thy keeper, the Lord is thy shade upon thy right hand. The sun shall not smite thee by day, nor the moon by night. The Lord shall preserve thee from all evil, he shall preserve thy soul. The Lord shall preserve thy going out and thy coming in from this time forth, and even for evermore.

PSALM 122
A Song of degrees of David.

I was glad when they said unto me, Let us go into the house of the Lord. Our feet shall stand within thy gates, O Jerusalem. Jerusalem is builded as a city that is compact together whither the tribes go up, the tribes of the Lord, unto the testimony of Israel, to give thanks unto the name of the Lord. For there are set thrones of judgment, the thrones of the house of David. Pray for the peace of Jerusalem, they shall prosper that love thee. Peace be within thy walls and prosperity within thy palaces. For my brethren and companions' sakes I will now say, Peace be within thee. Because of the house of the Lord our God I will seek thy good.

PSALM 123
A Song of degrees.

Unto thee lift I up mine eyes, O thou that dwellest in the heavens. Behold, as the eyes of servants look unto the hand of their masters and as the eyes of a maiden unto the hand of her mistress, so our eyes wait upon the Lord our God until that he have mercy upon us. Have mercy upon us, O Lord, have mercy upon us, for we are exceedingly filled with contempt. Our soul is exceedingly filled with the scorning of those that are at ease and with the contempt of the proud.

PSALM 124
A Song of degrees of David.

Now may Israel say, If the Lord was not on our side when men rose up against us, then they had swallowed us up quick when their wrath was kindled against us. Then the waters had overwhelmed us, the stream had gone over our soul, then the proud waters had gone over our soul. Blessed be the Lord who hath not given us as a prey to their teeth. Our soul is escaped as a bird out of the snare of the fowlers: the snare is broken and we are escaped. Our help is in the name of the Lord who made Heaven and Earth.

PSALM 125
A Song of degrees.

They that trust in the Lord in mount Zion cannot be removed, but abide forever. As the mountains are round about Jerusalem, so the Lord is round about his people from henceforth even forever. For the rod of the wicked shall not rest upon the lot of the righteous, lest the righteous put forth their hands unto iniquity. Do good, O Lord, unto the good and unto the upright in their hearts. As for such as turn aside unto their crooked ways, the Lord shall lead them forth with the workers of iniquity, but peace shall be upon Israel.

PSALM 126
A Song of degrees.

When the Lord turned again the captivity of Zion we were like them that dream. Then was our mouth filled with laughter and our tongues with singing, then said they among the heathen, The Lord hath done great things for them. The Lord hath done great things for us whereof we are glad. Turn again our captivity, O Lord, as the streams in the south. They that sow in tears shall reap in joy. He that goeth forth and weepeth bearing precious seed shall doubtless come again with rejoicing, bringing his sheaves with him.

PSALM 127
A Song of degrees for Solomon.

Except the Lord build the house, they labor in vain that build it, except the Lord keep the city, the watchman waketh but in vain. It is vain for you to rise up early, to sit up late, to eat the bread of sorrows, for so he giveth his beloved sleep. Lo, children are a heritage of the Lord and the fruit of the womb is his reward. As arrows are in the hand of a mighty man, so are children of the youth. Happy is the man that hath his quiver full of them, they shall not be ashamed, but they shall speak with the enemies in the gate.

PSALM 128
A Song of degrees.

Blessed is everyone that feareth the Lord, that walketh in his ways. For thou shalt eat the labor of thine hands, happy shalt thou be and it shall be well with thee. Thy wife shall be as a fruitful vine by the sides of thine house, thy children like olive plants round about thy table. Behold, that thus shall the man be blessed that feareth the Lord. The Lord shall bless thee out of Zion and thou shalt see the good of Jerusalem all the days of thy life. Yea, thou shalt see thy children's children and peace upon Israel.

PSALM 129
A Song of degrees.

Many a time have they afflicted me from my youth, may Israel now say, many a time have they afflicted me from my youth, yet they have not prevailed against me. The ploughers ploughed upon my back, they made long their furrows. The Lord is righteous, he hath cut asunder the cords of the wicked. Let them all be confounded and turned back that hate Zion. Let them be as the grass upon the housetops which withereth afore it groweth up. Wherewith the mower filleth not his hand, nor he that bindeth sheaves his bosom. Neither do they which go by say, The blessing of the Lord be upon you, we bless you in the name of the Lord.

PSALM 130
A Song of degrees.

Out of the depths have I cried unto thee, O Lord. Lord, hear my voice, let thine ears be attentive to the voice of my supplications. If thou, Lord, shouldest mark iniquities, O Lord, who shall stand? But there is forgiveness with thee, that thou mayest be feared. I wait for the Lord, my soul doth wait and in his word do I hope. My soul waiteth for the Lord more than they that watch for the morning, I say more than they that watch for the morning. Let Israel hope in the Lord, for with the Lord there is mercy and with him is plenteous redemption. And he shall redeem Israel from all his iniquities.

PSALM 131
A Song of degrees of David.

Lord, my heart is not haughty, nor mine eyes lofty, neither do I exercise myself in great matters, or in things too high for me. Surely I have behaved and quieted myself as a child that is weaned of his mother; my soul is even as a weaned child. Let Israel hope in the Lord from henceforth and forever.

PSALM 132
A Song of degrees.

Lord, remember David and all his afflictions, how he sware unto the Lord and vowed unto the mighty God of Jacob, Surely I will not come into the tabernacle of my house nor go up into my bed, I will not give sleep to mine eyes or slumber to mine eyelids until I find out a place for the Lord, a habitation for the mighty God of Jacob. Lo, we heard of it at Ephratah, we found it in the fields of the wood. We will go into his tabernacles, we will worship at his footstool. Arise, O Lord, into thy rest, thou and the ark of thy strength. Let thy priests be clothed with righteousness and let thy saints shout for joy. For thy servant David's sake turn not away the face of thine anointed. The Lord hath sworn in truth unto David, he will not turn from it, Of the fruit of thy body will I set upon thy throne. If thy children will keep my covenant and my testimony that I shall teach them, their children shall also sit upon thy throne for evermore. For the Lord hath chosen Zion, he hath desired it for his habitation. This is my rest forever, here will I dwell for I have desired it. I will abundantly bless her provision, I will satisfy her poor with bread. I will also clothe her priests with salvation and her saints shall shout aloud for joy. There will I make the horn of David to bud, I have ordained a lamp for mine anointed. His enemies will I clothe with shame, but upon himself shall his crown flourish.

PSALM 133
A Song of degrees of David.
Behold, how good and how pleasant it is for brethren to dwell together in unity. It is like the precious ointment upon the head that ran down upon the beard, even Aaron's beard that went down to the skirts of his garments, as the dew of Hermon and as the dew that descended upon the mountains of Zion, for there the Lord commanded the blessing, even life for evermore.

PSALM 134
A Song of degrees.
Behold, bless ye the Lord, all ye servants of the Lord which by night stand in the house of the Lord. Lift up your hands in the sanctuary and bless the Lord. The Lord that made Heaven and earth bless thee out of Zion.

PSALM 135
Praise ye the Lord. Praise ye the name of the Lord, praise him, O ye servants of the Lord. Ye that stand in the house of the Lord, in the courts of the house of our God, praise the Lord for the Lord is good, sing praises unto his name for it is pleasant. For the Lord hath chosen Jacob unto himself and Israel for his peculiar treasure. For I know that the Lord is great and that our Lord is above all gods. Whatsoever the Lord pleased, that did he in Heaven, and in Earth, in the seas, and all deep places. He causeth the vapors to ascend from the ends of the Earth, he maketh lightnings for the rain, he bringeth the wind out of his treasuries. Who smote the firstborn of Egypt both of man and beast, who sent tokens and wonders into the midst of thee, O Egypt, upon Pharaoh and upon all his servants, who smote great nations and slew mighty kings, Sihon king of the Amorites, and Og king of Bashan, and all the kingdoms of Canaan, and gave their land for a heritage, a heritage unto Israel his people. Thy name, O Lord, endureth for ever and thy memorial, O Lord, throughout all generations. For the Lord will judge his people and he will not repent himself concerning his servants. The idols of the heathen are silver and gold, the work of men's hands. They have mouths, but they speak not, eyes have they, but they see not, they have ears, but they hear not, neither is there any breath in their mouths. They that make them are like unto them, so is everyone that trusteth in them. Bless the Lord, O house of Israel, bless the Lord, O house of Aaron, bless the Lord, O house of Levi, ye that fear the Lord, bless the Lord. Blessed be the Lord out of Zion, Blessed be the Lord out of Jerusalem. Praise ye the Lord.

PSALM 136

O Give thanks unto the Lord, for he is good, for his mercy endureth forever. O give thanks unto the God of gods, for his mercy endureth forever. O give thanks to the Lord of lords, for his mercy endureth forever. To him who alone doeth great wonders, for his mercy endureth forever. To him that by wisdom made the Heavens, for his mercy endureth forever. To him that stretched out the Earth above the waters, for his mercy endureth forever. To him that made great lights, for his mercy endureth forever, the sun to rule by day, for his mercy endureth forever, the moon and stars to rule by night, for his mercy endureth forever. To him that smote Egypt in their firstborn, for his mercy endureth forever, and brought out Israel from among them, for his mercy endureth forever, with a strong hand and with a stretched out arm, for his mercy endureth forever. To him which divided the Red Sea into parts, for his mercy endureth forever, and made Israel to pass through the midst of it, for his mercy endureth forever, but overthrew Pharaoh and his host in the Red Sea, for his mercy endureth forever. To him which led his people through the wilderness, for his mercy endureth forever. To him which smote great kings, for his mercy endureth forever, and slew famous kings, for his mercy endureth forever, Sihon king of the Amorites, for his mercy endureth forever, and Og the king of Bashan, for his mercy endureth forever, and gave their land for a heritage, for his mercy endureth forever, even a heritage unto Israel his servant, for his mercy endureth forever. Who remembered us in our low estate, for his mercy endureth forever, and hath redeemed us from our enemies, for his mercy endureth forever. Who giveth food to all flesh, for his mercy endureth forever. O give thanks unto the God of Heaven, for his mercy endureth forever.

PSALM 137

By the rivers of Babylon, there we sat down, yea, we wept when we remembered Zion. We hanged our harps upon the willows in the midst thereof. For there they that carried us away captive required of us a song and they that wasted us required of us mirth saying, Sing us one of the songs of Zion. How shall we sing the Lord's song in a strange land? If I forget thee, O Jerusalem, let my right hand forget its cunning. If I do not remember thee, let my tongue cleave to the roof of my mouth, if I prefer not Jerusalem above my chief joy. Remember, O Lord, the children of Edom in the day of Jerusalem who said, Raze it, even to the foundation thereof. O daughter of Babylon, who art to be destroyed, happy shall he be that rewardeth thee as thou hast served us. Happy shall he be that taketh and dasheth thy little ones against the stones.

PSALM 138

I will praise thee with my whole heart, before the gods will I sing praise unto thee. I will worship toward thy holy temple and praise thy name for thy lovingkindness and for thy truth, for that hast magnified thy word above all thy name. In the day when I cried thou answeredst me and strengthenedst me with strength in my soul. All the kings of the earth shall praise thee, O Lord, when they hear the words of thy mouth. Yea, they shall sing in the ways of the Lord, for great is the glory of the Lord. Though the Lord be high, yet hath he respect unto the lowly, but the proud he knoweth afar off. Though I walk in the midst of trouble, thou wilt revive me, thou shalt stretch forth thine hand against the wrath of mine enemies and thy right hand shall save me. The Lord will perfect me in knowledge concerning his kingdom. I will praise thee O Lord forever, for thou art merciful, and wilt not forsake the works of thine own hands.

PSALM 139
To the chief Musician, A Psalm of David.

O Lord, thou hast searched me, and known me. Thou knowest my downsitting and mine uprising, thou understandest my thought afar off. Thou compassest my path and my lying down and art acquainted with all my ways. For there is not a word in my tongue, but lo, O Lord, thou knowest it altogether. Thou hast beset me behind and before, and laid thine hand upon me. Such knowledge is too wonderful for me, it is high, I cannot attain unto it. Whither shall I go from thy Spirit? Or whither shall I flee from thy presence? If I ascend up into Heaven, thou art there, if I make my bed in hell, behold, thou art there. If I take the wings of the morning and dwell in the uttermost parts of the sea, even there shall thy hand lead me and thy right hand shall hold me. If I say, Surely the darkness shall cover me, even the night shall be light about me. Yea, the darkness hideth not from thee, but the night shineth as the day, the darkness and the light are both alike to thee. For thou hast possessed my reins, thou hast covered me in my mother's womb. I will praise thee, for I am fearfully and wonderfully made, marvelous are thy works, and that my soul knoweth right well. My substance was not hid from thee when I was made in secret and curiously wrought in the lowest parts of the Earth. Thine eyes did see my substance, yet being imperfect, and in thy book all my members were written, which in continuance were fashioned when as yet I knew none of them. How precious also are thy thoughts unto me, O God! How great is the sum of them! If I should count them, they are more in number than the sand, when I awake I am still with thee. Surely thou wilt slay the wicked, O God, depart from me therefore, ye bloody men. For they speak against thee wickedly and thine enemies take thy name in vain. Do not I hate them, O Lord, that hate thee? And am not I grieved with those that rise up against thee? I hate them with perfect hatred, I count them mine enemies. Search me, O God, and know my heart, try me and know my thoughts, and see if there be any wicked way in me, and lead me in the way everlasting.

PSALM 140
To the chief Musician, A Psalm of David.

Deliver me, O Lord, from the evil man, preserve me from the violent man which imagine mischiefs in their heart, continually are they gathered together for war. They have sharpened their tongues like a serpent, adders' poison is under their lips. Selah. Keep me, O Lord, from the hands of the wicked, preserve me from the violent man who have purposed to overthrow my goings. The proud have hid a snare for me and cords, they have spread a net by the wayside, they have set gins for me. Selah. I said unto the Lord, Thou art my God, hear the voice of my supplications, O Lord. O God the Lord, the strength of my salvation, thou hast covered my head in the day of battle. Grant not, O Lord, the desires of the wicked, further not his wicked device lest they exalt themselves. Selah. As for the head of those that compass me about, let the mischief of their own lips cover them. Let burning coals fall upon them, let them be cast into the fire, into deep pits, that they rise not up again. Let not an evil speaker be established in the earth, evil shall hunt the violent man to overthrow him. I know that the Lord will maintain the cause of the afflicted and the right of the poor. Surely the righteous shall give thanks unto thy name, the upright shall dwell in thy presence.

PSALM 141
A Psalm of David.

Lord, I cry unto thee, make haste unto me, give ear unto my voice when I cry unto thee. Let my prayer be set forth before thee as incense and the lifting up of my hands as the evening sacrifice. Set a watch, O Lord, before my mouth, keep the door of my lips. Incline not my heart to any evil thing, to practice wicked works with men that work iniquity and let me not eat of their dainties. When the righteous smite me with the word of the Lord it is a kindness and when they reprove me, it shall be an excellent oil and shall not destroy my faith, for yet my prayer also shall be for them. I delight not in their calamities. When their judges are overthrown in stony places, they shall hear my words for they are sweet. Our bones are scattered at the grave's mouth, as when one cutteth and cleaveth wood upon the Earth. But mine eyes are unto thee, O God the Lord, in thee is my trust, leave not my soul destitute. Keep me from the snares which they have laid for me and the gins of the workers of iniquity. Let the wicked fall into their own nets whilst that I withal escape.

PSALM 142
Maschil of David, A prayer when he was in the cave.
I cried unto the Lord with my voice, with my voice unto the Lord did I make my supplication. I poured out my complaint before him, I showed before him my trouble. When my spirit was overwhelmed within me, then thou knewest my path. In the way wherein I walked have they privily laid a snare for me. I looked on my right hand and behold, but there was no man that would know me, refuge failed me, no man cared for my soul. I cried unto thee, O Lord, I said, Thou art my refuge and my portion in the land of the living. Attend unto my cry, for I am brought very low, deliver me from my persecutors, for they are stronger than I. Bring my soul out of prison that I may praise thy name, the righteous shall compass me about for thou shalt deal bountifully with me.

PSALM 143
A Psalm of David.
Hear my prayer, O Lord, give ear to my supplications, in thy faithfulness answer me and in thy righteousness. And enter not into judgment with thy servant, for in thy sight shall no man living be justified. For the enemy hath persecuted my soul, he hath smitten my life down to the ground, he hath made me to dwell in darkness as those that have long been dead. Therefore is my spirit overwhelmed within me, my heart within me is desolate. I remember the days of old, I meditate on all thy works, I muse on the work of thy hands. I stretch forth my hands unto thee, my soul thirsteth after thee as a thirsty land. Selah. Hear me speedily, O Lord, my spirit faileth, hide not thy face from me, lest I be like unto them that go down into the pit. Cause me to hear thy lovingkindness in the morning, for in thee do I trust, cause me to know the way wherein I should walk, for I lift up my soul unto thee. Deliver me, O Lord, from mine enemies, I flee unto thee to hide me. Teach me to do thy will, for thou art my God, thy Spirit is good, lead me into the land of uprightness. Quicken me, O Lord, for thy name's sake, for thy righteousness' sake bring my soul out of trouble. And of thy mercy cut off mine enemies and destroy all them that afflict my soul, for I am thy servant.

PSALM 144
A Psalm of David.
Blessed be the Lord my strength, which teacheth my hands to war and my fingers to fight, my goodness, and my fortress, my high tower, and my deliverer, my shield, and he in whom I trust, who subdueth my people under me. Lord, what is man, that thou takest knowledge of him? Or the son of man, that thou makest account of him? Man is like to vanity, his days are as a shadow that passeth away. Bow thy heavens, O Lord, and come down, touch the mountains,

and they shall smoke. Cast forth lightning and scatter them, shoot out thine arrows and destroy them. Send thine hand from above, rid me, and deliver me out of great waters, from the hand of strange children whose mouth speaketh vanity and their right hand is a right hand of falsehood. I will sing a new song unto thee, O God, upon a psaltery and an instrument of ten strings will I sing praises unto thee. It is he that giveth salvation unto kings, who delivereth David his servant from the hurtful sword. Rid me and deliver me from the hand of strange children, whose mouth speaketh vanity and their right hand is a right hand of falsehood, that our sons may be as plants grown up in their youth, that our daughters may be as cornerstones, polished after the similitude of a palace, that our garners may be full, affording all manner of store, that our sheep may bring forth thousands and ten thousands in our streets, that our oxen may be strong to labor, that there be no breaking in nor going out, that there be no complaining in our streets. Happy is that people that is in such a case, yea, happy is that people whose God is the Lord.

PSALM 145

I will extol thee, my God, O King, and I will bless thy name for ever and ever. Every day will I bless thee, and I will praise thy name for ever and ever. Great is the Lord and greatly to be praised and his greatness is unsearchable. One generation shall praise thy works to another and shall declare thy mighty acts. I will speak of the glorious honor of thy majesty and of thy wondrous works. And men shall speak of the might of thy terrible acts and I will declare thy greatness. They shall abundantly utter the memory of thy great goodness and shall sing of thy righteousness. The Lord is gracious and full of compassion, slow to anger and of great mercy. The Lord is good to all and his tender mercies are over all his works. All thy works shall praise thee, O Lord, and thy saints shall bless thee. They shall speak of the glory of thy kingdom and talk of thy power, to make known to the sons of men his mighty acts and the glorious majesty of his kingdom. Thy kingdom is an everlasting kingdom and thy dominion endureth throughout all generations. The Lord upholdeth all that fall, and raiseth up all those that be bowed down. The eyes of all wait upon thee and thou givest them their meat in due season. Thou openest thine hand and satisfiest the desire of every living thing. The Lord is righteous in all his ways and holy in all his works. The Lord is nigh unto all them that call upon him, to all that call upon him in truth. He will fulfill the desire of them that fear him, he also will hear their cry and will save them. The Lord preserveth all them that love him, but all the wicked will he destroy. My mouth shall speak the praise of the Lord and let all flesh bless his holy name for ever and ever.

PSALM 146

Praise ye the Lord. Praise the Lord, O my soul. While I live will I praise the Lord, I will sing praises unto my God while I have any being. Put not your trust in princes, nor in the son of man in whom there is no help. His breath goeth forth, he returneth to his earth, in that very day his thoughts perish. Happy is he that hath the God of Jacob for his help, whose hope is in the Lord his God. Which made Heaven, and Earth, the sea, and all that therein is, which keepeth truth forever, which executeth judgment for the oppressed, which giveth food to the hungry. The Lord looseth the prisoners, the Lord openeth the eyes of the blind, the Lord raiseth them that are bowed down, the Lord loveth the righteous, the Lord preserveth the strangers, he relieveth the fatherless and widow, but the way of the wicked he turneth upside down. The Lord shall reign forever, even thy God, O Zion, unto all generations. Praise ye the Lord.

PSALM 147

Praise ye the Lord, for it is good to sing praises unto our God, for it is pleasant and praise is comely. The Lord doth build up Jerusalem, he gathereth together the outcasts of Israel. He healeth the broken in heart and bindeth up their wounds. He telleth the number of the stars, he calleth them all by their names. Great is our Lord and of great power his understanding is infinite. The Lord lifteth up the meek he casteth the wicked down to the ground. Sing unto the Lord with thanksgiving, sing praise upon the harp unto our God, who covereth the Heaven with clouds, who prepareth rain for the Earth, who maketh grass to grow upon the mountains. He giveth to the beast his food and to the young ravens which cry. He delighteth not in the strength of the horse, he taketh not pleasure in the legs of a man. The Lord taketh pleasure in them that fear him, in those that hope in his mercy. Praise the Lord, O Jerusalem, praise thy God, O Zion. For he hath strengthened the bars of thy gates, he hath blessed thy children within thee. He maketh peace in thy borders and filleth thee with the finest of the wheat. He sendeth forth his commandment upon earth, his word runneth very swiftly. He giveth snow like wool, he scattereth the hoarfrost like ashes. He casteth forth his ice like morsels, who can stand before his cold? He sendeth out his word and melteth them, he causeth his wind to blow and the waters flow. He showeth his word unto Jacob, his statutes and his judgments unto Israel. He hath not dealt so with any nation, and as for his judgments, they have not known them. Praise ye the Lord.

PSALM 148

Praise ye the Lord. Praise ye the Lord from the heavens, praise him in the heights. Praise ye him all his angels, praise ye him all his hosts. Praise ye him, sun and moon, praise him, all ye stars of light. Praise him, ye Heavens of Heavens, and ye waters that be above the Heavens. Let them praise the name of the Lord, for he commanded and they were created. He hath also established them for ever and ever, he hath made a decree which shall not pass. Praise the Lord from the earth, ye dragons and all deeps. Fire, and hail, snow and vapor, stormy wind fulfilling his word, mountains and all hills, fruitful trees and all cedars, beasts and all cattle, creeping things, and flying fowl, kings of the earth and all people, princes and all judges of the earth, both young men and maidens, old men and children, let them praise the name of the Lord, for his name alone is excellent, his glory is above the earth and Heaven. He also exalteth the horn of his people, the praise of all his saints, even of the children of Israel, a people near unto him. Praise ye the Lord.

PSALM 149

Praise ye the Lord. Sing unto the Lord a new song and his praise in the congregation of saints. Let Israel rejoice in him that made him, let the children of Zion be joyful in their King. Let them praise his name in the dance, let them sing praises unto him with the timbrel and harp. For the Lord taketh pleasure in his people, he will beautify the meek with salvation. Let the saints be joyful in glory, let them sing aloud upon their beds. Let the high praises of God be in their mouth and a two-edged sword in their hand, to execute vengeance upon the heathen and punishments upon the people, to bind their kings with chains and their nobles with fetters of iron, to execute upon them the judgment written, this honor have all his saints. Praise ye the Lord.

PSALM 150

Praise ye the Lord. Praise God in his sanctuary, praise him in the firmament of his power. Praise him for his mighty acts, praise him according to his excellent greatness. Praise him with the sound of the trumpet, praise him with the psaltery and harp. Praise him with the timbrel and dance, praise him with stringed instruments and organs. Praise him upon the loud cymbals, praise him upon the high-sounding cymbals. Let everything that hath breath praise the Lord. Praise ye the Lord.

THE PROVERBS

The Proverbs of Solomon the son of David king of Israel, to know wisdom and instruction, to perceive the words of understanding, to receive the instruction of wisdom, justice, and judgment, and equity, to give subtilty to the simple, to the young man knowledge and discretion. A wise man will hear, and will increase learning, and a man of understanding shall attain unto wise counsels to understand a proverb and the interpretation, the words of the wise, and their dark sayings.

THE fear of the Lord is the beginning of knowledge, but fools despise wisdom and instruction. My son, hear the instruction of thy father and forsake not the law of thy mother, for they shall be an ornament of grace unto thy head and chains about thy neck. My son, if sinners entice thee, consent thou not. If they say, Come with us, let us lay wait for blood, let us lurk privily for the innocent without cause, let us swallow them up alive as the grave, and whole, as those that go down into the pit, we shall find all precious substance, we shall fill our houses with spoil, cast in thy lot among us, let us all have one purse, my son walk not thou in the way with them, refrain thy foot from their path, for their feet run to evil and make haste to shed blood. Surely in vain the net is spread in the sight of any bird. And they lay wait for their own blood, they lurk privily for their own lives. So are the ways of everyone that is greedy of gain, which taketh away the life of the owners thereof.

Wisdom crieth without, she uttereth her voice in the streets, she crieth in the chief place of concourse, in the openings of the gates, in the city she uttereth her words, saying, How long, ye simple ones, will ye love simplicity? And the scorners delight in their scorning and fools hate knowledge? Turn you at my reproof, behold, I will pour out my spirit unto you, I will make known my words unto you.

Because I have called and ye refused, I have stretched out my hand and no man regarded, but ye have set at naught all my counsel and would none of my reproof, I also will laugh at your calamity, will mock when your fear cometh, when your fear cometh as desolation and your destruction cometh as a whirlwind, when distress and anguish cometh upon you. Then shall they call upon me, but I will not answer, they shall seek me early, but they shall not fined me, for that they hated knowledge and did not choose the fear of the Lord, they would none of my counsel, they despised all my reproof. Therefore shall they eat of the fruit of their own way, and be filled with their own devices. For the turning away of the simple shall slay them and the prosperity of fools shall destroy them. But whoso hearkeneth unto me shall dwell safely and shall be quiet from fear of evil.

My son, if thou wilt receive my words and hide my commandments with thee so that thou incline thine ear unto wisdom and apply thine heart to understanding, yea, if thou criest after knowledge and liftest up thy voice for understanding, if thou seekest her as silver and searchest for her as for hid treasures, then shalt thou understand the fear of the Lord and find the knowledge of God. For the Lord giveth wisdom, out of his mouth cometh knowledge and understanding.

He layeth up sound wisdom for the righteous, he is a buckler to them that walk uprightly. He keepeth the paths of judgment and preserveth the way of his saints. Then shalt thou understand righteousness, and judgment, and equity, yea, every good path.

When wisdom entereth into thine heart and knowledge is pleasant unto thy soul, discretion shall preserve thee, understanding shall keep thee, to deliver thee from the way of the evil man, from the man that speaketh froward things, who leave the paths of uprightness to walk in the ways of darkness, who rejoice to do evil and delight in the frowardness of the wicked, whose ways are crooked and they froward in their paths, to deliver thee from the strange woman, even from the stranger which flattereth with her words, which forsaketh the guide of her youth and forgetteth the covenant of her God. For her house inclineth unto death and her paths unto the dead. None that go unto her return again, neither take they hold of the paths of life. That thou mayest walk in the way of good men and keep the paths of the righteous. For the upright shall dwell in the land and the perfect shall remain in it. But the wicked shall be cut off from the earth and the transgressors shall be rooted out of it.

My son, forget not my law, but let thine heart keep my commandments, for length of days, and long life, and peace shall they add to thee. Let not mercy and truth forsake thee, bind them about thy neck, write them upon the table of thine heart so shalt thou find favor and good understanding in the sight of God and man.

Trust in the Lord with all thine heart and lean not unto thine own understanding. In all thy ways acknowledge him and he shall direct thy paths. Be not wise in thine own eyes, fear the Lord and depart from evil. It shall be health to thy navel and marrow to thy bones.

Honor the Lord with thy substance and with the firstfruits of all thine increase, so shall thy barns be filled with plenty and thy presses shall burst out with new wine.

My son, despise not the chastening of the Lord neither be weary of his correction, for whom the Lord loveth he correcteth, even as a father the son in whom he delighteth.

Happy is the man that findeth wisdom and the man that getteth understanding, for the merchandise of it is better than the merchandise of silver and the gain thereof than fine gold. She is more precious than rubies and all the things thou canst desire are not to be compared unto her. Length of days is in her right hand and in her left hand riches and honor. Her ways are ways of pleasantness and all her paths are peace. She is a tree of life to them that lay hold upon her and happy is everyone that retaineth her. The Lord by wisdom hath founded the Earth, by understanding hath he established the heavens. By his knowledge the depths are broken up and the clouds drop down the dew.

My son, let not them depart from thine eyes, keep sound wisdom and discretion, so shall they be life unto thy soul and grace to thy neck. Then shalt thou walk in thy way safely and thy foot shall not stumble. When thou liest down, thou shalt not be afraid, yea, thou shalt lie down and thy sleep shall be sweet. Be not afraid of sudden fear, neither of the desolation of the wicked when it cometh. For the Lord shall be thy confidence and shall keep thy foot from being taken.

Withhold not good from them to whom it is due when it is in the power of thine hand to do it. Say not unto thy neighbor, Go, and come again, and tomorrow I will give, when thou hast it by thee. Devise not evil against thy neighbor, seeing he dwelleth securely by thee. Strive not with a man without cause, if he have done thee no harm. Envy thou not the oppressor and choose none of his ways. For the froward is abomination to the Lord, but his secret is with the righteous. The curse of the Lord is in the house of the wicked, but he blesseth the habitation of the just. Surely he scorneth the scorners, but he giveth grace unto the lowly. The wise shall inherit glory, but shame shall be the promotion of fools.

Hear, ye children, the instruction of a father and attend to know understanding. For I give you good doctrine, forsake ye not my law. For I was my father's son, tender and only beloved in the sight of my mother. He taught me also and said unto me, Let thine heart retain my words, keep my commandments, and live. Get wisdom, get understanding, forget it not, neither decline from the words of my mouth. Forsake her not and she shall preserve thee, love her and she shall keep thee. Wisdom is the principal thing, therefore get wisdom and with all thy getting get understanding. Exalt her and she shall promote thee, she shall bring thee to honor when thou dost embrace her. She shall give to thine head an ornament of grace, a crown of glory shall she deliver to thee.

Hear, O my son, and receive my sayings, and the years of thy life shall be many. I have taught thee in the way of wisdom, I have led thee in right paths. When thou goest, thy steps shall not be straitened and when thou runnest, thou shalt not stumble. Take fast hold of instruction, let her not go, keep her, for she is thy life.

Enter not into the path of the wicked and go not in the way of evil men. Avoid it, pass not by it, turn from it, and pass away. For they sleep not, except they have done mischief and their sleep is taken away unless they cause some to fall. For they eat the bread of wickedness and drink the wine of violence. But the path of the just is as the shining light that shineth more and more unto the perfect day. The way of the wicked is as darkness, they know not at what they stumble.

My son, attend to my words, incline thine ear unto my sayings. Let them not depart from thine eyes, keep them in the midst of thine heart. For they are life unto those that find them and health to all their flesh. Keep thy heart with all diligence, for out of it are the issues of life. Put away from thee a froward mouth and perverse lips put far from thee. Let thine eyes look right on and let thine eyelids look straight before thee. Ponder the path of thy feet and let all thy ways be established. Turn not to the right hand nor to the left, remove thy foot from evil.

My son, attend unto my wisdom and bow thine ear to my understanding, that thou mayest regard discretion and that thy lips may keep knowledge. For the lips of a strange woman drop as a honeycomb and her mouth is smoother than oil, but her end is bitter as wormwood, sharp as a two-edged sword. Her feet go down to death, her steps take hold on hell. Lest thou shouldest ponder the path of life, her ways are moveable that thou canst not know them. Hear me now therefore, O ye children, and depart not from the words of my mouth. Remove thy way far from her and come not nigh the door of her house, lest thou give thine honor unto others and thy years unto the cruel, lest strangers be filled with thy wealth and thy labors be in the house of a stranger, and thou mourn at the last when thy flesh and thy body are consumed and say, How have I hated instruction, and my heart despised reproof, and have not obeyed the voice of my teachers, nor inclined mine ear to them that instructed me. I was almost in all evil in the midst of the congregation and assembly.

Drink waters out of thine own cistern and running waters out of thine own well. Let thy fountains be dispersed abroad and rivers of waters in the streets. Let them be only thine own and not strangers' with thee. Let thy fountain be blessed and rejoice with the wife of thy youth. Let her be as the loving hind and pleasant roe, let her breasts satisfy thee at all times, and be thou ravished always with her love. And why wilt thou, my son, be ravished with a strange woman and embrace the bosom of a stranger? For the ways of man are before the eyes of the Lord and he pondereth all his goings. His own iniquities shall take the wicked himself and he shall be holden with the cords of his sins. He shall die without instruction and in the greatness of his folly he shall go astray.

My son, if thou be surety for thy friend, if thou hast stricken thy hand with a stranger, thou art snared with the words of thy mouth, thou art taken with the words of thy mouth. Do this now, my son, and deliver thyself, when thou art come into the hand of thy friend, go, humble thyself and make sure thy friend. Give not sleep to thine eyes, nor slumber to thine eyelids. Deliver thyself as a roe from the hand of the hunter and as a bird from the hand of the fowler.

Go to the ant, thou sluggard, consider her ways and be wise, which having no guide, overseer, or ruler, provideth her meat in the summer and gathereth her food in the harvest. How long wilt thou sleep, O sluggard? When wilt thou arise out of thy sleep? Yet a little sleep, a little slumber, a little folding of the hands to sleep, so shall thy poverty come as one that traveleth and thy want as an armed man.

A naughty person, a wicked man, walketh with a froward mouth. He winketh with his eyes, he speaketh with his feet, he teacheth with his fingers, frowardness is in his heart, he deviseth mischief continually, he soweth discord. Therefore shall his calamity come suddenly, suddenly shall he be broken without remedy.

These six things doth the Lord hate, yea, seven are an abomination unto him: a proud look, a lying tongue, and hands that shed innocent blood, a heart that deviseth wicked imaginations, feet that be swift in running to mischief, a false witness that speaketh lies, and he that soweth discord among brethren.

2 MY son, keep thy father's commandment and forsake not the law of thy mother, bind them continually upon thine heart and tie them about thy neck. When thou goest, it shall lead thee, when thou sleepest, it shall keep thee, and when thou awakest, it shall talk with thee. For the commandment is a lamp, and the law is light, and reproofs of instruction are the way of life, to keep thee from the evil woman, from the flattery of the tongue of a strange women. Lust not after her beauty in thine heart, neither let her take thee with her eyelids. For by means of a whorish woman a man is brought to a piece of bread and the adulteress will hunt for the precious life. Can a man take fire in his bosom and his clothes not be burned? Can one go upon hot coals and his feet not be burned? So he that goeth into his neighbor's wife, whosoever toucheth her shall not be innocent. Men do not despise a thief, if he steal to satisfy his soul when he is hungry, but if he be found, he shall restore sevenfold, he shall give all the substance of his house. But whoso committeth adultery with a woman lacketh understanding, he that doeth it destroyeth his own soul. A wound and dishonor shall he get and his reproach shall not be wiped away. For jealousy is the rage of a man, therefore he will not spare in the day of vengeance. He will not regard any ransom, neither will he rest content, though thou givest many gifts.

My son, keep my words, and lay up my commandments with thee. Keep my commandments and live, and my law as the apple of thine eye. Bind them upon thy fingers, write them upon the table of thine heart. Say unto wisdom, Thou art my sister, and call understanding thy kinswoman, that they may keep thee from the strange woman, from the stranger which flattereth with her words. For at the window of my house I looked through my casement, and beheld among the simple ones, I discerned among the youths a young man void of understanding, passing through the street near her corner, and he went the way to her house. In the twilight, in the evening, in the black and dark night, and, behold, there met him a woman with the attire of a harlot, and subtle of heart (She is loud and stubborn, her feet abide not in her house, now is she without, now in the streets and lieth in wait at every corner). So she caught him and kissed him, and with an impudent face said unto him, I have peace offerings with me, this day have I paid my vows. Therefore came

I forth to meet thee, diligently to seek thy face, and I have found thee. I have decked my bed with coverings of tapestry, with carved works, with fine linen of Egypt. I have perfumed my bed with myrrh, aloes, and cinnamon. Come, let us take our fill of love until the morning, let us solace ourselves with loves. For the goodman is not at home, he is gone a long journey, he hath taken a bag of money with him and will come home at the day appointed. With her much fair speech she caused him to yield, with the flattering of her lips she forced him. He goeth after her straightway, as an ox goeth to the slaughter or as a fool to the correction of the stocks, till a dart strike through his liver, as a bird hasteth to the snare and knoweth not that it is for his life.

3 HEARKEN unto me now therefore, O ye children, and attend to the words of my mouth. Let not thine heart decline to her ways, go not astray in her paths. For she hath cast down many wounded, yea, many strong men have been slain by her. Her house is the way to hell, going down to the chambers of death.

Doth not wisdom cry and understanding put forth her voice? She standeth in the top of high places, by the way in the places of the paths. She crieth at the gates, at the entry of the city, at the coming in at the doors. Unto you, O men, I call and my voice is to the sons of man. O ye simple, understand wisdom, and ye fools, be ye of an understanding heart. Hear, for I will speak of excellent things and the opening of my lips shall be right things. For my mouth shall speak truth and wickedness is an abomination to my lips. All the words of my mouth are in righteousness, there is nothing froward or perverse in them. They are all plain to him that understandeth and right to them that find knowledge. Receive my instruction and not silver, and knowledge rather than choice gold. For wisdom is better than rubies and all the things that may be desired are not to be compared to it.

I, wisdom, dwell with prudence and find out knowledge of witty inventions. The fear of the Lord is to hate evil, pride, and arrogancy, and the evil way and the froward mouth do I hate. Counsel is mine and sound wisdom, I am understanding, I have strength. By me kings reign and princes decree justice. By me princes rule and nobles, even all the judges of the earth. I love them that love me and those that seek me early shall find me. Riches and honor are with me, yea, durable riches and righteousness. My fruit is better than gold, yea, than fine gold and my revenue than choice silver. I lead in the way of righteousness, in the midst of the paths of judgment. That I may cause those that love me to inherit substance and I will fill their treasures.

The Lord possessed me in the beginning of his way before his works of old. I was set up from everlasting, from the beginning, or ever the Earth was. When there were no depths I was brought forth, when there were no fountains abounding with water. Before the mountains were settled, before the hills was I brought forth, while as yet he had not made the Earth, nor the fields, nor the highest part of the dust of the world. When he prepared the heavens I was there, when he set a compass upon the face of the depth, when he established the clouds above, when he strengthened the fountains of the deep, when he gave to the sea his decree that the waters should not pass his commandment, when he appointed the foundations of the Earth, then I was by him, as one brought up with him, and I was daily his delight, rejoicing always before him, rejoicing in the habitable part of his Earth and my delights were with the sons of men.

Now therefore hearken unto me, O ye children, for blessed are they that keep my ways. Hear instruction, and be wise, and refuse it not. Blessed is the man that heareth me, watching daily at my gates, waiting at the posts of my doors. For whoso findeth me findeth life and shall obtain favor of the Lord. But he that sinneth against me wrongeth his own soul, all they that hate me love death.

Wisdom hath builded her house, she hath hewn out her seven pillars, she hath killed her beasts, she hath mingled her wine, she hath also furnished her table. She hath sent forth her maidens, she crieth upon the highest places of the city. Whoso is simple, let him turn in hither, as for him that wanteth understanding, she saith to him, Come, eat of my bread and drink of the wine which I have mingled. Forsake the foolish and live, and go in the way of understanding. He that reproveth a scorner getteth to himself shame and he that rebuketh a wicked man getteth himself a blot. Reprove not a scorner, lest he hate thee, rebuke a wise man and he will love thee. Give instruction to a wise man and he will be yet wiser, teach a just man and he will increase in learning. The fear of the Lord is the beginning of wisdom and the knowledge of the Holy is understanding. For by me thy days shall be multiplied and the years of thy life shall be increased. If thou be wise, thou shalt be wise for thyself, but if thou scornest, thou alone shalt bear it.

A foolish woman is clamorous, she is simple and knoweth nothing. For she sitteth at the door of her house, on a seat in the high places of the city, to call passengers who go right on their ways, Whoso is simple, let him turn in hither, and as for him that wanteth understanding, she saith to him, Stolen waters are sweet and bread eaten in secret is pleasant. But he knoweth not that the dead are there and that her guests are in the depths of hell.

4 *The Proverbs of Solomon*

1 A wise son maketh a glad father, but a foolish son is the heaviness of his mother.
2 Treasures of wickedness profit nothing, but righteousness delivereth from death.
3 The Lord will not suffer the soul of the righteous to famish, but he casteth away the substance of the wicked.
4 He becometh poor that dealeth with a slack hand, but the hand of the diligent maketh rich.
5 He that gathereth in summer is a wise son, but he that sleepeth in harvest is a son that causeth shame.
6 Blessings are upon the head of the just, but violence covereth the mouth of the wicked.
7 The memory of the just is blessed, but the name of the wicked shall rot.
8 The wise in heart will receive commandments, but a prating fool shall fall.
9 He that walketh uprightly walketh surely, but he that perverteth his ways shall be known.
10 He that winketh with the eye causeth sorrow, but a prating fool shall fall.
11 The mouth of a righteous man is a well of life, but violence covereth the mouth of the wicked.
12 Hatred stirreth up strifes, but love covereth all sins.
13 In the lips of him that hath understanding wisdom is found, but a rod is for the back of him that is void of understanding.
14 Wise men lay up knowledge, but the mouth of the foolish is near destruction.
15 The rich man's wealth is his strong city, the destruction of the poor is their poverty.
16 The labor of the righteous tendeth to life, the fruit of the wicked to sin.
17 He is in the way of life that keepeth instruction, but he that refuseth reproof erreth.
18 He that hideth hatred with lying lips and he that uttereth a slander is a fool.
19 In the multitude of words there wanteth not sin, but he that refraineth his lips is wise.

20 The tongue of the just is as choice silver, the heart of the wicked is little worth.
21 The lips of the righteous feed many, but fools die for want of wisdom.
22 The blessing of the Lord, it maketh rich, and he addeth no sorrow with it.
23 It is as sport to a fool to do mischief, but a man of understanding hath wisdom.
24 The fear of the wicked, it shall come upon him, but the desire of the righteous shall be granted.
25 As the whirlwind passeth, so is the wicked no more, but the righteous is an everlasting foundation.
26 As vinegar to the teeth and as smoke to the eyes, so is the sluggard to them that send him.
27 The fear of the Lord prolongeth days, but the years of the wicked shall be shortened.
28 The hope of the righteous shall be gladness, but the expectation of the wicked shall perish.
29 The way of the Lord is strength to the upright, but destruction shall be to the workers of iniquity.
30 The righteous shall never be removed, but the wicked shall not inhabit the earth.
31 The mouth of the just bringeth forth wisdom, but the froward tongue shall be cut out.
32 The lips of the righteous know what is acceptable, but the mouth of the wicked speaketh frowardness.
33 A false balance is an abomination to the Lord, but a just weight is his delight.
34 When pride cometh, then cometh shame, but with the lowly is wisdom.
35 The integrity of the upright shall guide them, but the perverseness of transgressors shall destroy them.
36 Riches profit not in the day of wrath, but righteousness delivereth from death.
37 The righteousness of the perfect shall direct his way, but the wicked shall fall by his own wickedness.
38 The righteousness of the upright shall deliver them, but transgressors shall be taken in their own naughtiness.
39 When a wicked man dieth, his expectation shall perish and the hope of unjust men perisheth.
40 The righteous is delivered out of trouble, and the wicked cometh in his stead.
41 A hypocrite with his mouth destroyeth his neighbor, but through knowledge shall the just be delivered.
42 When it goeth well with the righteous, the city rejoiceth, and when the wicked perish, there is shouting.
43 By the blessing of the upright the city is exalted, but it is overthrown by the mouth of the wicked.
44 He that is void of wisdom despiseth his neighbor, but a man of understanding holdeth his peace.
45 A talebearer revealeth secrets, but he that is of a faithful spirit concealeth the matter.
46 Where no counsel is, the people fall, but in the multitude of counselors there is safety.
47 He that is surety for a stranger shall smart for it, and he that hateth suretyship is sure.
48 A gracious woman retaineth honor, and strong men retain riches.
49 The merciful man doeth good to his own soul, but he that is cruel troubleth his own flesh.
50 The wicked worketh a deceitful work, but to him that soweth righteousness shall be a sure reward.

51 As righteousness tendeth to life, so he that pursueth evil pursueth it to his own death.
52 They that are of a froward heart are an abomination to the Lord, but such as are upright in their way are his delight.
53 Though hand join in hand, the wicked shall not be unpunished, but the seed of the righteous shall be delivered.
54 As a jewel of gold in a swine's snout, so is a fair woman which is without discretion.
55 The desire of the righteous is only good, but the expectation of the wicked is wrath.
56 There is that scattereth, and yet increaseth, and there is that withholdeth more than is meet, but it tendeth to poverty.
57 The liberal soul shall be made fat, and he that watereth shall be watered also himself.
58 He that withholdeth corn, the people shall curse him, but blessing shall be upon the head of him that selleth it.
59 He that diligently seeketh good procureth favor, but he that seeketh mischief, it shallcome unto him.
60 He that trusteth in his riches shall fall, but the righteous shall flourish as a branch.
61 He that troubleth his own house shall inherit the wind, and the fool shall be servant to the wise of heart.
62 The fruit of the righteous is a tree of life, and he that winneth souls is wise.
63 Behold, the righteous shall be recompensed in the earth, much more the wicked and the sinner.
64 Whoso loveth instruction loveth knowledge, but he that hateth reproof is brutish.
65 A good man obtaineth favor of the Lord, but a man of wicked devices will he condemn.
66 A man shall not be established by wickedness, but the root of the righteous shall not be moved.
67 A virtuous woman is a crown to her husband, but she that maketh ashamed is as rottenness in his bones.
68 The thoughts of the righteous are right, but the counsels of the wicked are deceit.
69 The words of the wicked are to lie in wait for blood, but the mouth of the upright shall deliver them.
70 The wicked are overthrown and are not, but the house of the righteous shall stand.
71 A man shall be commended according to his wisdom, but he that is of a perverse heart shall be despised.
72 He that is despised and hath a servant is better than he that honoreth himself and lacketh bread.
73 A righteous man regardeth the life of his beast, but the tender mercies of the wicked are cruel.
74 He that tilleth his land shall be satisfied with bread, but he that followeth vain persons is void of understanding.
75 The wicked desireth the net of evil men, but the root of the righteous yieldeth fruit.
76 The wicked is snared by the transgression of his lips, but the just shall come out of trouble.
77 A man shall be satisfied with good by the fruit of his mouth, and the recompense of a man's hands shall be rendered unto him.

78 The way of a fool is right in his own eyes, but he that hearkeneth unto counsel is wise.
79 A fool's wrath is presently known, but a prudent man covereth shame.
80 He that speaketh truth showeth forth righteousness, but a false witness deceit.
81 There is that speaketh like the piercings of a sword, but the tongue of the wise is health.
82 The lip of truth shall be established forever, but a lying tongue is but for a moment.
83 Deceit is in the heart of them that imagine evil, but to the counselors of peace is joy.
84 There shall no evil happen to the just, but the wicked shall be filled with mischief.
85 Lying lips are abomination to the Lord, but they that deal truly are his delight.
86 A prudent man concealeth knowledge, but the heart of fools proclaimeth foolishness.
87 The hand of the diligent shall bear rule, but the slothful shall be under tribute.
88 Heaviness in the heart of man maketh it stoop, but a good word maketh it glad.
89 The righteous is more excellent than his neighbor, but the way of the wicked seduceth them.
90 The slothful man roasteth not that which he took in hunting, but the substance of a diligent man is precious.
91 In the way of righteousness is life, and in the pathway thereof there is no death.
92 A wise son heareth his father's instruction, but a scorner heareth not rebuke.
93 A man shall eat good by the fruit of his mouth, but the soul of the transgressors shall eat violence.
94 He that keepeth his mouth keepeth his life, but he that openeth wide his lips shall have destruction.
95 The soul of the sluggard desireth, and hath nothing, but the soul of the diligent shall be made fat.
96 A righteous man hateth lying, but a wicked man is loathsome and cometh to shame.
97 Righteousness keepeth him that is upright in the way, but wickedness overthroweth the sinner.
98 There is that maketh himself rich, yet hath nothing, there is that maketh himself poor, yet hath great riches.
99 The ransom of a man's life are his riches, but the poor heareth not rebuke.
100 The light of the righteous rejoiceth, but the lamp of the wicked shall be put out.
101 Only by pride cometh contention, but with the well-advised is wisdom.
102 Wealth gotten by vanity shall be diminished, but he that gathereth by labor shall increase.
103 Hope deferred maketh the heart sick, but when the desire cometh it is a tree of life.
104 Whoso despiseth the word shall be destroyed, but he that feareth the commandment shall be rewarded.
105 The law of the wise is a fountain of life, to depart from the snares of death.
106 Good understanding giveth favor, but the way of transgressors is hard.
107 Every prudent man dealeth with knowledge, but a fool layeth open his folly.
108 A wicked messenger falleth into mischief, but a faithful ambassador is health.

109 Poverty and shame shall be to him that refuseth instruction, but he that regardeth reproof shall be honored.
110 The desire accomplished is sweet to the soul, but it is a abomination to fools to depart from evil.
111 He that walketh with wise men shall be wise, but a companion of fools shall be destroyed.
112 Evil pursueth sinners, but to the righteous good shall be repaid.
113 A good man leaveth an inheritance to his children's children, and the wealth of the sinner is laid up for the just.
114 Much food is in the tillage of the poor, but there is that is destroyed for want of judgment.
115 He that spareth his rod hateth his son, but he that loveth him chasteneth him betimes.
116 The righteous eateth to the satisfying of his soul, but the belly of the wicked shall want.
117 Every wise woman buildeth her house, but the foolish plucketh it down with her hands.
118 He that walketh in his uprightness feareth the Lord, but he that is perverse in his ways despiseth him.
119 In the mouth of the foolish is a rod of pride, but the lips of the wise shall preserve them.
120 Where no oxen are, the crib is clean, but much increase is by the strength of the ox.
121 A faithful witness will not lie, but a false witness will utter lies.
122 A scorner seeketh wisdom, and findeth it not, but knowledge is easy unto him that understandeth.
123 Go from the presence of a foolish man, when thou perceivest not in him the lips of knowledge.
124 The wisdom of the prudent is to understand his way, but the folly of fools is deceit.
125 Fools make a mock at sin, but among the righteous there is favor.
126 The heart knoweth his own bitterness and a stranger doth not intermeddle with his joy.
127 The house of the wicked shall be overthrown, but the tabernacle of the upright shall flourish.
128 There is a way which seemeth right unto a man, but the end thereof are the ways of death.
129 Even in laughter the heart is sorrowful and the end of that mirth is heaviness.
130 The backslider in heart shall be filled with his own ways and a good man shall be satisfied from himself.
131 The simple believeth every word, but the prudent man looketh well to his going.
132 A wise man feareth, and departeth from evil, but the fool rageth and is confident.
133 He that is soon angry dealeth foolishly and a man of wicked devices is hated.
134 The simple inherit folly, but the prudent are crowned with knowledge.
135 The evil bow before the good and the wicked at the gates of the righteous.
136 The poor is hated even of his own neighbor, but the rich hath many friends.
137 He that despiseth his neighbor sinneth, but he that hath mercy on the poor, happy is he.
138 Do they not err that devise evil? But mercy and truth shall be to them that devise good.
139 In all labor there is profit, but the talk of the lips tendeth only to penury.

140 The crown of the wise is their riches, but the foolishness of fools is folly.
141 A true witness delivereth souls, but a deceitful witness speaketh lies.
142 In the fear of the Lord is strong confidence and his children shall have a place of refuge.
143 The fear of the Lord is a fountain of life, to depart from the snares of death.
144 In the multitude of people is the king's honor, but in the want of people is the destruction of the prince.
145 He that is slow to wrath is of great understanding, but he that is hasty of spirit exalteth folly.
146 A sound heart is the life of the flesh, but envy the rottenness of the bones.
147 He that oppresseth the poor reproacheth his Maker, but he that honor him hath mercy on the poor.
148 The wicked is driven away in his wickedness, but the righteous hath hope in his death.
149 Wisdom resteth in the heart of him that hath understanding, but that which is in the midst of fools is made known.
150 Righteousness exalteth a nation, but sin is a reproach to any people.
151 The king's favor is toward a wise servant, but his wrath is against him that causeth shame.
152 A soft answer turneth away wrath, but grievous words stir up anger.
153 The tongue of the wise useth knowledge aright, but the mouth of fools poureth out foolishness.
154 The eyes of the Lord are in every place beholding the evil and the good.
155 A wholesome tongue is a tree of life, but perverseness therein is a breach in the spirit.
156 A fool despiseth his father's instruction, but he that regardeth reproof is prudent.
157 In the house of the righteous is much treasure, but in the revenues of the wicked is trouble.
158 The lips of the wise disperse knowledge, but the heart of the foolish doeth not so.
159 The sacrifice of the wicked is an abomination to the Lord, but the prayer of the upright is his delight.
160 The way of the wicked is an abomination unto the Lord, but he loveth him that followeth after righteousness.
161 Correction is grievous unto him that forsaketh the way, and he that hateth reproof shall die.
162 Hell and destruction are before the Lord, how much more then the hearts of the children of men?
163 A scorner loveth not one that reproveth him, neither will he go unto the wise.
164 A merry heart maketh a cheerful countenance, but by sorrow of the heart the spirit is broken.
165 The heart of him that hath understanding seeketh knowledge, but the mouth of fools feedeth on foolishness.
166 All the days of the afflicted are evil, but he that is of a merry heart hath a continual feast.
167 Better is little with the fear of the Lord, than great treasure and trouble therewith.
168 Better is a dinner of herbs where love is, than a stalled ox and hatred therewith.
169 A wrathful man stirreth up strife, but he that is slow to anger appeaseth strife.
170 The way of the slothful man is as a hedge of thorns, but the way of the righteous is made plain.
171 A wise son maketh a glad father, but a foolish man despiseth his mother.

172 Folly is joy to him that is destitute of wisdom, but a man of understanding walketh uprightly.
173 Without counsel purposes are disappointed, but in the multitude of counselors they are established.
174 A man hath joy by the answer of his mouth, and a word spoken in due season, how good is it!
175 The way of life is above to the wise, that he may depart from hell beneath.
176 The Lord will destroy the house of the proud, but he will establish the border of the widow.
177 The thoughts of the wicked are an abomination to the Lord, but the words of the pure are pleasant words.
178 He that is greedy of gain troubleth his own house, but he that hateth gifts shall live.
179 The heart of the righteous studieth to answer, but the mouth of the wicked poureth out evil things.
180 The Lord is far from the wicked, but he heareth the prayer of the righteous.
181 The light of the eyes rejoiceth the heart, and a good report maketh the bones fat.
182 The ear that heareth the reproof of life abideth among the wise.
183 He that refuseth instruction despiseth his own soul, but he that heareth reproof getteth understanding.
184 The fear of the Lord is the instruction of wisdom and before honor is humility.
185 The preparations of the heart in man and the answer of the tongue is from the Lord.
186 All the ways of a man are clean in his own eyes, but the Lord weigheth the spirits.
187 Commit thy works unto the Lord and thy thoughts shall be established.
188 The Lord hath made all things for himself, yea, even the wicked for the day of evil.
189 Everyone that is proud in heart is an abomination to the Lord, though hand join in hand, he shall not be unpunished.
190 By mercy and truth iniquity is purged and by the fear of the Lord men depart from evil.
191 When a man's ways please the Lord, he maketh even his enemies to be at peace with him.
192 Better is a little with righteousness, than great revenues without right.
193 A man's heart deviseth his way, but the Lord directeth his steps.
194 A divine sentence is in the lips of the king, his mouth transgresseth not in judgment.
195 A just weight and balance are the Lord's, all the weights of the bag are his work.
196 It is an abomination to kings to commit wickedness, for the throne is established by righteousness.
197 Righteous lips are the delight of kings and they love him that speaketh right.
198 The wrath of a king is as messengers of death, but a wise man will pacify it.
199 In the light of the king's countenance is life, and his favor is as a cloud of the latter rain.
200 How much better is it to get wisdom than gold and to get understanding rather to be chosen than silver!
201 The highway of the upright is to depart from evil, he that keepeth his way preserveth his soul.
202 Pride goeth before destruction, and a haughty spirit before a fall.

203 Better it is to be of an humble spirit with the lowly, than to divide the spoil with the proud.
204 He that handleth a matter wisely shall find good and whoso trusteth in the Lord, happy is he.
205 The wise in heart shall be called prudent and the sweetness of the lips increaseth learning.
206 Understanding is a wellspring of life unto him that hath it, but the instruction of fools is folly.
207 The heart of the wise teacheth his mouth and addeth learning to his lips.
208 Pleasant words are as a honeycomb, sweet to the soul and health to the bones.
209 There is a way that seemeth right unto a man, but the end thereof are the ways of death.
210 He that laboreth laboreth for himself, for his mouth craveth it of him.
211 An ungodly man diggeth up evil and in his lips there is as a burning fire.
212 A froward man soweth strife and a whisperer separateth chief friends.
213 A violent man enticeth his neighbor and leadeth him into a way that is not good.
214 He shutteth his eyes to devise froward things, moving his lips he bringeth evil to pass.
215 The hoary head is a crown of glory, if it be found in the way of righteousness.
216 He that is slow to anger is better than the mighty and he that ruleth his spirit than he that taketh a city.
217 The lot is cast into the lap, but the whole disposing thereof is of the Lord.
218 Better is a dry morsel and quietness therewith than a house full of sacrifices with strife.
219 A wise servant shall have rule over a son that causeth shame and shall have part of the inheritance among the brethren.
220 The fining pot is for silver and the furnace for gold, but the Lord trieth the hearts.
221 A wicked doer giveth heed to false lips and a liar giveth ear to a naughty tongue.
222 Whoso mocketh the poor reproacheth his Maker and he that is glad at calamities shall not be unpunished.
223 Children's children are the crown of old men and the glory of children are their fathers.
224 Excellent speech becometh not a fool, much less do lying lips a prince.
225 A gift is as a precious stone in the eyes of him that hath it, whithersoever it turneth, it prospereth.
226 He that covereth a transgression seeketh love, but he that repeateth a matter separateth very friends.
227 A reproof entereth more into a wise man than a hundred stripes into a fool.
228 An evil man seeketh only rebellion, therefore a cruel messenger shall be sent against him.
229 Let a bear robbed of her whelps meet a man rather than a fool in his folly.
230 Whoso rewardeth evil for good, evil shall not depart from his house.
231 The beginning of strife is as when one letteth out water, therefore leave off contention before it be meddled with.
232 He that justifieth the wicked and he that condemneth the just, even they both are abomination to the Lord.
233 Wherefore is there a price in the hand of a fool to get wisdom, seeing he hath no heart to it?
234 A friend loveth at all times and a brother is born for adversity.
235 A man void of understanding striketh hands, and becometh surety in the presence of his friend.

236 He loveth transgression that loveth strife and he that exalteth his gate seeketh destruction.
237 He that hath a froward heart findeth no good, and he that hath a perverse tongue falleth into mischief.
238 He that begetteth a fool doeth it to his sorrow, and the father of a fool hath no joy.
239 A merry heart doeth good like a medicine, but a broken spirit drieth the bones.
240 A wicked man taketh a gift out of the bosom to pervert the ways of judgment.
241 Wisdom is before him that hath understanding, but the eyes of a fool are in the ends of the Earth.
242 A foolish son is a grief to his father and bitterness to her that bare him.
243 Also to punish the just is not good, nor to strike princes for equity.
244 He that hath knowledge spareth his words and a man of understanding is of an excellent spirit.
245 Even a fool, when he holdeth his peace, is counted wise and he that shutteth his lips is esteemed a man of understanding.
246 Through desire, a man, having separated himself, seeketh and intermeddleth with all wisdom.
247 A fool hath no delight in understanding but that his heart may discover itself.
248 When the wicked cometh, then cometh also contempt and with ignominy reproach.
249 The words of a man's mouth are as deep waters and the wellspring of wisdom as a flowing brook.
250 It is not good to accept the person of the wicked, to overthrow the righteous in judgement.
251 A fool's lips enter into contention and his mouth calleth for strokes.
252 A fool's mouth is his destruction and his lips are the snare of his soul.
253 The words of a talebearer are as wounds and they go down into the innermost parts of the belly.
254 He also that is slothful in his work is brother to him that is a great waster.
255 The name of the Lord is a strong tower, the righteous runneth into it and is safe.
256 The rich man's wealth is his strong city and as a high wall in his own conceit.
257 Before destruction the heart of man is haughty and before honor is humility.
258 He that answereth a matter before he heareth it, it is folly and shame unto him.
259 The spirit of a man will sustain his infirmity, but a wounded spirit who can bear?
260 The heart of the prudent getteth knowledge and the ear of the wise seeketh knowledge.
261 A man's gift maketh room for him and bringeth him before great men.
252 He that is first in his own cause seemeth just, but his neighbor cometh and searcheth him.
263 The lot causeth contentions to cease and parteth between the mighty.
264 A brother offended is harder to be won than a strong city and their contentions are like the bars of a castle.
265 A man's belly shall be satisfied with the fruit of his mouth and with the increase of his lips shall he be filled.
266 Death and life are in the power of the tongue and they that love it shall eat the fruit thereof.

267 Whoso findeth a good wife hath obtained favor of the Lord.
268 The poor useth entreaties, but the rich answereth roughly.
269 Better is the poor that walketh in his integrity than he that is perverse in his lips and is a fool.
270 Also, that the soul be without knowledge, it is not good and he that hasteth with his feet sinneth.
271 The foolishness of man perverteth his way and his heart fretteth against the Lord.
272 Wealth maketh many friends, but the poor is separated from his neighbor.
273 A false witness shall not be unpunished and he that speaketh lies shall not escape.
274 Many will entreat the favor of the prince and every man is a friend to him that giveth gifts.
275 All the brethren of the poor do hate him, how much more do his friends go far from him? He pursueth them with words, yet they are wanting to him.
276 He that getteth wisdom loveth his own soul he that keepeth understanding shall find good.
277 A false witness shall not be unpunished and he that speaketh lies shall perish.
278 Delight is not seemly for a fool, much less for a servant to have rule over princes.
279 The discretion of a man deferreth his anger and it is his glory to pass over a transgression.
280 The king's wrath is as the roaring of a lion, but his favor is as dew upon the grass.
281 A foolish son is the calamity of his father and the contentions of a wife are a continual dropping.
282 House and riches are the inheritance of fathers and a prudent wife is from the Lord.
283 Slothfulness casteth into a deep sleep and an idle soul shall suffer hunger.
284 He that keepeth the commandment keepeth his own soul, but he that despiseth his ways shall die.
285 He that hath pity upon the poor lendeth unto the Lord and that which he hath given will he pay him again.
286 Chasten thy son while there is hope and let not thy soul spare for his crying.
287 A man of great wrath shall suffer punishment, for if thou deliver him, yet thou must do it again.
288 Hear counsel, and receive instruction that thou mayest be wise in thy latter end.
289 There are many devices in a man's heart, nevertheless the counsel of the Lord, that shall stand.
290 The desire of a man is his kindness and a poor man is better than a liar.
291 The fear of the Lord tendeth to life and he that hath it shall abide satisfied, he shall not be visited with evil.
292 A slothful man hideth his hand in his bosom and will not so much as bring it to his mouth again.
293 Smite a scorner and the simple will beware and reprove one that hath understanding and he will understand knowledge.
294 He that wasteth his father and chaseth away his mother is a son that causeth shame and bringeth reproach.
295 Cease, my son, to hear the instruction that causeth to err from the words of knowledge.
296 An ungodly witness scorneth judgment and the mouth of the wicked devoureth iniquity.
297 Judgments are prepared for scorners and stripes for the back of fools.

298 Wine is a mocker, strong drink is raging and whosoever is deceived thereby is not wise.
299 The fear of a king is as the roaring of a lion, whoso provoketh him to anger sinneth against his own soul.
300 It is an honor for a man to cease from strife, but every fool will be meddling.
301 The sluggard will not plough by reason of the cold, therefore shall he beg in harvest and have nothing.
302 Counsel in the heart of man is like deep water, but a man of understanding will draw it out.
303 Most men will proclaim everyone his own goodness, but a faithful man who can find?
304 The just man walketh in his integrity, his children are blessed after him.
305 A king that sitteth in the throne of judgment scattereth away all evil with his eyes.
306 Who can say, I have made my heart clean, I am pure from my sin?
307 Divers weights and divers measures, both of them are alike abomination to the Lord.
308 Even a child is known by his doings, whether his work be pure and whether it be right.
309 The hearing ear and the seeing eye, the Lord hath made even both of them.
310 Love not sleep, lest thou come to poverty, open thine eyes and thou shalt be satisfied with bread.
311 It is naught, it is naught, saith the buyer, but when he is gone his way, then he boasteth.
312 There is gold, and a multitude of rubies, but the lips of knowledge are a precious jewel.
313 Take his garment that is surety for a stranger and take a pledge of him for a strange women.
314 Bread of deceit is sweet to a man, but afterwards his mouth shall be filled with gravel.
315 Every purpose is established by counsel and with good advice make war.
316 He that goeth about as a talebearer revealeth secrets, therefore meddle not with him that flattereth with his lips.
317 Whoso curseth his father or his mother, his lamp shall be put out in obscure darkness.
318 An inheritance may be gotten hastily at the beginning, but the end thereof shall not be blessed.
319 Say not thou, I will recompense evil, but wait on the Lord and he shall save thee.
320 Divers weights are an abomination unto the Lord and a false balance is not good.
321 Men's goings are of the Lord, how can a man then understand his own way?
322 It is a snare to the man who devoureth that which is holy and after vows to make inquiry.
323 A wise king scattereth the wicked and bringeth the wheel over them.
324 The spirit of man is the candle of the Lord, searching all the inward parts of the belly.
325 Mercy and truth preserve the king and his throne is upholden by mercy.
326 The glory of young men is their strength and the beauty of old men is the gray head.
327 The blueness of a wound cleanseth away evil, so do stripes the inward parts of the belly.
328 The king's heart is in the hand of the Lord as the rivers of water, he turneth it whithersoever he will.

329 Every way of a man is right in his own eyes, but the Lord pondereth the hearts.
330 To do justice and judgment is more acceptable to the Lord than sacrifice.
331 A high look, and a proud heart, and the ploughing of the wicked is sin.
332 The thoughts of the diligent tend only to plenteousness, but of everyone that is hasty only to want.
333 The getting of treasures by a lying tongue is a vanity tossed to and fro of them that seek death.
334 The robbery of the wicked shall destroy them because they refuse to do judgment.
335 The way of man is froward and strange, but as for the pure, his work is right.
336 It is better to dwell in a corner of the housetop, than with a brawling woman in a wide house.
337 The soul of the wicked desireth evil, his neighbor findeth no favor in his eyes.
338 When the scorner is punished, the simple is made wise, and when the wise is instructed he receiveth knowledge.
339 The righteous man wisely considereth the house of the wicked, but God overthroweth the wicked for their wickedness.
340 Whoso stoppeth his ears at the cry of the poor, he also shall cry himself, but shall not be heard.
341 A gift in secret pacifieth anger and a reward in the bosom, strong wrath.
342 It is joy to the just to do judgment, but destruction shall be to the workers of iniquity.
343 The man that wandereth out of the way of understanding shall remain in the congregation of the dead.
344 He that loveth pleasure shall be a poor man, he that loveth wine and oil shall not be rich.
345 The wicked shall be a ransom for the righteous and the transgressor for the upright.
346 It is better to dwell in the wilderness than with a contentious and an angry woman.
347 There is treasure to be desired and oil in the dwelling of the wise, but a foolish man spendeth it up.
348 He that followeth after righteousness and mercy findeth life, righteousness, and honor.
349 A wise man scaleth the city of the mighty and casteth down the strength of the confidence thereof.
350 Whoso keepeth his mouth and his tongue keepeth his soul from troubles.
351 Proud and haughty scorner is his name who dealeth in proud wrath.
352 The desire of the slothful killeth him, for his hands refuse to labor. He coveteth greed-ily all the day long, but the righteous giveth and spareth not.
353 The sacrifice of the wicked is abomination; how much more when he bringeth it with a wicked mind?
354 A false witness shall perish, but the man that heareth speaketh constantly.
355 A wicked man hardeneth his face, but as for the upright, he directeth his way.
356 There is no wisdom nor understanding nor counsel against the Lord.
357 The horse is prepared against the day of battle, but safety is of the Lord.
358 A good name is rather to be chosen than great riches and loving favor rather than silver and gold.
359 The rich and poor meet together, the Lord is the maker of them all.
360 A prudent man foreseeth the evil and hideth himself, but the simple pass on and are punished.
361 By humility and the fear of the Lord are riches, and honor, and life.
362 Thorns and snares are in the way of the froward, he that doth keep his soul shall be far from them.

363 Train up a child in the way he should go and when he is old, he will not depart from it.
364 The rich ruleth over the poor and the borrower is servant to the lender.
365 He that soweth iniquity shall reap vanity and the rod of his anger shall fail.
366 He that hath a bountiful eye shall be blessed, for he giveth of his bread to the poor.
367 Cast out the scorner and contention shall go out, yea, strife and reproach shall cease.
368 He that loveth pureness of heart, for the grace of his lips the king shall be his friend.
369 For the eyes of the Lord preserve knowledge, but he overthroweth the words of the transgressor.
370 The slothful man saith, There is a lion without, I shall be slain in the streets.
371 The mouth of strange women is a deep pit, he that is abhorred of the Lord shall fall therein.
372 Foolishness is bound in the heart of a child, but the rod of correction shall drive it far from him.
373 He that oppresseth the poor to increase his riches, and he that giveth to the rich shall surely come to want.
374 Bow down thine ear, and hear the words of the wise, and apply thine heart unto my knowledge. For it is a pleasant thing if thou keep them within thee, they shall withal be fitted in thy lips. That thy trust may be in the Lord I have made known to thee this day, even to thee. Have not I written to thee excellent things in counsels and knowledge that I might make thee know the certainty of the words of truth, that thou mightest answer the words of truth to them that send unto thee?
375 Rob not the poor because he is poor, neither oppress the afflicted in the gate, for the Lord will plead their cause and spoil the soul of those that spoiled them.
376 Make no friendship with an angry man and with a furious man thou shalt not go, lest thou learn his ways and get a snare to thy soul.
377 Be not thou one of them that strike hands or of them that are sureties for debts.
378 If thou hast nothing to pay, why should he take away thy bed from under thee?
379 Remove not the ancient landmark which thy fathers have set.
380 Seest thou a man diligent in his business? He shall stand before kings, he shall not stand before mean men.
381 When thou sittest to eat with a ruler, consider diligently what is before thee and put a knife to thy throat, if thou be a man given to appetite. Be not desirous of his dainties, for they are deceitful meat.
382 Labor not to be rich, cease from thine own wisdom.
383 Wilt thou set thine eyes upon that which is not? For riches certainly make themselves wings, they fly away as an eagle toward Heaven.
384 Eat thou not the bread of him that hath an evil eye, neither desire thou his dainty meats, for as he thinketh in his heart so is he. Eat and drink saith he to thee, but his heart is not with thee. The morsel which thou hast eaten shalt thou vomit up and lose thy sweet words.
385 Speak not in the ears of a fool, for he will despise the wisdom of thy words.
386 Remove not the old landmark and enter not into the fields of the fatherless, for their Redeemer is mighty, he shall plead their cause with thee.
387 Apply thine heart unto instruction and thine ears to the words of knowledge.

388 Withhold not correction from the child, for if thou beatest him with the rod, he shall not die. Thou shalt beat him with the rod and shalt deliver his soul from hell.

5 MY son, if thine heart be wise, my heart shall rejoice, even mine. Yea, my reins shall rejoice when thy lips speak right things. Let not thine heart envy sinners, but be thou in the fear of the Lord all the day long. For surely there is an end and thine expectation shall not be cut off. Hear thou, my son, and be wise and guide thine heart in the way. Be not among winebibbers, among riotous eaters of flesh, for the drunkard and the glutton shall come to poverty and drowsiness shall clothe a man with rags.

Hearken unto thy father that begat thee and despise not thy mother when she is old. Buy the truth, and sell it not, also wisdom, and instruction, and understanding. The father of the righteous shall greatly rejoice and he that begetteth a wise child shall have joy of him. Thy father and thy mother shall be glad and she that bare thee shall rejoice. My son, give me thine heart and let thine eyes observe my ways. For a whore is a deep ditch and a strange woman is a narrow pit. She also lieth in wait as for a prey and increaseth the transgressors among men.

Who hath wo? Who hath sorrow? Who hath contentions? Who hath babbling? Who hath wounds without cause? Who hath redness of eyes? They that tarry long at the wine, they that go to seek mixed wine. Look not thou upon the wine when it is red, when it giveth his color in the cup, when it moveth itself aright. At the last it biteth like a serpent, and stingeth like an adder. Thine eyes shall behold strange women and thine heart shall utter perverse things. Yea, thou shalt be as he that lieth down in the midst of the sea or as he that lieth upon the top of a mast. They have stricken me, shalt thou say, and I was not sick, they have beaten me and I felt it not; when shall I awake? I will seek it yet again.

389 Be not thou envious against evil men, neither desire to be with them, for their heart studieth destruction, and their lips talk of mischief.

390 Through wisdom is a house builded, and by understanding it is established, and by knowledge shall the chambers be filled with all precious and pleasant riches.

391 A wise man is strong, yea, a man of knowledge increaseth strength. For by wise counsel thou shalt make thy war, and in multitude of counselors there is safety.

392 Wisdom is too high for a fool, he openeth not his mouth in the gate.

393 He that deviseth to do evil shall be called a mischievous person.

394 The thought of foolishness is sin, and the scorner is an abomination to men.

395 If thou faint in the day of adversity, thy strength is small.

If thou forbear to deliver them that are drawn unto death and those that are ready to be slain, if thou sayest, Behold, we knew it not, doth not he that pondereth the heart consider it? And he that keepeth thy soul, doth not he know it? And shall not he render to every man according to his works? My son, eat thou honey, because it is good, and the honeycomb, which is sweet to thy taste, so shall the knowledge of wisdom be unto thy soul when thou hast found it, then there shall be a reward and thy expectation shall not be cut off. Lay not wait, O wicked man, against the dwelling of the righteous, spoil not his resting-place, for a just man falleth seven times, and riseth up again, but the wicked shall fall into mischief. Rejoice not when thine enemy falleth, and let not thine heart be glad when he stumbleth, lest the Lord see it, and it displease him, and he turn away his wrath from him. Fret not thyself because of evil men, neither be thou envious at the wicked, for there shall be no reward to the evil man, the candle of the wicked shall be put out. My son, fear thou the Lord and the king and meddle not with them that are given to change. For their calamity shall rise suddenly, and who knoweth the ruin of them both?

These things also belong to the wise:
It is not good to have respect of persons in judgment. He that saith unto the wicked, Thou art righteous, him shall the people curse, nations shall abhor him. But to them that rebuke him shall be delight and a good blessing shall come upon them. Every man shall kiss his lips that giveth a right answer. Prepare thy work without, and make it fit for thyself in the field, and afterwards build thine house. Be not a witness against thy neighbor without cause, and deceive not with thy lips. Say not, I will do so to him as he hath done to me, I will render to the man according to his work.

I went by the field of the slothful, and by the vineyard of the man void of understanding and lo, it was all grown over with thorns, and nettles had covered the face thereof, and the stone wall thereof was broken down. Then I saw, and considered it well, I looked upon it, and received instruction. Yet a little sleep, a little slumber, a little folding of the hands to sleep, so shall thy poverty come as one that traveleth and thy want as an armed man.

6 THESE are also proverbs of Solomon which the men of Hezekiah king of Judah copied out.

396 It is the glory of God to conceal a thing, but the honor of kings is to search out a matter.
397 The Heaven for height, and the earth for depth, and the heart of kings is unsearchable.
398 Take away the dross from the silver, and there shall come forth a vessel for the finer.
399 Take away the wicked from before the king and his throne shall be established in righteousness.
400 Put not forth thyself in the presence of the king and stand not in the place of great men, for better it is that it be said unto thee, Come up hither, than that thou shouldest be put lower in the presence of the prince whom thine eyes have seen.
401 Go not forth hastily to strive, lest thou know not what to do in the end thereof, when thy neighbor hath put thee to shame. Debate thy cause with thy neighbor himself and discover not a secret to another, lest he that heareth it put thee to shame, and thine infamy turn not away.
402 A word fitly spoken is like apples of gold in pictures of silver.
403 As an earring of gold and an ornament of fine gold, so is a wise reprover upon an obedient ear.
404 As the cold of snow in the time of harvest, so is a faithful messenger to them that send him, for he refresheth the soul of his masters.
405 Whoso boasteth himself of a false gift is like clouds and wind without rain.
406 By long forbearing is a prince persuaded and a soft tongue breaketh the bone.
407 Hast thou found honey? Eat so much as is sufficient for thee, lest thou be filled therewith and vomit it.
408 Withdraw thy foot from thy neighbor's house, lest he be weary of thee and so hate thee.
409 A man that beareth false witness against his neighbor is a maul, and a sword, and a sharp arrow.
410 Confidence in an unfaithful man in time of trouble is like a broken tooth and a foot out of joint.

411 As he that taketh away a garment in cold weather and as vinegar upon nitre, so is he that singeth songs to a heavy heart.
412 If thine enemy be hungry, give him bread to eat, and if he be thirsty, give him water to drink, for thou shalt heap coals of fire upon his head and the Lord shall reward thee.
413 The north wind driveth away rain, so doth an angry countenance a backbiting tongue.
414 It is better to dwell in the corner of the housetop than with a brawling woman and in a wide house.
415 As cold waters to a thirsty soul, so is good news from a far country.
416 A righteous man falling down before the wicked is as a troubled fountain and a corrupt spring.
417 It is not good to eat much honey, so for men to search their own glory is not glory.
418 He that hath no rule over his own spirit is like a city that is broken down and without walls.
419 As snow in summer and as rain in harvest, so honor is not seemly for a fool.
420 As the bird by wandering, as the swallow by flying, so the curse causeless shall not come.
421 A whip for the horse, a bridle for the ass, and a rod for the fool's back.
422 Answer not a fool according to his folly, lest thou also be like unto him.
423 Answer a fool according to his folly, lest he be wise in his own conceit.
424 He that sendeth a message by the hand of a fool cutteth off the feet and drinketh damage.
425 The legs of the lame are not equal, so is a parable in the mouth of fools.
426 As he that bindeth a stone in a sling, so is he that giveth honor to a fool.
427 As a thorn goeth up into the hand of a drunkard, so is a parable in the mouth of fools.
428 The great God that formed all things both rewardeth the fool and rewardeth transgressors.
429 As a dog returneth to his vomit, so a fool returneth to his folly.
430 Seest thou a man wise in his own conceit? There is more hope of a fool than of him.
431 The slothful man saith, There is a lion in the way, a lion is in the streets.
432 As the door turneth upon his hinges, so doth the slothful upon his bed.
433 The slothful hideth his hand in his bosom, it grieveth him to bring it again to his mouth.
434 The sluggard is wiser in his own conceit than seven men that can render a reason.
435 He that passeth by and meddleth with strife belonging not to him, is like one that taketh a dog by the ears.
436 As a mad man who casteth firebrands, arrows, and death, so is the man that deceiveth his neighbor, and saith, Am not I in sport?
437 Where no wood is, there the fire goeth out, so where there is no talebearer, the strife ceaseth.
438 As coals are to burning coals, and wood to fire, so is a contentious man to kindle strife.
439 The words of a talebearer are as wounds, and they go down into the innermost parts of the belly.
440 Burning lips and a wicked heart are like a potsherd covered with silver dross.
441 He that hateth dissembleth with his lips and layeth up deceit within him; when he speaketh fair, believe him not, for there are seven abominations in his heart.

442 Whose hatred is covered by deceit, his wickedness shall be showed before the whole congregation.
443 Whoso diggeth a pit shall fall therein and he that rolleth a stone, it will return upon him.
444 A lying tongue hateth those that are afflicted by it and a flattering mouth worketh ruin.
445 Boast not thyself of tomorrow, for thou knowest not what a day may bring forth.
446 Let another man praise thee and not thine own mouth, a stranger and not thine own lips.
447 A stone is heavy, and the sand weighty, but a fool's wrath is heavier than them both.
448 Wrath is cruel and anger is outrageous, but who is able to stand before envy.
449 Open rebuke is better than secret love.
450 Faithful are the wounds of a friend, but the kisses of an enemy are deceitful.
451 The full soul loatheth a honeycomb, but to the hungry soul every bitter thing is sweet.
452 As a bird that wandereth from her nest, so is a man that wandereth from his place.
453 Ointment and perfume rejoice the heart, so doth the sweetness of a man's friend by hearty counsel.
454 Thine own friend and thy father's friend forsake not, neither go into thy brother's house in the day of thy calamity, for better is a neighbor that is near than a brother far off.
455 My son, be wise and make my heart glad, that I may answer him that reproacheth me.
456 A prudent man foreseeth the evil and hideth himself, but the simple pass on and are punished.
457 Take his garment that is surety for a stranger and take a pledge of him for a strange woman.
458 He that blesseth his friend with a loud voice, rising early in the morning, it shall be counted a curse to him.
459 A continual dropping in a very rainy day and a contentious woman are alike. Whosoever hideth her hideth the wind and the ointment of his right hand, which betrayeth itself.
460 Iron sharpeneth iron, so a man sharpeneth the countenance of his friend.
461 Whoso keepeth the fig tree shall eat the fruit thereof, so he that waiteth on his master shall be honored.
462 As in water face answereth to face, so the heart of man to man.
463 Hell and destruction are never full, so the eyes of man are never satisfied.
464 As the fining pot for silver and the furnace for gold, so is a man to his praise.
465 Though thou shouldest bray a fool in a mortar among wheat with a pestle, yet will not his foolishness depart from him.
466 Be thou diligent to know the state of thy flocks, and look well to thy herds, for riches are not for ever and doth the crown endure to every generation?
467 The hay appeareth, and the tender grass showeth itself, and herbs of the mountains are gathered.
468 The lambs are for thy clothing, and the goats are the price of the field. And thou shalt have goats' milk enough for thy food, for the food of thy household, and for the maintenance for thy maidens.
469 The wicked flee when no man pursueth, but the righteous are bold as a lion.
470 For the transgression of a land many are the princes thereof, but by a man of understanding and knowledge the state thereof shall be prolonged.

471 A poor man that oppresseth the poor is like a sweeping rain which leaveth no food.
472 They that forsake the law praise the wicked, but such as keep the law contend with them.
473 Evil men understand not judgment, but they that seek the Lord understand all things.
474 Better is the poor that walketh in his uprightness, than he that is perverse in his ways, though he be rich.
475 Whoso keepeth the law is a wise son, but he that is a companion of riotous men shameth his father.
476 He that by usury and unjust gain increaseth his substance, he shall gather it for him that will pity the poor.
477 He that turneth away his ear from hearing the law, even his prayer shall be abomination.
478 Whoso causeth the righteous to go astray in an evil way, he shall fall himself into his own pit, but the upright shall have good things in possession.
479 The rich man is wise in his own conceit, but the poor that hath understanding searcheth him out.
480 When righteous men do rejoice, there is great glory, but when the wicked rise, a man is hidden.
481 He that covereth his sins shall not prosper, but whoso confesseth and forsaketh them shall have mercy.
482 Happy is the man that feareth always, but he that hardeneth his heart shall fall into mischief.
483 As a roaring lion and a ranging bear, so is a wicked ruler over the poor people.
484 The prince that wanteth understanding is also a great oppressor, but he that hateth covetousness shall prolong his days.
485 A man that doeth violence to the blood of any person shall flee to the pit, let no man stay him.
486 Whoso walketh uprightly shall be saved, but he that is perverse in his ways shall fall at once.
487 He that tilleth his land shall have plenty of bread, but he that followeth after vain persons shall have poverty enough.
488 A faithful man shall abound with blessings, but he that maketh haste to be rich shall not be innocent.
489 To have respect of persons is not good, for, for a piece of bread that man will transgress.
490 He that hasteth to be rich hath an evil eye, and considereth not that poverty shall come upon him.
491 He that rebuketh a man, afterwards shall find more favor than he that flattereth with the tongue.
492 Whoso robbeth his father or his mother and saith, It is no transgression, the same is the companion of a destroyer.
493 He that is of a proud heart stirreth up strife, but he that putteth his trust in the Lord shall be made fat.
494 He that trusteth in his own heart is a fool, but whoso walketh wisely, he shall be delivered.
495 He that giveth unto the poor shall not lack, but he that hideth his eyes shall have many a curse.
496 When the wicked rise men hide themselves, but when they perish, the righteous increase.
497 He that being often reproved hardeneth his neck shall suddenly be destroyed and that without remedy.

PROVERBS 7

498 When the righteous are in authority the people rejoice, but when the wicked beareth rule the people mourn.

499 Whoso loveth wisdom rejoiceth his father, but he that keepeth company with harlots spendeth his substance.

500 The king by judgment establisheth the land, but he that receiveth gifts overthroweth it.

501 A man that flattereth his neighbor spreadeth a net for his feet.

502 In the transgression of an evil man there is a snare, but the righteous doth sing and rejoice.

503 The righteous considereth the cause of the poor, but the wicked regardeth not to know it.

504 Scornful men bring a city into a snare, but wise men turn away wrath.

505 If a wise man contendeth with a foolish man, whether he rage or laugh there is no rest.

506 The bloodthirsty hate the upright, but the just seek his soul.

507 A fool uttereth all his mind, but a wise man keepeth it in till afterwards.

508 If a ruler hearken to lies, all his servants are wicked.

509 The poor and the deceitful man meet together, the Lord lighteneth both their eyes.

510 The king that faithfully judgeth the poor, his throne shall be established forever.

511 The rod and reproof give wisdom, but a child left to himself bringeth his mother to shame.

512 When the wicked are multiplied transgression increaseth, but the righteous shall see their fall.

513 Correct thy son and he shall give thee rest, yea, he shall give delight unto thy soul.

514 Where there is no vision the people perish, but he that keepeth the law, happy is he.

515 A servant will not be corrected by words, for though he understand he will not answer.

516 Seest thou a man that is hasty in his words? There is more hope of a fool than of him.

517 He that delicately bringeth up his servant from a child shall have him become his son at the length.

518 An angry man stirreth up strife and a furious man aboundeth in transgression.

519 A man's pride shall bring him low, but honor shall uphold the humble in spirit.

520 Whoso is partner with a thief hateth his own soul, he heareth cursing and bewrayeth it not.

521 The fear of man bringeth a snare, but whoso putteth his trust in the Lord shall be safe.

522 Many seek the ruler's favor, but every man's judgment cometh from the Lord.

523 An unjust man is an abomination to the just and he that is upright in the way is abomination to the wicked.

7 THE words of Agur the son of Jakeh, even the prophecy the man spake unto Ithiel, even unto Ithiel and Ucal:

Surely I am more brutish than any man and have not the understanding of a man. I neither learned wisdom, nor have the knowledge of the holy. Who hath ascended up into Heaven or descended? Who hath gathered the wind in his fists? Who hath bound the waters in a garment? Who hath established all the ends of the earth? What is his name and what is his son's name, if thou canst tell?

Every word of God is pure, he is a shield unto them that put their trust in him. Add thou not unto his words, lest he reprove thee and thou be found a liar.

Two things have I required of thee, deny me them not before I die: remove far from me vanity and lies, give me neither poverty nor riches, feed me with food convenient for me lest I be full, and deny thee and say, Who is the Lord? Or lest I be poor, and steal, and take the name of my God in vain.

Accuse not a servant unto his master lest he curse thee and thou be found guilty. There is a generation that curseth their father and doth not bless their mother. There is a generation that are pure in their own eyes and yet is not washed from their filthiness. There is a generation, O how lofty are their eyes! and their eyelids are lifted up. There is a generation whose teeth are as swords and their jaw teeth as knives, to devour the poor from off the earth and the needy from among men.

The horseleech hath two daughters, crying, Give, give.

There are three things that are never satisfied, yea, four things say not, It is enough: the grave, and the barren womb, the Earth that is not filled with water, and the fire that saith not, It is enough.

The eye that mocketh at his father, and despiseth to obey his mother, the ravens of the valley shall pick it out and the young eagles shall eat it. There be three things which are too wonderful for me, yea, four which I know not: the way of an eagle in the air, the way of a serpent upon a rock, the way of a ship in the midst of the sea, and the way of a man with a maid. Such is the way of an adulterous woman: she eateth and wipeth her mouth, and saith, I have done no wickedness.

For three things the earth is disquieted, and for four which it cannot bear: for a servant when he reigneth, and a fool when he is filled with meat, for an odious woman when she is married, and a handmaid that is heir to her mistress.

There be four things which are little upon the earth, but they are exceeding wise: the ants are a people not strong, yet they prepare their meat in the summer; the conies are but a feeble folk, yet make they their houses in the rocks; the locusts have no king, yet go they forth all of them by bands; the spider taketh hold with her hands and is in kings' palaces.

There be three things which go well, yea, four are comely in going: a lion which is strongest among beasts and turneth not away from any, a greyhound, a he goat also, and a king, against whom there is no rising up.

If thou hast done foolishly in lifting up thyself or if thou hast thought evil, lay thine hand upon thy mouth. Surely the churning of milk bringeth forth butter and the wringing of the nose bringest forth blood, so the forcing of wrath bringeth forth strife.

8 THE *words of king Lemuel: the prophecy that his mother taught him.*
What, my son? And what, the son of my womb? And what, the son of my vows? Give not thy strength unto women, nor thy ways to that which destroyeth kings. It is not for kings, O Lemuel, it is not for kings to drink wine, nor for princes strong drink, lest they drink and forget the law and pervert the judgment of any of the afflicted. Give strong drink unto him that is ready to perish and wine unto those that be of heavy hearts. Let him drink and forget his poverty and remember his misery no more. Open thy mouth for the dumb in the cause of all such as are appointed to destruction. Open thy mouth, judge righteously, and plead the cause of the poor and needy.

Who can find a virtuous woman? For her price is far above rubies. The heart of her husband doth safely trust in her so that he shall have no need of spoil. She will do him good and not evil all the days of her life. She seeketh wool, and flax, and worketh willingly with her hands. She is like the merchants' ships: she bringeth her food from afar. She riseth also while it is yet night and giveth meat to her household and a portion to her maidens. She considereth a field and buyeth it, with the fruit of her hands she planteth a vineyard. She girdeth her loins with strength and strengtheneth her arms. She perceiveth that her merchandise is good, her candle goeth not out by night. She layeth her hands to the spindle and her hands hold the distaff. She stretcheth out her hand to the poor, yea, she reacheth forth her hands to the needy. She is not afraid of the snow for her household, for all her household are clothed with scarlet. She maketh herself coverings of tapestry, her clothing is silk and purple. Her husband is known in the gates when he sitteth among the elders of the land. She maketh fine linen, and selleth it, and delivereth girdles unto the merchant. Strength and honor are her clothing and she shall rejoice in time to come. She openeth her mouth with wisdom and in her tongue is the law of kindness. She looketh well to the ways of her household and eateth not the bread of idleness. Her children arise up and call her blessed, her husband also, and he praiseth her. Many daughters have done virtuously, but thou excellest them all. Favor is deceitful and beauty is vain, but a woman that feareth the Lord, she shall be praised. Give her of the fruit of her hands and let her own works praise her in the gates.

9 *The Proverbs of Joseph Smith, Jr.*

1. Never exact of a friend in adversity what you would require in prosperity.
2. If a man prove himself to be honest in his deal and an enemy come upon him wickedly, through fraud or false pretences and because he is stronger than he, maketh him his prisoner and spoil him with his goods, never say unto that man in the day of his adversity, Pay me what thou owest, for if thou doest it, thou addest a deeper wound and condemnation shall come upon thee and thy riches shall be justified in the days of thine adversity if they mock at thee.
3. Never afflict thy soul for what an enemy hath put it out of thy power to do, if thy desires are ever so just.
4. Let thy hand never fail to hand out that that thou owest while it is yet within thy grasp to do so, but when thy stocks fails, say to thy heart, Be strong, and to thine anxieties, Cease, for man, what is he? He is but dung upon the earth and although he demand of thee the cattle of a thousand hills, he cannot possess himself of his own life. God made him and thee and gave all things in common.
5. There is one thing under the sun which I have learned and that is that the righteousness of man is sin because it exacteth over much. Nevertheless, the righteousness of God is just because it exacteth nothing at all, but sendeth the rain on the just and the unjust, seed time and harvest, for all of which man is ungrateful.

10 *The Proverbs of Denver Snuffer, Jr.*

1. The things of God really are of deep import. Only time, experience, and careful, ponderous and solemn thoughts can find them out, provided, of course, there is a real desire to know the things of God accompanied by obedience to His commandments. If you don't desire them, you won't ask and won't receive. And if you do desire them, you will ask and you will obey. It is self-regulated, in that sense. Everyone decides for themselves just how much of an advantage in the world to come they are willing to acquire here.
2. Freedom of agency really means accountability. That is its chief meaning. Unfortunately, because of political debate, it has assumed a much less

rigorous meaning. We are free, therefore we are accountable before God for all our acts. The Atonement alone affords us relief from that accountability. Taking advantage of the Atonement for that purpose requires us to obey Christ's conditions.

3. It is not true that "seeing is believing." Rather, believing is to see. Belief will open your eyes. The Voice, three levels removed from us, is regained by your election to remove the veil that bars your hearing and your sight.
4. It is a veil and not a wall you must pass through. You elect whether or not you will pass through.
5. There is no one, other than you, who can make the decision to go forward, It is far more frightening to persist through the veil than to remain without a view of Heaven.
6. Revelation from Heaven is also a revelation of yourself. For as you see Him, you see most clearly how very limited and dependent you are upon Him. You cannot be prideful after seeing yourself alongside Him.
7. Heaven is steeped in ceremonial rites intended to preserve and declare the Glory of God and the wisdom of His acts. The depth, heights and majesty of His undertakings are beyond man's comprehension. Words fail in the attempt. It is best understood by seeing and not to be otherwise understood.
8. God wants for us to understand Him. He is eager to meet with and touch us, as we should be to know and touch Him.
9. God loves His children equally, but we love Him unequally in return. If we would love Him as He loves us, we would leap into His open arms and rejoice in the touch of our Lord.
10. He bears seven wounds on His person: Two in His wrists, two in His palms, two in His feet, and one in His side. Seven is the symbolic number of completion or perfection. Seven wounds reflect the completion of His sacrifice and of that sacrifice's complete perfection.
11. Christ's sacrifice has completely healed all that the Fall of Adam brought to pass. As Adam went before, So Christ came after, the one the antithesis of the other, and both making this creation a chiasm of Fall and Redemption. We stand in the center, where it is all in balance about us.
12. The balance between Adam's Fall and Christ's sacrifice provides a neutral balance of opposites. We choose what we are willing to do with this balanced universe.
13. We tip the scales by our choices, and by so doing, we change all eternity. We change eternity by the choices we make here.
14. There is an Eternal balance, with infinite results, hanging on our every choice. We stand in peril or stand in glory depending on our every thought and deed.
15. Five minutes of mortality are more precious than all the prior eternities of pre-earth life. Only here can you demonstrate the faith from which creation itself was born.
16. Our failures are mourned in the corridors of Heaven with groans for our shortcom-ings. We have angels and gods wishing our choices were always tipping the scale of balance in this life in favor of obedience to God.
17. Our noble acts and righteous deeds are celebrated in joy and song in the corridors of Heaven. As we choose God and His ways, the Hosanna Shout rings out in heaven for such choices. We are the place where eternity's conflicts are now being played out. We are the battleground between infinite good and infinite failure.
18. Life is an open book test. We only need to realize the test is underway to be able to pass it.
19. Joy cannot be found by subordinating the spirit to the flesh. Joy, peace and freedom come only by subordinating the flesh to the spirit.

20 The meekness of the Lord as He supplicates us to follow Him is because of the great worth of souls. That great worth has been poured into us by the bitter cup from which He drank. Every person who has ever lived is an infinite creation.
21 Within the coupling of the man and woman in the Lord there is found all eternity. Together they are infinite. The temple rites are intended to establish this infinite and Eternal union.
22 Adam and Eve were given by God to each other before death entered into creation. Had there been no Fall, the man and woman would have remained together forever.
23 The Eternal union of man and woman is a return to Eden before the Fall. The Temple and the ordinances found there are, for us, the return to Eden before the Fall and the completion of creation through the union of man and woman in an infinite covenant.
24 Heaven does not need to await the afterlife, but you can be redeemed from the Fall here and now. Receiving the presence of God is to be redeemed from the Fall.
25 The millennium will happen as people prepare themselves for it. When the wheat is fully ripe, the Lord will return. You can receive millennial blessings through the Second Comforter now.
26 It would do little good to have the Lord return if there were not people prepared and awaiting His presence. If that were to occur before people are prepared, the whole earth would be wasted at His coming.
27 If you would have Him return, then you must prepare individually to abide His coming. When you are ready, He will return.
28 There is nothing hidden but what will be made known, but it is up to you to be willing to see and receive what is hidden.
29 God hides most things in plain sight. It is up to you to be willing to draw back the veil and see them.
30 The religiously blind refuse to see. Blindness born from religious error is the most recalcitrant form of the disease.
31 Knowledge of the mysteries of godliness is obtained only through obedience to God. He ordained this method to make His greatest truths universally available to all His training for the ministry.
32 Education is no real advantage in receiving light and truth from God. Humility is the only real, great advantage that any soul ever possesses.
33 Since God is no respecter of persons, He has ordained truth to come to us without respect to persons. Whatever truths may exist, His true followers seek after these things and find they are freely given.
34 In order to go forward, you must go back. Without a return to the humility and faith of childhood you will not be able to see Him.
35 When we elect to receive Him, He elects at that moment to receive us. We determine whether we are "elect" by our own election to receive Him.
36 The proud will fail. Their failure will come as a natural consequence of their unfitness to be in God's presence. Their pride will keep them from doing what is required to be in His presence. Had Naaman not returned to wash himself seven times in the Jordan River, he would have died a leper. Many of us die lepers because we find such things as dipping in rivers childish. Too often we join Naaman in asking, "Are not Abana and Pharpar, river of Damascus, better than all the waters of Israel? May I not wash in them, and be clean?" and join him too in reacting, "So he turned and went his way in a rage." Be humble enough to do as true prophets ask you and submit to the laws and ordinances of the Gospel. You will be healed if you do.

37 You must choose your world: this one or the next. You cannot choose both.
38 Your past controls your now. You can only control the future by what you do now. But what you do 'now' controls all of eternity.
39 The most important lessons in life, shedding the greatest light, are almost invariably the most painful. That is as it should be. Christ learned the most because of what He suffered.
40 Things which seem perfectly normal here in mortality are completely mad when viewed from eternity. Had the rich man of the parable a broader view of things, he would have treated his beggar Lazarus more kindly. By the time his omission became clear to him, it was too late to repair.
41 While mortal we are all rich because it lies within each of us to help others.
42 We are better off taking advice and instruction from God than giving it to Him. Most of mankind is unwilling to accept advice and instruction from Him, and therefore they never hear Him.
43 The restoration of the gospel through Joseph Smith contains His tools for approaching Him.
44 We are told to study out of "the best books." In this dispensation, apart from the scriptures themselves, very few have been written.

ECCLESIASTES or THE PREACHER

The words of the Preacher, the son of David, king in Jerusalem.

VANITY of vanities, saith the Preacher, vanity of vanities, all is vanity. What profit hath a man of all his labor which he taketh under the sun?
One generation passeth away and another generation cometh, but the Earth abideth forever. The sun also ariseth and the sun goeth down and hasteth to his place where he arose. The wind goeth toward the south and turneth about unto the north, it whirleth about continually and the wind returneth again according to his circuits. All the rivers run into the sea, yet the sea in not full, unto the place from whence the rivers come, thither they return again. All things are full of labor, man cannot utter it, the eye is not satisfied with seeing, nor the ear filled with hearing. The thing that hath been, it is that which shall be, and that which is done is that which shall be done and there is no new thing under the sun. Is there anything whereof it may be said, See, this is new? It hath been already of old time which was before us. There is no remembrance of former things, neither shall there be any remembrance of things that are to come with those that shall come after.

I, the Preacher, was king over Israel in Jerusalem. And I gave my heart to seek and search out by wisdom concerning all things that are done under Heaven, this sore travail hath God given to the sons of man to be exercised therewith. I have seen all the works that are done under the sun and behold, all is vanity and vexation of spirit. That which is crooked cannot be made straight and that which is wanting cannot be numbered. I communed with mine own heart saying, Lo, I am come to great estate and have gotten more wisdom than all they that have been before me in Jerusalem, yea, my heart had great experience of wisdom and knowledge. And I gave my heart to know wisdom and to know madness and folly; I perceived that this also is vexation of spirit. For in much wisdom is much grief and he that increaseth knowledge increaseth sorrow.

I said in mine heart, Go to now, I will prove thee with mirth, therefore enjoy pleasure and behold, this also is vanity. I said of laughter, It is mad, and of mirth, What doeth it? I sought in mine heart to give myself unto wine, yet acquainting mine heart with wisdom, and to lay hold on folly till I might see what was that good for the sons of men which they should do under the Heaven all the days of their life. I made me great works, I builded me houses, I planted me vineyards, I made me gardens and orchards, and I planted trees in them of all kind of fruits. I made me pools of water to water therewith the wood that bringeth forth trees, I got me servants and maidens and had servants born in my house, also I had great possessions of great and small cattle above all that were in Jerusalem before me. I gathered me also silver and gold and the peculiar treasure of kings and of the provinces, I gat me men singers and women singers, and the delights of the sons of men, as musical instruments, and that of all sorts. So I was great, and increased more than all that were before me in Jerusalem, also my wisdom remained with me. And whatsoever mine eyes desired I kept not from them, I withheld not my heart from any joy, for my heart rejoiced in all my labor and this was my portion of all my labor. Then I looked on all the works that my hands had wrought and on the labor that I had labored to do and behold, all was vanity and vexation of spirit and there was no profit under the sun.

And I turned myself to behold wisdom, and madness, and folly, for what can the man do that cometh after the king? Even that which hath been already done. Then I saw that wisdom excelleth folly as far as light excelleth darkness. The wise man's eyes are in his head, but the fool walketh in darkness and I myself perceived also that one event happeneth to them all. Then said I in my heart, As it happeneth to the fool, so it happeneth even to me and why was I then more wise? Then I said in my heart that this also is vanity. For there is no remembrance of the wise more than of the fool forever, seeing that which now is in the days to come shall all be forgotten. And how dieth the wise man? As the fool. Therefore I hated life, because the work that is wrought under the sun is grievous unto me, for all is vanity and vexation of spirit. Yea, I hated all my labor which I had taken under the sun because I should leave it unto the man that shall be after me. And who knoweth whether he shall be a wise man or a fool? Yet shall he have rule over all my labor wherein I have labored and wherein I have showed myself wise under the sun. This is also vanity. Therefore I went about to cause my heart to despair of all the labor which I took under the sun. For there is a man whose labor is in wisdom, and in knowledge, and in equity, yet to a man that hath not labored therein shall he leave it for his portion. This also is vanity and a great evil. For what hath man of all his labor and of the vexation of his heart wherein he hath labored under the sun? For all his days are sorrows and his travail grief, yea, his heart taketh not rest in the night. This is also vanity.

2 THERE is nothing better for a man than that he should eat and drink and that he should make his soul enjoy good in his labor. This also I saw, that it was from the hand of God. For who can eat or who else can hasten hereunto more than I? For God giveth to a man that is good in his sight, wisdom, and knowledge, and joy, but to the sinner he giveth travail, to gather, and to heap up, that he may give to him that is good before God. This also is vanity and vexation of spirit.

> To everything there is a season and a time to every purpose under Heaven:
> A time to be born and a time to die,
> a time to plant and a time to pluck up that which is planted,
> a time to kill and a time to heal,
> a time to break down and a time to build up,
> a time to weep and a time to laugh,
> a time to mourn and a time to dance,

a time to cast away stones and a time to gather stones together,
a time to embrace and a time to refrain from embracing,
a time to get and a time to lose,
a time to keep and a time to cast away,
a time to rend and a time to sew,
a time to keep silence and a time to speak,
a time to love and a time to hate,
a time of war and a time of peace.

What profit hath he that worketh in that wherein he laboreth?
I have seen the travail, which God hath given to the sons of men to be exercised in it. He hath made everything beautiful in his time, also he hath set the world in their heart so that no man can find out the work that God maketh from the beginning to the end. I know that there is no good in them but for a man to rejoice and to do good in his life. And also that every man should eat and drink and enjoy the good of all his labor, it is the gift of God. I know that whatsoever God doeth it shall be forever, nothing can be put to it, nor anything taken from it, and God doeth it that men should fear before him. That which hath been is now, and that which is to be hath already been, and God requireth that which is past.

And moreover I saw under the sun the place of judgment, that wickedness was there, and the place of righteousness, that iniquity was there. I said in mine heart, God shall judge the righteous and the wicked, for there is a time there for every purpose and for every work.

I said in mine heart concerning the estates of the sons of men that God might manifest them and that they might see that they themselves are beasts. For that which befalleth the sons of men befalleth beasts, even one thing befalleth them: as the one dieth, so dieth the other, yea, they have all one breath so that a man hath no pre-eminence above a beast, for all is vanity. All go unto one place, all are of the dust, and all turn to dust again. Who knoweth the spirit of man that goeth upward and the spirit of the beast that goeth downward to the Earth? Wherefore I perceive that there is nothing better than that a man should rejoice in his own works, for that is his portion, for who shall bring him to see what shall be after him?

3 SO I returned and considered all the oppressions that are done under the sun, and behold the tears of such as were oppressed, and they had no comforter, and on the side of their oppressors there was power, but they had no comforter. Wherefore I praised the dead which are already dead, more than the living which are yet alive. Yea, better is he than both they, which hath not yet been, who hath not seen the evil work that is done under the sun.

Again, I considered all travail and every right work, that for this a man is envied of his neighbor. This is also vanity and vexation of spirit. The fool foldeth his hands together and eateth his own flesh. Better is a handful with quietness than both the hands full with travail and vexation of spirit.

Then I returned and I saw vanity under the sun. There is one alone and there is not a second, yea, he hath neither child nor brother, yet is there no end of all his labor, neither is his eye satisfied with riches, neither saith he, For whom do I labor and bereave my soul of good? This is also vanity, yea, it is a sore travail. Two are better than one because they have a good reward for their labor. For if they fall, the one will lift up his fellow, but wo to him that is alone when he falleth, for he hath not another to help him up. Again, if two lie together, then they have heat, but how can one be warm alone? And if one prevail against him, two shall withstand him and a threefold cord is not quickly broken.

Better is a poor and a wise child than an old and foolish king who will no more be admonished. For out of prison he cometh to reign, whereas also he that is born in his kingdom becometh poor. I considered all the living which walk under the sun with the second child that shall stand up in his stead. There is no end of all the people, even of all that have been before them, they also that come after shall not rejoice in him. Surely this also is vanity and vexation of spirit.

Keep thy foot when thou goest to the house of God and be more ready to hear than to give the sacrifice of fools, for they consider not that they do evil. Be not rash with thy mouth and let not thine heart be hasty to utter anything before God, for God is in Heaven and thou upon Earth, therefore let thy words be few. For a dream cometh through the multitude of business and a fool's voice is known by multitude of words. When thou vowest a vow unto God, defer not to pay it, for he hath no pleasure in fools; pay that which thou hast vowed. Better is it that thou shouldest not vow than that thou shouldest vow and not pay. Suffer not thy mouth to cause thy flesh to sin, neither say thou before the angel that it was an error; wherefore should God be angry at thy voice and destroy the work of thine hands? For in the multitude of dreams and many words there are also divers vanities, but fear thou God.

If thou seest the oppression of the poor and violent perverting of judgment and justice in a province, marvel not at the matter, for he that is higher than the highest regardeth and there be higher than they.

Moreover the profit of the Earth is for all, the king himself is served by the field. He that loveth silver shall not be satisfied with silver, nor he that loveth abundance with increase, this is also vanity. When goods increase they are increased that eat them, and what good is there to the owners thereof saving the beholding of them with their eyes? The sleep of a laboring man is sweet, whether he eat little or much, but the abundance of the rich will not suffer him to sleep.

There is a sore evil which I have seen under the sun, namely riches kept for the owners thereof to their hurt. But those riches perish by evil travail, and he begetteth a son and there is nothing in his hand. As he came forth of his mother's womb, naked shall he return to go as he came and shall take nothing of his labor which he may carry away in his hand. And this also is a sore evil, that in all points as he came so shall he go, and what profit hath he that hath labored for the wind? All his days also he eateth in darkness and he hath much sorrow and wrath with his sickness.

Behold that which I have seen, it is good and comely for one to eat and to drink and to enjoy the good of all his labor that he taketh under the sun all the days of his life which God giveth him, for it is his portion. Every man also to whom God hath given riches and wealth, and hath given him power to eat thereof, and to take his portion, and to rejoice in his labor, this is the gift of God. For he shall not much remember the days of his life because God answereth him in the joy of his heart.

There is an evil which I have seen under the sun and it is common among men, a man to whom God hath given riches, wealth, and honor, so that he wanteth nothing for his soul of all that he desireth, yet God giveth him not power to eat thereof, but a stranger eateth it, this is vanity and it is an evil disease. If a man beget a hundred children, and live many years so that the days of his years be many, and his soul be not filled with good, and also that he have no burial, I say that an untimely birth is better than he. For he cometh in with vanity and departeth in darkness, and his name shall be covered with darkness. Moreover he hath not seen the sun, nor known anything, this hath more rest than the other. Yea, though he live a thousand years twice told, yet hath he seen no good; do not all go to one place?

All the labor of man is for his mouth and yet the appetite is not filled. For what hath the wise more than the fool? What hath the poor, that knoweth to walk before the living? Better is the sight of the eyes than the wandering of the desire, this is also vanity and vexation of spirit. That which hath been is named already and it is known that it is man, neither may he contend with him that is mightier than he. Seeing there be many things that increase vanity, what is man the better? For who knoweth what is good for man in this life, all the days of his vain life which he spendeth as a shadow? For who can tell a man what shall be after him under the sun?

A good name is better than precious ointment and the day of death than the day of one's birth. It is better to go to the house of mourning than to go to the house of feasting, for that is the end of all men and the living will lay it to his heart. Sorrow is better than laughter, for by the sadness of the countenance the heart is made better. The heart of the wise is in the house of mourning, but the heart of fools is in the house of mirth. It is better to hear the rebuke of the wise than for a man to hear the song of fools, for as the crackling of thorns under a pot, so is the laughter of the fool; this also is vanity.

Surely oppression maketh a wise man mad and a gift destroyeth the heart. Better is the end of a thing than the beginning thereof and the patient in spirit is better than the proud in spirit. Be not hasty in thy spirit to be angry, for anger resteth in the bosom of fools. Say not thou, What is the cause that the former days were better than these? For thou dost not inquire wisely concerning this. Wisdom is good with an inheritance and by it there is profit to them that see the sun. For wisdom is a defense and money is a defense, but the excellency of knowledge is that wisdom giveth life to them that have it. Consider the work of God, for who can make that straight which he hath made crooked? In the day of prosperity be joyful, but in the day of adversity consider; God also hath set the one over against the other to the end that man should find nothing after him.

All things have I seen in the days of my vanity, there is a just man that perisheth in his righteousness and there is a wicked man that prolongeth his life in his wickedness. Be not righteous overmuch, neither make thyself overwise; why shouldest thou destroy thyself? Be not overmuch wicked, neither be thou foolish; why shouldest thou die before thy time? It is good that thou shouldest take hold of this, yea, also from this withdraw not thine hand, for he that feareth God shall come forth of them all. Wisdom strengtheneth the wise more than ten mighty men which are in the city. For there is not a just man upon Earth that doeth good and sinneth not. Also take no heed unto all words that are spoken, lest thou hear thy servant curse thee, for oftentimes also thine own heart knoweth that thou thyself likewise hast cursed others.

All this have I proved by wisdom, I said, I will be wise, but it was far from me. That which is far off and exceeding deep, who can find it out? I applied mine heart to know, and to search, and to seek out wisdom, and the reason of things, and to know the wickedness of folly, even of foolishness and madness, and I find more bitter than death the woman whose heart is snares and nets, and her hands as bands; whoso pleaseth God shall escape from her, but the sinner shall be taken by her. Behold, this have I found, saith the Preacher, counting one by one to find out the account which yet my soul seeketh, but I find not one man among a thousand have I found, but a woman among all those have I not found. Lo, this only have I found, that God hath made man upright, but they have sought out many inventions.

Who is as the wise man? And who knoweth the interpretation of a thing? A man's wisdom maketh his face to shine and the boldness of his face shall be changed. I counsel thee to keep the king's commandment, and that in regard of the oath of God. Be not hasty to go out of his sight, stand not in an evil thing, for he doeth whatsoever pleaseth him. Where the word of a king is, there is power, and who may say unto him, What doest thou? Whoso keepeth the commandment shall feel no evil thing and a wise man's heart discerneth both time and judgment.

Because to every purpose there is time and judgment, therefore the misery of man is great upon him. For he knoweth not that which shall be, for who can tell him when it shall be? There is no man that hath power over the spirit to retain the spirit, neither hath he power in the day of death, and there is no discharge in that war, neither shall wickedness deliver those that are given to it. All this have I seen and applied my heart unto every work that is done under the sun, there is a time wherein one man ruleth over another to his own hurt. And so I saw the wicked buried who had come and gone from the place of the holy and they were forgotten in the city where they had so done, this is also vanity.

Because sentence against an evil work is not executed speedily, therefore the heart of the sons of men is fully set in them to do evil. Though a sinner do evil a hundred times and his days be prolonged, yet surely I know that it shall be well with them that fear God which fear before him, but it shall not be well with the wicked, neither shall he prolong his days which are as a shadow because he feareth not before God.

There is a vanity which is done upon the earth, that there be just men unto whom it happeneth according to the work of the wicked, again, there be wicked men, to whom it happeneth according to the work of the righteous; I said that this also is vanity. Then I commended mirth because a man hath no better thing under the sun than to eat, and to drink, and to be merry, for that shall abide with him of his labor the days of his life which God giveth him under the sun.

When I applied mine heart to know wisdom and to see the business that is done upon the earth (for also there is that neither day nor night seeth sleep with his eyes), then I beheld all the work of God, that a man cannot find out the work that is done under the sun because though a man labor to seek it out, yet he shall not find it, yea further, though a wise man think to know it, yet shall he not be able to find it.

For all this I considered in my heart even to declare all this, that the righteous, and the wise, and their works are in the hand of God, no man knoweth either love or hatred by all that is before them. All things come alike to all: there is one event to the righteous and to the wicked, to the good and to the clean and to the unclean, to him that sacrificeth, and to him that sacrificeth not, as is the good so is the sinner, and he that sweareth as he that feareth an oath. This is an evil among all things that are done under the sun, that there is one event unto all, yea, also the heart of the sons of men is full of evil, and madness is in their heart while they live, and after that they go to the dead. For to him that is joined to all the living there is hope, for a living dog is better than a dead lion. For the living know that they shall die, but the dead know not anything, neither have they anymore a reward, for the memory of them is forgotten. Also their love, and their hatred, and their envy is now perished, neither have they anymore a portion for ever in anything that is done under the sun.

Go thy way, eat thy bread with joy, and drink thy wine with a merry heart, for God now accepteth thy works. Let thy garments be always white and let thy head lack no ointment. Live joyfully with the wife whom thou lovest all the days of the life of thy vanity which he hath given thee under the sun, all the days of thy vanity, for that is thy portion in this life and in thy labor which thou takest under the sun. Whatsoever thy hand findeth to do, do it with thy might, for there is no work, nor device, nor knowledge, nor wisdom in the grave whither thou goest.

I returned and saw under the sun that the race is not to the swift, nor the battle to the strong, neither yet bread to the wise, nor yet riches to men of understanding, nor yet favor to men of skill, but time and chance happeneth to them all. For man also knoweth not his time, as the fishes that are taken in an evil net, and as the birds that are caught in the snare, so are the sons of men snared in an evil time when it falleth suddenly upon them.

This wisdom have I seen also under the sun and it seemed great unto me: there was a little city and few men within it and there came a great king against it, and besieged it, and built great bulwarks against it. Now there was found in it a poor wise man and he by his wisdom delivered the city, yet no man remembered that same poor man. Then said I, Wisdom is better than strength, nevertheless the poor man's wisdom is despised and his words are not heard. The words of wise men are heard in quiet more than the cry of him that ruleth among fools. Wisdom is better than weapons of war, but one sinner destroyeth much good.

Dead flies cause the ointment of the apothecary to send forth a stinking savor, so doth a little folly him that is in reputation for wisdom and honor.

A wise man's heart is at his right hand, but a fool's heart at his left. Yea also, when he that is a fool walketh by the way, his wisdom faileth him and he saith to everyone that he is a fool.

If the spirit of the ruler rise up against thee, leave not thy place, for yielding pacifieth great offenses.

There is an evil which I have seen under the sun as an error which proceedeth from the ruler, folly is set in great dignity and the rich sit in low place. I have seen servants upon horses and princes walking as servants upon the Earth.

He that diggeth a pit shall fall into it and whoso breaketh a hedge, a serpent shall bite him. Whoso removeth stones shall be hurt therewith and he that cleaveth wood shall be endangered thereby.

If the iron be blunt and he do not whet the edge, then must he put to more strength, but wisdom is profitable to direct.

Surely the serpent will bite without enchantment and a babbler is no better. The words of a wise man's mouth are gracious, but the lips of a fool will swallow up himself. The beginning of the words of his mouth is foolishness and the end of his talk is mischievous madness. A fool also is full of words, a man cannot tell what shall be, and what shall be after him, who can tell him? The labor of the foolish wearieth every one of them because he knoweth not how to go to the city.

Wo to thee, O land, when thy king is a child and thy princes eat in the morning. Blessed art thou, O land, when thy king is the son of nobles and thy princes eat in due season, for strength and not for drunkenness.

By much slothfulness the building decayeth and through idleness of the hands the house droppeth through.

A feast is made for laughter and wine maketh merry, but money answereth all things.

Curse not the king, no not in thy thought and curse not the rich in thy bedchamber, for a bird of the air shall carry the voice and that which hath wings shall tell the matter.

Cast thy bread upon the waters, for thou shalt find it after many days. Give a portion to seven and also to eight, for thou knowest not what evil shall be upon the earth. If the clouds be full of rain, they empty themselves upon the Earth, and if the tree fall toward the south or toward the north, in the place where the tree falleth there it shall be. He that observeth the wind shall not sow and he that regardeth the clouds shall not reap. As thou knowest not what is the way of the spirit, nor how the bones do grow in the womb of her that is with child, even so thou knowest not the works of God who maketh all. In the morning sow thy seed and in the evening withhold not thine hand, for thou knowest not whether shall prosper either this or that, or whether they both shall be alike good.

Truly the light is sweet and a pleasant thing it is for the eyes to behold the sun, but if a man live many years and rejoice in them all, yet let him remember the days of darkness, for they shall be many. All that cometh is vanity.

Rejoice, O young man, in thy youth and let thy heart cheer thee in the days of thy youth, and walk in the ways of thine heart, and in the sight of thine eyes, but know thou that for all these things God will bring thee into judgment. Therefore remove sorrow from thy heart and put away evil from thy flesh, for childhood and youth are vanity.

Remember now thy Creator in the days of thy youth while the evil days come not, nor the years draw nigh, when thou shalt say, I have no pleasure in them while the sun, or the light, or the moon, or the stars be not darkened, nor the clouds return after the rain, in the day when the keepers of the house shall tremble and the strong men shall bow themselves, and the grinders cease because they are few, and those that look out of the windows be darkened. And the doors shall be shut in the streets when the sound of the grinding is low, and he shall rise up at the voice of the bird and all the daughters of music shall be brought low, also when they shall be afraid of that which is high, and fears shall be in the way, and the almond tree shall flourish, and the grasshopper shall be a burden and desire shall fail, because man goeth to his long home and the mourners go about the streets, or ever the silver cord be loosed, or the golden bowl be broken, or the pitcher be broken at the fountain, or the wheel broken at the cistern. Then shall the dust return to the earth as it was and the spirit shall return unto God who gave it.

Vanity of vanities, saith the Preacher, all is vanity.

And moreover, because the Preacher was wise, he still taught the people knowledge, yea, he gave good heed, and sought out, and set in order many proverbs. The Preacher sought to find out acceptable words, and that which was written was upright, even words of truth. The words of the wise are as goads and as nails fastened by the masters of assemblies which are given from one shepherd. And further, by these, my son, be admonished, of making many books there is no end and much study is a weariness of the flesh.

Let us hear the conclusion of the whole matter: Fear God and keep his commandments, for this is the whole duty of man. For God shall bring every work into judgment with every secret thing, whether it be good or whether it be evil.

THE BOOK OF THE PROPHET ISAIAH

THE vision of Isaiah the son of Amoz, which he saw concerning Judah and Jerusalem in the days of Uzziah, Jotham, Ahaz, and Hezekiah, kings of Judah. Hear, O heavens, and give ear, O earth, for the Lord hath spoken, I have nourished and brought up children, and they have rebelled against me. The ox knoweth his owner, and the ass his master's crib, but Israel doth not know, my people doth not consider. Ah sinful nation, a people laden with iniquity, a seed of evildoers, children that are corrupters, they have forsaken the Lord, they have provoked the Holy One of Israel unto anger, they are gone away backward. Why should ye be stricken anymore? ye will revolt more and more, the whole head is sick, and the whole heart faint. From the sole of the foot even unto the head there is no soundness in it, but wounds, and bruises, and putrifying sores, they have not been closed, neither bound up, neither mollified with ointment. Your country is desolate, your cities are burned with fire, your land, strangers devour it in your presence, and it is desolate, as overthrown by strangers. And the daughter of Zion is left as a cottage in a vineyard, as a lodge in a garden of cucumbers, as a besieged city. Except the Lord of hosts had left unto us a very small remnant, we should have been as Sodom, and we should have been like unto Gomorrah.

Hear the word of the Lord, ye rulers of Sodom, give ear unto the law of our God, ye people of Gomorrah. To what purpose is the multitude of your sacrifices unto me? saith the Lord, I am full of the burnt offerings of rams, and the fat of fed beasts, and I delight not in the blood of bullocks, or of lambs, or of he goats. When ye come to appear before me, who hath required this at your hand, to tread my courts? Bring no more vain oblations, incense is an abomination unto me, the new moons and sabbaths, the calling of assemblies, I cannot away with, it is iniquity, even the solemn meeting. Your new moons and your appointed feasts my soul hateth, they are a trouble unto me, I am weary to bear them. And when ye spread forth your hands, I will hide mine eyes from you, yea, when ye make many prayers, I will not hear, your hands are full of blood.

Wash ye, make you clean, put away the evil of your doings from before mine eyes, cease to do evil, learn to do well, seek judgment, relieve the oppressed, judge the fatherless, plead for the widow. Come now, and let us reason together, saith the Lord, though your sins be as scarlet, they shall be as white as snow, though they be red like crimson, they shall be as wool. If ye be willing and obedient, ye shall eat the good of the land, but if ye refuse and rebel, ye shall be devoured with the sword, for the mouth of the Lord hath spoken it.

How is the faithful city become a harlot! it was full of judgment, righteousness lodged in it, but now murderers. Thy silver is become dross, thy wine mixed with water, thy princes are rebellious, and companions of thieves, everyone loveth gifts, and followeth after rewards, they judge not the fatherless, neither doth the cause of the widow come unto them. Therefore saith the Lord, the Lord of hosts, the Mighty One of Israel, Ah, I will ease me of mine adversaries, and avenge me of mine enemies. And I will turn my hand upon thee, and purely purge away thy dross, and take away all thy tin, and I will restore thy judges as at the first, and thy counselors as at the beginning, afterward thou shalt be called, The city of righteousness the faithful city. Zion shall be redeemed with judgment, and her converts with righteousness. And the destruction of the transgressors and of the sinners shall be together, and they that forsake the Lord shall be consumed. For they shall be ashamed of the oaks which ye have desired, and ye shall be confounded for the gardens that ye have chosen. For ye shall be as an oak whose leaf fadeth, and as a garden that hath no water. And the strong shall be as tow, and the maker of it as a spark, and they shall both burn together, and none shall quench them.

The word that Isaiah the son of Amoz saw concerning Judah and Jerusalem. And it shall come to pass in the last days when the mountain of the Lord's house shall be established in the top of the mountains, and shall be exalted above the hills, and all nations shall flow unto it, and many people shall go and say, Come ye, and let us go up to the mountain of the Lord, to the house of the God of Jacob, and he will teach us of his ways, and we will walk in his paths, for out of Zion shall go forth the law, and the word of the Lord from Jerusalem, and he shall judge among the nations, and shall rebuke many people, and they shall beat their swords into ploughshares, and their spears into pruning hooks, nation shall not lift up sword against nation, neither shall they learn war anymore.

O house of Jacob, come ye, and let us walk in the light of the Lord, yea, come, for ye have all gone astray, everyone to his wicked ways. Therefore, O Lord, thou hast forsaken thy people the house of Jacob, because they be replenished from the east, and hearken unto the soothsayers like the Philistines, and they please themselves in the children of strangers. Their land also is full of silver and gold, neither is there any end of their treasures, their land is also full of horses, neither is there any end of their chariots, their land also is full of idols, they worship the work of their own hands, that which their own fingers have made. And the mean man boweth not down, and the great man humbleth himself not, therefore forgive them not.

O ye wicked ones, enter into the rock, and hide ye in the dust, for the fear of the Lord and his majesty shall smite thee. And it shall come to pass that the lofty looks of man shall be humbled, and the haughtiness of man shall be bowed down, and the Lord alone shall be exalted in that day. For the day of the Lord of hosts soon cometh upon all nations, yea, upon everyone, yea, upon the proud and lofty, and upon everyone who is lifted up, and he shall be brought low. Yea, and the day of the Lord shall come upon all the cedars of Lebanon, for they are high and lifted up, and upon all the oaks of Bashan, and upon all the high mountains, and upon all the hills, and upon all the nations which are lifted up, and upon every people, and upon every high tower, and upon every fenced wall, and upon all the ships of the sea, and upon all the ships of Tarshish, and upon all pleasant pictures. And the loftiness of man shall be bowed down, and the haughtiness of men shall be made low, and the Lord alone shall be exalted in that day. And the idols he shall utterly abolish. And they shall go into the holes of the rocks, and into the caves of the Earth, for the fear of the Lord shall come upon them, and the glory of his majesty shall smite them, when he ariseth to shake terribly the earth. In that day a man shall cast his idols of silver, and his idols of gold, which he hath made for himself to worship, to the moles and to the bats, to go into the clefts of the rocks, and into the tops of the ragged rocks, for the fear of the Lord shall come upon them, and the majesty of the Lord shall smite them, when he ariseth to shake terribly the earth.

Cease ye from man, whose breath is in his nostrils, for wherein is he to be accounted of? For, behold, the Lord, the Lord of hosts, doth take away from Jerusalem and from Judah the stay and the staff, the whole staff of bread, and the whole stay of water, the mighty man, and the man of war, the judge, and the prophet, and the prudent, and the ancient, the captain of fifty, and the honorable man, and the counselor, and the cunning artificer, and the eloquent orator. And I will give children unto them to be their princes, and babes shall rule over them. And the people shall be oppressed, everyone by another, and everyone by his neighbor, the child shall behave himself proudly against the ancient, and the base against the honorable. When a man shall take hold of his brother of the house of his father, and shall say, Thou hast clothing, be thou our ruler, and let not this ruin come under thy hand, in that day shall he swear, saying, I will not be a healer, for in my house there is neither bread nor clothing, make me not a ruler of the people. For Jerusalem is ruined, and Judah is fallen, because their tongues and their doings have been against the Lord, to provoke the eyes of his glory. The show of their countenance doth witness against them, and doth declare their sin to be even as Sodom, they cannot hide it. Wo unto their souls! for they have rewarded evil unto themselves. Say unto the righteous, that it is well with them, for they shall eat the fruit of their doings. Wo unto the wicked! for they shall perish, for the reward of their hands shall be upon them. And as for my people, children are their oppressors, and women rule over them. O my people, they who lead thee cause thee to err, and destroy the way of thy paths.

The Lord standeth up to plead, and standeth to judge the people. The Lord will enter into judgment with the ancients of his people, and the princes thereof, for ye have eaten up the vineyard, and the spoil of the poor is in your houses. What mean ye? Ye beat my people to pieces, and grind the faces of the poor, saith the Lord God of hosts.

Moreover the Lord saith, Because the daughters of Zion are haughty, and walk with stretched-forth necks and wanton eyes, walking and mincing as they go, and making a tinkling with their feet, therefore the Lord will smite with a scab the crown of the head of the daughters of Zion, and the Lord will discover their secret parts. In that day the Lord will take away the bravery of tinkling ornaments, and cauls, and round tires like the moon, the chains, and the bracelets, and the mufflers, the bonnets, and the ornaments of the legs, and the headbands, and the tablets, and the earrings, the rings, and nose jewels, the changeable suits of apparel, and the mantles, and the wimples, and the crisping pins, the glasses, and the fine linen, and the hoods, and the veils. And it shall come to pass, instead of sweet smell there shall be stink, and instead of a girdle a rent, and instead of well-set hair, baldness, and instead of a stomacher a girding of sackcloth, burning instead of beauty. Thy men shall fall by the sword, and thy mighty in the war. And her gates shall lament and mourn, and she shall be desolate, and shall sit upon the ground.

And in that day seven women shall take hold of one man, saying, We will eat our own bread, and wear our own apparel, only let us be called by thy name, to take away our reproach.

In that day shall the branch of the Lord be beautiful and glorious, and the fruit of the Earth shall be excellent and comely to them that are escaped of Israel. And it shall come to pass, they that are left in Zion, and he that remaineth in Jerusalem, shall be called holy, even everyone that is written among the living in Jerusalem, when the Lord shall have washed away the filth of the daughters of Zion, and shall have purged the blood of Jerusalem from the midst thereof by the spirit of judgment, and by the spirit of burning. And the Lord will create upon every dwelling place of mount Zion, and upon her assemblies, a cloud and smoke by day, and the shining of a flaming fire by night, for upon all the glory of Zion shall be a defense. And there shall be a tabernacle for a shadow in the daytime from the heat, and for a place of refuge, and for a covert from storm and from rain.

And then will I sing to my well-beloved a song of my beloved touching his vineyard. My well-beloved hath a vineyard in a very fruitful hill, and he fenced it, and gathered out the stones thereof, and planted it with the choicest vine, and built a tower in the midst of it, and also made a winepress therein, and he looked that it should bring forth grapes, and it brought forth wild grapes. And now, O inhabitants of Jerusalem, and men of Judah, judge, I pray you, betwixt me and my vineyard. What could have been done more to my vineyard, that I have not done in it? wherefore, when I looked that it should bring forth grapes, it brought forth wild grapes. And now go to, I will tell you what I will do to my vineyard, I will take away the hedge thereof, and it shall be eaten up, and I will break down the wall thereof, and it shall be trodden down, and I will lay it waste, it shall not be pruned, nor digged, but there shall come up briers and thorns, I will also command the clouds that they rain no rain upon it. For the vineyard of the Lord of hosts is the house of Israel, and the men of Judah his pleasant plant, and he looked for judgment, but behold oppression, for righteousness, but behold a cry.

Wo unto them that join house to house, that lay field to field, till there can be no place, that they may be placed alone in the midst of the earth. In mine ears said the Lord of hosts, Of a truth many houses shall be desolate, and great and fair cities without inhabitant. Yea, ten acres of vineyard shall yield one bath, and the seed of a homer shall yield an ephah. Wo unto them that rise up early in the morning, that they may follow strong drink, and that continue until night, and wine inflame them! And the harp and the viol, the tabret and pipe, and wine, are in their feasts, but they regard not the work of the Lord, neither consider the operation of his hands. Therefore my people are gone into captivity, because they have no knowledge, and their honorable men are famished, and their multitude dried up with thirst. Therefore hell hath enlarged herself, and opened her mouth without measure, and their glory, and their multitude, and their pomp, and he that rejoiceth, shall descend into it. And the mean man shall be brought down, and the mighty man shall be humbled, and the eyes of the lofty shall be humbled, but the Lord of hosts shall be exalted in judgment, and God that is holy shall be sanctified in righteousness. Then shall the lambs feed after their manner, and the waste places of the fat ones shall strangers eat.

Wo unto them that draw iniquity with cords of vanity, and sin as it were with a cart rope, that say, Let him make speed, and hasten his work, that we may see it, and let the counsel of the Holy One of Israel draw nigh and come, that we may know it.

Wo unto them that call evil good, and good evil, that put darkness for light, and light for darkness, that put bitter for sweet, and sweet for bitter.

Wo unto the wise in their own eyes, and prudent in their own sight! Wo unto the mighty to drink wine, and men of strength to mingle strong drink, which justify the wicked for reward, and take away the righteousness of the righteous from him.

Therefore as the fire devoureth the stubble, and the flame consumeth the chaff, so their root shall be as rottenness, and their blossom shall go up as dust, because they have cast away the law of the Lord of hosts, and despised the word of the Holy One of Israel. Therefore is the anger of the Lord kindled against his people, and he hath stretched forth his hand against them, and hath smitten them, and the hills did tremble, and their carcasses were torn in the midst of the streets. For all this his anger is not turned away, but his hand is stretched out still.

And he will lift up an ensign to the nations from far, and will hiss unto them from the end of the earth, and, behold, they shall come with speed swiftly, none shall be weary nor stumble among them, none shall slumber nor sleep, neither shall the girdle of their loins be loosed, nor the latchet of their shoes be broken, whose arrows shall be sharp, and all their bows bent, and their horses' hooves shall be counted like flint, and their wheels like a whirlwind, their roaring shall be like a lion. They shall roar like young lions, yea, they shall roar, and lay hold of the prey, and shall carry away safe, and none shall deliver. And in that day they shall roar against them like the roaring of the sea, and if they look unto the land, behold darkness and sorrow, and the light is darkened in the heavens thereof.

2 IN the year that king Uzziah died I saw also the Lord sitting upon a throne, high and lifted up, and his train filled the temple. Above it stood the seraphim, each one had six wings, with twain he covered his face, and with twain he covered his feet, and with twain he did fly. And one cried unto another, and said,
> Holy, holy, holy, is the Lord of hosts,
> the whole earth is full of his glory.

And the posts of the door moved at the voice of him that cried, and the house was filled with smoke. Then said I, Wo is me! For I am undone, because I am a man of unclean lips, and I dwell in the midst of a people of unclean lips, for mine eyes have seen the King, the Lord of hosts. Then flew one of the seraphim unto me, having a live coal in his hand, which he had taken with the tongs from off the altar, and he laid it upon my mouth, and said, Lo, this has touched thy lips, and thine iniquity is taken away, and thy sin purged. Also I heard the voice of the Lord, saying, Whom shall I send, and who will go for us? Then said I, Here am I, send me.

And he said, Go, and tell this people, Hear ye indeed, but they understood not, and see ye indeed, but they perceived not. Make the heart of this people fat, and make their ears heavy, and shut their eyes, lest they see with their eyes, and hear with their ears, and understand with their hearts, and convert, and be healed.

Then said I, Lord, how long? And he said, Until the cities be wasted without inhabitant, and the houses without man, And the land be utterly desolate. And the Lord have removed men far away, for there shall be a great forsaking in the midst of the land. But yet in it there shall be a tenth, and they shall return, and shall be eaten, as a teil tree, and as an oak, whose substance is in them, when they cast their leaves, so the holy seed shall be the substance thereof.

3 AND it came to pass in the days of Ahaz the son of Jotham, the son of Uzziah, king of Judah, that Rezin the king of Syria, and Pekah the son of Remaliah, king of Israel, went up toward Jerusalem to war against it, but could not prevail against it. And it was told the house of David, saying, Syria is confederate with Ephraim. And his heart was moved, and the heart of his people, as the trees of the wood are moved with the wind.

Then said the Lord unto Isaiah, Go forth now to meet Ahaz, thou, and Shear-jashub thy son, at the end of the conduit of the upper pool, in the highway of the fuller's field, and say unto him, Take heed, and be quiet, fear not, neither be faint-hearted for the two tails of these smoking firebrands, for the fierce anger of Rezin with Syria, and of the son of Remaliah. Because Syria, Ephraim, and the son of Remaliah, have taken evil counsel against thee, saying, Let us go up against Judah, and vex it, and let us make a breach therein for us, and set a king in the midst of it, yea, even the son of Tabeal, thus saith the Lord God, It shall not stand, neither shall it come to pass. For the head of Syria is Damascus, and the head of Damascus is Rezin, and within threescore and five years shall Ephraim be broken, that it be not a people. And the head of Ephraim is Samaria, and the head of Samaria is Remaliah's son. If ye will not believe, surely ye shall not be established.

Moreover the Lord spake again unto Ahaz, saying, Ask thee a sign of the Lord thy God, ask it either in the depth, or in the height above. But Ahaz said, I will not ask, neither will I tempt the Lord.

And he said, Hear ye now, O house of David, Is it a small thing for you to weary men, but will ye weary my God also? Therefore the Lord himself shall give you a sign: Behold, a virgin shall conceive, and shall bear a son, and shall call his name Immanuel. Butter and honey shall he eat, that he may know to refuse the evil, and to choose the good. For before the child shall know to refuse the evil, and choose the good, the land that thou abhorrest shall be forsaken of both her kings. The Lord shall bring upon thee, and upon thy people, and upon thy father's house, days that have not come, from the day that Ephraim departed from Judah, even the king of Assyria. And it shall come to pass in that day, that the Lord shall hiss for the fly that is in the uttermost part of the rivers of Egypt, and for the bee that is in the land of Assyria. And they shall come, and shall rest all of them in the desolate valleys, and in the holes of the rocks, and upon all thorns, and upon all bushes. In the same day shall the Lord shave with a razor that is hired, namely, by them beyond the river, by the king of Assyria, the head, and the hair of the feet, and it shall also consume the beard. And it shall come to pass in that day, that a man shall nourish a young cow and two sheep. And it shall come to pass, for the abundance of milk that they shall give, he shall eat butter, for butter and honey shall everyone eat that is left in the land. And it shall come to pass in that day that every place shall be, where there were a thousand vines at a thousand silverlings, which shall even be for briers and thorns. With arrows and with bows shall men come thither, because all the land shall become briers and thorns. And on all hills that shall be digged with the mattock, there shall not come thither the fear of briers and thorns, but it shall be for the sending forth of oxen, and for the treading of lesser cattle.

Moreover the word of the Lord said unto me, Take thee a great roll, and write in it with a man's pen concerning Maher-shalal-hash-baz. And I took unto me faithful witnesses to record, Uriah the priest, and Zechariah the son of Jeberechiah. And I went unto the prophetess, and she conceived, and bare a son. Then said the Lord to me, Call his name Maher-shalal-hash-baz. For behold, the child shall not have knowledge to cry, My father, and, My mother, before the riches of Damascus and the spoil of Samaria shall be taken away before the king of Assyria.

The Lord spake also unto me again, saying, Forasmuch as this people refuseth the waters of Shiloah that go softly and rejoice in Rezin and Remaliah's son, now therefore, behold, the Lord bringeth up upon them the waters of the river, strong and many, even the king of Assyria, and all his glory. And he shall come up over all his channels, and go over all his banks, and he shall pass through Judah. He shall overflow and go over, he shall reach even to the neck, and the stretching out of his wings shall fill the breadth of thy land, O Immanuel. Associate yourselves, O ye people, and ye shall be broken in pieces, and give ear, all ye of far countries, gird yourselves, and ye shall be broken in pieces, gird yourselves, and ye shall be broken in pieces. Take counsel together, and it shall come to naught, speak the word, and it shall not stand, for God is with us.

For the Lord spake thus to me with a strong hand, and instructed me that I should not walk in the way of this people, saying, Say ye not, A confederacy, to all them to whom this people shall say, A confederacy, neither fear ye their fear, nor be afraid. Sanctify the Lord of hosts himself, and let him be your fear, and let him be your dread. And he shall be for a sanctuary, but for a stone of stumbling and for a rock of offense to both the houses of Israel, for a gin and for a snare to the inhabitants of Jerusalem. And many among them shall stumble, and fall, and be broken, and be snared, and be taken. Bind up the testimony, seal the law among my disciples. And I will wait upon the Lord, that hideth his face from the house of Jacob, and I will look for him. Behold, I and the children whom the Lord hath given me are for signs and for wonders in Israel from the Lord of hosts, which dwelleth in mount Zion. And when they shall say unto you, Seek unto them that have familiar spirits, and unto wizards that peep and that mutter, should not a people seek unto their God for the living to hear from the dead? To the law and to the testimony, and if they speak not according to this word, it is because there is no light in them. And they shall pass through it, hardly bestead and hungry, and it shall come to pass, that when they shall be hungry, they shall fret themselves, and curse their king and their God, and look upward. And they shall look unto the earth, and behold trouble and darkness, dimness of anguish, and they shall be driven to darkness.

4 NEVERTHELESS the dimness shall not be such as was in her vexation, when at the first he lightly afflicted the land of Zebulun, and the land of Naphtali, and afterward did more grievously afflict her by the way of the Red Sea, beyond Jordan, in Galilee of the nations. The people that walked in darkness have seen a great light, they that dwell in the land of the shadow of death, upon them hath the light shined. Thou hast multiplied the nation, and increased the joy, and they joy before thee, according to the joy in harvest, and as men rejoice when they divide the spoil. For thou hast broken the yoke of his burden, and the staff of his shoulder, the rod of his oppressor, as in the day of Midian. For every battle of the warrior is with confused noise, and garments rolled in blood,

but this shall be with burning and fuel of fire. For unto us a child is born, unto us a son is given, and the government shall be upon his shoulder, and his name shall be called Wonderful Counselor, The mighty God, The everlasting Father, The Prince of Peace. Of the increase of his government and peace there is no end, upon the throne of David, and upon his kingdom, to order it, and to establish it with judgment and with justice from henceforth even forever. The zeal of the Lord of hosts will perform this.

The Lord sent his word unto Jacob and it hath lighted upon Israel. And all the people shall know, even Ephraim and the inhabitant of Samaria, that say in the pride and stoutness of heart, The bricks are fallen down, but we will build with hewn stones, the sycamores are cut down, but we will change them into cedars. Therefore the Lord shall set up the adversaries of Rezin against him, and join his enemies together, the Syrians before, and the Philistines behind, and they shall devour Israel with open mouth. For all this his anger is not turned away, but his hand is stretched out still.

For the people turneth not unto him that smiteth them, neither do they seek the Lord of hosts. Therefore the Lord will cut off from Israel head and tail, branch and rush, in one day. The ancient and honorable, he is the head, and the prophet that teacheth lies, he is the tail. For the leaders of this people cause them to err, and they that are led of them are destroyed. Therefore the Lord shall have no joy in their young men, neither shall have mercy on their fatherless and widows, for every one of them is a hypocrite and an evildoer, and every mouth speaketh folly. For all this his anger is not turned away, but his hand is stretched out still. For wickedness burneth as the fire, it shall devour the briers and thorns, and shall kindle in the thickets of the forest, and they shall mount up like the lifting up of smoke. Through the wrath of the Lord of hosts is the land darkened, and the people shall be as the fuel of the fire, no man shall spare his brother. And he shall snatch on the right hand, and be hungry, and he shall eat on the left hand, and they shall not be satisfied, they shall eat every man the flesh of his own arm, Manasseh, Ephraim, and Ephraim, Manasseh, and they together shall be against Judah. For all this his anger is not turned away, but his hand is stretched out still.

Wo unto them that decree unrighteous decrees, and that write grievousness which they have prescribed, to turn aside the needy from judgment, and to take away the right from the poor of my people, that widows may be their prey, and that they may rob the fatherless! And what will ye do in the day of visitation, and in the desolation which shall come from far? To whom will ye flee for help? and where will ye leave your glory? Without me they shall bow down under the prisoners, and they shall fall under the slain. For all this his anger is not turned away, but his hand is stretched out still.

O Assyrian, the rod of mine anger, and the staff in their hand is mine indignation. I will send him against a hypocritical nation, and against the people of my wrath will I give him a charge, to take the spoil, and to take the prey, and to tread them down like the mire of the streets. Howbeit he meaneth not so, neither doth his heart think so, but in his heart it is to destroy and cut off nations not a few. For he saith, Are not my princes altogether kings? Is not Calno as Carchemish? Is not Hamath as Arpad? is not Samaria as Damascus? As my hand hath founded the kingdoms of the idols, and whose graven images did excel them of Jerusalem and of Samaria, shall I not, as I have done unto Samaria and her idols, so do to Jerusalem and to her idols? Wherefore it shall come to pass, that, when the Lord hath performed his whole work upon Mount Zion and upon Jerusalem, I will punish the fruit of the stout heart of the king of Assyria, and the glory of his high looks. For he saith, By the strength of my hand, and by my wisdom I have done these things, for I am prudent, and I have moved the borders of the people, and have robbed their treasures, and I have put down the inhabitants like a valiant man. And my hand hath found as a nest the riches of the people, and as one gathereth eggs that are left, have I gathered all the earth, and there was none that moved the wing, or opened the mouth, or peeped.

Shall the axe boast itself against him that heweth therewith? Or shall the saw magnify itself against him that shaketh it? As if the rod should shake itself against them that lift it up, or as if the staff should lift up itself, as if it were no wood. Therefore shall the Lord, the Lord of hosts, send among his fat ones leanness, and under his glory he shall kindle a burning like the burning of a fire. And the light of Israel shall be for a fire, and his Holy One for a flame, and it shall burn and devour his thorns and his briers in one day, and shall consume the glory of his forest, and of his fruitful field, both soul and body, and they shall be as when a standard-bearer fainteth. And the rest of the trees of his forest shall be few, that a child may write them.

5 AND it shall come to pass in that day, that the remnant of Israel, and such as are escaped of the house of Jacob, shall no more again stay upon him that smote them, but shall stay upon the Lord, the Holy One of Israel, in truth. The remnant shall return, yea even the remnant of Jacob, unto the mighty God. For though thy people Israel be as the sand of the sea, yet a remnant of them shall return, the consumption decreed shall overflow with righteousness. For the Lord God of hosts shall make a consumption, even determined, in all the land. Therefore thus saith the Lord God of Hosts, O my people that dwellest in Zion, be not afraid of the Assyrian, he shall smite thee with a rod, and shall lift up his staff against thee, after the manner of Egypt. For yet a very little while, and the indignation shall cease, and mine anger in their destruction. And the Lord of hosts shall stir up a scourge for him according to the slaughter of Midian at the rock of Oreb, and as his rod was upon the sea, so shall he lift it up after the manner of Egypt. And it shall come to pass in that day, that his burden shall be taken away from off thy shoulder, and his yoke from off thy neck, and the yoke shall be destroyed because of the anointing.

He is come to Aiath, he is passed to Migron, at Michmash he hath laid up his carriages, they are gone over the passage, they have taken up their lodging at Geba, Ramah is afraid, Gibeah of Saul is fled. Lift up thy voice, O daughter of Gallim, cause it to be heard unto Laish, O poor Anathoth. Madmenah is removed, the inhabitants of Gebim gather themselves to flee. As yet shall he remain at Nob that day, he shall shake his hand against the mount of the daughter of Zion, the hill of Jerusalem. Behold, the Lord, the Lord of hosts, shall lop the bough with terror, and the high ones of stature shall be hewn down, and the haughty shall be humbled. And he shall cut down the thickets of the forest with iron, and Lebanon shall fall by a mighty one.

And there shall come forth a rod out of the stem of Jesse, and a Branch shall grow out of his roots, and the Spirit of the Lord shall rest upon him, the spirit of wisdom and understanding, the spirit of counsel and might, the spirit of knowledge and of the fear of the Lord, and shall make him of quick understanding in the fear of the Lord, and he shall not judge after the sight of his eyes, neither reprove after the hearing of his ears, but with righteousness shall he judge the poor, and reprove with equity for the meek of the earth, and he shall smite the earth with the rod of his mouth, and with the breath of his lips shall he slay the wicked. And righteousness shall be the girdle of his loins, and faithfulness the girdle of his reins. The wolf also shall dwell with the lamb, and the leopard shall lie down with the kid, and the calf and the young lion and the fatling together, and a little child shall lead them. And the cow and the bear shall feed, their young ones shall lie down together, and the lion shall eat straw like the ox. And the sucking child shall play on the hole of the asp, and the weaned child shall put his hand on the cockatrice' den. They shall not hurt nor destroy in all my holy mountain, for the earth shall be full of the knowledge of the Lord, as the waters cover the sea. And in that day there shall be a root of Jesse, which shall stand for an ensign of the people, to it shall the Gentiles seek, and his rest shall be glorious. And it shall come to pass in that day, that the Lord shall set his hand again the second time to recover the remnant of his people, which shall be left, from Assyria, and from Egypt, and from Pathros, and from Cush, and from Elam, and from Shinar, and from Hamath, and from the islands of the sea. And he shall set up an ensign for the nations, and shall assemble the outcasts of Israel, and gather together the dispersed of Judah from the four corners of the earth. The envy also of Ephraim shall depart, and the adversaries of Judah shall be cut off, Ephraim shall not envy Judah, and Judah shall not vex Ephraim. But they shall fly upon the shoulders of the Philistines toward the west, they shall spoil them of the east together, they shall lay their hand upon Edom and Moab, and the children of Ammon shall obey them. And the Lord shall utterly destroy the tongue of the Egyptian sea, and with his mighty wind shall he shake his hand over the river, and shall smite it in the seven streams, and make men go over dry-shod. And there shall be a highway for the remnant of his people, which shall be left from Assyria, like as it was to Israel in the day that he came up out of the land of Egypt.

And in that day thou shalt say, O Lord, I will praise thee, though thou wast angry with me, thine anger is turned away, and thou comfortedst me. Behold, God is my salvation, I will trust, and not be afraid, for the Lord JEHOVAH is my strength and my song, he also is become my salvation. Therefore with joy shall ye draw water out of the wells of salvation. And in that day shall ye say, Praise the Lord, call upon his name, declare his doings among the people, make mention that his name is exalted. Sing unto the Lord, for he hath done excellent things, this is known in all the earth. Cry out and shout, thou inhabitant of Zion, for great is the Holy One of Israel in the midst of thee.

6 THE burden of Babylon, which Isaiah the son of Amoz did see. Lift ye up my banner upon the high mountain, exalt the voice unto them, shake the hand, that they may go into the gates of the nobles. I have commanded my sanctified ones, I have also called my mighty ones, for mine anger is not upon them that rejoice in my highness. The noise of the multitude in the mountains, like as of a great people, a tumultuous noise of the kingdoms of nations gathered together, the Lord of hosts mustereth the hosts of the battle. They come from a far country, from the end of Heaven, yea, the Lord, and the weapons of his indignation, to destroy the whole land.

Howl ye, for the day of the Lord is at hand, it shall come as a destruction from the Almighty. Therefore shall all hands be faint, and every man's heart shall melt, and they shall be afraid, pangs and sorrows shall take hold of them, they shall be in pain as a woman that travaileth, they shall be amazed one at another, their faces shall be as flames.

Behold, the day of the Lord cometh, cruel both with wrath and fierce anger, to lay the land desolate, and he shall destroy the sinners thereof out of it. For the stars of Heaven and the constellations thereof shall not give their light, the sun shall be darkened in his going forth, and the moon shall not cause her light to shine. And I will punish the world for their evil, and the wicked for their iniquity, and I will cause the arrogancy of the proud to cease, and will lay low the haughtiness of the terrible. I will make a man more precious than fine gold, even a man than the golden wedge of Ophir. Therefore I will shake the heavens, and the Earth shall remove out of her place, in the wrath of the Lord of hosts, and in the day of his fierce anger. And it shall be as the chased roe, and as a sheep that no man taketh up, they shall every man turn to his own people, and flee everyone into his own land. Everyone that is proud shall be thrust through, and everyone that is joined to the wicked shall fall by the sword. Their children also shall be dashed to pieces before their eyes, their houses shall be spoiled, and their wives ravished. Behold, I will stir up the Medes against them, which shall not regard silver, and as for gold, they shall not delight in it. Their bows also shall dash the young men to pieces, and they shall have no pity on the fruit of the womb, their eye shall not spare children. And Babylon, the glory of kingdoms, the beauty of the Chaldees' excellency, shall be as when God overthrew Sodom and Gomorrah. It shall never be inhabited, neither shall it be dwelt in from generation to generation, neither shall the Arabian pitch tent there, neither shall the shepherds make their fold there. But wild beasts of the desert shall lie there, and their houses shall be full of doleful creatures, and owls shall dwell there, and satyrs shall dance there. And the wild beasts of the islands shall cry in their desolate houses, and dragons in their pleasant palaces, and her time is near to come, and her days shall not be prolonged, for I will destroy her speedily, yea, for I will be merciful unto my people, but the wicked shall perish.

For the Lord will have mercy on Jacob, and will yet choose Israel, and set them in their own land, and the strangers shall be joined with them, and they shall cleave to the house of Jacob. And the people shall take them, and bring them to their place, yea, from far, unto the end of the earth, and they shall return to their land of promise, and the house of Israel shall possess them in the land of the Lord for servants and handmaids, and they shall take them captives, whose captives they were, and they shall rule over their oppressors.

And it shall come to pass in that day that the Lord shall give thee rest from thy sorrow and from thy fear, and from the hard bondage wherein thou wast made to serve. And it shall come to pass in that day that thou shalt take up this proverb against the king of Babylon, and say, How hath the oppressor ceased! the golden city ceased! The Lord hath broken the staff of the wicked and the scepters of the rulers. He who smote the people in wrath with a continual stroke, he that ruled the nations in anger, is persecuted, and none hindereth. The whole Earth is at rest, and is quiet, they break forth into singing. Yea, the fir trees rejoice at thee, and also the cedars of Lebanon, saying, Since thou art laid down, no feller is come up against us. Hell from beneath is moved for thee to meet thee at thy coming, it stirreth up the dead for thee, even all the chief ones of the earth, it hath raised up from their thrones all the kings of the nations. All they shall speak and say unto thee, Art thou also become weak as we? Art thou become like unto us? Thy pomp is brought down to the grave, and the noise of thy viols, the worm is spread under thee, and the worms cover thee.

How art thou fallen from Heaven, O Lucifer, son of the morning! How art thou cut down to the ground, which didst weaken the nations! For thou hast said in thine heart, I will ascend into Heaven, I will exalt my throne above the stars of God, I will sit also upon the mount of the congregation, in the sides of the north, I will ascend above the heights of the clouds, I will be like the Most High. Yet thou shalt be brought down to hell, to the sides of the pit.

They that see thee shall narrowly look upon thee, and shall consider thee, and shall say, Is this the man that made the earth to tremble, that did shake kingdoms, and made the world as a wilderness, and destroyed the cities thereof, and opened not the house of his prisoners? All the kings of the nations, yea all of them, lie in glory, every one of them in his own house. But thou art cast out of thy grave like an abominable branch, and the remnant of those that are slain, thrust through with a sword, that go down to the stones of the pit, as a carcass trodden under feet. Thou shalt not be joined with them in burial, because thou hast destroyed thy land, and slain thy people, the seed of evildoers shall never be renowned. Prepare slaughter for his children for the iniquities of their fathers, that they do not rise, nor possess the land, nor fill the face of the world with cities. For I will rise up against them, saith the Lord of hosts, and cut off from Babylon the name, and remnant, and son, and nephew, saith the Lord. I will also make it a possession for the bittern, and pools of water, and I will sweep it with the besom of destruction, saith the Lord of hosts. The Lord of hosts hath sworn, saying, Surely as I have thought, so shall it come to pass, and as I have purposed, so shall it stand, that I will break the Assyrian in my land, and upon my mountains tread him underfoot, then shall his yoke depart from off them, and his burden depart from off their shoulders. This is the purpose that is purposed upon the whole earth, and this is the hand that is stretched out upon all the nations. For the Lord of hosts hath purposed, and who shall disannul it? and his hand is stretched out, and who shall turn it back?

In the year the king Ahaz died was this burden. Rejoice not thou, whole Palestina, because the rod of him that smote thee is broken, for out of the serpent's root shall come forth a cockatrice, and his fruit shall be a fiery flying serpent. And the firstborn of the poor shall feed, and the needy shall lie down in safety, and I will kill thy root with famine, and he shall slay thy remnant. Howl, O gate, cry, O city, thou, whole Palestina, art dissolved, for there shall come from the north a smoke, and none shall be alone in his appointed times. What shall then answer the messengers of the nation? That the Lord hath founded Zion, and the poor of his people shall trust in it.

The burden of Moab. Because in the night Ar of Moab is laid waste, and brought to silence, because in the night Kir of Moab is laid waste, and brought to silence, he is gone up to Bajith, and to Dibon, the high places, to weep, Moab shall howl over Nebo, and over Medeba, on all their heads shall be baldness, and every beard cut off. In their streets they shall gird themselves with sackcloth, on the tops of their houses, and in their streets, everyone shall howl, weeping abundantly. And Heshbon shall cry, and Elealeh, their voice shall be heard even unto Jahaz, therefore the armed soldiers of Moab shall cry out, his life shall be grievous unto him. My heart shall cry out for Moab, his fugitives shall flee unto Zoar, a heifer of three years old, for by the mounting up of Luhith with weeping shall they go it up, for in the way of Horonaim they shall raise up a cry of destruction. For the waters of Nimrim shall be desolate, for the hay is withered away, the grass faileth, there is no green thing. Therefore the abundance they have gotten, and that which they have laid up, shall they carry away to the brook of the willows. For the cry is gone round about the borders of Moab, the howling thereof unto Eglaim, and the howling thereof unto Beer-elim. For the waters of Dimon shall be full of blood, for I will bring more upon Dimon, lions upon him that escapeth of Moab, and upon the remnant of the land.

Send ye the lamb to the ruler of the land from Sela to the wilderness, unto the mount of the daughter of Zion. For it shall be, that, as a wandering bird cast out of the nest, so the daughters of Moab shall be at the fords of Arnon. Take counsel, execute judgment, make thy shadow as the night in the midst of the noonday, hide the outcasts, bewray not him that wandereth. Let mine outcasts dwell with thee, Moab, be thou a covert to them from the face of the spoiler, for the extortioner is at an end, the spoiler ceaseth, the oppressors are consumed out of the land. And in mercy shall the throne be established, and he shall sit upon it in truth in the tabernacle of David, judging, and seeking judgment, and hasting righteousness. We have heard of the pride of Moab, of his haughtiness and his pride, for he is very proud, and his wrath, his lies, and all his evil works. Therefore shall Moab howl for Moab, everyone shall howl, for the foundations of Kir-hareseth shall ye mourn, surely they are stricken. For the fields of Heshbon languish, and the vine of Sibmah, the lords of the heathen have broken down the principal plants thereof, they are come even unto Jazer, they wandered through the wilderness, her branches are stretched out, they are gone over the sea. Therefore I will bewail with the weeping of Jazer the vine of Sibmah, I will water thee with my tears, O Heshbon, and Elealeh, for the shouting for thy summer fruits and for thy harvest is fallen. And gladness is taken away, and joy out of the plentiful field, and in the vineyards there shall be no singing, neither shall there be shouting, the treaders shall tread out no wine in their presses, I have made their vintage shouting to cease. Wherefore my bowels shall sound like a harp for Moab, and mine inward parts for Kir-haresh. And it shall come to pass, when it is seen that Moab is weary on the high place, that he shall come to his sanctuary to pray, but he shall not prevail.

This is the word that the Lord hath spoken concerning Moab since that time. But now the Lord hath spoken, saying, Within three years, as the years of a hireling, and the glory of Moab shall be contemned, with all that great multitude, and the remnant shall be very small and feeble.

The burden of Damascus. Behold, Damascus is taken away from being a city, and it shall be a ruinous heap. The cities of Aroer are forsaken, they shall be for flocks, which shall lie down, and none shall make them afraid. The fortress also shall cease from Ephraim, and the kingdom from Damascus, and the remnant of Syria, they shall be as the glory of the children of Israel, saith the Lord of hosts. And in that day it shall come to pass, that the glory of Jacob shall be made thin, and the fatness of his flesh shall wax lean. And it shall be as when the harvestman gathereth the corn, and reapeth the ears with his arm, and it shall be as he that gathereth ears in the valley of Rephaim. Yet gleaning grapes shall be left in it, as the shaking of an olive tree, two or three berries in the top of the uppermost bough, four or five in the outmost fruitful branches thereof, saith the Lord God of Israel. At that day shall a man look to his Maker, and his eyes shall have respect to the Holy One of Israel. And he shall not look to the altars, the work of his hands, neither shall respect that which his fingers have made, either the groves, or the images. In that day shall his strong cities be as a forsaken bough, and an uppermost branch, which they left because of the children of Israel, and there shall be desolation. Because thou hast forgotten the God of thy salvation, and hast not been mindful of the Rock of thy strength, therefore shalt thou plant pleasant plants, and shalt set it with strange slips, in the day shalt thou make thy plant to grow, and in the morning shalt thou make thy seed to flourish, but the harvest shall be a heap in the day of grief and of desperate sorrow.

Wo to the multitude of many people, which make a noise like the noise of the seas, and to the rushing of nations, that make a rushing like the rushing of mighty waters! The nations shall rush like the rushing of many waters, but God shall rebuke them, and they shall flee far off, and shall be chased as the chaff of the mountains before the wind, and like a rolling thing before the whirlwind. And behold at eveningtide trouble, and before the morning he is not. This is the portion of them that spoil us, and the lot of them that rob us.

Wo to the land shadowing with wings, which is beyond the rivers of Ethiopia, that sendeth ambassadors by the sea, even in vessels of bulrushes upon the waters, saying, Go, ye swift messengers, to a nation scattered and peeled, to a people terrible from their beginning hitherto, a nation meted out and trodden down, whose land the rivers have spoiled! All ye inhabitants of the world and dwellers on the Earth, see ye, when he lifteth up an ensign on the mountains, and when he bloweth a trumpet, hear ye. For so the Lord said unto me, I will take my rest, and I will consider in my dwelling place like a clear heat upon herbs, and like a cloud of dew in the heat of harvest. For afore the harvest, when the bud is perfect, and the sour grape is ripening in the flower, he shall both cut off the sprigs with pruning hooks, and take away and cut down the branches. They shall be left together unto the fowls of the mountains, and to the beasts of the Earth, and the fowls shall summer upon them, and all the beasts of the Earth shall winter upon them. In that time shall the present be brought unto the Lord of hosts of a people scattered and peeled, and from a people terrible from their beginning hitherto, a nation meted out and trodden underfoot, whose land the rivers have spoiled, to the place of the name of the Lord of hosts, the mount Zion.

The burden of Egypt. Behold, the Lord rideth upon a swift cloud, and shall come into Egypt, and the idols of Egypt shall be moved at his presence and the heart of Egypt shall melt in the midst of it. And I will set the Egyptians against the Egyptians, and they shall fight everyone against his brother, and everyone against his neighbor, city against city, and kingdom against kingdom. And the spirit of Egypt shall fail in the midst thereof, and I will destroy the counsel thereof, and they shall seek to the idols, and to the charmers, and to them that have familiar spirits, and to the wizards. And the Egyptians will I give over into the hand of a cruel lord, and a fierce king shall rule over them, saith the Lord, the Lord of hosts. And the waters shall fail from the sea, and the river shall be wasted and dried up. And they shall turn the rivers far away, and the brooks of defense shall be emptied and dried up, the reeds and flags shall wither. The paper reeds by the brooks, by the mouth of the brooks, and everything sown by the brooks, shall wither, be driven away, and be no more. The fishers also shall mourn, and all they that cast angle into the brooks shall lament, and they that spread nets upon the waters shall languish. Moreover they that work in fine flax, and they that weave networks, shall be confounded. And they shall be broken in the purposes thereof, all that make sluices and ponds for fish.

Surely the princes of Zoan are fools, the counsel of the wise counselors of Pharaoh is become brutish, how say ye unto Pharaoh, I am the son of the wise, the son of ancient kings? Where are they? Where are thy wise men? And let them tell thee now, and let them know what the Lord of hosts hath purposed upon Egypt. The princes of Zoan are become fools, the princes of Noph are deceived, they have also seduced Egypt, even they that are the stay of the tribes thereof. The Lord hath mingled a perverse spirit in the midst thereof, and they have caused Egypt to err in every work thereof, as a drunken man staggereth in his vomit. Neither shall there be any work for Egypt, which the head or tail, branch or rush, may do. In that day shall Egypt be like unto women, and it shall be afraid and fear because of the shaking of the hand of the Lord of hosts, which he shaketh over it. And the land of Judah shall be a terror unto Egypt, everyone that maketh mention thereof shall be afraid in himself, because of the counsel of the Lord of hosts, which he hath determined against it.

In that day shall five cities in the land of Egypt speak the language of Canaan and swear to the Lord of hosts, One shall be called, The city of destruction. In that day shall there be an altar to the Lord in the midst of the land of Egypt, and a pillar at the border thereof to the Lord. And it shall be for a sign and for a witness unto the Lord of hosts in the land of Egypt, for they shall cry unto the Lord because of the oppressors, and he shall send them a savior, and a great one, and he shall deliver them. And the Lord shall be known to Egypt, and the Egyptians shall know the Lord in that day, and shall do sacrifice and oblation, yea, they shall vow a vow unto the Lord, and perform it. And the Lord shall smite Egypt, he shall smite and heal it, and they shall return even to the Lord, and he shall be entreated of them, and shall heal them. In that day shall there be a highway out of Egypt to Assyria, and the Assyrian shall come into Egypt, and the Egyptian into Assyria, and the Egyptians shall serve with the Assyrians. In that day shall Israel be the third with Egypt and with Assyria, even a blessing in the midst of the land, whom the Lord of hosts shall bless, saying, Blessed be Egypt my people, and Assyria the work of my hands, and Israel mine inheritance.

In the year that Tartan came unto Ashdod (when Sargon the king of Assyria sent him), and fought against Ashdod, and took it, at the same time spake the Lord by Isaiah the son of Amoz, saying, Go and loose the sackcloth from off thy loins, and put off thy shoe from thy foot.

And he did so, walking naked and barefoot. And the Lord said, Like as my servant Isaiah hath walked naked and barefoot three years for a sign and wonder upon Egypt and upon Ethiopia, so shall the king of Assyria lead away the Egyptians prisoners, and the Ethiopians captives, young and old, naked and barefoot, even with their buttocks uncovered, to the shame of Egypt. And they shall be afraid and ashamed of Ethiopia their expectation, and of Egypt their glory. And the inhabitant of this isle shall say in that day, Behold, such is our expectation, whither we flee for help to be delivered from the king of Assyria, and how shall we escape?

The burden of the desert of the sea. As whirlwinds in the south pass through, so it cometh from the desert, from the terrible land. A grievous vision is declared unto me, The treacherous dealer dealeth treacherously and the spoiler spoileth. Go up, O Elam, besiege, O Media, all the sighing thereof have I made to cease. Therefore are my loins filled with pain, pangs have taken hold upon me, as the pangs of a woman that travaileth, I was bowed down at the hearing of it, I was dismayed at the seeing of it. My heart panted, fearfulness affrighted me, the night of my pleasure hath he turned into fear unto me. Prepare the table, watch in the watchtower, eat, drink, arise, ye princes, and anoint the shield. For thus hath the Lord said unto me, Go, set a watchman, let him declare what he seeth. And he saw a chariot with a couple of horsemen, a chariot of asses, and a chariot of camels, and he hearkened diligently with much heed, and he cried, A lion. My lord, I stand continually upon the watchtower in the daytime, and I am set in my ward whole nights, and, behold, here cometh a chariot of men, with a couple of horsemen. And he answered and said, Babylon is fallen, is fallen, and all the graven images of her gods he hath broken unto the ground. O my threshing, and the corn of my floor, that which I have heard of the Lord of hosts, the God of Israel, have I declared unto you.

The burden of Dumah. He calleth to me out of Seir, Watchman, what of the night? Watchman, what of the night? The watchman said, The morning cometh, and also the night, if ye will inquire, inquire ye, return, come. The burden upon Arabia. In the forest in Arabia shall ye lodge, O ye traveling companies of Dedanim. The inhabitants of the land of Tema brought water to him that was thirsty, they prevented with their bread him that fled. For they fled from the swords, from the drawn sword, and from the bent bow, and from the grievousness of war. For thus hath the Lord said unto me, Within a year, according to the years of a hireling, and all the glory of Kedar shall fail, and the residue of the number of archers, the mighty men of the children of Kedar, shall be diminished, for the Lord God of Israel hath spoken it.

The burden of the valley of vision. What aileth thee now, that thou art wholly gone up to the housetops? Thou that art full of stirs, a tumultuous city, a joyous city, thy slain men are not slain with the sword, nor dead in battle. All thy rulers are fled together, they are bound by the archers, all that are found in thee are bound together, which have fled from far. Therefore said I, Look away from me, I will weep bitterly, labor not to comfort me, because of the spoiling of the daughter of my people. For it is a day of trouble, and of treading down, and of perplexity by the Lord God of hosts in the valley of vision, breaking down the walls, and of crying to the mountains. And Elam bare the quiver with chariots of men and horsemen, and Kir uncovered the shield. And it shall come to pass, that thy choicest valleys shall be full of chariots, and the horsemen shall set themselves in array at the gate. And he discovered the covering of Judah, and thou didst look in that day to the armor of the house of the forest. Ye have seen also the breaches of the city of David, that they are many, and ye gathered together the waters of the lower pool. And ye have numbered the houses of Jerusalem, and the houses have ye broken down to fortify the wall. Ye made also a ditch between the two walls for the water of the old pool, but ye have not looked unto the maker thereof, neither had respect unto him that fashioned it long ago. And in that day did the Lord God of hosts call to weeping, and to mourning, and to baldness, and to girding with sackcloth, and behold joy and gladness, slaying oxen, and killing sheep, eating flesh, and drinking wine, let us eat and drink, for tomorrow we shall die. And it was revealed in mine ears by the Lord of hosts, Surely this iniquity shall not be purged from you till ye die, saith the Lord God of hosts.

Thus saith the Lord God of hosts, Go, get thee unto this treasurer, even unto Shebna, which is over the house, and say, What hast thou here, and whom hast thou here, that thou hast hewed thee out a sepulcher here, as he that heweth him out a sepulcher on high, and that graveth a habitation for himself in a rock? Behold, the Lord will carry thee away with a mighty captivity, and will surely cover thee. He will surely violently turn and toss thee like a ball into a large country, there shalt thou die, and there the chariots of thy glory shall be the shame of thy lord's house. And I will drive thee from thy station, and from thy state shall he pull thee down. And it shall come to pass in that day, that I will call my servant Eliakim the son of Hilkiah, and I will clothe him with thy robe, and strengthen him with thy girdle, and I will commit thy government into his hand, and he shall be a father to the inhabitants of Jerusalem, and to the house of Judah. And the key of the house of David will I lay upon his shoulder, so he shall open, and none shall shut, and he shall shut, and none shall open. And I will fasten him as a nail in a sure place, and he shall be for a glorious throne to his father's house. And they shall hang upon him all the glory of his father's house, the offspring and the issue, all vessels of small quantity, from the vessels of cups, even to all the vessels of flagons. In that day saith the Lord of hosts, shall the nail that is fastened in the sure place be removed, and be cut down, and fall, and the burden that was upon it shall be cut off, for the Lord hath spoken it.

The burden of Tyre. Howl, ye ships of Tarshish, for it is laid waste, so that there is no house, no entering in, from the land of Chittim it is revealed to them. Be still, ye inhabitants of the isle, thou whom the merchants of Zidon, that pass over the sea, have replenished. And by great waters the seed of Sihor, the harvest of the river, is her revenue, and she is a mart of nations. Be thou ashamed, O Zidon, for the sea hath spoken, even the strength of the sea, saying, I travail not, nor bring forth children, neither do I nourish up young men, nor bring up virgins. As at the report concerning Egypt, so shall they be sorely pained at the report of Tyre. Pass ye over to Tarshish, howl, ye inhabitants of the isle. Is this your joyous city, whose antiquity is of ancient days? her own feet shall carry her afar off to sojourn. Who hath taken this counsel against Tyre, the crowning city, whose merchants are princes, whose traffickers are the honorable of the earth? The Lord of hosts hath purposed it, to stain the pride of all glory, and to bring into contempt all the honorable of the earth. Pass through thy land as a river, O daughter of Tarshish, there is no more strength in thee. He stretched out his hand over the sea, he shook the kingdoms, the Lord hath given a commandment against the merchant city, to destroy the strongholds thereof.

And he said, Thou shalt no more rejoice, O thou oppressed virgin, daughter of Zidon, arise, pass over to Chittim, there also shalt thou have no rest. Behold the land of the Chaldeans, this people was not, till the Assyrian founded it for them that dwell in the wilderness, they set up the towers thereof, they raised up the palaces thereof, and he brought it to ruin.

Howl, ye ships of Tarshish, for your strength is laid waste. And it shall come to pass in that day, that Tyre shall be forgotten seventy years, according to the days of one king, after the end of seventy years shall Tyre sing as a harlot. Take a harp, go about the city, thou harlot that hast been forgotten, make sweet melody, sing many songs, that thou mayest be remembered. And it shall come to pass after the end of seventy years, that the Lord will visit Tyre, and she shall turn to her hire, and shall commit fornication with all the kingdoms of the world upon the face of the Earth. And her merchandise and her hire shall be holiness to the Lord, it shall not be treasured nor laid up, for her merchandise shall be for them that dwell before the Lord, to eat sufficiently, and for durable clothing.

7 BEHOLD, the Lord maketh the Earth empty, and maketh it waste, and turneth it upside down, and scattereth abroad the inhabitants thereof. And it shall be, as with the people, so with the priest, as with the servant, so with his master, as with the maid, so with her mistress, as with the buyer, so with the seller, as with the lender, so with the borrower, as with the taker of usury, so with the giver of usury to him. The land shall be utterly emptied, and utterly spoiled, for the Lord hath spoken this word. The earth mourneth and fadeth away, the world languisheth and fadeth away, the haughty people of the earth do languish. The Earth also is defiled under the inhabitants thereof, because they have transgressed the laws, changed the ordinance, broken the everlasting covenant. Therefore hath the curse devoured the Earth, and they that dwell therein are desolate, therefore the inhabitants of the Earth are burned, and few men left. The new wine mourneth, the vine languisheth, all the merryhearted do sigh. The mirth of tabrets ceaseth, the noise of them that rejoice endeth, the joy of the harp ceaseth. They shall not drink wine with a song, strong drink shall be bitter to them that drink it. The city of confusion is broken down, every house is shut up, that no man may come in. There is a crying for wine in the streets, all joy is darkened, the mirth of the land is gone. In the city is left desolation, and the gate is smitten with destruction. When thus it shall be in the midst of the land among the people, there shall be as the shaking of an olive tree, and as the gleaning grapes when the vintage is done. They shall lift up their voice, they shall sing for the majesty of the Lord, they shall cry aloud from the sea. Wherefore glorify ye the Lord in the fires, even the name of the Lord God of Israel in the isles of the sea.

From the uttermost part of the earth have we heard songs, even glory to the righteous. But I said, My leanness, my leanness, wo unto me! the treacherous dealers have dealt treacherously, yea, the treacherous dealers have dealt very treacherously. Fear, and the pit, and the snare, are upon thee, O inhabitant of the Earth. And it shall come to pass, that he who fleeth from the noise of the fear shall fall into the pit, and he that cometh up out of the midst of the pit shall be taken in the snare, for the windows from on high are open, and the foundations of the Earth do shake. The Earth is utterly broken down, the Earth is clean dissolved, the Earth is moved exceedingly. The Earth shall reel to and fro like a drunkard, and shall be removed like a cottage, and the transgression thereof shall be heavy upon it, and it shall fall, and not rise again. And it shall come to pass in that day, that the Lord shall punish the host of the high ones that are on high, and the kings of the earth upon the Earth. And they shall be gathered together, as prisoners are gathered in the pit, and shall be shut up in the prison, and after many days shall they be visited. Then the moon shall be confounded, and the sun ashamed, when the Lord of hosts shall reign in mount Zion and in Jerusalem, and before his ancients gloriously.

O Lord, thou art my God, I will exalt thee, I will praise thy name, for thou hast done wonderful things, thy counsels of old are faithfulness and truth. For thou hast made of a city a heap, of a defensed city a ruin, a palace of strangers to be no city, it shall never be built. Therefore shall the strong people glorify thee, the city of the terrible nations shall fear thee. For thou hast been a strength to the poor, a strength to the needy in his distress, a refuge from the storm, a shadow from the heat, when the blast of the terrible ones is as a storm against the wall. Thou shalt bring down the noise of strangers, as the heat in a dry place, even the heat with the shadow of a cloud, the branch of the terrible ones shall be brought low. And in this mountain shall the Lord of hosts make unto all people a feast of fat things, a feast of wines on the lees, of fat things full of marrow, of wines on the lees well refined. And he will destroy in this mountain the face of the covering cast over all people, and the veil that is spread over all nations. He will swallow up death in victory, and the Lord God will wipe away tears from off all faces, and the rebuke of his people shall he take away from off all the earth, for the Lord hath spoken it. And it shall be said in that day, Lo, this is our God, we have waited for him, and he will save us, this is the Lord, we have waited for him, we will be glad and rejoice in his salvation. For in this mountain shall the hand of the Lord rest, and Moab shall be trodden down under him, even as straw is trodden down for the dunghill. And he shall spread forth his hands in the midst of them, as he that swimmeth spreadeth forth his hands to swim, and he shall bring down their pride together with the spoils of their hands. And the fortress of the high fort of thy walls shall he bring down, lay low, and bring to the ground, even to the dust.

In that day shall this song be sung in the land of Judah, We have a strong city, salvation will God appoint for walls and bulwarks. Open ye the gates, that the righteous nation which keepeth the truth may enter in. Thou wilt keep him in perfect peace, whose mind is stayed on thee, because he trusteth in thee. Trust ye in the Lord forever, for in the Lord JEHOVAH is everlasting strength. For he bringeth down them that dwell on high, the lofty city he layeth it low, he layeth it low, even to the ground, he bringeth it even to the dust. The foot shall tread it down, even the feet of the poor, and the steps of the needy. The way of the just is uprightness, thou, most upright, dost weigh the path of the just. Yea, in the way of thy judgments, O Lord, have we waited for thee, the desire of our soul is to thy name, and to the remembrance of thee. With my soul have I desired thee in the night, yea, with my spirit within me will I seek thee early, for when thy judgments are in the Earth, the inhabitants of the world will learn righteousness. Let favor be showed to the wicked, yet will he not learn righteousness, in the land of uprightness will he deal unjustly, and will not behold the majesty of the Lord. Lord, when thy hand is lifted up, they will not see, but they shall see, and be ashamed for their envy at the people, yea, the fire of thine enemies shall devour them. Lord, thou wilt ordain peace for us, for thou also hast wrought all our works in us. O Lord our God, other lords besides thee have had dominion over us, but by thee only will we make mention of thy name. They are dead, they shall not live, they are deceased, they shall not rise, therefore hast thou visited and destroyed them, and made all their memory to perish. Thou hast increased the nation, O Lord, thou hast increased the nation, thou art glorified, thou hadst removed it far unto all the ends of the earth.

Lord, in trouble have they visited thee, they poured out a prayer when thy chastening was upon them. Like as a woman with child, that draweth near the time of her delivery, is in pain, and crieth out in her pangs, so have we been in thy sight, O Lord. We have been with child, we have been in pain, we have as it were brought forth wind, we have not wrought any deliverance in the Earth, neither have the inhabitants of the world fallen.

Thy dead men shall live, together with my dead body shall they arise. Awake and sing, ye that dwell in dust, for thy dew is as the dew of herbs, and the Earth shall cast out the dead. Come, my people, enter thou into thy chambers, and shut thy doors about thee, hide thyself as it were for a little moment, until the indignation be overpast. For, behold, the Lord cometh out of his place to punish the inhabitants of the Earth for their iniquity, the Earth also shall disclose her blood, and shall no more cover her slain.

In that day the Lord with his sore and great and strong sword shall punish leviathan the piercing serpent, even leviathan that crooked serpent, and he shall slay the dragon that is in the sea.

In that day sing ye unto her, A vineyard of red wine. I the Lord do keep it, I will water it every moment, lest any hurt it, I will keep it night and day. Fury is not in me, who would set the briers and thorns against me in battle, I would go through them, I would burn them together. Or let him take hold of my strength, that he may make peace with me, and he shall make peace with me. He shall cause them that come of Jacob to take root, Israel shall blossom and bud, and fill the face of the world with fruit. Hath he smitten him, as he smote those that smote him? or is he slain according to the slaughter of them that are slain by him? In measure, when it shooteth forth, thou wilt debate with it, he stayeth his rough wind in the day of the east wind. By this therefore shall the iniquity of Jacob be purged, and this is all the fruit to take away his sin, when he maketh all the stones of the altar as chalkstones that are beaten in sunder, the groves and images shall not stand up. Yet the defensed city shall be desolate, and the habitation forsaken, and left like a wilderness, there shall the calf feed, and there shall he lie down, and consume the branches thereof. When the boughs thereof are withered, they shall be broken off, the women come, and set them on fire, for it is a people of no understanding, therefore he that made them will not have mercy on them, and he that formed them will show them no favor. And it shall come to pass in that day, that the Lord shall beat off from the channel of the river unto the stream of Egypt, and ye shall be gathered one by one, O ye children of Israel. And it shall come to pass in that day, that the great trumpet shall be blown, and they shall come which were ready to perish in the land of Assyria, and the outcasts in the land of Egypt, and shall worship the Lord in the holy mount at Jerusalem.

8 WO to the crown of pride, to the drunkards of Ephraim, whose glorious beauty is a fading flower, which are on the head of the fat valleys of them that are overcome with wine! Behold, the Lord hath a mighty and strong one, which as a tempest of hail and a destroying storm, as a flood of mighty waters overflowing, shall cast down to the Earth with the hand. The crown of pride, the drunkards of Ephraim, shall be trodden under feet, and the glorious beauty, which is on the head of the fat valley, shall be a fading flower, and as the hasty fruit before the summer, which when he that looketh upon it seeth, while it is yet in his hand he eateth it up.

In that day shall the Lord of hosts be for a crown of glory, and for a diadem of beauty unto the residue of his people, and for a spirit of judgment to him that sitteth in judgment, and for strength to them that turn the battle to the gate. But they also have erred through wine, and through strong drink are out of the way, the priest and the prophet have erred through strong drink, they are swallowed up of wine, they are out of the way through strong drink, they err in vision, they stumble in judgment. For all tables are full of vomit and filthiness, so that there is no place clean.

Whom shall he teach knowledge? And whom shall he make to understand doctrine? Them that are weaned from the milk, and drawn from the breasts. For precept must be upon precept, precept upon precept, line upon line, line upon line, here a little, and there a little, for with stammering lips and another tongue will he speak to this people. To whom he said, This is the rest wherewith ye may cause the weary to rest, and this is the refreshing, yet they would not hear. But the word of the Lord was unto them precept upon precept, precept upon precept, line upon line, line upon line, here a little, and there a little, that they might go, and fall backward, and be broken, and snared, and taken.

Wherefore hear the word of the Lord, ye scornful men, that rule this people which is in Jerusalem. Because ye have said, We have made a covenant with death, and with hell are we at agreement, when the overflowing scourge shall pass through, it shall not come unto us, for we have made lies our refuge, and under falsehood have we hid ourselves, therefore thus saith the Lord God, Behold, I lay in Zion for a foundation a stone, a tried stone, a precious cornerstone, a sure foundation, he that believeth shall not make haste. Judgment also will I lay to the line, and righteousness to the plummet, and the hail shall sweep away the refuge of lies, and the water shall overflow the hiding place. And your covenant with death shall be disannulled, and your agreement with hell shall not stand, when the overflowing scourge shall pass through, then ye shall be trodden down by it. From the time that it goeth forth it shall take you, for morning by morning shall it pass over, by day and by night, and it shall be a vexation only to understand the report. For the bed is shorter than that a man can stretch himself on it, and the covering narrower than that he can wrap himself in it. For the Lord shall rise up as in mount Perazim, he shall be wroth as in the valley of Gibeon, that he may do his work, his strange work, and bring to pass his act, his strange act. Now therefore be ye not mockers, lest your bands be made strong, for I have heard from the Lord God of hosts a consumption, even determined upon the whole earth.

Give ye ear, and hear my voice, hearken, and hear my speech. Doth the ploughman plough all day to sow? doth he open and break the clods of his ground? When he hath made plain the face thereof, doth he not cast abroad the fitches, and scatter the cummin, and cast in the principal wheat and the appointed barley and the rye in their place? For his God doth instruct him to discretion, and doth teach him. For the fitches are not threshed with a threshing instrument, neither is a cartwheel turned about upon the cummin, but the fitches are beaten out with a staff, and the cummin with a rod. Bread corn is bruised, because he will not ever be threshing it, nor break it with the wheel of his cart, nor bruise it with his horsemen. This also cometh forth from the Lord of hosts, which is wonderful in counsel, and excellent in working.

Wo to Ariel, to Ariel, the city where David dwelt. Add ye year to year, let them kill sacrifices. Yet I will distress Ariel, and there shall be heaviness and sorrow, for thus hath the Lord said unto me, It shall be unto Ariel, that I the Lord will camp against her round about, and will lay siege against her with a mount, and I will raise forts against her. And she shall be brought down, and shall speak out of the ground and her speech shall be low out of the dust, and her voice shall be as of one that hath a familiar spirit out of the ground, and her speech shall whisper out of the dust. Moreover the multitude of her strangers shall be like small dust, and the multitude of the terrible ones shall be as chaff that passeth away, yea, it shall be at an instant suddenly. For they shall be visited of the Lord of hosts with thunder, and with earthquake, and great noise, with storm and tempest, and the flame of devouring fire. And the multitude of all the nations that fight against Ariel, even all that fight against her and her munition, and that distress her, shall be as a dream of a night vision. Yea, it shall be unto them even as unto a hungry man who dreameth, and behold, he eateth, but he awaketh and his soul is empty, or like unto a thirsty man who dreameth, and behold, he drinketh, but he awaketh, and behold, he is faint, and his soul hath appetite. Yea, even so shall the multitude of all the nations be that fight against mount Zion.

For, behold, all ye that do iniquity, stay yourselves, and wonder, for ye shall cry out, and cry, yea, ye shall be drunken, but not with wine, ye shall stagger, but not with strong drink. For, behold, the Lord hath poured out upon you the spirit of deep sleep. For, behold, ye have closed your eyes, and ye have rejected the prophets, and your rulers, and the seers hath he covered because of your iniquities.

9 AND it shall come to pass, that the Lord God shall bring forth unto you the words of a book, and they shall be the words of them which have slumbered. And behold, the book shall be sealed, and in the book shall be a revelation from God, from the beginning of the world to the ending thereof. Wherefore because of the things which are sealed up, the things which are sealed shall not be delivered in the day of the wickedness and abominations of the people. Wherefore, the book shall be kept from them. But the book shall be delivered unto a man, and he shall deliver the words of the book, which are the words of those who have slumbered in the dust, and he shall deliver these words unto another, but the words that are sealed he shall not deliver, neither shall he deliver the book. For the book shall be sealed by the power of God, and the revelation which was sealed shall be kept in the book until the own due time of the Lord, that they may come forth, for behold, they reveal all things from the foundation of the world unto the end thereof.

And the day cometh, that the words of the book which were sealed shall be read upon the housetops, and they shall be read by the power of Christ, and all things shall be revealed unto the children of men which ever have been among the children of men, and which ever will be, even unto the end of the earth. Wherefore, at that day when the book shall be delivered unto the man of whom I have spoken, the book shall be hid from the eyes of the world, that the eyes of none shall behold it, save it be that three witnesses shall behold it by the power of God, besides him to whom the book shall be delivered, and they shall testify to the truth of the book and the things therein. And there is none other which shall view it, save it be a few according to the will of God, to bear testimony of his word unto the children of men, for the Lord God hath said that the words of the faithful should speak as it were from the dead.

Wherefore, the Lord God will proceed to bring forth the words of the book, and in the mouth of as many witnesses as seemeth him good will he establish his word, and wo be unto him that rejecteth the word of God. But, behold, it shall come to pass, that the Lord God shall say unto him to whom he shall deliver the book, Take these words which are not sealed and deliver them to another, that he may show them unto the learned, saying, Read this, I pray thee. And the learned shall say, Bring hither the book and I will read them, and now because of the glory of the world, and to get gain will they say this, and not for the glory of God. And the man shall say, I cannot bring the book for it is sealed. Then shall the learned say, I cannot read it. Wherefore it shall come to pass, that the Lord God will deliver again the book and the words thereof to him that is not learned, and the man that is not learned shall say, I am not learned.

Then shall the Lord God say unto him, The learned shall not read them, for they have rejected them, and I am able to do mine own work, wherefore thou shalt read the words which I shall give unto thee. Touch not the things which are sealed, for I will bring them forth in mine own due time, for I will show unto the children of men that I am able to do mine own work. Wherefore, when thou hast read the words which I have commanded thee, and obtained the witnesses which I have promised unto thee, then shalt thou seal up the book again, and hide it up unto me, that I may preserve the words which thou hast not read until I shall see fit in mine own wisdom to reveal all things unto the children of men. For behold, I am God, and I am a God of miracles, and I will show unto the world that I am the same yesterday, today, and forever, and I work not among the children of men, save it be according to their faith.

And again it shall come to pass, that the Lord shall say unto him that shall read the words that shall be delivered him, Forasmuch as this people draw near unto me with their mouth, and with their lips do honor me, but have removed their hearts far from me, and their fear toward me is taught by the precepts of men, therefore I will proceed to do a marvelous work among this people, yea, a marvelous work and a wonder, for the wisdom of their wise and learned shall perish, and the understanding of their prudent shall be hid.

And wo unto them that seek deep to hide their counsel from the Lord. And their works are in the dark, and they say, Who seeth us and who knoweth us? And they also say, Surely, your turning of things upside down shall be esteemed as the potter's clay. But behold, I will show unto them, saith the Lord of hosts, that I know all their works. For, shall the work say of him that made it, He made me not? or shall the thing framed say of him that framed it, He had no understanding? But behold, saith the Lord of hosts, I will show unto the children of men, that it is not yet a very little while, and Lebanon shall be turned into a fruitful field, and the fruitful field shall be esteemed as a forest. And in that day shall the deaf hear the words of the book, and the eyes of the blind shall see out of obscurity and out of darkness, and the meek also shall increase, and their joy shall be in the Lord, and the poor among men shall rejoice in the Holy One of Israel. For, assuredly as the Lord liveth, they shall see that the terrible one is brought to naught, and the scorner is consumed, and all that watch for iniquity are cut off, and they that make a man an offender for a word, and lay a snare for him that reproveth in the gate, and turn aside the just for a thing of naught. Therefore, thus saith the Lord who redeemed Abraham concerning the house of Jacob, Jacob shall not now be ashamed, neither shall his face now wax pale, but when he seeth his children, the work of my hands, in the midst of him, they shall sanctify my name, and sanctify the Holy One of Jacob, and shall fear the God of Israel. They also that erred in spirit shall come to understanding, and they that murmured shall learn doctrine.

Wo to the rebellious children, saith the Lord, that take counsel, but not of me, and that cover with a covering, but not of my Spirit, that they may add sin to sin, that walk to go down into Egypt, and have not asked at my mouth, to strengthen themselves in the strength of Pharaoh, and to trust in the shadow of Egypt. Therefore shall the strength of Pharaoh be your shame, and the trust in the shadow of Egypt your confusion. For his princes were at Zoan, and his ambassadors came to Hanes. They were all ashamed of a people that could not profit them, nor be a help nor profit, but a shame, and also a reproach.

The burden of the beasts of the south, into the land of trouble and anguish, from whence come the young and old lion, the viper and fiery flying serpent, they will carry their riches upon the shoulders of young asses, and their treasures upon the bunches of camels, to a people that shall not profit them. For the Egyptians shall help in vain, and to no purpose, therefore have I cried concerning this, Their strength is to sit still.

Now go, write it before them in a table, and note it in a book, that it may be for the time to come for ever and ever, that this is a rebellious people, lying children, children that will not hear the law of the Lord, which say to the seers, See not, and to the prophets, Prophesy not unto us right things; speak unto us smooth things, prophesy deceits, Get you out of the way, turn aside out of the path, cause the Holy One of Israel to cease from before us. Wherefore thus saith the Holy One of Israel, Because ye despise this word, and trust in oppression and perverseness, and stay thereon, therefore this iniquity shall be to you as a breach ready to fall, swelling out in a high wall, whose breaking cometh suddenly at an instant. And he shall break it as the breaking of the potters' vessel that is broken in pieces, he shall not spare, so that there shall not be found in the bursting of it a sherd to take fire from the hearth, or to take water withal out of the pit. For thus saith the Lord God, the Holy One of Israel, In returning and rest shall ye be saved, in quietness and in confidence shall be your strength, and ye would not. But ye said, No, for we will flee upon horses, therefore shall ye flee, and, We will ride upon the swift, therefore shall they that pursue you be swift. One thousand shall flee at the rebuke of one, at the rebuke of five shall ye flee, till ye be left as a beacon upon the top of a mountain, and as an ensign on a hill.

And therefore will the Lord wait that he may be gracious unto you, and therefore will he be exalted that he may have mercy upon you, for the Lord is a God of judgment, blessed are all they that wait for him. For the people shall dwell in Zion at Jerusalem, thou shalt weep no more, he will be very gracious unto thee at the voice of thy cry, when he shall hear it, he will answer thee. And though the Lord give you the bread of adversity, and the water of affliction, yet shall not thy teachers be removed into a corner anymore, but thine eyes shall see thy teachers, and thine ears shall hear a word behind thee, saying, This is the way, walk ye in it, when ye turn to the right hand and when ye turn to the left. Ye shall defile also the covering of thy graven images of silver and the ornament of thy molten images of gold, thou shalt cast them away as a menstruous cloth; thou shalt say unto it, Get thee hence. Then shall he give the rain of thy seed, that thou shalt sow the ground withal, and bread of the increase of the Earth, and it shall be fat and plenteous, in that day shall thy cattle feed in large pastures. The oxen likewise and the young asses that ear the ground shall eat clean provender, which hath been winnowed with the shovel and with the fan. And there shall be upon every high mountain, and upon every high hill, rivers and streams of waters in the day of the great slaughter, when the towers fall. Moreover the light of the moon shall be as the light of the sun, and the light of the sun shall be sevenfold, as the light of seven days, in the day that the Lord bindeth up the breach of his people, and healeth the stroke of their wound.

10 BEHOLD, the name of the Lord cometh from far, burning with his anger, and the burden thereof is heavy, his lips are full of indignation and his tongue as a devouring fire, and his breath, as an overflowing stream, shall reach to the midst of the neck, to sift the nations with the sieve of vanity, and there shall be a bridle in the jaws of the people, causing them to err. Ye shall have a song, as in the night when a holy solemnity is kept, and gladness of heart, as when one goeth with a pipe to come unto the mountain of the Lord, to the Mighty One of Israel. And the Lord shall cause his glorious voice to be heard, and shall show the lighting down of his arm, with the indignation of his anger, and with the flame of a devouring fire, with scattering, and tempest, and hailstones. For through the voice of the Lord shall the Assyrian be beaten down, which smote with a rod. And in every place where the grounded staff shall pass, which the Lord shall lay upon him, it shall be with tabrets and harps, and in battles of shaking will he fight with it. For Topheth is ordained of old, yea, for the king it is prepared, he hath made it deep and large, the pile thereof is fire and much wood, the breath of the Lord, like a stream of brimstone, doth kindle it.

Wo to them that go down to Egypt for help, and stay on horses, and trust in chariots, because they are many, and in horsemen, because they are very strong, but they look not unto the Holy One of Israel, neither seek the Lord. Yet he also is wise, and will bring evil, and will not call back his words, but will arise against the house of the evildoers, and against the help of them that work iniquity, now the Egyptians are men, and not God, and their horses flesh, and not spirit. When the Lord shall stretch out his hand, both he that helpeth shall fall, and he that is holpen shall fall down, and they all shall fail together. For thus hath the Lord spoken unto me, Like as the lion and the young lion roaring on his prey, when a multitude of shepherds is called forth against him, he will not be afraid of their voice, nor abase himself for the noise of them, so shall the Lord of hosts come down to fight for mount Zion, and for the hill thereof. As birds flying, so will the Lord of hosts defend Jerusalem, defending also he will deliver it, and passing over he will preserve it.

Turn ye unto him from whom the children of Israel have deeply revolted. For in that day every man shall cast away his idols of silver, and his idols of gold, which your own hands have made unto you for a sin. Then shall the Assyrian fall with the sword, not of a mighty man, and the sword, not of a mean man, shall devour him, but he shall flee from the sword, and his young men shall be discomfited. And he shall pass over to his stronghold for fear, and his princes shall be afraid of the ensign, saith the Lord, whose fire is in Zion, and his furnace in Jerusalem.

11 BEHOLD, a King shall reign in righteousness, and princes shall rule in judgment. And a man shall be as a hiding place from the wind, and a covert from the tempest, as rivers of water in a dry place, as the shadow of a great rock in a weary land. And the eyes of them that see shall not be dim, and the ears of them that hear shall hearken. The heart also of the rash shall understand knowledge, and the tongue of the stammerers shall be ready to speak plainly. The vile person shall be no more called liberal, nor the churl said to be bountiful. For the vile person will speak villany, and his heart will work iniquity, to practice hypocrisy, and to utter error against the Lord, to make empty the soul of the hungry, and he will cause the drink of the thirsty to fail. The instruments also of the churl are evil, he deviseth wicked devices to destroy the poor with lying words, even when the needy speaketh right. But the liberal deviseth liberal things, and by liberal things shall he stand.

Rise up, ye women that are at ease, hear my voice, ye careless daughters, give ear unto my speech. Many days and years shall ye be troubled, ye careless women, for the vintage shall fail, the gathering shall not come. Tremble, ye women that are at ease, be troubled, ye careless ones, strip you, and make you bare, and gird sackcloth upon your loins. They shall lament for the teats, for the pleasant fields, for the fruitful vine. Upon the land of my people shall come up thorns and briers, yea, upon all the houses of joy in the joyous city. Because the palaces shall be forsaken, the houses of the city shall be left desolate, the forts and towers shall be for dens forever, a joy of wild asses, a pasture of flocks, until the Spirit be poured upon us from on high, and the wilderness be a fruitful field, and the fruitful field be counted for a forest. Then judgment shall dwell in the wilderness, and righteousness remain in the fruitful field. And the work of righteousness shall be peace, and the effect of righteousness, quietness and assurance forever. And my people shall dwell in a peaceable habitation, and in sure dwellings, and in quiet resting places, when it shall hail, coming down on the forest, and the city shall be low in a low place. Blessed are ye that sow beside all waters, that send forth thither the feet of the ox and the ass.

Wo to thee that spoilest, and thou wast not spoiled, and dealest treacherously, and they dealt not treacherously with thee! when thou shalt cease to spoil, thou shalt be spoiled, and when thou shalt make an end to deal treacherously, they shall deal treacherously with thee.

O Lord, be gracious unto us, we have waited for thee, be thou their arm every morning, their salvation also in the time of trouble. At the noise of the tumult the people fled, at the lifting up of thyself the nations were scattered. And your spoil shall be gathered like the gathering of the caterpillar, as the running to and fro of locusts shall he run upon them. The Lord is exalted, for he dwelleth on high, he hath filled Zion with judgment and righteousness. And wisdom and knowledge shall be the stability of thy times, and strength of salvation, the fear of the Lord is his treasure. Behold, their valiant ones shall cry without, the ambassadors of peace shall weep bitterly. The highways lie waste, the wayfaring man ceaseth, he hath broken the covenant, he hath despised the cities, he regardeth no man. The earth mourneth and languisheth, Lebanon is ashamed and hewn down, Sharon is like a wilderness, and Bashan and Carmel shake off their fruits.

Now will I rise, saith the Lord, now will I be exalted, now will I lift up myself. Ye shall conceive chaff, ye shall bring forth stubble, your breath, as fire, shall devour you. And the people shall be as the burnings of lime, as thorns cut up shall they be burned in the fire. Hear, ye that are far off, what I have done, and ye that are near, acknowledge my might. The sinners in Zion are afraid, fearfulness hath surprised the hypocrites. Who among us shall dwell with the devouring fire? who among us shall dwell with everlasting burnings? He that walketh righteously, and speaketh uprightly, he that despiseth the gain of oppressions, that shaketh his hands from holding of bribes, that stoppeth his ears from hearing of blood, and shutteth his eyes from seeing evil, he shall dwell on high, his place of defense shall be the munitions of rocks, bread shall be given him, his waters shall be sure. Thine eyes shall see the King in his beauty, they shall behold the land that is very far off. Thine heart shall meditate in terror. Where is the scribe? Where is the receiver? Where is he that counted the towers? Thou shalt not see a fierce people, a people of a deeper speech than thou canst perceive, of a stammering tongue, that thou canst not understand. Look upon Zion, the city of our solemnities, thine eyes shall see Jerusalem a quiet habitation, a tabernacle that shall not be taken down, not one of the stakes thereof shall ever be removed, neither shall any of the cords thereof be broken. But there the glorious Lord will be unto us a place of broad rivers and streams, wherein shall go no galley with oars, neither shall gallant ship pass thereby. For the Lord is our judge, the Lord is our lawgiver, the Lord is our King, he will save us. Thy tacklings are loosed, they could not well strengthen their mast, they could not spread the sail, then is the prey of a great spoil divided, the lame take the prey. And the inhabitant shall not say, I am sick, the people that dwell therein shall be forgiven their iniquity.

12 COME near, ye nations, to hear, and hearken, ye people, let the earth hear, and all that is therein, the world, and all things that come forth of it. For the indignation of the Lord is upon all nations, and his fury upon all their armies, he hath utterly destroyed them, he hath delivered them to the slaughter. Their slain also shall be cast out, and their stink shall come up out of their carcasses, and the mountains shall be melted with their blood. And all the host of Heaven shall be dissolved, and the heavens shall be rolled together as a scroll, and all their host shall fall down, as the leaf falleth off from the vine, and as a falling fig from the fig tree. For my sword shall be bathed in Heaven, behold, it shall come down upon Idumea, and upon the people of my curse, to judgment. The sword of the Lord is filled with blood, it is made fat with fatness, and with the blood of lambs and goats, with the fat of the kidneys of rams, for the Lord hath a sacrifice in Bozrah, and a great slaughter in the land of Idumea.

And the reem shall come down with them, and the bullocks with the bulls, and their land shall be soaked with blood, and their dust made fat with fatness. For it is the day of the Lord's vengeance, and the year of recompenses for the controversy of Zion. And the streams thereof shall be turned into pitch, and the dust thereof into brimstone, and the land thereof shall become burning pitch. It shall not be quenched night nor day, the smoke thereof shall go up forever, from generation to generation it shall lie waste, none shall pass through it for ever and ever. But the cormorant and the bittern shall possess it, the owl also and the raven shall dwell in it, and he shall stretch out upon it the line of confusion, and the stones of emptiness. They shall call the nobles thereof to the kingdom, but none shall be there, and all her princes shall be nothing. And thorns shall come up in her palaces, nettles and brambles in the fortresses thereof, and it shall be a habitation of dragons, and a court for owls. The wild beasts of the desert shall also meet with the wild beasts of the island, and the satyr shall cry to his fellow, the screech owl also shall rest there, and find for herself a place of rest. There shall the great owl make her nest, and lay, and hatch, and gather under her shadow, there shall the vultures also be gathered, everyone with her mate.

Seek ye out of the book of the Lord and read the names written therein: no one of these shall fail, none shall want their mate, for my mouth it hath commanded and my Spirit it hath gathered them. And I have cast the lot for them, and I have divided it unto them by line, they shall possess it forever, from generation to generation they shall dwell therein.

The wilderness and the solitary place shall be glad for them, and the desert shall rejoice, and blossom as the rose. It shall blossom abundantly, and rejoice even with joy and singing, the glory of Lebanon shall be given unto it, the excellency of Carmel and Sharon, they shall see the glory of the Lord, and the excellency of our God.

Strengthen ye the weak hands, and confirm the feeble knees. Say to them that are of a fearful heart, Be strong, fear not, behold, your God will come with vengeance, even God with a recompense, he will come and save you. Then the eyes of the blind shall be opened, and the ears of the deaf shall be unstopped. Then shall the lame man leap as a hart, and the tongue of the dumb sing, for in the wilderness shall waters break out, and streams in the desert. And the parched ground shall become a pool, and the thirsty land springs of water, in the habitation of dragons, where each lay, shall be grass with reeds and rushes. And a highway shall be there, for a way shall be cast up, and it shall be called the way of holiness. The unclean shall not pass over upon it, but it shall be cast up for those who are clean, and the wayfaring men, though they are accounted fools, shall not err therein. No lion shall be there, nor any ravenous beast shall go up thereon, it shall not be found there, but the redeemed shall walk there, and the ransomed of the Lord shall return, and come to Zion with songs and everlasting joy upon their heads, they shall obtain joy and gladness, and sorrow and sighing shall flee away.

13 NOW it came to pass in the fourteenth year of king Hezekiah, the Sennacherib king of Assyria came up against all the defensed cities of Judah, and took them. And the king of Assyria sent Rabshakeh from Lachish to Jerusalem unto king Hezekiah with a great army. And he stood by the conduit of the upper pool in the highway of the fuller's field. Then came forth unto him Eliakim, Hilkiah's son, which was over the house, and Shebna the scribe, and Joah, Asaph's son, the recorder.

And Rabshakeh said unto them, Say ye now to Hezekiah, Thus saith the great king, the king of Assyria, What confidence is this wherein thou trustest? I say, Thy words are but vain when thou sayest, I have counsel and strength for war. Now, on whom dost thou trust that thou rebellest against me? Lo, thou trustest in the staff of this broken reed, on Egypt, whereon if a man lean, it will go into his hand, and pierce it, so is Pharaoh king of Egypt to all that trust in him. But if thou say to me, We trust in the Lord our God, is it not he, whose high places and whose altars Hezekiah hath taken away, and said to Judah and to Jerusalem, Ye shall worship before this altar? Now therefore give pledges, I pray thee, to my master the king of Assyria, and I will give thee two thousand horses, if thou be able on thy part to set riders upon them. How then wilt thou turn away the face of one captain of the least of my master's servants, and put thy trust on Egypt for chariots and for horsemen? And am I now come up without the Lord against this land to destroy it? the Lord said unto me, Go up against this land, and destroy it.

Then said Eliakim and Shebna and Joah unto Rabshakeh, Speak, I pray thee, unto thy servants in the Syrian language, for we understand it, and speak not to us in the Jews' language, in the ears of the people that are on the wall. But Rabshakeh said, Hath my master sent me to thy master and to thee to speak these words? hath he not sent me to the men that sit upon the wall, that they may eat their own dung, and drink their own piss with you?

Then Rabshakeh stood, and cried with a loud voice in the Jews' language, and said, Hear ye the words of the great king, the king of Assyria. Thus saith the king, Let not Hezekiah deceive you, for he shall not be able to deliver you. Neither let Hezekiah make you trust in the Lord, saying, The Lord will surely deliver us, this city shall not be delivered into the hand of the king of Assyria. Hearken not to Hezekiah, for thus saith the king of Assyria, Make an agreement with me by a present, and come out to me, and eat ye everyone of his vine, and everyone of his fig tree, and drink ye everyone the waters of his own cistern, until I come and take you away to a land like your own land, a land of corn and wine, a land of bread and vineyards. Beware lest Hezekiah persuade you, saying, The Lord will deliver us. Hath any of the gods of the nations delivered his land out of the hand of the king of Assyria? Where are the gods of Hamath and Arpad? Where are the gods of Sepharvaim? And have they delivered Samaria out of my hand? Who are they among all the gods of these lands, that have delivered their land out of my hand, that the Lord should deliver Jerusalem out of my hand?

But they held their peace, and answered him not a word, for the king's commandment was, saying, Answer him not. Then came Eliakim, the son of Hilkiah, that was over the household, and Shebna the scribe, and Joah, the son of Asaph, the recorder, to Hezekiah with their clothes rent, and told him the words of Rabshakeh.

And it came to pass, when king Hezekiah heard it, that he rent his clothes, and covered himself with sackcloth, and went into the house of the Lord. And he sent Eliakim, who was over the household, and Shebna the scribe, and the elders of the priests, covered with sackcloth, unto Isaiah the prophet the son of Amoz. And they said unto him, Thus said Hezekiah, This day is a day of trouble, and of rebuke, and of blasphemy, for the children are come to the birth, and there is not strength to bring forth. It may be the Lord thy God will hear the words of Rabshakeh, whom the king of Assyria his master hath sent to reproach the living God, and will reprove the words which the Lord thy God hath heard, wherefore lift up thy prayer for the remnant that is left.

So the servants of King Hezekiah came to Isaiah. And Isaiah said unto them, Thus shall ye say unto your master, Thus saith the Lord, Be not afraid of the words that thou hast heard, wherewith the servants of the king of Assyria have blasphemed me. Behold, I will send a blast upon him, and he shall hear a rumor, and return to his own land, and I will cause him to fall by the sword in his own land.

So Rabshakeh returned, and found the king of Assyria warring against Libnah, for he had heard that he was departed from Lachish. And he heard say concerning Tirhakah king of Ethiopia, He is come forth to make war with thee. And when he heard it, he sent messengers to Hezekiah, saying, Thus shall ye speak to Hezekiah king of Judah, saying, Let not thy God, in whom thou trustest, deceive thee, saying, Jerusalem shall not be given into the hand of the king of Assyria. Behold, thou hast heard what the kings of Assyria have done to all lands by destroying them utterly, and shalt thou be delivered? Have the gods of the nations delivered them which my fathers have destroyed, as Gozan, and Haran, and Rezeph, and the children of Eden which were in Telassar? Where is the king of Hamath, and the king of Arpad? and the king of the city of Sepharvaim, Hena, and Ivah?

And Hezekiah received the letter from the hand of the messengers, and read it, and Hezekiah went up unto the house of the Lord, and spread it before the Lord. And Hezekiah prayed unto the Lord, saying, O Lord of hosts, God of Israel, that dwellest between the cherubim, thou art the God, even thou alone, of all the kingdoms of the earth, thou hast made Heaven and Harth. Incline thine ear, O Lord, and hear, open thine eyes, O Lord, and see, and hear all the words of Sennacherib, which he hath sent to reproach the living God. Of a truth, Lord, the kings of Assyria have laid waste all the nations, and their countries, and have cast their gods into the fire, for they were no gods, but the work of men's hands, wood and stone, therefore they have destroyed them. Now therefore, O Lord our God, save us from his hand, that all the kingdoms of the earth may know that thou art the Lord, even thou only.

Then Isaiah the son of Amoz sent unto Hezekiah, saying, Thus saith the Lord God of Israel, whereas thou hast prayed to me against Sennacherib king of Assyria, this is the word which the Lord hath spoken concerning him, The virgin, the daughter of Zion, hath despised thee, and laughed thee to scorn, the daughter of Jerusalem hath shaken her head at thee. Whom hast thou reproached and blasphemed? And against whom hast thou exalted thy voice, and lifted up thine eyes on high? Even against the Holy One of Israel. By thy servants hast thou reproached the Lord, and hast said, By the multitude of my chariots am I come up to the height of the mountains, to the sides of Lebanon, and I will cut down the tall cedars thereof, and the choice fir trees thereof, and I will enter into the height of his border, and the forest of his Carmel. I have digged, and drunk water, and with the sole of my feet have I dried up all the rivers of the besieged places. Hast thou not heard long ago, how I have done it, and of ancient times, that I have formed it? Now have I brought to pass, that thou shouldest be to lay waste defensed cities into ruinous heaps. Therefore their inhabitants were of small power, they were dismayed and confounded, they were as the grass of the field, and as the green herb, as the grass on the housetops, and as corn blasted before it be grown up. But I know thy abode, and thy going out, and thy coming in, and thy rage against me. Because thy rage against me, and thy tumult, is come up into mine ears, therefore will I put my hook in thy nose, and my bridle in thy lips, and I will turn thee back by the way by which thou camest.

And this shall be a sign unto thee, Ye shall eat this year such as groweth of itself, and the second year that which springeth of the same, and in the third year sow ye, and reap, and plant vineyards, and eat the fruit thereof. And the remnant that is escaped of the house of Judah shall again take root downward, and bear fruit upward, for out of Jerusalem shall go forth a remnant, and they that escape out of Jerusalem shall come up upon mount Zion, the zeal of the Lord of hosts shall do this.

Therefore thus saith the Lord concerning the king of Assyria, He shall not come into this city, nor shoot an arrow there, nor come before it with shields, nor cast a bank against it. By the way that he came, by the same shall he return, and shall not come into this city, saith the Lord. For I will defend this city to save it for mine own sake, and for my servant David's sake.

Then the Angel of the Lord went forth, and smote in the camp of the Assyrians a hundred and fourscore and five thousand, and when they who were left arose early in the morning, behold, they were all dead corpses. So Sennacherib king of Assyria departed, and went and returned, and dwelt at Nineveh. And it came to pass, as he was worshiping in the house of Nisroch his god, that Adrammelech and Sharezer his sons smote him with the sword, and they escaped into the land of Armenia, and Esar-haddon his son reigned in his stead.

In those days was Hezekiah sick unto death. And Isaiah the prophet the son of Amoz came unto him, and said unto him, Thus saith the Lord, Set thine house in order, for thou shalt die, and not live. Then Hezekiah turned his face toward the wall, and prayed unto the Lord, and said, Remember now, O Lord, I beseech thee, how I have walked before thee in truth and with a perfect heart, and have done that which is good in thy sight. And Hezekiah wept sore. Then came the word of the Lord to Isaiah, saying, Go, and say to Hezekiah, Thus saith the Lord, the God of David thy father, I have heard thy prayer, I have seen thy tears, behold, I will add unto thy days fifteen years. And I will deliver thee and this city out of the hand of the king of Assyria, and I will defend this city. And this shall be a sign unto thee from the Lord, that the Lord will do this thing that he hath spoken, behold, I will bring again the shadow of the degrees, which is gone down in the sundial of Ahaz, ten degrees backward. So the sun returned ten degrees, by which degrees it was gone down.

The writing of Hezekiah king of Judah, when he had been sick, and was recovered of his sickness, I said in the cutting off of my days, I shall go to the gates of the grave, I am deprived of the residue of my years. I said, I shall not see the Lord, even the Lord, in the land of the living, I shall behold man no more with the inhabitants of the world. Mine age is departed, and is removed from me as a shepherd's tent, I have cut off like a weaver my life, he will cut me off with pining sickness, from day even to night wilt thou make an end of me. I reckoned till morning, that, as a lion, so will he break all my bones, from day even to night wilt thou make an end of me. Like a crane or swallow, so did I chatter, I did mourn as a dove, mine eyes fail with looking upward, O Lord, I am oppressed, undertake for me. What shall I say? He hath both spoken unto me, and himself hath healed me. I shall go softly all my years, that I may not walk in the bitterness of my soul. O Lord, thou who art the life of my spirit, in whom I live, so wilt thou recover me, and make me to live, and in all these things I will praise thee. Behold, I had great bitterness instead of peace, but thou hast in love to my soul, saved me from the pit of corruption, for thou hast cast all my sins behind thy back. For the grave cannot praise thee, death cannot celebrate thee, they that go down into the pit cannot hope for thy truth. The living, the living, he shall praise thee, as I do this day, the father to the children shall make known thy truth. The Lord was ready to save me, therefore we will sing my songs to the stringed instruments all the days of our life in the house of the Lord.

For Isaiah had said, Let them take a lump of figs, and lay it for a plaster upon the boil, and he shall recover. Hezekiah also had said, What is the sign that I shall go up to the house of the Lord?

At that time Merodach-baladan, the son of Baladan, king of Babylon, sent letters and a present to Hezekiah, for he had heard that he had been sick, and was recovered. And Hezekiah was glad of them, and showed them the house of his precious things, the silver, and the gold, and the spices, and the precious ointment, and all the house of his armor, and all that was found in his treasures, there was nothing in his house, nor in all his dominion, that Hezekiah showed him not. Then came Isaiah the prophet unto king Hezekiah, and said unto him, What said these men? and from whence came they unto thee? And Hezekiah said, They are come from a far country unto me, even from Babylon. Then said he, What have they seen in thine house? And Hezekiah answered, All that is in mine house have they seen, there is nothing among my treasures that I have not showed them. Then said Isaiah to Hezekiah, Hear the word of the Lord of hosts, behold, the days come, that all that is in thine house, and that which thy fathers have laid up in store until this day, shall be carried to Babylon, nothing shall be left, saith the Lord. And of thy sons that shall issue from thee, which thou shalt beget, shall they take away, and they shall be eunuchs in the palace of the king of Babylon. Then said Hezekiah to Isaiah, Good is the word of the Lord which thou hast spoken. He said moreover, For there shall be peace and truth in my days.

Comfort ye, comfort ye my people, saith your God. Speak ye comfortably to Jerusalem, and cry unto her, that her warfare is accomplished, that her iniquity is pardoned, for she hath received of the Lord's hand double for all her sins.

14 THE voice of him that crieth in the wilderness, Prepare ye the way of the Lord, make straight in the desert a highway for our God. Every valley shall be exalted, and every mountain and hill shall be made low, and the crooked shall be made straight, and the rough places plain, and the glory of the Lord shall be revealed, and all flesh shall see it together, for the mouth of the Lord hath spoken it. The voice said, Cry. And he said, What shall I cry? All flesh is grass, and all the goodliness thereof is as the flower of the field, the grass withereth, the flower fadeth, because the Spirit of the Lord bloweth upon it, surely the people is grass. The grass withereth, the flower fadeth, but the word of our God shall stand forever.

O Zion, that bringest good tidings, get thee up into the high mountain, O Jerusalem, that bringest good tidings, lift up thy voice with strength, lift it up, be not afraid, say unto the cities of Judah, Behold your God! Behold, the Lord God will come with strong hand, and his arm shall rule for him, behold, his reward is with him, and his work before him. He shall feed his flock like a shepherd, he shall gather the lambs with his arm, and carry them in his bosom, and shall gently lead those that are with young.

Who hath measured the waters in the hollow of his hand, and meted out Heaven with the span, and comprehended the dust of the earth in a measure, and weighed the mountains in scales, and the hills in a balance? Who hath directed the Spirit of the Lord, or being his counselor hath taught him? With whom took he counsel, and who instructed him, and taught him in the path of judgment, and taught him knowledge, and showed to him the way of understanding? Behold, the nations are as a drop of a bucket, and are counted as the small dust of the balance, behold, he taketh up the isles as a very little thing. And Lebanon is not sufficient to burn, nor the beasts thereof sufficient for a burnt offering. All nations before him are as nothing, and they are counted to him less than nothing, and vanity.

To whom then will ye liken God? Or what likeness will ye compare unto him? The workman melteth a graven image, and the goldsmith spreadeth it over with gold, and casteth silver chains. He that is so impoverished that he hath no oblation chooseth a tree that will not rot, he seeketh unto him a cunning workman to prepare a graven image, that shall not be moved.

Have ye not known? Have ye not heard? Hath it not been told you from the beginning? Have ye not understood from the foundations of the earth, it is he that sitteth upon the circle of the Earth, and the inhabitants thereof are as grasshoppers? That stretcheth out the heavens as a curtain, and spreadeth them out as a tent to dwell in, that bringeth the princes to nothing, he maketh the judges of the earth as vanity. Yea, they shall not be planted, yea, they shall not be sown, yea, their stock shall not take root in the earth, and he shall also blow upon them, and they shall wither, and the whirlwind shall take them away as stubble.

To whom then will ye liken me or shall I be equal? saith the Holy One. Lift up your eyes on high, and behold who hath created these things, that bringeth out their host by number, he calleth them all by names by the greatness of his might, for that he is strong in power, not one faileth. Why sayest thou, O Jacob, and speakest, O Israel, My way is hid from the Lord, and my judgment is passed over from my God? Hast thou not known? Hast thou not heard, that the everlasting God, the Lord, the Creator of the ends of the Earth, fainteth not, neither is weary? There is no searching of his understanding. He giveth power to the faint, and to them that have no might he increaseth strength. Even the youths shall faint and be weary, and the young men shall utterly fall, but they that wait upon the Lord shall renew their strength, they shall mount up with wings as eagles, they shall run, and not be weary, and they shall walk, and not faint.

15 KEEP silence before me, O islands, and let the people renew their strength, let them come near, then let them speak, let us come near together to judgment. Who raised up the righteous man from the east, called him to his foot, gave the nations before him, and made him rule over kings? he gave them as the dust to his sword, and as driven stubble to his bow. He pursued them, and passed safely, even by the way that he had not gone with his feet.

Who hath wrought and done it, calling the generations from the beginning? I the Lord, the first, and with the last, I am he. The isles saw it, and feared, the ends of the earth were afraid, drew near, and came. They helped everyone his neighbor, and everyone said to his brother, Be of good courage. So the carpenter encouraged the goldsmith, and he that smootheth with the hammer him that smote the anvil, saying, It is ready for the soldering, and he fastened it with nails, that it should not be moved.

But, thou, Israel, art my servant, Jacob whom I have chosen, the seed of Abraham my friend. Thou whom I have taken from the ends of the earth, and called thee from the chief men thereof, and said unto thee, Thou art my servant, I have chosen thee, and not cast thee away. Fear thou not, for I am with thee, be not dismayed, for I am thy God, I will strengthen thee, yea, I will help thee, yea, I will uphold thee with the right hand of my righteousness. Behold, all they that were incensed against thee shall be ashamed and confounded, they shall be as nothing, and they that strive with thee shall perish. Thou shalt seek them, and shalt not find them, even them that contended with thee, they that war against thee shall be as nothing, and as a thing of naught. For I the Lord thy God will hold thy right hand, saying unto thee, Fear not, I will help thee. Fear not, thou worm Jacob, and ye men of Israel, I will help thee, saith the Lord, and thy Redeemer, the Holy One of Israel. Behold, I will make thee a new sharp threshing instrument having teeth, thou shalt thresh the mountains, and beat them small, and shalt make the hills as chaff. Thou shalt fan them, and the wind shall carry them away, and the whirlwind shall scatter them, and thou shalt rejoice in the Lord, and shalt glory in the Holy One of Israel.

When the poor and needy seek water, and there is none, and their tongue faileth for thirst, I the Lord will hear them, I the God of Israel will not forsake them. I will open rivers in high places, and fountains in the midst of the valleys, I will make the wilderness a pool of water, and the dry land springs of water. I will plant in the wilderness the cedar, the shittah tree, and the myrtle, and the oil tree, I will set in the desert the fir tree, and the pine, and the box tree together, that they may see and know, and consider, and understand together, that the hand of the Lord hath done this, and the Holy One of Israel hath created it.

Produce your cause, saith the Lord, bring forth your strong reasons, saith the King of Jacob. Let them bring them forth, and show us what shall happen, let them show the former things, what they be, that we may consider them, and know the latter end of them, or declare us things for to come. Show the things that are to come hereafter, that we may know that ye are gods, yea, do good or do evil, that we may be dismayed, and behold it together. Behold, ye are of nothing, and your work of naught, an abomination is he that chooseth you. I have raised up one from the north, and he shall come, from the rising of the sun shall he call upon my name, and he shall come upon princes as upon mortar, and as the potter treadeth clay.

Who hath declared from the beginning, that we may know, and beforetime, that we may say, He is righteous? Yea, there is none that showeth, yea, there is none that declareth, yea, there is none that heareth your words. The first shall say to Zion, Behold, behold them, and I will give to Jerusalem one that bringeth good tidings. For I beheld, and there was no man, even among men, and there was no counselor that, when I asked of them, could answer a word. Behold, they are all vanity, their works are nothing, their molten images are wind and confusion.

Behold my servant, whom I uphold, mine elect, in whom my soul delighteth, I have put my Spirit upon him, he shall bring forth judgment to the Gentiles. He shall not cry, nor lift up, nor cause his voice to be heard in the street. A bruised reed shall he not break, and the smoking flax shall he not quench, he shall bring forth judgment unto truth. He shall not fail nor be discouraged, till he have set judgment in the earth, and the isles shall wait for his law.

Thus saith God the Lord, he that created the heavens, and stretched them out, he that spread forth the Earth, and that which cometh out of it, he that giveth breath unto the people upon it, and spirit to them that walk therein, I the Lord have called thee in righteousness, and will hold thine hand, and will keep thee, and give thee for a covenant of the people, for a light of the Gentiles, to open the blind eyes, to bring out the prisoners from the prison, and them that sit in darkness out of the prison house. I am the Lord, that is my name, and my glory will I not give to another, neither my praise to graven images. Behold, the former things are come to pass, and new things do I declare, before they spring forth I tell you of them.

Sing unto the Lord a new song, and his praise from the end of the earth, ye that go down to the sea, and all that is therein, the isles, and the inhabitants thereof. Let the wilderness and the cities thereof lift up their voice, the villages that Kedar doth inhabit, let the inhabitants of the rock sing, let them shout from the top of the mountains. Let them give glory unto the Lord, and declare his praise in the islands. The Lord shall go forth as a mighty man, he shall stir up jealousy like a man of war, he shall cry, yea, roar, he shall prevail against his enemies. I have long time holden my peace, I have been still, and refrained myself, now will I cry like a travailing woman, I will destroy and devour at once. I will make waste mountains and hills, and dry up all their herbs, and I will make the rivers islands, and I will dry up the pools. And I will bring the blind by a way that they knew not, I will lead them in paths that they have not known, I will make darkness light before them, and crooked things straight. These things will I do unto them, and not forsake them. They shall be turned back, they shall be greatly ashamed, that trust in graven images, that say to the molten images, Ye are our gods.

Hear, ye deaf, and look, ye blind, that ye may see. For I will send my servant unto you who are blind, yea, a messenger to open the eyes of the blind, and unstop the ears of the deaf, and they shall be made perfect notwithstanding their blindness, if they will hearken unto the messenger, the Lord's servant. Thou art a people, seeing many things, but thou observest not, opening the ears to hear, but thou hearest not. The Lord is not well pleased with such a people, but for his righteousness' sake he will magnify the law and make it honorable. Thou art a people robbed and spoiled, thine enemies, all of them, have snared thee in holes, and they have hid thee in prison houses, they have taken thee for a prey, and none delivereth, for a spoil, and none saith, Restore. Who among them will give ear unto thee, or hearken and hear thee for the time to come, And who gave Jacob for a spoil, and Israel to the robbers? Did not the Lord, he against whom they have sinned? For they would not walk in his ways, neither were they obedient unto his law, therefore he hath poured upon them the fury of his anger, and the strength of battle, and they have set them on fire round about, yet they know not, and it burned them, yet they laid it not to heart.

But now thus saith the Lord that created thee, O Jacob, and he that formed thee, O Israel, Fear not, for I have redeemed thee, I have called thee by thy name, thou art mine. When thou passest through the waters, I will be with thee, and through the rivers, they shall not overflow thee, when thou walkest through the fire, thou shalt not be burned, neither shall the flame kindle upon thee. For I am the Lord thy God, the Holy One of Israel, thy Savior, I gave Egypt for thy ransom, Ethiopia and Seba for thee. Since thou wast precious in my sight, thou hast been honorable, and I have loved thee, therefore will I give men for thee, and people for thy life. Fear not, for I am with thee, I will bring thy seed from the east, and gather thee from the west, I will say to the north, Give up, and to the south, Keep not back, bring my sons from far, and my daughters from the ends of the earth, even everyone that is called by my name, for I have created him for my glory, I have formed him, yea, I have made him.

Bring forth the blind people that have eyes, and the deaf that have ears. Let all the nations be gathered together, and let the people be assembled, who among them can declare this, and show us former things? let them bring forth their witnesses, that they may be justified, or let them hear, and say, It is truth. Ye are my witnesses, saith the Lord, and my servant whom I have chosen, that ye may know and believe me, and understand that I am he, before me there was no God formed, neither shall there be after me. I, even I, am the Lord, and beside me there is no savior. I have declared, and have saved, and I have showed, when there was no strange god among you, therefore ye are my witnesses, saith the Lord, that I am God. Yea, before the day was I am he, and there is none that can deliver out of my hand, I will work, and who shall let it?

Thus saith the Lord, your Redeemer, the Holy One of Israel, For your sake I have sent to Babylon, and have brought down all their nobles, and the Chaldeans, whose cry is in the ships. I am the Lord, your Holy One, the Creator of Israel, your King. Thus saith the Lord, which maketh a way in the sea and a path in the mighty waters, which bringeth forth the chariot and horse, the army and the power, They shall lie down together, they shall not rise, they are extinct, they are quenched as tow. Remember ye not the former things, neither consider the things of old. Behold, I will do a new thing, now it shall spring forth, shall ye not know it? I will even make a way in the wilderness, and rivers in the desert. The beast of the field shall honor me, the dragons and the owls, because I give waters in the wilderness, and rivers in the desert, to give drink to my people, my chosen. This people have I formed for myself, they shall show forth my praise.

But thou hast not called upon me, O Jacob, but thou hast been weary of me, O Israel. Thou hast not brought me the small cattle of thy burnt offerings, neither hast thou honored me with thy sacrifices. I have not caused thee to serve with an offering, nor wearied thee with incense. Thou hast bought me no sweet cane with money, neither hast thou filled me with the fat of thy sacrifices, but thou hast made me to serve with thy sins, thou hast wearied me with thine iniquities. I, even I, am he that blotteth out thy transgressions for mine own sake, and will not remember thy sins. Put me in remembrance, let us plead together, declare thou, that thou mayest be justified. Thy first father hath sinned, and thy teachers have transgressed against me. Therefore I have profaned the princes of the sanctuary, and have given Jacob to the curse, and Israel to reproaches.

Yet now hear, O Jacob my servant, and Israel, whom I have chosen, thus saith the Lord that made thee and formed thee from the womb, which will help thee, Fear not, O Jacob, my servant, and thou, Jeshurun, whom I have chosen. For I will pour water upon him that is thirsty, and floods upon the dry ground, I will pour my Spirit upon thy seed, and my blessing upon thine offspring, and they shall spring up as among the grass, as willows by the watercourses. One shall say, I am the Lord's, and another shall call himself by the name of Jacob, and another shall subscribe with his hand unto the Lord, and surname himself by the name of Israel.

Thus saith the Lord the King of Israel and his Redeemer the Lord of hosts, I am the first and I am the last, and besides me there is no God. And who, as I, shall call and shall declare it, and set it in order for me, since I appointed the ancient people? And the things that are coming, and shall come, let them show unto them. Fear ye not, neither be afraid, have not I told thee from that time, and have declared it? Ye are even my witnesses. Is there a God besides me? Yea, there is no God, I know not any. They that make a graven image are all of them vanity, and their delectable things shall not profit, and they are their own witnesses, they see not, nor know, that they may be ashamed. Who hath formed a god, or molten a graven image that is profitable for nothing? Behold, all his fellows shall be ashamed, and the workmen, they are of men, let them all be gathered together, let them stand up, yet they shall fear, and they shall be ashamed together. The smith with the tongs both worketh in the coals, and fashioneth it with hammers, and worketh it with the strength of his arms, yea, he is hungry, and his strength faileth, he drinketh no water, and is faint. The carpenter stretcheth out his rule, he marketh it out with a line, he fitteth it with planes, and he marketh it out with the compass, and maketh it after the figure of a man, according to the beauty of a man, that it may remain in the house. He heweth him down cedars, and taketh the cypress and the oak, which he strengtheneth for himself among the trees of the forest, he planteth an ash, and the rain doth nourish it. Then shall it be for a man to burn, for he will take thereof, and warm himself, yea, he kindleth it, and baketh bread, yea, he maketh a god, and worshipeth it, he maketh it a graven image, and falleth down thereto. He burneth part thereof in the fire, with part thereof he eateth flesh, he roasteth roast, and is satisfied, yea, he warmeth himself, and saith, Aha, I am warm, I have seen the fire, and the residue thereof he maketh a god, even his graven image, he falleth down unto it, and worshipeth it, and prayeth unto it, and saith, Deliver me, for thou art my god. They have not known nor understood, for he hath shut their eyes, that they cannot see, and their hearts, that they cannot understand. And none considereth in his heart, neither is there knowledge nor understanding to say, I have burned part of it in the fire, yea, also I have baked bread upon the coals thereof, I have roasted flesh, and eaten it, and shall I make the residue thereof an abomination? shall I fall down to the stock of a tree? He feedeth on ashes, a deceived heart hath turned him aside, that he cannot deliver his soul, nor say, Is there not a lie in my right hand? Remember these, O Jacob and Israel, for thou art my servant, I have formed thee, thou art my servant, O Israel, thou shalt not be forgotten of me. I have blotted out, as a thick cloud, thy transgressions, and, as a cloud, thy sins, return unto me, for I have redeemed thee.

Sing, O ye heavens, for the Lord hath done it, shout, ye lower parts of the Earth, break forth into singing, ye mountains, O forest, and every tree therein, for the Lord hath redeemed Jacob, and glorified himself in Israel. Thus saith the Lord, thy Redeemer, and he that formed thee from the womb, I am the Lord that maketh all things, that stretcheth forth the heavens alone, that spreadeth abroad the Earth by myself. That frustrateth the tokens of the liars and maketh diviners mad, that turneth wise men backward and maketh their knowledge foolish, that confirmeth the word of his servant and performeth the counsel of his messengers, that saith to Jerusalem, Thou shalt be inhabited, and to the cities of Judah, Ye shall be built, and I will raise up the decayed places thereof, that saith to the deep, Be dry, and I will dry up thy rivers, that saith of Cyrus, He is my shepherd, and shall perform all my pleasure, even saying to Jerusalem, Thou shalt be built, and to the temple, Thy foundation shall be laid.

Thus saith the Lord to his anointed, to Cyrus, whose right hand I have holden, to subdue nations before him, and I will loose the loins of kings, to open before him the two-leaved gates, and the gates shall not be shut, I will go before thee, and make the crooked places straight, I will break in pieces the gates of brass, and cut in sunder the bars of iron, and I will give thee the treasures of darkness, and hidden riches of secret places, that thou mayest know that I, the Lord, which call thee by thy name, am the God of Israel. For Jacob my servant's sake, and Israel mine elect, I have even called thee by thy name, I have surnamed thee, though thou hast not known me. I am the Lord, and there is none else, there is no God besides me, I girded thee, though thou hast not known me, that they may know from the rising of the sun, and from the west, that there is none besides me. I am the Lord, and there is none else. I form the light, and create darkness, I make peace, and create evil, I the Lord do all these things. Drop down, ye heavens, from above, and let the skies pour down righteousness, let the Earth open, and let them bring forth salvation, and let righteousness spring up together, I the Lord have created it. Wo unto him that striveth with his Maker! Let the potsherd strive with the potsherds of the earth. Shall the clay say to him that fashioneth it, What makest thou? or thy work, He hath no hands? Wo unto him that saith unto his father, What begettest thou? or to the woman, What hast thou brought forth? Thus saith the Lord, the Holy One of Israel, and his Maker, Ask me of things to come concerning my sons, and concerning the work of my hands command ye me. I have made the Earth, and created man upon it, I, even my hands, have stretched out the heavens, and all their hosts have I commanded. I have raised him up in righteousness, and I will direct all his ways, he shall build my city, and he shall let go my captives, not for price nor reward, saith the Lord of hosts. Thus saith the Lord, The labor of Egypt and merchandise of Ethiopia and of the Sabeans, men of stature, shall come over unto thee, and they shall be thine, they shall come after thee, in chains they shall come over, and they shall fall down unto thee, they shall make supplication unto thee, saying, Surely God is in thee, and there is none else, there is no God. Verily thou art a God that hidest thyself, O God of Israel, the Savior. They shall be ashamed, and also confounded, all of them, they shall go to confusion together, that are makers of idols. But Israel shall be saved in the Lord with an everlasting salvation, ye shall not be ashamed nor confounded world without end.

For thus saith the Lord that created the heavens, God himself that formed the Earth and made it, he hath established it, he created it not in vain, he formed it to be inhabited, I am the Lord, and there is none else. I have not spoken in secret, in a dark place of the Earth, I said not unto the seed of Jacob, Seek ye me in vain, I the Lord speak righteousness, I declare things that are right. Assemble yourselves and come, draw near together, ye that are escaped of the nations, they have no knowledge that set up the wood of their graven image, and pray unto a god that cannot save. Tell ye, and bring them near, yea, let them take counsel together, who hath declared this from ancient time? Who hath told it from that time? Have not I the Lord? And there is no god else beside me, a just God, and a Savior, there is none beside me. Look unto me, and be ye saved, all the ends of the earth, for I am God, and there is none else. I have sworn by myself, the word is gone out of my mouth in righteousness, and shall not return, That unto me every knee shall bow, every tongue shall swear. Surely shall one say, In the Lord have I righteousness and strength, even to him shall men come, and all that are incensed against him shall be ashamed. In the Lord shall all the seed of Israel be justified, and shall glory.

Bel boweth down, Nebo stoopeth, their idols were upon the beasts, and upon the cattle, your carriages were heavy laden, they are a burden to the weary beast. They stoop, they bow down together, they could not deliver the burden, but themselves are gone into captivity.

Hearken unto me, O house of Jacob, and all the remnant of the house of Israel, which are borne by me from the belly, which are carried from the womb, and even to your old age I am he, and even to hoar hairs will I carry you, I have made, and I will bear, even I will carry, and will deliver you. To whom will ye liken me, and make me equal and compare me, that we may be like? They lavish gold out of the bag, and weigh silver in the balance, and hire a goldsmith, and he maketh it a god, they fall down, yea, they worship. They bear him upon the shoulder, they carry him, and set him in his place, and he standeth, from his place shall he not remove, yea, one shall cry unto him, yet can he not answer, nor save him out of his trouble. Remember this, and show yourselves men, bring it again to mind, O ye transgressors. Remember the former things of old, for I am God, and there is none else, I am God, and there is none like me. Declaring the end from the beginning, and from ancient times the things that are not yet done, saying, My counsel shall stand, and I will do all my pleasure, calling a ravenous bird from the east, the man that executeth my counsel from a far country, yea, I have spoken it, I will also bring it to pass, I have purposed it, I will also do it. Hearken unto me, ye stouthearted, that are far from righteousness, I bring near my righteousness, it shall not be far off, and my salvation shall not tarry, and I will place salvation in Zion for Israel my glory.

16 COME down, and sit in the dust, O virgin daughter of Babylon, sit on the ground, there is no throne, O daughter of the Chaldeans, for thou shalt no more be called tender and delicate. Take the millstones, and grind meal, uncover thy locks, make bare the leg, uncover the thigh, pass over the rivers. Thy nakedness shall be uncovered, yea, thy shame shall be seen, I will take vengeance, and I will not meet thee as a man. As for our Redeemer, the Lord of hosts is his name, the Holy One of Israel. Sit thou silent, and get thee into darkness, O daughter of the Chaldeans, for thou shalt no more be called, The lady of kingdoms. I was wroth with my people, I have polluted mine inheritance, and given them into thine hand, thou didst show them no mercy, upon the ancient hast thou very heavily laid thy yoke. And thou saidst, I shall be a lady forever, so that thou didst not lay these things to thy heart, neither didst remember the latter end of it. Therefore hear now this, thou that art given to pleasures, that dwellest carelessly, that sayest in thine heart, I am, and none else besides me, I shall not sit as a widow, neither shall I know the loss of children, but these two things shall come to thee in a moment in one day, the loss of children, and widowhood, they shall come upon thee in their perfection for the multitude of thy sorceries, and for the great abundance of thine enchantments. For thou hast trusted in thy wickedness, thou hast said, None seeth me. Thy wisdom and thy knowledge, it hath perverted thee, and thou hast said in thine heart, I am, and none else besides me. Therefore shall evil come upon thee, thou shalt now know from whence it riseth, and mischief shall fall upon thee, thou shalt not be able to put it off, and desolation shall come upon thee suddenly, which thou shalt not know. Stand now with thine enchantments, and with the multitude of thy sorceries, wherein thou hast labored from thy youth, if so be thou shalt be able to profit, if so be thou mayest prevail. Thou art wearied in the multitude of thy counsels. Let now the astrologers, the stargazers, the monthly prognosticators, stand up, and save thee from these things that shall come upon thee. Behold, they shall be as stubble, the fire shall burn them, they shall not deliver themselves from the power of the flame, there shall not be a coal to warm at, nor fire to sit before it. Thus shall they be unto thee with whom thou hast labored, even thy merchants, from thy youth, they shall wander everyone to his quarter, none shall save thee.

17 HEAR ye this, O house of Jacob, which are called by the name of Israel, and are come forth out of the waters of Judah, which swear by the name of the Lord, and make mention of the God of Israel, but not in truth, nor in righteousness. For they call themselves of the holy city, and stay themselves upon the God of Israel, The Lord of hosts is his name. I have declared the former things from the beginning, and they went forth out of my mouth, and I showed them, I did them suddenly, and they came to pass. Because I knew that thou art obstinate, and thy neck is an iron sinew, and thy brow brass, I have even from the beginning declared it to thee, before it came to pass I showed it thee, lest thou shouldest say, Mine idol hath done them, and my graven image, and my molten image, hath commanded them. Thou hast heard, see all this, and will not ye declare it? I have showed thee new things from this time, even hidden things, and thou didst not know them. They are created now, and not from the beginning, even before the day when thou heardest them not, lest thou shouldest say, Behold, I knew them. Yea, thou heardest not, yea, thou knewest not, yea, from that time that thine ear was not opened, for I knew that thou wouldest deal very treacherously, and wast called a transgressor from the womb. For my name's sake will I defer mine anger, and for my praise will I refrain for thee, that I cut thee not off. Behold, I have refined thee, but not with silver, I have chosen thee in the furnace of affliction. For mine own sake, even for mine own sake, will I do it, for how should my name be polluted? And I will not give my glory unto another.

Hearken unto me, O Jacob and Israel, my called, I am he, I am the first, I also am the last. Mine hand also hath laid the foundation of the Earth, and my right hand hath spanned the heavens, when I call unto them, they stand up together. All ye, assemble yourselves, and hear, which among them hath declared these things? The Lord hath loved him, he will do his pleasure on Babylon, and his arm shall be on the Chaldeans. I, even I, have spoken, yea, I have called him, I have brought him, and he shall make his way prosperous.

Come ye near unto me, hear ye this, I have not spoken in secret from the beginning, from the time that it was, there am I, and now the Lord God, and his Spirit, hath sent me. Thus saith the Lord, thy Redeemer, the Holy One of Israel, I am the Lord thy God which teacheth thee to profit, which leadeth thee by the way that thou shouldest go. O that thou hadst hearkened to my commandments! Then had thy peace been as a river, and thy righteousness as the waves of the sea, thy seed also had been as the sand, and the offspring of thy bowels like the gravel thereof, his name should not have been cut off nor destroyed from before me.

Go ye forth of Babylon, flee ye from the Chaldeans, with a voice of singing declare ye, tell this, utter it even to the end of the earth, say ye, The Lord hath redeemed his servant Jacob. And they thirsted not when he led them through the deserts, he caused the waters to flow out of the rock for them, he clave the rock also, and the waters gushed out. There is no peace, saith the Lord, unto the wicked.

Listen, O isles, unto me, and hearken, ye people, from far, The Lord hath called me from the womb, from the bowels of my mother hath he made mention of my name. And he hath made my mouth like a sharp sword, in the shadow of his hand hath he hid me, and made me a polished shaft, in his quiver hath he hid me, and said unto me, Thou art my servant, O Israel, in whom I will be glorified. Then I said, I have labored in vain, I have spent my strength for naught, and in vain, yet surely my judgment is with the Lord, and my work with my God. And now, saith the Lord that formed me from the womb to be his servant, to bring Jacob again to him, Though Israel be not gathered, yet shall I be glorious in the eyes of the Lord, and my God shall be my strength. And he said, It is a light thing that thou shouldest be my servant to raise up the tribes of Jacob, and to restore the preserved of Israel, I will also give thee for a light to the Gentiles, that thou mayest be my salvation unto the end of the earth. Thus saith the Lord, the Redeemer of Israel, and his Holy One, to him whom man despiseth, to him whom the nation abhorreth, to a servant of rulers, Kings shall see and arise, princes also shall worship, because of the Lord that is faithful, and the Holy One of Israel, and he shall choose thee. Thus saith the Lord, In an acceptable time have I heard thee, and in a day of salvation have I helped thee, and I will preserve thee, and give thee for a covenant of the people, to establish the earth, to cause to inherit the desolate heritages, that thou mayest say to the prisoners, Go forth, to them that are in darkness, Show yourselves. They shall feed in the ways, and their pastures shall be in all high places. They shall not hunger nor thirst, neither shall the heat nor sun smite them, for he that hath mercy on them shall lead them, even by the springs of water shall he guide them. And I will make all my mountains a way, and my highways shall be exalted. Behold, these shall come from far, and, lo, these from the north and from the west, and these from the land of Sinim.

Sing, O heavens, and be joyful, O earth, and break forth into singing, O mountains, for the Lord hath comforted his people, and will have mercy upon his afflicted. But Zion said, The Lord hath forsaken me, and my Lord hath forgotten me. Can a woman forget her sucking child, that she should not have compassion on the son of her womb? Yea, they may forget, yet will I not forget thee. Behold, I have graven thee upon the palms of my hands, thy walls are continually before me. Thy children shall make haste, thy destroyers and they that made thee waste shall go forth of thee.

Lift up thine eyes round about, and behold, all these gather themselves together, and come to thee. As I live, saith the Lord, thou shalt surely clothe thee with them all, as with an ornament, and bind them on thee, as a bride doeth. For thy waste and thy desolate places, and the land of thy destruction, shall even now be too narrow by reason of the inhabitants, and they that swallowed thee up shall be far away. The children which thou shalt have, after thou hast lost the other, shall say again in thine ears,

The place is too strait for me, give place to me that I may dwell. Then shalt thou say in thine heart, Who hath begotten me these, seeing I have lost my children, and am desolate, a captive, and removing to and fro? And who hath brought up these? Behold, I was left alone, these, where had they been? Thus saith the Lord God, Behold, I will lift up mine hand to the Gentiles, and set up my standard to the people, and they shall bring thy sons in their arms, and thy daughters shall be carried upon their shoulders. And kings shall be thy nursing fathers, and their queens thy nursing mothers, they shall bow down to thee with their faces toward the Earth, and lick up the dust of thy feet, and thou shalt know that I am the Lord, for they shall not be ashamed that wait for me. Shall the prey be taken from the mighty, or the lawful captive delivered? But thus saith the Lord, even the captives of the mighty shall be taken away, and the prey of the terrible shall be delivered, for the mighty God shall deliver his covenant people. For thus saith the Lord, I will contend with them that contend with thee, and I will save thy children. And I will feed them that oppress thee with their own flesh, and they shall be drunken with their own blood, as with sweet wine, and all flesh shall know that I the Lord am thy Savior and thy Redeemer, the Mighty One of Jacob.

Yea, for thus saith the Lord, Have I put thee away, or have I cast thee off forever? For thus saith the Lord, Where is the bill of your mother's divorcement? To whom have I put thee away, or to which of my creditors have I sold you, yea, to whom have I sold you? Behold, for your iniquities have ye sold yourselves, and for your transgressions is your mother put away, wherefore, when I came there was no man, when I called there was none to answer. O house of Israel, is my hand shortened at all, that it cannot redeem, or have I no power to deliver? Behold, at my rebuke I dry up the sea, I make their rivers a wilderness, and their fish to stink, because the waters are dried up, and they die because of thirst. I clothe the heavens with blackness, and I make sackcloth their covering.

18 THE Lord God hath given me the tongue of the learned, that I should know how to speak a word in season unto thee, O house of Israel, when ye are weary. He waketh morning by morning, he waketh mine ear to hear as the learned. The Lord God hath appointed mine ears, and I was not rebellious, neither turned away back. I gave my back to the smiters, and my cheeks to them that plucked off the hair. I hid not my face from shame and spitting, for the Lord God will help me, therefore shall I not be confounded, therefore have I set my face like a flint, and I know that I shall not be ashamed, and the Lord is near and he justifieth me. Who will contend with me? let us stand together. Who is mine adversary? Let him come near me, and I will smite him with the strength of my mouth, for the Lord God will help me, and all they which shall condemn me, behold all they shall wax old as a garment, and the moth shall eat them up.

Who is among you that feareth the Lord, that obeyeth the voice of his servant, that walketh in darkness and hath no light? Let him trust in the name of the Lord, and stay upon his God. Behold all ye that kindleth fire, that compass yourselves about with sparks, walk in the light of your fire, and in the sparks which ye have kindled, this shall ye have of mine hand, ye shall lie down in sorrow.

Hearken unto me, ye that follow after righteousness, ye that seek the Lord, look unto the rock from whence ye were hewn, and to the hole of the pit from whence ye are digged. Look unto Abraham your father, and unto Sarah that bare you, for I called him alone, and blessed him, and increased him. For the Lord shall comfort Zion, he will comfort all her waste places, and he will make her wilderness like Eden, and her desert like the garden of the Lord, joy and gladness shall be found therein, thanksgiving, and the voice of melody. Hearken unto me, my people, and give ear unto me, O my nation, for a law shall proceed from me, and I will make my judgment to rest for a light of the people. My righteousness is near, my salvation is gone forth, and mine arms shall judge the people, the isles shall wait upon me, and on mine arm shall they trust. Lift up your eyes to the heavens, and look upon the Earth beneath, for the heavens shall vanish away like smoke, and the Earth shall wax old like a garment, and they that dwell therein shall die in like manner, but my salvation shall be forever, and my righteousness shall not be abolished. Hearken unto me, ye that know righteousness, the people in whose heart I have written my law, fear ye not the reproach of men, neither be ye afraid of their revilings. For the moth shall eat them up like a garment, and the worm shall eat them like wool, but my righteousness shall be forever, and my salvation from generation to generation.

Awake, awake, put on strength, O arm of the Lord, awake, as in the ancient days, in the generations of old. Art thou not it that hath cut Rahab, and wounded the dragon? Art thou not it which hath dried the sea, the waters of the great deep that hath made the depths of the sea a way for the ransomed to pass over? Therefore the redeemed of the Lord shall return, and come with singing unto Zion, and everlasting joy and holiness shall be upon their heads, they shall obtain gladness and joy, and sorrow and mourning shall flee away. I am he, yea, I am he that comforteth you, behold, who art thou, that thou shouldest be afraid of a man that shall die, and of the son of man which shall be made as grass, and forgettest the Lord thy Maker, that hath stretched forth the heavens, and laid the foundations of the Earth, and hast feared continually every day because of the fury of the oppressor, as if he were ready to destroy? And where is the fury of the oppressor? The captive exile hasteneth that he may be loosed, and that he should not die in the pit, nor that his bread should fail. But I am the Lord thy God, that divided the sea, whose waves roared, The Lord of hosts is his name. And I have put my words in thy mouth, and I have covered thee in the shadow of mine hand, that I may plant the heavens, and lay the foundations of the Earth, and say unto Zion, Behold, thou art my people.

Awake, awake, stand up, O Jerusalem, which hast drunk at the hand of the Lord the cup of his fury, thou hast drunken the dregs of the cup of trembling, and wrung them out. And there is none to guide her among all the sons whom she hath brought forth, neither is there any that taketh her by the hand of all the sons that she hath brought up. These two sons are come unto thee, they shall be sorry for thee, thy desolation, and destruction, and the famine, and the sword, and by whom shall I comfort thee? Thy sons have fainted save these two, they lie at the head of all the streets, as a wild bull in a net, they are full of the fury of the Lord, the rebuke of thy God. Therefore hear now this, thou afflicted, and drunken, but not with wine, thus saith thy Lord the Lord, and thy God that pleadeth the cause of his people, Behold, I have taken out of thine hand the cup of trembling, even the dregs of the cup of my fury, thou shalt no more drink it again, but I will put it into the hand of them that afflict thee, which have said to thy soul, Bow down, that we may go over, and thou hast laid thy body as the ground, and as the street, to them that went over.

Awake, awake, put on thy strength, O Zion, put on thy beautiful garments, O Jerusalem, the holy city, for henceforth there shall no more come into thee the uncircumcised and the unclean. Shake thyself from the dust, arise, and sit down, O Jerusalem, loose thyself from the bands of thy neck, O captive daughter of Zion. For thus saith the Lord, Ye have sold yourselves for naught, and ye shall be redeemed without money. For thus saith the Lord God, My people went down aforetime into Egypt to sojourn there, and the Assyrian oppressed them without cause. Now therefore, what have I here, saith the Lord, that my people is taken away for naught? They that rule over them make them to howl, saith the Lord, and my name continually every day is blasphemed. Therefore, my people shall know my name, yea, in that day they shall know that I am he that doth speak, behold, it is I.

And then shall they say, How beautiful upon the mountains are the feet of him that bringeth good tidings unto them, that publisheth peace, that bringeth good tidings unto them of good, that publisheth salvation, that saith unto Zion, Thy God reigneth! Thy watchmen shall lift up the voice, with the voice together shall they sing, for they shall see eye to eye, when the Lord shall bring again Zion. Break forth into joy, sing together, ye waste places of Jerusalem, for the Lord hath comforted his people, he hath redeemed Jerusalem. The Lord hath made bare his holy arm in the eyes of all the nations, and all the ends of the earth shall see the salvation of our God. Depart ye, depart ye, go ye out from thence, touch no unclean thing, go ye out of the midst of her, be ye clean, that bear the vessels of the Lord. For ye shall not go out with haste, nor go by flight, for the Lord will go before you, and the God of Israel will be your rearward.

19 BEHOLD, my servant shall deal prudently, he shall be exalted and extolled, and be very high. As many were astonished at thee, his visage was so marred more than any man, and his form more than the sons of men, so shall he gather many nations, the kings shall shut their mouths at him, for that which had not been told them shall they see, and that which they had not heard shall they consider.

Who hath believed our report? And to whom is the arm of the Lord revealed? For he shall grow up before him as a tender plant, and as a root out of a dry ground, he hath no form nor comeliness, and when we shall see him, there is no beauty that we should desire him. He is despised and rejected of men, a man of sorrows, and acquainted with grief, and we hid as it were our faces from him, he was despised, and we esteemed him not. Surely he hath borne our griefs, and carried our sorrows, yet we did esteem him stricken, smitten of God, and afflicted. But he was wounded for our transgressions, he was bruised for our iniquities, the chastisement of our peace was upon him, and with his stripes we are healed. All we like sheep have gone astray, we have turned every one to his own way, and the Lord hath laid on him the iniquity of us all. He was oppressed, and he was afflicted, yet he opened not his mouth, he is brought as a lamb to the slaughter, and as a sheep before her shearers is dumb, so he openeth not his mouth. He was taken from prison and from judgment, and who shall declare his generation? for he was cut off out of the land of the living, for the transgression of my people was he stricken. And he made his grave with the wicked, and with the rich in his death, because he had done no violence, neither was any deceit in his mouth. Yet it pleased the Lord to bruise him, he hath put him to grief, when thou shalt make his soul an offering for sin, he shall see his seed, he shall prolong his days, and the pleasure of the Lord shall prosper in his hand. He shall see of the travail of his soul, and shall be satisfied, by his knowledge shall my righteous servant justify many, for he shall bear their iniquities. Therefore will I divide him a portion with the great, and he shall divide the spoil with the strong, because he hath poured out his soul unto death, and he was numbered with the transgressors, and he bare the sin of many, and made intercession for the transgressors.

Sing, O barren, thou that didst not bear, break forth into singing and cry aloud, thou that didst not travail with child, for more are the children of the desolate than the children of the married wife, saith the Lord. Enlarge the place of thy tent, and let them stretch forth the curtains of thine habitations, spare not, lengthen thy cords, and strengthen thy stakes, for thou shalt break forth on the right hand and on the left, and thy seed shall inherit the Gentiles, and make the desolate cities to be inhabited. Fear not, for thou shalt not be ashamed, neither be thou confounded, for thou shalt not be put to shame, for thou shalt forget the shame of thy youth, and shalt not remember the reproach of thy widowhood anymore. For thy Maker is thine husband, The Lord of hosts is his name, and thy Redeemer the Holy One of Israel, The God of the whole earth shall he be called. For the Lord hath called thee as a woman forsaken and grieved in spirit, and a wife of youth, when thou wast refused, saith thy God. For a small moment have I forsaken thee, but with great mercies will I gather thee. In a little wrath I hid my face from thee for a moment, but with everlasting kindness will I have mercy on thee, saith the Lord thy Redeemer. For this is as the waters of Noah unto me, for as I have sworn that the waters of Noah should no more go over the earth, so have I sworn that I would not be wroth with thee, nor rebuke thee. For the mountains shall depart, and the hills be removed, but my kindness shall not depart from thee, neither shall the covenant of my people be removed, saith the Lord that hath mercy on thee. O thou afflicted, tossed with tempest, and not comforted, behold, I will lay thy stones with fair colors, and lay thy foundations with sapphires. And I will make thy windows of agates, and thy gates of carbuncles, and all thy borders of pleasant stones. And all thy children shall be taught of the Lord, and great shall be the peace of thy children. In righteousness shalt thou be established, thou shalt be far from oppression, for thou shalt not fear, and from terror, for it shall not come near thee. Behold, they shall surely gather together against thee, but not by me, whosoever shall gather together against thee shall fall for thy sake. Behold, I have created the smith that bloweth the coals in the fire, and that bringeth forth an instrument for his work, and I have created the waster to destroy. No weapon that is formed against thee shall prosper, and every tongue that shall rise against thee in judgment thou shalt condemn. This is the heritage of the servants of the Lord, and their righteousness is of me, saith the Lord.

20 HO, everyone that thirsteth, come ye to the waters, and he that hath no money, come ye, buy, and eat, yea, come, buy wine and milk without money and without price. Wherefore do ye spend money for that which is not bread and your labor for that which satisfieth not? Hearken diligently unto me, and eat ye that which is good, and let your soul delight itself in fatness. Incline your ear, and come unto me, hear, and your soul shall live, and I will make an everlasting covenant with you, even the sure mercies of David. Behold, I have given him for a witness to the people, a leader and commander to the people. Behold, thou shalt call a nation that thou knowest not, and nations that knew not thee shall run unto thee, because of the Lord thy God, and for the Holy One of Israel, for he hath glorified thee.

Seek ye the Lord while he may be found, call ye upon him while he is near, let the wicked forsake his way, and the unrighteous man his thoughts, and let him return unto the Lord, and he will have mercy upon him, and to our God, for he will abundantly pardon. For my thoughts are not your thoughts, neither are your ways my ways, saith the Lord. For as the heavens are higher than the Earth, so are my ways higher than your ways, and my thoughts than your thoughts. For as the rain cometh down, and the snow from Heaven, and returneth not thither, but watereth the Earth, and maketh it bring forth and bud, that it may give seed to the sower, and bread to the eater, so shall my word be that goeth forth out of my mouth, it shall not return unto me void, but it shall accomplish that which I please, and it shall prosper in the thing whereto I sent it. For ye shall go out with joy, and be led forth with peace, the mountains and the hills shall break forth before you into singing, and all the trees of the field shall clap their hands. Instead of the thorn shall come up the fir tree, and instead of the brier shall come up the myrtle tree, and it shall be to the Lord for a name, for an everlasting sign that shall not be cut off.

Thus saith the Lord, Keep ye judgment, and do justice, for my salvation is near to come, and my righteousness to be revealed. Blessed is the man that doeth this, and the son of man that layeth hold on it, that keepeth the sabbath from polluting it, and keepeth his hand from doing any evil. Neither let the son of the stranger, that hath joined himself to the Lord, speak, saying, The Lord hath utterly separated me from his people, neither let the eunuch say, Behold, I am a dry tree. For thus saith the Lord unto the eunuchs that keep my sabbaths, and choose the things that please me, and take hold of my covenant, even unto them will I give in mine house and within my walls a place and a name better than of sons and of daughters, I will give them an everlasting name that shall not be cut off. Also the sons of the stranger that join themselves to the Lord, to serve him, and to love the name of the Lord, to be his servants, everyone that keepeth the sabbath from polluting it, and taketh hold of my covenant, even them will I bring to my holy mountain, and make them joyful in my house of prayer, their burnt offerings and their sacrifices shall be accepted upon mine altar, for mine house shall be called a house of prayer for all people. The Lord God which gathereth the outcasts of Israel saith, Yet will I gather others to him, besides those that are gathered unto him.

All ye beasts of the field, come to devour, yea, all ye beasts in the forest. His watchmen are blind, they are all ignorant, they are all dumb dogs, they cannot bark, sleeping, lying down, loving to slumber. Yea, they are greedy dogs, which can never have enough, and they are shepherds that cannot understand, they all look to their own way, everyone for his gain, from his quarter. Come ye, say they, I will fetch wine, and we will fill ourselves with strong drink, and tomorrow shall be as this day, and much more abundant.

The righteous perisheth, and no man layeth it to heart, and merciful men are taken away, none considering that the righteous is taken away from the evil to come. He shall enter into peace, they shall rest in their beds, each one walking in his uprightness.

But draw near hither, ye sons of the sorceress, the seed of the adulterer and the whore. Against whom do ye sport yourselves? against whom make ye a wide mouth, and draw out the tongue? Are ye not children of transgression, a seed of falsehood, inflaming yourselves with idols under every green tree, slaying the children in the valleys under the clefts of the rocks? Among the smooth stones of the stream is thy portion, they, they are thy lot, even to them hast thou poured a drink offering, thou hast offered a meat offering. Should I receive comfort in these? Upon a lofty and high mountain hast thou set thy bed, even thither wentest thou up to offer sacrifice. Behind the doors also and the posts hast thou set up thy remembrance, for thou hast discovered thyself to another than me, and art gone up, thou hast enlarged thy bed, and made thee a covenant with them, thou lovedst their bed where thou sawest it. And thou wentest to the king with ointment, and didst increase thy perfumes, and didst send thy messengers far off, and didst debase thyself even unto hell. Thou art wearied in the greatness of thy way, yet saidst thou not. There is no hope, thou hast found the life of thine hand, therefore thou wast not grieved. And of whom hast thou been afraid or feared, that thou hast lied, and hast not remembered me, nor laid it to thy heart? Have not I held my peace even of old, and thou fearest me not? I will declare thy righteousness, and thy works, for they shall not profit thee. When thou criest, let thy companies deliver thee, but the wind shall carry them all away, vanity shall take them, but he that putteth his trust in me shall possess the land, and shall inherit my holy mountain, and shall say, Cast ye up, cast ye up, prepare the way, take up the stumbling block out of the way of my people. For thus saith the high and lofty One that inhabiteth eternity, whose name is Holy, I dwell in the high and holy place with him also that is of a contrite and humble spirit, to revive the spirit of the humble and to revive the heart of the contrite ones. For I will not contend forever, neither will I be always wroth, for the spirit should fail before me, and the souls which I have made. For the iniquity of his covetousness was I wroth, and smote him, I hid me and was wroth, and he went on frowardly in the way of his heart. I have seen his ways, and will heal him, I will lead him also, and restore comforts unto him and to his mourners. I create the fruit of the lips, Peace, peace to him that is far off, and to him that is near, saith the Lord, and I will heal him. But the wicked are like the troubled sea, when it cannot rest, whose waters cast up mire and dirt. There is no peace, saith my God, to the wicked.

Cry aloud, spare not, lift up thy voice like a trumpet, and show my people their transgression, and the house of Jacob their sins. Yet they seek me daily, and delight to know my ways, as a nation that did righteousness, and forsook not the ordinance of their God, they ask of me the ordinances of justice, they take delight in approaching to God. Wherefore have we fasted, say they, and thou seest not? Wherefore have we afflicted our soul, and thou takest no knowledge?

Behold, in the day of your fast ye find pleasure, and exact all your labors. Behold, ye fast for strife and debate, and to smite with the fist of wickedness, ye shall not fast as ye do this day, to make your voice to be heard on high. Is it such a fast that I have chosen: a day for a man to afflict his soul? Is it to bow down his head as a bulrush and to spread sackcloth and ashes under him? Wilt thou call this a fast and an acceptable day to the Lord? Is not this the fast that I have chosen: to loose the bands of wickedness, to undo the heavy burdens, and to let the oppressed go free, and that ye break every yoke? Is it not to deal thy bread to the hungry, and that thou bring the poor that are cast out to thy house? When thou seest the naked, that thou cover him, and that thou hide not thyself from thine own flesh? Then shall thy light break forth as the morning, and thine health shall spring forth speedily, and thy righteousness shall go before thee, the glory of the Lord shall be thy rearward. Then shalt thou call, and the Lord shall answer, thou shalt cry, and he shall say, Here I am. If thou take away from the midst of thee the yoke, the putting forth of the finger, and speaking vanity, and if thou draw out thy soul to the hungry, and satisfy the afflicted soul, then shall thy light rise in obscurity, and thy darkness be as the noonday, and the Lord shall guide thee continually, and satisfy thy soul in drought, and make fat thy bones, and thou shalt be like a watered garden, and like a spring of water, whose waters fail not. And they that shall be of thee shall build the old waste places, thou shalt raise up the foundations of many generations, and thou shalt be called, The repairer of the breach, The restorer of paths to dwell in. If thou turn away thy foot from the sabbath, from doing thy pleasure on my holy day, and call the sabbath a delight, the holy of the Lord, honorable, and shalt honor him, not doing thine own ways, nor finding thine own pleasure, nor speaking thine own words, then shalt thou delight thyself in the Lord, and I will cause thee to ride upon the high places of the Earth, and feed thee with the heritage of Jacob thy father, for the mouth of the Lord hath spoken it.

21 BEHOLD, the Lord's hand is not shortened, that it cannot save, neither his ear heavy, that it cannot hear, but your iniquities have separated between you and your God, and your sins have hid his face from you, that he will not hear. For your hands are defiled with blood, and your fingers with iniquity, your lips have spoken lies, your tongue hath muttered perverseness. None calleth for justice, nor any pleadeth for truth, they trust in vanity, and speak lies, they conceive mischief, and bring forth iniquity. They hatch cockatrice eggs, and weave the spider's web, he that eateth of their eggs dieth, and that which is crushed breaketh out into a viper. Their webs shall not become garments, neither shall they cover themselves with their works, their works are works of iniquity, and the act of violence is in their hands. Their feet run to evil, and they make haste to shed innocent blood, their thoughts are thoughts of iniquity, wasting and destruction are in their paths. The way of peace they know not, and there is no judgment in their goings, they have made them crooked paths, whosoever goeth therein shall not know peace.

Therefore is judgment far from us, neither doth justice overtake us, we wait for light, but behold obscurity, for brightness, but we walk in darkness. We grope for the wall like the blind, and we grope as if we had no eyes, we stumble at noonday as in the night, we are in desolate places as dead men. We roar all like bears, and mourn sore like doves, we look for judgment, but there is none, for salvation, but it is far off from us. For our transgressions are multiplied before thee, and our sins testify against us, for our transgressions are with us, and as for our iniquities, we know them, in transgressing and lying against the Lord, and departing away from our God, speaking oppression and revolt, conceiving and uttering from the heart words of falsehood. And judgment is turned away backward, and justice standeth afar off, for truth is fallen in the street, and equity cannot enter. Yea, truth faileth, and he that departeth from evil maketh himself a prey, and the Lord saw it, and it displeased him that there was no judgment. And he saw that there was no man, and wondered that there was no intercessor, therefore his arm brought salvation unto him, and his righteousness, it sustained him. For he put on righteousness as a breastplate, and a helmet of salvation upon his head, and he put on the garments of vengeance for clothing, and was clad with zeal as a cloak. According to their deeds, accordingly he will repay, fury to his adversaries, recompense to his enemies, to the islands he will repay recompense. So shall they fear the name of the Lord from the west, and his glory from the rising of the sun. When the enemy shall come in like a flood, the Spirit of the Lord shall lift up a standard against him. And the Redeemer shall come to Zion, and unto them that turn from transgression in Jacob, saith the Lord. As for me, this is my covenant with them, saith the Lord, my Spirit that is upon thee and my words which I have put in thy mouth shall not depart out of thy mouth, nor out of the mouth of thy seed, nor out of the mouth of thy seed's seed, saith the Lord, from henceforth and for ever.

22 ARISE, shine, for thy light is come, and the glory of the Lord is risen upon thee. For, behold, the darkness shall cover the earth, and gross darkness the people, but the Lord shall arise upon thee, and his glory shall be seen upon thee. And the Gentiles shall come to thy light, and kings to the brightness of thy rising. Lift up thine eyes round about, and see, all they gather themselves together, they come to thee, thy sons shall come from far, and thy daughters shall be nursed at thy side. Then thou shalt see, and flow together, and thine heart shall fear, and be enlarged, because the abundance of the sea shall be converted unto thee, the forces of the Gentiles shall come unto thee. The multitude of camels shall cover thee, the dromedaries of Midian and Ephah, all they from Sheba shall come, they shall bring gold and incense, and they shall show forth the praises of the Lord. All the flocks of Kedar shall be gathered together unto thee, the rams of Nebaioth shall minister unto thee, they shall come up with acceptance on mine altar, and I will glorify the house of my glory. Who are these that fly as a cloud, and as the doves to their windows? Surely the isles shall wait for me, and the ships of Tarshish first, to bring thy sons from far, their silver and their gold with them, unto the name of the Lord thy God, and to the Holy One of Israel, because he hath glorified thee. And the sons of strangers shall build up thy walls, and their kings shall minister unto thee, for in my wrath I smote thee, but in my favor have I had mercy on thee. Therefore thy gates shall be open continually, they shall not be shut day nor night, that men may bring unto thee the forces of the Gentiles, and that their kings may be brought. For the nation and kingdom that will not serve thee shall perish, yea, those nations shall be utterly wasted. The glory of Lebanon shall come unto thee, the fir tree, the pine tree, and the box together, to beautify the place of my sanctuary, and I will make the place of my feet glorious. The sons also of them that afflicted thee shall come bending unto thee, and all they that despised thee shall bow themselves down at the soles of thy feet, and they shall call thee, The city of the Lord, The Zion of the Holy One of Israel. Whereas thou hast been forsaken and hated, so that no man went through thee, I will make thee an Eternal excellency, a joy of many generations. Thou shalt also suck the milk of the Gentiles, and shalt suck the breast of kings, and thou shalt know that I the Lord am thy Savior and thy Redeemer, the Mighty One of Jacob. For brass I will bring gold, and for iron I will bring silver, and for wood brass, and for stones iron, I will also make thy officers peace, and thine exactors righteousness. Violence shall no more be heard in thy land, wasting nor destruction within thy borders, but thou shalt call thy walls Salvation, and thy gates Praise. The sun shall be no more thy

light by day, neither for brightness shall the moon give light unto thee, but the Lord shall be unto thee an everlasting light, and thy God thy glory. Thy sun shall no more go down, neither shall thy moon withdraw itself, for the Lord shall be thine everlasting light, and the days of thy mourning shall be ended. Thy people also shall be all righteous, they shall inherit the land forever, the branch of my planting, the work of my hands, that I may be glorified. A little one shall become a thousand, and a small one a strong nation, I the Lord will hasten it in my time.

23 THE Spirit of the Lord God is upon me, because the Lord hath anointed me to preach good tidings unto the meek, he hath sent me to bind up the brokenhearted, to proclaim liberty to the captives, and the opening of the prison to them that are bound, to proclaim the acceptable year of the Lord, and the day of vengeance of our God, to comfort all that mourn, to appoint unto them that mourn in Zion, to give unto them beauty for ashes, the oil of joy for mourning, the garment of praise for the spirit of heaviness, that they might be called trees of righteousness, the planting of the Lord, that he might be glorified. And they shall build the old wastes, they shall raise up the former desolations, and they shall repair the waste cities, the desolations of many generations. And strangers shall stand and feed your flocks, and the sons of the alien shall be your ploughmen and your vinedressers. But ye shall be named the Priests of the Lord, men shall call you the Ministers of our God, ye shall eat the riches of the Gentiles, and in their glory shall ye boast yourselves. For your shame ye shall have double, and for confusion they shall rejoice in their portion, therefore in their land they shall possess the double, everlasting joy shall be unto them. For I the Lord love judgment, I hate robbery for burnt offering, and I will direct their work in truth, and I will make an everlasting covenant with them. And their seed shall be known among the Gentiles, and their offspring among the people, all that see them shall acknowledge them, that they are the seed which the Lord hath blessed. I will greatly rejoice in the Lord, my soul shall be joyful in my God, for he hath clothed me with the garments of salvation, he hath covered me with the robe of righteousness, as a bridegroom decketh himself with ornaments, and as a bride adorneth herself with her jewels. For as the Earth bringeth forth her bud, and as the garden causeth the things that are sown in it to spring forth, so the Lord God will cause righteousness and praise to spring forth before all the nations.

24 FOR Zion's sake will I not hold my peace, and for Jerusalem's sake I will not rest, until the righteousness thereof go forth as brightness, and the salvation thereof as a lamp that burneth. And the Gentiles shall see thy righteousness, and all kings thy glory, and thou shalt be called by a new name, which the mouth of the Lord shall name. Thou shalt also be a crown of glory in the hand of the Lord, and a royal diadem in the hand of thy God. Thou shalt no more be termed Forsaken, neither shall thy land any more be termed Desolate, but thou shall be called Delightful, and thy land Union, for the Lord delighteth in thee, and thy land shall be married. For as a young man marrieth a virgin, so shall thy God marry thee, and as the bridegroom rejoiceth over the bride, so shall thy God rejoice over thee. I have set watchmen upon thy walls, O Jerusalem, which shall never hold their peace day nor night, ye that make mention of the Lord, keep not silence, and give him no rest, till he establish, and till he make Jerusalem a praise in the earth. The Lord hath sworn by his right hand, and by the arm of his strength, Surely I will no more give thy corn to be meat for thine enemies, and the sons of the stranger shall not drink thy wine, for the which thou hast labored, but they that have gathered it shall eat it, and praise the Lord, and they that have brought it together shall drink it in the courts of my holiness.

Go through, go through the gates, prepare ye the way of the people, cast up, cast up the highway, gather out the stones, lift up a standard for the people. Behold, the Lord hath proclaimed unto the end of the world, Say ye to the daughter of Zion, Behold, thy salvation cometh, behold, his reward is with him, and his work before him. And they shall call them, The holy people, The redeemed of the Lord, and thou shalt be called, Sought out, A city not forsaken.

Who is this that cometh from Edom, with dyed garments from Bozrah? This that is glorious in his apparel, traveling in the greatness of his strength? I that speak in righteousness, mighty to save. Wherefore art thou red in thine apparel, and thy garments like him that treadeth in the winefat? I have trodden the winepress alone, and of the people there was none with me, for I will tread them in mine anger, and trample them in my fury, and their blood shall be sprinkled upon my garments, and I will stain all my raiment. For the day of vengeance is in mine heart, and the year of my redeemed is come. And I looked, and there was none to help, and I wondered that there was none to uphold, therefore mine own arm brought salvation unto me, and my fury, it upheld me. And I will tread down the people in mine anger, and make them drunk in my fury, and I will bring down their strength to the earth.

I will mention the lovingkindnesses of the Lord, and the praises of the Lord, according to all that the Lord hath bestowed on us, and the great goodness toward the house of Israel, which he hath bestowed on them according to his mercies, and according to the multitude of his lovingkindnesses. For he said, Surely they are my people, children that will not lie, so he was their Savior. In all their affliction he was afflicted, and the angel of his presence saved them, in his love and in his pity he redeemed them, and he bare them, and carried them all the days of old. But they rebelled, and vexed his Holy Spirit, therefore he was turned to be their enemy, and he fought against them. Then he remembered the days of old, Moses, and his people, saying, Where is he that brought them up out of the sea with the shepherd of his flock? where is he that put his Holy Spirit within him? That led them by the right hand of Moses with his glorious arm, dividing the water before them, to make himself an everlasting name? That led them through the deep, as a horse in the wilderness, that they should not stumble? As a beast goeth down into the valley, the Spirit of the Lord caused him to rest, so didst thou lead thy people, to make thyself a glorious name.

Look down from Heaven, and behold from the habitation of thy holiness and of thy glory, Where is thy zeal and thy strength, the sounding of thy bowels and of thy mercies toward me? Are they restrained? Doubtless thou art our Father, though Abraham be ignorant of us, and Israel acknowledge us not, thou, O Lord, art our Father, our Redeemer, thy name is from everlasting. O Lord, why hast thou suffered us to err from thy ways, and to harden our heart from thy fear? Return for thy servants' sake, the tribes of thine inheritance. The people of thy holiness have possessed it but a little while, our adversaries have trodden down thy sanctuary. We are thine, thou never barest rule over them, they were not called by thy name.

Oh that thou wouldest rend the heavens, that thou wouldest come down, that the mountains might flow down at thy presence, as when the melting fire burneth, the fire causeth the waters to boil, to make thy name known to thine adversaries, that the nations may tremble at thy presence! When thou didst terrible things which we looked not for, thou camest down, the mountains flowed down at thy presence. For since the beginning of the world men have not heard, nor perceived by the ear, neither hath the eye seen, O God, besides thee, what he hath prepared for him that waiteth for him. Thou meetest him that worketh righteousness, and rejoiceth him that remembereth thee in thy ways, in righteousness there is continuance, and such shall be saved. But we have sinned, we are all as an unclean thing, and all our righteousnesses are as filthy rags, and we all do fade as a leaf, and our iniquities, like the wind, have taken us away. And there is none that calleth upon thy name, that stirreth up himself to take hold of thee, for thou hast hid thy face from us, and hast consumed us, because of our iniquities. But now, O Lord, thou art our Father, we are the clay, and thou our potter, and we all are the work of thy hand. Be not wroth very sore, O Lord, neither remember iniquity forever, behold, see, we beseech thee, we are all thy people. Thy holy cities are a wilderness, Zion is a wilderness, Jerusalem a desolation. Our holy and our beautiful house, where our fathers praised thee, is burned up with fire, and all our pleasant things are laid waste. Wilt thou refrain thyself for these things, O Lord? Wilt thou hold thy peace and afflict us very sore?

I am found of them who seek after me, I give unto all them that ask of me, I am not found of them that sought me not, or that inquireth not after me. I said unto my servant, Behold me, look upon me, I will send you unto a nation that is not called after my name, for I have spread out my hands all the day to a people who walketh not in my ways, and their works are evil and not good, and they walk after their own thoughts. A people that provoketh me to anger continually to my face, that sacrificeth in gardens, and burneth incense upon altars of brick, which remain among the graves, and lodge in the monuments, which eat swine's flesh, and broth of abominable beasts, and pollute their vessels, which say, Stand by thyself, come not near to me, for I am holier than thou. These are a smoke in my nose, a fire that burneth all the day. Behold, it is written before me, I will not keep silence, but will recompense, even recompense into their bosom, your iniquities, and the iniquities of your fathers together, saith the Lord, which have burned incense upon the mountains, and blasphemed me upon the hills, therefore will I measure their former work into their bosom.

Thus saith the Lord, As the new wine is found in the cluster and one saith, Destroy it not, for a blessing is in it, so will I do for my servants' sake, that I may not destroy them all. And I will bring forth a seed out of Jacob, and out of Judah an inheritor of my mountains, and mine elect shall inherit it, and my servants shall dwell there. And Sharon shall be a fold of flocks, and the valley of Achor a place for the herds to lie down in, for my people that have sought me.

But ye are they that forsake the Lord, that forget my holy mountain, that prepare a table for that troop, and that furnish the drink offering unto that number. Therefore will I number you to the sword, and ye shall all bow down to the slaughter, because when I called, ye did not answer, when I spake, ye did not hear, but did evil before mine eyes, and did choose that wherein I delighted not. Therefore thus saith the Lord God, Behold, my servants shall eat, but ye shall be hungry, behold, my servants shall drink, but ye shall be thirsty, behold, my servants shall rejoice, but ye shall be ashamed. Behold, my servants shall sing for joy of heart, but ye shall cry for sorrow of heart, and shall howl for vexation of spirit. And ye shall leave your name for a curse unto my chosen, for the Lord God shall slay thee, and call his servants by another name, that he who blesseth himself in the earth shall bless himself in the God of truth, and he that sweareth in the earth shall swear by the God of truth, because the former troubles are forgotten, and because they are hid from mine eyes.

For, behold, I create new heavens and a new Earth, and the former shall not be remembered, nor come into mind. But be ye glad and rejoice for ever in that which I create, for, behold, I create Jerusalem a rejoicing, and her people a joy. And I will rejoice in Jerusalem, and joy in my people, and the voice of weeping shall be no more heard in her, nor the voice of crying. In those days there shall be no more thence an infant of days, nor an old man that hath not filled his days, for the child shall not die, but shall live to be an hundred years old, but the sinner, living to be an hundred years old, shall be accursed. And they shall build houses, and inhabit them, and they shall plant vineyards, and eat the fruit of them. They shall not build, and another inhabit, they shall not plant, and another eat, for as the days of a tree are the days of my people, and mine elect shall long enjoy the work of their hands. They shall not labor in vain, nor bring forth for trouble, for they are the seed of the blessed of the Lord, and their offspring with them. And it shall come to pass, that before they call, I will answer, and while they are yet speaking, I will hear. The wolf and the lamb shall feed together, and the lion shall eat straw like the bullock, and dust shall be the serpent's meat. They shall not hurt nor destroy in all my holy mountain, saith the Lord.

25 THUS saith the Lord, The Heaven is my throne, and the Earth is my footstool, where is the house that ye build unto me, and where is the place of my rest? For all those things hath mine hand made, and all those things have been, saith the Lord, but to this man will I look, even to him that is poor and of a contrite spirit, and trembleth at my word. He that killeth an ox is as if he slew a man, he that sacrificeth a lamb, as if he cut off a dog's neck, he that offereth an oblation, as if he offered swine's blood, he that burneth incense, as if he blessed an idol. Yea, they have chosen their own ways, and their soul delighteth in their abominations. I also will choose their delusions, and will bring their fears upon them, because when I called, none did answer, when I spake, they did not hear, but they did evil before mine eyes, and chose that in which I delighted not.

Hear the word of the Lord, ye that tremble at his word, Your brethren that hated you, that cast you out for my name's sake said, Let the Lord be glorified, but he shall appear to your joy, and they shall be ashamed. A voice of noise from the city, a voice from the temple, a voice of the Lord that rendereth recompense to his enemies. Before she travailed, she brought forth, before her pain came, she was delivered of a man-child. Who hath heard such a thing? Who hath seen such things? Shall the Earth be made to bring forth in one day? Or shall a nation be born at once? For as soon as Zion travailed, she brought forth her children. Shall I bring to the birth, and not cause to bring forth?, saith the Lord. Shall I cause to bring forth, and shut the womb?, saith thy God. Rejoice ye with Jerusalem, and be glad with her, all ye that love her, rejoice for joy with her, all ye that mourn for her, that ye may suck, and be satisfied with the breasts of her consolations, that ye may milk out, and be delighted with the abundance of her glory. For thus saith the Lord, Behold, I will extend peace to her like a river, and the glory of the Gentiles like a flowing stream, then shall ye suck, ye shall be borne upon her sides, and be dandled upon her knees. As one whom his mother comforteth, so will I comfort you, and ye shall be comforted in Jerusalem. And when ye see this, your heart shall rejoice, and your bones shall flourish like an herb, and the hand of the Lord shall be known toward his servants, and his indignation toward his enemies. For, behold, the Lord will come with fire, and with his chariots like a whirlwind, to render his anger with fury, and his rebuke with flames of fire. For by fire and by his sword will the Lord plead with all flesh, and the slain of the Lord shall be many. They that sanctify themselves, and purify themselves in the gardens behind one tree in the midst, eating swine's flesh, and the abomination, and the mouse, shall be consumed together, saith the Lord. For I know their works and their thoughts, it shall come, that I will gather all nations and tongues, and they shall come, and see my glory. And I will set a sign among them, and I will send those that escape of them unto the nations, to Tarshish, Pul, and Lud, that draw the bow, to Tubal and Javan, to the isles afar off, that have not heard my fame, neither have seen my glory, and they shall declare my glory among the Gentiles. And they shall bring all your brethren for an offering unto the Lord out of all nations upon horses, and in chariots, and in litters, and upon mules, and upon swift beasts, to my holy mountain Jerusalem, saith the Lord, as the children of Israel bring an offering in a clean vessel into the house of the Lord. And I will also take of them for priests and for Levites, saith the Lord. For as the new heavens and the new Earth, which I will make, shall remain before me, saith the Lord, so shall your seed and your name remain. And it shall come to pass, that from one new moon to another, and from one sabbath to another, shall all flesh come to worship before me, saith the Lord. And they shall go forth, and look upon the carcasses of the men that have transgressed against me, for their worm shall not die, neither shall their fire be quenched, and they shall be an abhorring unto all flesh.

THE BOOK OF THE PROPHET JEREMIAH

THE words of Jeremiah the son of Hilkiah of the priests that were in Anathoth in the land of Benjamin, to whom the word of the Lord came in the days of Josiah the son of Amon king of Judah, in the thirteenth year of his reign. It came also in the days of Jehoiakim the son of Josiah king of Judah unto the end of the eleventh year of Zedekiah the son of Josiah king of Judah unto the carrying away of Jerusalem captive in the fifth month.

Then the word of the Lord came unto me, saying, Before I formed thee in the belly I knew thee, and before thou camest forth out of the womb I sanctified thee and I ordained thee a prophet unto the nations. Then said I, Ah, Lord God! Behold, I cannot speak for I am a child. But the Lord said unto me, Say not, I am a child, for thou shalt go to all that I shall send thee and whatsoever I command thee thou shalt speak. Be not afraid of their faces, for I am with thee to deliver thee, saith the Lord. Then the Lord put forth his hand and touched my mouth. And the Lord said unto me, Behold, I have put my words in thy mouth. See, I have this day set thee over the nations and over the kingdoms, to root out, and to pull down, and to destroy, and to throw down, to build, and to plant.

Moreover the word of the Lord came unto me saying, Jeremiah, what seest thou? And I said, I see a rod of an almond tree. Then said the Lord unto me, Thou hast well seen, for I will hasten my word to perform it. And the word of the Lord came unto me the second time, saying, What seest thou? And I said, I see a seething pot and the face thereof is toward the north. Then the Lord said unto me, Out of the north an evil shall break forth upon all the inhabitants of the land. For lo, I will call all the families of the kingdoms of the north, saith the Lord, and they shall come and they shall set everyone his throne at the entering of the gates of Jerusalem, and against all the walls thereof round about, and against all the cities of Judah. And I will utter my judgments against them touching all their wickedness who have forsaken me, and have burned incense unto other gods, and worshipped the works of their own hands. Thou therefore gird up thy loins and arise, and speak unto them all that I command thee, be not dismayed at their faces lest I confound thee before them. For, behold, I have made thee this day a defensed city, and an iron pillar, and brazen walls against the whole land, against the kings of Judah, against the princes thereof, against the priests thereof, and against the people of the land. And they shall fight against thee, but they shall not prevail against thee, for I am with thee, saith the Lord, to deliver thee.

Moreover the word of the Lord came to me, saying, Go and cry in the ears of Jerusalem saying, Thus saith the Lord, I remember thee, the kindness of thy youth, the love of thine espousals, when thou wentest after me in the wilderness in a land that was not sown. Israel was holiness unto the Lord, and the firstfruits of his increase, all that devour him shall offend, evil shall come upon them, saith the Lord. Hear ye the word of the Lord, O house of Jacob and all the families of the house of Israel, thus saith the Lord, What iniquity have your fathers found in me that they are gone far from me, and have walked after vanity, and are become vain? Neither said they, Where is the Lord that brought us up out of the land of Egypt, that led us through the wilderness, through a land of deserts and of pits, through a land of drought and of the shadow of death, through a land that no man passed through and where no man dwelt? And I brought you into a plentiful country to eat the fruit thereof and the goodness thereof, but when ye entered, ye defiled my land and made mine heritage an abomination. The priests said not, Where is the Lord? And they that handle the law knew me not; the pastors also transgressed against me, and the prophets prophesied by Baal, and walked after things that do not profit. Wherefore I will yet plead with you, saith the Lord, and with your children's children will I plead. For pass over the isles of Chittim and see, and send unto Kedar and consider diligently, and see if there be such a thing. Hath a nation changed their gods which are yet no gods? But my people have changed their glory for that which doth not profit. Be astonished, O ye heavens, at this and be horribly afraid; be ye very desolate, saith the Lord. For my people have committed two evils: they have forsaken me, the fountain of living waters, and hewed them out cisterns, broken cisterns, that can hold no water.

Is Israel a servant? Is he a homeborn slave? Why is he spoiled? The young lions roared upon him and yelled, and they made his land waste, his cities are burned without inhabitant. Also the children of Noph and Tahapanes have broken the crown of thy head. Hast thou not procured this unto thyself in that thou hast forsaken the Lord thy God when he led thee by the way? And now what hast thou to do in the way of Egypt, to drink the waters of Sihor? Or what hast thou to do in the way of Assyria, to drink the waters of the river? Thine own wickedness shall correct thee and thy backslidings shall reprove thee, know therefore and see that it is an evil thing and bitter that thou hast forsaken the Lord thy God, and that my fear is not in thee, saith the Lord God of hosts. For of old time I have broken thy yoke and burst thy bands, and thou saidst, I will not transgress, when upon every high hill and under every green tree thou wanderest playing the harlot. Yet I had planted thee a noble vine, wholly a right seed, how then art thou turned into the degenerate plant of a strange vine unto me? For though thou wash thee with nitre and take thee much soap, yet thine iniquity is marked before me, saith the Lord God. How canst thou say, I am not polluted, I have not gone after Baalim? See thy way in the valley, know what thou hast done, thou art a swift dromedary traversing her ways, a wild ass used to the wilderness, that snuffeth up the wind at her pleasure, in her occasion who can turn her away? All they that seek her will weary themselves, in her month they shall not find her. Withhold thy foot from being unshod and thy throat from thirst, but thou saidst, There is no hope, no, for I have loved strangers and after them will I go. As the thief is ashamed when he is found, so is the house of Israel ashamed, they, their kings, their princes, and their priests, and their prophets, saying to a stock, Thou art my father, and to a stone, Thou hast brought me forth, for they have turned their back unto me and not their face, but in the time of their trouble they will say, Arise and save us. But where are thy gods that thou hast made thee? Let them arise, if they can save thee in the time of thy trouble, for according to the number of thy cities are thy gods, O Judah. Wherefore will ye plead with me? Ye all have transgressed against me, saith the Lord. In vain have I smitten your children, they received no correction; your own sword hath devoured your prophets like a destroying lion.

O generation, see ye the word of the Lord. Have I been a wilderness unto Israel? A land of darkness? Wherefore say my people, We are lords, we will come no more unto thee? Can a maid forget her ornaments or a bride her attire? Yet my people have forgotten me days without number. Why trimmest thou thy way to seek love? Therefore hast thou also taught the wicked ones thy ways. Also in thy skirts is found the blood of the souls of the poor innocents, I have not found it by secret search, but upon all these. Yet thou sayest, Because I am innocent, surely his anger shall turn from me. Behold, I will plead with thee because thou sayest, I have not sinned. Why gaddest thou about so much to change thy way? Thou also shalt be ashamed of Egypt as thou wast ashamed of Assyria. Yea, thou shalt go forth from him and thine hands upon thine head, for the Lord hath rejected thy confidences and thou shalt not prosper in them.

They say, If a man put away his wife, and she go from him and become another man's, shall he return unto her again? Shall not that land be greatly polluted? But thou hast played the harlot with many lovers yet return again to me, saith the Lord. Lift up thine eyes unto the high places and see where thou hast not been lain with. In the ways hast thou sat for them as the Arabian in the wilderness, and thou hast polluted the land with thy whoredoms and wickedness. Therefore thy showers have been withholden and there hath been no latter rain, and thou hadst a whore's forehead, thou refusedst to be ashamed. Wilt thou not from this time cry unto me, My father, thou art the guide of my youth? Will he reserve his anger forever? Will he keep it to the end? Behold, thou hast spoken and done evil things as thou couldst.

2 THE Lord said also unto me in the days of Josiah the king, Hast thou seen that which backsliding Israel hath done? She is gone up upon every high mountain and under every green tree and there hath played the harlot. And I said after she had done all these things, Turn thou unto me. But she returned not. And her treacherous sister Judah saw it. And I saw, when for all the causes whereby backsliding Israel committed adultery, I had put her away and given her a bill of divorce, yet her treacherous sister Judah feared not, but went and played the harlot also. And it came to pass through the lightness of her whoredom that she defiled the land and committed adultery with stones and with stocks. And yet, for all this her treacherous sister Judah hath not turned unto me with her whole heart, but feignedly, saith the Lord. And the Lord said unto me, The backsliding Israel hath justified herself more than treacherous Judah. Go and proclaim these words toward the north and say, Return, thou backsliding Israel, saith the Lord, and I will not cause mine anger to fall upon you, for I am merciful, saith the Lord, and I will not keep anger forever. Only acknowledge thine iniquity, that thou hast transgressed against the Lord thy God, and hast scattered thy ways to the strangers under every green tree, and ye have not obeyed my voice, saith the Lord. Turn, O backsliding children, saith the Lord, for I am married unto you, and I will take you one of a city and two of a family, and I will bring you to Zion, and I will give you pastors according to mine heart which shall feed you with knowledge and understanding. And it shall come to pass when ye be multiplied and increased in the land in those days, saith the Lord, they shall say no more, The ark of the covenant of the Lord, neither shall it come to mind, neither shall they remember it, neither shall they visit it, neither shall that be done anymore. At that time they shall call Jerusalem the throne of the Lord, and all the nations shall be gathered unto it, to the name of the Lord, to Jerusalem, neither shall they walk anymore after the imagination of their evil heart. In those days the house of Judah shall walk with the house of Israel and they shall come together out of the land of the north to the land that I have given for an inheritance unto your fathers. But I said, How shall I put thee among the children and give thee a pleasant land, a goodly heritage of the hosts of nations? And I said, Thou shalt call me, My father, and shalt not turn away from me. Surely as a wife treacher-

ously departeth from her husband, so have ye dealt treacherously with me, O house of Israel, saith the Lord.

A voice was heard upon the high places, weeping and supplications of the children of Israel, for they have perverted their way and they have forgotten the Lord their God. Return, ye backsliding children, and I will heal your backslidings. Behold, we come unto thee, for thou art the Lord our God. Truly in vain is salvation hoped for from the hills and from the multitude of mountains; truly in the Lord our God is the salvation of Israel. For shame hath devoured the labor of our fathers from our youth, their flocks and their herds, their sons and their daughters. We lie down in our shame and our confusion covereth us, for we have sinned against the Lord our God, we and our fathers, from our youth even unto this day, and have not obeyed the voice of the Lord our God.

If thou wilt return, O Israel, saith the Lord, return unto me and if thou wilt put away thine abominations out of my sight, then shalt thou not remove. And thou shalt swear, The Lord liveth, in truth, in judgment, and in righteousness, and the nations shall bless themselves in him, and in him shall they glory. For thus saith the Lord to the men of Judah and Jerusalem, Break up your fallow ground and sow not among thorns. Circumcise yourselves to the Lord and take away the foreskins of your heart, ye men of Judah and inhabitants of Jerusalem, lest my fury come forth like a fire, and burn that none can quench it, because of the evil of your doings. Declare ye in Judah and publish in Jerusalem and say, Blow ye the trumpet in the land, cry, gather together and say, Assemble yourselves and let us go into the defensed cities. Set up the standard toward Zion, retire, stay not, for I will bring evil from the north and a great destruction. The lion is come up from his thicket and the destroyer of the Gentiles is on his way, he is gone forth from his place to make thy land desolate, and thy cities shall be laid waste, without an inhabitant. For this gird you with sackcloth, lament and howl, for the fierce anger of the Lord is not turned back from us. And it shall come to pass at that day, saith the Lord, that the heart of the king shall perish and the heart of the princes and the priests shall be astonished and the prophets shall wonder.

Then said I, Ah, Lord God! Surely thou hast greatly deceived this people and Jerusalem saying, Ye shall have peace, whereas the sword reacheth unto the soul. At that time shall it be said to this people and to Jerusalem, A dry wind of the high places in the wilderness toward the daughter of my people, not to fan, nor to cleanse, even a full wind from those places shall come unto me, now also will I give sentence against them. Behold, he shall come up as clouds, and his chariots shall be as a whirlwind, his horses are swifter than eagles. Wo unto us, for we are spoiled. O Jerusalem, wash thine heart from wickedness that thou mayest be saved. How long shall thy vain thoughts lodge within thee? For a voice declareth from Dan and publisheth affliction from mount Ephraim. Make ye mention to the nations, behold, publish against Jerusalem that watchers come from a far country and give out their voice against the cities of Judah. As keepers of a field are they against her round about because she hath been rebellious against me, saith the Lord. Thy way and thy doings have procured these things unto thee, this is thy wickedness because it is bitter, because it reacheth unto thine heart.

3 MY bowels, my bowels! I am pained at my very heart, my heart maketh a noise in me, I cannot hold my peace because thou hast heard, O my soul, the sound of the trumpet, the alarm of war. Destruction upon destruction is cried, for the whole land is spoiled, suddenly are my tents spoiled and my curtains in a moment. How long shall I see the standard and hear the sound of the trumpet? For my people is foolish, they have not known me, they are sottish children

and they have none understanding, they are wise to do evil, but to do good they have no knowledge. I beheld the Earth and lo, it was empty and desolate, and the heavens, and they had no light. I beheld the mountains, and lo, they trembled and all the hills moved lightly. I beheld and lo, there was no man and all the birds of the heavens were fled. I beheld and lo, the fruitful place was a wilderness and all the cities thereof were broken down at the presence of the Lord and by his fierce anger.

For thus hath the Lord said, The whole land shall be desolate, yet will I not make a full end. For this shall the earth mourn and the heavens above be black, because I have spoken it, I have purposed it, and will not repent, neither will I turn back from it. The whole city shall flee for the noise of the horsemen and bowmen, they shall go into thickets and climb up upon the rocks, every city shall be forsaken and not a man dwell therein. And when thou art spoiled, what wilt thou do? Though thou clothest thyself with crimson, though thou deckest thee with ornaments of gold, though thou rentest thy face with painting, in vain shalt thou make thyself fair; thy lovers will despise thee, they will seek thy life. For I have heard a voice as of a woman in travail, and the anguish as of her that bringeth forth her first child, the voice of the daughter of Zion that bewaileth herself, that spreadeth her hands, saying, Wo is me now, for my soul is wearied because of murderers.

Run ye to and fro through the streets of Jerusalem, and see now and know, and seek in the broad places thereof; if ye can find a man, if there be any that executeth judgment, that seeketh the truth, and I will pardon it. And though they say, The Lord liveth, surely they swear falsely. O Lord, are not thine eyes upon the truth? Thou hast stricken them, but they have not grieved, thou hast consumed them, but they have refused to receive correction, they have made their faces harder than a rock, they have refused to return. Therefore I said, Surely these are poor, they are foolish, for they know not the way of the Lord nor the judgment of their God. I will get me unto the great men and will speak unto them, for they have known the way of the Lord and the judgment of their God, but these have altogether broken the yoke and burst the bonds. Wherefore a lion out of the forest shall slay them, and a wolf of the evenings shall spoil them, a leopard shall watch over their cities, everyone that goeth out thence shall be torn in pieces because their transgressions are many and their backslidings are increased. How shall I pardon thee for this? Thy children have forsaken me and sworn by them that are no gods; when I had fed them to the full they then committed adultery and assembled themselves by troops in the harlots' houses. They were as fed horses in the morning, everyone neighed after his neighbor's wife. Shall I not visit for these things, saith the Lord, and shall not my soul be avenged on such a nation as this?

Go ye up upon her walls and destroy, but make not a full end, take away her battlements, for they are not the Lord's. For the house of Israel and the house of Judah have dealt very treacherously against me, saith the Lord. They have belied the Lord and said, It is not he, neither shall evil come upon us, neither shall we see sword nor famine, and the prophets shall become wind and the word is not in them; thus shall it be done unto them. Wherefore thus saith the Lord God of hosts, Because ye speak this word, behold, I will make my words in thy mouth fire and this people wood and it shall devour them. Lo, I will bring a nation upon you from far, O house of Israel, saith the Lord, it is a mighty nation, it is an ancient nation, a nation whose language thou knowest not, neither understandest what they say. Their quiver is as an open sepulcher, they are all mighty men. And they shall eat up thine harvest and thy bread which thy sons and thy daughters should eat, they shall eat up thy flocks and thine herds, they shall eat up thy vines and thy fig trees, they shall impoverish thy fenced cities wherein thou trustedst with the sword. Nevertheless in those days, saith the Lord, I will not make a full end with you.

And it shall come to pass when ye shall say, Wherefore doeth the Lord our God all these things unto us? Then shalt thou answer them, Like as ye have forsaken me and served strange gods in your land, so shall ye serve strangers in the land that is not yours. Declare this in the house of Jacob and publish it in Judah saying, Hear now this, O foolish people and without understanding, which have eyes and see not, which have ears and hear not, fear ye not me? saith the Lord. Will ye not tremble at my presence, which have placed the sand for the bound of the sea by a perpetual decree that it cannot pass it, and though the waves thereof toss themselves, yet can they not prevail, though they roar, yet can they not pass over it? But this people hath a revolting and rebellious heart, they are revolted and gone. Neither say they in their heart, Let us now fear the Lord our God, that giveth rain, both the former and the latter, in his season, he reserveth unto us the appointed weeks of the harvest. Your iniquities have turned away these things and your sins have withholden good things from you. For among my people are found wicked men, they lay wait as he that setteth snares, they set a trap, they catch men. As a cage as full of birds so are their houses full of deceit, therefore they are become great and waxen rich. They are waxen fat, they shine; yea, they overpass the deeds of the wicked, they judge not the cause, the cause of the fatherless, yet they prosper and the right of the needy do they not judge. Shall I not visit for these things? saith the Lord. Shall not my soul be avenged on such a nation as this?

A wonderful and horrible thing is committed in the land: the prophets prophesy falsely, and the priests bear rule by their means, and my people love to have it so, and what will ye do in the end thereof?

O ye children of Benjamin, gather yourselves to flee out of the midst of Jerusalem, and blow the trumpet in Tekoa, and set up a sign of fire in Beth-haccerem, for evil appeareth out of the north and great destruction. I have likened the daughter of Zion to a comely and delicate woman. The shepherds with their flocks shall come unto her, they shall pitch their tents against her round about, they shall feed everyone in his place. Prepare ye war against her, arise and let us go up at noon. Wo unto us, for the day goeth away, for the shadows of the evening are stretched out. Arise and let us go by night and let us destroy her palaces. For thus hath the Lord of hosts said, Hew ye down trees and cast a mount against Jerusalem, this is the city to be visited, she is wholly oppression in the midst of her. As a fountain casteth out her waters, so she casteth out her wickedness, violence and spoil is heard in her, before me continually is grief and wounds. Be thou instructed, O Jerusalem, lest my soul depart from thee, lest I make thee desolate and a land not inhabited.

Thus saith the Lord of hosts, They shall thoroughly glean the remnant of Israel as a vine, turn back thine hand as a grape-gatherer into the baskets. To whom shall I speak and give warning that they may hear? Behold, their ear is uncircumcised and they cannot hearken, behold, the word of the Lord is unto them a reproach, they have no delight in it. Therefore I am full of the fury of the Lord, I am weary with holding in, I will pour it out upon the children abroad and upon the assembly of young men together, for even the husband with the wife shall be taken, the aged with him that is full of days. And their houses shall be turned unto others with their fields and wives together, for I will stretch out my hand upon the inhabitants of the land, saith the Lord. For from the least of them even unto the greatest of them everyone is given to covetousness, and from the prophet even unto the priest everyone dealeth falsely. They have healed also the hurt of the daughter of my people slightly, saying, Peace, peace, when there is no peace. Were they ashamed when they had committed abomination? Nay, they were not at all ashamed, neither could they blush, therefore they shall fall among them that fall, at the time that I visit them they shall be cast down, saith the Lord. Thus saith the Lord, Stand ye in the ways and see, and ask for the old paths where is the good way and walk therein and ye shall find rest for your souls. But they said, We will not walk therein. Also I set watchmen over you, saying, Hearken to the sound of the trumpet. But they said, We will not hearken. Therefore hear, ye nations, and know, O congregation, what is among them. Hear, O earth, behold, I will bring evil upon this people, even the fruit of their thoughts, because they have not hearkened unto my words nor to my law, but rejected it. To what purpose cometh there to me incense from Sheba and the sweet cane from a far country? Your burnt offerings are not acceptable nor your sacrifices sweet unto me. Therefore thus saith the Lord, Behold, I will lay stumbling blocks before this people and the fathers and the sons together shall fall upon them, the neighbor and his friend shall perish. Thus saith the Lord, Behold, a people cometh from the north country and a great nation shall be raised from the sides of the earth. They shall lay hold on bow and spear, they are cruel and have no mercy, their voice roareth like the sea and they ride upon horses, set in array as men for war against thee, O daughter of Zion. We have heard the fame thereof, our hands wax feeble, anguish hath taken hold of us, and pain as of a woman in travail. Go not forth into the field nor walk by the way, for the sword of the enemy and fear is on every side. O daughter of my people, gird thee with sackcloth and wallow thyself in ashes, make thee mourning as for an only son, most bitter lamentations, for the spoiler shall suddenly come upon us. I have set thee for a tower and a fortress among my people that thou mayest know and try their way. They are all grievous revolters, walking with slanders, they are brass and iron, they are all corrupters. The bellows are burned, the lead is consumed of the fire, the founder melteth in vain for the wicked are not plucked away. Reprobate silver shall men call them because the Lord hath rejected them.

4 THE word that came to Jeremiah from the Lord, saying, Stand in the gate of the Lord's house and proclaim there this word and say, Hear the word of the Lord all ye of Judah that enter in at these gates to worship the Lord. Thus saith the Lord of hosts, the God of Israel, Amend your ways and your doings and I will cause you to dwell in this place. Trust ye not in lying words, saying, The temple of the Lord, The temple of the Lord, The temple of the Lord are these. For if ye thoroughly amend your ways and your doings, if ye thoroughly execute judgment between a man and his neighbor, if ye oppress not the stranger, the fatherless, and the widow, and shed not innocent blood in this place, neither walk after other gods to your hurt, then will I cause you to dwell in this place, in the land that I gave to your fathers, for ever and ever.

Behold, ye trust in lying words that cannot profit. Will ye steal, murder, and commit adultery, and swear falsely, and burn incense unto Baal, and walk after other gods whom ye know not, and come and stand before me in this house which is called by my name and say, We are delivered to do all these abominations? Is this house, which is called by my name, become a den of robbers in your eyes? Behold, even I have seen it, saith the Lord. But go ye now unto my place which was in Shiloh, where I set my name at the first, and see what I did to it for the wickedness of my people Israel. And now, because ye have done all these works, saith the Lord, and I spake unto you, rising up early and speaking, but ye heard not, and I called you, but ye answered not, therefore will I do unto this house, which is called by my name, wherein ye trust, and unto the place which I gave to you and to your fathers as I have done to Shiloh. And I will cast you out of my sight, as I have cast out all your brethren, even the whole seed of Ephraim. Therefore pray not thou for this people, neither lift up cry nor prayer for them, neither make intercession to me, for I will not hear thee. Seest thou not what they do in the cities of Judah and in the streets of Jerusalem? The children gather wood, and the fathers kindle the fire, and the women knead their dough to make cakes to the queen of Heaven, and to pour out drink offerings unto other gods that they may provoke me to anger. Do they provoke me to anger? saith the Lord. Do they not provoke themselves to the confusion of their own faces? Therefore thus saith the Lord God, Behold, mine anger and my fury shall be poured out upon this place, upon man, and upon beast, and upon the trees of the field, and upon the fruit of the ground, and it shall burn and shall not be quenched.

Thus saith the Lord of hosts, the God of Israel, Put your burnt offerings unto your sacrifices and eat flesh. For I spake not unto your fathers, nor commanded them in the day that I brought them out of the land of Egypt concerning burnt offerings or sacrifices, but this thing commanded I them, saying, Obey my voice and I will be your God, and ye shall be my people, and walk ye in all the ways that I have commanded you that it may be well unto you. But they hearkened not nor inclined their ear, but walked in the counsels and in the imagination of their evil heart, and went backward and not forward. Since the day that your fathers came forth out of the land of Egypt unto this day I have even sent unto you all my servants the prophets, daily rising up early and sending them. Yet they hearkened not unto me, nor inclined their ear, but hardened their neck, they did worse than their fathers. Therefore thou shalt speak all these words unto them, but they will not hearken to thee, thou shalt also call unto them, but they will not answer thee. But thou shalt say unto them, This is a nation that obeyeth not the voice of the Lord their God, nor receiveth correction, truth is perished and is cut off from their mouth.

Cut off thine hair, O Jerusalem, and cast it away and take up a lamentation on high places, for the Lord hath rejected and forsaken the generation of his wrath. For the children of Judah have done evil in my sight, saith the Lord, they have set their abominations in the house which is called by my name to pollute it. And they have built the high places of Tophet, which is in the valley of the son of Hinnom, to burn their sons and their daughters in the fire which I commanded them not, neither came it into my heart. Therefore behold, the days come, saith the Lord, that it shall no more be called Tophet nor the valley of the son of Hinnom, but the valley of slaughter, for they shall bury in Tophet till there be no place. And the carcasses of this people shall be meat for the fowls of the Heaven and for the beasts of the earth and none shall fray them away. Then will I cause to cease from the cities of Judah and from the streets of Jerusalem the voice of mirth, and the voice of gladness, the voice of the bridegroom, and the voice of the bride, for the land shall be desolate.

At that time, saith the Lord, they shall bring out the bones of the kings of Judah, and the bones of his princes, and the bones of the priests, and the bones of the prophets, and the bones of the inhabitants of Jerusalem out of their graves, and they shall spread them before the sun, and the moon, and all the host of Heaven whom they have loved, and whom they have served, and after whom they have walked, and whom they have sought, and whom they have worshiped; they shall not be gathered nor be buried, they shall be for dung upon the face of the Earth. And death shall be chosen rather than life by all the residue of them that remain of this evil family which remain in all the places whither I have driven them, saith the Lord of hosts.

Moreover thou shalt say unto them, Thus saith the Lord, Shall they fall and not arise? Shall he turn away and not return? Why then is this people of Jerusalem slidden back by a perpetual backsliding? They hold fast deceit, they refuse to return. I hearkened and heard, but they spake not aright, no man repented him of his wickedness saying, What have I done? Everyone turned to his course, as the horse rusheth into the battle. Yea, the stork in the Heaven knoweth her appointed times, and the turtle and the crane and the swallow observe the time of their coming, but my people know not the judgment of the Lord. How do ye say, We are wise and the law of the Lord is with us? Lo, certainly in vain made he it, the pen of the scribes is in vain. The wise men are ashamed, they are dismayed and taken, lo, they have rejected the word of the Lord and what wisdom is in them, therefore will I give their wives unto others and their fields to them that shall inherit them, for everyone from the least even unto the greatest is given to covetousness, from the prophet even unto the priest everyone dealeth falsely. For they have healed the hurt of the daughter of my people slightly, saying, Peace, peace, when there is no peace. Were they ashamed when they had committed abomination? Nay, they were not at all ashamed, neither could they blush, therefore shall they fall among them that fall, in the time of their visitation they shall be cast down, saith the Lord. I will surely consume them, saith the Lord, there shall be no grapes on the vine nor figs on the fig tree, and the leaf shall fade and the things that I have given them shall pass away from them. Why do we sit still? Assemble yourselves and let us enter into the defensed cities and let us be silent there, for the Lord our God hath put us to silence and given us water of gall to drink because we have sinned against the Lord. We looked for peace, but no good came, and for a time of health and behold trouble. The snorting of his horses was heard from Dan, the whole land trembled at the sound of the neighing of his strong ones, for they are come and have devoured the land and all that is in it, the city and those that dwell therein. For, behold, I will send serpents, cockatrices among you, which will not be charmed, and they shall bite you, saith the Lord.

When I would comfort myself against sorrow my heart is faint in me. Behold the voice of the cry of the daughter of my people because of them that dwell in a far country, Is not the Lord in Zion? Is not her king in her? Why have they provoked me to anger with their graven images and with strange vanities? The harvest is past, the summer is ended, and we are not saved. For the hurt of the daughter of my people am I hurt, I am black, astonishment hath taken hold on me. Is there no balm in Gilead? Is there no physician there? Why then is not the health of the daughter of my people recovered?

Oh that my head were waters and mine eyes a fountain of tears, that I might weep day and night for the slain of the daughter of my people! O that I had in the wilderness a lodging place of wayfaring men that I might leave my people and go from them! For they be all adulterers, an assembly of treacherous men. And they bend their tongues like their bow for lies, but they are not valiant for the truth upon the earth, for they proceed from evil to evil and they know not me, saith the Lord. Take ye heed everyone of his neighbor and trust ye not in any brother, for every brother will utterly supplant and every neighbor will walk with slanders. And they will deceive everyone his neighbor and will not speak the truth, they have taught their tongue to speak lies and weary themselves to commit iniquity. Thine habitation is in the midst of deceit, through deceit they refuse to know me, saith the Lord. Therefore thus saith the Lord of hosts, Behold, I will melt them and try them, for how shall I do for the daughter of my people? Their tongue is as an arrow shot out, it speaketh deceit, one speaketh peaceably to his neighbor with his mouth, but in heart he layeth his wait. Shall I not visit them for these things? saith the Lord. Shall not my soul be avenged on such a nation as this?

For the mountains will I take up a weeping and wailing and for the habitations of the wilderness a lamentation, because they are burned up so that none can pass through them, neither can men hear the voice of the cattle, both the fowl of the heavens and the beast are fled, they are gone. And I will make Jerusalem heaps and a den of dragons, and I will make the cities of Judah desolate, without an inhabitant. Who is the wise man that may understand this? And who is he to whom the mouth of the Lord hath spoken that he may declare it, for what the land perisheth and is burned up like a wilderness that none passeth through? And the Lord saith, Because they have forsaken my law which I set before them, and have not obeyed my voice, neither walked therein, but have walked after the imagination of their own heart and after Baalim which their fathers taught them, therefore thus saith the Lord of hosts, the God of Israel, Behold, I will feed them, even this people, with wormwood and give them water of gall to drink. I will scatter them also among the heathen, whom neither they nor their fathers have known, and I will send a sword after them till I have consumed them.

Thus saith the Lord of hosts, Consider ye and call for the mourning women that they may come, and send for cunning women that they may come. And let them make haste and take up a wailing for us, that our eyes may run down with tears and our eyelids gush out with waters. For a voice of wailing is heard out of Zion, How are we spoiled! We are greatly confounded because we have forsaken the land, because our dwellings have cast us out. Yet hear the word of the Lord, O ye women, and let your ear receive the word of his mouth and teach your daughters wailing and everyone her neighbor lamentation. For death is come up into our windows and is entered into our palaces, to cut off the children from without and the young men from the streets. Speak, Thus saith the Lord, Even the carcasses of men shall fall as dung upon the open field and as the handful after the harvestman and none shall gather them.

Thus saith the Lord, Let not the wise man glory in his wisdom neither let the mighty man glory in his might, let not the rich man glory in his riches, but let him that glorieth glory in this, that he understandeth and knoweth me, that I am the Lord which exercise lovingkindness, judgment, and righteousness in the earth, for in these things I delight, saith the Lord. Behold, the days come, saith the Lord, that I will punish all them which are circumcised with the uncircumcised, Egypt, and Judah, and Edom, and the children of Ammon, and Moab, and all that are in the utmost corners, that dwell in the wilderness, for all these nations are uncircumcised and all the house of Israel are uncircumcised in the heart.

Hear ye the word which the Lord speaketh unto you, O house of Israel, thus saith the Lord, Learn not the way of the heathen and be not dismayed at the signs of Heaven, for the heathen are dismayed at them. For the customs of the people are vain, for one cutteth a tree out of the forest, the work of the hands of the workman, with the axe. They deck it with silver and with gold, they fasten it with nails and with hammers that it move not. They are upright as the palm tree, but speak not, they must needs be borne because they cannot go. Be not afraid of them for they cannot do evil, neither also is it in them to do good. Forasmuch as there is none like unto thee, O Lord, thou art great and thy name is great in might. Who would not fear thee, O King of nations? For to thee doth it appertain, forasmuch as among all the wise men of the nations and in all their kingdoms there is none like unto thee. But they are altogether brutish and foolish, the stock is a doctrine of vanities. Silver spread into plates is brought from Tarshish and gold from Uphaz, the work of the workman and of the hands of the founder, blue and purple is their clothing, they are all the work of cunning men. But the Lord is the true God, he is the living God and an everlasting King, at his wrath the Earth shall tremble and the nations shall not be able to abide his indignation. Thus shall ye say unto them, The gods that have not made the heavens and the Earth, even they shall perish from the Earth, and from under these heavens. He hath made the Earth by his power, he hath established the world by his wisdom and hath stretched out the heavens by his discretion. When he uttereth his voice there is a multitude of waters in the heavens, and he causeth the vapors to ascend from the ends of the Earth, he maketh lightnings with rain and bringeth forth the wind out of his treasures. Every man is brutish in his knowledge, every founder is confounded by the graven image, for his molten image is falsehood and there is no breath in them. They are vanity and the work of errors, in the time of their visitation they shall perish. The portion of Jacob is not like them, for he is the former of all things and Israel is the rod of his inheritance, The Lord of hosts is his name.

Gather up thy wares out of the land, O inhabitant of the fortress. For thus saith the Lord, Behold, I will sling out the inhabitants of the land at this once and will distress them that they may find it so. Wo is me for my hurt, my wound is grievous, but I said, Truly this is a grief and I must bear it. My tabernacle is spoiled and all my cords are broken, my children are gone forth of me and they are not, there is none to stretch forth my tent anymore and to set up my curtains. For the pastors are become brutish and have not sought the Lord, therefore they shall not prosper and all their flocks shall be scattered. Behold, the noise of the noise is come and a great commotion out of the north country, to make the cities of Judah desolate and a den of dragons.

O Lord, I know that the way of man is not in himself, it is not in man that walketh to direct his steps. O Lord, correct me, but with judgment, not in thine anger, lest thou bring me to nothing. Pour out thy fury upon the heathen that know thee not and upon the families that call not on thy name, for they have eaten up Jacob, and devoured him, and consumed him, and have made his habitation desolate.

5 THE word that came to Jeremiah from the Lord saying, Hear ye the words of this covenant, and speak unto the men of Judah and to the inhabitants of Jerusalem and say thou unto them, Thus saith the Lord God of Israel, Cursed be the man that obeyeth not the words of this covenant which I commanded your fathers in the day that I brought them forth out of the land of Egypt, from the iron furnace, saying, Obey my voice and do them according to all which I command you, so shall ye be my people and I will be your God, that I may perform the oath which I have sworn unto your fathers, to give them a land flowing with milk and honey as it is this day. Then answered I and said, So be it, O Lord. Then the Lord said unto me, Proclaim all these words in the cities of Judah and in the streets of Jerusalem saying, Hear ye the words of this covenant and do them. For I earnestly protested unto your fathers in the day that I brought them up out of the land of Egypt even unto this day, rising early and protesting, saying, Obey my voice. Yet they obeyed not nor inclined their ear, but walked everyone in the imagination of their evil heart, therefore I will bring upon them all the words of this covenant which I commanded them to do, but they did them not. And the Lord said unto me, A conspiracy is found among the men of Judah and among the inhabitants of Jerusalem. They are turned back to the iniquities of their forefathers which refused to hear my words and they went after other gods to serve them; the house of Israel and the house of Judah have broken my covenant which I made with their fathers. Therefore thus saith the Lord, Behold, I will bring evil upon them which they shall not be able to escape, and though they shall cry unto me, I will not hearken unto them. Then shall the cities of Judah and inhabitants of Jerusalem go and cry unto the gods unto whom they offer incense, but they shall not save them at all in the time of their trouble. For according to the number of thy cities were thy gods, O Judah, and according to the number of the streets of Jerusalem have ye set up altars to that shameful thing, even altars to burn incense unto Baal. Therefore pray not thou for this people neither lift up a cry or prayer for them, for I will not hear them in the time that they cry unto me for their trouble.

What hath my beloved to do in mine house, seeing she hath wrought lewdness with many and the holy flesh is passed from thee? When thou doest evil, then thou rejoicest. The Lord called thy name, A green olive tree, fair and of goodly fruit, with the noise of a great tumult he hath kindled fire upon it and the branches of it are broken. For the Lord of hosts that planted thee hath pronounced evil against thee, for the evil of the house of Israel and of the house of Judah which they have done against themselves to provoke me to anger in offering incense unto Baal. And the Lord hath given me knowledge of i, and I know it, then thou showedst me their doings. But I was like a lamb or an ox that is brought to the slaughter and I knew not that they had devised devices against me saying, Let us destroy the tree with the fruit thereof, and let us cut him off from the land of the living that his name may be no more remembered. But, O Lord of hosts, that judgest righteously, that triest the reins and the heart, let me see thy vengeance on them, for unto thee have I revealed my cause.

Therefore thus saith the Lord of the men of Anathoth that seek thy life saying, Prophesy not in the name of the Lord that thou die not by our hand, therefore thus saith the Lord of hosts, Behold, I will punish them, the young men shall die by the sword, their sons and their daughters shall die by famine and there shall be no remnant of them, for I will bring evil upon the men of Anathoth, even the year of their visitation.

Righteous art thou, O Lord, when I plead with thee, yet let me talk with thee of thy judgments, Wherefore doth the way of the wicked prosper? Wherefore are all they happy that deal very treacherously? Thou hast planted them, yea, they have taken root, they grow, yea, they bring forth fruit, thou art near in their mouth and far from their reins. But thou, O Lord, knowest me, thou hast seen me and tried mine heart toward thee, pull them out like sheep for the slaughter and prepare them for the day of slaughter. How long shall the land mourn and the herbs of every field wither for the wickedness of them that dwell therein? The beasts are consumed and the birds, because they said, He shall not see our last end.

If thou hast run with our footmen and they have wearied thee, then how canst thou contend with horses? And if in the land of peace wherein thou trustedst they wearied thee, then how wilt thou do in the swelling of Jordan? For even thy brethren and the house of thy father, even they have dealt treacherously with thee, yea, they have called a multitude after thee; believe them not though they speak fair words unto thee.

I have forsaken mine house, I have left mine heritage, I have given the dearly beloved of my soul into the hand of her enemies. Mine heritage is unto me as a lion in the forest: it crieth out against me, therefore have I hated it. Mine heritage is unto me as a speckled bird: the birds round about are against her, come ye, assemble all the beasts of the field, come to devour. Many pastors have destroyed my vineyard, they have trodden my portion under foot, they have made my pleasant portion a desolate wilderness. They have made it desolate, and being desolate it mourneth unto me; the whole land is made desolate because no man layeth it to heart. The spoilers are come upon all high places through the wilderness, for the sword of the Lord shall devour from the one end of the land even to the other end of the land; no flesh shall have peace. They have sown wheat, but shall reap thorns, they have put themselves to pain, but shall not profit, and they shall be ashamed of your revenues because of the fierce anger of the Lord.

Thus saith the Lord against all mine evil neighbors that touch the inheritance which I have caused my people Israel to inherit, Behold, I will pluck them out of their land and pluck out the house of Judah from among them. And it shall come to pass after that I have plucked them out I will return and have compassion on them and will bring them again, every man to his heritage and every man to his land. And it shall come to pass if they will diligently learn the ways of my people, to swear by my name, The Lord liveth, as they taught my people to swear by Baal, then shall they be built in the midst of my people. But if they will not obey I will utterly pluck up and destroy that nation, saith the Lord.

Thus saith the Lord unto me, Go and get thee a linen girdle and put it upon thy loins and put it not in water. So I got a girdle according to the word of the Lord and put it on my lions. And the word of the Lord came unto me the second time saying, Take the girdle that thou hast got which is upon thy loins and arise, go to Euphrates and hide it there in a hole of the rock. So I went and hid it by Euphrates as the Lord commanded me. And it came to pass after many days that the Lord said unto me, Arise, go to Euphrates and take the girdle from thence which I commanded thee to hide there. Then I went to Euphrates and digged and took the girdle from the place where I had hit it and behold, the girdle was marred, it was profitable for nothing. Then the word of the Lord came unto me saying, Thus saith the Lord, After this manner will I mar the pride of Judah and the great pride of Jerusalem. This evil people which refuse to hear my words, which walk in the imagination of their heart, and walk after other gods to serve them and to worship them, shall even be as this girdle which is good for nothing. For as the girdle cleaveth to the loins of a man, so have I caused to cleave unto me the whole house of Israel and the whole house of Judah, saith the Lord, that they might be unto me for a people, and for a name, and for a praise, and for a glory, but they would not hear.

Therefore thou shalt speak unto them this word, Thus saith the Lord God of Israel, Every bottle shall be filled with wine and they shall say unto thee, Do we not certainly know that every bottle shall be filled with wine? Then shalt thou say unto them, Thus saith the Lord, Behold, I will fill all the inhabitants of this land, even the kings that sit upon David's throne, and the priests, and the prophets, and all the inhabitants of Jerusalem, with drunkenness. And I will dash them one against another, even the fathers and the sons together, saith the Lord, I will not pity, nor spare, nor have mercy, but destroy them. Hear ye and give ear, be not proud, for the Lord hath spoken. Give glory to the Lord your God, before he cause darkness and before your feet stumble upon the dark mountains, and while ye look for light, he turn it into the shadow of death and make it gross darkness. But if ye will not hear it, my soul shall weep in secret places for your pride and mine eye shall weep sore and run down with tears because the Lord's flock is carried away captive. Say unto the king and to the queen, Humble yourselves, sit down, for your principalities shall come down, even the crown of your glory. The cities of the south shall be shut up and none shall open them, Judah shall be carried away captive all of it, it shall be wholly carried away captive. Lift up your eyes and behold them that come from the north, where is the flock that was given thee, thy beautiful flock? What wilt thou say when he shall punish thee? For thou hast taught them to be captains, and as chief over thee shall not sorrows take thee as a woman in travail? And if thou say in thine heart, Wherefore come these things upon me? For the greatness of thine iniquity are thy skirts discovered and thy heels made bare. Can the Ethiopian change his skin or the leopard his spots? Then may ye also do good that are accustomed to do evil. Therefore will I scatter them as the stubble that passeth away by the wind of the wilderness. This is thy lot, the portion of thy measures from me, saith the Lord, because thou hast forgotten me and trusted in falsehood. Therefore will I discover thy skirts upon thy face that thy shame may appear. I have seen thine adulteries and thy neighings, the lewdness of thy whoredom and thine abominations on the hills in the fields. Wo unto thee, O Jerusalem. Wilt thou not be made clean? When shall it once be?

6 THE word of the Lord that came to Jeremiah concerning the dearth. Judah mourneth and the gates thereof languish, they are black unto the ground and the cry of Jerusalem is gone up. And their nobles have sent their little ones to the waters, they came to the pits and found no water, they returned with their vessels empty, they were ashamed and confounded and covered their heads. Because the ground is chapped, for there was no rain in the Earth, the ploughmen were ashamed, they covered their heads. Yea, the hind also calved in the field and forsook it because there was no grass. And the wild asses did stand in the high places, they snuffed up the wind like dragons, their eyes did fail because there was no grass.

O Lord, though our iniquities testify against us, do thou it for thy name's sake, for our backslidings are many, we have sinned against thee. O the hope of Israel, the Savior thereof in time of trouble, why shouldest thou be as a stranger in the land and as a wayfaring man that turneth aside to tarry for a night? Why shouldest thou be as a man astonished, as a mighty man that cannot save? Yet thou, O Lord, art in the midst of us and we are called by thy name, leave us not. Thus saith the Lord unto this people, Thus have they loved to wander, they have not refrained their feet, therefore the Lord doth not accept them, he will now remember their iniquity and visit their sins. Then said the Lord unto me, Pray not for this people for their good. When they fast I will not hear their cry and when they offer burnt offering and an oblation I will not accept them, but I will consume them by the sword, and by the famine, and by the pestilence.

Then said I, Ah, Lord God! Behold, the prophets say unto them, Ye shall not see the sword neither shall ye have famine, but I will give you assured peace in this place. Then the Lord said unto me, The prophets prophesy lies in my name; I sent them not, neither have I commanded them, neither spake unto them. They prophesy unto you a false vision and divination, and a thing of naught, and the deceit of their heart. Therefore thus saith the Lord concerning the prophets that prophesy in my name, and I sent them not, yet they say, Sword and famine shall not be in this land, By sword and famine shall those prophets be consumed. And the people to whom they prophesy shall be cast out in the streets of Jerusalem because of the famine and the sword, and they shall have none to bury them, them, their wives, nor their sons, nor their daughters, for I will pour their wickedness upon them. Therefore thou shalt say this word unto them, Let mine eyes run down with tears night and day and let them not cease, for the virgin daughter of my people is broken with a great breach, with a very grievous blow. If I go forth into the field, then behold the slain with the sword, and if I enter into the city, then behold them that are sick with famine. Yea, both the prophet and the priest go about into a land that they know not. Hast thou utterly rejected Judah? Hath thy soul loathed Zion? Why hast thou smitten us and there is no healing for us? We looked for peace and there is no good, and for the time of healing and behold trouble. We acknowledge, O Lord, our wickedness and the iniquity of our fathers, for we have sinned against thee. Do not abhor us, for thy name's sake do not disgrace the throne of thy glory, remember, break not thy covenant with us. Are there any among the vanities of the Gentiles that can cause rain? Or can the heavens give showers? Art not thou he, O Lord our God? Therefore we will wait upon thee, for thou hast made all these things.

Then said the Lord unto me, Though Moses and Samuel stood before me, yet my mind could not be toward this people; cast them out of my sight and let them go forth. And it shall come to pass if they say unto thee, Whither shall we go forth?, then thou shalt tell them, Thus saith the Lord, Such as are for death, to death, and such as are for the sword, to the sword, and such as are for the famine, to the famine, and such as are for the captivity, to the captivity. And

I will appoint over them four kinds, saith the Lord, the sword to slay, and the dogs to tear, and the fowls of the Heaven, and the beasts of the Earth to devour and destroy. And I will cause them to be removed into all kingdoms of the earth because of Manasseh the son of Hezekiah king of Judah, for that which he did in Jerusalem. For who shall have pity upon thee, O Jerusalem? Or who shall bemoan thee? Or who shall go aside to ask how thou doest? Thou hast forsaken me, saith the Lord, thou art gone backward, therefore will I stretch out my hand against thee and destroy thee, I am weary with repenting. And I will fan them with a fan in the gates of the land, I will bereave them of children, I will destroy my people since they return not from their ways. Their widows are increased to me above the sand of the seas, I have brought upon them against the mother of the young men a spoiler at noonday, I have caused him to fall upon it suddenly, and terrors upon the city. She that hath borne seven languisheth, she hath given up the ghost, her sun is gone down while it was yet day, she hath been ashamed and confounded, and the residue of them will I deliver to the sword before their enemies, saith the Lord.

Wo is me, my mother, that thou hast borne me a man of strife and a man of contention to the whole earth. I have neither lent on usury nor men have lent to me on usury, yet everyone of them doth curse me. The Lord said, Verily it shall be well with thy remnant, verily I will cause the enemy to entreat thee well in the time of evil and in the time of affliction. Shall iron break the northern iron and the steel? Thy substance and thy treasures will I give to the spoil without price and that for all thy sins, even in all thy borders. And I will make thee to pass with thine enemies into a land which thou knowest not, for a fire is kindled in mine anger, which shall burn upon you.

O Lord, thou knowest, remember me and visit me, and revenge me of my persecutors, take me not away in thy longsuffering, know that for thy sake I have suffered rebuke. Thy words were found and I did eat them, and thy word was unto me the joy and rejoicing of mine heart, for I am called by thy name, O Lord God of hosts. I sat not in the assembly of the mockers nor rejoiced, I sat alone because of thy hand, for thou hast filled me with indignation. Why is my pain perpetual and my wound incurable, which refuseth to be healed? Wilt thou be altogether unto me as a liar and as waters that fail?

Therefore thus saith the Lord, If thou return, then will I bring thee again and thou shalt stand before me, and if thou take forth the precious from the vile thou shalt be as my mouth; let them return unto thee, but return not thou unto them. And I will make thee unto this people a fenced brazen wall and they shall fight against thee, but they shall not prevail against thee, for I am with thee to save thee and to deliver thee, saith the Lord. And I will deliver thee out of the hand of the wicked and I will redeem thee out of the hand of the terrible.

The word of the Lord came also unto me, saying, Thou shalt not take thee a wife neither shalt thou have sons nor daughters in this place. For thus saith the Lord concerning the sons and concerning the daughters that are born in this place, and concerning their mothers that bare them, and concerning their fathers that begat them in this land, they shall die of grievous deaths, they shall not be lamented, neither shall they be buried, but they shall be as dung upon the face of the Earth, and they shall be consumed by the sword, and by famine, and their carcasses shall be meat for the fowls of Heaven and for the beasts of the Earth. For thus saith the Lord, Enter not into the house of mourning neither go to lament nor bemoan them, for I have taken away my peace from this people, saith the Lord, even lovingkindness and mercies. Both the great and the small shall die in this land, they shall not be buried, neither shall men lament for them, nor cut themselves, nor make themselves bald for them. Neither shall men tear themselves for them in mourning to comfort them for the dead, neither shall men give them the cup of consolation to drink for their father or for their mother. Thou shalt not also go into the house of feasting to sit with them to eat and to drink. For thus saith the Lord of hosts, the God of Israel, Behold, I will cause to cease out of this place in your eyes and in your days the voice of mirth, and the voice of gladness, the voice of the bridegroom, and the voice of the bride. And it shall come to pass when thou shalt show this people all these words and they shall say unto thee, Wherefore hath the Lord pronounced all this great evil against us? Or what is our iniquity? Or what is our sin that we have committed against the Lord our God? Then shalt thou say unto them, Because your fathers have forsaken me, saith the Lord, and have walked after other gods, and have served them, and have worshipped them, and have forsaken me, and have not kept my law, and ye have done worse than your fathers, for behold, ye walk everyone after the imagination of his evil heart that they may not hearken unto me, therefore will I cast you out of this land into a land that ye know not, neither ye nor your fathers, and there shall ye serve other gods day and night where I will not show you favor.

Therefore behold, the days come, saith the Lord, that it shall no more be said, The Lord liveth that brought up the children of Israel out of the land of Egypt, but, The Lord liveth, that brought up the children of Israel from the land of the north and from all the lands whither he had driven them, and I will bring them again into their land that I gave unto their fathers. Behold, I will send for many fishers, saith the Lord, and they shall fish them, and after will I send for many hunters and they shall hunt them from every mountain, and from every hill, and out of the holes of the rocks. For mine eyes are upon all their ways, they are not hid from my face, neither is their iniquity hid from mine eyes. And first I will recompense their iniquity and their sin double because they have defiled my land, they have filled mine inheritance with the carcasses of their detestable and abominable things. O Lord, my strength, and my fortress, and my refuge in the day of affliction, the Gentiles shall come unto thee from the ends of the Earth and shall say, Surely our fathers have inherited lies, vanity, and things wherein there is no profit. Shall a man make gods unto himself and they are no gods? Therefore, behold, I will this once cause them to know, I will cause them to know mine hand and my might, and they shall know that my name is The Lord.

The sin of Judah is written with a pen of iron and with the point of a diamond, it is graven upon the table of their heart and upon the horns of your altars, whilst their children remember their altars and their groves by the green trees upon the high hills. O my mountain in the field, I will give thy substance and all thy treasures to the spoil, and thy high places for sin throughout all thy borders. And thou, even thyself, shalt discontinue from thine heritage that I gave thee, and I will cause thee to serve thine enemies in the land which thou knowest not, for ye have kindled a fire in mine anger, which shall burn forever.

Thus saith the Lord, Cursed be the man that trusteth in man, and maketh flesh his arm, and the man whose heart departeth from the Lord. For he shall be like the heath in the desert and shall not see when good cometh, but shall inhabit the parched places in the wilderness, in a salt land and not inhabited. Blessed is the man that trusteth in the Lord and whose hope the Lord is. For he shall be as a tree planted by the waters, and that spreadeth out her roots by the river, and shall not see when heat cometh, but her leaf shall be green, and shall not be careful in the year of drought, neither shall cease from yielding fruit.

The heart is deceitful above all things and desperately wicked; who can know it? I the Lord search the heart, I try the reins, even to give every man according to his ways and according to the fruit of his doings. As the partridge sitteth on eggs and hatcheth them not, so he that getteth riches, and not by right, shall leave them in the midst of his days and at his end shall be a fool.

7 A glorious high throne from the beginning is the place of our sanctuary. O Lord, the hope of Israel, all that forsake thee shall be ashamed and they that depart from me shall be written in the earth because they have forsaken the Lord, the fountain of living waters. Heal me, O Lord, and I shall be healed, save me and I shall be saved, for thou art my praise. Behold, they say unto me, Where is the word of the Lord? Let it come now. As for me, I have not hastened from being a pastor to follow thee, neither have I desired the woeful day, thou knowest, that which came out of my lips was right before thee. Be not a terror unto me, thou art my hope in the day of evil. Let them be confounded that persecute me, but let not me be confounded, let them be dismayed, but let not me be dismayed, bring upon them the day of evil and destroy them with double destruction.

Thus said the Lord unto me, Go and stand in the gate of the children of the people whereby the kings of Judah come in, and by the which they go out, and in all the gates of Jerusalem, and say unto them, Hear ye the word of the Lord, ye kings of Judah, and all Judah, and all the inhabitants of Jerusalem that enter in by these gates, thus saith the Lord, Take heed to yourselves, and bear no burden on the sabbath day, nor bring it in by the gates of Jerusalem, neither carry forth a burden out of your houses on the sabbath day, neither do ye any work, but hallow ye the sabbath day as I commanded your fathers. But they obeyed not neither inclined their ear, but made their neck stiff that they might not hear nor receive instruction. And it shall come to pass if ye diligently hearken unto me, saith the Lord, to bring in no burden through the gates of this city on the sabbath day, but hallow the sabbath day to do no work therein, then shall there enter into the gates of this city kings and princes sitting upon the throne of David, riding in chariots and on horses, they and their princes, the men of Judah and the inhabitants of Jerusalem, and this city shall remain forever. And they shall come from the cities of Judah, and from the places about Jerusalem, and from the land of Benjamin, and from the plain, and from the mountains, and from the south, bringing burnt offerings, and sacrifices, and meat offerings, and incense, and bringing sacrifices of praise unto the house of the Lord. But if ye will not hearken unto me to hallow the sabbath day and not to bear a burden, even entering in at the gates of Jerusalem on the sabbath day, then will I kindle a fire in the gates thereof, and it shall devour the palaces of Jerusalem, and it shall not be quenched.

8 THE word which came to Jeremiah from the Lord, saying, Arise and go down to the potter's house and there I will cause thee to hear my words. Then I went down to the potter's house and behold, he wrought a work on the wheels. And the vessel that he made of clay was marred in the hand of the potter, so he made it again another vessel as seemed good to the potter to make it. Then the word of the Lord came to me, saying, O house of Israel, cannot I do with you as this potter? saith the Lord. Behold, as the clay is in the potter's hand, so are ye in mine hand, O house of Israel. At what instant I shall speak concerning a nation and concerning a kingdom, to pluck up, and to pull down, and to destroy it, if that nation against whom I have pronounced turn from their evil I will withhold the evil that I thought to do unto them. And at what instant I shall speak concerning a nation and concerning a kingdom, to build and to plant it, if it do evil in my sight that it obey not my voice, then I will withhold the good wherewith I said I would benefit them. Now therefore go to, speak to the men of Judah and to the inhabitants of Jerusalem saying, Thus saith the Lord, Behold, I frame evil against you and devise a device against you, return ye now everyone from his

evil way and make your ways and your doings good. And they said, There is no hope, but we will walk after our own devices and we will everyone do the imagination of his evil heart. Therefore thus saith the Lord, Ask ye now among the heathen who hath heard such things; the virgin of Israel hath done a very horrible thing. Will you not leave the snow of the fields of Lebanon; shall not the cold flowing waters that come from another place from the rock be forsaken? Because my people hath forgotten me, they have burned incense to vanity, and they have caused them to stumble in their ways from the ancient paths, to walk in paths in a way not cast up, to make their land desolate and a perpetual hissing, everyone that passeth thereby shall be astonished and wag his head. I will scatter them as with an east wind before the enemy, I will show them the back and not the face in the day of their calamity.

Then said they, Come, and let us devise devices against Jeremiah, for the law shall not perish from the priest, nor counsel from the wise, nor the word from the prophet. Come and let us smite him with the tongue and let us not give heed to any of his words. Give heed to me, O Lord, and hearken to the voice of them that contend with me. Shall evil be recompensed for good? For they have digged a pit for my soul. Remember that I stood before thee to speak good for them and to turn away thy wrath from them. Therefore deliver up their children to the famine, and pour out their blood by the force of the sword, and let their wives be bereaved of their children and be widows, and let their men be put to death, let their young men be slain by the sword in battle. Let a cry be heard from their houses when thou shalt bring a troop suddenly upon them, for they have digged a pit to take me and hid snares for my feet. Yet, Lord, thou knowest all their counsel against me to slay me, forgive not their iniquity neither blot out their sin from thy sight, but let them be overthrown before thee, deal thus with them in the time of thine anger.

Thus saith the Lord, Go and get a potter's earthen bottle and take of the ancients of the people, and of the ancients of the priests, and go forth unto the valley of the son of Hinnom which is by the entry of the east gate, and proclaim there the words that I shall tell thee and say, Hear ye the word of the Lord, O kings of Judah and inhabitants of Jerusalem, Thus saith the Lord of hosts, the God of Israel, Behold, I will bring evil upon this place, the which whosoever heareth his ears shall tingle. Because they have forsaken me, and have estranged this place, and have burned incense in it unto other gods, whom neither they nor their fathers have known, nor the kings of Judah, and have filled this place with the blood of innocents. They have built also the high places of Baal, to burn their sons with fire for burnt offerings unto Baal, which I commanded not, nor spake it, neither came it into my mind, therefore behold, the days come, saith the Lord, that this place shall no more be called Tophet, nor The valley of the son of Hinnom, but The valley of slaughter. And I will make void the counsel of Judah and Jerusalem in this place, and I will cause them to fall by the sword before their enemies and by the hands of them that seek their lives, and their carcasses will I give to be meat for the fowls of Heaven and for the beasts of the Earth. And I will make this city desolate and a hissing, everyone that passeth thereby shall be astonished and hiss because of all the plagues thereof. And I will cause them to eat the flesh of their sons and the flesh of their daughters, and they shall eat everyone the flesh of his friend in the siege and straitness wherewith their enemies, and they that seek their lives, shall straiten them. Then shalt thou break the bottle in the sight of the men that go with thee and shalt say unto them, Thus saith the Lord of hosts, Even so will I break this people and this city as one breaketh a potter's vessel that cannot be made whole again, and they shall bury them in Tophet till there be no place to bury. Thus will I do unto this place, saith the Lord, and to the inhabitants thereof, and even make this city as Tophet, and the houses of Jerusalem, and the houses of the kings of Judah shall be defiled as the place of Tophet because of all the houses upon whose roofs they have burned incense unto all the host of Heaven, and have poured out drink offerings unto other gods.

Then came Jeremiah from Tophet, whither the Lord had sent him to prophesy, and he stood in the court of the Lord's house and said to all the people, Thus saith the Lord of hosts, the God of Israel, Behold, I will bring upon this city and upon all her towns all the evil that I have pronounced against it because they have hardened their necks that they might not hear my words.

Now Pashur the son of Immer the priest who was also chief governor in the house of the Lord, heard that Jeremiah prophesied these things. Then Pashur smote Jeremiah the prophet and put him in the stocks that were in the high gate of Benjamin which was by the house of the Lord. And it came to pass on the morrow that Pashur brought forth Jeremiah out of the stocks. Then said Jeremiah unto him, The Lord hath not called thy name Pashur, but Magor-missabib. For thus saith the Lord, Behold, I will make thee a terror to thyself and to all thy friends, and they shall fall by the sword of their enemies, and thine eyes shall behold it, and I will give all Judah into the hand of the king of Babylon, and he shall carry them captive into Babylon and shall slay them with the sword. Moreover I will deliver all the strength of this city, and all the labors thereof, and all the precious things thereof, and all the treasures of the kings of Judah will I give into the hand of their enemies, which shall spoil them, and take them, and carry them to Babylon. And thou, Pashur, and all that dwell in thine house, shall go into captivity, and thou shalt come to Babylon, and there thou shalt die and shalt be buried there, thou, and all thy friends to whom thou hast prophesied lies.

O Lord, thou hast deceived me and I was deceived, thou art stronger than I and hast prevailed, I am in derision daily, everyone mocketh me. For since I spake, I cried out, I cried violence and spoil because the word of the Lord was made a reproach unto me and a derision daily. Then I said, I will not make mention of him nor speak anymore in his name. But his word was in mine heart as a burning fire shut up in my bones, and I was weary with forbearing and I could not stay. For I heard the defaming of many, fear on every side. Report, say they, and we will report it. All my familiars watched for my halting saying, Peradventure he will be enticed, and we shall prevail against him, and we shall take our revenge on him. But the Lord is with me as a mighty terrible one, therefore my persecutors shall stumble and they shall not prevail, they shall be greatly ashamed, for they shall not prosper, their everlasting confusion shall never be forgotten. But, O Lord of hosts, that triest the righteous and seest the reins and the heart, let me see thy vengeance on them, for unto thee have I opened my cause. Sing unto the Lord, praise ye the Lord, for he hath delivered the soul of the poor from the hand of evildoers.

Cursed be the day wherein I was born, let not the day wherein my mother bare me be blessed. Cursed be the man who brought tidings to my father saying, A man-child is born unto thee, making him very glad. And let that man be as the cities which the Lord overthrew and repented not, and let him hear the cry in the morning and the shouting at noontide, because he slew me not from the womb, or that my mother might have been my grave and her womb to be always great with me. Wherefore came I forth out of the womb to see labor and sorrow, that my days should be consumed with shame?

The word which came unto Jeremiah from the Lord when king Zedekiah sent unto him Pashur the son of Melchiah and Zephaniah the son of Maaseiah the priest saying, Inquire, I pray thee, of the Lord for us, for Nebuchadnezzar king of Babylon maketh war against us, if so be that the Lord will deal with us according to all his wondrous works, that he may go up from us. Then said Jeremiah unto them, Thus shall ye say to Zedekiah, Thus saith the Lord God of Israel, Behold, I will turn back the weapons of war that are in your hands wherewith ye fight against the king of Babylon, and against the Chaldeans which besiege you without the walls, and I will assemble them into the midst of this city. And I myself will fight against you with an outstretched hand and with a strong arm, even in anger, and in fury, and in great wrath. And I will smite the inhabitants of this city, both man and beast, they shall die of a great pestilence. And afterward, saith the Lord, I will deliver Zedekiah king of Judah, and his servants, and the people, and such as are left in this city from the pestilence, from the sword, and from the famine, into the hand of Nebuchadnezzar king of Babylon, and into the hand of their enemies, and into the hand of those that seek their life, and he shall smite them with the edge of the sword, he shall not spare them neither have pity nor have mercy.

And unto this people thou shalt say, Thus saith the Lord, Behold, I set before you the way of life and the way of death. He that abideth in this city shall die by the sword, and by the famine, and by the pestilence, but he that goeth out and falleth to the Chaldeans that besiege you, he shall live and his life shall be unto him for a prey. For I have set my face against this city for evil and not for good, saith the Lord, it shall be given into the hand of the king of Babylon and he shall burn it with fire.

And touching the house of the king of Judah, say, Hear ye the word of the Lord, O house of David, thus saith the Lord, Execute judgment in the morning and deliver him that is spoiled out of the hand of the oppressor, lest my fury go out like fire and burn that none can quench it because of the evil of your doings. Behold, I am against thee, O inhabitant of the valley and rock of the plain, saith the Lord, which say, Who shall come down against us? Or who shall enter into our habitations? But I will punish you according to the fruit of your doings, saith the Lord, and I will kindle a fire in the forest thereof, and it shall devour all things round about it. Thus saith the Lord, Go down to the house of the king of Judah and speak there this word and say, Hear the word of the Lord, O King of Judah, that sittest upon the throne of David, thou, and thy servants, and thy people that enter in by these gates, thus saith the Lord, Execute ye judgment and righteousness, and deliver the spoiled out of the hand of the oppressor, and do no wrong, do no violence to the stranger, the fatherless, nor the widow, neither shed innocent blood in this place. For if ye do this thing indeed, then shall there enter in by the gates of this house kings sitting upon the throne of David, riding in chariots and on horses, he, and his servants, and his people. But if ye will not hear these words, I swear by myself, saith the Lord, that this house shall become a desolation. For thus saith the Lord unto the King's house of Judah, Thou art Gilead unto me and the head of Lebanon, yet surely I will make thee a wilderness and cities which are not inhabited. And I will prepare destroyers against thee, everyone with his weapons, and they shall cut down thy choice cedars and cast them into the fire. And many nations shall pass by this city and they shall say every man to his neighbor, Wherefore hath the Lord done thus unto this great city? Then they shall answer, Because they have forsaken the covenant of the Lord their God, and worshiped other gods, and served them.

Weep ye not for the dead neither bemoan him, but weep sore for him that goeth away, for he shall return no more, nor see his native country. For thus saith the Lord touching Shallum the son of Josiah king of Judah, which reigned instead of Josiah his father, which went forth out of this place, He shall not return thither anymore, but he shall die in the place whither they have led him captive and shall see this land no more.

Wo unto him that buildeth his house by unrighteousness and his chambers by wrong, that useth his neighbor's service without wages and giveth him not for his work, that saith, I will build me a wide house and large chambers, and cutteth him out windows, and it is ceiled with cedar, and painted with vermilion. Shalt thou reign because thou closest thyself in cedar? Did not thy father eat and drink and do judgment and justice and then it was well with him? He judged the cause of the poor and needy, then it was well with him; was not this to know me? saith the Lord. But thine eyes and thine heart are not but for thy covetousness, and for to shed innocent blood, and for oppression, and for violence to do it. Therefore thus saith the Lord concerning Jehoiakim the son of Josiah king of Judah, They shall not lament for him saying, Ah my brother! or, Ah sister! They shall not lament for him, saying, Ah lord! or, Ah his glory! He shall be buried with the burial of an ass drawn and cast forth beyond the gates of Jerusalem. Go up to Lebanon and cry, and lift up thy voice in Bashan, and cry from the passages, for all thy lovers are destroyed. I spake unto thee in thy prosperity, but thou saidst, I will not hear. This hath been thy manner from thy youth, that thou obeyedst not my voice. The wind shall eat up all thy pastors and thy lovers shall go into captivity, surely then shalt thou be ashamed and confounded for all thy wickedness. O inhabitant of Lebanon, that makest thy nest in the cedars, how gracious shalt thou be when pangs come upon thee, the pain as of a woman in travail.

As I live, saith the Lord, though Coniah the son of Jehoiakim king of Judah were the signet upon my right hand, yet would I pluck thee thence, and I will give thee into the hand of them that seek thy life and into the hand of them whose face thou fearest, even into the hand of Nebuchadnezzar king of Babylon and into the hand of the Chaldeans. And I will cast thee out and thy mother that bare thee into another country where ye were not born, and there shall ye die. But to the land whereunto they desire to return, thither shall they not return. Is this man Coniah a despised broken idol? Is he a vessel wherein is no pleasure? Wherefore are they cast out, he and his seed, and are cast into a land which they know not? O earth, earth, earth, hear the word of the Lord. Thus saith the Lord, Write ye this man childless, a man that shall not prosper in his days, for no man of his seed shall prosper sitting upon the throne of David and ruling anymore in Judah.

Wo be unto the pastors that destroy and scatter the sheep of my pasture, saith the Lord. Therefore thus saith the Lord God of Israel against the pastors that feed my people, Ye have scattered my flock, and driven them away, and have not visited them, behold, I will visit upon you the evil of your doings, saith the Lord. And I will gather the remnant of my flock out of all countries whither I have driven them, and will bring them again to their folds, and they shall be fruitful and increase. And I will set up shepherds over them which shall feed them, and they shall fear no more, nor be dismayed, neither shall they be lacking, saith the Lord.

Behold, the days come, saith the Lord, that I will raise unto David a righteous Branch, and a King shall reign and prosper, and shall execute judgment and justice in the earth. In his days Judah shall be saved and Israel shall dwell safely, and this is his name whereby he shall be called: THE LORD OUR RIGHTEOUSNESS. Therefore behold, the days come, saith the Lord, that they shall no more say, The Lord liveth which brought up the children of Israel out of the land of Egypt, but, The Lord liveth which brought up and which led the seed of the house of Israel out of the north country, and from all countries whither I had driven them, and they shall dwell in their own land.

Mine heart within me is broken because of the prophets, all my bones shake, I am like a drunken man and like a man whom wine hath overcome, because of the Lord and because of the words of his holiness. For the land is full of adulterers, for because of swearing the land mourneth, the pleasant places of the wilderness are dried up, and their course is evil, and their force is not right. For both prophet and priest are profane, yea, in my house have I found their wickedness, saith the Lord. Wherefore their way shall be unto them as slippery ways in the darkness, they shall be driven on and fall therein, for I will bring evil upon them, even the year of their visitation, saith the Lord. And I have seen folly in the prophets of Samaria, they prophesied in Baal and caused my people Israel to err. I have seen also in the prophets of Jerusalem a horrible thing: they commit adultery and walk in lies, they strengthen also the hands of evildoers that none doth return from his wickedness, they are all of them unto me as Sodom and the inhabitants thereof as Gomorrah.

Therefore thus saith the Lord of hosts concerning the prophets, Behold, I will feed them with wormwood and make them drink the water of gall, for from the prophets of Jerusalem is profaneness gone forth into all the land. Thus saith the Lord of hosts, Hearken not unto the words of the prophets that prophesy unto you, they make you vain, they speak a vision of their own heart and not out of the mouth of the Lord. They say still unto them that despise me, The Lord hath said, Ye shall have peace, and they say unto everyone that walketh after the imagination of his own heart, No evil shall come upon you. For who hath stood in the counsel of the Lord, and hath perceived and heard his word? Who hath marked his word and heard it? Behold, a whirlwind of the Lord is gone forth in fury, even a grievous whirlwind, it shall fall grievously upon the head of the wicked. The anger of the Lord shall not return until he have executed, and till he have performed the thoughts of his heart, in the latter days ye shall consider it perfectly. I have not sent these prophets, yet they ran, I have not spoken to them, yet they prophesied. But if they had stood in my counsel and had caused my people to hear my words, then they should have turned them from their evil way and from the evil of their doings. Am I a God at hand, saith the Lord, and not a God afar off? Can any hide himself in secret places that I shall not see him? saith the Lord. Do not I fill Heaven and Earth? saith the Lord. I have heard what the prophets said, that prophesy lies in my name saying, I have dreamed, I have dreamed. How long shall this be in the heart of the prophets that prophesy lies? Yea, they are prophets of the deceit of their own heart, which think to cause my people to forget my name by their dreams which they tell every man to his neighbor, as their fathers have forgotten my name for Baal. The prophet that hath a dream, let him tell a dream, and he that hath my word, let him speak my word faithfully. What is the chaff to the wheat? saith the Lord. Is not my word like as a fire, saith the Lord, and like a hammer that breaketh the rock in pieces? Therefore behold, I am against the prophets, saith the Lord, that steal my words, everyone from his neighbor. Behold, I am against the prophets, saith the Lord, that use their tongues and say, He saith. Behold, I am against them that prophesy false dreams, saith the Lord, and do tell them and cause my people to err by their lies, and by their lightness, yet I sent them not nor commanded them, therefore they shall not profit this people at all, saith the Lord.

And when this people, or the prophet, or a priest shall ask thee, saying, What is the burden of the Lord? Thou shalt then say unto them, What burden? I will even forsake you, saith the Lord. And as for the prophet, and the priest, and the people that shall say, The burden of the Lord, I will even punish that man and his house. Thus shall ye say everyone to his neighbor and everyone to his brother, What hath the Lord answered? and, What hath the Lord spoken? And the burden of the Lord shall ye mention no more, for every man's word shall be his burden, for ye have perverted the words of the living God, of the Lord of hosts our God. Thus shalt thou say to the prophet, What hath the Lord answered thee? and, What hath the Lord spoken? But since ye say, The burden of the Lord, therefore thus saith the Lord, Because ye say this word, The burden of the Lord, and I have sent unto you saying, Ye shall not say, The burden of the Lord, therefore behold, I, even I, will utterly forget you, and I will forsake you and the city that I gave you and your fathers, and cast you out of my presence, and I will bring an everlasting reproach upon you, and a perpetual shame which shall not be forgotten.

The Lord showed me and behold, two baskets of figs were set before the temple of the Lord, after that Nebuchadnezzar king of Babylon had carried away captive Jeconiah the son of Jehoiakim king of Judah and the princes of Judah, with the carpenters and smiths from Jerusalem and had brought them to Babylon. One basket had very good figs, even like the figs that are first ripe, and the other basket had very naughty figs, which could not be eaten they were so bad. Then said the Lord unto me, What seest thou, Jeremiah? And I said, Figs, the good figs, very good, and the evil, very evil, that cannot be eaten they are so evil. Again the word of the Lord came unto me, saying, Thus saith the Lord, the God of Israel, Like these good figs, so will I acknowledge them that are carried away captive of Judah whom I have sent out of this place into the land of the Chaldeans for their good. For I will set mine eyes upon them for good, and I will bring them again to this land, and I will build them and not pull them down, and I will plant them and not pluck them up. And I will give them a heart to know me, that I am the Lord, and they shall be my people and I will be their God, for they shall return unto me with their whole heart. And as the evil figs, which cannot be eaten they are so evil, surely thus saith the Lord, So will I give Zedekiah the king of Judah, and his princes, and the residue of Jerusalem that remain in this land, and them that dwell in the land of Egypt, and I will deliver them to be removed into all the kingdoms of the earth for their hurt, to be a reproach and a proverb, a taunt and a curse, in all places whither I shall drive them. And I will send the sword, the famine, and the pestilence among them till they be consumed from off the land that I gave unto them and to their fathers.

9 THE word that came to Jeremiah concerning all the people of Judah, in the fourth year of Jehoiakim the son of Josiah king of Judah that was the first year of Nebuchadnezzar king of Babylon, the which Jeremiah the prophet spake unto all the people of Judah and to all the inhabitants of Jerusalem saying, From the thirteenth year of Josiah the son of Amon king of Judah, even unto this day that is the three and twentieth year, the word of the Lord hath come unto me and I have spoken unto you, rising early and speaking, but ye have not hearkened. And the Lord hath sent unto you all his servants the prophets, rising early and sending them, but ye have not hearkened nor inclined your ear to hear. They said, Turn ye again now everyone from his evil way and from the evil of your doings, and dwell in the land that the Lord hath given unto you and to your fathers for ever and ever, and go not after other gods to serve them, and to worship them, and provoke me not to anger with the works of your hands, and I will do you no hurt. Yet ye have not hearkened unto me, saith the Lord, that ye might provoke me to anger with the works of your hands to your own hurt.

Therefore thus saith the Lord of hosts, Because ye have not heard my words, behold, I will send and take all the families of the north, saith the Lord, and Nebuchadnezzar the king of Babylon, my servant, and will bring them against this land and against the inhabitants thereof, and against all these nations round about, and will utterly destroy them, and make them an astonishment, and a hissing, and perpetual desolations. Moreover I will take from them the voice of mirth, and the voice of gladness, the voice of the bridegroom, and the voice of the bride, the sound of the millstones, and the light of the candle. And this whole land shall be a desolation and an astonishment, and these nations shall serve the king of Babylon seventy years. And it shall come to pass when seventy years are accomplished that I will punish the king of Babylon and that nation, saith the Lord, for their iniquity and the land of the Chaldeans, and will make it perpetual desolations. And I will bring upon that land all my words which I have pronounced against it, even all that is written in this book which Jeremiah hath prophesied against all the nations. For many nations and great kings shall serve themselves of them also, and I will recompense them according to their deeds and according to the works of their own hands.

For thus saith the Lord God of Israel unto me, Take the wine cup of this fury at my hand, and cause all the nations to whom I send thee to drink it. And they shall drink and be moved and be mad because of the sword that I will send among them. Then took I the cup at the Lord's hand and made all the nations to drink, unto whom the Lord had sent me, to wit, Jerusalem, and the cities of Judah, and the kings thereof, and the princes thereof, to make them a desolation, an astonishment, a hissing, and a curse, as it is this day, Pharaoh king of Egypt, and his servants, and his princes, and all his people, and all the mingled people, and all the kings of the land of Uz, and all the kings of the land of the Philistines, and Ashkelon, and Azzah, and Ekron, and the remnant of Ashdod, Edom, and Moab, and the children of Ammon, and all the kings of Tyrus, and all the kings of Zidon, and the kings of the isles which are beyond the sea, Dedan, and Tema, and Buz, and all that are in the utmost corners, and all the kings of Arabia, and all the kings of the mingled people that dwell in the desert, and all the kings of Zimri, and all the kings of Elam, and all the kings of the Medes, and all the kings of the north, far and near, one with another, and all the kingdoms of the world, which are upon the face of the Earth, and the king of Sheshach shall drink after them. Therefore thou shalt say unto them, Thus saith the Lord of hosts, the God of Israel, Drink ye and be drunken, and spew, and fall, and rise no more, because of the sword which I will send among you. And it shall be, if they refuse to take the cup at thine hand to drink, then shalt thou say unto them, Thus saith the Lord of hosts, Ye shall certainly drink. For lo, I begin to bring evil on the city which is called by my name and should ye be utterly unpunished? Ye shall not be unpunished, for I will call for a sword upon all the inhabitants of the earth, saith the Lord of hosts.

Therefore prophesy thou against them all these words and say unto them, The Lord shall roar from on high and utter his voice from his holy habitation, he shall mightily roar upon his habitation, he shall give a shout as they that tread the grapes against all the inhabitants of the earth. A noise shall come even to the ends of the earth, for the Lord hath a controversy with the nations, he will plead with all flesh, he will give the wicked to the sword, saith the Lord. Thus saith the Lord of hosts, Behold, evil shall go forth from nation to nation and a great whirlwind shall be raised up from the coasts of the earth. And the slain of the Lord shall be at that day from one end of the Earth even unto the other end of the Earth, they shall not be lamented, neither gathered, nor buried, they shall be dung upon the ground. Howl, ye shepherds and cry, and wallow yourselves in the ashes, ye principal of the flock, for the days of your slaughter and of your dispersions are accomplished, and ye shall fall like a pleasant vessel. And the shepherds shall have no way to flee nor the principal of the flock to escape. A voice of the cry of the shepherds and a howling of the principal of the flock shall be heard, for the Lord hath spoiled their pasture. And the peaceable habitations are cut down because of the fierce anger of the Lord. He hath forsaken his covert as the lion, for their land is desolate because of the fierceness of the oppressor and because of his fierce anger.

10 IN the beginning of the reign of Jehoiakim the son of Josiah king of Judah came this word from the Lord, saying, Thus saith the Lord, Stand in the court of the

Lord's house, and speak unto all the cities of Judah which come to worship in the Lord's house, all the words that I command thee to speak unto them, diminish not a word. If so be they will hearken, and turn every man from his evil way, and repent, I will turn away the evil which I purpose to do unto them because of the evil of their doings. And thou shalt say unto them, Thus saith the Lord, If ye will not hearken to me, to walk in my law which I have set before you, to hearken to the words of my servants the prophets whom I sent unto you, commanding them to rise up early and sending them, then will I make this house like Shiloh and will make this city a curse to all the nations of the earth, for ye have not hearkened unto my servants the prophets.

So the priests and the prophets and all the people heard Jeremiah speaking these words in the house of the Lord. Now it came to pass when Jeremiah had made an end of speaking all that the Lord had commanded him to speak unto all the people, that the priests and the prophets and all the people took him saying, Thou shalt surely die. Why hast thou prophesied in the name of the Lord, saying, This house shall be like Shiloh and this city shall be desolate without an inhabitant? And all the people were gathered against Jeremiah in the house of the Lord. When the princes of Judah heard these things, then they came up from the king's house unto the house of the Lord and sat down in the entry of the new gate of the Lord's house. Then spake the priests and the prophets unto the princes and to all the people saying, This man is worthy to die, for he hath prophesied against this city as ye have heard with your ears. Then spake Jeremiah unto all the princes and to all the people saying, The Lord sent me to prophesy against this house and against this city all the words that ye have heard. Therefore now, amend your ways and your doings, and obey the voice of the Lord your God, and repent, and the Lord will turn away the evil that he hath pronounced against you. As for me, behold, I am in your hand, do with me as seemeth good and meet unto you. But know ye for certain, that if ye put me to death, ye shall surely bring innocent blood upon yourselves, and upon this city, and upon the inhabitants thereof, for of a truth the Lord hath sent me unto you to speak all these words in your ears.

Then said the princes and all the people unto the priests and to the prophets, This man is not worthy to die, for he hath spoken to us in the name of the Lord our God. Then rose up certain of the elders of the land and spake to all the assembly of the people saying, Micah the Morasthite prophesied in the days of Hezekiah king of Judah and spake to all the people of Judah saying, Thus saith the Lord of hosts, Zion shall be ploughed like a field, and Jerusalem shall become heaps, and the mountain of the house of the Lord as the high places of a forest.

Did Hezekiah, king of Judah, and all Judah put him at all to death? Did he not fear the Lord and beseech the Lord and repent and the Lord turned away the evil which he had pronounced against them? Thus by putting Jeremiah to death we might procure great evil against our souls. But there was a man among the priests, rose up and said that Urijah the son of Shemaiah of Kirjath-jearim prophesied in the name of the Lord, who also prophesied against this city and against this land, according to all the words of Jeremiah, and when Jehoiakim the king with all his mighty men and all the princes heard his words, the king sought to put him to death, but when Urijah heard it he was afraid, and fled, and went into Egypt, and Jehoiakim the king sent men into Egypt, namely Elnathan the son of Achbor and certain men with him into Egypt. And they fetched forth Urijah out of Egypt and brought him unto Jehoiakim the king, who slew him with the sword and cast his dead body into the graves of the common people. Nevertheless, the hand of Ahikam the son of Shaphan was with Jeremiah that they should not give him into the hand of the people to put him to death.

In the beginning of the reign of Jehoiakim the son of Josiah king of Judah came this word unto Jeremiah from the Lord saying, Thus saith the Lord to me, Make thee bonds and yokes and put them upon thy neck, and send them to the king of Edom, and to the king of Moab, and to the king of the Ammonites, and to the king of Tyrus, and to the king of Zidon, by the hand of the messengers which come to Jerusalem unto Zedekiah king of Judah, and command them to say unto their masters, Thus saith the Lord of hosts, the God of Israel, Thus shall ye say unto your masters, I have made the earth, the man and the beast that are upon the ground, by my great power and by my outstretched arm, and have given it unto whom it seemed meet unto me. And now have I given all these lands into the hand of Nebuchadnezzar the king of Babylon, my servant, and the beasts of the field have I given him also to serve him. And all nations shall serve him, and his son, and his son's son, until the very time of their end come, and after that many nations and great kings shall serve themselves of them. And it shall come to pass that the nation and kingdom which will not serve the same Nebuchadnezzar the king of Babylon and that will not put their neck under the yoke of the king of Babylon, that nation will I punish, saith the Lord, with the sword, and with the famine, and with the pestilence, until I have consumed them by his hand. Therefore hearken not ye to your prophets, nor to your diviners, nor to your dreamers, nor to your enchanters, nor to your sorcerers which speak unto you saying, Ye shall not serve the king of Babylon, for they prophesy a lie unto you to remove you far from your land, and that I should drive you out, and ye should perish. But the nations that bring their neck under the yoke of the king of Babylon and serve him, those will I let still remain in their own land, saith the Lord, and they shall till it and dwell therein.

I spake also to Zedekiah king of Judah according to all these words, saying, Bring your necks under the yoke of the king of Babylon, and serve him and his people and live. Why will ye die, thou and thy people, by the sword, by the famine, and by the pestilence, as the Lord hath spoken against the nation that will not serve the king of Babylon? Therefore hearken not unto the words of the prophets that speak unto you, saying, Ye shall not serve the king of Babylon, for they prophesy a lie unto you. For I have not sent them, saith the Lord, yet they prophesy a lie in my name, that I might drive you out and that ye might perish, ye, and the prophets that prophesy unto you. Also I spake to the priests and to all this people saying, Thus saith the Lord, Hearken not to the words of your prophets that prophesy unto you, saying, Behold, the vessels of the Lord's house shall now shortly be brought again from Babylon, for they prophesy a lie unto you. Hearken not unto them, serve the king of Babylon and live, wherefore should this city be laid waste? But if they be prophets, and if the word of the Lord be with them, let them now make intercession to the Lord of hosts that the vessels which are left in the house of the Lord, and in the house of the king of Judah, and at Jerusalem, go not to Babylon. For thus saith the Lord of hosts concerning the pillars, and concerning the sea, and concerning the bases, and concerning the residue of the vessels that remain in this city which Nebuchadnezzar king of Babylon took not when he carried away captive Jeconiah the son of Jehoiakim king of Judah from Jerusalem to Babylon and all the nobles of Judah and Jerusalem, yea, thus saith the Lord of hosts, the God of Israel, concerning the vessels that remain in the house of the Lord and in the house of the king of Judah and of Jerusalem, they shall be carried to Babylon, and there shall they be until the day that I visit them, saith the Lord, then will I bring them up and restore them to this place.

And it came to pass the same year, in the beginning of the reign of Zedekiah king of Judah, in the fourth year, and in the fifth month, that Hananiah the son of Azur the prophet which was of Gibeon, spake unto me in the house of the

Lord in the presence of the priests and of all the people, saying, Thus speaketh the Lord of hosts, the God of Israel, saying, I have broken the yoke of the king of Babylon. Within two full years will I bring again into this place all the vessels of the Lord's house that Nebuchadnezzar king of Babylon took away from this place and carried them to Babylon, and I will bring again to this place Jeconiah the son of Jehoiakim king of Judah with all the captives of Judah that went into Babylon, saith the Lord, for I will break the yoke of the king of Babylon. Then the prophet Jeremiah said unto the prophet Hananiah in the presence of the priests and in the presence of all the people that stood in the house of the Lord, even the prophet Jeremiah said, Amen, the Lord do so, the Lord perform thy words which thou hast prophesied, to bring again the vessels of the Lord's house and all that is carried away captive from Babylon into this place. Nevertheless, hear thou now this word that I speak in thine ears and in the ears of all the people, the prophets that have been before me and before thee of old prophesied both against many countries and against great kingdoms, of war, and of evil, and pestilence. The prophet which prophesieth of peace, when the word of the prophet shall come to pass then shall the prophet be known that the Lord hath truly sent him. Then Hananiah the prophet took the yoke from off the prophet Jeremiah's neck and brake it. And Hananiah spake in the presence of all the people, saying, Thus saith the Lord, Even so will I break the yoke of Nebuchadnezzar king of Babylon from the neck of all nations within the space of two full years. And the prophet Jeremiah went his way.

Then the word of the Lord came unto Jeremiah the prophet, after that Hananiah the prophet had broken the yoke from off the neck of the prophet Jeremiah, saying, Go and tell Hananiah saying, Thus saith the Lord, Thou hast broken the yokes of wood, but thou shalt make for them yokes of iron. For thus saith the Lord of hosts, the God of Israel, I have put a yoke of iron upon the neck of all these nations that they may serve Nebuchadnezzar king of Babylon, and they shall serve him, and I have given him the beasts of the field also. Then said the prophet Jeremiah unto Hananiah the prophet, Hear now, Hananiah, The Lord hath not sent thee, but thou makest this people to trust in a lie. Therefore thus saith the Lord, Behold, I will cast thee from off the face of the earth, this year thou shalt die because thou hast taught rebellion against the Lord. So Hananiah the prophet died the same year in the seventh month.

Now these are the words of the letter that Jeremiah the prophet sent from Jerusalem unto the residue of the elders which were carried away captives, and to the priests, and to the prophets, and to all the people whom Nebuchadnezzar had carried away captive from Jerusalem to Babylon (after that Jeconiah the king, and the queen, and the eunuchs, the princes of Judah and Jerusalem, and the carpenters, and the smiths, were departed from Jerusalem), by the hand of Elasah the son of Shaphan and Gemariah the son of Hilkiah (whom Zedekiah king of Judah sent unto Babylon to Nebuchadnezzar king of Babylon) saying, Thus saith the Lord of hosts, the God of Israel, unto all that are carried away captives whom I have caused to be carried away from Jerusalem unto Babylon, build ye houses and dwell in them, and plant gardens, and eat the fruit of them, take ye wives, and beget sons and daughters, and take wives for you sons, and give your daughters to husbands, that they may bear sons and daughters, that ye may be increased there and not diminished. And seek the peace of the city whither I have caused you to be carried away captives, and pray unto the Lord for it, for in the peace thereof shall ye have peace. For thus saith the Lord of hosts, the God of Israel, let not your prophets and your diviners, that be in the midst of you, deceive you, neither hearken to your dreams which ye cause to be dreamed. For they prophesy falsely unto you in my name, I have not sent them, saith the Lord. For thus saith the Lord, that after seventy years be accomplished at Babylon I will visit you and perform my good word toward you in causing you to return to this place. For I know the thoughts that I think toward you, saith the Lord, thoughts of peace and not of evil, to give you an expected end. Then shall ye call unto me, and ye shall go and pray unto me, and I will hearken unto you. And ye shall seek me and find me when ye shall search for me with all your heart. And I will be found of you, saith the Lord, and I will turn away your captivity, and I will gather you from all the nations, and from all the places whither I have driven you, saith the Lord, and I will bring you again into the place whence I caused you to be carried away captive.

Because ye have said, The Lord hath raised us up prophets in Babylon, know that thus saith the Lord of the king that sitteth upon the throne of David, and of all the people that dwelleth in this city, and of your brethren that are not gone forth with you into captivity, thus saith the Lord of hosts, Behold, I will send upon them the sword, the famine, and the pestilence, and will make them like vile figs that cannot be eaten they are so evil. And I will persecute them with the sword, with the famine, and with the pestilence, and will deliver them to be removed to all the kingdoms of the earth, to be a curse, and an astonishment, and a hissing, and a reproach among all the nations whither I have driven them because they have not hearkened to my words, saith the Lord, which I sent unto them by my servants the prophets, commanding them to rise early and sending them, but ye would not hear, saith the Lord. Hear ye therefore the word of the Lord, all ye of the captivity whom I have sent from Jerusalem to Babylon, thus saith the Lord of hosts, the God of Israel, of Ahab the son of Kolaiah and of Zedekiah the son of Maaseiah, which prophesy a lie unto you in my name, Behold, I will deliver them into the hand of Nebuchadnezzar king of Babylon, and he shall slay them before your eyes, and of them shall be taken up a curse by all the captivity of Judah which are in Babylon, saying, The Lord make thee like Zedekiah and like Ahab, whom the king of Babylon roasted in the fire, because they have committed villany in Israel, and have committed adultery with their neighbors' wives, and have spoken lying words in my name which I have not commanded them, even I know and am a witness, saith the Lord.

Thus shalt thou also speak to Shemaiah the Nehelamite, saying, Thus speaketh the Lord of hosts, the God of Israel saying, Because thou hast sent letters in thy name unto all the people that are at Jerusalem, and to Zephaniah the son of Maaseiah the priest, and to all the priests saying, The Lord hath made thee priest in the stead of Jehoiada the priest that ye should be officers in the house of the Lord, for every man that is mad and maketh himself a prophet, that thou shouldest put him in prison and in the stocks. Now therefore why hast thou not reproved Jeremiah of Anathoth, which maketh himself a prophet to you? For therefore he sent unto us in Babylon, saying, This captivity is long, build ye houses and dwell in them, and plant gardens and eat the fruit of them. And Zephaniah the priest read this letter in the ears of Jeremiah the prophet. Then came the word of the Lord unto Jeremiah saying, Send to all them of the captivity, saying, Thus saith the Lord concerning Shemaiah the Nehelamite, Because that Shemaiah hath prophesied unto you and I sent him not and he caused you to trust in a lie, therefore thus saith the Lord, Behold, I will punish Shemaiah the Nehelamite and his seed: he shall not have a man to dwell among this people neither shall he behold the good that I will do for my people, saith the Lord, because he hath taught rebellion against the Lord.

11 THE word that came to Jeremiah from the Lord, saying, Thus speaketh the Lord God of Israel, saying, Write thee all the words that I have spoken unto thee in a book. For lo, the days come, saith the Lord, that I will bring again the captivity of my people Israel and Judah, saith the Lord, and I will cause them

to return to the land that I gave to their fathers and they shall possess it. And these are the words that the Lord spake concerning Israel and concerning Judah.

For thus saith the Lord, We have heard a voice of trembling, of fear, and not of peace. Ask ye now, and see whether a man doth travail with child? Wherefore do I see every man with his hands on his loins as a woman in travail and all faces are turned into paleness? Alas! For that day is great so that none is like it, it is even the time of Jacob's trouble, but he shall be saved out of it. For it shall come to pass in that day, saith the Lord of hosts, that I will break his yoke from off thy neck and will burst thy bonds, and strangers shall no more serve themselves of him, but they shall serve the Lord their God and David their king whom I will raise up unto them.

Therefore fear thou not O my servant Jacob, saith the Lord, neither be dismayed O Israel, for lo, I will save thee from afar, and thy seed from the land of their captivity, and Jacob shall return, and shall be in rest and be quiet, and none shall make him afraid. For I am with thee, saith the Lord, to save thee; though I make a full end of all nations whither I have scattered thee, yet will I not make a full end of thee, but I will correct thee in measure and will not leave thee altogether unpunished. For thus saith the Lord, thy bruise is not incurable although thy wounds are grievous. Is there none to plead thy cause, that thou mayest be bound up? Hast thou no healing medicines? Have all thy lovers forgotten thee, do they not seek thee? For I have wounded thee with the wound of an enemy, with the chastisement of a cruel one, for the multitude of thine iniquities because thy sins are increased. Why criest thou for thine affliction? Is thy sorrow incurable? It was for the multitude of thine iniquities and because thy sins are increased I have done these things unto thee. But all they that devour thee shall be devoured, and all thine adversaries, every one of them, shall go into captivity, and they that spoil thee shall be a spoil, and all that prey upon thee will I give for a prey. For I will restore health unto thee and I will heal thee of thy wounds, saith the Lord, because they called thee an Outcast, saying, This is Zion whom no man seeketh after.

Thus saith the Lord, Behold, I will bring again the captivity of Jacob's tents and have mercy on his dwelling places, and the city shall be builded upon her own heap and the palace shall remain after the manner thereof. And out of them shall proceed thanksgiving and the voice of them that make merry, and I will multiply them and they shall not be few, I will also glorify them and they shall not be small. Their children also shall be as aforetime, and their congregation shall be established before me, and I will punish all that oppress them. And their nobles shall be of themselves, and their governor shall proceed from the midst of them, and I will cause him to draw near and he shall approach unto me, for who is this that engaged his heart to approach unto me? saith the Lord. And ye shall be my people and I will be your God. Behold, the whirlwind of the Lord goeth forth with fury, a continuing whirlwind, it shall fall with pain upon the head of the wicked. The fierce anger of the Lord shall not return until he have done it and until he have performed the intents of his heart, in the latter days ye shall consider it.

At the same time, saith the Lord, will I be the God of all the families of Israel and they shall be my people. Thus saith the Lord, The people which were left of the sword found grace in the wilderness, even Israel, when I went to cause him to rest. The Lord hath appeared of old unto me, saying, Yea, I have loved thee with an everlasting love, therefore with lovingkindness have I drawn thee. Again I will build thee and thou shalt be built, O virgin of Israel, thou shalt again be adorned with thy tabrets and shalt go forth in the dances of them that make merry. Thou shalt yet plant vines upon the mountains of Samaria, the planters shall plant and shall eat them as common things. For there shall be a day that the watchmen upon the mount Ephraim shall cry, Arise ye, and let us go up to Zion unto the Lord our God. For thus saith the Lord, Sing with gladness for Jacob and shout among the chief of the nations, publish ye, praise ye, and say, O Lord, save thy people, the remnant of Israel. Behold, I will bring them from the north country and gather them from the coasts of the Earth, and with them the blind and the lame, the woman with child and her that travaileth with child together, a great company shall return thither. They shall come with weeping and with supplications will I lead them, I will cause them to walk by the rivers of waters in a straight way wherein they shall not stumble, for I am a father to Israel and Ephraim is my firstborn.

Hear the word of the Lord, O ye nations, and declare it in the isles afar off and say, He that scattered Israel will gather him and keep him as a shepherd doth his flock. For the Lord hath redeemed Jacob and ransomed him from the hand of him that was stronger than he. Therefore they shall come and sing in the height of Zion, and shall flow together to the goodness of the Lord, for wheat, and for wine, and for oil, and for the young of the flock and of the herd, and their soul shall be as a watered garden, and they shall not sorrow anymore at all. Then shall the virgin rejoice in the dance, both young men and old together, for I will turn their mourning into joy, and will comfort them, and make them rejoice from their sorrow. And I will satiate the soul of the priests with fatness and my people shall be satisfied with my goodness, saith the Lord.

Thus saith the Lord, A voice was heard in Ramah, lamentation and bitter weeping, Rachel weeping for her children refused to be comforted for her children, because they were not. Thus saith the Lord, Refrain thy voice from weeping and thine eyes from tears, for thy work shall be rewarded, saith the Lord, and they shall come again from the land of the enemy. And there is hope in thine end, saith the Lord, that thy children shall come again to their own border. I have surely heard Ephraim bemoaning himself thus, Thou hast chastised me and I was chastised as a bullock unaccustomed to the yoke, turn thou me and I shall be turned, for thou art the Lord my God. Surely after that I was turned, I repented, and after that I was instructed, I smote upon my thigh, I was ashamed, yea, even confounded, because I did bear the reproach of my youth. Is Ephraim my dear son? Is he a pleasant child? For since I spake against him, I do earnestly remember him still, therefore my bowels are troubled for him, I will surely have mercy upon him, saith the Lord. Set thee up waymarks, make thee high heaps, set thine heart toward the highway, even the way which thou wentest, turn again, O virgin of Israel, turn again to these thy cities. How long wilt thou go about, O thou backsliding daughter? For the Lord hath created a new thing in the earth: a woman shall compass a man. Thus saith the Lord of hosts, the God of Israel, As yet they shall use this speech in the land of Judah and in the cities thereof when I shall bring again their captivity, The Lord bless thee, O habitation of justice and mountain of holiness. And there shall dwell in Judah itself, and in all the cities thereof together, husbandmen, and they that go forth with flocks. For I have satiated the weary soul and I have replenished every sorrowful soul. Upon this I awaked and beheld, and my sleep was sweet unto me.

Behold, the days come, saith the Lord, that I will sow the house of Israel and the house of Judah with the seed of man and with the seed of beast. And it shall come to pass, that like as I have watched over them, to pluck up, and to break down, and to throw down, and to destroy, and to afflict, so will I watch over them, to build, and to plant, saith the Lord. In those days they shall say no more, The fathers have eaten a sour grape and the children's teeth are set on edge. But everyone shall die for his own iniquity, every man that eateth the sour grape, his teeth shall be set on edge. Behold, the days come, saith the Lord, that I will make a new covenant with the house of Israel, and with the house of Judah, not according to the covenant that I made with their fathers in the day that I took them by the hand to bring them out of the land of Egypt, which my covenant they brake although I was a husband unto them, saith the Lord. But this shall be the covenant that I will make with the house of Israel: After those days, saith the Lord, I will put my law in their inward parts, and write it in their hearts, and will be their God and they shall be my people. And they shall teach no more every man his neighbor and every man his brother saying, Know the Lord, for they shall all know me, from the least of them unto the greatest of them, saith the Lord, for I will forgive their iniquity and I will remember their sin no more.

Thus saith the Lord, which giveth the sun for a light by day and the ordinances of the moon and of the stars for a light by night, which divideth the sea when the waves thereof roar, The Lord of hosts is his name. If those ordinances depart from before me, saith the Lord, then the seed of Israel also shall cease from being a nation before me forever. Thus saith the Lord, If Heaven above can be measured and the foundations of the Earth searched out beneath, I will also cast off all the seed of Israel for all that they have done, saith the Lord. Behold, the days come, saith the Lord, that the city shall be built to the Lord from the tower of Hananeel unto the gate of the corner. And the measuring line shall yet go forth over against it upon the hill Gareb and shall compass about to Goath. And the whole valley of the dead bodies and of the ashes, and all the fields unto the brook of Kidron unto the corner of the horse gate toward the east, shall be holy unto the Lord, it shall not be plucked up nor thrown down anymore forever.

12 THE word that came to Jeremiah from the Lord in the tenth year of Zedekiah king of Judah, which was the eighteenth year of Nebuchadnezzar. For then the king of Babylon's army besieged Jerusalem, and Jeremiah the prophet was shut up in the court of the prison which was in the king of Judah's house. For Zedekiah king of Judah had shut him up saying, Wherefore dost thou prophesy and say, Thus saith the Lord, Behold, I will give this city into the hand of the king of Babylon and he shall take it, and Zedekiah king of Judah shall not escape out of the hand of the Chaldeans, but shall surely be delivered into the hand of the king of Babylon, and shall speak with him mouth to mouth, and his eyes shall behold his eyes, and he shall lead Zedekiah to Babylon, and there shall he be until I visit him, saith the Lord, though ye fight with the Chaldeans ye shall not prosper.

And Jeremiah said, The word of the Lord came unto me, saying, Behold, Hanameel the son of Shallum thine uncle shall come unto thee saying, Buy thee my field that is in Anathoth, for the right of redemption is thine to buy it. So Hanameel mine uncle's son came to me in the court of the prison according to the word of the Lord and said unto me, Buy my field, I pray thee, that is in Anathoth which is in the country of Benjamin, for the right of inheritance is thine and the redemption is thine, buy it for thyself. Then I knew that this was the word of the Lord. And I bought the field of Hanameel my uncle's son that was in Anathoth, and weighed him the money, even seventeen shekels of silver. And I subscribed the evidence and sealed it, and took witnesses, and weighed him the money in the balances. So I took the evidence of the purchase, both that which was sealed according to the law and custom and that which was open, and I gave the evidence of the purchase unto Baruch the son of Neriah the son of Maaseiah in the sight of Hanameel mine uncle's son and in the presence of the witnesses that subscribed the book of the purchase, before all the Jews that sat in the court of the prison. And I charged Baruch before them saying, Thus saith the Lord of hosts, the God of Israel, Take these evidences, this evidence of the purchase, both which is sealed and this evidence which is open, and put them in an earthen vessel that they may continue many days. For thus saith the Lord of hosts, the God of Israel, Houses and fields and vineyards shall be possessed again in this land.

Now when I had delivered the evidence of the purchase unto Baruch the son of Neriah, I prayed unto the Lord saying, Ah Lord God! Behold, thou hast made the Heaven and the Earth by thy great power and stretched out arm, and there is nothing too hard for thee. Thou showest lovingkindness unto thousands, and recompensest the iniquity of the fathers into the bosom of their children after them. The Great, The Mighty God, The Lord of hosts is his name, great in counsel and mighty in work, for thine eyes are open upon all the ways of the sons of men, to give everyone according to his ways, and according to the fruit of his doings, which hast set signs and wonder in the land of Egypt even unto this day, and in Israel and among other men, and hast made thee a name as at this day, and hast brought forth thy people Israel out of the land of Egypt with signs, and with wonders, and with a strong hand, and with a stretched out arm, and with great terror, and hast given them this land, which thou didst swear to their fathers to give them, a land flowing with milk and honey, and they came in and possessed it. But they obeyed not thy voice neither walked in thy law, they have done nothing of all that thou commandedst them to do, therefore thou hast caused all this evil to come upon them. Behold the mounts, they are come unto the city to take it, and the city is given into the hand of the Chaldeans that fight against it because of the sword, and of the famine, and of the pestilence, and what thou hast spoken is come to pass and behold, thou seest it. And thou hast said unto me, O Lord God, Buy thee the field for money and take witnesses, for the city is given into the hand of the Chaldeans.

Then came the word of the Lord unto Jeremiah, saying, Behold, I am the Lord, the God of all flesh, is there anything too hard for me? Therefore thus saith the Lord, Behold, I will give this city into the hand of the Chaldeans and into the hand of Nebuchadnezzar king of Babylon, and he shall take it, and the Chaldeans that fight against this city shall come and set fire on this city and burn it with the houses, upon whose roofs they have offered incense unto Baal, and poured out drink offerings unto other gods to provoke me to anger. For the children of Israel and the children of Judah have only done evil before me from their youth, for the children of Israel have only provoked me to anger with the work of their hands, saith the Lord. For this city hath been to me as a provocation of mine anger and of my fury from the day that they built it even unto this day, that I should remove it from before my face because of all the evil of the children of Israel and of the children of Judah which they have done to provoke me to anger, they, their kings, their princes, their priests, and their prophets, and the men of Judah, and the inhabitants of Jerusalem. And they have turned unto me the back and not the face, though I taught them, rising up early and teaching them, yet they have not hearkened to receive instruction. But they set their abominations in the house which is called by my name to defile it. And they built the high places of Baal which are in the valley of the son of Hinnom to cause their sons and their daughters to pass through the fire unto Molech, which I commanded them not, neither came it into my mind that they should do this abomination to cause Judah to sin.

And now therefore thus saith the Lord, the God of Israel, concerning this city whereof ye say, It shall be delivered into the hand of the king of Babylon by the sword, and by the famine, and by the pestilence, Behold, I will gather them out of all countries, whither I have driven them in mine anger, and in my fury, and in great wrath, and I will bring them again unto this place, and I will cause them to dwell safely, and they shall be my people and I will be their God, and I will give them one heart and one way, that they may fear me forever, for the good of them and of their children after them, and I will make an everlasting covenant with them, that I will not turn away from them to do them good, but I will put my fear in their hearts that they shall not depart from me. Yea, I will rejoice over them to do them good and I will plant them in this land assuredly with my whole heart and with my whole soul. For thus saith the Lord, Like as I have brought all this great evil upon this people, so will I bring upon them all the good that I have promised them. And fields shall be bought in this land whereof ye say, It is desolate without man or beast, it is given into the hand of the Chaldeans. Men shall buy fields for money, and subscribe evidences, and seal them, and take witnesses in the land of Benjamin, and in the places about Jerusalem, and in the cities of Judah, and in the cities of the mountains, and in the cities of the valley, and in the cities of the south, for I will cause their captivity to return, saith the Lord.

Moreover the word of the Lord came unto Jeremiah the second time, while he was yet shut up in the court of the prison, saying, Thus saith the Lord the maker thereof, the Lord that formed it, to establish it, The Lord is his name, Call unto me and I will answer thee and show thee great and mighty things which thou knowest not. For thus saith the Lord, the God of Israel, concerning the houses of this city, and concerning the houses of the kings of Judah which are thrown down by the mounts, and by the sword. They come to fight with the Chaldeans, but it is to fill them with the dead bodies of men whom I have slain in mine anger and in my fury, and for all whose wickedness I have hid my face from his city. Behold, I will bring it health and cure, and I will cure them and will reveal unto them the abundance of peace and truth. And I will cause the captivity of Judah and the captivity of Israel to return, and will build them as at the first. And I will cleanse them from all their iniquity whereby they have sinned against me, and I will pardon all their iniquities whereby they have sinned and whereby they have transgressed against me. And it shall be to me a name of joy, a praise and an honor before all the nations of the earth, which shall hear all the good that I do unto them, and they shall fear and tremble for all the goodness and for all the prosperity that I procure unto it. Thus saith the Lord, Again there shall be heard in this place - which ye say shall be desolate without man and without beast, even in the cities of Judah and in the streets of Jerusalem that are desolate, without man, and without inhabitant, and without beast - the voice of joy and the voice of gladness, the voice of the bridegroom and the voice of the bride, the voice of them that shall say, Praise the Lord of hosts for the Lord is good, for his mercy endureth for ever unto them that shall bring the sacrifice of praise into the house of the Lord. For I will cause to return the captivity of the land as at the first, saith the Lord. Thus saith the Lord of hosts, Again in this place, which is desolate without man and without beast, and in all the cities thereof shall be a habitation of shepherds causing their flocks to lie down. In the cities of the mountains, in the cities of the vale, and in the cities of the south, and in the land of Benjamin, and in the places about Jerusalem, and in the cities of Judah shall the flocks pass again under the hands of him that telleth them, saith the Lord.

Behold, the days come, saith the Lord, that I will perform that good thing which I have promised unto the house of Israel and to the house of Judah. In those days and at that time will I cause the Branch of righteousness to grow up unto David and he shall execute judgment and righteousness in the land. In those days shall Judah be saved and Jerusalem shall dwell safely, and this is the name wherewith she shall be called: The Lord our Righteousness. For thus saith the Lord, David shall never want a man to sit upon the throne of the house of Israel, neither shall the priests the Levites want a man before me to offer burnt offerings, and to kindle meat offerings, and to do sacrifice continually.

And the word of the Lord came unto Jeremiah, saying, Thus saith the Lord, If ye can break my covenant of the day, and my covenant of the night, and that there should not be day and night in their season, then may also my covenant be broken with David my servant, that he should not have a son to reign upon his throne, and with the Levites the priests, my ministers. As the host of Heaven cannot be numbered, neither the sand of the sea measured, so will I multiply the seed of David my servant, and the Levites that minister unto me.

Moreover the word of the Lord came to Jeremiah, saying, Considerest thou not what this people have spoken saying, The two families which the Lord hath chosen, he hath even cast them off. Thus they have despised my people that they should be no more a nation before them. Thus saith the Lord, if my covenant be not with day and night, and if I have not appointed the ordinances of Heaven and earth, then will I cast away the seed of Jacob and David my servant so that I will not take any of his seed to be rulers over the seed of Abraham, Isaac, and Jacob, for I will cause their captivity to return and have mercy on them.

13 THE word which came unto Jeremiah from the Lord when Nebuchadnezzar king of Babylon, and all his army, and all the kingdoms of the earth of his dominion, and all the people, fought against Jerusalem and against all the cities thereof, saying, Thus saith the Lord, the God of Israel, Go and speak to Zedekiah king of Judah and tell him, Thus saith the Lord, Behold, I will give this city into the hand of the king of Babylon, and he shall burn it with fire, and thou shalt not escape out of his hand, but shalt surely be taken and delivered into his hand, and thine eyes shall behold the eyes of the king of Babylon, and he shall speak with thee mouth to mouth, and thou shalt go to Babylon. Yet hear the word of the Lord, O Zedekiah king of Judah, Thus saith the Lord of thee, Thou shalt not die by the sword, but thou shalt die in peace and with the burnings of thy fathers, the former kings which were before thee, so shall they burn odors for thee, and they will lament thee saying, Ah lord! For I have pronounced the word, saith the Lord. Then Jeremiah the prophet spake all these words unto Zedekiah king of Judah in Jerusalem, when the king of Babylon's army fought against Jerusalem, and against all the cities of Judah that were left, against Lachish, and against Azekah, for these defensed cities remained of the cities of Judah.

This is the word that came unto Jeremiah from the Lord after that the king Zedekiah had made a covenant with all the people which were at Jerusalem to proclaim liberty unto them, that every man should let his manservant, and every man his maidservant, being a Hebrew or a Hebrewess, go free, that none should serve himself of them, to wit of a Jew his brother. Now when all the princes and all the people which had entered into the covenant heard that everyone should let his manservant and everyone his maidservant go free, that none should serve themselves of them anymore, then they obeyed and let them go. But afterwards they turned and caused the servants and the handmaids whom they had let go free to return and brought them into subjection for servants and for handmaids.

Therefore the word of the Lord came to Jeremiah from the Lord, saying, Thus saith the Lord, the God of Israel, I made a covenant with your fathers in the day that I brought them forth out of the land of Egypt, out of the house of bondmen saying, At the end of seven years let ye go every man his brother a Hebrew which hath been sold unto thee, and when he hath served thee six years thou shalt let him go free from thee, but your fathers hearkened not unto me neither inclined their ear. But ye were now turned and had done right in my sight, in proclaiming liberty every man to his neighbor, and ye had made a covenant before me in the house which is called by my name. But ye turned and polluted my name and caused every man his servant and every man his handmaid whom he had set at liberty at their pleasure to return, and brought them into subjection to be unto you for servants and for handmaids.

Therefore thus saith the Lord, Ye have not hearkened unto me in proclaiming liberty, everyone to his brother and every man to his neighbor, behold, I proclaim a liberty for you, saith the Lord, to the sword, to the pestilence, and to the famine, and I will make you to be removed into all the kingdoms of the earth. And I will give the men that have transgressed my covenant, which have not performed the words of the covenant which they had made before me, when they cut the calf in twain and passed between the parts thereof the princes of Judah, and the princes of Jerusalem, the eunuchs, and the priests, and all the people of the land which passed between the parts of the calf, I will even give them into the hand of their enemies and into the hand of them that seek their life, and their dead bodies shall be for meat unto the fowls of the Heaven, and to the beasts of the Earth. And Zedekiah king of Judah and his princes will I give into the hand of their enemies, and into the hand of them that seek their life, and into the hand of the king of Babylon's army which are gone up from you. Behold, I will command, saith the Lord, and cause them to return to this city, and they shall fight against it, and take it and burn it with fire, and I will make the cities of Judah a desolation without an inhabitant.

The word which came unto Jeremiah from the Lord, in the days of Jehoiakim the son of Josiah king of Judah saying, Go unto the house of the Rechabites and speak unto them, and bring them into the house of the Lord, into one of the chambers, and give them wine to drink. Then I took Jaazaniah the son of Jeremiah the son of Habaziniah, and his brethren, and all his sons, and the whole house of Rechabites, and I brought them into the house of the Lord, into the chamber of the sons of Hanan the son of Igdaliah, a man of God, which was by the chamber of the princes which was above the chamber of Maaseiah the son of Challum the keeper of the door, and I set before the sons of the house of the Rechabites pots full of wine and cups, and I said unto them, Drink ye wine. But they said, We will drink no wine, for Jonadab the son of Rechab our father commanded us, saying, Ye shall drink no wine, neither ye, nor your sons forever, neither shall ye build house, nor sow seed, nor plant vineyard, nor have any, but all your days ye shall dwell in tents that ye may live many days in the land where ye be strangers. Thus have we obeyed the voice of Jonadab the son of Rechab our father in all that he hath charged us, to drink no wine all our days, we, our wives, our sons, nor our daughters, nor to build houses for us to dwell in, neither have we vineyard, nor field, nor seed, but we have dwelt in tents and have obeyed and done according to all that Jonadab our father commanded us. But it came to pass when Nebuchadnezzar king of Babylon came up into the land that we said, Come and let us go to Jerusalem for fear of the army of the Chaldeans, and for fear of the army of the Syrians, so we dwell at Jerusalem.

Then came the word of the Lord unto Jeremiah, saying, Thus saith the Lord of hosts, the God of Israel, Go and tell the men of Judah and the inhabitants of Jerusalem, Will ye not receive instruction to hearken to my words? saith the Lord. The words of Jonadab the son of Rechab that he commanded his sons not to drink wine, are performed, for unto this day they drink none, but obey their father's commandment, notwithstanding I have spoken unto you, commanding you to rise early, and speaking to you, but ye hearkened not unto me. I have sent also unto you all my servants the prophets, commanding them to rise up early, and sending them saying, Return ye now every man from his evil way, and amend your doings, and go not after other gods to serve them, and ye shall dwell in the land which I have given to you and to your fathers, but ye have not inclined your ear nor hearkened unto me. Because the sons of Jonadab the son of Rechab have performed the commandment of their father, which he commanded them, but this people hath not hearkened unto me, therefore thus saith the Lord God of hosts, the God of Israel, Behold, I will bring upon Judah and upon all the inhabitants of Jerusalem all the evil that I have pronounced against them, because I have spoken unto them, but they have not heard, and I have called unto them, but they have not answered.

And Jeremiah said unto the house of the Rechabites, Thus saith the Lord of hosts, the God of Israel, Because ye have obeyed the commandment of Jonadab your father, and kept all his precepts, and done according unto all that he hath commanded you, therefore thus saith the Lord of hosts, the God of Israel, Jonadab the son of Rechab shall not want a man to stand before me forever.

14 AND it came to pass in the fourth year of Jehoiakim the son of Josiah king of Judah that this word came unto Jeremiah from the Lord, saying, Take thee a roll of a book and write therein all the words that I have spoken unto thee against Israel, and against Judah, and against all the nations, from the day I spake unto thee, from the days of Josiah even unto this day. It may be that the house of Judah will hear all the evil which I purpose to do unto them, that they may return every man from his evil way, that I may forgive their iniquity and their sin.

Then Jeremiah called Baruch the son of Neriah, and Baruch wrote from the mouth of Jeremiah all the words of the Lord which he had spoken unto him, upon a roll of a book. And Jeremiah commanded Baruch, saying, I am shut up, I cannot go into the house of the Lord, therefore go thou and read in the roll which thou hast written from my mouth the words of the Lord in the ears of the people in the Lord's house upon the fasting day, and also thou shalt read them in the ears of all Judah that come out of their cities. It may be they will present their supplication before the Lord and will return everyone from his evil way, for great is the anger and the fury that the Lord hath pronounced against this people. And Baruch the son of Neriah did according to all that Jeremiah the prophet commanded him, reading in the book the words of the Lord in the Lord's house.

And it came to pass in the fifth year of Jehoiakim the son of Josiah king of Judah, in the ninth month, that they proclaimed a fast before the Lord to all the people in Jerusalem and to all the people that came from the cities of Judah unto Jerusalem. Then read Baruch in the book the words of Jeremiah in the house of the Lord, in the chamber of Gemariah the son of Shaphan the scribe in the higher court, at the entry of the new gate of the Lord's house, in the ears of all the people.

When Michaiah the son of Gemariah the son of Shaphan had heard out of the book all the words of the Lord, then he went down into the king's house, into the scribe's chamber and lo, all the princes sat there, even Elishama the scribe, and Delaiah the son of Shemaiah, and Elnathan the son of Achbor, and Gemariah the son of Shaphan, and Zedekiah the son of Hananiah, and all the princes. Then Michaiah declared unto them all the words that he had heard when Baruch read the book in the ears of the people. Therefore all the princes sent Jehudi the son of Nethaniah the son of Shelemiah the son of Cushi, unto Baruch saying, Take in thine hand the roll wherein thou hast read in the ears of the people and come. So Baruch the son of Neriah took the roll in his hand and came unto them. And they said unto him, Sit down now and read it in our ears. So Baruch read it in their ears. Now it came to pass when they had heard all the words, they were afraid both one and other and said unto Baruch, We will surely tell the king of all these words. And they asked Baruch saying, Tell us now, How didst thou write all these words at his mouth? Then Baruch answered them, He pronounced all these words unto me with his mouth and

I wrote them with ink in the book. Then said the princes unto Baruch, Go, hide thee, thou and Jeremiah, and let no man know where ye be.

And they went into the king into the court, but they laid up the roll in the chamber of Elishama the scribe and told all the words in the ears of the king. So the king sent Jehudi to fetch the roll and he took it out of Elishama the scribe's chamber. And Jehudi read it in the ears of the king and in the ears of all the princes which stood beside the king. Now the king sat in the winter house in the ninth month and there was a fire on the hearth burning before him. And it came to pass that when Jehudi had read three or four leaves, he cut it with the penknife, and cast it into the fire that was on the hearth until all the roll was consumed in the fire that was on the hearth. Yet they were not afraid, nor rent their garments, neither the king, nor any of his servants that heard all these words. Nevertheless Elnathan and Delaiah and Gemariah had made intercession to the king that he would not burn the roll, but he would not hear them. But the king commanded Jerahmeel the son of Hammelech, and Seraiah the son of Azriel, and Shelemiah the son of Abdeel to take Baruch the scribe and Jeremiah the prophet, but the Lord hid them.

Then the word of the Lord came to Jeremiah after that the king had burned the roll, and the words which Baruch wrote at the mouth of Jeremiah saying, Take thee again another roll, and write in it all the former words that were in the first roll which Jehoiakim the king of Judah hath burned. And thou shalt say to Jehoiakim king of Judah, Thus saith the Lord, Thou hast burned this roll saying, Why hast thou written therein, saying, The king of Babylon shall certainly come and destroy this land and shall cause to cease from thence man and beast? Therefore thus saith the Lord unto Jehoiakim king of Judah, He shall have none to sit upon the throne of David, and his dead body shall be cast out in the day to the heat and in the night to the frost. And I will punish him and his seed and his servants for their iniquity, and I will bring upon them, and upon the inhabitants of Jerusalem, and upon the men of Judah, all the evil that I have pronounced against them, but they hearkened not.

Then took Jeremiah another roll and gave it to Baruch the scribe the son of Neriah, who wrote therein from the mouth of Jeremiah all the words of the book which Jehoiakim king of Judah had burned in the fire, and there were added besides unto them many like words.

And king Zedekiah the son of Josiah reigned instead of Coniah the son of Jehoiakim, whom Nebuchadnezzar king of Babylon made king in the land of Judah. But neither he, nor his servants, nor the people of the land did hearken unto the words of the Lord which he spake by the prophet Jeremiah.

And Zedekiah the king sent Jehucal the son of Shelemiah and Zephaniah the son of Maaseiah the priest to the prophet Jeremiah, saying, Pray now unto the Lord our God for us. Now Jeremiah came in and went out among the people, for they had not put him in prison. Then Pharaoh's army was come forth out of Egypt and when the Chaldeans that besieged Jerusalem heard tidings of them, they departed from Jerusalem.

Then came the word of the Lord unto the prophet Jeremiah saying, Thus saith the Lord, the God of Israel, Thus shall ye say to the king of Judah that sent you unto me to inquire of me, Behold, Pharaoh's army, which is come forth to help you, shall return to Egypt into their own land. And the Chaldeans shall come again, and fight against this city, and take it, and burn it with fire. Thus saith the Lord, Deceive not yourselves saying, The Chaldeans shall surely depart from us, for they shall not depart. For though ye had smitten the whole army of the Chaldeans that fight against you and there remained but wounded men among them, yet should they rise up every man in his tent and burn this city with fire.

And it came to pass that when the army of the Chaldeans was broken up from Jerusalem for fear of Pharaoh's army, then Jeremiah went forth out of Jerusalem to go into the land of Benjamin, to separate himself thence in the midst of the people. And when he was in the gate of Benjamin, a captain of the ward was there whose name was Irijah the son of Shelemiah the son of Hananiah and he took Jeremiah the prophet saying, Thou fallest away to the Chaldeans. Then said Jeremiah, It is false; I fall not away to the Chaldeans. But he hearkened not to him, so Irijah took Jeremiah and brought him to the princes. Wherefore the princes were wroth with Jeremiah, and smote him, and put him in prison in the house of Jonathan the scribe, for they had made that the prison. And Jeremiah was entered into the dungeon and into the cabins and he remained there many days.

Then Zedekiah the king sent and took him out, and the king asked him secretly in his house and said, Is there any word from the Lord? And Jeremiah said, There is, for said he, thou shalt be delivered into the hand of the king of Babylon. Moreover Jeremiah said unto king Zedekiah, What have I offended against thee, or against thy servants, or against this people, that ye have put me in prison? Where are now your prophets which prophesied unto you, saying, The king of Babylon shall not come against you nor against this land? Therefore hear now, I pray thee, O my lord the king, let my supplication, I pray thee, be accepted before thee that thou cause me not to return to the house of Jonathan the scribe, lest I die there. Then Zedekiah the king commanded that they should commit Jeremiah into the court of the prison and that they should give him daily a piece of bread out of the bakers street until all the bread in the city were spent. Thus Jeremiah remained in the court of the prison.

Then Shephatiah the son of Mattan, and Gedaliah the son of Pashur, and Jucal the son of Shelemiah, and Pashur the son of Malchiah heard the words that Jeremiah had spoken unto all the people, saying, Thus saith the Lord, He that remaineth in this city shall die by the sword, by the famine, and by the pestilence, but he that goeth forth to the Chaldeans shall live, for he shall have his life for a prey and shall live. Thus saith the Lord, This city shall surely be given into the hand of the king of Babylon's army which shall take it. Therefore the princes said unto the king, We beseech thee, let this man be put to death, for thus he weakeneth the hands of the men of war that remain in this city, and the hands of all the people in speaking such words unto them, for this man seeketh not the welfare of this people, but the hurt. Then Zedekiah the king said, Behold, he is in your hand, for the king is not he that can do anything against you. Then took they Jeremiah, and cast him into the dungeon of Malchiah the son of Hammelech that was in the court of the prison, and they let down Jeremiah with cords. And in the dungeon there was no water, but mire, so Jeremiah sunk in the mire.

Now when Ebed-melech the Ethiopian, one of the eunuchs which was in the king's house, heard that they had put Jeremiah in the dungeon, the king then sitting in the gate of Benjamin, Ebed-melech went forth out of the king's house and spake to the king saying, My lord the king, these men have done evil in all that they have done to Jeremiah the prophet whom they have cast into the dungeon, and he is like to die for hunger in the place where he is, for there is no more bread in the city. Then the king commanded Ebed-melech the Ethiopian saying, Take from hence thirty men with thee and take up Jeremiah the prophet out of the dungeon before he die. So Ebed-melech took the men with him and went into the house of the king under the treasury, and took thence old cast clouts and old rotten rags, and let them down by cords into the dungeon to Jeremiah. And Ebed-melech the Ethiopian said unto Jeremiah, Put now these old cast clouts and rotten rags under thine armholes under the cords.

And Jeremiah did so. So they drew up Jeremiah with cords, and took him up out of the dungeon, and Jeremiah remained in the court of the prison.

Then Zedekiah the king sent and took Jeremiah the prophet unto him into the third entry that is in the house of the Lord, and the king said unto Jeremiah, I will ask thee a thing, hide nothing from me. Then Jeremiah said unto Zedekiah, If I declare it unto thee, wilt thou not surely put me to death? And if I give thee counsel, wilt thou not hearken unto me? So Zedekiah the king sware secretly unto Jeremiah, saying, As the Lord liveth, that made us this soul, I will not put thee to death neither will I give thee into the hand of these men that seek thy life.

Then said Jeremiah unto Zedekiah, Thus saith the Lord, the God of hosts, the God of Israel, If thou wilt assuredly go forth unto the king of Babylon's princes, then thy soul shall live, and this city shall not be burned with fire, and thou shalt live, and thine house, but if thou wilt not go forth to the king of Babylon's princes, then shall this city be given into the hand of the Chaldeans, and they shall burn it with fire, and thou shalt not escape out of their hand. And Zedekiah the king said unto Jeremiah, I am afraid of the Jews that are fallen to the Chaldeans, lest they deliver me into their hand and they mock me. But Jeremiah said, They shall not deliver thee. Obey, I beseech thee, the voice of the Lord which I speak unto thee, so it shall be well unto thee, and thy soul shall live. But if thou refuse to go forth, this is the word that the Lord hath showed me, And, behold, all the women that are left in the king of Judah's house shall be brought forth to the king of Babylon's princes, and those women shall say, Thy friends have set thee on and have prevailed against thee, thy feet are sunk in the mire and they are turned away back. So they shall bring out all thy wives and thy children to the Chaldeans, and thou shalt not escape out of their hand, but shalt be taken by the hand of the king of Babylon, and thou shalt cause this city to be burned with fire.

Then said Zedekiah unto Jeremiah, Let no man know of these words, and thou shalt not die. But if the princes hear that I have talked with thee, and they come unto thee and say unto thee, Declare unto us now what thou hast said unto the king, hide it not from us, and we will not put thee to death, also what the king said unto thee, then thou shalt say unto them, I presented my supplication before the king that he would not cause me to return to Jonathan's house to die there. Then came all the princes unto Jeremiah and asked him, and he told them according to all these words that the king had commanded. So they left off speaking with him, for the matter was not perceived. So Jeremiah abode in the court of the prison until the day that Jerusalem was taken and he was there when Jerusalem was taken. In the ninth year of Zedekiah king of Judah, in the tenth month, came Nebuchadnezzar king of Babylon and all his army against Jerusalem and they besieged it. And in the eleventh year of Zedekiah, in the fourth month, the ninth day of the month, the city was broken up. And all the princes of the king of Babylon came in, and sat in the middle gate, even Nergal-sharezer, Samgar-nebo, Sarsechim, Rab-saris, Nergal-sharezer, Rab-mag, with all the residue of the princes of the king of Babylon. And it came to pass, that when Zedekiah the king of Judah saw them and all the men of war, then they fled and went forth out of the city by night, by the way of the king's garden, by the gate betwixt the two walls, and he went out the way of the plain. But the Chaldeans' army pursued after them, and overtook Zedekiah in the plains of Jericho, and when they had taken him, they brought him up to Nebuchadnezzar king of Babylon to Riblah in the land of Hamath, where he gave judgment upon him. Then the king of Babylon slew the sons of Zedekiah in Riblah before his eyes, also the king of Babylon slew all the nobles of Judah. Moreover he put out Zedekiah's eyes and bound him with chains to carry him to Babylon. And the Chaldeans burned the king's house and the houses of the people with fire and brake down the walls of Jerusalem. Then Nebuzar-adan the captain of the guard carried away captive into Babylon the remnant of the people that remained in the city and those that fell away, that fell to him with the rest of the people that remained. But Nebuzar-adan the captain of the guard left of the poor of the people, which had nothing, in the land of Judah and gave them vineyards and fields at the same time.

Now Nebuchadnezzar king of Babylon gave charge concerning Jeremiah to Nebuzar-adan the captain of the guard saying, Take him and look well to him, and do him no harm, but do unto him even as he shall say unto thee. So Nebuzar-adan the captain of the guard sent, and Nebushas-ban, Rab-saris, and Nergal-sharezer, Rabmag, and all the king of Babylon's princes, even they sent, and took Jeremiah out of the court of the prison, and committed him unto Gedaliah the son of Ahikam the son of Shaphan, that he should carry him home, so he dwelt among the people.

15 NOW the word of the Lord came unto Jeremiah while he was shut up in the court of the prison saying, Go and speak to Ebed-melech the Ethiopian saying, Thus saith the Lord of hosts, the God of Israel, Behold, I will bring my words upon this city for evil and not for good, and they shall be accomplished in that day before thee. But I will deliver thee in that day, saith the Lord, and thou shalt not be given into the hand of the men of whom thou art afraid. For I will surely deliver thee, and thou shalt not fall by the sword, but thy life shall be for a prey unto thee because thou hast put thy trust in me, saith the Lord.

The word which came to Jeremiah from the Lord, after that Nebuzar-adan the captain of the guard had let him go from Ramah, when he had taken him being bound in chains among all that were carried away captive of Jerusalem and Judah, which were carried away captive unto Babylon. And the captain of the guard took Jeremiah and said unto him, The Lord thy God hath pronounced this evil upon this place. Now the Lord hath brought it and done according as he hath said because ye have sinned against the Lord and have not obeyed his voice, therefore this thing is come upon you. And now, behold, I loose thee this day from the chains which were upon thine hand. If it seem good unto thee to come with me into Babylon, come, and I will look well unto thee, but if it seem ill unto thee to come with me into Babylon, forbear. Behold, all the land is before thee, whither it seemeth good and convenient for thee to go, thither go. Now while he was not yet gone back, he said, Go back also to Gedaliah the son of Ahikam the son of Shaphan, whom the king of Babylon hath made governor over the cities of Judah, and dwell with him among the people, or go wheresoever it seemeth convenient unto thee to go. So the captain of the guard gave him victuals and a reward and let him go. Then went Jeremiah unto Gedaliah the son of Ahikam to Mizpah, and dwelt with him among the people that were left in the land.

Now when all the captains of the forces which were in the fields, even they and their men, heard that the king of Babylon had made Gedaliah the son of Ahikam governor in the land, and had committed unto him men, and women, and children, and of the poor of the land, of them that were not carried away captive to Babylon, then they came to Gedaliah to Mizpah, even Ishmael the son of Nethaniah, and Johanan and Jonathan the sons of Kareah, and Seraiah the son of Tanhumeth, and the sons of Ephai the Netophathite, and Jezaniah the son of a Maachathite, they and their men. And Gedaliah the son of Ahikam the son of Shaphan sware unto them and to their men, saying, Fear not to serve the Chaldeans, dwell in the land, and serve the king of Babylon, and it shall be well with you. As for me, behold, I will dwell at Mizpah, to serve the Chaldeans, which will come unto us, but ye, gather ye wine, and summer fruits, and oil, and put them in your vessels, and dwell in your cities that ye have taken. Likewise when all the Jews that were in Moab, and among the Ammonites, and in Edom and that were in all the countries heard that the king of Babylon had left a remnant of Judah, and that he had set over them Gedaliah the son of Ahikam the son of Shaphan, even all the Jews returned out of all places whither they were driven and came to the land of Judah, to Gedaliah, unto Mizpah, and gathered wine and summer fruits very much.

Moreover Johanan the son of Kareah and all the captains of the forces that were in the fields came to Gedaliah to Mizpah and said unto him, Dost thou certainly know that Baalis the king of the Ammonites hath sent Ishmael the son of Nethaniah to slay thee? But Gedaliah the son of Ahikam believed them not. Then Johanan the son of Kareah spake to Gedaliah in Mizpah secretly saying, Let me go, I pray thee, and I will slay Ishmael the son of Nethaniah and no man shall know it; wherefore should he slay thee, that all the Jews which are gathered unto thee should be scattered, and the remnant in Judah perish? But Gedaliah the son of Ahikam said unto Johanan the son of Kareah, Thou shalt not do this thing, for thou speakest falsely of Ishmael.

Now it came to pass in the seventh month, that Ishmael the son of Nethaniah the son of Elishama of the seed royal, and the princes of the king, even ten men with him, came unto Gedaliah the son of Ahikam to Mizpah and there they did eat bread together in Mizpah. Then arose Ishmael the son of Nethaniah and the ten men that were with him, and smote Gedaliah the son of Ahikam the son of Shaphan with the sword and slew him whom the king of Babylon had made governor over the land. Ishmael also slew all the Jews that were with him, even with Gedaliah at Mizpah, and the Chaldeans that were found there, and the men of war.

And it came to pass the second day after he had slain Gedaliah, and no man knew it, that there came certain from Shechem, from Shiloh, and from Samaria, even fourscore men, having their beards shaven, and their clothes rent, and having cut themselves, with offerings and incense in their hand, to bring them to the house of the Lord. And Ishmael the son of Nethaniah went forth from Mizpah to meet them, weeping all along as he went, and it came to pass as he met them he said unto them, Come to Gedaliah the son of Ahikam. And it was so when they came into the midst of the city that Ishmael the son of Nethaniah slew them and cast them into the midst of the pit, he and the men that were with him. But ten men were found among them that said unto Ishmael, Slay us not, for we have treasures in the field, of wheat, and of barley, and of oil, and of honey. So he forbare, and slew them not among their brethren.

Now the pit wherein Ishmael had cast all the dead bodies of the men whom he had slain because of Gedaliah, was it which Asa the king had made for fear of Baasha king of Israel, and Ishmael the son of Nethaniah filled it with them that were slain. Then Ishmael carried away captive all the residue of the people that were in Mizpah, even the king's daughters, and all the people that remained in Mizpah whom Nebuzar-adan the captain of the guard had committed to Gedaliah the son of Ahikam, and Ishmael the son of Nethaniah carried them away captive and departed to go over to the Ammonites.

But when Johanan the son of Kareah, and all the captains of the forces that were with him, heard of all the evil that Ishmael the son of Nethaniah had done, then they took all the men and went to fight with Ishmael the son of Nethaniah and found him by the great waters that are in Gibeon. Now it came to pass, that when all the people which were with Ishmael saw Johanan the son of Kareah and all the captains of the forces that were with him, then they were glad. So all the people that Ishmael had carried away captive from Mizpah cast about and returned, and went unto Johanan the son of Kareah. But Ishmael the son of Nethaniah escaped from Johanan with eight men and went to the Ammonites. Then took Johanan the son of Kareah and all the captains of the forces that were with him all the remnant of the people whom he had recovered from Ishmael the son of Nethaniah from Mizpah, after that he had slain Gedaliah the son of Ahikam, even mighty men of war, and the women, and the children, and the eunuchs whom he had brought again from Gibeon, and they departed and dwelt in the habitation of Chimham which is by Bethlehem, to go to enter into Egypt because of the Chaldeans, for they were afraid of them because Ishmael the son of Nethaniah had slain Gedaliah the son of Ahikam whom the king of Babylon made governor in the land.

Then all the captains of the forces, and Johanan the son of Kareah, and Jezaniah the son of Hoshaiah, and all the people from the least even unto the greatest, came near and said unto Jeremiah the prophet, Let, we beseech thee, our supplication be accepted before thee, and pray for us unto the Lord thy God, even for all this remnant (for we are left but a few of many, as thine eyes do behold us), that the Lord thy God may show us the way wherein we may walk and the thing that we may do. Then Jeremiah the prophet said unto them, I have heard you; behold, I will pray unto the Lord your God according to your words and it shall come to pass that whatsoever thing the Lord shall answer you, I will declare it unto you. I will keep nothing back from you. Then they said to Jeremiah, The Lord be a true and faithful witness between us if we do not even according to all things for the which the Lord thy God shall send thee to us. Whether it be good or whether it be evil, we will obey the voice of the Lord our God to whom we send thee, that it may be well with us when we obey the voice of the Lord our God.

And it came to pass after ten days, that the word of the Lord came unto Jeremiah. Then called he Johanan the son of Kareah, and all the captains of the forces which were with him, and all the people from the least even to the greatest, and said unto them, Thus saith the Lord, the God of Israel, unto whom ye sent me to present your supplication before him, if you will still abide in this land, then will I build you and not pull down, I will plant you and not pluck up, and I will turn away the evil that I have done unto you. Be not afraid of the king of Babylon of whom ye are afraid, be not afraid of him, saith the Lord, for I am with you to save you and to deliver you from his hand. And I will show mercies unto you that he may have mercy upon you and cause you to return to your own land. But if ye say, We will not dwell in this land, neither obey the voice of the Lord your God saying, No, but we will go into the land of Egypt where we shall see no war, nor hear the sound of the trumpet, nor have hunger for want of bread, and there will we dwell, and now therefore hear the word of the Lord, ye remnant of Judah. Thus saith the Lord of hosts, the God of Israel, If ye wholly set your faces to enter into Egypt and go to sojourn there, then it shall come to pass that the sword which ye feared shall overtake you there in the land of Egypt, and the famine whereof ye were afraid shall follow close after you there in Egypt and there ye shall die. So shall it be with all the men that set their faces to go into Egypt to sojourn there, they shall die by the sword, by the famine, and by the pestilence, and none of them shall remain or escape from the evil that I will bring upon them.

For thus saith the Lord of hosts, the God of Israel, As mine anger and my fury hath been poured forth upon the inhabitants of Jerusalem, so shall my fury be poured forth upon you when ye shall enter into Egypt, and ye shall be an execration, and an astonishment, and a curse, and a reproach, and ye shall see this place no more. The Lord hath said concerning you, O ye remnant of Judah, Go ye not into Egypt, know certainly that I have admonished you this day. For ye dissembled in your hearts, when ye sent me unto the Lord your God saying, Pray for us unto the Lord our God, and according unto all that the Lord our God shall say, so declare unto us and we will do it. And now I have this day declared it to you, that ye have not obeyed the voice of the Lord your God, nor anything for the which he hath sent me unto you. Now therefore know certainly that ye shall die by the sword, by the famine, and by the pestilence, in the place whither ye desire to go and to sojourn.

And it came to pass, that when Jeremiah had made an end of speaking unto all the people all the words of the Lord their God, for which the Lord their God had sent him to them, even all these words, then spake Azariah the son of Hoshaiah, and Johanan the son of Kareah, and all the proud men, saying unto Jeremiah, Thou speakest falsely; the Lord our God hath not sent thee to say, Go not into Egypt to sojourn there, but Baruch the son of Neriah setteth thee on against us for to deliver us into the hand of the Chaldeans, that they might put us to death and carry us away captives into Babylon. So Johanan the son of Kareah, and all the captains of the forces, and all the people obeyed not the voice of the Lord to dwell in the land of Judah. But Johanan the son of Kareah, and all the captains of the forces, took all the remnant of Judah that were returned from all nations whither they had been driven, to dwell in the land of Judah, even men, and women, and children, and the king's daughters, and every person that Nebuzar-adan the captain of the guard had left with Gedaliah the son of Ahikam the son of Shaphan, and Jeremiah the prophet, and Baruch the son of Neriah. So they came into the land of Egypt, for they obeyed not the voice of the Lord, thus came they even to Tahpanhes.

Then came the word of the Lord unto Jeremiah in Tahpanhes, saying, Take great stones in thine hand, and hide them in the clay in the brick kiln, which is at the entry of Pharaoh's house in Tahpanhes, in the sight of the men of Judah and say unto them, Thus saith the Lord of hosts, the God of Israel, Behold, I will send and take Nebuchadnezzar the king of Babylon, my servant, and will set his throne upon these stones that I have hid, and he shall spread his royal pavilion over them. And when he cometh, he shall smite the land of Egypt and deliver such as are for death to death, and such as are for captivity to captivity, and such as are for the sword to the sword. And I will kindle a fire in the houses of the gods of Egypt, and he shall burn them, and carry them away captives, and he shall array himself with the land of Egypt as a shepherd putteth on his garment, and he shall go forth from thence in peace. He shall break also the images of Beth-shemesh that is in the land of Egypt, and the houses of the gods of the Egyptians shall he burn with fire.

The word that came to Jeremiah concerning all the Jews which dwell in the land of Egypt, which dwell at Migdol, and at Tahpanhes, and at Noph, and in the country of Pathros saying, Thus saith the Lord of hosts, the God of Israel, Ye have seen all the evil that I have brought upon Jerusalem and upon all the cities of Judah and behold, this day they are a desolation and no man dwelleth therein because of their wickedness which they have committed to provoke me to anger in that they went to burn incense and to serve other gods whom they knew not, neither they, ye, nor your fathers. Howbeit I sent unto you all my servants the prophets, commanding them to rise early, and sending them saying, Oh, do not this abominable thing that I hate. But they hearkened not nor inclined their ear to turn from their wickedness, to burn no incense unto other gods. Wherefore my fury and mine anger was poured forth and was kindled in the cities of Judah and in the streets of Jerusalem, and they are wasted and desolate as at this day. Therefore now thus saith the Lord, the God of hosts, the God of Israel, Wherefore commit ye this great evil against your souls, to cut off from you man and woman, child and suckling out of Judah, to leave you none to remain. In that ye provoke me unto wrath with the works of your hands, burning incense unto other gods in the land of Egypt whither ye be gone to dwell, that ye might cut yourselves off and that ye might be a curse and a reproach among all the nations of the earth?

Have ye forgotten the wickedness of your fathers, and the wickedness of the kings of Judah, and the wickedness of their wives, and your own wickedness, and the wickedness of your wives which they have committed in the land of Judah and in the streets of Jerusalem? They are not humbled even unto this day, neither have they feared, nor walked in my law, nor in my statutes, that I set before you and before your fathers.

Therefore thus saith the Lord of hosts, the God of Israel, Behold, I will set my face against you for evil and to cut off all Judah. And I will take the remnant of Judah that have set their faces to go into the land of Egypt to sojourn there and they shall all be consumed and fall in the land of Egypt; they shall even be consumed by the sword and by the famine and they shall die, from the least even unto the greatest, by the sword and by the famine, and they shall be an execration, and an astonishment, and a curse, and a reproach. For I will punish them that dwell in the land of Egypt as I have punished Jerusalem, by the sword, by the famine, and by the pestilence, so that none of the remnant of Judah which are gone into the land of Egypt to sojourn there shall escape or remain, that they should return into the land of Judah to the which they have a desire to return to dwell there, for none shall return but such as shall escape.

Then all the men which knew that their wives had burned incense unto other gods and all the women that stood by, a great multitude, even all the people that dwelt in the land of Egypt, in Pathros, answered Jeremiah saying, As for the word that thou hast spoken unto us in the name of the Lord, we will not hearken unto thee. But we will certainly do whatsoever thing goeth forth out of our own mouth, to burn incense unto the queen of Heaven, and to pour out drink offerings unto he, as we have done, we, and our fathers, our kings, and our princes, in the cities of Judah, and in the streets of Jerusalem, for then had we plenty of victuals, and were well, and saw no evil, but since we left off to burn incense to the queen of Heaven, and to pour out drink offerings unto her, we have wanted all things, and have been consumed by the sword and by the famine. And when we burned incense to the queen of Heaven and poured out drink offerings unto her, did we make her cakes to worship her and pour out drink offerings unto her without our men?

Then Jeremiah said unto all the people, to the men and to the women, and to all the people which had given him that answer saying, The incense that ye burned in the cities of Judah and in the streets of Jerusalem, ye and your fathers, your kings, and your princes, and the people of the land, did not the Lord remember them and came it not into his mind? So that the Lord could no longer bear, because of the evil of your doings and because of the abominations which ye have committed, therefore is your land a desolation, and an astonishment, and a curse, without an inhabitant as at this day. Because ye have burned incense, and because ye have sinned against the Lord, and have not obeyed the voice of the Lord, nor walked in his law, nor in his statutes, nor in his testimonies, therefore this evil is happened unto you, as at this day.

Moreover Jeremiah said unto all the people and to all the women, Hear the word of the Lord, all Judah that are in the land of Egypt, thus saith the Lord of hosts, the God of Israel saying, Ye and your wives have both spoken with your mouths and fulfilled with your hand saying, We will surely perform our vows that we have vowed, to burn incense to the queen of Heaven and to pour out drink offerings unto her, ye will surely accomplish your vows and surely perform your vows. Therefore hear ye the word of the Lord, all Judah that dwell in the land of Egypt, Behold, I have sworn by my great name, saith the Lord, that my name shall no more be named in the mouth of any man of Judah in all the land of Egypt saying, The Lord God liveth. Behold, I will watch over them for evil and not for good, and all the men of Judah that are in the land of

Egypt shall be consumed by the sword and by the famine, until there be an end of them. Yet a small number that escape the sword shall return out of the land of Egypt into the land of Judah, and all the remnant of Judah that are gone into the land of Egypt to sojourn there shall know whose words shall stand: mine or theirs. And this shall be a sign unto you, saith the Lord, that I will punish you in this place, that ye may know that my words shall surely stand against you for evil; thus saith the Lord, Behold, I will give Pharaoh-hophra king of Egypt into the hand of his enemies and into the hand of them that seek his life as I gave Zedekiah king of Judah into the hand of Nebuchadnezzar king of Babylon, his enemy, and that sought his life.

16 THE word that Jeremiah the prophet spake unto Baruch the son of Neriah, when he had written these words in a book at the mouth of Jeremiah, in the fourth year of Jehoiakim the son of Josiah king of Judah saying, Thus saith the Lord, the God of Israel, unto thee, O Baruch, thou didst say, Wo is me now, for the Lord hath added grief to my sorrow; I fainted in my sighing and I find no rest. Thus shalt thou say unto him, The Lord saith thus, Behold, that which I have built will I break down and that which I have planted I will pluck up, even this whole land. And seekest thou great things for thyself? Seek them not, for behold, I will bring evil upon all flesh, saith the Lord, but thy life will I give unto thee for a prey in all the places whither thou goest.

The word of the Lord which came to Jeremiah the prophet against the Gentiles, against Egypt, against the army of Pharaoh-necho king of Egypt, which was by the river Euphrates in Charchemish, which Nebuchadnezzar king of Babylon smote in the fourth year of Jehoiakim the son of Josiah king of Judah: Order ye the buckler and shield and draw near to battle. Harness the horses and get up, ye horsemen, and stand forth with your helmets, furbish the spears and put on the brigandines. Wherefore have I seen them dismayed and turned away back? And their mighty ones are beaten down, and are fled apace, and look not back, for fear was round about, saith the Lord. Let not the swift flee away, nor the mighty man escape, they shall stumble and fall toward the north by the river Euphrates. Who is this that cometh up as a flood, whose waters are moved as the rivers? Egypt riseth up like a flood, and his waters are moved like the rivers, and he saith, I will go up and will cover the earth, I will destroy the city and the inhabitants thereof. Come up, ye horses, and rage, ye chariots, and let the mighty men come forth, the Ethiopians and the Libyans that handle the shield, and the Lydians that handle and bend the bow. For this is the day of the Lord God of hosts, a day of vengeance, that he may avenge him of his adversaries, and the sword shall devour, and it shall be satiated and made drunk with their blood, for the Lord God of hosts hath a sacrifice in the north country by the river Euphrates. Go up into Gilead and take balm, O virgin, the daughter of Egypt, in vain shalt thou use many medicines, for thou shalt not be cured. The nations have heard of thy shame, and thy cry hath filled the land, for the mighty man hath stumbled against the mighty and they are fallen both together.

The word that the Lord spake to Jeremiah the prophet, how Nebuchadnezzar king of Babylon should come and smite the land of Egypt: Declare ye in Egypt, and publish in Migdol, and publish in Noph and in Tahpanhes, say ye, Stand fast and prepare thee, for the sword shall devour round about thee. Why are thy valiant men swept away? They stood not because the Lord did drive them. He made many to fall, yea, one fell upon another, and they said, Arise and let us go again to our own people and to the land of our nativity, from the oppressing sword. They did cry there, Pharaoh king of Egypt is but a noise, he hath passed the time appointed. As I live, saith the King, whose name is the Lord of hosts, Surely as Tabor is among the mountains and as Carmel by the sea, so shall he come. O thou daughter dwelling in Egypt, furnish thyself to go into captivity, for Noph shall be waste and desolate without an inhabitant. Egypt is like a very fair heifer, but destruction cometh, it cometh out of the north. Also her hired men are in the midst of her like fatted bullocks, for they also are turned back and are fled away together, they did not stand because the day of their calamity was come upon them and the time of their visitation. The voice thereof shall go like a serpent, for they shall march with an army, and come against her with axes as hewers of wood. They shall cut down her forest, saith the Lord, though it cannot be searched, because they are more than the grasshoppers and are innumerable. The daughter of Egypt shall be confounded, she shall be delivered into the hand of the people of the north. The Lord of hosts, the God of Israel, saith, Behold, I will punish the multitude of No, and Pharaoh, and Egypt, with their gods, and their kings, even Pharaoh, and all them that trust in him, and will deliver them into the hand of those that seek their lives, and into the hand of Babylon, and into the hand of his servants, and afterward it shall be inhabited as in the days of old, saith the Lord. But fear not thou, O my servant Jacob, and be not dismayed, O Israel, for, behold, I will save thee from afar off and thy seed from the land of their captivity, and Jacob shall return and be in rest and at ease, and none shall make him afraid. Fear thou not, O Jacob my servant, saith the Lord, for I am with thee, for I will make a full end of all the nations whither I have driven thee, but I will not make a full end of thee, but correct thee in measure, yet will I not leave thee wholly unpunished.

The word of the Lord that came to Jeremiah the prophet against the Philistines, before that Pharaoh smote Gaza. Thus saith the Lord, Behold, waters rise up out of the north, and shall be an overflowing flood, and shall overflow the land and all that is therein, the city and them that dwell therein, then the men shall cry and all the inhabitants of the land shall howl. At the noise of the stamping of the hooves of his strong horses, at the rushing of his chariots, and at the rumbling of his wheels, the father shall not look back to their children for feebleness of hands, because of the day that cometh to spoil all the Philistines and to cut off from Tyrus and Zidon every helper that remaineth, for the Lord will spoil the Philistines, the remnant of the country of Caphtor. Baldness is come upon Gaza, Ashkelon is cut off with the remnant of their valley; how long wilt thou cut thyself? O thou sword of the Lord, how long will it be ere thou be quiet? Put up thyself into thy scabbard, rest and be still. How can it be quiet, seeing the Lord hath given it a charge against Ashkelon and against the seashore? There hath he appointed it. Against Moab, thus saith the Lord of hosts, the God of Israel, Wo unto Nebo, for it is spoiled, Kiriathaim is confounded and taken, Misgab is confounded and dismayed. There shall be no more praise of Moab, in Heshbon they have devised evil against it; come, and let us cut it off from being a nation. Also thou shalt be cut down, O Madmen, the sword shall pursue thee. A voice of crying shall be from Horonaim, spoiling and great destruction. Moab is destroyed, her little ones have caused a cry to be heard. For in the going up of Luhith continual weeping shall go up, for in the going down of Horonaim the enemies have heard a cry of destruction. Flee, save your lives, and be like the heath in the wilderness. For because thou hast trusted in thy works and in thy treasures, thou shalt also be taken, and Chemosh shall go forth into captivity with his priests and his princes together. And the spoiler shall come upon every city and no city shall escape, the valley also shall perish and the plain shall be destroyed as the Lord hath spoken. Give wings unto Moab that it may flee and get away, for the cities thereof shall be desolate, without any to dwell therein. Cursed be he that doeth the work of the Lord deceitfully and cursed be he that keepeth back his sword from blood.

Moab hath been at ease from his youth, and he hath settled on his lees, and hath not been emptied from vessel to vessel, neither hath he gone into captivity, therefore his taste remained in him and his scent is not changed. Therefore behold, the days come, saith the Lord, that I will send unto him wanderers that shall cause him to wander, and shall empty his vessels, and break their bottles. And Moab shall be ashamed of Chemosh as the house of Israel was ashamed of Beth-el their confidence. How say ye, We are mighty and strong men for the war? Moab is spoiled and gone up out of her cities, and his chosen young men are gone down to the slaughter, saith the King, whose name is the Lord of hosts. The calamity of Moab is near to come and his affliction hasteth fast. All ye that are about him, bemoan him, and all ye that know his name, say, How is the strong staff broken and the beautiful rod! Thou daughter that dost inhabit Dibon, come down from thy glory and sit in thirst, for the spoiler of Moab shall come upon thee and he shall destroy thy strongholds. O inhabitant of Aroer, stand by the way and espy, ask him that fleeth and her that escapeth and say, What is done? Moab is confounded, for it is broken down, howl and cry, tell ye it in Arnon that Moab is spoiled and judgment is come upon the plain country, upon Holon, and upon Jahazah, and upon Mephaath, and upon Dibon, and upon Nebo, and upon Beth-diblathaim, and upon Kiriathaim, and upon Beth-gamul, and upon Beth-meon, and upon Kerioth, and upon Bozrah, and upon all the cities of the land of Moab, far or near. The horn of Moab is cut off and his arm is broken, saith the Lord.

Make ye him drunken, for he magnified himself against the Lord; Moab also shall wallow in his vomit and he also shall be in derision. For was not Israel a derision unto thee? Was he found among thieves? For since thou spakest of him, thou skippedst for joy. O ye that dwell in Moab, leave the cities and dwell in the rock, and be like the dove that maketh her nest in the sides of the hole's mouth. We have heard the pride of Moab (he is exceeding proud), his loftiness and his arrogance, and his pride, and the haughtiness of his heart. I know his wrath, saith the Lord, but it shall not be so, his lies shall not so affect it. Therefore will I howl for Moab, and I will cry out for all Moab, mine heart shall mourn for the men of Kir-heres. O vine of Sibmah, I will weep for thee with the weeping of Jazer, thy plants are gone over the sea, they reach even to the Sea of Jazer, the spoiler is fallen upon thy summer fruits and upon thy vintage. And joy and gladness is taken from the plentiful field and from the land of Moab, and I have caused wine to fail from the wine presses, none shall tread with shouting, their shouting shall be no shouting. From the cry of Heshbon even unto Elealeh, and even unto Jahaz have they uttered their voice, from Zoar even unto Horonaim as a heifer of three years old, for the waters also of Nimrim shall be desolate. Moreover I will cause to cease in Moab, saith the Lord, him that offereth in the high places and him that burneth incense to his gods. Therefore mine heart shall sound for Moab like pipes, and mine heart shall sound like pipes for the men of Kir-heres, because the riches that he hath gotten are perished. For every head shall be bald and every beard clipped, upon all the hands shall be cuttings and upon the loins sackcloth. There shall be lamentation generally upon all the housetops of Moab and in the streets thereof, for I have broken Moab like a vessel wherein is no pleasure, saith the Lord. They shall howl, saying, How is it broken down! How hath Moab turned the back with shame! So shall Moab be a derision and a dismaying to all them about him. For thus saith the Lord, Behold, he shall fly as an eagle, and shall spread his wings over Moab. Kerioth is taken, and the strongholds are surprised, and the mighty men's hearts in Moab at that day shall be as the heart of a woman in her pangs. And Moab shall be destroyed from being a people because he hath magnified himself against the Lord. Fear, and the pit, and the snare shall be upon thee, O inhabitant of Moab, saith the Lord. He that fleeth from the fear shall fall into the pit, and he that getteth up out of the pit shall be taken in the snare, for I will bring upon it, even upon Moab, the year of their visitation, saith the Lord. They that fled stood under the shadow of Heshbon because of the force, but a fire shall come forth out of Heshbon, and a flame from the midst of Sihon, and shall devour the corner of Moab, and the crown of the head of the tumultuous ones. Wo be unto thee, O Moab. The people of Chemosh perisheth, for thy sons are taken captives and thy daughters captives. Yet will I bring again the captivity of Moab in the latter days, saith the Lord. Thus far is the judgment of Moab.

Concerning the Ammonites, thus saith the Lord, Hath Israel no sons? Hath he no heir? Why then doth their king inherit Gad, and his people dwell in his cities? Therefore, behold, the days come, saith the Lord, that I will cause an alarm of war to be heard in Rabbah of the Ammonites, and it shall be a desolate heap, and her daughters shall be burned with fire, then shall Israel be heir unto them that were his heirs, saith the Lord. Howl, O Heshbon, for Ai is spoiled; cry, ye daughters of Rabbah, gird you with sackcloth, lament, and run to and fro by the hedges, for their king shall go into captivity, and his priests and his princes together. Wherefore gloriest thou in the valleys, thy flowing valley, O backsliding daughter, that trusted in her treasures, saying, Who shall come unto me? Behold, I will bring a fear upon thee, saith the Lord God of hosts, from all those that be about thee, and ye shall be driven out every man right forth, and none shall gather up him that wandereth. And afterward I will bring again the captivity of the children of Ammon, saith the Lord.

Concerning Edom, thus saith the Lord of hosts, Is wisdom no more in Teman? is counsel perished from the prudent? is there wisdom vanished? Flee ye, turn back, dwell deep, O inhabitants of Dedan, for I will bring the calamity of Esau upon him, the time that I will visit him. If grape-gatherers come to thee, would they not leave some gleaning grapes? If thieves by night, they will destroy till they have enough. But I have made Esau bare, I have uncovered his secret places and he shall not be able to hide himself, his seed is spoiled, and his brethren, and his neighbors, and he is not. Leave thy fatherless children, I will preserve them alive, and let thy widows trust in me. For thus saith the Lord, Behold, they whose judgment was not to drink of the cup have assuredly drunken, and art thou he that shall altogether go unpunished? Thou shalt not go unpunished, but thou shalt surely drink of it. For I have sworn by myself, saith the Lord, that Bozrah shall become a desolation, a reproach, a waste, and a curse, and all the cities thereof shall be perpetual wastes. I have heard a rumor from the Lord, and an ambassador is sent unto the heathen, saying, Gather ye together and come against her, and rise up to the battle. For lo, I will make thee small among the heathen and despised among men. Thy terribleness hath deceived thee, and the pride of thine heart, O thou that dwellest in the clefts of the rock, that holdest the height of the hill; though thou shouldest make thy nest as high as the eagle, I will bring thee down from thence, saith the Lord. Also Edom shall be a desolation, everyone that goeth by it shall be astonished and shall hiss at all the plagues thereof. As in the overthrow of Sodom and Gomorrah and the neighbor cities thereof, saith the Lord, no man shall abide there neither shall a son of man dwell in it. Behold, he shall come up like a lion from the swelling of Jordan against the habitation of the strong, but I will suddenly make him run away from her, and who is a chosen man that I may appoint over her? For who is like me? And who will appoint me the time? And who is that shepherd that will stand before me? Therefore hear the counsel of the Lord that he hath taken against Edom, and his purposes that he hath purposed against the inhabitants of Teman: Surely the least of the flock shall draw them out, surely he shall make their habitations desolate with them. The Earth is moved at the noise of their fall, at the cry the noise thereof was heard in the Red Sea. Behold, he shall come up and fly as the eagle, and spread his wings over Bozrah, and at that day shall the heart of the mighty men of Edom be as the heart of a woman in her pangs.

Concerning Damascus. Hamath is confounded, and Arpad, for they have heard evil tidings, they are faint-hearted, there is sorrow on the sea, it cannot be quiet. Damascus is waxed feeble and turneth herself to flee, and fear hath seized on her, anguish and sorrows have taken her as a woman in travail. How is the city of praise not left, the city of my joy! Therefore her young men shall fall in her streets, and all the men of war shall be cut off in that day, saith the Lord of hosts. And I will kindle a fire in the wall of Damascus and it shall consume the palaces of Ben-hadad.

Concerning Kedar, and concerning the kingdoms of Hazor which Nebuchadnezzar king of Babylon shall smite, thus saith the Lord, Arise ye, go up to Kedar and spoil the men of the east. Their tents and their flocks shall they take away, they shall take to themselves their curtains, and all their vessels, and their camels, and they shall cry unto them, Fear is on every side. Flee, get you far off, dwell deep, O ye inhabitants of Hazor, saith the Lord, for Nebuchadnezzar king of Babylon hath taken counsel against you and hath conceived a purpose against you. Arise, get you up unto the wealthy nation that dwelleth without care, saith the Lord, which have neither gates nor bars, which dwell alone. And their camels shall be a booty, and the multitude of their cattle a spoil, and I will scatter into all winds them that are in the utmost corners, and I will bring their calamity from all sides thereof, saith the Lord. And Hazor shall be a dwelling for dragons, and a desolation forever, there shall no man abide there, nor any son of man dwell in it.

17 THE word of the Lord that came to Jeremiah the prophet against Elam in the beginning of the reign of Zedekiah king of Judah, saying, Thus saith the Lord of hosts, Behold, I will break the bow of Elam, the chief of their might. And upon Elam will I bring the four winds from the four quarters of Heaven and will scatter them toward all those winds, and there shall be no nation whither the outcasts of Elam shall not come. For I will cause Elam to be dismayed before their enemies, and before them that seek their life, and I will bring evil upon them, even my fierce anger, saith the Lord, and I will send the sword after them, till I have consumed them, and I will set my throne in Elam, and will destroy from thence the king and the princes, saith the Lord. But it shall come to pass in the latter days, that I will bring again the captivity of Elam, saith the Lord.

The word that the Lord spake against Babylon and against the land of the Chaldeans by Jeremiah the prophet: Declare ye among the nations, and publish and set up a standard, publish and conceal not, say, Babylon is taken, Bel is confounded, Merodach is broken in pieces, her idols are confounded, her images are broken in pieces. For out of the north there cometh up a nation against her which shall make her land desolate, and none shall dwell therein, they shall remove, they shall depart, both man and beast. In those days and in that time, saith the Lord, the children of Israel shall come, they and the children of Judah together, going and weeping, they shall go and seek the Lord their God. They shall ask the way to Zion with their faces thitherward saying, Come and let us join ourselves to the Lord in a perpetual covenant that shall not be forgotten. My people have been lost sheep, their shepherds have caused them to go astray, they have turned them away on the mountains, they have gone from mountain to hill, they have forgotten their resting place. All that found them have devoured them, and their adversaries said, We offend not because they have sinned against the Lord, the habitation of justice, even the Lord, the hope of their fathers.

Remove out of the midst of Babylon, and go forth out of the land of the Chaldeans, and be as the he goats before the flocks. For lo, I will raise and cause to come up against Babylon an assembly of great nations from the north country, and they shall set themselves in array against her, from thence she shall be taken, their arrows shall be as of a mighty expert man, none shall return in vain. And Chaldea shall be a spoil, all that spoil her shall be satisfied, saith the Lord. Because ye were glad, because ye rejoiced, O ye destroyers of mine heritage, because ye are grown fat as the heifer at grass and bellow as bulls, your mother shall be sore confounded, she that bare you shall be ashamed, behold, the hindermost of the nations shall be a wilderness, a dry land, and a desert. Because of the wrath of the Lord it shall not be inhabited, but it shall be wholly desolate, everyone that goeth by Babylon shall be astonished and hiss at all her plagues. Put yourselves in array against Babylon round about, all ye that bend the bow, shoot at her, spare no arrows, for she hath sinned against the Lord. Shout against her round about, she hath given her hand, her foundations are fallen, her walls are thrown down, for it is the vengeance of the Lord. Take vengeance upon her; as she hath done, do unto her. Cut off the sower from Babylon and him that handleth the sickle in the time of harvest, for fear of the oppressing sword they shall turn everyone to his people, and they shall flee everyone to his own land.

Israel is a scattered sheep, the lions have driven him away, first the king of Assyria hath devoured him and last this Nebuchadnezzar king of Babylon hath broken his bones. Therefore thus saith the Lord of hosts, the God of Israel, Behold, I will punish the king of Babylon and his land, as I have punished the king of Assyria. And I will bring Israel again to his habitation, and he shall feed on Carmel and Bashan, and his soul shall be satisfied upon mount Ephraim and Gilead. In those days and in that time, saith the Lord, the iniquity of Israel shall be sought for and there shall be none, and the sins of Judah and they shall not be found, for I will pardon them whom I reserve.

Go up against the land of Merathaim, even against it and against the inhabitants of Pekod, waste and utterly destroy after them, saith the Lord, and do according to all that I have commanded thee. A sound of battle is in the land and of great destruction. How is the hammer of the whole earth cut asunder and broken! How is Babylon become a desolation among the nations! I have laid a snare for thee and thou art also taken, O Babylon, and thou wast not aware, thou art found and also caught because thou hast striven against the Lord. The Lord hath opened his armory, and hath brought forth the weapons of his indignation, for this is the work of the Lord God of hosts in the land of the Chaldeans. Come against her from the utmost border, open her storehouses, cast her up as heaps and destroy her utterly, let nothing of her be left. Slay all her bullocks, let them go down to the slaughter, wo unto them. For their day is come, the time of their visitation, the voice of them that flee and escape out of the land of Babylon, to declare in Zion the vengeance of the Lord our God, the vengeance of his temple. Call together the archers against Babylon, all ye that bend the bow, camp against it round about, let none thereof escape, recompense her according to her work, according to all that she hath done, do unto her, for she hath been proud against the Lord, against the Holy One of Israel. Therefore shall her young men fall in the streets, and all her men of war shall be cut off in that day, saith the Lord. Behold, I am against thee, O thou most proud, saith the Lord God of hosts, for thy day is come, the time that I will visit thee. And the most proud shall stumble and fall and none shall raise him up, and I will kindle a fire in his cities and it shall devour all round about him.

Thus saith the Lord of hosts, The children of Israel and the children of Judah were oppressed together, and all that took them captives held them fast, they refused to let them go. Their Redeemer is strong, The Lord of hosts is his name, he shall thoroughly plead their cause, that he may give rest to the land

and disquiet the inhabitants of Babylon. A sword is upon the Chaldeans, saith the Lord, and upon the inhabitants of Babylon, and upon her princes, and upon her wise men. A sword is upon the liars and they shall dote, a sword is upon her mighty men and they shall be dismayed. A sword is upon their horses, and upon their chariots, and upon all the mingled people that are in the midst of her, and they shall become as women, a sword is upon her treasures, and they shall be robbed. A drought is upon her waters and they shall be dried up, for it is the land of graven images and they are mad upon their idols. Therefore the wild beasts of the desert with the wild beasts of the islands shall dwell there, and the owls shall dwell therein, and it shall be no more inhabited forever, neither shall it be dwelt in from generation to generation. As God overthrew Sodom and Gomorrah and the neighbor cities thereof, saith the Lord, so shall no man abide there, neither shall any son of man dwell therein.

Behold, a people shall come from the north, and a great nation, and many kings shall be raised up from the coasts of the earth. They shall hold the bow and the lance, they are cruel and will not show mercy, their voice shall roar like the sea, and they shall ride upon horses, everyone put in array, like a man to the battle, against thee, O daughter of Babylon. The king of Babylon hath heard the report of them, and his hands waxed feeble, anguish took hold of him, and pangs as of a woman in travail.

Behold, he shall come up like a lion from the swelling of Jordan unto the habitation of the strong, but I will make them suddenly run away from her, and who is a chosen man, that I may appoint over her? For who is like me? And who will appoint me the time? And who is that shepherd that will stand before me? Therefore hear ye the counsel of the Lord that he hath taken against Babylon, and his purposes, that he hath purposed against the land of the Chaldeans, Surely the least of the flock shall draw them out, surely he shall make their habitation desolate with them. At the noise of the taking of Babylon the Earth is moved, and the cry is heard among the nations.

Thus saith the Lord, Behold, I will raise up against Babylon and against them that dwell in the midst of them that rise up against me a destroying wind, and will send unto Babylon fanners that shall fan her and shall empty her land, for in the day of trouble they shall be against her round about. Against him that bendeth let the archer bend his bow and against him that lifteth himself up in his brigandine, and spare ye not her young men, destroy ye utterly all her host. Thus the slain shall fall in the land of the Chaldeans and they that are thrust through in her streets. For Israel hath not been forsaken nor Judah of his God, of the Lord of hosts, though their land was filled with sin against the Holy One of Israel. Flee out of the midst of Babylon, and deliver every man his soul, be not cut off in her iniquity, for this is the time of the Lord's vengeance, he will render unto her a recompense. Babylon hath been a golden cup in the Lord's hand, that made all the earth drunken, the nations have drunken of her wine, therefore the nations are mad. Babylon is suddenly fallen and destroyed, howl for her, take balm for her pain if so be she may be healed. We would have healed Babylon, but she is not healed, forsake her and let us go everyone into his own country, for her judgment reacheth unto Heaven and is lifted up even to the skies. The Lord hath brought forth our righteousness, come and let us declare in Zion the work of the Lord our God. Make bright the arrows, gather the shields, the Lord hath raised up the spirit of the kings of the Medes, for his device is against Babylon, to destroy it because it is the vengeance of the Lord, the vengeance of his temple. Set up the standard upon the walls of Babylon, make the watch strong, set up the watchmen, prepare the ambushes, for the Lord hath both devised and done that which he spake against the inhabitants of Babylon. O thou that dwellest upon many waters, abundant in treasures, thine end is come and the measure of thy covetousness. The Lord of hosts hath sworn by himself, saying, Surely I will fill thee with men as with caterpillars, and they shall lift up a shout against thee.

He hath made the Earth by his power, he hath established the world by his wisdom, and hath stretched out the Heaven by his understanding. When he uttereth his voice, there is a multitude of waters in the heavens, and he causeth the vapors to ascend from the ends of the Earth, he maketh lightnings with rain and bringeth forth the wind out of his treasures. Every man is brutish by his knowledge, every founder is confounded by the graven image, for his molten image is falsehood and there is no breath in them. They are vanity, the work of errors, in the time of their visitation they shall perish. The portion of Jacob is not like them, for he is the former of all things and Israel is the rod of his inheritance, the Lord of hosts is his name.

Thou art my battle axe and weapons of war, for with thee will I break in pieces the nations, and with thee will I destroy kingdoms. And with thee will I break in pieces the horse and his rider, and with thee will I break in pieces the chariot and his rider, with thee also will I break in pieces man and woman, and with thee will I break in pieces old and young, and with thee will I break in pieces the young man and the maid. I will also break in pieces with thee the shepherd and his flock, and with thee will I break in pieces the husbandman and his yoke of oxen, and with thee will I break in pieces captains and rulers. And I will render unto Babylon and to all the inhabitants of Chaldea all their evil that they have done in Zion in your sight, saith the Lord. Behold, I am against thee, O destroying mountain, saith the Lord, which destroyest all the earth, and I will stretch out mine hand upon thee and roll thee down from the rocks, and will make thee a burnt mountain. And they shall not take of thee a stone for a corner, nor a stone for foundations, but thou shalt be desolate forever, saith the Lord. Set ye up a standard in the land, blow the trumpet among the nations, prepare the nations against her, call together against her the kingdoms of Ararat, Minni, and Ashchenaz, appoint a captain against her, cause the horses to come up as the rough caterpillars. Prepare against her the nations with the kings of the Medes, the captains thereof, and all the rulers thereof, and all the land of his dominion. And the land shall tremble and sorrow, for every purpose of the Lord shall be performed against Babylon, to make the land of Babylon a desolation without an inhabitant. The mighty men of Babylon have forborne to fight, they have remained in their holds, their might hath failed, they became as women, they have burned her dwelling places, her bars are broken. One post shall run to meet another and one messenger to meet another, to show the king of Babylon that his city is taken at one end, and that the passages are stopped, and the reeds they have burned with fire, and the men of war are affrighted. For thus saith the Lord of hosts, the God of Israel, The daughter of Babylon is like a threshing floor, it is time to thresh her, yet a little while and the time of her harvest shall come. Nebuchadnezzar the king of Babylon hath devoured me, he hath crushed me, he hath made me an empty vessel, he hath swallowed me up like a dragon, he hath filled his belly with my delicates, he hath cast me out. The violence done to me and to my flesh be upon Babylon, shall the inhabitant of Zion say, and my blood upon the inhabitants of Chaldea, shall Jerusalem say. Therefore thus saith the Lord, Behold, I will plead thy cause, and take vengeance for thee, and I will dry up her sea, and make her springs dry. And Babylon shall become heaps, a dwelling place for dragons, an astonishment, and a hissing, without an inhabitant. They shall roar together like lions, they shall yell as lions' whelps. In their heat I will make their feasts, and I will make them drunken, that they may rejoice and sleep a perpetual sleep and not wake, saith the Lord. I will bring them down like lambs to the slaughter, like rams with he goats. How is Sheshach taken! And how is the praise of the whole earth surprised! How is Babylon become an astonishment among the nations! The sea is come up upon Babylon, she is covered with the multitude of the waves thereof. Her cities are a desolation, a dry land and a wilderness, a land wherein no man dwelleth, neither doth any son of man pass thereby. And I will punish Bel in Babylon, and I will bring forth out of his mouth that which he hath swallowed up, and the nations shall not flow together anymore unto him, yea, the wall of Babylon shall fall. My people, go ye out of the midst of her and deliver ye every man his soul from the fierce anger of the Lord. And lest your heart faint and ye fear for the rumor that shall be heard in the land, a rumor shall both come one year, and after that in another year shall come a rumor, and violence in the land, ruler against ruler. Therefore, behold, the days come that I will do judgment upon the graven images of Babylon, and her whole land shall be confounded, and all her slain shall fall in the midst of her. Then the Heaven and the Earth, and all that is therein, shall sing for Babylon, for the spoilers shall come unto her from the north, saith the Lord. As Babylon hath caused the slain of Israel to fall, so at Babylon shall fall the slain of all the earth. Ye that have escaped the sword, go away, stand not still, remember the Lord afar off and let Jerusalem come into your mind. We are confounded because we have heard reproach, shame hath covered our faces, for strangers are come into the sanctuaries of the Lord's house. Wherefore, behold the days come, saith the Lord, that I will do judgment upon her graven images and through all her land the wounded shall groan. Though Babylon should mount up to Heaven and though she should fortify the height of her strength, yet from me shall spoilers come unto her, saith the Lord. A sound of a cry cometh from Babylon, and great destruction from the land of the Chaldeans, because the Lord hath spoiled Babylon and destroyed out of her the great voice, when her waves do roar like great waters, a noise of their voice is uttered because the spoiler is come upon her, even upon Babylon, and her mighty men are taken, every one of their bows is broken, for the Lord God of recompenses shall surely requite. And I will make drunk her princes, and her wise men, her captains, and her rulers, and her mighty men, and they shall sleep a perpetual sleep and not wake, saith the King, whose name is the Lord of hosts. Thus saith the Lord of hosts, The broad walls of Babylon shall be utterly broken, and her high gates shall be burned with fire, and the people shall labor in vain, and the folk in the fire, and they shall be weary.

18 THE word which Jeremiah the prophet commanded Seraiah the son of Neriah, the son of Maaseiah, when he went with Zedekiah the king of Judah into Babylon in the fourth year of his reign. And this Seraiah was a quiet prince. So Jeremiah wrote in a book all the evil that should come upon Babylon, even all these words that are written against Babylon. And Jeremiah said to Seraiah, When thou comest to Babylon and shalt see and shalt read all tese words, then shalt thou say, O Lord, thou hast spoken against this place to cut it off, that none shall remain in it, neither man nor beast, but that it shall be desolate forever. And it shall be when thou hast made an end of reading this book that thou shalt bind a stone to it and cast it into the midst of Euphrates and thou shalt say, Thus shall Babylon sink and shall not rise from the evil that I will bring upon her, and they shall be weary. Thus far are the words of Jeremiah.

Zedekiah was one and twenty years old when he began to reign, and he reigned eleven years in Jerusalem. And his mother's name was Hamutal the daughter of Jeremiah of Libnah. And he did that which was evil in the eyes of the Lord, according to all that Jehoiakim had done. For through the anger of the Lord it came to pass in Jerusalem and Judah, till he had cast them out from his presence, that Zedekiah rebelled against the king of Babylon. And it came to pass in the ninth year of his reign, in the tenth month, in the tenth day of the month, that

Nebuchadnezzar king of Babylon came, he and all his army, against Jerusalem, and pitched against it, and built forts against it round about. So the city was besieged unto the eleventh year of king Zedekiah. And in the fourth month, in the ninth day of the month, the famine was sore in the city, so that there was no bread for the people of the land. Then the city was broken up, and all the men of war fled, and went forth out of the city by night by the way of the gate between the two walls which was by the king's garden (now the Chaldeans were by the city round about) and they went by the way of the plain. But the army of the Chaldeans pursued after the king and overtook Zedekiah in the plains of Jericho, and all his army was scattered from him. Then they took the king and carried him up unto the king of Babylon to Riblah in the land of Hamath, where he gave judgment upon him. And the king of Babylon slew the sons of Zedekiah before his eyes, he slew also all the princes of Judah in Riblah. Then he put out the eyes of Zedekiah, and the king of Babylon bound him in chains and carried him to Babylon and put him in prison till the day of his death.

Now in the fifth month, in the tenth day of the month, which was the nineteenth year of Nebuchadnezzar king of Babylon came Nebuzar-adan captain of the guard, which served the king of Babylon into Jerusalem and burned the house of the Lord, and the king's house, and all the houses of Jerusalem, and all the houses of the great men burned he with fire, and all the army of the Chaldeans that were with the captain of the guard brake down all the walls of Jerusalem round about. Then Nebuzar-adan the captain of the guard carried away captive certain of the poor of the people, and the residue of the people that remained in the city, and those that fell away, that fell to the king of Babylon, and the rest of the multitude. But Nebuzar-adan the captain of the guard left certain of the poor of the land for vinedressers and for husbandmen.

Also the pillars of brass that were in the house of the Lord, and the bases, and the brazen sea that was in the house of the Lord, the Chaldeans brake and carried all the brass of them to Babylon. The caldrons also, and the shovels, and the snuffers, and the bowls, and the spoons, and all the vessels of brass wherewith they ministered took they away. And the basins, and the firepans, and the bowls, and the caldrons, and the candlesticks, and the spoons, and the cups, that which was of gold in gold, and that which was of silver in silver, took the captain of the guard away. The two pillars, one sea, and twelve brazen bulls that were under the bases, which king Solomon had made in the house of the Lord, the brass of all these vessels was without weight. And concerning the pillars, the height of one pillar was eighteen cubits, and a fillet of twelve cubits did compass it, and the thickness thereof was four fingers; it was hollow. And a chapiter of brass was upon it, and the height of one chapiter was five cubits, with network and pomegranates upon the chapiters round about, all of brass. The second pillar also and the pomegranates were like unto these. And there were ninety and six pomegranates on a side, and all the pomegranates upon the network were a hundred round about.

And the captain of the guard took Seraiah the chief priest, and Zephaniah the second priest, and the three keepers of the door, he took also out of the city a eunuch, which had the charge of the men of war, and seven men of them that were near the king's person, which were found in the city, and the principal scribe of the host who mustered the people of the land, and threescore men of the people of the land that were found in the midst of the city. So Nebuzar-adan the captain of the guard took them and brought them to the king of Babylon to Riblah. And the king of Babylon smote them and put them to death in Riblah in the land of Hamath. Thus Judah was carried away captive out of his own land.

This is the people whom Nebuchadnezzar carried away captive: in the seventh year three thousand Jews and three and twenty; in the eighteenth year of

Nebuchadnezzar he carried away captive from Jerusalem eight hundred thirty and two persons; in the three and twentieth year of Nebuchadnezzar, Nebuzar-adan the captain of the guard carried away captive of the Jews seven hundred forty and five persons; all the persons were four thousand and six hundred.

And it came to pass in the seven and thirtieth year of the captivity of Jehoiachin king of Judah, in the twelfth month, in the five and twentieth day of the month, that Evilmerodach king of Babylon, in the first year of his reign, lifted up the head of Jehoiachin king of Judah, and brought him forth out of prison, and spake kindly unto him, and set his throne above the throne of the kings that were with him in Babylon. And changed his prison garments, and he did continually eat bread before him all the days of his life. And for his diet there was a continual diet given him of the king of Babylon, every day a portion until the day of his death, all the days of his life.

THE LAMENTATIONS OF JEREMIAH

HOW doth the city sit solitary, that was full of people! How is she become as a widow! She that was great among the nations and princess among the provinces, how is she become tributary! She weepeth sore in the night and her tears are on her cheeks, among all her lovers she hath none to comfort her, all her friends have dealt treacherously with her, they are become her enemies. Judah is gone into captivity because of affliction and because of great servitude, she dwelleth among the heathen, she findeth no rest, all her persecutors overtook her between the straits.

The ways of Zion do mourn because none come to the solemn feasts, all her gates are desolate, her priests sigh, her virgins are afflicted, and she is in bitterness. Her adversaries are the chief, her enemies prosper, for the Lord hath afflicted her for the multitude of her transgressions, her children are gone into captivity before the enemy. And from the daughter of Zion all her beauty is departed, her princes are become like harts that find no pasture and they are gone without strength before the pursuer.

Jerusalem remembered in the days of her affliction and of her miseries all her pleasant things that she had in the days of old; when her people fell into the hand of the enemy and none did help her, the adversaries saw her and did mock at her sabbaths. Jerusalem hath grievously sinned therefore she is removed, all that honored her despise her because they have seen her nakedness, yea, she sigheth and turneth backward. Her filthiness is in her skirts, she remembereth not her last end, therefore she came down wonderfully, she had no comforter. O Lord, behold my affliction, for the enemy hath magnified himself. The adversary hath spread out his hand upon all her pleasant things, for she hath seen that the heathen entered into her sanctuary whom thou didst command that they should not enter into thy congregation.

All her people sigh, they seek bread, they have given their pleasant things for meat to relieve the soul. See, O Lord, and consider, for I am become vile. Is it nothing to you, all ye that pass by? Behold and see if there be any sorrow like unto my sorrow which is done unto me, wherewith the Lord hath afflicted me in the day of his fierce anger. From above hath he sent fire into my bones and it prevaileth against them, he hath spread a net for my feet, he hath turned me back, he hath made me desolate and faint all the day. The yoke of my transgressions is bound by his hand, they are wreathed and come up upon my neck, he hath made my strength to fall, the Lord hath delivered me into their hands, from whom I am not able to rise up. The Lord hath trodden under foot all my mighty men in the midst of me, he hath called an assembly against me to crush my young men, the Lord hath trodden the virgin, the daughter of Judah, as in a winepress. For these things I weep, mine eye, mine eye runneth down with water because the comforter that should relieve my soul is far from me, my children are desolate because the enemy prevailed. Zion spreadeth forth her hands and there is none to comfort her, the Lord hath commanded concerning Jacob, that his adversaries should be round about him; Jerusalem is as a menstruous woman among them.

The Lord is righteous, for I have rebelled against his commandments; hear, I pray you, all people, and behold my sorrow: my virgins and my young men are gone into captivity. I called for my lovers, but they deceived me, my priests and mine elders gave up the ghost in the city while they sought their meat to relieve their souls. Behold, O Lord, for I am in distress, my bowels are troubled, mine heart is turned within me for I have grievously rebelled; abroad the sword bereaveth, at home there is as death. They have heard that I sigh, there is none to comfort me, all mine enemies have heard of my trouble, they are glad that thou hast done it, thou wilt bring the day that thou hast called and they shall be like unto me. Let all their wickedness come before thee, and do unto them as thou hast done unto me for all my transgressions, for my sighs are many and my heart is faint.

How hath the Lord covered the daughter of Zion with a cloud in his anger, and cast down from Heaven unto the earth the beauty of Israel, and remembered not his footstool in the day of his anger! The Lord hath swallowed up all the habitations of Jacob and hath not pitied, he hath thrown down in his wrath the strongholds of the daughter of Judah, he hath brought them down to the ground, he hath polluted the kingdom and the princes thereof.

He hath cut off in his fierce anger all the horn of Israel, he hath drawn back his right hand from before the enemy, and he burned against Jacob like a flaming fire which devoureth round about. He hath bent his bow like an enemy, he stood with his right hand as an adversary and slew all that were pleasant to the eye in the tabernacle of the daughter of Zion; he poured out his fury like fire. The Lord was as an enemy, he hath swallowed up Israel, he hath swallowed up all her palaces, he hath destroyed his strongholds and hath increased in the daughter of Judah mourning and lamentation. And he hath violently taken away his tabernacle as if it were of a garden, he hath destroyed his places of the assembly.

The Lord hath caused the solemn feasts and sabbaths to be forgotten in Zion and hath despised in the indignation of his anger the king and the priest. The Lord hath cast off his altar, he hath abhorred his sanctuary, he hath given up into the hand of the enemy the walls of her palaces; they have made a noise in the house of the Lord as in the day of a solemn feast. The Lord hath purposed to destroy the wall of the daughter of Zion, he hath stretched out a line, he hath not withdrawn his hand from destroying, therefore he made the rampart and the wall to lament, they languished together. Her gates are sunk into the ground, he hath destroyed and broken her bars, her king and her princes are among the Gentiles, the law is no more, her prophets also find no vision from the Lord. The elders of the daughter of Zion sit upon the ground and keep silence, they have cast up dust upon their heads, they have girded themselves with sackcloth, the virgins of Jerusalem hang down their heads to the ground. Mine eyes do fail with tears, my bowels are troubled, my liver is poured upon the earth, for the destruction of the daughter of my people because the children and the sucklings swoon in the streets of the city. They say to their mothers, Where is corn and wine? when they swooned as the wounded in the streets of the city, when their soul was poured out into their mothers' bosom. What thing shall I take to witness for thee? What thing shall I liken to thee, O daughter of

Jerusalem? What shall I equal to thee that I may comfort thee, O virgin daughter of Zion? For thy breach is great like the sea; who can heal thee?

Thy prophets have seen vain and foolish things for thee, and they have not discovered thine iniquity, to turn away thy captivity, but have seen for thee false burdens and causes of banishment. All that pass by clap their hands at thee, they hiss and wag their head at the daughter of Jerusalem, saying, Is this the city that men call The perfection of beauty, The joy of the whole earth? All thine enemies have opened their mouth against thee, they hiss and gnash the teeth, they say, We have swallowed her up, certainly this is the day that we looked for, we have found, we have seen it.

The Lord hath done that which he had devised, he hath fulfilled his word that he had commanded in the days of old, he hath thrown down and hath not pitied, and he hath caused thine enemy to rejoice over thee; he hath set up the horn of thine adversaries. Their heart cried unto the Lord, O wall of the daughter of Zion, let tears run down like a river day and night, give thyself no rest, let not the apple of thine eye cease. Arise, cry out in the night, in the beginning of the watches pour out thine heart like water before the face of the Lord. Llift up thy hands toward him for the life of thy young children that faint for hunger in the top of every street. Behold, O Lord, and consider to whom thou hast done this. Shall the women eat their fruit and children of a span long? Shall the priest and the prophet be slain in the sanctuary of the Lord? The young and the old lie on the ground in the streets, my virgins and my young men are fallen by the sword, thou hast slain them in the day of thine anger, thou hast killed and not pitied. Thou hast called as in a solemn day my terrors round about so that in the day of the Lord's anger none escaped nor remained, those that I have swaddled and brought up hath mine enemy consumed.

I am the man that hath seen affliction by the rod of his wrath. He hath led me and brought me into darkness, but not into light. Surely against me is he turned, he turneth his hand against me all the day. My flesh and my skin hath he made old, he hath broken my bones. He hath builded against me and compassed me with gall and travail. He hath set me in dark places as they that be dead of old. He hath hedged me about that I cannot get out, he hath made my chain heavy. Also when I cry and shout he shutteth out my prayer. He hath enclosed my ways with hewn stone, he hath made my paths crooked. He was unto me as a bear lying in wait and as a lion in secret places. He hath turned aside my ways and pulled me in pieces, he hath made me desolate. He hath bent his bow and set me as a mark for the arrow. He hath caused the arrows of his quiver to enter into my reins. I was a derision to all my people and their song all the day. He hath filled me with bitterness, he hath made me drunken with wormwood. He hath also broken my teeth with gravel stones, he hath covered me with ashes. And thou hast removed my soul far off from peace, I forgat prosperity. And I said, My strength and my hope is perished from the Lord, remembering mine affliction and my misery, the wormwood and the gall. My soul hath them still in remembrance and is humbled in me. This I recall to my mind, therefore have I hope. It is of the Lord's mercies that we are not consumed because his compassions fail not.

They are new every morning, great is thy faithfulness. The Lord is my portion, saith my soul, therefore will I hope in him. The Lord is good unto them that wait for him, to the soul that seeketh him. It is good that a man should both hope and quietly wait for the salvation of the Lord. It is good for a man that he bear the yoke in his youth. He sitteth alone and keepeth silence because he hath borne it upon him. He putteth his mouth in the dust, if so be there may be hope. He giveth his cheek to him that smiteth him, he is filled full with reproach. For the Lord will not cast off forever, but though he cause grief, yet will he have compassion according to the multitude of his mercies. For he doth not afflict willingly nor grieve the children of men. To crush under his feet all the prisoners of the earth, to turn aside the right of a man before the face of the Most High, to subvert a man in his cause, the Lord approveth not.

Who is he that saith and it cometh to pass when the Lord commandeth it not? Out of the mouth of the Most High proceedeth not evil and good. Wherefore doth a living man complain, a man for the punishment of his sins? Let us search and try our ways and turn again to the Lord. Let us lift up our heart with our hands unto God in the heavens. We have transgressed and have rebelled, thou hast not pardoned. Thou hast covered with anger and persecuted us, thou hast slain, thou hast not pitied. Thou hast covered thyself with a cloud that our prayer should not pass through. Thou hast made us as the offscouring and refuse in the midst of the people. All our enemies have opened their mouths against us. Fear and a snare is come upon us, desolation and destruction. Mine eye runneth down with rivers of water for the destruction of the daughter of my people. Mine eye trickleth down and ceaseth not, without any intermissions, till the Lord look down and behold from Heaven. Mine eye affecteth mine heart because of all the daughters of my city. Mine enemies chased me sore like a bird, without cause. They have cut off my life in the dungeon and cast a stone upon me. Waters flowed over mine head, then I said, I am cut off.

I called upon thy name, O Lord, out of the low dungeon. Thou hast heard my voice, hide not thine ear at my breathing, at my cry. Thou drewest near in the day that I called upon thee, thou saidst, Fear not. O Lord, thou hast pleaded the causes of my soul, thou hast redeemed my life. O Lord, thou hast seen my wrong, judge thou my cause. Thou hast seen all their vengeance and all their imaginations against me. Thou hast heard their reproach, O Lord, and all their imaginations against me, the lips of those that rose up against me and their device against me all the day. Behold their sitting down and their rising up, I am their music. Render unto them a recompense, O Lord, according to the work of their hands. Give them sorrow of heart, thy curse unto them. Persecute and destroy them in anger from under the heavens of the Lord.

How is the gold become dim! How is the most fine gold changed! The stones of the sanctuary are poured out in the top of every street. The precious sons of Zion, comparable to fine gold, how are they esteemed as earthen pitchers, the work of the hands of the potter! Even the sea monsters draw out the breast, they give suck to their young ones, the daughter of my people is become cruel like the ostriches in the wilderness. The tongue of the sucking child cleaveth to the roof of his mouth for thirst, the young children ask bread and no man breaketh it unto them. They that did feed delicately are desolate in the streets, they that were brought up in scarlet embrace dunghills.

For the punishment of the iniquity of the daughter of my people is greater than the punishment of the sin of Sodom that was overthrown as in a moment and no hands stayed on her. Her Nazarites were purer than snow, they were whiter than milk, they were more ruddy in body than rubies, their polishing was of sapphire. Their visage is blacker than a coal, they are not known in the streets, their skin cleaveth to their bones, it is withered, it is become like a stick. They that be slain with the sword are better than they that be slain with hunger, for these pine away, stricken through for want of the fruits of the field. The hands of the pitiful women have sodden their own children, they were their meat in the destruction of the daughter of my people.

The Lord hath accomplished his fury, he hath poured out his fierce anger and hath kindled a fire in Zion and it hath devoured the foundations thereof. The kings of the Earth and all the inhabitants of the world would not have believed that the adversary and the enemy should have entered into the gates of Jerusalem. For the sins of her prophets and the iniquities of her priests, that have shed the blood of the just in the midst of her, they have wandered as blind men in the streets, they have polluted themselves with blood so that men could not touch their garments. They cried unto them, Depart ye, it is unclean, depart, depart, touch not, when they fled away and wandered. They said among the heathen, They shall no more sojourn there. The anger of the Lord hath divided them, he will no more regard them, they respected not the persons of the priests, they favored not the elders.

As for us, our eyes as yet failed for our vain help, in our watching we have watched for a nation that could not save us. They hunt our steps that we cannot go in our streets, our end is near, our days are fulfilled for our end is come. Our persecutors are swifter than the eagles of the Heaven, they pursued us upon the mountains, they laid wait for us in the wilderness. The breath of our nostrils, the anointed of the Lord, was taken in their pits, of whom we said, Under his shadow we shall live among the heathen.

Rejoice and be glad, O daughter of Edom, that dwellest in the land of Uz, the cup also shall pass through unto thee, thou shalt be drunken and shalt make thyself naked. The punishment of thine iniquity is accomplished, O daughter of Zion, he will no more carry thee away into captivity, he will visit thine iniquity, O daughter of Edom, he will discover thy sins.

Remember, O Lord, what is come upon us, consider and behold our reproach. Our inheritance is turned to strangers, our houses to aliens. We are orphans and fatherless, our mothers are as widows. We have drunken our water for money, our wood is sold unto us. Our necks are under persecution, we labor and have no rest. We have given the hand to the Egyptians and to the Assyrians to be satisfied with bread. Our fathers have sinned and are not, and we have borne their iniquities. Servants have ruled over us, there is none that doth deliver us out of their hand. We gat our bread with the peril of our lives because of the sword of the wilderness. Our skin was black like an oven because of the terrible famine. They ravished the women in Zion and the maids in the cities of Judah. Princes are hanged up by their hand, the faces of elders were not honored. They took the young men to grind and the children fell under the wood. The elders have ceased from the gate, the young men from their music. The joy of our heart is ceased, our dance is turned into mourning. The crown is fallen from our head, wo unto us that we have sinned. For this our heart is faint, for these things our eyes are dim. Because of the mountain of Zion which is desolate, the foxes walk upon it.

Thou, O Lord, remainest forever, thy throne from generation to generation. Wherefore dost thou forget us for ever and forsake us so long time? Turn thou us unto thee, O Lord, and we shall be turned, renew our days as of old. But thou hast utterly rejected us, thou art very wroth against us.

THE BOOK OF THE PROPHET EZEKIEL

NOW it came to pass in the thirtieth year, in the fourth month, in the fifth day of the month, as I was among the captives by the river of Chebar, that the heavens were opened and I saw visions of God. In the fifth day of the month, which was the fifth year of king Jehoiachin's captivity, the word of the Lord came expressly unto Ezekiel the priest, the son of Buzi, in the land of the Chaldeans by the river Chebar and the hand of the Lord was there upon him.

And I looked and behold, a whirlwind came out of the north, a great cloud and a fire infolding itself, and a brightness was about it, and out of the midst thereof as the color of amber, out of the midst of the fire. Also out of the midst thereof came the likeness of four living creatures. And this was their appearance: they had the likeness of a man. And every one had four faces, and every one had four wings. And their feet were straight feet, and the sole of their feet was like the sole of a calf's foot, and they sparkled like the color of burnished brass. And they had the hands of a man under their wings on their four sides, and they four had their faces and their wings. Their wings were joined one to another, they turned not when they went, they went every one straight forward. As for the likeness of their faces, they four had the face of a man, and the face of a lion on the right side, and they four had the face of an ox on the left side, they four also had the face of an eagle. Thus were their faces, and their wings were stretched upward, two wings of every one were joined one to another, and two covered their bodies. And they went every one straight forward, whither the spirit was to go they went and they turned not when they went. As for the likeness of the living creatures, their appearance was like burning coals of fire and like the appearance of lamps; it went up and down among the living creatures, and the fire was bright, and out of the fire went forth lightning. And the living creatures ran and returned as the appearance of a flash of lightning.

Now as I beheld the living creatures, behold one wheel upon the earth by the living creatures with his four faces. The appearance of the wheels and their work was like unto the color of a beryl, and they four had one likeness and their appearance and their work was as it were a wheel in the middle of a wheel. When they went, they went upon their four sides and they turned not when they went. As for their rings, they were so high that they were dreadful, and their rings were full of eyes round about them four. And when the living creatures went, the wheels went by them, and when the living creatures were lifted up from the Earth the wheels were lifted up. Whithersoever the spirit was to go, they went, thither was their spirit to go, and the wheels were lifted up over against them, for the spirit of the living creature was in the wheels. When those went, these went, and when those stood, these stood, and when those were lifted up from the Earth, the wheels were lifted up over against them, for the spirit of the living creature was in the wheels. And the likeness of the firmament upon the heads of the living creature was as the color of the terrible crystal stretched forth over their heads above. And under the firmament were their wings straight, the one toward the other; every one had two which covered on this side, and every one had two which covered on that side, their bodies. And when they went I heard the noise of their wings like the noise of great waters, as the voice of the Almighty, the voice of speech as the noise of a host; when they stood, they let down their wings. And there was a voice from the firmament that was over their heads when they stood and had let down their wings.

And above the firmament that was over their heads was the likeness of a throne as the appearance of a sapphire stone, and upon the likeness of the throne was the likeness as the appearance of a man above upon it. And I saw as the color of amber, as the appearance of fire round about within it, from the appearance of his loins even upward and from the appearance of his loins even downward I saw as it were the appearance of fire, and it had brightness round about. As the appearance of the bow that is in the cloud in the day of rain so was the appearance of the brightness round about. This was the appearance of the likeness of the glory of the Lord. And when I saw it I fell upon my face and I heard a voice of one that spake.

And he said unto me, Son of man, stand upon thy feet and I will speak unto thee. And the Spirit entered into me when he spake unto me and set me upon my feet that I heard him that spake unto me. And he said unto me, Son of man, I send thee to the children of Israel, to a rebellious nation that hath rebelled against me; they and their fathers have transgressed against me even unto this very day. For they are impudent children and stiff-hearted. I do send thee unto them and thou shalt say unto them, Thus saith the Lord God. And they, whether they will hear or whether they will forbear (for they are a rebellious house), yet shall know that there hath been a prophet among them. And thou, son of man, be not afraid of them, neither be afraid of their words; though briers and thorns be with thee and thou dost dwell among scorpions, be not afraid of their words nor be dismayed at their looks, though they be a rebellious house. And thou shalt speak my words unto them whether they will hear or whether they will forbear, for they are most rebellious. But thou, son of man, hear what I say unto thee, be not thou rebellious like that rebellious house, open thy mouth, and eat that I give thee.

And when I looked, behold, a hand was sent unto me and lo, a roll of a book was therein, and he spread it before me, and it was written within and without and there was written therein lamentations, and mourning, and woe.

Moreover he said unto me, Son of man, eat that thou findest, eat this roll and go speak unto the house of Israel. So I opened my mouth and he caused me to eat that roll. And he said unto me, Son of man, cause thy belly to eat and fill thy bowels with this roll that I give thee. Then did I eat it and it was in my mouth as honey for sweetness.

And he said unto me, Son of man, go, get thee unto the house of Israel and speak with my words unto them. For thou art not sent to a people of a strange speech and of a hard language, but to the house of Israel, not to many people of a strange speech and of a hard language whose words thou canst not understand. Surely had I sent thee to them they would have hearkened unto thee. But the house of Israel will not hearken unto thee, for they will not hearken unto me, for all the house of Israel are impudent and hardhearted. Behold, I have made thy face strong against their faces and thy forehead strong against their foreheads. As an adamant harder than flint have I made thy forehead; fear them not, neither be dismayed at their looks, though they be a rebellious house. Moreover he said unto me, Son of man, all my words that I shall speak unto thee receive in thine heart and hear with thine ears. And go, get thee to them of the captivity, unto the children of thy people, and speak unto them and tell them, Thus saith the Lord God, whether they will hear or whether they will forbear. Then the Spirit took me up and I heard behind me a voice of a great rushing saying, Blessed be the glory of the Lord from his place. I heard also the noise of the wings of the living creatures that touched one another, and the noise of the wheels over against them, and a noise of a great rushing. So the Spirit lifted me up and took me away and I went in bitterness, in the heat of my spirit, but the hand of the Lord was strong upon me.

Then I came to them of the captivity at Tel-abab, that dwelt by the river of Chebar, and I sat where they sat and remained there astonished among them seven days. And it came to pass at the end of seven days that the word of the Lord came unto me saying, Son of man, I have made thee a watchman unto the house of Israel, therefore hear the word at my mouth and give them warning from me. When I say unto the wicked, Thou shalt surely die, and thou givest him not warning, nor speakest to warn the wicked from his wicked way to save his life, the same wicked man shall die in his iniquity, but his blood will I require at thine hand. Yet if thou warn the wicked and he turn not from his wickedness, nor from his wicked way, he shall die in his iniquity, but thou hast delivered thy soul. Again, when a righteous man doth turn from his righteousness and commit iniquity and I lay a stumbling block before him, he shall die; because thou hast not given him warning, he shall die in his sin, and his righteousness which he hath done shall not be remembered, but his blood will I require at thine hand. Nevertheless, if thou warn the righteous man, that the righteous sin not and he doth not sin, he shall surely live because he is warned, also thou hast delivered thy soul.

And the hand of the Lord was there upon me and he said unto me, Arise, go forth into the plain and I will there talk with thee. Then I arose and went forth into the plain and behold, the glory of the Lord stood there as the glory which I saw by the river of Chebar, and I fell on my face. Then the Spirit entered into me and set me upon my feet, and spake with me, and said unto me, Go, shut thyself within thine house. But thou, O son of man, behold, they shall put bands upon thee and shall bind thee with them, and thou shalt not go out among them, and I will make thy tongue cleave to the roof of thy mouth, that thou shalt be dumb and shalt not be to them a reprover, for they are a rebellious house. But when I speak with thee, I will open thy mouth and thou shalt say unto them, Thus saith the Lord God, He that heareth, let him hear, and he that forbeareth, let him forbear, for they are a rebellious house.

Thou also, son of man, take thee a tile and lay it before thee and portray upon it the city, even Jerusalem, and lay siege against it, and build a fort against it, and cast a mount against it, set the camp also against it, and set battering rams against it round about. Moreover take thou unto thee an iron pan and set it for a wall of iron between thee and the city, and set thy face against it and it shall be besieged, and thou shalt lay siege against it. This shall be a sign to the house of Israel.

Lie thou also upon thy left side and lay the iniquity of the house of Israel upon it; according to the number of the days that thou shalt lie upon it thou shalt bear their iniquity. For I have laid upon thee the years of their iniquity; according to the number of the days, three hundred and ninety days, so shalt thou bear the iniquity of the house of Israel. And when thou hast accomplished them, lie again on thy right side, and thou shalt bear the iniquity of the house of Judah forty days; I have appointed thee each day for a year. Therefore thou shalt set thy face toward the siege of Jerusalem, and thine arm shall be uncovered, and thou shalt prophesy against it. And, behold, I will lay bands upon thee and thou shalt not turn thee from one side to another till thou hast ended the days of thy siege.

Take thou also unto thee wheat, and barley, and beans, and lentils, and millet, and fitches, and put them in one vessel, and make thee bread thereof, according to the number of the days that thou shalt lie upon thy side: three hundred and ninety days shalt thou eat thereof. And thy meat which thou shalt eat shall be by weight twenty shekels a day, from time to time shalt thou eat it. Thou shalt drink also water by measure, the sixth part of a hin, from time to time shalt thou drink. And thou shalt eat it as barley cakes, and thou shalt bake it with dung that cometh out of man, in their sight. And the Lord said, Even thus shall the children of Israel eat their defiled bread among the Gentiles whither I will drive them. Then said I, Ah Lord God! behold, my soul hath not been polluted, for from my youth up even till now have I not eaten of that which dieth of itself, or is torn in pieces, neither came there abominable flesh into my mouth. Then he said unto me, Lo, I have given thee cow's dung for man's dung and thou shalt prepare thy bread therewith. Moreover he said unto me, Son of man, behold, I will break the staff of bread in Jerusalem, and they shall eat bread by weight and with care, and they shall drink water by measure and with astonishment, that they may want bread and water, and be astonished one with another, and consume away for their iniquity.

And thou, son of man, take thee a sharp knife, take thee a barber's razor, and cause it to pass upon thine head and upon thy beard, then take thee balances to weigh, and divide the hair. Thou shalt burn with fire a third part in the midst of the city when the days of the siege are fulfilled, and thou shalt take a third part and smite about it with a knife, and a third part thou shalt scatter in the wind, and I will draw out a sword after them. Thou shalt also take thereof a few in number and bind them in thy skirts. Then take of them again, and cast them into the midst of the fire, and burn them in the fire, for thereof shall a fire come forth into all the house of Israel.

Thus saith the Lord God, This is Jerusalem, I have set it in the midst of the nations and countries that are round about her. And she hath changed my judgments into wickedness more than the nations, and my statutes more than the countries that are round about her, for they have refused my judgments and my statutes, they have not walked in them. Therefore thus saith the Lord God, Because ye multiplied more than the nations that are round about you and have not walked in my statutes, neither have kept my judgments, neither have done according to the judgments of the nations that are round about you, therefore thus saith the Lord God, Behold I, even I, am against thee and will execute judgments in the midst of thee in the sight of the nations. And I will do in thee that which I have not done, and whereunto I will not do anymore the like, because of all thine abominations. Therefore the fathers shall eat the sons in the midst of thee, and the sons shall eat their fathers, and I will execute judgments in thee, and the whole remnant of thee will I scatter into all the winds. Wherefore, as I live, saith the Lord God, surely because thou hast defiled my sanctuary with all thy detestable things and with all thine abominations, therefore will I also diminish thee, neither shall mine eye spare, neither will I have any pity. A third part of thee shall die with the pestilence and with famine shall they be consumed in the midst of thee, and a third part shall fall by the sword round about thee, and I will scatter a third part into all the winds, and I will draw out a sword after them. Thus shall mine anger be accomplished and I will cause my fury to rest upon them, and I will be comforted, and they shall know that I the Lord have spoken it in my zeal when I have accomplished my fury in them. Moreover I will make thee waste and a reproach among the nations that are round about thee in the sight of all that pass by. So it shall be a reproach and a taunt, and instruction, and an astonishment unto the nations that are round about thee when I shall execute judgments in thee in anger and in fury and in furious rebukes. I the Lord have spoken it. When I shall send upon them the evil arrows of famine, which shall be for their destruction and which I will send to destroy you, and I will increase the famine upon you and will break your staff of bread, so will I send upon you famine and evil beasts, and they shall bereave thee, and pestilence and blood shall pass through thee, and I will bring the sword upon thee. I the Lord have spoken it.

2 AND the word of the Lord came unto me, saying, Son of man, set thy face toward the mountains of Israel, and prophesy against them, and say, Ye mountains of Israel, hear the word of the Lord God: Thus saith the Lord God to the mountains and to the hills, to the rivers and to the valleys, Behold, I, even I will bring a sword upon you and I will destroy your high places. And your altars shall be desolate, and your images shall be broken, and I will cast down your slain men before your idols. And I will lay the dead carcasses of the children of Israel before their idols and I will scatter your bones round about your altars. In all your dwelling places the cities shall be laid waste and the high places shall be desolate, that your altars may be laid waste and made desolate, and your idols may be broken and cease, and your images may be cut down, and your works may be abolished. And the slain shall fall in the midst of you and ye shall know that I am the Lord.

Yet will I leave a remnant, that ye may have some that shall escape the sword among the nations when ye shall be scattered through the countries. And they that escape of you shall remember me among the nations whither they shall be carried captives, because I am broken with their whorish heart which hath departed from me, and with their eyes which go a whoring after their idols, and they shall loathe themselves for the evils which they have committed in all their abominations. And they shall know that I am the Lord and that I have not said in vain that I would do this evil unto them.

Thus saith the Lord God, Smite with thine hand, and stamp with thy foot, and say, Alas for all the evil abominations of the house of Israel! For they shall fall by the sword, by the famine, and by the pestilence. He that is far off shall die of the pestilence, and he that is near shall fall by the sword, and he that remaineth and is besieged shall die by the famine, thus will I accomplish my fury upon them. Then shall ye know that I am the Lord, when their slain men shall be among their idols round about their altars, upon every high hill, in all the tops of the mountains, and under every green tree, and under every thick oak, the place where they did offer sweet savor to all their idols. So will I stretch out my hand upon them and make the land desolate, yea, more desolate than the wilderness toward Diblath in all their habitations and they shall know that I am the Lord.

Moreover the word of the Lord came unto me, saying, Also, thou son of man, thus saith the Lord God unto the land of Israel, An end, the end is come upon the four corners of the land. Now is the end come upon thee and I will send mine anger upon thee, and will judge thee according to thy ways, and will recompense upon thee all thine abominations. And mine eye shall not spare thee neither will I have pity, but I will recompense thy ways upon thee, and thine abominations shall be in the midst of thee, and ye shall know that I am the Lord.

Thus saith the Lord God, An evil, an only evil, behold, is come. An end is come, the end is come, it watcheth for thee; behold, it is come. The morning is come unto thee, O thou that dwellest in the land, the time is come, the day of trouble is near and not the sounding again of the mountains. Now will I shortly pour out my fury upon thee and accomplish mine anger upon thee, and I will judge thee according to thy ways, and will recompense thee for all thine abominations. And mine eye shall not spare, neither will I have pity, I will recompense thee according to thy ways and thine abominations that are in the midst of thee and ye shall know that I am the Lord that smiteth. Behold the day, behold, it is come, the morning is gone forth, the rod hath blossomed, pride hath budded. Violence is risen up into a rod of wickedness, none of them shall remain, nor of their multitude, nor of any of theirs, neither shall there be wailing for them. The time is come, the day draweth near, let not the buyer rejoice nor the seller mourn, for wrath is upon all the multitude thereof. For the seller shall not return to that which is sold, although they were yet alive, for the vision is touching the whole multitude thereof which shall not return, neither shall any strengthen himself in the iniquity of his life.

They have blown the trumpet, even to make all ready, but none goeth to the battle for my wrath is upon all the multitude thereof. The sword is without and the pestilence and the famine within, he that is in the field shall die with the sword and he that is in the city, famine and pestilence shall devour him. But they that escape of them shall escape and shall be on the mountains like doves of the valleys, all of them mourning, everyone for his iniquity. All hands shall be feeble and all knees shall be weak as water. They shall also gird themselves with sackcloth, and horror shall cover them, and shame shall be upon all faces, and baldness upon all their heads. They shall cast their silver in the streets, and their gold shall be removed, their silver and their gold shall not be able to deliver them in the day of the wrath of the Lord, they shall not satisfy their souls neither fill their bowels because it is the stumbling block of their iniquity.

As for the beauty of his ornament, he set it in majesty, but they made the images of their abominations and of their detestable things therein, therefore have I set it far from them. And I will give it into the hands of the strangers for a prey and to the wicked of the earth for a spoil and they shall pollute it. My face will I turn also from them and they shall pollute my secret place, for the robbers shall enter into it and defile it. Make a chain, for the land is full of bloody crimes and the city is full of violence. Wherefore I will bring the worst of the heathen and they shall possess their houses, I will also make the pomp of the strong to cease and their holy places shall be defiled. Destruction cometh and they shall seek peace and there shall be none. Mischief shall come upon mischief and rumor shall be upon rumor, then shall they seek a vision of the prophet, but the law shall perish from the priest and counsel from the ancients. The king shall mourn, and the prince shall be clothed with desolation, and the hands of the people of the land shall be troubled; I will do unto them after their way and according to their deserts will I judge them and they shall know that I am the Lord.

3 AND it came to pass in the sixth year, in the sixth month, in the fifth day of the month, as I sat in mine house and the elders of Judah sat before me, that the hand of the Lord God fell there upon me. Then I beheld, and lo a likeness as the appearance of fire, from the appearance of his loins even downward, fire, and from his loins even upward, as the appearance of brightness, as the color of amber. And he put forth the form of a hand and took me by a lock of mine head, and the Spirit lifted me up between the earth and the Heaven, and brought me in the visions of God to Jerusalem, to the door of the inner gate that looketh toward the north where was the seat of the image of jealousy which provoketh to jealousy. And, behold, the glory of the God of Israel was there according to the vision that I saw in the plain.

Then said he unto me, Son of man, lift up thine eyes now the way toward the north. So I lifted up mine eyes the way toward the north and behold, northward at the gate of the altar this image of jealousy in the entry. He said furthermore unto me, Son of man, seest thou what they do? Even the great abominations that the house of Israel committeth here, that I should go far off from my sanctuary? But turn thee yet again, and thou shalt see greater abominations. And he brought me to the door of the court and when I looked, behold a hole in the wall. Then said he unto me, Son of man, dig now in the wall, and when I had digged in the wall, behold a door. And he said unto me, Go in and behold the wicked abominations that they do here. So I went in and saw, and behold every form of creeping things, and abominable beasts, and all the idols of the house of Israel portrayed upon the wall round about. And there stood before them seventy men of the ancients of the house of Israel, and in the midst of them stood Jaazaniah the son of Shaphan, with every man his censer in his hand, and a thick cloud of incense went up. Then said he unto me, Son of man, hast thou seen what the ancients of the house of Israel do in the dark, every man in the chambers of his imagery? For they say, The Lord seeth us not, the Lord hath forsaken the earth. He said also unto me, Turn thee yet again and thou shalt see greater abominations that they do.

Then he brought me to the door of the gate of the Lord's house which was toward the north and behold, there sat women weeping for Tammuz. Then said he unto me, Hast thou seen this, O son of man? Turn thee yet again and thou shalt see greater abominations than these. And he brought me into the inner court of the Lord's house and behold, at the door of the temple of the Lord, between the porch and the altar, were about five and twenty men, with their backs toward the temple of the Lord and their faces toward the east and they worshiped the sun toward the east. Then he said unto me, Hast thou seen this, O son of man? Is it a light thing to the house of Judah that they commit the abominations which they commit here? For they have filled the land with violence and have returned to provoke me to anger and lo, they put the branch to their nose. Therefore will I also deal in fury, mine eye shall not spare, neither will I have pity, and though they cry in mine ears with a loud voice, yet will I not hear them.

He cried also in mine ears with a loud voice saying, Cause them that have charge over the city to draw near, even every man with his destroying weapon in his hand. And behold, six men came from the way of the higher gate which lieth toward the north, and every man a slaughter weapon in his hand, and one man among them was clothed with linen, with a writer's inkhorn by his side, and they went in and stood beside the brazen altar. And the glory of God of Israel was gone up from the cherub whereupon he was to the threshold of the house. And he called to the man clothed with linen, which had the writer's inkhorn by his side, and the Lord said unto him, Go through the midst of the city, through the midst of Jerusalem and set a mark upon the foreheads of the men that sigh and that cry for all the abominations that be done in the midst thereof. And to the others he said in mine hearing, Go ye after him through the city and smite, let not your eye spare, neither have ye pity, slay utterly old and young, both maids, and little children, and women, but come not near any man upon whom is the mark, and begin at my sanctuary. Then they began at the ancient men which were before the house. And he said unto them, Defile the house and fill the courts with the slain, go ye forth. And they went forth and slew in the city.

And it came to pass, while they were slaying them, and I was left, that I fell upon my face and cried and said, Ah Lord God. Wilt thou destroy all the residue of Israel in thy pouring out of thy fury upon Jerusalem? Then said he unto me, The iniquity of the house of Israel and Judah is exceeding great, and the land is full of blood, and the city full of perverseness, for they say, The Lord hath forsaken the earth and the Lord seeth not. And as for me also, mine eye shall not spare neither will I have pity, but I will recompense their way upon their head. And, behold, the man clothed with linen, which had the inkhorn by his side, reported the matter, saying, I have done as thou hast commanded me.

Then I looked, and, behold, in the firmament that was above the head of the cherubim there appeared over them as it were a sapphire stone, as the appearance of the likeness of a throne. And he spake unto the man clothed with linen and said, Go in between the wheels, even under the cherub, and fill thine hand with coals of fire from between the cherubim, and scatter them over the city. And he went in in my sight. Now the cherubim stood on the right side of the house when the man went in and the cloud filled the inner court. Then the glory of the Lord went up from the cherub and stood over the threshold of the house, and the house was filled with the cloud and the court was full of the brightness of the Lord's glory. And the sound of the cherubim's wings was heard even to the outer court, as the voice of the Almighty God when he speaketh. And it came to pass that when he had commanded the man clothed with linen, saying, Take fire from between the wheels, from between the cherubim, then he went in and stood beside the wheels. And one cherub stretched forth his hand from between the cherubim unto the fire that was between the cherubim, and took thereof and put it into the hands of him that was clothed with linen, who took it and went out.

And there appeared in the cherubim the form of a man's hand under their wings. And when I looked, behold the four wheels by the cherubim, one wheel by one cherub and another wheel by another cherub, and the appearance of the wheels was as the color of a beryl stone. And as for their appearances, they four had one likeness, as if a wheel had been in the midst of a wheel. When they went, they went upon their four sides, they turned not as they went, but to the place whither the head looked, they followed it, they turned not as they went. And their whole body, and their backs, and their hands, and their wings, and the wheels, were full of eyes round about, even the wheels that they four had. As for the wheels, it was cried unto them in my hearing, O wheel. And everyone had four faces, the first face was the face of a cherub, and the second face was the face of a man, and the third the face of a lion, and the fourth the face of an eagle. And the cherubim were lifted up. This is the living creature that I saw by the river of Chebar. And when the cherubim went, the wheels went by them, and when the cherubim lifted up their wings to mount up from the Earth, the same wheels also turned not from beside them. When they stood, these stood, and when they were lifted up, these lifted up themselves also, for the spirit of the living creature was in them.

Then the glory of the Lord departed from off the threshold of the house and stood over the cherubim. And the cherubim lifted up their wings and mounted up from the earth in my sight; when they went out, the wheels also were beside them and every one stood at the door of the east gate of the Lord's house and the glory of the God of Israel was over them above. This is the living creature that I saw under the God of Israel by the river of Chebar and I knew that they were the cherubim. Every one had four faces apiece, and every one four wings, and the likeness of the hands of a man was under their wings. And the likeness of their faces was the same faces which I saw by the river of Chebar, their appearances and themselves, they went every one straight forward.

Moreover the Spirit lifted me up and brought me unto the east gate of the Lord's house which looketh eastward and behold, at the door of the gate five and twenty men, among whom I saw Jaazaniah the son of Azur and Pelatiah the son of Benaiah, princes of the people. Then said he unto me, Son of man, these are the men that devise mischief and give wicked counsel in this city, which say, It is not near, let us build houses, this city is the caldron and we be the flesh. Therefore prophesy against them, prophesy, O son of man. And the Spirit of the Lord fell upon me and said unto me, Speak, Thus saith the Lord, Thus have ye said, O house of Israel, for I know the things that come into your mind, every one of them. Ye have multiplied your slain in this city and ye have filled the streets thereof with the slain. Therefore thus saith the Lord God, Your slain whom ye have laid in the midst of it, they are the flesh and this city is the caldron, but I will bring you forth out of the midst of it. Ye have feared the sword and I will bring a sword upon you, saith the Lord God. And I will bring you out of the midst thereof, and deliver you into the hands of strangers, and will execute judgments among you. Ye shall fall by the sword, I will judge you in the border of Israel, and ye shall know that I am the Lord. This city shall not be your caldron, neither shall ye be the flesh in the midst thereof, but I will judge you in the border of Israel, and ye shall know that I am the Lord, for ye have not walked in my statutes neither executed my judgments, but have done after the manners of the heathen that are round about you.

And it came to pass, when I prophesied, that Pelatiah the son of Benaiah died. Then fell I down upon my face and cried with a loud voice and said, Ah Lord God! Wilt thou make a full end of the remnant of Israel? Again the word of the Lord came unto me saying, Son of man, thy brethren, even thy brethren, the men of thy kindred and all the house of Israel wholly, are they unto whom the inhabitants of Jerusalem have said, Get you far from the Lord, unto us is this land given in possession. Therefore say, Thus saith the Lord God, Although I have cast them far off among the heathen and although I have scattered them among the countries, yet will I be to them as a little sanctuary in the countries where they shall come. Therefore say, Thus saith the Lord God, I will even gather you from the people and assemble you out of the countries where ye have been scattered, and I will give you the land of Israel. And they shall come thither and they shall take away all the detestable things thereof and all the abominations thereof from thence.

And I will give them one heart, and I will put a new spirit within you, and I will take the stony heart out of their flesh and will give them a heart of flesh, that they may walk in my statutes, and keep mine ordinances and do them, and they shall be my people and I will be their God. But as for them whose heart walketh after the heart of their detestable things and their abominations, I will recompense their way upon their own heads, saith the Lord God.

Then did the cherubim lift up their wings, and the wheels beside them, and the glory of the God of Israel was over them above. And the glory of the Lord went up from the midst of the city and stood upon the mountain which is on the east side of the city. Afterwards the Spirit took me up and brought me in a vision by the Spirit of God into Chaldea, to them of the captivity. So the vision that I had seen went up from me. Then I spake unto them of the captivity all the things that the Lord had showed me.

4 THE word of the Lord also came unto me, saying, Son of man, thou dwellest in the midst of a rebellious house, which have eyes to see and see not, they have ears to hear and hear not, for they are a rebellious house. Therefore, thou son of man, prepare thee stuff for removing, and remove by day in their sight, and thou shalt remove from thy place to another place in their sight, it may be they will consider, though they be a rebellious house. Then shalt thou bring forth thy stuff by day in their sight as stuff for removing, and thou shalt go forth at even in their sight as they that go forth into captivity. Dig thou through the wall in their sight and carry out thereby. In their sight shalt thou bear it upon thy shoulders and carry it forth in the twilight, thou shalt cover thy face that thou see not the ground, for I have set thee for a sign unto the house of Israel. And I did so as I was commanded, I brought forth my stuff by day as stuff for captivity, and in the even I digged through the wall with mine hand, I brought it forth in the twilight, and I bare it upon my shoulder in their sight.

And in the morning came the word of the Lord unto me saying, Son of man, hath not the house of Israel, the rebellious house, said unto thee, What doest thou? Say thou unto them, Thus saith the Lord God, This burden concerneth the prince in Jerusalem and all the house of Israel that are among them. Say, I am your sign, like as I have done so shall it be done unto them, they shall remove and go into captivity. And the prince that is among them shall bear upon his shoulder in the twilight and shall go forth, they shall dig through the wall to carry out thereby, he shall cover his face that he see not the ground with his eyes. My net also will I spread upon him, and he shall be taken in my snare, and I will bring him to Babylon to the land of the Chaldeans, yet shall he not see it though he shall die there. And I will scatter toward every wind all that are about him to help him, and all his bands, and I will draw out the sword after them. And they shall know that I am the Lord when I shall scatter them among the nations, and disperse them in the countries. But I will leave a few men of them from the sword, from the famine, and from the pestilence, that they may declare all their abominations among the heathen whither they come and they shall know that I am the Lord.

Moreover the word of the Lord came to me, saying, Son of man, eat thy bread with quaking, and drink thy water with trembling and with carefulness, and say unto the people of the land, Thus saith the Lord God of the inhabitants of Jerusalem and of the land of Israel, They shall eat their bread with carefulness, and drink their water with astonishment, that her land may be desolate from all that is therein because of the violence of all them that dwell therein. And the cities that are inhabited shall be laid waste, and the land shall be desolate, and ye shall know that I am the Lord.

5 AND the word of the Lord came unto me, saying, Son of man, what is that proverb that ye have in the land of Israel saying, The days are prolonged and every vision faileth? Tell them therefore, Thus saith the Lord God, I will make this proverb to cease and they shall no more use it as a proverb in Israel, but say unto them, The days are at hand and the effect of every vision. For there shall be no more any vain vision nor flattering divination within the house of Israel. For I am the Lord, I will speak and the word that I shall speak shall come to pass, it shall be no more prolonged, for in your days, O rebellious house will I say the word and will perform it, saith the Lord God.

Again the word of the Lord came to me, saying, Son of man, behold, they of the house of Israel say, The vision that he seeth is for many days to come and he prophesieth of the times that are far off. Therefore say unto them, Thus saith the Lord God, There shall none of my words be prolonged anymore, but the word which I have spoken shall be done, saith the Lord God.

And the word of the Lord came unto me, saying, Son of man, prophesy against the prophets of Israel that prophesy, and say thou unto them that prophesy out of their own hearts, Hear ye the word of the Lord, thus saith the Lord God, Wo unto the foolish prophets that follow their own spirit, and have seen nothing. O Israel, thy prophets are like the foxes in the deserts. Ye have not gone up into the gaps, neither made up the hedge for the house of Israel to stand in the battle in the day of the Lord. They have seen vanity and lying divination, saying, The Lord saith, and the Lord hath not sent them, and they have made others to hope that they would confirm the word. Have ye not seen a vain vision and have ye not spoken a lying divination, whereas ye say, The Lord saith it, albeit I have not spoken?

Therefore thus saith the Lord God, Because ye have spoken vanity and seen lies, therefore behold, I am against you, saith the Lord God. And mine hand shall be upon the prophets that see vanity and that divine lies, they shall not be in the assembly of my people, neither shall they be written in the writing of the house of Israel, neither shall they enter into the land of Israel, and ye shall know that I am the Lord God. Because, even because they have seduced my people saying, Peace, and there was no peace, and one built up a wall and lo, others daubed it with untempered mortar, say unto them which daub it with untempered mortar that it shall fall, there shall be an overflowing shower, and ye, O great hailstones, shall fall, and a stormy wind shall rend it. Lo, when the wall is fallen, shall it not be said unto you, Where is the daubing wherewith ye have daubed it? Therefore thus saith the Lord God, I will even rend it with a stormy wind in my fury, and there shall be an overflowing shower in mine anger, and great hailstones in my fury to consume it. So will I break down the wall that ye have daubed with untempered mortar and bring it down to the ground so that the foundation thereof shall be discovered, and it shall fall, and ye shall be consumed in the midst thereof, and ye shall know that I am the Lord. Thus will I accomplish my wrath upon the wall, and upon them that have daubed it with untempered mortar, and will say unto you, The wall is no more, neither they that daubed it, to wit the prophets of Israel which prophesy concerning Jerusalem, and which see visions of peace for her and there is no peace, saith the Lord God.

Likewise, thou son of man, set thy face against the daughters of thy people which prophesy out of their own heart and prophesy thou against them. And say, Thus saith the Lord God, Wo to the women that sew pillows to all armholes and make kerchiefs upon the head of every stature to hunt souls. Will ye hunt the souls of my people and will ye save the souls alive that come unto you? And will ye pollute me among my people for handfuls of barley and for pieces of bread, to slay the souls that should not die, and to save the souls alive that should not live, by your lying to my people that hear your lies?

Wherefore thus saith the Lord God, Behold, I am against your pillows wherewith ye there hunt the souls to make them fly, and I will tear them from your arms and will let the souls go, even the souls that ye hunt to make them fly. Your kerchiefs also will I tear and deliver my people out of your hand, and they shall be no more in your hand to be hunted, and ye shall know that I am the Lord. Because with lies ye have made the heart of the righteous sad whom I have not made sad, and strengthened the hands of the wicked that he should not return from his wicked way by promising him life, therefore ye shall see no more vanity, nor divine divinations, for I will deliver my people out of your hand and ye shall know that I am the Lord.

6 THEN came certain of the elders of Israel unto me, and sat before me. And the word of the Lord came unto me saying, Son of man, these men have set up their idols in their heart and put the stumbling block of their iniquity before their face; should I be inquired of at all by them? Therefore speak unto them and say unto them, Thus saith the Lord God, Every man of the house of Israel that setteth up his idols in his heart, and putteth the stumbling block of his iniquity before his face, and cometh to the prophet, I the Lord will answer him that cometh according to the multitude of his idols that I may take the house of Israel in their own heart because they are all estranged from me through their idols. Therefore say unto the house of Israel, Thus saith the Lord God, Repent and turn yourselves from your idols and turn away your faces from all your abominations. For everyone of the house of Israel, or of the stranger that sojourneth in Israel, which separateth himself from me, and setteth up his idols in his heart, and putteth the stumbling block of his iniquity before his face, and cometh to a prophet to inquire of him concerning me, I the Lord will answer him by myself, and I will set my face against that man, and will make him a sign and a proverb, and I will cut him off from the midst of my people, and ye shall know that I am the Lord. And if the prophet be deceived when he hath spoken a thing, I the Lord have not deceived that prophet, therefore I will stretch out my hand upon him, and will destroy him from the midst of my people Israel. And they shall bear the punishment of their iniquity, the punishment of the prophet shall be even as the punishment of him that seeketh unto him, that the house of Israel may go no more astray from me neither be polluted anymore with all their transgressions, but that they may be my people and I may be their God, saith the Lord God.

The word of the Lord came again to me, saying, Son of man, when the land sinneth against me by trespassing grievously, then I will stretch out mine hand upon it, and will break the staff of the bread thereof, and will send famine upon it, and will cut off man and beast from it; though these three men, Noah, Daniel, and Job were in it they should deliver but their own souls by their righteousness, saith the Lord God. If I cause noisome beasts to pass through the land and they spoil it so that it be desolate that no man may pass through because of the beasts, though these three men were in it, as I live, saith the Lord God, they shall deliver neither sons nor daughters, they only shall be delivered, but the land shall be desolate. Or if I bring a sword upon that land, and say, Sword, go through the land, so that I cut off man and beast from it, though these three men were in it, as I live, saith the Lord God, they shall deliver neither sons nor daughters, but they only shall be delivered themselves. Or if I send a pestilence into that land and pour out my fury upon it in blood to cut off from it man and beast, though Noah, Daniel, and Job were in it, as I live, saith the Lord God, they shall deliver neither son nor daughter, they shall but deliver their own souls by their righteousness. For thus saith the Lord God, How much more when I send my four sore judgments upon Jerusalem, the sword, and the famine, and the noisome beast, and the pestilence, to cut off from it man and beast? Yet, behold, therein shall be left a remnant that shall be brought forth, both sons and daughters, behold, they shall come forth unto you, and ye shall see their way and their doings, and ye shall be comforted concerning the evil that I have brought upon Jerusalem, even concerning all that I have brought upon it. And they shall comfort you when ye see their ways and their doings and ye shall know that I have not done without cause all that I have done in it, saith the Lord God.

And the word of the Lord came unto me, saying, Son of man, What is the vine tree more than any tree or than a branch which is among the trees of the forest? Shall wood be taken thereof to do any work? Or will men take a pin of it to hang any vessel thereon? Behold, it is cast into the fire for fuel, the fire devoureth both the ends of it and the midst of it is burned. Is it meet for any work? Behold, when it was whole it was meet for no work; how much less shall it be meet yet for any work when the fire hath devoured it and it is burned? Therefore thus saith the Lord God, As the vine tree among the trees of the forest which I have given to the fire for fuel, so will I give the inhabitants of Jerusalem. And I will set my face against them, they shall go out from one fire and another fire shall devour them, and ye shall know that I am the Lord when I set my face against them. And I will make the land desolate because they have committed a trespass, saith the Lord God.

Again the word of the Lord came unto me, saying, Son of man, cause Jerusalem to know her abominations and say, Thus saith the Lord God unto Jerusalem, Thy birth and thy nativity is of the land of Canaan, thy father was an Amorite and thy mother a Hittite. And as for thy nativity, in the day thou wast born thy navel was not cut, neither wast thou washed in water to supple thee, thou wast not salted at all nor swaddled at all. None eye pitied thee to do any of these unto thee, to have compassion upon thee, but thou wast cast out in the open field, to the loathing of thy person in the day that thou wast born.

And when I passed by thee, and saw thee polluted in thine own blood I said unto thee when thou wast in thy blood, Live. Yea, I said unto thee when thou wast in thy blood, Live. I have caused thee to multiply as the bud of the field, and thou hast increased and waxen great, and thou art come to excellent ornaments, thy breasts are fashioned, and thine hair is grown, whereas thou wast naked and bare. Now when I passed by thee and looked upon thee, behold, thy time was the time of love, and I spread my skirt over thee and covered thy nakedness, yea, I sware unto thee and entered into a covenant with thee, saith the Lord God, and thou becamest mine. Then washed I thee with water, yea, I thoroughly washed away thy blood from thee and I anointed thee with oil. I clothed thee also with broidered work and shod thee with badgers' skin, and I girded thee about with fine linen and I covered thee with silk. I decked thee also with ornaments, and I put bracelets upon thy hands, and a chain on thy neck. And I put a jewel on thy forehead, and earrings in thine ears, and a beautiful crown upon thine head. Thus wast thou decked with gold and silver, and thy raiment was of fine linen and silk and broidered work; thou didst eat fine flour, and honey, and oil, and thou wast exceeding beautiful, and thou didst prosper into a kingdom. And thy renown went forth among the heathen for thy beauty, for it was perfect through my comeliness which I had put upon thee, saith the Lord God.

But thou didst trust in thine own beauty, and playedst the harlot because of thy renown, and pouredst out thy fornications on everyone that passed by; his it was. And of thy garments thou didst take, and deckedst thy high places with divers colors, and playedst the harlot thereupon, the like things shall not come neither shall it be so. Thou hast also taken thy fair jewels of my gold and of my silver which I had given thee and madest to thyself images of men, and didst commit whoredom with them, and tookest thy broidered garments and coveredst them, and thou hast set mine oil and mine incense before them. My meat also which I gave thee, fine flour, and oil, and honey wherewith I fed thee, thou hast even set it before them for a sweet savor, and thus it was saith the Lord God. Moreover thou hast taken thy sons and thy daughters whom thou hast born unto me, and these hast thou sacrificed unto them to be devoured. Is this of thy whoredoms a small matter, that thou hast slain my children and delivered them to cause them to pass through the fire for them? And in all thine abominations and thy whoredoms thou hast not remembered the days of thy youth when thou wast naked and bare and wast polluted in thy blood.

And it came to pass after all thy wickedness (wo, wo unto thee, saith the Lord God), that thou hast also built unto thee an eminent place and hast made thee a high place in every street. Thou hast built thy high place at every head of the way, and hast made thy beauty to be abhorred, and hast opened thy feet to everyone that passed by, and multiplied thy whoredoms. Thou hast also committed fornication with the Egyptians thy neighbors great of flesh and hast increased thy whoredoms to provoke me to anger. Behold, therefore I have stretched out my hand over thee and have diminished thine ordinary food, and delivered thee unto the will of them that hate thee, the daughters of the Philistines, which are ashamed of thy lewd way. Thou hast played the whore also with the Assyrians because thou wast unsatiable, yea, thou hast played the harlot with them and yet couldst not be satisfied. Thou hast moreover multiplied thy fornication in the land of Canaan unto Chaldea and yet thou wast not satisfied herewith.

How weak is thine heart, saith the Lord God, seeing thou doest all these things, the work of an imperious whorish woman, in that thou buildest thine eminent place in the head of every way, and makest thine high pace in every street, and hast not been as a harlot, in that thou scornest hire, but as a wife that committeth adultery which taketh strangers instead of her husband. They give gifts to all whores, but thou givest thy gifts to all thy lovers and hirest them that they may come unto thee on every side for thy whoredom. And the contrary is in thee from other women in thy whoredoms, whereas none followeth thee to commit whoredoms, and in that thou givest a reward and no reward is given unto thee, therefore thou art contrary.

Wherefore, O harlot, hear the word of the Lord: Thus saith the Lord God, Because thy filthiness was poured out and thy nakedness discovered through thy whoredoms with thy lovers, and with all the idols of thy abominations, and by the blood of thy children which thou didst give unto them, behold, therefore I will gather all thy lovers with whom thou hast taken pleasure, and all them that thou hast loved, with all them that thou hast hated, I will even gather them round about against thee and will discover thy nakedness unto them that they may see all thy nakedness. And I will judge thee as women that break wedlock and shed blood are judged, and I will give thee blood in fury and jealousy. And I will also give thee into their hand and they shall throw down thine eminent place, and shall break down thy high places, they shall strip thee also of thy clothes, and shall take thy fair jewels, and leave thee naked and bare. They shall also bring up a company against thee, and they shall stone thee with stones, and thrust thee through with their swords. And they shall burn thine houses with fire, and execute judgments upon thee in the sight of many women, and I will cause thee to cease from playing the harlot, and thou also shalt give no hire anymore. So will I make my fury toward thee to rest and my jealousy shall depart from thee, and I will be quiet and will be no more angry. Because thou hast not remembered the days of thy youth, but hast fretted me in all these things, behold, therefore I also will recompense thy way upon thine head, saith the Lord God, and thou shalt not commit this lewdness above all thine abominations.

Behold, everyone that useth proverbs shall use this proverb against thee, saying, As is the mother, so is her daughter. Thou art thy mother's daughter that loatheth her husband and her children, and thou art the sister of thy sisters which loathed their husbands and their children; your mother was a Hittite and your father an Amorite. And thine elder sister is Samaria, she and her daughters that dwell at thy left hand, and thy younger sister that dwelleth at thy right hand is Sodom and her daughters. Yet hast thou not walked after their ways nor done after their abominations, but, as if that were a very little thing, thou wast corrupted more than they in all thy ways. As I live, saith the Lord God, Sodom thy sister hath not done, she nor her daughters, as thou hast done, thou and thy daughters. Behold, this was the iniquity of thy sister Sodom: pride, fullness of bread, and abundance of idleness was in her and in her daughters, neither did she strengthen the hand of the poor and needy. And they were haughty and committed abomination before me, therefore I took them away as I saw good. Neither hath Samaria committed half of thy sins, but thou hast multiplied thine abominations more than they and hast justified thy sisters in all thine abominations which thou hast done. Thou also, which hast judged thy sisters, bear thine own shame for thy sins that thou hast committed more abominable than they; they are more righteous than thou, yea, be thou confounded also and bear thy shame in that thou hast justified thy sisters.

When I shall bring again their captivity, the captivity of Sodom and her daughters and the captivity of Samaria and her daughters, then will I bring again the captivity of thy captives in the midst of them, that thou mayest bear thine own shame, and mayest be confounded in all that thou hast done in that thou art a comfort unto them. When thy sisters, Sodom and her daughters, shall return to their former estate, and Samaria and her daughters shall return to their former estate, then thou and thy daughters shall return to your former estate. For thy sister Sodom was not mentioned by thy mouth in the day of thy pride, before thy wickedness was discovered, as at the time of thy reproach of the daughters of Syria and all that are round about her, the daughters of the Philistines, which despise thee round about. Thou hast borne thy lewdness and thine abominations, saith the Lord.

For thus saith the Lord God, I will even deal with thee as thou hast done, which hast despised the oath in breaking the covenant. Nevertheless, I will remember my covenant with thee in the days of thy youth and I will establish unto thee an everlasting covenant. Then thou shalt remember thy ways and be ashamed, when thou shalt receive thy sisters, thine elder and thy younger, and I will give them unto thee for daughters, but not by thy covenant. And I will establish my covenant with thee and thou shalt know that I am the Lord, that thou mayest remember and be confounded and never open thy mouth anymore because of thy shame when I am pacified toward thee for all that thou hast done, saith the Lord God.

7 AND the word of the Lord came unto me, saying, Son of man, put forth a riddle and speak a parable unto the house of Israel and say, Thus saith the Lord God, A great eagle with great wings, long winged, full of feathers which had divers colors, came unto Lebanon and took the highest branch of the cedar, he cropped off the top of his young twigs and carried it into a land of traffic; he set it in a city of merchants. He took also the seed of the land and planted it in a fruitful field, he placed it by great waters and set it as a willow tree. And it grew and became a spreading vine of low stature whose branches turned toward him, and the roots thereof were under him so it became a vine, and brought forth branches, and shot forth sprigs.

There was also another great eagle with great wings and many feathers, and, behold, this vine did bend her roots toward him and shot forth her branches toward him that he might water it by the furrows of her plantation. It was planted in a good soil by great waters that it might bring forth branches and that it might bear fruit, that it might be a goodly vine. Say thou, Thus saith the Lord God, shall it prosper? Shall he not pull up the roots thereof and cut off the fruit thereof that it wither? It shall wither in all the leaves of her spring, even without great power or many people to pluck it up by the roots thereof. Yea, behold, being planted, shall it prosper? Shall it not utterly wither when the east wind toucheth it? It shall wither in the furrows where it grew.

Moreover the word of the Lord came unto me, saying, Say now to the rebellious house, know ye not what these things mean? Tell them, Behold, the king of Babylon is come to Jerusalem and hath taken the king thereof, and the princes thereof, and led them with him to Babylon. And hath taken of the king's seed and made a covenant with him, and hath taken an oath of him. He hath also taken the mighty of the land, that the kingdom might be base, that it might not lift itself up, but that by keeping of his covenant it might stand. But he rebelled against him in sending his ambassadors into Egypt that they might give him horses and much people. Shall he prosper? Shall he escape that doeth such things? Or shall he break the covenant and be delivered? As I live, saith the Lord God, surely in the place where the king dwelleth that made him king, whose oath he despised and whose covenant he brake, even with him in the midst of Babylon he shall die. Neither shall Pharaoh with his mighty army and great company make for him in the war by casting up mounts and building forts to cut off many persons, seeing he despised the oath by breaking the covenant when lo, he had given his hand and hath done all these things, he shall not escape. Therefore thus saith the Lord God, As I live, surely mine oath that he hath despised and my covenant that he hath broken, even it will I recompense upon his own head. And I will spread my net upon him and he shall be taken in my snare, and I will bring him to Babylon and will plead with him there for his trespass that he hath trespassed against me. And all his fugitives with all his bands shall fall by the sword, and they that remain shall be scattered toward all winds, and ye shall know that I the Lord have spoken it.

Thus saith the Lord God, I will also take of the highest branch of the high cedar, and will set it, I will crop off from the top of his young twigs a tender one and will plant it upon a high mountain and eminent. In the mountain of the height of Israel will I plant it, and it shall bring forth boughs, and bear fruit, and be a goodly cedar, and under it shall dwell all fowl of every wing; in the shadow of the branches thereof shall they dwell. And all the trees of the field shall know that I the Lord have brought down the high tree, have exalted the low tree, have dried up the green tree, and have made the dry tree to flourish; I the Lord have spoken and have done it.

8 THE word of the Lord came unto me again, saying, What mean ye, that ye use this proverb concerning the land of Israel saying, The fathers have eaten sour grapes and the children's teeth are set on edge? As I live, saith the Lord God, ye shall not have occasion anymore to use this proverb in Israel. Behold, all souls are mine, as the soul of the father, so also the soul of the son is mine, the soul that sinneth, it shall die.

But if a man be just, and do that which is lawful and right and hath not eaten upon the mountains, neither hath lifted up his eyes to the idols of the house of Israel, neither hath defiled his neighbor's wife, neither hath come near to a menstruous woman, and hath not oppressed any, but hath restored to the debtor his pledge, hath spoiled none by violence, hath given his bread to the hungry, and hath covered the naked with a garment, he that hath not given forth upon usury, neither hath taken any increase, that hath withdrawn his hand from iniquity, hath executed true judgment between man and man, hath walked in my statutes and hath kept my judgments to deal truly, he is just, he shall surely live, saith the Lord God.

If he beget a son that is a robber, a shedder of blood, and that doeth the like to any one of these things, and that doeth not any of those duties, but even hath eaten upon the mountains, and defiled his neighbor's wife, hath oppressed the poor and needy, hath spoiled by violence, hath not restored the pledge and hath lifted up his eyes to the idols, hath committed abomination, hath given forth upon usury and hath taken increase, shall he then live? He shall not live, he hath done all these abominations, he shall surely die, his blood shall be upon him.

Now lo, if he beget a son that seeth all his father's sins which he hath done, and considereth and doeth not such like, that hath not eaten upon the mountains, neither hath lifted up his eyes to the idols of the house of Israel, hath not defiled his neighbor's wife, neither hath oppressed any, hath not withholden the pledge, neither hath spoiled by violence, but hath given his bread to the hungry and hath covered the naked with a garment, that hath taken off his hand from the poor, that hath not received usury nor increase, hath executed my judgments, hath walked in my statutes, he shall not die for the iniquity of his father, he shall surely live. As for his father, because he cruelly oppressed, spoiled his brother by violence, and did that which is not good among his people, lo, even he shall die in his iniquity.

Yet say ye, Why? Doth not the son bear the iniquity of the father? When the son hath done that which is lawful and right, and hath kept all my statutes and hath done them, he shall surely live. The soul that sinneth, it shall die. The son shall not bear the iniquity of the father, neither shall the father bear the iniquity of the son, the righteousness of the righteous shall be upon him, and the wickedness of the wicked shall be upon him. But if the wicked will turn from all his sins that he hath committed, and keep all my statutes, and do that which is lawful and right, he shall surely live, he shall not die. All his transgressions that he hath committed, they shall not be mentioned unto him, in his righteousness that he hath done he shall live. Have I any pleasure at all that the wicked should die? saith the Lord God, and not that he should return from his ways and live?

But when the righteous turneth away from his righteousness, and committeth iniquity and doeth according to all the abominations that the wicked man doeth, shall he live? All his righteousness that he hath done shall not be mentioned in his trespass that he hath trespassed and in his sin that he hath sinned, in them shall he die. Yet ye say, The way of the Lord is not equal. Hear now, O house of Israel, Is not my way equal? Are not your ways unequal? When a righteous man turneth away from his righteousness and committeth iniquity, and dieth in them, for his iniquity that he hath done shall he die. Again, when the wicked man turneth away from his wickedness that he hath committed and doeth that which is lawful and right, he shall save his soul alive. Because he considereth and turneth away from all his transgressions that he hath committed, he shall surely live, he shall not die. Yet saith the house of Israel, The way of the Lord is not equal. O house of Israel, are not my ways equal? are not your ways unequal?

Therefore I will judge you, O house of Israel, everyone according to his ways, saith the Lord God. Repent and turn yourselves from all your transgressions so iniquity shall not be your ruin. Cast away from you all your transgressions whereby ye have transgressed and make you a new heart and a new spirit, for why will ye die, O house of Israel? For I have no pleasure in the death of him that dieth, saith the Lord God, wherefore turn ye and live.

Moreover, take thou up a lamentation for the princes of Israel, and say, What is thy mother? A lioness, she lay down among lions, she nourished her whelps among young lions. And she brought up one of her whelps: it became a young lion, and it learned to catch the prey, it devoured men. The nations also heard of him, he was taken in their pit and they brought him with chains unto the land of Egypt. Now when she saw that she had waited and her hope was lost, then she took another of her whelps and made him a young lion. And he went up and down among the lions, he became a young lion and learned to catch the prey and devoured men. And he knew their desolate palaces, and he laid waste their cities, and the land was desolate, and the fullness thereof by the noise of his roaring. Then the nations set against him on every side from the provinces and spread their net over him, he was taken in their pit. And they put him in ward in chains, and brought him to the king of Babylon, they brought him into holds, that his voice should no more be heard upon the mountains of Israel.

Thy mother is like a vine, in my blood, planted by the waters, she was fruitful and full of branches by reason of many waters. And she had strong rods for the scepters of them that bare rule, and her stature was exalted among the thick branches, and she appeared in her height with the multitude of her branches. But she was plucked up in fury, she was cast down to the ground and the east wind dried up her fruit, her strong rods were broken and withered, the fire consumed them. And now she is planted in the wilderness, in a dry and thirsty ground. And fire is gone out of a rod of her branches, which hath devoured her fruit, so that she hath no strong rod to be a scepter to rule. This is a lamentation and shall be for a lamentation.

9 AND it came to pass in the seventh year, in the fifth month, the tenth day of the month, that certain of the elders of Israel came to inquire of the Lord, and sat before me. Then came the word of the Lord unto me, saying, Son of man speak unto the elders of Israel and say unto them, Thus saith the Lord God, Are ye come to inquire of me? As I live, saith the Lord God, I will not be inquired of by you. Wilt thou judge them, son of man, wilt thou judge them? Cause them to know the abominations of their fathers and say unto them, Thus saith the Lord God, In the day when I chose Israel, and lifted up mine hand unto the seed of the house of Jacob, and made myself known unto them in the land of Egypt, when I lifted up mine hand unto them, saying, I am the Lord your God, in the day that I lifted up mine hand unto them to bring them forth of the land of Egypt into a land that I had espied for them, flowing with milk and honey which is the glory of all lands, then said I unto them, Cast ye away every man the abominations of his eyes and defile not yourselves with the idols of Egypt, I am the Lord your God. But they rebelled against me and would not hearken unto me, they did not every man cast away the abominations of their eyes, neither did they forsake the idols of Egypt, then I said, I will pour out my fury upon them, to accomplish my anger against them in the midst of the land of Egypt. But I wrought for my name's sake that it should not be polluted before the heathen among whom they were, in whose sight I made myself known unto them in bringing them forth out of the land of Egypt. Wherefore I caused them to go forth out of the land of Egypt, and brought them into the wilderness. And I gave them my statutes and showed them my judgments, which if a man do, he shall even live in them. Moreover also I gave them my sabbaths to be a sign between me and them, that they might know that I am the Lord that sanctify them. But the house of Israel rebelled against me in the wilderness, they walked not in my statutes and they despised my judgments, which if a man do, he shall even live in them. And my sabbaths they greatly polluted, then I said I would pour out my fury upon them in the wilderness to

consume them. But I wrought for my name's sake, that it should not be polluted before the heathen, in whose sight I brought them out. Yet also I lifted up my hand unto them in the wilderness, that I would not bring them into the land which I had given them, flowing with milk and honey, which is the glory of all lands, because they despised my judgments and walked not in my statutes, but polluted my sabbaths, for their heart went after their idols. Nevertheless mine eyes spared them from destroying them, neither did I make an end of them in the wilderness. But I said unto their children in the wilderness, Walk ye not in the statutes of your fathers, neither observe their judgments, nor defile yourselves with their idols,

I am the Lord your God, walk in my statutes, and keep my judgments, and do them, and hallow my sabbaths, and they shall be a sign between me and you, that ye may know that I am the Lord your God. Notwithstanding, the children rebelled against me, they walked not in my statutes, neither kept my judgments to do them, which if a man do, he shall even live in them, they polluted my sabbaths, then I said I would pour out my fury upon them to accomplish my anger against them in the wilderness. Nevertheless I withdrew mine hand, and wrought for my name's sake that it should not be polluted in the sight of the heathen, in whose sight I brought them forth. I lifted up mine hand unto them also in the wilderness, that I would scatter them among the heathen and disperse them through the countries because they had not executed my judgments, but had despised my statutes, and had polluted my sabbaths, and their eyes were after their fathers' idols. Wherefore I gave them also statutes that were not good, and judgments whereby they should not live, and I polluted them in their own gifts, in that they caused to pass through the fire all that openeth the womb, that I might make them desolate, to the end that they might know that I am the Lord.

Therefore, son of man, speak unto the house of Israel and say unto them, Thus saith the Lord God, Yet in this your fathers have blasphemed me, in that they have committed a trespass against me. For when I had brought them into the land, for the which I lifted up mine hand to give it to them, then they saw every high hill and all the thick trees and they offered there their sacrifices, and there they presented the provocation of their offering; there also they made their sweet savor and poured out there their drink offerings. Then I said unto them, What is the high place whereunto ye go? And the name thereof is called Bamah unto this day. Wherefore say unto the house of Israel, Thus saith the Lord God, Ye are polluted after the manner of your fathers and ye commit whoredom after their abominations. For when ye offer your gifts, when ye make your sons to pass through the fire, ye pollute yourselves with all your idols even unto this day, and shall I be inquired of by you, O house of Israel? As I live, saith the Lord God, I will not be inquired of by you. And that which cometh into your mind shall not be at all, that ye say, We will be as the heathen, as the families of the countries, to serve wood and stone.

As I live, saith the Lord God, surely with a mighty hand and with a stretched out arm, and with fury poured out will I rule over you, and I will bring you out from the people and will gather you out of the countries wherein ye are scattered, with a mighty hand, and with a stretched out arm, and with fury poured out. And I will bring you into the wilderness of the people and there will I plead with you face to face. Like as I pleaded with you fathers in the wilderness of the land of Egypt so will I plead with you, saith the Lord God. And I will cause you to pass under the rod, and I will bring you into the bond of the covenant, and I will purge out from among you the rebels and them that transgress against me. I will bring them forth out of the country where they sojourn, and they shall not enter into the land of Israel, and ye shall know that I am the Lord.

As for you, O house of Israel, thus saith the Lord God, Go ye, serve ye everyone his idols and hereafter also if ye will not hearken unto me, but pollute ye my holy name no more with your gifts and with your idols. For in mine holy mountain, in the mountain of the height of Israel, saith the Lord God, there shall all the house of Israel, all of them in the land, serve me; there will I accept them and there will I require your offerings, and the firstfruits of your oblations with all your holy things. I will accept you with your sweet savor when I bring you out from the people, and gather you out of the countries wherein ye have been scattered, and I will be sanctified in you before the heathen. And ye shall know that I am the Lord when I shall bring you into the land of Israel, into the country for the which I lifted up mine hand to give it to your fathers. And there shall ye remember your ways and all your doings wherein ye have been defiled, and ye shall loathe yourselves in your own sight for all your evils that ye have committed. And ye shall know that I am the Lord when I have wrought with you for my name's sake, not according to your wicked ways, nor according to your corrupt doings, O ye house of Israel, saith the Lord God.

Moreover the word of the Lord came unto me, saying, Son of man, set thy face toward the south, and drop thy word toward the south, and prophesy against the forest of the south field, and say to the forest of the south, Hear the word of the Lord. Thus saith the Lord God, Behold, I will kindle a fire in thee, and it shall devour every green tree in thee, and every dry tree, the flaming flame shall not be quenched and all faces from the south to the north shall be burned therein. And all flesh shall see that I the Lord have kindled it, it shall not be quenched. Then said I, Ah Lord God, they say of me, Doth he not speak parables?

And the word of the Lord came unto me, saying, Son of man, set thy face toward Jerusalem and drop thy word toward the holy places, and prophesy against the land of Israel and say to the land of Israel, Thus saith the Lord, Behold, I am against thee and will draw forth my sword out of his sheath and will cut off from thee the righteous and the wicked. Seeing then that I will cut off from thee the righteous and the wicked, therefore shall my sword go forth out of his sheath against all flesh from the south to the north, that all flesh may know that I the Lord have drawn forth my sword out of his sheath; it shall not return anymore. Sigh therefore, thou son of man, with the breaking of thy loins and with bitterness sigh before their eyes. And it shall be when they say unto thee, Wherefore sighest thou? that thou shalt answer, For the tidings, because it cometh, and every heart shall melt, and all hands shall be feeble, and every spirit shall faint, and all knees be weak as water; behold, it cometh and shall be brought to pass, saith the Lord God.

Again the word of the Lord came unto me, saying, Son of man, prophesy and say, Thus saith the Lord, Say, A sword, a sword is sharpened and also furbished, it is sharpened to make a sore slaughter, it is furbished that it may glitter, should we then make mirth? It contemneth the rod of my son, as every tree. And he hath given it to be furbished that it may be handled; this sword is sharpened and it is furbished to give it into the hand of the slayer. Cry and howl, son of man, for it shall be upon my people, it shall be upon all the princes of Israel, terrors by reason of the sword shall be upon my people, smite therefore upon thy thigh. Because it is a trial, and what if the sword contemn even the rod? it shall be no more, saith the Lord God. Thou therefore, son of man, prophesy, and smite thine hands together, and let the sword be doubled the third time, the sword of the slain, it is the sword of the great men that are slain which entereth into their privy chambers. I have set the point of the sword against all their gates, that their heart may faint and their ruins be multiplied, ah! It is made bright, it is wrapped up for the slaughter. Go thee one way or other, either on the right hand or on the left, whithersoever thy face is set. I will also smite mine hands together and I will cause my fury to rest. I the Lord have said it.

The word of the Lord came unto me again, saying, Also, thou son of man, appoint thee two ways, that the sword of the king of Babylon may come, both twain shall come forth out of one land, and choose thou a place, choose it at the head of the way to the city. Appoint a way, that the sword may come to Rabbath of the Ammonites and to Judah in Jerusalem the defensed. For the king of Babylon stood at the parting of the way, at the head of the two ways, to use divination, he made his arrows bright, he consulted with images, he looked in the liver. At his right hand was the divination for Jerusalem, to appoint captains, to open the mouth in the slaughter, to lift up the voice with shouting, to appoint battering rams against the gates, to cast a mount, and to build a fort. And it shall be unto them as a false divination in their sight, to them that have sworn oaths, but he will call to remembrance the iniquity that they may be taken. Therefore thus saith the Lord God, Because ye have made your iniquity to be remembered in that your transgressions are discovered so that in all your doings your sins do appear because, I say, that ye are come to remembrance, ye shall be taken with the hand.

And thou, profane wicked prince of Israel whose day is come when iniquity shall have an end, thus saith the Lord God, Remove the diadem and take off the crown, this shall not be the same; exalt him that is low and abase him that is high. I will overturn, overturn, overturn it, and it shall be no more until he come whose right it is and I will give it him.

10 AND thou, son of man, prophesy and say, Thus saith the Lord God concerning the Ammonites and concerning their reproach; even say thou, The sword, the sword is drawn, for the slaughter it is furbished, to consume because of the glittering, while they see vanity unto thee, while they divine a lie unto thee, to bring thee upon the necks of them that are slain, of the wicked whose day is come when their iniquity shall have an end. Shall I cause it to return into his sheath? I will judge thee in the place where thou wast created, in the land of thy nativity. And I will pour out mine indignation upon thee, I will blow against thee in the fire of my wrath and deliver thee into the hand of brutish men and skillful to destroy. Thou shalt be for fuel to the fire, thy blood shall be in the midst of the land, thou shalt be no more remembered, for I the Lord have spoken it.

Moreover the word of the Lord came unto me, saying, Now, thou son of man, wilt thou judge, wilt thou judge the bloody city? Yea, thou shalt show her all her abominations. Then say thou, Thus saith the Lord God, The city sheddeth blood in the midst of it that her time may come and maketh idols against herself to defile herself. Thou art become guilty in thy blood that thou hast shed, and hast defiled thyself in thine idols which thou hast made, and thou hast caused thy days to draw near, and art come even unto thy years, therefore have I made thee a reproach unto the heathen and a mocking to all countries. Those that be near and those that be far from thee shall mock thee which art infamous and much vexed. Behold, the princes of Israel, everyone were in thee to their power to shed blood. In thee have they set light by father and mother, in the midst of thee have they dealt by oppression with the stranger, in thee have they vexed the fatherless and the widow. Thou hast despised mine holy things and hast profaned my sabbaths. In thee are men that carry tales to shed blood, and in thee they eat upon the mountains, in the midst of thee they commit lewdness. In thee have they discovered their fathers' nakedness, in thee have they humbled her that was set apart for pollution. And one hath committed abomination with his neighbor's wife, and another hath lewdly defiled his daughter-in-law, in thee hath humbled his sister, his father's daughter. In thee have they taken gifts to shed blood, thou hast taken usury and increase, and thou hast greedily gained of thy neighbors by extortion and hast forgotten me, saith the Lord God. Behold, therefore I have smitten mine hand at thy dishonest gain which thou hast made and at thy blood which hath been in the midst of thee. Can thine heart endure, or can thine hands be strong, in the days that I shall deal with thee? I the Lord have spoken it and will do it. And I will scatter thee among the heathen, and disperse thee in the countries and will consume thy filthiness out of thee. And thou shalt take thine inheritance in thyself in the sight of the heathen, and thou shalt know that I am the Lord.

11 AND the word of the Lord came unto me, saying, Son of man, the house of Israel is to me become dross, all they are brass, and tin, and iron, and lead; in the midst of the furnace they are even the dross of silver. Therefore thus saith the Lord God, Because ye are all become dross, behold, therefore I will gather you into the midst of Jerusalem. As they gather silver, and brass, and iron, and lead, and tin, into the midst of the furnace, to blow the fire upon it to melt it, so will I gather you in mine anger and in my fury and I will leave you there and melt you. Yea, I will gather you and blow upon you in the fire of my wrath, and ye shall be melted in the midst thereof. As silver is melted in the midst of the furnace, so shall ye be melted in the midst thereof and ye shall know that I the Lord have poured out my fury upon you.

And the word of the Lord came unto me, saying, Son of man, say unto her, Thou art the land that is not cleansed nor rained upon in the day of indignation. There is a conspiracy of her prophets in the midst thereof; like a roaring lion ravening the prey they have devoured souls, they have taken the treasure and precious things, they have made her many widows in the midst thereof. Her priests have violated my law and have profaned mine holy things, they have put no difference between the holy and profane, neither have they showed difference between the unclean and the clean, and have hid their eyes from my sabbaths, and I am profaned among them. Her princes in the midst thereof are like wolves ravening the prey to shed blood and to destroy souls, to get dishonest gain. And her prophets have daubed them with untempered mortar, seeing vanity and divining lies unto them, saying, Thus saith the Lord God when the Lord hath not spoken. The people of the land have used oppression, and exercised robbery, and have vexed the poor and needy, yea, they have oppressed the stranger wrongfully. And I sought for a man among them that should make up the hedge and stand in the gap before me for the land, that I should not destroy it, but I found none. Therefore have I poured out mine indignation upon them, I have consumed them with the fire of my wrath, their own way have I recompensed upon their heads, saith the Lord God.

The word of the Lord came again unto me, saying, Son of man, there were two women, the daughters of one mother, and they committed whoredoms in Egypt, they committed whoredoms in their youth, there were their breasts pressed and there they bruised the teats of their virginity. And the names of them were Aholah the elder and Aholibah her sister, and they were mine, and they bare sons and daughters. Thus were their names: Samaria is Aholah, and Jerusalem Aholibah.

And Aholah played the harlot when she was mine and she doted on her lovers, on the Assyrians her neighbors hich were clothed with blue, captains and rulers, all of them desirable young men, horsemen riding upon horses. Thus she committed her whoredoms with them, with all them that were the chosen men of Assyria, and with all on whom she doted, with all their idols she defiled herself. Neither left she her whoredoms brought from Egypt, for in her youth they lay with her and they bruised the breasts of her virginity, and poured their whoredom upon her. Wherefore I have delivered her into the hand of her lovers, into the hand of the Assyrians upon whom she doted. These discovered her nakedness, they took her sons and her daughters, and slew her with the sword, and she became famous among women, for they had executed judgment upon her.

And when her sister Aholibah saw this, she was more corrupt in her inordinate love than she, and in her whoredoms more than her sister in her whoredoms. She doted upon the Assyrians her neighbors, captains and rulers clothed most gorgeously, horsemen riding upon horses, all of them desirable young men. Then I saw that she was defiled, that they took both one way, and that she increased her whoredoms, for when she saw men portrayed upon the walls, the images of the Chaldeans portrayed with vermilion, girded with girdles upon their loins, exceeding in dyed attire upon their heads, all of them princes to look to after the manner of the Babylonians of Chaldea, the land of their nativity, and as soon as she saw them with her eyes she doted upon them and sent messengers unto them into Chaldea. And the Babylonians came to her into the bed of love, and they defiled her with their whoredom, and she was polluted with them, and her mind was alienated from me by them. So she discovered her whoredoms and discovered her nakedness, then my mind was alienated from her like as my mind was alienated from her sister. Yet she multiplied her whoredoms, in calling to remembrance the days of her youth wherein she had played the harlot in the land of Egypt. For she doted upon their paramours, whose flesh is as the flesh of asses, and whose issue is like the issue of horses. Thus thou calledst to remembrance the lewdness of thy youth in bruising thy teats by the Egyptians for the paps of thy youth.

Therefore, O Aholibah, thus saith the Lord God, Behold, I will raise up thy lovers against thee by whom thy mind is alienated from me, and I will bring them against thee on every side, the Babylonians, and all the Chaldeans, Pekod, and Shoa, and Koa, and all the Assyrians with them, all of them desirable young men, captains and rulers, great lords and renowned, all of them riding upon horses. And they shall come against thee with chariots, wagons, and wheels, and with an assembly of people which shall set against thee buckler and shield and helmet round about, and I will set judgment before them, and they shall judge thee according to their judgments. And I will set my jealousy against thee and they shall deal furiously with thee, they shall take away thy nose and thine ears, and thy remnant shall fall by the sword; they shall take thy sons and thy daughters and thy residue shall be devoured by the fire. They shall also strip thee out of thy clothes and take away thy fair jewels. Thus will I make thy lewdness to cease from thee, and thy whoredom brought from the land of Egypt, so that thou shalt not lift up thine eyes unto them nor remember Egypt anymore. For thus saith the Lord God, Behold, I will deliver thee into the hand of them whom thou hatest, into the hand of them by whom thy mind is alienated, and they shall deal with thee hatefully, and shall take away all thy labor, and shall leave thee naked and bare, and the nakedness of thy whoredoms shall be discovered, both thy lewdness and thy whoredoms. I will do these things unto thee because thou hast gone a whoring after the heathen and because thou art polluted with their idols. Thou hast walked in the way of thy sister, therefore will I give her cup into thine hand. Thus saith the Lord God, Thou shalt drink of thy sister's cup deep and large, thou shalt be laughed to scorn and had in derision, it containeth much. Thou shalt be filled with drunkenness and sorrow, with the cup of astonishment and desolation, with the cup of thy sister Samaria. Thou shalt even drink it and suck it out, and thou shalt break the shreds thereof, and pluck off thine own breasts, for I have spoken it, saith the Lord God. Therefore thus saith the Lord God, Because thou hast forgotten me and cast me behind thy back, therefore bear thou also thy lewdness and thy whoredoms.

The Lord said moreover unto me, Son of man, wilt thou judge Aholah and Aholibah? Yea, declare unto them their abominations, that they have committed adultery and blood is in their hands, and with their idols have they committed adultery and have also caused their sons whom they bare unto me to pass for them through the fire, to devour them. Moreover this they have done unto me, they have defiled my sanctuary in the same day and have profaned my sabbaths. For when they had slain their children to their idols, then they came the same day into my sanctuary to profane it and lo, thus have they done in the midst of mine house. And furthermore, that ye have sent for men to come from far, unto whom a messenger was sent, and, lo, they came, for whom thou didst wash thyself, paintedst thy eyes, and deckedst thyself with ornaments. And satest upon a stately bed, and a table prepared before it, whereupon thou hast set mine incense and mine oil. And a voice of a multitude being at ease was with her, and with the men of the common sort were brought Sabeans from the wilderness, which put bracelets upon their hands and beautiful crowns upon their heads. Then said I unto her that was old in adulteries, Will they now commit whoredoms with her and she with them? Yet they went in unto her, as they go in unto a woman that playeth the harlot so went they in unto Aholah and unto Aholibah, the lewd women.

And the righteous men, they shall judge them after the manner of adulteresses and after the manner of women that shed blood because they are adulteresses and blood is in their hands. For thus saith the Lord God, I will bring up a company upon them and will give them to be removed and spoiled. And the company shall stone them with stones and dispatch them with their swords, they shall slay their sons and their daughters and burn up their houses with fire. Thus will I cause lewdness to cease out of the land that all women may be taught not to do after your lewdness. And they shall recompense your lewdness upon you and ye shall bear the sins of your idols and ye shall know that I am the Lord God.

Again in the ninth year, in the tenth month, in the tenth day of the month, the word of the Lord came unto me, saying, Son of man, write thee the name of the day, even of this same day, the king of Babylon set himself against Jerusalem this same day. And utter a parable unto the rebellious house, and say unto them, Thus saith the Lord God, Set on a pot, set it on, and also pour water into it, gather the pieces thereof into it, even every good piece, the thigh, and the shoulder, fill it with the choice bones. Take the choice of the flock, and burn also the bones under it, and make it boil well, and let them seethe the bones of it therein.

Wherefore thus saith the Lord God, Wo to the bloody city, to the pot whose scum is therein and whose scum is not gone out of it. Bring it out piece by piece, let no lot fall upon it. For her blood is in the midst of her, she set it upon the top of a rock, she poured it not upon the ground, to cover it with dust, that it might cause fury to come up to take vengeance, I have set her blood upon the top of a rock, that it should not be covered. Therefore thus saith the Lord God, Wo to the bloody city. I will even make the pile for fire great. Heap on wood, kindle the fire, consume the flesh, and spice it well, and let the bones be burned. Then set it empty upon the coals thereof, that the brass of it may be hot and may burn, and that the filthiness of it may be molten in it, that the scum of it may be consumed. She hath wearied herself with lies and her great scum went not forth out of her, her scum shall be in the fire. In thy filthiness is lewdness, because I have purged thee and thou wast not purged, thou shalt not be purged from thy filthiness anymore till I have caused my fury to rest upon thee. I, the Lord, have spoken it, it shall come to pass and I will do it, I will not go back, neither will I spare, neither will I repent, according to thy ways, and according to thy doings shall they judge thee, saith the Lord God.

Also the word of the Lord came unto me, saying, Son of man, behold, I take away from thee the desire of thine eyes with a stroke, yet neither shalt thou mourn nor weep, neither shall thy tears run down. Forbear to cry, make no mourning for the dead, bind the tire of thine head upon thee, and put on thy shoes upon thy feet, and cover not thy lips, and eat not the bread of men. So I spake unto the people in the morning, and at even my wife died, and I did in the morning as I was commanded.

And the people said unto me, Wilt thou not tell us what these things are to us that thou doest so? Then I answered them, The word of the Lord came unto me, saying, Speak unto the house of Israel, Thus saith the Lord God, Behold, I will profane my sanctuary, the excellency of your strength, the desire of your eyes, and that which your soul pitieth, and your sons and your daughters whom ye have left shall fall by the sword. And ye shall do as I have done, ye shall not cover your lips nor eat the bread of men. And your tires shall be upon your heads, and your shoes upon your feet, ye shall not mourn nor weep, but ye shall pine away for your iniquities and mourn one toward another. Thus Ezekiel is unto you a sign, according to all that he hath done shall ye do, and when this cometh, ye shall know that I am the Lord God.

Also, thou Son of man, shall it not be in the day when I take from them their strength, the joy of their glory, the desire of their eyes, and that whereupon they set their minds, their sons and their daughters, that he that escapeth in that day shall come unto thee, to cause thee to hear it with thine ears? In that day shall thy mouth be opened to him which is escaped, and thou shalt speak and be no more dumb, and thou shalt be a sign unto them, and they shall know that I am the Lord.

The word of the Lord came again unto me saying, Son of man, set thy face against the Ammonites, and prophesy against them and say unto the Ammonites, Hear the word of the Lord God: Thus saith the Lord God, Because thou saidst, Aha, against my sanctuary when it was profaned, and against the land of Israel when it was desolate, and against the house of Judah when they went into captivity, behold, therefore I will deliver thee to the men of the east for a possession, and they shall set their palaces in thee and make their dwellings in thee, they shall eat thy fruit and they shall drink thy milk. And I will make Rabbah a stable for camels, and the Ammonites a couching place for flocks, and ye shall know that I am the Lord. For thus saith the Lord God, Because thou hast clapped thine hands, and stamped with the feet, and rejoiced in heart with all thy despite against the land of Israel, behold, therefore I will stretch out mine hand upon thee, and will deliver thee for a spoil to the heathen, and I will cut thee off from the people, and I will cause thee to perish out of the countries, I will destroy thee, and thou shalt know that I am the Lord.

Thus saith the Lord God, Because that Moab and Seir do say, Behold, the house of Judah is like unto all the heathen, therefore, behold, I will open the side of Moab from the cities, from his cities which are on his frontiers, the glory of the country, Beth-jeshimoth, Baal-meon, and Kiria-thaim, unto the men of the east with the Ammonites, and will give them in possession, that the Ammonites may not be remembered among the nations. And I will execute judgments upon Moab, and they shall know that I am the Lord.

Thus saith the Lord God, Because that Edom hath dealt against the house of Judah by taking vengeance, and hath greatly offended, and revenged himself upon them, therefore thus saith the Lord God, I will also stretch out mine hand upon Edom and will cut off man and beast from it, and I will make it desolate from Teman, and they of Dedan shall fall by the sword. And I will lay my vengeance upon Edom by the hand of my people Israel, and they shall do in Edom according to mine anger and according to my fury, and they shall know my vengeance, saith the Lord God.

Thus saith the Lord God, Because the Philistines have dealt by revenge and have taken vengeance with a despiteful heart to destroy it for the old hatred, therefore thus saith the Lord God, Behold I will stretch out mine hand upon the Philistines, and I will cut off the Cherethim, and destroy the remnant of the seacoast. And I will execute great vengeance upon them with furious rebukes, and they shall know that I am the Lord when I shall lay my vengeance upon them.

12 AND it came to pass in the eleventh year, in the first day of the month, that the word of the Lord came unto me, saying, Son of man, because that Tyrus hath said against Jerusalem, Aha, she is broken that was the gates of the people, she is turned unto me, I shall be replenished, now she is laid waste, therefore thus saith the Lord God, Behold, I am against thee, O Tyrus, and will cause many nations to come up against thee as the sea causeth his waves to come up. And they shall destroy the walls of Tyrus and break down her towers, I will also scrape her dust from her and make her like the top of a rock. It shall be a place for the spreading of nets in the midst of the sea, for I have spoken it, saith the Lord God, and it shall become a spoil to the nations. And her daughters which are in the field shall be slain by the sword and they shall know that I am the Lord.

For thus saith the Lord God, Behold, I will bring upon Tyrus, Nebuchadrezzar king of Babylon, a king of kings, from the north with horses, and with chariots, and with horsemen, and companies, and much people. He shall slay with the sword thy daughters in the field, and he shall make a fort against thee, and cast a mount against thee, and lift up the buckler against thee. And he shall set engines of war against thy walls and with his axes he shall break down thy towers. By reason of the abundance of his horses their dust shall cover thee, thy walls shall shake at the noise of the horsemen, and of the wheels, and of the chariots, when he shall enter into thy gates as men enter into a city wherein is made a breach. With the hooves of his horses shall he tread down all thy streets, he shall slay thy people by the sword, and thy strong garrisons shall go down to the ground. And they shall make a spoil of thy riches and make a prey of thy merchandise, and they shall break down thy walls and destroy thy pleasant houses, and they shall lay thy stones and thy timber and thy dust in the midst of the water. And I will cause the noise of thy songs to cease and the sound of thy harps shall be no more heard. And I will make thee like the top of a rock, thou shalt be a place to spread nets upon, thou shalt be built no more, for I the Lord have spoken it, saith the Lord God.

Thus saith the Lord God to Tyrus, Shall not the isles shake at the sound of thy fall when the wounded cry, when the slaughter is made in the midst of thee? Then all the princes of the sea shall come down from their thrones, and lay away their robes, and put off their broidered garments. They shall clothe themselves with trembling, they shall sit upon the ground, and shall tremble at every moment, and be astonished at thee. And they shall take up a lamentation for thee and say to thee, How art thou destroyed, that wast inhabited of seafaring men, the renowned city which wast strong in the sea, she and her inhabitants, which cause their terror to be on all that haunt it! Now shall the isles tremble in the day of thy fall, yea, the isles that are in the sea shall be troubled at thy departure. For thus saith the Lord God, When I shall make thee a desolate city like the cities that are not inhabited, when I shall bring up the deep upon thee and great waters shall cover thee, when I shall bring thee down with them that descend into the pit with the people of old time, and shall set thee in the low parts of the earth, in places desolate of old with them that go down to the pit that thou be not inhabited, and I shall set glory in the land of the living, I will make thee a terror and thou shalt be no more, though thou be sought for, yet shalt thou never be found again, saith the Lord God.

The word of the Lord came again unto me, saying, Now, thou Son of man, take up a lamentation for Tyrus and say unto Tyrus, O thou that art situate at the entry of the sea, which art a merchant of the people for many isles, Thus saith the Lord God, O Tyrus, thou hast said, I am of perfect beauty. Thy borders are in the midst of the seas, thy builders have perfected thy beauty. They have made all thy ship boards of fir trees of Senir, they have taken cedars from Lebanon to make masts for thee. Of the oaks of Bashan have they made thine oars, the company of the Ashurites have made thy benches of ivory, brought out of the isles of Chittim. Fine linen with broidered work from Egypt was that which thou spreadest forth to be thy sail, blue and purple from the isles of Elishah was that which covered thee. The inhabitants of Zidon and Arvad were thy mariners, thy wise men, O Tyrus, that were in thee, were thy pilots. The ancients of Gebal and the wise men thereof were in thee thy caulkers, all the ships of the sea with their mariners were in thee to occupy thy merchandise. They of Persia and of Lud and of Phut were in thine army, thy men of war, they hanged the shield and helmet in thee, they set forth thy comeliness. The men of Arvad with thine army were upon thy walls round about, and the Gammadim were in thy towers, they hanged their shields upon thy walls round about, they have made thy beauty perfect.

Tarshish was thy merchant by reason of the multitude of all kinds of riches, with silver, iron, tin, and lead, they traded in thy fairs. Javan, Tubal, and Meshech, they were thy merchants, they traded the persons of men and vessels of brass in thy market. They of the house of Togarmah traded in thy fairs with horses and horsemen and mules. The men of Dedan were thy merchants, many isles were the merchandise of thine hand, they brought thee for a present, horns of ivory and ebony. Syria was thy merchant by reason of the multitude of the wares of thy making, they occupied in thy fairs with emeralds, purple, and broidered work, and fine linen, and coral, and agate. Judah, and the land of Israel, they were thy merchants, they traded in thy market wheat of Minnith, and Pannag, and honey, and oil, and balm. Damascus was thy merchant in the multitude of the wares of thy making, for the multitude of all riches, in the wine of Helbon, and white wool. Dan also and Javan going to and fro occupied in thy fairs, bright iron, cassia, and calamus, were in thy market. Dedan was thy merchant in precious clothes for chariots. Arabia, and all the princes of Kedar, they occupied with thee in lambs, and rams, and goats, in these were they thy merchants. The merchants of Sheba and Raamah, they were thy merchants, they occupied in thy fairs with chief of all spices, and with all precious stones, and gold. Haran, and Canneh, and Eden, the merchants of Sheba, Asshur, and Chilmad, were thy merchants. These were thy merchants in all sorts of things, in blue clothes, and broidered work, and in chests of rich apparel, bound with cords, and made of cedar, among thy merchandise.

The ships of Tarshish did sing of thee in thy market, and thou wast replenished, and made very glorious in the midst of the seas. Thy rowers have brought thee into great waters, the east wind hath broken thee in the midst of the seas. Thy riches and thy fairs, thy merchandise, thy mariners and thy pilots, thy caulker and the occupiers of thy merchandise, and all thy men of war, that are in thee and in all thy company which is in the midst of thee, shall fall into the midst of the seas in the day of thy ruin. The suburbs shall shake at the sound of the cry of thy pilots. And all that handle the oar, the mariners and all the pilots of the sea, shall come down from their ships, they shall stand upon the land, and shall cause their voice to be heard against thee, and shall cry bitterly, and shall cast up dust upon their heads, they shall wallow themselves in the ashes, and they shall make themselves utterly bald for thee, and gird them with sackcloth, and they shall weep for thee with bitterness of heart and bitter wailing. And in their wailing they shall take up a lamentation for thee, and lament over thee saying, What city is like Tyrus, like the destroyed in the midst of the sea? When thy wares went forth out of the seas, thou filledst many people, thou didst enrich the kings of the earth with the multitude of thy riches and of thy merchandise. In the time when thou shalt be broken by the seas in the depths of the waters, thy merchandise and all thy company in the midst of thee shall fall. All the inhabitants of the isles shall be astonished at thee, and their kings shall be sore afraid, they shall be troubled in their countenance. The merchants among the people shall hiss at thee, thou shalt be a terror and never shalt be anymore.

The word of the Lord came again unto me saying, Son of man, say unto the prince of Tyrus, Thus saith the Lord God, Because thine heart is lifted up and thou hast said, I am a god, I sit in the seat of God, in the midst of the seas, yet thou art a man, and not God, though thou set thine heart as the heart of God, behold, thou art wiser than Daniel, there is no secret that they can hide from thee, with thy wisdom and with thine understanding thou hast gotten thee riches, and hast gotten gold and silver into thy treasures. By thy great wisdom and by thy traffic hast thou increased thy riches, and thine heart is lifted up because of thy riches, therefore thus saith the Lord God, Because thou hast set thine heart as the heart of God, behold, therefore I will bring strangers upon thee, the terrible of the nations, and they shall draw their swords against the beauty of thy wisdom, and they shall defile thy brightness. They shall bring thee down to the pit, and thou shalt die the deaths of them that are slain in the midst of the seas. Wilt thou yet say before him that slayeth thee, I am God? But thou shalt be a man and no God in the hand of him that slayeth thee. Thou shalt die the deaths of the uncircumcised by the hand of strangers, for I have spoken it, saith the Lord God.

Moreover the word of the Lord came unto me, saying, Son of man, take up a lamentation upon the king of Tyrus, and say unto him, Thus saith the Lord God, Thou sealest up the sum, full of wisdom and perfect in beauty. Thou hast been in Eden, the garden of God, every precious stone was thy covering: the sardius, topaz, and the diamond, the beryl, the onyx, and the jasper, the sapphire, the emerald, and the carbuncle, and gold. The workmanship of thy tabrets and of thy pipes was prepared in thee in the day that thou wast created. Thou art the anointed cherub that covereth and I have set thee so, thou wast upon the holy mountain of God, thou hast walked up and down in the midst of the stones of fire. Thou wast perfect in thy ways from the day that thou wast created till iniquity was found in thee. By the multitude of thy merchandise they have filled the midst of thee with violence and thou hast sinned, therefore I will cast thee as profane out of the mountain of God and I will destroy thee, O covering cherub, from the midst of the stones of fire. Thine heart was lifted up because of thy beauty, thou hast corrupted thy wisdom by reason of thy brightness, I will cast thee to the ground, I will lay thee before kings that they may behold thee. Thou hast defiled thy sanctuaries by the multitude of thine iniquities, by the iniquity of thy traffic, therefore will I bring forth a fire from the midst of thee, it shall devour thee, and I will bring thee to ashes upon the earth in the sight of all them that behold thee. All they that know thee among the people shall be astonished at thee, thou shalt be a terror, and never shalt thou be anymore.

Again the word of the Lord came unto me, saying, Son of man, set thy face against Zidon, and prophesy against it and say, Thus saith the Lord God, Behold, I am against thee, O Zidon, and I will be glorified in the midst of thee, and they shall know that I am the Lord when I shall have executed judgments in her and shall be sanctified in her. For I will send into her pestilence, and blood into her streets, and the wounded shall be judged in the midst of her by the sword upon her on every side, and they shall know that I am the Lord. And there shall be no more a pricking brier unto the house of Israel, nor any grieving thorn of all that are round about them that despised them, and they shall know that I am the Lord God. Thus saith the Lord God, When I shall have gathered the house of Israel from the people among whom they are scattered and shall be sanctified in them in the sight of the heathen, then shall they dwell in their land that I have given to my servant Jacob. And they shall dwell safely therein, and shall build houses, and plant vineyards, yea, they shall dwell with confidence when I have executed judgments upon all those that despise them round about them, and they shall know that I am the Lord their God.

13 IN the tenth year, in the tenth month, in the twelfth day of the month, the word of the Lord came unto me, saying, Son of man, set thy face against Pharaoh king of Egypt and prophesy against him and against all Egypt, speak and say, Thus saith the Lord God, Behold, I am against thee, Pharaoh king of Egypt, the great dragon that lieth in the midst of his rivers which hath said, My river is mine own and I have made it for myself. But I will put hooks in thy jaws, and I will cause the fish of thy rivers to stick unto thy scales, and I will bring thee up out of the midst of thy rivers, and all the fish of thy rivers shall stick unto thy scales. And I will leave thee thrown into the wilderness, thee and all the fish of thy rivers, thou shalt fall upon the open fields, thou shalt not be brought together nor gathered, I have given thee for meat to the beasts of the field and to the fowls of the Heaven. And all the inhabitants of Egypt shall know that I am the Lord because they have been a staff of reed to the house of Israel. When they took hold of thee by thy hand, thou didst break and rend all their shoulder, and when they leaned upon thee, thou brakest and madest all their loins to be at a stand.

Therefore thus saith the Lord God, Behold, I will bring a sword upon thee, and cut off man and beast out of thee. And the land of Egypt shall be desolate and waste, and they shall know that I am the Lord, because he hath said, The river is mine and I have made it. Behold, therefore I am against thee and against thy rivers, and I will make the land of Egypt utterly waste and desolate, from the tower of Syene even unto the border of Ethiopia. No foot of man shall pass through it, nor foot of beast shall pass through it, neither shall it be inhabited forty years. And I will make the land of Egypt desolate in the midst of the countries that are desolate, and her cities among the cities that are laid waste shall be desolate forty years, and I will scatter the Egyptians among the nations, and will disperse them through the countries.

Yet thus saith the Lord God, At the end of forty years will I gather the Egyptians from the people whither they were scattered, and I will bring again the captivity of Egypt, and will cause them to return into the land of Pathros, into the land of their habitation, and they shall be there a base kingdom. It shall be the basest of the kingdoms, neither shall it exalt itself any more above the nations, for I will diminish them that they shall no more rule over the nations. And it shall be no more the confidence of the house of Israel which bringeth their iniquity to remembrance when they shall look after them, but they shall know that I am the Lord God.

And it came to pass in the seven and twentieth year, in the first month, in the first day of the month, the word of the Lord came unto me, saying, Son of man, Nebuchadrezzar king of Babylon caused his army to serve a great service against Tyrus, every head was made bald, and every shoulder was peeled, yet had he no wages nor his army, for Tyrus, for the service that he had served against it, therefore thus saith the Lord God, Behold, I will give the land of Egypt unto Nebuchadrezzar king of Babylon, and he shall take her multitude, and take her spoil, and take her prey, and it shall be the wages for his army. I have given him the land of Egypt for his labor wherewith he served against it, because they wrought for me, saith the Lord God.

In that day will I cause the horn of the house of Israel to bud forth, and I will give thee the opening of the mouth in the midst of them, and they shall know that I am the Lord.

The word of the Lord came again unto me, saying, Son of man, prophesy and say, Thus saith the Lord God, Howl ye, Wo worth the day. For the day is near, even the day of the Lord is near, a cloudy day, it shall be the time of the heathen. And the sword shall come upon Egypt, and great pain shall be in Ethiopia when the slain shall fall in Egypt, and they shall take away her multitude, and her foundations shall be broken down. Ethiopia, and Libya, and Lydia, and all the mingled people, and Chub, and the men of the land that is in league, shall fall with them by the sword. Thus saith the Lord, They also that uphold Egypt shall fall, and the pride of her power shall come down, from the tower of Syene shall they fall in it by the sword, saith the Lord God. And they shall be desolate in the midst of the countries that are desolate, and her cities shall be in the midst of the cities that are wasted. And they shall know that I am the Lord when I have set a fire in Egypt and when all her helpers shall be destroyed. In that day shall messengers go forth from me in ships to make the careless Ethiopians afraid, and great pain shall come upon them as in the day of Egypt, for lo, it cometh. Thus saith the Lord God, I will also make the multitude of Egypt to cease by the hand of Nebuchadnezzar king of Babylon. He and his people with him, the terrible of the nations, shall be brought to destroy the land, and they shall draw their swords against Egypt, and fill the land with the slain. And I will make the rivers dry, and sell the land into the hand of the wicked, and I will make the land waste, and all that is therein, by the hand of strangers, I the Lord have spoken it. Thus saith the Lord God, I will also destroy the idols and I will cause their images to cease out of Noph, and there shall be no more a prince of the land of Egypt, and I will put a fear in the land of Egypt. And I will make Pathros desolate, and will set fire in Zoan, and will execute judgments in No. And I will pour my fury upon Sin, the strength of Egypt, and I will cut off the multitude of No. And I will set fire in Egypt, Sin shall have great pain, and No shall be rent asunder, and Noph shall have distresses daily. The young men of Aven and of Pi-beseth shall fall by the sword, and these cities shall go into captivity. At Tehaphnehes also the day shall be darkened when I shall break there the yokes of Egypt, and the pomp of her strength shall cease in her, as for her, a cloud shall cover her and her daughters shall go into captivity. Thus will I execute judgments in Egypt, and they shall know that I am the Lord.

And it came to pass in the eleventh year, in the first month, in the seventh day of the month, that the word of the Lord came unto me, saying, Son of man, I have broken the arm of Pharaoh king of Egypt and lo, it shall not be bound up to be healed, to put a roller to bind it, to make it strong to hold the sword. Therefore thus saith the Lord God, Behold, I am against Pharaoh king of Egypt and will break his arms, the strong and that which was broken, and I will cause the sword to fall out of his hand. And I will scatter the Egyptians among the nations and will disperse them through the countries. And I will strengthen the arms of the king of Babylon and put my sword in his hand, but I will break Pharaoh's arms and he shall groan before him with the groanings of a deadly wounded man. But I will strengthen the arms of the king of Babylon, and the arms of Pharaoh shall fall down, and they shall know that I am the Lord when I shall put my sword into the hand of the king of Babylon, and he shall stretch it out upon the land of Egypt. And I will scatter the Egyptians among the nations, and disperse them among the countries, and they shall know that I am the Lord.

And it came to pass in the eleventh year, in the third month, in the first day of the month, that the word of the Lord came unto me, saying, Son of man, speak unto Pharaoh king of Egypt and to his multitude, Whom art thou like in thy greatness? Behold, the Assyrian was a cedar in Lebanon with fair branches, and with a shadowing shroud, and of a high stature, and his top was among the thick boughs. The waters made him great, the deep set him up on high with her rivers running round about his plants, and sent out her little rivers unto all the trees of the field. Therefore his height was exalted above all the trees of the field, and his boughs were multiplied, and his branches became long because of the multitude of waters when he shot forth. All the fowls of Heaven made their nests in his boughs, and under his branches did all the beasts of the field bring forth their young, and under his shadow dwelt all great nations. Thus was he fair in his greatness, in the length of his branches, for his root was by great waters. The cedars in the garden of God could not hide him, the fir trees were not like his boughs, and the chestnut trees were not like his branches, not any tree in the garden of God was like unto him in his beauty. I have made him fair by the multitude of his branches so that all the trees of Eden that were in the garden of God envied him.

Therefore thus saith the Lord God, Because thou hast lifted up thyself in height, and he hath shot up his top among the thick boughs, and his heart is lifted up in his height, I have therefore delivered him into the hand of the mighty one of the heathen, he shall surely deal with him, I have driven him out for his wickedness. And strangers, the terrible of the nations, have cut him off and have left him, upon the mountains and in all the valleys his branches are fallen, and his boughs are broken by all the rivers of the land, and all the people of the earth are gone down from his shadow and have left him. Upon his ruin shall all the fowls of the Heaven remain and all the beasts of the field shall be upon his branches, to the end that none of all the trees by the waters exalt themselves for their height, neither shoot up their top among the thick boughs, neither their trees stand up in their height, all that drink water, for they are all delivered unto death, to the nether parts of the earth in the midst of the children of men with them that go down to the pit.

Thus saith the Lord God, In the day when he went down to the grave I caused a mourning, I covered the deep for him and I restrained the floods thereof, and the great waters were stayed, and I caused Lebanon to mourn for him, and all the trees of the field fainted for him. I made the nations to shake at the sound of his fall when I cast him down to hell with them that descend into the pit, and all the trees of Eden, the choice and best of Lebanon, all that drink water, shall be comforted in the nether parts of the earth. They also went down into hell with him, unto them that be slain with the sword, and they that were his arm, that dwelt under his shadow in the midst of the heathen. To whom art thou thus like in glory and in greatness among the trees of Eden? Yet shalt thou be brought down with the trees of Eden unto the nether parts of the earth, thou shalt lie in the midst of the uncircumcised with them that be slain by the sword. This is Pharaoh and all his multitude, saith the Lord God.

And it came to pass in the twelfth year, in the twelfth month, in the first day of the month, that the word of the Lord came unto me, saying, Son of man, take up a lamentation for Pharaoh king of Egypt and say unto him, Thou art like a young lion of the nations, and thou art as a whale in the seas, and thou camest forth with thy rivers, and troubledst the waters with thy feet, and fouledst their rivers. Thus saith the Lord God, I will therefore spread out my net over thee with a company of many people and they shall bring thee up in my net. Then will I leave thee upon the land, I will cast thee forth upon the open field, and will cause all the fowls of the Heaven to remain upon thee, and I will fill the beasts of the whole earth with thee. And I will lay thy flesh upon the mountains and fill the valleys with thy height. I will also water with thy blood the land wherein thou swimmest, even to the mountains, and the rivers shall be full of thee. And when I shall put thee out, I will cover the Heaven and make the stars thereof dark, I will cover the sun with a cloud and the moon shall not give her light. All the bright lights of Heaven will I make dark over thee and set darkness upon thy land, saith the Lord God. I will also vex the hearts of many people, when I shall bring thy destruction among the nations, into the countries which thou hast not known. Yea, I will make many people amazed at thee, and their kings shall be horribly afraid for thee when I shall brandish my sword before them, and they shall tremble at every moment, every man for his own life in the day of thy fall.

For thus saith the Lord God, The sword of the king of Babylon shall come upon thee. By the swords of the mighty will I cause thy multitude to fall, the terrible of the nations, all of them, and they shall spoil the pomp of Egypt, and all the multitude thereof shall be destroyed. I will destroy also all the beasts thereof from beside the great waters, neither shall the foot of man trouble them anymore, nor the hooves of beasts trouble them. Then will I make their waters deep and cause their rivers to run like oil, saith the Lord God. When I shall make the land of Egypt desolate, and the country shall be destitute of that whereof it was full when I shall smite all them that dwell therein, then shall they know that I am the Lord. This is the lamentation wherewith they shall lament her, the daughters of the nations shall lament her, they shall lament for her, even for Egypt, and for all her multitude, saith the Lord God.

It came to pass also in the twelfth year, in the fifteenth day of the month, that the word of the Lord came unto me, saying, Son of man, wail for the multitude of Egypt and cast them down, even her, and the daughters of the famous nations, unto the nether parts of the earth, with them that go down into the pit. Whom dost thou pass in beauty? Go down and be thou laid with the uncircumcised. They shall fall in the midst of them that are slain by the sword, she is delivered to the sword, draw her and all her multitudes. The strong among the mighty shall speak to him out of the midst of hell with them that help him, they are gone down, they lie uncircumcised, slain by the sword. Asshur is there and all her company, his graves are about him, all of them slain, fallen by the sword, whose graves are set in the sides of the pit, and her company is round about her grave, all of them slain, fallen by the sword, which caused terror in the land of the living. There is Elam and all her multitude round about her grave, all of them slain, fallen by the sword, which are gone down uncircumcised into the nether parts of the earth, which caused their terror in the land of the living, yet have they borne their shame with them that go down to the pit. They have set her a bed in the midst of the slain with all her multitude, her graves are round about him, all of them uncircumcised, slain by the sword; though their terror was caused in the land of the living, yet have they borne their shame with them that go down to the pit, he is put in the midst of them that be slain. There is Meshech, Tubal, and all her multitude, her graves are round about him, all of them uncircumcised, slain by the sword, though they caused their terror in the land of the living. And they shall not lie with the mighty that are fallen of the uncircumcised, which are gone down to hell with their weapons of war, and they have laid their swords under their heads, but their iniquities shall be upon their bones, though they were the terror of the mighty in the land of the living. Yea, thou shalt be broken in the midst of the uncircumcised, and shalt lie with them that are slain with the sword. There is Edom, her kings and all her princes, which with their might are laid by them that were slain by the sword, they shall lie with the uncircumcised and with them that go down to the pit. There be the princes of the north, all of them, and all the Zidonians which are gone down with the slain, with their terror they are ashamed of their might, and they lie uncircumcised with them that be slain by the sword, and bear their shame with them that go down to the pit. Pharaoh shall see them and shall be comforted over all his multitude, even Pharaoh and all his army slain by the sword, saith the Lord God. For I have caused my terror in the land of the living, and he shall be laid in the midst of the uncircumcised with them that are slain with the sword, even Pharaoh and all his multitude, saith the Lord God.

14 AGAIN the word of the Lord came unto me, saying, Son of man, speak to the children of thy people, and say unto them, When I bring the sword upon a land, if the people of the land take a man of their coasts and set him for their watchman, if when he seeth the sword come upon the land he blow the trumpet and warn the people, then whosoever heareth the sound of the trumpet and taketh not warning, if the sword come and take him away, his blood shall be upon his own head. He heard the sound of the trumpet and took not warning, his blood shall be upon him. But he that taketh warning shall deliver his soul. But if the watchman see the sword come and blow not the trumpet and the people be not warned, if the sword come and take any person from among them, he is taken away in his iniquity, but his blood will I require at the watchman's hand. So thou, O son of man, I have set thee a watchman unto the house of Israel, therefore thou shalt hear the word at my mouth, and warn them from me. When I say unto the wicked, O wicked man, thou shalt surely die, if thou dost not speak to warn the wicked from his way, that wicked man shall die in his iniquity, but his blood will I require at thine hand. Nevertheless, if thou warn the wicked of his way to turn from it, if he do not turn from his way, he shall die in his iniquity, but thou hast delivered thy soul.

Therefore, O thou son of man, speak unto the house of Israel, Thus ye speak saying, If our transgressions and our sins be upon us and we pine away in them, how should we then live? Say unto them, As I live, saith the Lord God, I have no pleasure in the death of the wicked, but that the wicked turn from his way and live; turn ye, turn ye from your evil ways, for why will ye die, O house of Israel? Therefore, thou son of man, say unto the children of thy people, The righteousness of the righteous shall not deliver him in the day of his transgression, as for the wickedness of the wicked, he shall not fall thereby in the day that he turneth from his wickedness, neither shall the righteous be able to live for his righteousness in the day that he sinneth. When I shall say to the righteous that he shall surely live, if he trust to his own righteousness and commit iniquity, all his righteousness shall not be remembered, but for his iniquity that he hath committed, he shall die for it. Again, when I say unto the wicked, Thou shalt surely die, if he turn from his sin and do that which is lawful and right, if the wicked restore the pledge, give again that he had robbed, walk in the statutes of life without committing iniquity, he shall surely live, he shall not die. None of his sins that he hath committed shall be mentioned unto him, he hath done that which is lawful and right, he shall surely live. Yet the children of thy people say, The way of the Lord is not equal, but as for them, their way is not equal. When the righteous turneth from his righteousness and committeth iniquity, he shall even die thereby. But if the wicked turn from his wickedness and do that which is lawful and right, he shall live thereby. Yet ye say, The way of the Lord is not equal. O ye house of Israel, I will judge you everyone after his ways.

And it came to pass in the twelfth year of our captivity, in the tenth mount, in the fifth day of the month, that one that had escaped out of Jerusalem came unto me, saying, The city is smitten. Now the hand of the Lord was upon me in the evening, afore he that was escaped came and had opened my mouth, until he came to me in the morning and my mouth was opened and I was no more dumb. Then the word of the Lord came unto me saying, Son of man, they that inhabit those wastes of the land of Israel speak saying, Abraham was one and he inherited the land, but we are many, the land is given us for inheritance. Wherefore say unto them, Thus saith the Lord God, Ye eat with the blood, and lift up your eyes toward your idols, and shed blood, and shall ye possess the land? Ye stand upon your sword, ye work abominations, and ye defile everyone his neighbor's wife, and shall ye possess the land? Say thou thus unto them, Thus saith the Lord God, As I live, surely they that are in the wastes shall fall by the sword, and him that is in the open field will I give to the beasts to be devoured, and they that be in the forts and in the caves shall die of the pestilence. For I will lay the land most desolate, and the pomp of her strength shall cease, and the mountains of Israel shall be desolate that none shall pass through. Then shall they know that I am the Lord, when I have laid the land most desolate because of all their abominations which they have committed.

Also, thou son of man, the children of thy people still are talking against thee by the walls and in the doors of the houses and speak one to another, everyone to his brother, saying, Come, I pray you, and hear what is the word that cometh forth from the Lord. And they come unto thee as the people cometh, and they sit before thee as my people, and they hear thy words, but they will not do them, for with their mouth they show much love, but their heart goeth after their covetousness. And lo, thou art unto them as a very lovely song of one that hath a pleasant voice and can play well on an instrument, for they hear thy words, but they do them not. And when this cometh to pass (lo, it will come), then shall they know that a prophet hath been among them.

And the word of the Lord came unto me, saying, Son of man, prophesy against the shepherds of Israel, prophesy and say unto them, Thus saith the Lord God unto the shepherds, Wo be to the shepherds of Israel that do feed themselves. Should not the shepherds feed the flocks? Ye eat the fat and ye clothe you with the wool, ye kill them that are fed, but ye feed not the flock. The diseased have ye not strengthened, neither have ye healed that which was sick, neither have ye bound up that which was broken, neither have ye brought again that which was driven away, neither have ye sought that which was lost, but with force and with cruelty have ye ruled them. And they were scattered because there is no shepherd and they became meat to all the beasts of the field when they were scattered. My sheep wandered through all the mountains and upon every high hill, yea, my flock was scattered upon all the face of the earth and none did search or seek after them.

Therefore, ye shepherds, hear the word of the Lord, As I live, saith the Lord God, surely because my flock became a prey and my flock became meat to every beast of the field because there was no shepherd neither did my shepherds search for my flock, but the shepherds fed themselves and fed not my flock, therefore, O ye shepherds, hear the word of the Lord: Thus saith the Lord God, Behold, I am against the shepherds and I will require my flock at their hand, and cause them to cease from feeding the flock neither shall the shepherds feed themselves anymore, for I will deliver my flock from their mouth, that they may not be meat for them.

For thus saith the Lord God, Behold, I, even I will both search my sheep and seek them out. As a shepherd seeketh out his flock in the day that he is among his sheep that are scattered, so will I seek out my sheep and will deliver them out of all places where they have been scattered in the cloudy and dark day. And I will bring them out from the people and gather them from the countries, and will bring them to their own land and feed them upon the mountains of Israel by the river and in all the inhabited places of the country. I will feed them in a good pasture, and upon the high mountains of Israel shall their fold be, there shall they lie in a good fold, and in a fat pasture shall they feed upon the mountains of Israel. I will feed my flock and I will cause them to lie down, saith the Lord God. I will seek that which was lost, and bring again that which was driven away, and will bind up that which was broken, and will strengthen that which was sick, but I will destroy the fat and the strong; I will feed them with judgment.

And as for you, O my flock, thus saith the Lord God, Behold, I judge between cattle and cattle, between the rams and the he goats. Seemeth it a small thing unto you to have eaten up the good pasture but ye must tread down with your feet the residue of your pastures? And to have drunk of the deep waters, but ye must foul the residue with your feet? And as for my flock, they eat that which ye have trodden with your feet and they drink that which ye have fouled with your feet.

Therefore thus saith the Lord God unto them, Behold, I, even I will judge between the fat cattle and between the lean cattle. Because ye have thrust with side and with shoulder and pushed all the diseased with your horns till ye have scattered them abroad, therefore will I save my flock, and they shall no more be a prey and I will judge between cattle and cattle. And I will set up one shepherd over them and he shall feed them, even my servant David, he shall feed them and he shall be their shepherd. And I the Lord will be their God and my servant David a prince among them, I the Lord have spoken it. And I will make with them a covenant of peace and will cause the evil beasts to cease out of the land, and they shall dwell safely in the wilderness and sleep in the woods. And I will make them and the places round about my hill a blessing, and I will cause the shower to come down in his season; there shall be showers of blessing. And the tree of the field shall yield her fruit, and the Earth shall yield her increase, and they shall be safe in their land, and shall know that I am the Lord when I have broken the bands of their yoke and delivered them out of the hand of those that served themselves of them. And they shall no more be a prey to the heathen, neither shall the beasts of the land devour them, but they shall dwell safely and none shall make them afraid. And I will raise up for them a plant of renown, and they shall be no more consumed with hunger in the land, neither bear the shame of the heathen anymore. Thus shall they know that I the Lord their God am with them and that they, even the house of Israel, are my people, saith the Lord God. And ye my flock, the flock of my pasture, are men and I am your God, saith the Lord God.

15 MOREOVER the word of the Lord came unto me, saying, Son of man, set thy face against mount Seir and prophesy against it and say unto it, Thus saith the Lord God, Behold, O mount Seir, I am against thee and I will stretch out mine hand against thee and I will make thee most desolate. I will lay thy cities waste and thou shalt be desolate and thou shalt know that I am the Lord.

Because thou hast had a perpetual hatred and hast shed the blood of the children of Israel by the force of the sword in the time of their calamity, in the time that their iniquity had an end, therefore, as I live, saith the Lord God, I will prepare thee unto blood and blood shall pursue thee, since thou hast not hated blood even blood shall pursue thee. Thus will I make mount Seir most desolate and cut off from it him that passeth out and him that returneth. And I will fill his mountains with his slain men, in thy hills, and in thy valleys, and in all thy rivers shall they fall that are slain with the sword. I will make thee perpetual desolations and thy cities shall not return, and ye shall know that I am the Lord.

Because thou hast said, These two nations and these two countries shall be mine and we will possess it, whereas the Lord was there, therefore, as I live, saith the Lord God, I will even do according to thine anger and according to thine envy which thou hast used out of thy hatred against them, and I will make myself known among them when I have judged thee. And thou shalt know that I am the Lord, and that I have heard all thy blasphemies which thou hast spoken against the mountains of Israel saying, They are laid desolate, they are given us to consume. Thus with your mouth ye have boasted against me and have multiplied your words against me; I have heard them. Thus saith the Lord God, When the whole earth rejoiceth, I will make thee desolate. As thou didst rejoice at the inheritance of the house of Israel because it was desolate, so will I do unto thee: thou shalt be desolate, O mount Seir, and all Idumea, even all of it, and they shall know that I am the Lord.

Also, thou son of man, prophesy unto the mountains of Israel, and say, Ye mountains of Israel hear the word of the Lord: Thus saith the Lord God, Because the enemy hath said against you, Aha, even the ancient high places are ours in possession, therefore prophesy and say, Thus saith the Lord God, Because they have made you desolate and swallowed you up on every side that ye might be a possession unto the residue of the heathen, and ye are taken up in the lips of talkers and are an infamy of the people, therefore, ye mountains of Israel, hear the word of the Lord God: Thus saith the Lord God to the mountains and to the hills, to the rivers and to the valleys, to the desolate wastes and to the cities that are forsaken, which became a prey and derision to the residue of the heathen that are round about, therefore thus saith the Lord God, Surely in the fire of my jealousy have I spoken against the residue of the heathen and against all Idumea which have appointed my land into their possession with the joy of all their heart, with despiteful minds to cast it out for a prey. Prophesy therefore concerning the land of Israel and say unto the mountains and to the hills, to the rivers and to the valleys, Thus saith the Lord God, Behold, I have spoken in my jealousy and in my fury because ye have borne the shame of the heathen, therefore thus saith the Lord God, I have lifted up mine hand, Surely the heathen that are about you, they shall bear their shame. But ye, O mountains of Israel, ye shall shoot forth your branches and yield your fruit to my people of Israel, for they are at hand to come. For behold, I am for you, and I will turn unto you, and ye shall be tilled and sown, and I will multiply men upon you, all the house of Israel, even all of it, and the cities shall be inhabited, and the wastes shall be builded, and I will multiply upon you man and beast, and they shall increase and bring fruit, and I will settle you after your old estates, and will do better unto you than at your beginnings, and ye shall know that I am the Lord. Yea, I will cause men to walk upon you, even my people Israel, and they shall possess thee and thou shalt be their inheritance, and thou shalt no more henceforth bereave them of men.

Thus saith the Lord God, Because they say unto you, Thou land devourest up men and hast bereaved thy nations, therefore thou shalt devour men no more neither bereave thy nations anymore, saith the Lord God. Neither will I cause men to hear in thee the shame of the heathen anymore, neither shalt thou bear the reproach of the people anymore, neither shalt thou cause thy nations to fall anymore, saith the Lord God.

Moreover the word of the Lord came unto me, saying, Son of man, when the house of Israel dwelt in their own land, they defiled it by their own way and by their doings, their way was before me as the uncleanness of a removed woman. Wherefore I poured my fury upon them for the blood that they had shed upon the land and for their idols wherewith they had polluted it, and I scattered them among the heathen and they were dispersed through the countries, according to their way and according to their doings I judged them. And when they entered unto the heathen whither they went, they profaned my holy name when they said to them, These are the people of the Lord and are gone forth out of this land. But I had pity for mine holy name which the house of Israel had profaned among the heathen whither they went.

Therefore say unto the house of Israel, Thus saith the Lord God, I do not this for your sakes, O house of Israel, but for mine holy name's sake which ye have profaned among the heathen whither ye went. And I will sanctify my great name, which was profaned among the heathen which ye have profaned in the midst of them, and the heathen shall know that I am the Lord, saith the Lord God, when I shall be sanctified in you before their eyes. For I will take you from among the heathen, and gather you out of all countries, and will bring you into your own land. Then will I sprinkle clean water upon you and ye shall be clean, from all your filthiness and from all your idols will I cleanse you. A new heart also will I give you and a new spirit will I put within you, and I will take away the stony heart out of your flesh and I will give you a heart of flesh. And I will put my Spirit within you and cause you to walk in my statutes, and ye shall keep my judgments and do them. And ye shall dwell in the land that I gave to your fathers, and ye shall be my people and I will be your God. I will also save you from all your uncleanness, and I will call for the corn and will increase it and lay no famine upon you. And I will multiply the fruit of the tree and the increase of the field that ye shall receive no more reproach of famine among the heathen. Then shall ye remember your own evil ways and your doings that were not good and shall loathe yourselves in your own sight for your iniquities and for your abominations. Not for your sakes do I this, saith the Lord God, be it known unto you, be ashamed and confounded for your own ways, O house of Israel.

Thus saith the Lord God, In the day that I shall have cleansed you from all your iniquities I will also cause you to dwell in the cities and the wastes shall be builded. And the desolate land shall be tilled whereas it lay desolate in the sight of all that passed by. And they shall say, This land that was desolate is become like the garden of Eden, and the waste and desolate and ruined cities are become fenced and are inhabited. Then the heathen that are left round about you shall know that I the Lord build the ruined places and plant that which was desolate, I the Lord have spoken it, and I will do it.

Thus saith the Lord God, I will yet for this be inquired of by the house of Israel, to do it for them I will increase them with men like a flock. As the holy flock, as the flock of Jerusalem in her solemn feasts, so shall the waste cities be filled with flocks of men, and they shall know that I am the Lord.

The hand of the Lord was upon me and carried me out in the Spirit of the Lord, and set me down in the midst of the valley which was full of bones, and caused me to pass by them round about, and behold, there were very many in the open valley, and lo, they were very dry. And he said unto me, Son of man, can these bones live? And I answered, O Lord God, thou knowest. Again he said unto me, Prophesy upon these bones and say unto them, O ye dry bones, hear the word of the Lord: Thus saith the Lord God unto these bones, Behold, I will cause breath to enter into you and ye shall live, and I will lay sinews upon you and will bring up flesh upon you, and cover you with skin, and put breath in you, and ye shall live, and ye shall know that I am the Lord.

So I prophesied as I was commanded, and as I prophesied, there was a noise and behold a shaking, and the bones came together, bone to his bone. And when I beheld lo, the sinews and the flesh came up upon them, and the skin covered them above, but there was no breath in them. Then said he unto me, Prophesy unto the wind, prophesy, son of man, and say to the wind, Thus saith the Lord God, Come from the four winds, O breath, and breathe upon these slain, that they may live. So I prophesied as he commanded me and the breath came into them, and they lived, and stood up upon their feet, an exceeding great army.

Then he said unto me, Son of man, these bones are the whole house of Israel. Behold, they say, Our bones are dried and our hope is lost, we are cut off for our parts. Therefore prophesy and say unto them, Thus saith the Lord God, Behold,

O my people, I will open your graves and cause you to come up out of your graves and bring you into the land of Israel. And ye shall know that I am the Lord when I have opened your graves, O my people, and brought you up out of your graves and shall put my Spirit in you, and ye shall live and I shall place you in your own land, then shall ye know that I the Lord have spoken it, and performed it, saith the Lord.

The word of the Lord came again unto me, saying, Moreover, thou son of man, take thee one stick and write upon it, For Judah and for the children of Israel his companions; then take another stick, and write upon it, For Joseph, the stick of Ephraim, and for all the house of Israel his companions, and join them one to another into one stick, and they shall become one in thine hand. And when the children of thy people shall speak unto thee saying, Wilt thou not show us what thou meanest by these? Say unto them, Thus saith the Lord God, Behold, I will take the stick of Joseph which is in the hand of Ephraim, and the tribes of Israel his fellows, and will put them with him, even with the stick of Judah, and make them one stick, and they shall be one in mine hand. And the sticks whereon thou writest shall be in thine hand before their eyes. And say unto them, Thus saith the Lord God, Behold, I will take the children of Israel from among the heathen whither they be gone, and will gather them on every side and bring them into their own land, and I will make them one nation in the land upon the mountains of Israel, and one king shall be king to them all and they shall be no more two nations, neither shall they be divided into two kingdoms anymore at all, neither shall they defile themselves anymore with their idols, nor with their detestable things, nor with any of their transgressions, but I will save them out of all their dwelling places wherein they have sinned and will cleanse them, so shall they be my people and I will be their God.

And David my servant shall be king over them and they all shall have one shepherd; they shall also walk in my judgments and observe my statutes and do them. And they shall dwell in the land that I have given unto Jacob my servant wherein your fathers have dwelt, and they shall dwell therein, even they and their children and their children's children forever, and my servant David shall be their prince forever. Moreover I will make a covenant of peace with them: it shall be an everlasting covenant with them, and I will place them, and multiply them, and will set my sanctuary in the midst of them for evermore. My tabernacle also shall be with them, yea, I will be their God and they shall be my people. And the heathen shall know that I the Lord do sanctify Israel when my sanctuary shall be in the midst of them for evermore.

16 AND the word of the Lord came unto me, saying, Son of man, set thy face against Gog, the land of Magog, the chief prince of Meshech and Tubal, and prophesy against him and say, Thus saith the Lord God, Behold, I am against thee, O Gog, the chief prince of Meshech and Tubal, and I will turn thee back and put hooks into thy jaws, and I will bring thee forth and all thine army, horses and horsemen, all of them clothed with all sorts of armor, even a great company with bucklers and shields, all of them handling swords: Persia, Ethiopia, and Libya with them, all of them with shield and helmet, Gomer, and all his bands, the house of Togarmah of the north quarters and all his bands, and many people with thee.

Be thou prepared, and prepare for thyself, thou and all thy company that are assembled unto thee, and be thou a guard unto them. After many days thou shalt be visited, in the latter years thou shalt come into the land that is brought back from the sword and is gathered out of many people, against the mountains of Israel which have been always waste, but it is brought forth out of the nations and they shall dwell safely all of them. Thou shalt ascend and come like a storm, thou shalt be like a cloud to cover the land, thou and all thy bands and many people with thee.

Thus saith the Lord God, It shall also come to pass, that at the same time shall things come into thy mind, and thou shalt think an evil thought and thou shalt say, I will go up to the land of unwalled villages, I will go to them that are at rest, that dwell safely, all of them dwelling without walls and having neither bars nor gates, to take a spoil, and to take a prey, to turn thine hand upon the desolate places that are now inhabited and upon the people that are gathered out of the nations which have gotten cattle and goods, that dwell in the midst of the land. Sheba, and Dedan, and the merchants of Tarshish, with all the young lions thereof, shall say unto thee, Art thou come to take a spoil? Hast thou gathered thy company to take a prey? To carry away silver and gold, to take away cattle and goods, to take a great spoil?

Therefore, son of man, prophesy and say unto Gog, Thus saith the Lord God, In that day when my people of Israel dwelleth safely, shalt thou not know it? And thou shalt come from thy place out of the north parts, thou and many people with thee, all of them riding upon horses, and great company and a mighty army, and thou shalt come up against my people of Israel, as a cloud to cover the land; it shall be in the latter days, and I will bring thee against my land that the heathen may know me, when I shall be sanctified in thee, O Gog, before their eyes.

Thus saith the Lord God, Art thou he of whom I have spoken in old time by my servants the prophets of Israel, which prophesied in those days many years that I would bring thee against them? And it shall come to pass at the same time when Gog shall come against the land of Israel, saith the Lord God, that my fury shall come up in my face. For in my jealousy and in the fire of my wrath have I spoken, surely in that day there shall be a great shaking in the land of Israel so that the fishes of the sea, and the fowls of the Heaven, and the beasts of the field, and all creeping things that creep upon the Earth, and all the men that are upon the face of the Earth shall shake at my presence, and the mountains shall be thrown down, and the steep places shall fall, and every wall shall fall to the ground. And I will call for a sword against him throughout all my mountains, saith the Lord God, every man's sword shall be against his brother. And I will plead against him with pestilence and with blood, and I will rain upon him, and upon his bands, and upon the many people that are with him, an overflowing rain and great hailstones, fire and brimstone. Thus will I magnify myself and sanctify myself, and I will be known in the eyes of many nations and they shall know that I am the Lord.

Therefore, thou son of man, prophesy against Gog, and say, Thus saith the Lord God, Behold, I am against thee, O Gog, the chief prince of Meshech and Tubal, and I will turn thee back and leave but the sixth part of thee, and will cause thee to come up from the north parts, and will bring thee upon the mountains of Israel, and I will smite thy bow out of thy left hand and will cause thine arrows to fall out of thy right hand. Thou shalt fall upon the mountains of Israel, thou and all thy bands and the people that is with thee, I will give thee unto the ravenous birds of every sort, and to the beasts of the field to be devoured. Thou shalt fall upon the open field for I have spoken it, saith the Lord God. And I will send a fire on Magog and among them that dwell carelessly in the isles, and they shall know that I am the Lord.

So will I make my holy name known in the midst of my people Israel, and I will not let them pollute my holy name anymore, and the heathen shall know that I am the Lord, the Holy One in Israel. Behold, it is come and it is done, saith the Lord God, this is the day whereof I have spoken.

And they that dwell in the cities of Israel shall go forth and shall set on fire and burn the weapons, both the shields and the bucklers, the bows and the arrows, and the hand-staves and the spears, and they shall burn them with fire seven years so that they shall take no wood out of the field, neither cut down any out of the forests, for they shall burn the weapons with fire, and they shall spoil those that spoiled them, and rob those that robbed them, saith the Lord God.

And it shall come to pass in that day that I will give unto Gog a place there of graves in Israel, the valley of the passengers on the east of the sea, and it shall stop the noses of the passengers, and there shall they bury Gog and all his multitude, and they shall call it, The valley of Hamon-gog. And seven months shall the house of Israel be burying of them that they may cleanse the land. Yea, all the people of the land shall bury them, and it shall be to them a renown the day that I shall be glorified, saith the Lord God. And they shall sever out men of continual employment, passing through the land, to bury with the passengers those that remain upon the face of the earth to cleanse it; after the end of seven months shall they search. And the passengers that pass through the land, when any seeth a man's bone, then shall he set up a sign by it till the buriers have buried it in the valley of Hamon-gog. And also the name of the city shall be Hamonah. Thus shall they cleanse the land.

And, thou son of man, thus saith the Lord God, Speak unto every feathered fowl, and to every beast of the field, Assemble yourselves, and come gather yourselves on every side to my sacrifice that I do sacrifice for you, even a great sacrifice upon the mountains of Israel, that ye may eat flesh and drink blood. Ye shall eat the flesh of the mighty and drink the blood of the princes of the earth, of rams, of lambs, and of goats, of bullocks, all of them fatlings of Bashan. And ye shall eat fat till ye be full, and drink blood till ye be drunken of my sacrifice which I have sacrificed for you. Thus ye shall be filled at my table with horses and chariots, with mighty men and with all men of war, saith the Lord God.

And I will set my glory among the heathen, and all the heathen shall see my judgment that I have executed, and my hand that I have laid upon them. So the house of Israel shall know that I am the Lord their God from that day and forward. And the heathen shall know that the house of Israel went into captivity for their iniquity because they trespassed against me, therefore hid I my face from them and gave them into the hand of their enemies, so fell they all by the sword. According to their uncleanness and according to their transgressions have I done unto them and hid my face from them.

Therefore thus saith the Lord God, Now will I bring again the captivity of Jacob and have mercy upon the whole house of Israel, and will be jealous for my holy name, after that they have borne their shame and all their trespasses whereby they have trespassed against me when they dwelt safely in their land and none made them afraid. When I have brought them again from the people, and gathered them out of their enemies' lands, and am sanctified in them in the sight of many nations, then shall they know that I am the Lord their God which caused them to be led into captivity among the heathen, but I have gathered them unto their own land and have left none of them anymore there. Neither will I hide my face anymore from them, for I have poured out my Spirit upon the house of Israel, saith the Lord God.

17 IN the five and twentieth year of our captivity, in the beginning of the year, in the tenth day of the month, in the fourteenth year after that the city was smitten, in the selfsame day the hand of the Lord was upon me and brought me thither. In the visions of God brought he me into the land of Israel and set me upon a very high mountain, by which was as the frame of a city on the south. And he brought me thither and, behold, there was a man whose appearance was like the appearance of brass, with a line of flax in his hand and a measuring reed, and he stood in the gate. And the man said unto me, Son of man, behold with

thine eyes and hear with thine ears and set thine heart upon all that I shall show thee, for to the intent that I might show them unto thee art thou brought hither; declare all that thou seest to the house of Israel.

And behold a wall on the outside of the house round about, and in the man's hand a measuring reed of six cubits long by the cubit and a handbreadth, so he measured the breadth of the building, one reed, and the height, one reed. Then came he unto the gate which looketh toward the east, and went up the stairs thereof, and measured the threshold of the gate which was one reed broad, and the other threshold of the gate which was one reed broad. And every little chamber was one reed long, and one reed broad, and between the little chambers were five cubits, and the threshold of the gate by the porch of the gate within was one reed. He measured also the porch of the gate within, one reed. Then measured he the porch of the gate, eight cubits, and the posts thereof, two cubits, and the porch of the gate was inward. And the little chambers of the gate eastward were three on this side and three on that side, they three were of one measure, and the posts had one measure on this side and on that side. And he measured the breadth of the entry of the gate, ten cubits, and the length of the gate, thirteen cubits. The space also before the little chambers was one cubit on this side, and the space was one cubit on that side, and the little chambers were six cubits on this sid, and six cubits on that side. He measured then the gate from the roof of one little chamber to the roof of another, the breadth was five and twenty cubits, door against door. He made also posts of threescore cubits, even unto the post of the court round about the gate. And from the face of the gate of the entrance unto the face of the porch of the inner gate were fifty cubits. And there were narrow windows to the little chambers and to their posts within the gate round about, and likewise to the arches, and windows were round about inward, and upon each post were palm trees.

Then brought he me into the outward court and lo, there were chambers and a pavement made for the court round about; thirty chambers were upon the pavement. And the pavement by the side of the gates over against the length of the gates was the lower pavement. Then he measured the breadth from the forefront of the lower gate unto the forefront of the inner court without, a hundred cubits eastward and northward.

And the gate of the outward court that looked toward the north he measured the length thereof and the breadth thereof. And the little chambers thereof were three on this side and three on that side, and the posts thereof and the arches thereof were after the measure of the first gate, the length thereof was fifty cubits, and the breadth five and twenty cubits. And their windows, and their arches, and their palm trees were after the measure of the gate that looketh toward the east, and they went up unto it by seven steps, and the arches thereof were before them. And the gate of the inner court was over against the gate toward the north, and toward the east, and he measured from gate to gate a hundred cubits.

After that he brought me toward the south, and behold a gate toward the south, and he measured the posts thereof and the arches thereof, according to these measures. And there were windows in it and in the arches thereof round about, like those windows, the length was fifty cubits and the breadth five and twenty cubits. And there were seven steps to go up to it, and the arches thereof were before them and it had palm trees, one on this side and another on that side, upon the posts thereof. And there was a gate in the inner court toward the south, and he measured from gate to gate toward the south a hundred cubits.

And he brought me to the inner court by the south gate, and he measured the south gate according to these measures, and the little chambers thereof, and the posts thereof, and the arches thereof, according to these measures, and there were windows in it and in the arches thereof round about, it was fifty cubits long, and five and twenty cubits broad. And the arches round about were five and twenty cubits long, and five cubits broad. And the arches thereof were toward the outer court, and palm trees were upon the posts thereof, and the going up to it had eight steps.

And he brought me into the inner court toward the east, and he measured the gate according to these measures. And the little chambers thereof, and the posts thereof, and the arches thereof, were according to these measures, and there were windows therein and in the arches thereof round about, it was fifty cubits long, and five and twenty cubits broad. And the arches thereof were toward the outward court, and palm trees were upon the posts thereof, on this side, and on that side, and the going up to it had eight steps.

And he brought me to the north gate and measured it according to these measures: the little chambers thereof, the posts thereof, and the arches thereof, and the windows to it round about, the length was fifty cubits and the breadth five and twenty cubits. And the posts thereof were toward the outer court, and palm trees were upon the posts thereof, on this side and on that side, and the going up to it had eight steps. And the chambers and the entries thereof were by the posts of the gates where they washed the burnt offering. And in the porch of the gate were two tables on this side, and two tables on that side, to slay thereon the burnt offering and the sin offering and trespass offering. And at the side without, as one goeth up to the entry of the north gate, were two tables, and on the other side which was at the porch of the gate, were two tables. Four tables were on this side and four tables on that side, by the side of the gate, eight tables whereupon they slew their sacrifices. And the four tables were of hewn stone for the burnt offering, of a cubit and a half long, and a cubit and a half broad, and one cubit high, whereupon also they laid the instruments wherewith they slew the burnt offering and the sacrifice. And within were hooks, a hand broad, fastened round about, and upon the tables was the flesh of the offering.

And without the inner gate were the chambers of the singers in the inner court which was at the side of the north gate, and their prospect was toward the south, one at the side of the east gate having the prospect toward the north. And he said unto me, This chamber, whose prospect is toward the south, is for the priests, the keepers of the charge of the house. And the chamber whose prospect is toward the north is for the priests, the keepers of the charge of the altar; these are the sons of Zadok among the sons of Levi, which come near to the Lord to minister unto him.

So he measured the court, a hundred cubits long and a hundred cubits broad, foursquare, and the altar that was before the house. And he brought me to the porch of the house and measured each post of the porch, five cubits on this side and five cubits on that side, and the breadth of the gate was three cubits on this side and three cubits on that side. The length of the porch was twenty cubits and the breadth eleven cubits, and he brought me by the steps whereby they went up to it, and there were pillars by the posts, one on this side and another on that side.

Afterward he brought me to the temple, and measured the posts, six cubits broad on the one side and six cubits broad on the other side, which was the breadth of the tabernacle. And the breadth of the door was ten cubits, and the sides of the door were five cubits on the one side and five cubits on the other side, and he measured the length thereof, forty cubits, and the breadth, twenty cubits. Then went he inward and measured the post of the door, two cubits, and the door, six cubits, and the breadth of the door, seven cubits. So he measured the length thereof, twenty cubits, and the breadth, twenty cubits, before the temple and he said unto me, This is the most holy place.

After he measured the wall of the house, six cubits, and the breadth of every side chamber, four cubits, round about the house on every side. And the side chambers were three, one over another and thirty in order, and they entered into the wall which was of the house for the side chambers roundabout that they might have hold, but they had not hold in the wall of the house. And there was an enlarging and a winding about still upward to the side chambers, for the winding about of the house went still upward round about the house, therefore the breadth of the house was still upward, and so increased from the lowest chamber to the highest by the midst. I saw also the height of the house round about, the foundations of the side chambers were a full reed of six great cubits. The thickness of the wall which was for the side chamber without was five cubits, and that which was left was the place of the side chambers that were within. And between the chambers was the wideness of twenty cubits round about the house on every side. And the doors of the side chambers were toward the place that was left, one door toward the north and another door toward the south, and the breadth of the place that was left was five cubits round about.

Now the building that was before the separate place at the end toward the west was seventy cubits broad, and the wall of the building was five cubits thick round about, and the length thereof ninety cubits. So he measured the house, a hundred cubits long, and the separate plac, and the building, with the walls thereof, a hundred cubits long; also the breadth of the face of the house and of the separate place toward the east, a hundred cubits. And he measured the length of the building over against the separate place which was behind it and the galleries thereof on the one side and on the other side, a hundred cubits, with the inner temple and the porches of the court, the doorposts and the narrow windows, and the galleries round about on their three stories, over against the door, ceiled with wood round about, and from the ground up to the windows, and the windows were covered to that above the door, even unto the inner house and without, and by all the wall round about within and without, by measure. And it was made with cherubim and palm trees, so that a palm tree was between a cherub and a cherub, and every cherub had two faces, so that the face of a man was toward the palm tree on the one side, and the face of a young lion toward the palm tree on the other side, it was made through all the house round about. From the ground unto above the door were cherubim and palm trees made, and on the wall of the temple.

The posts of the temple were squared and the face of the sanctuary, the appearance of the one as the appearance of the other. The altar of wood was three cubits high, and the length thereof two cubits, and the corners thereof, and the length thereof, and the walls thereof, were of wood, and he said unto me, This is the table that is before the Lord. And the temple and the sanctuary had two doors. And the doors had two leaves apiece, two turning leaves, two leaves for the one door, and two leaves for the other door. And there were made on them, on the doors of the temple, cherubim and palm trees, like as were made upon the walls, and there were thick planks upon the face of the porch without. And there were narrow windows and palm trees on the one side and on the other side, on the sides of the porch and upon the side chambers of the house, and thick planks.

Then he brought me forth into the outer court, the way toward the north, and he brought me into the chamber that was over against the separate place and which was before the building toward the north. Before the length of a hundred cubits was the north door and the breadth was fifty cubits. Over against the twenty cubits which were for the inner court and over against the pavement which was for the outer court was gallery against gallery in three stories. And before the chambers was a walk of ten cubits breadth inward, a way of one cubit, and their doors toward the north. Now the upper chambers were shorter, for the galleries were higher than these, than the lower, and than the middlemost of the building. For they were in three stories, but had not pillars as the pillars of the courts, therefore the building was straitened more than the lowest and the middlemost from the ground. And the wall that was without over against the chambers toward the outer court on the forepart of the chambers, the length thereof was fifty cubits. For the length of the chambers that were in the outer court was fifty cubits and lo, before the temple were a hundred cubits. And from under these chambers was the entry on the east side as one goeth into them from the outer court. The chambers were in the thickness of the wall of the court toward the east, over against the separate place and over against the building. And the way before them was like the appearance of the chambers which were toward the north, as long as they and as broad as they, and all their goings out were both according to their fashions and according to their doors. And according to the doors of the chambers that were toward the south was a door in the head of the way, even the way directly before the wall toward the east as one entereth into them.

Then said he unto me, The north chambers and the south chambers which are before the separate place, they be holy chambers where the priests that approach unto the Lord shall eat the most holy things, there shall they lay the most holy things, and the meat offering, and the sin offering, and the trespass offering, for the place is holy. When the priests enter therein, then shall they not go out of the holy place into the outer court, but there they shall lay their garments wherein they minister, for they are holy, and shall put on other garments, and shall approach to those things which are for the people.

Now when he had made an end of measuring the inner house he brought me forth toward the gate whose prospect is toward the east and measured it round about. He measured the east side with the measuring reed, five hundred reeds, with the measuring reed round about. He measured the north side, five hundred reeds, with the measuring reed round about. He measured the south side, five hundred reeds, with the measuring reed. He turned about to the west side, and measured five hundred reeds with the measuring reed. He measured it by the four sides, it had a wall round about, five hundred reeds long and five hundred broad, to make a separation between the sanctuary and the profane place.

Afterward he brought me to the gate, even the gate that looketh toward the east and behold, the glory of the God of Israel came from the way of the east, and his voice was like a noise of many waters, and the Earth shined with his glory. And it was according to the appearance of the vision which I saw, even according to the vision that I saw when I came to destroy the city, and the visions were like the vision that I saw by the river Chebar, and I fell upon my face. And the glory of the Lord came into the house by the way of the gate whose prospect is toward the east. So the Spirit took me up and brought me into the inner court and behold, the glory of the Lord filled the house. And I heard him speaking unto me out of the house and the man stood by me. And he said unto me, Son of man, the place of my throne and the place of the soles of my feet where I will dwell in the midst of the children of Israel forever, and my holy name, shall the house of Israel no more defile, neither they nor their kings, by their whoredom, nor by the carcasses of their kings in their high places. In their setting of their threshold by my thresholds, and their post by my posts, and the wall between me and them, they have even defiled my holy name by their abominations that they have committed, wherefore I have consumed them in mine anger. Now let them put away their whoredom and the carcasses of their kings far from me and I will dwell in the midst of them forever.

Thou son of man, show the house to the house of Israel, that they may be ashamed of their iniquities and let them measure the pattern. And if they be ashamed of all that they have done, show them the form of the house, and the fashion thereof, and the goings out thereof, and the comings in thereof, and all the forms thereof, and all the ordinances thereof, and all the forms thereof, and all the laws thereof, and write it in their sight that they may keep the whole form thereof, and all the ordinances thereof, and do them. This is the law of the house; upon the top of the mountain the whole limit thereof round about shall be most holy. Behold, this is the law of the house.

And these are the measures of the altar after the cubits, The cubit is a cubit and a handbreadth, even the bottom shall be a cubit, and the breadth a cubit, and the border thereof by the edge thereof round about shall be a span, and this shall be the higher place of the altar. And from the bottom upon the ground even to the lower settle shall be two cubits, and the breadth, one cubit, and from the lesser settle even to the greater settle shall be four cubits, and the breadth, one cubit. So the altar shall be four cubits, and from the altar and upward shall be four horns. And the altar shall be twelve cubits long, twelve broad, square in the four squares thereof. And the settle shall be fourteen cubits long and fourteen broad in the four squares thereof, and the border about it shall be half a cubit, and the bottom thereof shall be a cubit about, and his stairs shall look toward the east.

18 AND he said unto me, Son of man, thus saith the Lord God, These are the ordinances of the altar in the day when they shall make it, to offer burnt offerings thereon and to sprinkle blood thereon. And thou shalt give to the priests, the Levites that be of the seed of Zadok which approach unto me to minister unto me, saith the Lord God, a young bullock for a sin offering. And thou shalt take of the blood thereof and put it on the four horns of it, and on the four corners of the settle, and upon the border round about; thus shalt thou cleanse and purge it. Thou shalt take the bullock also of the sin offering and he shall burn it in the appointed place of the house without the sanctuary. And on the second day thou shalt offer a kid of the goats without blemish for a sin offering, and they shall cleanse the altar as they did cleanse it with the bullock. When thou hast made an end of cleansing it, thou shalt offer a young bullock without blemish and a ram out of the flock without blemish. And thou shalt offer them before the Lord, and the priests shall cast salt upon them, and they shall offer them up for a burnt offering unto the Lord. Seven days shalt thou prepare every day a goat for a sin offering, they shall also prepare a young bullock and a ram out of the flock without blemish. Seven days shall they purge the altar and purify it and they shall consecrate themselves. And when these days are expired, it shall be that upon the eighth day, and so forward, the priests shall make your burnt offerings upon the altar and your peace offerings, and I will accept you, saith the Lord God.

Then he brought me back the way of the gate of the outward sanctuary which looketh toward the east and it was shut. Then said the Lord unto me, This gate shall be shut, it shall not be opened and no man shall enter in by it, because the Lord the God of Israel hath entered in by it therefore it shall be shut. It is for the prince, the prince, he shall sit in it to eat bread before the Lord, he shall enter by the way of the porch of that gate and shall go out by the way of the same.

Then brought he me the way of the north gate before the house, and I looked and behold, the glory of the Lord filled the house of the Lord and I fell upon my face. And the Lord said unto me, Son of man, mark well and behold with thine eyes, and hear with thine ears all that I say unto thee concerning all the ordinances of the house of the Lord, and all the laws thereof, and mark well the entering in of the house with every going forth of the sanctuary. And thou shalt say to the rebellious, even to the house of Israel, Thus saith the Lord God, O ye house of

Israel, let it suffice you of all your abominations in that ye have brought into my sanctuary strangers, uncircumcised in heart and uncircumcised in flesh, to be in my sanctuary, to pollute it, even my house, when ye offer my bread, the fat and the blood, and they have broken my covenant because of all your abominations. Ye have not kept the charge of mine holy things, but ye have set keepers of my charge in my sanctuary for yourselves.

Thus saith the Lord God, No stranger, uncircumcised in heart nor uncircumcised in flesh, shall enter into my sanctuary, of any stranger that is among the children of Israel. And the Levites that are gone away far from me when Israel went astray, which went astray away from me after their idols, they shall even bear their iniquity. Yet they shall be ministers in my sanctuary, having charge at the gates of the house and ministering to the house, they shall slay the burnt offering and the sacrifice for the people and they shall stand before them to minister unto them. Because they ministered unto them before their idols and caused the house of Israel to fall into iniquity, therefore have I lifted up mine hand against them, saith the Lord God, and they shall bear their iniquity. And they shall not come near unto me to do the office of a priest unto me, nor to come near to any of my holy things in the most holy place, but they shall bear their shame and their abominations which they have committed. But I will make them keepers of the charge of the house, for all the service thereof, and for all that shall be done therein. But the priests, the Levites, the sons of Zadok, that kept the charge of my sanctuary when the children of Israel went astray from me, they shall come near to me to minister unto me and they shall stand before me to offer unto me the fat and the blood, saith the Lord God; they shall enter into my sanctuary, and they shall come near to my table to minister unto me, and they shall keep my charge.

And it shall come to pass, that when they enter in at the gates of the inner court they shall be clothed with linen garments, and no wool shall come upon them while they minister in the gates of the inner court and within. They shall have linen bonnets upon their heads and shall have linen breeches upon their loins; they shall not gird themselves with anything that causeth sweat. And when they go forth into the outer court, even into the outer court to the people, they shall put off their garments wherein they ministered and lay them in the holy chambers, and they shall put on other garments, and they shall not sanctify the people with their garments. Neither shall they shave their heads, nor suffer their locks to grow long, they shall only poll their heads. Neither shall any priest drink wine when they enter into the inner court. Neither shall they take for their wives a widow nor her that is put away, but they shall take maidens of the seed of the house of Israel or a widow that had a priest before. And they shall teach my people the difference between the holy and profane and cause them to discern between the unclean and the clean. And in controversy they shall stand in judgment and they shall judge it according to my judgments, and they shall keep my laws and my statutes in all mine assemblies, and they shall hallow my sabbaths. And they shall come at no dead person to defile themselves, but for father, or for mother, or for son, or for daughter, for brother, or for sister that hath had no husband they may defile themselves. And after he is cleansed, they shall reckon unto him seven days. And in the day that he goeth into the sanctuary unto the inner court to minister in the sanctuary he shall offer his sin offering, saith the Lord God.

And it shall be unto them for an inheritance: I am their inheritance, and ye shall give them no possession in Israel: I am their possession. They shall eat the meat offering, and the sin offering, and the trespass offering, and every dedicated thing in Israel shall be theirs. And the first of all the firstfruits of all things, and every oblation of all, of every sort of your oblations, shall be the priest's; ye shall also give unto the priest the first of your dough, that he may cause the blessing to rest in thine house. The priests shall not eat of anything that is dead of itself or torn, whether it be fowl or beast.

Moreover, when ye shall divide by lot the land for inheritance, ye shall offer an oblation unto the Lord, a holy portion of the land, the length shall be the length of five and twenty thousand reeds, and the breadth shall be ten thousand. This shall be holy in all the borders thereof round about. Of this there shall be for the sanctuary five hundred in length, with five hundred in breadth, square round about, and fifty cubits round about for the suburbs thereof. And of this measure shalt thou measure the length of five and twenty thousand, and the breadth of ten thousand, and in it shall be the sanctuary and the most holy place. The holy portion of the land shall be for the priests, the ministers of the sanctuary which shall come near to minister unto the Lord, and it shall be a place for their houses and a holy place for the sanctuary. And the five and twenty thousand of length and the ten thousand of breadth shall also the Levites, the ministers of the house, have for themselves for a possession for twenty chambers. And ye shall appoint the possession of the city five thousand broad, and five and twenty thousand long, over against the oblation of the holy portion; it shall be for the whole house of Israel.

And a portion shall be for the prince on the one side and on the other side of the oblation of the holy portion and of the possession of the city, before the oblation of the holy portion, and before the possession of the city, from the west side westward and from the east side eastward, and the length shall be over against one of the portions, from the west border unto the east border. In the land shall be his possession in Israel and my princes shall no more oppress my people, and the rest of the land shall they give to the house of Israel according to their tribes. Thus saith the Lord God, Let it suffice you, O princes of Israel, remove violence and spoil, and execute judgment and justice, take away your exactions from my people, saith the Lord God. Ye shall have just balances, and a just ephah, and a just bath. The ephah and the bath shall be of one measure, that the bath may contain the tenth part of a homer and the ephah the tenth part of a homer; the measure thereof shall be after the homer. And the shekel shall be twenty gerahs, twenty shekels, five and twenty shekels, fifteen shekels, shall be your maneh.

This is the oblation that ye shall offer: the sixth part of an ephah of a homer of wheat, and ye shall give the sixth part of an ephah of a homer of barley. Concerning the ordinance of oil, the bath of oil, ye shall offer the tenth part of a bath out of the cor, which is a homer of ten baths, for ten baths are a homer, and one lamb out of the flock, out of two hundred, out of the fat pastures of Israel, for a meat offering, and for a burnt offering, and for peace offerings, to make reconciliation for them, saith the Lord God. All the people of the land shall give this oblation for the prince in Israel. And it shall be the prince's part to give burnt offerings, and meat offerings, and drink offerings, in the feasts, and in the new moons, and in the sabbaths, in all solemnities of the house of Israel he shall prepare the sin offering, and the meat offering, and the burnt offering, and the peace offerings, to make reconciliation for the house of Israel.

Thus saith the Lord God, In the first month, in the first day of the month, thou shalt take a young bullock without blemish and cleanse the sanctuary, and the priest shall take of the blood of the sin offering and put it upon the posts of the house, and upon the four corners of the settle of the altar, and upon the posts of the gate of the inner court. And so thou shalt do the seventh day of the month for every one that erreth, and for him that is simple so shall ye reconcile the house.

In the first month, in the fourteenth day of the month, ye shall have the Passover, a feast of seven days; unleavened bread shall be eaten. And upon that day shall the prince prepare for himself and for all the people of the land a bullock for a sin offering. And seven days of the feast he shall prepare a burnt offering to the Lord, seven bullocks and seven rams without blemish daily the seven days, and a kid of the goats daily for a sin offering. And he shall prepare a meat offering of an ephah for a bullock, and an ephah for a ram, and a hin of oil for an ephah. In the seventh month, in the fifteenth day of the month, shall he do the like in the feast of the seven days, according to the sin offering, according to the burnt offering, according to the meat offering, and according to the oil.

Thus saith the Lord God, The gate of the inner court that looketh toward the east shall be shut the six working days, but on the sabbath it shall be opened and in the day of the new moon it shall be opened. And the prince shall enter by the way of the porch of that gate without and shall stand by the post of the gate, and the priests shall prepare his burnt offering and his peace offerings, and he shall worship at the threshold of the gate, then he shall go forth, but the gate shall not be shut until the evening. Likewise the people of the land shall worship at the door of this gate before the Lord in the sabbaths and in the new moons. And the burnt offering that the prince shall offer unto the Lord in the sabbath day shall be six lambs without blemish and a ram without blemish. And the meat offering shall be an ephah for a ram, and the meat offering for the lambs as he shall be able to give, and a hin of oil to an ephah. And in the day of the new moon it shall be a young bullock without blemish, and six lambs, and a ram; they shall be without blemish. And he shall prepare a meat offering: an ephah for a bullock, and an ephah for a ram, and for the lambs according as his hand shall attain unto and a hin of oil to an ephah. And when the prince shall enter he shall go in by the way of the porch of that gate and he shall go forth by the way thereof.

But when the people of the land shall come before the Lord in the solemn feasts, he that entereth in by the way of the north gate to worship shall go out by the way of the south gate, and he that entereth by the way of the south gate shall go forth by the way of the north gate, he shall not return by the way of the gate whereby he came in, but shall go forth over against it. And the prince in the midst of them, when they go in, shall go in, and when they go forth, shall go forth. And in the feasts and in the solemnities, the meat offering shall be an ephah to a bullock, and an ephah to a ram, and to the lambs as he is able to give, and a hin of oil to an ephah. Now when the prince shall prepare a voluntary burnt offering or peace offerings voluntarily unto the Lord, one shall then open him the gate that looketh toward the east, and he shall prepare his burnt offering and his peace offerings as he did on the sabbath day; then he shall go forth and after his going forth one shall shut the gate. Thou shalt daily prepare a burnt offering unto the Lord of a lamb of the first year without blemish; thou shalt prepare it every morning. And thou shalt prepare a meat offering for it every morning, the sixth part of an ephah, and the third part of a hin of oil, to temper with the fine flour, a meat offering continually by a perpetual ordinance unto the Lord. Thus shall they prepare the lamb, and the meat offering, and the oil, every morning for a continual burnt offering.

Thus saith the Lord God, If the prince give a gift unto any of his sons, the inheritance thereof shall be his sons', it shall be their possession by inheritance. But if he give a gift of his inheritance to one of his servants, then it shall be his to the year of liberty, after, it shall return to the prince, but his inheritance shall be his sons' for them. Moreover the prince shall not take of the people's inheritance by oppression to thrust them out of their possession, but he shall give his sons inheritance out of his own possession that my people be not scattered every man from his possession.

After he brought me through the entry which was at the side of the gate into the holy chambers of the priests which looked toward the north, and behold, there was a place on the two sides westward. Then said he unto me, This is the place where the priests shall boil the trespass offering and the sin offering, where they shall bake the meat offering, that they bear them not out into the outer court to sanctify the people. Then he brought me forth into the outer court and caused me to pass by the four corners of the court, and behold, in every corner of the court there was a court. In the four corners of the court there were courts joined of forty cubits long and thirty broad; these four corners were of one measure. And there was a row of building round about in them, round about them four, and it was made with boiling places under the rows round about. Then said he unto me, These are the places of them that boil, where the ministers of the house shall boil the sacrifice of the people.

Afterward he brought me again unto the door of the house, and behold, waters issued out from under the threshold of the house eastward, for the forefront of the house stood toward the east and the waters came down from under, from the right side of the house at the south side of the altar. Then brought he me out of the way of the gate northward and led me about the way without unto the outer gate by the way that looketh eastward, and behold, there ran out waters on the right side. And when the man that had the line in his hand went forth eastward, he measured a thousand cubits and he brought me through the waters; the waters were to the ankles. Again he measured a thousand and brought me through the waters; the waters were to the knees. Again he measured a thousand and brought me through; the waters were to the loins. Afterward he measured a thousand and it was a river that I could not pass over, for the waters were risen, waters to swim in, a river that could not be passed over.

And he said unto me, Son of man, hast thou seen this? Then he brought me and caused me to return to the brink of the river. Now when I had returned, behold, at the bank of the river were very many trees on the one side and on the other. Then said he unto me, These waters issue out toward the east country and go down into the desert and go into the sea, which being brought forth into the sea, the waters shall be healed. And it shall come to pass that everything that liveth which moveth, whithersoever the rivers shall come, shall live, and there shall be a very great multitude of fish because these waters shall come thither, for they shall be healed and everything shall live whither the river cometh. And it shall come to pass that the fishers shall stand upon it from En-gedi even unto En-eglaim, they shall be a place to spread forth nets; their fish shall be according to their kinds as the fish of the great sea, exceeding many. But the miry places thereof and the marshes thereof shall not be healed, they shall be given to salt. And by the river upon the bank thereof, on this side and on that side, shall grow all trees for meat, whose leaf shall not fade neither shall the fruit thereof be consumed; it shall bring forth new fruit according to his months because their waters they issued out of the sanctuary, and the fruit thereof shall be for meat and the leaf thereof for medicine.

Thus saith the Lord God, This shall be the border, whereby ye shall inherit the land according to the twelve tribes of Israel; Joseph shall have two portions. And ye shall inherit it, one as well as another, concerning the which I lifted up mine hand to give it unto your fathers, and this land shall fall unto you for inheritance. And this shall be the border of the land toward the north side, from the great sea, the way of Hethlon, as men go to Zedad, Hamath, Berothah, Sibraim, which is between the border of Damascus and the border of Hamath, Hazar-hatticon, which is by the coast of Hauran. And the border from the sea shall be Hazar-enan, the border of Damascus, and the north northward, and the border of Hamath. And this is the north side. And the east side ye shall measure from Hauran, and from Damascus, and from Gilead, and from the land of Israel by Jordan, from the border unto the east sea. And this is the east side. And the south side southward, from Tamar even to the waters of strife in Kadesh, the river to the great sea. And this is the south side southward. The west side also shall be the great sea from the border till a man come over against Hamath. This is the west side. So shall ye divide this land unto you according to the tribes of Israel.

And it shall come to pass, that ye shall divide it by lot for an inheritance unto you, and to the strangers that sojourn among you which shall beget children among you, and they shall be unto you as born in the country among the children of Israel; they shall have inheritance with you among the tribes of Israel. And it shall come to pass that in what tribe the stranger sojourneth, there shall ye give him his inheritance, saith the Lord God.

Now these are the names of the tribes: From the north end to the coast of the way of Hethlon, as one goeth to Hamath, Hazar-enan, the border of Damascus northward, to the coast of Hamath, for these are his sides east and west, a portion for Dan. And by the border of Dan, from the east side unto the west side, a portion for Asher. And by the border of Asher, from the east side even unto the west side, a portion for Naphtali. And by the border of Naphtali, from the east side unto the west side, a portion for Manasseh. And by the border of Manasseh, from the east side unto the west side, a portion for Ephraim. And by the border of Ephraim, from the east side even unto the west side, a portion for Reuben. And by the border of Reuben, from the east side unto the west side, a portion for Judah.

And by the border of Judah, from the east side unto the west side, shall be the offering which ye shall offer of five and twenty thousand reeds in breadth, and in length as one of the other parts, from the east side unto the west side, and the sanctuary shall be in the midst of it. The oblation that ye shall offer unto the Lord shall be of five and twenty thousand in length and of ten thousand in breadth. And for them, even for the priests, shall be this holy oblation, toward the north five and twenty thousand in length, and toward the west ten thousand in breadth, and toward the east ten thousand in breadth, and toward the south five and twenty thousand in length, and the sanctuary of the Lord shall be in the midst thereof. It shall be for the priests that are sanctified of the sons of Zadok which have kept my charge, which went not astray when the children of Israel went astray as the Levites went astray. And this oblation of the land that is offered shall be unto them a thing most holy by the border of the Levites. And over against the border of the priests the Levites shall have five and twenty thousand in length and ten thousand in breadth, all the length shall be five and twenty thousand and the breadth ten thousand. And they shall not sell of it, neither exchange, nor alienate the firstfruits of the land, for it is holy unto the Lord.

And the five thousand that are left in the breadth over against the five and twenty thousand shall be a profane place for the city, for dwelling and for suburbs, and the city shall be in the midst thereof. And these shall be the measures thereof, the north side four thousand and five hundred, and the south side four thousand and five hundred, and on the east side four thousand and five hundred, and the west side four thousand and five hundred. And the suburbs of the city shall be toward the north two hundred and fifty, and toward the south two hundred and fifty, and toward the east two hundred and fifty, and toward the west two hundred and fifty. And the residue in length over against the oblation of the holy portion shall be ten thousand eastward, and ten thousand westward, and it shall be over against the oblation of the holy portion, and the increase thereof shall be for food unto them that serve the city. And they that serve the city shall serve it out of all the tribes of Israel. All the oblation shall be five and twenty thousand by five and twenty thousand; ye shall offer the holy oblation foursquare with the possession of the city. And the residue shall be for the prince, on the one side and on the other of the holy oblation, and of the possession of the city, over against the five and twenty thousand of the oblation toward the east border, and westward over against the five and twenty thousand toward the west border, over against the portion for the prince, and it shall be the holy oblation, and the sanctuary of the house shall be in the midst thereof. Moreover, from the possession of the Levites and from the possession of the city, being in the midst of that which is the prince's, between the border of Judah and the border of Benjamin, shall be for the prince.

As for the rest of the tribes, from the east side unto the west side, Benjamin shall have a portion. And by the border of Benjamin, from the east side unto the west side, Simeon shall have a portion. And by the border of Simeon, from the east side unto the west side, Issachar a portion. And by the border of Issachar, from the east side unto the west side, Zebulun a portion. And by the border of Zebulun, from the east side unto the west side, Gad a portion. And by the border of Gad, at the south side southward, the border shall be even from Tamar unto the waters of strife in Kadesh and to the river toward the great sea. This is the land which ye shall divide by lot unto the tribes of Israel for inheritance and these are their portions, saith the Lord God.

And these are the goings out of the city on the north side, four thousand and five hundred measures. And the gates of the city shall be after the names of the tribes of Israel, three gates northward, one gate of Reuben, one gate of Judah, one gate of Levi. And at the east side four thousand and five hundred, and three gates, and one gate of Joseph, one gate of Benjamin, one gate of Dan. And at the south side four thousand and five hundred measures, and three gates, one gate of Simeon, one gate of Issachar, one gate of Zebulun. At the west side four thousand and five hundred, with their three gates, one gate of Gad, one gate of Asher, one gate of Naphtali. It was round about eighteen thousand measures, and the name of the city from that day shall be called Holy, for the Lord shall be there.

THE BOOK OF DANIEL

IN the third year of the reign of Jehoiakim, king of Judah, came Nebuchadnezzar king of Babylon unto Jerusalem, and besieged it. And the Lord gave Jehoiakim king of Judah into his hand, with part of the vessels of the house of God which he carried into the land of Shinar to the house of his god, and he brought the vessels into the treasure house of his god.

And the king spake unto Ashpenaz, the master of his eunuchs, that he should bring certain of the children of Israel, and of the king's seed, and of the princes, children in whom was no blemish, but well favored and skillful in all wisdom, and cunning in knowledge, and understanding science, and such as had ability in them to stand in the king's palace, and whom they might teach the learning and the tongue of the Chaldeans. And the king appointed them a daily provision of the king's meat and of the wine which he drank, so nourishing them three years, that at the end thereof they might stand before the king. Now among these were of the children of Judah, Daniel, Hananiah, Mishael, and Azariah, unto whom the prince of the eunuchs gave names, for he gave unto Daniel the name of Beltheshazzar, and to Hananiah, of Shadrach, and to Mishael, of Meshach, and to Azariah, of Abed-nego.

But Daniel purposed in his heart that he would not defile himself with the portion of the king's meat, nor with the wine which he drank, therefore he requested of the prince of the eunuchs that he might not defile himself. Now God had brought Daniel into favor and tender love with the prince of the eunuchs. And the prince of the eunuchs said unto Daniel, I fear my lord the king, who hath appointed your meat and your drink, for why should he see your faces worse liking than the children which are of your sort? Then shall ye make me endanger my head to the king. Then said Daniel to Melzar, whom the prince of the eunuchs had set over Daniel, Hananiah, Mishael, and Azariah, Prove thy servants, I beseech thee, ten days, and let them give us pulse to eat and water to drink. Then let our countenances be looked upon before thee and the countenance of the children that eat of the portion of the king's meat, and as thou seest, deal with thy servants. So he consented to them in this matter and proved them ten days. And at the end of ten days their countenances appeared fairer and fatter in flesh than all the children which did eat the portion of the king's meat. Thus Melzar took away the portion of their meat and the wine that they should drink and gave them pulse.

As for these four children, God gave them knowledge and skill in all learning and wisdom, and Daniel had understanding in all visions and dreams. Now at the end of the days that the king had said he should bring them in, then the prince of the eunuchs brought them in before Nebuchadnezzar. And the king communed with them and among them all was found none like Daniel, Hananiah, Mishael, and Azariah, therefore stood they before the king. And in all matters of wisdom and understanding that the king inquired of them, he found them ten times better than all the magicians and astrologers that were in all his realm. And Daniel continued even unto the first year of king Cyrus.

2 AND in the second year of the reign of Nebuchadnezzar, Nebuchadnezzar dreamed dreams wherewith his spirit was troubled and his sleep brake from him. Then the king commanded to call the magicians, and the astrologers, and the sorcerers, and the Chaldeans, for to show the king his dreams. So they came and stood before the king. And the king said unto them, I have dreamed a dream and my spirit was troubled to know the dream. Then spake the Chaldeans to the king in Syriac, O king, live forever, tell thy servants the dream and we will show the interpretation. The king answered and said to the Chaldeans, The thing is gone from me, if ye will not make known unto me the dream with the interpretation thereof, ye shall be cut in pieces, and your houses shall be made a dunghill. But if ye show the dream and the interpretation thereof, ye shall receive of me gifts and rewards and great honor; therefore show me the dream and the interpretation thereof. They answered again and said, Let the king tell his servants the dream and we will show the interpretation of it. The king answered and said, I know of certainty that ye would gain the time because ye see the thing is gone from me. But if ye will not make known unto me the dream, there is but one decree for you, for ye have prepared lying and corrupt words to speak before me till the time be changed; therefore tell me the dream and I shall know that ye can show me the interpretation thereof. The Chaldeans answered before the king and said, There is not a man upon the earth that can show the king's matter, therefore there is no king, lord, nor ruler that asked such things at any magician, or astrologer, or Chaldean. And it is a rare thing that the king requireth and there is none other that can show it before the king, except the gods whose dwelling is not with flesh. For this cause the king was angry and very furious and commanded to destroy all the wise men of Babylon. And the decree went forth that the wise men should be slain and they sought Daniel and his fellows to be slain.

Then Daniel answered with counsel and wisdom to Arioch the captain of the king's guard, which was gone forth to slay the wise men of Babylon, he answered and said to Arioch the king's captain, Why is the decree so hasty from the king? Then Arioch made the thing known to Daniel. Then Daniel went in and desired of the king that he would give him time and that he would show the king the interpretation. Then Daniel went to his house and made the thing known to Hananiah, Mishael, and Azariah, his companions, that they would desire mercies of the God of Heaven concerning this secret, that Daniel and his fellows should not perish with the rest of the wise men of Babylon.

Then was the secret revealed unto Daniel in a night vision. Then Daniel blessed the God of Heaven. Daniel answered and said, Blessed be the name of God for ever and ever, for wisdom and might are his and he changeth the times and the seasons, he removeth kings and setteth up kings, he giveth wisdom unto the wise and knowledge to them that know understanding, he revealeth the deep and secret things, he knoweth what is in the darkness and the light dwelleth with him. I thank thee and praise thee, O thou God of my fathers, who hast given me wisdom and might and hast made known unto me now what we desired of thee, for thou hast now made known unto us the king's matter.

Therefore Daniel went in unto Arioch, whom the king had ordained to destroy the wise men of Babylon, he went and said thus unto him, Destroy not the wise men of Babylon; bring me in before the king and I will show unto the king the interpretation. Then Arioch brought in Daniel before the king in haste, and said thus unto him, I have found a man of the captives of Judah that will make known unto the king the interpretation. The king answered and said to Daniel whose name was Belteshazzar, Art thou able to make known unto me the dream which I have seen and the interpretation thereof? Daniel answered in the presence of the king and said, The secret which the king hath demanded cannot the wise men, the astrologers, the magicians, the soothsayers show unto the king, but there is a God in Heaven that revealeth secrets and maketh known to the king Nebuchadnezzar what shall be in the latter days. Thy dream and the visions of thy head upon thy bed are these: as for thee, O king, thy thoughts came into thy mind upon thy bed what should come to pass hereafter, and he that revealeth secrets maketh known to thee what shall come to pass. But as for me, this secret is not revealed to me for any wisdom that I have more than any living, but for their sakes that shall make known the interpretation to the king and that thou mightest know the thoughts of thy heart.

Thou, O king, sawest, and behold a great image. This great image, whose brightness was excellent, stood before thee and the form thereof was terrible. This image's head was of fine gold, his breast and his arms of silver, his belly and his thighs of brass, his legs of iron, his feet part of iron and part of clay. Thou sawest till that a stone was cut out without hands, which smote the image upon his feet that were of iron and clay and brake them to pieces. Then was the iron, the clay, the brass, the silver, and the gold, broken to pieces together and became like the chaff of the summer threshing floors, and the wind carried them away that no place was found for them, and the stone that smote the image became a great mountain and filled the whole earth.

This is the dream, and we will tell the interpretation thereof before the king. Thou, O king, art a king of kings, for the God of Heaven hath given thee a kingdom, power, and strength, and glory. And wheresoever the children of men dwell, the beasts of the field and the fowls of the Heaven hath he given into thine hand and hath made thee ruler over them all. Thou art this head of gold. And after thee shall arise another kingdom inferior to thee, and another third kingdom of brass which shall bear rule over all the earth. And the fourth kingdom shall be strong as iron, forasmuch as iron breaketh in pieces and subdueth all things, and as iron that breaketh all these shall it break in pieces and bruise. And whereas thou sawest the feet and toes, part of potters' clay and part of iron, the kingdom shall be divided, but there shall be in it of the strength of the iron forasmuch as thou sawest the iron mixed with miry clay. And as the toes of the feet were part of iron and part of clay, so the kingdom shall be partly strong and partly broken. And whereas thou sawest iron mixed with miry clay, they shall mingle themselves with the seed of men, but they shall not cleave one to another even as iron is not mixed with clay. And in the days of these kings shall the God of Heaven set up a kingdom which shall never be destroyed, and the kingdom shall not be left to other people, but it shall break in pieces and consume all these kingdoms and it shall stand forever. Forasmuch as thou sawest that the stone was cut out of the mountain without hands and that it brake in pieces the iron, the brass, the clay, the silver, and the gold, the great God hath made known to the king what shall come to pass hereafter, and the dream is certain and the interpretation thereof sure.

Then the king Nebuchadnezzar fell upon his face and worshiped Daniel and commanded that they should offer an oblation and sweet odors unto him. The king answered unto Daniel and said, Of a truth it is that your God is a God of gods, and a Lord of kings, and a revealer of secrets, seeing thou couldest reveal this secret. Then the king made Daniel a great man and he gave him many great gifts, and made him ruler over the whole province of Babylon and chief of the governors over all the wise men of Babylon. Then Daniel requested of the king and he set Shadrach, Meshach, and Abed-nego, over the affairs of the province of Babylon, but Daniel sat in the gate of the king.

3 NEBUCHADNEZZAR the king made an image of gold, whose height was threescore cubits and the breadth thereof six cubits, he set it up in the plain of Dura in the province of Babylon. Then Nebuchadnezzar the king sent to gather together the princes, the governors, and the captains, the judges, the treasurers, the counselors, the sheriffs, and all the rulers of the provinces, to come to the dedication of the image which Nebuchadnezzar the king had set up. Then the princes, the governors, and captains, the judges, the treasurers, the counselors, the sheriffs, and all the rulers of the provinces were gathered together unto the dedication of the image that Nebuchadnezzar the king had set up and they stood before the image that Nebuchadnezzar had set up. Then a herald cried aloud, To you it is commanded, O people, nations, and languages, that at what time ye hear the sound of the cornet, flute, harp, sackbut, psaltery, dulcimer, and all kinds of music, ye fall down and worship the golden image that Nebuchadnezzar the king hath set up, and whoso falleth not down and worshipeth shall the same hour be cast into the midst of a burning fiery furnace. Therefore at that time when all the people heard the sound of the cornet, flute, harp, sackbut, psaltery, and all kinds of music, all the people, the nations, and the languages, fell down and worshiped the golden image that Nebuchadnezzar the king had set up.

Wherefore at that time certain Chaldeans came near and accused the Jews. They spake and said to the king Nebuchadnezzar, O king, live forever. Thou, O king, hast made a decree that every man that shall hear the sound of the cornet, flute, harp, sackbut, psaltery, and dulcimer, and all kinds of music, shall fall down and worship the golden image, and whoso falleth not down and worshipeth, that he should be cast into the midst of a burning fiery furnace. There are certain Jews whom thou hast set over the affairs of the province of Babylon, Shadrach, Meshach, and Abed-nego; these men, O king, have not regarded thee, they serve not thy gods nor worship the golden image which thou hast set up.

Then Nebuchadnezzar in his rage and fury commanded to bring Shadrach, Meshach, and Abed-nego. Then they brought these men before the king. Nebuchadnezzar spake and said unto them, Is it true, O Shadrach, Meshach, and Abed-nego, do not ye serve my god, nor worship the golden image which I have set up? Now if ye be ready that at what time ye hear the sound of the cornet, flute, harp, sackbut, psaltery, and dulcimer, and all kinds of music, ye fall down and worship the image which I have made, well, but if ye worship not, ye shall be cast the same hour into the midst of a burning fiery furnace, and who is that God that shall deliver you out of my hands? Shadrach, Meshach, and Abed-nego answered and said to the king, O Nebuchadnezzar, we are not careful to answer thee in this matter. If it be so, our God whom we serve is able to deliver us from the burning fiery furnace and he will deliver us out of thine hand, O king. But if not, be it known unto thee, O king, that we will not serve thy gods nor worship the golden image which thou hast set up.

Then was Nebuchadnezzar full of fury and the form of his visage was changed against Shadrach, Meshach, and Abed-nego, therefore he spake and commanded that they should heat the furnace one seven times more than it was wont to be heated. And he commanded the most mighty men that were in his army to bind Shadrach, Meshach, and Abed-nego and to cast them into the burning fiery furnace. Then these men were bound in their coats, their hosen, and their hats, and their other garments, and were cast into the midst of the burning fiery furnace. Therefore because the king's commandment was urgent, and the furnace exceeding hot, the flame of the fire slew those men that took up Shadrach, Meshach, and Abed-nego. And these three men, Shadrach, Meshach, and Abed-nego, fell down bound into the midst of the burning fiery furnace.

Then Nebuchadnezzar the king was astonished, and rose up in haste and spake and said unto his counselors, Did not we cast three men bound into the midst of the fire? They answered and said unto the king, True, O king. He answered and said Lo, I see four men loose, walking in the midst of the fire and they have no hurt and the form of the fourth is like the Son of God. Then Nebuchadnezzar came near to the mouth of the burning fiery furnace and spake and said, Shadrach, Meshach, and Abed-nego, ye servants of the Most High God, come forth and come hither. Then Shadrach, Meshach, and Abed-nego came forth of the midst of the fire. And the princes, governors, and captains, and the king's counselors, being gathered together, saw these men upon whose bodies the fire had no power, nor was a hair of their head singed, neither were their coats changed, nor the smell of fire had passed on them. Then Nebuchadnezzar spake and said, Blessed be the God of Shadrach, Meshach, and Abed-nego, who hath sent his angel and delivered his servants that trusted in him, and have changed the king's word, and yielded their bodies that they might not serve nor worship any god except their own God. Therefore I make a decree that every people, nation, and language, which speak anything amiss against the God of Shadrach, Meshach, and Abed-nego shall be cut in pieces and their houses shall be made a dunghill, because there is no other God that can deliver after this sort. Then the king promoted Shadrach, Meshach, and Abed-nego, in the province of Babylon.

Nebuchadnezzar the king, unto all people, nations, and languages that dwell in all the earth, Peace be multiplied unto you. I thought it good to show the signs and wonders that the high God hath wrought toward me. How great are his signs and how mighty are his wonders! His kingdom is an everlasting kingdom and his dominion is from generation to generation.

I, Nebuchadnezzar, was at rest in mine house and flourishing in my palace. I saw a dream which made me afraid and the thoughts upon my bed and the visions of my head troubled me. Therefore made I a decree to bring in all the wise men of Babylon before me that they might make known unto me the interpretation of the dream. Then came in the magicians, the astrologers, the Chaldeans, and the soothsayers, and I told the dream before them, but they did not make known unto me the interpretation thereof. But at the last Daniel came in before me, whose name was Belteshazzar, according to the name of my god and in whom is the spirit of the holy gods, and before him I told the dream, saying, O Belteshazzar, master of the magicians, because I know that the spirit of the holy gods is in thee and no secret troubleth thee, tell me the visions of my dream that I have seen, and the interpretation thereof.

Thus were the visions of mine head in my bed: I saw, and behold a tree in the midst of the Earth, and the height thereof was great. The tree grew and was strong, and the height thereof reached unto Heaven, and the sight thereof to the end of all the Earth, the leaves thereof were fair, and the fruit thereof much, and in it was meat for all, the beasts of the field had shadow under it, and the fowls of the Heaven dwelt in the boughs thereof, and all flesh was fed of it. I saw in the visions of my head upon my bed, and behold, a watcher and a holy one came down from Heaven, he cried aloud and said thus, Hew down the tree and cut off his branches, shake off his leaves and scatter his fruit, let the beasts get away from under it and the fowls from his branches, nevertheless, leave the stump of his roots in the earth, even with a band of iron and brass, in the tender grass of the field, and let it be wet with the dew of Heaven, and let his portion be with the beasts in the grass of the Earth, let his heart be changed from man's and let a beast's heart be given unto him, and let seven times pass over him. This matter is by the decree of the watchers and the demand by thy word of the holy ones, to the intent that the living may know that the Most High ruleth in the kingdom of men, and giveth it to whomsoever he will, and setteth up over it the basest of men. This dream I king Nebuchadnezzar have seen. Now thou, O Belteshazzar, declare the interpretation thereof, forasmuch as all the wise men of my kingdom are not able to make known unto me the interpretation, but thou art able, for the spirit of the holy gods is in thee.

Then Daniel, whose name was Belteshazzar, was astonished for one hour and his thoughts troubled him. The king spake and said, Belteshazzar, let not the dream, or the interpretation thereof, trouble thee. Belteshazzar answered and said, My lord, the dream be to them that hate thee and the interpretation thereof to thine enemies. The tree that thou sawest, which grew and was strong, whose height reached unto the Heaven and the sight thereof to all the Earth, whose leaves were fair and the fruit thereof much, and in it was meat for all, under which the beasts of the field dwelt and upon whose branches the fowls of the Heaven had their habitation, it is thou, O king, that art grown and become strong, for thy greatness is grown and reacheth unto Heaven, and thy dominion to the end of the earth. And whereas the king saw a watcher and a holy one coming down from Heaven and saying, Hew the tree down and destroy it, yet leave the stump of the roots thereof in the Earth, even with a band of iron and brass, in the tender grass of the field, and let it be wet with the dew of Heaven, and let his portion be with the beasts of the field, till seven times pass over him, this is the interpretation, O king, and this is the decree of the Most High which is come upon my lord the king, that they shall drive thee from men, and thy dwelling shall be with the beasts of the field, and they shall make thee to eat grass as oxen, and they shall wet thee with the dew of Heaven, and seven times shall pass over thee till thou know that the Most High ruleth in the kingdom of men and giveth it to whomsoever he will. And whereas they commanded to leave the stump of the tree roots, thy kingdom shall be sure unto thee, after that thou shalt have known that the heavens do rule. Wherefore, O king, let my counsel be acceptable unto thee, and break off thy sins by righteousness, and thine iniquities by showing mercy to the poor, if it may be a lengthening of thy tranquility.

All this came upon the king Nebuchadnezzar. At the end of twelve months he walked in the palace of the kingdom of Babylon. The king spake and said, Is not this great Babylon that I have built for the house of the kingdom by the might of my power and for the honor of my majesty? While the word was in the king's mouth, there fell a voice from Heaven saying, O king Nebuchadnezzar, to thee it is spoken, The kingdom is departed from thee. And they shall drive thee from men, and thy dwelling shall be with the beasts of the field, they shall make thee to eat grass as oxen, and seven times shall pass over thee until thou know that the Most High ruleth in the kingdom of men and giveth it to whomsoever he will. The same hour was the thing fulfilled upon Nebuchadnezzar, and he was driven from men, and did eat grass as oxen, and his body was wet with the dew of Heaven, till his hairs were grown like eagles' feathers and his nails like birds' claws.

And at the end of the days I, Nebuchadnezzar, lifted up mine eyes unto Heaven, and mine understanding returned unto me, and I blessed the Most High, and I praised and honored him that liveth forever, whose dominion is an everlasting dominion, and his kingdom is from generation to generation, and all the inhabitants of the earth are reputed as nothing, and he doeth according to his will in the army of Heaven and among the inhabitants of the earth, and none can stay his hand or say unto him, What doest thou? At the same time my reason returned unto me, and for the glory of my kingdom, mine honor and brightness returned unto me, and my counselors and my lords sought unto me, and I was established in my kingdom, and excellent majesty was added unto me. Now I Nebuchadnezzar praise and extol and honor the King of Heaven, all whose works are truth, and his ways judgment, and those that walk in pride he is able to abase.

4 BELSHAZZAR the king made a great feast to a thousand of his lords, and drank wine before the thousand. Belshazzar, while he tasted the wine, commanded to bring the golden and silver vessels which his father Nebuchadnezzar had taken out of the temple which was in Jerusalem, that the king and his princes, his wives and his concubines, might drink therein. Then they brought the golden vessels that were taken out of the temple of the house of God which was at Jerusalem, and the king and his princes, his wives and his concubines, drank in them. They drank wine and praised the gods of gold, and of silver, of brass, of iron, of wood, and of stone.

In the same hour came forth fingers of a man's hand and wrote over against the candlestick upon the plaster of the wall of the king's palace, and the king saw the part of the hand that wrote. Then the king's countenance was changed and his thoughts troubled him, so that the joints of his loins were loosed and his knees smote one against another. The king cried aloud to bring in the astrologers, the Chaldeans, and the soothsayers. And the king spake and said to the wise men of Babylon, Whosoever shall read this writing and show me the interpretation thereof shall be clothed with scarlet, and have a chain of gold about his neck, and shall be the third ruler in the kingdom. Then came in all the king's wise men, but they could not read the writing, nor make known to the king the interpretation thereof. Then was king Belshazzar greatly troubled, and his countenance was changed in him, and his lords were astonished.

Now the queen, by reason of the words of the king and his lords, came into the banquet house, and the queen spake and said, O king, live forever, let not thy thoughts trouble thee, nor let thy countenance be changed; there is a man in thy kingdom in whom is the spirit of the holy gods, and in the days of thy father light and understanding and wisdom, like the wisdom of the gods, was found in him, whom the king Nebuchadnezzar thy father, the king, I say, thy father made master of the magicians, astrologers, Chaldeans, and soothsayers, forasmuch as an excellent spirit, and knowledge and understanding, interpreting of dreams, and showing of hard sentences, and dissolving of doubts, were found in the same Daniel, whom the king named Belteshazzar, now let Daniel be called and he will show the interpretation. Then was Daniel brought in before the king. And the king spake and said unto Daniel, Art thou that Daniel which art of the children of the captivity of Judah whom the king my father brought out of Jewry? I have even heard of thee, that the spirit of the gods is in thee and that light and understanding and excellent wisdom is found in thee. And now the wise men, the astrologers, have been brought in before me that they should read this writing and make known unto me the interpretation thereof, but they could not show the interpretation of the thing. And I have heard of thee, that thou canst make interpretations, and dissolve doubts. Now if thou canst read the writing and make known to me the interpretation thereof, thou shalt be clothed with scarlet, and have a chain of gold about thy neck, and shall be the third ruler in the kingdom. Then Daniel answered and said before the king, Let thy gifts be to thyself and give thy rewards to another, yet I will read the writing unto the king and make known to him the interpretation.

O thou king, the Most High God gave Nebuchadnezzar thy father a kingdom, and majesty, and glory, and honor, and for the majesty that he gave him, all people, nations, and languages, trembled and feared before him, whom he would he slew, and whom he would he kept alive, and whom he would he set up, and whom he would he put down. But when his heart was lifted up and his mind hardened in pride, he was deposed from his kingly throne, and they took his glory from him, and he was driven from the sons of men, and his heart was made like the beasts, and his dwelling was with the wild asses, they fed him with grass like oxen, and his body was wet with the dew of Heaven till he knew that the Most High God ruled in the kingdom of men and that he appointeth over it whomsoever he will. And thou his son, O Belshazzar, hast not humbled thine heart, though thou knewest all this, but hast lifted up thyself against the Lord of Heaven, and they have brought the vessels of his house before thee, and thou and thy lords, thy wives and thy concubines, have drunk wine in them, and thou hast praised the gods of silver and gold, of brass, iron, wood, and stone, which see not, nor hear, nor know, and the God in whose hand thy breath is, and whose are all thy ways hast thou not glorified, then was the part of the hand sent from him, and this writing was written. And this is the writing that was written, MENE, MENE, TEKEL, UPHARSIN. This is the interpretation of the thing, MENE, God hath numbered thy kingdom, and finished it. TEKEL, Thou art weighed in the balances and art found wanting. UPHARSIN, Thy kingdom is divided and given to the Medes and Persians.

Then commanded Belshazzar, and they clothed Daniel with scarlet, and put a chain of gold about his neck, and made a proclamation concerning him, that he should be the third ruler in the kingdom. In that night was Belshazzar the king of the Chaldeans slain. And Darius the Median took the kingdom, being about threescore and two years old.

It pleased Darius to set over the kingdom a hundred and twenty princes, which should be over the whole kingdom and over these three presidents, of whom Daniel was first, that the princes might give accounts unto them and the king should have no damage. Then this Daniel was preferred above the presidents and princes because an excellent spirit was in him, and the king thought to set him over the whole realm.

Then the presidents and princes sought to find occasion against Daniel concerning the kingdom, but they could find none occasion nor fault, forasmuch as he was faithful, neither was there any error or fault found in him. Then said these men, We shall not find any occasion against this Daniel except we find it against him concerning the law of his God. Then these presidents and princes assembled together to the king and said thus unto him, King Darius, live forever. All the presidents of the kingdom, the governors, and the princes, the counselors, and the captains, have consulted together to establish a royal statute and to make a firm decree, that whosoever shall ask a petition of any God or man for thirty days, save of thee O king, he shall be cast into the den of lions. Now, O king, establish the decree and sign the writing, that it be not changed, according to the law of the Medes and Persians, which altereth not. Wherefore King Darius signed the writing and the decree.

Now when Daniel knew that the writing was signed, he went into his house and, his windows being open in his chamber toward Jerusalem, he kneeled upon his knees three times a day and prayed, and gave thanks before his God as he did aforetime. Then these men assembled and found Daniel praying and making supplication before his God. Then they came near and spake before the king concerning the king's decree, Hast thou not signed a decree, that every man that shall ask a petition of any God or man within thirty days, save of thee O king, shall be cast into the den of lions? The king answered and said, The thing is true, according to the law of Medes and Persians, which altereth not. Then answered they and said before the king, That Daniel, which is of the children of the captivity of Judah, regardeth not thee, O king, nor the decree that thou hast signed, but maketh his petition three times a day. Then the king, when he heard these words, was sore displeased with himself, and set his heart on Daniel to deliver him, and he labored till the going down of the sun to deliver him. Then these men assembled unto the king and said unto the king, Know, O king, that the law of the Medes and Persians is, That no decree nor statute which the king establisheth may be changed. Then the king commanded, and they brought Daniel, and cast him into the den of lions. Now the king spake and said unto Daniel, Thy God whom thou servest continually, he will deliver thee. And a stone was brought and laid upon the mouth of the den, and the king sealed it with his own signet and with the signet of his lords, that the purpose might not be changed concerning Daniel.

Then the king went to his palace, and passed the night fasting, neither were instruments of music brought before him, and his sleep went from him. Then the king arose very early in the morning and went in haste unto the den of lions. And when he came to the den, he cried with a lamentable voice unto Daniel and the king spake and said to Daniel, O Daniel, servant of the living God, is thy God, whom thou servest continually, able to deliver thee from the lions? Then said Daniel unto the king, O king, live forever. My God hath sent his angel, and hath shut the lions' mouths that they have not hurt me, forasmuch as before him innocency was found in me, and also before thee, O king, have I done no hurt. Then was the king exceeding glad for him and commanded that they should take Daniel up out of the den. So Daniel was taken up out of the den and no manner of hurt was found upon him, because he believed in his God. And the king commanded and they brought those men which had accused Daniel, and they cast them into the den of lions, them, their children, and their wives, and the lions had the mastery of them and brake all their bones in pieces or ever they came at the bottom of the den.

Then king Darius wrote unto all people, nations, and languages, that dwell in all the Earth, Peace be multiplied unto you. I make a decree, That in every dominion of my kingdom men tremble and fear before the God of Daniel, for he is the living God and steadfast forever, and his kingdom, that which shall not be destroyed, and his dominion shall be even unto the end. He delivereth and rescueth, and he worketh signs and wonders in Heaven and in Earth, who hath delivered Daniel from the power of the lions. So this Daniel prospered in the reign of Darius and in the reign of Cyrus the Persian.

5 IN the first year of Belshazzar king of Babylon, Daniel had a dream and visions of his head upon his bed, then he wrote the dream and told the sum of the matters. Daniel spake and said, I saw in my vision by night and behold, the four winds of the Heaven strove upon the great sea. And four great beasts came up from the

sea, diverse one from another. The first was like a lion and had eagle's wings, I beheld till the wings thereof were plucked, and it was lifted up from the Earth and made stand upon the feet as a man and a man's heart was given to it. And behold another beast, a second, like to a bear, and it raised up itself on one side, and it had three ribs in the mouth of it between the teeth of it, and they said thus unto it, Arise, devour much flesh. After this I beheld and lo another, like a leopard which had upon the back of it four wings of a fowl, the beast had also four heads, and dominion was given to it. After this I saw in the night visions and behold a fourth beast, dreadful and terrible, and strong exceedingly and it had great iron teeth, it devoured and brake in pieces, and stamped the residue with the feet of it, and it was diverse from all the beasts that were before it, and it had ten horns. I considered the horns and behold, there came up among them another little horn, before whom there were three of the first horns plucked up by the roots and behold, in this horn were eyes like the eyes of man and a mouth speaking great things.

I beheld till the thrones were cast down, and the Ancient of days did sit, whose garment was white as snow and the hair of his head like the pure wool, his throne was like the fiery flame and his wheels as burning fire. A fiery stream issued and came forth from before him, thousand thousands ministered unto him and ten thousand times ten thousand stood before him; the judgment was set and the books were opened. I beheld then, because of the voice of the great words which the horn spake, I beheld even till the beast was slain and his body destroyed and given to the burning flame. As concerning the rest of the beasts, they had their dominion taken away, yet their lives were prolonged for a season and time. I saw in the night visions and behold, one like the Son of man came with the clouds of Heaven and came to the Ancient of days, and they brought him near before him. And there was given him dominion, and glory, and a kingdom, that all people, nations, and languages should serve him; his dominion is an everlasting dominion which shall not pass away and his kingdom that which shall not be destroyed.

I, Daniel, was grieved in my spirit in the midst of my body and the visions of my head troubled me. I came near unto one of them that stood by and asked him the truth of all this. So he told me and made me know the interpretation of the things.

These great beasts, which are four, are four kings which shall arise out of the earth. But the saints of the Most High shall take the kingdom, and possess the kingdom forever, even for ever and ever. Then I would know the truth of the fourth beast which was diverse from all the other, exceeding dreadful, whose teeth were of iron, and his nails of brass, which devoured, brake in pieces, and stamped the residue with his feet, and of the ten horns that were in his head, and of the other which came up, and before whom three fell, even of that horn that had eyes, and a mouth that spake very great things, whose look was more stout than his fellows. I beheld, and the same horn made war with the saints, and prevailed against them until the Ancient of days came, and judgment was given to the saints of the Most High and the time came that the saints possessed the kingdom. Thus he said, The fourth beast shall be the fourth kingdom upon earth, which shall be diverse from all kingdoms and shall devour the whole earth, and shall tread it down, and break it in pieces. And the ten horns out of this kingdom are ten kings that shall arise, and another shall rise after them and he shall be diverse from the first, and he shall subdue three kings. And he shall speak great words against the Most High, and shall wear out the saints of the Most High, and think to change times and laws, and they shall be given into his hand until a time and times and the dividing of time. But the judgment shall sit, and they shall take away his dominion, to consume and to destroy it unto the end. And the kingdom and dominion and the greatness of the kingdom under the whole Heaven shall be given to the people of the saints of the Most High, whose kingdom is an everlasting kingdom, and all dominions shall serve and obey him. Hitherto is the end of the matter. As for me Daniel, my cogitations much troubled me and my countenance changed in me, but I kept the matter in my heart.

In the third year of the reign of king Belshazzar a vision appeared unto me, even unto me Daniel, after that which appeared unto me at the first. And I saw in a vision, and it came to pass when I saw that I was at Shushan in the palace, which is in the province of Elam, and I saw in a vision and I was by the river Ulai. Then I lifted up mine eyes and saw and behold, there stood before the river a ram which had two horns, and the two horns were high, but one was higher than the other and the higher came up last. I saw the ram pushing westward, and northward, and southward, so that no beasts might stand before him, neither was there any that could deliver out of his hand, but he did according to his will and became great.

And as I was considering, behold, a he goat came from the west on the face of the whole Earth and touched not the ground, and the goat had a notable horn between his eyes. And he came to the ram that had two horns, which I had seen standing before the river and ran unto him in the fury of his power. And I saw him come close unto the ram, and he was moved with choler against him, and smote the ram, and brake his two horns, and there was no power in the ram to stand before him, but he cast him down to the ground, and stamped upon him, and there was none that could deliver the ram out of his hand. Therefore the he goat waxed very great, and when he was strong the great horn was broken, and for it came up four notable ones toward the four winds of Heaven.

And out of one of them came forth a little horn which waxed exceeding great, toward the south, and toward the east, and toward the pleasant land. And it waxed great, even to the host of Heaven, and it cast down some of the host and of the stars to the ground and stamped upon them. Yea, he magnified himself even to the prince of the host, and by him the daily sacrifice was taken away and the place of his sanctuary was cast down. And a host was given him against the daily sacrifice by reason of transgression, and it cast down the truth to the ground, and it practiced and prospered. Then I heard one saint speaking and another saint said unto that certain saint which spake, How long shall be the vision concerning the daily sacrifice, and the transgression of desolation, to give both the sanctuary and the host to be trodden underfoot? And he said unto me, Unto two thousand and three hundred days, then shall the sanctuary be cleansed.

And it came to pass when I, even I Daniel, had seen the vision and sought for the meaning, then behold, there stood before me as the appearance of a man. And I heard a man's voice between the banks of Ulai, which called and said, Gabriel, make this man to understand the vision. So he came near where I stood, and when he came I was afraid and fell upon my face, but he said unto me, Understand, O son of man, for at the time of the end shall be the vision. Now as he was speaking with me I was in a deep sleep on my face toward the ground, but he touched me and set me upright. And he said, Behold, I will make thee know what shall be in the last end of the indignation, for at the time appointed the end shall be. The ram which thou sawest having two horns are the kings of Media and Persia. And the rough goat is the king of Grecia, and the great horn that is between his eyes is the first king. Now that being broken, whereas four stood up for it, four kingdoms shall stand up out of the nation, but not in his power. And in the latter time of their kingdom, when the transgressors are come to the full, a king of fierce countenance and understanding dark sentences shall stand up. And his power shall be mighty, but not by his own power, and he shall destroy wonderfully, and shall prosper, and practice, and shall destroy the mighty and the holy people. And through his policy also he shall cause craft to prosper in his hand, and he shall magnify himself in his heart, and by peace shall destroy many, he shall also stand up against the Prince of princes, but he shall be broken without hand. And the vision of the evening and the morning which was told is true, wherefore shut thou up the vision, for it shall be for many days. And I, Daniel, fainted and was sick certain days, afterward I rose up and did the king's business, and I was astonished at the vision, but none understood it.

In the first year of Darius the son of Ahasuerus, of the seed of the Medes, which was made king over the realm of the Chaldeans, in the first year of his reign, I, Daniel, understood by books the number of the years whereof the word of the Lord came to Jeremiah the prophet, that he would accomplish seventy years in the desolations of Jerusalem. And I set my face unto the Lord God, to seek by prayer and supplications, with fasting, and sackcloth and ashes, and I prayed unto the Lord my God and made my confession and said, O Lord, the great and dreadful God, keeping the covenant and mercy to them that love him and to them that keep his commandments, we have sinned and have committed iniquity, and have done wickedly and have rebelled, even by departing from thy precepts and from thy judgments, neither have we hearkened unto thy servants the prophets, which spake in thy name to our kings, our princes, and our fathers, and to all the people of the land.

O Lord, righteousness belongeth unto thee, but unto us confusion of faces as at this day, to the men of Judah, and to the inhabitants of Jerusalem, and unto all Israel that are near and that are far off, through all the countries whither thou hast driven them because of their trespass that they have trespassed against thee. O Lord, to us belongeth confusion of face, to our kings, to our princes, and to our fathers, because we have sinned against thee. To the Lord our God belong mercies and forgivenesses, though we have rebelled against him, neither have we obeyed the voice of the Lord our God to walk in his laws which he set before us by his servants the prophets. Yea, all Israel have transgressed thy law even by departing, that they might not obey thy voice, therefore the curse is poured upon us and the oath that is written in the law of Moses the servant of God because we have sinned against him. And he hath confirmed his words which he spake against us and against our judges that judged us by bringing upon us a great evil, for under the whole Heaven hath not been done as hath been done upon Jerusalem. As it is written in the law of Moses, all this evil is come upon us, yet made we not our prayer before the Lord our God that we might turn from our iniquities and understand thy truth. Therefore hath the Lord watched upon the evil and brought it upon us, for the Lord our God is righteous in all his works which he doeth, for we obeyed not his voice.

And now, O Lord our God that hast brought thy people forth out of the land of Egypt with a mighty hand and hast gotten thee renown as at this day, we have sinned, we have done wickedly. O Lord, according to all thy righteousness I beseech thee, let thine anger and thy fury be turned away from thy city Jerusalem, thy holy mountain, because for our sins and for the iniquities of our fathers Jerusalem and thy people are become a reproach to all that are about us. Now therefore, O our God, hear the prayer of thy servant and his supplications, and cause thy face to shine upon thy sanctuary that is desolate for the Lord's sake. O my God, incline thine ear and hear, open thine eyes and behold our desolations and the city which is called by thy name, for we do not present our supplications before thee for our righteousnesses, but for thy great mercies. O Lord, hear, O Lord, forgive, O Lord, hearken and do, defer not for thine own sake, O my God, for thy city and thy people are called by thy name.

And while I was speaking and praying, and confessing my sin and the sin of my people Israel, and presenting my supplication before the Lord my God for the holy mountain of my God, yea, while I was speaking in prayer, even the man Gabriel whom I had seen in the vision at the beginning, being caused to fly swiftly, touched me about the time of the evening oblation. And he informed me and talked with me and said, O Daniel, I am now come forth to give thee skill and understanding. At the beginning of thy supplications the commandment came forth and I am come to show thee, for thou art greatly beloved, therefore understand the matter and consider the vision. Seventy weeks are determined upon thy people and upon thy holy city to finish the transgression, and to make an end of sins, and to make reconciliation for iniquity, and to bring in everlasting righteousness, and to seal up the vision and prophecy, and to anoint the Most Holy. Know therefore and understand that from the going forth of the commandment to restore and to build Jerusalem, unto the Messiah the Prince, shall be seven weeks and threescore and two weeks, the street shall be built again and the wall, even in troublous times. And after threescore and two weeks shall Messiah be cut off, but not for himself, and the people of the prince that shall come shall destroy the city and the sanctuary, and the end thereof shall be with a flood, and unto the end of the war desolations are determined. And he shall confirm the covenant with many for one week, and in the midst of the week he shall cause the sacrifice and the oblation to cease, and for the overspreading of abominations he shall make it desolate, even until the consummation and that determined shall be poured upon the desolate.

6 IN the third year of Cyrus king of Persia a thing was revealed unto Daniel whose name was called Belteshazzar, and the thing was true, but the time appointed was long, and he understood the thing and had understanding of the vision.

In those days I, Daniel, was mourning three full weeks. I ate no pleasant bread, neither came flesh nor wine in my mouth, neither did I anoint myself at all, till three whole weeks were fulfilled. And in the four and twentieth day of the first month, as I was by the side of the great river which is Hiddekel, then I lifted up mine eyes and looked, and behold a certain man clothed in linen, whose loins were girded with fine gold of Uphaz, his body also was like the beryl and his face as the appearance of lightning, and his eyes as lamps of fire, and his arms and his feet like in color to polished brass, and the voice of his words like the voice of a multitude. And I, Daniel, alone saw the vision, for the men that were with me saw not the vision, but a great quaking fell upon them so that they fled to hide themselves. Therefore I was left alone and saw this great vision, and there remained no strength in me, for my comeliness was turned in me into corruption and I retained no strength. Yet heard I the voice of his words, and when I heard the voice of his words, then was I in a deep sleep on my face and my face toward the ground.

And, behold, a hand touched me which set me upon my knees and upon the palms of my hands. And said unto me, O Daniel, a man greatly beloved, understand the words that I speak unto thee, and stand upright, for unto thee am I now sent. And when he had spoken this word unto me I stood trembling. Then said he unto me, Fear not, Daniel, for from the first day that thou didst set thine heart to understand and to chasten thyself before thy God, thy words were heard and I am come for thy words. But the prince of the kingdom of Persia withstood me one and twenty days, but lo, Michael, one of the chief princes came to help me and I remained there with the kings of Persia. Now I am come to make thee understand what shall befall thy people in the latter days, for yet the vision is for many days.

And when he had spoken such words unto me I set my face toward the ground and I became dumb. And, behold, one like the similitude of the sons of men touched my lips, then I opened my mouth and spake and said unto him that stood before me, O my lord, by the vision my sorrows are turned upon me and I have retained no strength. For how can the servant of this my lord talk with this my lord? For as for me, straightway there remained no strength in me, neither is there breath left in me.

Then there came again and touched me one like the appearance of a man, and he strengthened me, and said, O man greatly beloved, fear not, peace be unto thee, be strong, yea, be strong. And when he had spoken unto me I was strengthened and said, Let my lord speak, for thou hast strengthened me. Then said he, Knowest thou wherefore I come unto thee? And now will I return to fight with the prince of Persia, and when I am gone forth lo, the prince of Grecia shall come. But I will show thee that which is noted in the scripture of truth, and there is none that holdeth with me in these things but Michael your prince. Also I in the first year of Darius the Mede, even I stood to confirm and to strengthen him.

And now will I show thee the truth. Behold, there shall stand up yet three kings in Persia, and the fourth shall be far richer than they all, and by his strength through his riches he shall stir up all against the realm of Grecia. And a mighty king shall stand up that shall rule with great dominion and do according to his will. And when he shall stand up, his kingdom shall be broken and shall be divided toward the four winds of Heaven, and not to his posterity, nor according to his dominion which he ruled, for his kingdom shall be plucked up, even for others besides those.

And the king of the south shall be strong and one of his princes, and he shall be strong above him and have dominion; his dominion shall be a great dominion. And in the end of years they shall join themselves together, for the king's daughter of the south shall come to the king of the north to make an agreement, but she shall not retain the power of the arm, neither shall he stand, nor his arm, but she shall be given up and they that brought her, and he that begat her, and he that strengthened her in these times. But out of a branch of her roots shall one stand up in his estate which shall come with an army and shall enter into the fortress of the king of the north, and shall deal against them, and shall prevail, and shall also carry captives into Egypt their gods, with their princes and with their precious vessels of silver and of gold, and he shall continue more years than the king of the north. So the king of the south shall come into his kingdom and shall return into his own land.

But his sons shall be stirred up and shall assemble a multitude of great forces, and one shall certainly come and overflow and pass through, then shall he return and be stirred up, even to his fortress. And the king of the south shall be moved with choler and shall come forth and fight with him, even with the king of the north, and he shall set forth a great multitude, but the multitude shall be given into his hand. And when he hath taken away the multitude, his heart shall be lifted up and he shall cast down many ten thousands, but he shall not be strengthened by it. For the king of the north shall return, and shall set forth a multitude greater than the former and shall certainly come after certain years with a great army and with much riches.

And in those times there shall many stand up against the king of the south, also the robbers of thy people shall exalt themselves to establish the vision, but they shall fall. So the king of the north shall come, and cast up a mount and take the most fenced cities, and the arms of the south shall not withstand, neither his chosen people, neither shall there be any strength to withstand. But he that cometh against him shall do according to his own will and none shall stand before him, and he shall stand in the glorious land which by his hand shall be consumed. He shall also set his face to enter with the strength of his whole kingdom and upright ones with him, thus shall he do, and he shall give him the daughter of women, corrupting her, but she shall not stand on his side, neither be for him. After this shall he turn his face unto the isles and shall take many, but a prince for his own behalf shall cause the reproach offered by him to cease, without his own reproach he shall cause it to turn upon him. Then he shall turn his face toward the fort of his own land, but he shall stumble and fall and not be found. Then shall stand up in his estate a raiser of taxes in the glory of the kingdom, but within few days he shall be destroyed, neither in anger, nor in battle.

And in his estate shall stand up a vile person to whom they shall not give the honor of the kingdom, but he shall come in peaceably and obtain the kingdom by flatteries. And with the arms of a flood shall they be overflown from before him and shall be broken, yea, also the prince of the covenant. And after the league made with him he shall work deceitfully, for he shall come up and shall become strong with a small people. He shall enter peaceably even upon the fattest places of the province, and he shall do that which his fathers have not done, nor his fathers' fathers: he shall scatter among them the prey, and spoil, and riches, yea, and he shall forecast his devices against the strongholds, even for a time. And he shall stir up his power and his courage against the king of the south with a great army, and the king of the south shall be stirred up to battle with a very great and mighty army, but he shall not stand, for they shall forecast devices against him. Yea, they that feed of the portion of his meat shall destroy him, and his army shall overflow and many shall fall down slain. And both these kings' hearts shall be to do mischief, and they shall speak lies at one table, but it shall not prosper, for yet the end shall be at the time appointed. Then shall he return into his land with great riches, and his heart shall be against the holy covenant, and he shall do exploits and return to his own land. At the time appointed he shall return and come toward the south, but it shall not be as the former or as the latter.

For the ships of Chittim shall come against him, therefore he shall be grieved and return and have indignation against the holy covenant, so shall he do, he shall even return and have intelligence with them that forsake the holy covenant. And arms shall stand on his part, and they shall pollute the sanctuary of strength and shall take away the daily sacrifice, and they shall place the abomination that maketh desolate. And such as do wickedly against the covenant shall be corrupt by flatteries, but the people that do know their God shall be strong and do exploits. And they that understand among the people shall instruct many, yet they shall fall by the sword, and by flame, by captivity, and by spoil, many days. Now when they shall fall, they shall be holpen with a little help, but many shall cleave to them with flatteries. And some of them of understanding shall fall, to try them, and to purge and to make them white, even to the time of the end, because it is yet for a time appointed. And the king shall do according to his will, and he shall exalt himself and magnify himself above every god, and shall speak marvelous things against the God of gods, and shall prosper till the indignation be accomplished, for that that is determined shall be done. Neither shall he regard the God of his fathers, nor the desire of women, nor regard any god, for he shall magnify himself above all. But in his estate shall he honor the God of forces, and a god whom his fathers knew not shall he honor with gold, and silver, and with precious stones, and pleasant things. Thus shall he do in the most strongholds with a strange god whom he shall acknowledge and increase with glory, and he shall cause them to rule over many and shall divide the land for gain.

And at the time of the end shall the king of the south push at him, and the king of the north shall come against him like a whirlwind, with chariots, and with horsemen, and with many ships, and he shall enter into the countries and shall overflow and pass over. He shall enter also into the glorious land and many countries shall be overthrown, but these shall escape out of his hand, even Edom, and Moab, and the chief of the children of Ammon. He shall stretch forth his hand also upon the countries and the land of Egypt shall not escape. But he shall have power over the treasures of gold and of silver, and over all the precious things of Egypt, and the Libyans and the Ethiopians shall be at his steps. But tidings out of the east and out of the north shall trouble him, therefore he shall go forth with great fury to destroy and utterly to make away many. And he shall plant the tabernacles of his palace between the seas in the glorious holy mountain, yet he shall come to his end and none shall help him.

And at that time shall Michael stand up, the great prince which standeth for the children of thy people, and there shall be a time of trouble such as never was since there was a nation even to that same time, and at that time thy people shall be delivered, everyone that shall be found written in the book. And many of them that sleep in the dust of the earth shall awake, some to everlasting life, and some to shame and everlasting contempt. And they that be wise shall shine as the brightness of the firmament, and they that turn many to righteousness as the stars for ever and ever. But thou, O Daniel, shut up the words and seal the book even to the time of the end; many shall run to and fro and knowledge shall be increased.

Then I, Daniel, looked and behold, there stood other two, the one on this side of the bank of the river and the other on that side of the bank of the river. And one said to the man clothed in linen which was upon the waters of the river, How long shall it be to the end of these wonders? And I heard the man clothed in linen which was upon the waters of the river, when he held up his right hand and his left hand unto Heaven and sware by him that liveth forever, that it shall be for a time, times, and a half, and when he shall have accomplished to scatter the power of the holy people, all these things shall be finished. And I heard, but I understood not, then said I, O my Lord, what shall be the end of these things? And he said, Go thy way, Daniel, for the words are closed up and sealed till the time of the end. Many shall be purified, and made white and tried, but the wicked shall do wickedly, and none of the wicked shall understand, but the wise shall understand. And from the time that the daily sacrifice shall be taken away and the abomination that maketh desolate set up, there shall be a thousand two hundred and ninety days. Blessed is he that waiteth and cometh to the thousand three hundred and five and thirty days. But go thou thy way till the end be, for thou shalt rest and stand in thy lot at the end of the days.

HOSEA

THE word of the Lord that came unto Hosea, the son of Beeri, in the days of Uzziah, Jotham, Ahaz, and Hezekiah, kings of Judah, and in the days of Jeroboam the son of Joash, king of Israel.

The beginning of the word of the Lord by Hosea. And the Lord said to Hosea, Go, take unto thee a wife of whoredoms and children of whoredoms for the land hath committed great whoredom, departing from the Lord. So he went and took Gomer the daughter of Diblaim, which conceived, and bare him a son. And the Lord said unto him, Call his name Jezreel, for yet a little while and I will avenge the blood of Jezreel upon the house of Jehu and will cause to cease the kingdom of the house of Israel. And it shall come to pass at that day that I will break the bow of Israel in the valley of Jezreel.

And she conceived again and bare a daughter. And God said unto him, Call her name Lo-ruhamah, for I will no more have mercy upon the house of Israel, but I will utterly take them away. But I will have mercy upon the house of Judah and will save them by the Lord their God and will not save them by bow, nor by sword, nor by battle, by horses, nor by horsemen.

Now when she had weaned Lo-ruhamah she conceived and bare a son. Then said God, call his name Lo-ammi, for ye are not my people and I will not be your God. Yet the number of the children of Israel shall be as the sand of the sea which cannot be measured nor numbered, and it shall come to pass that in the place where it was said unto them, ye are not my people, there it shall be said unto them, Ye are the sons of the living God. Then shall the children of Judah and the children of Israel be gathered together and appoint themselves one head and they shall come up out of the land, for great shall be the day of Jezreel.

Say ye unto your brethren, Ammi, and to your sisters, Ruhamah. Plead with your mother, plead, for she is not my wife, neither am I her husband; let her therefore put away her whoredoms out of her sight and her adulteries from between her breasts, lest I strip her naked and set her as in the day that she was born, and make her as a wilderness, and set her like a dry land, and slay her with thirst.

And I will not have mercy upon her children, for they be the children whoredoms. For their mother hath played the harlot, she that conceived them hath done shamefully for she said, I will go after my lovers that give me my bread and my water, my wool and my flax, mine oil and my drink. Therefore, behold, I will hedge up thy way with thorns, and make a wall, that she shall not find her paths.

And she shall follow after her lovers, but she shall not overtake them, and she shall seek them, but shall not find them; then shall she say, I will go and return to my first husband, for then was it better with me than now. For she did not know that I gave her corn, and wine, and oil, and multiplied her silver and gold, which they prepared for Baal. Therefore will I return and take away my corn in the time thereof, and my wine in the season thereof, and will recover my wool and my flax given to cover her nakedness. And now will I discover her lewdness in the sight of her lovers and none shall deliver her out of mine hand. I will also cause all her mirth to cease, her feast days, her new moons, and her sabbaths, and all her solemn feasts. And I will destroy her vines and her fig trees whereof she hath said, These are my rewards that my lovers have given me, and I will make them a forest, and the beasts of the field shall eat them. And I will visit upon her the days of Baalim wherein she burned incense to them, and she decked herself with her earrings and her jewels, and she went after her lovers, and forgat me, saith the Lord.

Therefore behold, I will allure her, and bring her into the wilderness, and speak comfortably unto her. And I will give her her vineyards from thence, and the valley of Achor for a door of hope, and she shall sing there as in the days of her youth, and as in the day when she came up out of the land of Egypt.

And it shall be at that day, saith the Lord, that thou shalt call me Ishi and shalt call me no more Baali. For I will take away the names of Baalim out of her mouth and they shall no more be remembered by their name. And in that day will I make a covenant for them with the beasts of the field, and with the fowls of Heaven, and with the creeping things of the ground, and I will break the bow and the sword and the battle out of the earth and will make them to lie down safely. And I will betroth thee unto me forever, yea, I will betroth thee unto me in righteousness, and in judgment, and in lovingkindness, and in mercies. I will even betroth thee unto me in faithfulness and thou shalt know the Lord. And it shall come to pass in that day I will hear, saith the Lord, I will hear the heavens, and they shall hear the earth, and the earth shall hear the corn, and the wine, and the oil, and they shall hear Jezreel. And I will sow her unto me in the earth, and I will have mercy upon her that had not obtained mercy, and I will say to them which were not my people, Thou art my people, and they shall say, Thou art my God.

Then said the Lord unto me, Go, yet love a woman beloved of her friend, yet an adulteress, according to the love of the Lord toward the children of Israel, who look to other gods and love flagons of wine. So I bought her to me for fifteen pieces of silver, and for a homer of barley, and a half homer of barley, and I said unto her, Thou shalt abide for me many days, thou shalt not play the harlot, and thou shalt not be for another man, so will I also be for thee. For the children of Israel shall abide many days without a king, and without a prince, and without a sacrifice, and without an image, and without an ephod, and without teraphim; afterward shall the children of Israel return and seek the Lord their God, and David their king, and shall fear the Lord and his goodness in the latter days.

2 HEAR the word of the Lord, ye children of Israel, for the Lord hath a controversy with the inhabitants of the land because there is no truth, nor mercy, nor knowledge of God in the land. By swearing, and lying, and killing, and stealing and committing adultery they break out and blood toucheth blood. Therefore shall the land mourn, and everyone that dwelleth therein shall languish with the beasts of the field, and with the fowls of Heaven, yea, the fishes of the sea also shall be taken away, yet let no man strive nor reprove another, for thy people are as they that strive with the priest. Therefore shalt thou fall in the day, and the prophet also shall fall with thee in the night, and I will destroy thy mother. My people are destroyed for lack of knowledge; because thou hast rejected knowledge, I will also reject thee that thou shalt be no priest to me; seeing thou hast forgotten the law of thy God I will also forget thy children. As they were increased, so they sinned against me, therefore will I change their glory into shame. They eat up the sin of my people and they set their heart on their iniquity. And there shall be like people, like priest, and I will punish them for their ways and reward them their doings. For they shall eat and not have enough, they shall commit whoredom and shall not increase because they have left off to take heed to the Lord. Whoredom and wine and new wine take away the heart. My people ask counsel at their stocks, and their staff declareth unto them, for the spirit of whoredoms hath caused them to err and they have gone a whoring from under their God. They sacrifice upon the tops of the mountains, and burn incense upon the hills, under oaks and poplars and elms because the shadow thereof is good, therefore your daughters shall commit whoredom and your spouses shall commit adultery. I will not punish your daughters when they commit whoredom, nor your spouses when they commit adultery, for themselves are separated with whores, and they sacrifice with harlots, therefore the people that doth not understand shall fall.

Though thou, Israel, play the harlot, yet let not Judah offend, and come not ye unto Gilgal, neither go ye up to Beth-aven, nor swear, The Lord liveth. For Israel slideth back as a backsliding heifer, now the Lord will feed them as a lamb in a large place. Ephraim is joined to idols, let him alone. Their drink is sour, they have committed whoredom continually, her rulers with shame do love, Give ye. The wind hath bound her up in her wings, and they shall be ashamed because of their sacrifices.

Hear ye this, O priests, and hearken, ye house of Israel, and give ye ear, O house of the king, for judgment is toward you because ye have been a snare on Mizpah and a net spread upon Tabor. And the revolters are profound to make slaughter though I have been a rebuker of them all. I know Ephraim, and Israel is not hid from me, for now, O Ephraim, thou committest whoredom and Israel is defiled. They will not frame their doings to turn unto their God, for the spirit of whoredoms is in the midst of them and they have not known the Lord. And the pride of Israel doth testify to his face, therefore shall Israel and

Ephraim fall in their iniquity; Judah also shall fall with them. They shall go with their flocks and with their herds to seek the Lord, but they shall not find him, he hath withdrawn himself from them. They have dealt treacherously against the Lord, for they have begotten strange children, now shall a month devour them with their portions.

Blow ye the cornet in Gibeah, and the trumpet in Ramah, cry aloud at Bethaven after thee, O Benjamin. Ephraim shall be desolate in the day of rebuke; among the tribes of Israel have I made known that which shall surely be. The princes of Judah were like them that remove the bound, therefore I will pour out my wrath upon them like water. Ephraim is oppressed and broken in judgment because he willingly walked after the commandment. Therefore will I be unto Ephraim as a moth and to the house of Judah as rottenness. When Ephraim saw his sickness and Judah saw his wound, then went Ephraim to the Assyrian and sent to king Jareb, yet could he not heal you nor cure you of your wound. For I will be unto Ephraim as a lion and as a young lion to the house of Judah, I, even I, will tear and go away, I will take away and none shall rescue him. I will go and return to my place till they acknowledge their offense and seek my face; in their affliction they will seek me early.

Come, and let us return unto the Lord, for he hath torn and will heal us, he hath smitten and he will bind us up. After two days will he revive us, in the third day he will raise us up and we shall live in his sight. Then shall we know, if we follow on to know the Lord, his going forth is prepared as the morning, and he shall come unto us as the rain, as the latter and former rain unto the earth.

O Ephraim, what shall I do unto thee? O Judah, what shall I do unto thee? For your goodness is as a morning cloud and as the early dew it goeth away. Therefore have I hewed them by the prophets, I have slain them by the words of my mouth, and thy judgments are as the light that goeth forth. For I desired mercy and not sacrifice, and the knowledge of God more than burnt offerings. But they like men have transgressed the covenant, there have they dealt treacherously against me. Gilead is a city of them that work iniquity and is polluted with blood. And as troops of robbers wait for a man, so the company of priests murder in the way by consent, for they commit lewdness. I have seen a horrible thing in the house of Israel: there is the whoredom of Ephraim, Israel is defiled. Also, O Judah, he hath set a harvest for thee when I returned the captivity of my people.

When I would have healed Israel, then the iniquity of Ephraim was discovered and the wickedness of Samaria, for they commit falsehood, and the thief cometh in, and the troop of robbers spoileth without. And they consider not in their hearts that I remember all their wickedness, now their own doings have beset them about, they are before my face. They make the king glad with their wickedness and the princes with their lies. They are all adulterers, as an oven heated by the baker who ceaseth from raising after he hath kneaded the dough until it be leavened. In the day of our king, the princes have made him sick with bottles of wine, he stretched out his hand with scorners. For they have made ready their heart like an oven: while they lie in wait, their baker sleepeth all the night, in the morning it burneth as a flaming fire. They are all hot as an oven and have devoured their judges, all their kings are fallen, there is none among them that called unto me. Ephraim, he hath mixed himself among the people, Ephraim is a cake not turned. Strangers have devoured his strength and he knoweth it not, yea, gray hairs are here and there upon him yet he knoweth not. And the pride of Israel testifieth to his face, and they do not return to the Lord their God, nor seek him for all this.

Ephraim also is like a silly dove without heart; they call to Egypt, they go to Assyria. When they shall go I will spread my net upon them, I will bring them down as the fowls of the Heaven, I will chastise them as their congregation hath heard. Wo unto them, for they have fled from me. Destruction unto them because they have transgressed against me; though I have redeemed them, yet they have spoken lies against me. And they have not cried unto me with their heart; when they howled upon their beds they assemble themselves for corn and wine and they rebel against me. Though I have bound and strengthened their arms, yet do they imagine mischief against me. They return, but not to the Most High; they are like a deceitful bow, their princes shall fall by the sword for the rage of their tongue, this shall be their derision in the land of Egypt.

Set the trumpet to thy mouth. He shall come as an eagle against the house of the Lord because they have transgressed my covenant and trespassed against my law. Israel shall cry unto me, My God, we know thee. Israel hath cast off the thing that is good, the enemy shall pursue him. They have set up kings, but not by me, they have made princes and I knew it not, of their silver and their gold have they made them idols that they may be cut off. Thy calf, O Samaria, hath cast thee off, mine anger is kindled against them, how long will it be ere they attain to innocency? For from Israel was it also, the workman made it, therefore it is not God, but the calf of Samaria shall be broken in pieces. For they have sown the wind and they shall reap the whirlwind, it hath no stalk, the bud shall yield no meal, if so be it yield, the strangers shall swallow it up.

Israel is swallowed up, now shall they be among the Gentiles as a vessel wherein is no pleasure. For they are gone up to Assyria, a wild ass alone by himself, Ephraim hath hired lovers. Yea, though they have hired among the nations, now will I gather them and they shall sorrow a little for the burden of the king of princes. Because Ephraim hath made many altars to sin, altars shall be unto him to sin.

I have written to him the great things of my law, but they were counted as a strange thing. They sacrifice flesh for the sacrifices of mine offerings, and eat it, but the Lord accepteth them not: now will he remember their iniquity, and visit their sins, they shall return to Egypt. For Israel hath forgotten his Maker and buildeth temples, and Judah hath multiplied fenced cities, but I will send a fire upon his cities and it shall devour the palaces thereof.

Rejoice not, O Israel, for joy, as other people, for thou hast gone a whoring from thy God, thou hast loved a reward upon every cornfloor. The floor and the winepress shall not feed them and the new wine shall fail in her. They shall not dwell in the Lord's land, but Ephraim shall return to Egypt and they shall eat unclean things in Assyria. They shall not offer wine offerings to the Lord, neither shall they be pleasing unto him, their sacrifices shall be unto them as the bread of mourners, all that eat thereof shall be polluted, for their bread for their soul shall not come into the house of the Lord.

What will ye do in the solemn day and in the day of the feast of the Lord? For lo, they are gone because of destruction, Egypt shall gather them up, Memphis shall bury them, the pleasant places for their silver, nettles shall possess them, thorns shall be in their tabernacles.

The days of visitation are come, the days of recompense are come, Israel shall know it, the prophet is a fool, the spiritual man is mad, for the multitude of thine iniquity and the great hatred. The watchman of Ephraim was with my God, but the prophet is a snare of a fowler in all his ways and hatred in the house of his God. They have deeply corrupted themselves as in the days of Gibeah, therefore he will remember their iniquity, he will visit their sins.

I found Israel like grapes in the wilderness, I saw your fathers as the first ripe in the fig tree at her first time, but they went to Baal-peor and separated themselves unto that shame, and their abominations were according as they loved. As for Ephraim, their glory shall fly away like a bird, from the birth, and from the womb, and from the conception. Though they bring up their children, yet will I bereave them, that there shall not be a man left, yea, wo also to them when I depart from them. Ephraim, as I saw Tyrus, is planted in a pleasant place, but Ephraim shall bring forth his children to the murderer.

Give them, O Lord, what wilt thou give? Give them a miscarrying womb and dry breasts. All their wickedness is in Gilgal, for there I hated them, for the wickedness of their doings I will drive them out of mine house, I will love them no more, all their princes are revolters. Ephraim is smitten, their root is dried up, they shall bear no fruit, yea, though they bring forth, yet will I slay even the beloved fruit of their womb. My God will cast them away because they did not hearken unto him, and they shall be wanderers among the nations.

Israel is an empty vine, he bringeth forth fruit unto himself, according to the multitude of his fruit he hath increased the altars, according to the goodness of his land they have made goodly images. Their heart is divided, now shall they be found faulty, he shall break down their altars, he shall spoil their images.

For now they shall say, We have no king, because we feared not the Lord, what then should a king do to us? They have spoken words, swearing falsely in making a covenant, thus judgment springeth up as hemlock in the furrows of the field. The inhabitants of Samaria shall fear because of the calves of Beth-aven, for the people thereof shall mourn over it, and the priests thereof that rejoiced on it for the glory thereof, because it is departed from it. It shall also be carried unto Assyria for a present to king Jareb, Ephraim shall receive shame and Israel shall be ashamed of his own counsel.

As for Samaria, her king is cut off as the foam upon the water. The high places also of Aven, the sin of Israel, shall be destroyed, the thorn and the thistle shall come up on their altars, and they shall say to the mountains, Cover us, and to the hills, Fall on us.

O Israel, thou hast sinned from the days of Gibeah, there they stood, the battle in Gibeah against the children of iniquity did not overtake them. It is in my desire that I should chastise them, and the people shall be gathered against them, when they shall bind themselves in their two furrows. And Ephraim is as a heifer that is taught and loveth to tread out the corn, but I passed over upon her fair neck, I will make Ephraim to ride, Judah shall plough, and Jacob shall break his clods.

Sow to yourselves in righteousness, reap in mercy, break up your fallow ground, for it is time to seek the Lord till he come and rain righteousness upon you. Ye have ploughed wickedness, ye have reaped iniquity, ye have eaten the fruit of lies because thou didst trust in thy way, in the multitude of thy mighty men. Therefore shall a tumult arise among thy people, and all thy fortresses shall be spoiled, as Shalman spoiled Beth-arbel in the day of battle, the mother was dashed in pieces upon her children. So shall Beth-el do unto you because of your great wickedness, in a morning shall the king of Israel utterly be cut off.

When Israel was a child, then I loved him and called my son out of Egypt. As they called them, so they went from them, they sacrificed unto Baalim and burned incense to graven images. I taught Ephraim also to go, taking them by their arms, but they knew not that I healed them. I drew them with the cords of a man, with bands of love, and I was to them as they that take off the yoke on their jaws and I laid meat unto them.

He shall not return unto the land of Egypt, but the Assyrian shall be his king because they refused to return. And the sword shall abide on his cities, and shall consume his branches, and devour them because of their own counsels. And my people are bent to backsliding from me, though they called them to the Most High, none at all would exalt him. How shall I give thee up, Ephraim? How shall I deliver thee, Israel? How shall I make thee as Admah? How shall I set thee as Zeboim? My heart is turned toward thee and my mercies are extended to gather thee. I will not execute the fierceness of mine anger, I will not return to destroy Ephraim, for I am God and not man, the Holy One in the midst of thee, and I will not enter into the city. They shall walk after the Lord, he shall roar like a lion; when he shall roar, then the children shall tremble from the west. They shall tremble as a bird out of Egypt, and as a dove out of the land of Assyria, and I will place them in their houses, saith the Lord. Ephraim compasseth me about with lies, and the house of Israel with deceit, but Judah yet ruleth with God and is faithful with the saints.

Ephraim feedeth on wind and followeth after the east wind, he daily increaseth lies and desolation, and they do make a covenant with the Assyrians, and oil is carried into Egypt. The Lord hath also a controversy with Judah and will punish Jacob according to his ways according to his doings will he recompense him.

He took his brother by the heel in the womb and by his strength he had power with God. Yea, he had power over the angel and prevailed, he wept and made supplication unto him, he found him in Beth-el and there he spake with us, even the Lord God of hosts, the Lord is his memorial. Therefore turn thou to thy God, keep mercy and judgment, and wait on thy God continually.

He is a merchant, the balances of deceit are in his hand, he loveth to oppress. And Ephraim said, Yet I am become rich, I have found me out substance, in all my labors they shall find none iniquity in me that were sin. And I that am the Lord thy God from the land of Egypt will yet make thee to dwell in tabernacles as in the days of the solemn feast. I have also spoken by the prophets, and I have multiplied visions, and used similitudes by the ministry of the prophets. Is there iniquity in Gilead? Surely they are vanity; they sacrifice bullocks in Gilgal, yea, their altars are as heaps in the furrows of the fields. And Jacob fled into the country of Syria and Israel served for a wife, and for a wife he kept sheep. And by a prophet the Lord brought Israel out of Egypt and by a prophet was he preserved. Ephraim provoked him to anger most bitterly, therefore shall he leave his blood upon him and his reproach shall his Lord return unto him.

When Ephraim spake trembling he exalted himself in Israel, but when he offended in Baal he died. And now they sin more and more and have made them molten images of their silver and idols according to their own understanding, all of it the work of the craftsmen; they say of them, Let the men that sacrifice kiss the calves. Therefore they shall be as the morning cloud and as the early dew that passeth away, as the chaff that is driven with the whirlwind out of the floor and as the smoke out of the chimney.

Yet I am the Lord thy God from the land of Egypt, and thou shalt know no god but me, for there is no savior beside me. I did know thee in the wilderness, in the land of great drought. According to their pasture, so were they filled; they were filled and their heart was exalted, therefore have they forgotten me. Therefore I will be unto them as a lion, as a leopard by the way will I observe them. I will meet them as a bear that is bereaved of her whelps, and will rend the caul of their heart, and there will I devour them like a lion, the wild beast shall tear them.

O Israel, thou hast destroyed thyself, but in me is thine help. I will be thy king, where is any other that may save thee in all thy cities? And thy judges of whom thou saidst, Give me a king and princes? I gave thee a king in mine anger and took him away in my wrath. The iniquity of Ephraim is bound up, his sin is hid. The sorrows of a travailing woman shall come upon him, he is an unwise son for he should not stay long in the place of the breaking forth of children. I will ransom them from the power of the grave, I will redeem them from death,

O death, I will be thy plagues, O grave, I will be thy destruction, repentance shall be hid from mine eyes. Though he be fruitful among his brethren, an east wind shall come, the wind of the Lord shall come up from the wilderness, and his spring shall become dry, and his fountain shall be dried up; he shall spoil the treasure of all pleasant vessels. Samaria shall become desolate for she hath rebelled against her God: they shall fall by the sword, their infants shall be dashed in pieces, and their women with child shall be ripped up.

O Israel, return unto the Lord thy God, for thou hast fallen by thine iniquity. Take with you words and turn to the Lord, say unto him, Take away all iniquity and receive us graciously, so will we render the calves of our lips. Asshur shall not save us, we will not ride upon horses, neither will we say anymore to the work of our hands, Ye are our gods, for in thee the fatherless findeth mercy. I will heal their backsliding, I will love them freely, for mine anger is turned away from him. I will be as the dew unto Israel, he shall grow as the lily and cast forth his roots as Lebanon. His branches shall spread, and his beauty shall be as the olive tree, and his smell as Lebanon. They that dwell under his shadow shall return: they shall revive as the corn, and grow as the vine, the scent thereof shall be as the wine of Lebanon. Ephraim shall say, What have I to do anymore with idols? I have heard him and observed him, I am like a green fir tree. From me is thy fruit found. Who is wise, and he shall understand these things? Prudent, and he shall know them? For the ways of the Lord are right and the just shall walk in them, but the transgressors shall fall therein.

JOEL

THE word of the Lord that came to Joel, the son of Pethuel. Hear this ye old men, and give ear all ye inhabitants of the land. Hath this been in your days or even in the days of your fathers? Tell ye your children of it, and let your children tell their children, and their children another generation. That which the palmerworm hath left hath the locust eaten and that which the locust hath left hath the cankerworm eaten, and that which the cankerworm hath left hath the caterpillar eaten.

Awake, ye drunkards, and weep and howl, all ye drinkers of wine because of the new wine, for it is cut off from your mouth. For a nation is come up upon my land, strong and without number, whose teeth are as the teeth of a lion, and he hath the cheek teeth of a great lion. He hath laid my vine waste and barked my fig tree, he hath made it clean bare and cast it away, the branches thereof are made white.

Lament like a virgin girded with sackcloth for the husband of her youth. The meat offering and the drink offering is cut off from the house of the Lord, the priests, the Lord's ministers, mourn. The field is wasted, the land mourneth, for the corn is wasted, the new wine is dried up, the oil languisheth. Be ye ashamed, O ye husbandmen, howl, O ye vinedressers, for the wheat and for the barley because the harvest of the field is perished. The vine is dried up and the fig tree languisheth, the pomegranate tree, the palm tree also, and the apple tree, even all the trees of the field are withered because joy is withered away from the sons of men.

Gird yourselves and lament, ye priests, howl ye ministers of the altar, come lie all night in sackcloth ye ministers of my God, for the meat offering and the drink offering is withholden from the house of your God. Sanctify ye a fast, call a solemn assembly, gather the elders and all the inhabitants of the land into the house of the Lord your God, and cry unto the Lord, Alas for the day! For the day of the Lord is at hand and as a destruction from the Almighty shall it come. Is not the meat cut off before our eyes, yea, joy and gladness from the house of our God? The seed is rotten under their clods, the garners are laid desolate, the barns are broken down for the corn is withered. How do the beasts groan! The herds of cattle are perplexed because they have no pasture, yea, the flocks of sheep are made desolate. O Lord, to thee will I cry, for the fire hath devoured the pastures of the wilderness and the flame hath burned all the trees of the field. The beasts of the field cry also unto thee, for the rivers of water are dried up and the fire hath devoured the pastures of the wilderness.

Blow ye the trumpet in Zion and sound an alarm in my holy mountain, let all the inhabitants of the land tremble, for the day of the Lord cometh, for it is nigh at hand, a day of darkness and of gloominess, a day of clouds and of thick darkness as the morning spread upon the mountains, a great people and a strong there hath not been ever the like, neither shall be anymore after it, even to the years of many generations. A fire devoureth before them and behind them a flame burneth, the land is as the garden of Eden before them and behind them a desolate wilderness, yea, and nothing shall escape them. The appearance of them is as the appearance of horses, and as horsemen so shall they run. Like the noise of chariots on the tops of mountains shall they leap, like the noise of a flame of fire that devoureth the stubble, as a strong people set in battle array. Before their face the people shall be much pained, all faces shall gather blackness. They shall run like mighty men, they shall climb the wall like men of war, and they shall march everyone on his ways, and they shall not break their ranks, neither shall one thrust another, they shall walk everyone in his path, and when they fall upon the sword they shall not be wounded. They shall run to and fro in the city, they shall run upon the wall, they shall climb up upon the houses, they shall enter in at the windows like a thief. The earth shall quake before them, the heavens shall tremble, the sun and the moon shall be dark and the stars shall withdraw their shining, and the Lord shall utter his voice before his army, for his camp is very great, for he is strong that executeth his word, for the day of the Lord is great and very terrible and who can abide it?

Therefore also now saith the Lord, turn ye even to me with all your heart, and with fasting, and with weeping, and with mourning, and rend your heart and not your garments, and repent and turn unto the Lord your God, for he is gracious and merciful, slow to anger and of great kindness, and he will turn away the evil from you. Therefore repent, and who knoweth but he will return and leave a blessing behind him that you may offer a meat offering and a drink offering unto the Lord your God.

Blow the trumpet in Zion, sanctify a fast, call a solemn assembly, gather the people, sanctify the congregation, assemble the elders, gather the children and those that suck the breasts, let the bridegroom go forth of his chamber and the bride out of her closet. Let the priests, the ministers of the Lord, weep between the porch and the altar and let them say, Spare thy people, O Lord, and give not thine heritage to reproach that the heathen should rule over them, wherefore should they say among the people, Where is their God? Then will the Lord be jealous for his land and pity his people. Yea, the Lord will answer and say unto his people, Behold, I will send you corn, and wine, and oil, and ye shall be satisfied therewith, and I will no more make you a reproach among the heathen, but I will remove far off from you the northern army, and will drive him into a land barren and desolate, with his face toward the east sea and his hinder part toward the utmost sea, and his stink shall come up and his ill savor shall come up because he hath done great things.

Fear not, O land, be glad and rejoice, for the Lord will do great things. Be not afraid, ye beasts of the field, for the pastures of the wilderness do spring, for the tree beareth her fruit, the fig tree and the vine do yield their strength. Be glad then, ye children of Zion and rejoice in the Lord your God, for he hath given you the former rain moderately, and he will cause to come down for you the rain, the former rain, and the latter rain in the first month. And the floors shall be full of wheat, and the fats shall overflow with wine and oil. And I will restore to you the years that the locust hath eaten, the cankerworm, and the caterpillar, and the palmerworm, my great army which I sent among you. And ye shall eat in plenty and be satisfied, and praise the name of the Lord your God that hath dealt wondrously with you, and my people shall never be ashamed. And ye shall know that I am in the midst of Israel, and that I am the Lord your God and none else, and my people shall never be ashamed.

And it shall come to pass afterward that I will pour out my Spirit upon all flesh, and your sons and your daughters shall prophesy, your old men shall dream dreams, your young men shall see visions, and also upon the servants and upon the handmaids in those days will I pour out my Spirit. And I will show wonders in the heavens and in the Earth, blood, and fire, and pillars of smoke. The sun shall be turned into darkness and the moon into blood before the great and the terrible day of the Lord come. And it shall come to pass that whosoever shall call on the name of the Lord shall be delivered, for in mount Zion and in Jerusalem shall be deliverance as the Lord hath said and in the remnant whom the Lord shall call.

For behold, in those days and in that time when I shall bring again the captivity of Judah and Jerusalem I will also gather all nations, and will bring them down into the valley of Jehoshaphat, and will plead with them there for my people and for my heritage Israel whom they have scattered among the nations and parted my land. And they have cast lots for my people, and have given a boy for a harlot, and sold a girl for wine that they might drink. Yea, and what have ye to do with me, O Tyre and Zidon and all the coasts of Palestine? Will ye render me a recompense? And if ye recompense me, swiftly and speedily will I return your recompense upon your own head because ye have taken my silver and my gold and have carried into your temples my goodly pleasant things; the children also of Judah and the children of Jerusalem have ye sold unto the Grecians that ye might remove them far from their border. Behold, I will raise them out of the place whither ye have sold them, and will return your recompense upon your own head, and I will sell your sons and your daughters into the hand of the children of Judah, and they shall sell them to the Sabeans, to a people far off, for the Lord hath spoken it.

Proclaim ye this among the Gentiles, Prepare war, wake up the mighty men, let all the men of war draw near, let them come up, beat your ploughshares into swords and your pruning hooks into spears, let the weak say, I am strong. Assemble yourselves, and come, all ye heathen, and gather yourselves together round about; thither cause thy mighty ones to come down, O Lord. Let the heathen be wakened and come up to the valley of Jehoshaphat, for there will I sit to judge all the heathen round about. Put ye in the sickle, for the harvest is ripe, come, get you down, for the press is full, the fats overflow for their wickedness is great. Multitudes, multitudes in the valley of decision, for the day of the Lord is near in the valley of decision. The sun and the moon shall be darkened and the stars shall withdraw their shining. The Lord also shall roar out of Zion and utter his voice from Jerusalem, and the Heavens and the Earth shall shake, but the Lord will be the hope of his people and the strength of the children of Israel. So shall ye know that I am the Lord your God dwelling in Zion, my holy mountain, then shall Jerusalem be holy and there shall no strangers pass through her anymore.

And it shall come to pass in that day, that the mountains shall drop down new wine, and the hills shall flow with milk, and all the rivers of Judah shall flow with waters, and a fountain shall come forth of the house of the Lord and shall water the valley of Shittim. Egypt shall be a desolation and Edom shall be a desolate wilderness for the violence against the children of Judah, because they have shed innocent blood in their land. But Judah shall dwell for ever and

Jerusalem from generation to generation. For I will cleanse their blood that I have not cleansed, for the Lord dwelleth in Zion.

AMOS

THE words of Amos, who was among the herdmen of Tekoa, which he saw concerning Israel in the days of Uzziah king of Judah, and in the days of Jeroboam, the son of Joash king of Israel, two years before the earthquake. And he said, The Lord will roar from Zion and utter his voice from Jerusalem, and the habitations of the shepherds shall mourn, and the top of Carmel shall wither. Thus saith the Lord, For three transgressions of Damascus and for four I will not turn away the punishment thereof, because they have threshed Gilead with threshing instruments of iron, but I will send a fire into the house of Hazael which shall devour the palaces of Ben-hadad. I will break also the bar of Damascus, and cut off the inhabitant from the plain of Aven, and him that holdeth the scepter from the house of Eden, and the people of Syria shall go into captivity unto Kir, saith the Lord.

Thus saith the Lord, For three transgressions of Gaza and for four, I will not turn away the punishment thereof, because they carried away captive the whole captivity to deliver them up to Edom, but I will send a fire on the wall of Gaza which shall devour the palaces thereof, and I will cut off the inhabitant from Ashdod, and him that holdeth the scepter from Ashkelon, and I will turn mine hand against Ekron, and the remnant of the Philistines shall perish, saith the Lord God.

Thus saith the Lord, For three transgressions of Tyrus and for four I will not turn away the punishment thereof, because they delivered up the whole captivity to Edom and remembered not the brotherly covenant, but I will send a fire on the wall of Tyrus which shall devour the palaces thereof.

Thus saith the Lord, For three transgressions of Edom and for four I will not turn away the punishment thereof, because he did pursue his brother with the sword, and did cast off all pity, and his anger did tear perpetually, and he kept his wrath forever, but I will send a fire upon Teman which shall devour the palaces of Bozrah.

Thus saith the Lord, For three transgressions of the children of Ammon and for four I will not turn away the punishment thereof, because they have ripped up the women with child of Gilead that they might enlarge their border, but I will kindle a fire in the wall of Rabbah and it shall devour the palaces thereof, with shouting in the day of battle, with a tempest in the day of the whirlwind, and their king shall go into captivity, he and his princes together, saith the Lord.

Thus saith the Lord, For three transgressions of Moab and for four I will not turn away the punishment thereof, because he burned the bones of the king of Edom into lime, but I will send a fire upon Moab and it shall devour the palaces of Kirioth, and Moab shall die with tumult, with shouting, and with the sound of the trumpet, and I will cut off the judge from the midst thereof and will slay all the princes thereof with him, saith the Lord.

Thus saith the Lord, For three transgressions of Judah and for four I will not turn away the punishment thereof, because they have despised the law of the Lord and have not kept his commandments, and their lies caused them to err after the which their fathers have walked, but I will send a fire upon Judah, and it shall devour the palaces of Jerusalem.

Thus saith the Lord, For three transgressions of Israel and for four I will not turn away the punishment thereof, because they sold the righteous for silver and the poor for a pair of shoes, that pant after the dust of the earth on the head of the poor and turn aside the way of the meek, and a man and his father will go in unto the same maid to profane my holy name, and they lay themselves down upon clothes laid to pledge by every altar, and they drink the wine of the condemned in the house of their god. Yet destroyed I the Amorite before them, whose height was like the height of the cedars, and he was strong as the oaks, yet I destroyed his fruit from above and his roots from beneath. Also I brought you up from the land of Egypt and led you forty years through the wilderness to possess the land of the Amorite. And I raised up of your sons for prophets and of your young men for Nazarites. Is it not even thus, O ye children of Israel? saith the Lord. But ye gave the Nazarites wine to drink and commanded the prophets saying, Prophesy not. Behold, I am pressed under you as a cart is pressed that is full of sheaves. Therefore the flight shall perish from the swift and the strong shall not strengthen his force, neither shall the mighty deliver himself, neither shall he stand that handleth the bow, and he that is swift of foot shall not deliver himself, neither shall he that rideth the horse deliver himself. And he that is courageous among the mighty shall flee away naked in that day, saith the Lord.

Hear this word that the Lord hath spoken against you, O children of Israel, against the whole family which I brought up from the land of Egypt saying, You only have I known of all the families of the earth, therefore I will punish you for all your iniquities. Can two walk together except they be agreed? Will a lion roar in the forest when he hath no prey? Will a young lion cry out of his den if he have taken nothing? Can a bird fall in a snare upon the Earth where no gin is for him? Shall one take up a snare from the Earth and have taken nothing at all? Shall a trumpet be blown in the city and the people not be afraid? Shall there be evil in a city and the Lord hath not known it? Surely the Lord God will do nothing, until he revealeth the secret unto his servants the prophets. The lion hath roared, who will not fear? The Lord God hath spoken, who can but prophesy?

Publish in the palaces at Ashdod and in the palaces in the land of Egypt and say, Assemble yourselves upon the mountains of Samaria, and behold the great tumults in the midst thereof, and the oppressed in the midst thereof. For they know not to do right, saith the Lord, who store up violence and robbery in their palaces. Therefore thus saith the Lord God, An adversary there shall be even round about the land, and he shall bring down thy strength from thee, and thy palaces shall be spoiled. Thus saith the Lord, As the shepherd taketh out of the mouth of the lion two legs or a piece of an ear, so shall the children of Israel be taken out that dwell in Samaria in the corner of a bed and in Damascus in a couch. Hear ye, and testify in the house of Jacob, saith the Lord God, the God of hosts, that in the day that I shall visit the transgressions of Israel upon him, I will also visit the altars of Beth-el and the horns of the altar shall be cut off and fall to the ground. And I will smite the winter house with the summer house, and the houses of ivory shall perish, and the great houses shall have an end, saith the Lord.

Hear this word, ye kine of Bashan that are in the mountain of Samaria, which oppress the poor, which crush the needy, which say to their masters, Bring and let us drink. The Lord God hath sworn by his holiness that lo, the days shall come upon you that he will take you away with hooks and your posterity with fishhooks. And ye shall go out at the breaches, everyone before his enemy, and ye shall be cast out of your palaces, saith the Lord.

Come to Beth-el, and transgress, at Gilgal multiply transgression, and bring your sacrifices every morning, and your tithes after three years, and offer a sacrifice of thanksgiving with leaven, and proclaim and publish the free offerings, for thus do ye, O ye children of Israel, saith the Lord God. Therefore I also have given you cleanness of teeth in all your cities and want of bread in all your places, yet have ye not returned unto me, saith the Lord. And also I have withholden the rain from you when there were yet three months to the harvest, and I caused it to rain upon one city and caused it not to rain upon another city: one piece was rained upon and the piece whereupon it rained not withered. So two or three cities wandered unto one city to drink water, but they were not satisfied, yet have ye not returned unto me, saith the Lord. I have smitten you with blasting and mildew, when your gardens and your vineyards and your fig trees and your olive trees increased, the palmerworm devoured them, yet have ye not returned unto me, saith the Lord. I have sent among you the pestilence after the manner of Egypt, your young men have I slain with the sword, and have taken away your horses, and I have made the stink of your camps to come up unto your nostrils, yet have ye not returned unto me, saith the Lord. I have overthrown some of you, as God overthrew Sodom and Gomorrah, and ye were as a firebrand plucked out of the burning, yet have ye not returned unto me, saith the Lord. Therefore thus will I do unto thee, O Israel, and because I will do this unto thee, prepare to meet thy God, O Israel. For lo, he that formeth the mountains, and createth the wind, and declareth unto man what is his thought, that maketh the morning darkness, and treadeth upon the high places of the earth, the Lord, the God of hosts is his name.

Hear ye this word which I take up against you, even a lamentation, O house of Israel. The virgin of Israel is fallen, she shall no more rise, she is forsaken upon her land, there is none to raise her up. For thus saith the Lord God, The city that went out by a thousand shall leave a hundred, and that which went forth by a hundred shall leave ten to the house of Israel.

For thus saith the Lord unto the house of Israel, Seek ye me and ye shall live. But seek not Beth-el, nor enter into Gilgal, and pass not to Beer-sheba, for Gilgal shall surely go into captivity and Beth-el shall come to naught. Seek the Lord and ye shall live, lest he break out like fire in the house of Joseph, and devour it, and there be none to quench it in Beth-el. Ye who turn judgment to wormwood and leave off righteousness in the earth, seek him that maketh the seven stars and Orion, and turneth the shadow of death into the morning, and maketh the day dark with night, that calleth for the waters of the sea and poureth them out upon the face of the earth; The Lord is his name. That strengtheneth the spoiled against the strong so that the spoiled shall come against the fortress. They hate him that rebuketh in the gate and they abhor him that speaketh uprightly. Forasmuch therefore as your treading is upon the poor and ye take from him burdens of wheat, ye have built houses of hewn stone, but ye shall not dwell in them, ye have planted pleasant vineyards, but ye shall not drink wine of them. For I know your manifold transgressions and your mighty sins: they afflict the just, they take a bribe, and they turn aside the poor in the gate from their right. Therefore the prudent shall keep silence in that time for it is an evil time. Seek good and not evil, that ye may live, and so the Lord, the God of hosts, shall be with you as ye have spoken. Hate the evil and love the good, and establish judgment in the gate; it may be that the Lord God of hosts will be gracious unto the remnant of Joseph.

Therefore the Lord, the God of hosts, the Lord saith thus, Wailing shall be in all streets, and they shall say in all the highways, Alas, alas! And they shall call the husbandman to mourning, and such as are skillful of lamentation to wailing. And in all vineyards shall be wailing, for I will pass through thee, saith the Lord. Wo unto you that desire the day of the Lord. To what end is it for you? The day of the Lord is darkness and not light. As if a man did flee from a lion and a bear met him, or went into the house and leaned his hand on the wall and a serpent bit him. Shall not the day of the Lord be darkness and not light? Even very dark and no brightness in it?

I hate, I despise your feast days, and I will not smell in your solemn assemblies. Though ye offer me burnt offering and your meat offerings, I will not accept them, neither will I regard the peace offerings of your fat beasts. Take thou away from me the noise of thy songs, for I will not hear the melody of thy viols. But let judgment run down as waters and righteousness as a mighty stream. Have ye offered unto me sacrifices and offerings in the wilderness forty years, O house of Israel? But ye have borne the tabernacle of your Moloch and Chiun your images, the star of your god, which ye made to yourselves. Therefore will I cause you to go into captivity beyond Damascus, saith the Lord, whose name is The God of hosts.

Wo to them that are at ease in Zion, and trust in the mountain of Samaria, which are named chief of the nations, to whom the house of Israel came. Pass ye unto Calneh and see, and from thence go ye to Hamath the great, then go down to Gath of the Philistines; be they better than these kingdoms? Or their border greater than your border? Ye that put far away the evil day and cause the seat of violence to come near, that lie upon beds of ivory and stretch themselves upon their couches, and eat the lambs out of the flock and the calves out of the midst of the stall, that chant to the sound of the viol and invent to themselves instruments of music like David, that drink wine in bowls and anoint themselves with the chief ointments, but they are not grieved for the affliction of Joseph.

Therefore now shall they go captive with the first that go captive and the banquet of them that stretched themselves shall be removed. The Lord God hath sworn by himself, saith the Lord the God of hosts, I abhor the excellency of Jacob and hate his palaces, therefore will I deliver up the city with all that is therein. And it shall come to pass if there remain ten men in one house, that they shall die. And a man's uncle shall take him up, and he that burneth him, to bring out the bones out of the house, and that say unto him that is by the sides of the house, Is there yet any with thee? And he shall say, No. Then shall he say, Hold thy tongue, for we may not make mention of the name of the Lord. For, behold, the Lord commandeth and he will smite the great house with breaches and the little house with clefts.

Shall horses run upon the rock? Will one plough there with oxen? For ye have turned judgment into gall, and the fruit of righteousness into hemlock, ye which rejoice in a thing of naught, which say, Have we not taken to us horns by our own strength? But, behold, I will raise up against you a nation, O house of Israel, saith the Lord the God of hosts, and they shall afflict you from the entering in of Hamath unto the river of the wilderness.

Thus hath the Lord God showed unto me and behold, he formed grasshoppers in the beginning of the shooting up of the latter growth and lo, it was the latter growth after the king's mowings. And it came to pass that when they had made an end of eating the grass of the land, then I said, O Lord God, forgive, I beseech thee, by whom shall Jacob arise, for he is small? And the Lord said, concerning Jacob, Jacob shall repent for this, therefore I will not utterly destroy him, saith the Lord.

Thus hath the Lord God showed unto me and behold, the Lord God called to contend by fire, and it devoured the great deep and did eat up a part. Then said I, O Lord God, cease, I beseech thee, by whom shall Jacob arise, for he is small? And the Lord said, concerning Jacob, Jacob shall repent of his wickedness, therefore I will not utterly destroy him, saith the Lord God.

Thus he showed me and behold, the Lord stood upon a wall made by a plumb line with a plumb line in his hand. And the Lord said unto me, Amos, what seest thou? And I said, A plumb line. Then said the Lord, Behold, I will set a plumb line in the midst of my people Israel, I will not again pass by them anymore, and the high places of Isaac shall be desolate, and the sanctuaries of Israel shall be laid waste, and I will rise against the house of Jeroboam with the sword.

Then Amaziah the priest of Beth-el sent to Jeroboam king of Israel saying, Amos hath conspired against thee in the midst of the house of Israel, the land is not able to bear all his words. For thus Amos saith, Jeroboam shall die by the sword and Israel shall surely be led away captive out of their own land.

Also Amaziah said unto Amos, O thou seer, go, flee thee away into the land of Judah and there eat bread and prophesy there, but prophesy not again anymore at Beth-el, for it is the king's chapel and it is the king's court. Then answered Amos and said to Amaziah, I was no prophet, neither was I a prophet's son, but I was a herdman and a gatherer of sycamore fruit, and the Lord took me as I followed the flock and the Lord said unto me, Go prophesy unto my people Israel. Now therefore hear thou the word of the Lord: Thou sayest, Prophesy not against Israel and drop not thy word against the house of Isaac. Therefore thus saith the Lord, Thy wife shall be a harlot in the city, and thy sons and thy daughters shall fall by the sword, and thy land shall be divided by line, and thou shalt die in a polluted land, and Israel shall surely go into captivity forth of his land.

Thus hath the Lord God showed unto me, and behold a basket of summer fruit. And he said, Amos, what seest thou? And I said, A basket of summer fruit. Then said the Lord with me, The end is come upon my people of Israel, I will not again pass by them anymore. And the songs of the temple shall be howlings in that day, saith the Lord God, there shall be many dead bodies in every place, they shall cast them forth with silence. Hear this, O ye that swallow up the needy, even to make the poor of the land to fail saying, When will the new moon be gone, that we may sell corn? And the sabbath, that we may set forth wheat, making the ephah small, and the shekel great, and falsifying the balances by deceit? That we may buy the poor for silver, and the needy for a pair of shoes, yea, and sell the refuse of the wheat? The Lord hath sworn by the excellency of Jacob, Surely I will never forget any of their works. Shall not the land tremble for this and everyone mourn that dwelleth therein? And it shall rise up wholly as a flood and it shall be cast out and drowned as by the flood of Egypt. And it shall come to pass in that day, saith the Lord God, that I will cause the sun to go down at noon, and I will darken the earth in the clear day, and I will turn your feasts into mourning, and all your songs into lamentation, and I will bring up sackcloth upon all loins, and baldness upon every head, and I will make it as the mourning of an only son, and the end thereof as a bitter day.

Behold, the days come, saith the Lord God, that I will send a famine in the land, not a famine of bread, nor a thirst for water, but of hearing the words of the Lord, and they shall wander from sea to sea and from the north even to the east, they shall run to and fro to seek the word of the Lord and shall not find it. In that day shall the fair virgins and young men faint for thirst. They that swear by the sin of Samaria and say, Thy god, O Dan, liveth, and, The manner of Beer-sheba liveth, even they shall fall and never rise up again.

I saw the Lord standing upon the altar and he said, Smite the lintel of the door, that the posts may shake, and cut them in the head, all of them, and I will slay the last of them with the sword; he that fleeth of them shall not flee away and he that escapeth of them shall not be delivered. Though they dig into hell, thence shall mine hand take them, though they climb up to Heaven, thence will I bring them down, and though they hide themselves in the top of Carmel, I will search and take them out thence, and though they be hid from my sight in the bottom of the sea, thence will I command the serpent and he shall bite them, and though they go into captivity before their enemies, thence will I command the sword and it shall slay them, and I will set mine eyes upon them for evil and not for good. And the Lord God of hosts is he that toucheth the land and it shall melt, and all that dwell therein shall mourn, and it shall rise up wholly like a flood, and shall be drowned as by the flood of Egypt. It is he that buildeth his stories in the Heaven, and hath founded his troop in the

Earth, he that calleth for the waters of the sea and poureth them out upon the face of the Earth, The Lord is his name. Are ye not as children of the Ethiopians unto me, O children of Israel? saith the Lord. Have not I brought up Israel out of the land of Egypt? And the Philistines from Caphtor, and the Syrians from Kir? Behold, the eyes of the Lord God are upon a sinful kingdom and I will destroy it from off the face of the earth, saving that I will not utterly destroy the house of Jacob, saith the Lord. For lo, I will command and I will sift the house of Israel among all nations like as corn is sifted in a sieve, yet shall not the least grain fall upon the Earth. All the sinners of my people shall die by the sword which say, The evil shall not overtake nor prevent us.

In that day will I raise up the tabernacle of David that is fallen and close up the breaches thereof, and I will raise up his ruins and I will build it as in the days of old, that they may possess the remnant of Edom and of all the heathen which are called by my name, saith the Lord that doeth this. Behold, the days come, saith the Lord, that the ploughman shall overtake the reaper, and the treader of grapes him that soweth seed, and the mountains shall drop sweet wine, and all the hills shall melt. And I will bring again the captivity of my people of Israel, and they shall build the waste cities and inhabit them, and they shall plant vineyards and drink the wine thereof, they shall also make gardens and eat the fruit of them. And I will plant them upon their land and they shall no more be pulled up out of their land which I have given them, saith the Lord thy God.

OBADIAH

THE vision of Obadiah. Thus saith the Lord God concerning Edom, We have heard a rumor from the Lord and an ambassador is sent among the heathen, Arise ye, and let us rise up against her in battle. Behold, I have made thee small among the heathen, thou art greatly despised. The pride of thine heart hath deceived thee, thou that dwellest in the clefts of the rock, whose habitation is high, that saith in his heart, Who shall bring me down to the ground? Though thou exalt thyself as the eagle and though thou set thy nest among the stars, thence will I bring thee down, saith the Lord. If thieves came to thee, if robbers by night (how art thou cut off!), would they not have stolen till they had enough? If the grape gatherers came to thee, would they not leave some grapes? How are the things of Esau searched out! How are his hidden things sought up! All the men of thy confederacy have brought thee even to the border, the men that were at peace with thee have deceived thee and prevailed against thee, they that eat thy bread have laid a wound under thee, there is none understanding in him. Shall I not in that day, saith the Lord, even destroy the wise men out of Edom and understanding out of the mount of Esau? And thy mighty men, O Teman, shall be dismayed to the end that every one of the mount of Esau may be cut off by slaughter.

For thy violence against thy brother Jacob, shame shall cover thee and thou shalt be cut off forever. In the day that thou stoodest on the other side, in the day that the strangers carried away captive his forces, and foreigners entered into his gates and cast lots upon Jerusalem, even thou wast as one of them, But thou shouldest not have looked on the day of thy brother in the day that he became a stranger, neither shouldest thou have rejoiced over the children of Judah in the day of their destruction, neither shouldest thou have spoken proudly in the day of distress. Thou shouldest not have entered into the gate of my people in the day of their calamity, yea, thou shouldest not have looked on their affliction in the day of their calamity, nor have laid hands on their substance in the day of their calamity, neither shouldest thou have stood in the crossway to cut off those of his that did escape, neither shouldest thou have delivered up those of his that did remain in the day of distress. For the day of the Lord is near upon all the heathen, as thou hast done it shall be done unto thee, thy reward shall return upon thine own head. For as ye have drunk upon my holy mountain, so shall all the heathen drink continually, yea, they shall drink, and they shall swallow down, and they shall be as though they had not been.

But upon mount Zion shall be deliverance, and there shall be holiness, and the house of Jacob shall possess their possessions. And the house of Jacob shall be a fire, and the house of Joseph a flame, and the house of Esau for stubble, and they shall kindle in them and devour them, and there shall not be any remaining of the house of Esau, for the Lord hath spoken it. And they of the south shall possess the mount of Esau, and they of the plain, the Philistines, and they shall possess the fields of Ephraim and the fields of Samaria, and Benjamin shall possess Gilead. And the captivity of this host of the children of Israel shall possess that of the Canaanites, even unto Zarephath, and the captivity of Jerusalem which is in Sepharad shall possess the cities of the south. And saviors shall come up on mount Zion to judge the mount of Esau, and the kingdom shall be the Lord's.

JONAH

NOW the word of the Lord came unto Jonah, the son of Amittai, saying, Arise, go to Nineveh, that great city, and cry against it, for their wickedness is come up before me. But Jonah rose up to flee unto Tarshish from the presence of the Lord and went down to Joppa; and he found a ship going to Tarshish, so he paid the fare thereof and went down into it, to go with them unto Tarshish from the presence of the Lord.

But the Lord sent out a great wind into the sea and there was a mighty tempest in the sea so that the ship was like to be broken. Then the mariners were afraid and cried every man unto his god, and cast forth the wares that were in the ship into the sea to lighten it of them. But Jonah was gone down into the sides of the ship, and he lay and was fast asleep. So the shipmaster came to him and said unto him, What meanest thou, O sleeper? Arise, call upon thy God, if so be that God will think upon us that we perish not.

And they said everyone to his fellow, Come, and let us cast lots that we may know for whose cause this evil is upon us. So they cast lots and the lot fell upon Jonah. Then said they unto him, Tell us, we pray thee, for whose cause this evil is upon us. What is thine occupation? And whence comest thou? What is thy country and of what people art thou? And he said unto them, I am a Hebrew and I fear the Lord, the God of Heaven, which hath made the sea and the dry land. Then were the men exceedingly afraid and said unto him, Why hast thou done this? For the men knew that he fled from the presence of the Lord because he had told them. Then said they unto him, What shall we do unto thee that the sea may be calm unto us? For the sea wrought and was tempestuous. And he said unto them, Take me up and cast me forth into the sea; so shall the sea be calm unto you, for I know that for my sake this great tempest is upon you. Nevertheless the men rowed hard to bring it to the land, but they could not, for the sea wrought and was tempestuous against them. Wherefore they cried unto the Lord and said, We beseech thee, O Lord, we beseech thee, let us not perish for this man's life and lay not upon us innocent blood, for thou, O Lord, hast done as it pleased thee. So they took up Jonah and cast him forth into the sea and the sea ceased from her raging. Then the men feared the Lord exceedingly and offered a sacrifice unto the Lord and made vows.

Now the Lord had prepared a great fish to swallow up Jonah. And Jonah was in the belly of the fish three days and three nights.

Then Jonah prayed unto the Lord his God out of the fish's belly and said, I cried by reason of mine affliction unto the Lord and he heard me, out of the belly of hell cried I and thou heardest my voice. For thou hadst cast me into the deep, in the midst of the seas and the floods compassed me about, all thy billows and thy waves passed over me. Then I said, I am cast out of thy sight, yet I will look again toward thy holy temple. The waters compassed me about even to the soul, the depth closed me round about, the weeds were wrapped about my head. I went down to the bottoms of the mountains, the Earth with her bars was about me forever, yet hast thou brought up my life from corruption, O Lord my God. When my soul fainted within me I remembered the Lord, and my prayer came in unto thee, into thine holy temple. They that observe lying vanities forsake their own mercy. But I will sacrifice unto thee with the voice of thanksgiving, I will pay that that I have vowed. Salvation is of the Lord. And the Lord spake unto the fish, and it vomited out Jonah upon the dry land.

2 AND the word of the Lord came unto Jonah the second time saying, Arise, go unto Nineveh, that great city, and preach unto it the preaching that I bid thee. So Jonah arose, and went unto Nineveh according to the word of the Lord. Now Nineveh was an exceeding great city of three days' journey. And Jonah began to enter into the city a day's journey and he cried and said, Yet forty days and Nineveh shall be overthrown.

So the people of Nineveh believed God and proclaimed a fast and put on sackcloth, from the greatest of them even to the least of them. For word came unto the king of Nineveh, and he arose from his throne, and he laid his robe from him, and covered him with sackcloth, and sat in ashes. And he caused it to be proclaimed and published through Nineveh by the decree of the king and his nobles, saying, Let neither man nor beast, herd nor flock taste anything; let them not feed, nor drink water, but let man and beast be covered with sackcloth and cry mightily unto God, yea, let them turn everyone from his evil way and from the violence that is in their hands. Who can tell, if we will repent and turn unto God, but he will turn away from us his fierce anger that we perish not?

And God saw their works that they turned from their evil way and repented and God turned away the evil that he had said he would bring upon them. But it displeased Jonah exceedingly and he was very angry. And he prayed unto the lord, and said, I pray thee, O Lord, was not this my saying when I was yet in my country? Therefore I fled before unto Tarshish, for I knew that thou art a gracious God and merciful, slow to anger and of great kindness, and repentest thee of the evil. Therefore now, O Lord, take, I beseech thee, my life from me, for it is better for me to die than to live. Then said the Lord, Doest thou well to be angry?

So Jonah went out of the city, and sat on the east side of the city, and there made him a booth, and sat under it in the shadow till he might see what would become of the city. And the Lord God prepared a gourd and made it to come up over Jonah that it might be a shadow over his head to deliver him from his grief. So Jonah was exceeding glad of the gourd. But God prepared a worm when the morning rose the next day and it smote the gourd that it withered. And it came to pass when the sun did arise that God prepared a vehement east wind, and the sun beat upon the head of Jonah that he fainted and wished in himself to die and said, It is better for me to die than to live.

And God said to Jonah, Doest thou well to be angry for the gourd? And he said, I do well to be angry even unto death. Then said the Lord, Thou hast had pity on the gourd, for the which thou hast not labored neither madest it grow, which came up in a night and perished in a night; and should not I spare Nineveh, that great city wherein are more than sixscore thousand persons that cannot discern between their right hand and their left hand, and also much cattle?

MICAH

THE word of the Lord that came to Micah the Morasthite in the days of Jotham, Ahaz, and Hezekiah, kings of Judah, which he saw concerning Samaria and Jerusalem. Hear, all ye people, hearken, O earth, and all that therein iS and let the Lord God be witness against you, the Lord from his holy temple. For, behold, the Lord cometh forth out of his place and will come down and tread upon the high places of the earth. And the mountains shall be molten under him and the valleys shall be cleft as wax before the fire and as the waters that are poured down a steep place. For the transgression of Jacob is all this and for the sins of the house of Israel. What is the transgression of Jacob? is it not Samaria? And what are the high places of Judah? Are they not Jerusalem? Therefore I will make Samaria as a heap of the field and as plantings of a vineyard, and I will pour down the stones thereof into the valley, and I will discover the foundations thereof. And all the graven images thereof shall be beaten to pieces, and all the hires thereof shall be burned with the fire, and all the idols thereof will I lay desolate, for she gathered it of the hire of a harlot and they shall return to the hire of a harlot. Therefore I will wail and howl, I will go stripped and naked, I will make a wailing like the dragons and mourning as the owls. For her wound is incurable, for it is come unto Judah, he is come unto the gate of my people, even to Jerusalem.

Declare ye it not at Gath, weep ye not at all, in the house of Aphrah roll thyself in the dust. Pass ye away, thou inhabitant of Saphir having thy shame naked, the inhabitant of Zaanan came not forth in the mourning of Beth-ezel, he shall receive of you his standing. For the inhabitant of Maroth waited carefully for good, but evil came down from the Lord unto the gate of Jerusalem. O thou inhabitant of Lachish, bind the chariot to the swift beast, she is the beginning of the sin to the daughter of Zion, for the transgressions of Israel were found in thee. Therefore shalt thou give presents to Moresheth-gath, the houses of Achzib shall be a lie to the kings of Israel. Yet will I bring an heir unto thee, O inhabitant of Mareshah, he shall come unto Adullam the glory of Israel. Make thee bald, and poll thee for thy delicate children, enlarge thy baldness as the eagle, for they are gone into captivity from thee.

Woe to them that devise iniquity and work evil upon their beds. When the morning is light they practice it because it is in the power of their hand. And they covet fields and take them by violence, and houses and take them away, so they oppress a man and his house, even a man and his heritage. Therefore thus saith the Lord, Behold, against this family do I devise an evil from which ye shall not remove your necks, neither shall ye go haughtily, for this time is evil.

In that day shall one take up a parable against you and lament with a doleful lamentation and say, We be utterly spoiled, he hath changed the portion of my people, how hath he removed it from me; turning away he hath divided our fields. Therefore thou shalt have none that shall cast a cord by lot in the congregation of the Lord. Prophesy ye not, say they to them that prophesy, they shall not prophesy to them that they shall not take shame. O thou that art named The house of Jacob, is the Spirit of the Lord straitened? Are these his doings? Do not my words do good to him that walketh uprightly? Even of late my people is risen up as an enemy, ye pull off the robe with the garment from them that pass by securely as men averse from war. The women of my people have ye cast out from their pleasant houses, from their children have ye taken away my glory forever. Arise ye and depart, for this is not your rest because it is polluted, it shall destroy you even with a sore destruction. If a man walking in the spirit and falsehood do lie saying, I will prophesy unto thee of wine and of strong drink, he shall even be the prophet of this people.

I will surely assemble, O Jacob, all of thee, I will surely gather the remnant of Israel, I will put them together as the sheep of Bozrah, as the flock in the midst of their fold they shall make great noise by reason of the multitude of men. The breaker is come up before them, they have broken up, and have passed through the gate, and are gone out by it, and their king shall pass before them, and the Lord on the head of them.

And I said, Hear, I pray you, O heads of Jacob and ye princes of the house of Israel, Is it not for you to know judgment? Who hate the good and love the evil, who pluck off their skin from off them and their flesh from off their bones, who also eat the flesh of my people and flay their skin from off them, and they break their bones and chop them in pieces, as for the pot, and as flesh within the caldron. Then shall they cry unto the Lord, but he will not hear them, he will even hide his face from them at that time as they have behaved themselves ill in their doings.

Thus saith the Lord concerning the prophets that make my people err, that bite with their teeth and cry, Peace, and he that putteth not into their mouths, they even prepare war against him, Therefore night shall be unto you that ye shall not have a vision, and it shall be dark unto you that ye shall not divine, and the sun shall go down over the prophets, and the day shall be dark over them. Then shall the seers be ashamed and the diviners confounded, yea, they shall all cover their lips, for there is no answer of God. But truly I am full of power by the Spirit of the Lord, and of judgment and of might, to declare unto Jacob his transgression and to Israel his sin. Hear this, I pray you, ye heads of the house of Jacob and princes of the house of Israel, that abhor judgment and pervert all equity. They build up Zion with blood and Jerusalem with iniquity. The heads thereof judge for reward, and the priests thereof teach for hire, and the prophets thereof divine for money, yet will they lean upon the Lord and say, Is not the Lord among us? None evil can come upon us. Therefore shall Zion for your sake be ploughed as a field, and Jerusalem shall become heaps, and the mountain of the house as the high places of the forest.

But in the last days it shall come to pass that the mountain of the house of the Lord shall be established in the top of the mountains, and it shall be exalted above the hills, and people shall flow unto it. And many nations shall come and say, Come, and let us go up to the mountain of the Lord and to the house of the God of Jacob, and he will teach us of his ways and we will walk in his paths, for the law shall go forth of Zion and the word of the Lord from Jerusalem. And he shall judge among many people and rebuke strong nations afar off, and they shall beat their swords into ploughshares and their spears into pruning hooks; nation shall not lift up a sword against nation, neither shall they learn war anymore. But they shall sit every man under his vine and under his fig tree and none shall make them afraid, for the mouth of the Lord of Hosts hath spoken it. For all people will walk every one in the name of his god, and we will walk in the name of the Lord our God for ever and ever. In that day, saith the Lord, will I assemble her that halteth, and I will gather her that is driven out, and her that I have afflicted, and I will make her that halted a remnant, and her that was cast far off a strong nation, and the Lord shall reign over them in mount Zion from henceforth, even forever. And thou, O tower of the flock, the stronghold of the daughter of Zion, unto thee shall it come, even the first dominion, the kingdom shall come to the daughter of Jerusalem.

Now why dost thou cry out aloud, is there no king in thee? Is thy counselor perished? For pangs have taken thee as a woman in travail. Be in pain and labor to bring forth, O daughter of Zion, like a woman in travail, for now shalt thou go forth out of the city and thou shalt dwell in the field, and thou shalt go even to Babylon, there shalt thou be delivered, there the Lord shall redeem thee from the hand of thine enemies. Now also many nations are gathered against thee that say, Let her be defiled and let our eye look upon Zion. But they know not the thoughts of the Lord, neither understand they his counsel, for he shall gather them as the sheaves into the floor. Arise and thresh, O daughter of Zion, for I will make thine horn iron, and I will make thy hoofs brass, and thou shalt beat in pieces many people, and I will consecrate their gain unto the Lord, and their substance unto the Lord of the whole earth.

Now gather thyself in troops, O daughter of troops, he hath laid siege against us; they shall smite the judge of Israel with a rod upon the cheek. But thou, Bethlehem Ephratah, though thou be little among the thousands of Judah, yet out of thee shall he come forth unto me that is to be ruler in Israel, whose goings forth have been from of old, from everlasting. Therefore will he give them up, until the time that she which travaileth hath brought forth, then the remnant of his brethren shall return unto the children of Israel. And he shall stand and feed in the strength of the Lord, in the majesty of the name of the Lord his God, and they shall abide, for now shall he be great unto the ends of the earth. And this man shall be the peace when the Assyrian shall come into our land, and when he shall tread in our palaces, then shall we raise against him seven shepherds and eight principal men. And they shall waste the land of Assyria with the sword, and the land of Nimrod in the entrances thereof, thus shall he deliver us from the Assyrian when he cometh into our land and when he treadeth within our borders. And the remnant of Jacob shall be in the midst of many people as a dew from the Lord, as the showers upon the grass that tarrieth not for man nor waiteth for the sons of man. And the remnant of Jacob shall be among the Gentiles in the midst of many people, as a lion among the beasts of the forest, as a young lion among the flocks of sheep, who, if he go through, both treadeth down and teareth in pieces and none can deliver. Thine hand shall be lifted up upon thine adversaries and all thine enemies shall be cut off.

And it shall come to pass in that day, saith the Lord, that I will cut off thy horses out of the midst of thee, and I will destroy thy chariots, and I will cut off the cities of thy land, and throw down all thy strongholds, and I will cut off witchcrafts out of thine hand, and thou shalt have no more soothsayers. Thy graven images also will I cut off and thy standing images out of the midst of thee, and thou shalt no more worship the work of thine hands. And I will pluck up thy groves out of the midst of thee, so will I destroy thy cities. And I will execute vengeance in anger and fury upon the heathen such as they have not heard.

Hear ye now what the Lord saith, Arise, contend thou before the mountains and let the hills hear thy voice. Hear ye, O mountains, the Lord's controversy, and ye strong foundations of the earth, for the Lord hath a controversy with his people and he will plead with Israel. O my people, what have I done unto thee? And wherein have I wearied thee? Testify against me. For I brought thee up out of the land of Egypt, and redeemed thee out of the house of servants, and I sent before thee Moses, Aaron, and Miriam. O my people, remember now what Balak king of Moab consulted, and what Balaam the son of Beor answered him from Shittim unto Gilgal, that ye may know the righteousness of the Lord. Wherewith shall I come before the Lord and bow myself before the high God? Shall I come before him with burnt offerings, with calves of a year old? Will the Lord be pleased with thousands of rams, or with ten thousands of rivers of oil? Shall I give my firstborn for my transgression, the fruit of my body for the sin of my soul? He hath showed thee, O man, what is good, and what doth the Lord require of thee but to do justly, and to love mercy, and to walk humbly with thy God.

The Lord's voice crieth unto the city, and the man of wisdom shall see thy name; hear ye the rod and who hath appointed it. Are there yet the treasures of wickedness in the house of the wicked and the scant measure that is abominable? Shall I count them pure with the wicked balances and with the bag of deceitful weights? For the rich men thereof are full of violence, and the inhabitants thereof have spoken lies, and their tongue is deceitful in their mouth. Therefore also will I make thee sick in smiting thee, in making thee desolate because of thy sin. Thou shalt eat, but not be satisfied, and thy casting down shall be in the midst of thee, and thou shalt take hold, but shalt not deliver, and that which thou deliverest will I give up to the sword. Thou shalt sow, but thou shalt not reap, thou shalt tread the olives, but thou shalt not anoint thee with oil, and sweet wine, but shalt not drink wine. For the statutes of Omri are kept, and all the works of the house of Ahab, and ye walk in their counsels that I should make thee a desolation and the inhabitants thereof a hissing, therefore ye shall bear the reproach of my people.

Woe is me. For I am as when they have gathered the summer fruits, as the grape gleanings of the vintage there is no cluster to eat; my soul desired the first ripe fruit. The good man is perished out of the earth and there is none upright among men, they all lie in wait for blood, they hunt every man his brother with a net. That they may do evil with both hands earnestly, the prince asketh and the judge asketh for a reward, and the great man, he uttereth his mischievous desire so they wrap it up. The best of them is as a brier, the most upright is sharper than a thorn hedge, the day of thy watchman and thy visitation cometh, now shall be their perplexity. Trust ye not in a friend, put ye not confidence in a guide, keep the doors of thy mouth from her that lieth in thy bosom. For the son dishonoreth the father, the daughter riseth up against her mother, the daughter-in-law against her mother-in-law, a man's enemies are the men of his own house. Therefore I will look unto the Lord, I will wait for the God of my salvation, my God will hear me.

2 REJOICE not against me, O mine enemy, when I fall, I shall arise; when I sit in darkness, the Lord shall be a light unto me. I will bear the indignation of the Lord because I have sinned against him, until he plead my cause and execute judgment for me, he will bring me forth to the light and I shall behold his righteousness. Then she that is mine enemy shall see it, and shame shall cover her which said unto me, Where is the Lord thy God? Mine eyes shall behold her, now shall she be trodden down as the mire of the streets. In the day that thy walls are to be built, in that day shall the decree be far removed. In that day also he shall come even to thee from Assyria, and from the fortified cities, and from the fortress even to the river, and from sea to sea, and from mountain to mountain. Notwithstanding, the land shall be desolate because of them that dwell therein for the fruit of their doings. Feed thy people with thy rod, the flock of thine heritage which dwell solitarily in the wood, in the midst of Carmel, let them feed in Bashan and Gilead as in the days of old. According to the days of thy coming out of the land of Egypt will I show unto him marvelous things. The nations shall see and be confounded at all their might, they shall lay their hand upon their mouth, their ears shall be deaf. They shall lick the dust like a serpent, they shall move out of their holes like worms of the earth, they shall be afraid of the Lord our God, and shall fear because of thee.

Who is a God like unto thee, that pardoneth iniquity and passeth by the transgression of the remnant of his heritage? He retaineth not his anger for ever because he delighteth in mercy. He will turn again, he will have compassion upon us, he will subdue our iniquities, and thou wilt cast all their sins into the depths of the sea. Thou wilt perform the truth to Jacob and the mercy to Abraham which thou hast sworn unto our fathers from the days of old.

NAHUM

THE burden of Nineveh. The book of the vision of Nahum the Elkoshite. God is jealous and the Lord revengeth, the Lord revengeth and is furious, The Lord will take vengeance on his adversaries and he reserveth wrath for his enemies. The Lord is slow to anger, and great in power, and will not at all acquit the wicked; the Lord hath his way in the whirlwind, and in the storm, and the clouds are the dust of his feet. He rebuketh the sea and maketh it dry, and drieth up all the rivers: Bashan languisheth, and Carmel, and the flower of Lebanon languisheth. The mountains quake at him and the hills melt, and the earth is burned at his presence, yea, the world and all that dwell therein. Who can stand before his indignation? And who can abide in the fierceness of his anger? His fury is poured out like fire and the rocks are thrown down by him. The Lord is good, a stronghold in the day of trouble, and he knoweth them that trust in him. But with an ever running flood he will make an utter end of the place thereof and darkness shall pursue his enemies.

What do ye imagine against the Lord? He will make an utter end, affliction shall not rise up the second time. For while they be folded together as thorns and while they are drunken as drunkards, they shall be devoured as stubble fully dry. There is one come out of thee that imagineth evil against the Lord, a wicked counselor. Thus saith the Lord, Though they be quiet and likewise many, yet thus shall they be cut down when he shall pass through. Though I have afflicted thee, I will afflict thee no more. For now will I break his yoke from off thee and will burst thy bonds in sunder. And the Lord hath given a commandment concerning thee, that no more of thy name be sown; out of the house of thy gods will I cut off the graven image and the molten image; I will make thy grave, for thou art vile.

Behold upon the mountains the feet of him that bringeth good tidings, that publisheth peace, O Judah, keep thy solemn feasts, perform thy vows, for the wicked shall no more pass through thee, he is utterly cut off.

He that dasheth in pieces is come up before thy face; keep the munition, watch the way, make thy loins strong, fortify thy power mightily. For the Lord hath turned away the excellency of Jacob as the excellency of Israel, for the emptiers have emptied them out and marred their vine branches. The shield of his mighty men is made red, the valiant men are in scarlet, the chariots shall be with flaming torches in the day of his preparation, and the fir trees shall be terribly shaken. The chariots shall rage in the streets, they shall jostle one against another in the broad ways, they shall seem like torches, they shall run like the lightnings. He shall recount his worthies, they shall stumble in their walk, they shall make haste to the wall thereof, and the defense shall be prepared. The gates of the rivers shall be opened and the palace shall be dissolved. And Huzzab shall be led away captive, she shall be brought up, and her maids shall lead her as with the voice of doves, tabering upon their breasts. But Nineveh is of old like a pool of water, yet they shall flee away. Stand, stand, shall they cry, but none shall look back. Take ye the spoil of silver, take the spoil of gold, for their is none end of the store and glory out of all the pleasant furniture. She is empty, and void, and waste, and the heart melteth, and the knees smite together, and much pain is in all loins, and the faces of them all gather blackness. Where is the dwelling of the lions, and the feeding place of the young lions where the lion, even the old lion, walked, and the lion's whelp and none made them afraid? The lion did tear in pieces enough for his whelps, and strangled for his lionesses, and filled his holes with prey, and his dens with ravin. Behold, I am against thee, saith the Lord of hosts, and I will burn her chariots in the smoke, and the sword shall devour thy young lions, and I will cut off thy prey from the earth, and the voice of thy messengers shall no more be heard.

Woe to the bloody city. It is all full of lies and robbery, the prey departeth not, the noise of a whip, and the noise of the rattling of the wheels, and of the prancing horses, and of the jumping chariots. The horseman lifteth up both the bright sword and the glittering spear, and there is a multitude of slain, and a great number of carcasses, and there is none end of their corpses; they stumble upon their corpses because of the multitude of the whoredoms of the well-favored harlot, the mistress of witchcrafts that selleth nations through her whoredoms and families through her witchcrafts.

Behold, I am against thee, saith the Lord of hosts and I will discover thy skirts upon thy face, and I will show the nations thy nakedness and the kingdoms thy shame. And I will cast abominable filth upon thee and make thee vile, and will set thee as a gazing-stock. And it shall come to pass that all they that look upon thee shall flee from thee and say, Nineveh is laid waste, who will bemoan her? Whence shall I seek comforters for thee?

Art thou better than populous No that was situate among the rivers, that had the waters round about it, whose rampart was the sea and her wall was from the sea? Ethiopia and Egypt were her strength and it was infinite, Put and Lubim were thy helpers. Yet was she carried away, she went into captivity, her young children also were dashed in pieces at the top of all the streets, and they cast lots for her honorable men, and all her great men were bound in chains. Thou also shalt be drunken, thou shalt be hid, thou also shalt seek strength because of the enemy. All thy strongholds shall be like fig trees with the first ripe figs: if they be shaken, they shall even fall into the mouth of the eater.

Behold, thy people in the midst of thee are women, the gates of thy land shall be set wide open unto thine enemies, the fire shall devour thy bars. Draw thee waters for the siege, fortify thy strongholds, go into clay and tread the mortar, make strong the brickkiln. There shall the fire devour thee, the sword shall cut thee off, it shall eat thee up like the cankerworms; make thyself many as the cankerworm, make thyself many as the locusts. Thou hast multiplied thy merchants above the stars of heavens, the cankerworm spoileth and fleeth away. Thy crowned are as the locusts, and thy captains as the great grasshoppers which camp in the hedges in the cold day, but when the sun ariseth they flee away and their place is not known where they are.

Thy shepherds slumber, O king of Assyria, thy nobles shall dwell in the dust, thy people is scattered upon the mountains and no man gathereth them. There is no healing of thy bruise, thy wound is grievous: all that hear the noise of thee shall clap the hands over thee, for upon whom hath not thy wickedness passed continually?

HABAKKUK

THE burden which Habakkuk the prophet did see. O Lord, how long shall I cry and thou wilt not hear? Even cry out unto thee of violence and thou wilt not save? Why dost thou show me iniquity and cause me to behold grievances? For spoiling and violence are before me and there are that raise up strife and contention. Therefore the law is slacked and judgment doth never go forth, for the wicked doth compass about the righteous, therefore wrong judgment proceedeth.

Behold ye among the heathen, and regard, and wonder marvelously, for I will work a work in your days which ye will not believe, though it be told you. For, lo, I raise up the Chaldeans, that bitter and hasty nation, which shall march through the breadth of the land, to possess the dwelling-places that are not theirs. They are terrible and dreadful, their judgment and their dignity shall proceed of themselves. Their horses also are swifter than the leopards and are more fierce than the evening wolves, and their horsemen shall spread themselves, and their horsemen shall come from far, they shall fly as the eagle that hasteth to eat. They shall come all for violence, their faces shall sup up as the east wind and they shall gather the captivity as the sand. And they shall scoff at the kings, and the princes shall be a scorn unto them, they shall deride every stronghold, for they shall heap dust and take it. Then shall his mind change, and he shall pass over and offend, imputing this his power unto his god.

Art thou not from everlasting, O Lord my God, mine Holy One? We shall not die. O Lord, thou hast ordained them for judgment, and O mighty God, thou hast established them for correction. Thou art of purer eyes than to behold evil and canst not look on iniquity, wherefore lookest thou upon them that deal treacherously, and holdest thy tongue when the wicked devoureth the man that is more righteous than he? And maketh men as the fishes of the sea, as the creeping things that have no ruler over them? They take up all of them with the angle, they catch them in their net, and gather them in their drag, therefore they rejoice and are glad. Therefore they sacrifice unto their net, and burn incense unto their drag, because by them their portion is fat and their meat plenteous. Shall they therefore empty their net, and not spare continually to slay the nations? I will stand upon my watch, and set me upon the tower, and will watch to see what he will say unto me and what I shall answer when I am reproved.

And the Lord answered me and said, Write the vision and make it plain upon tables that he may run that readeth it. For the vision is yet for an appointed time, but at the end it shall speak and not lie; though it tarry, wait for it because it will surely come, it will not tarry. Behold his soul which is lifted up is not upright in him, but the just shall live by his faith.

Yea also, because he transgresseth by wine he is a proud man, neither keepeth at home, who enlargeth his desire as hell and is as death, and cannot be satisfied, but gathereth unto him all nations and heapeth unto him all people; shall not all these take up a parable against him and a taunting proverb against him and say, Wo to him that increaseth that which is not his. How long? And to him that ladeth himself with thick clay. Shall they not rise up suddenly that shall bite thee, and awake that shall vex thee, and thou shalt be for booties unto them? Because thou hast spoiled many nations, all the remnant of the people shall spoil thee because of men's blood and for the violence of the land, of the city, and of all that dwell therein. Wo to him that coveteth an evil covetousness to his house that he may set his nest on high, that he may be delivered from the power of evil. Thou hast consulted shame to thy house by cutting off many people and hast sinned against thy soul. For the stone shall cry out of the wall and the beam out of the timber shall answer it.

Woe to him that buildeth a town with blood and establisheth a city by iniquity. Behold, is it not of the Lord of hosts that the people shall labor in the very fire and the people shall weary themselves for very vanity? For the earth shall be filled with the knowledge of the glory of the Lord, as the waters cover the sea.

Woe unto him that giveth his neighbor drink, that puttest thy bottle to him, and makest him drunken also, that thou mayest look on their nakedness. Thou art filled with shame for glory, drink thou also, and let thy foreskin be uncovered; the cup of the Lord's right hand shall be turned unto thee and shameful spewing shall be on thy glory. For the violence of Lebanon shall cover thee, and the spoil of beasts which made them afraid because of men's blood, and for the violence of the land, of the city, and of all that dwell therein.

What profiteth the graven image that the maker thereof hath graven it, the molten image, and a teacher of lies, that the maker of his work trusteth therein, to make dumb idols? Wo unto him that saith to the wood, Awake, to the dumb stone, Arise, it shall teach. Behold, it is laid over with gold and silver and there is no breadth at all in the midst of it. But the Lord is in his holy temple; let all the earth keep silence before him.

2 A prayer of Habakkuk the prophet upon Shigionoth. O Lord, I have heard thy speech, and was afraid; O Lord, revive thy work in the midst of the years, in the midst of the years make known, in wrath remember mercy.

God came from Teman, and the Holy One from mount Paran. Selah. His glory covered the heavens, and the earth was full of his praise. And his brightness was as the light; he had horns coming out of his hand and there was the hiding of his power. Before him went the pestilence and burning coals went forth at his feet. He stood and measured the earth, he beheld and drove asunder the nations, and the everlasting mountains were scattered, the perpetual hills did bow; his ways are everlasting. I saw the tents of Cushan in affliction and the curtains of the land of Midian did tremble. Was the Lord displeased against the rivers? Was thine anger against the rivers? Was thy wrath against the sea that thou didst ride upon thine horses and thy chariots of salvation? Thy bow was made quite naked, according to the oaths of the tribes, even thy word. Selah. Thou didst cleave the earth with rivers. The mountains saw thee and they trembled, the overflowing of the water passed by, the deep uttered his voice and lifted up his hands on high. The sun and moon stood still in their habitation, at the light of thine arrows they went, and at the shining of thy glittering spear. Thou didst march through the land in indignation, thou didst thresh the heathen in anger. Thou wentest forth for the salvation of thy people, even for salvation with thine anointed, thou woundedest the head out of the house of the wicked, by discovering the foundation unto the neck. Selah. Thou didst strike through with his staves the head of his villages; they came out as a whirlwind to scatter me, their rejoicing was as to devour the poor secretly. Thou didst walk through the sea with thine horses, through the heap of great waters. When I heard, my belly trembled, my lips quivered at the voice, rottenness entered into my bones and I trembled in myself that I might rest in the day of trouble; when he cometh up unto the people he will invade them with his troops.

Although the fig tree shall not blossom neither shall fruit be in the vines, the labor of the olive shall fail and the fields shall yield no meat. The flock shall be cut off from the fold and there shall be no herd in the stalls, yet I will rejoice in the Lord, I will joy in the God of my salvation. The Lord God is my strength and he will make my feet like hinds' feet and he will make me to walk upon mine high places. To the chief singer on my stringed instruments.

ZEPHANIAH

THE word of the Lord which came unto Zephaniah the son of Cushi, the son of Gedaliah, the son of Amariah, the son of Hizkiah, in the days of Josiah, the son of Amon king of Judah. I will utterly consume all things from off the land, saith the Lord. I will consume man and beast, I will consume the fowls of the Heaven, and the fishes of the sea, and the stumbling-blocks with the wicked, and I will cut off man from off the land, saith the Lord. I will also stretch out mine hand upon Judah and upon all the inhabitants of Jerusalem, and I will cut off the remnant of Baal from this place, and the name of the Chemarim with the priests, and them that worship the host of Heaven upon the housetops, and them that worship and that swear by the Lord, and that swear by Malcham, and them that are turned back from the Lord, and those that have not sought the Lord nor inquired for him.

Hold thy peace at the presence of the Lord God, for the day of the Lord is at hand, for the Lord hath prepared a sacrifice, he hath bid his guests. And it shall come to pass in the day of the Lord's sacrifice that I will punish the princes, and the king's children, and all such as are clothed with strange apparel. In the same day also will I punish all those that leap on the threshold, which fill their masters' houses with violence and deceit. And it shall come to pass in that day, saith the Lord, that there shall be the noise of a cry from the fish gate, and a howling from the second, and a great crashing from the hills. Howl, ye inhabitants of Maktesh, for all the merchant people are cut down, all they that bear silver are cut off. And it shall come to pass at that time that I will search Jerusalem with candles, and punish the men that are settled on their lees, that say in their heart, The Lord will not do good neither will he do evil. Therefore their goods shall become a booty and their houses a desolation, they shall also build houses, but not inhabit them, and they shall plant vineyards, but not drink the wine thereof.

The great day of the Lord is near, it is near and hasteth greatly, even the voice of the day of the Lord; the mighty man shall cry there bitterly. That day is a day of wrath, a day of trouble and distress, a day of wasteness and desolation, a day of darkness and gloominess, a day of clouds and thick darkness. A day of the trumpet and alarm against the fenced cities and against the high towers. And I will bring distress upon men, that they shall walk like blind men because they have sinned against the Lord, and their blood shall be poured out as dust and their flesh as the dung. Neither their silver nor their gold shall be able to deliver them in the day of the Lord's wrath, but the whole land shall be devoured by the fire of his jealousy, for he shall make even a speedy riddance of all them that dwell in the land.

Gather yourselves together, yea, gather together, O nation not desired, before the decree bring forth, before the day pass as the chaff, before the fierce anger of the Lord come upon you, before the day of the Lord's anger come upon you. Seek ye the Lord all ye meek of the earth which have wrought his judgment, seek righteousness, seek meekness, it may be ye shall be hid in the day of the Lord's anger.

For Gaza shall be forsaken and Ashkelon a desolation, they shall drive out Ashdod at the noonday and Ekron shall be rooted up. Wo unto the inhabitants of the sea coast, the nation of the Cherethites. The word of the Lord is against you, O Canaan, the land of the Philistines, I will even destroy thee that there shall be no inhabitant. And the sea coast shall be dwellings and cottages for shepherds and folds for flocks. And the coast shall be for the remnant of the house of Judah, they shall feed thereupon, in the houses of Ashkelon shall they lie down in the evening, for the Lord their God shall visit them and turn away their captivity. I have heard the reproach of Moab and the revilings of the children of Ammon whereby they have reproached my people and magnified themselves against their border. Therefore as I live, saith the Lord of hosts, the God of Israel, surely Moab shall be as Sodom, and the children of Ammon as Gomorrah, even the breeding of nettles, and salt pits, and a perpetual desolation, the residue of my people shall spoil them and the remnant of my people shall possess them. This shall they have for their pride because they have reproached and magnified themselves against the people of the Lord of hosts. The Lord will be terrible unto them for he will famish all the gods of the earth and men shall worship him, everyone from his place, even all the isles of the heathen.

Ye Ethiopians also, ye shall be slain by my sword. And he will stretch out his hand against the north, and destroy Assyria, and will make Nineveh a desolation and dry like a wilderness. And flocks shall lie down in the midst of her, all the beasts of the nations, both the cormorant and the bittern shall lodge in the upper lintels of it, their voice shall sing in the windows, desolation shall be in the thresholds, for he shall uncover the cedar work. This is the rejoicing city that dwelt carelessly, that said in her heart, I am and there is none besides me; how is she become a desolation, a place for beasts to lie down in. Everyone that passeth by her shall hiss and wag his hand.

Woe to her that is filthy and polluted: to the oppressing city. She obeyed not the voice, she received not correction, she trusted not in the Lord, she drew not near to her God. Her princes within her are roaring lions, her judges are evening wolves, they gnaw not the bones till the morrow. Her prophets are light and treacherous persons, her priests have polluted the sanctuary, they have done violence to the law. The just Lord is in the midst thereof, he will not do iniquity, every morning doth he bring his judgment to light, he faileth not, but the unjust knoweth no shame. I have cut off the nations, their towers are desolate, I made their streets waste that none passeth by, their cities are destroyed, so that there is no man, that there is none inhabitant. I said, Surely thou wilt fear me, thou wilt receive instruction, so their dwelling should not be cut off, howsoever I punished them, but they rose early and corrupted all their doings.

Therefore wait ye upon me, saith the Lord, until the day that I rise up to the prey, for my determination is to gather the nations that I may assemble the kingdoms to pour upon them mine indignation, even all my fierce anger, for all the earth shall be devoured with the fire of my jealousy. For then will I turn to the people a pure language that they may all call upon the name of the Lord to serve him with one consent. From beyond the rivers of Ethiopia my suppliants, even the daughter of my dispersed, shall bring mine offering. In that day shalt thou not be ashamed for all thy doings wherein thou hast transgressed against me, for then I will take away out of the midst of thee them that rejoice in thy pride and thou shalt no more be haughty because of my holy mountain. I will also leave in the midst of thee an afflicted and poor people and they shall trust in the name of the Lord. The remnant of Israel shall not do iniquity, nor speak lies, neither shall a deceitful tongue be found in their mouth, for they shall feed and lie down, and none shall make them afraid.

Sing, O daughter of Zion, shout, O Israel, be glad and rejoice with all the heart, O daughter of Jerusalem. The Lord hath taken away thy judgments, he hath cast out thine enemy, the King of Israel, even the Lord, is in the midst of thee; thou shalt not see evil any more. In that day it shall be said to Jerusalem, Fear thou not, and to Zion, Let not thine hands be slack. The Lord thy God in the midst of thee is mighty, he will save, he will rejoice over thee with joy, he will rest in his love, he will joy over thee with singing. I will gather them that are sorrowful for the solemn assembly, who are of thee, to whom the reproach of it was a burden. Behold, at that time I will undo all that afflict thee, and I will save her that halteth, and gather her that was driven out, and I will get them praise and fame in every land where they have been put to shame. At that time will I bring you again, even in the time that I gather you, for I will make you a name and a praise among all people of the earth when I turn back your captivity before your eyes, saith the Lord.

HAGGAI

IN the second year of Darius the king, in the sixth month, in the first day of the month, came the word of the Lord by Haggai the prophet unto Zerubbabel the son of Shealtiel, governor of Judah, and to Joshua, the son of Josedech the high priest, saying, Thus speaketh the Lord of hosts saying, This people say, The time is not come, the time that the Lord's house should be built. Then came the word of the Lord by Haggai the prophet, saying, Is it time for you, O ye, to dwell in your ceiled houses and this house lie waste? Now therefore thus saith the Lord of hosts, Consider your ways. Ye have sown much and bring in little, ye eat, but ye have not enough, ye drink, but ye are not filled with drink, ye clothe you, but there is none warm, and he that earneth wages earneth wages to put it into a bag with holes. Thus saith the Lord of hosts, Consider your ways. Go up to the mountain and bring wood and build the house, and I will take pleasure in it, and I will be glorified, saith the Lord. Ye looked for much, and, lo, it came to little and when ye brought it home I did blow upon it. Why? saith the Lord of hosts. Because of mine house that is waste, and ye run every man unto his own house. Therefore the Heaven over you is stayed from dew and the earth is stayed from her fruit. And I called for a drought upon the land, and upon the mountains, and upon the corn, and upon the new wine, and upon the oil, and upon that which the ground bringeth forth, and upon men, and upon cattle, and upon all the labor of the hands.

Then Zerubbabel, the son of Shealtiel, and Joshua, the son of Josedech the high priest, with all the remnant of the people obeyed the voice of the Lord their God and the words of Haggai the prophet as the Lord their God had sent him, and the people did fear before the Lord. Then spake Haggai the Lord's messenger in the Lord's message unto the people, saying, I am with you saith the Lord. And the Lord stirred up the spirit of Zerubbabel, the son of Shealtiel, governor of Judah, and the spirit of Joshua, the son of Josedech the high priest, and the spirit of all the remnant of the people, and they came and did work in the house of the Lord of hosts their God, in the four and twentieth day of the sixth month, in the second year of Darius the king.

In the seventh month, in the one and twentieth day of the month, came the word of the Lord by the prophet Haggai, saying, Speak now to Zerubbabel, the son of Shealtiel, governor of Judah, and to Joshua, the son of Josedech the high priest, and to the residue of the people, saying, Who is left among you that saw this house in her first glory? And how do ye see it now? Is it not in your eyes in comparison of it as nothing? Yet now be strong, O Zerubbabel, saith the Lord, and be strong, O Joshua, son of Josedech the high priest, and be strong, all ye people of the land, saith the Lord, and work, for I am with you, saith the Lord of hosts, according to the word that I covenanted with you when ye came out of Egypt; so my spirit remaineth among you, fear ye not. For thus saith the Lord of hosts, Yet once it is a little while and I will shake the heavens, and the earth, and the sea, and the dry land, and I will shake all nations, and the desire of all nations shall come and I will fill this house with glory, saith the Lord of hosts. The silver is mine, and the gold is mine, saith the Lord of hosts. The glory of this latter house shall be greater than of the former, saith the Lord of hosts, and in this place will I give peace, saith the Lord of hosts.

In the four and twentieth day of the ninth month, in the second year of Darius, came the word of the Lord by Haggai the prophet saying, Thus saith the Lord of hosts, Ask now the priests concerning the law saying, If one bear holy flesh in the skirt of his garment and with his skirt do touch bread, or pottage, or wine, or oil, or any meat, shall it be holy? And the priests answered and said, No. Then said Haggai, If one that is unclean by a dead body touch any of these, shall it be unclean? And the priests answered and said, It shall be unclean. Then answered Haggai, and said, So is this people and so is this nation before me, saith the Lord, and so is every work of their hands and that which they offer there is unclean. And now, I pray you, consider from this day and upward, from before a stone was laid upon a stone in the temple of the Lord: since those days were, when one came to a heap of twenty measures, there were but ten; when one came to the pressfat for to draw out fifty vessels out of the press, there were but twenty. I smote you with blasting and with mildew and with hail in all the labors of your hands, yet ye turned not to me, saith the Lord. Consider now from this day and upward, from the four and twentieth day of the ninth month, even from the day that the foundation of the Lord's temple was laid, consider it. Is the seed yet in the barn? Yea, as yet the vine, and the fig tree, and the pomegranate, and the olive tree hath not brought forth, from this day will I bless you.

And again the word of the Lord came unto Haggai in the four and twentieth day of the month, saying, Speak to Zerubbabel, governor of Judah saying, I will shake the heavens and the Earth, and I will overthrow the throne of kingdoms, and I will destroy the strength of the kingdoms of the heathen, and I will overthrow the chariots and those that ride in them, and the horses and their riders shall come down, every one by the sword of his brother. In that day, saith the Lord of hosts, will I take thee, O Zerubbabel my servant, the son of Shealtiel, saith the Lord, and will make thee as a signet, for I have chosen thee, saith the Lord of hosts.

ZECHARIAH

1 In the eighth month, in the second year of Darius, came the word of the Lord unto Zechariah, the son of Berechiah, the son of Iddo the prophet, saying, The Lord hath been sore displeased with your fathers. Therefore say thou unto them, Thus saith the Lord of hosts, Turn ye unto me, saith the Lord of hosts, and I will turn unto you, saith the Lord of hosts. Be ye not as your fathers unto whom the former prophets have cried, saying, Thus saith the Lord of hosts, Turn ye now from your evil ways and from your evil doings, but they did not hear nor hearken unto me, saith the Lord. Your fathers, where are they? And the prophets, do they live forever? But my words and my statutes, which I commanded my servants the prophets, did they not take hold of your fathers? And they returned and said, Like as the Lord of hosts thought to do unto us according to our ways and according to our doings, so hath he dealt with us.

Upon the four and twentieth day of the eleventh month, which is the month Sebat, in the second year of Darius, came the word of the Lord unto Zechariah, the son of Berechiah, the son of Iddo the prophet, saying, I saw by night and behold, a man riding upon a red horse, and he stood among the myrtle trees that were in the bottom, and behind him were there red horses, speckled and white. Then said I, O my lord, what are these? And the angel that talked with me said unto me, I will shew thee what these be. And the man that stood among the myrtle trees answered and said, These are they whom the Lord hath sent to walk to and fro through the earth. And they answered the Angel of the LORD that stood among the myrtle trees and said, We have walked to and fro through the earth and, behold, all the earth sitteth still and is at rest. Then the Angel of the Lord answered and said, O Lord of hosts, how long wilt thou not have mercy on Jerusalem and on the cities of Judah, against which thou hast had indignation these threescore and ten years? And the Lord answered the angel that talked with me with good words and comfortable words.

So the angel that communed with me said unto me, Cry thou, saying, Thus saith the Lord of hosts, I am jealous for Jerusalem and for Zion with a great jealousy. And I am very sore displeased with the heathen that are at ease, for I was but a little displeased and they helped forward the affliction. Therefore thus saith the Lord, I am returned to Jerusalem with mercies; my house shall be built in it, saith the Lord of hosts, and a line shall be stretched forth upon Jerusalem. Cry yet, saying, Thus saith the Lord of hosts, My cities through prosperity shall yet be spread abroad, and the Lord shall yet comfort Zion, and shall yet choose Jerusalem.

Then lifted I up mine eyes and saw, and behold four horns. And I said unto the angel that talked with me, What be these? And he answered me, These are the horns which have scattered Judah, Israel, and Jerusalem. And the Lord shewed me four carpenters. Then said I, What come these to do? And he spake saying, These are the horns which have scattered Judah so that no man did lift up his head, but these are come to fray them, to cast out the horns of the Gentiles which lifted up their horn over the land of Judah to scatter it.

I lifted up mine eyes again and looked, and behold a man with a measuring line in his hand. Then said I, Whither goest thou? And he said unto me, To measure Jerusalem, to see what is the breadth thereof and what is the length thereof. And behold, the angel that talked with me went forth, and another angel went out to meet him, and said unto him, Run, speak to this young man, saying, Jerusalem shall be inhabited as towns without walls for the multitude of men and cattle therein, for I, saith the Lord, will be unto her a wall of fire round about and will be the glory in the midst of her.

Ho, ho, come forth and flee from the land of the north, saith the Lord, for I have spread you abroad as the four winds of the heaven, saith the Lord. Deliver thyself, O Zion, that dwellest with the daughter of Babylon. For thus saith the Lord of hosts, After the glory hath he sent me unto the nations which spoiled you, for he that toucheth you toucheth the apple of his eye. For behold, I will shake mine hand upon them and they shall be a spoil to their servants and ye shall know that the Lord of hosts hath sent me.

Sing and rejoice, O daughter of Zion, for lo, I come and I will dwell in the midst of thee, saith the Lord. And many nations shall be joined to the Lord in that day and shall be my people, and I will dwell in the midst of thee, and thou shalt know that the Lord of hosts hath sent me unto thee. And the Lord shall inherit Judah his portion in the holy land and shall choose Jerusalem again. Be silent, O all flesh before the Lord, for he is raised up out of his holy habitation.

And he showed me Joshua the high priest standing before the Angel of the Lord and Satan standing at his right hand to resist him. And the Lord said unto Satan, The Lord rebuke thee, O Satan, even the Lord that hath chosen Jerusalem rebuke thee; is not this a brand plucked out of the fire?

Now Joshua was clothed with filthy garments, and stood before the angel. And he answered and spake unto those that stood before him, saying, Take away the filthy garments from him. And unto him he said, Behold, I have caused thine iniquity to pass from thee and I will clothe thee with change of raiment. And I said, Let them set a fair mitre upon his head. So they set a fair mitre upon his head and clothed him with garments. And the Angel of the Lord stood by. And the Angel of the Lord protested unto Joshua, saying, Thus saith the Lord of hosts, If thou wilt walk in my ways and if thou wilt keep my charge, then thou shalt also judge my house and shalt also keep my courts, and I will give thee places to walk among these that stand by. Hear now, O Joshua the high priest, thou and thy fellows that sit before thee, for they are men wondered at, for behold, I will bring forth my servant the BRANCH. For behold the stone that I have laid before Joshua: upon one stone shall be seven eyes; behold, I will engrave the graving thereof, saith the Lord of hosts, and I will remove the iniquity of that land in one day. In that day, saith the Lord of hosts, shall ye call every man his neighbor under the vine and under the fig tree.

And the angel that talked with me came again and waked me as a man that is wakened out of his sleep, and said unto me, What seest thou? And I said, I have looked and behold a candlestick all of gold with a bowl upon the top of it, and his seven lamps thereon, and seven pipes to the seven lamps which are upon the top thereof, and two olive trees by it, one upon the right side of the bowl and the other upon the left side thereof. So I answered and spake to the angel that talked with me saying, What are these, my lord? Then the angel that talked with me answered and said unto me, Knowest thou not what these be? And I said, No, my lord.

Then he answered and spake unto me saying, This is the word of the Lord unto Zerubbabel, saying, Not by might nor by power, but by my spirit, saith the Lord of hosts. Who art thou, O great mountain? Before Zerubbabel thou shalt become a plain, and he shall bring forth the headstone thereof with shoutings, crying, Grace, grace unto it. Moreover the word of the Lord came unto me, saying, The hands of Zerubbabel have laid the foundation of this house, his hands shall also finish it and thou shalt know that the Lord of hosts hath sent me unto you. For who hath despised the day of small things? For they shall rejoice and shall see the plummet in the hand of Zerubbabel with those seven; they are the servants of the Lord, which run to and fro through the whole earth.

Then answered I and said unto him, What are these two olive trees upon the right side of the candlestick and upon the left side thereof? And I answered again and said unto him, What be these two olive branches which through the two golden pipes empty the golden oil out of themselves? And he answered me and said, Knowest thou not what these be? And I said, No, my lord. Then said he, These are the two anointed ones that stand before the Lord of the whole earth.

Then I turned and lifted up mine eyes and looked, and behold a flying roll. And he said unto me, What seest thou? And I answered, I see a flying roll, the length thereof is twenty cubits and the breadth thereof ten cubits. Then said he unto me, This is the curse that goeth forth over the face of the whole earth, for every one that stealeth shall be cut off as on this side according to it, and every one that sweareth shall be cut off as on that side according to it. I will bring it forth, saith the Lord of hosts, and it shall enter into the house of the thief, and into the house of him that sweareth falsely by my name, and it shall remain in the midst of his house, and shall consume it with the timber thereof and the stones thereof.

Then the angel that talked with me went forth and said unto me, Lift up now thine eyes and see what is this that goeth forth. And I said, What is it? And he said, This is an ephah that goeth forth. He said moreover, This is their resemblance through all the earth. And behold, there was lifted up a talent of lead, and this is a woman that sitteth in the midst of the ephah. And he said, This is wickedness. And he cast it into the midst of the ephah and he cast the weight of lead upon the mouth thereof. Then lifted I up mine eyes and looked and behold, there came out two women, and the wind was in their wings for they had wings like the wings of a stork, and they lifted up the ephah between the earth and the Heaven. Then said I to the angel that talked with me, Whither do these bear the ephah? And he said unto me, To build it a house in the land of Shinar and it shall be established and set there upon her own base.

And I turned and lifted up mine eyes and looked and behold, there came four chariots out from between two mountains and the mountains were mountains of brass. In the first chariot were red horses, and in the second chariot black horses, and in the third chariot white horses, and in the fourth chariot grisled and bay horses. Then I answered and said unto the angel that talked with me, What are these, my lord? And the angel answered and said unto me, These are the four servants of the heavens which go forth from standing before the Lord of all the earth. The black horses which are therein go forth unto the north country, and the white go forth after them, and the grisled go forth toward the south country. And the bay went forth and sought to go that they might walk to and fro through the earth, and he said, Get ye hence, walk to and fro through the earth. So they walked to and fro through the earth. Then cried he upon me and spake unto me, saying, Behold, these that go toward the north country have quieted my spirit in the north country.

And the word of the Lord came unto me, saying, Take of them of the captivity, even of Heldai, of Tobijah, and of Jedaiah, which are come from Babylon, and come thou the same day and go into the house of Josiah the son of Zephaniah, then take silver and gold and make crowns and set them upon the head of Joshua the son of Josedech the high priest and speak unto him, saying, Thus speaketh the Lord of hosts saying, Behold the man whose name is The BRANCH, and he shall grow up out of his place and he shall build the temple of the Lord, even he shall build the temple of the Lord, and he shall bear the glory and shall sit and rule upon his throne, and he shall be a priest upon his throne, and the counsel of peace shall be between them both.

And the crowns shall be to Helem, and to Tobijah, and to Jedaiah, and to Hen the son of Zephaniah, for a memorial in the temple of the Lord. And they that are far off shall come and build in the temple of the Lord and ye shall know that the Lord of hosts hath sent me unto you. And this shall come to pass if ye will diligently obey the voice of the Lord your God.

And it came to pass in the fourth year of king Darius that the word of the Lord came unto Zechariah in the fourth day of the ninth month, even in Chisleu, when they had sent unto the house of God Sherezer and Regem-melech and their men, to pray before the Lord and to speak unto the priests which were in the house of the Lord of hosts and to the prophets, saying, Should I weep in the fifth month, separating myself as I have done these so many years?

Then came the word of the Lord of hosts unto me, saying, Speak unto all the people of the land and to the priests saying, When ye fasted and mourned in the fifth and seventh month, even those seventy years, did ye at all fast unto me, even to me? And when ye did eat and when ye did drink, did not ye eat for yourselves and drink for yourselves? Should ye not hear the words which the Lord hath cried by the former prophets, when Jerusalem was inhabited and in prosperity and the cities thereof round about her, when men inhabited the south and the plain?

And the word of the Lord came unto Zechariah, saying, Thus speaketh the Lord of hosts saying, Execute true judgment and shew mercy and compassions every man to his brother, and oppress not the widow, nor the fatherless, the stranger, nor the poor, and let none of you imagine evil against his brother in your heart. But they refused to hearken, and pulled away the shoulder, and stopped their ears that they should not hear. Yea, they made their hearts as an adamant stone lest they should hear the law, and the words which the Lord of hosts hath sent in his spirit by the former prophets; therefore came a great wrath from the Lord of hosts. Therefore it is come to pass that as he cried and they would not hear, so they cried and I would not hear, saith the Lord of hosts, but I scattered them with a whirlwind among all the nations whom they knew not. Thus the land was desolate after them that no man passed through nor returned, for they laid the pleasant land desolate.

Again the word of the Lord of hosts came to me saying, Thus saith the Lord of hosts, I was jealous for Zion with great jealousy and I was jealous for her with great fury. Thus saith the Lord, I am returned unto Zion and will dwell in the midst of Jerusalem, and Jerusalem shall be called a city of truth and the mountain of the Lord of hosts, the holy mountain. Thus saith the Lord of hosts, There shall yet old men and old women dwell in the streets of Jerusalem and every man with his staff in his hand for very age. And the streets of the city shall be full of boys and girls playing in the streets thereof. Thus saith the Lord of hosts, If it be marvelous in the eyes of the remnant of this people in these days, should it also be marvelous in mine eyes? saith the Lord of hosts.

Thus saith the Lord of hosts, Behold, I will gather my people from the east country and from the west country and I will bring them, and they shall dwell in the midst of Jerusalem, and they shall be my people and I will be their God in truth and in righteousness.

Thus saith the Lord of hosts, Let your hands be strong, ye that hear in these days these words by the mouth of the prophets which were in the day that the foundation of the house of the Lord of hosts was laid that the temple might be built. For before these days there was no hire for man, nor any hire for beast, neither was there any peace to him that went out or came in because of the affliction, for I set all men every one against his neighbor. But now I will not be unto the residue of this people as in the former days, saith the Lord of hosts. For the seed shall be prosperous, the vine shall give her fruit, and the ground shall give her increase, and the heavens shall give their dew, and I will cause the remnant of this people to possess all these things. And it shall come to pass, that as ye were a curse among the heathen, O house of Judah and house of Israel, so will I gather you and ye shall be a blessing; fear not, but let your hands be strong. For thus saith the Lord of hosts, As I thought to punish you when your fathers provoked me to wrath, saith the Lord of hosts, and I repented not, so again have I thought in these days to do well unto Jerusalem and to the house of Judah; fear ye not. These are the things that ye shall do: Speak ye every man the truth to his neighbor, execute the judgment of truth and peace in your gates, and let none of you imagine evil in your hearts against his neighbor, and love no false oath, for all these are things that I hate, saith the Lord.

And the word of the Lord of hosts came unto me, saying, Thus saith the Lord of hosts, The fast of the fourth month, and the fast of the fifth, and the fast of the seventh, and the fast of the tenth, shall be to the house of Judah joy and gladness, and cheerful feasts, therefore love the truth and peace.

Thus saith the Lord of hosts, It shall yet come to pass that there shall come people and the inhabitants of many cities, and the inhabitants of one city shall go to another saying, Let us go speedily to pray before the Lord and to seek the Lord of hosts; I will go also. Yea, many people and strong nations shall come to seek the Lord of hosts in Jerusalem and to pray before the Lord.

Thus saith the Lord of hosts, In those days it shall come to pass that ten men shall take hold out of all languages of the nations, even shall take hold of the skirt of him that is a Jew, saying, We will go with you, for we have heard that God is with you.

The burden of the word of the Lord in the land of Hadrach and Damascus shall be the rest thereof when the eyes of man, as of all the tribes of Israel, shall be toward the Lord. And Hamath also shall border thereby, Tyrus, and Zidon, though it be very wise. And Tyrus did build herself a stronghold and heaped up silver as the dust and fine gold as the mire of the streets. Behold, the Lord will cast her out, and he will smite her power in the sea and she shall be devoured with fire. Ashkelon shall see it and fear, Gaza also shall see it and be very sorrowful, and Ekron for her expectation shall be ashamed, and the king shall perish from Gaza, and Ashkelon shall not be inhabited. And a bastard shall dwell in Ashdod, and I will cut off the pride of the Philistines. And I will take away his blood out of his mouth and his abominations from between his teeth, but he that remaineth, even he shall be for our God, and he shall be as a governor in Judah and Ekron as a Jebusite. And I will encamp about mine house because of the army, because of him that passeth by, and because of him that returneth, and no oppressor shall pass through them anymore, for now have I seen with mine eyes.

Rejoice greatly, O daughter of Zion, shout, O daughter of Jerusalem, behold, thy King cometh unto thee: he is just, and having salvation, lowly and riding upon an ass, and upon a colt, the foal of an ass. And I will cut off the chariot from Ephraim, and the horse from Jerusalem, and the battle bow shall be cut off, and he shall speak peace unto the heathen, and his dominion shall be from sea even to sea, and from river even to the ends of the earth. As for thee also by the blood of thy covenant I have sent forth thy prisoners out of the pit wherein is no water. Turn you to the stronghold, ye prisoners of hope, even today do I declare that I will render double unto thee when I have bent Judah for me, filled the bow with Ephraim, and raised up thy sons, O Zion, against thy sons, O Greece, and made thee as the sword of a mighty man. And the Lord shall be seen over them and his arrow shall go forth as the lightning, and the Lord God shall blow the trumpet and shall go with whirlwinds of the south. The Lord of hosts shall defend them, and they shall devour and subdue with sling stones, and they shall drink, and make a noise as through wine, and they shall be filled like bowls, and as the corners of the altar. And the Lord their God shall save them in that day as the flock of his people, for they shall be as the stones of a crown lifted up as an ensign upon his land. For how great is his goodness, and how great is his beauty; corn shall make the young men cheerful and new wine the maids.

Ask ye of the Lord rain in the time of the latter rain, so the Lord shall make bright clouds and give them showers of rain, to every one grass in the field. For the idols have spoken vanity, and the diviners have seen a lie and have told false dreams, they comfort in vain; therefore they went their way as a flock, they were troubled because there was no shepherd.

Mine anger was kindled against the shepherds, and I punished the goats, for the Lord of hosts hath visited his flock, the house of Judah, and hath made them as his goodly horse in the battle. Out of him came forth the corner, out of him the nail, out of him the battle bow, out of him every oppressor together. And they shall be as mighty men which tread down their enemies in the mire of the streets in the battle, and they shall fight because the Lord is with them, and the riders on horses shall be confounded. And I will strengthen the house of Judah, and I will save the house of Joseph, and I will bring them again to place them for I have mercy upon them, and they shall be as though I had not cast them off, for I am the Lord their God and will hear them.

And they of Ephraim shall be like a mighty man and their heart shall rejoice as through wine, yea, their children shall see it and be glad, their heart shall rejoice in the Lord. I will hiss for them and gather them, for I have redeemed them, and they shall increase as they have increased. And I will sow them among the people, and they shall remember me in far countries, and they shall live with their children and turn again. I will bring them again also out of the land of Egypt and gather them out of Assyria, and I will bring them into the land of Gilead and Lebanon and place shall not be found for them. And he shall pass through the sea with affliction, and shall smite the waves in the sea, and all the deeps of the river shall dry up, and the pride of Assyria shall be brought down, and the sceptre of Egypt shall depart away. And I will strengthen them in the Lord and they shall walk up and down in his name, saith the Lord.

Open thy doors, O Lebanon, that the fire may devour thy cedars. Howl, fir tree, for the cedar is fallen because the mighty are spoiled. Howl, O ye oaks of Bashan, for the forest of the vintage is come down. There is a voice of the howling of the shepherds for their glory is spoiled, a voice of the roaring of young lions for the pride of Jordan is spoiled. Thus saith the Lord my God, Feed the flock of the slaughter, whose possessors slay them and hold themselves not guilty, and they that sell them say, Blessed be the Lord for I am rich, and their own shepherds pity them not. For I will no more pity the inhabitants of the land, saith the Lord, but, lo, I will deliver the men every one into his neighbor's hand and into the hand of his king, and they shall smite the land and out of their hand I will not deliver them.

And I will feed the flock of slaughter, even you, O poor of the flock. And I took unto me two staves, the one I called Beauty, and the other I called Bands, and I fed the flock. Three shepherds also I cut off in one month, and my soul lothed them, and their soul also abhorred me. Then said I, I will not feed you; that that dieth, let it die, and that that is to be cut off, let it be cut off, and let the rest eat every one the flesh of another. And I took my staff, even Beauty, and cut it asunder that I might break my covenant which I had made with all the people. And it was broken in that day, and so the poor of the flock that waited upon me knew that it was the word of the Lord. And I said unto them, If ye think good, give me my price, and if not, forbear. So they weighed for my price thirty pieces of silver. And the Lord said unto me, Cast it unto the potter, a goodly price that I was prised at of them. And I took the thirty pieces of silver and cast them to the potter in the house of the Lord. Then I cut asunder mine other staff, even Bands, that I might break the brotherhood between Judah and Israel.

And the Lord said unto me, Take unto thee yet the instruments of a foolish shepherd. For, lo, I will raise up a shepherd in the land which shall not visit those that be cut off, neither shall seek the young one, nor heal that that is broken, nor feed that that standeth still, but he shall eat the flesh of the fat, and tear their claws in pieces. Wo to the idol shepherd that leaveth the flock. The sword shall be upon his arm and upon his right eye, his arm shall be clean dried up and his right eye shall be utterly darkened.

The burden of the word of the Lord for Israel, saith the Lord, which stretcheth forth the heavens, and layeth the foundation of the Earth, and formeth the spirit of man within him.

Behold, I will make Jerusalem a cup of trembling unto all the people round about, when they shall be in the siege both against Judah and against Jerusalem. And in that day will I make Jerusalem a burdensome stone for all people; all that burden themselves with it shall be cut in pieces though all the people of the earth be gathered together against it. In that day, saith the Lord, I will smite every horse with astonishment, and his rider with madness, and I will open mine eyes upon the house of Judah, and will smite every horse of the people with blindness. And the governors of Judah shall say in their heart, The inhabitants of Jerusalem shall be my strength in the Lord of hosts their God.

In that day will I make the governors of Judah like a hearth of fire among the wood and like a torch of fire in a sheaf, and they shall devour all the people round about, on the right hand and on the left, and Jerusalem shall be inhabited again in her own place, even in Jerusalem. The Lord also shall save the tents of Judah first, that the glory of the house of David and the glory of the inhabitants of Jerusalem do not magnify themselves against Judah. In that day shall the Lord defend the inhabitants of Jerusalem, and he that is feeble among them at that day shall be as David, and the house of David shall be as God, as the Angel of the Lord before them. And it shall come to pass in that day, that I will seek to destroy all the nations that come against Jerusalem.

And I will pour upon the house of David and upon the inhabitants of Jerusalem the spirit of grace and of supplications, and they shall look upon me whom they have pierced and they shall mourn for him as one mourneth for his only son, and shall be in bitterness for him as one that is in bitterness for his firstborn. In that day shall there be a great mourning in Jerusalem, as the mourning of Hadadrimmon in the valley of Megiddon. And the land shall mourn, every family apart, the family of the house of David apart and their wives apart, the family of the house of Nathan apart and their wives apart, the family of the house of Levi apart and their wives apart, the family of Shimei apart and their wives apart, all the families that remain, every family apart and their wives apart.

In that day there shall be a fountain opened to the house of David and to the inhabitants of Jerusalem for sin and for uncleanness. And it shall come to pass in that day, saith the Lord of hosts, that I will cut off the names of the idols out of the land and they shall no more be remembered, and also I will cause the prophets and the unclean spirit to pass out of the land. And it shall come to pass that when any shall yet prophesy, then his father and his mother that begat him shall say unto him, Thou shalt not live, for thou speakest lies in the name of the Lord, and his father and his mother that begat him shall thrust him through when he prophesieth. And it shall come to pass in that day that the prophets shall be ashamed every one of his vision when he hath prophesied, neither shall they wear a rough garment to deceive, but he shall say, I am no prophet, I am a husbandman, for man taught me to keep cattle from my youth. And one shall say unto him, What are these wounds in thine hands? Then he shall answer, Those with which I was wounded in the house of my friends.

Awake, O sword, against my shepherd and against the man that is my fellow, saith the Lord of hosts. Smite the shepherd and the sheep shall be scattered and I will turn mine hand upon the little ones. And it shall come to pass that in all the land, saith the Lord, two parts therein shall be cut off and die, but the third shall be left therein. And I will bring the third part through the fire and will refine them as silver is refined and will try them as gold is tried; they shall call on my name and I will hear them; I will say, It is my people, and they shall say, The Lord is my God.

Behold, the day of the Lord cometh and thy spoil shall be divided in the midst of thee. For I will gather all nations against Jerusalem to battle, and the city shall be taken, and the houses rifled, and the women ravished, and half of the city shall go forth into captivity, and the residue of the people shall not be cut off from the city. Then shall the Lord go forth and fight against those nations, as when he fought in the day of battle. And his feet shall stand in that day upon the mount of Olives which is before Jerusalem on the east, and the mount of Olives shall cleave in the midst thereof toward the east and toward the west, and there shall be a very great valley, and half of the mountain shall remove toward the north and half of it toward the south. And ye shall flee to the valley of the mountains, for the valley of the mountains shall reach unto Azal. Yea, ye shall flee like as ye fled from before the earthquake in the days of Uzziah king of Judah, and the Lord my God shall come and all the saints with thee.

And it shall come to pass in that day that the light shall not be clear nor dark, but it shall be one day which shall be known to the Lord, not day nor night, but it shall come to pass that at evening time it shall be light. And it shall be in that day that living waters shall go out from Jerusalem, half of them toward the former sea and half of them toward the hinder sea, in summer and in winter shall it be. And the Lord shall be king over all the earth; in that day shall there be one Lord and his name one. All the land shall be turned as a plain from Geba to Rimmon south of Jerusalem, and it shall be lifted up and inhabited in her place, from Benjamin's gate unto the place of the first gate, unto the corner gate, and from the tower of Hananeel unto the king's wine presses. And men shall dwell in it, and there shall be no more utter destruction, but Jerusalem shall be safely inhabited.

And this shall be the plague wherewith the Lord will smite all the people that have fought against Jerusalem: Their flesh shall consume away while they stand upon their feet, and their eyes shall consume away in their holes, and their tongue shall consume away in their mouth. And it shall come to pass in that day that a great tumult from the Lord shall be among them, and they shall lay hold everyone on the hand of his neighbor and his hand shall rise up against the hand of his neighbor. And Judah also shall fight at Jerusalem, and the wealth of all the heathen round about shall be gathered together, gold, and silver, and apparel, in great abundance. And so shall be the plague of the horse, of the mule, of the camel, and of the ass, and of all the beasts that shall be in these tents, as this plague.

And it shall come to pass, that every one that is left of all the nations which came against Jerusalem shall even go up from year to year to worship the King, the LORD of hosts, and to keep the feast of tabernacles. And it shall be that whoso will not come up of all the families of the earth unto Jerusalem to worship the King, the Lord of hosts, even upon them shall be no rain. And if the family of Egypt go not up, and come not that have no rain, there shall be the plague wherewith the Lord will smite the heathen that come not up to keep the feast of tabernacles. This shall be the punishment of Egypt, and the punishment of all nations that come not up to keep the feast of tabernacles.

In that day shall there be upon the bells of the horses, HOLINESS UNTO THE LORD, and the pots in the Lord's house shall be like the bowl's before the altar. Yea, every pot in Jerusalem and in Judah shall be holiness unto the Lord of hosts, and all they that sacrifice shall come and take of them, and seethe therein, and in that day there shall be no more the Canaanite in the house of the Lord of hosts.

MALACHI

1 The burden of the word of the Lord to Israel by Malachi. I have loved you, saith the Lord, yet ye say, Wherein hast thou loved us? Was not Esau Jacob's brother? saith the Lord, yet I loved Jacob. And I hated Esau and laid his mountains and his heritage waste for the dragons of the wilderness. Whereas Edom saith, We are impoverished, but we will return and build the desolate places, thus saith the Lord of hosts, They shall build, but I will throw down; and they shall call them, The border of wickedness, and, The people against whom the Lord hath indignation forever. And your eyes shall see and ye shall say, The Lord will be magnified from the border of Israel.

A son honoreth his father and a servant his master; if then I be a father, where is mine honor? And if I be a master, where is my fear? saith the Lord of hosts unto you, O priests that despise my name. And ye say, Wherein have we despised thy name? Ye offer polluted bread upon mine altar and ye say, Wherein have we polluted thee? In that ye say, The table of the Lord is contemptible. And if ye offer the blind for sacrifice, is it not evil? And if ye offer the lame and sick, is it not evil? Offer it now unto thy governor; will he be pleased with thee or accept thy person? saith the Lord of hosts. And now I pray you, beseech God that he will be gracious unto us; this hath been by your means, will he regard your persons? saith the Lord of hosts. Who is there even among you that would shut the doors for naught? Neither do ye kindle fire on mine altar for naught. I have no pleasure in you, saith the Lord of hosts, neither will I accept an offering at your hand. For from the rising of the sun even unto the going down of the same my name shall be great among the Gentiles, and in every place incense shall be offered unto my name, and a pure offering for my name shall be great among the heathen, saith the Lord of hosts. But ye have profaned it in that ye say, The table of the Lord is polluted and the fruit thereof, even his meat is contemptible. Ye said also, Behold, what a weariness is it, and ye have snuffed at it, saith the Lord of hosts, and ye brought that which was torn, and the lame, and the sick; thus ye brought an offering, should I accept this of your hand? saith the Lord. But cursed be the deceiver which hath in his flock a male, and voweth and sacrificeth unto the Lord a corrupt thing, for I am a great King, saith the Lord of hosts, and my name is dreadful among the heathen.

And now, O ye priests, this commandment is for you. If ye will not hear and if ye will not lay it to heart to give glory unto my name, saith the Lord of hosts, I will even send a curse upon you and I will curse your blessings. Yea, I have cursed them already because ye do not lay it to heart. Behold, I will corrupt your seed and spread dung upon your faces, even the dung of your solemn feasts, and one shall take you away with it. And ye shall know that I have sent this commandment unto you that my covenant might be with Levi, saith the Lord of hosts. My covenant was with him of life and peace and I gave them to him for the fear wherewith he feared me and was afraid before my name. The law of truth was in his mouth and iniquity was not found in his lips, he walked with me in peace and equity and did turn many away from iniquity. For the priest's lips should keep knowledge and they should seek the law at his mouth, for he is the messenger of the Lord of hosts. But ye are departed out of the way, ye have caused many to stumble at the law, ye have corrupted the covenant of Levi, saith the Lord of hosts. Therefore have I also made you contemptible and base before all the people, according as ye have not kept my ways, but have been partial in the law.

Have we not all one father? Hath not one God created us? Why do we deal treacherously every man against his brother by profaning the covenant of our fathers? Judah hath dealt treacherously and an abomination is committed in Israel and in Jerusalem, for Judah hath profaned the holiness of the Lord which he loved and hath married the daughter of a strange god. The Lord will cut off the man that doeth this, the master and the scholar, out of the tabernacles of Jacob and him that offereth an offering unto the Lord of hosts. And this have ye done again, covering the altar of the Lord with tears, with weeping, and with crying out, insomuch that he regardeth not the offering anymore or receiveth it with good will at your hand. Yet ye say, Wherefore? Because the Lord hath been witness between thee and the wife of thy youth against whom thou hast dealt treacherously, yet is she thy companion and the wife of thy covenant. And did not he make one? Yet had he the residue of the Spirit. And wherefore one? That he might seek a godly seed. Therefore take heed to your spirit and let none deal treacherously against the wife of his youth. For the Lord, the God of Israel, saith that he hateth putting away, for one covereth violence with his garment, saith the Lord of hosts, therefore take heed to your spirit that ye deal not treacherously.

Ye have wearied the Lord with your words. Yet ye say, Wherein have we wearied him? When ye say, Everyone that doeth evil is good in the sight of the Lord and he delighteth in them, or, Where is the God of judgment?

Behold, I will send my messenger and he shall prepare the way before me, and the Lord whom ye seek shall suddenly come to his temple; even the messenger of the covenant whom ye delight in, behold, he shall come, saith the Lord of hosts. But who may abide the day of his coming? And who shall stand when he appeareth? For he is like a refiner's fire and like fullers' soap, and he shall sit as a refiner and purifier of silver, and he shall purify the sons of Levi, and purge them as gold and silver that they may offer unto the Lord an offering in righteousness. Then shall the offering of Judah and Jerusalem be pleasant unto the Lord, as in the days of old and as in former years. And I will come near to you to judgment and I will be a swift witness against the sorcerers, and against the adulterers, and against false swearers, and against those that oppress the hireling in his wages, the widow, and the fatherless, and that turn aside the stranger from his right, and fear not me, saith the Lord of hosts. For I am the Lord, I change not; therefore ye sons of Jacob are not consumed.

Even from the days of your fathers ye are gone away from mine ordinances and have not kept them. Return unto me and I will return unto you, saith the Lord of hosts. But ye said, Wherein shall we return? Will a man rob God? Yet ye have robbed me. But ye say, Wherein have we robbed thee? In tithes and offerings. Ye are cursed with a curse for ye have robbed me, even this whole nation. Bring ye all the tithes into the storehouse that there may be meat in mine house and prove me now herewith, saith the Lord of hosts, if I will not open you the windows of Heaven and pour you out a blessing that there shall not be room enough to receive it. And I will rebuke the devourer for your sakes, and he shall not destroy the fruits of your ground, neither shall your vine cast her fruit before the time in the field, saith the Lord of hosts. And all nations shall call you blessed for ye shall be a delightsome land, saith the Lord of hosts. Your words have been stout against me, saith the Lord. Yet ye say, What have we spoken so much against thee? Ye have said, It is vain to serve God and what profit is it that we have kept his ordinance and that we have walked mournfully before the Lord of hosts? And now we call the proud happy, yea, they that work wickedness are set up, yea, they that tempt God are even delivered.

Then they that feared the Lord spake often one to another and the Lord hearkened and heard it, and a book of remembrance was written before him for them that feared the Lord and that thought upon his name. And they shall be mine, saith the Lord of hosts, in that day when I make up my jewels, and I will spare them as a man spareth his own son that serveth him. Then shall ye return and discern between the righteous and the wicked, between him that serveth God and him that serveth him not.

For, behold, the day cometh that shall burn as an oven and all the proud, yea, and all that do wickedly shall be stubble, and the day that cometh shall burn them up, saith the Lord of hosts, that it shall leave them neither root nor branch. But unto you that fear my name shall the Sun of righteousness arise with healing in his wings, and ye shall go forth and grow up as calves of the stall. And ye shall tread down the wicked, for they shall be ashes under the soles of your feet in the day that I shall do this, saith the Lord of hosts.

Remember ye the law of Moses my servant which I commanded unto him in Horeb for all Israel, with the statutes and judgments.

Behold, I will send you Elijah the prophet before the coming of the great and dreadful day of the Lord, and he shall bind the heart of the fathers to the children and the heart of the children to their fathers lest I come and smite the earth with a curse.